# Lecture Notes in Computer Science    9636

Commenced Publication in 1973
Founding and Former Series Editors:
Gerhard Goos, Juris Hartmanis, and Jan van Leeuwen

## Advanced Research in Computing and Software Science

Subline of Lecture Notes in Computer Science

More information about this series at http://www.springer.com/series/7407

Marsha Chechik · Jean-François Raskin (Eds.)

# Tools and Algorithms for the Construction and Analysis of Systems

22nd International Conference, TACAS 2016
Held as Part of the European Joint Conferences
on Theory and Practice of Software, ETAPS 2016
Eindhoven, The Netherlands, April 2–8, 2016
Proceedings

Springer

*Editors*
Marsha Chechik
University of Toronto
Toronto, ON
Canada

Jean-François Raskin
Université Libre de Bruxelles
Brussels
Belgium

ISSN 0302-9743                    ISSN 1611-3349   (electronic)
Lecture Notes in Computer Science
ISBN 978-3-662-49673-2       ISBN 978-3-662-49674-9   (eBook)
DOI 10.1007/978-3-662-49674-9

Library of Congress Control Number: 2016933319

LNCS Sublibrary: SL1 – Theoretical Computer Science and General Issues

This Springer imprint is published by Springer Nature
The registered company is Springer-Verlag GmbH Berlin Heidelberg

# ETAPS Foreword

Welcome to the proceedings of ETAPS 2016, which was held in Eindhoven, located in "the world's smartest region," also known as the Dutch Silicon Valley. Since ETAPS' second edition held in Amsterdam (1999), ETAPS returned to The Netherlands this year.

ETAPS 2016 was the 19th instance of the European Joint Conferences on Theory and Practice of Software. ETAPS is an annual federated conference established in 1998, consisting of five constituting conferences (ESOP, FASE, FoSSaCS, TACAS, and POST) this year. Each conference has its own Programme Committee and its own Steering Committee. The conferences cover various aspects of software systems, ranging from theoretical computer science to foundations to programming language developments, analysis tools, formal approaches to software engineering, and security. Organizing these conferences in a coherent, highly synchronized conference program, enables attendees to participate in an exciting event, having the possibility to meet many researchers working in different directions in the field, and to easily attend the talks of various conferences. Before and after the main conference, numerous satellite workshops took place and attracted many researchers from all over the globe.

The ETAPS conferences received 474 submissions in total, 143 of which were accepted, yielding an overall acceptance rate of 30.2 %. I thank all authors for their interest in ETAPS, all reviewers for their peer-reviewing efforts, the Program Committee members for their contributions, and in particular the program co-chairs for their hard work in running this intensive process. Last but not least, my congratulations to all the authors of the accepted papers!

ETAPS 2016 was greatly enriched by the unifying invited speakers Andrew Gordon (MSR Cambridge and University of Edinburgh, UK), and Rupak Majumdar (MPI Kaiserslautern, Germany), as well as the conference-specific invited speakers (ESOP) Cristina Lopes (University of California at Irvine, USA), (FASE) Oscar Nierstrasz (University of Bern, Switzerland), and (POST) Vitaly Shmatikov (University of Texas at Austin, USA). Invited tutorials were organized by Lenore Zuck (Chicago) and were provided by Grigore Rosu (University of Illinois at Urbana-Champaign, USA) on software verification and Peter Ryan (University of Luxembourg, Luxembourg) on security. My sincere thanks to all these speakers for their inspiring and interesting talks!

ETAPS 2016 took place in Eindhoven, The Netherlands. It was organized by the Department of Computer Science of the Eindhoven University of Technology. It was further supported by the following associations and societies: ETAPS e.V., EATCS (European Association for Theoretical Computer Science), EAPLS (European Association for Programming Languages and Systems), and EASST (European Association of Software Science and Technology). The local organization team consisted of Mark van den Brand, Jan Friso Groote (general chair), Margje Mommers, Erik Scheffers, Julien Schmaltz, Erik de Vink, Anton Wijs, Tim Willemse, and Hans Zantema.

The overall planning for ETAPS is the main responsibility of the Steering Committee, and in particular of its Executive Board. The ETAPS Steering Committee consists of an Executive Board and representatives of the individual ETAPS conferences, as well as representatives of EATCS, EAPLS, and EASST. The Executive Board consists of Gilles Barthe (Madrid), Holger Hermanns (Saarbrücken), Joost-Pieter Katoen (chair, Aachen and Twente), Gerald Lüttgen (Bamberg), Vladimiro Sassone (Southampton), and Tarmo Uustalu (Tallinn). Other members of the Steering Committee are: Parosh Abdulla (Uppsala), David Basin (Zurich), Giuseppe Castagna (Paris), Marsha Chechik (Toronto), Javier Esparza (Munich), Jan Friso Groote (Eindhoven), Reiko Heckel (Leicester), Marieke Huisman (Twente), Bart Jacobs (Nijmegen), Paul Klint (Amsterdam), Jens Knoop (Vienna), Kim G. Larsen (Aalborg), Axel Legay (Rennes), Christof Löding (Aachen), Matteo Maffei (Saarbrücken), Pasquale Malacaria (London), Tiziana Margaria (Limerick), Andrzej Murawski (Warwick), Catuscia Palamidessi (Palaiseau), Frank Piessens (Leuven), Jean-Francois Raskin (Brussels), Mark Ryan (Birmingham), Julia Rubin (Massachussetts), Don Sannella (Edinburgh), Perdita Stevens (Edinburgh), Gabriele Taentzer (Marburg), Peter Thiemann (Freiburg), Luca Vigano (London), Igor Walukiewicz (Bordeaux), Andrzej Wąsowski (Copenhagen), and Hongseok Yang (Oxford).

I sincerely thank all ETAPS Steering Committee members for all their work in making the 19th edition of ETAPS a success. Moreover, thanks to all speakers, attendees, organizers of the satellite workshops, and Springer for their support. Finally, a big thanks to Jan Friso and his local organization team for all their enormous efforts enabling ETAPS to take place in Eindhoven!

January 2016

Joost-Pieter Katoen
ETAPS SC Chair
ETAPS e.V. President

# Preface

TACAS 2016 was the 22nd edition of the International Conference on Tools and Algorithms for the Construction and Analysis of Systems conference series. The conference took place during April, 2016, on the campus of the Eindhoven University of Technology as part of the 19th European Joint Conferences on Theory and Practice of Software (ETAPS 2016).

TACAS is a forum for researchers, developers, and users interested in rigorously based tools and algorithms for the construction and analysis of systems. The conference aims to bridge the gaps between different communities with this common interest and to support them in their quest to improve the utility, reliability, flexibility, and efficiency of tools and algorithms for building systems.

The research areas covered by TACAS 2016 include specification and verification techniques; software and hardware verification; analytical techniques for real-time, hybrid, or stochastic systems; analytical techniques for safety, security, or dependability; model-checking; theorem-proving; SAT and SMT solving; static and dynamic program analysis; testing; abstraction techniques for modeling and verification; compositional and refinement-based methodologies; system construction and transformation techniques; tool environments and architectures; tool demonstrations, as well as applications and case studies.

As in former years, TACAS 2016 solicited four types of submissions:

- Research papers, identifying and justifying a principled advance to the theoretical foundations for the construction and analysis of systems, where applicable supported by experimental validation
- Case study papers, reporting on case studies and providing information about the system being studied, the goals of the study, the challenges the system poses to automated analysis, research methodologies and approaches used, the degree to which goals were attained, and how the results can be generalized to other problems and domains
- Regular tool papers, presenting a new tool, a new tool component, or novel extensions to an existing tool, with an emphasis on design and implementation concerns, including software architecture and core data structures, practical applicability, and experimental evaluations
- Short tool demonstration papers, focusing on the usage aspects of tools

This year, 175 papers were submitted to TACAS, among which 157 were research, case study, or tool papers, and 18 were tool demonstration papers. After a rigorous review process followed by an online discussion, the Program Committee accepted 44 full papers and nine tool demonstration papers.

This volume also includes an invited paper by the ETAPS unifying speaker Rupak Majumdar titled "Robots at the Edge of the Cloud."

TACAS 2016 also hosted the 5th International Competition on Software Verification (SV-COMP), chaired and organized by Dirk Beyer. The competition had a record number of participants: 35 verification tools from 16 countries were submitted for the systematic comparative evaluation. This volume includes an overview of the competition results, and short papers describing 14 of the participating tools. These papers were reviewed by a separate Program Committee (PC); each of the papers was assessed by four reviewers. Two sessions in the TACAS program were reserved for the presentation of the results: the summary by the SV-COMP chair and the participating tools by the developer teams.

Many people worked hard and offered their valuable time generously to make TACAS 2016 successful. First of all, the PC chairs would like to thank the 493 researchers from 30 countries who worked hard to complete and submit papers to the conference. In all, 525 reviews (three for each submission) were written by PC members and their 227 external reviewers in order to select the papers to be presented at the conference. Steering Committee members also deserve a special recognition. Without them, a competitive and peer-reviewed international symposium like TACAS simply could not take place. Also, we would like to express a special thanks to Joost-Pieter Katoen, who answered many of our questions during the preparation of TACAS 2016.

Finally, we thank EasyChair for providing us with the infrastructure to manage the submissions, the reviewing process, the PC discussion, and the preparation of the proceedings.

January 2016

Marsha Chechik (TACAS PC Co-chair)
Jean-Francois Raskin (TACAS PC Co-chair)
Radu Mateescu (TACAS Tools Chair)
Dirk Beyer (SV-COMP Chair)

# Organization

## Program Committee

Parosh Aziz Abdulla     Uppsala University, Sweden
Aws Albarghouthi     University of Wisconsin, USA
Christel Baier     Technical University of Dresden, Germany
Nathalie Bertrand     Inria Rennes Bretagne Atlantique, France
Derk Beyer     University of Passau, Germany
Patricia Bouyer     LSV, CNRS and ENS Cachan, France
Radu Calinescu     University of York, UK
Franck Cassez     NICTA, Australia
Pavol Cerny     University of Colorado Boulder, USA
Krishnendu Chatterjee     Institute of Science and Technology (IST)
Marsha Chechik     University of Toronto, Canada (PC Co-chair)
Rance Cleaveland     University of Maryland, USA
Javier Esparza     Technische Universität München, Germany
Pierre Ganty     IMDEA Software Institute, Spain
Radu Grosu     Stony Brook University, USA
Orna Grumberg     Technion and Israel Institute of Technology, Israel
Kim Guldstrand Larsen     Aalborg University, Denmark
Arie Gurfinkel     Carnegie Mellon University, USA
Holger Hermanns     Saarland University, Germany
Zachary Kincaid     University of Toronto, Canada
Daniel Kroening     University of Oxford, UK
Akash Lal     Microsoft Research India
Rupak Majumdar     MPI-SWS
Tiziana Margaria     University of Potsdam, Germany
Nicolas Markey     LSV, CNRS and ENS Cachan, France
Radu Mateescu     Inria Grenoble, France (Tools Chair)
Roland Meyer     University of Kaiserslautern, Germany
Corina Pasareanu     CMU and NASA Ames Research Center, USA
Nir Piterman     University of Leicester, UK
Jean-Francois Raskin     Université Libre de Bruxelles, Belgium (PC Co-chair)
Grigore Rosu     University of Illinois at Urbana-Champaign, USA
Natasha Sharygina     University of Lugano, Switzerland
Bernhard Steffen     University of Dortmund, Germany
Cesare Tinelli     University of Iowa, USA

# Additional Reviewers

Abate, Alessandro
Abraham, Erika
Alberti, Francesco
Alt, Leonardo
Andreychenko, Alexander
André, Étienne
Arbel, Eli
Aronis, Stavros
Artho, Cyrille
Artho, Cyrille Valentin
Atig, Mohamed Faouzi
Avni, Guy
Bacci, Giorgio
Bacci, Giovanni
Badouel, Eric
Bae, Kyungmin
Bainczyk, Alexander
Barbot, Benoit
Ben Sassi, Mohamed Amin
Benes, Nikola
Bogomolov, Sergiy
Botterweck, Goetz
Bozzelli, Laura
Brain, Martin
Brenguier, Romain
Broadbent, Christopher
Brockschmidt, Marc
Brunner, Julian
Bui, Diep
Butkova, Yuliya
Cachera, David
Calin, Georgel
Cattaruzza, Dario
Champion, Adrien
Chen, Yu-Fang
Chini, Peter
Chonev, Ventsislav
Christakis, Maria
Ciobaca, Stefan
Costa Silva, Gabriel
D'Antoni, Loris
D'Osualdo, Emanuele
David, Amélie

David, Cristina
De Boer, Frank
Deligiannis, Pantazis
Dimitrova, Rayna
Doyen, Laurent
Dragoi, Cezara
Dragomir, Iulia
Ellison, Martyn
Emmi, Michael
Farzan, Azadeh
Fedyukovich, Grigory
Felderer, Michael
Ferrer Fioriti, Luis María
Fijalkow, Nathanaël
Finkbeiner, Bernd
Fox, Gereon
Fränzle, Martin
Frömel, Bernhard
Fu, Hongfei
Fuhs, Carsten
Furbach, Florian
Genaim, Samir
Gerasimou, Simos
Giacobbe, Mirco
Giannini, Paola
Golden, Bat-Chen
González De Aledo, Pablo
Gorla, Alessandra
Graf-Brill, Alexander
Griggio, Alberto
Hadarean, Liana
Hague, Matthew
Hashemi, Vahid
Hatefi, Hassan
Heindel, Tobias
Heizmann, Matthias
Herbreteau, Frédéric
Heußner, Alexander
Hoenicke, Jochen
Hoffmann, Philipp
Hojjat, Hossein
Holik, Lukas
Horn, Florian

Howar, Falk
Hyvärinen, Antti
Höftberger, Oliver
Ibsen-Jensen, Rasmus
Ignatiev, Alexey
Isberner, Malte
Jasper, Marc
Jensen, Peter Gjøl
Johnson, Kenneth
Jonsson, Bengt
Jovanović, Dejan
Kahsai, Temesghen
Kanade, Aditya
Kern-Isberner, Gabriele
Kersten, Rody
Khlaaf, Heidy
Kikuchi, Shinji
Klebanov, Vladimir
Klein, Gerwin
Klein, Joachim
Klüppelholz, Sascha
Komuravelli, Anvesh
Kraehmann, Daniel
Krcal, Jan
Krena, Bohuslav
Kuester, Jan-Christoph
Kuperberg, Denis
Lahiri, Shuvendu
Lammich, Peter
Lamprecht, Anna-Lena
Lange, Martin
Laurent, Fribourg
Legunsen, Owolabi
Leonardsson, Carl
Lhote, Nathan
Li, Yi
Li, Yilong
Lime, Didier
Lu, Tianhan
Lucanu, Dorel
Luckow, Kasper
Lukina, Anna
Marescotti, Matteo
Marinescu, Paul
Mayr, Richard
McClurg, Jedidiah

Mebsout, Alain
Meier, Shawn
Meller, Yael
Meyer, Philipp J.
Miculan, Marino
Mikučionis, Marius
Miné, Antoine
Mjeda, Anila
Mohammad Hasani, Ramin
Moore, Brandon
Morgan, Carroll
Mover, Sergio
Mukherjee, Rajdeep
Mullins, John
Muskalla, Sebastian
Müller, Christian
Müller, David
Navas, Jorge A.
Neville, Daniel
Ngo, Tuan Phong
Niksic, Filip
Novotny, Petr
Nyman, Ulrik
Olesen, Mads Chr.
Olsen, Petur
Oualhadj, Youssouf
Park, Daejun
Paskevich, Andrei
Paterson, Colin
Pavlogiannis, Andreas
Pek, Edgar
Phan, Quoc-Sang
Poulsen, Danny Bøgsted
Pérez, Diego
Radhakrishna, Arjun
Rafiq, Yasmeen
Rakamaric, Zvonimir
Rasin, Dan
Rastogi, Aseem
Reynier, Pierre-Alain
Reynolds, Andrew
Rezine, Ahmed
Rezine, Othmane
Rodionova, Alena
Rodriguez, Cesar
Ruemmer, Philipp

Rungta, Neha
Ryzhyk, Leonid
Rüthing, Oliver
S., Krishna
Sadrzadeh, Mehrnoosh
Saivasan, Prakash
Sanchez, Cesar
Sankaranarayanan, Sriram
Sankur, Ocan
Schewe, Sven
Schordan, Markus
Schrammel, Peter
Schwoon, Stefan
Seceleanu, Cristina
Serbanuta, Traian Florin
Serwe, Wendelin
Sharma, Subodh
Sheinvald, Sarai
Sickert, Salomon
Sloane, Tony
Smith, Calvin
Sosnovich, Adi
Srba, Jiri
Srinivasan, Venkatesh Karthik
Stefanescu, Andrei

Stefanescu, Gheorghe
Steffen, Bernhard
Strichman, Ofer
Taankvist, Jakob Haahr
Tarrach, Thorsten
Tizpaz Niari, Saeid
Trivedi, Ashutosh
Trostanetski, Anna
Urban, Caterina
Van Der Meyden, Ron
Velner, Yaron
Vizel, Yakir
Wang, Guodong
Wijs, Anton
Wimmer, Ralf
Wintersteiger, Christoph M.
Wolf, Karsten
Wolff, Sebastian
Woodhouse, Steven
Worrell, James
Xiao, He
Yuan, Yifei
Yuwen, Shijiao
Zetzsche, Georg
Zhang, Yi

# Contents

## Probabilistic and Stochastic Systems II

## Tool Papers I

## Tool Papers II

## Concurrency

## Tool Demos

## Abstraction and Verification II

## Abstraction and Verification III

## Languages and Automata

## Security

## Optimization

## Competition on Software Verification: SV-COMP

# Unifying Talk

# Robots at the Edge of the Cloud

Rupak Majumdar[✉]

Max Planck Institute for Software Systems (MPI-SWS),
Kaiserslautern, Saarbrücken, Germany
rupak@mpi-sws.org

**Abstract.** Computers have come a long way from their roots as fast calculating devices. We live in a world in which computers collect, store, and analyze huge volumes of data. We are seeing the beginnings of a new revolution in the use of computers. In addition to collecting and analyzing data, computers are influencing the physical world and interacting autonomously, and in complex ways, with large groups of humans. These *cyber-physical-social* systems have the potential to dramatically alter the way we lead our lives. However, designing these systems in a reliable way is a difficult problem. In this paper, we enumerate a set of research challenges that have to be overcome in order to realize the potential of cyber-physical-social systems.

## 1 Motivation

The computer has come a long way from its initial role as a fast calculating device. We live in a world where a large number of geographically distributed and physically embedded computing devices increasingly participate in our everyday actions. Our digital activities generate and consume data at unprecedented volumes. This data is collected, stored, and combined in novel ways. Storage, communication, and processing of this data has moved out of individual workstations into large ensembles of geographically distributed computers ("cloud computers") connected via the Internet and dynamically managed for data processing tasks. Data processing in the cloud has revolutionized the way we approach large-scale design and deployment of software systems. Over the past decade, a similar revolution is happening in the monitoring of the physical world through large swarms of sensors wirelessly connected with each other and with a cloud computing backbone (called variously "Internet of Things" (IoT) or "sensory swarm" [31]).

The next wave in this progression is in large-scale interaction with the physical world through autonomous systems with actuation capabilities and symbiotic relationships of these autonomous systems with large groups of humans. These autonomous systems, call them *robots*, will connect wirelessly with each other as well as with the cloud and the sensor swarm. They will interact with large groups of people, and their actuation capabilities will allow them to modify the state of the physical world. For the purposes of this paper, and keeping with marketing practice, let us call this next progression the "Internet of Robots" (IoR).

© Springer-Verlag Berlin Heidelberg 2016
M. Chechik and J.-F. Raskin (Eds.): TACAS 2016, LNCS 9636, pp. 3–13, 2016.
DOI: 10.1007/978-3-662-49674-9_1

The notion of "closing the control loop" on sensor networks is not novel (see, e.g., [44]), and indeed, the whole field of cyber-physical systems studies the interaction between software and the physical world. However, the potential for IoR today, with the computing and sensing infrastructure available through the cloud and IoT, is much greater. On the one hand, we can expect systems with a large number of dynamically interacting autonomous agents co-ordinating through the cloud. On the other hand, we can expect systems in which software agents and humans co-operate towards a common goal. In contrast to the "traditional" view where the human is in charge and the machines perform his or her bidding, the IoR vision is that human agents and software or robotic agents interact equally, or even with robots in charge.

While the IoR vision holds enormous promise, as with other grand visions, realizing it requires overcoming a number of very hard research problems. In this paper, we discuss some challenges for IoR, and posit that implementing the IoR vision is a grand challenge for computer science. We structure the problems in three core directions: challenges in the correct design of core algorithmic components (controller synthesis), challenges in software engineering, and challenges in human-robot interaction.

## 2    Formal Design of Control Systems

At the core of IoR is the notion of *feedback control* of mixed discrete-continuous dynamical systems. Feedback control has a long history in both the continuous world of dynamical systems and in the discrete world of automata theory.

In continuous control, one starts with a model of the system in continuous time, where the continuous state of the system evolves based on the current state, a control input, and a disturbance input. The goal is to provide *feedback* to the system through the control input, that depends on the sensed value of the state, so that the controlled system has "good" properties. Typically, the properties studied in control are stability or performance. When restricted to these properties, under suitable restrictions on the dynamics, methods from continuous control theory show how to synthesize the feedback controller.

In control of discrete systems, usually called *reactive synthesis*, one models the system as a two-player game on graphs, and the goal is to come up with a strategy, a state machine that looks at the history of the game and defines the next move in the game, so that the outcome satisfies "good" properties. Properties are typically specified in a temporal logic such as linear-time temporal logic (LTL) or using automata [17].

The combination of continuous and discrete dynamics leads to *cyber-physical* systems (CPS). In a cyber-physical system, the discrete component ranges over nodes of a graph —as in reactive synthesis— and for each node of the graph, there is a separate continuous dynamics. Cyber-physical systems arise in control problems when one mixes the higher-level logical decision making (e.g., planning a trajectory to reach a goal while avoiding obstacles) with lower-level dynamics (e.g., navigation). At the level of the continuous dynamics, the specification is, as before, related to stability and performance. At the level of the discrete state, the specification is, as in reactive synthesis, given as a temporal logic formula.

The controller for a cyber-physical system combines a strategy at the discrete level with strategies at the continuous level. Traditionally, such controllers would be designed "by hand" and verified through extensive simulation or through symbolic techniques such as model checking. Recent research attempts to synthesize controllers directly from the specification and the model [30,34,46]. Typically, these synthesis techniques compute a finite-state abstraction of the continuous dynamical system and apply reactive synthesis to the abstraction. One step of the discrete strategy —for example, a request to go from one abstract state to the next— can be refined to a continuous controller in the original continuous system. Under certain assumptions on the dynamics, one can show that the original and the abstracted systems are related by an $\varepsilon$-bisimulation relation [24,46]. This guarantees that controllers synthesized on the abstraction can be implemented on the original system.

While initial results on controller synthesis through abstractions is encouraging, there are several difficult technical challenges before the techniques can be applied more widely and to larger classes of systems. We outline some key research questions.

*Scalability of Synthesis.* The major challenge in using formal synthesis techniques is their scalability. The abstraction of a continuous system yields a discrete system which is exponential in the dimension. In addition, reactive synthesis algorithms, even with symbolic implementations, are expensive (cubic for broad classes of properties [13], but doubly exponential for full linear temporal logic [37]). When the modeling paradigm is extended to include probabilities or other numerical parameters, the problem is even harder.

Recent approaches attempt to get around the scalability by adapting receding horizon control techniques for temporal logic [52]. There are also some interesting initial approaches based on deductive approaches [20], compositional synthesis [38,41] and hierarchical decompositions [43]. In addition to techniques for state-space reduction, an important open direction is to handle dynamically changing specifications in open environments.

*Notions of Robustness.* A system is *robust* if small changes to its inputs cause small changes in its outputs. Robustness is a classical notion in control theory and a natural requirement when designing control systems. However, appropriate notions of robustness are difficult to obtain for cyber-physical systems. Physical systems are modeled and analyzed using continuous mathematics and concepts such as continuity are readily available to help describe robustness. On the other hand, discrete systems are modeled and analyzed using discrete mathematics for which it is far less obvious what a meaningful notion of robustness can be. There are several current attempts to define notions of robustness [11,47]. However, a challenge is to come up with a definition that is broadly applicable and has good algorithmic properties.

*Quantitative Properties.* Related to robustness are *quantitative* specification languages for synthesis. A specification in LTL classifies system behaviors as "true" or "false." In many cases, such specifications are too strict, and it is preferable to use a quantitative formalism that associates a numerical score with system behaviors. Recent work in the theory of quantitative languages and synthesis [12,14,16], in quantitative logics such as signal temporal logic (STL) [21], and in metrics on systems such as the Skorokhod metric [19,35], move in this direction. The use of quantitative specifications also opens the door to more data-driven approaches that optimize or learn system parameters [23,51]. Combinations of learning with synthesis is an interesting emerging area.

*System Co-design.* The controller is one component of a complex stack integrating sensing, computation, communication, and actuation running several control loops at various different levels of granularity. An end-to-end design, which co-designs the controller along with other components of the system can achieve better resource usage than one which designs each component in isolation. For example, by designing a controller robust to intermittent steps in which the control input is not computed, one can schedule more processes in the same processor without sacrificing control performance [36,42,45]. At the same time, co-design techniques may involve loss of modularity in the design. It is a challenging question whether tradeoffs between design choices of different components can be captured in an abstract interface —controller-scheduler co-design is one example where this is possible [42].

Co-design also requires reasoning about the underlying architecture. For example, in order to guarantee a certain system performance, it may be necessary to provide bounds on worst case execution times or worst case latencies. This is a hard problem, and may require a fundamental redesign of architectural elements for cyber-physical systems [7,33].

Co-design considers the various algorithmic components of a system together. A new set of challenges arise when we consider the software implementation of a system, which we describe next.

## 3   Programming Model and the Software Stack

Formal synthesis and verification is a key step towards more reliable and large-scale IoR systems. However, synthesis of controllers is only the "core" algorithm. For end-to-end development, these algorithms must be embedded in a software stack. We now discuss the challenges of developing programming models and software infrastructure for IoR applications.

We start with an analogy in the cloud computing scenario. Cloud computing abstracts the computing, distribution, communication, and storage needs of a large-scale, distributed application. The end user can write computational tasks focusing on the functionality. The cloud infrastructure manages physical resources for the computation such as compute-servers, distribution, and fault tolerance. The cloud can dynamically provision additional resources for computation and storage, or distribute or replicate a data structure across geographically separated infrastructure. However, for the most part, this is transparent to the user application.

A dominant application on the cloud is statistical analysis of large data sets. For this application, there is a declarative programming model (querying data in specialized languages such as Pig Latin [5] or HiveQL [4]) that compiles into a computational model (map-reduce [3,18] or Spark [6]) for fast execution on parallel machines. The programmer's view of the data is abstracted to centralized database tables, and the query is made at a logical level. The infrastructure takes care of executing the "program" on distributed and dynamic infrastructure. This includes not only scheduling parallel jobs for low latency but also fault tolerance and replication. While not a panacea for all applications, the abstraction enables the separation between the programming abstraction (logical operations on a dataset) and the infrastructure on which the operations are performed.

We lack a corresponding "programming model" for large-scale IoR applications. Currently, applications are written in low level programming languages and use ad hoc mechanisms to implement layering between logical task models and the underlying continuous controllers. Communication is mediated through middleware such as ROS [39], but the resulting message-passing programs are difficult to design and verify, especially when the number of components grow large and when components can dynamically enter or leave the system.

A key design challenge for IoR is to develop programming tools for cyber-physical systems. We outline some research challenges in this direction.

*Programming Models and Run-time Systems.* One major success of programming models we use today is that they abstract from the real world. The "step" of a Turing machine is a purely logical step. When we program, we do not, for most applications, reason about the details of the physical world. This abstraction breaks when we design cyber-physical systems where the controller must react to events within a given (real) time bound. Indeed, dealing with the real world and real time is one reason designing and verifying these systems is so difficult. The difficulty is compounded when we consider large ensembles of autonomous agents concurrently sensing and actuating the physical world. It is yet unclear what programming models will enable ordinary developers design large-scale IoR applications. One possibility is the programming idiom of actors [1], extended to faithfully represent interactions in the physical world. A different possibility is a specialized programming model such as the globally asynchronous locally synchronous (GALS) model that abstracts out the part of the timing behavior that the underlying compiler and run time systems enforce [9,15,49]. Very likely, declarative techniques to specify controller behaviors —e.g., in LTL or STL— will be integrated within the programming model; the compiler will be expected to generate the code that enforces these behaviors at run time.

Developing languages, compilers, and run-time systems for large-scale sensing, co-ordination, computing, and actuation is an outstanding open problem.

*Managing Uncertainty.* A second challenge is to incorporate uncertainty as a first-class construct in the language. IoR applications will necessarily work in environments that are not completely specified, or whose behaviors may change over time in unexpected ways. There is a lot of recent work on introducing uncertainty and probabilistic reasoning in programming languages [26,27]. Integration of uncertainty management with controller synthesis in a programming model is likely to be the next step.

*Managing Dynamic Resources.* Embedded control systems are currently programmed with well-defined resource requirements at compile time. Since their correctness depends on real-time requirements, a conservative static analysis bounds required resources and pre-allocates these resources. Such a programming model can be overly pessimistic in dynamic environments where requirements change and resources can be provisioned dynamically. It is a challenge to set up a programming model and run-time where critical resources are statically allocated (to ensure basic safety) but other resources can be dynamically provisioned.

## 4    Cyber-Physical-Social Systems

In many IoR applications, groups of autonomous agents interact with humans. For example, in an autonomous vehicle, the human may be kept in the loop to compensate for driving conditions not familiar to the autonomous driver. In a traffic management scenario involving both autonomous and human drivers, a central server may provide route suggestions to ensure optimal flow of traffic based on dynamically collected data, while individual drivers —human and autonomous— may decide to follow the suggestions or not, based on individual rational preferences. In an energy distribution scenario, human-operated electric vehicles may be used to store energy and redistribute it in the grid. In these and many other emerging scenarios, humans interact closely with computers and controllers in a dynamic fashion [29]. These systems raise a number of new challenges in design, implementation, and analysis.

First, the interaction between humans and computers may not be "one way" —the human initiating a task that the controller implements— but involve cooperation between the two, and even be initiated by the controller. Second, formal reasoning about such systems requires understanding social behavior and the incentives that enable human participants to act in a way that optimizes the overall system behavior. Third, these systems must implement infrastructure to manage privacy, accountability, compliance, and reputation. We focus on two directions.

*Specification Challenges.* Computers can follow algorithms that enforce logically-specified behaviors. Unfortunately, it is hard to enforce similar logical specifications for human behaviors. Instead, humans participate in activities motivated by incentives, such as the desire for a particular beneficial outcome, or extrinsic motivations such as money or reputation. Thus, the design of cyber-social systems requires not only logical specifications but also incentive mechanisms that ensure the participants engage in behaviors that are beneficial to the system. There is some initial work on the modeling of human participants in human-in-the-loop control (see, e.g., [22,32]), but a unified science for formal design of cyber-physical-social systems remains a big challenge. Traditionally, design of protocols for rational agents is the realm of (algorithmic) mechanism design. An open question is whether approaches to synthesis from control, reactive synthesis, and mechanism design can be combined profitably.

At the programming level, human-agent collectives also introduce new challenges. First, the natural interaction of humans with robots is not at the level of code or of logical specifications but at the level of natural languages or gestural user interfaces. Second, the programming model has to support incentive mechanisms that allow groups of humans to come together for a system task, in cooperation with autonomous participants. Designing such programming abstractions that interoperate between code, natural user interfaces, and incentive mechanisms is a hard problem.

We are encouraged by some programming abstractions that are emerging in projects such as participatory sensing [40,48] and crowd-sourced computation (such as the Mechanical Turk API [2] and its embedding in programming platforms [10,50]). It remains to be seen how such platforms can be integrated with control and co-ordination capabilities.

*Privacy, Accountability, and Trust.* A system that allows large scale interaction between humans and autonomous agents also leads to social and ethical problems. Human social actions often follow incentives such as social responsibility and reputation: we behave in the way we do because we care about how our actions are perceived by others, and we are held accountable for our interactions with other humans. It is unclear how norms of social behavior change when we interact with robots. Can we "hurt the feelings" of an autonomous controller by ignoring its suggestion? Moreover, when things go wrong, due to errors or malicious behavior, how is accountability shared between human participants and autonomous ones? Many of these questions involve social sciences or law in addition to engineering and computer science.

Related to the problem of accountability is the problem of privacy. The use of information relating to individuals may be necessary to engineer a system to its optimal outcomes, but revealing personal information may not be allowed due to individual preferences or regulatory limitations. The tradeoff between accountability and privacy, or related tradeoffs between privacy and trust, must be understood as we design more complex systems [8]. This problem is already relevant in social computing systems without physical controllers; it takes a larger role in complex applications where robots actuate the physical world.

## 5   Conclusion

IoR applications have the potential to transform the way we interact with computers and with each other. The road to reliable and massive-scale IoR applications is long, and has many exciting research challenges, both technical and social. While the list of problems in this paper is partial, they already demonstrate the richness of the research landscape.

**Acknowledgements..** This work is partially funded by the ERC Synergy grant ImPACT. Thanks to Dmitry Chistikov, Samira Farahani, and Anne-Kathrin Schmuck for useful discussions on these topics. I was inspired by several excellent overview articles on the topic of this paper [28,29,31].

# References

1. Agha, G.A.: ACTORS - A Model of Concurrent Computation in Distributed Systems. MIT Press series in artificial intelligence. MIT Press, Cambridge (1990)
2. Amazon mechanical turk. https://aws.amazon.com/documentation/mturk/
3. Apache hadoop. https://hadoop.apache.org/
4. Apache hive. https://hive.apache.org/
5. Apache pig. https://pig.apache.org/
6. Apache spark. https://spark.apache.org/
7. Axer, P., Ernst, R., Falk, H., Girault, A., Grund, D., Guan, N., Jonsson, B., Marwedel, P., Reineke, J., Rochange, C., Sebastian, M., von Hanxleden, R., Wilhelm, R., Yi, W.: Building timing predictable embedded systems. ACM Trans. Embedded Comput. Syst. **13**(4), 82:1–82:37 (2014)
8. Backes, M., Druschel, P., Majumdar, R., Weikum, G.: Impact: privacy, accountability, compliance, and trust in tomorrow's Internet. ERC Synergy Grant White Paper (2015). http://www.impact-erc.eu/src/doc/imPACT-whitepaper.pdf
9. Balarin, F., Chiodo, M., Giusto, P., Hsieh, H., Jurecska, A., Lavagno, L., Passerone, C., Sangiovanni-Vincentelli, A., Sentovich, E., Suzuki, K., Tabbara, B.: The Polis Approach. The Springer International Series in Engineering and Computer Science, vol. 404. Kluwer Academic, Dordrecht (1997)
10. Bernstein, M.S., Chi, E.H., Chilton, L.B., Hartmann, B., Kittur, A., Miller, R.C.: Crowdsourcing, human computation: systems, studies and platforms. In: Tan, D.S., Amershi, S., Begole, B., Kellogg, W.A., Tungare, M. (eds.) Proceedings of the International Conference on Human Factors in Computing Systems, CHI 2011, Extended Abstracts Volume, Vancouver, BC, Canada, 7–12 May, 2011, pp. 53–56. ACM (2011)
11. Bloem, R., Chatterjee, K., Greimel, K., Henzinger, T.A., Hofferek, G., Jobstmann, B., Könighofer, B., Könighofer, R.: Synthesizing robust systems. Acta Inf. **51**(3–4), 193–220 (2014)
12. Bloem, R., Chatterjee, K., Henzinger, T.A., Jobstmann, B.: Better quality in synthesis through quantitative objectives. In: Bouajjani, A., Maler, O. (eds.) CAV 2009. LNCS, vol. 5643, pp. 140–156. Springer, Heidelberg (2009)
13. Bloem, R., Jobstmann, B., Piterman, N., Pnueli, A., Sa'ar, Y.: Synthesis of reactive(1) designs. J. Comput. Syst. Sci. **78**(3), 911–938 (2012)
14. Cerný, P., Henzinger, T.A., Radhakrishna, A.: Simulation distances. Theor. Comput. Sci. **413**(1), 21–35 (2012)
15. Chapiro, D.M.: Globally asynchronous locally synchronous systems. PhD thesis (1984)
16. Chatterjee, K., Doyen, L., Henzinger, T.A.: Quantitative languages. ACM Trans. Comput. Log. **11**(4), 23 (2010)

17. Clarke, E.M., Grumberg, O., Peled, D.: Model Checking. MIT Press, Cambridge (1999)
18. Dean, J., Ghemawat, S.: Mapreduce: simplified data processing on large clusters. Commun. ACM **51**(1), 107–113 (2008)
19. Deshmukh, J.V., Majumdar, R., Prabhu, V.S.: Quantifying conformance using the skorokhod metric. In: Kroening, D., Păsăreanu, C.S. (eds.) CAV 2015. LNCS, vol. 9207, pp. 234–250. Springer, Heidelberg (2015)
20. Dimitrova, R., Majumdar, R.: Deductive control synthesis for alternating-time logics. In: Mitra, T., Reineke, J. (eds.) 2014 International Conference on Embedded Software, EMSOFT 2014, New Delhi, India, 12–17 October, 2014, pp. 14:1–14:10. ACM (2014)
21. Donzé, A., Maler, O.: Robust satisfaction of temporal logic over real-valued signals. In: Chatterjee, K., Henzinger, T.A. (eds.) FORMATS 2010. LNCS, vol. 6246, pp. 92–106. Springer, Heidelberg (2010)
22. Feng, L., Wiltsche, C., Humphrey, L., Topcu, U.: Controller synthesis for autonomous systems interacting with human operators. In: Bayen, A.M., Branicky, M.S. (eds.) Proceedings of the ACM/IEEE Sixth International Conference on Cyber-Physical Systems, Seattle, WA, USA, 14–16 April, pp. 70–79. ACM (2015)
23. Fu, J., Topcu, U.: Probably approximately correct MDP learning, control with temporal logic constraints. In: Fox, D., Kavraki, L.E., Kurniawati, H. (eds.) Robotics: Science and Systems X, University of California, Berkeley, USA, 12–16 July, 2014 (2014)
24. Girard, A., Pappas, G.J.: Approximate bisimulation: a bridge between computer science and control theory. Eur. J. Control **17**(5–6), 568–578 (2011)
25. Girard, A., Sankaranarayanan, S. (eds.) Proceedings of the 18th International Conference on Hybrid Systems: Computation and Control, HSCC 2015, Seattle, WA, USA, 14–16 April, 2015. ACM (2015)
26. Gordon, A.D., Aizatulin, M., Borgström, J., Claret, G., Graepel, T., Nori, A.V., Rajamani, S.K., Russo, C.V.: A model-learner pattern for bayesian reasoning. In: Giacobazzi, R., Cousot, R. (eds.) The 40th Annual ACM SIGPLAN-SIGACT Symposium on Principles of Programming Languages, POPL 2013, Rome, Italy - 23–25 January, pp. 403–416. ACM (2013)
27. Gordon, A.D., Henzinger, T.A., Nori, A.V., Rajamani, S.K.: Probabilistic programming. In: Herbsleb, J.D., Dwyer, M.B. (eds.) Proceedings of the on Future of Software Engineering, FOSE 2014, Hyderabad, India, 31 May - 7 June, 2014, pp. 167–181. ACM (2014)
28. Henzinger, T.A., Sifakis, J.: The discipline of embedded systems design. IEEE Comput. **40**(10), 32–40 (2007)
29. Jennings, N.R., Moreau, L., Nicholson, D., Ramchurn, S.D., Roberts, S.J., Rodden, T., Rogers, A.: Human-agent collectives. Commun. ACM **57**(12), 80–88 (2014)
30. Kress-Gazit, H., Fainekos, G.E., Pappas, G.J.: Temporal-logic-based reactive mission and motion planning. IEEE Trans. Robot. **25**(6), 1370–1381 (2009)
31. Lee, E.A., Hartmann, B., Kubiatowicz, J., Rosing, T.S., Wawrzynek, J., Wessel, D., Rabaey, J.M., Pister, K., Sangiovanni-Vincentelli, A.L., Seshia, S.A., Blaauw, D., Dutta, P., Fu, K., Guestrin, C., Taskar, B., Jafari, R., Jones, D.L., Kumar, V., Mangharam, R., Pappas, G.J., Murray, R.M., Rowe, A.: The swarm at the edge of the cloud. IEEE Des. Test **31**(3), 8–20 (2014)
32. Li, W., Sadigh, D., Sastry, S.S., Seshia, S.A.: Synthesis for human-in-the-loop control systems. In: Ábrahám, E., Havelund, K. (eds.) TACAS 2014 (ETAPS). LNCS, vol. 8413, pp. 470–484. Springer, Heidelberg (2014)

33. Liu, I., Reineke, J., Broman, D., Zimmer, M., Lee, E.A.: A PRET microarchitecture implementation with repeatable timing and competitive performance. In: 30th International IEEE Conference on Computer Design, ICCD 2012, Montreal, QC, Canada, 30 September- 3 October, 2012, pp. 87–93. IEEE Computer Society (2012)

34. Liu, J., Ozay, N., Topcu, U., Murray, R.M.: Synthesis of reactive switching protocols from temporal logic specifications. IEEE Trans. Automat. Contr. **58**(7), 1771–1785 (2013)

35. Majumdar, R., Prabhu, V.S.: Computing the skorokhod distance between polygonal traces. In: Girard, A., Sankaranarayanan, S. (eds.) [25], pp. 199–208

36. Majumdar, R., Saha, I., Zamani, M.: Synthesis of minimal-error control software. In: Jerraya, A., Carloni, L.P., Maraninchi, F., Regehr, J. (eds.) Proceedings of the 12th International Conference on Embedded Software, EMSOFT 2012, part of the Eighth Embedded Systems Week, ESWeek 2012, Tampere, Finland, 7–12 October, 2012, pp. 123–132. ACM (2012)

37. Pnueli, A., Rosner, R.: On the synthesis of a reactive module. In: Conference Record of the Sixteenth Annual ACM Symposium on Principles of Programming Languages, Austin, Texas, USA, 11–13 January, pp. 179–190. ACM (1989)

38. Pola, G., Pepe, P., Di Benedetto, M.D.: Compositional symbolic models for networks of incrementally stable control systems. CoRR, abs/1404.0048 (2015)

39. Quigley, M., Conley, K., Gerkey, B.P., Faust, J., Foote, T., Leibs, J., Wheeler, R., Andrew, Y. Ng. ROS: an open-source robot operating system. In: ICRA Workshop on Open Source Software (2009)

40. Reddy, S., Mun, M.Y., Burke, J., Estrin, D., Hansen, M.H., Srivastava, M.B.: Using mobile phones to determine transportation modes. TOSN **6**(2), 23 (2010)

41. Rungger, M., Zamani, M.: Compositional construction of approximate abstractions. In: Girard, A., Sankaranarayanan, S. (eds.) [25], pp. 68–77

42. Saha, I., Baruah, S., Majumdar, R.: Dynamic scheduling for networked control systems. In: Girard, A., Sankaranarayanan, S. (eds.) [25], pp. 98–107

43. Schmuck, A.-K., Majumdar, R.: Dynamic hierarchical reactive controller synthesis. CoRR, abs/1510.07246 (2015)

44. Sinopoli, B., Sharp, C., Schenato, L., Schaffert, S., Sastry, S.: Distributed control applications within sensor networks. IEEE Proc. **91**(8), 1235–1246 (2003)

45. Soudbakhsh, D., Phan, L.T.X., Sokolsky, O., Lee, I., Annaswamy, A.: Co-design of control and platform with dropped signals. In: Lu, C., Kumar, P.R., Stoleru, R. (eds.) ACM/IEEE 4th International Conference on Cyber-Physical Systems (with CPS Week ), ICCPS 2013, Philadelphia, PA, USA, 8–11 April, 2013, pp. 129–140. ACM (2013)

46. Tabuada, P.: Verification and Control of Hybrid Systems - A Symbolic Approach. Springer, Heidelberg (2009)

47. Tabuada, P., Caliskan, S.Y., Rungger, M., Majumdar, R.: Towards robustness for cyber-physical systems. IEEE Trans. Automat. Contr. **59**(12), 3151–3163 (2014)

48. Tangmunarunkit, H., Hsieh, C.-K., Longstaff, B., Nolen, S., Jenkins Ketcham, J., Ketcham, C., Selsky, J., Alquaddoomi, F., George, D., Kang, J., Khalapyan, Z., Ooms, J., Ramanathan, N., Estrin, D.: Ohmage: a general and extensible end-to-end participatory sensing platform. ACM TIST **6**(3), 38 (2015)

49. Tripakis, S., Pinello, C., Benveniste, A., Sangiovanni-Vincentelli, A.L., Caspi, P., Di Natale, M.: Implementing synchronous models on loosely time triggered architectures. IEEE Trans. Comput. **57**(10), 1300–1314 (2008)

50. Trushkowsky, B., Kraska, T., Sarkar, P.: Answering enumeration queries with the crowd. Commun. ACM **59**(1), 118–127 (2016)

51. Wen, M., Ehlers, R., Topcu, U.: Correct-by-synthesis reinforcement learning with temporal logic constraints. CoRR, abs/1503.01793 (2015)
52. Wongpiromsarn, T., Topcu, U., Murray, R.M.: Receding horizon control for temporal logic specifications. In: Johansson, K.H., Yi, W. (eds.) Proceedings of the 13th ACM International Conference on Hybrid Systems: Computation and Control, HSCC 2010, Stockholm, Sweden, 12–15 April, 2010, pp. 101–110. ACM (2010)

# Abstraction and Verification I

# Finding Recurrent Sets with Backward Analysis and Trace Partitioning

Alexey Bakhirkin$^{(\boxtimes)}$ and Nir Piterman

Department of Computer Science, University of Leicester, Leicester, UK
abakhirkin@gmail.com, nir.piterman@le.ac.uk

**Abstract.** We propose an abstract-interpretation-based analysis for recurrent sets. A recurrent set is a set of states from which the execution of a program cannot or might not (as in our case) escape. A recurrent set is a part of a program's non-termination proof (that needs to be complemented by reachability analysis). We find recurrent sets by performing a potentially over-approximate backward analysis that produces an initial candidate. We then perform over-approximate forward analysis on the candidate to check and refine it and ensure soundness. In practice, the analysis relies on trace partitioning that predicts future paths through the program that non-terminating executions will take. Using our technique, we were able to find recurrent sets in many benchmarks found in the literature including some that, to our knowledge, cannot be handled by existing tools. In addition, we note that typically, analyses that search for recurrent sets are applied to linear under-approximations of programs or employ some form of non-approximate numeric reasoning. In contrast, our analysis uses standard abstract-interpretation techniques and is potentially applicable to a larger class of abstract domains (and therefore – programs).

## 1 Introduction

Termination is a fundamental property of software routines. The majority of code is required to terminate (e.g., dispatch routines of device drivers or other event-driven code, GPU programs) and the existence of a non-terminating behavior is a severe bug that might freeze a device, an entire system [1], or cause a multi-region cloud service disruption [2]. The problem of proving *termination* has seen much attention lately [15,16,33], but the techniques are sound and hence necessarily incomplete. That is, failure to prove termination does not imply the existence of non-terminating behaviors. Hence, proving *non-termination* is an interesting complementary problem.

Several modern analyses [8,13,14,26] characterize non-terminating behaviors with a notion of *recurrent set*, i.e., a set of states from which an execution of the program or fragment cannot or might not escape (there exist multiple definitions). In this paper, we focus on the notion of an *existential recurrent set* – a set of states, s.t., from every state in the set there exists at least one non-terminating execution. Typically, the analyses that find existential recurrent

© Springer-Verlag Berlin Heidelberg 2016
M. Chechik and J.-F. Raskin (Eds.): TACAS 2016, LNCS 9636, pp. 17–35, 2016.
DOI: 10.1007/978-3-662-49674-9_2

sets and/or prove non-termination are applied to linear *under*-approximations of programs [13] and/or employ some form of non-approximate numeric reasoning, e.g., using an SMT-solver as in [12], or applying Farkas' lemma as (to our knowledge) in [10]. This allows the analyses to produce genuine recurrent sets. In the context of abstract interpretation (that may go beyond numeric reasoning), under-approximation is problematic. For example, as we show later, fixed-point characterization of an existential recurrent set involves set union, and in most abstract domains it is hard to define an under-approximate join operation.

In this paper, we propose a sound abstract-interpretation-based analysis that finds existential recurrent sets via approximate reasoning. The proposed analysis works in two steps. First, we perform approximate (potentially, over-approximate) backward analysis to find a *candidate recurrent set*. An important technique that allows finding successful candidates is *trace partitioning* (for trace partitioning in forward analysis, see [29]). Then, we perform over-approximate forward analysis on the candidate to check and refine it and ensure soundness. We define the analysis for imperative programs without procedures, and we apply it separately for every loop of the program (i.e., every strongly connected component of the program graph). We evaluated the analysis on the test set [3] of Invel [35], on non-terminating programs from the SV-COMP 2015 [4] termination category, and on a set of non-deterministic numeric programs that we produced ourselves. In this paper, we make a number of assumptions on the memory domain. In particular, we assume that there exists a meet operation that allows backward analysis to build a descending chain; then, we use lower widening to ensure convergence of backward analysis. Non-numeric domains may employ different techniques. For example, in shape analysis with 3-valued logic [31], convergence is due to the use of a finite domain of *bounded structures*. Our backward analysis would need to be modified to be applicable to this and similar domains.

Finally, we note that finding a recurrent set is a *sub-problem* of proving non-termination (in this paper, by proving non-termination we mean proving the existence of at least one non-terminating execution). To prove non-termination, we would need to show that a recurrent set is reachable from the program entry which we *do not* address in this paper for practical reasons. In theory, our analysis may find a recurrent set in any program or fragment (not necessarily strongly connected), and if the inferred set contains an initial program state, this proves the existence of non-terminating behaviours. In practice, we have so far obtained satisfactory results only with finding recurrent sets of individual loops. There also exists work on showing feasibility of abstract counterexamples (including, for non-numeric abstract domains [9]), and techniques from that area would also be applicable to show reachability of a recurrent set.

## 2    Background

We use 1 and 0 to mean logical truth and falsity respectively. We use Kleene's 3-valued logic [25] to represent truth values of state formulas in abstract states and sets of concrete states. The logic uses a set of three values $\mathcal{K} = \{0, {}^1\!/_2, 1\}$ meaning *false*, *maybe*, and *true* respectively. $\mathcal{K}$ is arranged in partial *information order* $\sqsubseteq_{\mathcal{K}}$, s.t. 0 and 1 are incomparable, $0 \sqsubseteq_{\mathcal{K}} {}^1\!/_2$, and $1 \sqsubseteq_{\mathcal{K}} {}^1\!/_2$. For $k_1, k_2 \in \mathcal{K}$, the least upper bound $\sqcup_{\mathcal{K}}$ is s.t. $k_1 \sqcup_{\mathcal{K}} k_2 = k_1$ if $k_1 = k_2$, and ${}^1\!/_2$ otherwise. For a lattice $\mathcal{L}$ ordered by $\preccurlyeq$ and a monotonic function $F\colon \mathcal{L} \to \mathcal{L}$, we use $\mathrm{lfp}_{\preccurlyeq} F$ to denote the least fixed point of $F$ and $\mathrm{gfp}_{\preccurlyeq} F$ to denote the greatest fixed point.

**States, Statements, and Programs.** Let $\mathbb{M}$ be the set of *memory states*. A memory state may map program variables to their values, describe the shape of the heap, etc. A *memory-state formula* $\theta$ denotes a set of memory states $[\![\theta]\!] \subseteq \mathbb{M}$. In this paper, the formulas will usually be conjunctions of linear inequalities over the program variables. E.g., the formula $x > 0$ will denote the set of memory states where $x$ is positive. We say that a memory state $m \in \mathbb{M}$ satisfies $\theta$ if $m \in [\![\theta]\!]$. For a memory-state formula $\theta$ and a set of memory states $M \subseteq \mathbb{M}$, the *value* of $\theta$ over $M$ is defined as: $\mathrm{eval}(\theta, M) = 1$ if $M \subseteq [\![\theta]\!]$; $\mathrm{eval}(\theta, M) = 0$ if $M \neq \varnothing \wedge M \cap [\![\theta]\!] = \varnothing$; $\mathrm{eval}(\theta, M) = {}^1\!/_2$ otherwise. That is, a formula evaluates to 1 in a *set* of memory states if all the memory states in the set satisfy the formula; to 0 if the set is non-empty and no memory states in the set satisfy the formula; and to ${}^1\!/_2$ if some memory states satisfy the formula and some do not.

Let $\mathbb{C}$ be the set of *atomic statements*. For a statement $C \in \mathbb{C}$, its *input-output relation* is $T_{\mathbb{M}}(C) \subseteq \mathbb{M} \times \mathbb{M}$. A pair of memory states $(m, m') \in T_{\mathbb{M}}(C)$, iff it is possible to produce $m'$ by executing $C$ in $m$. We assume that $\mathbb{C}$ includes (but is not limited to):

(i) a passive statement *skip* with $T_{\mathbb{M}}(skip) = \{(m, m) \mid m \in \mathbb{M}\}$; and
(ii) an assumption statement $[\theta]$ for every memory-state formula $\theta$, with $T_{\mathbb{M}}([\theta]) = \{(m, m) \mid m \in [\![\theta]\!]\}$. The main use of assumption statements is to represent branch and loop conditions.

What other the statements are in $\mathbb{C}$ depends on the class of programs we're working with; e.g., for numeric programs, $\mathbb{C}$ may include assignments of the form $x = expr$.

We assume that for other atomic statements, their input-output relations are given. We require that for every non-assumption statement $C \in \mathbb{C}$, the input-output relation of $C$ is left-total, i.e., for every memory state $m \in \mathbb{M}$, there exists a successor state $m' \in \mathbb{M}$, s.t., $(m, m') \in T_{\mathbb{M}}(C)$. In this paper, we do not discuss the analysis of unsafe programs, but if executing $C$ in some $m \in \mathbb{M}$ may *fail*, we assume that there exists a distinguished *error memory state* $\varepsilon$, s.t. $(m, \varepsilon) \in T_{\mathbb{M}}(C)$. In this paper, we work with programs that manipulate numeric variables, most often (but not necessarily) integer-valued. Thus, given the set of program variables $\mathbb{V}$, we can assume $\mathbb{M} = (\mathbb{V} \to \mathbb{Z}) \cup \{\varepsilon\}$.

A *program* $\mathbb{P}$ is a graph $(\mathbb{L}, \vdash, \mathbb{E}, \mathfrak{c})$ where $\mathbb{L}$ is a finite set of *program locations* that are vertices of the graph; $\vdash \in \mathbb{L}$ is a distinguished *initial location*; $\mathbb{E} \subseteq \mathbb{L} \times \mathbb{L}$ is a set of *edges*; and $\mathfrak{c}\colon \mathbb{E} \to \mathbb{C}$ labels edges with atomic statements. A location without outgoing edges is a *final location*. Intuitively, an execution of the program terminates iff it reaches a final location. For a location $l \in \mathbb{L}$, the *successors* of $l$

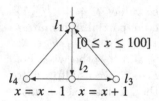

**Fig. 1.** Loop with non-deterministic branching.

is the set $succ(l) = \{l' \in \mathbb{L} \mid (l, l') \in \mathbb{E}\}$. Note that for $l, l' \in \mathbb{L}$, we allow at most one edge from $l$ to $l'$. This simplifies the presentation, but does not restrict the allowed class of programs.

An example of a program is shown in Fig. 1. It is a loop where in every iteration, the execution makes a non-deterministic choice: whether to increment or decrement the variable $x$ (thus, $\mathbb{V} = \{x\}$). The set of location $\mathbb{L} = \{l_1, \cdots, l_4\}$, the initial location $l_\vdash = l_1$.

The program does not have a final location and can be assumed to be a fragment of a larger program (as discussed later, our analysis works with such fragments). Also note how we cannot have multiple edges from $l_2$ to $l_1$, and we use locations $l_3$ and $l_4$ to work around that (for the edges displayed without a label, we assume the label *skip*).

Set $\mathbb{S} = \mathbb{L} \times \mathbb{M}$ is the set of *program states*. We say that a program state $s \in \mathbb{S}$ is final iff $s = (l, m)$ for a final location $l \in \mathbb{L}$ and some memory state $m \in \mathbb{M}$. For a program $\mathbb{P}$, the *transition relation on program states* $T_{\mathbb{S}}(\mathbb{P}) \subseteq \mathbb{S} \times \mathbb{S}$ is s.t. a pair of program states $((l, m), (l', m')) \in T_{\mathbb{S}}(\mathbb{P})$ iff one of the following holds: (i) $(l, l') \in \mathbb{E}$ and $(m, m') \in T_{\mathbb{M}}(\mathfrak{c}(l, l'))$; or (ii) $l$ is final, $l' = l$, and $m' = m$. That is, the transition relation consists of pairs of program states $(s, s')$, s.t. it is possible to reach $s'$ by executing an atomic statement from $s$ or by staying in the same final state.

**Traces and Executions.** To use trace partitioning, we need to be able to reason not only about memory states and locations, but also about traces. A *path* is a pair $(p, i) \in \mathbb{L}^{\mathbb{N}} \times \mathbb{N}$, where $p = \langle l_0, l_1, l_2, \ldots \rangle \in \mathbb{L}^{\mathbb{N}}$ is an *infinite* sequence of locations, and $i \geq 0$ is a (current) *position*. Intuitively, a path is a sequence of locations that is visited by a potential run of the program, together with a point in the run where we currently are. We denote the set of paths by $\Pi$. For a path $\pi = (p, i) \in \Pi$, $p_{(0)}$ and $\pi_{(0)}$ denote the first location in the path; $p_{(j)}$ and $\pi_{(j)}$ denote the $j+1$-th location.

A *trace* is a pair $(t, i) \in \mathbb{S}^{\mathbb{N}} \times \mathbb{N}$, where $t = \langle s_0, s_1, s_2, \ldots \rangle \in \mathbb{S}^{\mathbb{N}}$ is an infinite sequence of program states, and $i \geq 0$ is a (current) position. Intuitively, a trace is a sequence of program states that is visited by a potential run of the program, together with a point in the run where we currently are. We denote the set of traces by $\Sigma$. For a trace $\tau \in \Sigma$, $t_{(0)}$ and $\tau_{(0)}$ denote the first state of the trace; $t_{(j)}$ and $\tau_{(j)}$ denote the $j+1$-th state. For a location $l \in \mathbb{L}$, the set of all traces *at* $l$ is $\Sigma|_l = \{(t, i) \in \Sigma \mid \exists m \in \mathbb{M}.\ t_{(i)} = (l, m)\}$. The set of all traces at $l$ and position $i$ is $\Sigma|_{l,i} = \{(t, i) \in \Sigma \mid \exists m \in \mathbb{M}.\ t_{(i)} = (l, m)\}$. For example, $\Sigma|_{l_\vdash, 0}$ is the set of traces, s.t. they start at the initial program location $l_\vdash$, and the current position is 0. For a trace $\tau \in \Sigma$, its path $\mathfrak{p}(\tau) \in \Pi$ is produced by removing information about the memory states. For $\tau = (\langle (l_0, m_0), (l_1, m_1), (l_2, m_2), \ldots \rangle, i) \in \Sigma$, $\mathfrak{p}(\tau) = (\langle l_0, l_1, l_2, \ldots \rangle, i) \in \Pi$. We say that a trace is *terminating* iff there exists $j \geq 0$, a final location $l \in \mathbb{L}$, and a memory state $m \in \mathbb{M}$, s.t., for every $k \geq j$, $\tau_{(k)} = (l, m)$. We say that a trace is *non-terminating* iff it is not terminating.

Given a program $\mathbb{P}$, not every trace can be produced by it. A trace $\tau \in \Sigma$ is a *semi-execution* of $\mathbb{P}$ iff for every $j \geq 0$, $(\tau_{(j)}, \tau_{(j+1)}) \in T_{\mathbb{S}}(\mathbb{P})$. A trace $\tau \in \Sigma$ is an *execution*, if it is a semi-execution and $\tau_{(0)} = (\vdash, m)$ for some memory state $m \in \mathbb{M}$. Intuitively, an execution, as its first component, has a sequence of program states that is produced by starting in the initial program location in some memory state, and running the program either infinitely (producing a non-terminating execution) or until it terminates in a final location (producing a terminating one). For the program in Fig. 1, we can produce a non-terminating execution by, e.g., alternating the increment and decrement of $x$: $(\langle\langle\langle(l_1, x \mapsto 0), (l_2, x \mapsto 0), (l_3, x \mapsto 1), (l_1, x \mapsto 1), (l_2, x \mapsto 1), (l_4, x \mapsto 0)\rangle^{\mathbb{N}}\rangle, i)$. A trace $(t, i) \in \Sigma$ is an *execution prefix* iff $t_{(0)} = (\vdash, m)$ for some memory state $m \in \mathbb{M}$, and for every $j$, s.t. $0 \leq j < i$, $(t_{(j)}, t_{(j+1)}) \in T_{\mathbb{S}}(\mathbb{P})$. Intuitively, for an *execution prefix* $(t, i)$, the prefix of $t$ up to position $i$ is produced by starting in the initial location in some memory state and making $i$ steps through the program. A trace $(t, i) \in \Sigma$ is an execution postfix iff for every $j \geq i$, $(t_{(j)}, t_{(j+1)}) \in T_{\mathbb{S}}(\mathbb{P})$. We lift the program transition relation to traces and paths. The transition relation on traces is $T_{\Sigma}(\mathbb{P}) = \{((t, i), (t, i+1)) \in \Sigma \times \Sigma \mid (t_{(i)}, t_{(i+1)}) \in T_{\mathbb{S}}(\mathbb{P})\}$. The transition relation on paths is $T_{\Pi}(\mathbb{P}) = \{((p, i), (p, i+1)) \in \Pi \times \Pi \mid (p_{(i)}, p_{(i+1)}) \in \mathbb{E}\}$.

**Non-Termination Analysis and Set-of-States Abstraction.** For a set of traces $S \subseteq \Sigma$, the *closed subset* $(\!|S|\!) = \{(t, i) \in S \mid \forall j \geq 0. \ (t, j) \in S\}$. That is, $(\!|S|\!)$ is the largest subset of $S$ closed under shifting the position.

Given some set $S_0$ and a transition relation $T \subseteq S_0 \times S_0$, the *post-condition* and *pre-condition* of a set $S \subseteq S_0$ via $T$ are the sets:

$$\text{post}(T, S) = \{s' \in S_0 \mid \exists s \in S. \ (s, s') \in T\}, \quad \text{pre}(T, S) = \{s \in S_0 \mid \exists s' \in S. \ (s, s') \in T\}$$

For a program $\mathbb{P}$, *non-termination* analysis of $\mathbb{P}$ is the greatest fixed point:

$$\text{gfp}_{\subseteq} \lambda X. ((\bigcup \{\Sigma|_l \text{ for non-final } l \in \mathbb{L}\}) \cap \text{pre}(T_{\Sigma}(\mathbb{P}), X)) \tag{1}$$

**Lemma 1.** *For a program $\mathbb{P}$ the closed subset of its non-termination analysis gives the set of all non-terminating semi-executions of the program.*

*Proof idea.* Intuitively, non-termination analysis retains non-terminating execution postfixes. Taking closed subset keeps only the traces that also are execution prefixes: if $(t, i)$ is in the closed subset, then for every $j$, s.t., $0 \leq j < i$, $(t, j)$ must be in the closed subset and thus must be an execution postfix, i.e., $(t, i)$ must be a semi-execution. $\qquad\square$

Note that usually, a pre-condition through the whole program is computed as a *union* of pre-conditions through the program statements. This makes it hard to define a sound computable non-termination analysis, since in most abstract domains it is hard to define an under-approximate join operation.

For a set of traces $S \subseteq \Sigma$, the *set-of-states abstraction* $\alpha_s(S) \in \mathbb{S}$ collects current program states of every trace: $\alpha_s(S) = \{s' \in \mathbb{S} \mid \exists (t, i) \in S. \ t_{(i)} = s'\}$. The corresponding concretization $\gamma_s$, for $S' \subseteq \mathbb{S}$ produces the set of traces that have an element of $S'$ at the current position: $\gamma_{\mathfrak{s}}(S') = \{(t, i) \in \Sigma \mid t_{(i)} \in S'\}$. For $S' \subseteq \mathbb{S}$, $(\!(\gamma_{\mathfrak{s}}(S'))\!) = \{(t, i) \in \Sigma \mid \forall j \geq 0. \, t_{(j)} \in S'\}$. This is the set of traces that only visit program states from $S'$.

**Existential Recurrent Set.** For a program $\mathbb{P}$, a set of program states $S_\exists \subseteq \mathbb{S}$ is an *existential recurrent set* if for every $s \in S_\exists$, $s$ is not final and there exists $s' \in S_\exists$, s.t., $(s, s') \in T_{\mathbb{S}}(\mathbb{P})$. Intuitively, this is a set of program states, from which the program *may* run forever. Note that by this definition, an empty set is trivially existentially recurrent. The authors of [13] use a similar (but stronger) notion of *open recurrent set*, requiring that all the states in the open recurrent set are reachable. In this paper, by just *recurrent set* we mean existential recurrent set.

**Lemma 2.** *Set-of-states abstraction of non-termination analysis gives the largest existential recurrent set.*

*Proof idea.* Intuitively a recurrent set $S_\exists$ is s.t. from every element of $S_\exists$ we can start a non-terminating semi-execution that only visits elements of $S_\exists$. Non-termination analysis produces the set of all non-terminating execution postfixes, and by applying set-of-states abstraction to it, we produce the set of all program states from which we can start a non-terminating semi-execution, i.e., the maximal recurrent set. □

The problem of finding a recurrent set is a sub-problem of proving non-termination. To prove non-termination (i.e., the existence of at least one non-terminating execution), we would need to find a recurrent set and show that it is reachable from an initial state. In this paper, though, we focus on finding a recurrent set only.

**Memory and Path Abstraction.** From the set-of-states abstraction of an analysis, one can produce a computable over-approximate analysis by performing further memory abstraction, which is standard in abstract interpretation. We introduce *memory abstract domain* $\mathbb{D}_{\mathfrak{m}}$, with least element $\perp_{\mathfrak{m}}$, greatest element $\top_{\mathfrak{m}}$, partial order $\sqsubseteq_{\mathfrak{m}}$, and join $\sqcup_{\mathfrak{m}}$. Every *element*, or abstract memory state, $a \in \mathbb{D}_{\mathfrak{m}}$ represents a set of memory states $\gamma_{\mathfrak{m}}(a) \subseteq \mathbb{M}$. For the analysis of numeric programs, $\mathbb{D}_{\mathfrak{m}}$ can be a polyhedral domain where an element is a conjunction of linear inequalities over the program variables.

We lift *concretization* to sets of abstract memory states: for $A \subseteq \mathbb{D}_{\mathfrak{m}}, \gamma_{\mathfrak{m}}(A) = \bigcup\{\gamma_{\mathfrak{m}}(a) \mid a \in A\}$. We introduce over-approximate versions of post, pre, and eval, s.t. for a statement $C \in \mathbb{C}$, an element $a \in \mathbb{D}_{\mathfrak{m}}$, and a memory-state formula $\theta$,

$$\gamma_{\mathfrak{m}}(\text{post}^{\mathrm{m}}(C, a)) \supseteq \text{post}(T_{\mathbb{M}}(C), \gamma_{\mathfrak{m}}(a)) \qquad \text{eval}^{\mathrm{m}}(\theta, a) \sqsupseteq_{\mathcal{K}} \text{eval}(\theta, \gamma(a))$$
$$\gamma_{\mathfrak{m}}(\text{pre}^{\mathrm{m}}(C, a)) \supseteq \text{pre}(T_{\mathbb{M}}(C), \gamma_{\mathfrak{m}}(a))$$

Normally, $\text{eval}^{\mathrm{m}}$ is given for atomic formulas; for arbitrary formulas it is defined by induction over the formula structure, using 3-valued logical operators, possibly over-approximate w.r.t. $\sqsubseteq_{\mathcal{K}}$. In this paper, we make additional assumptions on $\mathbb{D}_{\mathfrak{m}}$. We assume there exists meet operation, s.t., for $a_1, a_2 \in \mathbb{D}_{\mathfrak{m}}, a_1 \sqcap_{\mathfrak{m}} a_2 \sqsubseteq_{\mathfrak{m}} a_1$ and $a_1 \sqcap_{\mathfrak{m}} a_2 \sqsubseteq_{\mathfrak{m}} a_2$. This allows producing descending chains in $\mathbb{D}_{\mathfrak{m}}$

and performing approximation of greatest fixed points even with non-monotonic abstract transformers. If $\mathbb{D}_m$ admits infinite descending chains, we assume there exists *lower widening* operation $\underline{\nabla}_m$. Similarly, if $\mathbb{D}_m$ admits infinite ascending chains, we assume there exists *widening* operation $\nabla_m$. To produce a standard over-approximate analysis one transitions to the domain $\mathbb{L} \to \mathbb{D}_m$, where every element represents a set of program states partitioned with locations.

We are going to use trace partitioning and we take an additional step to introduce what we call a *path abstract domain* $\mathbb{D}_p$, with least element $\perp_p$, greatest element $\top_p$, partial order $\sqsubseteq_p$, join $\sqcup_p$ and meet $\sqcap_p$. Every *element*, or abstract path, $q \in \mathbb{D}_p$ represents a set of paths $\gamma_p(q) \subseteq \Pi$. We introduce over-approximate versions of post and pre, s.t. for an edge $e \in \mathbb{E}$ and an element $q \in \mathbb{D}_p$,

$$\gamma_p(\mathrm{post}^p(e, q)) \supseteq \mathrm{post}(T_\Pi(\mathbb{P})|_e, \gamma_p(q)) \qquad \gamma_p(\mathrm{pre}^p(e, q)) \supseteq \mathrm{pre}(T_\Pi(\mathbb{P})|_e, \gamma_p(q))$$

where $T_\Pi(\mathbb{P})|_e = \{((p, i), (p, i+1)) \in \Pi \times \Pi \mid (p_{(i)}, p_{(i+1)}) = e\}$, i.e., it restricts the transition relation on paths to an edge $e \in E$. For our purposes, we also assume that $\mathbb{D}_p$ is finite, and there exists abstraction function $\alpha_p$ that, together with $\gamma_p$ forms a Galois connection between $\mathbb{D}_p$ and $\mathcal{P}(\Pi)$. This allows to partition memory states with elements of $\mathbb{L} \times \mathbb{D}_p$, similarly to how a standard analysis partitions memory states with locations.

**Abstract Domain of the Analysis.** Given a memory abstract domain $\mathbb{D}_m$ and path abstract domain $\mathbb{D}_p$ with required properties, we can construct the abstract domain $\mathbb{D}_\sharp \subseteq \mathbb{D}_p \rightharpoonup \mathbb{D}_m$ (where $\rightharpoonup$ denotes a partial function). We require that every element $D \in \mathbb{D}_\sharp$ is what we call *reduced*: for every $q \in \mathrm{dom}(D)$, $q \neq \perp_p$ and $D(q) \neq \perp_m$; and for every pair of abstract paths $q_1, q_2 \in \mathrm{dom}(D)$, $q_1 \sqcap_p q_2 = \perp_p$. Intuitively, $D$ is a collection of abstract memory states partitioned with *disjoint* abstract paths.

*Idea of the Construction.* $\mathbb{D}_\sharp$ is ordered by $\sqsubseteq_\sharp$ point-wise, $\top_\sharp = \{\top_p \mapsto \top_m\}$, and $\perp_\sharp$ is the empty partial function. For every partial function $D' : \mathbb{D}_p \rightharpoonup \mathbb{D}_m$, we can produce a reduced element $D \in \mathbb{D}_\sharp$: we remove "bottoms" and then repeatedly join the pairs from $D'$ (thinking of a function as of a set of pairs) that have non-disjoint abstract paths. From this point, it is straightforward to construct join $\sqcup_\sharp$, abstract post-condition $\mathrm{post}^\sharp(e, d)$, and abstract pre-condition $\mathrm{pre}^\sharp(e, d)$, $e \in \mathbb{E}$ and $d \in \mathbb{D}_\sharp$. When taking meet of $D_1, D_2 \in \mathbb{D}_\sharp$, we meet the tuples from $D_1$ and $D_2$ pair-wise. As both $D_1$ and $D_2$ are reduced, it follows that $D_1 \sqcap_\sharp D_2$ is reduced; and $D_1 \sqcap_\sharp D_2 \sqsubseteq_\sharp D_1$ and $D_1 \sqcap_\sharp D_2 \sqsubseteq_\sharp D_2$. Widening and lower widening are defined point-wise.

Then, we transition from $\mathbb{D}_\sharp$ to $\mathbb{D}_{l\sharp} = \mathbb{L} \to \mathbb{D}_\sharp$ in which backward analysis is performed. Such transition is standard in abstract interpretation (usually, it is from $\mathbb{D}_m$ to $\mathbb{L} \to \mathbb{D}_m$) and we do not describe it. We only note that in $\mathbb{D}_{l\sharp}$, the post-condition $\mathrm{post}^{l\sharp}(\mathbb{P}, \cdot)$ and pre-condition $\mathrm{pre}^{l\sharp}(\mathbb{P}, \cdot)$ are taken with respect to the whole program. We prefer to think of an element $D_l \in \mathbb{D}_{l\sharp}$ as of a collection of abstract program states partitioned by location and abstract path.

# 3   Finding a Recurrent Set

In this section we describe the main analysis steps: a backward analysis for a candidate recurrent set that is performed below the set of reachable states; followed by a forward refinement step that produces a genuine recurrent set.

We start by performing a standard forward pre-analysis of the whole program $\mathbb{P}$ to find the over-approximation of the set of reachable program states $F \in \mathbb{D}_{l\sharp}$. $F$ is the stable limit of the sequence of $\{f_i\}_{i \geq 0}$ where $f_0 = \{l_{\vdash} \mapsto \top_{\sharp}; l \neq l_{\vdash} \mapsto \bot_{\sharp}\}$; for $i \geq 1$, $f_i = f_{i-1} \nabla_{l\sharp} (f_{i-1} \sqcup_{l\sharp} \text{post}^{l\sharp}(\mathbb{P}, f_{i-1}))$; and $\nabla_{l\sharp}$ is a widening operator.

## 3.1   Backward Analysis for a Candidate

Next, we perform approximate (possibly, over-approximate) backward analysis to find candidate recurrent sets. We do it separately for every strongly connected sub-program $\mathbb{P}_s$ that represents a loop of the original program $\mathbb{P}$. More formally, we perform the analysis for every *strongly connected component* [32] $\mathbb{P}_s = (\mathbb{L}_s, l_{s\vdash}, \mathbb{E}_s, c|_{\mathbb{E}_s})$ where $\mathbb{L}_s \subseteq \mathbb{L}$; $\mathbb{E}_s \subseteq (\mathbb{L}_s \times \mathbb{L}_s) \cap \mathbb{E}$; $|\mathbb{L}_s| > 1$ or $(l_{s\vdash}, l_{s\vdash}) \in \mathbb{E}_s$ (i.e., the component represents a loop in the program); $c|_{\mathbb{E}_s}$ is the restriction of $c$ to the edges of $\mathbb{P}_s$; and $l_{s\vdash} \in \mathbb{L}_s$ is the *head* of the strongly connected component which is usually selected as the first location of the component encountered in $\mathbb{P}$ by a depth-first search. We can restrict the notion of successors to a sub-program: for $l \in \mathbb{L}_s$, $\text{succ}(l)|_{\mathbb{P}_s} = \{l' \in \mathbb{L}_s \mid (l, l') \in \mathbb{E}_s\}$. Note that since $\mathbb{P}_s$ is strongly connected, it does not have final locations.

For every strongly connected sub-program $\mathbb{P}_s$, we find the candidate recurrent set $W_s \in \mathbb{D}_{l\sharp}$ as the stable limit of the sequence of elements $\{w_i\}_{i \geq 0}$ that approximates non-termination analysis below $F$. Here, $w_0 = F|_{\mathbb{L}_s}$ (the restriction of $F$ to the locations of $\mathbb{P}_s$); for $i \geq 1$, $w_i = w_{i-1} \underline{\nabla}_{l\sharp} (w_{i-1} \sqcap_{l\sharp} \text{pre}^{l\sharp}(\mathbb{P}_s, w_{i-1}))$; and $\underline{\nabla}_{l\sharp}$ is a lower widening operator. Note that we use over-approximate operations (join, backward transformers) to compute $W_s$, and hence $W_s$ may over-approximate non-termination analysis and might not represent a genuine recurrent set. Although formally an element of $\mathbb{D}_{l\sharp}$ concretizes to a set of traces, we can think that $W_s$ represents a candidate recurrent set $\alpha_s(\gamma_{l\sharp}(W_s)) = \{(l, m) \in \mathbb{S} \mid \exists q \in \mathbb{D}_p. \ m \in \gamma_m(W_s(l)(q))\}$. In the next step, we will produce a refined element $R_s \sqsubseteq_{l\sharp} W_s$ representing a genuine recurrent set.

In theory, a recurrent set does not have to be below $F$, but in practice, a combination of backward and forward analyses is known to be more precise than just, e.g., backward analysis [17], and we found that performing backward analysis below $F$ (rather than below $\top_{l\sharp}$) better directs the search for a recurrent set. Intuitively, some information (e.g., conditions of assumption statements) is better propagated by forward analysis, and this information may be important to find a genuine recurrent set. Another feature important for precision is trace partitioning. We observe that for many imperative programs, non-terminating executions take a specific path through the loop. When we perform backward analysis with trace partitioning, abstract memory states in $W_s$ are partitioned by the path through the loop that the program run would take from them. If the path domain is precise enough, s.t., (states, from which exist) non-terminating semi-executions get collected in separate partitions, the analysis is more likely to find a genuine recurrent set.

## 3.2   Checking and Refining the Candidate

Approximate backward analysis for every strongly connected component $\mathbb{P}_s$ of the original program, produces an element $W_s \in \mathbb{D}_{l\sharp}$, which represents a candidate recurrent set. We use over-approximate operations (join, backward transformers) to compute $W_s$, and hence $W_s$ may over-approximate non-termination analysis and might not represent a genuine recurrent set. We refine $W_s$ to a (possibly, bottom) element $R_s \sqsubseteq_{l\sharp} W_s$ representing a genuine recurrent set of $\mathbb{P}_s$ and hence of the original program $\mathbb{P}$. That is, we produce such $R_s$ that $\forall s \in \alpha_s(\gamma_{l\sharp}(R_s))$. $\exists s' \in \alpha_s(\gamma_{l\sharp}(R_s))$. $(s, s') \in T_{\mathbb{S}}(\mathbb{P}_s)$. To do so, we define a predicate CONT, s.t. for an abstract memory state $a \in \mathbb{D}_m$, a set of abstract memory states $A \subseteq \mathbb{D}_m$, and an atomic statement $C \in \mathbb{C}$, if CONT$(a, C, A)$ holds (we say that the run of the program can continue from $a$ to $A$ through $C$) then $\forall m \in \gamma_m(a)$. $\exists m' \in \gamma_m(A)$. $(m, m') \in T_M(C)$. We define CONT separately for different kinds of atomic statements. In this paper, we consider numeric programs, which, apart from passive and assumption statements, can use:

(i)  a *deterministic assignment* $x = expr$, which assigns the value of an expression *expr* to a program *variable* $x$;

(ii) a *nondeterministic assignment*, or *forget operation*, $x = *$, which assigns a non-deterministically selected value to a program variable $x$.

For the memory abstract domain, let us introduce an additional *coverage* operation $\sqsubseteq_m^+$ that generalizes abstract order. For an abstract memory state $a \in \mathbb{D}_m$ and a set $A \subseteq \mathbb{D}_m$, it should be that if $a \sqsubseteq_m^+ A$ (we say that $a$ is *covered* by $A$) then $\gamma_m(a) \subseteq \gamma_m(A)$. For an arbitrary domain, coverage can be defined via Hoare order: $a \sqsubseteq_m^+ A$ iff $\exists a' \in A$. $a \sqsubseteq_m a'$. For a numeric domain, it is usually possible to define a more precise coverage operation. For example, the Parma Polyhedra Library [6] defines a specialized coverage operation for finite sets of convex polyhedra.

We define CONT as follows. For $a \in \mathbb{D}_m, A \subseteq \mathbb{D}_m$,

(i)  For the passive statement *skip*, CONT$(a, skip, A) \equiv a \sqsubseteq_m^+ A$. Indeed, if $a \sqsubseteq_m^+ A$ then $\gamma_m(a) \subseteq \gamma_m(A)$, and hence $\forall m \in \gamma_m(a)$. $\exists m' = m \in \gamma_m(A)$. $(m, m') = (m, m) \in T_M(skip)$.

(ii) For an assumption statement $[\theta]$, CONT$(a, [\theta], A) \equiv eval^m(\theta, a) = 1 \wedge a \sqsubseteq_m^+ A$. Indeed, if $eval^m(\theta, a) = 1$, then $\gamma_m(a) \subseteq [\![\theta]\!]$, and if additionally $a \sqsubseteq_m^+ A$ then $\forall m \in \gamma_m(a)$. $\exists m' = m \in \gamma_m(A)$. $(m, m') = (m, m) \in T_M([\theta])$.

(iii) For a nondeterministic assignment $x = *$, we use the fact that in many numeric domains (including the polyhedral domain) the pre-condition of $x = *$ can be computed precisely (via *cylindrification* operation [24]). That is, for $a \in \mathbb{D}_m$, $\gamma_m(\text{pre}^m(x = *, a)) = \{m \in \mathbb{M} \mid \exists m' \in \gamma_m(a). (m, m') \in T_M(x = *)\}$. In this case, CONT$(a, x = *, A) \equiv a \sqsubseteq_m^+ \{\text{pre}^m(x = *, a') \mid a' \in A\}$.

(iv) Finally, for every other atomic statement $C$ with left-total input-output relation $T_M(C)$ (e.g., a deterministic assignment), $\text{CONT}(a, C, A) \equiv \text{post}^m(C, a) \sqsubseteq_m^+ A$. Indeed, in this case $\gamma_m(A) \supseteq \gamma_m(\text{post}^m(C, a)) \supseteq \text{post}(C, \gamma_m(a))$. Since additionally, $T_M(C)$ is left-total then for every $m \in \gamma_m(a)$. $\exists m' \in \gamma_m(A)$. $(m, m') \in T_M(C)$.

Another way to look at it is that (iv) represents a general case that allows handling atomic statements with left-total input-output relations. Then, we specialize CONT for non-deterministic statements and for statements with non-left-total input-output relations. Case (iii) specializes CONT for non-deterministic assignments. It allows us to detect a situation where there exists a *specific* non-deterministic choice (i.e., a specific new value of a variable) that keeps the execution inside the recurrent set. Case (ii) specializes CONT for assumption statements (with non-left-total input-output relations). By extending the definition of CONT, we can extend our analysis to support more kinds of atomic statements. Note that the predicate CONT is defined using operations that are standard in program analysis.

**Theorem 1.** *Let $R_s \in \mathbb{D}_{l\sharp}$ be an element of $\mathbb{D}_{l\sharp}$ and $\mathbb{P}_s$ be a sub-program. Let it be that for every location $l \in \mathbb{L}_s$, abstract path $q \in \mathbb{D}_p$, and an abstract memory state $a \in \mathbb{D}_m$, s.t., $R_s(l)(q) = a$, there exists a successor location $l' \in \text{succ}(l)|_{\mathbb{P}_s}$, s.t. $\text{CONT}(a, \mathfrak{c}(l, l'), \{a' \mid \exists q' \in \mathbb{D}_p. \ a' = R_s(l')(q')\})$. Then, $R_s$ represents a recurrent set of $\mathbb{P}_s$ and hence the whole program $\mathbb{P}$.*

*Proof idea.* The proof is a straightforward application of the definitions of CONT and $T_\mathbb{S}$. Intuitively, if $R_s \in \mathbb{D}_{l\sharp}$ satisfies the condition of the lemma, from every program state in $\alpha_s(\gamma_{l\sharp}(R_s))$ we can form a non-terminating semi-execution that only visits the elements of $\alpha_s(\gamma_{l\sharp}(R_s))$ – by executing the statements of $\mathbb{P}_s$ in a specific order. □

Thus, in the refinement step, we start with an element $W_s \in \mathbb{D}_{l\sharp}$ produced by the backward analysis, and from every location $l \in \mathbb{L}_s$, we repeatedly exclude the tuples $(q, a) \in W_s(l)$ that do not satisfy the condition of Theorem 1. Eventually, we arrive at an element $R_s \sqsubseteq_{l\sharp} W_s$ that satisfies Theorem 1 and hence, represents a recurrent set. Note that the refinement step that we implement in this paper is coarse. For some disjunct $(q, a) \in W_s(l)$, we either keep it unchanged or remove it as a whole. In particular, an empty set is trivially recurrent, and it is still sound to produce $R_s = \bot_{l\sharp}$. This is acceptable, as the main purpose of the refinement step is to ensure soundness, and the form of the recurrent set in our current implementation is inferred by the preceding backward and forward analyses. Although, the analysis would benefit from the ability to modify individual disjuncts during refinement (we leave this for future work).

Theorem 1 requires that for every location $l \in \mathbb{L}_s$ and abstract memory state $a = R_s(l)(q)$ (for some $q \in \mathbb{D}_p$), there is at least one edge $(l, l') \in \mathbb{E}_s$, s.t., for every program state $s \in \{(l, m) \in \mathbb{S} \mid m \in \gamma_m(a)\}$ there exists $s' \in \{(l', m') \mid \exists q \in \mathbb{D}_p. \ m' \in \gamma_m(R_s(l')(q))\}$, s.t. $(s, s') \in T_\mathbb{S}(\mathbb{P}_s)$. That is, for every abstract memory state in $R_s$, there exists at least one edge, s.t. taking this edge from any corresponding concrete state keeps the execution inside the recurrent set. This is viable in practice because of the choice of path domain $\mathbb{D}_p$ (which is described in the following section). Our path domain ensures that at every branching point, backward analysis always partitions the memory states by the branch that they are going to take at this branching point.

Finally, note that Theorem 1 can be used to find a recurrent set of the whole program (not necessarily a strongly connected sub-program $\mathbb{P}_s$) and this way, prove non-termination. If $\gamma_\sharp(R_s(\sharp)) \neq \varnothing$, then there exists at least one non-terminating program execution (a non-terminating semi-execution starting in the initial location). Unfortunately, so far, we have not had practical success with this approach. Our path domain $\mathbb{D}_p$, while sufficient to capture non-terminating paths through loops (esp., non-nested loops), is not precise enough to capture non-terminating paths through the whole program. Thus, for practical reasons, we search for recurrent sets of individual loops and assume that reachability analysis will be used to complete the non-termination proof.

### 3.3  Path Domain

For the path domain, in this paper, we use finite sequences of *future branching choices*. A *branching point* is a location $l \in \mathbb{L}$, s.t., there exists at least two edges from $l$. A *branching choice* is an edge $(l, l') \in \mathbb{E}$, s.t., $l$ is a branching point. We denote the set of all branching choices by $\mathbb{E}_\flat \subseteq \mathbb{E}$. For every non-bottom element $q \in \mathbb{D}_p$, $q$ is a finite sequence of branching choices: $q = \langle e_0, e_1, \ldots, e_n \rangle \in \mathbb{E}_\flat^*$; top element $\top_p$ is the empty sequence $\langle \rangle$; and bottom is a distinguished element $\bot_p \notin \mathbb{E}_\flat^*$. E.g., for our running example in Fig. 1, $l_2$ is a branching point, and the branching choices are $(l_2, l_3)$ and $(l_2, l_4)$ For $q_1, q_2 \in \mathbb{D}_p$, $q_1 \sqsubseteq_p q_2$ if $q_1 = \bot_p$ or $q_2$ is a prefix of $q_1$. For $q_1, q_2 \in \mathbb{D}_p$, join $q_1 \sqcup_p q_2$ is $q_2$ if $q_1 = \bot_p$, $q_1$ if $q_2 = \bot_p$, or the longest common prefix of $q_1$ and $q_2$ otherwise. For $q_1, q_2 \in \mathbb{D}_p$, meet $q_1 \sqcap_p q_2 = q_1$ if $q_1 \sqsubseteq_p q_2$, $q_2$ if $q_2 \sqsubseteq_p q_1$, and $\bot_p$ otherwise. Additionally, we require that every element $q \in \mathbb{D}_p$ is *bounded*, i.e., every branching choice $e \in \mathbb{E}_\flat$ appears in $q$ at most $k$ times for a parameter $k \geq 1$. For a sequence of branching choices $q' \in \mathbb{E}_\flat^*$ (or $\in \mathbb{E}_\flat^\mathbb{N}$), we can produce a bounded element $\flat_k(q') \in \mathbb{D}_p$ by keeping the longest bounded prefix of the sequence. An element $q = \langle e_0, e_1, \ldots, e_n \rangle \in \mathbb{E}_\flat^*$ represents the set of paths $\gamma_p(q) \subseteq \Pi$, s.t. $\pi = (\langle l_0, l_1, \ldots \rangle, i) \in \gamma_p(q)$ iff for $j = 0..n$, there exists a strictly increasing sequence of indices $\{x_j\} : i \leq x_0 < \ldots < x_n$, s.t., every $\pi_{(x_j)}$ is a branching point, $(\pi_{(x_j)}, \pi_{((x_j)+1)}) = e_j$, and for every index $z$, s.t. $i \leq z < x_n$, if $z \notin \{x_j\}$, then $\pi_{(z)}$ is not a branching point. Let us define a corresponding abstraction function. For a path $\pi = (\langle l_0, l_1, \ldots \rangle, i) \in \Pi$ and $j \geq 0$ let $\{y_j\}$ be a strictly increasing sequence of indices of branching points at or after position $i$: $i \leq y_0 < y_1 < \ldots$, every $\pi_{(y_j)}$ is a branching point, and for every index $z \geq i$, if $z \notin \{y_j\}$, then $\pi_{(z)}$ is not a branching point. Then, the abstraction of $\pi$ is $\alpha_p(\pi) = \flat_k(\langle (\pi_{(y_0)}, \pi_{((y_0)+1)}), (\pi_{(y_1)}, \pi_{((y_1)+1)}), \ldots \rangle)$. For a set of paths $V$, $\alpha_p(V) = \bigsqcup_p \{\alpha_p(\pi) \mid \pi \in V\}$. For an edge $e \in \mathbb{E}$ and $q \in \mathbb{D}_p$, $\mathrm{pre}^p(e, q) = \bot_p$ if $q = \bot_p$; $\flat_k(e \cdot q)$ if $q \neq \bot_p$ and $e$ is a branching choice; and $q$ otherwise. Here $\cdot$ denotes concatenation. Respectively, $\mathrm{post}^p(e, q) = q'$ if $q = e \cdot q'$

for some $q' \in \mathbb{D}_p$; $\perp_p$ if $q = e' \cdot q'$ for some $q' \in \mathbb{D}_p$ and $e' \neq e$; $\top_p$ if $q = \top_p$; and $\perp_p$ if $q = \perp_p$.

Intuitively, an abstract path $q \in \mathbb{D}_p$ predicts a bounded number of branching choices that an execution would make. For our running example in Fig. 1, if we take $k = 1$ then the abstraction of the infinite path $\langle (l_1, l_2, l_3)^{\mathbb{N}} \rangle$ is $\langle (l_2, l_3) \rangle$. We observe that our path domain works well for non-nested loops, and the bound $k$ is the number of loop iterations for which we keep the branching choices. In most our experiments, $k = 1$ or $2$ was enough to find a recurrent set. Note that the forward transformer post$^p$ leaves $\top_p$ unchanged. Thus, our backward analysis does use trace partitioning, but the forward pre-analysis does not (with the current path domain). The forward pre-analysis, is initialized with $f_0 = \{l_\vdash \mapsto \top_\sharp; l \neq l_\vdash \mapsto \perp_\sharp\}$ where $\top_\sharp = \{\top_p \mapsto \top_m\}$, i.e., during the forward pre-analysis, every location is mapped either to $\perp_\sharp$ or to $\{\top_p \mapsto m\}$ for some $m \in \mathbb{D}_m$.

## 4   Examples of Handling Non-Determinism

In this section, we present numeric examples that demonstrate how different components of the analysis (trace partitioning, CONT, lower widening) are important for different kinds of non-terminating behaviors. In all examples, we assume that program variables are unbounded integers, and the analysis uses the polyhedral domain [19]. In Examples 1, 2 and 3, we focus on a single loop and ignore that it can be a part of a larger program: e.g., we omit the branch that exits a loop, although it would usually be present in a program.

**Example 1 — Non-deterministic Branches.** For the program in Fig. 1, a non-terminating execution in every iteration needs to make the choice depending on the current value of $x$, so that it does not go outside the range $[0, 100]$. This is captured by our path domain with $k = 1$ (the bound on the occurrences of the same branching choice in the abstract path). The first two steps (pre-analysis and backward analysis) yield the candidate recurrent set $W_s$. We do not describe these steps in detail, but $W_s(l_1) = \{\langle (l_2, l_3) \rangle \mapsto (0 \leq x \leq 99); \langle (l_2, l_4) \rangle \mapsto (1 \leq x \leq 100)\}$, $W_s(l_2) = W_s(l_1)$, $W_s(l_3) = \{\langle (l_2, l_3) \rangle \mapsto (1 \leq x \leq 99); \langle (l_2, l_4) \rangle \mapsto (1 \leq x \leq 100)\}$, and $W_s(l_4) = \{\langle (l_2, l_3) \rangle \mapsto (0 \leq x \leq 99); \langle (l_2, l_4) \rangle \mapsto (1 \leq x \leq 99)\}$.

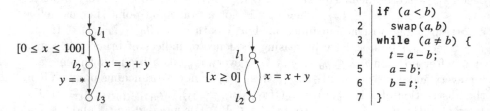

**Fig. 2.** Loop that assigns a non-deterministic value to a variable in every iteration.

**Fig. 3.** Loop that requires a specific range of $y$ for non-termination.

**Fig. 4.** GCD algorithm with an introduced bug.

This can be interpreted as follows. If the execution is at location $l_1$ and, as the next branching choice, is going to increment $x$ (by taking the edge $(l_2, l_3)$), then, for the execution to not leave the loop, it must be that $0 \leq x \leq 99$. Indeed, if $x < 0$, the execution will not enter the loop, and if $x > 99$, the execution will exit the loop after incrementing $x$. Similarly, if the execution is going to decrement $x$, it must be that $1 \leq x \leq 100$. That is, if the execution is at location $l_1$, and $0 \leq x \leq 100$, there exists a branching choice at location $l_2$ that keeps $x$ in range $[0, 100]$. This way we can construct a non-terminating execution. Note that $W_s$ represents a genuine recurrent set, and the final (refinement) step of the analysis yields $R_s = W_s$.

**Example 2 — Non-deterministic Assignment in the Loop.** Figure 2 shows a loop that in every iteration, first assigns a non-deterministic value to $y$ and then adds it to $x$. Intuitively, if at location $l_1$ $x$ is in range $[0, 100]$, then for the edge $(l_2, l_3)$, there is always a choice of $y$, s.t. $x + y$ is still in the range $[0, 100]$. This way, we can construct a non-terminating execution. The way we specialize the predicate CONT to non-deterministic assignments allows us to handle such cases. The first two steps (pre-analysis and backward analysis) yield the candidate recurrent set $W_s$, s.t. $W_s(l_1) = \{\langle\rangle \mapsto (0 \leq x \leq 100)\}$, $W_s(l_2) = W_s(l_1)$, and $W_s(l_3) = \{\langle\rangle \mapsto (0 \leq x \leq 100 \wedge 0 \leq x + y \leq 100)\}$. We show that $W_s$ satisfies Theorem 1 and thus represents a genuine recurrent set. Indeed. For location $l_1$, the successor location is $l_2$, and $(0 \leq x \leq 100)$ satisfies the memory-state formula of the assumption statement that labels $(l_1, l_2)$. That is, for every state at location $l_1$ with $0 \leq x \leq 100$, we will stay in the recurrent set after executing the assumption statement. This corresponds to case (ii) of the predicate CONT. For location $l_2$, the successor location is $l_3$ and $c(l_2, l_3)$ is the non-deterministic assignment $y = *$. Note that for every value of $x$ it is possible to choose a value of $y$, s.t. $0 \leq x + y \leq 100$ holds. Or, more formally, $\mathrm{pre}^m(y = *, (0 \leq x \leq 100 \wedge 0 \leq x + y \leq 100)) = (0 \leq x \leq 100)$ which corresponds to case (iii) of the predicate CONT. Finally, for location $l_3$, the successor location is $l_1$ and $c(l_3, l_1)$ is $x = x + y$. Also, $\mathrm{post}^m(x = x + y, (0 \leq x \leq 100 \wedge 0 \leq x + y \leq 100)) = (0 \leq x - y \leq 100 \wedge 0 \leq x \leq 100) \sqsubseteq (0 \leq x \leq 100)$ which corresponds to case (iv) of the predicate CONT. Therefore, $W_s$ represents a genuine recurrent set, and the final step of the analysis yields $R_s = W_s$.

**Example 3 — Non-deterministic Assignment Before the Loop.** Figure 3 shows a loop that in every iteration adds $y$ to $x$. Both $x$ and $y$ are not initialized before the loop, and are thus assumed to take non-deterministic values. If at location $l_1$, $x \geq 0$ and $y \geq 0$, it is possible to continue the execution forever. Let us see how the constraint $y \geq 0$ can be inferred with lower widening. For this program, the pre-analysis produces the invariant $F$, s.t., $F(l_1) = \{\langle\rangle \mapsto \top\}$, and $F(l_2) = \{\langle\rangle \mapsto x \geq 0\}$. Then, consider a sequence of approximants $\{w_i\}_{i \geq 0}$ where $w_0 = F$ and for $i \geq 1$, $w_i = w_{i-1} \sqcap_{\sharp} \mathrm{pre}^{\sharp}(\mathbb{P}, w_{i-1})$ which corresponds to running the backward analysis without lower widening. Then, we will observe that the $i$-th approximant at location $l_1$ represents the condition that ensures that the execution will make at least $i$ iterations through the loop. For $i \geq 0$, let $w_i' = w_i(l_1)(\langle\rangle)$. Then, $w_0' = \top$, $w_1' = x \geq 0$, $w_2' = (x \geq 0 \wedge x+y \geq 0)$, $w_3' = (x \geq 0 \wedge x+2y \geq 0)$, $w_4' = (x \geq 0 \wedge x+3y \geq 0)$, and so on. That is, for $i \geq 1$, $w_i' = (x \geq 0 \wedge x + iy \geq 0)$ (a polyhedron with a "rotating" constraint), and we would like a lower widening technique that would produce an extrapolated polyhedron $(x \geq 0 \wedge y \geq 0)$ which is the limit of the chain $\{w_i'\}_{i\geq 0}$. Notice how this limit is below $w_i'$ for every $i \geq 0$. This explains why we use lower widening (and not, e.g., narrowing) to ensure convergence of the backward analysis. Here, we use lower widening as proposed by A. Miné [30]. Intuitively, it works by retaining stable generators (which can be seen as dual to standard widening that retains stable constraints). Additionally, we use widening delay of 2 and a technique of threshold rays (also described in [30]), adding the coordinate vectors and their negations to the set of thresholds. Alternatively, instead of using threshold rays, one could adapt to lower widening the technique of evolving rays [7]. This allows the backward analysis to produce the extrapolated polyhedron $(x \geq 0 \wedge y \geq 0)$. Eventually, backward analysis produces the candidate $W_s$ where $W_s(l_1) = \{\langle\rangle \mapsto (x \geq 0 \wedge y \geq 0)\}$ and $W_s(l_2) = W_s(l_1)$. $W_s$ represents a genuine recurrent set, and the final (refinement) step of the analysis yields $R_s = W_s$.

**Example 4.** This example is a program "GCD" from the test set [3] of Invel [35]. The program given in pseudocode in Fig. 4 is based on the basic algorithm that computes the greatest common divisor of two numbers: $a$ and $b$ – but has an introduced bug that produces non-terminating behaviors. For the loop in this program, our analysis (with $k = 2$) is able to show that if at line 3, it is the case that $(a > b \wedge a > 2b)$ or $(b > a \wedge 2b > a)$, the execution will never terminate and will alternate between these two regions. This example demonstrates how the interaction between the components of the analysis allows finding non-trivial non-terminating behaviors. In a program graph, the condition $a \neq b$ will be represented by a pair of edges, labelled by assumption statements: $[a > b]$ and $[a < b]$. Thus, these assumption statements become branching choices at line 3. Then, the path domain (with $k$ at least 2) allows the analysis to distinguish the executions that alternate between these two assumption statements for the first $k$ loop iterations. By doing numeric reasoning, one can check that there exist non-terminating executions that alternate between the two assumption statements indefinitely.

The example also demonstrates a non-trivial refinement step. At line 3, backwards analysis actually yields two additional disjuncts, one of those being $(a > b \wedge 2b > a \wedge 3b - a > 4)$. These are the states that take the branching choice $[a > b]$ for at least two first loop iterations. But from some of the concrete states in the disjunct, e.g., $(a = 6, b = 4)$, the loop eventually terminates. As currently implemented, the refinement step has to remove the whole disjunct from the final result.

Finally, note how for this example, recurrent set cannot be represented by a single convex polyhedron (per program location). Our approach allows to keep multiple polyhedra per location, corresponding to different abstract paths.

**To Summarize,** the components of the analysis are responsible for handling different features of non-terminating executions. Trace partitioning allows predicting paths that non-terminating executions take; predicate CONT deals with non-deterministic statements in a loop; lower widening infers the required values of variables that are non-deterministically set outside of a loop.

## 5   Experiments

Our prototype implementation supports numeric programs (with some restrictions) and uses the product of polyhedra and congruences (via Parma Polyhedra Library [6]) as the memory domain. We applied our tool to the test set [3] of Invel [35], to non-terminating programs from SV-COMP 2015 [4] termination category (manually converted to our tool's input language), and additionally, to a set of non-deterministic numeric programs that we produced ourselves (all test programs are non-terminating, i.e., every program has at least one non-terminating behavior). Table 1 summarizes the results for the Invel and SV-COMP non-terminating programs and compares our tool to 3 existing tools: AProVE [20], Automizer [22], and HipTNT+ [27], and additionally to the authors' previous work on finding universal recurrent sets with forward analysis [8], column "SAS15". For Automizer and HipTNT+, we do not have the results for Invel programs, and for [8], there are no results for SV-COMP benchmarks. For AProVE, we give results for Invel programs as reported by [12] and for SV-COMP programs, as reported by the Non-Termination competition 2015 [5] (the version of AProVE that participated in SV-COMP did not include a non-termination prover for C programs). For our tool, column "OK" is the number of programs for which our tool finds a recurrent set. In most cases $k = 1$ or 2 was enough to find a recurrent set. In some cases, we need $k = 4$. The sets were later checked *manually* for reachability. Most test programs consist of a single non-terminating loop and a stem that gives initial values to program variables; and to check reachability, we only needed to intersect the inferred recurrent set with the produced set of initial states. Column "M" is the number of programs that originally fall outside of the class that our tool can handle, but after we introduced small modifications (e.g., replaced a non-linear condition with an equivalent linear one), our tool finds a recurrent set for them. Column "U" is the number of programs for which no recurrent set could be found due to technical limitations of our tool that does not support arrays, pointers, some instances of modular arithmetic, etc. Column "X" is the number of programs for which no recurrent set could be found for other reasons. This is usually due to overly aggressive lower widening, which could be improved in the future by introducing relevant widening heuristics. Note that our tool always terminates, i.e., failure means that it produced an empty recurrent set. For the other tools, the columns "OK" and "X" give the number of programs for which the tools were able, and respectively failed to prove non-termination. In brackets, we give the number of programs for which our tool gives the opposite outcome. Column "?" gives the number of programs for which we did not find reported results.

Table 1 should not be interpreted as a *direct* comparison of our tool or approach with the other tools. On one hand, our results are not subsumed by other

**Table 1.** Experimental results

| | Tot. | This paper | | | | APROVE | | | Automizer | | HipTNT+ | | SAS15 | | |
|---|---|---|---|---|---|---|---|---|---|---|---|---|---|---|---|
| | | OK | M | U | X | OK | ? | X | OK | X | OK | X | OK | ? | X |
| Invel | 53 | 46 | 5 | 2 | - | 51 | - | 2 | - | - | - | - | 39(+1) | 1 | 13(+12) |
| SVCOMP | 44 | 32 | - | 9 | 3 | 30(+6) | 4 | 10(+6) | 37(+11) | 7(+6) | 35(+7) | 9(+4) | - | - | - |

tools, and we were able to find recurrent sets for some programs, where other tools failed to prove non-termination. On the other hand, the tools prove different things about the programs. Our tool finds recurrent sets of loops; APROVE and Automizer prove the existence of at least one non-terminating execution; the analysis of [8] and HipTNT+ (to our knowledge) prove that from some initial states, all executions are non-terminating. Also, the analysis of [8] is not optimized for numeric programs: e.g., it uses interval domain, while the analysis that we present uses the more expressive polyhedral domain.

## 6 Related Work

The idea of proving non-termination by looking at paths of a certain form appears in multiple existing approaches. An early analysis by Gupta et al. [21] produces proofs of non-termination from lasso-shaped symbolic executions using Farkas' lemma. Automizer [22,23] decomposes the original program into a set of lasso-programs (a stem and a loop with no branches) to separately infer termination or non-termination [28] arguments for them. APROVE [20] implements a range of techniques. One of those [12], from a set of paths through a loop, produces a formula that is unsatisfiable if there is a set of states that cannot be escaped by following these paths. In a similar way, our approach uses trace partitioning to identify a path through a loop that a non-terminating execution takes. This does not have to be the same path segment repeated infinitely often, but may be an alternation of different segments. We see a strength of our approach in that it is parameterized by a path domain. That is, the partitioning scheme can be improved in future work and/or specialized for different classes of programs.

Chen et al. [13] use a combination of forward and backward analysis, but in a different way. With forward analysis, they identify terminating abstract traces; then using backward analysis over a single trace, they restrict the program (by adding assumption statements) to remove this trace. In contrast, our approach uses backward analysis to produce a candidate recurrent set, by computing an approximation of its fixed point characterization. Then, they show that the restricted program has at least one execution (non-terminating by construction). This is similar to the final step of our analysis.

A number of approaches prove that from some input states, a program does not have terminating behaviors (in contrast to proving the existence of at least one non-terminating behavior). That is, they find a set of states from which a program cannot escape. This can be done using Farkas' lemma [14], forward

[8] or backward [34] abstract interpretation based analysis, or by encoding the search as a max-SMT problem [26]. Le et al. propose a specification logic and an inference algorithm [27] (implemented in HipTNT+) that can capture the absence of terminating behaviors. Invel [35] uses a template and a refinement scheme to infer invariants proving that final states of a program are unreachable.

A distinctive approach implemented in E-HSF [10] allows to specifying the semantics of programs and expressing verified properties (including the existence of different kinds of recurrent sets) in the form of $\forall\exists$ quantified Horn clauses.

Finally, [29] presents a different formalization of trace partitioning (in the context of standard forward analysis), and [18] – of trace semantics.

# 7    Conclusion and Future Work

We proposed an analysis that finds existential recurrent sets of the loops in imperative programs. The analysis is based on the combination of forward and backward abstract interpretation and an important technique that we use is trace partitioning. To our knowledge, this is the first application of trace partitioning to backward analysis. The implementation of our approach for numeric programs demonstrated results that are comparable to those of state-of-the-art tools. As directions of future work we see: first, to develop a more precise path domain. Having a domain that can represent, e.g., lasso-shaped paths would allow better handling of nested loops and extending our technique to proving non-termination (rather than finding recurrent sets). Second, to extend our prototype to support additional memory domains (e.g., for shape analysis). Finally, the analysis of numeric programs will benefit from a specialized numeric refinement step.

**Acknowledgements.** A. Bakhirkin is supported by a Microsoft Research Scholarship.

# References

1. http://www.zuneboards.com/forums/showthread.php?t=38143. Last accessed in October 2015
2. http://azure.microsoft.com/blog/2014/11/19/update-on-azure-storage-service-interruption. Last accessed in October 2015
3. http://www.key-project.org/nonTermination/. Last accessed in October2015
4. http://sv-comp.sosy-lab.org/2015/. Last accessed in October 2015
5. http://www.termination-portal.org/wiki/Termination_Competition_2015. Last accessed in October 2015
6. Bagnara, R., Hill, P.M., Zaffanella, E.: The parma polyhedra library: toward a complete set of numerical abstractions for the analysis and verification of hardware and software systems. Sci. Comput. Program. **72**(1–2), 3–21 (2008)
7. Bagnara, R., Hill, P.M., Ricci, E., Zaffanella, E.: Precise widening operators for convex polyhedra. Sci. Comput. Program. **58**(1–2), 28–56 (2005)
8. Bakhirkin, A., Berdine, J., Piterman, N.: A forward analysis for recurrent sets. In: Blazy, S., Jensen, T. (eds.) SAS 2015. LNCS, vol. 9291, pp. 293–311. Springer, Heidelberg (2015)

9. Berdine, J., Bjørner, N., Ishtiaq, S., Kriener, J.E., Wintersteiger, C.M.: Resourceful reachability as HORN-LA. In: McMillan, K., Middeldorp, A., Voronkov, A. (eds.) LPAR-19 2013. LNCS, vol. 8312, pp. 137–146. Springer, Heidelberg (2013)
10. Beyene, T.A., Popeea, C., Rybalchenko, A.: Solving existentially quantified Horn clauses. In: Sharygina, N., Veith, H. (eds.) CAV 2013. LNCS, vol. 8044, pp. 869–882. Springer, Heidelberg (2013)
11. Biere, A., Bloem, R. (eds.): CAV 2014. LNCS, vol. 8559. Springer, Heidelberg (2014)
12. Brockschmidt, M., Ströder, T., Otto, C., Giesl, J.: Automated detection of non-termination and NullPointerExceptions for JavaBytecode. In: Beckert, B., Damiani, F., Gurov, D. (eds.) FoVeOOS 2011. LNCS, vol. 7421, pp. 123–141. Springer, Heidelberg (2012)
13. Chen, H.-Y., Cook, B., Fuhs, C., Nimkar, K., O'Hearn, P.: Proving nontermination via safety. In: Ábrahám, E., Havelund, K. (eds.) TACAS 2014 (ETAPS). LNCS, vol. 8413, pp. 156–171. Springer, Heidelberg (2014)
14. Cook, B., Fuhs, C., Nimkar, K., O'Hearn, P.W.: Disproving termination with over-approximation. In: FMCAD, pp. 67–74. IEEE (2014)
15. Cook, B., Podelski, A., Rybalchenko, A.: Proving program termination. Commun. ACM 54(5), 88–98 (2011)
16. Cook, B., See, A., Zuleger, F.: Ramsey vs. lexicographic termination proving. In: Piterman, N., Smolka, S.A. (eds.) TACAS 2013 (ETAPS 2013). LNCS, vol. 7795, pp. 47–61. Springer, Heidelberg (2013)
17. Cousot, P., Cousot, R.: Refining model checking by abstract interpretation. Autom. Softw. Eng. 6(1), 69–95 (1999)
18. Cousot, P., Cousot, R.: An abstract interpretation framework for termination. In: Field, J., Hicks, M. (eds.) POPL, pp. 245–258. ACM (2012)
19. Cousot, P., Halbwachs, N.: Automatic discovery of linear restraints among variables of a program. In: Aho, A.V., Zilles, S.N., Szymanski, T.G. (eds.) POPL, pp. 84–96. ACM Press (1978)
20. Giesl, J., et al.: Proving termination of programs automatically with AProVE. In: Demri, S., Kapur, D., Weidenbach, C. (eds.) IJCAR 2014. LNCS, vol. 8562, pp. 184–191. Springer, Heidelberg (2014)
21. Gupta, A., Henzinger, T.A., Majumdar, R., Rybalchenko, A., Xu, R.G.: Proving non-termination. In: Necula, G.C., Wadler, P. (eds.) POPL, pp. 147–158. ACM (2008)
22. Heizmann, M., Dietsch, D., Leike, J., Musa, B., Podelski, A.: ULTIMATE AUTOMIZER with array interpolation. In: Baier, C., Tinelli, C. (eds.) TACAS 2015. LNCS, vol. 9035, pp. 455–457. Springer, Heidelberg (2015)
23. Heizmann, M., Hoenicke, J., Podelski, A.: Termination analysis by learning terminating programs. In: Biere, Bloem (eds.) [11], pp. 797–813
24. Henkin, L., Monk, J.D., Tarski, A.: Cylindric Algebras: Part I. North-Holland, Amsterdam (1971)
25. Kleene, S.: Introduction to Metamathematics, 2nd edn. North-Holland, Amsterdam (1987)
26. Larraz, D., Nimkar, K., Oliveras, A., Rodríguez-Carbonell, E., Rubio, A.: Proving non-termination using max-smt. In: Biere, Bloem (eds.) [11], pp. 779–796
27. Le, T.C., Qin, S., Chin, W.: Termination and non-termination specification inference. In: Grove, D., Blackburn, S. (eds.) PLDI, pp. 489–498. ACM (2015)
28. Leike, J., Heizmann, M.: Geometric series as nontermination arguments for linear lasso programs. CoRR abs/1405.4413 (2014)

29. Mauborgne, L., Rival, X.: Trace partitioning in abstract interpretation based static analyzers. In: Sagiv, M. (ed.) ESOP 2005. LNCS, vol. 3444, pp. 5–20. Springer, Heidelberg (2005)

30. Miné, A.: Backward under-approximations in numeric abstract domains to automatically infer sufficient program conditions. Sci. Comput. Program., 33, October 2013

31. Sagiv, S., Reps, T.W., Wilhelm, R.: Parametric shape analysis via 3-valued logic. ACM Trans. Program. Lang. Syst. **24**(3), 217–298 (2002)

32. Tarjan, R.E.: Depth-first search and linear graph algorithms. SIAM J. Comput. **1**(2), 146–160 (1972)

33. Urban, C., Miné, A.: A decision tree abstract domain for proving conditional termination. In: Müller-Olm, M., Seidl, H. (eds.) Static Analysis. LNCS, vol. 8723, pp. 302–318. Springer, Heidelberg (2014)

34. Urban, C., Miné, A.: Proving guarantee and recurrence temporal properties by abstract interpretation. In: D'Souza, D., Lal, A., Larsen, K.G. (eds.) VMCAI 2015. LNCS, vol. 8931, pp. 190–208. Springer, Heidelberg (2015)

35. Velroyen, H., Rümmer, P.: Non-termination checking for imperative programs. In: Beckert, B., Hähnle, R. (eds.) TAP 2008. LNCS, vol. 4966, pp. 154–170. Springer, Heidelberg (2008)

# Tactics for the Dafny Program Verifier

Gudmund Grov[✉] and Vytautas Tumas[✉]

School of Mathematical and Computer Sciences,
Heriot-Watt University, Edinburgh, UK
{G.Grov,vt50}@hw.ac.uk

**Abstract.** Many modern program verifiers are based on automated theorem provers, which enable full hiding of proof details and allow users to focus all their effort on the program text. This has the advantage that the additional expertise of theorem provers is not required, but has the drawback that when the prover fails to verify a valid program, the user has to annotate the program text with guidance for the verifier. This can be tedious, low-level and repetitive, and may impact on the annotation overhead, readability of the program text and overall development time. Inspired by proof tactics for interactive theorem provers [19], a notion of 'tactics' for the state-of-the-art Dafny program verifier, called *Tacny*, is developed. With only minor extensions to the Dafny syntax, a user can encode high-level proof patterns as *Dafny tactics*, liberating herself from low-level and repetitive search tasks, whilst still working with familiar Dafny programming constructs. Manual search and guidance can be replaced with calls to such tactics, which will automate this task. We provide syntax and semantics for Tacny, and show feasibility through a prototype implementation, applied to several examples.

## 1  Introduction

Properties that programs should satisfy are commonly expressed by *contracts*: given a precondition the program guarantees that a given postcondition holds. Many modern *program verifiers* can then be used to verify that a program satisfies its contract by automatically generating verification conditions (VCs), which are sent to an automated theorem prover. Failure to prove VCs will then be highlighted in the program text, and the user must then update the code with *auxiliary annotations* to guide the proof. A feature of this approach is that all interaction, including proof guidance, is conducted in the program text using a single programming language. Spec# [6], VCC [9], Verifast [24], Dafny [27], and SPARK 2014 [34] are program verifiers that follow this approach.

The ability of users to guide the prover for the cases where the underlying theorem prover fails to verify a *correct* program is crucial. Such guidance involves

This work has been supported by EPSRC grants EP/M018407/1 and EP/J001058/1. We would like to the anonymous reviewers for excellent suggestions, thank our collaborators Rustan Leino (who suggested the tactic and one case study), Rosemary Monahan, Altran and Escher.

© Springer-Verlag Berlin Heidelberg 2016
M. Chechik and J.-F. Raskin (Eds.): TACAS 2016, LNCS 9636, pp. 36–53, 2016.
DOI: 10.1007/978-3-662-49674-9_3

changing, and in most cases adding, auxiliary annotations, and, in many cases, manipulation of a *ghost state*: a state that can be updated and used as normal, but is only used for verification purposes and will not be compiled.

With the exception of generic *lemmas* that can be reused in e.g. Dafny, the support for reuse of previous verification tasks in order to reduce the required user interaction is limited. In particular, there is no support for users to encode knowledge of common "proof" steps used for verification tasks. Some trial-and-error is involved as several known "verification patterns" may be attempted, and there could be multiple options for each of them. For these cases, the verification guidance process can be unnecessarily tedious and cost-ineffective.

This paper presents a novel extension to program verifiers, by extending the Dafny program verifier with a *tactic* language where users can encode more abstract and reusable verification patterns. Our hypothesis is that

*it is possible to abstract over low-level manual proof guidance by encoding high-level and reusable verification patterns in the program text of Dafny.*

The work is inspired by *proof tactics* for *interactive theorem provers* (ITPs), which allow users to encode re-usable proof patterns [19], and our main contribution is the introduction of such a tactic language on top of Dafny. A high-level introduction is given in Sect. 2 before giving the details of the syntactic extension and semantics in Sect. 3, and the implementation as the Tacny system in Sect. 4. We believe that Dafny tactics can be used to (*i*) *reduce the annotation overhead*[1]; (*ii*) *reduce development time*; and (*iii*) *increase readability* of the program text by abstracting low-level proof details. Based upon experiments in Tacny, Sect. 5 provides some evidence for (*i*), Sect. 6 contains related work; while we conclude and discuss future work, including how we plan to address (*ii*) and (*iii*), in Sect. 7.

## 2 Dafny Tactics by Example

Dafny [27] is a programming language and program verifier for the .NET platform, developed by Microsoft Research. The language is an imperative object-oriented language, containing both methods and proper functions (i.e. without side-effects). It also supports advanced features such as inductive [28] and co-inductive [29] datatypes and higher-order types [26]. It uses familiar notations for assignment (x := e), declarations (**var** x := e;), conditionals (**if** and **if-else**) and loops (e.g. **while**). It also supports pattern matching (**match**) and a 'such as' operator, where x :| p means that x is assigned a value such that p holds[2].

Dafny has been designed for verification. Properties are specified by *contracts* for methods/functions in terms of preconditions (**requires**) and postconditions (**ensures**). To verify a program, Dafny translates it into an *intermediate verification language* (IVL)[3] called Boogie [5]. From Boogie a set of VCs is generated

---

[1] To illustrate, [37] reported on 4.8 Lines of Annotation for each Line of Code.

[2] Full details of all examples and results in the paper available from [2].

[3] An IVL can be seen as a layer to ease the process of generating new program verifiers.

and sent to the Z3 SMT solver [35]. If it fails, then the failure is translated back to the Dafny code, via Boogie.

In the case of failure, a user must provide guidance in the program text[4]. The simplest form is to add assertions (**assert**) of true properties in the program text. In the case of loops, we might also provide loop invariants (**invariant**). Loops and recursion have to be shown to terminate and for advanced cases a user needs to provide a variant (**decreases**) to help Dafny prove this.

For more advanced verification tasks, one can make use of the *ghost state*. A ghost variable (**ghost var**) or ghost method can be introduced and used by the verifier. A lemma (**lemma**) is a type of ghost method that can be used to express richer properties, where assumptions are preconditions, and the conclusion becomes the postcondition. The proof is a method body that satisfies the postcondition, given the precondition. We will see examples of this below, but note that standard programming language elements are used in the body of the lemma, which illustrates the close correspondence between proofs and programs.

To illustrate Dafny, consider a simple compiler for arithmetic expressions[5]. Here, an inductive data type is used to capture arithmetic expressions as numbers, variables or addition:

```
datatype aexp = N(n: int) | V(x: vname) | Plus(0: aexp, 1: aexp)
```

A state s is a Dafny map from vnames to integers; Total(s) states that the state s is total; aval(a,s) is the evaluation of the arithmetic expression a over the state s; while asimp_const(a) performs constant folding of arithmetic expression a: constants added together are recursively replaced by their sum. The following lemma proves that constant•folding preserves the behaviour for a total state:

```
lemma AsimpConst(a: aexp, s: state)
   requires Total(s);
   ensures aval(asimp_const(a),s) = aval(a,s);
{   match a
     case N(n) ⇒
     case V(x) ⇒
     case Plus(a0,a1) ⇒ AsimpConst(a0,s); AsimpConst(a1,s); }
```

The proof follows by structural induction: using pattern matching, a case is introduced for each constructor and for the recursive case the lemma is applied recursively for each argument. Next, consider another example[6] where a list of expressions is defined as:

```
datatype List = Nil | Cons(Expr, List)
```

SubstL(l,v,val) is a function that replaces variable v with value val for each expression in list l. The following lemma proves that SubstL is idempotent:

---

[4] We assume correct programs: verification may also fail because the program is incorrect and in this case the program (or specification) needs to change.

[5] This example is taken from NipkowKlein-chapter3.dfy on the Dafny webpage.

[6] Substitution.dfy, also taken from the Dafny webpage; both examples available at [2].

```
lemma Lemma( l : List , v : int , val : int )
  ensures SubstL ( SubstL ( l , v , val ) , v , val ) = SubstL ( l , v , val ); {
{ match l
    case Nil ⇒
    case Cons( e , tail ) ⇒ Theorem ( e , v , val ); Lemma( tail , v , val ); }
```

This proof follows more or less the same pattern, with the difference that a separate lemma Theorem is applied for the first case, which shows idempotence for substitution of a single expression. Theorem is not discussed further here.

AsimpConst and Lemma illustrate two Dafny verification tasks that exhibit the same verification pattern: a case analysis for each constructor of an inductive data type, with two possible lemma applications. Still, a user has to spell out all the proof details. To abstract over such details, we introduce a *tactic* construct that allows the user to encode the *verification pattern*. The proof details of the lemmas can then be replaced by a single tactic application. This is achieved by extending Dafny with a new ghost method called **tactic**, without any contracts. The following tactic captures the proofs of AsimpConst and Lemma:

```
tactic CasePerm ( v : Element )
{ solved {
    var lem1 : | lem1 in lemmas ();
    var lem2 : | lem2 in lemmas ();
    cases( v ){ var vars := variables ();
                perm ( lem1 , vars ); perm ( lem2 , vars ); } } }
```

The tactic takes an input v, expected to be a variable of an inductive data type. It then picks two lemma names, lem1 and lem2. Here, all possible combinations of lemma names will be generated as separate branches of the search space. Then for each branch, cases(v) will generate a match statement with a case for each constructor ofv. Within each case the "body" of cases is evaluated. Here, all variables in scope are found (vars). The invocation of perm(lem1,vars) generates all possible permutations of applying lemma lem1 with arguments found in any sub-set of vars in separate branches of the search space. The second application of perm does the same for lem2. The keyword solved{ body } states that the program has to verify when body has been evaluated. This is required here as a tactic may be used to progress a proof without completing it, which is desirable in certain cases. Note that the tactic will stop evaluating when a proof is found, thus the body will not be applied for cases such as Nil above. For that reason, CasePerm(b) will also work for the following lemma found in the first example:

```
lemma BsimpCorrect ( b : bexp , s : state )
  requires Total ( s );
  ensures bval ( bsimp ( b ) , s ) = bval ( b , s ); {
{ match b
  case Bc( v ) ⇒
  case Not( b0 ) ⇒ BsimpCorrect ( b0 , s );
  case And( b0 , b1 ) ⇒ BsimpCorrect ( b0 , s ); BsimpCorrect ( b1 , s );
  case Less( a0 , a1 ) ⇒ AsimpCorrect ( a0 , s ); AsimpCorrect ( a1 , s ); }
```

This lemma states a similar property to AsimpConst, with the difference that it is applied to boolean expressions. It works for the Not(b0) case as it will stop evaluating when the case verifies. Thus, in the Not(b0) case the second call to perm will not be applied as BsimpCorrect(b0,s) is sufficient. To apply a tactic the body is replaced by a call to it, illustrated for Lemma:

```
lemma Lemma2( l : List , v : int , val : int )
   ensures  SubstL ( SubstL ( l , v , val ) , v , val ) = SubstL ( l , v , val );
{    CasePerm ( l ); }
```

The tactic language is *metalanguage* for Dafny, where tactic evaluation works at the Dafny level: it takes a Dafny program with tactics and tactic applications, evaluates the tactics and produces a new valid Dafny program, where tactic calls are replaced by Dafny constructs generated by the tactics. The advantages of working on the Dafny level are: (*i*) *iterative development and debugging* is supported as a user can partly develop a tactic, inspect the result and then extend or modify it; (*ii*) *soundness* as users can inspect and validate the result and the tool is independent of its encoding into Boogie; (*iii*) *modularity* as it becomes easier to adapt to new versions of Dafny.

While we can rely on the soundness of Dafny for the actual verification, a program transformation could in principle make changes to both the program and its specification. A tactic should not make such changes to Dafny programs as this is changing what we are attempting to prove:

**Definition 1 (Contract Preserving Transformation).** *A* contract preserving transformation *is a program transformation that preserves the behaviour and the contract of a method (or lemma or function).*

The evaluation of a tactic call will transform the code by replacing the call with the code the tactic generates. To illustrate, the evaluation of Lemma2 should generate the same body as Lemma (or similar verifiable code that fits the pattern encoded by the tactic). As a lemma is a ghost construct, and the contract is unchanged, the transformation is contract preserving.

By reusing Dafny constructs, users can develop schematic and intuitive tactics, comparable to *declarative* or *schematic* tactics found in some modern ITP tactic languages, e.g. [4]. To illustrate, a proof by 'mathematical induction' over a variable n, where we assume existence of tactic base_tac(), which handles the base case (when n is 0), and tactic step_tac(), which is used for the step case, can be written as follows:

```
tactic InductTac ( n : Element )
{ if  n = 0 { . base_tac (); }
   else { var curr := current ();   curr ( n−1 );  step_tac (); } }
```

Variable curr will point to the "current" method or lemma in which the tactic was called from (and the generated code will be added). curr(n-1) is therefore an application of the induction hypothesis before the step case is handled.

The **if** statement of InductTac is at the *object level*, i.e. it will be part of the generated Dafny code after applying the tactic. Statements such as **if** (and **while**) are also used at the *meta-level*, i.e. used by Tacny and will not be generated. These levels are distinguished by whether the tactic evaluator can evaluate the condition. If it cannot be evaluated then it is an object-level feature. In this case, we do not know the value of n hence we cannot resolve whether n = 0 is true or false.

Such schematic tactics provide a very elegant way of composing tactics, a well known problem for ITP tactics [3]. cases(v){ body } illustrated another example of composition where { body } is used to separate tactics applied within each case, from tactics that should follow the match statement.

Both CasePerm and InductTac have a parameter of type *Element*. This is a Tacny-specific type denoting the name of an element of the Dafny program text, such as a variable, method name or lemma name. For CasePerm this is assumed to be a variable of an inductively defined datatype while for InductTac it should be a variable that is a natural number. To simplify, we are using a single type to refer to this; *type safety* is handled by Dafny which will fail when we try to verify a wrongly typed program. This is another example of *modularity*, albeit at the expense of efficiency in this case. Note that for InductTac we cannot use **nat** as this refers to a number and not a variable of **nat** type.

## 3   The Tacny Language

The Tacny language is designed to be as familiar for Dafny users as possible. A tactic definition is a type of Dafny ghost method, with the following syntax:

**tactic** *Id(Params)*{ *TStmts* }

where a parameter *Param* has the syntax *Id* : *Type*. A type here is any Dafny type [26], with two additional types: *Element*, already discussed; and *Term*, the term representation of a Dafny expression. A Tacny statement *TStmt* is:

$$TStmt := Atom \mid Id(TExprs); \mid var\ Id := TExpr; \mid Id := TExpr;$$
$$\mid \textbf{var}\ Id : \mid TExpr; \mid Id : \mid TExpr; \mid \{\ TStmts\ \}$$
$$\mid \textbf{if}\ TExpr\ \{\ TStmts\ \} \mid \textbf{if}\ TExpr\ \{\ TStmts\ \}\ \textbf{else}\{\ TStmts\ \}$$
$$\mid \textbf{while}\ TExpr\ Invs\ \{\ TStmts\ \} \mid TStmt \mid\mid TStmt;$$

With the exception of || and *Atom*, these constructs are part of the Dafny language. However, within a tactic they have different semantics: e.g. a declared variable in a tactic will not appear in the Dafny program resulting from tactic evaluation. *Atom* refers to the *atomic tactics* of the Tacny language. These are the hard-coded building blocks of Tacny, and all tactics are compositions of them. The set of atomic tactics is expected to change and develop, but hopefully converge. So far, we have identified the following atomic tactics:

$$Atom := id(); \mid fail (); \mid \textbf{invariant}\ TExpr; \mid \textbf{decreases}\ TExpr;$$
$$\mid \textbf{assert}\ TExpr; \mid \textbf{fresh var}\ Id := TExpr; \mid \textbf{fresh var}\ Id : \mid TExpr;$$
$$\mid try\{\ TStmts\ \}catch\{\ TStmts\ \} \mid cases(Element)\{\ TStmts\ \}$$
$$\mid solved\{\ TStmts\ \} \mid perm(Element,\textbf{seq}<Element>);$$

Dafny's contract and loop (in)variant *Inv* is extended with tactic calls *Id(TExprs)*, with the syntax definition omitted for space reasons. A *TExpr* is an extension of Dafny's expression *Expr*:

$$TExpr := Expr \mid current() \mid variables() \mid lemmas() \mid params() \mid \cdots$$

Note that to understand the evaluation of Tacny expressions, the full details of Dafny expressions are not required and thus omitted. To evaluate a Tacny expression, a context $C$, containing relevant details of the program at the point a tactic call was made, and a state $s$, which holds a map from Tacny-specific variables to values, are given. These may be updated during evaluation. The evaluation of an expression is given by $[\![-]\!]_{\langle C,s \rangle}$, with the following semantics:

$$[\![e_1 \; op \; e_2]\!]_{\langle C,s \rangle} := \qquad \text{when } op \in \{+,-,*,/\}$$
$$\qquad [\![e_1]\!]_{\langle C,s \rangle} \; op \; [\![e_2]\!]_{\langle C,s \rangle} \text{ and } [\![e_1]\!]_{\langle C,s \rangle} \text{ and } [\![e_2]\!]_{\langle C,s \rangle} \text{ are numbers.}$$
$$[\![!e]\!]_{\langle C,s \rangle} := \neg[\![e]\!]_{\langle C,s \rangle} \qquad \text{when } [\![e]\!]_{\langle C,s \rangle} \neq \bot$$
$$[\![|e|]\!]_{\langle C,s \rangle} := length([\![e]\!]_{\langle C,s \rangle}) \text{ when } [\![e]\!]_{\langle C,s \rangle} \neq \bot$$
$$[\![e]\!]_{\langle C,s \rangle} := true \qquad \text{when } tautology(e)$$
$$[\![e]\!]_{\langle C,s \rangle} := false \qquad \text{when } tautology(!e)$$
$$[\![n]\!]_{\langle C,s \rangle} := s(n) \qquad \text{when } n \in dom(s)$$
$$[\![v]\!]_{\langle C,s \rangle} := v \qquad \text{when } v \text{ is a value}$$
$$[\![f()]\!]_{\langle C,s \rangle} := C.f \qquad \text{when } f \in \{current, variables, lemmas, params\}$$
$$[\![e]\!]_{\langle C,s \rangle} := \bot \qquad \text{otherwise}$$

*tautology* is a simple tautology checker for proposition logic with (in)-equality; *length* returns the length of a sequence, and a dot-notation is used to project values from the context. If an expression cannot be evaluated, then $\bot$ is returned. In that case, the expression is treated as *object* level. E.g. if we cannot evaluate the condition of an **if**-statement, then an **if**-statement will be generated, which enables us to write declarative/schematic tactics in Tacny. In such cases, Tacny-level variables need to be instantiated (using the state $s$) and Tacny-level expressions (current, variables, lemmas, params) unfolded (using the context $C$). This is achieved by $[-]_{\langle C,s \rangle}$, which we do not provide further details of. In the semantics we often try $[\![e]\!]_{\langle C,s \rangle}$ first, applying $[-]_{\langle C,s \rangle}$ if it fails (i.e. returns $\bot$):

$$[\![e]\!]^{?}_{\langle C,s \rangle} := \begin{cases} [\![e]\!]_{\langle C,s \rangle} & \text{when } [\![e]\!]_{\langle C,s \rangle} \neq \bot \\ [e]_{\langle C,s \rangle} & \text{otherwise} \end{cases}$$

We give Plotkin-style big-step operational semantics [38], using a nondeterministic relation $\longrightarrow$. $\langle C, s, c, stmt \rangle \longrightarrow \langle C', s', c' \rangle$ should be read as: given context $C$, state $s$, generated Dafny code $c$ and Tacny statement $stmt$, evaluation will produce a new context $C'$, state $s'$ and Dafny code $c'$. The inference rules are given in Figs. 1 and 2. For space reasons we do not provide a full set of rules[7]. We focus on the interesting cases, omitting rules for generating context and evaluating methods and lemmas, where tactics are called from, which is only briefly discussed.

---

[7] For full details we refer to the 'Tacny system working document' [21].

$$\frac{\langle C, s, c, stmt_1 \rangle \longrightarrow \langle C', s', c' \rangle}{\langle C, s, c, stmt_1 \parallel stmt_2 \rangle \longrightarrow \langle C', s', c' \rangle} \qquad \frac{\langle C, s, c, stmt_2 \rangle \longrightarrow \langle C', s', c' \rangle}{\langle C, s, c, stmt_1 \parallel stmt_2 \rangle \longrightarrow \langle C', s', c' \rangle}$$

$$\frac{\langle C, s, c, stmt \rangle \longrightarrow \langle C'', s'', c'' \rangle \qquad C''.vcs \neq \{\} \qquad \langle C'', s'', c'', stmts \rangle \longrightarrow \langle C', s', c' \rangle}{\langle C, s, c, stmt\ stmts \rangle \longrightarrow \langle C', s', c' \rangle}$$

$$\frac{\langle C, s, c, stmt \rangle \longrightarrow \langle C', s', c' \rangle \qquad C'.vcs = \{\}}{\langle C, s, c, stmt\ stmts \rangle \longrightarrow \langle C', s', c' \rangle}$$

$$\frac{\langle C, s, c, B \rangle \longrightarrow \langle C, s', c' \rangle}{\langle C, s, c, \{B\} \rangle \longrightarrow \langle C[vcs := C'.vcs], dom(s) \triangleleft s', c' \rangle}$$

$$\frac{x \notin dom(s) \cup C.v \cup C.p \qquad [\![e]\!]^{?}_{\langle C,s \rangle} = v}{\langle C, s, c, \mathbf{var}\ x := e; \rangle \longrightarrow \langle C, s[x := v], c \rangle} \qquad \frac{x \in dom(s) \qquad [\![e]\!]^{?}_{\langle C,s \rangle} = v}{\langle C, s, c, x := e; \rangle \longrightarrow \langle C, s[x := v], c \rangle}$$

$$\frac{x \notin dom(s) \cup C.v \cup C.p \qquad [\![P(n)]\!]_{\langle C,s \rangle} = true}{\langle C, s, c, \mathbf{var}\ x : \mid P(x); \rangle \longrightarrow \langle C, s[x := n], c \rangle} \qquad \frac{C' = C[vcs := verify(C.M[c])]}{\langle C, s, c, \mathsf{id}(); \rangle \longrightarrow \langle C', s, c \rangle}$$

$$\frac{x \in dom(s) \qquad [\![P(n)]\!]_{\langle C,s \rangle} = true}{\langle C, s, c, x : \mid P(x); \rangle \longrightarrow \langle C, s[x := n], c \rangle} \qquad \frac{[\![b]\!]_{\langle C,s \rangle} = false}{\langle C, s, c, \mathbf{while}\ b\ I\{B\} \rangle \longrightarrow \langle C, s, c \rangle}$$

$$\frac{[\![b]\!]_{\langle C,s \rangle} = true \qquad \langle C, s, c, \mathsf{id}(); B \rangle \longrightarrow \langle C', s', c' \rangle \qquad C'.vcs = \{\}}{\langle C, s, c, \mathbf{while}\ b\ I\{B\} \rangle \longrightarrow \langle C', dom(s) \triangleleft s', c' \rangle}$$

$$\frac{\begin{array}{c}[\![b]\!]_{\langle C,s \rangle} = true \qquad \langle C, s, c, \mathsf{id}(); B \rangle \longrightarrow \langle C'', s'', c'' \rangle \\ C''.vcs \neq \{\} \qquad \langle C'', s'', c'', \mathbf{while}\ b\ I\{B\} \rangle \longrightarrow \langle C', s', c' \rangle \end{array}}{\langle C, s, c, \mathbf{while}\ b\ I\{B\} \rangle \longrightarrow \langle C', dom(s) \triangleleft s', c' \rangle}$$

$$\frac{\begin{array}{c}\langle C[mode := annot], s, \epsilon, I \rangle \longrightarrow \langle C'', s'', I' \rangle \qquad M = \lambda x.\ C.M[\mathbf{while}\ [\![b]\!]_{\langle C,s \rangle}\ I'\{x\}] \\ [\![b]\!]_{\langle C,s \rangle} = \bot \qquad \langle C[M := M], s, \epsilon, B \rangle \longrightarrow \langle C', s', B' \rangle \end{array}}{\langle C, s, c, \mathbf{while}\ b\ I\{B\} \rangle \longrightarrow \langle C[vcs := C'.vcs], s, c \cdot \mathbf{while}\ [\![b]\!]_{\langle C,s \rangle}\ I'\{B'\} \rangle}$$

**Fig. 1.** Operational semantics for Tacny statements [1/2]

To evaluate $\parallel$, as shown in Fig. 1, either the statement on the left or on the right is evaluated. Sequential composition depends on whether the program verifies after the first statement is completed. If the set of verification conditions $vcs$ is empty, the evaluation stops; if not, it continues to the next statement. When a block is evaluated then only changes to the given state $s$ are kept and the context is only updated with the VCs[8]. A declaration or assignment will update $s$, and the expression $e$ is evaluated by $[\![e]\!]^{?}_{\langle C,s \rangle}$, meaning it may not evaluate fully. The projections $C.v$ and $C.p$ are the set of declared variables and parameters, respectively, of the method the tactic was called from. To evaluate the $: \mid$ operator

---

[8] $S \triangleleft R$ restricts the domain of relation/map $R$ to the set $S$.

$$\frac{C.tac[t] = t(a_1, \cdots, a_n)\{B\} \quad \langle C, [a_1, \cdots, a_n := [\![e_1]\!]^?_{\langle C,s \rangle}, \cdots, [\![e_n]\!]^?_{\langle C,s \rangle}], c, B \rangle \longrightarrow \langle C', s', c' \rangle}{\langle C, s, c, t(e_1, \cdots, e_n) \rangle \longrightarrow \langle C, s, c' \rangle}$$

$$\frac{\langle C, s, c, B \rangle \longrightarrow \langle C', s', c' \rangle \quad C'.vcs = \{\}}{\langle C, s, c, \mathsf{solved}\{B\} \rangle \longrightarrow \langle C[vcs := C'.vcs], dom(s) \lhd s', c' \rangle}$$

$$\frac{mode = annot}{\langle C, s, c, \mathbf{decreases}\ e; \rangle \longrightarrow \langle C, s, c \cdot \mathbf{decreases}\ [e]_{\langle C,s \rangle}; \rangle}$$

$$\frac{mode = code \quad C' = C[vcs := verify(C.M[c \cdot \mathbf{assert}\ [e]_{\langle C,s \rangle};])]}{\langle C, s, c, \mathbf{assert}\ e; \rangle \longrightarrow \langle C', s, c \cdot \mathbf{assert}\ [e]_{\langle C,s \rangle}; \rangle}$$

$$\frac{a_1 \in as \quad \cdots \quad a_n \in xs \quad m(a_1, \cdots, a_n)\_\{\_\} \in C.m \cup C.l \cup C.f}{ghost(m) \quad C' = C[vcs := verify(C.M[c \cdot m(a_1, \cdots, a_n);])] \quad C.mode = code}{\langle C, s, c, \mathsf{perm}(m, as); \rangle \longrightarrow \langle C', s, c \cdot m(a_1, \cdots, a_n); \rangle}$$

$$\frac{\begin{array}{c} x : T \quad T = C_1(x_{10}, \cdots, x_{1i}) \mid \cdots \mid C_n(x_{n0}, \cdots, x_{nj}) \quad x_{ij} \notin C.v \cup C.p \\ M_1 = \lambda y.\ C.M[\mathsf{match}\ x\ \mathsf{case}\ C_1(x_{10}, \cdots, x_{1i}) \Rightarrow y \quad \mathsf{case}\ \_ \Rightarrow \mathsf{assume\ false};] \cdots \\ M_n = \lambda y.\ C.M[\mathsf{match}\ x\ \mathsf{case}\ C_n(x_{n0}, \cdots, x_{nj}) \Rightarrow y \quad \mathsf{case}\ \_ \Rightarrow \mathsf{assume\ false};] \\ \langle C[v := C.v \cup \{x_{10}, \cdots, x_{1i}\}, M = M_1], s, \epsilon, \mathsf{id}(); B \rangle \longrightarrow \langle C'_1, s_1, c_1 \rangle \cdots \\ \langle C[v := C.v \cup \{x_{n0}, \cdots, x_{nj}\}, M = M_n], s, \epsilon, \mathsf{id}(); B \rangle \longrightarrow \langle C'_n, s_n, c_n \rangle \\ m_1 = \mathsf{case}\ C_1(x_{10}, \cdots, x_{1i}) \Rightarrow c_1 \quad \cdots \quad m_n = \mathsf{case}\ C_n(x_{n0}, \cdots, x_{nj}) \Rightarrow c_n \\ C' = C[vcs := verify(C.M[c \cdot \mathsf{match}\ x\ m_1 \cdots m_n])] \quad C.mode = code \end{array}}{\langle C, s, c, \mathsf{cases}(x)\{\ B\ \} \rangle \longrightarrow \langle C', s, c \cdot \mathsf{match}\ x\ m_1 \cdots m_n \rangle}$$

**Fig. 2.** Operational semantics for Tacny statements [2/2]

we find a value where the property holds. This has to be enumerable, and $P$ has to have the syntactic form $x$ in $X$, possibly followed by further constraints on $x$. $X$ must be a collection that can be derived from $s$ and/or $C$.

The identity atomic tactic id() only changes the context, by attempting to *verify* the program using Dafny. In order to apply Dafny to verify it, the code surrounding a tactic call (or other construct as seen below) must be given. This is provided by $C.M$ in the context, with a "hole" $[-]$ where the code generated by the tactic can be "plugged in", as illustrated by $C.M[c]$ in the identity tactic. *verify* is used to represent a call to Dafny, returning a set of open VCs. If Dafny fails to execute, e.g. due to type errors, then the rule will fail. fail() always fails and is therefore not given an inference rule following a closed world assumption.

We will only discuss the **while** control structure as this is the most interesting and complicated; conditionals (**if** and **if-else**) have comparable semantics but are omitted for space reasons. **while** is captured by 4 inference rules. The first is the trivial case where the condition is *false* and nothing is changed. The second case is when the condition is *true* and the resulting program verifies, in which case the loop is terminated. Note that the body is prefixed by a call to the identity tactic to enforce a call to the verifier before a tactic is applied. The third case is the "step case" where the program does not verify and the loop is recursively applied. The final case is the most interesting one. This is an example of a schematic tactic, where the **while** loop will be generated in the Dafny code. Here, it is not possible to evaluate the condition, meaning $[-]_{\langle C,s\rangle}$ is applied to the generated condition. As the loop annotations (loop invariants and decrease clauses) may have tactic calls, this is first evaluated in an *annot* mode we will return to below. We then evaluate the body. Note that $C.M$ is updated with the loop (using $\lambda$ notation for the hole) as the verifier has to know about the loop when applied within the body; this change is local to the loop and is discarded afterwards. $\epsilon$ denotes empty code, and $\cdot$ concatenates code.

The rule to make a call to another tactic is shown in Fig. 2. The input state of the method only contains the parameters, meaning there is no shared state between tactics. These are evaluated as far as possible. A tactic call within a lemma or method has the same semantics, with $c$ set to $\epsilon$. $C.tac$ maps tactic names to their definition. The **solved** tactic is similar to a block, but requires that the program verifies on termination of the block; **decreases** statements are only valid in the *annot* mode, i.e. contract or loop annotations. Note that the expression is simplified by $[-]_{\langle C,s\rangle}$ which e.g. allows us to write more generic tactics by including Tacny level variables. Note that the verifier is not applied in the annotations, however it is after an **assert**ion is added. This requires a *code* mode, i.e. generation of Dafny statements.

The perm$(m, as)$ tactic generates all possible ways of applying $m$ with arguments taken from $as$. Here, $m$ is first found in the context among the methods, lemmas and functions, and checked that it is a ghost construct. The rule allows all possible combinations, while Dafny is used to ensure type checking as part of the verification. The **cases** tactic has the most involved semantics. The given variable has to of an inductively-defined type and the constructors (with fresh argument names) are created. Each case is evaluated separately, and to control the verifier the other cases are assumed to be false[9].

Most state-of-the-art ITP systems follow the LCF-approach [19] which reduces soundness to a small "trusted kernel" of axioms and inference rules. The following proposition states a similar feature for Tacny without proof:

**Proposition 1.** $\longrightarrow$ *is a contract preserving transformation if the atomics are contract preserving.*

To increase soundness, our aim is to converge to a small "trusted kernel" of atomic tactics we can show are contract preserving. This is straightforward to show for the atomic tactics discussed here:

**Proposition 2.** *id(), fail(), perm, cases, **decreases**, **assert**, solved are contract preserving.*

---

[9] The underscore '_' is not valid Dafny syntax in pattern matching but used for brevity.

## 4    The Tacny System

The Tacny tool provides a proof-of-concept implementation of the semantics. The architecture of this tool is shown in Fig. 3, where the shaded boxes represent Dafny components. The tool accepts a Dafny program extended with tactics (.tacny) and the Dafny PARSER has therefore been updated with the grammar discussed in the previous section.

   The parsed program is then sent to the INTERPRETER, which is discussed in detail below. It uses the GENERATOR, which removes all tactics and tactic calls from the source program, thus making it a valid Dafny (.dfy) program. This is used at the end, to generate "a proof", in terms of a valid Dafny program, and during interpretation. In the latter case, the DAFNY RESOLVER performs *type checking* and prepares the program for translation to BOOGIE, which is conducted by the VERIFIER. As with the PARSER, this is a minor update of the existing Dafny code, with some additional book-keeping. The result from BOOGIE is then sent back to the INTERPRETER.

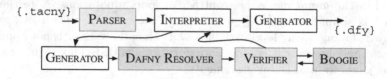

**Fig. 3.** Tacny tool architecture

**procedure** INTERPRETER($prog$ : Tacny)
  $r \leftarrow$ INITTASK($prog$)
  $r \leftarrow r\big[pc := \text{NEXTTAC}(r)\big]$
  **if** ENDOFFILE($r.pc$) **then**
    **return** $[r]$
  $res, solutions \leftarrow [r], []$
  **repeat**
    **for** each $r \in$ MAPS(TAC, $res$) **do**
      $r \leftarrow r\big[pc := \text{NEXTTAC}(r)\big]$
      **if** $r.vcs = \{\} \vee$ ENDOFFILE($r.pc$) **then**
        $solutions \leftarrow solutions + r$
      **else** $res \leftarrow res + r$
  **until** $res = []$
  **return** solutions

**procedure** TAC($t$ : Task)
  $res \leftarrow [t]$
  **repeat**
    **for** each $r \in$ MAPS(STEP, $res$) **do**
      **if** $r.vcs = \{\}$ **then return** $[r]$
      $res \leftarrow res + r'$
  **until** ENDOFTAC($t.pc$)
  **return** res

**procedure** STEP($t$ : Task)
  $res \leftarrow []$
  **for** each $r \in$ TACSTEP($t$) **do**
    $dfy \leftarrow$ GENERATE($r$)
    **if** $dfy =$ NULL **then return** $[]$
    $bgy \leftarrow$ BOOGIE($dfy$)
    **if** PROVEN($bgy$) **then**
      **return** $[r[vcs := \{\}]]$
    **if** SUBGOALS($bgy$) **then**
      $res \leftarrow res + [r[vcs := bgy]]$
  **return** res

**Fig. 4.** Tacny interpreter

The main work of Tacny happens in the INTERPRETER, and the algorithm is given in Fig. 4. It first generates an initial task by INITTASK. A task is a record containing a state, context and Tacny program similar to the input of $\longrightarrow$ from Sect. 3. In addition, it contains a program counter. INITTASK will generate the context, and initialise the state to empty. NEXTTAC will then find the next tactic call, or reach the end of the file (ENDOFFILE) if there are no more calls.

In the main loop, the INTERPRETER keeps track of intermediate results *res* and completed *solutions*. It then applies a *breadth-first* search strategy by applying a single tactic application, represented by the undefined TACSTEP procedure, for each element of the result list. This continues until either there are no "open" VCs or there are no more tactic calls. Each tactic evaluation involves a step by step evaluation where after each step a Dafny program is generated. Tacny works on a method-by-method basis, and to focus verification on the current method, the body of all other methods is removed, and all tactics and tactic calls are removed to make it a valid Dafny program. The DAFNY RESOLVER may fail, e.g. if the program does not type check, returning NULL; in that case that particular task is aborted. If not, BOOGIE is applied and the result is returned. If BOOGIE can prove that the program is correct, then the task is completed. This modularity has the advantage that extensions to Dafny and Boogie can be easily integrated: Tacny is a layer on top of Dafny. Currently, some features of Sect. 3 are not supported, such as object level (schematic) loops.

## 5   Experiments

In Sect. 2 we introduced the CasePerm tactic and showed that it was applicable for multiple examples. Table 1 shows the results from our experiments[10], with results from running CasePerm above the double line (1). **Calls** refers to the number of tactic calls for each file; **TLoC** and **DLoC** are the LoC for the respective Tacny and (analysed) Dafny programs; **Vars** is the highest number of variables in a branch; **#B** is the number of branches; **#DB** is the number of discarded branches before a solution was found; **T** is the running time for Tacny in seconds.

A user must often provide a variant in form of a **decreases** clause to prove that a loop or recursive method terminates. This can often be a trial-and-error process, where the user may have some ideas in hand. Here, we give a generic tactic to generate either a single variable or a subtraction of two variables:

```
tactic VariantGen(){
  solved{ var x :| x in params() + variables();
        decreases x ||
        { var y :| x in params() + variables() ∧ x ≠ y;
        decreases x−y }; }
}
```

---

[10] All examples are taken from the Dafny repo [1], with code used available from [2].
Experiments conducted running Windows 8.1 on Intel i7 2.4 GHz with 4GB RAM.

**Table 1.** Results from executing: CasePerm (1) and VariantGen (2).

| Tac | Program | Calls | TLoC | DLoC | Vars | #B | #DB | T(sec) |
|-----|---------|-------|------|------|------|-----|------|--------|
| (1) | NipkowKlein-chapter3.dfy | 2 | 186 | 192 | 4 | 1473 | 506 | 113 |
|     | Substitution.dfy | 2 | 52 | 84 | 5 | 21739 | 4758 | 190 |
|     | InductionVsCoinduction.dfy | 1 | 74 | 70 | 5 | 1137 | 544 | 30 |
|     | Streams.dfy | 7 | 221 | 228 | 3 | 62 | 0 | 37 |
|     | CoqArt-InsertionSort.dfy | 2 | 201 | 198 | 2 | 58 | 0 | 15 |
| (2) | Dijkstra.dfy | 1 | 126 | 117 | | 19 | 4 | 8 |
|     | SchorrWaite.dfy | 1 | 204 | 195 | | 34 | 7 | 11 |
|     | Prime.dfy | 1 | 232 | 224 | | 54 | 9 | 20 |
|     | SetIterator.dfy | 1 | 82 | 63 | | 48 | 6 | 20 |
|     | SimpleInduction.dfy | 1 | 66 | 65 | | 11 | 0 | 5 |

The results from applying this to a set of examples can be seen below the double line (2) in Table 1. The number of variables are omitted as they are not relevant.

The fact that a single tactic can be applied to several examples (14 and 5) and, for CasePerm several lemmas within each example, provides evidence for our hypothesis that tactics for Dafny are feasible. In most cases, CasePerm reduces the annotation overhead. For the other cases, the size has not reduced for 2 reasons: (i) the proofs replaced where short; and (ii) although the tactic is the same for all examples, it had to be copied into each example for technical reasons. This is the reason why VariantGen increased the LoC: each variant is a single line, thus replacing it with a tactic call will have the same LoC. For this tactic, we cannot argue reduced annotation overhead, however the manual search task is replaced by a tactic, thus development time should decrease.

For some examples CasePerm has a very high branching factor, in particular when there are 4 or more variables. This is due to the naivety of the perm tactic, and we are working on improvements to this. We believe that this has potential for a very generic tactic if we can extend it and, at the same time, improve on the branching factor. VariantGen is discussed further in Sect. 7.

## 6    Related Work

An alternative approach to Dafny tactics is the more traditional approach of proving the generated VCs in an interactive prover and developing tactics at this level. This has the following drawbacks: users have to (additionally) learn how to use and develop tactics in the interactive prover[11]; and certain tactics, such as adding an invariant, precede VC generation. Thus, a richer set of tactics can be developed in the program text. Most tactic languages for ITP systems,

---

[11] It commonly takes at least six months just to become a proficient user of an ITP system (see e.g. [30]), and even longer to have sufficient expertise to develop tactics.

dating back to the seminal LCF system [19], contain a *combinator* language to compose tactics into larger and more powerful ones. For example, the **solved** tactic is common. As far as possible, we have attempted to use Dafny's constructs to compose tactics to keep them as familiar as possible. Within ITP, there is also a trend towards building tactic languages at the *proof script* level, compared with the *implementation language* of the system. LTac for Coq [14] and EisBach for Isabelle [33] are examples of such languages. Non-trivial tactic compositions are hard to get right for tactic languages due to their procedural nature; see e.g. [18] for a discussion. Inspired by *declarative proof scripts*, with Mizar [36] and Isabelle/Isar [40] probably the most well-known, [4] develops a *declarative tactic language*, where a tactic is given a more schematic description. Such schematics are also supported in Tacny, and provide a more intuitive mechanism for tactic composition. Most of the popular ITPs follow the so-called LCF approach [19], where soundness is ensured by a small "trusted kernel" of axioms and inference rules. The type system ensures that all proof steps go through this kernel. We are following this approach by reducing our correctness property (contract preserving transformation) to the atomic tactics, where all the code is generated. We hope the set of atomics will converge into a small kernel. These resemblences to ITP tactics are the reason that we have adopted the 'tactic' name for our language. It is also considered good practice that each refactoring should only make small changes to the code as this is easier to analyse [17]. [41] applies refactoring to proof scripts to improve existing proofs; however, it is not used to support the proof process of open conjectures, as is the case for Tacny.

We are not familiar with any other work attempting to develop a tactic language at the program text level for program verifiers[12]. Chen [7] describes a simple imperative language that includes verification constructs. This may provide the foundations to encode a tactic language, similar to ours, but it is not clear how this can be done. Moreover, our goal is to work with existing program verifiers. The Aris project [32] uses case-based reasoning to re-use specifications from a large corpus of existing proofs in Spec# [6], and it would be interesting to see if the Tacny language could be used as a target language for the generalisation of such specifications. There has also been work at "lower-levels": Leino [28] has developed an "induction tactic" for Dafny. This is an optimisation of the encoding into Boogie, and requires deep understanding of the underlying Dafny implementation. Moreover, working at this level one has to be very careful not to introduce inconsistencies in the logic. At an even lower-level, a tactic language has been developed for the underlying Z3 prover [13] – again, this requires expertise in SMT solving and Z3.

To *improve readability* of the program text, Dafny supports Dijkstra-style calculational proofs (**calc**) [30], comparable to declaritive proofs in e.g. Mizar or Isabelle/Isar. A considerable amount of work has been done using *static analysis* techniques on the program text in order to *reduce the number of required annotations* by automatically generating these (in particular loop invariants) [16,22,23,39]. Techniques include abstract interpretation [12], constraint-based

---

[12] Unpublished early ideas for tactics by the first author is available on ArXiV [20].

techniques [10], inductive logic programming [16], and declarative machine learning [31]. Stretching our "ITP analogy", comparing this work to Tacny, is like comparing tactic languages to decision procedures: we are not proposing a new technique to improve automation, but a language in which users can encode patterns so *they* can improve automation. Note that Dafny uses abstract interpretation at the Boogie level [5].

The perm tactic can seen as a limited form of *term synthesis* at the Dafny level. This technique is used in theory exploration tools, such as IsaCosy [25] and HipSpec [8]. The perm tactic can also be seen as a form of a *brute-force* tactic that essentially tries various combinations without an overall proof pattern. The cases tactic introduces 'proof by cases' for inductive data types. This can easily be extended to support structural induction, by adding recursive calls. The CasePerm tactic is a generalisation of this and similar to how one would prove simple inductive lemmas in ITPs: apply induction followed by a powerful tactic. The VariantGen tactic is used to guide the search for a termination measure. There is a considerable amount of work on proving termination (see e.g. [11]), which is beyond the discussion here.

## 7    Conclusion and Future Work

We have extended the Dafny program verifier by adding support for users to encode reusable verification patterns using a novel *tactic language* in the program text. We have provided formal syntax and semantics for this extension, implemented as the Tacny tool. Our experiments have shown that *it is possible to encode Dafny tactics and reuse them accross verification tasks*. This has been illustrated by two tactics, used to automate 19 lemmas that required interaction. 10 different Dafny programs were used in order to illustrate generality.

We are continously developing, re-engineering and analysing Dafny programs, in order to extract common verification patterns, and use this to develop new (atomic) tactics, which we hope will converge as a result of this work. Based upon ITP kernels we hope that around $15 - 20$ will be sufficient. We are currently investigating better integration of the proof failure information into the language, e.g. the solved condition of VariantGen could be weakened to 'no termination VCs'. We are also starting to incorporate (dynamic) contracts to rule out invalid branches earlier. We also plan to extend the language to: allow function definitions at the Tacny level for more readable tactics; allow "a tactic body" as an "argument" for user defined tactics (as is used for the cases atomic tactic); and use of the recently added higher order features in Dafny [26] to allow tactics as arguments, e.g. allow us to write **tactic** Maybe(t : Tactic){id() || t(); }. Through user evaluations, we would like to validate if/when users find the program text more readable when low-level proofs are replaced by tactics.

The perm tactic is a starting point for a generic brute force tactic, and we are working on extending it to support richer parameters (e.g. constructors and operators which themselves have parameters), and support for assignments, control structures and use within calculations [30]. We would also like to create a more generic **VariantGen** tactic, with better control of the execution: e.g. only use variables that change, and determine in which cases one variant is more likely to work, thus replacing non-deterministic choice with a conditional.

The Tacny tool is only a proof-of-concept and not particularly fast and we have identified multiple improvements. Firstly, some of the tactics have an ad-hoc implementation and we plan to refactor the code into a more generic framework, where it is easy to extend it with new atomic tactics and expressions and the ability to explore different search strategies. Ideally, tactics should be able to tailor their search strategy. We also plan to explore the use of lazy lists and lazy evaluation to improve memory consumption, and data parallelisation to improve speed. We would also like to see how calls to Dafny/Boogie can be reduced, possibly adding such control to the user via e.g. a form of **atomic** statement.

Longer term we would like to have a closer integration with Dafny and added support for Tacny in the Visual Studio Dafny IDE. We would also like to investigate how general the approach is by exploring tactics for other program verifiers. "Dafny style proof" has been shown to be feasible in Spark 2014 [15], and we would like to try to develop tactics for Spark 2014 and other program verifiers.

# References

1. Dafny. research.microsoft.com/dafny
2. The Tacny projectd: TACAS 2016 information. https://sites.google.com/site/tacnyproject/tacas-2016. Accessed 16 October 2015
3. Asperti, A., Ricciotti, W., Sacerdoti, C., Tassi, C.: A new type for tactics. In: PLMMS 2009, pp. 229–232 (2009)
4. Autexier, S., Dietrich, D.: A tactic language for declarative proofs. In: Kaufmann, M., Paulson, L.C. (eds.) ITP 2010. LNCS, vol. 6172, pp. 99–114. Springer, Heidelberg (2010)
5. Barnett, M., Chang, B.-Y.E., DeLine, R., Jacobs, B., M. Leino, K.R.: Boogie: a modular reusable verifier for object-oriented programs. In: Boer, F.S., Bonsangue, M.M., Graf, S., Roever, W.-P. (eds.) FMCO 2005. LNCS, vol. 4111, pp. 364–387. Springer, Heidelberg (2006)
6. Barnett, M., M. Leino, K.R., Schulte, W.: The Spec# programming system: an overview. In: Barthe, G., Burdy, L., Huisman, M., Lanet, J.-L., Muntean, T. (eds.) CASSIS 2004. LNCS, vol. 3362, pp. 49–69. Springer, Heidelberg (2005)
7. Chen, Y.: Programmable verifiers in imperative programming. In: Qin, S. (ed.) UTP 2010. LNCS, vol. 6445, pp. 172–187. Springer, Heidelberg (2010)
8. Claessen, K., Johansson, M., Rosén, D., Smallbone, N.: Automating inductive proofs using theory exploration. In: Bonacina, M.P. (ed.) CADE 2013. LNCS, vol. 7898, pp. 392–406. Springer, Heidelberg (2013)
9. Cohen, E., Dahlweid, M., Hillebrand, M., Leinenbach, D., Moskal, M., Santen, T., Schulte, W., Tobies, S.: VCC: a practical system for verifying concurrent C. In: Berghofer, S., Nipkow, T., Urban, C., Wenzel, M. (eds.) TPHOLs 2009. LNCS, vol. 5674, pp. 23–42. Springer, Heidelberg (2009)
10. Colón, M.A., Sankaranarayanan, S., Sipma, H.B.: Linear invariant generation using non-linear constraint solving. In: Hunt Jr., W.A., Somenzi, F. (eds.) CAV 2003. LNCS, vol. 2725, pp. 420–432. Springer, Heidelberg (2003)

11. Cook, B., Podelski, A., Rybalchenko, A.: Proving program termination. Commun. ACM **54**(5), 88–98 (2011)
12. Cousot, P., Halbwachs, N.: Automatic discovery of linear restraints among variables of a program. In: Proceedings of the 5th ACM SIGACT-SIGPLAN Symposium on Principles of Programming Languages, pp. 84–96. ACM (1978)
13. de Moura, L., Passmore, G.O.: The strategy challenge in SMT solving. In: Bonacina, M.P., Stickel, M.E. (eds.) Automated Reasoning and Mathematics. LNCS, vol. 7788, pp. 15–44. Springer, Heidelberg (2013)
14. Delahaye, D.: A tactic language for the system Coq. In: Parigot, M., Voronkov, A. (eds.) LPAR 2000. LNCS (LNAI), vol. 1955, pp. 85–95. Springer, Heidelberg (2000)
15. Dross, C.: Manual Proof with Ghost Code in SPARK (2014). http://www.spark-2014.org/entries/detail/manual-proof-in-spark-2014. Accessed 01 October 2015
16. Ernst, M.D., Perkins, J.H., Guo, P.J., McCamant, S., Pacheco, C., Tschantz, A.S., Xiao, C.: The Daikon system for dynamic detection of likely invariants. Sci. Comput. Program. **69**(1), 35–45 (2007)
17. Fowler, M.: Refactoring: Improving the Design of Existing Code. Addison-Wesley, Menlo Park (1999)
18. Giero, M., Wiedijk, F.: MMode, a Mizar Mode for the proof assistant Coq. Technical report, 07 January 2004
19. Gordon, M.J., Milner, R., Wadsworth, C.P.: Edinburgh LCF. Springer, Heidelberg (1979)
20. Grov, G.: Some Ideas for Program Verifier Tactics. arxiv:1406.2824
21. Grov, G., Tumas, V.: The Tacny system (working document). Version generated, 16 October 2015. Available from [2]
22. Gupta, A., Rybalchenko, A.: InvGen: an efficient invariant generator. In: Bouajjani, A., Maler, O. (eds.) CAV 2009. LNCS, vol. 5643, pp. 634–640. Springer, Heidelberg (2009)
23. Hoder, K., Kovács, L., Voronkov, A.: Invariant generation in vampire. In: Abdulla, P.A., Leino, K.R.M. (eds.) TACAS 2011. LNCS, vol. 6605, pp. 60–64. Springer, Heidelberg (2011)
24. Jacobs, B., Smans, J., Piessens, F.: A quick tour of the verifast program verifier. In: Ueda, K. (ed.) APLAS 2010. LNCS, vol. 6461, pp. 304–311. Springer, Heidelberg (2010)
25. Johansson, M., Dixon, L., Bundy, A.: Conjecture synthesis for inductive theories. J. Autom. Reasoning **47**(3), 251–289 (2011)
26. Leino, K.R.M.: Types in Dafny. http://research.microsoft.com/en-us/um/people/leino/papers/krml243.html. Manuscript KRML 243, 27 February 2015
27. Leino, K.R.M.: Dafny: an automatic program verifier for functional correctness. In: Clarke, E.M., Voronkov, A. (eds.) LPAR-16 2010. LNCS, vol. 6355, pp. 348–370. Springer, Heidelberg (2010)
28. Leino, K.R.M.: Automating induction with an SMT solver. In: Kuncak, V., Rybalchenko, A. (eds.) VMCAI 2012. LNCS, vol. 7148, pp. 315–331. Springer, Heidelberg (2012)
29. Leino, K.R.M., Moskal, M.: Co-induction simply. In: Jones, C., Pihlajasaari, P., Sun, J. (eds.) FM 2014. LNCS, vol. 8442, pp. 382–398. Springer, Heidelberg (2014)
30. Leino, K.R.M., Polikarpova, N.: Verified calculations. In: Cohen, E., Rybalchenko, A. (eds.) VSTTE 2013. LNCS, vol. 8164, pp. 170–190. Springer, Heidelberg (2014)
31. Llano, M.T., Ireland, A., Pease, A.: Discovery of invariants through automated theory formation. FAoC **26**, 203–249 (2014)

32. Pitu, M., Grijincu, D., Li, P., Saleem, A., Monahan, R., O'Donoghue, D.P.: Aris : Analogical reasoning for reuse of implementation & specification. In: AI4FM 2013 (2013)

33. Matichuk, D., Wenzel, M., Murray, T.: An Isabelle proof method language. In: Klein, G., Gamboa, R. (eds.) ITP 2014. LNCS, vol. 8558, pp. 390–405. Springer, Heidelberg (2014)

34. McCormick, J.W., Chapin, P.C.: Building High Integrity Applications with SPARK. Cambridge University Press, Cambridge (2015)

35. de Moura, L., Bjørner, N.S.: Z3: an efficient SMT solver. In: Ramakrishnan, C.R., Rehof, J. (eds.) TACAS 2008. LNCS, vol. 4963, pp. 337–340. Springer, Heidelberg (2008)

36. Naumowicz, A., Korniłowicz, A.: A brief overview of MIZAR. In: Berghofer, S., Nipkow, T., Urban, C., Wenzel, M. (eds.) TPHOLs 2009. LNCS, vol. 5674, pp. 67–72. Springer, Heidelberg (2009)

37. Penninckx, W., Mühlberg, J.T., Smans, J., Jacobs, B., Piessens, F.: Sound formal verification of linux's USB BP keyboard driver. In: Goodloe, A.E., Person, S. (eds.) NFM 2012. LNCS, vol. 7226, pp. 210–215. Springer, Heidelberg (2012)

38. Plotkin, G.D.: The origins of structural operational semantics. J. Logic Algebraic Program. **60–61**, 3–15 (2004)

39. Srivastava, S., Gulwani, S.: Program verification using templates over predicate abstraction. In: ACM Sigplan Notices, vol. 44, pp. 223–234. ACM (2009)

40. Wenzel, M.: Structured induction proofs in Isabelle/Isar. In: Borwein, J.M., Farmer, W.M. (eds.) MKM 2006. LNCS (LNAI), vol. 4108, pp. 17–30. Springer, Heidelberg (2006)

41. Whiteside, I., Aspinall, D., Dixon, L., Grov, G.: Towards formal proof script refactoring. In: Farmer, W.M., Urban, J., Rabe, F., Davenport, J.H. (eds.) MKM 2011 and Calculemus 2011. LNCS, vol. 6824, pp. 260–275. Springer, Heidelberg (2011)

# Synthesizing Ranking Functions
# from Bits and Pieces

Caterina Urban[1,2]([✉]), Arie Gurfinkel[2], and Temesghen Kahsai[2,3]

[1] ETH Zürich, Zürich, Switzerland
caterina.urban@inf.ethz.ch
[2] Carnegie Mellon University, Pittsburgh, USA
[3] NASA Ames Research Center, Moffett Field, USA

**Abstract.** In this work, we present a novel approach based on recent advances in software model checking to synthesize ranking functions and prove termination (and non-termination) of imperative programs.

Our approach incrementally refines a termination argument from an under-approximation of the terminating program state. Specifically, we learn *bits* of information from terminating executions, and from these we extrapolate ranking functions over-approximating the number of loop iterations needed for termination. We combine these *pieces* into piecewise-defined, lexicographic, or multiphase ranking functions.

The proposed technique has been implemented in SeaHorn – an LLVM based verification framework – targeting C code. Preliminary experimental evaluation demonstrated its effectiveness in synthesizing ranking functions and proving termination of C programs.

## 1 Introduction

The traditional method for proving program *termination* and other *liveness* properties is based on the synthesis of *ranking functions*, that is, for any potentially looping computation, proving that some well-founded metric strictly decreases every time around the loop.

State-of-the-art termination provers (e.g., [5,10,16]) reduce termination to the *safety* property that no program state is repeatedly visited (and it is not covered by the current termination argument), and compose termination arguments by repeatedly invoking ranking function synthesis tools (e.g., [4,8,26]).

In this work, we present a novel approach based on recent advances in *software model checking* to synthesize ranking functions and prove termination (and non-termination) of imperative programs. The core of our approach lies on an innovative use of *safety* verification techniques to build termination arguments.

This material is based upon work funded and supported by NSF Award No. 1136008 the Department of Defense under Contract No. FA8721-05-C-0003 with Carnegie Mellon University for the operation of the Software Engineering Institute, a federally funded research and development center. This material has been approved for public release and unlimited distribution. DM-0002915.

© Springer-Verlag Berlin Heidelberg 2016
M. Chechik and J.-F. Raskin (Eds.): TACAS 2016, LNCS 9636, pp. 54–70, 2016.
DOI: 10.1007/978-3-662-49674-9_4

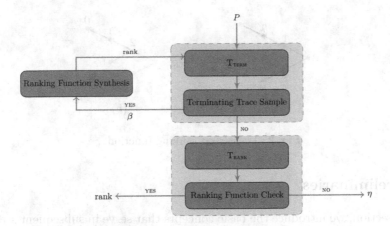

**Fig. 1.** Overview of our approach.

We use a safety verifier to systematically sample *terminating* program executions and extrapolate from these a candidate ranking function for the program, or to otherwise provide a witness for program non-termination. More specifically, rather than verifying that no program state is repeatedly visited, we verify the safety property that no program state is terminating (and it is not covered by the current termination argument). The counterexamples are terminating program executions which provide an *under-approximation* of the terminating program states. From these we extrapolate a candidate ranking function which *over-approximates* the number of loop iterations to termination and is possibly valid also for other terminating program executions. The candidate ranking function can be an *affine* function, or a *piecewise-defined, lexicographic,* or *multiphase* combination of affine functions. We then use the safety verifier to validate that the candidate ranking function is indeed a ranking function, or to provide a counterexample non-terminating program state.

The proposed approach has been implemented in SEAHORN [15] targeting C code. We show empirically that it performs well on a wide variety of benchmarks collected from SV-COMP 2015[1], is competitive with the state-of-the-art and is able to analyze programs that are out of the reach of existing techniques.

*Overview.* Figure 1 provides an overview of our approach for proving termination via safety verification. The overall algorithm is presented in Sect. 3.2. A program $P$ systematically undergoes a transformation $T_{TERM}$ described in Sect. 4.1 which allows sampling terminating executions $\beta$ not covered by the current candidate ranking function *rank*. The candidate *rank* is systematically refined as described in Sect. 4.2 until no terminating execution $\beta$ is left uncovered. Finally, $P$ undergoes a final transformation $T_{RANK}$ described in Sect. 4.1 which allows validating the ranking function *rank* or providing a counterexample non-terminating state $\eta$.

---

[1] http://sv-comp.sosy-lab.org/2015/.

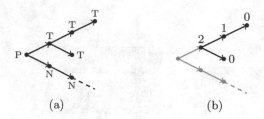

Fig. 2. Traces and ranking function.

## 2 Preliminaries

In this section, we introduce the basic concepts that serve in subsequent sections and we establish the notation used throughout the paper.

*Transition Systems.* We formalize programs using *transition systems* $\langle \Sigma, \tau \rangle$ where $\Sigma$ is the set of program states and $\tau \subseteq \Sigma \times \Sigma$ defines the transition relation. Note that this model allows representing programs with (possibly unbounded) non-determinism. In the following, a program state $s \in \Sigma$ is a pair $\langle l, \bar{x} \rangle$ consisting of a program control point $l \in \mathcal{L}$ and a vector $\bar{x}$ of integers representing the values of the program variables at that control point. We write $\tau(s, s')$ for $\langle s, s' \rangle \in \tau$. The set of initial states is $\mathcal{I} \overset{\text{def}}{=} \{ \langle i, \bar{x} \rangle \mid i \in \mathcal{L} \} \subseteq \Sigma$, where $i \in \mathcal{L}$ is the program initial control point, and the set of final states is $\mathcal{F} \overset{\text{def}}{=} \{ \langle f, \bar{x} \rangle \mid f \in \mathcal{L} \} \subseteq \Sigma$, where $f \in \mathcal{L}$ is the program final control point.

Given a transition system $\langle \Sigma, \tau \rangle$, a *trace* is a non-empty sequence of states in $\Sigma$ determined by the transition relation $\tau$, that is $\tau(s, s')$ for each pair of consecutive states $s, s' \in \Sigma$ in the sequence. A state $s' \in \Sigma$ is *reachable* from another state $s \in \Sigma$ if and only if there exists a trace from $s$ to $s'$. In the following, we write $\tau^*(s, s')$ to denote the existence of a trace from $s$ to $s'$. A state $s' \in \Sigma$ is reachable if and only if it is reachable from an initial state $s \in \mathcal{I}$.

A state $s \in \Sigma$ is *terminating* if and only if all traces to which it belongs are finite, *potentially non-terminating* if and only if it belongs to at least one infinite trace. Dually, it is *non-terminating* if and only if all traces to which it belongs are infinite, and *potentially terminating* if and only if it belongs to at least one finite trace. Note that, terminating states are also potentially terminating states, and non-terminating states are also potentially non-terminating states. For instance, consider the traces depicted in Fig. 2a: the states labeled with T are terminating, the states labeled with N are non-terminating, and the state labeled with P is potentially non-terminating and potentially terminating.

*Ranking Functions.* The traditional method for proving termination dates back to Turing [29] and Floyd [14] and it requires finding a *ranking function*:

**Definition 1 (Ranking Function).** *Given a transition system* $\langle \Sigma, \tau \rangle$*, a ranking function is a partial function* rank *whose domain* $\text{dom}(rank)$ *is a subset*

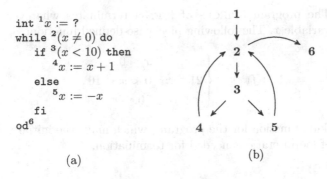

```
        int ¹x := ?
        while ²(x ≠ 0) do
            if ³(x < 10) then
                ⁴x := x + 1
            else
                ⁵x := -x
            fi
        od⁶
```

(a)                                    (b)

**Fig. 3.** Terminating program 3PIECES (a) and its control flow graph (b).

*of the program states and whose value (i) strictly decreases through transitions between program states, that is $\forall s, s' \in \text{dom}(rank) : \tau(s, s') \Rightarrow rank(s') < rank(s)$, and (ii) is bounded from below, that is $\forall s \in \text{dom}(rank) : rank(s) \geq 0$.*

For instance, an obvious ranking function maps each program state to some well-chosen upper bound on the number of transitions until termination. Figure 2b shows a ranking function labeling the terminating states of Fig. 2a.

*Control Flow Graphs.* The *control flow graph* (CFG) induced by a transition system $\langle \Sigma, \tau \rangle$ is a graph whose nodes are the program control points $\mathcal{L}$ and whose edges $\mathcal{E} \subseteq \mathcal{L} \times \mathcal{L}$ are pairs of control points corresponding to transitions in the transition system: $\forall \langle l, \bar{x} \rangle, \langle l, \bar{x}' \rangle \in \Sigma : \tau(\langle l, \bar{x} \rangle, \langle l, \bar{x}' \rangle) \Rightarrow \langle l, l' \rangle \in \mathcal{E}$. In the following, we restrict our attention to *reducible* control flow graphs. A *loop* is a strongly connected component of the CFG with a single entry node $h$ called *loop header*. The loops nested within a loop are the strongly connected components of the loop after removing the loop header. A loop *entry edge* is an edge whose source is outside the loop and whose target is inside the loop, a *loop edge* is an edge whose source and target are within the loop, and a loop *exit edge* is an edge whose source is inside the loop and whose target is outside the loop. Similarly, we can partition the corresponding transitions in the transition system into loop *entry transitions*, *loop transitions*, and loop *exit transition*.

*Example 1.* Consider the program in Fig. 3a: the integer variable $x$ is initialized non-deterministically; then, at each loop iteration, the value of $x$ is increased by one or negated when it becomes greater than or equal to ten, until $x$ becomes zero. The control flow graph of the program is depicted in Fig. 3b. The program while loop corresponds to the strongly connected component of the CFG formed by the nodes 2, 3, 4 and 5. The loop header is the node 2. There is a single entry edge $\langle 1, 2 \rangle$ and a single exit edge $\langle 2, 6 \rangle$.

*Remark 1.* Note that it is not necessary for a ranking function to strictly decrease at each transition but only around each loop iteration [11]: $\forall \langle h, \bar{x} \rangle, \langle h, \bar{x}' \rangle \in \text{dom}(rank) : \tau^*(\langle h, \bar{x} \rangle, \langle h, \bar{x}' \rangle) \Rightarrow rank(\langle h, \bar{x}' \rangle) < rank(\langle h, \bar{x} \rangle)$.

*Example 2.* The program 3PIECES of Fig. 3a terminates whatever the initial value of the variable $x$. The following piecewise-defined function:

$$f(x) = \begin{cases} -x & x \leq 0 \\ 21 - x & 0 < x < 10 \\ x + 1 & 10 \leq x \end{cases}$$

is a valid ranking function for the program, which maps the initial value of $x$ to the number of loop iterations needed for termination.

# 3   Verifying Termination via Safety

In the late 1970s, Lamport suggested a classification of program properties into the classes of *safety* and *liveness* properties [20]. Safety properties represent requirements that should be continuously maintained by the program. On the other hand, liveness properties represent requirements that need not hold continuously but whose eventual or repeated realization must be guaranteed. Thus, a counterexample to a safety property is a *finite* (prefix of a) program execution, while for a liveness property a counterexample is an *infinite* execution on which an event of interest does not occur. A prominent example of a liveness property is *termination*. Instead, *non-termination* is a safety property since any terminating (and, thus, finite) program execution is a witness against non-termination.

## 3.1   Verifying Safety Properties

The verification of safety properties often amounts to checking the reachability of an *error* location: *a program is safe when the error location is unreachable*; otherwise, the program is unsafe. In the former case, safety provers often provide an *invariant* testifying the validity of the property. In the latter case, safety provers usually provide a *counterexample* trace violating the safety property. In the following, we propose some examples to informally illustrate how safety properties can be verified by checking the (un)-reachability of an error.

*Verifying Non-Termination* [6]. Consider the program in Fig. 4a: the integer variables $x$ and $y$ are initialized with value zero and nine, respectively; then, at each iteration, $x$ and $y$ are increased by one, until $x$ becomes equal to $y$. Since safety provers report counterexample traces reaching an error location, in order to verify that the program is non-terminating, we turn terminating traces into counterexamples to be found. In Fig. 4b, we added an error location — defined as assert(false) — before the end of the program of Fig. 4a: only terminating traces would execute assert(false), thus the program is non-terminating since in this case the error location is in fact unreachable.

$$\text{int } {}^1x := 0, \, y := 9$$
$$\text{while } {}^2(x \neq y) \text{ do}$$
$$\quad {}^3x := x + 1$$
$$\quad {}^4y := y + 1$$
$$\text{od}^5$$

(a)

$$\text{int } {}^1x := 0, \, y := 9$$
$$\text{while } {}^2(x \neq y) \text{ do}$$
$$\quad {}^3x := x + 1$$
$$\quad {}^4y := y + 1$$
$$\text{od}$$
$$\text{assert (false)}^5$$

(b)

**Fig. 4.** Non-terminating program (a) annotated with an error location (b).

$$\text{int } {}^1x := \text{?}, \, r := \max\{-x, 21 - x, x + 1\}$$
$$\text{while } {}^2(x \neq 0) \text{ do}$$
$$\quad r := r - 1$$
$$\quad \text{assert } (r \geq 0)$$
$$\quad \text{if } {}^3(x < 10) \text{ then } {}^4x := x + 1 \text{ else } {}^5x := -x \text{ fi}$$
$$\text{od}^6$$

**Fig. 5.** Program 3PIECES annotated with a ranking function.

*Verifying a Ranking Function.* Safety provers can also be used to verify whether a given function is a ranking function for a program. For instance, to check wether $\max\{-x, 21 - x, x + 1\}$ is a ranking function for the program 3PIECES shown in Fig. 3a, we instrument the program as shown in Fig. 5: we add a variable $r$ initialized with the given function $\max\{-x, 21 - x, x + 1\}$; then, within the loop, according to Definition 1 and Remark 1 (i) we strictly decrease the value of $r$ (i.e., we decrease $r$ by one), and (ii) we assert that the value of $r$ is bounded from below (i.e., we assert that $r$ is greater than or equal to zero). Note that the counterexample traces that would violate the assertion are either (prefixes of) non-terminating traces, or (prefixes of) traces that are terminating but require a higher number of loop iterations with respect to the initial value of $r$. In this case, since the assertion is never violated, the given function $\max\{-x, 21 - x, x + 1\}$ is a valid ranking function for the program 3PIECES.

## 3.2   Verifying Termination via Safety

In the following, we describe the overall algorithm for proving termination via safety. We detail our specific implementation choices in Sect. 4.

The overall algorithm is illustrated by Algorithm 1. We verify termination of each loop in a program, implicitly constructing a lexicographic ranking function for nested sets of loops [1]. The function ISTERMINATING takes as input a transition system $\langle \Sigma, \tau \rangle$ and returns either TRUE: $R$, meaning that the program is terminating and $R$ is a ranking function, or FALSE: $\rho$, meaning that the program is potentially non-terminating and $\rho$ is a counterexample potentially non-terminating initial state. Specifically, ISTERMINATING invokes the function ISLOOPTERMINATING for each loop in the program (identified by the function GETLOOPS, cf. Line 4) and maps each loop header $h$ (cf. Line 3) to the

**Algorithm 1.** Program Termination

1: **function** IsTERMINATING($\langle \Sigma, \tau \rangle$)
2:     $R \leftarrow \emptyset$
3:     **for** $h \in$ GETLOOPS($\langle \Sigma, \tau \rangle$) **do**       ▷ $h$ is a loop header in the program
4:         $r : \rho \leftarrow$ ISLOOPTERMINATING($h, \langle \Sigma, \tau \rangle$)
5:         **if** $r$ **then**                     ▷ the loop is terminating
6:             $R \leftarrow R[h \mapsto \rho]$
7:         **else return** FALSE: $\rho$        ▷ $\rho$ is a potentially non-terminating state
8:     **return** TRUE : $R$        ▷ $R$ is a ranking function for the program

**Algorithm 2.** Loop Termination

1: **function** IsLOOPTERMINATING($h, \langle \Sigma, \tau \rangle$)              ▷ $h$ is the loop header
2:     $rank \leftarrow 0$              ▷ candidate ranking function initialization
3:     $B \leftarrow \emptyset$
4:     **while** TRUE **do**
5:         $\beta \leftarrow$ GETTERMINATINGTRACE($h, \langle \Sigma, \tau \rangle, rank$)
6:         **if** $\beta$ **then**              ▷ there are terminating traces violating $rank$
7:             $B \leftarrow B \cup \beta$
8:             $rank \leftarrow$ GETCANDIDATERANKINGFUNCTION($rank, B$)
9:         **else**              ▷ there are no terminating traces violating $rank$
10:             $\eta \leftarrow$ ISRANKINGFUNCTION($rank$)
11:             **if** $\eta$ **then**              ▷ $\eta$ is a potentially non-terminating state
12:                 **return** FALSE: $\eta$
13:             **else**              ▷ $rank$ is a ranking function for the loop
14:                 **return** TRUE: $rank$

returned ranking function (cf. Line 6), or returns as soon as a counterexample non-terminating state $\rho$ is found (cf. Line 7). The function GETLOOPS implements a standard control-flow analysis to identify (natural) loops within the CFG induced by the transition system $\langle \Sigma, \tau \rangle$. We omit its pseudocode due to space limitations. The identified program loops are analyzed in no specific order.

The function ISLOOPTERMINATING is shown in Algorithm 2. Initially, ISLOOPTERMINATING assumes that all program states within the loop are non-terminating and looks for a counterexample, that is, a terminating trace $\beta$ (cf. Line 5). Then, the call to the function GETCANDIDATERANKINGFUNCTION computes a candidate ranking function $rank$ for the (potentially terminating) states along this trace (cf. Line 8). The original non-termination property is weakened to only search for terminating traces violating the candidate $rank$, and the process starts over. The information provided by the collected terminating traces is used to incrementally refine the candidate $rank$ with further ranking function pieces. In case no further terminating traces violating $rank$ are found (cf. Line 9), the call to the function ISRANKINGFUNCTION checks wether all program states within the loop are terminating (cf. Line 10): if so, $rank$ is a ranking function for the loop (cf. Line 14); if not, a counterexample potentially non-terminating initial state $\eta$ (that is, $\eta$ belongs to at least one infinite trace) is returned (cf. Line 12). Note that ISLOOPTERMINATING might also not terminate (cf. Line 4).

# 4 Counterexample-Guided Ranking Function Synthesis

We now detail our implementation choices for the functions GETTERMINATING-TRACE, ISRANKINGFUNCTION and GETCANDIDATERANKINGFUNCTIONS. We omit their pseudocode due to space limitations.

## 4.1 Search for Ranking Function Counterexamples

In Sect. 3.1, we have seen how to use a safety prover for verifying non-termination by turning terminating traces into counterexamples (cf. Fig. 4). In our approach, we use a similar intuition to systematically detect terminating traces violating a given candidate ranking function $rank$.

In the following, we consider a generic candidate $rank$ and we introduce two program transformations $T_{TERM}$ and $T_{RANK}$ implemented by the functions GET-TERMINATINGTRACE and ISRANKINGFUNCTION, respectively. We detail these transformations with respect to a specific candidate $rank$ in Sect. 4.2.

$T_{TERM}$ **Transformation.** Let $h$ be a loop header within a program $\langle \Sigma, \tau \rangle$ and let $rank$ be a candidate ranking function for the loop. We modify the program in order to turn terminating traces violating $rank$ into counterexamples to be found. Specifically, we modify $\Sigma$ in order to include the value of $rank$ and we add an error state $\omega \notin \Sigma$: $(\Sigma \times \mathbb{Z}) \cup \{\omega\}$. In the following, $s$, $s'$, and $\langle h, \bar{x} \rangle$ denote program states in $\Sigma$. We also define the modified transition relation $\tau$ as follows:

- for each loop *entry transition* $\tau(s, \langle h, \bar{x} \rangle)$ there exists an entry transition $\tau^{rank}$ which also includes the candidate $rank$:

$$\tau^{rank}(\langle s, r \rangle, \langle \langle h, \bar{x} \rangle, r' \rangle) \Leftrightarrow \tau(s, \langle h, \bar{x} \rangle) \wedge r' = rank(\bar{x})$$

- for each *loop transition* $\tau(\langle h, \bar{x} \rangle, s)$ whose source is the loop header $h$ there exists a loop transition $\tau^{\ominus}$ which also strictly decreases the value of $rank$:

$$\tau^{\ominus}(\langle \langle h, \bar{x} \rangle, r \rangle, \langle s, r' \rangle) \Leftrightarrow \tau(\langle h, \bar{x} \rangle, s) \wedge r' = r \ominus 1$$

- for each loop *exit transition* $\tau(s, s')$ there exists transition $\tau^{\lhd}$ to the error state $\omega$ when the candidate ranking function is negative:

$$\tau^{\lhd}(\langle s, r \rangle, \omega) \stackrel{\text{def}}{=} r \lhd 0$$

For every other transition $\tau(s, s')$ there exists a transition $\tau'(\langle s, r \rangle, \langle s', r' \rangle) \Leftrightarrow \tau(s, s') \wedge r' = r$. The counterexample traces that reach the error state are traces that are leaving the considered loop but violate the candidate $rank$ since they require a higher number of loop iterations with respect to the initial value of $rank$. The function GETTERMINATINGTRACE returns any of these counterexamples.

```
int ¹x := ?, r := rank
while ²(x ≠ 0) do
    r := r − 1
    if ³(x < 10) then ⁴x := x + 1 else ⁵x := −x fi
od
assert (r ≥ 0)⁶
```

**Fig. 6.** Program 3PIECES annotated with a candidate ranking function *rank*.

**Theorem 1.** *Let h be a loop header of a program $\langle \Sigma, \tau \rangle$ and let $\langle \Sigma', \tau' \rangle$ be the program resulting from the $T_{\text{TERM}}$ transformation for a given candidate ranking function rank. Then, $\tau'^*(\langle\langle h, \bar{x}\rangle, rank(\bar{x})\rangle, \langle s, r\rangle) \wedge \tau(\langle s, r\rangle, \omega)$ if and only if there exist $s' \in \Sigma$ $\tau(s, s')$ and the transition is an exit transition, and $\tau^*(s, s')$ and the trace visits the loop header h strictly more than $rank(\bar{x})$ times.*

*Example 3.* Consider again the program 3PIECES of Fig. 3a. The transformation that we have just described intuitively corresponds to modifying 3PIECES as illustrated in Fig. 6: we add a variable $r$ initialized with the candidate *rank* within the entry transition $\langle 1, 2 \rangle$; then, within the loop transition $\langle 2, 3 \rangle$, we decrease the value of $r$ by one and, after the loop, we assert that the value of $r$ is greater than or equal to zero. The assertion is equivalent to adding an error transition $\langle 2, \omega \rangle$ when $r$ is negative. The counterexample traces that violate the assertion are traces that leave the loop after $rank - r$ loop iterations, where $r$ is the (negative) value of the variable $r$ after the loop.

$T_{\text{RANK}}$ **Transformation.** Note that traces that never leave the considered loop are not counterexamples since they never reach the error state. For this reason Algorithm 2 includes a final validation of the ranking function (cf. Lines 10–14). We implement this using an analogous program transformation: we define entry transitions $\tau^{rank}$ and loop transitions $\tau^{\ominus}$ as before:

$$\tau^{rank}(\langle s, r\rangle, \langle\langle h, \bar{x}\rangle, r'\rangle) \Leftrightarrow \tau(s, \langle h, \bar{x}\rangle) \wedge r' = rank(\bar{x})$$

$$\tau^{\ominus}(\langle\langle h, \bar{x}\rangle, r\rangle, \langle s, r'\rangle) \Leftrightarrow \tau(\langle h, \bar{x}\rangle, s) \wedge r' = r \ominus 1$$

unlike before, for each *loop transition* $\tau(s, s')$ we also define a transition $\tau^{\triangleleft}$ to the error state $\omega$ when the candidate ranking function is negative:

$$\tau^{\triangleleft}(\langle s, r\rangle, \omega) \stackrel{\text{def}}{=} r \triangleleft 0$$

Other transitions are again defined as $\tau'(\langle s, r\rangle, \langle s', r'\rangle) \stackrel{\text{def}}{=} \tau(s, s') \wedge r' = r$. The counterexample traces that violate the assertion are necessarily (prefixes of) non-terminating traces, since the $T_{\text{TERM}}$ transformation has excluded all terminating traces violating the candidate ranking function. The function ISRANKINGFUNCTION returns the initial state of any of these counterexamples.

**Theorem 2.** *Let $h$ be a loop header of a program $\langle \Sigma, \tau \rangle$ and let $\langle \Sigma', \tau' \rangle$ be the program resulting from the $\mathrm{T_{RANK}}$ transformation for a given candidate ranking function rank. Then, $\tau'^*(\langle \langle h, \bar{x} \rangle, rank(\bar{x}) \rangle, \langle s, r \rangle) \wedge \tau(\langle s, r \rangle, \omega)$ if and only if $\tau^*(\langle \langle h, \bar{x} \rangle, s)$ and the trace is the prefix of an infinite trace and visits the loop header $h$ strictly more than $rank(\bar{x})$ times.*

*Example 4.* The transformation that we have just described intuitively corresponds to modifying the program 3PIECES of Fig. 3a as illustrated in Fig. 5 and described in Sect. 3.1.

## 4.2  Synthesis of Candidate Ranking Functions

The function GETCANDIDATERANKINGFUNCTION uses the terminating traces collected by GETTERMINATINGTRACE to extrapolate ranking function pieces which are combined into a candidate loop ranking function. We only consider *affine* pieces and leave the extrapolation of non-linear pieces for future work.

In Algorithm 2, the initial candidate is the constant function equal to zero (cf. Line 2). Then, the candidate ranking function is systematically updated in order to be valid for the newly discovered terminating traces, and possibly for other terminating traces not explicitly enumerated.

We extrapolate an affine ranking function piece from terminating traces mapping the initial states of these traces to the number of loop iterations needed for termination, and then finding an affine ranking function which fits these bits of information. More specifically, let $\{ \langle \bar{x}_1, r_1 \rangle, \langle \bar{x}_2, r_2 \rangle, \ldots \}$ be the set of pairs mapping the initial states $\bar{x}_1, \bar{x}_2, \ldots$ of the collected terminating traces to the number $r_1, r_2, \ldots$ of loop iterations needed for termination. We find a fitting affine function $\bar{m} \cdot \bar{x} + q$ of the program variables $\bar{x}$ by *linear interpolation*, that is by solving the system of equations:

$$\bar{m} \cdot \bar{x}_1 + q = r_1$$
$$\bar{m} \cdot \bar{x}_2 + q = r_2$$

$$\vdots$$

for the unknowns $\bar{m}$ and $q$.

*Example 5.* Let $\{ \langle 9, 12 \rangle, \langle 4, 17 \rangle \}$ be the set of pairs mapping some initial states of the program 3PIECES of Fig. 3a to the number of loop iterations needed for termination: the initial state with $x = 9$ needs 12 loop iterations, and the initial state with $x = 4$ needs 17 loop iterations. Solving the system of equations:

$$m \cdot 9 + q = 12$$
$$m \cdot 4 + q = 17$$

yields the affine function $21 - x$ of the program variable $x$. Note that this is a valid ranking function for all initial states with $0 < x < 10$, and not only for the given initial states with $x = 9$ and $x = 4$ (cf. Example 2).

When the system is unsatisfiable, we discard all collected states and we start over by building a new ranking function piece. The ranking function pieces are alternatively combined into *piecewise-defined, lexicographic,* or *multiphase* ranking functions [24]. These combinations have complementary strengths: piecewise-defined combinations are well-suited when multiple paths are present within loops (cf. Fig. 3a), lexicographic combinations are convenient for loops featuring unbounded non-determinism (cf. Fig. 7), and multiphase combinations target loops that go through a number of phases in their executions [3]. The choice of the combination is a parameter of the analysis.

*Piecewise-Defined Ranking Functions.* We represent piecewise-defined affine ranking functions using *max* combinations of affine ranking functions [25]:

$$\max\{rank_1, \ldots, rank_n\}$$

where $rank_1, \ldots, rank_n$ are the affine ranking function pieces.

In the transformations $T_{\text{TERM}}$ and $T_{\text{RANK}}$ described in Sect. 4.1, the modified loop transitions $\tau^\ominus$ strictly decrease a *max* combination of ranking functions by strictly decreasing all its pieces:

$$\max\{r_1, \ldots, r_n\} \ominus 1 = \max\{r_1 - 1, \ldots, r_n - 1\}$$

In the added error transitions $\tau^\lhd$ a *max* combination of ranking functions is negative when all its pieces are negative:

$$\max\{r_1, \ldots, r_n\} \lhd 0 \Leftrightarrow r_1 < 0 \wedge \cdots \wedge r_n < 0$$

*Example 6.* The transformations $T_{\text{TERM}}$ and $T_{\text{RANK}}$ of the program 3PIECES of Fig. 3a are shown in Figs. 5 and 6, respectively.

*Lexicographic Ranking Functions.* Lexicographic ranking functions are tuples:

$$(rank_1, \ldots, rank_n)$$

where $rank_1, \ldots, rank_n$ are affine ranking function pieces.

In the transformations $T_{\text{TERM}}$ and $T_{\text{RANK}}$, the modified loop transitions $\tau^\ominus$ strictly decrease a lexicographic ranking function resetting the less significant pieces to their initial affine expression:

$$(r_1, \ldots, r_i, r_{i+1}, \ldots, r_n) \ominus 1 = (r_1, \ldots, r_i - 1, rank_{i+1}, \ldots rank_n)$$

were $r_{i+1}, \ldots, r_n$ are negative and get reset to the initial $rank_{i+1}, \ldots, rank_n$. In the added error transitions $\tau^\lhd$ a lexicographic combination of ranking functions is negative when the first of its pieces is negative:

$$(r_1, \ldots, r_n) \lhd 0 \Leftrightarrow r_1 < 0$$

```
int ¹x := ?, y := ?, r := (x, y)
while ²(x > 0 ∧ y > 0) do
    if (snd(r) < 0) then r := (fst(r) − 1, y) else r := (fst(r), snd(r) − 1) fi
    assert (fst(r) ≥ 0)
    if ³(?) then ⁴x := x − 1; ⁵y := ? else ⁶y := y − 1 fi
od⁷
```

**Fig. 7.** Program annotated with a lexicographic ranking function.

*Example 7.* Consider the program in Fig. 7: the integer variables $x$ and $y$ are initialized non-deterministically; then, at each iteration, either the value of $y$ is decreased by one or the value of $x$ is decreased by one and the value of $y$ is reset non-deterministically, until either variable is less than or equal to zero. The program terminates whatever the initial value of $x$ and $y$. Let $(x, y)$ be a candidate lexicographic ranking function for the program. In this case, the transformation $T_{RANK}$ intuitively corresponds to adding a variable $r$ initialized with $(x, y)$ within the entry transition $\langle 1, 2 \rangle$; then, within the loop transition $\langle 2, 3 \rangle$, decreasing the value of $r$ lexicographically *resetting* its second component $snd(r)$ when negative, and asserting that its first component $fst(r)$ is greater than or equal to zero. The assertion is equivalent to adding an error transition $\langle 2, \omega \rangle$ when $fst(r)$ is negative. In this case, since the assertion is never violated, $(x, y)$ is a valid lexicographic ranking function for the program.

*Multiphase Ranking Functions.* Multiphase ranking functions specify ranking functions that proceed through a certain number of phases during program execution [24]. They are represented as tuples:

$$(rank_1, \ldots, rank_n)$$

where $rank_1, \ldots, rank_n$ are affine ranking function pieces. Each piece represents a phase of the ranking function. In the transformations $T_{TERM}$ and $T_{RANK}$, the modified loop transitions $\tau^\ominus$ strictly decrease a multiphase combination of ranking functions as follows:

$$(r_1, \ldots, r_i, r_{i+1}, \ldots, r_n) \ominus 1 = (r_1, \ldots, r_i - 1, r_{i+1}, \ldots r_n)$$

were $r_{i+1}, \ldots, r_n$ are negative (and, unlike in the lexicographic combination, are never reset). In the added error transitions $\tau^\triangleleft$ a multiphase combination of ranking functions is negative when the first of its pieces is negative:

$$(r_1, \ldots, r_n) \triangleleft 0 \Leftrightarrow r_1 < 0$$

In summary, our approach systematically collects terminating program executions and searches for a function that uniformly captures the termination argument of the program. The function can be an affine ranking function, or a piecewise, lexicographic, or multiphase combination of affine functions. Then, we either manage to validate the candidate ranking function or we provide a witness for program non-termination.

|         | Tot | Time |
|---------|-----|------|
| SEAHORN | 135 | 1.71s |
| APROVE [28] | 129 | 10.77s |
| FUNCTION [30] | 111 | 0.55s |
| HIPTNT+ [22] | 152 | 0.62s |
| ULTIMATE [16] | 109 | 8.45s |

(a)

| | SEAHORN | | | |
|---------|-----|-----|-----|-----|
| | ■ | ● | ✕ | ▲ |
| APROVE [28] | 39 | 33 | 96 | 22 |
| FUNCTION [30] | 50 | 26 | 85 | 29 |
| HIPTNT+ [22] | 16 | 33 | 119 | 22 |
| ULTIMATE [16] | 55 | 29 | 80 | 26 |

(b)

**Fig. 8.** Overview of the experimental evaluation.

# 5    Implementation

Our approach is implemented in SEAHORN[2], an LLVM [21] based safety verification framework. SEAHORN verifies user-supplied assertions as well as a number of built-in safety properties (e.g., buffer and signed integer overflows). It can also be used to check for inconsistent code in C programs [18].

SEAHORN is parameterized by the semantic representation of the program using Constrained Horn Clauses (CHCs), and by the verification engine that leverages the latest advances made in SMT-based Model Checking and Abstract Interpretation. Detailed information about SEAHORN can be found in [15]. The transformations $T_{TERM}$ and $T_{RANK}$ presented in Sect. 4.1 are used to enhance the CHCs passed to the verification engine. SEAHORN employs several SMT-based model checking engines based on PDR/IC3 [2], including SPACER [19]. The synthesis of candidate ranking functions presented in Sect. 4.2 uses Z3 [12] to find affine functions fitting the collected terminating states.

*Experimental Evaluation.* We compared SEAHORN to the participants in the termination division of SV-COMP 2015: APROVE [28], FUNCTION [30], HIPTNT+ [22], and ULTIMATE AUTOMIZER [16]. We evaluated the tools against 190 terminating C programs collected from the SV-COMP 2015 benchmarks. Specifically, we selected only the programs that *all* tools could analyze (e.g., without parse errors or other clear issues) among the two most populated verification tasks of the termination category (i.e., crafted-lit and memory alloca). Note that other tools (e.g., FUNCTION) provide a very limited support for arrays and pointers. Therefore, we were not able to analyze 30 % of the considered benchmarks. The experiments were performed on a machine with a 2.90 GHz 64-bit Dual-Core CPU (Intel i5-5287U) and 4 GB of RAM, and running Ubuntu 14.04.

In the evaluation, we run in parallel three instances of SEAHORN parameterized with the different ranking function combinations presented in Sect. 4.2, halting the analysis as soon as one instance reported a result. Figure 8 summarizes our experimental evaluation and Fig. 9 shows a detailed comparison of SEAHORN against each other tool. In Fig. 8a, the first column reports the total

---

[2] http://seahorn.github.io/.

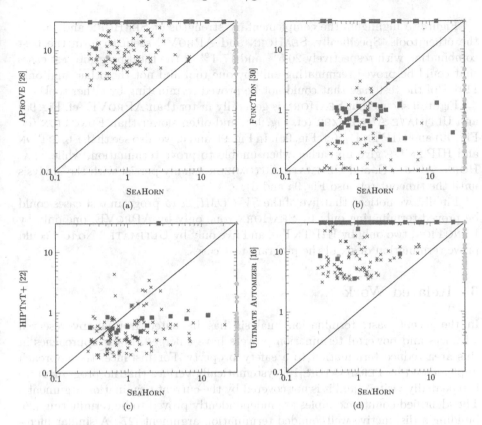

**Fig. 9.** Detailed comparison of SEAHORN against APROVE [28] (a), FUNCTION [30] (b), HIPTNT+ [22] (c), and ULTIMATE AUTOMIZER [16] (d).

number of programs that each tool could prove terminating, and the second column reports the average running time in seconds for the programs where the tool proved termination. We used a time limit of 30 s for each program. In Fig. 8b, the first column (■) lists the total number of programs that the tool was not able to prove termination for and that SEAHORN could prove terminating, the second column (●) reports the total number of programs that SEAHORN was not able to prove termination for and that the tool could prove terminating, and the last two columns report the total number of programs that both the tool and SEAHORN were able (✗) or unable (▲) to prove terminating. The same symbols are used in Fig. 9.

Figure 8a shows that SEAHORN is able to prove termination of 3.2 % more programs than APROVE, 12.6 % more programs than FUNCTION, and 13.7 % more programs than ULTIMATE AUTOMIZER. HIPTNT+ is able to prove termination of 8.9 % more programs than SEAHORN, but SEAHORN can prove termination of 42.1 % of the programs that HIPTNT+ is not able to prove terminating (8.4 % of the total program test cases, cf. Fig. 8b).

Figure 8b highlights the complementary strengths of SEAHORN and each of the other tools. Specifically, SEAHORN and APROVE seem to form the best combination with respectively 20.5 % and 17.4 % of the total program test cases that could be proved terminating only by one tool and not the other, and only 11.6 % of the test case that could not be proved terminating by either tool.

Figure 9 shows that SEAHORN is generally faster than APROVE (cf. Fig. 9a) and ULTIMATE AUTOMIZER (cf. Fig. 9d), and often slower than FUNCTION (cf. Fig. 9b) and HIPTNT+ (cf. Fig. 9c). In Fig. 9b and c, we also see that FUNCTION and HIPTNT+ give up earlier when unable to prove termination, while SEA-HORN, APROVE, and ULTIMATE AUTOMIZER usually persist with the analysis until the timeout (cf. also Fig. 9a and d).

Finally, we noticed that five of the *SV-COMP 2015* program test cases could be proved terminating only by SEAHORN (one only by APROVE, one only by FUNCTION, two only by HIPTNT+, and five only by ULTIMATE). No tool could prove termination of six of the program test cases.

# 6   Related Work

In the recent past, termination analysis has benefited from many research advances and powerful termination provers have emerged. Many approaches in this area reduce termination to a safety property. For instance, the approach implemented in TERMINATOR [10] systematically verifies that no program state is repeatedly visited (and it is not covered by the current termination argument). The identified counterexamples are independently proved to be terminating [26] building a disjunctive well-founded termination argument [27]. A similar incremental approach is used in T2 [5] for the construction of lexicographic ranking functions. An automata-based incremental approach is described in [17] and implemented in ULTIMATE [16]. An approach based on conflict-driven learning is used in [13] to enhance the abstract interpretation-based termination analysis [31] implemented in FUNCTION [30].

The incremental approach that we have proposed in this paper uses safety verifiers for proving termination in a fundamentally different way than existing methods: rather than systematically verifying that no program state is visited repeatedly, we systematically verify that no program state is terminating. Thus, our counterexamples are finite traces and do not need to be proven terminating.

The counterexample finite traces identified by our approach are used to extrapolate affine ranking functions. The linear interpolation that we use resembles the widening operator described in [31]. The extrapolated ranking functions are combined into a piecewise-defined, lexicographic, or multiphase ranking function for a program. Thus, our method provides more valuable information than just a positive or inconclusive answer like the methods based on the size-change termination principle [23] and implemented in APROVE [28], or like the already cited methods based on disjunctive well-foundedness and implemented in TERMI-NATOR. Finally, compared to the incomplete methods implemented in APROVE and FUNCTION, our method is also able to prove program non-termination.

# 7    Conclusion and Future Work

This paper provides a new perspective on the use of safety verifiers for proving program (non-)termination. We have proposed a novel incremental approach, which uses a safety verifier to systematically sample *terminating* program executions and synthesize from these a ranking function for the program, or to otherwise provide a witness for program non-termination.

It remains for future work to adapt the approach in order to infer sufficient preconditions for program termination [7,31]. We also plan to extend the approach to other liveness properties [9,32].

# References

1. Ben-Amram, A.M.: Ranking functions for linear-constraint loops. In: VPT, pp. 1–8 (2013)
2. Bradley, A.R.: IC3 and beyond: incremental, inductive verification. In: Madhusudan, P., Seshia, S.A. (eds.) CAV 2012. LNCS, vol. 7358, p. 4. Springer, Heidelberg (2012)
3. Bradley, A.R., Manna, Z., Sipma, H.B.: The polyranking principle. In: Caires, L., Italiano, G.F., Monteiro, L., Palamidessi, C., Yung, M. (eds.) ICALP 2005. LNCS, vol. 3580, pp. 1349–1361. Springer, Heidelberg (2005)
4. Bradley, A.R., Manna, Z., Sipma, H.B.: Termination analysis of integer linear loops. In: Abadi, M., de Alfaro, L. (eds.) CONCUR 2005. LNCS, vol. 3653, pp. 488–502. Springer, Heidelberg (2005)
5. Brockschmidt, M., Cook, B., Fuhs, C.: Better termination proving through cooperation. In: Sharygina, N., Veith, H. (eds.) CAV 2013. LNCS, vol. 8044, pp. 413–429. Springer, Heidelberg (2013)
6. Chen, H.-Y., Cook, B., Fuhs, C., Nimkar, K., O'Hearn, P.W.: Proving nontermination via safety. In: Ábrahám, E., Havelund, K. (eds.) TACAS 2014. LNCS, vol. 8413, pp. 156–171. Springer, Heidelberg (2014)
7. Chen, H.Y., David, C., Kroening, D., Schrammel, P., Wachter, B.: Synthesising interprocedural bit-precise termination proofs. In: ASE (2015)
8. Colón, M.A., Sipma, H.B.: Synthesis of linear ranking functions. In: Margaria, T., Yi, W. (eds.) TACAS 2001. LNCS, vol. 2031, pp. 67–81. Springer, Heidelberg (2001)
9. Cook, B., Khlaaf, H., Piterman, N.: On automation of CTL* verification for infinite-state systems. In: Kroening, D., Păsăreanu, C.S. (eds.) CAV 2015, Part I. LNCS, vol. 9206, pp. 13–29. Springer, Heidelberg (2015)
10. Cook, B., Podelski, A., Rybalchenko, A.: Termination proofs for systems code. In: PLDI, pp. 415–426 (2006)
11. Cousot, P., Cousot, R.: An abstract interpretation framework for termination. In: POPL, pp. 245–258 (2012)
12. de Moura, L., Bjørner, N.S.: Z3: an efficient SMT solver. In: Ramakrishnan, C.R., Rehof, J. (eds.) TACAS 2008. LNCS, vol. 4963, pp. 337–340. Springer, Heidelberg (2008)
13. D'Silva, V., Urban, C.: Conflict-driven conditional termination. In: Kroening, D., Păsăreanu, C.S. (eds.) CAV 2015, Part II. LNCS, vol. 9207, pp. 271–286. Springer, Heidelberg (2015)

14. Floyd, R.W.: Assigning meanings to programs. Proc. Symp. Appl. Math. **19**, 19–32 (1967)
15. Gurfinkel, A., Kahsai, T., Komuravelli, A., Navas, J.A.: The seahorn verification framework. In: Kroening, D., Păsăreanu, C.S. (eds.) CAV 2015, Part I. LNCS, vol. 9206, pp. 343–361. Springer, Heidelberg (2015)
16. Heizmann, M., Dietsch, D., Leike, J., Musa, B., Podelski, A.: Ultimate automizer with array interpolation (competition contribution). In: Baier, C., Tinelli, C. (eds.) TACAS 2015. LNCS, vol. 9035, pp. 455–457. Springer, Heidelberg (2015)
17. Heizmann, M., Hoenicke, J., Podelski, A.: Software model checking for people who love automata. In: Sharygina, N., Veith, H. (eds.) CAV 2013. LNCS, vol. 8044, pp. 36–52. Springer, Heidelberg (2013)
18. Kahsai, T., Navas, J.A., Jovanovic, D., Schäf, M.: Finding inconsistencies in programs with loops. In: Davis, M., et al. (eds.) LPAR-20 2015. LNCS, vol. 9450, pp. 499–514. Springer, Heidelberg (2015). doi:10.1007/978-3-662-48899-7_35
19. Komuravelli, A., Gurfinkel, A., Chaki, S.: SMT-based model checking for recursive programs. In: Biere, A., Bloem, R. (eds.) CAV 2014. LNCS, vol. 8559, pp. 17–34. Springer, Heidelberg (2014)
20. Lamport, L.: Proving the correctness of multiprocess programs. IEEE Trans. Softw. Eng. **3**(2), 125–143 (1977)
21. Lattner, C., Adve, V.S.: LLVM: a compilation framework for lifelong program analysis & transformation. In: CGO, pp. 75–88 (2004)
22. Le, T.-C., Qin, S., Chin, W.-N.: Termination and non-termination specification inference. In: PLDI, pp. 489–498 (2015)
23. Lee, C.S., Jones, N.D., Ben-Amram, A.M.: The size-change principle for program termination. In: POPL, pp. 81–92 (2001)
24. Leike, J., Heizmann, M.: Ranking templates for linear loops. In: Ábrahám, E., Havelund, K. (eds.) TACAS 2014. LNCS, vol. 8413, pp. 172–186. Springer, Heidelberg (2014)
25. Ovchinnikov, S.: Max-min representation of piecewise linear functions. Contrib. Algebra Geom. **42**(1), 297–302 (2002)
26. Podelski, A., Rybalchenko, A.: A complete method for the synthesis of linear ranking functions. In: Steffen, B., Levi, G. (eds.) VMCAI 2004. LNCS, vol. 2937, pp. 239–251. Springer, Heidelberg (2004)
27. Podelski, A., Rybalchenko, A.: Transition invariants. In: LICS, pp. 32–41 (2004)
28. Ströder, T., Aschermann, C., Frohn, F., Hensel, J., Giesl, J.: AProVE: termination and memory safety of C programs (competition contribution). In: Baier, C., Tinelli, C. (eds.) TACAS 2015. LNCS, vol. 9035, pp. 417–419. Springer, Heidelberg (2015)
29. Turing, A.: Checking a large routine. In: Report of a Conference on High Speed Automatic Calculating Machines, pp. 67–69 (1948)
30. Urban, C.: FuncTion: an abstract domain functor for termination (competition contribution). In: Baier, C., Tinelli, C. (eds.) TACAS 2015. LNCS, vol. 9035, pp. 464–466. Springer, Heidelberg (2015)
31. Urban, C., Miné, A.: A decision tree abstract domain for proving conditional termination. In: Müller-Olm, M., Seidl, H. (eds.) SAS 2014. LNCS, vol. 8723, pp. 302–318. Springer, Heidelberg (2014)
32. Urban, C., Miné, A.: Proving guarantee and recurrence temporal properties by abstract interpretation. In: D'Souza, D., Lal, A., Larsen, K.G. (eds.) VMCAI 2015. LNCS, vol. 8931, pp. 190–208. Springer, Heidelberg (2015)

# Abstraction Refinement and Antichains for Trace Inclusion of Infinite State Systems

Radu Iosif[1], Adam Rogalewicz[2(✉)], and Tomáš Vojnar[2]

[1] University Grenoble Alpes, CNRS, VERIMAG, Grenoble, France
iosif@imag.fr
[2] FIT, IT4Innovations Centre of Excellence, Brno University of Technology,
Brno, Czech Republic
{rogalew,vojnar}@fit.vutbr.cz

**Abstract.** A *data automaton* is a finite automaton equipped with variables (counters or registers) ranging over infinite data domains. A trace of a data automaton is an alternating sequence of alphabet symbols and values taken by the counters during an execution of the automaton. The problem addressed in this paper is the inclusion between the sets of traces (data languages) recognized by such automata. Since the problem is undecidable in general, we give a semi-algorithm based on abstraction refinement, which is proved to be sound and complete modulo termination. Due to the undecidability of the trace inclusion problem, our procedure is not guaranteed to terminate. We have implemented our technique in a prototype tool and show promising results on several nontrivial examples.

## 1 Introduction

In this paper, we address a *trace inclusion* problem for infinite-state systems. Given (i) a network of *data automata* $\mathcal{A} = \langle A_1, \ldots, A_N \rangle$ that communicate via a set of shared variables $\mathbf{x}_{\mathcal{A}}$, ranging over an infinite data domain, and a set of input events $\Sigma_{\mathcal{A}}$, and (ii) a data automaton $B$ whose set of variables $\mathbf{x}_B$ is a subset of $\mathbf{x}_{\mathcal{A}}$, does the set of (finite) traces of $B$ contain the traces of $\mathcal{A}$? Here, by a *trace*, we understand an alternating sequence of valuations of the variables from the set $\mathbf{x}_B$ and input events from the set $\Sigma_{\mathcal{A}} \cap \Sigma_B$, starting and ending with a valuation. Typically, the network of automata $\mathcal{A}$ is an implementation of a concurrent system and $B$ is a specification of the set of good behaviors of the system.

Consider, for instance, the network $\langle A_1, \ldots, A_N \rangle$ of data automata equipped with the integer-valued variables $x$ and $\nu$ shown in Fig. 1 (left). The automata synchronize on the **init** symbol and interleave their $\mathbf{a}_{1,\ldots,N}$ actions. Each automaton $A_i$ increases the shared variable $x$ and writes its identifier $i$ into the shared

R. Iosif—Supported by the French National Research Agency project VECOLIB (ANR-14-CE28-0018).

A. Rogalewicz and T. Vojnar—Supported by the Czech Science Foundation project 14-11384S, the IT4IXS: IT4Innovations Excellence in Science project (LQ1602), and the internal BUT project FIT-S-14-2486.

M. Chechik and J.-F. Raskin (Eds.): TACAS 2016, LNCS 9636, pp. 71–89, 2016.
DOI: 10.1007/978-3-662-49674-9_5

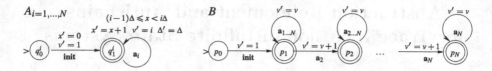

**Fig. 1.** An instance of the trace inclusion problem.

variable $\nu$ as long as the value of $x$ is in the interval $[(i-1)\Delta, i\Delta - 1]$, and it is inactive outside this interval, where $\Delta \geqslant 1$ is an unbounded parameter of the network. A possible specification for this network might require that each firing sequence is of the form **init** $\mathbf{a}_{1,\ldots,N}^* \mathbf{a}_2 \mathbf{a}_{2,\ldots,N}^* \cdots \mathbf{a}_i \mathbf{a}_i^*$ for some $1 \leqslant i \leqslant N$, and that $\nu$ is increased only on the first occurrence of the events $\mathbf{a}_2, \ldots, \mathbf{a}_i$, in this order. This condition is encoded by the automaton $B$ (Fig. 1, right). Observe that only the $\nu$ variable is shared between the network $\langle A_1, \ldots, A_N \rangle$ and the specification automaton $B$—we say that $\nu$ is *observable* in this case. An example of a trace, for $\Delta = 2$ and $N \geqslant 3$, is: $(v = 0)$ **init** $(v = 1)$ $\mathbf{a}_1$ $(v = 1)$ $\mathbf{a}_1$ $(v = 1)$ $\mathbf{a}_2$ $(v = 2)$ $\mathbf{a}_2$ $(v = 2)$ $\mathbf{a}_3$ $(v = 3)$. Our problem is to check that this, and all other traces of the network, are included in the language of the specification automaton, called the *observer*.

The trace inclusion problem has several applications, some of which we detail next. As the first potential application domain, we mention decision procedures for logics describing array structures in imperative programs [16,17] that use a translation of array formulae to integer counter automata, which encode the set of array models of a formula. The expressiveness of such logics is currently limited by the decidability of the emptiness (reachability) problem for counter automata. If we give up on decidability, we can reduce an entailment between two array formulae to the trace inclusion of two integer counter automata, and use the method presented in this paper as a semi-decision procedure. To assess this claim, we have applied our trace inclusion method to several verification conditions for programs with unbounded arrays of integers [7].

Another application is within the theory of timed automata and regular specifications of timed languages [2] that can be both represented by finite automata extended with real-valued variables [14]. The verification problem boils down to the trace inclusion of two real-valued data automata. Our method has been tested on several timed verification problems, including communication protocols and boolean circuits [27].

When developing a method for checking the inclusion between trace languages of automata extended with variables ranging over infinite data domains, the first problem is the lack of determinization and/or complementation results. In fact, certain classes of infinite state systems, such as timed automata [2], cannot be determinized and are provably not closed under complement. This is the case due to the fact that the clock variables of a timed automaton are not observable in its timed language, which records only the time lapses between successive events. However, if we require that the values of all variables of a data automaton be part of its trace language, we obtain a determinization result, which generalizes the classical subset construction by taking into account the data valuations. Building on this first result, we define the complement of a data language and reduce the trace inclusion problem to the emptiness of a product data automaton $\mathcal{L}(A \times \overline{B}) = \varnothing$. It is crucial, for this reduction, that the variables $\mathbf{x}_B$ of the right-hand side data automaton $B$ (the one being determinized) are also controlled by the left-hand side data automaton $A$, in other words, that $B$ has no hidden variables.

The language emptiness problem for data automata is, in general, undecidable [23]. Nevertheless, several semi-algorithms and tools for this problem (better known as the *reachability* problem) have been developed [3,15,19,22]. Among those, the technique of *lazy predicate abstraction* [19] combined with *counterexample-driven refinement* using *interpolants* [22] has been shown to be particularly successful in proving emptiness of rather large infinite-state systems. Moreover, this technique shares similar aspects with the antichain-based algorithm for language inclusion in the case of a finite alphabet [1]. An important similarity is that both techniques use a partial order on states, to prune the state space during the search.

The main result of this paper is a semi-algorithm that combines the principle of the antichain-based language inclusion algorithm [1] with the interpolant-based abstraction refinement semi-algorithm [22], via a general notion of language-based subsumption relation. We have implemented our semi-algorithm in a prototype tool and carried out a number of experiments, involving hardware, real-time systems, and array logic problems. Since our procedure tests inclusion within a set of good traces, instead of empty intersection with a set of error traces, we can encode rather complex verification conditions concisely, by avoiding the blowup caused by an a-priori complementation of the automaton encoding the property.

## 1.1 Overview

We introduce the reader to our trace inclusion method by means of an example. For space reasons, all proofs are given in an extended version of the paper [21].

Let us consider the network of data automata $\langle A_1, A_2 \rangle$ and the data automaton $B$ from Fig. 1. We prove that, for any value of $\Delta$, any trace of the network $\langle A_1, A_2 \rangle$, obtained as an interleaving of the actions of $A_1$ and $A_2$, is also a trace of the observer $B$. To this end, our procedure will fire increasingly longer sequences of input events, in

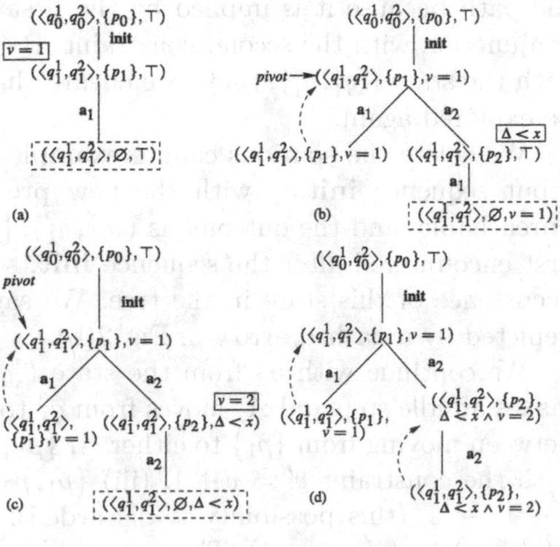

Fig. 2. Sample run of our semi-algorithm.

search for a counterexample trace. We keep a set of predicates associated with each state $(\langle q_1, q_2 \rangle, P)$ of the product automaton where $q_i$ is a state of $A_i$ and $P$ is a set of states of $B$. These predicates are formulae that define over-approximations of the data values reached simultaneously by the network, when $A_i$ is the state $q_i$, and by the observer $B$, in every state from $P$.

The first input event is **init**, on which $A_1$ and $A_2$ synchronize, moving together from the initial state $\langle q_0^1, q_0^2 \rangle$ to $\langle q_1^1, q_1^2 \rangle$. In response, $B$ can chose to either (i) move from $\{p_0\}$ to $\{p_1\}$, matching the only transition rule from $p_0$, or (ii) ignore the transition rule and move to the empty set. In the first case, the values of $\nu$ match the relation of the rule $p_0 \xrightarrow{\text{init}, v'=1} p_1$, while in the second case, these values match the negated relation $\neg(v' = 1)$. The second case is impossible because the action of the network requires $x' = 0 \wedge v' = 1$. The only successor state is thus $(\langle q_1^1, q_1^2 \rangle, \{p_1\})$ in Fig. 2(a). Since no predicates are initially available at this state, the best over-approximation of the set of reachable data valuations is the universal set ($\top$).

The second input event is $\mathbf{a}_1$, on which $A_1$ moves from $q_1^1$ back to itself, while $A_2$ makes an idle step because no transition with $\mathbf{a}_1$ is enabled from $q_1^2$. Again, $B$ has the choice between moving from $\{p_1\}$ either to $\varnothing$ or $\{p_1\}$. Let us consider the first case, in which the successor state is $(\langle q_1^1, q_1^2 \rangle, \varnothing, \top)$. Since $q_1^1$ and $q_1^2$ are final states of $A_1$ and $A_2$, respectively, and no final state of $B$ is present in $\varnothing$, we say that the state is accepting. If the accepting state (in dashed boxes in Fig. 2) is reachable according to the transition constraints along the input sequence **init.a₁**, we have found a counterexample trace that is in the language of $\langle A_1, A_2 \rangle$ but not in the language of $B$.

To verify the reachability of the accepting state, we check the satisfiability of the path formula corresponding to the composition of the transition constraints $x' = 0 \wedge v' = 1$ (**init**) and $0 \leqslant x < \Delta \wedge x' = x + 1 \wedge v' = 1 \wedge \neg(v' = v)$ ($\mathbf{a}_1$) in Fig. 2(a). This formula is unsatisfiable, and the proof of infeasibility provides the interpolant $\langle v = 1 \rangle$. This formula is an explanation for the infeasibility of the path because it is implied by the first constraint and it is unsatisfiable in conjunction with the second constraint. By associating the new predicate $v = 1$ with the state $(\langle q_1^1, q_1^2 \rangle, \{p_1\})$, we ensure that the same spurious path will never be explored again.

We delete the spurious counterexample and recompute the states along the input sequence **init.a₁** with the new predicate. In this case, $(\langle q_1^1, q_1^2 \rangle, \varnothing)$ is unreachable, and the outcome is $(\langle q_1^1, q_1^2 \rangle, \{p_1\}, v = 1)$. However, this state was first encountered after the sequence **init**, so there is no need to store a second occurrence of this state in the tree. We say that **init.a₁** is subsumed by **init**, depicted by a dashed arrow in Fig. 2(b).

We continue with $\mathbf{a}_2$ from the state $(\langle q_1^1, q_1^2 \rangle, \{p_1\}, v = 1)$. In this case, $A_1$ makes an idle step and $A_2$ moves from $q_1^2$ to itself. In response, $B$ has the choice between moving from $\{p_1\}$ to either (i) $\{p_1\}$ with the constraint $v' = v$, (ii) $\{p_2\}$ with the constraint $v' = v + 1$, (iii) $\{p_1, p_2\}$ with the constraint $v' = v \wedge v' = v + 1 \rightarrow \perp$ (this possibility is discarded), (iv) $\varnothing$ for data values that satisfy $\neg(v' = v) \wedge \neg(v' = v + 1)$. The last case is also discarded because the value of $\nu$

after **init** constrained to 1 and the $A_2$ imposes further the constraint $v' = 2$ and $v = 1 \wedge v' = 2 \wedge \neg(v' = v) \wedge \neg(v' = v + 1) \rightarrow \bot$. Hence, the only $\mathbf{a}_2$-successor of $(\langle q_1^1, q_1^2 \rangle, \{p_1\}, v = 1)$ is $(\langle q_1^1, q_1^2 \rangle, \{p_2\}, \top)$, in Fig. 2(b).

By firing the event $\mathbf{a}_1$ from this state, we reach $(\langle q_1^1, q_1^2 \rangle, \varnothing, v = 1)$, which is, again, accepting. We check whether the path **init**.$\mathbf{a}_2$.$\mathbf{a}_1$ is feasible, which turns out not to be the case. For efficiency reasons, we find the shortest suffix of this path that can be proved infeasible. It turns out that the sequence $\mathbf{a}_2$.$\mathbf{a}_1$ is infeasible starting from the state $(\langle q_1^1, q_1^2 \rangle, \{p_1\}, v = 1)$, which is called the *pivot*. This proof of infeasibility yields the interpolant $\langle v = 1, \Delta < x \rangle$, and a new predicate $\Delta < x$ is associated with $(\langle q_1^1, q_1^2 \rangle, \{p_2\})$. The refinement phase rebuilds only the subtree rooted at the pivot state, in Fig. 2(b).

The procedure then builds the tree on Fig. 2(c) starting from the pivot node and finds the accepting state $(\langle q_1^1, q_1^2 \rangle, \varnothing, \Delta < x)$ as the result of firing the sequence **init**.$\mathbf{a}_2$.$\mathbf{a}_2$. This path is spurious, and the new predicate $v = 2$ is associated with the location $(\langle q_1^1, q_1^2 \rangle, \{p_2\})$. The pivot node is the same as in Fig. 2(b), and, by recomputing the subtree rooted at this node with the new predicates, we obtain the tree in Fig. 2(d), in which all frontier nodes are subsumed by their predecessors. Thus, no new event needs to be fired, and the procedure can stop reporting that the trace inclusion holds.

**Related Work.** The trace inclusion problem has been previously addressed in the context of timed automata [25]. Although the problem is undecidable in general, decidability is recovered when the left-hand side automaton has at most one clock, or the only constant appearing in the clock constraints is zero. These are essentially the only known decidable cases of language inclusion for timed automata.

The study of *data automata* [5,6] usually deals with decision problems in logics describing data languages for simple theories, typically infinite data domains with equality. Although our notions of data words and data languages are similar to the classical ones in the literature [5,6], the data automata defined in this paper are different from [5], as well as [6]. The main difference consists in the fact that the existing notions of data automata are controlled by equivalence relations of finite index, whereas in our case, the transitions are defined by unrestricted formulae in the first-order theory of the data domain. Moreover, the emptiness problems [5,6] are decidable, whereas we consider an undecidable model that subsumes the existing ones.

Data words are also studied in the context of *symbolic visibly pushdown automata* (SVPA) [11]. Language inclusion is decidable for SVPAs with transition guards from a decidable theory because SVPAs are closed under complement and the emptiness can be reduced to a finite number of queries expressible in the underlying theory of guards. Decidability comes here at the cost of reducing the expressiveness and forbidding comparisons between adjacent positions in the input (only comparisons between matching call/return positions of the input nested words are allowed).

Another related model is that of *predicate automata* [13], which recognize languages over integer data by labeling the words with conjunctions of uninterpreted predicates. The emptiness problem is undecidable for this model and becomes decidable when all predicates are monadic. Exploring further the connection between predicate automata and our definition of data automata could also provide interesting examples for our method, stemming from verification problems for parallel programs.

Finally, several works on model checking infinite-state systems against CTL [4] and CTL* [9] specifications are related to our problem as they check inclusion between the set of computation trees of an infinite-state system and the set of trees defined by a branching temporal logic specification. The verification of existential CTL formulae [4] is reduced to solving forall-exists quantified Horn clauses by applying counterexample guided refinement to discover witnesses for existentially quantified variables. The work [9] on CTL* verification of infinite systems is based on partial symbolic determinization, using prophecy variables to summarize the future program execution. For finite-state systems, automata are a strictly more expressive formalism than temporal logics[1]. Such a comparison is, however, non-trivial for infinite-state systems. Nevertheless, we found the data automata considered in this paper to be a natural tool for specifying verification conditions of array programs [7,16,17] and regular properties of timed languages [2].

## 2    Data Automata

Let $\mathbb{N}$ denote the set of non-negative integers including zero. For any $k, \ell \in \mathbb{N}$, $k \leqslant \ell$, we write $[k, \ell]$ for the set $\{k, k+1, \ldots, \ell\}$. We write $\bot$ and $\top$ for the boolean constants *false* and *true*, respectively. Given a possibly infinite data domain $\mathcal{D}$, we denote by $\text{Th}(\mathcal{D}) = \langle \mathcal{D}, p_1, \ldots, p_n, f_1, \ldots, f_m \rangle$ the set of syntactically correct first-order formulae with predicate symbols $p_1, \ldots, p_n$ and function symbols $f_1, \ldots, f_m$. A variable $x$ is said to be *free* in a formula $\phi$, denoted as $\phi(x)$, iff it does not occur under the scope of a quantifier.

Let $\mathbf{x} = \{x_1, \ldots, x_n\}$ be a finite set of variables. A *valuation* $\nu : \mathbf{x} \to \mathcal{D}$ is an assignment of the variables in $\mathbf{x}$ with values from $\mathcal{D}$. We denote by $\mathcal{D}^{\mathbf{x}}$ the set of such valuations. For a formula $\phi(\mathbf{x})$, we denote by $\nu \models_{\text{Th}(\mathcal{D})} \phi$ the fact that substituting each variable $x \in \mathbf{x}$ by $\nu(x)$ yields a valid formula in the theory $\text{Th}(\mathcal{D})$. In this case, $\nu$ is said to be a *model* of $\phi$. A formula is said to be *satisfiable* iff it has a model. For a formula $\phi(\mathbf{x}, \mathbf{x}')$ where $\mathbf{x}' = \{x' \mid x \in \mathbf{x}\}$ and two valuations $\nu, \nu' \in \mathcal{D}^{\mathbf{x}}$, we denote by $(\nu, \nu') \models_{\text{Th}(\mathcal{D})} \phi$ the fact that the formula obtained from $\phi$ by substituting each $x$ with $\nu(x)$ and each $x'$ with $\nu'(x')$ is valid in $\text{Th}(\mathcal{D})$.

**Data Automata.** *Data Automata* (DA) are extensions of non-deterministic finite automata with variables ranging over an infinite data domain $\mathcal{D}$, equipped with a first order theory $\text{Th}(\mathcal{D})$. Formally, a DA is a tuple $A = \langle \mathcal{D}, \Sigma, \mathbf{x}, Q, \iota, F, \Delta \rangle$, where:

---

[1] For (in)finite words, the class of LTL-definable languages coincides with the star-free languages, which are a strict subclass of ($\omega$-)regular languages.

- $\Sigma$ is a finite alphabet of input events and $\diamond \in \Sigma$ is a special padding symbol,
- $\mathbf{x} = \{x_1, \dots, x_n\}$ is a set of variables,
- $Q$ is a finite set of *states*, $\iota \in Q$ is an *initial* state, $F \subseteq Q$ are *final* states, and
- $\Delta$ is a set of *rules* of the form $q \xrightarrow{\sigma, \phi(\mathbf{x}, \mathbf{x}')} q'$ where $\sigma \in \Sigma$ is an alphabet symbol and $\phi(\mathbf{x}, \mathbf{x}')$ is a formula in $\mathrm{Th}(\mathcal{D})$.

A *configuration* of $A$ is a pair $(q, \nu) \in Q \times \mathcal{D}^{\mathbf{x}}$. We say that a configuration $(q', \nu')$ is a *successor* of $(q, \nu)$ if and only if there exists a rule $q \xrightarrow{\sigma, \phi} q' \in \Delta$ and $(\nu, \nu') \models_{\mathrm{Th}(\mathcal{D})} \phi$. We denote the successor relation by $(q, \nu) \xrightarrow{\sigma, \phi} {}_A (q', \nu')$, and we omit writing $\phi$ and $A$ when no confusion may arise. We denote by $succ_A(q, \nu) = \{(q', \nu') \mid (q, \nu) \to {}_A (q', \nu')\}$ the set of successors of a configuration $(q, \nu)$.

A *trace* is a finite sequence $w = (\nu_0, \sigma_0), \dots, (\nu_{n-1}, \sigma_{n-1}), (\nu_n, \diamond)$ of pairs $(\nu_i, \sigma_i)$ taken from the infinite alphabet $\mathcal{D}^{\mathbf{x}} \times \Sigma$. A *run* of $A$ over the *trace* $w$ is a sequence of configurations $\pi : (q_0, \nu_0) \xrightarrow{\sigma_0} (q_1, \nu_1) \xrightarrow{\sigma_1} \dots \xrightarrow{\sigma_{n-1}} (q_n, \nu_n)$. We say that the run $\pi$ is *accepting* if and only if $q_n \in F$, in which case $A$ *accepts* $w$. The *language* of $A$, denoted $\mathcal{L}(A)$, is the set of traces accepted by $A$.

**Data Automata Networks.** A *data automata network* (DAN) is a non-empty tuple $\mathcal{A} = \langle A_1, \dots, A_N \rangle$ of data automata $A_i = \langle \mathcal{D}, \Sigma_i, \mathbf{x}_i, Q_i, \iota_i, F_i, \Delta_i \rangle$, $i \in [1, N]$ whose sets of states are pairwise disjoint. A DAN is a succinct representation of an exponentially larger DA $\mathcal{A}^e = \langle \mathcal{D}, \Sigma_{\mathcal{A}}, \mathbf{x}_{\mathcal{A}}, Q_{\mathcal{A}}, \iota_{\mathcal{A}}, F_{\mathcal{A}}, \Delta_{\mathcal{A}} \rangle$, called the *expansion* of $\mathcal{A}$, where:

- $\Sigma_{\mathcal{A}} = \Sigma_1 \cup \dots \cup \Sigma_N$ and $\mathbf{x}_{\mathcal{A}} = \mathbf{x}_1 \cup \dots \cup \mathbf{x}_N$,
- $Q_{\mathcal{A}} = Q_1 \times \dots \times Q_N$, $\iota_{\mathcal{A}} = \langle \iota_1, \dots, \iota_N \rangle$ and $F_{\mathcal{A}} = F_1 \times \dots \times F_N$,
- $\langle q_1, \dots, q_N \rangle \xrightarrow{\sigma, \varphi} \langle q'_1, \dots, q'_N \rangle$ if and only if (i) for each $i \subset I$, there exists $\varphi_i \in \mathrm{Th}(\mathcal{D})$ such that $q_i \xrightarrow{\sigma, \varphi_i} q'_i \in \Delta_i$, (ii) for all $i \notin I$, $q_i = q'_i$, and (iii) $\varphi \equiv \bigwedge_{i \in I} \varphi_i \wedge \bigwedge_{j \notin I} \tau_j$, where $I = \{i \in [1, N] \mid q_i \xrightarrow{\sigma, \varphi_i} q'_i \in \Delta_i\}$ is the set of DA that can move from $q_i$ to $q'_i$ while reading the input symbol $\sigma$, and $\tau_j \equiv \bigwedge_{x \in \mathbf{x}_j \setminus (\bigcup_{i \in I} \mathbf{x}_i)} x' = x$ propagates the values of the local variables in $A_j$ that are not updated by $\{A_i\}_{i \in I}$.

Intuitively, all automata that can read an input symbol synchronize their actions on that symbol whereas the rest of the automata make an idle step and copy the values of their local variables which are not updated by the active automata. The language of the DAN $\mathcal{A}$ is defined as the language of its expansion DA, i.e. $\mathcal{L}(\mathcal{A}) = \mathcal{L}(\mathcal{A}^e)$.

**Trace Inclusion.** Let $\mathcal{A}$ be a DAN and $\mathcal{A}^e = \langle \mathcal{D}, \Sigma, \mathbf{x}_{\mathcal{A}}, Q_{\mathcal{A}}, \iota_{\mathcal{A}}, F_{\mathcal{A}}, \Delta_{\mathcal{A}} \rangle$ be its expansion. For a set of variables $\mathbf{y} \subseteq \mathbf{x}_{\mathcal{A}}$, we denote by $\nu \downarrow_{\mathbf{y}}$ the restriction of a valuation $\nu \in \mathcal{D}^{\mathbf{x}_{\mathcal{A}}}$ to the variables in $\mathbf{y}$. For a trace $w = (\nu_0, \sigma_0), \dots, (\nu_n, \diamond) \in (\mathcal{D}^{\mathbf{x}_{\mathcal{A}}} \times \Sigma_{\mathcal{A}})^*$, we denote by $w \downarrow_{\mathbf{y}}$ the trace $(\nu_0 \downarrow_{\mathbf{y}}, \sigma_0), \dots, (\nu_{n-1} \downarrow_{\mathbf{y}}, \sigma_{n-1})$, $(\nu_n \downarrow_{\mathbf{y}}, \diamond) \in (\mathcal{D}^{\mathbf{y}} \times \Sigma)^*$. We lift this notion to sets of words in the natural way, by defining $\mathcal{L}(\mathcal{A}) \downarrow_{\mathbf{y}} = \{w \downarrow_{\mathbf{y}} \mid w \in \mathcal{L}(\mathcal{A})\}$.

We are now ready to define the trace inclusion problem on which we focus in this paper. Given a DAN $\mathcal{A}$ as before and a DA $B = \langle \mathcal{D}, \Sigma, \mathbf{x}_B, Q_B, \iota_B, F_B, \Delta_B \rangle$

such that $\mathbf{x}_B \subseteq \mathbf{x}_{\mathcal{A}}$, the *trace inclusion problem* asks whether $\mathcal{L}(\mathcal{A}) \downarrow_{\mathbf{x}_B} \subseteq \mathcal{L}(B)$? The right-hand side DA $B$ is called *observer*, and the variables in $\mathbf{x}_B$ are called *observable* variables.

## 2.1 Boolean Closure Properties of Data Automata

Let $A = \langle \mathcal{D}, \Sigma, \mathbf{x}, Q, \iota, F, \Delta \rangle$ be a DA for the rest of this section. $A$ is said to be *deterministic* if and only if, for each trace $w \in \mathcal{L}(A)$, $A$ has at most one run over $w$. The first result of this section is that, interestingly, any DA can be determinized while preserving its language. The determinization procedure is a generalization of the classical subset construction for Rabin-Scott word automata on finite alphabets. The reason why determinization is possible for automata over an infinite data alphabet $\mathcal{D}^{\mathbf{x}} \times \Sigma$ is that the successive values taken by *each variable* $x \in \mathbf{x}$ are tracked by the language $\mathcal{L}(A) \subseteq (\mathcal{D}^{\mathbf{x}} \times \Sigma)^*$. This assumption is crucial: a typical example of automata over an infinite alphabet, that cannot be determinized, are timed automata [2], where only the elapsed time is reflected in the language, and not the values of the variables (clocks).

Formally, the *deterministic* DA accepting the language $\mathcal{L}(A)$ is defined as $A^d = \langle \mathcal{D}, \Sigma, \mathbf{x}, Q^d, \iota^d, F^d, \Delta^d \rangle$, where $Q^d = 2^Q$, $\iota^d = \{\iota\}$, $F^d = \{P \subseteq Q \mid P \cap F \neq \varnothing\}$ and $\Delta^d$ is the set of rules $P \xrightarrow{\sigma, \theta} P'$ such that:

- for all $p' \in P'$ there exists $p \in P$ and a rule $p \xrightarrow{\sigma, \psi} p' \in \Delta$,
- $\theta(\mathbf{x}, \mathbf{x}') \equiv \bigwedge_{p' \in P'} \bigvee_{\substack{p \xrightarrow{\sigma, \psi} p' \in \Delta \\ p \in P}} \psi \wedge \bigwedge_{p' \in Q \setminus P'} \bigwedge_{\substack{p \xrightarrow{\sigma, \varphi} p' \in \Delta \\ p \in P}} \neg\varphi$ .

The main difference with the classical subset construction for Rabin-Scott automata is that here we consider *all sets* $P'$ of states that have a predecessor in $P$, not just the maximal such set. The reason is that a set $P'$ is not automatically subsumed by the union of all such sets due to the data constraints on the variables $\mathbf{x}$. Observe, moreover, that $A^d$ can be built for any theory $\mathrm{Th}(\mathcal{D})$ that is closed under conjunction and negation.

**Lemma 1.** *Given a DA* $A = \langle \mathcal{D}, \Sigma, \mathbf{x}, Q, \iota, F, \Delta \rangle$, *(1) for any* $w \in (\mathcal{D}^{\mathbf{x}} \times \Sigma)^*$ *and* $P \in Q^d$, $A^d$ *has exactly one run on* $w$ *that starts in* $P$, *and (2)* $\mathcal{L}(A) = \mathcal{L}(A^d)$.

The construction of a deterministic DA recognizing the language of $A$ is key to defining a DA that recognizes the complement of $A$. Let $\overline{A} = \langle \mathcal{D}, \Sigma, \mathbf{x}, Q^d, \iota^d, Q^d \setminus F^d, \Delta^d \rangle$. In other words, $\overline{A}$ has the same structure as $A^d$, and the set of final states consists of those subsets that contain no final state, i.e. $\{P \subseteq Q \mid P \cap F = \varnothing\}$. Using Lemma 1, it is not difficult to show that $\mathcal{L}(\overline{A}) = (\mathcal{D}^{\mathbf{x}} \times \Sigma)^* \setminus \mathcal{L}(A)$.

Next, we show closure of DA under intersection. Let $B = \langle \mathcal{D}, \Sigma, \mathbf{x}, Q', \iota', F', \Delta' \rangle$ be a DA and define $A \times B = \langle \mathcal{D}, \Sigma, \mathbf{x}, Q \times Q', (\iota, \iota'), F \times F', \Delta^\times \rangle$, where $(q, q') \xrightarrow{\sigma, \varphi} (p, p') \in \Delta^\times$ if and only if $q \xrightarrow{\sigma, \phi} p \in \Delta$, $q' \xrightarrow{\sigma, \psi} p' \in \Delta'$ and $\varphi \equiv \phi \wedge \psi$. It is easy to show that $\mathcal{L}(A \times B) = \mathcal{L}(A) \cap \mathcal{L}(B)$. DA are also closed under union, since $\mathcal{L}(A) \cup \mathcal{L}(B) = \mathcal{L}(\overline{\overline{A} \times \overline{B}})$.

Let us turn now to the trace inclusion problem. The following lemma shows that this problem can be effectively reduced to an equivalent language emptiness problem. However, note that this reduction does not work when the trace inclusion problem is generalized by removing the condition $\mathbf{x}_B \subseteq \mathbf{x}_A$. In other words, if the observer uses local variables not shared with the network[2], i.e. $\mathbf{x}_B \backslash \mathbf{x}_A \neq \varnothing$, the generalized trace inclusion problem $L(A) \downarrow_{\mathbf{x}_A \cap \mathbf{x}_B} \subseteq L(B) \downarrow_{\mathbf{x}_A \cap \mathbf{x}_B}$ has a negative answer iff *there exists a trace* $w = (\nu_0, \sigma_0), \ldots, (\nu_n, \diamond) \in L(A)$ such that, *for all valuations* $\mu_0, \ldots, \mu_n \in \mathcal{D}^{\mathbf{x}_B \backslash \mathbf{x}_A}$, we have $w' = (\nu_0 \downarrow_{\mathbf{x}_A \cap \mathbf{x}_B} \cup \mu_0, \sigma_0), \ldots, (\nu_n \downarrow_{\mathbf{x}_A \cap \mathbf{x}_B} \cup \mu_n, \diamond) \notin L(B)$. This kind of quantifier alternation cannot be easily accommodated within the framework of language emptiness, in which only one type of (existential) quantifier occurs.

**Lemma 2.** *Given* DA $A = \langle \mathcal{D}, \Sigma, \mathbf{x}_A, Q_A, \iota_A, F_A, \Delta_A \rangle$ *and* $B = \langle \mathcal{D}, \Sigma, \mathbf{x}_B, Q_B, \iota_B, F_B, \Delta_B \rangle$ *such that* $\mathbf{x}_B \subseteq \mathbf{x}_A$. *Then* $L(A) \downarrow_{\mathbf{x}_B} \subseteq L(B)$ *if and only if* $L(A \times \overline{B}) = \varnothing$.

The trace inclusion problem is undecidable, which can be shown by reduction from the language emptiness problem for DA (take $B$ such that $L(B) = \varnothing$). However the above lemma shows that any semi-decision procedure for the language emptiness problem can also be used to deal with the trace inclusion problem.

# 3   Abstract, Check, and Refine for Trace Inclusion

This section describes our semi-algorithm for checking the trace inclusion between a given network $\mathcal{A}$ and an observer $B$. Let $\mathcal{A}^e$ denote the expansion of $\mathcal{A}$, defined in the previous. In the light of Lemma 2, the trace inclusion problem $L(\mathcal{A}) \downarrow_{\mathbf{x}_B} \subseteq L(B)$, where the set of observable variables $\mathbf{x}_B$ is included in the set of network variables, can be reduced to the language emptiness problem $L(\mathcal{A}^e \times \overline{B}) = \varnothing$.

Although language emptiness is undecidable for data automata [23], several cost-effective semi-algorithms and tools [3,15,18,22] have been developed, showing that it is possible, in many practical cases, to provide a yes/no answer to this problem. However, to apply one of the existing off-the-shelf tools to our problem, one needs to build the product automaton $\mathcal{A}^e \times \overline{B}$ prior to the analysis. Due to the inherent state explosion caused by the interleaving semantics of the network as well as by the complementation of the observer, such a solution would not be efficient in practice.

To avoid building the product automaton, our procedure builds *on-the-fly* an over-approximation of the (possibly infinite) set of reachable configurations of $\mathcal{A}^e \times \overline{B}$. This over-approximation is defined using the approach of *lazy predicate abstraction* [18], combined with *counterexample-driven abstraction refinement* using *interpolants* [22]. We store the explored abstract states in a structure

---

[2] For timed automata, this is the case since the only shared variable is the time, and the observer may have local clocks.

called an *antichain tree*. In general, antichain-based algorithms [28] store only states which are incomparable w.r.t. a partial order called *subsumption*. Our method can be thus seen as an extension of the antichain-based language inclusion algorithm [1] to infinite-state systems by means of predicate abstraction and interpolation-based refinement. Since the trace inclusion problem is undecidable in general, termination of our procedure is not guaranteed; in the following, we shall, however, call our procedure an algorithm for the sake of brevity.

### 3.1 Antichain Trees

We define antichain trees, which are the main data structure of the trace inclusion procedure. Let $\mathcal{A} = \langle A_1, \ldots, A_N \rangle$ be a network of automata where $A_i = \langle \mathcal{D}, \Sigma_i, \mathbf{x}_i, Q_i, \iota_i, F_i, \Delta_i \rangle$, for all $i \in [1, N]$, and let $B = \langle \mathcal{D}, \Sigma, \mathbf{x}_B, Q_B, \iota_B, F_B, \Delta_B \rangle$ be an observer such that $\mathbf{x}_B \subseteq \bigcup_{i=1}^{N} \mathbf{x}_i$. We also denote by $\mathcal{A}^e = \langle \mathcal{D}, \Sigma_{\mathcal{A}}, \mathbf{x}_{\mathcal{A}}, Q_{\mathcal{A}}, \iota_{\mathcal{A}}, F_{\mathcal{A}}, \Delta_{\mathcal{A}} \rangle$ the expansion of the network $\mathcal{A}$ and by $\mathcal{A}^e \times \overline{B} = \langle \mathcal{D}, \Sigma_{\mathcal{A}}, \mathbf{x}_{\mathcal{A}}, Q^p, \iota^p, F^p, \Delta^p \rangle$ the product automaton used for checking language inclusion.

An *antichain tree* for the network $\mathcal{A}$ and the observer $B$ is a tree whose nodes are labeled by *product states* (see Fig. 2 for examples). Intuitively, a product state is an over-approximation of the set of configurations of the product automaton $\mathcal{A}^e \times \overline{B}$ that share the same control state. Formally, a *product state for $\mathcal{A}$ and $B$* is a tuple $s = (\mathbf{q}, P, \Phi)$ where (i) $(\mathbf{q}, P)$ is a state of $\mathcal{A}^e \times \overline{B}$ with $\mathbf{q} = \langle q_1, \ldots, q_N \rangle$ being a state of the network expansion $\mathcal{A}^e$ and $P$ being a set of states of the observer $B$, and (ii) $\Phi(\mathbf{x}_{\mathcal{A}}) \in \mathrm{Th}(\mathcal{D})$ is a formula which defines an over-approximation of the set of valuations of the variables $\mathbf{x}_{\mathcal{A}}$ that reach the state $(\mathbf{q}, P)$ in $\mathcal{A}^e \times \overline{B}$. A product state $s = (\mathbf{q}, P, \Phi)$ is a finite representation of a possibly infinite set of configurations of $\mathcal{A}^e \times \overline{B}$, denoted as $[\![s]\!] = \{(\mathbf{q}, P, \nu) \mid \nu \models_{\mathrm{Th}(\mathcal{D})} \Phi\}$.

To build an over-approximation of the set of reachable states of the product automaton, we need to compute, for a product state $s$, an over-approximation of the set of configurations that can be reached in one step from $s$. To this end, we define first a finite abstract domain of product states, based on the notion of *predicate map*. A predicate map is a partial function that associates sets of facts about the values of the variables used in the product automaton, called *predicates*, with components of a product state, called *substates*. The reason behind the distribution of predicates over substates is two-fold. First, we would like the abstraction to be *local*, i.e. the predicates needed to define a certain subtree in the antichain must be associated with the labels of that subtree only. Second, once a predicate appears in the context of a substate, it should be subsequently reused whenever that same substate occurs as part of another product state.

Formally, a *substate* of a state $(\langle q_1, \ldots, q_N \rangle, P) \in Q^p$ of the product automaton $\mathcal{A}^e \times \overline{B}$ is a pair $(\langle q_{i_1}, \ldots, q_{i_k} \rangle, S)$ such that (i) $\langle q_{i_1}, \ldots, q_{i_k} \rangle$ is a subsequence of $\langle q_1, \ldots, q_N \rangle$, and (ii) $S \neq \varnothing$ only if $S \cap P \neq \varnothing$. We denote the substate relation by $(\langle q_{i_1}, \ldots, q_{i_k} \rangle, S) \lhd (\langle q_1, \ldots, q_N \rangle, P)$. The substate relation requires the automata $A_{i_1}, \ldots, A_{i_k}$ of the network $\mathcal{A}$ to be in the control states

$q_{i_1}, \ldots, q_{i_k}$ simultaneously, and the observer $B$ to be in at least some state of $S$ provided $S \neq \varnothing$ (if $S = \varnothing$, the state of $B$ is considered to be irrelevant). Let $S_{\langle \mathcal{A}, B \rangle} = \{r \mid \exists q \in Q^p \ . \ r \lhd q\}$ be the set of substates of a state of $\mathcal{A}^e \times \overline{B}$.

A *predicate map* $\Pi : S_{\langle \mathcal{A}, B \rangle} \to 2^{\mathrm{Th}(\mathcal{D})}$ associates each substate $(\mathbf{r}, S) \in Q_{i_1} \times \ldots \times Q_{i_k} \times 2^{Q_B}$ with a set of formulae $\pi(\mathbf{x})$ where (i) $\mathbf{x} = \mathbf{x}_{i_1} \cup \ldots \cup \mathbf{x}_{i_k} \cup \mathbf{x}_B$ if $S \neq \varnothing$, and (ii) $\mathbf{x} = \mathbf{x}_{i_1} \cup \ldots \cup \mathbf{x}_{i_k}$ if $S = \varnothing$. Notice that a predicate associated with a substate refers only to the local variables of those network components $A_{i_1}, \ldots, A_{i_k}$ and of the observer $B$ that occur in the particular substate.

We are now ready to define the abstract semantics of the product automaton $\mathcal{A}^e \times \overline{B}$, induced by a given predicate map. For convenience, we define first a set $Post(s)$ of *concrete successors* of a product state $s = (\mathbf{q}, P, \Phi)$ such that $(\mathbf{r}, S, \Psi) \in Post(s)$ if and only if (i) the product automaton $\mathcal{A}^e \times \overline{B}$ has a rule $(\mathbf{q}, P) \xrightarrow{\sigma, \theta} (\mathbf{r}, S) \in \Delta^p$ and $\Psi(\mathbf{x}_{\mathcal{A}}) \not\to \bot$, where $\Psi(\mathbf{x}_{\mathcal{A}}) \equiv \exists \mathbf{x}'_{\mathcal{A}} \ . \ \Phi(\mathbf{x}'_{\mathcal{A}}) \wedge \theta(\mathbf{x}'_{\mathcal{A}}, \mathbf{x}_{\mathcal{A}})$. The set of concrete successors does not contain states with empty set of valuations; these states are unreachable in $\mathcal{A}^e \times \overline{B}$.

Given a predicate map $\Pi$, the set $Post_\Pi(s)$ of *abstract successors* of a product state $s$ is defined as follows: $(\mathbf{r}, S, \Psi^\sharp) \in Post_\Pi(s)$ if and only if (i) there exists a product state $(\mathbf{r}, S, \Psi) \in Post(s)$ and (ii) $\Psi^\sharp(\mathbf{x}_{\mathcal{A}}) \equiv \bigwedge_{r \lhd (\mathbf{r}, S)} \bigwedge \{\pi \in \Pi(r) \mid \Psi \to \pi\}$. In other words, the set of data valuations that are reachable by an abstract successor is the tightest over-approximation of the concrete set of reachable valuations, obtained as the conjunction of the available predicates from the predicate map that over-approximate this set.

Finally, an *antichain tree* (or, simply antichain) $\mathcal{T}$ for $\mathcal{A}$ and $B$ is a tree whose nodes are labeled with product states and whose edges are labeled by input symbols and concrete transition relations. Let $\mathbb{N}^*$ be the set of finite sequences of natural numbers that denote the positions in the tree. For a tree position $p \in \mathbb{N}^*$ and $i \in \mathbb{N}$, the position $p.i$ is a *child* of $p$. A set $S \subseteq \mathbb{N}^*$ is said to be *prefix-closed* if and only if, for each $p \in S$ and each prefix $q$ of $p$, we have $q \in S$ as well. The root is denoted by the empty sequence $\varepsilon$.

Formally, an antichain $\mathcal{T}$ is a set of pairs $\langle s, p \rangle$, where $s$ is a product state and $p \in \mathbb{N}^*$ is a tree position, such that (1) for each position $p \in \mathbb{N}^*$ there exists at most one product state $s$ such that $\langle s, p \rangle \in \mathcal{T}$, (2) the set $\{p \mid \langle s, p \rangle \in \mathcal{T}\}$ is prefix-closed, (3) $(root_{\langle \mathcal{A}, B \rangle}, \varepsilon) \in \mathcal{T}$ where $root_{\langle \mathcal{A}, B \rangle} = (\langle \iota_1, \ldots, \iota_N \rangle, \{\iota_B\}, \top)$ is the label of the root, and (4) for each edge $(\langle s, p \rangle, \langle t, p.i \rangle)$ in $\mathcal{T}$, there exists a predicate map $\Pi$ such that $t \in Post_\Pi(s)$. For the latter condition, if $s = (\mathbf{q}, P, \Phi)$ and $t = (\mathbf{r}, S, \Psi)$, there exists a unique rule $(\mathbf{q}, P) \xrightarrow{\sigma, \theta} (\mathbf{r}, S) \in \Delta^p$, and we shall sometimes denote the edge as $s \xrightarrow{\sigma, \theta} t$ or simply $s \xrightarrow{\theta} t$ when the tree positions are not important.

Each antichain node $n = (s, d_1 \ldots d_k) \in \mathcal{T}$ is naturally associated with a path from the root to itself $\rho \colon n_0 \xrightarrow{\sigma_1, \theta_1} n_1 \xrightarrow{\sigma_2, \theta_2} \ldots \xrightarrow{\sigma_2, \theta_k} n_k$. We denote by $\rho_i$ the node $n_i$ for each $i \in [0, k]$, and by $|\rho| = k$ the length of the path. The *path formula* associated with $\rho$ is $\Theta(\rho) \equiv \bigwedge_{i=1}^{k} \theta(\mathbf{x}_{\mathcal{A}}^{i-1}, \mathbf{x}_{\mathcal{A}}^i)$ where $\mathbf{x}_{\mathcal{A}}^i = \{x^i \mid x \in \mathbf{x}_{\mathcal{A}}\}$ is a set of indexed variables.

## 3.2   Counterexample-Driven Abstraction Refinement

A *counterexample* is a path from the root of the antichain to a node which is labeled by an *accepting* product state. A product state $(\mathbf{q}, P, \Phi)$ is said to be *accepting* iff $(\mathbf{q}, P)$ is an accepting state of the product automaton $\mathcal{A}^e \times \overline{B}$, i.e. $\mathbf{q} \in F_{\mathcal{A}}$ and $P \cap F_B = \varnothing$. A counterexample is said to be *spurious* if its path formula is unsatisfiable, i.e. the path does not correspond to a concrete execution of $\mathcal{A}^e \times \overline{B}$. In this case, we need to (i) remove the path $\rho$ from the current antichain and (ii) refine the abstract domain in order to exclude the occurrence of $\rho$ from future state space exploration.

Let $\rho : root_{\langle \mathcal{A}, B \rangle} = (\mathbf{q}_0, P_0, \Phi_0) \xrightarrow{\theta_1} (\mathbf{q}_1, P_1, \Phi_1) \xrightarrow{\theta_2} \ldots \xrightarrow{\theta_k} (\mathbf{q}_k, P_k, \Phi_k)$ be a spurious counterexample in the following. For efficiency reasons, we would like to save as much work as possible and remove only the smallest suffix of $\rho$ which caused the spuriousness. For some $j \in [0, k]$, let $\Theta^j(\rho) \equiv \Phi_j(\mathbf{x}_{\mathcal{A}}^0) \wedge \bigwedge_{i=j}^{k} \theta_i(\mathbf{x}_{\mathcal{A}}^{i-j}, \mathbf{x}_{\mathcal{A}}^{i-j+1})$ be the formula defining all sequences of data valuations that start in the set $\Phi_j$ and proceed along the suffix $(\mathbf{q}_j, P_j, \Phi_j) \rightarrow \ldots \rightarrow (\mathbf{q}_k, P_k, \Phi_k)$ of $\rho$. The *pivot* of a path $\rho$ is the maximal position $j \in [0, k]$ such that $\Theta^j(\rho) = \bot$, and $-1$ if $\rho$ is not spurious.

Finally, we describe the refinement of the predicate map, which ensures that a given spurious counterexample will never be found in a future iteration of the abstract state space exploration. The refinement is based on the notion of *interpolant* [22].

**Definition 1.** *Given a formula $\Phi(\mathbf{x})$ and a sequence $\langle \theta_1(\mathbf{x}, \mathbf{x}'), \ldots, \theta_k(\mathbf{x}, \mathbf{x}') \rangle$ of formulae, an* interpolant *is a sequence of formulae $\mathbf{I} = \langle I_0(\mathbf{x}), \ldots, I_k(\mathbf{x}) \rangle$ where: (1) $\Phi \rightarrow I_0$, (2) $I_k \rightarrow \bot$, and (3) $I_{i-1}(\mathbf{x}) \wedge \theta_i(\mathbf{x}, \mathbf{x}') \rightarrow I_i(\mathbf{x}')$ for all $i \in [1, k]$.*

Any given interpolant is a witness for the unsatisfiability of a (suffix) path formula $\Theta^j(\rho)$. Dually, if *Craig's Interpolation Lemma* [10] holds for the considered first-order data theory $\mathrm{Th}(\mathcal{D})$, any infeasible path formula is guaranteed to have an interpolant.

Given a spurious counterexample $\rho$ with pivot $j \geqslant 0$, an interpolant $\mathbf{I} = \langle I_0, \ldots, I_{k-j} \rangle$ for the infeasible path formula $\Theta^j(\rho)$ can be used to refine the abstract domain by augmenting the predicate map $\Pi$. As an effect of this refinement, the antichain construction algorithm will avoid every path with the suffix $(\mathbf{q}_j, P_j, \Phi_j) \rightarrow \ldots \rightarrow (\mathbf{q}_k, P_k, \Phi_k)$ in a future iteration. If $I_i \iff C_i^1(\mathbf{y}_1) \wedge \ldots \wedge C_i^{m_i}(\mathbf{y}_{m_i})$ is a conjunctive normal form (CNF) of the $i$-th component of the interpolant, we consider the substate $(\mathbf{r}_i^\ell, S_i^\ell)$ for each $C_i^\ell(\mathbf{y}_\ell)$ where $l \in [1, m_i]$:

- $\mathbf{r}_i^\ell = \langle q_{i_1}, \ldots, q_{i_n} \rangle$ where $1 \leqslant i_1 < \ldots < i_h \leqslant N$ is the largest sequence of indices such that $\mathbf{x}_{i_g} \cap \mathbf{y}_\ell \neq \varnothing$ for each $g \in [1, h]$ and the set $\mathbf{x}_{i_g}$ of variables of the network component DA $A_{i_g}$,
- $S_i^\ell = P_j$ if $\mathbf{x}_B \cap \mathbf{y}_\ell \neq \varnothing$, and $S_i^\ell = \varnothing$, otherwise.

A predicate map $\Pi$ is said to be *compatible* with a spurious path $\rho : s_0 \xrightarrow{\theta_1} \ldots \xrightarrow{\theta_k} s_k$ with pivot $j \geqslant 0$ if $s_j = (\mathbf{q}_j, P_j, \Phi_j)$ and there is an interpolant

$\mathbf{I} = \langle I_0, \ldots, I_{k-j} \rangle$ of the suffix $\langle \theta_1, \ldots, \theta_k \rangle$ wrt. $\Phi_j$ such that, for each clause $C$ of some equivalent CNF of $I_i$, $i \in [0, k-j]$, it holds that $C \in \Pi(r)$ for some substate $r \lhd s_{i+j}$. The following lemma proves that, under a predicate map compatible with a spurious path $\rho$, the antichain construction will exclude further paths that share the suffix of $\rho$ starting with its pivot.

**Lemma 3.** *Let* $\rho : (q_0, P_0, \Phi_0) \xrightarrow{\theta_0} (q_1, P_1, \Phi_1) \xrightarrow{\theta_1} \cdots \xrightarrow{\theta_{k-1}} (q_k, P_k, \Phi_k)$ *be a spurious counterexample and* $\Pi$ *be a predicate map compatible with* $\rho$. *Then, there is no sequence of product states* $(q_j, P_j, \Psi_0), \ldots, (q_k, P_k, \Psi_{k-j})$ *such that: (1)* $\Psi_0 \rightarrow \Phi_j$ *and (2)* $(q_{i+1}, P_{i+1}, \Psi_{i-j+1}) \in Post_\Pi((q_i, P_i, \Psi_{i-j}))$ *for all* $i \in [j, k-1]$.

Observe that the refinement induced by interpolation is *local* since $\Pi$ associates sets of predicates with substates of the states in $\mathcal{A}^e \times \overline{B}$, and the update impacts only the states occurring within the suffix of that particular spurious counterexample.

### 3.3   Subsumption

The main optimization of antichain-based algorithms [1] for checking language inclusion of automata over finite alphabets is that product states that are *subsets* of already visited states are never stored in the antichain. On the other hand, language emptiness semi-algorithms, based on *predicate abstraction* [22] use a similar notion to cover newly generated abstract successor states by those that were visited sooner and that represent larger sets of configurations. In this case, state coverage does not only increase efficiency but also ensures termination of the semi-algorithm in many practical cases.

In this section, we generalize the subset relation used in classical antichain algorithms with the notion of coverage from predicate abstraction, and we define a more general notion of *subsumption* for data automata. Given a state $(q, P)$ of the product automaton $\mathcal{A}^e \times \overline{B}$ and a valuation $\nu \in \mathcal{D}^{x_\mathcal{A}}$, the *residual language* $\mathcal{L}_{(q,P,\nu)}(\mathcal{A}^e \times \overline{B})$ is the set of traces $w$ accepted by $\mathcal{A}^e \times \overline{B}$ from the state $(q, P)$ such that $\nu$ is the first valuation which occurs on $w$. This notion is then lifted to product states as follows: $\mathcal{L}_s(\mathcal{A}^e \times \overline{B}) = \bigcup_{(q,P,\nu) \in [\![s]\!]} \mathcal{L}_{(q,P,\nu)}(\mathcal{A}^e \times \overline{B})$ where $[\![s]\!]$ is the set of configurations of the product automaton $\mathcal{A}^e \times \overline{B}$ represented by the given product state $s$.

**Definition 2.** *Given a DAN* $\mathcal{A}$ *and a DA* $B$, *a partial order* $\sqsubseteq$ *is a subsumption provided that, for any two product states* $s$ *and* $t$, *we have* $s \sqsubseteq t$ *only if* $\mathcal{L}_s(\mathcal{A}^e \times \overline{B}) \subseteq \mathcal{L}_t(\mathcal{A}^e \times \overline{B})$.

A procedure for checking the emptiness of $\mathcal{A}^e \times \overline{B}$ needs not continue the search from a product state $s$ if it has already visited a product state $t$ that subsumes $s$. The intuition is that any counterexample discovered from $s$ can also be discovered from $t$. The trace inclusion semi-algorithm described below in Sect. 3.4 works, in principle, with any given subsumption relation. In practice, our implementation uses the subsumption relation defined by the lemma below:

**Lemma 4.** *The relation defined s.t.* $(\mathbf{q}, P, \Phi) \sqsubseteq_{img} (\mathbf{r}, S, \Psi) \iff \mathbf{q} = \mathbf{r}, \ P \supseteq S,$ *and* $\Phi \to \Psi$ *is a subsumption.*

### 3.4  The Trace Inclusion Semi-algorithm

With the previous definitions, Algorithm 1 describes the procedure for checking trace inclusion. It uses a classical work-list iteration loop (lines 2-30) that builds an antichain tree by simultaneously unfolding the expansion $\mathcal{A}^e$ of the network $\mathcal{A}$ and the complement $\overline{B}$ of the observer $B$, while searching for a counterexample trace $w \in \mathcal{L}(\mathcal{A}^e \times \overline{B})$. Both $\mathcal{A}^e$ and $\overline{B}$ are built on-the-fly, during the abstract state space exploration.

The processed antichain nodes are kept in the set Visited, and their abstract successors, not yet processed, are kept in the set Next. Initially, Visited $= \varnothing$ and Next $= \{root_{\mathcal{A},B}\}$. The algorithm uses a predicate map $\Pi$, which is initially empty (line 1). We keep a set of subsumption edges Subsume $\subseteq$ Visited $\times$ (Visited $\cup$ Next) with the following meaning: $(\langle s, p \rangle, \langle t, q \rangle) \in$ Subsume for two antichain nodes, where $s, t$ are product states and $p, q \in \mathbb{N}^*$ are tree positions, if and only if there exists an abstract successor $s' \in Post_{\Pi}(s)$ such that $s' \sqsubseteq t$

---

**Algorithm 1.** Trace Inclusion Semi-algorithm

input:
　　1. a DAN $\mathcal{A} = \langle A_1, \ldots, A_N \rangle$ such that $A_i = \langle \mathcal{D}, \Sigma_i, \mathbf{x}_i, Q_i, \iota_i, F_i, \Delta_i \rangle$ for all $i \in [1, N]$,
　　2. a DA $B = \langle \mathcal{D}, \Sigma, \mathbf{x}_B, Q_B, \iota_B, F_B, \Delta_B \rangle$ such that $\mathbf{x}_B \subseteq \bigcup_{i=1}^{N} \mathbf{x}_i$.
output: true if $\mathcal{L}(\mathcal{A}) \downarrow_{\mathbf{x}_B} \subseteq \mathcal{L}(B)$, otherwise a trace $\tau \in \mathcal{L}(\mathcal{A}) \downarrow_{\mathbf{x}_B} \setminus \mathcal{L}(B)$ .

```
 1:  Π ← ∅, Visited ← ∅, Next ← ⟨root⟨𝒜,B⟩, ε⟩, Subsume ← ∅
 2:  while Next ≠ ∅ do
 3:      choose curr ∈ Next and move curr from Next to Visited
 4:      match curr with ⟨s, p⟩
 5:      if s is an accepting product state then
 6:          let ρ be the path from the root to curr and k be the pivot of ρ
 7:          if k ⩾ 0 then
 8:              Π ← REFINEPREDICATEMAPBYINTERPOLATION(Π, ρ, k)
 9:              rem ← SUBTREE(ρk)
10:              for (n, m) ∈ Subsume such that m ∈ rem do
11:                  move n from Visited to Next
12:              remove rem from (Visited, Next, Subsume)
13:              add ρk to Next
14:          else
15:              return EXTRACTCOUNTEREXAMPLE(ρ)
16:      else
17:          i ← 0
18:          for t ∈ Postᴨ(s) do
19:              if there exists m = ⟨t', p'⟩ ∈ Visited such that t ⊑ t' then
20:                  add (curr, m) to Subsume
21:              else
22:                  rem ← {n ∈ Next | n = ⟨t', p'⟩ and t' ⊑ t}
23:                  succ ← ⟨t, p.i⟩
24:                  i ← i + 1
25:                  for n ∈ Visited such that n has a successor m ∈ rem do
26:                      add (n, succ) to Subsume
27:                  for (n, m) ∈ Subsume such that m ∈ rem do
28:                      add (n, succ) to Subsume
29:                  remove rem from (Visited, Next, Subsume)
30:                  add succ to Next
```

(Definition 2). Observe that we do not explicitly store a subsumed successor of a product state $s$ from the antichain; instead, we add a subsumption edge between the node labeled with $s$ and the node that subsumes that particular successor. The algorithm terminates when each abstract successors of a node from Next is subsumed by some node from Visited.

An iteration of Algorithm 1 starts by choosing an antichain node curr $= \langle s, p \rangle$ from Next and moving it to Visited (line 3). If the product state $s$ is accepting (line 5) we check the counterexample path $\rho$, from the root of the antichain to curr, for spuriousness, by computing its pivot $k$. If $k \geqslant 0$, then $\rho$ is a spurious counterexample (line 7), and the path formula of the suffix of $\rho$, which starts with position $k$, is infeasible. In this case, we compute an interpolant for the suffix and refine the current predicate map $\Pi$ by adding the predicates from the interpolant to the corresponding substates of the product states from the suffix (line 8).

The computation of the interpolant and the update of the predicate map are done by the REFINEPREDICATEMAPBYINTERPOLATION function using the approach described in Sect. 3.2. Subsequently, we remove (line 12) from the current antichain the subtree rooted at the pivot node $\rho_k$, i.e. the $k$-th node on the path $\rho$ (line 9), and add $\rho_k$ to Next in order to trigger a recomputation of this subtree with the new predicate map. Moreover, all nodes with a successor previously subsumed by a node in the removed subtree are moved from Visited back to Next in order to reprocess them (line 11).

On the other hand, if the counterexample $\rho$ is found to be real ($k = -1$), any valuation $\nu \in \bigcup_{i=0}^{|\rho|} \mathcal{D}^{\mathbf{x}_\mathcal{A}^i}$ that satisfies the path formula $\Theta(\rho)$ yields a counterexample trace $w \in \mathcal{L}(\mathcal{A}) \downarrow_{\mathbf{x}_B} \setminus \mathcal{L}(B)$, obtained by ignoring all variables from $\mathbf{x}_\mathcal{A} \setminus \mathbf{x}_B$ (line 15).

If the current node is not accepting, we generate its abstract successors (line 18). In order to keep in the antichain only nodes that are incomparable w.r.t. the subsumption relation $\sqsubseteq$, we add a successor $t$ of $s$ to Next (lines 23 and 30) only if it is not subsumed by another product state from a node $m \in$ Visited. Otherwise, we add a subsumption edge (curr, $m$) to the set Subsume (line 20). Furthermore, if $t$ is not subsumed by another state in Visited, we remove from Next all nodes $\langle t', p' \rangle$ such that $t$ strictly subsumes $t'$ (lines 22 and 29) and add subsumption edges to the node storing $t$ from all nodes with a removed successor (line 26) or a removed subsumption edge (line 28).

The following theorem shows completeness modulo termination.

**Theorem 1.** *Let $\mathcal{A} = \langle A_1, \ldots, A_N \rangle$ be a DAN such that $A_i = \langle \mathcal{D}, \Sigma_i, \mathbf{x}_i, Q_i, \iota_i, F_i, \Delta_i \rangle$ for all $i \in [1, N]$, and let $B = \langle \mathcal{D}, \Sigma, \mathbf{x}_B, Q_B, \iota_B, F_B, \Delta_B \rangle$ be a DA such that $\mathbf{x}_B \subseteq \bigcup_{i=1}^{N} \mathbf{x}_i$. If Algorithm 1 terminates and returns true on input $\mathcal{A}$ and $B$, then $\mathcal{L}(\mathcal{A}) \downarrow_{\mathbf{x}_B} \subseteq \mathcal{L}(B)$.*

The soundness question "if there exists a counterexample trace $w \in \mathcal{L}(\mathcal{A}) \downarrow_{\mathbf{x}_B} \setminus \mathcal{L}(B)$, will Algorithm 1 discover it?" has a positive answer, when exploring paths

in breadth-first order[3]. The reason is that any real counterexample corresponds
to a finite path in the antichain, which will be eventually processed. Moreover, a
real counterexample always results in an abstract counterexample, for any given
predicate map.

## 4    Experimental Results

We have implemented Algorithm 1 in a prototype tool[4] using the MATHSAT SMT
solver [8] for answering the satisfiability queries and computing the interpolants.
The results of the experiments are given in Tables 1 and 2. The results were
obtained on an Intel i7-4770 CPU @ 3.40 GHz machine with 32 GB RAM.

Table 1 contains
experiments where the
network $\mathcal{A}$ consists of
a single component.
We applied the tool
on several verification
conditions generated
from imperative pro-
grams with arrays [7]
(Array shift, Array
rotation 1+2, Array
split) available online
[24]. Then, we applied

**Table 1.** Experiments with single-component networks.

| Example | $A$ $(|Q|/|\Delta|)$ | $B$ $(|Q|/|\Delta|)$ | Vars | Res | Time |
|---|---|---|---|---|---|
| Arrays shift | 3/3 | 3/4 | 5 | ok | < 0.1s |
| Array rotation 1 | 4/5 | 4/5 | 7 | ok | 0.1s |
| Array rotation 2 | 8/21 | 6/24 | 11 | ok | 34s |
| Array split | 20/103 | 6/26 | 14 | ok | 4m32s |
| HW counter 1 | 2/3 | 1/2 | 2 | ok | 0.2s |
| HW counter 2 | 6/12 | 1/2 | 2 | ok | 0.4s |
| Synchr. LIFO | 4/34 | 2/15 | 4 | ok | 2.5s |
| ABP-error | 14/20 | 2/6 | 14 | cex | 2s |
| ABP-correct | 14/20 | 2/6 | 14 | ok | 3s |

it on models of hardware circuits (HW Counter 1+2, Synchronous LIFO) [26].
Finally, we checked two versions (correct and faulty) of the timed Alternating
Bit Protocol [29].

Table 2 provides a list of experiments where the network $\mathcal{A}$ has $N > 1$
components. First, we have the example of Fig. 1 (Running). Next, we have
several examples of real-time verification problems [27]: a controller of a rail-
road crossing [20] (Train) with $T$ trains, the Fischer Mutual Exclusion protocol
with deadlines $\Delta$ and $\Gamma$ (Fischer), and a hardware communication circuit with
$K$ stages, composed of timed NOR gates (Stari). Third, we have modelled a
Producer-Consumer example [12] with a fixed buffer size $B$. Fourth, we have
experimented with several models of parallel programs that manipulate arrays
(Array init, Array copy, Array join) with window size $\Delta$.

For the time being, our implementation is a proof-of-concept prototype that
leaves plenty of room for optimization (e.g. caching intermediate computation results) likely to improve the performance on more complicated examples.
Despite that, we found the results from Tables 1 and 2 rather encouraging.

---

[3] In fact, our implementation uses a queue to represent the Next set.
[4] http://www.fit.vutbr.cz/research/groups/verifit/tools/includer/.

**Table 2.** Experiments with multiple-component networks (e.g., $2 \times 2/2 + 2 \times 3/3$ in column $\mathcal{A}$ means that $\mathcal{A}$ is a network with 4 components, of which 2 DA with 2 states and 2 rules, and 2 DA with 3 states and 3 rules).

| Example | N | $\mathcal{A}$ ($|Q|/|\Delta|$) | $B$ ($|Q|/|\Delta|$) | Vars | Res | Time |
|---|---|---|---|---|---|---|
| Running | 2 | $2 \times 2/2$ | 3/4 | 3 | ok | $0.2s$ |
| Running | 10 | $10 \times 2/2$ | 11/20 | 3 | ok | $25s$ |
| Train ($T = 5$) | 7 | $5 \times 3/3 + 4/4 + 4/4$ | 2/38 | 1 | ok | $4s$ |
| Train ($T = 20$) | 22 | $20 \times 3/3 + 4/4 + 4/4$ | 2/128 | 1 | ok | $6m26s$ |
| Fischer ($\Delta = 1$, $\Gamma = 2$) | 2 | $2 \times 5/6$ | 1/10 | 4 | ok | $8s$ |
| Fischer ($\Delta = 1$, $\Gamma = 2$) | 3 | $3 \times 5/6$ | 1/15 | 4 | ok | $2m48s$ |
| Fischer ($\Delta = 2$, $\Gamma = 1$) | 2 | $2 \times 5/6$ | 1/10 | 4 | cex | $3s$ |
| Fischer ($\Delta = 2$, $\Gamma = 1$) | 3 | $3 \times 5/6$ | 1/15 | 4 | cex | $32s$ |
| Stari ($K = 1$) | 5 | $4/5 + 2/4 + 5/7 + 5/7 + 5/7$ | 3/6 | 3 | ok | $0.5s$ |
| Stari ($K = 2$) | 8 | $4/5 + 2/4 + 2 \times 5/7 + 2 \times 5/7 + 2 \times 5/7$ | 3/6 | 3 | ok | $0.5s$ |
| Prod-Cons ($B = 3$) | 2 | $4/4 + 4/4$ | 2/7 | 2 | ok | $10s$ |
| Prod-Cons ($B = 6$) | 2 | $4/4 + 4/4$ | 2/7 | 2 | ok | $2m32s$ |
| Array init ($\Delta = 2$) | 5 | $5 \times 2/2$ | 2/6 | 2 | ok | $3s$ |
| Array init ($\Delta = 2$) | 15 | $15 \times 2/2$ | 2/16 | 2 | ok | $3m15s$ |
| Array copy ($\Delta = 20$) | 20 | $20 \times 2/2$ | 2/21 | 3 | ok | $0.3s$ |
| Array copy ($\Delta = 20$) | 150 | $150 \times 2/2$ | 2/151 | 3 | ok | $43s$ |
| Array join ($\Delta = 10$) | 4 | $2 \times 2/2 + 2 \times 3/3$ | 2/3 | 2 | ok | $6s$ |
| Array join ($\Delta = 20$) | 6 | $3 \times 2/2 + 3 \times 3/3$ | 2/4 | 2 | ok | $1m9s$ |

# 5    Conclusions

We have presented an interpolation-based abstraction refinement method for trace inclusion between a network of data automata and an observer where the variables used by the observer are a subset of those used by the network. The procedure builds on a new determinization result for DAs and combines in a novel way predicate abstraction and interpolation with antichain-based inclusion checking. The procedure has been successfully applied to several examples, including verification problems for array programs, real-time systems, and hardware designs. Future work includes an extension of the method to data tree automata and its application to logics for heaps with data. Also, we foresee an extension of the method to handle infinite traces.

# References

1. Abdulla, P.A., Chen, Y.-F., Holík, L., Mayr, R., Vojnar, T.: When simulation meets antichains. In: Esparza, J., Majumdar, R. (eds.) TACAS 2010. LNCS, vol. 6015, pp. 158–174. Springer, Heidelberg (2010)
2. Alur, R., Dill, D.L.: A theory of timed automata. Theor. Comput. Sci. **126**(2), 183–235 (1994)
3. Bardin, S., Finkel, A., Leroux, J., Petrucci, L.: FAST: Fast acceleration of symbolic transition systems. In: Hunt Jr., W.A., Somenzi, F. (eds.) CAV 2003. LNCS, vol. 2725, pp. 118–121. Springer, Heidelberg (2003)

4. Beyene, T.A., Popeea, C., Rybalchenko, A.: Solving existentially quantified horn clauses. In: Sharygina, N., Veith, H. (eds.) CAV 2013. LNCS, vol. 8044, pp. 869–882. Springer, Heidelberg (2013)
5. Bojańczyk, M., David, C., Muscholl, A., Schwentick, T., Segoufin, L.: Two-variable logic on data words. ACM Trans. Comput. Logic 12(4), 27:1–27:26 (2011)
6. Bouyer, P., Petit, A., Thrien, D.: An algebraic approach to data languages and timed languages. Inf. Comput. 182(2), 137–162 (2003)
7. Bozga, M., Habermehl, P., Iosif, R., Konečný, F., Vojnar, T.: Automatic verification of integer array programs. In: Bouajjani, A., Maler, O. (eds.) CAV 2009. LNCS, vol. 5643, pp. 157–172. Springer, Heidelberg (2009)
8. Cimatti, A., Griggio, A., Schaafsma, B.J., Sebastiani, R.: The mathSAT5 SMT solver. In: Piterman, N., Smolka, S.A. (eds.) TACAS 2013 (ETAPS 2013). LNCS, vol. 7795, pp. 93–107. Springer, Heidelberg (2013)
9. Cook, B., Khlaaf, H., Piterman, N.: On automation of CTL* verification for infinite-state systems. In: Kroening, D., Păsăreanu, C.S. (eds.) CAV 2015. LNCS, vol. 9206, pp. 13–29. Springer, Heidelberg (2015)
10. Craig, W.: Three uses of the herbrand-gentzen theorem in relating model theory and proof theory. J. Symb. Log. 22(3), 269–285 (1957)
11. D'Antoni, L., Alur, R.: Symbolic visibly pushdown automata. In: Biere, A., Bloem, R. (eds.) CAV 2014. LNCS, vol. 8559, pp. 209–225. Springer, Heidelberg (2014)
12. Dhar, A.: Algorithms For Model-Checking Flat Counter Systems. Ph.D. thesis, Univ. Paris 7 (2014)
13. Farzan, A., Kincaid, Z., Podelski, A.: Proof spaces for unbounded parallelism. SIGPLAN Not. 50(1), 407–420 (2015)
14. Fribourg, L.: A closed-form evaluation for extended timed automata. Technical report, CNRS et Ecole Normale Supérieure de Cachan (1998)
15. Grebenshchikov, S., Lopes, N.P., Popeea, C., Rybalchenko, A.: Synthesizing software verifiers from proof rules. In: ACM SIGPLAN Conference on Programming Language Design and Implementation, PLDI 2012, Beijing, China, 11–16 June 2012, pp. 405–416 (2012)
16. Habermehl, P., Iosif, R., Vojnar, T.: A logic of singly indexed arrays. In: Cervesato, I., Veith, H., Voronkov, A. (eds.) LPAR 2008. LNCS (LNAI), vol. 5330, pp. 558–573. Springer, Heidelberg (2008)
17. Habermehl, P., Iosif, R., Vojnar, T.: What else is decidable about integer arrays? In: Amadio, R.M. (ed.) FOSSACS 2008. LNCS, vol. 4962, pp. 474–489. Springer, Heidelberg (2008)
18. Henzinger, T.A., Jhala, R., Majumdar, R., Sutre, G.: Lazy abstraction. In: Proceedings of POPL 2002. ACM (2002)
19. Henzinger, T.A., Jhala, R., Majumdar, R., Sutre, G.: Software verification with BLAST. In: Ball, T., Rajamani, S.K. (eds.) SPIN 2003. LNCS, vol. 2648, pp. 235–239. Springer, Heidelberg (2003)
20. Henzinger, T.A., Nicollin, X., Sifakis, J., Yovine, S.: Symbolic model checking for real-time systems. Inf. Comput. 111, 394–406 (1992)
21. Iosif, R., Rogalewicz, A., Vojnar, T.: Abstraction refinement for trace inclusion of data automata. CoRR abs/1410.5056 (2014). http://arxiv.org/abs/1410.5056
22. McMillan, K.L.: Lazy abstraction with interpolants. In: Ball, T., Jones, R.B. (eds.) CAV 2006. LNCS, vol. 4144, pp. 123–136. Springer, Heidelberg (2006)
23. Minsky, M.: Computation: Finite and Infinite Machines. Prentice-Hall, Upper Saddle River (1967)
24. Numerical Transition Systems Repository (2012). http://nts.imag.fr/index.php/ Flata

25. Ouaknine, J., Worrell, J.: On the language inclusion problem for timed automata: Closing a decidability gap. In: Proceedings of LICS 2004. IEEE Computer Society (2004)
26. Smrčka, A., Vojnar, T.: Verifying parametrised hardware designs via counter automata. In: Yorav, K. (ed.) HVC 2007. LNCS, vol. 4899, pp. 51–68. Springer, Heidelberg (2008)
27. Tripakis, S.: The analysis of timed systems in practice. Ph.D. thesis, Universite Joseph Fourier, Grenoble, December 1998
28. De Wulf, M., Doyen, L., Henzinger, T.A., Raskin, J.-F.: Antichains: a new algorithm for checking universality of finite automata. In: Ball, T., Jones, R.B. (eds.) CAV 2006. LNCS, vol. 4144, pp. 17–30. Springer, Heidelberg (2006)
29. Zbrzezny, A., Polrola, A.: Sat-based reachability checking for timed automata with discrete data. Fundam. Informaticae **79**, 1–15 (2007)

# Probabilistic and Stochastic Systems I

# Efficient Syntax-Driven Lumping
# of Differential Equations

Luca Cardelli[1,2](✉), Mirco Tribastone[3](✉), Max Tschaikowski[3](✉),
and Andrea Vandin[3](✉)

[1] Microsoft Research, Cambridge, UK
luca@microsoft.com
[2] University of Oxford, Oxford, UK
[3] IMT Institute for Advanced Studies Lucca, Lucca, Italy
{mirco.tribastone,max.tschaikowski,andrea.vandin}@imtlucca.it

**Abstract.** We present an algorithm to compute exact aggregations of
a class of systems of ordinary differential equations (ODEs). Our approach consists in an extension of Paige and Tarjan's seminal solution
to the coarsest refinement problem by encoding an ODE system into a
suitable discrete-state representation. In particular, we consider a simple
extension of the syntax of elementary chemical reaction networks because
(i) it can express ODEs with derivatives given by polynomials of degree
at most two, which are relevant in many applications in natural sciences
and engineering; and (ii) we can build on two recently introduced bisimulations, which yield two complementary notions of ODE lumping. Our
algorithm computes the largest bisimulations in $O(r \cdot s \cdot \log s)$ time, where
$r$ is the number of monomials and $s$ is the number of variables in the
ODEs. Numerical experiments on real-world models from biochemistry,
electrical engineering, and structural mechanics show that our prototype
is able to handle ODEs with millions of variables and monomials, providing significant model reductions.

## 1 Introduction

Ordinary differential equations (ODEs) are widespread in many disciplines
including chemistry, epidemiology, systems biology, electrical engineering, and
control theory. Often, due to the complexity of the system under consideration,
the state space size (intended as the number of ODE variables) is so large that it
makes the numerical solution intractable (e.g., in protein-based interaction networks [1,2]). Formal kinds of analyses such as reachability computation suffer
from the curse of dimensionality, particularly for nonlinear systems (e.g., [3,4]).
It is therefore an important goal to be able to obtain reduced size models that
appropriately preserve the original dynamics.

For discrete-state quantitative models based on labeled transition systems,
the notion of bisimilarity has played a key role for model reduction, with efficient
algorithms [5–7] based on Paige and Tarjan's celebrated solution to the coarsest
refinement problem [8]. The main contribution of this paper is to lift this approach to ODE systems. In particular we focus on a class of *polynomial systems*,

© Springer-Verlag Berlin Heidelberg 2016
M. Chechik and J.-F. Raskin (Eds.): TACAS 2016, LNCS 9636, pp. 93–111, 2016.
DOI: 10.1007/978-3-662-49674-9_6

where the time derivatives are multivariate polynomials of degree at most two in the ODE variables. This class is quite general because it incorporates models frequently used in (bio-)chemistry (cf. [9]) as well as the ubiquitous linear ODEs.

We reconcile the established approaches based on discrete-state models with the continuous-state semantics of ODEs by reasoning at the level of a discrete-state *syntactic* representation of the ODE system. In particular, our class of interest can be encoded into a variant of elementary chemical reaction networks (CRNs). This consists of species (the ODE variables) interacting through unary or binary reactions that are appropriately mapped onto monomials that govern the derivative of the species involved. To be able to encode an arbitrary polynomial ODE system (with degree at most two), we slightly extend the CRN syntax by allowing negative rates. This has important repercussions on the applicability of established results of CRN theory (e.g., [10]). Hence, to disambiguate, we refer to this extension as Reaction Networks (RN). Instead, all the results for exact quantitative bisimulations for CRNs, recently proposed by these authors in [11] (cf. Sect. 2), do carry over to RN. The *forward* bisimulation (FB) gives a partition of the ODE variables such that the sum of the ODEs can be written as an explicit function of the sum of the variables. With *backward* bisimulation (BB) species in the same block have the same ODE solution, provided that they start with the same initial condition.

Our key idea is to exploit the fact that the *syntactic* conditions for an equivalence relation over species to be either bisimulation can be expressed in the Larsen-Skou style of probabilistic bisimulation [12]. (Actually, while this is immediate for FB, in this paper we provide a novel characterization of BB tailored to that format, cf. Sect. 3.1.) Thus, we can approach the problem of computing the largest bisimulations by developing a variant of Paige and Tarjan's algorithm, along the lines of the efficient partition refinement algorithms of [6] and [7] for Markov chain lumping [13], and of [5] for probabilistic transition systems. In particular, for technical reasons that will be clarified later, we build on the Markov chain lumping algorithm of [7].

Our algorithm, presented in Sects. 3 and 4, runs in $O(r \cdot s \cdot \log s)$ time, where $s$ is the number of variables and $r$ is the number of monomials in the ODEs. Interestingly, this can be related to continuous-time Markov chain (CTMC) lumping. The time complexity of our algorithm is a tight increase, in the following sense: Since RNs can encode arbitrary affine ODEs, *a fortiori* they can encode a CTMC through its Kolmogorov equations (cf. Sect. 5). For this encoding we show that FB and BB correspond to the well-known notions of ordinary and exact lumpability for CTMCs, respectively. In the affine ODE case, the time complexity of our algorithm collapses to $\mathcal{O}(r \cdot \log s)$, which is equivalent to that of the most efficient CTMC lumpability algorithms [6,7].

We show the practical usefulness of our algorithm by means of numerical experiments (in Sect. 6), with a prototype available at http://sysma.imtlucca.it/crnreducer/. Using the benchmark biochemical models of [11], we measure run-time speed-ups of up to four orders of magnitude over our own more straightforward $\mathcal{O}(r^2 \cdot s^5)$ algorithm used in [11]. We are now able to reduce the largest benchmark biochemical model within a few seconds on commodity hardware, as opposed to almost one day as reported in [11]. To evaluate the effectiveness on affine systems, we propose an application of the bisimulations beyond ODEs: we consider linear systems of equations $Ax = b$. Stationary iterative methods such as Jacobi's (e.g., [14]) can be interpreted as an affine dynamical system in *discrete time*, to which case the bisimulations carry over. For these, we report considerable aggregations for real-world applications in atmospheric modeling, structural mechanics, and electrical engineering, taken from the Sparse Matrix Collection [15].

***Further Related Work.*** FB is a special case of the theory of ODE lumping [16,17], which is more general because it considers an arbitrary linear transformation of the state space, as opposed to a sum of variables for FB. While the theory is established, no algorithm is available to compute such aggregations. BB is a generalization of a behavioral equivalence originally defined for Markovian process algebra [18]. FB and BB have been recently put in a unifying algorithmic context in [19], using the notions of *forward* and *backward differential equivalences* for a low-level syntax describing a more general class of nonlinear ODE systems. A symbolic partition-refinement algorithm to compute the largest differential equivalences is provided through a satisfiability modulo theories encoding. Clearly, unlike this approach, the algorithm of [19] is independent of the restriction of the RN language, and is not a variant of Paige and Tarjan's approach. As a result, it is more general but less efficient. Indeed, the runtimes reported in [19] are at best only comparable to those of our earlier algorithm [11].

This is the first application of Paige and Tarjan's seminal idea for a general class of ODE systems, whereas automatic exact ODE reduction algorithms are available for domain specific languages such as rule-based models of biochemical networks [1] and Markovian process algebra using FB-like (though not BB-like) conditions [20].

## 2   Background

***Reaction Networks.*** An RN $(S, R)$ is a pair of a finite set of *species* $S$ and a finite set of *reactions* $R$. A reaction is a triple written in the form $\rho \xrightarrow{\alpha} \pi$, where $\rho$ and $\pi$ are multisets of species, called *reactants* and *products*, respectively, and $\alpha \neq 0$ is the *reaction rate*. We restrict to *elementary* reactions where $|\rho| \leq 2$ (while no restriction is posed on the products). We denote by $\rho(X)$ the multiplicity of species $X$ in the multiset $\rho$, and by $\mathcal{MS}(S)$ the set of finite multisets of species in $S$. The operator $+$ denotes multiset union, e.g., $X + Y + Y$ (or just $X + 2Y$) is the multiset $\{\!|X, Y, Y|\!\}$. We also use $X$ to denote either the species $X$ or the singleton $\{\!|X|\!\}$.

The *semantics* of an RN $(S, R)$ is given by the (autonomous) ODE system $\dot{V} = F(V)$, with $F : \mathbb{R}^S \to \mathbb{R}^S$, where each component $F_X$, with $X \in S$ is defined as:

$$F_X(V) := \sum_{\rho \xrightarrow{\alpha} \pi \in R} (\pi(X) - \rho(X)) \cdot \alpha \cdot \prod_{Y \in S} V_Y^{\rho(Y)}.$$

This ODE satisfies a unique solution $V(t) = (V_X(t))_{X \in S}$ for any initial condition $V(0)$.

The restriction to elementary reactions ensures that the monomials are of degree at most 2; unary reactions give degree-one monomials; a *nullary* reaction, $\emptyset \xrightarrow{c} X$, adds a constant $c$ to $F_X(V)$. (The encoding of an arbitrary polynomial ODE system is shown in Sect. 5.) Finally, we remark that a standard CRN with mass-action semantics (where reactions speeds are proportional to the product of the concentrations of the reactants) is recovered by restricting to positive reaction rates and nonnegative initial conditions.

*Example 1.* We now provide a simple RN, $(S_e, R_e)$, with $S_e = \{A, B, C, D, E\}$ and $R_e = \{A + C \xrightarrow{\alpha} C + E, B + C \xrightarrow{\alpha} C + E, C \xrightarrow{\beta} A, D \xrightarrow{\beta} B\}$, which will be used as a running example in this section. Its ODE system is

$$\dot{V}_A = -\alpha V_A V_C + \beta V_C \qquad \dot{V}_C = -\beta V_C \qquad \dot{V}_E = \alpha V_A V_C + \alpha V_B V_C$$
$$\dot{V}_B = -\alpha V_B V_C + \beta V_D \qquad \dot{V}_D = -\beta V_D$$

We now overview the main definitions of [11], restating them in terms of an RN.

**Forward Bisimulation.** FB induces a partition associating an ODE with each block, representing the sum of the species in that block. It is defined in terms of *reaction* and *production* rates.

**Definition 1 (Reaction and Production rates).** *Let $(S, R)$ be an RN, $X, Y \in S$, and $\rho \in S \cup \{\emptyset\}$. The $\rho$-reaction rate of $X$, and the $\rho$-production rate of Y-elements by $X$ are defined respectively as*

$$\mathbf{crr}[X, \rho] := (\rho(X) + 1) \sum_{X + \rho \xrightarrow{\alpha} \pi \in R} \alpha, \quad \mathbf{pr}(X, Y, \rho) := (\rho(X) + 1) \sum_{X + \rho \xrightarrow{\alpha} \pi \in R} \alpha \cdot \pi(Y)$$

*Finally, for $H \subseteq S$ we define $\mathbf{pr}[X, H, \rho] := \sum_{Y \in H} \mathbf{pr}(X, Y, \rho)$.*

**Definition 2.** *Let $(S, R)$ be an RN, $\mathcal{R}$ an equivalence relation over $S$ and $\mathcal{H} = S/\mathcal{R}$. Then, $\mathcal{R}$ is a forward RN bisimulation (FB) if for all $(X, Y) \in \mathcal{R}$, all $\rho \in S \cup \{\emptyset\}$, and all $H \in \mathcal{H}$ it holds that*

$$\mathbf{crr}[X, \rho] = \mathbf{crr}[Y, \rho] \quad and \quad \mathbf{pr}[X, H, \rho] = \mathbf{pr}[Y, H, \rho] \qquad (1)$$

For instance, it can be shown that $\mathcal{H}_F = \{\{A, B\}, \{C\}, \{D\}, \{E\}\}$ for Example 1 is an FB. Indeed, the ODEs can be reduced by writing them in terms of $V_{AB} := V_A + V_B$:

$$\dot{V}_{AB} = -\alpha V_{AB} V_C + \beta V_C + \beta V_D \quad \dot{V}_C = -\beta V_C \quad \dot{V}_D = -\beta V_D \quad \dot{V}_E = \alpha V_{AB} V_C$$

**Backward Bisimulation.** BB leads to partitions where species in the same block have the same solution when starting with the same initial condition. It is defined according to the notion of *flux rates*.

**Definition 3 (Cumulative flux rate).** *Let $(S, R)$ be an RN, $X \in S$, $\rho \in MS(S)$, and $M \subseteq MS(S)$. Then, we define*

$$\mathbf{fr}(X, \rho) := \sum_{\rho \xrightarrow{\alpha} \pi \in R} (\pi(X) - \rho(X)) \cdot \alpha, \qquad \mathbf{fr}[X, M] := \sum_{\rho \in M} \mathbf{fr}(X, \rho).$$

*We call $\mathbf{fr}(X, \rho)$ and $\mathbf{fr}[X, M]$ $\rho$-flux rate and cumulative $M$-flux rate of $X$, respectively.*

**Definition 4.** *Let $(S, R)$ be an RN, $\mathcal{R}$ an equivalence relation over $S$, and $\mathcal{H} = S/\mathcal{R}$. Then, $\mathcal{R}$ is a backward RN bisimulation (BB) if for any $(X, Y) \in \mathcal{R}$ it holds that*

$$\mathbf{fr}[X, M] = \mathbf{fr}[Y, M] \quad \text{for all} \quad M \in \{\rho \mid \rho \xrightarrow{\alpha} \pi \in R\}/\approx_{\mathcal{H}},$$

*where any two $\rho, \sigma \in MS(S)$ satisfy $\rho \approx_{\mathcal{H}} \sigma$ when $\sum_{Y \in H} \rho(Y) = \sum_{Y \in H} \sigma(Y)$ for all $H \in \mathcal{H}$.*

It can be shown that $\mathcal{H}_B = \{\{A, B\}, \{C, D\}, \{E\}\}$ is a BB for the running example. Indeed, it is easy to see that $V_A(t) = V_B(t)$ and $V_C(t) = V_D(t)$ at all time points $t \geq 0$ whenever $V_A(0) = V_B(0)$ and $V_C(0) = V_D(0)$. So, one can remove the ODEs of $\dot{V}_B, \dot{V}_D$ and replace each $V_B$ with $V_A$ and each $V_D$ by $V_C$, yielding the reduced ODE:

$$\dot{V}_A = -\alpha V_A V_C + \beta V_C \qquad \dot{V}_C = -\beta V_C \qquad \dot{V}_E = 2\alpha V_A V_C$$

In [11] it is discussed how to additionally obtain a reduced network up to a bisimulation $\mathcal{H}$, having one species per block of $\mathcal{H}$. For example, it can be shown that $\mathcal{H}_F$ induces the FB-reduced RN $S_e^F = \{A, C, D, E\}$ and $R_e^F = \{A + C \xrightarrow{\alpha} C + E, C \xrightarrow{\beta} A, D \xrightarrow{\beta} A\}$.

## 3 Computing the Coarsest RN Bisimulations

As introduced in Sect. 1, we exploit the fact that the conditions for FB and BB are in the Larsen-Skou style of probabilistic bisimulation, whereby, roughly speaking, two states are equivalent if their behavior toward any equivalence class is the same.

For FB, the notion of $\mathbf{pr}[X, H, \rho]$ in Definition 2 is already in such desired format: $X$ is the species for which the equivalence is being checked, $H$ is an equivalence class of "target" states, while $\rho$ plays the role of a "label", identifying partner species reacting with $X$ (akin to an action type in a probabilistic transition system). This is the intuitive correspondence that suggests us to employ a partition refinement approach based on Paige and Tarjan's algorithm, iteratively refining an input partition based on a *splitter* block that tells apart the behavior of two species toward that block, for some label $\rho$. One fundamental aspect of such an approach is that, at each iteration, the blocks of the current partition are used as potential splitters. This ensures that the list of splitters can be updated at essentially no additional cost while splitting the blocks.

For BB, instead, the situation is more delicate because the equivalence condition is based on the flux rate $\mathbf{fr}[X, \mathcal{M}]$. Unlike FB, here $\mathcal{M}$ does not represent an equivalence class of the species, but it is an equivalence class of *multi-sets* of species (all the possible reagents in the RN), which are equal up to $\approx_{\mathcal{H}}$, i.e., the equivalence induced by the current partition $\mathcal{H}$. Within this setting Paige and Tarjan's approach cannot be used directly because the splitters are not the partition blocks of the equivalence relation of interest. Thus, we first provide an alternative characterization of BB which allows to use (species) partition blocks as splitters. Then, we discuss a parameterized algorithm that can compute the coarsest refinement of a given partition of species up to FB or BB.

### 3.1 Splitter-Based Characterization of Backward Bisimulation

The alternative characterization of BB is based on the following.

**Definition 5 (Cumulative splitter flux rate).** *Let $(S, R)$ be an RN, $X, Y \in S$, $\mathcal{H}$ a partition of $S$, $H \in \mathcal{H}$ and $H' \in \mathcal{H} \cup \{\{\emptyset\}\}$. We define*

$$\mathbf{sr}(X, Y, H') := \sum_{\rho' \in H'} \sum_{\substack{\rho \xrightarrow{\alpha} \pi \in R \\ \rho = Y + \rho'}} (\pi(X) - \rho(X)) \cdot \alpha', \quad \mathbf{sr}[X, H, H'] := \sum_{Y \in H} \mathbf{sr}(X, Y, H').$$

*with $\alpha' = \frac{\alpha}{2}$ if $Y \neq \rho'$ and $Y \in H'$, or $\alpha' = \alpha$ otherwise. We call the quantity $\mathbf{sr}[X, H, H']$ the cumulative $(H, H')$-splitter flux rate of $X$.*

Note that we account for summands that are counted twice due to the summation over $H$ and $H'$ in $\mathbf{sr}[X, H, H']$ by choosing $\alpha' \in \{\alpha, \frac{\alpha}{2}\}$ in the above definition.

**Theorem 1.** *Let $(S, R)$ be an RN, $\mathcal{R}$ an equivalence relation over $S$ and $\mathcal{H} = S/\mathcal{R}$. Then $\mathcal{R}$ is a BB if and only if for all $(X, Y) \in \mathcal{R}$, all $H \in \mathcal{H}$ and all $H' \in \mathcal{H} \cup \{\{\emptyset\}\}$ it holds that $\mathbf{sr}[X, H, H'] = \mathbf{sr}[Y, H, H']$.* [1]

With this characterization both **pr** and **sr** have three arguments, with analogous meaning, as discussed. In particular, the third argument of **sr** can now be also interpreted as a *label*. However, while in FB this ranges over the set of species (together with the distinguished species $\emptyset$ to indicate unary reactions), in BB it ranges over blocks of the candidate BB partition to be checked (again, together with the distinguished set $\{\emptyset\}$ for unary reactions). When used within the partition refinement algorithm, splitting a partition block leads to a refinement of the BB labels. In other words, unlike for FB the set of labels must be updated at every iteration. However, differently from the original definition of **fr**, this only requires splitting a block rather than computing an equivalence relation over the species multi-sets appearing as reaction products. As we will see, this can be done at no additional cost.

---

*Remark 1.* The analogy with the probabilistic-bisimulation condition (where a label corresponds to an action type and the rates correspond to probabilities) may suggest to use a variant of the algorithm for probabilistic bisimilarity developed in [5]. Indeed, by suitably encoding an RN into a hyper-graph, the largest FB can be computed with [5]. However, a similar algorithm cannot be straightforwardly adapted to BB because the set of labels changes at every iteration. In particular, the bounds of Lemma 4.5 in [5] would not carry over if the labels were not kept fixed. For this reason, in this paper we consider an extension of the more recent [7], which also has the advantage of a simpler implementation because it does not require the intertwining between two classes of splitters like [5], or splay trees like [6].

## 3.2 Data Structures

We introduce the data structures used in our algorithm for computing the coarsest RN bisimulations. To achieve tight time and space bounds, we make use of pointer-based data structures only. Furthermore, we assume that species, partition blocks and reactions are stored once and then referred by other data structures via pointers.

*Notation.* Fix an RN $(S, R)$, set $s := |S|$, $r := |R|$ and let $\mathcal{L}(R) := \{X \mid \exists X + Y \xrightarrow{\alpha} \pi \in R\} \cup \{\emptyset\}$ be the set of all *labels*. Set $l := |\mathcal{L}(R)|$ which can be bounded by $\mathcal{O}(\min(s, r))$. Finally, use $p := \max\{\sum_{X \in S} \mathbb{1}_{\{\pi(X)>0\}} \mid \rho \xrightarrow{\alpha} \pi \in R\}$ to denote the maximum number of different species which appear as products of a reaction. We will also use the fact that $s$ is bounded by $(2 + p) \cdot r$. This is because each reaction can have at most 2 and $p$ different species as reagents and products, respectively.[2]

We remark that, in general, $p$ is bounded by $s$. However, we prefer to explicitly use this parameter because in the main application of this paper, i.e., the encoding of an arbitrary polynomial ODE system, $p$ becomes a constant (i.e., 3). Instead, when an RN is used *directly* as the input specification to describe a model, as is the case in CRNs, $p$ is typically small. For instance, in most reactions of biological processes the number of distinct products is typically one (e.g., for binding and internal state modification) or two (for unbinding or catalytic reactions). Indeed, across all the benchmark CRNs considered in Sect. 6, $p$ never exceeds 3. This is due, for instance, to unbinding reactions favored by a catalyst, in the form $AB + C \rightarrow A + B + C$.

*RN Representation.* Species are stored in a list. We assume that the set $\mathcal{L}(R)$ is given and stored as a list of pointers to species (plus one entry for $\emptyset$), requiring $\mathcal{O}(l)$ space. However, its computation requires $\mathcal{O}(r)$ time because the reactions have to be scanned only once, assuming that a vector with a boolean entry per species is used to check (in constant time) if it has been already added to the list. Indices from 0 to $s - 1$ and from 0 and $l - 1$ are implicitly assigned to each species and label, respectively. A reaction is a structure with two fields, one for

---

[2] We implicitly disregard pathological cases with species not appearing in any reaction.

each possible reagent, and a list of pairs in the form (species, multiplicity) for the products. Storing $R$ requires $\mathcal{O}(p \cdot r)$ space.

We make use of two vectors, inc and out, indexed by species. Each inc[$X$] entry points to a list of pairs (reaction, multiplicity) containing all reactions with $X$ in their products, accompanied by the corresponding product multiplicity of $X$ for each reaction. Note that each reaction may appear in inc[$X$] for at most $p$ species, thus requiring $\mathcal{O}(p \cdot r)$ to store inc. The vector out is similar, but each out[$X$] entry points to a list of reactions having $X$ in their reagents. The space required by out is thus $\mathcal{O}(r)$.

In the algorithm we build sets of elements. However, insertions in sets can be implemented in constant time because an element is never added to a set more than once.

**Refinable Partition.** A partition is stored as a doubly linked list of pointers to its blocks. Each block record contains an integer to store its size and pointers to two doubly linked lists that divide the species into marked and unmarked (as a result of operations that are used to split blocks, discussed later). Each species has a pointer to its block in the current partition. Thus, finding the block for a species, marking, and unmarking take constant time. Also, it is possible to scan the species of a block in time linear with respect to its size, and to split it in time proportional to the number of marked states.

The operation of splitting a block $H$ creates a new block $H_1$ containing the marked species of $H$, while $H$ maintains those that are not marked. This requires to assign the list pointed by $H$.marked to $H_1$.unmarked and to assign an empty list to $H$.marked. These operations are done in constant time, while a time proportional to originally marked species of $H$ is necessary to update their reference to the new block $H_1$. If instead $H$ originally contained just marked or unmarked species, then no split is actually performed, and marked species get unmarked at no further cost.

**Splitters.** The list of pointers spls refers to the blocks of the current partition that will be used as splitters. An $s \times l$ matrix M of real numbers is maintained to efficiently compute conditional, production and flux rates. A possible majority candidate (pmc) of an array A of size $s$ is either the value which appears more than $\lfloor s/2 \rfloor$ times in A, or any other value if it does not exist. We calculate the pmc row of M by extending the algorithm from [7] to vectors in a straightforward manner.

We denote the row of species $X$ in M by M[$X$], that is M[$X$] $\in \mathbb{R}^l$. In the course of splitting, we sort species according to the lexicographical order on their rows in M. Clearly, sorting a set $H \in \mathcal{H}$ takes $\mathcal{O}(l \cdot |H| \cdot \log |H|)$ time, as $\mathcal{O}(|H| \cdot \log |H|)$ comparisons are needed, each requiring $\mathcal{O}(l)$ time.

This leads to an overall $\mathcal{O}(p \cdot r + l \cdot s) \leq \mathcal{O}(s \cdot r + r \cdot s) = \mathcal{O}(r \cdot s)$ space complexity. Other auxiliary lists and sets of pointers presented in the remainder of the section will respect the space bound given above.

```
1   CoarsestRNBisimulation(χ,S,R,H) :=
2       M = build an s × l matrix of reals
3       if(χ = FB)
4           H = RefineCRR(S,R,M,H)
5       spls = shallow copy of H
6       while(spls ≠ ∅)
7           H_sp = pop(spls)
8           Split(χ,S,R,M,H,H_sp,spls)
```

**Algorithm 1.** Computation of the coarsest bisimulations.

## 3.3 Overview

Algorithm 1 provides the parametric procedure `CoarsestRNBisimulation` for computing the coarsest RN bisimulations that refine a given initial partition $\mathcal{H}$ of species of an RN $(S, R)$. The first argument $(\chi)$ specifies either FB or BB.

We first observe that the **crr**-condition of FB can be implemented as an initialization step that pre-partitions the species according to the values of **crr**. This is because **crr** is a "global" property of the RN, i.e., it does not depend on the current partition. Instead, the conditions on **pr** and **sr** for FB and BB, respectively, require the iterative partition-refinement treatment. Consequently, our algorithm starts (Lines 3–4) by invoking, if necessary, the `RefineCRR` procedure.

*RefineCRR* (Algorithm 2). This procedure provides the coarsest refinement of $\mathcal{H}$ which satisfies the **crr**-condition of FB. It refines $\mathcal{H}$ according to the $\rho$-reaction rates for each species $X$ and label $\rho$. In particular, in this procedure each entry $M[X][\rho]$ is used to store $\mathbf{crr}(X, \rho)$, and is assumed to be initialized with 0. We can thus compute the values of **crr** for all labels and species in one iteration of $R$ only (Lines 3–7), requiring $\mathcal{O}(r)$ time. Then, we refine $\mathcal{H}$ (Lines 10–12). This can be done, for each initial block $H \in \mathcal{H}$, by sorting the species $X \in H$ according to a lexicographical ordering on their $M[X]$ row. After sorting, all species belonging to the same sub-block will be alongside each other, and it is easy to transform them into new blocks in $\mathcal{O}(|H|)$ time. As discussed, the sorting of each block requires $\mathcal{O}(l \cdot |H| \cdot \log|H|)$ time, and the total time spent in sorting is thus $\mathcal{O}(l \cdot \sum_{H \in \mathcal{H}} |H| \cdot \log|H|) \leq \mathcal{O}(l \cdot \sum_{H \in \mathcal{H}} |H| \cdot \log s) = \mathcal{O}(l \cdot s \cdot \log s)$. Finally, Line 13 resets to 0 all entries of M, requiring $\mathcal{O}(l \cdot s)$ time.

Overall, this yields $\mathcal{O}(r + l \cdot s \cdot \log s)$ time complexity. Given that $s \leq (2+p) \cdot r$, this can be bounded by $\mathcal{O}(r \cdot p \cdot l \cdot \log s)$.

*Iterative Refinement* (Algorithm 1, *Lines 5–8*). The procedure performs the iterative partition refinement required by our bisimulations as an extension of the algorithm for Markov chains of [7], as discussed. If $\chi = FB$, blocks of $\mathcal{H}$ are *split* into sub-blocks of species with same $\rho$-production rates towards the block $H_{sp}$ for all $\rho \in \mathcal{L}(R)$. Instead, if $\chi = BB$, blocks are split with respect to their $(H_{sp}, H')$-splitter flux rates with respect to all labels $H' \in \mathcal{H} \cup \{\{\emptyset\}\}$.

Line 5 creates the linked list `spls` of initial candidate splitters containing pointers to each $H \in \mathcal{H}$: all blocks of $\mathcal{H}$ are considered as (initial) candidate

```
1   RefineCRR(S,R,M,H) :=
2     //Iterate once R to compute crr[X,ρ] for all ρ and X
3     forall(X →α→ π ∈ R)
4       M[X][0] = M[X][0] + α
5     forall(X + Y →α→ π ∈ R)
6       M[X][Y] = M[X][Y] + α
7       M[Y][X] = M[Y][X] + α
8     //Refine H according to the M rows, and store it in H'
9     H' = ∅
10    forall(H ∈ H)
11      Sort and split H wrt crr[X], for all X ∈ H, yielding H₁,...,Hb
12      Add H₁,...,Hb to H'
13    CleanRowsOfMatrix(M,S)
14    return H'
15
16  CleanRowsOfMatrix(M,H) :=
17    forall(X ∈ H and ρ ∈ L(R))
18      M[X][ρ]=0
```

**Algorithm 2.** Pre-partitioning according to the condition of FB on **crr**.

splitters. Then, Lines 6–8 iterate while there are candidate splitters to be considered: after selecting a splitter $(H_{sp})$ and removing it from spls, the procedure Split is invoked to refine each block of $\mathcal{H}$ with respect to $H_{sp}$.

We now provide an overview of the Split procedure (Algorithm 3). A detailed presentation is given in Sect. 4, together with the complexity results. Split first computes either $\mathbf{pr}[X, H_{sp}, \rho]$ for all $X \in S$ and $\rho \in \mathcal{L}(R)$ (FB case) or $\mathbf{sr}[X, H_{sp}, H']$, for all $X \in S$ and $H' \in \mathcal{H} \cup \{\{\emptyset\}\}$ (BB case). The rates are computed for all labels at once and are stored in M similarly to RefineCRR. We remark that BB uses different labels than FB. Nevertheless, as will be discussed in Sect. 4, the number of labels used by BB is bounded by $l$ as well, and hence we can safely use M also in the BB case.

Then, we iterate over the set of blocks containing a species for which at least one non-zero rate has been computed. Each partition block $H$ is split in sub-blocks with either same $\mathbf{pr}[\cdot, H_{sp}, \rho]$ for all $\rho \in \mathcal{L}(R)$ (FB), or same $\mathbf{sr}[\cdot, H_{sp}, H']$ for all $H' \in \mathcal{H} \cup \{\{\emptyset\}\}$ (BB), updating the list spls. Following the usual approach of Paige and Tarjan [8], a sub-block with maximal size is not added to spls. However, this is done only if the block that is split (i.e., $H$) has been already used as a splitter, as otherwise the algorithm would be incorrect (see the discussion in [7]).

## 4    The Split Procedure

We now provide a detailed description of the Split procedure shown in Algorithm 3. It begins (Line 2) by initializing the set of pointers $S_T$ that will refer to all species $X$ for which either there exists a $\rho$ such that $\mathbf{pr}[X, H_{sp}, \rho] \neq 0$ if $\chi = FB$, or for which there exists a block $H'$ (or $\{\emptyset\}$) such that $\mathbf{sr}[X, H_{sp}, H'] \neq 0$ if $\chi = BB$. Similarly, Line 3 initializes the set $H_T$ which will point to the blocks of the species in $S_T$. We remark that only the blocks in $H_T$ may be split due

```
1   Split(χ,S,R,M,H,H_sp,spls) :=
2     S_T = ∅ //Set of species X with at least a non-zero pr/sr[X,H_sp,·]
3     H_T = ∅ //Set of blocks containing the species in S_T
4     forall(Y ∈ H_sp)
5       if(χ = FB)
6         ComputePR(Y,M) //Compute pr[X,Y,ρ] for all X and ρ. Populate S_T
7       else
8         ComputeSR(Y,H_sp,M) //Compute sr[X,Y,H'] for all X and H'. Populate S_T
9     //Now each M[X][ρ] stores pr[X,H_sp,ρ] (or sr[X,H_sp,H'], with ρ = H'.label)
10      forall(X ∈ S_T)
11        H = get block of X
12        Discard label of H, if any
13        if(M[X] is not a zero row) //Discard spurious species from S_T
14          if(H contains no marked states) //Add only once H to H_T
15            Add H to H_T
16          Mark X in H
17      while(H_T ≠ ∅)
18        H = pop(H_T)
19        H_1 = marked states of H
20        H = not marked states of H
21        if(H = ∅)
22          Give the identity of H to H_1
23        else
24          Make H_1 a new block
25        pmc = PMCRow(H_1,M)
26        H_2 = {X ∈ H_1 | M[X] not equal to the pmc-row}
27        H_1 = H_1 \ H_2
28        if(H_2 = ∅)
29          b = 1 //No need to split H_1.
30        else
31          Sort and split H_2 according to M[X], yielding H_2,...,H_b
32          Make each of H_2,...,H_b a new block
33        if(H ∈spls)
34          Add H_1,...,H_b except H to spls
35        else
36          Add [H,]^?H_1,...,H_b to spls except a sub-block of maximal size
37      while(S_T ≠ ∅)
38        X = pop(S_T)
39        touched[X]=false
40        CleanRowsOfMatrix(M,X)
```

**Algorithm 3.** The Split procedure.

to the current splitter $H_{sp}$. If $\chi = FB$, Line 4–8 compute $\mathbf{pr}[X, H_{sp}, \rho]$ and store it in $M[X][\rho]$ for each $X$ and $\rho$. This is done by ComputePR in Algorithm 4. The procedure scans all the reactions in the inc list of each $Y \in H_{sp}$. We can have either unary or binary reactions (Lines 2–3 or 4–6, respectively). In the latter case, if the two reagents are equal (i.e., $X = X'$) we add $\alpha \cdot \pi(Y)$ twice to $M[X][X]$. This corresponds to the $\rho(X) + 1$ factor of Definition 1. The actual updates on the entries of M are performed by the simple sub-routine Update in Lines 9–13 of Algorithm 4 which also updates $S_T$ if necessary.

If $\chi = BB$, Lines 4–8 of Algorithm 3 compute $\mathbf{sr}[X, H_{sp}, H']$ and store it in $M[X, \rho_{H'}]$ for each $X \in S$ and $H' \in \mathcal{H} \cup \{\{\emptyset\}\}$, with $\mathcal{H}$ the current partition. The symbol $\rho_{H'}$ denotes a label in $\mathcal{L}(R)$ which identifies $H'$ and is discussed below. The flux rates are computed by ComputeSR of Algorithm 5. It is similar to ComputePR, but it scans the reactions in the out lists of each species $Y \in H_{sp}$.

By Definition 5, unary reactions contribute to splitter flux rates with $\{\emptyset\}$ as third parameter. Here we associate the label $\emptyset \in \mathcal{L}(R)$ to unary reactions. For each unary reaction $Y \xrightarrow{\alpha} \pi \in \text{out}[Y]$ (Lines 2–5), $\text{M}[Y][\emptyset]$ is decreased by $\alpha$ and we increase $\text{M}[X][\emptyset]$ of each species $X$ in $\pi$ by $\alpha \cdot \pi(X)$. Instead, each binary reaction $Y + Y' \xrightarrow{\alpha} \pi \in \text{out}[Y]$ contributes to those with the block of $Y'$ as third parameter. As depicted in Lines 6–15, we provide each block $H'$ with a field label used to point to the label in $\mathcal{L}(R)$ assigned to $H'$. This will be a species in $H' \cap \mathcal{L}(R)$. In particular, in Line 7 we get the block of $Y'$ ($H'$). Then, if no label is currently assigned to $H'$, we set $Y'$ as label of $H'$. Finally, the entries of M are updated by Update similarly to the FB case, but using $H'$.label as label. Note that all reactions involving species $Y'$ of a block $H'$ will contribute to the same $H'$.label entries of M, thus computing the summation over the elements of $H'$ of Definition 5. We remark that we may have blocks $H'' \in \mathcal{H}$ with $H'' \cap \mathcal{L}(R) = \emptyset$. Those do not contribute to ComputeSR as both reagents of an arbitrary binary reaction are elements of $\mathcal{L}(R)$. Finally, we note that in Lines 10–11 we halve the rate of reactions with two different reagents $Y + Y'$ belonging to the splitter block $H_{sp}$, as done in Definition 5.

Now that $S_T$ and M have been populated, Lines 10–16 of Algorithm 3 build $H_T$ and mark all species in $S_T$ as discussed in Sect. 3.2. The marking operation could have not been done in Lines 4–8 because it changes the order of species in a block, and hence might interfere with the iteration of the forall statement of Line 4. Note that Line 13 discards species in $S_T$ whose M-rows have only zeros. This can happen because positive and negative values can sum up to zero (see, e.g., lines 3 and 5 and of Algorithm 5). In addition, Line 12 reinitializes all label fields of the blocks in $H_T$, a super-set of those to which ComputeSR might have assigned a label.

```
1  ComputePR(Y,M):=
2     forall((X --α--> π,π(Y)) ∈ inc[Y])
3        Update(M,X,∅,π(Y),α)
4     forall((X+X' --α--> π,π(Y)) ∈ inc[Y
          ])
5        Update(M,X,X',π(Y),α)
6        Update(M,X',X,π(Y),α)\\
7
8     //Sub-routine to update M and S_T
9     Update(M,X,ρ,mult,α):=
10       if(!touched[X])
11          touched[X] = true
12          add X to S_T
13       M[X][ρ] = M[X][ρ] + α·mult
```

**Algorithm 4.** Compute **pr** wrt the splitters.

```
1  ComputeSR(Y,H_sp,M):=
2     forall(Y --α--> π ∈ out[Y])
3        Update(M,Y,∅,1,-α)
4        forall(X ∈ π)
5           Update(M,X,∅,π(X),α)
6     forall(Y+Y' --α--> π ∈ out[Y])
7        H' = get block of Y'
8        if(H' does not have a label)
9           H'.label = Y'
10       if(Y ≠ Y' and H' = H_sp)
11          α = α/2
12       Update(M,Y,H'.label,1,-α)
13       Update(M,Y',H'.label,1,-α)
14       forall(X ∈ π)
15          Update(M,X,H'.label,π(X),α)
```

**Algorithm 5.** Compute **sr** wrt the splitters.

It is now possible to refine $\mathcal{H}$ and update the list of candidate splitters by splitting each block $H \in H_T$ according to the **pr** or **sr** values (Lines 17–36). Lines 19–20 perform the split operation discussed in Sect. 3.2. They split (in constant time) the species in $H$ which appear in $H_T$ (the marked ones) from those which do not appear in $H_T$ (the unmarked ones). Those $X \in H$ that yield

M[X][·] ≠ 0 form the block $H_1$, while the other remain in $H$. If the new $H$ is empty, $H_1$ contains the elements originally present in $H$ and thus receives its identity. Otherwise $H_1$ is made to a new block in $O(|H_1|)$ time.

Lines 25–27 further split $H_1$ by moving some of its elements in a new block $H_2$ in $O(|H_1|)$ time. In particular, we calculate the pmc-row in order to split $H_1$ into (a new) $H_1$ and $H_2$. In case more than half of the species of the original $H_1$ have their M-row equal, the new block $H_1$ will contain those species with the pmc-row; otherwise, it will contain any sub-set of $H_1$ with same row in M. In both cases the obtained $H_1$ does not need to be further split. Instead $H_2$ might need to be split further. We note that $H_2$ might be empty, meaning that there was no need in splitting $H_1$. In such case $H_1$ remains unchanged; in the opposite case, instead, $H_2$ is split in Lines 31–32 and the obtained sub-blocks are added to $\mathcal{H}$. We remark that we are guaranteed that each sub-block of $H_2$ has at most half the elements originally in $H$. Moreover, it is worth noting that splitting blocks in $\mathcal{H}$ affects spls because spls stores pointers to the elements of $\mathcal{H}$.

Finally, we add the so obtained sub-blocks to spls by storing the corresponding pointers in spls. As discussed, we do not add a sub-block with maximal size if the original $H$ has already been used as splitter (Line 36). Note that $[H,]^? H_1$ means that we add only one of the two blocks to spls if Line 22 gave the identity of $H$ to $H_1$. Instead, in Line 34 there is no need to add the new $H$ to spls because it is already there (i.e., the original $H$ was there, and hence the refined $H$ inherited its presence).

The procedure terminates by resetting the vector touched, used to build $S_T$, and the rows of M regarding the species in $S_T$.

**Theorem 2.** *Algorithm 1 calculates the coarsest RN bisimulations that refine a partition $\mathcal{H}$. Its time complexity is $\mathcal{O}(r \cdot p \cdot l \cdot \log s)$, while its space complexity is $\mathcal{O}(r \cdot s)$.*

The proof lifts the ideas of [7] to RNs. As discussed previously, the complexity stated above relates to an arbitrary RN. We shall see next that in the encoding of a polynomial ODE system the factor $p \cdot l$ simplifies to $s$, while it becomes a constant for CTMCs.

## 5    Applications

We discuss how to encode into an RN an arbitrary polynomial ODE system of degree at most two. Based on this, we consider the special case of an affine ODE system, which gives reduced time and space complexities; here, we will show an application of RN bisimulations for the numerical solution of systems of linear equations using stationary iterative methods. Finally, we relate RN bisimulations to CTMC lumpability [13].

It is easy to see that the encoding of polynomials ODEs to RNs is not unique (cf. [21] for CRNs). Here, we propose one for which the algorithmic complexity can be directly related to the number of monomials appearing in the ODE system, leaving the question of investigating minimality issues to future work.

**Polynomial Systems.** We consider the ODE system $\dot{y} = G(y)$ with components

$$\dot{y}_k = G_k(y) := \sum_{1 \le i,j \le n} \alpha_{i,j}^{(k)} \cdot y_i \cdot y_j + \sum_{1 \le i \le n} \alpha_i^{(k)} \cdot y_i + \beta^{(k)}, \quad 1 \le k \le n, \qquad (2)$$

and with $\alpha_{i,j}^{(k)}, \alpha_i^{(k)}, \beta^{(k)} \in \mathbb{R}$.

**Lemma 1.** *The RN* $(S_G, R_G)$, *with* $S_G := \{1, \ldots, n\}$ *and*

$$R_G := \left\{ i + j \xrightarrow{\alpha_{i,j}^{(k)}} i + j + k \mid \alpha_{i,j}^{(k)} \ne 0 \right\}$$

$$\cup \left\{ i \xrightarrow{\alpha_i^{(k)}} i + k \mid \alpha_i^{(k)} \ne 0 \right\} \cup \left\{ \emptyset \xrightarrow{\beta^{(k)}} k \mid \beta^{(k)} \ne 0 \right\},$$

*has ODEs* $\dot{V}_k = G_k(V)$, *for* $1 \le k \le n$.

Note that with this encoding $r$ relates to the number of monomials used in the ODEs (while $s$ is the number of ODE variables). As anticipated in Sect. 1, Theorem 2 and Lemma 1 imply that Algorithm 1 gives the coarsest FB and BB partitions of an arbitrary polynomial ODE system in $\mathcal{O}(r \cdot s \cdot \log s)$ time and $\mathcal{O}(r \cdot s)$ space.

**Affine Systems.** Equation (2) also subsumes the interesting case of affine ODE systems where $G(y) = Cy + d$ for some $C \in \mathbb{R}^{n \times n}$ and $d \in \mathbb{R}^n$. In this case, Theorem 2 and Lemma 1 imply that the complexity reduces to $\mathcal{O}(r \cdot \log s)$ time and $\mathcal{O}(r + s)$ space. Here we consider the problem of computing a solution of a linear system of equations $Ax = b$, with $A \in \mathbb{R}^{n \times n}$ and $x, b \in \mathbb{R}^n$. Stationary iterative methods approximate a solution with updates in the form $x(k + 1) = F(x(k))$ where $k$ is the iteration index and $F$ is affine. For instance, Jacobi's method is written as $x(k + 1) = -Rx(k) + D^{-1}b$, with $x(0) = 0$, where $D, R$ are such that $D$ is a diagonal matrix and $A = D + R$. Under the assumption of strict diagonal dominance for $A$, it converges to the solution of $Ax = b$ (e.g., [14]). We interpret this sequence as a dynamical system, but in *discrete time*, and observe that the bisimulations carry over to the discrete time case. We denote the encoding of the Jacobi iterations by the RN $(S_{A,b}, R_{A,b})$. Then, the following holds.

**Theorem 3.** *An RN bisimulation* $\mathcal{H} = \{H_1, \ldots, H_m\}$ *on* $(S_{A,b}, R_{A,b})$ *induces a reduced discrete-time model* $\hat{x}(k+1) = \hat{A}\hat{x}(k) + \hat{b}$, *with* $\hat{A} \in \mathbb{R}^{m \times m}$ *and* $\hat{x}(k), \hat{b} \in \mathbb{R}^m$. *If* $\mathcal{H}$ *is an FB then,* $\hat{x}_i(k) = \sum_{l \in H_i} x_l(k)$ *for all* $1 \le i \le m$ *and* $k \ge 0$. *If* $\mathcal{H}$ *is a BB then,* $\hat{x}_i(k) = x_l(k)$ *for all* $1 \le i \le m$, $l \in H_i$ *and* $k \ge 0$.

Here, $\hat{A}$ and $\hat{b}$ can be obtained by constructing the reduced RN up to FB/BB [11].

**Continuous-time Markov Chains.** Let us fix a CTMC with transition rate matrix $Q = (q_{i,j})_{1 \le i,j \le n}$. Then the probability distribution $\pi = (\pi_i)_{1 \le i \le n}$ solves the Kolmogorov linear ODEs $\dot{\pi} = \pi Q$.

**Lemma 2.** *Let $Q$ be the transition matrix of a CTMC and $(S_Q, R_Q)$ be the RN encoding according to (2) of its Kolmogorov ODEs. Then, $\mathcal{H}$ is an ordinarily (resp., exactly) lumpable partition for $Q$ if and only if $\mathcal{H}$ is an FB (resp., a BB) for $(S_Q, R_Q)$.*

By Theorem 2 and Lemma 1, Algorithm 1 calculates the coarsest ordinarily and exactly lumpable partitions of $Q$ in $\mathcal{O}(r \cdot \log s)$ time and $\mathcal{O}(r + s)$ space. Thus, we recover the bounds of Markov-chain specific algorithms [6,7]. We also remark that, in the case of BB, Lemma 2 recovers a result from [19] using an alternative proof. Finally, it can be shown that Lemma 2 is still valid if the reactions are encoded via $R_Q = \{i \xrightarrow{q_{i,j}} j \mid q_{i,j} \neq 0\}$, using one-to-one reactions only. Though not affecting asymptotic complexity, this reduces memory and time consumption, and thus we will use it in our prototype.

# 6  Evaluation

We evaluate our algorithm using (i) the biochemical networks evaluated in [11] as case studies for degree-two polynomial systems; (ii) $Ax = b$ systems from [15]; and (iii) selected CTMCs from the MRMC distribution [33]. Comparing against the reductions of [11] and MRMC also allowed us to validate the implementation of our algorithm.

   The results are presented in Table 1. To ease layout, we label the models with short identifiers (first column), and refer to the publications in the second column for details. Headers $|R|$ and $|S|$ give the number of reactions and species of the original and reduced RNs. Headers "*Red.* [11]" and "*Red.*" provide the runtimes of the algorithm considered in [11] and of the proposed approach, respectively. Measurements were taken on a 2.6 GHz Intel Core i5 machine with 4 GB of RAM. The experiments are replicable using a prototype available at http://sysma.imtlucca.it/crnreducer/.

*Biochemical Models* (M1–M13). For consistency, we computed the coarsest bisimulations that refine the same initial partitions as specified in [11]. Specifically, for each RN $(S, R)$, in the case of FB we considered the trivial partition $\{S\}$ (thus yielding the largest bisimulation); due to the side condition of BB, in that case the initial partition was chosen in agreement with the initial conditions — two species are in the same initial block if their initial conditions, read from the original model specification, are equal (thus ensuring that the reduction is a lossless simplification of the original one).

   We refer to [11] for a description of the models and the biological interpretation of the bisimulations therein computed. Here, we confirm the same reductions, at a much improved performance over that of [11]. For the largest model (M1) we registered a speedup of four orders of magnitude—now all cases can be reduced within seconds.

*Systems of Linear Equations* (F1–F5). These are encodings of the Jacobi iterative method to solve large-scale real-world linear systems from the Sparse Matrix Collection [15]. F1–F2 (original names *Bourchtein/atmosmodl* and

**Table 1.** FB and BB reductions. Entries labeled with "—" indicate that the reduction algorithm did not terminate within 24 hours. Greyed out entries indicate no reduction.

| | | Original model | | | FB reduction | | | | BB reduction | | |
|---|---|---|---|---|---|---|---|---|---|---|---|
| Id | Ref. | \|R\| | \|S\| | Red.(s) [11] | Red.(s) | \|R\| | \|S\| | Red.(s) [11] | Red.(s) | \|R\| | \|S\| |
| | | | | | | | **Biochemical reaction networks** | | | | |
| M1 | [22] | 3 538 944 | 262 146 | 4.61E+4 | 7.49E+0 | 990 | 222 | 7.65E+4 | 1.21E+1 | 2 614 | 222 |
| M2 | [22] | 786 432 | 65 538 | 1.92E+3 | 1.58E+0 | 720 | 167 | 3.68E+3 | 2.51E+0 | 1 873 | 167 |
| M3 | [22] | 172 032 | 16 386 | 8.15E+1 | 2.89E-1 | 504 | 122 | 1.77E+2 | 6.03E-1 | 1 305 | 122 |
| M4 | [22] | 48 | 18 | 1.00E-3 | 1.00E-3 | 24 | 12 | 2.00E-3 | 2.00E-3 | 44 | 12 |
| M5 | [23] | 194 054 | 14 531 | 3.72E+1 | 3.88E-1 | 142 165 | 10 855 | 1.32E+3 | 6.00E-1 | 91 001 | 6 634 |
| M6 | [24] | 187 468 | 10 734 | 3.07E+1 | 6.09E-1 | 57 508 | 3 744 | 2.71E+2 | 1.40E+0 | 145 650 | 5 575 |
| M7 | [24] | 32 776 | 2 506 | 1.26E+0 | 1.19E-1 | 16 481 | 1 281 | 1.66E+1 | 2.14E-1 | 32 776 | 2 506 |
| M8 | [25] | 41 233 | 2 562 | 1.12E+0 | 2.69E-1 | 33 075 | 1 897 | 1.89E+1 | 3.97E-1 | 41 233 | 2 562 |
| M9 | [25] | 5 033 | 471 | 1.91E-1 | 1.60E-2 | 4 068 | 345 | 4.35E-1 | 2.40E-2 | 5 033 | 471 |
| M10 | [26] | 5 797 | 796 | 1.61E-1 | 1.90E-2 | 4 210 | 503 | 7.37E-1 | 3.30E-2 | 5 797 | 796 |
| M11 | [27] | 5 832 | 730 | 3.89E-1 | 1.50E-2 | 1 296 | 217 | 6.00E-1 | 2.40E-2 | 237 | 217 |
| M12 | [28] | 487 | 85 | 2.00E-3 | 2.00E-3 | 264 | 56 | 6.00E-3 | 3.00E-3 | 431 | 56 |
| M13 | [29] | 24 | 18 | 1.20E-2 | 4.00E-3 | 24 | 18 | 7.00E-3 | 4.00E-3 | 7 | 3 |
| | | | | | | | **Affine systems** | | | | |
| F1 | [15] | 10 319 760 | 1 489 753 | 9.74E+3 | 8.70E+2 | 1 295 514 | 188 101 | — | 2.23E+2 | 10 319 760 | 1 489 753 |
| F2 | [15] | 8 814 880 | 1 270 433 | 8.86E+2 | 5.58E+2 | 1 108 224 | 160 951 | — | 1.55E+2 | 4 420 168 | 639 509 |
| F3 | [15] | 2 101 250 | 525 826 | 3.71E+2 | 1.24E+1 | 526 338 | 131 842 | — | 4.79E+1 | 2 101 250 | 525 826 |
| F4 | [15] | 4 706 074 | 143 572 | 6.72E+0 | 6.70E+0 | 565 288 | 47 858 | — | 1.47E+1 | 2 739 188 | 112 444 |
| F5 | [15] | 706 577 | 116 836 | 3.23E+0 | 3.11E+0 | 609 459 | 73 423 | — | 2.86E+0 | 609 307 | 73 348 |
| | | | | | | | **Continuous-time Markov chains** | | | | |
| C1 | [30] | 22 871 849 | 3 101 445 | 4.00E+4 | 2.01E+3 | 1 069 777 | 135 752 | — | 1.34E+3 | 1 166 931 | 148 092 |
| C2 | [31] | 11 583 520 | 2 373 652 | 1.73E+2 | 9.78E+1 | 5 792 531 | 1 187 597 | — | 3.07E+2 | 5 814 622 | 1 187 597 |
| C3 | [32] | 10 485 761 | 1 048 576 | 1.48E+1 | 1.76E+1 | 3 301 | 792 | — | 1.23E+1 | 5 083 | 792 |

*Bourchtein/atmosmodd*, respectively) arise from atmospheric modeling; F3 (*Wissgott/parabolicFEM*) is to be computed during a finite-element-method solution to a convection-diffusion reaction; F4 (*TTK/engine*) comes from a problem in structural mechanics; F5 (*IBMEDA/dc1*) arises from the simulation of an electrical circuit. For F1–F4 we verified (in $\mathcal{O}(r)$ steps) that the sparse matrix is strictly diagonal dominant, a known sufficient condition for the convergence of Jacobi's method. All cases enjoy significant reductions with either bisimulation, up to one order of magnitude fewer species and reactions for F1.

In some cases (i.e., F2, F4, and F5) the FB runtimes are comparable to those of [11]. This can be explained by noting that, in the encoding of affine ODEs, the splitting based on the "labels" cannot yield a significant improvement because the RN has only unary reactions (hence only one label, $\emptyset$). This is not the case in the biochemical benchmarks M1–M13, which as a matter of fact showed significant runtime differences.

Regarding BB, the algorithm of [11] was not able to compute any BB reduction within 24 hours. The remarkable performance improvement is due to the novel splitter-based characterization of BB (Sect. 3.1), while with [11] it was required to compute, at each iteration, the equivalence classes for multi-sets of species according to Definition 4.

*CTMCs* (C1–C3). These are the three largest CTMCs of the MRMC distribution [33], used in [34] to study the impact of ordinary CTMC lumpability in model checking. In particular, these are: a protocol for wireless group communication (C1, original model name *FDT3E3_PE16E4_S4OD40*); a cluster model (C2, *WORKSTATION_CLUSTER_N256*); and a peer-to-peer protocol (C3. *TORRENT_N04*). The initial partitions for both FB and BB are consistent with the atomic propositions on the CTMC states.

Being affine ODE systems, the above observations regarding the runtime comparisons with [11] carry over to these models. Instead, a thorough comparison against MRMC is difficult because of the different languages were used for the implementation (C with specialized data structures for sparse matrices for MRMC, vs. Java with plain data structures from its API in our prototype) and because MRMC is CTMC-specific. However, MRMC ran one order of magnitude faster and was less memory demanding, indicating the potential in improving performance in optimized versions of our prototype.

## 7  Conclusion

The main advantage in aggregating dynamical systems from a chemical reaction network syntax lies in adapting established and efficient bisimulation algorithms for discrete-state models. The numerical benchmarks have demonstrated scalability as well as the effectiveness of exact aggregations in non-synthetic models. Future work will concern the equivalences and related algorithms to handle higher-degree polynomial nonlinearities.

**Acknowledgment.** This work was partially supported by the EU project QUANTI-COL, 600708. L. Cardelli is partially funded by a Royal Society Research Professorship.

## References

1. Danos, V., Feret, J., Fontana, W., Harmer, R., Krivine, J.: Abstracting the differential semantics of rule-based models: exact and automated model reduction. In: LICS, pp. 362–381 (2010)
2. Blinov, M.L., Faeder, J.R., Goldstein, B., Hlavacek, W.S.: BioNetGen: software for rule-based modeling of signal transduction based on the interactions of molecular domains. Bioinformatics **20**, 3289–3291 (2004)
3. Dang, T., Guernic, C.L., Maler, O.: Computing reachable states for nonlinear biological models. TCS **412**, 2095–2107 (2011)
4. Ben Sassi, M.A., Testylier, R., Dang, T., Girard, A.: Reachability analysis of polynomial systems using linear programming relaxations. In: Chakraborty, S., Mukund, M. (eds.) ATVA 2012. LNCS, vol. 7561, pp. 137–151. Springer, Heidelberg (2012)
5. Baier, C., Engelen, B., Majster-Cederbaum, M.E.: Deciding bisimilarity and similarity for probabilistic processes. J. Comput. Syst. Sci. **60**, 187–231 (2000)
6. Derisavi, S., Hermanns, H., Sanders, W.: Optimal state-space lumping in Markov chains. Inf. Process. Lett. **87**, 309–315 (2003)

7. Valmari, A., Franceschinis, G.: Simple $O(m \log n)$ time Markov chain lumping. In: Esparza, J., Majumdar, R. (eds.) TACAS 2010. LNCS, vol. 6015, pp. 38–52. Springer, Heidelberg (2010)

8. Paige, R., Tarjan, R.: Three partition refinement algorithms. SIAM J. Comput. **16**, 973–989 (1987)

9. Murray, J.D.: Mathematical Biology I: An Introduction, 3rd edn. Springer, Heidelberg (2002)

10. Feinberg, M.: Chemical reaction network structure and the stability of complex isothermal reactors – I. The deficiency zero and deficiency one theorems. Chem. Eng. Sci. **42**, 2229–2268 (1987)

11. Cardelli, L., Tribastone, M., Tschaikowski, M., Vandin, A.: Forward and backward bisimulations for chemical reaction networks. In: CONCUR, pp. 226–239 (2015)

12. Larsen, K.G., Skou, A.: Bisimulation through probabilistic testing. Inf. Comput. **94**, 1–28 (1991)

13. Buchholz, P.: Exact and ordinary lumpability in finite Markov chains. J. Appl. Probab. **31**, 59–75 (1994)

14. Saad, Y.: Iterative Methods for Sparse Linear Systems, 2nd edn. Society for Industrial and Applied Mathematics, Philadelphia (2003)

15. Davis, T.A., Hu, Y.: The University of Florida sparse matrix collection. ACM Trans. Math. Softw. **38**, 1–25 (2011)

16. Li, G., Rabitz, H.: A general analysis of exact lumping in chemical kinetics. Chem. Eng. Sci. **44**, 1413–1430 (1989)

17. Toth, J., Li, G., Rabitz, H., Tomlin, A.S.: The effect of lumping and expanding on kinetic differential equations. SIAM J. Appl. Math. **57**, 1531–1556 (1997)

18. Tschaikowski, M., Tribastone, M.: Exact fluid lumpability for Markovian process algebra. In: Koutny, M., Ulidowski, I. (eds.) CONCUR 2012. LNCS, vol. 7454, pp. 380–394. Springer, Heidelberg (2012)

19. Cardelli, L., Tribastone, M., Tschaikowski, M., Vandin, A.: Symbolic computation of differential equivalences. In: POPL (2016, to appear)

20. Iacobelli, G., Tribastone, M., Vandin, A.: Differential bisimulation for a Markovian process algebra. In: Italiano, G.F., Pighizzini, G., Sannella, D.T. (eds.) MFCS 2015. LNCS, vol. 9234, pp. 293–306. Springer, Heidelberg (2015)

21. Hars, V., Toth, J.: On the inverse problem of reaction kinetics. Colloquia Mathematica Societatis Janos Bolyai **30**, 363–379 (1979)

22. Sneddon, M.W., Faeder, J.R., Emonet, T.: Efficient modeling, simulation and coarse-graining of biological complexity with NFsim. Nat. Methods **8**, 177–183 (2011)

23. Suderman, R., Deeds, E.J.: Machines vs ensembles: effective MAPK signaling through heterogeneous sets of protein complexes. PLoS Comput. Biol. **9**, e1003278 (2013)

24. Faeder, J.R., Hlavacek, W.S., Reischl, I., Blinov, M.L., Metzger, H., Redondo, A., Wofsy, C., Goldstein, B.: Investigation of early events in Fc$\varepsilon$RI-mediated signaling using a detailed mathematical model. J. Immunol. **170**, 3769–3781 (2003)

25. Barua, D., Faeder, J.R., Haugh, J.M.: A bipolar clamp mechanism for activation of jak-family protein tyrosine kinases. PLoS Comput. Biol. **5**, e1000364 (2009)

26. Barua, D., Hlavacek, W.S.: Modeling the effect of apc truncation on destruction complex function in colorectal cancer cells. PLoS Comput. Biol. **9**, e1003217 (2013)

27. Colvin, J., Monine, M.I., Faeder, J.R., Hlavacek, W.S., Hoff, D.D.V., Posner, R.G.: Simulation of large-scale rule-based models. Bioinformatics **25**, 910–917 (2009)

28. Kocieniewski, P., Faeder, J.R., Lipniacki, T.: The interplay of double phosphorylation and scaffolding in MAPK pathways. J. Theor. Biol. **295**, 116–124 (2012)

29. Cardelli, L.: Morphisms of reaction networks that couple structure to function. BMC Syst. Biol. **8**, 84 (2014)
30. Massink, M., Katoen, J., Latella, D.: Model checking dependability attributes of wireless group communication. In: DSN, pp. 711–720 (2004)
31. Haverkort, B., Hermanns, H., Katoen, J.P.: On the use of model checking techniques for dependability evaluation. In: SRDS, pp. 228–237 (2000)
32. Kwiatkowska, M., Norman, G., Parker, D.: Symmetry reduction for probabilistic model checking. In: Ball, T., Jones, R.B. (eds.) CAV 2006. LNCS, vol. 4144, pp. 234–248. Springer, Heidelberg (2006)
33. Katoen, J., Khattri, M., Zapreev, I.: A Markov reward model checker. In: QEST, pp. 243–244 (2005)
34. Katoen, J.-P., Kemna, T., Zapreev, I., Jansen, D.N.: Bisimulation minimisation mostly speeds up probabilistic model checking. In: Grumberg, O., Huth, M. (eds.) TACAS 2007. LNCS, vol. 4424, pp. 87–101. Springer, Heidelberg (2007)

# Faster Statistical Model Checking
# for Unbounded Temporal Properties

Przemysław Daca[1]([✉]), Thomas A. Henzinger[1], Jan Křetínský[2],
and Tatjana Petrov[1]

[1] IST Austria, Klosterneuburg, Austria
przemek@ist.ac.at
[2] Institut Für Informatik, Technische Universität München, Munich, Germany

**Abstract.** We present a new algorithm for the statistical model checking of Markov chains with respect to unbounded temporal properties, including full linear temporal logic. The main idea is that we monitor each simulation run on the fly, in order to detect quickly if a bottom strongly connected component is entered with high probability, in which case the simulation run can be terminated early. As a result, our simulation runs are often much shorter than required by termination bounds that are computed a priori for a desired level of confidence on a large state space. In comparison to previous algorithms for statistical model checking our method is not only faster in many cases but also requires less information about the system, namely, only the minimum transition probability that occurs in the Markov chain. In addition, our method can be generalised to unbounded quantitative properties such as mean-payoff bounds.

## 1 Introduction

Traditional numerical algorithms for the verification of Markov chains may be computationally intense or inapplicable, when facing a large state space or limited knowledge about the chain. To this end, statistical algorithms are used as a powerful alternative. *Statistical model checking* (SMC) typically refers to approaches where (i) finite paths of the Markov chain are sampled a finite number of times, (ii) the property of interest is verified for each sampled path (e.g. state $r$ is reached), and (iii) hypothesis testing or statistical estimation is used to infer conclusions (e.g. state $r$ is reached with probability at most 0.5) and give statistical guarantees (e.g. the conclusion is valid with 99 % confidence). SMC approaches differ in (a) the class of properties they can verify (e.g. bounded or

---

This research was funded in part by the European Research Council (ERC) under grant agreement 267989 (QUAREM), the Austrian Science Fund (FWF) under grants project S11402-N23 (RiSE) and Z211-N23 (Wittgenstein Award), the People Programme (Marie Curie Actions) of the European Union's Seventh Framework Programme (FP7/2007-2013) REA Grant No 291734, the SNSF Advanced Postdoc. Mobility Fellowship – grant number P300P2_161067, and the Czech Science Foundation under grant agreement P202/12/G061.

© Springer-Verlag Berlin Heidelberg 2016
M. Chechik and J.-F. Raskin (Eds.): TACAS 2016, LNCS 9636, pp. 112–129, 2016.
DOI: 10.1007/978-3-662-49674-9_7

unbounded properties), (b) the strength of statistical guarantees they provide (e.g. confidence bounds, only asymptotic convergence of the method towards the correct value, or none), and (c) the amount of information they require about the Markov chain (e.g. the topology of the graph). In this paper, we provide an algorithm for SMC of unbounded properties, with confidence bounds, in the setting where only the minimum transition probability of the chain is known. Such an algorithm is particularly desirable in scenarios when the system is not known ("black box"), but also when it is too large to construct or fit into memory.

Most of the previous efforts in SMC has focused on the analysis of properties with bounded horizon [5,12,13,21,27,28]. For bounded properties (e.g. state $r$ is reached with probability at most 0.5 in the first 1000 steps) statistical guarantees can be obtained in a completely black-box setting, where execution runs of the Markov chain can be observed, but no other information about the chain is available. Unbounded properties (e.g. state $r$ is reached with probability at most 0.5 in any number of steps) are significantly more difficult, as a stopping criterion is needed when generating a potentially infinite execution run, and some information about the Markov chain is necessary for providing statistical guarantees (for an overview, see Table 1). On the one hand, some approaches require the knowledge of the full topology in order to preprocess the Markov chain. On the other hand, when the topology is not accessible, there are approaches where the correctness of the statistics relies on information ranging from the second eigenvalue $\lambda$ of the Markov chain, to knowledge of both the number $|S|$ of states and the minimum transition probability $p_{min}$.

**Table 1.** SMC approaches to Markov chain verification, organised by (i) the class of verifiable properties, and (ii) by the required information about the Markov chain, where $p_{min}$ is the minimum transition probability, $|S|$ is the number of states, and $\lambda$ is the second largest eigenvalue of the chain.

| LTL, mean payoff | $\times$ | **here** | [4] (LTL) | | |
| $\Diamond, \mathbf{U}$ | $\times$ | **here** | —"— | [26] | [26], [9] |
| bounded | e.g. [28, 21] | | | | |
| | no info | $p_{min}$ | $|S|, p_{min}$ | $\lambda$ | topology |

**Our contribution** is a new SMC algorithm for full linear temporal logic (LTL), as well as for unbounded quantitative properties (mean payoff), which provides strong guarantees in the form of confidence bounds. Our algorithm uses less information about the Markov chain than previous algorithms that provide confidence bounds for unbounded properties —we need to know only the minimum transition probability $p_{min}$ of the chain, and not the number of states nor the topology. Yet, experimentally, our algorithm performs in many cases better than these previous approaches (see Sect. 5). Our main idea is to *monitor each execution run on the fly in order to build statistical hypotheses about the structure of the Markov chain*. In particular, if from observing the current prefix of an execution run we can stipulate that with high probability a bottom strongly connected component (BSCC) of the chain has been entered, then we can terminate the current execution run. The information obtained from execution prefixes allows us to terminate executions as soon as the property is decided with the required confidence, which is usually much earlier than any bounds that can be computed a priori. As far as we know, this is the first SMC algorithm that uses information obtained from execution prefixes.

Finding $p_{min}$ is a light assumption in many realistic scenarios and often does not depend on the size of the chain – e.g. bounds on the rates for reaction kinetics in chemical reaction systems are typically known, from a PRISM language model they can be easily inferred without constructing the respective state space.

*Example 1.* Consider the property of reaching state $r$ in the Markov chain depicted in Fig. 1. While the execution runs reaching $r$ satisfy the property and can be stopped without ever entering any $v_i$, the finite execution paths without $r$, such as *stuttutuut*, are inconclusive. In other words, observing this path does not rule out the existence of a transition from, e.g., $u$ to $r$, which, if existing, would eventually be taken with probability 1. This transition could have arbitrarily low probability, rendering its detection arbitrarily unlikely, yet its presence would change the probability of satisfying the property from 0.5 to 1. However, knowing that if there exists such a transition leaving the set, its transition probability is at least $p_{min} = 0.01$, we can estimate the probability that the system is stuck in the set $\{t, u\}$ of states. Indeed, if existing, the exit transition was missed at least four times, no matter whether it exits $t$ or $u$. Consequently, the probability that there is no such transition and $\{t, u\}$ is a BSCC is at least $1 - (1 - p_{min})^4$.

This means that, in order to get 99 % confidence that $\{t, u\}$ is a BSCC, we only need to see both $t$ and $u$ around 500 times[1] on a run. This is in stark contrast to a priori bounds that provide the same level of confidence, such as

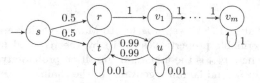

**Fig. 1.** A Markov chain.

the $(1/p_{min})^{|S|} = 100^{\mathcal{O}(m)}$ runs required by [4], which is infeasible for large $m$. In contrast, our method's performance is independent of $m$.    △

Monitoring execution prefixes allows us to design an SMC algorithm for complex unbounded properties such as full LTL. More precisely, we present a new SMC algorithm for LTL over Markov chains, specified as follows:

**Input:** we can sample finite runs of arbitrary length from an unknown finite-state discrete-time Markov chain $\mathcal{M}$ starting in the initial state[2], and we are given a lower bound $p_{min} > 0$ on the transition probabilities in $\mathcal{M}$, an LTL formula $\varphi$, a threshold probability $p$, an indifference region $\varepsilon > 0$, and two error bounds $\alpha, \beta > 0$,[3]

---

[1] $1 - (1 - p_{min})^{500} = 1 - 0.99^{500} \approx 0.993$.

[2] We have a black-box system in the sense of [21], different from e.g. [28] or [20], where simulations can be run from any state.

[3] Except for the transition probability bound $p_{min}$, all inputs are standard, as used in literature, e.g. [28].

**Output:** if $\mathbb{P}[\mathcal{M} \models \varphi] \geq p + \varepsilon$, return YES with probability at least $1 - \alpha$, and if $\mathbb{P}[\mathcal{M} \models \varphi] \leq p - \varepsilon$, return NO with probability at least $1 - \beta$.

In addition, we present the first SMC algorithm for computing the mean payoff of Markov chains whose states are labelled with rewards.

**Related Work.** To the best of our knowledge, we present the first SMC algorithm that provides confidence bounds for unbounded qualitative properties with access to only the minimum probability of the chain $p_{\mathsf{min}}$, and the first SMC algorithm for quantitative properties. For completeness, we survey briefly other related SMC approaches. SMC of unbounded properties, usually "unbounded until" properties, was first considered in [10] and the first approach was proposed in [22], but observed incorrect in [9]. Notably, in [26] two approaches are described. The first approach proposes to terminate sampled paths at every step with some probability $p_{\mathsf{term}}$. In order to guarantee the asymptotic convergence of this method, the second eigenvalue $\lambda$ of the chain must be computed, which is as hard as the verification problem itself. It should be noted that their method provides only asymptotic guarantees as the width of the confidence interval converges to zero. The correctness of [16] relies on the knowledge of the second eigenvalue $\lambda$, too. The second approach of [26] requires the knowledge of the chain's topology, which is used to transform the chain so that all potentially infinite paths are eliminated. In [9], a similar transformation is performed, again requiring knowledge of the topology. The (pre)processing of the state space required by the topology-aware methods, as well as by traditional numerical methods for Markov chain analysis, is a major practical hurdle for large (or unknown) state spaces. In [4] a priori bounds for the length of execution runs are calculated from the minimum transition probability and the number of states. However, without taking execution information into account, these bounds are exponential in the number of states and highly impractical, as illustrated in the example above. Another approach, limited to ergodic Markov chains, is taken in [20], based on coupling methods. There are also extensions of SMC to timed systems [7]. Our approach is also related to [8,18], where the product of a non-deterministic system and Büchi automaton is explored for accepting lassos. We are not aware of any method for detecting BSCCs by observing a single run, employing no directed search of the state space.

**Experimental Evaluation.** Our idea of inferring the structure of the Markov chain on the fly, while generating execution runs, allows for their early termination. In Sect. 5 we will see that for many chains arising in practice, such as the concurrent probabilistic protocols from the PRISM benchmark suite [15], the BSCCs are reached quickly and, even more importantly, can be small even for very large systems. Consequently, many execution runs can be stopped quickly. Moreover, since the number of execution runs necessary for a required precision and confidence is independent of the size of the state space, it needs not be very large even for highly confident results (a good analogy is that of the opinion polls: the precision and confidence of opinion polls is regulated by the sample size and is independent of the size of the population). It is therefore not surprising that, experimentally, in most cases from the benchmark suite, our method outperforms previous methods (often even the numerical methods) despite requiring much less knowledge of the Markov chain, and despite providing strong guarantees in the form of confidence bounds. In Sect. 6, we also provide theoretical bounds on the running time of our algorithm for classes of Markov chains on which it performs particularly well.

Due to space constraints, the proofs and further details can be found in [2].

## 2    Preliminaries

**Definition 1 (Markov chain).** *A Markov chain (MC) is a tuple* $\mathcal{M} = (S, \mathbf{P}, \mu)$, *where*

- $S$ *is a finite set of states,*
- $\mathbf{P}$ : $S \times S \to [0, 1]$ *is the transition probability matrix, such that for every* $s \in S$ *it holds* $\sum_{s' \in S} \mathbf{P}(s, s') = 1$,
- $\mu$ *is a probability distribution over* $S$.

We let $p_{\mathsf{min}} := \min(\{\mathbf{P}(s, s') > 0 \mid s, s' \in S\})$ denote the smallest positive transition probability in $\mathcal{M}$. A *run* of $\mathcal{M}$ is an infinite sequence $\rho = s_0 s_1 \ldots$ of states, such that for all $i \geq 0$, $\mathbf{P}(s_i, s_{i+1}) > 0$; we let $\rho[i]$ denote the state $s_i$. A *path* in $\mathcal{M}$ is a finite prefix of a run of $\mathcal{M}$. We denote the empty path by $\lambda$ and concatenation of paths $\pi_1$ and $\pi_2$ by $\pi_1 . \pi_2$. Each path $\pi$ in $\mathcal{M}$ determines the set of runs $\mathsf{Cone}(\pi)$ consisting of all runs that start with $\pi$. To $\mathcal{M}$ we assign the probability space $(\mathsf{Runs}, \mathcal{F}, \mathbb{P})$, where $\mathsf{Runs}$ is the set of all runs in $\mathcal{M}$, $\mathcal{F}$ is the $\sigma$-algebra generated by all $\mathsf{Cone}(\pi)$, and $\mathbb{P}$ is the unique probability measure such that $\mathbb{P}[\mathsf{Cone}(s_0 s_1 \ldots s_k)] = \mu(s_0) \cdot \prod_{i=1}^{k} \mathbf{P}(s_{i-1}, s_i)$, where the empty product equals 1. The respective expected value of a random variable $f$ : $\mathsf{Runs} \to \mathbb{R}$ is $\mathbb{E}[f] = \int_{\mathsf{Runs}} f \, d\mathbb{P}$.

A non-empty set $C \subseteq S$ of states is *strongly connected* (SC) if for every $s, s' \in C$ there is a path from $s$ to $s'$. A set of states $C \subseteq S$ is a *bottom strongly connected component* (BSCC) of $\mathcal{M}$, if it is a maximal SC, and for each $s \in C$ and $s' \in S \setminus C$ we have $\mathbf{P}(s, s') = 0$. The sets of all SCs and BSCCs in $\mathcal{M}$ are denoted by $\mathsf{SC}$ and $\mathsf{BSCC}$, respectively. Note that with probability 1, the set of states that appear infinitely many times on a run forms a BSCC. From now on, we use the standard notions of SC and BSCC for directed graphs as well.

## 3    Solution for Reachability

A fundamental problem in Markov chain verification is computing the probability that a certain set of goal states is reached. For the rest of the paper, let $\mathcal{M} = (S, \mathbf{P}, \mu)$ be a Markov chain and $G \subseteq S$ be the set of the goal states in $\mathcal{M}$. We let $\Diamond G := \{\rho \in \mathsf{Runs} \mid \exists i \geq 0 : \rho[i] \in G\}$ denote the event that "eventually a state in $G$ is reached." The event $\Diamond G$ is measurable and its probability $\mathbb{P}[\Diamond G]$

can be computed numerically or estimated using statistical algorithms. Since no bound on the number of steps for reaching $G$ is given, the major difficulty for any statistical approach is to decide how long each sampled path should be. We can stop extending the path either when we reach $G$, or when no more new states can be reached anyways. The latter happens if and only if we are in a BSCC and we have seen all of its states.

In this section, we first show how to monitor each simulation run on the fly, in order to detect quickly if a BSCC has been entered with high probability. Then, we show how to use hypothesis testing in order to estimate $\mathbb{P}[\Diamond G]$.

## 3.1 BSCC Detection

We start with an example illustrating how to measure probability of reaching a BSCC from one path observation.

*Example 2.* Recall Example 1 and Fig. 1. Now, consider an execution path *stuttutu*. Intuitively, does $\{t, u\}$ look as a good "candidate" for being a BSCC of $\mathcal{M}$? We visited both $t$ and $u$ three times; we have taken a transition from each $t$ and $u$ at least twice without leaving $\{t, u\}$. By the same reasoning as in Example 1, we could have missed some outgoing transition with probability at most $(1 - p_{\min})^2$. The structure of the system that can be deduced from this path is in Fig. 2 and is correct with probability at least $1 - (1 - p_{\min})^2$.  △

Now we formalise our intuition. Given a finite or infinite sequence $\rho = s_0 s_1 \ldots$, the *support* of $\rho$ is the set $\overline{\rho} = \{s_0, s_1, \ldots\}$. Further, the *graph of $\rho$* is given by vertices $\overline{\rho}$ and edges $\{(s_i, s_{i+1}) \mid i = 0, 1, \ldots\}$.

**Definition 2 (Candidate).** *If a path $\pi$ has a suffix $\kappa$ such that $\overline{\kappa}$ is a BSCC of the graph of $\pi$, we call $\overline{\kappa}$ the* candidate *of $\pi$. Moreover, for $k \in \mathbb{N}$, we call it a* k-candidate *(of $\pi$) if each $s \in \overline{\kappa}$ has at least $k$ occurrences in $\kappa$ and the last element of $\kappa$ has at least $k + 1$ occurrences. A* k-candidate *of a run $\rho$ is a k-candidate of some prefix of $\rho$.*

Note that for each path there is at most one candidate. Therefore, we write $K(\pi)$ to denote the candidate of $\pi$ if there is one, and $K(\pi) = \bot$, otherwise. Observe that each $K(\pi) \neq \bot$ is a SC in $\mathcal{M}$.

*Example 3.* Consider a path $\pi = stuttutu$, then $K(\pi) = \{t, u\}$. Observe that $\{t\}$ is not a candidate as it is not maximal. Further, $K(\pi)$ is a 2-candidate (and as such also a 1-candidate), but not a 3-candidate. Intuitively, the reason is that we only took a transition from $u$ (to the candidate) twice, cf. Example 2.  △

Intuitively, the higher the $k$ the more it looks as if the $k$-candidate is indeed a BSCC. Denoting by $Cand_k(K)$ the random predicate of $K$ being a $k$-candidate on a run, the probability of "unluckily" detecting any specific non-BSCC set of states $K$ as a $k$-candidate, can be bounded as follows.

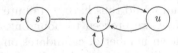

**Fig. 2.** A graph of a path *stuttutu*.

**Lemma 1.** *For every $K \subseteq S$ such that $K \notin \mathsf{BSCC}$, and every $s \in K$, $k \in \mathbb{N}$,*

$$\mathbb{P}[Cand_k(K) \mid \Diamond s] \leq (1 - p_{\min})^k.$$

*Example 4.* We illustrate how candidates "evolve over time" along a run. Consider a run $\rho = s_0 s_0 s_1 s_0 \ldots$ of the Markov chain in Fig. 3. The empty and one-letter prefix do not have the candidate defined, $s_0 s_0$ has a candidate $\{s_0\}$, then again $K(s_0 s_0 s_1) = \bot$, and $K(s_0 s_0 s_1 s_0) = \{s_0, s_1\}$. One can observe that subsequent candidates are either disjoint or contain some of the previous candidates. Consequently, there are at most $2|S| - 1$ candidates on every run, which is in our setting an unknown bound.    △

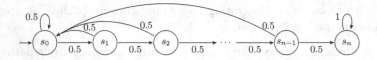

**Fig. 3.** A family (for $n \in \mathbb{N}$) of Markov chains with large eigenvalues.

While we have bounded the probability of detecting any specific non-BSCC set $K$ as a $k$-candidate, we need to bound the overall error for detecting a candidate that is not a BSCC. Since there can be many false candidates on a run before the real BSCC (e.g. Fig. 3), we need to bound the error of reporting any of them.

In the following, we first formalise the process of discovering candidates along the run. Second, we bound the error that any of the non-BSCC candidates becomes a $k$-candidate. Third, we bound the overall error of not detecting the real BSCC by increasing $k$ every time a different candidate is found.

We start with discovering the sequence of candidates on a run. For a run $\rho = s_0 s_1 \ldots$, consider the sequence of random variables defined by $K(s_0 \ldots s_j)$ for $j \geq 0$, and let $(K_i)_{i \geq 1}$ be the subsequence without undefined elements and with no repetition of consecutive elements. For example, for a run $\varrho = s_0 s_1 s_1 s_1 s_0 s_1 s_2 s_2 \ldots$, we have $K_1 = \{s_1\}$, $K_2 = \{s_0, s_1\}$, $K_3 = \{s_2\}$, etc. Let $K_j$ be the last element of this sequence, called the *final candidate*. Additionally, we define $K_\ell := K_j$ for all $\ell > j$. We describe the lifetime of a candidate. Given a non-final $K_i$, we write $\rho = \alpha_i \beta_i b_i \gamma_i d_i \delta_i$ so that $\overline{\alpha_i} \cap K_i = \emptyset$, $\overline{\beta_i b_i \gamma_i} = K_i$, $d_i \notin K_i$, and $K(\alpha_i \beta_i) \neq K_i$, $K(\alpha_i \beta_i b_i) = K_i$. Intuitively, we start exploring $K_i$ in $\beta_i$; $K_i$ becomes a candidate in $b_i$, the birthday of the $i$th candidate; it remains to be a candidate until $d_i$, the death of the $i$th candidate. For example, for the run $\varrho = s_0 s_1 s_1 s_1 s_0 s_1 s_2 s_2 \ldots$ and $i = 1$, $\alpha_1 = s_0$, $\beta_1 = s_1$, $b_1 = s_1$, $\gamma_1 = s_1$, $d_1 = s_0$, $\delta_1 = s_1 s_2 s_2 \varrho[8] \varrho[9] \ldots$. Note that the final candidate is almost surely a BSCC of $\mathcal{M}$ and would thus have $\gamma_j$ infinite.

Now, we proceed to bounding errors for each candidate. Since there is an unknown number of candidates on a run, we will need a slightly stronger definition. First, observe that $Cand_k(K_i)$ iff $K_i$ is a $k$-candidate of $\beta_i b_i \gamma_i$. We say $K_i$ is a *strong $k$-candidate*, written $SCand_k(K_i)$, if it is a $k$-candidate of $b_i \gamma_i$. Intuitively, it becomes a $k$-candidate even not counting the discovery phase. As

---

**Algorithm 1.** REACHEDBSCC

**Input:** path $\pi = s_0 s_1 \ldots s_n$, $p_{\min}, \delta \in (0,1]$
**Output:** Yes iff $K(\pi) \in \mathsf{BSCC}$
$\quad C \leftarrow \perp, i \leftarrow 0$
$\quad$ **for** $j = 0$ to $n$ **do**
$\qquad$ **if** $K(s_0 \ldots s_j) \neq \perp$ and $K(s_0 \ldots s_j) \neq C$ **then**
$\qquad\quad C \leftarrow K(s_0 \ldots s_j)$
$\qquad\quad i \leftarrow i + 1$
$\quad k_i \leftarrow \frac{i - \log \delta}{-\log(1 - p_{\min})}$
$\quad$ **if** $i \geq 1$ and $\mathrm{SCAND}_{k_i}(K(\pi), \pi)$ **then return Yes**
$\quad$ **else return No**

---

a result, even if we already assume there exists an $i$th candidate, its strong
$k$-candidacy gives the guarantees on being a BSCC as above in Lemma 1.

**Lemma 2.** *For every $i, k \in \mathbb{N}$, we have*

$$\mathbb{P}[SCand_k(K_i) \mid K_i \notin \mathsf{BSCC}] \leq (1 - p_{\min})^k.$$

Since the number of candidates can only be bounded with some knowledge
of the state space, e.g. its size, we assume no bounds and provide a method to
bound the error even for an unbounded number of candidates on a run.

**Lemma 3.** *For $(k_i)_{i=1}^{\infty} \in \mathbb{N}^{\mathbb{N}}$, let $\mathcal{E}rr$ be the set of runs such that for some
$i \in \mathbb{N}$, we have $SCand_{k_i}(K_i)$ despite $K_i \notin \mathsf{BSCC}$. Then*

$$\mathbb{P}[\mathcal{E}rr] < \sum_{i=1}^{\infty} (1 - p_{\min})^{k_i}.$$

In Algorithm 1 we present a procedure for deciding whether a BSCC inferred
from a path $\pi$ is indeed a BSCC with confidence greater than $1 - \delta$. We use notation $\mathrm{SCAND}_{k_i}(K, \pi)$ to denote the function deciding whether $K$ is a strong $k_i$-
candidate on $\pi$. The overall error bound is obtained by setting $k_i = \frac{i - \log \delta}{-\log(1 - p_{\min})}$.

**Theorem 1.** *For every $\delta > 0$, Algorithm 1 is correct with error probability at
most $\delta$.*

We have shown how to detect a BSCC of a single path with desired confidence. In Algorithm 2, we show how to use our BSCC detection method to
decide whether a given path reaches the set $G$ with confidence $1 - \delta$. The function $\mathsf{NextState}(\pi)$ randomly picks a state according to $\mu$ if the path is empty
($\pi = \lambda$); otherwise, if $\ell$ is the last state of $\pi$, it randomly chooses its successor
according to $\mathbf{P}(\ell, \cdot)$. The algorithm returns **Yes** when $\pi$ reaches a state in $G$,
and **No** when for some $i$, the $i$th candidate is a strong $k_i$-candidate. In the latter
case, with probability at least $1 - \delta$, $\pi$ has reached a BSCC not containing $G$.
Hence, with probability at most $\delta$, the algorithm returns **No** for a path that
could reach a goal.

## 3.2   Hypothesis Testing on a Bernoulli Variable Observed with Bounded Error

In the following, we show how to estimate the probability of reaching a set of goal states, by combining the BSCC detection and hypothesis testing. More specifically, we sample many paths of a Markov chain, decide for each whether it reaches the goal states (Algorithm 2), and then use hypothesis testing to estimate the event probability. The hypothesis testing is adapted to the fact that testing reachability on a single path may report false negatives.

Let $X_\Diamond^\delta$ be a Bernoulli random variable, such that $X_\Diamond^\delta = 1$ if and only if SINGLEPATHREACH$(G, p_{\min}, \delta) = $ **Yes**, describing the outcome of Algorithm 2. The following theorem establishes that $X_\Diamond^\delta$ estimates $\mathbb{P}[\Diamond G]$ with a bias bounded by $\delta$.

**Theorem 2.** *For every $\delta > 0$, we have $\mathbb{P}[\Diamond G] - \delta \leq \mathbb{E}[X_\Diamond^\delta] \leq \mathbb{P}[\Diamond G]$.*

In order to conclude on the value $\mathbb{P}[\Diamond G]$, the standard statistical model checking approach via hypothesis testing [28] decides between the hypothesis $H_0 : \mathbb{P}[\Diamond G] \geq p + \varepsilon$ and $H_1 : \mathbb{P}[\Diamond G] \leq p - \varepsilon$, where $\varepsilon$ is a desired indifference region. As we do not have precise observations on each path, we reduce this problem to a hypothesis testing on the variable $X_\Diamond^\delta$ with a narrower indifference region: $H_0' : \mathbb{E}[X_\Diamond^\delta] \geq p + (\varepsilon - \delta)$ and $H_1' : \mathbb{E}[X_\Diamond^\delta] \leq p - \varepsilon$, for some $\delta < \varepsilon$.

We define the reduction simply as follows. Given a statistical test $T'$ for $H_0', H_1'$ we define a test $T$ that accepts $H_0$ if $T'$ accepts $H_0'$, and $H_1$ otherwise. The following lemma shows that $T$ has the same strength as $T'$.

**Lemma 4.** *Suppose the test $T'$ decides between $H_0'$ and $H_1'$ with strength $(\alpha, \beta)$. Then the test $T$ decides between $H_0$ with $H_1$ with strength $(\alpha, \beta)$.*

Lemma 4 gives us the following algorithm to decide between $H_0$ and $H_1$. We generate samples $x_0, x_1, \ldots, x_n \sim X_\Diamond^\delta$ from SINGLEPATHREACH$(G, p_{\min}, \delta)$, and apply a statistical test to decide between $H_0'$ and $H_1'$. Finally, we accept $H_0$ if $H_0'$ was accepted by the test, and $H_1$ otherwise. In our implementation, we used the sequential probability ration test (SPRT) [24,25] for hypothesis testing.

---

**Algorithm 2.** SINGLEPATHREACH

---

**Input:** goal states $G$ of $\mathcal{M}$, $p_{\min}, \delta \in (0, 1]$
**Output: Yes** iff a run reaches $G$

  $\pi \leftarrow \lambda$
  **repeat**
    $s \leftarrow$ NextState$(\pi)$
    $\pi \leftarrow \pi . s$
    **if** $s \in G$ **then return Yes**            ▷ We have provably reached $G$
  **until** REACHEDBSCC$(\pi, p_{\min}, \delta)$
  **return No**                ▷ By Theorem 1, $\mathbb{P}[K(\pi) \in$ BSCC$] \geq 1 - \delta$

# 4    Extensions

In this section, we present how the on-the-fly BSCC detection can be used for verifying LTL and quantitative properties (mean payoff).

## 4.1    Linear Temporal Logic

We show how our method extends to properties expressible by linear temporal logic (LTL) [19] and, in the same manner, to all $\omega$-regular properties. Given a finite set $Ap$ of atomic propositions, a *labelled Markov chain* (LMC) is a tuple $\mathcal{M} = (S, \mathbf{P}, \mu, Ap, L)$, where $(S, \mathbf{P}, \mu)$ is a MC and $L : S \to 2^{Ap}$ is a labelling function. Definition of LTL formulae is standard and for reader's convenience recalled in the full version [2], along with other standard details omitted in this section. Given a labelled Markov chain $\mathcal{M}$ and an LTL formula $\varphi$, we are interested in the measure $\mathbb{P}[\mathcal{M} \models \varphi] := \mathbb{P}[\{\rho \in \mathsf{Runs} \mid L(\rho) \models \varphi\}]$, where $L$ is naturally extended to runs by $L(\rho)[i] = L(\rho[i])$ for all $i$.

For every LTL formula $\varphi$, one can construct a *deterministic Rabin automaton* (DRA) $\mathcal{A} = (Q, 2^{Ap}, \gamma, q_o, Acc)$ that accepts all runs that satisfy $\varphi$ [3]. Here $Q$ is a finite set of states, $\gamma : Q \times 2^{Ap} \to Q$ is the transition function, $q_o \in Q$ is the initial state, and $Acc \subseteq 2^Q \times 2^Q$ is the acceptance condition. Further, the product of a MC $\mathcal{M}$ and DRA $\mathcal{A}$ is the Markov chain $\mathcal{M} \otimes \mathcal{A} = (S \times Q, \mathbf{P}', \mu')$, where $\mathbf{P}'((s, q), (s', q')) = \mathbf{P}(s, s')$ if $q' = \gamma(q, L(s'))$ and $\mathbf{P}'((s, q), (s', q')) = 0$ otherwise, and $\mu'(s, q) = \mu(s)$ if $\gamma(q_o, L(s)) = q$ and $\mu'(s, q) = 0$ otherwise. Note that $\mathcal{M} \otimes \mathcal{A}$ has the same smallest transition probability $p_{\min}$ as $\mathcal{M}$.

The crux of LTL probabilistic model checking relies on the fact that the probability of satisfying an LTL property $\varphi$ in a Markov chain $\mathcal{M}$ equals the probability of reaching an accepting BSCC in the Markov chain $\mathcal{M} \otimes \mathcal{A}_\varphi$. Formally, a BSCC $C$ of $\mathcal{M} \otimes \mathcal{A}_\varphi$ is *accepting* if for some $(E, F) \in Acc$ we have $C \cap (S \times E) = \emptyset$ and $C \cap (S \times F) \neq \emptyset$. Let $\mathsf{AccBSCC}$ denote the union of all accepting BSCCs in $\mathcal{M}$. Then we obtain the following well-known fact [3]:

**Lemma 5.** *For every labelled Markov chain $\mathcal{M}$ and LTL formula $\varphi$, we have* $\mathbb{P}[\mathcal{M} \models \varphi] = \mathbb{P}[\Diamond \mathsf{AccBSCC}]$.

---

**Algorithm 3.** SINGLEPATHLTL

---

**Input:** DRA $\mathcal{A} = (Q, 2^{Ap}, \gamma, q_o, Acc)$, $p_{\min}, \delta \in (0, 1]$
**Output: Yes** iff the final candidate is an accepting BSCC
    $q \leftarrow q_o, \pi \leftarrow \lambda$
    **repeat**
        $s \leftarrow \mathsf{NextState}(\pi)$
        $q \leftarrow \gamma(q, L(s))$
        $\pi \leftarrow \pi . (s, q)$
    **until** REACHEDBSCC$(\pi, p_{\min}, \delta)$         $\triangleright \mathbb{P}[K(\pi) \in \mathsf{BSCC}] \geq 1 - \delta$
    **return** $\exists (E, F) \in Acc : K(\pi) \cap (S \times E) = \emptyset \wedge K(\pi) \cap (S \times F) \neq \emptyset$

---

Since the input used is a Rabin automaton, the method applies to all $\omega$-regular properties. Let $X_\varphi^\delta$ be a Bernoulli random variable, such that $X_\varphi^\delta = 1$ if and only if SINGLEPATHLTL$(\mathcal{A}_\varphi, p_{\min}, \delta) = \textbf{Yes}$. Since the BSCC must be reached and fully explored to classify it correctly, the error of the algorithm can now be both-sided.

**Theorem 3.** *For every $\delta > 0$, $\mathbb{P}[\mathcal{M} \models \varphi] - \delta \leq \mathbb{E}[X_\varphi^\delta] \leq \mathbb{P}[\mathcal{M} \models \varphi] + \delta$.*

Further, like in Sect. 3.2, we can reduce the hypothesis testing problem for

$$H_0 : \mathbb{P}[\mathcal{M} \models \varphi] \geq p + \varepsilon \qquad \text{and} \qquad H_1 : \mathbb{P}[\mathcal{M} \models \varphi] \leq p - \varepsilon$$

for any $\delta < \varepsilon$ to the following hypothesis testing problem on the observable $X_\varphi^\delta$

$$H_0' : \mathbb{E}[X_\varphi^\delta] \geq p + (\varepsilon - \delta) \qquad \text{and} \qquad H_1' : \mathbb{E}[X_\varphi^\delta] \leq p - (\varepsilon - \delta).$$

## 4.2   Mean Payoff

We show that our method extends also to quantitative properties, such as mean payoff (also called long-run average reward). Let $\mathcal{M} = (S, \mathbf{P}, \mu)$ be a Markov chain and $r : S \to [0, 1]$ be a *reward* function. Denoting by $S_i$ the random variable returning the $i$-th state on a run, the aim is to compute

$$\text{MP} := \lim_{n \to \infty} \mathbb{E}\left[\frac{1}{n} \sum_{i=1}^{n} r(S_i)\right].$$

This limit exists (see, e.g. [17]), and equals $\sum_{C \in \text{BSCC}} \mathbb{P}[\lozenge C] \cdot \text{MP}_C$, where $\text{MP}_C$ is the mean payoff of runs ending in $C$. Note that $\text{MP}_C$ can be computed from $r$ and transition probabilities in $C$ [17]. We have already shown how our method estimates $\mathbb{P}[\lozenge C]$. Now we show how it extends to estimating transition probabilities in BSCCs and thus the mean payoff.

First, we focus on a single path $\pi$ that has reached a BSCC $C = K(\pi)$ and show how to estimate the transition probabilities $\mathbf{P}(s, s')$ for each $s, s' \in C$. Let $X_{s,s'}$ be the random variable denoting the event that $\text{NextState}(s) = s'$. $X_{s,s'}$ is a Bernoulli variable with parameter $\mathbf{P}(s, s')$, so we use the obvious estimator $\hat{\mathbf{P}}(s, s') = \#_{ss'}(\pi)/\#_s(\pi)$, where $\#_\alpha(\pi)$ is the number of occurrences of $\alpha$ in $\pi$. If $\pi$ is long enough so that $\#_s(\pi)$ is large enough, the estimation is guaranteed to have desired precision $\xi$ with desired confidence $(1 - \delta_{s,s'})$. Indeed, using Höffding's inequality, we obtain

$$\mathbb{P}[\hat{\mathbf{P}}(s, s') - \mathbf{P}(s, s')| > \xi] \leq \delta_{s,s'} = 2e^{-2\#_s(\pi) \cdot \xi^2}. \tag{1}$$

Hence, we can extend the path $\pi$ with candidate $C$ until it is long enough so that we have a $1 - \delta_C$ confidence that all the transition probabilities in $C$ are in the $\xi$-neighbourhood of our estimates, by ensuring that $\sum_{s,s' \in C} \delta_{s,s'} < \delta_C$. These estimated transition probabilities $\hat{\mathbf{P}}$ induce a mean payoff $\hat{\text{MP}}_C$. Moreover, $\hat{\text{MP}}_C$ estimates the real mean payoff $\text{MP}_C$. Indeed, by [6,23],

$$|\hat{\text{MP}}_C - \text{MP}_C| \leq \zeta := \left(1 + \frac{\xi}{p_{\min}}\right)^{2 \cdot |C|} - 1. \tag{2}$$

Note that by Taylor's expansion, for small $\xi$, we have $\zeta \approx 2|C|\xi$.

---

**Algorithm 4.** SINGLEPATHMP

---

**Input:** reward function $r$, $p_{\mathsf{min}}, \zeta, \delta \in (0, 1]$,
**Output:** $\hat{\mathsf{MP}}_C$ such that $|\hat{\mathsf{MP}}_C - \mathsf{MP}_C| < \zeta$ where $C$ is the BSCC of the generated
    run
$\pi \leftarrow \lambda$
**repeat**
    $\pi \leftarrow \pi . \mathsf{NextState}(\pi)$
    **if** $K(\pi) \neq \perp$ **then**
        $\xi = p_{\mathsf{min}}((1 + \zeta)^{1/2|K(\pi)|} - 1)$         ▷ By Equation (2)
        $k \leftarrow \frac{\ln(2|K(\pi)|^2) - \ln(\delta/2)}{2\xi^2}$          ▷ By Equation (1)
    **until** REACHEDBSCC$(\pi, p_{\mathsf{min}}, \delta/2)$ and SCAND$_k(K(\pi), \pi)$
**return** $\hat{\mathsf{MP}}_{K(\pi)}$ computed from $\hat{\mathbf{P}}$ and $r$

---

Algorithm 4 extends Algorithm 2 as follows. It divides the confidence parameters $\delta$ into $\delta_{BSCC}$ (used as in Algorithm 2 to detect the BSCC) and $\delta_C$ (the total confidence for the estimates on transition probabilities). For simplicity, we set $\delta_{BSCC} = \delta_C = \delta/2$. First, we compute the bound $\xi$ required for $\zeta$-precision (by Eq. 2). Subsequently, we compute the required strength $k$ of the candidate guaranteeing $\delta_C$-confidence on $\hat{\mathbf{P}}$ (from Eq. 1). The path is prolonged until the candidate is strong enough; in such a case $\hat{\mathsf{MP}}_C$ is $\zeta$-approximated with $1 - \delta_C$ confidence. If the candidate of the path changes, all values are computed from scratch for the new candidate.

**Theorem 4.** *For every* $\delta > 0$, *the Algorithm 4 terminates correctly with probability at least* $1 - \delta$.

Let random variable $X_{\mathsf{MP}}^{\zeta, \delta}$ denote the value SINGLEPATHMP$(r, p_{\mathsf{min}}, \zeta, \delta)$. The following theorem establishes relation between the mean-payoff MP and the expected value of $X_{\mathsf{MP}}^{\zeta, \delta}$.

**Theorem 5.** *For every* $\delta, \zeta > 0$, $\mathsf{MP} - \zeta - \delta \leq \mathbb{E}[X_{\mathsf{MP}}^{\zeta, \delta}] \leq \mathsf{MP} + \zeta + \delta$.

As a consequence of Theorem 5, if we establish that with $(1 - \alpha)$ confidence $X_{\mathsf{MP}}^{\zeta, \delta}$ belongs to the interval $[a, b]$, then we can conclude with $(1 - \alpha)$ confidence that MP belongs to the interval $[a - \zeta - \delta, b + \zeta + \delta]$. Standard statistical methods can be applied to find the confidence bound for $X_{\mathsf{MP}}^{\zeta, \delta}$.

## 5  Experimental Evaluation

We implemented our algorithms in the probabilistic model checker PRISM [14], and evaluated them on the DTMC examples from the PRISM benchmark suite [15]. The benchmarks model communication and security protocols, distributed algorithms, and fault-tolerant systems. To demonstrate how our method performs depending on the topology of Markov chains, we also performed experiments on the generic DTMCs shown in Figs. 3 and 4, as well as on two CTMCs from the literature that have large BSCCs: "tandem" [11] and "gridworld" [27].

**Fig. 4.** A Markov chain with two transient parts consisting of $N$ strongly connected singletons, leading to BSCCs with the ring topology of $M$ states.

All benchmarks are parametrised by one or more values, which influence their size and complexity, e.g. the number of modelled components. We have made minor modifications to the benchmarks that could not be handled directly by the SMC component of PRISM, by adding self-loops to deadlock states and fixing one initial state instead of multiple.

Our tool can be downloaded at [1]. Experiments were done on a Linux 64-bit machine running an AMD Opteron 6134 CPU with a time limit of 15 min and a memory limit of 5GB. To increase performance of our tool, we check whether a candidate has been found every 1000 steps; this optimization does not violate correctness of our analysis. See the full version of this paper [2] for a discussion on this bound.

**Reachability.** The experimental results for unbounded reachability are shown in Table 2. The PRISM benchmarks were checked against their standard properties, when available. We directly compare our method to another topology-agnostic method of [26] (SimTermination), where at every step the sampled path is terminated with probability $p_{\text{term}}$. The approach of [4] with a priori bounds is not included, since it times out even on the smallest benchmarks. In addition, we performed experiments on two methods that are topology-aware: sampling with reachability analysis of [26] (SimAnalysis) and the numerical model-checking algorithm of PRISM (MC). The full version [2] contains detailed experimental evaluation of these methods.

The table shows the size of every example, its minimum probability, the number of BSCCs, and the size of the largest BSCC. Column "time" reports the total wall time for the respective algorithm, and "analysis" shows the time for symbolic reachability analysis in the SimAnalysis method. Highlights show the best result among the topology-agnostic methods. All statistical methods were used with the SPRT test for choosing between the hypothesis, and their results were averaged over five runs.

Finding the optimal termination probability $p_{\text{term}}$ for the SimTermination method is a non-trivial task. If the probability is too high, the method might never reach the target states, thus give an incorrect result, and if the value is too low, then it might sample unnecessarily long traces that never reach the target. For instance, to ensure a correct answer on the Markov chain in Fig. 3, $p_{\text{term}}$ has to decrease exponentially with the number of states. By experimenting we found that the probability $p_{\text{term}} = 0.0001$ is low enough to ensure correct results. See the full version [2] for experiments with other values of $p_{\text{term}}$.

On most examples, our method scales better than the SimTermination method. Our method performs well even on examples with large BSCCs, such

**Table 2.** Experimental results for unbounded reachability. Simulation parameters: $\alpha = \beta = \varepsilon = 0.01$, $\delta = 0.001$, $p_{term} = 0.0001$. TO means time-out, and MO means memory-out. Our approach is denoted by SimAdaptive here. Highlights show the best result the among topology-agnostic methods.

| name | size | $p_{min}$ | BSCC no., max. size | SimAdaptive time | SimTermination[26] time | SimAnalysis[26] time | analysis | MC time |
|---|---|---|---|---|---|---|---|---|
| bluetooth(4) | 149K | $7.8 \cdot 10^{-3}$ | 3K, 1 | 2.6s | 16.4s | 83.2s | 80.4s | 78.2s |
| bluetooth(7) | 569K | $7.8 \cdot 10^{-3}$ | 5.8K, 1 | 3.8s | 50.2s | 284.4s | 281.1s | 261.2s |
| bluetooth(10) | >569K | $7.8 \cdot 10^{-3}$ | >5.8K, 1 | 5.0s | 109.2s | TO | - | TO |
| brp(500,500) | 4.5M | 0.01 | 1.5K, 1 | 7.6s | 13.8s | 35.6s | 30.7s | 103.0s |
| brp(2K,2K) | 40M | 0.01 | 4.5K, 1 | 20.4s | 17.2s | 824.4s | 789.9s | TO |
| brp(10K,10K) | >40M | 0.01 | >4.5K, 1 | 89.2s | 15.8s | TO | - | TO |
| crowds(6,15) | 7.3M | 0.066 | >3K, 1 | 3.6s | 253.2s | 2.0s | 0.7s | 19.4s |
| crowds(7,20) | 17M | 0.05 | >3K, 1 | 4.0s | 283.8s | 2.6s | 1.1s | 347.8s |
| crowds(8,20) | 68M | 0.05 | >3K, 1 | 5.6s | 340.0s | 4.0s | 1.9s | TO |
| eql(15,10) | 616G | 0.5 | 1, 1 | 16.2s | TO | 151.8s | 145.1s | 110.4s |
| eql(20,15) | 1279T | 0.5 | 1, 1 | 28.8s | TO | 762.6s | 745.4s | 606.6s |
| eql(20,20) | 1719T | 0.5 | 1, 1 | 31.4s | TO | TO | - | TO |
| herman(17) | 129M | $7.6 \cdot 10^{-6}$ | 1, 34 | 23.0s | 33.6s | 21.6s | 0.1s | 1.2s |
| herman(19) | 1162M | $1.9 \cdot 10^{-6}$ | 1, 38 | 96.8s | 134.0s | 86.2s | 0.1s | 1.2s |
| herman(21) | 10G | $4.7 \cdot 10^{-7}$ | 1, 42 | 570.0s | TO | 505.2s | 0.1s | 1.4s |
| leader(6,6) | 280K | $2.1 \cdot 10^{-5}$ | 1, 1 | 5.0s | 5.4s | 536.6s | 530.3s | 491.4s |
| leader(6,8) | >280K | $3.8 \cdot 10^{-6}$ | 1, 1 | 23.0s | 26.0s | MO | - | MO |
| leader(6,11) | >280K | $5.6 \cdot 10^{-7}$ | 1, 1 | 153.0s | 174.8s | MO | - | MO |
| nand(50,3) | 11M | 0.02 | 51, 1 | 7.0s | 231.2s | 36.2s | 31.0s | 272.0s |
| nand(60,4) | 29M | 0.02 | 61, 1 | 6.0s | 275.2s | 60.2s | 56.3s | TO |
| nand(70,5) | 67M | 0.02 | 71, 1 | 6.8s | 370.2s | 148.2s | 144.2s | TO |
| tandem(500) | >1.7M | $2.4 \cdot 10^{-5}$ | 1, >501K | 2.4s | 6.4s | 4.6s | 3.0s | 3.4s |
| tandem(1K) | 1.7M | $9.9 \cdot 10^{-5}$ | 1, 501K | 2.6s | 19.2s | 17.0s | 12.7s | 13.0s |
| tandem(2K) | >1.7M | $4.9 \cdot 10^{-5}$ | 1, >501K | 3.4s | 72.4s | 62.4s | 59.8s | 59.4s |
| gridworld(300) | 162M | $1 \cdot 10^{-3}$ | 598, 89K | 8.2s | 81.6s | MO | - | MO |
| gridworld(400) | 384M | $1 \cdot 10^{-3}$ | 798, 160K | 8.4s | 100.6s | MO | - | MO |
| gridworld(500) | 750M | $1 \cdot 10^{-3}$ | 998, 250K | 5.8s | 109.4s | MO | - | MO |
| Fig.3(16) | 37 | 0.5 | 1, 1 | 58.6s | TO | 23.4s | 0.4s | 2.0s |
| Fig.3(18) | 39 | 0.5 | 1, 1 | TO | TO | 74.8.0s | 1.8s | 2.0s |
| Fig.3(20) | 41 | 0.5 | 1, 1 | TO | TO | 513.6s | 11.3s | 2.0s |
| Fig.4(1K,5) | 4022 | 0.5 | 2, 5 | 7.8s | 218.2s | 3.2s | 0.5s | 1.2s |
| Fig.4(1K,50) | 4202 | 0.5 | 2, 50 | 12.4s | 211.8s | 3.6s | 0.7s | 1.0s |
| Fig.4(1K,500) | 6002 | 0.5 | 2, 500, | 431.0s | 218.6s | 3.6s | 1.0s | 1.2s |
| Fig.4(10K,5) | 40K | 0.5 | 2, 5 | 52.2s | TO | 42.2s | 25.4s | 25.6s |
| Fig.4(100K,5) | 400K | 0.5 | 2, 5 | 604.2s | 5.4s | TO | - | TO |

as "tandem" and "gridworld," due to early termination when a goal state is reached. For instance, on the "gridworld" example, most BSCCs do not contain a goal state, thus have to be fully explored, however the probability of reaching such BSCC is low, and as a consequence full BSCC exploration rarely occurs. The SimTermination method performs well when the target states are unreachable or can be reached by short paths. When long paths are necessary to reach the target, the probability that an individual path reaches the target is small, hence many samples are necessary to estimate the real probability with high confidence.

Moreover, it turns out that our method compares well even with methods that have access to the topology of the system. In many cases, the running

**Table 3.** Experimental results for LTL and mean-payoff properties. Simulation parameters for LTL: $\alpha = \beta = \varepsilon = 0.01$, $\delta = 0.001$, for mean-payoff we computed 95%-confidence bound of size 0.22 with $\delta = 0.011, \zeta = 0.08$.

| | | LTL | | | Mean payoff | |
|---|---|---|---|---|---|---|
| name | property | SimAdaptive time | MC time | name | SimAdaptive time | MC time |
| bluetooth(10) | □◊ | 8.0s | TO | bluetooth(10) | 3.0s | TO |
| brp(10K,10K) | ◊□ | 90.0s | TO | brp(10K,10K) | 6.6s | TO |
| crowds(8,20) | ◊□ | 9.0s | TO | crowds(8,20) | 2.0s | TO |
| eql(20,20) | □◊ | 7.0s | MO | eql(20,20) | 2.6s | TO |
| herman(21) | □◊ | TO | 2.0s | herman(21) | MO | 3.0s |
| leader(6,5) | □◊ | 277.0s | 117.0s | leader(6,6) | 48.5 | 576.0 |
| nand(70,5) | □◊ | 4.0s | TO | nand(70,5) | 2.0s | 294.0s |
| tandem(2K) | □◊ | TO | 221.0s | tandem(500) | TO | 191.0s |
| gridworld(100) | □◊ → ◊□ | TO | 110.4s | gridworld(50) | TO | 58.1s |
| Fig.3(20) | □◊ → □◊ | TO | 3.4 | Fig.3(20) | TO | 1.8s |
| Fig.4(100K,5) | □◊ | 348.0s | TO | Fig.4(100K,5) | 79.6s | TO |
| Fig.4(1K,500) | □◊ | 827.0s | 2.0s | Fig.4(1K,500) | TO | 2.0s |

time of the numerical algorithm MC increases dramatically with the size of the system, while remaining almost constant in our method. The bottleneck of the SimAnalysis algorithm is the reachability analysis of states that cannot reach the target, which in practice can be as difficult as numerical model checking.

**LTL and Mean Payoff.** In the second experiment, we compared our algorithm for checking LTL properties and estimating the mean payoff with the numerical methods of PRISM; the results are shown in Table 3. We compare against PRISM, since we are not aware of any SMC-based or topology-agnostic approach for mean payoff, or full LTL. For mean payoff, we computed 95%-confidence bound of size 0.22 with parameters $\delta = 0.011, \zeta = 0.08$, and for LTL we used the same parameters as for reachability. Due to space limitations, we report results only on some models of each type, where either method did not time out. In general our method scales better when BSCCs are fairly small and are discovered quickly.

## 6    Discussion and Conclusion

As demonstrated by the experimental results, our method is fast on systems that are (1) shallow, and (2) with small BSCCs. In such systems, the BSCC is reached quickly and the candidate is built-up quickly. Further, recall that the BSCC is reported when a $k$-candidate is found, and that $k$ is increased with each candidate along the path. Hence, when there are many strongly connected sets, and thus many candidates, the BSCC is detected by a $k$-candidate for a large $k$. However, since $k$ grows linearly in the number of candidates, the most important and limiting factor is the size of BSCCs.

We state the dependency on the depth of the system and BSCC sizes formally. We pick $\delta := \frac{\varepsilon}{2}$ and let

$$sim = \frac{-\log \frac{\beta}{1-\alpha} \log \frac{1-\beta}{\alpha}}{\log \frac{p-\varepsilon+\delta}{p+\varepsilon-\delta} \log \frac{1-p-\varepsilon+\delta}{1-p+\varepsilon-\delta}} \quad \text{and} \quad k_i = \frac{i - \log \delta}{-\log(1 - p_{\min})}$$

denote the a priori upper bound on the number of simulations necessary for SPRT [24,25] and the strength of candidates as in Algorithm 2, respectively.

**Theorem 6.** *Let $R$ denote the expected number of steps before reaching a BSCC and $B$ the maximum size of a BSCC. Further, let $T :=$ $\max_{C \in \mathrm{BSCC}; s, s' \in C} \mathbb{E}[\mathit{time\,to\,reach}\, s'\, \mathit{from}\, s]$. In particular, $T \in \mathcal{O}(B/p_{\min}^B)$. Then the expected running time of Algorithms 2 and 3 is at most*

$$\mathcal{O}(sim \cdot k_{R+B} \cdot B \cdot T).$$

Systems that have large deep BSCCs require longer time to reach for the required level of confidence. However, such systems are often difficult to handle also for other methods agnostic of the topology. For instance, correctness of [26] on the example in Fig. 3 relies on the termination probability $p_{\mathrm{term}}$ being at most $1 - \lambda$, which is less than $2^{-n}$ here. Larger values lead to incorrect results and smaller values to paths of exponential length. Nevertheless, our procedure usually runs faster than the bound suggest; for detailed discussion see [2].

**Conclusion.** To the best of our knowledge, we propose the first statistical model-checking method that exploits the information provided by each simulation run on the fly, in order to detect quickly a potential BSCC, and verify LTL properties with the desired confidence. This is also the first application of SMC to quantitative properties such as mean payoff. We note that for our method to work correctly, the precise value of $p_{\min}$ is not necessary, but a lower bound is sufficient. This lower bound can come from domain knowledge, or can be inferred directly from description of white-box systems, such as the PRISM benchmark.

The approach we present is not meant to replace the other methods, but rather to be an addition to the repertoire of available approaches. Our method is particularly valuable for models that have small BSCCs and huge state space, such as many of the PRISM benchmarks.

In future work, we plan to investigate the applicability of our method to Markov decision processes, and to deciding language equivalence between two Markov chains.

# References

1. Tool for the paper. http://pub.ist.ac.at/~przemek/pa_tool.html
2. Daca, P., Henzinger, T.A., Kretínský, J., Petrov, T.: Faster statistical model checking for unbounded temporal properties. In: CoRR, abs/1504.05739 (2015)
3. Baier, C., Katoen, J.-P.: Principles of Model Checking. MIT Press, Cambridge (2008)
4. Brázdil, T., Chatterjee, K., Chmelík, M., Forejt, V., Křetínský, J., Kwiatkowska, M., Parker, D., Ujma, M.: Verification of Markov decision processes using learning algorithms. In: Cassez, F., Raskin, J.-F. (eds.) ATVA 2014. LNCS, vol. 8837, pp. 98–114. Springer, Heidelberg (2014)

5. Bulychev, P.E., David, A., Larsen, K.G., Mikucionis, M., Poulsen, D.B., Legay, A., Wang, Z.: UPPAAL-SMC: statistical model checking for priced timed automata. In: QAPL, pp. 1–16 (2012)
6. Chatterjee, K.: Robustness of structurally equivalent concurrent parity games. In: Birkedal, L. (ed.) FOSSACS 2012. LNCS, vol. 7213, pp. 270–285. Springer, Heidelberg (2012)
7. David, A., Larsen, K.G., Legay, A., Mikucionis, M., Poulsen, D.B.: Uppaal SMC tutorial. STTT **17**(4), 397–415 (2015)
8. Grosu, R., Smolka, S.A.: Monte carlo model checking. In: Halbwachs, N., Zuck, L.D. (eds.) TACAS 2005. LNCS, vol. 3440, pp. 271–286. Springer, Heidelberg (2005)
9. He, R., Jennings, P., Basu, S, Ghosh, A.P., Wu, H.: A bounded statistical approach for model checking of unbounded until properties. In: ASE, pp. 225–234 (2010)
10. Hérault, T., Lassaigne, R., Magniette, F., Peyronnet, S.: Approximate probabilistic model checking. In: Steffen, B., Levi, G. (eds.) VMCAI 2004. LNCS, vol. 2937, pp. 73–84. Springer, Heidelberg (2004)
11. Hermanns, H., Meyer-Kayser, J., Siegle, M.: Multi terminal binary decision diagrams to represent and analyse continuous time Markov chains. In: 3rd International Workshop on the Numerical Solution of Markov Chains, pp. 188–207. Citeseer (1999)
12. Jegourel, C., Legay, A., Sedwards, S.: A platform for high performance statistical model checking – PLASMA. In: Flanagan, C., König, B. (eds.) TACAS 2012. LNCS, vol. 7214, pp. 498–503. Springer, Heidelberg (2012)
13. Jha, S.K., Clarke, E.M., Langmead, C.J., Legay, A., Platzer, A., Zuliani, P.: A Bayesian approach to model checking biological systems. In: Degano, P., Gorrieri, R. (eds.) CMSB 2009. LNCS, vol. 5688, pp. 218–234. Springer, Heidelberg (2009)
14. Kwiatkowska, M., Norman, G., Parker, D.: PRISM 4.0: verification of probabilistic real-time systems. In: Gopalakrishnan, G., Qadeer, S. (eds.) CAV 2011. LNCS, vol. 6806, pp. 585–591. Springer, Heidelberg (2011)
15. Kwiatkowska, M.Z., Norman, G., Parker, D.: The PRISM benchmark suite. In: QUEST, pp. 203–204 (2012)
16. Lassaigne, R., Peyronnet, S.: Probabilistic verification and approximation. Ann. Pure Appl. Logic **152**(1–3), 122–131 (2008)
17. Norris, J.R.: Markov Chains. Cambridge University Press, Cambridge (1998)
18. Oudinet, J., Denise, A., Gaudel, M.-C., Lassaigne, R., Peyronnet, S.: Uniform monte-carlo model checking. In: Giannakopoulou, D., Orejas, F. (eds.) FASE 2011. LNCS, vol. 6603, pp. 127–140. Springer, Heidelberg (2011)
19. Pnueli, A.: The temporal logic of programs. In: FOCS, pp. 46–57 (1977)
20. El Rabih, D., Pekergin, N.: Statistical model checking using perfect simulation. In: Liu, Z., Ravn, A.P. (eds.) ATVA 2009. LNCS, vol. 5799, pp. 120–134. Springer, Heidelberg (2009)
21. Sen, K., Viswanathan, M., Agha, G.: Statistical model checking of black-box probabilistic systems. In: Alur, R., Peled, D.A. (eds.) CAV 2004. LNCS, vol. 3114, pp. 202–215. Springer, Heidelberg (2004)
22. Sen, K., Viswanathan, M., Agha, G.: On statistical model checking of stochastic systems. In: Etessami, K., Rajamani, S.K. (eds.) CAV 2005. LNCS, vol. 3576, pp. 266–280. Springer, Heidelberg (2005)
23. Solan, E.: Continuity of the value of competitive Markov decision processes. J. Theor. Probab. **16**(4), 831–845 (2003)
24. Wald, A.: Sequential tests of statistical hypotheses. Ann. Math. Stat. **16**(2), 117–186 (1945)

25. Younes, H.L.S.: Planning and verification for stochastic processes with asynchronous events. In: AAAI, pp. 1001–1002 (2004)
26. Younes, H.L.S., Clarke, E.M., Zuliani, P.: Statistical verification of probabilistic properties with unbounded until. In: Davies, J. (ed.) SBMF 2010. LNCS, vol. 6527, pp. 144–160. Springer, Heidelberg (2011)
27. Younes, H.L.S., Kwiatkowska, M.Z., Norman, G., Parker, D.: Numerical vs. statistical probabilistic model checking. STTT 8(3), 216–228 (2006)
28. Younes, H.L.S., Simmons, R.G.: Probabilistic verification of discrete event systems using acceptance sampling. In: Brinksma, E., Larsen, K.G. (eds.) CAV 2002. LNCS, vol. 2404, pp. 223–235. Springer, Heidelberg (2002)

# Safety-Constrained Reinforcement Learning for MDPs

Sebastian Junges[1], Nils Jansen[1,2]([⊠]), Christian Dehnert[1], Ufuk Topcu[2], and Joost-Pieter Katoen[1]

[1] RWTH Aachen University, Aachen, Germany
[2] University of Texas at Austin, Austin, USA
njansen@utexas.edu

**Abstract.** We consider controller synthesis for stochastic and partially unknown environments in which safety is essential. Specifically, we abstract the problem as a Markov decision process in which the expected performance is measured using a cost function that is *unknown* prior to run-time exploration of the state space. Standard learning approaches synthesize cost-optimal strategies without guaranteeing safety properties. To remedy this, we first compute safe, permissive strategies. Then, exploration is constrained to these strategies and thereby meets the imposed safety requirements. Exploiting an iterative learning procedure, the resulting strategy is safety-constrained and optimal. We show correctness and completeness of the method and discuss the use of several heuristics to increase its scalability. Finally, we demonstrate the applicability by means of a prototype implementation.

## 1 Introduction

*Probabilistic Model Checking.* Many formal system models are inherently stochastic, consider for instance randomized distributed algorithms (where randomization breaks the symmetry between processes), security (e.g., key generation at encryption), systems biology (where species randomly react depending on their concentration), or embedded systems (interacting with unknown and varying environments). These various applications made the *verification* of stochastic systems such as discrete-time Markov chains (MCs) or Markov decision processes (MDPs) an important research topic in the last decade, resulting in several tools like PRISM [1], LiQuoR [2], MRMC [3] or FMurphi [4]. The always growing set of case studies in the PRISM benchmark suite [5] witnesses the applicability of MDP and MC model checking.

*Controller Synthesis.* Contrarily, controller synthesis is a relatively new topic in this setting. Consider a controllable system like, e. g., a robot or some other

This work is supported by the Excellence Initiative of the German Research Council and the Sino-German project CAP. UT's work has been partly funded by the awards AFRL # FA8650-15-C-2546, ONR # N000141310778, ARO # W911NF-15-1-0592, NSF # 1550212 and DARPA # W911NF-16-1-0001.

M. Chechik and J.-F. Raskin (Eds.): TACAS 2016, LNCS 9636, pp. 130–146, 2016.
DOI: 10.1007/978-3-662-49674-9_8

machine which is embedded into an environment. Having a formal model of both the controllable entity and the environment, the goal is to synthesize a controller that satisfies certain requirements. Again, often faithful models are stochastic, imagine, e. g., sensor imprecisions of a robot, message loss, or unpredictable behavior of the environment. Moreover, it might be the case that certain information—such as cost caused by energy consumption—is not exactly known prior to exploring and observation.

*Our Problem.* Given an MDP with a cost structure, synthesize an optimal strategy subject to safety constraints, where optimality refers to expected performance (cost). This multi-objective model checking problem is studied in [6–8]. But what if the cost function is not known? Consider for instance the following motion planning scenario, placed in a grid-world where a robot wants to move to a certain position. Acting unpredictably, a janitor moves randomly through the grid. The robot reaches its goal *safely* if it moves according to a strategy that avoids the janitor. Moreover, each movement of the robot occasions cost depending on the surface. However, the robot only learns the actual costs during physically executing actions within the environment; this requires the exclusion of unsafe behavior prior to exploration. Consequently, a safe strategy for the robot which simultaneously induces minimal cost is to be found.

We model robot behavior by an MDP and the stochastic behavior of the environment by a MC. We are given a *safety condition* specified as a probabilistic reachability objective. Additionally, we have a *performance condition* bounding the *expected costs* for reaching a certain goal. A significant problem we are facing is that the costs of certain actions are not known before they are executed. This calls for using reinforcement learning [9] algorithms like Q-learning [10], where optimal strategies are obtained without prior knowledge about the system. While this is usually a suitable solution, in this case we have to ensure that no unsafe actions are taken during exploration to ensure an optimal and safe strategy.

*Our Approach.* The setting does neither allow for using plain verification nor direct reinforcement learning. On the one hand, verifying safety and performance properties—in the form of multi-objective model checking—is not possible because the costs of actions are not known. On the other hand, in practice learning means that the robot will explore parts of the system. Doing that, we need to ensure that all unsafe behavior is avoided *beforehand.* Our solution to these problems is to use the notion of *permissive schedulers.* In contrast to standard schedulers, where for each system run the next action to take is fixed, more permissiveness is given in the sense that several actions are allowed. The first step is to compute a *safe* permissive scheduler which allows only safe behavior. The system is then restricted according to this scheduler (or strategy) and fit for *safe exploration.*

It would be desirable to compute a permissive scheduler which encompasses the set of *all* safe schedulers. Having this would ensure that via reinforcement learning a safe scheduler inducing *optimal* cost would obtained. Unfortunately, there is no efficient representation of such a *maximal permissive scheduler.* Therefore, we propose an iterative approach utilizing SMT-solving where a safe permissive scheduler is computed. Out of this, reinforcement learning determines the *locally optimal* scheduler. In the next iteration, this scheduler is explicitly excluded and a new permissive scheduler is obtained. This is iterated until the performance criterion is satisfied or until the solution is determined to be globally optimal which can be done using known lower bounds on the occurring costs.

*Related Work.* In [11], the computation of permissive schedulers for stochastic 2-player games is proposed for reward properties without additional safety-constraints. A dedicated mixed-integer linear programming (MILP) encoding optimizes w. r. t. certain *penalties* for actions. In [12], permissive safe scheduling is investigated for transition systems and LTL properties. Safe or constrained (e.g., by temporal logic specifications) exploration has also been investigated in the learning literature. Some recent examples include [13,14]. In [15], safety guarantees are added via the usage of Gaussian processes. An overview on safe exploration using reinforcement learning can be found in [16].

*Summary of the Contributions.* We give the first approach to controller synthesis for stochastic systems regarding safety and performance in a setting where models are known but costs are not. This encompasses:

- an iterative approach to the computation of safe permissive schedulers based on SMT-solving;
- exploitation of permissive schedulers for reinforcement learning towards globally optimal solutions;
- a discussion of several heuristics to both speed up the computations and avoid too many iterations; and
- a prototype implementation showing promising results on several case studies.

The paper is structured as follows: First, we provide basic notations and formal prerequisites in Sect. 2. In Sect. 3 we introduce our notion of permissive schedulers, discuss efficient representations, and introduce technicalities that are needed afterwards. Section 4 presents our main results on computing safe and optimal schedulers. After presenting several case studies and benchmark results in Sect. 5, we finally draw a conclusion and point to future work in Sect. 6.

## 2    Preliminaries

In this section, we introduce the required models and specifications considered in this paper, and provide a formal problem statement.

*Models.* For a set $X$, let $2^X$ denote the power set of $X$. A *probability distribution* over a finite or countably infinite set $X$ is a function $\mu\colon X \to [0,1] \subseteq \mathbb{R}$ with $\sum_{x \in X} \mu(x) = \mu(X) = 1$. In this paper, all probabilities are taken from $\mathbb{Q}$. Let the set of all distributions on $X$ be denoted by $Distr(X)$. The set $supp(\mu) = \{x \in X \mid \mu(x) > 0\}$ is the *support* of $\mu \in Distr(X)$. If $\mu(x) = 1$ for $x \in X$ and $\mu(y) = 0$ for all $y \in X \setminus \{x\}$, $\mu$ is called a *Dirac distribution*.

**Definition 1 (MDP).** *A Markov decision process (MDP) $\mathcal{M} = (S, s_I, Act, \mathcal{P})$ is a tuple with a finite set $S$ of states, a unique initial state $s_I \in S$, a finite set Act of actions, and a (partial) probabilistic transition function $\mathcal{P} \colon S \times Act \to Distr(S)$.*

MDPs operate by means of *nondeterministic choices* of actions at each state, whose successors are then determined *probabilistically* w.r.t. the associated probability distribution. The set of *enabled* actions at state $s \in S$ is denoted by $Act(s) = \{a \in Act \mid \exists \mu \in Distr(S).\, \mu = \mathcal{P}(s, \alpha)\}$. To avoid deadlock states, we assume that $|Act(s)| \geq 1$ for all $s \in S$. A *cost function* $\rho \colon S \times Act \to \mathbb{R}_{\geq 0}$ for an MDP $\mathcal{M}$ adds a cost to each *transition* $(s, a) \in S \times Act$ with $a \in Act(s)$.

A *path* in an $\mathcal{M}$ is a finite (or infinite) sequence $\pi = s_0 a_0 s_1 a_1 \ldots$ with $\mathcal{P}(s_i, \alpha, s_{i+1}) > 0$ for all $i \geq 0$. The set of all paths in $\mathcal{M}$ is denoted by $Paths^{\mathcal{M}}$, all paths starting in state $s \in S$ by $Paths^{\mathcal{M}}(s)$. The cost of finite path $\pi$ is defined as the sum of the costs of all transitions in $\pi$, i.e., $\rho(\pi) = \sum_{i=0}^{n-1} \rho(s_i, a_i)$ where $n$ is the number of transitions in $\pi$.

If $|Act(s)| = 1$ for all $s \in S$, all actions can be disregarded and the MDP $\mathcal{M}$ reduces to a *discrete-time Markov chain (MC)*, sometimes denoted by $\mathcal{D}$, yielding a transition probability transition function of the form $\mathcal{P} \colon S \to Distr(S)$. The *unique probability measure* $\mathrm{Pr}^{\mathcal{D}}(\Pi)$ for set $\Pi$ of infinite paths of MC $\mathcal{D}$ can be defined by the usual cylinder set construction, see [17] for details. The *expected cost* of the set $\Pi$ of paths, denoted by $\mathrm{EC}^{\mathcal{D}}(\Pi)$, is defined as $\sum_{\pi \in \Pi} \mathrm{Pr}(\pi) \cdot \rho(\pi)$.

In order to define a probability measure and expected cost on MDPs, the non-deterministic choices of actions are resolved by so-called *schedulers*[1]. As in [11], for practical reasons we restrict ourselves to *memoryless* schedulers; more details about schedulers can be found in [17].

**Definition 2 (Scheduler).** *A scheduler for an MDP $\mathcal{M}$ is a function $\sigma \colon S \to Distr(Act)$ such that $\sigma(s)(a) > 0$ implies $a \in Act(s)$. Schedulers using only Dirac distributions are called* deterministic. *The set of all schedulers over $\mathcal{M}$ is denoted by $Sched^{\mathcal{M}}$.*

Deterministic schedulers are functions of the form $\sigma \colon S \to Act$ with $\sigma(s) \in Act(s)$. Schedulers that are not deterministic are also called *randomized*. Applying a scheduler to an MDP yields a so-called *induced Markov chain*, as all non-determinism is resolved.

**Definition 3 (Induced MC).** *Let MDP $\mathcal{M} = (S, s_I, Act, \mathcal{P})$ and scheduler $\sigma \in Sched^{\mathcal{M}}$. The MC induced by $\mathcal{M}$ and $\sigma$ is $\mathcal{M}^{\sigma} = (S, s_I, Act, \mathcal{P}^{\sigma})$ where*

$$\mathcal{P}^{\sigma}(s, s') = \sum_{a \in Act(s)} \sigma(s)(a) \cdot \mathcal{P}(s, a)(s') \quad \text{for all } s, s' \in S .$$

Intuitively, the transition probabilities in $\mathcal{M}^{\sigma}$ are obtained w.r.t. the random choices of action of the scheduler.

---

[1] Also referred to as strategies or policies.

*Remark 1. Deterministic schedulers* pick just one action at each state and the associated probability distribution determines the probabilities. In this case we write for all states $s \in S$ and $a \in Act$ with $\sigma(s)(a) = 1$:

$$\mathcal{P}^\sigma(s, s') = \mathcal{P}(s, a)(s') \ .$$

*Specifications.* Specifications are given by combining *reachability properties* and *expected cost properties*. A reachability property $\mathbb{P}_{\leq\lambda}(\Diamond T)$ with upper probability bound $\lambda \in [0, 1] \subseteq \mathbb{Q}$ and target set $T \subseteq S$ constrains the probability to finally reach $T$ from $s_I$ in $\mathcal{M}$ to be at most $\lambda$. Analogously, expected cost properties $\mathbb{E}_{\leq\kappa}(\Diamond G)$ impose an upper bound $\kappa \in \mathbb{Q}$ on the expected cost to reach goal states $G \subseteq S$. Combining both types of properties, the intuition is that a set of bad states $T$ shall only be reached with a certain probability $\lambda$ (safety specification) while the expected cost for reaching a set of goal states $G$ has to be below $\kappa$ (performance specification). This can be verified using multi-objective model checking [6–8], provided all problem data (i.e., probabilities and costs) are a-priori known.

We overload the notation $\Diamond T$ to denote both a reachability property and the set of all paths that finally reach $T$ from the initial state $s_I$ of an MC. The probability and the expected cost for reaching $T$ from $s_I$ are denoted by $\Pr(\Diamond T)$ and $\mathrm{EC}(\Diamond T)$, respectively. Hence, $\Pr^{\mathcal{D}}(\Diamond T) \leq \lambda$ and $\mathrm{EC}^{\mathcal{D}}(\Diamond G) \leq \kappa$ express that the properties $\mathbb{P}_{\leq\lambda}(\Diamond T)$ and $\mathbb{E}_{\leq\kappa}(\Diamond G)$ respectively are satisfied by MC $\mathcal{D}$.

An MDP $\mathcal{M}$ satisfies both reachability property $\varphi$ and expected cost property $\psi$, iff *for all* schedulers $\sigma$ it holds that the induced MC $\mathcal{M}^\sigma$ satisfies the properties $\varphi$ and $\psi$, i.e., $\mathcal{M}^\sigma \models \varphi$ and $\mathcal{M}^\sigma \models \psi$. In our setting, we are rather interested in the so-called *synthesis problem*, where the aim is to find a scheduler $\sigma$ such that both properties are satisfied (while this does not necessarily hold for all schedulers). If $\mathcal{M}^\sigma \models \varphi$, scheduler $\sigma$ is said to *admit* the property $\varphi$; this is denoted by $\sigma \models \varphi$.

*Formal Problem Statement.* Given an MDP $\mathcal{M}_1$ modeling possible controllable behaviors and an MC $\mathcal{D}$ modeling the stochastic behavior of an environment, the synchronous product (see e.g. [18]) is denoted by $\mathcal{M}_1 \times \mathcal{D} = \mathcal{M} = (S, s_I, Act, \mathcal{P})$. Let $\rho$ be a cost function over $\mathcal{M}$ that is *unknown* to the robot prior to exploring the state space. We assume that for each transition $(s, a)$, the cost is bounded from below and from above, i.e. $l_{(s,a)} \leq \rho(s, a) \leq u_{(s,a)}$ with $l_{(s,a)}, u_{(s,a)} \in \mathbb{Q}$ for any $(s, a) \in S \times Act$. Let safety specification $\varphi = \mathbb{P}_{\leq\lambda}(\Diamond T)$ and performance specification $\psi = \mathbb{E}_{\leq\kappa}(\Diamond G)$ for $\mathcal{M}$ with $T, G \subseteq S$.

The *synthesis problem* is to find a scheduler $\sigma \in Sched^{\mathcal{M}}$ such that $\mathcal{M}^\sigma \models \varphi$ and $\mathcal{M}^\sigma \models \psi$. The *optimal* synthesis problem is to find a scheduler $\sigma^* \in Sched^{\mathcal{M}}$ such that $\mathcal{M}^{\sigma^*} \models \varphi$ and $\sigma^*$ minimizes the expected cost to reach $G$.

## 3  Permissive Schedulers

As mentioned before, we will utilize the notion of *permissive* schedulers, where not all nondeterminism is to be resolved. A permissive scheduler may select a set of actions at each state, such that at a state there might be several possible actions or probability distributions over actions left open. In this sense, permissive schedulers can be seen as sets of schedulers. Here, we discuss properties and efficient representations that are needed later on. Analogously to schedulers, we consider only memoryless notions.

**Definition 4 (Permissive Scheduler).** *A permissive scheduler of MDP* $\mathcal{M} = (S, s_I, Act, \mathcal{P})$ *is a function* $\theta\colon S \to 2^{Distr(Act)} \setminus \emptyset$ *and* $\forall s \in S.\forall \mu \in \theta(s).\,supp(\mu) \subseteq Act(s)$. *The set of all permissive schedulers for* $\mathcal{M}$ *is* $PSched^{\mathcal{M}}$.

Intuitively, at each state there is not only one but several distributions over actions available. *Deterministic* permissive schedulers are functions of the form $S \to 2^{Act}$, i.e., there are different choices of action left open. We use the following notations for connections to (non-permissive) schedulers.

**Definition 5 (Compliance).** *A scheduler* $\sigma$ *for the MDP* $\mathcal{M}$ *is* compliant *with a permissive scheduler* $\theta$, *written* $\sigma \in \theta$, *iff for all* $s \in S$ *it holds that* $\sigma(s) \in \theta(s)$.

*A permissive scheduler* $\theta_S$ *for* $\mathcal{M}$ *is* induced *by a set of schedulers* $S \subseteq Sched^{\mathcal{M}}$, *iff for each state* $s \in S$ *and each distribution* $\mu \in \theta_S(s)$ *there is a scheduler* $\sigma \in S$ *with* $\sigma(s) = \mu$.

We are interested in sets of schedulers that admit our safety specification.

**Definition 6 (Safe and Maximal Permissive Scheduler).** *A permissive scheduler* $\theta \in PSched^{\mathcal{M}}$ *for the MDP* $\mathcal{M}$ *is* safe *for a reachability property* $\varphi = \mathbb{P}_{\leq\lambda}(\Diamond T)$ *iff for all* $\sigma \in \theta$ *it holds that* $\sigma \models \varphi$, *denoted by* $\theta \models \varphi$. *The permissive scheduler* $\theta$ *is called* maximal, *if there exists no scheduler* $\sigma \in Sched^{\mathcal{M}}$ *with* $\sigma \notin \theta$ *and* $\sigma \models \varphi$.

A safe permissive scheduler contains *only* schedulers that admit the safety specification while a maximal safe permissive scheduler contains *all* such schedulers (and probably more). Note that even for a set of safe schedulers, the induced permissive scheduler might be unsafe; contradicting choices might evolve, i.e., choosing a certain action (or distribution) at one state might rule out certain memoryless choices at other states; this is illustrated by the following example.

*Example 1.* Consider the MDP $\mathcal{M}$ depicted in Fig. 1, where the only nondeterministic choices occur at states $s_0$ and $s_1$. Assume a reachability property $\varphi = \mathbb{P}_{\leq 0.3}(\Diamond\{s_2\})$. This property is violated by the deterministic scheduler $\sigma_1 := \{s_0 \mapsto a, s_1 \mapsto c\}$ as $s_2$ is reached with probability 0.36 exceeding the threshold 0.3. This is the only unsafe scheduler; removing either action $a$ or $c$ from $\mathcal{M}$ leads to a *safe* MDP, i.e. the possible deterministic schedulers $\sigma_2 := \{s_0 \mapsto a, s_1 \mapsto d\}$, $\sigma_3 := \{s_0 \mapsto b, s_1 \mapsto c\}$, and $\sigma_4 := \{s_0 \mapsto b, s_1 \mapsto d\}$ are all safe. However, consider the induced permissive scheduler $\theta_{\sigma_2,\sigma_3,\sigma_4} \in PSched^{\mathcal{M}}$ with $\theta := \{s_0 \mapsto \{a, b\}, s_1 \mapsto \{b, c\}\}$, where in fact all nondeterministic choices are left open. Unfortunately, it holds that the unsafe scheduler $\sigma_1$ is compliant with $\theta_{\sigma_2,\sigma_3,\sigma_4}$, therefore $\theta$ is unsafe.

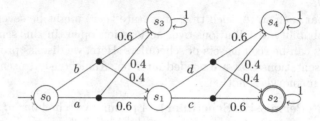

**Fig. 1.** Example MDP $\mathcal{M}$ illustrating conflicting schedulers

Example 1 shows that in order to form a safe permissive scheduler it is not sufficient to just consider the set of safe schedulers. Actually, one needs to keep track that the very same safe scheduler is used in every state. Theoretically, this can be achieved by adding finite memory to the scheduler in order to avoid conflicting actions.

A succinct representation of the maximal permissive scheduler can be gained by enumerating all *minimal* sets of conflicting action choices (now only considering deterministic schedulers), and excluding them from all possible schedulers. We investigate the worst case size of such a set. Assume without loss of generality that for all $s \in S$ the sets $Act(s)$ are pairwise disjoint.

**Definition 7 (Conflict Set).** $C \subseteq Act$ *is a conflict set for MDP* $\mathcal{M}$ *and property* $\varphi$ *iff there exists a deterministic scheduler* $\sigma \in Sched^{\mathcal{M}}$ *such that* $(\forall a \in C. \exists s \in S. \sigma(s) = a)$ *and* $\sigma \not\models \varphi$. *The set of all conflict sets for* $\mathcal{M}$ *and* $\varphi$ *is denoted by* $Conf_{\varphi}^{\mathcal{M}}$. $C \in Conf_{\varphi}^{\mathcal{M}}$ *is a minimal conflict set iff* $\forall C' \subsetneq C. C' \notin Conf_{\varphi}^{\mathcal{M}}$.

**Lemma 1.** *The size of the set of all minimal conflict sets for* $\mathcal{M}$ *and* $\varphi$ *potentially grows exponentially in the number of states of* $\mathcal{M}$.

*Proof Sketch.* Let $\mathcal{M}_n = (S, s_I, Act, \mathcal{P})$ be given by $S = \{s_0, \ldots, s_n, \bot\}$, $s_I = s_0$, $Act = \{a_0, \ldots, a_{n-1}, b_0, \ldots, b_{n-1}, c, d\}$ and

$$
\mathcal{P}(s, \alpha)(t) = \begin{cases}
0.5 & \text{if } i < n, \alpha = a_i, s = s_i, t = s_{i+1} \\
0.5 & \text{if } i < n, \alpha = a_i, s = s_i, t = \bot \\
1 & \text{if } i < n, \alpha = b_i, s = s_i, t = s_{i+1} \\
1 & \text{if } \alpha = c, s = s_n, t = s_n \\
1 & \text{if } \alpha = d, s = \bot, t = \bot \\
0 & \text{otherwise}
\end{cases}
$$

Figure 2 shows the instance $\mathcal{M}_4$ where several copies of the $\bot$-states have been drawn and the $d$ self-loops have been omitted for ease of presentation. Consider the property $\varphi = \mathbb{P}_{\leq\lambda}(\Diamond\{s_n\})$ with $\lambda = 0.5^{\frac{n}{2}+1}$. Choosing any combination of $\frac{n}{2}$

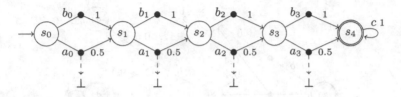

**Fig. 2.** MDP $\mathcal{M}_4$ inducing exponentially many (minimal) conflict sets

of the $b_i$ actions yields a minimal conflict set. Hence, there are at least

$$\binom{n}{\frac{n}{2}} \overset{n:=2m}{=} \frac{(2m)!}{2m!} = \underbrace{\frac{(m+1)}{1} \cdots \frac{2m}{m}}_{m \text{ factors} \geq 2} \geq 2^m \overset{m:=\frac{n}{2}}{=} 2^{\frac{n}{2}} \in \Omega\left(\left(\sqrt{2}\right)^n\right)$$

minimal conflict sets. □

This strongly indicates that an exact representation of the maximal permissive scheduler is not feasible. For algorithmic purposes, we strive for a more compact representation. It seems natural to investigate the possibilities of using MDPs as representation of permissive schedulers. Therefore, analogously to induced MCs for schedulers (cf. Definition 3), we define induced MDPs for permissive schedulers. For a permissive scheduler $\theta \in PSched^{\mathcal{M}}$, we will uniquely identify the nondeterministic choices of probability distributions $\mu \in \theta(s)$ at each state $s \in S$ of the MDP by new actions $a_{s,\mu}$.

**Definition 8 (Induced MDP).** *For an MDP* $\mathcal{M} = (S, s_I, Act, \mathcal{P})$ *and permissive scheduler* $\theta$ *for* $\mathcal{M}$*, the MDP induced by* $\mathcal{M}$ *and* $\theta$ *is* $\mathcal{M}^\theta = (S, s_I, Act^\theta, \mathcal{P}^\theta)$ *with* $Act^\theta = \{a_{s,\mu} \mid s \in S, \mu \in \theta(s)\}$ *and:*

$$\mathcal{P}^\theta(s, a_{s,\mu})(s') = \sum_{a \in Act(s)} \mu(s)(a) \cdot \mathcal{P}(s, a)(s') \quad \text{for } s, s' \in S \text{ and } a_{s,\mu} \in Act^\theta .$$

Intuitively, we nondeterministically choose between the distributions over actions induced by the permissive scheduler $\theta$. Note that if the permissive scheduler contains only one distribution for each state, i. e., in fact the permissive scheduler is just a scheduler, the actions can be discarded which yields an induced MC as in Definition 3, making this definition backward compatible.

*Remark 2.* Each deterministic scheduler $\sigma \in Sched^{\mathcal{M}^\theta}$ for the induced MDP $\mathcal{M}^\theta$ induces a *(randomized) scheduler* for the original MDP $\mathcal{M}$. In particular, $\sigma$ induces a scheduler $\sigma' \in \theta$ for $\mathcal{M}$ which is compliant with the permissive scheduler $\theta$: For all $s \in S$ there exists an action $a_{s,\mu} \in Act^\theta$ such that $\sigma(s) = a_{s,\mu}$. The randomized scheduler $\sigma'$ is then given by $\sigma'(s) = \mu$ and it holds that

$$\sum_{a \in Act(s)} \sigma'(s)(a) \cdot \mathcal{P}(s, a)(s') = \mathcal{P}^\theta(s, a_{s,\mu})(s') .$$

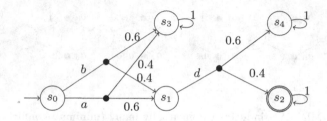

**Fig. 3.** Induced MDP $\mathcal{M}_{\theta_{safe}}$

*Remark 3.* A *deterministic permissive scheduler* $\theta_{\text{det}} \in PSched^{\mathcal{M}}$ for the MDP $\mathcal{M}$ simply *restricts* the nondeterministic choices of the original MDP to the ones that are chosen with probability one by $\theta_{\text{det}}$. The transition probability function $\mathcal{P}^{\theta_{\text{det}}}$ of the induced MDP $\mathcal{M}^{\theta_{\text{det}}}$ can be written as

$$\mathcal{P}^{\theta}(s, a_{s,\mu})(s') = \mathcal{P}(s,a)(s') \quad \text{for all } s \in S \text{ and } a_{s,\mu} \in Act^{\theta_{\text{det}}} \text{ with } \mu(a) = 1 \ .$$

The induced MDP $\mathcal{M}^{\theta}$ can be seen as a sub-MDP $\mathcal{M}^{sub} = (S, s_I, Act, \mathcal{P}^{sub})$ of $\mathcal{M}$ by omitting all actions that are not chosen. Hence, for all $s, s' \in S$:

$$\mathcal{P}^{sub}(s,a)(s') = \begin{cases} \mathcal{P}(s,a)(s') & \text{if } \exists \mu \in \theta(s). \, \mu(a) = 1 \\ 0 & \text{otherwise} \ . \end{cases}$$

*Example 2.* Recall Example 1 with $\varphi = \mathbb{P}_{\leq 0.3}(\lozenge\{s_2\})$. The MDP $\mathcal{M}^{\theta}$ induced by the permissive scheduler $\theta$ is the same as $\mathcal{M}$, as all available choices of actions are included (see Example 1). Note that we use the simplified notation from Remark 3. However, consider the safe (but not maximal) permissive scheduler $\theta_{safe}$ formed by $\{s_0 \mapsto a, s_1 \mapsto d\}$ and $\{s_0 \mapsto b, s_1 \mapsto d\}$. The induced MDP is the sub-MDP $\mathcal{M}^{\theta_{safe}}$ of $\mathcal{M}$ depicted in Fig. 3. This sub-MDP has no scheduler $\sigma$ with $\sigma \not\models \varphi$.

## 4    Safety-Constrained Reinforcement Learning

Recall that the synthesis problem amounts to determining a scheduler $\sigma^*$ of the MDP $\mathcal{M}$ such that $\sigma^*$ admits the safety specification $\varphi$ and minimizes the expected cost (of reaching $G$). A naive approach to this problem is to iterate over all safe schedulers $\sigma_1, \sigma_2, \sigma_3, \ldots$ of $\mathcal{M}$ and pursue in the $j$-th iteration as follows. Deploy the (safe) scheduler $\sigma_j$ on the robot. By letting the robot safely explore the environment (according to $\sigma_j$), one obtains the expected costs $c_j$, say, of reaching $G$ (under $\sigma_j$). By doing so for all safe schedulers, one obtains the minimum cost. After checking all safe schedulers, we have obtained a safe minimal one whenever some $c_n$ is below the threshold $\kappa$. The solution to the synthesis problem is then the scheduler $\sigma_n$ for which $c_n$ is minimal. Otherwise, we can conclude that the synthesis problem has no solution. Note that while

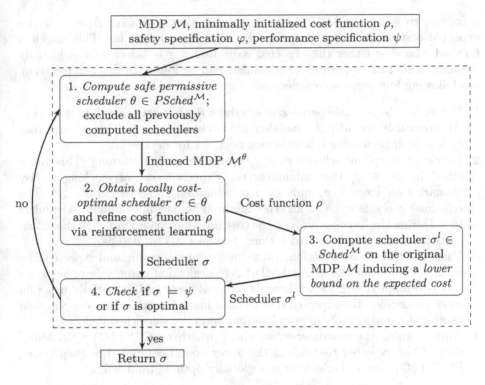

**Fig. 4.** Overview of safety-constrained reinforcement learning

deploying the safe schedulers, the robot explores more and more possible trajectories, thus becoming more knowledgeable about the (a-priori) unknown cost structure of the MDP.

Although this approach is evidently sound and complete, the number of deployments is excessive. Our approach avoids this by:

1. Testing permissive (i.e. *sets* of) schedulers rather than one scheduler at a time. This is done by employing reinforcement learning.
2. Using that the expected costs $c^*$ under $\sigma^*$ cannot be smaller than the minimal expected cost $c$ in the MDP $\mathcal{M}$ (possibly achieved by some unsafe scheduler). This allows for deciding minimality of scheduler $\sigma_j$ by checking $c_j = c$, possibly avoiding exploration of any further schedulers.
3. Preventing the deployment of safe scheduler $\sigma_j$ whenever the minimal expected cost $c_i$ of all schedulers checked so far $(i < j)$ is smaller than the expected cost under $\sigma_j$.

Let us now briefly explain our approach to synthesize a safe and optimal scheduler; further details are given in the rest of this section. Figure 4 surveys the approach. We initialize the cost function of the MDP by setting the cost of transition $(s, a)$ to its lower bound $l_{(s,a)}$. The synthesis of a safe and optimal scheduler is done by iteratively considering permissive schedulers $\theta_1, \theta_2, \theta_3, \ldots$

according to which the MDP $\mathcal{M}$ is explored. This yields a scheduler $\sigma$ whose expected cost is minimal among the schedulers deployed so far. This search is finished whenever either the expected costs under $\sigma$ is below $\kappa$, $\sigma$ is globally optimal, or no further permissive schedulers can be found. In the $j$-th iteration, the following four steps are carried out:

1. Determine the $j$-th safe permissive scheduler $\theta_j$ (if it exists) such that $\theta_j \models \varphi$. All previously considered schedulers are excluded from $\theta$. This ensures that $\theta_j$ is a fresh permissive scheduler; see Sect. 4.1 for details.
2. Check all compliant schedulers of $\theta_j$ by reinforcement learning. This yields scheduler $\sigma^j \in \theta_j$ that minimizes the expected cost of reaching $G$. By Remark 2 on Page 8, $\sigma_j$ induces a (randomized) scheduler $\sigma$ for $\mathcal{M}$. The scheduler $\sigma$ is safe w. r. t. $\varphi$ and cost-minimal among all compliant schedulers to $\theta$. During the learning process, the cost function $\rho$ is *refined* with the actual costs for the (newly) explored actions. See Sect. 4.2 for details.
3. Using the refined cost function, a scheduler $\sigma_l$ inducing minimal expected cost $c_l$ is computed for the original MDP $\mathcal{M}$ (neglecting being safe or not). As this is computed using lower bounds on local costs and potentially using an unsafe scheduler, the expected cost forms a lower bound on the cost obtained using full knowledge of the cost function and only safe schedulers.
4. After learning the scheduler $\sigma$, we check whether $\mathrm{EC}^{\mathcal{M}^\sigma}(\Diamond G) \leq \kappa$. Moreover, if the expected cost equals the lower bound computed in Step 3, i. e., $\mathrm{EC}^{\mathcal{M}^\sigma}(\Diamond G) = c_l$, the scheduler $\sigma$ is globally optimal (and safe).

Furthermore, the best scheduler found so far induces an *upper bound* on the performance as it is optimal for the already learned parts of the MDP. After computing a new candidate (permissive) scheduler, we can re-compute its performance using the lower bounds on actions on the original MDP. If it does not (potentially) admit a better performance, it does not need to be deployed at all.

Note that in the worst case, we actually enumerate all possible safe schedulers, i. e. the maximal permissive scheduler. However, the iterative nature of the procedure together with the optimizations allows for earlier termination as soon as the optimum is reached or the gap between the lower and upper bounds for the minimal expected cost is sufficiently small.

**Theorem 1.** *Safety-constrained reinforcement learning is sound and complete.*

The method is sound and complete because finally we iterate over all safe permissive schedulers and thereby over all possible safe schedulers.

## 4.1   Computing Permissive Schedulers

In the following, we discuss how to compute a safe deterministic permissive scheduler that induces a safe sub-MDP such as illustrated in Example 2. Moreover, we indicate how a safe permissive scheduler can be computed in general (for randomized schedulers). Recall that according to our setting we are given an MDP $\mathcal{M} = (S, s_I, Act, \mathcal{P})$ and a safety specification $\varphi = \mathbb{P}_{\leq \lambda}(\Diamond T)$ for $T \subseteq S$.

The computation will be performed by means of an SMT encoding. This is similar to the mixed linear integer programming (MILP) approach used in [11]. The intuition is that a satisfying assignment for the encoding induces a *safe* permissive scheduler according to Definition 6. We use the following variables.

$y_{s,a} \in \mathbb{B} = \{\texttt{true}, \texttt{false}\}$ for each state $s \in S$ and each action $a \in Act(s)$ is assigned $\texttt{true}$ iff action $a$ is allowed to be taken in state $s$ by the permissive scheduler. These variables form the permissive scheduler.

$p_s \in [0,1] \subseteq \mathbb{R}$ for each state $s \in S$ captures the *maximal* probability to reach the set of target states $T \subseteq S$ under each possible scheduler that is compliant to the permissive scheduler.

The SMT encoding reads as follows.

$$p_{s_I} \leq \lambda \tag{1}$$

$$\forall s \in S. \quad \bigvee_{a \in Act(s)} y_{s,a} \tag{2}$$

$$\forall s \in T. \quad p_s = 1 \tag{3}$$

$$\forall s \in S. \forall a \in Act(s). \quad y_{s,a} \rightarrow p_s \geq \sum_{s' \in S} \mathcal{P}(s,a)(s') \cdot p_{s'} \tag{4}$$

First, Constraint 1 ensures that the maximal probability at the initial state $s_I$ achieved by any scheduler that can be constructed according to the valuation of the $y_{s,a}$-variables does not exceed the given safety threshold $\lambda$. Due to Constraint 2, at least one action $a \in Act(s)$ is chosen by the permissive scheduler for every state $s \in S$ as at least one $y_{s,a}$-variable needs to be assigned $\texttt{true}$. The probability of target states is set to 1 by Constraint 3. Finally, Constraint 4 puts (multiple) lower bounds on each state's probability: For all $s \in S$ and $a \in Act$ with $y_{s,a} = \texttt{true}$, the probability to reach the target states is computed according to this particular choice and set as a lower bound. Therefore, only combinations of $y_{s,a}$-variables that induce safe schedulers can be assigned $\texttt{true}$.

**Theorem 2.** *The SMT encoding given by Constraints 1–4 is sound and complete.*

*Proof Sketch. Soundness* refers to the fact that each satisfying assignment for the encoding induces a safe deterministic permissive scheduler for MDP $\mathcal{M}$ and safety specification $\varphi$. This is shown by constructing a permissive scheduler according to an arbitrary assignment of $y_{s,a}$-variables. Applying the other (satisfied) constraints ensures that this scheduler is safe. *Completeness* means that for each safe deterministic permissive scheduler, a corresponding satisfying assignment of the constraints exists. This is done by assuming a safe deterministic permissive scheduler and constructing a corresponding assignment. Checking all the constraints ensures that this assignment is satisfying.

Now, consider a deterministic scheduler $\sigma \in Sched^{\mathcal{M}}$ which we want to *explicitly exclude* from the computation. It needs to be ensured that for a satisfying assignment at least for one state the corresponding $y_{s,\sigma(s)}$ variable is assigned `false` in order to at least make one different decision. This can be achieved by adding the disjunction $\bigvee_{s \in S} \neg y_{s,\sigma(s)}$ to the encoding.

Using an SMT solver like Z3, this encoding does not ensure a certain grade of permissiveness, i. e., that as many $y_{s,a}$-variables as possible are assigned `true`. While this is a typical setting for MAX-SMT [19], in the current stable version of Z3 this feature is not available yet. Certain schedulers inducing high probabilities or desired behavior can be included using the *assumptions* of the SMT solver. An alternative would be to use an MILP encoding like, e. g., in [11,20], and optimize towards a maximal number of available nondeterministic choices. However, in our setting it is crucial to ensure *incrementality* in the sense that if certain changes to the constraints are necessary this does not trigger a complete restart of the solving process.

Finally, there might be safe *randomized schedulers* that induce better optimal costs than all deterministic schedulers [7,8]. To compute *randomized permissive schedulers*, the difficulty is that there are arbitrarily (or even infinitely) many probability distributions over actions. A reasonable approach is to bound the number of possible distributions by a fixed number $n$ and introduce for each state $s$, distribution $\mu_i$, and action $a$ a real-valued variable $y_{s,\mu_i,a}$ for $1 \leq i \leq n$. Constraint 2 is modified such that for all states and actions the $y_{s,\mu_i,a}$-variables sum up to one and the probability computation in Constraint 4 has to take probabilities over actions into account. Note that the MILP approach from [11] cannot be adapted to randomized schedulers as non-linear constraints are involved.

## 4.2   Learning

In the learning phase, the main goal of this learning phase is the *exploration* of this MDP, as we thereby learn the cost function. In a more practical setting, we should balance this with *exploitation*, i. e., performing close to optimal—within the bounds of the permissive scheduler—during the learning. The algorithm we use for the reinforcement learning is *Q-learning* [10]. To favor the exploration, we initialize the learning with *overly-optimistic* expected rewards. Thereby, we explore large portions of the MDP while favoring promising regions of the MDP.

Proper balancing of exploration vs. exploitation depends on the exact scenario [21]. Here, the balance is heavily affected by the construction of permissive schedulers. For instance, if we try to find permissive schedulers which do not exclude the currently best known scheduler, then the exploitation during the learning phase might be higher, while we might severely restrict the exploration.

## 5   Experiments

We implemented a prototype of the aforementioned synthesis loop in C++ and conducted experiments using case studies motivated by robotic motion planning. Our prototype uses the SMT-based permissive scheduler computation described in Sect. 4.1 and seeks a *locally* maximal permissive scheduler by successively adding as many actions as possible.

Every MDP considered in the case studies has a set of bad states (that may only be reached with a certain probability) and a set of goal states that the system tries to reach. All case studies feature a relatively large number of nondeterministic choices in each state and a high amount of probabilistic branching to illustrate the applicability of our method to practically relevant models with a high number of schedulers that achieve various performances.

*Janitor.* This benchmark is loosely based on the grid world robot from [5]. It features a grid world with a controllable robot. In each step, the robot either changes its direction (while remaining on the same tile) or moves forward in the currently selected direction. Doing so, the robot consumes fuel depending on the surface it currently occupies. The goal is to minimize the fuel consumption for reaching the opposite corner of the grid world while simultaneously avoiding collision with a janitor that moves randomly across the board.

*Following a Line Fragment.* We consider a (discretized) variant of a machine that is bound to follow a straight line, e. g. a sawmill. In each step, there is a certain probability to deviate from the line depending on the speed the machine currently operates at. That is, higher speeds come at the price of an increased probability to deviate from the center. Given a fixed tolerable distance $d$, the system must avoid to reach states in which the distance from the center exceeds $d$. Also, the required time to complete the task or the required energy are to be minimized, both of which depend on the currently selected speed mode of the system.

*Communicating Explorer.* Finally, we use the model of a semi-autonomous explorer as described in e. g. [22]. Moving through a grid-like environment, the system communicates with its controller via two lossy channels for which the probability of a message loss depends on the location of the explorer. The explorer can choose between performing a limited number of attempts to communicate or moving in any direction in each time step. Similarly to the janitor case study, the system tries to reach the opposite corner of the grid while avoiding states in which the explorer moved too far without any (successful) intermediate communication. For this model, the cost to be optimized is the energy consumption of the electronic circuit, which induces cost for movement, e. g. by utilizing sensors, and (significantly higher) cost for utilizing the communcation channels.

*Benchmark Results.* Table 1 summarizes the results we obtained using our prototype on a MacBook Pro with an 2.67 GHz Intel Core i5 processor and a memory limit of 2 GB. As SMT-backend, we used Z3 [23] in version 4.4.0. For several instances of each case study, we list the number of states, transitions, and probabilistic branches (i. e., the size of the support set of the distributions). Furthermore, we give the bound $\lambda$ used in the safety property and the optimal performance over all safe schedulers. The following columns provide information about the progress of the synthesis procedure over several selected iterations. The first of these columns ($i$) shows the number of iterations performed thus far, i. e., the number of permissive schedulers on which we applied learning.

**Table 1.** Benchmark results

| Benchmark | | States | Trans. | Branch. | $\lambda$ | Opt. | $i$ | $t$ | Lower | Upper |
|---|---|---|---|---|---|---|---|---|---|---|
| Janitor | 5,5 | 625 | 1125 | 3545 | 0.1 | **88.6** | 1 | 813 | 84 | **88.6** |
| | | | | | | | 2 | 2578 | 84 | **88.6** |
| FolLine | 30,15 | 455 | 1265 | 3693 | 0.01 | **716.0** | 1 | 41 | 715.4 | **717.1** |
| | | | | | | | 3 | 85 | 715.62 | **716.83** |
| | | | | | | | 13 | 306 | 715.9 | **716.5** |
| | 40,15 | 625 | 1775 | 5223 | 0.12 | **966.0** | 1 | 304 | 964.8 | **968.2** |
| | | | | | | | 3 | 420 | 965.4 | **967.2** |
| | | | | | | | 8 | 738 | 965.6 | **966.7** |
| ComExp | 6,6,6 | 823 | 2603 | 3726 | 0.08 | **54.5** | 1 | 5 | 0.3 | **113.3** |
| | | | | | | | 2 | 26 | 0.3 | **74.9** |
| | | | | | | | 3 | 105 | 0.3 | **57.3** |
| | 8,8,6 | 1495 | 4859 | 6953 | 0.12 | **72.9** | 1 | 15 | 0.42 | **163.1** |
| | | | | | | | 2 | 80 | 0.42 | **122.0** |
| | | | | | | | 3 | 112 | 0.42 | **90.1** |
| | | | | | | | 7 | 1319 | 0.42 | **78.2** |

For iteration $i$, we give the cumulative time $t$ in seconds required for the computation of the permissive scheduler as well as the current lower and upper bound on the cost (w.r.t. the performance measure). The computation time for simulating deployment and reinforcement learning are negligible.

*Discussion of the Results.* For the Janitor and FolLine case studies, we observe that the investment of computing a locally maximal permissive scheduler pays off, meaning that we get very tight lower and upper bounds already after the first deployment. This investment comes at the cost of a higher computational effort (per iteration). This could be reduced by more elaborate heuristics which limit our search for (local) maximal permissiveness.

For the communicating explorer, the situation is more difficult. Since a scheduler that does not communicate at all has very low expected costs, a loose lower bound has been obtained. This bound could be severely improved upon by obtaining tighter lower bounds via multi-objective model checking.

*Lessons Learned.* Based on our experiments, we learned that quantifying permissiveness via the enabled number of actions yields counterintuitive results. Observe that for *unreachable states* literally *all actions* can be included in the scheduler without affecting the satisfaction of a property. This leads to the effect that—in order to achieve a high permissiveness—it is best to have only few reachable states and allow all actions for unreachable states. This effect is unmentioned by prior work in [11]. It thus follows that quantifying permissiveness should only consider actually reachable states. This observation is related to the general problem of forcing a solver to ensure reachability of certain states, which would also be beneficial for ensuring the reachability of, e. g., goal states. However, any guidance towards this proved to drastically decrease the solver performance.

## 6    Conclusion and Future Work

We presented the—to the best of our knowledge—first approach on iteratively computing safe and optimal strategies in a setting subject to random choices, unknown cost, and safety hazards. Our method was shown to work on practical benchmarks involving a high degree of nondeterminism. Future work will concern improving the scalability by employing multi-objective model checking in order to prove optimality at earlier iterations of the process. Moreover, extensions to stochastic 2-player games for modeling adversarial environment behavior or the investigation of unknown probability distributions seem very interesting.

**Acknowledgements.** We want to thank Benjamin Lucien Kaminski for the valuable discussion on the worst case size of conflicting sets.

## References

1. Kwiatkowska, M., Norman, G., Parker, D.: PRISM 4.0: verification of probabilistic real-time systems. In: Gopalakrishnan, G., Qadeer, S. (eds.) CAV 2011. LNCS, vol. 6806, pp. 585–591. Springer, Heidelberg (2011)
2. Ciesinski, F., Baier, C.: Liquor: A tool for qualitative and quantitative linear time analysis of reactive systems. In: Proceedings of QEST, pp. 131–132 (2006)
3. Katoen, J.P., Zapreev, I.S., Hahn, E.M., Hermanns, H., Jansen, D.N.: The ins and outs of the probabilistic model checker MRMC. Perform. Eval. **68**(2), 90–104 (2011)
4. Penna, G.D., Intrigila, B., Melatti, I., Tronci, E., Zilli, M.V.: Finite horizon analysis of Markov chains with the Murphi verifier. Softw. Tools Technol. Transf. **8**(4–5), 397–409 (2006)
5. Kwiatkowska, M., Norman, G., Parker, D.: The PRISM benchmark suite. In: Proceedings of QEST, pp. 203–204. IEEE CS (2012)
6. Forejt, V., Kwiatkowska, M., Parker, D.: Pareto curves for probabilistic model checking. In: Chakraborty, S., Mukund, M. (eds.) ATVA 2012. LNCS, vol. 7561, pp. 317–332. Springer, Heidelberg (2012)
7. Etessami, K., Kwiatkowska, M.Z., Vardi, M.Y., Yannakakis, M.: Multi-objective model checking of Markov decision processes. Logical Methods Comput. Sci. **4**(4), 1–21 (2008)
8. Baier, C., Dubslaff, C., Klüppelholz, S.: Trade-off analysis meets probabilistic model checking. In: Proceedings of CSL-LICS, pp. 1:1–1:10. ACM (2014)
9. Sutton, R., Barto, A.: Reinforcement Learning - An Introduction. MIT Press, Cambridge (1998)
10. Littman, M.L.: Markov games as a framework for multi-agent reinforcement learning. In: Proceedings of ICML, pp. 157–163. Morgan Kaufmann (1994)

11. Dräger, K., Forejt, V., Kwiatkowska, M., Parker, D., Ujma, M.: Permissive controller synthesis for probabilistic systems. In: Ábrahám, E., Havelund, K. (eds.) TACAS 2014. LNCS, vol. 8413, pp. 531–546. Springer, Heidelberg (2014)
12. Wen, M., Ehlers, R., Topcu, U.: Correct-by-synthesis reinforcement learning with temporal logic constraints. CoRR (2015)
13. Moldovan, T.M., Abbeel, P.: Safe exploration in Markov decision processes. In: Proceedings of ICML. icml.cc/Omnipress (2012)
14. Fu, J., Topcu, U.: Probably approximately correct MDP learning and control with temporal logic constraints. In: Proceedings of RSS (2014)
15. Akametalu, A., Fisac, J., Gillula, J., Kaynama, S., Zeilinger, M., Tomlin, C.: Reachability-based safe learning with Gaussian processes. In: Proceedings of CDC, pp. 1424–1431 (2014)
16. Pecka, M., Svoboda, T.: Safe exploration techniques for reinforcement learning – an overview. In: Hodicky, J. (ed.) MESAS 2014. LNCS, vol. 8906, pp. 357–375. Springer, Heidelberg (2014)
17. Baier, C., Katoen, J.P.: Principles of Model Checking. The MIT Press, Cambridge (2008)
18. Sokolova, A., de Vink, E.P.: Probabilistic automata: system types, parallel composition and comparison. In: Baier, C., Haverkort, B.R., Hermanns, H., Katoen, J.-P., Siegle, M. (eds.) Validation of Stochastic Systems. LNCS, vol. 2925, pp. 1–43. Springer, Heidelberg (2004)
19. Bjørner, N., Phan, A.: νZ - maximal satisfaction with Z3. In: Proceedings of SCSS. EPiC Series, vol. 30, pp. 1–9. EasyChair (2014)
20. Wimmer, R., Jansen, N., Ábrahám, E., Katoen, J.P., Becker, B.: Minimal counterexamples for linear-time probabilistic verification. Theor. Comput. Sci. **549**, 61–100 (2014)
21. Brafman, R.I., Tennenholtz, M.: R-MAX - a general polynomial time algorithm for near-optimal reinforcement learning. J. Mach. Learn. Res. **3**, 213–231 (2002)
22. Stückler, J., Schwarz, M., Schadler, M., Topalidou-Kyniazopoulou, A., Behnke, S.: Nimbro explorer: semiautonomous exploration and mobile manipulation in rough terrain. J. Field Robot. (2015, to appear)
23. de Moura, L., Bjørner, N.S.: Z3: an efficient SMT solver. In: Ramakrishnan, C.R., Rehof, J. (eds.) TACAS 2008. LNCS, vol. 4963, pp. 337–340. Springer, Heidelberg (2008)

# Safety Verification of Continuous-Space Pure Jump Markov Processes

Sadegh Esmaeil Zadeh Soudjani[1]($^{\boxtimes}$), Rupak Majumdar[2],
and Alessandro Abate[1]

[1] Department of Computer Science, University of Oxford, Oxford, UK
{Sadegh.Soudjani,Alessandro.Abate}@cs.ox.ac.uk
[2] Max Planck Institute for Software Systems,
Kaiserslautern and Saarbrücken, Germany
rupak@mpi-sws.org

**Abstract.** We study the probabilistic safety verification problem for pure jump Markov processes, a class of models that generalizes continuous-time Markov chains over continuous (uncountable) state spaces. Solutions of these processes are piecewise constant, right-continuous functions from time to states. Their jump (or reset) times are realizations of a Poisson process, characterized by a jump rate function that can be both time- and state-dependent. Upon jumping in time, the new state of the solution process is specified according to a (continuous) stochastic conditional kernel. After providing a full characterization of safety properties of these processes, we describe a formal method to abstract the process as a finite-state discrete-time Markov chain; this approach is formal in that it provides a-priori error bounds on the precision of the abstraction, based on the continuity properties of the stochastic kernel of the process and of its jump rate function. We illustrate the approach on a case study of thermostatically controlled loads.

## 1 Introduction

Stochastic processes evolving in continuous time are used to model many phenomena in science and engineering. In recent years, there has been a lot of work in the algorithmic analysis and formal verification of such models with respect to quantitative temporal specifications. For example, the verification of continuous-time Markov chains over finite state spaces has been widely addressed in the literature against properties expressed in temporal logics such as CSL [5–7], MTL [13], and timed-automata specifications [14], and there exist efficient software tools [24,27].

In this paper, we extend this line of work and study the class of continuous-space, pure jump Markov processes (cPJMP, for short). A cPJMP evolves in continuous time. The process starts at state $X_{t_0} = x_0$ at time $t = t_0$ and waits until a random time $t = T_1$, governed by a Poisson process depending on $x_0$ and possibly time-inhomogeneous, when it makes a jump to a new state $X_{T_1} = x_1$ based on a transition kernel that is conditional on the jumping time and on $x_0$.

© Springer-Verlag Berlin Heidelberg 2016
M. Chechik and J.-F. Raskin (Eds.): TACAS 2016, LNCS 9636, pp. 147–163, 2016.
DOI: 10.1007/978-3-662-49674-9_9

Then it waits until time $t = T_2$, when it makes another jump to state $X_{T_2} = x_2$ with probability that depends on the current time and on $x_1$, and so on. The states take values over a continuous domain, hence the transition kernel induces continuous measures.

cPJMPs generalize continuous-time, finite-state Markov chains (CTMCs) by allowing time-inhomogeneous behaviors (the waiting times and transition probabilities can depend on time) and allowing for general, continuous state spaces. Correspondingly, non-deterministic extensions of cPJMPs (not explicitly discussed in this work, but directly obtainable from cPJMPs) extend general-space MDPs [10] and LMPs [30] by allowing a random inter-arrival time in between stochastic resets over their continuous state space. cPJMPs can be employed in the definition and analysis of jump-diffusion processes [25]: of interest to this work, the jump component can capture event-driven uncertainties, such as corporate defaults, operational failures, or insured events [31]. It is likewise possible to obtain a cPJMP by random time sampling of a general stochastic differential equation (SDE) – indeed cPJMPs can be as well thought of as SDEs with jumps, with drift and diffusion terms that are equal to zero. This connection with diffusions driven by Wiener processes renders cPJMP relevant to areas including financial and economic modeling [31], systems biology [4], physics and chemistry [34].

We study the problem of approximately computing the bounded-time safety probability of a cPJMP by generalizing the corresponding algorithms for CTMCs. First, we show that a cPJMP can be embedded into a discrete-time, continuous-space Markov process (DTMP). In this process, we "compile away" the time inhomogeneity of the process by explicitly modeling the time as an additional state variable. Second, we characterize the bounded-time safety probability of the discrete-time Markov process as the least fixed point solution of a system of integral equations that generalize the Bellman equations for CTMCs. Finally, under Lipschitz continuity assumptions on the jump rate function and on the jump measure of the cPJMP, we show how the continuous-space discrete-time Markov process can be approximated by a finite-state discrete-time Markov chain (DTMC), up to any desired degree of precision. Our technical result shows a guaranteed upper bound on the error incurred in computing the bounded-time safety probability introduced by the finite-state approximation.

While we focus on bounded-time safety probability computation, our algorithms can be generalized to provide approximate model checking algorithms for more expressive temporal logics such as continuous-time stochastic logic (CSL) [5,9]. We demonstrate our results on a case study from energy systems, modeling thermostatically-controlled loads as a cPJMP.

## 2    Pure Jump Markov Processes in Continuous Time

### 2.1    Model Definition - Syntax and Semantics

Let $(K, \mathcal{K})$ be a measurable space, where $K$ is the (not necessarily finite) state space and $\mathcal{K}$ is a sigma-algebra on $K$. Let $\Omega$ be a sample space. Let $\mathbb{R}_{\geq 0}$ be the set of non-negative reals. We consider stochastic processes $X : \Omega \times \mathbb{R}_{\geq 0} \to K$

in continuous time. For any $t \in \mathbb{R}_{\geq 0}$, the function $X(\cdot, t) : \Omega \to K$ is a random variable, which we denote by $X_t$. For every $I \subseteq \mathbb{R}_{\geq 0}$ we write $\mathcal{F}_I = \sigma(X_t, t \in I)$ for the sigma-algebra on $\Omega$ generated by the stochastic process $X$ restricted to the index set $I$. We suppose that for every $t \in \mathbb{R}_{\geq 0}$ and $x \in K$, a probability $\mathbb{P}^{t,x}$ is given on $(\Omega, \mathcal{F}_{[t,\infty)})$. The stochastic process $X : \Omega \times \mathbb{R}_{\geq 0} \to K$ is a (pure) jump Markov process if the following conditions hold:

(a) $\mathcal{K}$ contains all one-point sets and $\mathbb{P}^{t,x}(X_t = x) = 1$ for every $t \in \mathbb{R}_{\geq 0}, x \in K$.
(b) For every $0 \leq t \leq s$ and $A \in \mathcal{K}$ the function $x \mapsto \mathbb{P}^{t,x}(X_s \in A)$ is $\mathcal{K}$-measurable.
(c) [**Markov property**] For every $0 \leq u \leq t \leq s$, $A \in \mathcal{K}$ we have $\mathbb{P}^{u,x}(X_s \in A | \mathcal{F}_{[u,t]}) = \mathbb{P}^{t,X_t}(X_s \in A)$, $\mathbb{P}^{u,x}$-a.s.
(d) [**Pure Jump property**] For every $\omega \in \Omega$ and $t \geq 0$ there exists $\delta > 0$ such that $X_s(\omega) = X_t(\omega)$ for $s \in [t, t + \delta]$; this is equivalent to requiring that all the trajectories of $X$ are càdlàg [11] when $K$ is given the discrete topology (where all subsets are open).
(e) [**Non-explosive property**] For every $\omega \in \Omega$ the number of jumps of the trajectory $t \mapsto X_t(\omega)$ is finite on every bounded interval.

Condition (a) enables us to assign probabilities to any points $x \in K$. In particular, the probability measure $\mathbb{P}^{t,x}$ assigns probability 1 to $x$, so that the process is initialized deterministically at $x$ at time $t$. Condition (b) is essential for transporting any probability measure on $X_t$ to the events $X_s \in A$, $A \in \mathcal{K}$, for any $t \leq s$.

Intuitively, a Markov process $X : \Omega \times \mathbb{R}_{\geq 0} \to K$ in continuous time is a pure jump process if, starting from any point $x \in K$, the process is right continuous, admits constant trajectories except at isolated jumps, and allows only for a finite number of isolated jumps within any bounded interval. A cPJMP is described by means of the joint law $Q$ of the first jump time $T_1$ and of the corresponding position $X_{T_1}$. To proceed formally, we first fix $t \geq 0$ and $x \in K$ and define the first jump time

$$T_1(\omega) = \inf\{s > t : X_s(\omega) \neq X_t(\omega)\}, \tag{1}$$

with the convention that $T_1(\omega) = \infty$ if the indicated set is empty. Clearly, the value of $T_1$ depends on $t$. Its associated probability measure also depends on $x$ through $\mathbb{P}^{t,x}$. Allowing this jump time to be equal to infinity requires extending the definition of the process $X$ as follows. Take an extra dummy point $\Delta \notin K$ and redefine $X : \Omega \times \mathbb{R}_{\geq 0} \cup \{\infty\} \to K \cup \{\Delta\}$ such that $X(\omega, \infty) = X_\infty(\omega) = \Delta$ for all $\omega \in \Omega$. Then $X_{T_1} : \Omega \to K \cup \{\Delta\}$ is well defined. Note that $X_{T_1}$ is associated with a probability measure first through the random variable $T_1$ (the first jump time) and then through the process $X$ conditioned on knowing this jump time.

On the extended space $S := (\mathbb{R}_{\geq 0} \times K) \cup \{(\infty, \Delta)\}$ we consider the smallest sigma-algebra, denoted by $\mathcal{S}$, containing $\{(\infty, \Delta)\}$ and all sets of $\mathcal{B}(\mathbb{R}_{\geq 0}) \otimes \mathcal{K}$ (here and in the following $\mathcal{B}(\Lambda)$ denotes the Borel sigma-algebra of a topological space $\Lambda$, and $Y \otimes Z$ is the product sigma-algebra of two sigma-algebras $Y, Z$, that is the smallest sigma-algebra generated by subsets of the form $A_1 \times A_2$, $A_1 \in Y, A_2 \in Z$). Note that this sigma-algebra $\mathcal{S}$ is smaller than the product of two sigma-algebras defined on $\mathbb{R}_{\geq 0} \cup \{\infty\}$ and $K \cup \{\Delta\}$. The extended process $X$ ensures that $\mathcal{S}$ is sufficient to contain the associated probability measure of $(T_1, X_{T_1})$. With these definitions, $(T_1, X_{T_1})$ is a random variable with values in $(S, \mathcal{S})$, and its law under $\mathbb{P}^{t,x}$ is denoted by $Q(t, x, \cdot)$.

We first construct $Q(t, x, \cdot)$ for the continuous part of $\mathcal{S}$ and later discuss how to assign probabilities to the single point $(\infty, \Delta)$. We will assume that $Q$ is constructed starting from a given transition measure from $\mathbb{R}_{\geq 0} \times K$ to $\mathcal{K}$, called *rate measure* and denoted by $\nu(t, x, A), t \in \mathbb{R}_{\geq 0}, x \in K, A \in \mathcal{K}$. We require that $A \mapsto \nu(t, x, A)$ is a positive measure on $\mathcal{K}$ for all $t \in \mathbb{R}_{\geq 0}$ and $x \in K$, and that $(t, x) \mapsto \nu(t, x, A)$ is $\mathcal{B}(\mathbb{R}_{\geq 0}) \otimes \mathcal{K}-$measurable for all $A \in \mathcal{K}$. We also assume that the rate measure $\nu$ satisfies the two conditions

(f)  $\sup\{\nu(t, x, K) | t \in \mathbb{R}_{\geq 0}, x \in K\} < \infty$ and
(g)  $\nu(t, x, \{x\}) = 0$ for all $t \in \mathbb{R}_{\geq 0}, x \in K$.

The condition (f) implies a finite number of jumps in a bounded interval, which satisfies the non-explosive condition (e) raised above. The condition (g) enforces no jump from a state to itself, which is in accordance with the definition of jump time in (1). Define

$$\lambda(t, x) = \nu(t, x, K), \quad \pi(t, x, A) = \begin{cases} \dfrac{\nu(t, x, A)}{\lambda(t, x)}, & \text{if } \lambda(t, x) > 0, \\ \mathbf{1}_A(x), & \text{if } \lambda(t, x) = 0, \end{cases}$$

where $\mathbf{1}_A(\cdot)$ is the indicator function of any set $A$. Therefore $\lambda$ is a nonnegative bounded measurable function and $\pi$ is a transition probability on $K$ satisfying

$$\pi(t, x, \{x\}) = \begin{cases} 0, & \text{if } \lambda(t, x) > 0, \\ \delta_x, & \text{if } \lambda(t, x) = 0, \end{cases}$$

where $\delta_x$ is the Dirac measure at $x$. Function $\lambda$ is called the *jump rate function*, and $\pi$ the *jump measure*. Note that we have $\nu(t, x, A) = \lambda(t, x)\pi(t, x, A), \forall t \in \mathbb{R}_{\geq 0}, x \in K, A \in \mathcal{K}$. Given the rate measure $\nu$, we require that for the Markov process $X$ we have, for $0 \leq t \leq a < b \leq \infty, x \in K, A \in \mathcal{K}$,

$$Q(t, x, (a, b) \times A) = \int_a^b \pi(s, x, A)\lambda(s, x) \exp\left[-\int_t^s \lambda(r, x)dr\right] ds, \qquad (2)$$

where $Q$ was described above as the law of $(T_1, X_{T_1})$ under $\mathbb{P}^{t,x}$. Note that (2) completely specifies the probability measure $Q(t, x, \cdot)$ on $(S, \mathcal{S})$: indeed simple computations show that

$$\mathbb{P}^{t,x}(T_1 = \infty) = Q(t, x, (\infty, \Delta))$$

$$:= 1 - Q(t, x, (t, \infty) \times K) = \exp\left[-\int_t^\infty \lambda(r, x)dr\right], \qquad (3)$$

$$\mathbb{P}^{t,x}(T_1 \in (s, \infty]) = 1 - Q(t, x, (t, s] \times K) = \exp\left[-\int_t^s \lambda(r, x)dr\right], \qquad (4)$$

for all $s \geq t$ and we clearly have $\mathbb{P}^{t,x}(T_1 \leq t) = Q(t,x,[0,t] \times K) = 0$. Note that (3) assigns probability to the single point $(\infty, \Delta)$, which completes the definition of $Q(t, x, \cdot)$ on $(S, \mathcal{S})$.

We may interpret (4) as the statement that $T_1$ has exponential distribution on $[t, \infty]$ with variable rate $\lambda(r, x), r \geq t$. Moreover, the probability $\pi(s, x, A)$ can be interpreted as the conditional probability that $X_{T_1}$ is in $A \in \mathcal{K}$, given that the jump time $T_1 = s$, or more precisely,

$$\mathbb{P}^{t,x}(X_{T_1} \in A, T_1 < \infty | T_1) = \pi(T_1, x, A)\mathbf{1}_{T_1 < \infty}, \quad \mathbb{P}^{t,x} - \text{a.s.}$$

## 2.2  Examples and Related Models

*Example 1* **Poisson-driven differential equation** [31, Section 1.7]. Let the process $\{\mathcal{N}_t \mid t \geq 0\}$ represent a standard Poisson process with homogeneous rate $\lambda$.[1] Consider a pure jump process $X = \{X_t, t \in \mathbb{R}_{\geq 0}, X_t \in \mathbb{R}\}$, driven by the Poisson process $\mathcal{N}_t$, where its value $X_t$ at time $t$ satisfies the SDE

$$dX_t = c(t, X_{t-})d\mathcal{N}_t \quad \forall t \in \mathbb{R}_{\geq 0},$$

with the deterministic initial value $X_0 \in \mathbb{R}$. The function $c : \mathbb{R}_{\geq 0} \times \mathbb{R} \to \mathbb{R}$ is called the *jump coefficient*. For the case of $c(t, x) = c_0 x$ with the constant $c_0 \in \mathbb{R}_{\geq 0}$ and initial value $X_0 > 0$, the process has an explicit representation[2]

$$X_t = X_0(c_0 + 1)^{\mathcal{N}_t}, \quad \text{for } t \in \mathbb{R}_{\geq 0}.$$

From this explicit representation, we can compute properties of the process $X_t$, such as the probability that the process does not exceed $\alpha_\hbar > 0$ within the time interval $[0, T]$. This probability is analytically computable for the above simple process: defining $\beta_\hbar = (\ln \alpha_\hbar - \ln X_0) / \ln(c_0 + 1)$, this probability is $\sum_{n=0}^{n \leq \beta_\hbar} e^{-\lambda T}(\lambda T)^n / n!$. $\qquad \square$

*Example 2* **Compound Poisson processes** [31, Section 1.1] represent a generalization of Poisson processes, with exponential waiting times between jumps but where jump sizes, rather than being deterministic, follow an arbitrary distribution. Let $\{y_n\}_{n \geq 1}$ be a sequence of independent random variables with distribution $\mu$ for all $n \geq 1$ and assume that the standard Poisson process $\{\mathcal{N}_t \mid t \geq 0\}$ with parameter $\lambda > 0$ is independent of $\{y_n\}_{n \geq 1}$. The compound Poisson process $X_t$ is represented in the form $X_t = \sum_{n=1}^{\mathcal{N}_t} y_n$. A typical application of compound Poisson processes is to model the aggregate claim up to time $t$ generated by a portfolio of insurance policies, where the individual claims are distributed according to $\mu$. Let us assume the gamma distribution $y_n \sim \Gamma(a, b)$ for the individual claims [35] and answer the same safety question as in the previous example: what

---

[1] Recall that a (homogeneous) Poisson process $\{\mathcal{N}_t \mid t \geq 0\}$ with rate $\lambda$ is a Lévy process with $\mathcal{N}_0 = 0$ and $\mathbb{P}\{\mathcal{N}_t = n\} = \frac{(\lambda t)^n}{n!}e^{-\lambda t}$.

[2] The solution can be derived observing that the process satisfies the recursive equation $X_{\tau_{n+1}} - X_{\tau_n} = c_0 X_{\tau_n}$, where the jumps occur at $\tau_n$, $n = 1, 2, 3, \ldots$ according to $\mathcal{N}_t$.

is the probability that the aggregate claim does not exceed $\alpha_{\mathfrak{h}} > 0$ in the time interval $[0, T]$? This probability is also analytically computable, and results in

$$e^{-\lambda T} + e^{-\lambda T} \sum_{n=1}^{\infty} \frac{\gamma\left(na, \alpha_{\mathfrak{h}}/b\right)}{\Gamma(na)} \frac{(\lambda T)^n}{n!},$$

where $\Gamma(\cdot)$ is the gamma function, and $\gamma(\cdot, \cdot)$ is the lower incomplete gamma function. $\qquad\square$

Notice that the safety probability is expressible analytically in the above two examples. This is first because the trajectories of the solution are always non-decreasing, and secondly since the distribution of the solution process conditioned on the value of the underlying Poisson process is computable analytically. Unfortunately in general trajectories of cPJMPs cannot be derived explicitly, and as such the safety probability is not analytically expressible. In Sect. 3 we provide a general characterization of the solution of the probabilistic safety problem. In Sect. 4 we also work out a formal approximation method to numerically compute the solution.

*Example 3* **Continuous-time Markov chains** [8]. The class of cPJMP we consider includes, as special cases, all the time-homogeneous, nonexplosive, jump Markov processes: these correspond to a function $\nu$ not depending on the time variable $t$. Within this time-homogeneous case we need to retain the boundedness assumption in (f) for the rate function. Assuming further that $K$ is a finite or countably infinite set, we obtain the class of continuous-time Markov chains characterized by the transition rates matrix $\nu(x, \{y\})_{x,y \in K}$, namely

$$\mathbb{P}^{t,x}(X_{T_1} = x', T_1 < \infty | T_1) = \frac{\nu(x, \{x'\})}{E(x)} \left[ 1 - e^{-E(x)t} \right] 1_{T_1 < \infty},$$

where $E(x) = \sum_{x' \in K} \nu(x, \{x'\})$. The probability that the system stays within a set $A \subseteq K$ in the interval $[0, T]$ can be expressed as the solution of a system of integral equations [7], which is a special case of the Bellman fixed-point equation developed in Sect. 3 for cPJMPs, but not expressible in closed form. $\qquad\square$

*Example 4* **cPJMP defined by dynamical systems.** Consider a process $X$ with piecewise-constant trajectories, which resets (or jumps) at time $t$ over a space $K$ according to a vector field $f : K \times \mathbb{R}^n \times \mathbb{R}_{\geq 0} \to K$, so that

$$x(t^+) = f(x(t^-), \zeta(t), t), \tag{5}$$

where $\zeta(\cdot)$ is a continuous-time stationary process with a given, time-independent density function. The resets for the process follow a Poisson process $\mathcal{N}_t, t \geq 0, \mathcal{N}_0 = 0$, with a rate $\lambda$ depending on time $t$ and on the continuous state of the process $x(t)$. Notice that the dependence of the vector field $f$ on time is in accordance with [25]. The map $f$, together with the distribution of the process $\zeta(\cdot)$, uniquely defines a jump measure $\pi(t, x, A)$, which gives the probability of jumping from any state $x$ at time $t$ to any (measurable) subset of the state space $A \subseteq K$ [26, Proposition 7.6]:

$$\pi(t, x, A) = T_\zeta \left( \zeta \in \mathbb{R}^n \ : \ f(x, \zeta, t) \in A \right),$$

where $T_\zeta$ is the distribution of the random vector $\zeta(0)$ (in fact, of any $\zeta(t)$ since the process is stationary and time-independent). $\qquad\square$

## 2.3   Embedded Discrete-Time Markov Process of a cPJMP

We have defined a cPJMP on a measurable space $(K, \mathcal{K})$ through the transition measure $\nu$. The trajectories of a cPJMP are piecewise constant, which makes them fully representable by their jump times and corresponding values. It is worth studying the properties of the random variables $(T_n(w), X_{T_n}(w))$, $n \in \mathbb{N} := \{0, 1, 2, \ldots\}$, where $T_n$ is the $n^{\text{th}}$ jump time and $X_{T_n}$ is the corresponding value of the process. The ensuing Theorem 1 states that $(T_n, X_{T_n})_{n \in \mathbb{N}}$ can be considered as a discrete-time Markov process (DTMP) by slight extension of the definition of $Q$. The discrete time is indexed by nonnegative natural numbers $n \in \mathbb{N}$, as opposed to continuous time indexed by $t \in \mathbb{R}_{\geq 0}$.

**Definition 1.** *A discrete-time Markov process* $(Y_n)_{n \in \mathbb{N}}$ *is uniquely defined by a triple* $\mathfrak{D} = (E_\mathfrak{y}, \mathcal{E}_\mathfrak{y}, P_\mathfrak{y})$, *where* $(E_\mathfrak{y}, \mathcal{E}_\mathfrak{y})$ *is a measurable space and* $P_\mathfrak{y} : E_\mathfrak{y} \times \mathcal{E}_\mathfrak{y} \to [0, 1]$ *is a transition kernel such that for any* $y \in E_\mathfrak{y}$ *and* $A \in \mathcal{E}_\mathfrak{y}$, $P_\mathfrak{y}(y, A)$ *gives the probability that* $Y_{n+1} \in A$, *conditioned on* $Y_n = y$. $E_\mathfrak{y}$ *is called the state space of the DTMP* $\mathfrak{D}$ *and the elements of* $E_\mathfrak{y}$ *are the states of* $\mathfrak{D}$. *The process is time-inhomogeneous if* $P_\mathfrak{y}$ *depends also on the time index* $n$.

We adapt the following result from [23, Chapter III, Section 1, Theorem 2].

**Theorem 1.** *Starting from* $T_0 = t$ *define inductively* $T_{n+1} = \inf\{s > T_n : X_s \neq X_{T_n}\}$, *with the convention that* $T_{n+1} = \infty$ *if the indicated set is empty. Under the probability* $\mathbb{P}^{t,x}$, *the sequence* $(T_n, X_{T_n})_{n \in \mathbb{N}}$ *is a DTMP in* $(S, \mathcal{S})$ *with transition kernel* $Q$, *provided we extend the definition of* $Q$ *making the state* $(\infty, \Delta)$ *absorbing, by defining* $Q(\infty, \Delta, \mathbb{R}_{\geq 0} \times K) = 0$, $Q(\infty, \Delta, \{(\infty, \Delta)\}) = 1$. *Note that* $(T_n, X_{T_n})_{n \in \mathbb{N}}$ *is time-homogeneous, although in general* $X$ *is not.*

Theorem 1 states that given the stochastic process $X : \Omega \times \mathbb{R}_{\geq 0} \to K$ with probability measure $\mathbb{P}^{t,x}$ as defined in Sect. 2, we can construct a DTMP on $(S, \mathcal{S})$ with the extended transition kernel $Q$, whose state includes jump times and jump values of $X$. The inverse is also true, as described next, which allows for a simple description of the process $X$. Suppose one starts with a DTMP $(\tau_n, \xi_n)_{n \in \mathbb{N}}$ in $S$ with transition probability kernel $Q$ and a given starting point $(t, x) \in \mathbb{R}_{\geq 0} \times K$. One can then define a process $Z$ in $K$ setting $Z_t = \sum_{n=0}^{N_\mathfrak{y}} \xi_n \mathbf{1}_{[\tau_n, \tau_{n+1})}(t)$, where $N_\mathfrak{y} := \sup\{n \in \mathbb{N} : \tau_n < \infty\}$. Then $Z$ has the same law as the process $X$ under $\mathbb{P}^{t,x}$.

*Example 5.* For a CTMC defined by its transition rate matrix $\nu(x, \{x'\})$, we get that $\pi(x, \{y\})_{x,y \in K}$ is the stochastic transition matrix of the corresponding embedded discrete-time Markov chain (DTMC). $\qquad\square$

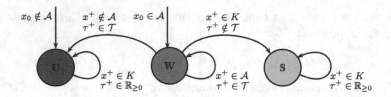

**Fig. 1.** Transition system for the safety problem.

## 3 Bounded-Time Safety Probability for cPJMPs

In this section, we characterize the bounded-time safety probability for a cPJMP $X$, that is the quantity

$$p_{\mathcal{A}}(t_0, x_0, T) = \mathbb{P}^{t_0, x_0}\{X_u \in \mathcal{A}, \text{ for all } u \in [t_0, T] | X_{t_0} = x_0\}, \tag{6}$$

for a given initial time $t_0 \in [0, T]$, $T < \infty$, and initial state $X_{t_0} = x_0$.[3] Note that in this setup we must account for the initial time $t_0$ alongside the initial state $x_0$ because the process is time-inhomogeneous.

For the characterization of $p_{\mathcal{A}}(t_0, x_0, T)$, we first construct the DTMP $\mathfrak{M} = (S, \mathcal{S}, Q)$ with state $s_n = (\tau_n, x_n) \in S$ according to Theorem 1. In order to formulate the safety problem over the new process $\mathfrak{M}$, we introduce a transition system with a set of states $\mathcal{Q} = \{\$, \mathrm{U}, \mathrm{W}\}$ representing *Safe, Unsafe,* and *Wait.* The transition system is initialized at $\mathrm{W}$ or $\mathrm{U}$ depending on whether the initial state of the process is in the safe set or not. A transition from $\mathrm{W}$ to $\$$ is activated if the next jump time $\tau^+$ is outside the interval $\mathcal{T} := [0, T]$ and the next state $x^+ \in K$. A transition $\mathrm{W} \to \mathrm{U}$ is activated if $\tau^+ \in \mathcal{T}$ and the next state is outside the safe set. Finally, the self loops at all the states of $\mathcal{Q}$ characterize all other dynamics of the transition system.

Based on the transition system in Fig. 1, the quantity $p_{\mathcal{A}}(t_0, x_0, T)$ can be characterized as the probability of reaching the state $\$$ in the transition system under the dynamics of $\mathfrak{M}$, which is equal to the likelihood associated to the set of words $\{\mathrm{W}^+\$\} = \{\mathrm{W}\$, \mathrm{W}^2\$, \mathrm{W}^3\$, \ldots\}$ (we have denoted by $\mathrm{W}^+$ the Kleene star without $\epsilon$). This can be written as the infinite series $p_{\mathcal{A}}(t_0, x_0, T) = \sum_{n=1}^{\infty} \mathbb{P}\{\mathrm{W}^n\$\}$, which equals to

$$p_{\mathcal{A}}(t_0, x_0, T) = \sum_{n=1}^{\infty} \mathbb{P}\{(s_0, s_1, \ldots, s_n) \in \mathcal{G}^n \mathcal{H} | s_0 = (t_0, x_0)\}, \tag{7}$$

where $\mathcal{G} := \mathcal{T} \times \mathcal{A}$ and $\mathcal{H} := (T, \infty) \times K \cup \{(\infty, \Delta)\}$. Note that the non-explosive condition posed in (e) and reinforced by assumption (f) on $\nu(\cdot)$ implies that $\lim_{n \to \infty} \mathbb{P}\{\mathrm{W}^n\$\} = 0$, which is a necessary condition for the series (7) to converge.

---

[3] A slight modification of the approach presented in this paper allows for verifying more general quantitative questions such as $\mathbb{P}_{\sim p}(\Phi \cup^{(T_1, T_2)} \Psi)$, defined over any state labels $\Psi, \Phi$ and over any (possibly unbounded) time interval $(T_1, T_2)$ – an adaptation is required on the construction of sets $\mathcal{G}, \mathcal{H}$ in (7).

We show in the rest of this section that the infinite series (7) converges and is approximately computable via its partial sums under a mild assumption on the jump rate function (a bound on the integral of $\lambda(\cdot)$ over the interval $T$).

The reformulation of $p_{\mathcal{A}}(t_0, x_0, T)$ as (7) indicates its close relationship with the infinite-horizon probabilistic reach-avoid specification over DTMPs. This problem is studied in [32,33], which formulate the solution as a Bellman equation and describe convergence properties of the series based on contractivity of the stochastic operator associated to the DTMP. The next theorem can be seen as an extension of [33, Section 3.1] and presents a Bellman equation for the characterization of the safety probability $p_{\mathcal{A}}(t_0, x_0, T)$, which is an equation for the infinite-horizon reach-avoid problem over the DTMP $\mathfrak{M}$ with the safe set $(\mathcal{G} \cup \mathcal{H}) \in \mathcal{S}$ and target set $\mathcal{H} \in \mathcal{S}$.

**Theorem 2.** *The solution of the probabilistic safety problem defined in (6) can be characterized as $p_{\mathcal{A}}(t_0, x_0, T) = V(t_0, x_0) - 1_{\mathcal{H}}(t_0, x_0)$, where the value function $V : S \rightarrow [0, 1]$ is the least solution of the fixed-point Bellman equation*

$$V(s) = 1_{\mathcal{H}}(s) + 1_{\mathcal{G}}(s) \int_S V(\bar{s})Q(s, d\bar{s}), \quad \forall s = (t, x) \in S. \tag{8}$$

In order to characterize the solution of the fixed-point equation (8), we consider the value functions $V_n : S \rightarrow [0, 1]$, $k \in \mathbb{N}$, for the finite-horizon reach-avoid probability $V_n(s) := \mathbb{P}\{\$, \mathrm{W}\$, \mathrm{W}^2\$, \ldots, \mathrm{W}^n\$\}$. These functions satisfy the Bellman recursion

$$V_{n+1}(s) = 1_{\mathcal{H}}(s) + 1_{\mathcal{G}}(s) \int_S V_n(\bar{s})Q(s, d\bar{s}), \quad V_0(s) = 1_{\mathcal{H}}(s). \tag{9}$$

Then we have that $V(s) = \lim_{n \to \infty} V_n(s)$, where the limit is point-wise non-decreasing [33, Section 3.1]. Equation (9) indicates that the support of the value functions $V_n(\cdot)$ is bounded by the set $\mathcal{G} \cup \mathcal{H}$. These value functions are equal to one over the set $\mathcal{H}$ and satisfy the following recursion for any $s = (t, x) \in \mathcal{G}$:

$$V_{n+1}(s) = g(s) + \int_{\mathcal{G}} V_n(\bar{s})Q(s, d\bar{s}), \quad g(t, x) := \exp\left[-\int_t^T \lambda(r, x)dr\right]. \tag{10}$$

In the following we provide an operator perspective to (10), show that the associated operator is contractive, and quantify an upper bound for the quantity $\|V - V_n\|$ as a function of $n$.

Let $\mathbb{B}$ denote the space of all real-valued, bounded and measurable functions on $\mathcal{G}$. Then $\mathbb{B}$ is a Banach space with a norm given by $\|f\| := \sup_{s \in \mathcal{G}} |f(s)|$ for $f \in \mathbb{B}$. An operator $\mathcal{J} : \mathbb{B} \rightarrow \mathbb{B}$ is called linear if

$$\mathcal{J}(\alpha_1 f_1 + \alpha_2 f_2) = \alpha_1 \mathcal{J}(f_1) + \alpha_2 \mathcal{J}(f_2), \quad \forall f_1, f_2 \in \mathbb{B}, \forall \alpha_1, \alpha_2 \in \mathbb{R}.$$

The quantity $\|\mathcal{J}\| = \sup_{\|f\| \leq 1} \|\mathcal{J}(f)\|$ is called the norm of the linear operator $\mathcal{J}$. We say that a linear operator $\mathcal{J}$ is a contraction whenever it holds that $\|\mathcal{J}\| < 1$. We define the linear operator $\mathcal{I}_{\mathcal{G}} f(s) := \int_{\mathcal{G}} f(\bar{s})Q(s, d\bar{s})$, which is associated with equation (10). The following lemma raises assumptions on the jump rate function $\lambda$ to render the operator $\mathcal{I}_{\mathcal{G}}$ contractive.

**Lemma 1.** *For a given set $\mathcal{G} = \mathcal{T} \times \mathcal{A}$, with $\mathcal{T} = [0, T]$ and bounded safe set $\mathcal{A}$, suppose there exists a finite constant $\kappa \geq \sup\left\{\int_0^T \lambda(r, x)dr,\ x \in \mathcal{A}\right\}$. Then the invariance operator $\mathcal{I}_\mathcal{G}$ is contractive with the norm $\|\mathcal{I}_\mathcal{G}\| \leq 1 - e^{-\kappa}$.*

**Theorem 3.** *Under the assumption of* Lemma 1 *the sequence $\{V_n\}_{n \in \mathbb{N}}$ satisfies*

$$V_{n+1}(s) = g(s) + \mathcal{I}_\mathcal{G} V_n(s), \quad \forall s \in \mathcal{G},$$

*and converges uniformly to $V(\cdot)$. Moreover, $\|V - V_n\| \leq (1 - e^{-\kappa})^n$ for all $n \in \mathbb{N}$.*

The previous result allows us to select a sufficiently large $n$ in order to make the difference between $V$ and $V_n$ smaller than a predefined threshold. For a given threshold, say $\epsilon_1$, one can select $N \geq \ln \epsilon_1 / \ln(1 - e^{-\kappa})$ and compute $V_N$. Theorem 3 then guarantees that $|V(s) - V_N(s)| \leq \epsilon_1$ for all $s \in S$. The next section is devoted to the precise computation of $V_N$ over the uncountable state space $S$, for a preselected $N$.

## 4   Finite DTMCs as Formal Approximations of cPJMPs

In the previous sections we have shown that the bounded-time safety verification of the given cPJMP can be approximated by a step-bounded reach-avoid verification of a DTMP, with guaranteed error bounds. Due to lack of analytical solutions, the verification of DTMPs against PCTL specifications (amongst which reach-avoid) is studied in the literature via finite abstractions [1,16], which result in the PCTL verification of discrete time, finite space Markov chains (DTMCs) [17,18]. In other words, the goal of the DTMC abstraction is to provide a discrete and automated computation of the reach-avoid probability. The approach is formal in that it allows for the computation of explicit bounds on the error associated with the abstraction.

The DTMC is obtained by state-space partitioning of the DTMP: equation (10) indicates that we only need to partition the bounded set $\mathcal{G}$. The abstraction procedure, presented in Algorithm 1, generates a DTMC $(S_a, P_a)$ with finite state space $S_a$ and transition probability matrix $P_a$. Over this DTMC we compute $p_a(s_i, N)$, which is the probability of reaching target state $s_{m+1}$, while avoiding the unsafe state $s_{m+2}$, during the step horizon $0, \ldots, N$, as a function of the initial state $s_i \in S_a$. This is obtained via a discrete version of equation (10), which boils down to via matrix manipulations [8].

We now introduce some regularity assumptions on the jump rate function $\lambda(\cdot)$ (Assumption 1) and on the jump measure $\pi(\cdot)$ (Assumption 2), which are needed to quantify the abstraction error resulting from the DTMC $(S_a, P_a)$.

**Assumption 1.** *Assume the space $K$ is endowed with a metric $\rho: K \times K \to \mathbb{R}$. Suppose the jump rate function $\lambda(\cdot)$ is bounded and Lipschitz-continuous, namely that there are finite constants $\Lambda$ and $h_\lambda$ such that $\lambda(t, x) \leq \Lambda$ and*

$$|\lambda(t, x) - \lambda(t, x')| \leq h_\lambda \rho(x, x'),$$

*for all $(t, x), (t, x') \in \mathcal{G}$.*

---

**Algorithm 1.** Finite-state abstraction of the DTMP $\mathfrak{M}$

---

**Require:** DTMP $\mathfrak{M} = (S, \mathcal{S}, Q)$, the sets $\mathcal{G} = [0, T] \times \mathcal{A}, \mathcal{H} = (T, \infty) \times K \cup \{(\infty, \Delta)\}$
1: Select an arbitrary finite partition of the set $\mathcal{G} = \cup_{i=1}^{m} \mathcal{D}_i$ ($\mathcal{D}_i$ are non-overlapping)

2: Define $\mathcal{D}_{m+1} := \mathcal{H}$, $\mathcal{D}_{m+2} := S \backslash (\mathcal{G} \cup \mathcal{H})$, to obtain a partition of $S = \cup_{i=1}^{m+2} \mathcal{D}_i$
3: For each $\mathcal{D}_i$, select one representative point $s_i \in \mathcal{D}_i$
4: Introduce DTMC $(S_a, P_a)$, with state space $S_a = \{s_1, s_2, \ldots, s_{m+2}\}$, and transition matrix $P_a$:
$$P_a(i, j) = \begin{cases} Q(s_i, \mathcal{D}_j) & 1 \leq i \leq m, 1 \leq j \leq m+2 \\ 1 & i = j \in \{m+1, m+2\} \\ 0 & \text{otherwise} \end{cases}$$

5: **return** DTMC $(S_a, P_a)$

---

Assumption 1 implies the Lipschitz continuity of $g(\cdot)$.

**Lemma 2.** *Under Assumption 1, the function $g(\cdot)$ in (10) is Lipschitz continuous, namely for all $s = (t, x), s' = (t', x') \in \mathcal{G}$,*

$$|g(t, x) - g(t', x')| \leq Th_\lambda \rho(x, x') + \Lambda |t - t'|.$$

The next assumption is on the regularity of the jump measure $\pi(\cdot)$ through its associated density function.

**Assumption 2.** *Let $\mathcal{K}$ be the Borel sigma-algebra on $K$. Assume that the jump measure $\pi$ on $(K, \mathcal{K})$ given $(\mathbb{R}_{\geq 0} \times K, \mathcal{B}(\mathbb{R}_{\geq 0}) \otimes \mathcal{K})$ is an integral kernel, i.e. that there exists a sigma-finite basis measure $\mu$ on $(K, \mathcal{K})$ and a jointly measurable function $p : \mathbb{R}_{\geq 0} \times K \times K \to \mathbb{R}_{\geq 0}$ such that $\pi(t, x, dy) = p(t, x, y)\mu(dy)$, i.e. $\pi(t, x, A) = \int_A p(t, x, y)\mu(dy)$ for any $(t, x) \in \mathbb{R}_{\geq 0} \times K, A \in \mathcal{K}$. Suppose further that the density function $p(\tau, x, y)$ is Lipschitz-continuous, namely that there exists a finite constant $h_p$, such that*

$$|p(\tau, x, y) - p(\tau, x', y)| \leq h_p \rho(x, x'), \quad \forall x, x', y \in \mathcal{A}, \tau \in \mathcal{T}.$$

*Example 6.* The density function $p(t, x, y)$ is computable for the dynamical system representation (5) in Example 4 under suitable assumptions on vector field $f$ given the density function of $\zeta(\cdot)$ [19,21]. □

*Remark 1.* Assumption 2 enables us to specify the conditional density function of the DTMP $(T_n, X_{T_n})_{n \in \mathbb{N}}$ as

$$t_s(\tau, y | t, x) = p(\tau, x, y)\lambda(\tau, x) \exp\left[-\int_t^\tau \lambda(r, x) dr\right] \mathbf{1}_{[t, \infty)}(\tau),$$

which gives the integral representation of the stochastic kernel of the process as $Q(t, x, (a, b), A) = \int_a^b \int_A t_s(\tau, y | t, x)\mu(dy) d\tau.$ □

Using Assumptions 1 and 2, and its consequences Theorem 3 and Lemmas 1, 2, we finally establish the following result for the error computation of the abstraction.

**Theorem 4.** *Under* Assumptions 1 and 2, *the following inequality holds:*

$$|p_{\mathcal{A}}(t_0, x_0, T) - p_a(s_\tau, N)| \leq (1 - e^{-\kappa})^N + N(h_x \delta_x + h_t \delta_t), \quad \forall (t_0, x_0) \in \mathcal{G},$$

*where* $h_x = h_p \mu(\mathcal{A}) + 3T h_\lambda$, $h_t = 3\Lambda$, *whereas* $\kappa$ *is defined in* Lemma 1. *The constants* $\delta_x, \delta_t$ *denote the partition diameters of state-space and time, namely*

$$\delta_x = \sup\{\rho(x, x'), \quad \forall (\tau, x), (\tau, x') \in \mathcal{D}_i, i = 1, 2, \ldots, m\},$$
$$\delta_t = \sup\{|\tau - \tau'|, \quad \forall (\tau, x), (\tau', x) \in \mathcal{D}_i, i = 1, 2, \ldots, m\}.$$

*In the inequality above,* $s_\tau$ *is the representative point of the partition set to which the state* $(t_0, x_0)$ *belongs, and* $p_a(s_\tau, N)$ *is the reach-avoid probability computed over the DTMC* $(S_a, P_a)$ *with finite step-horizon* $N$.

Notice that there are two terms contributing to the error in Theorem 4. The first term is caused by replacing the discrete infinite-step reach-avoid problem with an $N$-step one. The second term results from the DTMC abstraction. Augmenting the number of steps $N$ decreases the first term exponentially and increases the second term linearly: as such, this upper bound on the error can be tuned by selecting a sufficiently large step-horizon $N$, and accordingly small partition diameters $\delta_t, \delta_x$.

## 5    Case Study: Thermostatically Controlled Loads

*Thermostatically Controlled Loads* (TCLs) have shown potential to be engaged in power system services such as load shifting, peak shaving, and demand response programs. Recent studies have focused on the development of models for aggregated populations of TCLs [12,20,28]. Formal abstraction techniques have also been employed to verify properties of TCL models [2,20]. We employ the model of a TCL as the case study in this paper. The model describes the continuous-time evolution of the temperature in a TCL by a linear SDE. The value of the temperature is available to a thermostat for regulation via a network of independent asynchronous sensors [3,29]. We recast this model as a cPJMP and quantitatively verify user comfort as a probabilistic safety problem.

**Dynamical Model for the Case Study.** The continuous-time evolution of the temperature $\theta = \{\theta_t, t \in \mathbb{R}_{\geq 0}\}$ in a *cooling* TCL can be specified by the following linear SDE:

$$d\theta_t = \frac{dt}{RC}(\theta_a - q_t R P_{rate} - \theta_t) + \sigma dW_t, \tag{11}$$

where $\{W_t, t \in \mathbb{R}_{\geq 0}\}$ is the standard Brownian motion, $\theta_a$ is the ambient temperature, $C$ and $R$ indicate the thermal capacitance and resistance, $P_{rate}$ is the rate of energy transfer, and $\sigma$ is standard deviation of the noise term. The process $\{q_t,\ t \in \mathbb{R}_{\geq 0}\}$ represents the state of the thermostat at time $t$, $q_t \in \{0,1\}$ for OFF and ON modes (the latter meaning that the cooler is functioning), respectively. For a given temperature $\theta_t$ at time $t$ and a fixed mode $q_t$, the temperature at time $s \geq t$ is characterized by the solution of (11), namely

$$\theta_s = a\theta_t + (1-a)(\theta_a - q_t RP_{rate}) + w_s,$$

where $a = \exp[-(s-t)/RC]$ and $w_s \sim \mathcal{N}\left(0, \frac{1}{2}\sigma^2 RC(1-a^2)\right)$.

We assume the value of temperature is available to the thermostat via a network of sensors at possibly non-uniform time samples $\{\tau_n, n \in \mathbb{N}\}$. For a network of independent and asynchronous sensors, the time between two consecutive available values of temperature $(\tau_{n+1} - \tau_n)$, when the number of sensors is large, can be approximated by an exponential distribution [3, 29]. We assume that the associated rate depends on temperature, $\lambda(\theta_{\tau_n})$, where $\theta_{\tau_n}$ is the latest available temperature (at time $\tau_n$).

The temperature of the cooling TCL is regulated by updating the thermostat mode via the equation $q_{\tau_{n+1}} = f(q_{\tau_n}, \theta_{\tau_{n+1}})$, which is based on discrete switching

$$f(q, \theta) = \begin{cases} 0, & \theta < \theta_s - \delta_\eth/2 := \theta_- \\ 1, & \theta > \theta_s + \delta_\eth/2 := \theta_+ \\ q, & \text{else,} \end{cases} \tag{12}$$

where $\theta_s$ denotes a given temperature set-point and $\delta_\eth$ a dead-band, and together characterize the temperature operating range. Then the mode $q_t$ is a piecewise-constant and right-continuous function of time, which can change value from $q_{\tau_n}$ to $q_{\tau_{n+1}}$ at time $\tau_{n+1}$ according to the logic in (12).

**cPJMP for the Case Study.** The values of temperature and the mode of the thermostat evolve over the *hybrid* state space $K = \{0,1\} \times \mathbb{R}$, namely a space made up of discrete *and* continuous components [2]. The temperature space $\mathbb{R}$ is endowed with the Euclidean metric and with the Borel sigma-algebra. The jump measure of the process is an integral kernel (Assumption 2 is valid), with $\mu$ being the Lebesgue measure and with the density function

$$p(\tau - t, q, \theta, \bar{q}, \bar{\theta}) = \delta_\eth\left[\bar{q} - f(q, \bar{\theta})\right] \phi\left(\bar{\theta}; m_\eth(\tau - t, q, \theta), \sigma_\eth^2(\tau - t)\right),$$

where $\delta_\eth[\cdot]$ is the Kronecker delta function, $\phi(\cdot; \bar{m}, \bar{\sigma}^2)$ is the Gaussian density function with mean $\bar{m}$ and variance $\bar{\sigma}^2$, and

$$m_\eth(u, q, \theta) = a(u)\theta + (1 - a(u))(\theta_a - qRP_{rate}),$$
$$\sigma_\eth^2(u) = 2\sigma^2 RC(1 - a(u)^2), \quad a(u) = \exp[-u/RC].$$

We are interested in quantifying a proxy for user comfort: we quantify whether the likelihood of having the temperature inside a dead-band $[\theta_-, \theta_+]$ during the time interval $[0, T]$ is greater than a given threshold. This problem can be mathematically formulated as computing the safety probability of the model over the safe set $\mathcal{A} = \{0, 1\} \times [\theta_-, \theta_+]$.

Note that the density function $\pi(\cdot)$ is slightly different from the general formulation of cPJMPs in Sect. 2 in that it depends on $(\tau - t)$ (through $a(\cdot)$), instead of just the jump time $\tau$. This difference requires a slight modification of the abstraction error, which is presented next.

**Computation of Probabilistic Safety.** We consider a jump rate function $\lambda(t, \theta) = \lambda_0 e^{-\alpha t} \cosh[2\beta(\theta - \theta_s)]$ with positive constants $\lambda_0, \alpha$, and $\beta$. The term $e^{-\alpha t}$ models the reduction of the sampling rate of the sensors in time. The cosine hyperbolic function $\cosh[2\beta(\theta - \theta_s)]$ shows that more frequent temperature measurements are provided by the sensors for larger deviation of the temperature from the set-point. The assumption raised on the jump rate function in Lemma 1 holds with constant $\kappa = \lambda_0 \cosh(\beta\delta_\theta)/\alpha$, whereas Assumption 1 holds with $h_\lambda = 2\lambda_0\beta \sinh(\beta\delta_\theta)$ and $\Lambda = \lambda_0 \cosh(\beta\delta_\theta)$. The application of the abstraction technique presented in this paper to the case study leads to the error

$$E = (1 - e^{-\kappa})^N + N(h_1\delta_\theta + h_2\delta_t + h_3\sqrt{\delta_t}), \qquad (13)$$

with constants $h_1, h_2, h_3$ defined as

$$h_1 := 3Th_\lambda + \frac{\Lambda}{2\sigma}\sqrt{\pi RC}, \ \ h_2 := 3\Lambda + \frac{\Lambda\theta_+\sqrt{\pi}}{2\sigma\sqrt{RC}} + \frac{4\Lambda}{\sqrt{2\pi}}, \ \ h_3 := \frac{8\Lambda\sqrt{RC}}{\sqrt{\pi}}.$$

The additional terms contributing to the error, in comparison with the results of Theorem 4, are due to the dependence of the mean and variance of the Gaussian density function $\phi$ from the current time $t$. We use the values in Fig. 2 (left) for the parameters in the numerical simulation. The standard deviation of the process noise is $\sigma = 0.1 \, [°Cs^{-1/2}]$. The time bound for the safety specification is $T = 1 [h]$. The parameters of the jump rate functions are $\alpha = 1, \beta = 1, \lambda_0 = 1$, which means if the TCL is initialized at the set-point, the rate of temperature observations is 20 times higher than the decay rate of the TCL ($1/RC$).

We have implemented Algorithm 1 for the abstraction and computation of safety probability over the model using the software tool **FAUST**$^2$ [22]. Figure 2 (right) shows the error bound from (13), as a function of numbers of partition bins for the temperature $n_\theta$ and the time $n_t$, with a fixed step-horizon $N = 8$. One can see that for instance the abstraction algorithm guarantees an error bound of 0.23 by selecting $n_\theta = n_t = 4 \times 10^3$ ($\delta_\theta = 1.25 \times 10^{-4}, \delta_t = 2.5 \times 10^{-4}$), which generates a DTMC with $3.2 \times 10^7$ states. This indicates that meaningful error bounds (less than one) may lead to large DTMCs.

The derived error bounds can be in general conservative. To demonstrate the conservativeness of bounds, we perform the analysis with partition diameters $\delta_\theta = \delta_t = 0.0125$ ($n_\theta = 40, n_t = 80$), which result in a DTMC with 6400 states for which the error bounds are not meaningful. Figure 3 (top row) shows the computed safety probabilities as a function of initial temperature $\theta_0$ at initial time $t_0$, the left plot for ON mode and the right plot for OFF mode. Figure 3, bottom row, shows the safety likelihood estimated via Monte Carlo simulations

| Parameter | Interpretation | Value |
|-----------|----------------|-------|
| $\theta_s$ | temperature set-point | $20\,[^\circ C]$ |
| $\delta_{\bar{v}}$ | dead-band width | $0.5\,[^\circ C]$ |
| $\theta_a$ | ambient temperature | $32\,[^\circ C]$ |
| $R$ | thermal resistance | $2\,[^\circ C/kW]$ |
| $C$ | thermal capacitance | $10\,[kWh/^\circ C]$ |
| $P_{rate}$ | power | $14\,[kW]$ |

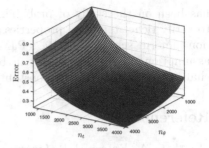

**Fig. 2.** Values of parameters for the TCL case study [20] (left). Error as a function of numbers of partition sets for temperature $n_\theta$ and time $n_t$ (right).

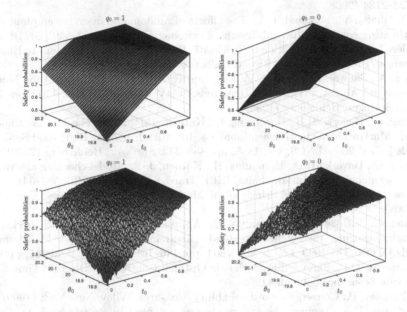

**Fig. 3.** Safety probabilities as a function of initial temperature $\theta_0$ and initial time $t_0$. Left and right columns for ON $q_0 = 1$ and OFF $q_0 = 0$ modes, respectively. First and second rows are computed via abstraction approach in this paper and via Monte Carlo simulations, respectively.

with 1000 runs initialized at the representative points used in Algorithm 1. The computation and the estimation are very close to each other with a maximum relative difference of 12 %. The results suggest that the error bounds can be reduced by employing advanced gridding techniques [18, 21].

## 6   Conclusions

We have presented an abstraction-based safety verification procedure for pure jump Markov processes with continuous states. While the focus of the work has been on the study of probabilistic safety, the technique can be extended to verify richer temporal properties. The errors can be sharpened via adaptive, non-uniform schemes [18,19]. cPJMP are a generalization of CTMC with an assumption of constant values in between jumps: we plan to investigate the challenging problem of non-constant dynamics between jumps [15].

# References

1. Abate, A., Katoen, J.-P., Lygeros, J., Prandini, M.: Approximate model checking of stochastic hybrid systems. Eur. J. Control **6**, 624–641 (2010)
2. Abate, A., Prandini, M., Lygeros, J., Sastry, S.: Probabilistic reachability and safety for controlled discrete time stochastic hybrid systems. Automatica **44**(11), 2724–2734 (2008)
3. Aït-Sahalia, Y., Mykland, P.A.: The effects of random and discrete sampling when estimating continuous-time diffusions. Econometrica **71**(2), 483–549 (2003)
4. Allen, L.J.S.: An Introduction to Stochastic Processes with Applications to Biology. Pearson/Prentice Hall, Englewood Cliffs (2003)
5. Aziz, A., Sanwal, K., Singhal, V., Brayton, R.: Verifying continuous time Markov chains. In: Alur, R., Henzinger, T.A. (eds.) CAV 1996. LNCS, vol. 1102, pp. 269–276. Springer, Heidelberg (1996)
6. Baier, C., Haverkort, B., Hermanns, H., Katoen, J.-P.: Model checking continuous-time Markov chains by transient analysis. In: Allen Emerson, E., Prasad Sistla, A. (eds.) CAV 2000. LNCS, vol. 1855, pp. 358–372. Springer, Heidelberg (2000)
7. Baier, C., Haverkort, B., Hermanns, H., Katoen, J.-P.: Model-checking algorithms for continuous-time Markov chains. IEEE Trans. Softw. Eng. **29**(6), 524–541 (2003)
8. Baier, C., Katoen, J.-P.: Principles of Model Checking. MIT Press, Cambridge (2008)
9. Baier, C., Katoen, J.-P., Hermanns, H.: Approximate symbolic model checking of continuous-time Markov chains (extended abstract). In: Baeten, J.C.M., Mauw, S. (eds.) CONCUR 1999. LNCS, vol. 1664, pp. 146–161. Springer, Heidelberg (1999)
10. Bertsekas, D.P., Shreve, S.E.: Stchastic Optimal Control: the Discrete-Time Case. Athena Scientific, Belmont (1996)
11. Billingsley, P.: Convergence of Probability Measures. Wiley, New York (1999)
12. Callaway, D.S.: Tapping the energy storage potential in electric loads to deliver load following and regulation, with application to wind energy. Ener. Convers. Manag. **50**(5), 1389–1400 (2009)
13. Chen, T., Diciolla, M., Kwiatkowska, M., Mereacre, A.: Time-bounded verification of CTMCs against real-time specifications. In: Fahrenberg, U., Tripakis, S. (eds.) FORMATS 2011. LNCS, vol. 6919, pp. 26–42. Springer, Heidelberg (2011)
14. Chen, T., Han, T., Katoen, J.-P., Mereacre, A.: Model checking of continuous-time Markov chains against timed automata specifications. Logical Methods Comput. Sci. **7**(1), 1–34 (2011)
15. Davis, M.H.A.: Markov Models and Optimization. Chapman & Hall/CRC Press, London (1993)
16. Esmaeil Zadeh Soudjani, S., Abate, A.: Adaptive gridding for abstraction and verification of stochastic hybrid systems. In: QEST, pp. 59–69 (2011)
17. Esmaeil Zadeh Soudjani, S., Abate, A.: Higher-order approximations for verification of stochastic hybrid systems. In: Chakraborty, S., Mukund, M. (eds.) ATVA 2012. LNCS, vol. 7561, pp. 416–434. Springer, Heidelberg (2012)

18. Esmaeil Zadeh Soudjani, S., Abate, A.: Adaptive and sequential gridding procedures for the abstraction and verification of stochastic processes. SIAM J. Appl. Dyn. Syst. **12**(2), 921–956 (2013)
19. Esmaeil Zadeh Soudjani, S., Abate, A.: Precise approximations of the probability distribution of a Markov process in time: an application to probabilistic invariance. In: Ábrahám, E., Havelund, K. (eds.) TACAS 2014 (ETAPS). LNCS, vol. 8413, pp. 547–561. Springer, Heidelberg (2014)
20. Esmaeil Zadeh Soudjani, S., Abate, A.: Aggregation and control of populations of thermostatically controlled loads by formal abstractions. IEEE Trans. Control Syst. Technol. **23**(3), 975–990 (2015)
21. Soudjani, S.E.Z., Abate, A.: Quantitative approximation of the probability distribution of a Markov process by formal abstractions. Logical Methods Comput. Sci **11**(3), 1–29 (2015)
22. Esmaeil Zadeh Soudjani, S., Gevaerts, C., Abate, A.: FAUST²: formal abstractions of uncountable-state stochastic processes. In: Baier, C., Tineli, C. (eds.) TACAS 2015. LNCS, vol. 9035, pp. 272–286. Springer, Heidelberg (2015)
23. Gihman, I.I., Skorokhod, A.V.: The Theory of Stochastic Processes: II. Die Grundlehren der mathematischen Wissenschaften, vol. 218. Springer, Heidelberg (1975)
24. Hinton, A., Kwiatkowska, M., Norman, G., Parker, D.: PRISM: a tool for automatic verification of probabilistic systems. In: Hermanns, H., Palsberg, J. (eds.) TACAS 2006. LNCS, vol. 3920, pp. 441–444. Springer, Heidelberg (2006)
25. Jacod, J., Shiryaev, A.: Limit Theorems for Stochastic Processes. Grundlehren der mathematischen Wissenschaften. Springer, Heidelberg (2010)
26. Kallenberg, O.: Foundations of Modern Probability. Probability and its Applications. Springer, New York (2002)
27. Katoen, J.-P., Khattri, M., Zapreev, I.S.: A Markov reward model checker. In: QEST, pp. 243–244. IEEE (2005)
28. Mathieu, J.L., Koch, S., Callaway, D.S.: State estimation and control of electric loads to manage real-time energy imbalance. IEEE Trans. Power Syst. **28**(1), 430–440 (2013)
29. Micheli, M., Jordan, M.: Random sampling of a continuous-time stochastic dynamical system. In: Proceedings of the 15th International Symposium on the Mathematical Theory of Networks and Systems (MTNS), pp. 1–15 (2002)
30. Panangaden, P.: Labelled Markov Processes. Imperial College Press, London (2009)
31. Platen, E., Bruti-Liberati, N.: Numerical Solution of Stochastic Differential Equations with Jumps in Finance. Stochastic Modelling and Applied Probability. Springer, Heidelberg (2010)
32. Tkachev, I., Abate, A.: On infinite-horizon probabilistic properties and stochastic bisimulation functions. In: Proceedings of the 50th IEEE Conference on Decision and Control and European Control Conference, pp. 526–531, Orlando, FL, December 2011
33. Tkachev, I., Abate, A.: Characterization and computation of infinite-horizon specifications over Markov processes. Theor. Comput. Sci. **515**, 1–18 (2014)
34. Van Kampen, N.G.: Stochastic Processes in Physics and Chemistry. North-Holland Personal Library. Elsevier Science, Amsterdam (2011)
35. Ziai, Y.: Statistical models of claim amount distributions in general insurance. Ph.D. thesis, School of Engineering and Maths, City University London (1979)

# Synthesis

# Abstract Learning Frameworks for Synthesis

Christof Löding[1], P. Madhusudan[2], and Daniel Neider[2,3](✉)

[1] RWTH Aachen, Aachen, Germany
[2] University of Illinois, Urbana-Champaign, Champaign, USA
[3] University of California, Los Angeles, USA
neider@ucla.edu

**Abstract.** We develop abstract learning frameworks for synthesis that embody the principles of the CEGIS (counterexample-guided inductive synthesis) algorithms in current literature. Our framework is based on iterative learning from a hypothesis space that captures synthesized objects, using counterexamples from an abstract sample space, and a concept space that abstractly defines the semantics of synthesis. We show that a variety of synthesis algorithms in current literature can be embedded in this general framework. We also exhibit three general recipes for convergent synthesis: the first two recipes based on finite spaces and Occam learners generalize all techniques of convergence used in existing engines, while the third, involving well-founded quasi-orderings, is new, and we instantiate it to concrete synthesis problems.

## 1 Introduction

The field of synthesis, which includes several forms of synthesis including synthesizing controllers [37], program expressions [43], program repairs [26], program translations [11,23], loop invariants [16,17], and even entire programs [25,32], has become a fundamental and vibrant subfield in programming languages. While classical studies of synthesis have focused on synthesizing entire programs or controllers from specifications [32,37], there is a surge of tractable methods that have emerged in recent years in synthesizing small program expressions. These expressions often are complex but small, and are applicable in niche domains such as program sketching [43] (finding program expressions that complete code), synthesizing Excel programs for string transformations [18], synthesizing super-optimized code [40], deobfuscating code [21], synthesizing invariants to help in verification [16,17], etc.

One prominent technique that has emerged in recent years for expression synthesis is based on *inductively learning expressions from samples*. Assume the synthesis problem is to synthesize an expression $e$ that satisfies some specification $\psi(e)$. The crux of this approach is to *ignore* the precise specification $\psi$, and instead synthesize an expression based on certain *facets* of the specification. These incomplete facets of the specification are often much simpler in structure and in logical complexity compared to the specification, and hence synthesizing an expression satisfying the constraints the facets impose is more tractable.

© Springer-Verlag Berlin Heidelberg 2016
M. Chechik and J.-F. Raskin (Eds.): TACAS 2016, LNCS 9636, pp. 167–185, 2016.
DOI: 10.1007/978-3-662-49674-9_10

The learning-based approach to synthesis hence happens in rounds— in each round, the learner synthesizes an expression that satisfies the current facets, and a *verification oracle* checks whether the expression satisfies the actual specification $\psi$, and if not, finds a new facet of the specification witnessing this. The learner then continues to synthesize by adding this new facet to its collection.

This counter-example guided inductive synthesis (CEGIS) approach [42] to synthesis in current literature philosophically advocates precisely this kind of inductive synthesis. The CEGIS approach has emerged as a powerful technique in several domains of both program synthesis as well as program verification ranging from synthesizing program invariants for verification [16,17] to specification mining [3], program expressions that complete sketches [43], superoptimization [40], control [22], string transformers for spreadsheets [18], protocols [45], etc.

The goal of this paper is to develop a *theory of iterative learning-based synthesis* through a formalism we call *abstract learning frameworks for synthesis*. The framework we develop aims to be general and abstract, encompassing several known CEGIS frameworks as well as several other synthesis algorithms not generally viewed as CEGIS. The goal of this line of work is to build a framework, with accompanying concepts, definitions, and vocabulary that can be used to understand and combine learning-based synthesis across different domains.

An abstract learning framework (ALF) (see Fig. 1) consists of three spaces: $\mathcal{H}$, $\mathcal{S}$, and $\mathcal{C}$. The *(semantic) concept space* $\mathcal{C}$ gives semantic descriptions of the concepts that we wish to synthesize, the *hypotheses space* $\mathcal{H}$ comprises restricted (typically syntactically restricted) forms of the concepts to synthesize, and the sample space $\mathcal{S}$ consists of samples (modeling facets of the specification) from which the learner synthesizes hypotheses. The spaces $\mathcal{H}$ and $\mathcal{S}$ are related by a variety of functions that give semantics to samples and semantics to hypotheses using the space $\mathcal{C}$. The conditions imposed on these relations capture the learning problem precisely, and their abstract formulation facilitates modeling a variety of synthesis frameworks in the literature.

The target for synthesis is specified as a *set* of semantic concepts. This is an important digression from classical learning frameworks, where often one can assume that there is a *particular* target concept that the learner is trying to learn. Note that in synthesis problems, we must *implement the teacher as well*, and hence the modeling of the target space is important. In synthesis problems, the teacher does not have a single target in mind nor does she know explicitly the target set (if she knew, there would be no reason to synthesize!). Rather, she knows the *properties* that capture the set of target concepts. For instance, in invariant synthesis, the teacher knows the properties of a set being an invariant for a loop, and this defines implicitly a *set* of invariants as target. The teacher needs to examine a hypothesis and check whether it satisfies the properties defining the target set. Consequently, we can view the teacher as a *verification oracle* that checks whether a hypothesis belongs to the implicitly defined target set.

We exhibit a variety of existing synthesis frameworks that can be naturally seen as instantiations of our abstract-learning framework, where the formulation shows the diversity in the instantiations of the spaces. These include

(a) a variety of CEGIS-based synthesis techniques for synthesizing program expressions in sketches (completing program sketches [43], synthesizing loop-free programs [19], mining specifications [22], synthesizing synchronization code for concurrent programs [10], etc.), (b) synthesis from input-output examples such as Flashfill [18], (c) the CEGIS framework applied to the concrete problem of solving synthesis problems expressed in the SMT-based SyGuS format [1,2], and three synthesis engines that use learning to synthesize solutions, (d) invariant synthesis frameworks, including Houdini [14] and the more recent ICE-learning model for synthesizing loop invariants [16], spanning a variety of domains from arithmetic [16,17] to quantified invariants over data structures [15], and (e) synthesizing fixed-points and abstract transformers in abstract interpretation settings [44].

Formalizing of synthesis algorithms as ALFs can help highlight the nuances of different learning-based synthesis algorithms, even for the *same* problem. One example comprises two inductive learning approaches for synthesizing program invariants— one based on the ICE learning model [16], and the second which is any synthesis engine for logically specified synthesis problems in the SyGuS format, which can express invariant synthesis. Though both can be seen as CEGIS-based synthesis algorithms, the sample space for them are very different, and hence the synthesis algorithms are also different— the significant performance differences between SyGuS-based solvers and ICE-based solvers (the latter performing better) in the recent SyGuS competition (invariant-synthesis track) suggest that this choice may be crucial [4]. Another example are two classes of CEGIS-based solvers for synthesizing linear integer arithmetic functions against SyGuS specifications— one based on a sample space that involves purely inputs to the function being synthesized [35,39], while the other is the more standard CEGIS algorithm based on valuations of quantified variables.

We believe that just describing an approach as a learning-based synthesis algorithm or a CEGIS algorithm does not convey the nuances of the approach— it is important to precisely spell out the sample space and the semantics of this space with respect to the space of hypotheses being learned. The ALF framework gives the vocabulary in phrasing these nuances, allowing us to compare and contrast different approaches.

**Convergence.** The second main contribution of this paper is to study *convergence* issues in the general abstract learning-based framework for synthesis. We first show that under the reasonable assumptions that the learner is consistent (always proposes a hypothesis consistent with the samples it has received) and the teacher is honest (gives a sample that distinguishes the current hypothesis from the target set without ruling out any of the target concepts), the iterative learning will always converge *in the limit* (though, not necessarily in finite time, of course). This theorem vouches for the correctness of our abstract formalism in capturing abstract learning, and utilizes all the properties that define ALFs.

We then turn to studying strategies for convergence in finite time. We propose three general techniques for ensuring successful termination for the learner.

First, when the hypothesis space is bounded, it is easy to show that any consistent learner (paired with an honest teacher) will converge in finite time. Several examples of these exist in learning— learning conjunctions as in the Houdini algorithm [14], etc., learning Boolean functions (like decision-tree learning with purely Boolean predicates as attributes) or functions over bit-vector domains (Sketch [43] and the SyGuS solvers that work on bit-vectors), and learning invariants using specialized forms of a finite class of automata that capture list/array invariants [15].

The second recipe is a formulation of the Occam's razor principle that uses parsimony/simplicity as the learning bias [6]. The idea of using Occam's principle in learning is prevalent (see Chap. 2 of [24] and [33]) though its universal appeal in generalizing concepts is debatable [13]. We show, however, that learning using Occam's principle helps in convergence. A learner is said to be an Occam learner if there is a *complexity ordering*, which needs to be a total quasi order where the set of elements below any element is finite, such that the learner always learns *a smallest* concept according to this order that is consistent with the sample. We can then show that any Occam learner will converge to some target concept, if one exists, in finite time. This result generalizes many convergent learning mechanisms that we know of in the literature (for example, the convergent ICE-learning algorithms for synthesizing invariants using constraint solvers [16], and the enumerative solvers in almost every domain of synthesis [26,28,36,45], including for SyGuS [1,2], that enumerate by dovetailing through expressions).

The first two recipes for finite convergence cover all the methods we know in the literature for convergent learning-based synthesis, to the best of our knowledge. The third recipe for finite convergence is a more complex one based on well-founded quasi orderings. This recipe is involved and calls for using clever initial queries that force the teacher to divulge information that then makes the learning space tractable. We do not know of any existing synthesis learning frameworks that use this natural recipe, but propose two new convergent learning algorithms following this recipe, one for intervals, and the other for conjunctive linear inequality constraints over a set of numerical attributes over integers.

## 2   Abstract Learning Frameworks for Synthesis

In this section we introduce our abstract learning framework for synthesis. Figure 1 gives an overview of the components and their relations that are introduced in the following (ignore the target $\mathcal{T}$, $\gamma^{-1}(\mathcal{T})$, and the maps $\tau$ and $\lambda$ for now). We explain these components in more detail after the formal definition.

**Definition 1 (Abstract Learning Frameworks).** *An abstract learning framework for synthesis (ALF, for short), is a tuple* $\mathcal{A} = (\mathcal{C}, \mathcal{H}, (\mathcal{S}, \sqsubseteq_s, \sqcup, \perp_s), \gamma, \kappa)$, *with*

- *A class $\mathcal{C}$, called the concept space,*
- *A class $\mathcal{H}$, called the hypothesis space,*

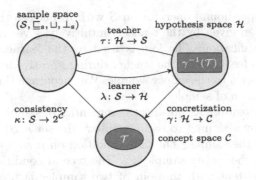

**Fig. 1.** Components of an ALF

- A class $\mathcal{S}$, called the sample space, with a join semi-lattice $(\mathcal{S}, \sqsubseteq_s, \sqcup, \perp_s)$ defined over it,
- A concretization function $\gamma : \mathcal{H} \to \mathcal{C}$, and
- A consistency function: $\kappa : \mathcal{S} \to 2^{\mathcal{C}}$ satisfying $\kappa(\perp_s) = \mathcal{C}$ and $\kappa(S_1 \sqcup S_2) = \kappa(S_1) \cap \kappa(S_2)$ for all $S_1, S_2 \in \mathcal{S}$. If the second condition is relaxed to $\kappa(S_1 \sqcup S_2) \subseteq \kappa(S_1) \cap \kappa(S_2)$, we speak of a general ALF.

We say an ALF has a complete sample space if the sample space $(\mathcal{S}, \sqsubseteq_s, \sqcup, \perp_s)$ is a complete join semi-lattice (i.e., if the join is defined for arbitrary subsets of $\mathcal{S}$). In this case, the consistency relation has to satisfy $\kappa(\bigsqcup(\mathcal{S}')) = \bigcap_{S \in \mathcal{S}'} \kappa(S)$ for each $\mathcal{S}' \subseteq \mathcal{S}$ (and $\kappa(\bigsqcup(\mathcal{S}')) \subseteq \bigcap_{S \in \mathcal{S}'} \kappa(S)$ for general ALFs).

As in computational learning theory, as presented in e.g., in [5] or [24], we consider a *concept space* $\mathcal{C}$, which contains the objects that we are interested in. For example, in an invariant synthesis setting in verification, an element $C \in \mathcal{C}$ would be a *set* of program configurations. In the synthesis setting, $\mathcal{C}$ could contain the objects we would like to synthesize, such as all functions from $\mathbb{Z}^n$ to $\mathbb{Z}$.

The *hypothesis space* $\mathcal{H}$ contains the objects that the learner produces. These are representations of (some) elements from the concept space. For example, if $\mathcal{C}$ consists of all functions from $\mathbb{Z}^n$ to $\mathbb{Z}$, then $\mathcal{H}$ could consist the set of all functions expressible in linear arithmetic.

The relation between hypotheses and concepts is given by a concretization function $\gamma : \mathcal{H} \to \mathcal{C}$ that maps hypotheses to concepts (their semantics).

In classical computational learning theory for classification [24,33], one often considers samples consisting of positive and negative examples. If learning is used to infer a target concept that is not uniquely defined but rather should satisfy certain properties, then samples consisting of positive and negative examples are sometimes not sufficient. As we will show later, samples can be quite complex (see Sect. 4 for such examples, including implication counterexamples and grounded formulas).

We work with a *sample space*, which is a bounded join-semilattice $(\mathcal{S}, \sqsubseteq_s, \sqcup, \perp_s)$ (i.e., $\sqsubseteq_s$ is a partial order over $\mathcal{S}$ with $\perp_s$ as the least element, and $\sqcup$ is the binary least upper-bound operator on $S$ with respect to this ordering). An element $S \in S$, when given by the teacher, intuitively, gives some information about a target specification. The join is used by the learner to combine the samples returned as feedback by the teacher during iterative learning. The least element $\perp_s$ corresponds to the empty sample. We encourage the reader to think of the join as the union of samples.

The *consistency relation* $\kappa$ captures the semantics of samples with respect to the concept space by assigning to each sample $S$ the set $\kappa(S)$ of concepts that are consistent with the sample. The first condition on $\kappa$ says that all concepts are consistent with the empty sample $\perp_s$. The second condition says that the set of samples consistent with the join of two samples is precisely the set of concepts that is consistent with both the samples. Intuitively, this means that joining samples does not introduce new inconsistencies, and existing inconsistencies transfer to bigger samples. The condition that $\kappa(S_1 \sqcup S_2) \subseteq \kappa(S_1) \cap \kappa(S_2)$ is natural, as it says that if a concept is consistent with the join of two samples, then the concept must be consistent with both of them individually. The condition that $\kappa(S_1 \sqcup S_2) \supseteq \kappa(S_1) \cap \kappa(S_2)$ is debatable; it claims that samples when taken together cannot eliminate a concept that they couldn't eliminate individually. We therefore mention the notion of *general ALF* in Definition 1. However, we have not found any natural example that requires such a generalization, and therefore prefer to work with ALFs instead of general ALFs in the rest of the paper. In Definition 4, we comment on what needs to be adapted to make the results of the paper go through for general ALFs.

Some other auxiliary definitions we will need: We define $\kappa_{\mathcal{H}}(S) := \{H \in \mathcal{H} \mid \gamma(H) \in \kappa(S)\}$ to be the set of hypotheses that are consistent with $S$. For a sample $S \in S$ we say that $S$ *is realizable* if there exists a hypothesis that is consistent with $S$ (i.e., $\kappa_{\mathcal{H}}(S) \neq \emptyset$).

*ALF Instances and Learners.* An instance of a learning task for an ALF is given by a specification that defines target concepts. The goal is to infer a hypothesis whose semantics is such a target concept. In classical computational learning theory, this target is a unique concept. In applications for synthesis, however, there can be many possible target concepts, for example, all inductive invariants of a program loop.

Formally, a *target specification* is just a set $\mathcal{T} \subseteq \mathcal{C}$ of concepts. An ALF instance combines an ALF and a target specification:

**Definition 2 (ALF Instance).** *An ALF instance is a pair* $(A, \mathcal{T})$ *where* $\mathcal{A} = (\mathcal{C}, \mathcal{H}, (S, \sqsubseteq_s, \sqcup, \perp_s), \gamma, \kappa)$ *is an ALF and* $\mathcal{T} \subseteq \mathcal{C}$ *is a target specification.*

The goal of learning-based synthesis is for the learner to synthesize *some* element $H \in \mathcal{H}$ such that $\gamma(H) \in \mathcal{T}$. Furthermore, the role of the teacher is to instruct the learner giving reasons why the hypothesis produced by the learner in the current round does not belong to the target set.

There is a subtle point here worth emphasizing. In synthesis frameworks, the teacher does not explicitly know the target space $\mathcal{T}$. Rather she knows a definition of the target space, and she can examine a hypothesis $H$ and check whether it satisfies the properties required of the target set. For instance, when synthesizing an invariant for a program, the teacher knows the properties of the invariant (inductiveness, etc.) and gives counterexample samples based on failed properties.

We say that the target specification is *realizable by a hypothesis*, or simply realizable, if there is some $H \in \mathcal{H}$ with $\gamma(H) \in \mathcal{T}$. For a hypothesis $H \in \mathcal{H}$, we often write $H \in \mathcal{T}$ instead of $\gamma(H) \in \mathcal{T}$.

As in classical computational learning theory, we define a *learner* (see Fig. 1) to be a function that maps samples to hypotheses, and a consistent learner to be a learner that only proposes consistent hypotheses for samples.

**Definition 3.** *A learner for an ALF* $\mathcal{A} = (\mathcal{C}, \mathcal{H}, (\mathcal{S}, \sqsubseteq_s, \sqcup, \perp_s), \gamma, \kappa)$ *is a map* $\lambda : \mathcal{S} \to \mathcal{H}$ *that assigns a hypothesis to every sample. A consistent learner is a learner* $\lambda$ *with* $\gamma(\lambda(S)) \in \kappa(S)$ *for all realizable samples* $S \in \mathcal{S}$.

*Iterative learning.* In the iterative learning setting, the learner produces a hypothesis starting from some initial sample (e.g., $\perp_s$). For each hypothesis provided by the learner that does not satisfy the target specification, a teacher (see Fig. 1) provides feedback by returning a sample witnessing that the hypothesis does not satisfy the target specification.

**Definition 4.** *Let* $(A, \mathcal{T})$ *be an ALF instance with* $\mathcal{A} = (\mathcal{C}, \mathcal{H}, (\mathcal{S}, \sqsubseteq_s, \sqcup, \perp_s),$ $\gamma, \kappa)$, *and* $\mathcal{T} \subseteq \mathcal{C}$. *A teacher for this ALF instance is a function* $\tau : \mathcal{H} \to \mathcal{S}$ *that satisfies the following two properties:*

(i) **Progress:** $\tau(H) = \perp_s$ *for each target element* $H \in \mathcal{T}$, *and* $\gamma(H) \notin \kappa(\tau(H))$ *for all* $H \notin \mathcal{T}$, *and*

(ii) **Honesty:** $\mathcal{T} \subseteq \kappa(\tau(H))$ *for each* $H \in \mathcal{H}$.[1]

Firstly, progress says that if the hypothesis is in the target set, then the teacher must return the "empty" sample $\perp_s$, signaling that the learner has learned a target; otherwise, the teacher must return a sample that rules out the current hypothesis. This ensures that a consistent learner can never propose the same hypothesis again, and hence makes progress. Secondly, honesty demands that the sample returned by the teacher is consistent with *all* target concepts. This ensures that the teacher does not eliminate any element of the target set arbitrarily.

When the learner and teacher interact iteratively, the learner produces a sequence of hypotheses, where in each round it proposes a hypothesis $\lambda(S)$ for the current sample $S \in \mathcal{S}$, and then adds the feedback $\tau(\lambda(S))$ of the teacher to obtain the new sample.

---

[1] For general ALFs one has to require that the least upper bound of all samples returned by the teacher is consistent with all targets (and for non-complete sample lattices the least upper bound of all possible finite sets of samples returned by the teacher).

**Definition 5.** *Let $(A, T)$ be an ALF instance with $A = (C, H, (S, \sqsubseteq_s, \sqcup, \bot_s), \gamma, \kappa)$, and $T \subseteq C$. Let $\lambda : S \to H$ be a learner, and let $\tau : H \to S$ be a teacher. The combined behavior of the learner $\lambda$ and teacher $\tau$ is the function $f_{\tau,\lambda} : S \to S$, where $f_{\tau,\lambda}(S) := S \sqcup \tau(\lambda(S))$.*

*The sequence of hypotheses generated by the learner $\lambda$ and teacher $\tau$ is the trans-finite sequence $\langle S^{\alpha}_{\tau,\lambda} \mid \alpha \in \mathbb{O} \rangle$, where $\mathbb{O}$ denotes the class of all ordinals, obtained by iterative application of $f_{\tau,\lambda}$:*

- $S^0_{\tau,\lambda} := \bot_s$;
- $S^{\alpha+1}_{\tau,\lambda} := f_{\tau,\lambda}(S^{\alpha}_{\tau,\lambda})$ *for successor ordinals; and*
- $S^{\alpha}_{\tau,\lambda} := \bigsqcup_{\beta < \alpha} S^{\beta}_{\tau,\lambda}$ *for limit ordinals.*

*If the sample lattice is not complete, the above definition is restricted to the first two items and yields a sequence indexed by natural numbers.*

The following lemma states that the teacher's properties of progress and honesty transfer to the iterative setting for consistent learners if the target specification is realizable. A proof can be found in the extended paper [31].

**Lemma 1.** *Let $T$ be realizable, $\lambda$ be a consistent learner, and $\tau$ be a teacher. If $S$ is a complete sample lattice, then*

(a) *the learner makes progress: for all $\alpha \in \mathbb{O}$, either $\kappa(S^{\alpha}_{\tau,\lambda}) \supsetneq \kappa(S^{\alpha+1}_{\tau,\lambda})$ and $\lambda(S^{\alpha}_{\tau,\lambda}) \notin \kappa(S^{\alpha+1}_{\tau,\lambda})$, or $\lambda(S^{\alpha}_{\tau,\lambda}) \in T$, and*
(b) *the sample sequence is consistent with the target specification: $T \subseteq \kappa(S^{\alpha}_{\tau,\lambda})$ for all $\alpha \in \mathbb{O}$.*

*If $S$ is a non-complete sample lattice, then (a) and (b) hold for all $\alpha \in \mathbb{N}$.*

We end with an example of an ALF. Consider the problem of synthesizing guarded affine functions that capture how a piece of code $P$ behaves, as in program deobfuscation. Then the concept class could be all functions from $\mathbb{Z}^n$ to $\mathbb{Z}$, the hypothesis space would be the set of all expressions describing a guarded affine function (in some fixed syntax). The target set (as a subset of $C$) would consist of a *single* function $\{f_t\}$, where $f_t$ is the function computed by the program $P$. For any hypothesis function $h$, let us assume we can build a teacher who can compare $h$ and $P$ for equivalence, and, if they differ, return a counterexample of the form $(i, o)$, which is a concrete input $i$ on which $h$ differs from $P$, and $o$ is the output of $P$ on $i$. Then the sample space would consist of sets of such pairs (with union for join and empty set for $\bot_s$). The set of functions consistent with a set of samples would be the those that map the inputs mentioned in the samples to their appropriate outputs. The iterative learning will then model the process of synthesis, using learning, a guarded affine function that is equivalent to $P$.

# 3 Convergence of Iterative Learning

In this section, we study convergence of the iterative learning process. We start with a general theorem on transfinite convergence (convergence in the limit) for complete sample lattices. We then turn to convergence in finite time and exhibit three recipes that guarantee convergence.

From Lemma 1 one can conclude that the transfinite sequence of hypotheses constructed by the learner converges to a target set (see the extended paper [31] for a proof).

**Theorem 1.** *Let $S$ be a complete sample lattice, $\mathcal{T}$ be realizable, $\lambda$ be a consistent learner, and $\tau$ be a teacher. Then there exists an ordinal $\alpha$ such that $\lambda(S_{\tau,\lambda}^{\alpha}) \in \mathcal{T}$.*

The above theorem ratifies the choice of our definitions, and the proof (relying on Lemma 1) crucially uses all aspects of our definitions (the honesty and progress properties of the teacher, the condition imposed on $\kappa$ in an ALF, the notion of consistent learners, etc.).

Convergence in finite time is clearly the more desirable notion, and we propose tactics for designing learners that converge in finite time. For an ALF instance $(\mathcal{A}, \mathcal{T})$, we say that a learner $\lambda$ *converges for a teacher* $\tau$ if there is an $n \in \mathbb{N}$ such that $\lambda(S_{\tau,\lambda}^{n}) \in \mathcal{T}$, which means that $\lambda$ produces a target hypothesis after $n$ steps. We say that $\lambda$ converges if it converges for every teacher. We say that $\lambda$ converges from a sample $S$ in case the learning process starts from a sample $S \neq \perp_s$ (i.e., if $S_{\lambda,\tau}^{0} = S$).

**Finite Hypothesis Spaces.** We first note that if the hypothesis space (or the concept space) is finite, then any consistent learner converges: by Lemma 1, the learner always makes progress, and hence never proposes two hypotheses that correspond to the same concept. Consequently, the learner only produces a finite number of hypotheses before finding one that is in the target (or declare that no such hypothesis exists).

There are several synthesis engines using learning that use finite hypothesis spaces. For example, Houdini [14] is a learner of *conjunctions* over a fixed finite set of predicates and, hence, has a finite hypothesis space. Learning decision trees over purely Boolean attributes (not numerical) [38] is also convergent because of finite hypothesis spaces, and this extends to the ICE learning model as well [17]. Invariant generation for arrays and lists using *elastic QDAs* [15] also uses a convergence argument that relies on a finite hypothesis space.

**Occam Learners.** We now discuss the most robust strategy we know for convergence, based on the Occam's razor principle. Occam's razor advocates parsimony or simplicity [6], that the simplest concept/theory that explains a set of observations is better, as a virtue in itself. There are several learning algorithms that use parsimony as a learning bias in machine learning (e.g., *pruning* in decision-tree learning [33]), though the general applicability of Occam's razor in machine learning as a sound means to generalize is debatable [13]. We now show that in *iterative* learning, following Occam's principle leads to convergence in finite time. However, the role of *simplicity* itself is not the technical reason for convergence, but that there is *some* ordering of concepts that biases the learning.

Enumerative learners are a good example of this. In enumerative learning, the learner enumerates hypotheses in some order, and always conjectures the first consistent hypothesis. In an iterative learning-based synthesis setting, such a learner always converges on some target concept, if one exists, in finite time.

Requiring a total order of the hypotheses is in some situations too strict. If, for example, the hypothesis space consists of deterministic finite automata (DFAs), we could build a learner that always produces a DFA with the smallest possible number of states that is consistent with the given sample. However, the relation $\preceq$ that compares DFAs w.r.t. their number of states is not an ordering because there are different DFAs with the same number of states.

In order to capture such situations, we work with a *total quasi-order* $\preceq$ on $\mathcal{H}$ instead of a total order. A quasi-order (also called preorder) is a transitive and reflexive relation. The relation being total means that $H \preceq H'$ or $H' \preceq H$ for all $H, H' \in \mathcal{H}$. The difference to an order relation is that $H \preceq H'$ and $H' \preceq H$ can hold in a quasi-order, even if $H \neq H'$.

In analogy to enumerations, we require that each hypothesis has only finitely many hypotheses "before" it w.r.t. $\preceq$, as expressed in the following definition.

**Definition 6.** *A complexity ordering is a total quasi-order $\preceq$ such that for each $x \in \mathcal{H}$ the set $\{y \in \mathcal{H} \mid y \preceq x\}$ is finite.*

The example of comparing DFAs with respect to their number of states is such a complexity ordering.

**Definition 7.** *A consistent learner that always constructs a smallest hypothesis with respect to a complexity ordering $\preceq$ on $\mathcal{H}$ is called an $\preceq$-Occam learner.*

*Example 1.* Consider $\mathcal{H} = \mathcal{C}$ to be the interval domain over the integers consisting of all intervals of the form $[l, r]$, where $l, r \in \mathbb{Z} \cup \{-\infty, \infty\}$ and $l \leq r$. We define $[l, r] \preceq [l', r']$ if either $[l, r] = [-\infty, \infty]$ or $\max\{|x| \mid x \in \{l, r\} \cap \mathbb{Z}\} \leq \max\{|x| \mid x \in \{l', r'\} \cap \mathbb{Z}\}$. For example, $[-4, \infty] \preceq [1, 7]$ because $4 \leq 7$. This ordering $\preceq$ satisfies the property that for each interval $[l, r]$ the set $\{[l', r'] \mid [l', r'] \preceq [l, r]\}$ is finite (because there are only finitely many intervals using integer constants with a bounded absolute value). A standard positive/negative sample $S = (P, N)$ with $P, N \subseteq \mathbb{N}$ is consistent with all intervals that contain the elements from $P$ and do not contain an element from $N$. A learner that maps $S$ to an interval that uses integers with the smallest possible absolute value (while being consistent with $S$) is an $\preceq$-Occam learner. For example, such a learner would map the sample $(P = \{-2, 5\}, N = \{-8\})$ to the interval $[-2, \infty]$. □

The next theorem shows that $\preceq$-Occam learners ensure convergence in finite time (see the extended paper [31] for a proof).

**Theorem 2.** *If $T$ is realizable and $\lambda$ is a $\preceq$-Occam learner, then $\lambda$ converges. Furthermore, the learner converges to a $\preceq$-minimal target element.*

There are several existing algorithms in the literature that use such orderings to ensure convergence. Several enumeration-based solvers are convergent because of the ordering of enumeration (e.g., the generic enumerative solver for SyGuS problems [1,2]). The invariant-generation ranging over conditional linear arithmetic expressions described in [16] ensures convergence using a total quasi-order based on the number of conditionals and the values of the coefficients. The learner uses templates to restrict the number of conditionals and a constraint-solver to find small coefficients for linear constraints.

**Convergence Using Tractable Well Founded Quasi-Orders.** The third strategy for convergence in finite time that we propose is based on well founded quasi-orders, or simply well-quasi-orders. Interestingly, we know of no existing learning algorithms in the literature that uses this recipe for convergence (a technique of similar flavor is used in [9]). We exhibit in this section a learning algorithm for intervals and for conjunctions of inequalities of numerical attributes based on this recipe. A salient feature of this recipe is that the convergence actually uses the samples returned by the teacher in order to converge (the first two recipes articulated above, on the other hand, would even guarantee convergence if the teacher just replies yes/no when asked whether the hypothesis is in the target set).

A binary relation $\preceq$ over some set $X$ is a well-quasi-order if it is transitive and reflexive, and for each infinite sequence $x_0, x_1, x_2, \ldots$ there are indices $i < j$ such that $x_i \preceq x_j$. In other words, there are no infinite descending chains and no infinite anti-chains for $\preceq$.

**Definition 8.** *Let $(\mathcal{A}, T)$ be an ALF instance with $\mathcal{A} = (\mathcal{C}, \mathcal{H}, (\mathcal{S}, \sqsubseteq_s, \sqcup, \perp_s), \gamma, \kappa)$. A subset of hypotheses $W \subseteq \mathcal{H}$ is called wqo-tractable if*

*(a) there is a well-quasi-order $\preceq_W$ on $W$, and*
*(b) for each realizable sample $S \in \mathcal{S}$ with $\kappa_{\mathcal{H}}(S) \subseteq W$, there is some $\preceq_W$-maximal hypothesis in $W$ that is consistent with $S$.*

*Example 2.* Consider again the example of intervals over $\mathbb{Z} \cup \{-\infty, \infty\}$ with samples of the form $S = (P, N)$ (see Example 1). Let $p \in \mathbb{Z}$ be a point and let $\mathcal{I}_p$ be the set of all intervals that contain the point $p$. Then, $\mathcal{I}_p$ is wqo-tractable with the standard inclusion relation for intervals, defined by $[\ell, r] \subseteq [\ell', r']$ iff $\ell \geq \ell'$ and $r \leq r'$. Restricted to intervals that contain the point $p$, this is the product of two well-founded orders on the sets $\{x \in \mathbb{Z} \mid x \leq p\}$ and $\{x \in \mathbb{Z} \mid x \geq p\}$, and as such is itself well-founded [20, Theorem 2.3]. Furthermore, for each realizable sample $(P, N)$, there is a unique maximal interval over $\mathbb{Z} \cup \{-\infty, \infty\}$ that contains $P$ and excludes $N$. Hence, the two conditions of wqo-tractability are satisfied. (Note that this ordering on the set of *all* intervals is not a well-quasi-order; the sequence $[-\infty, 0], [-\infty, -1], [-\infty, -2], \ldots$ witnesses this.) □

On a wqo-tractable $W \subseteq \mathcal{H}$ a learner can ensure convergence by always proposing a maximal consistent hypothesis, as stated in the following lemma (a proof can be found in the extended paper [31]).

**Lemma 2.** *Let $\mathcal{T}$ be realizable, $W \subseteq \mathcal{H}$ be wqo-tractable with well-quasi-order $\preceq_W$, and $S$ be a sample such that $\kappa_{\mathcal{H}}(S) \subseteq W$. Then, there exists a learner that converges from the sample $S$.*

As shown in Example 2, for each $p \in \mathbb{Z}$, the set $\mathcal{I}_p$ of intervals containing $p$ is wqo-tractable. Using this, we can build a convergent learner starting from the empty sample $\perp_s$. First, the learner starts by proposing the empty interval, the teacher must either confirm that this is a target or return a positive example, that is, a point $p$ that is contained in every target interval. Hence, the set of hypotheses consistent with this sample is wqo-tractable and the learner can converge from here on as stated in Lemma 2. In general, the strategy for the learner is to force in one step a sample $S$ such that the set $\kappa_{\mathcal{H}}(S) = \mathcal{I}_p$ is wqo-tractable. This is generalized in the following definition.

**Definition 9.** *We say that an ALF is wqo-tractable if there is a finite set $\{H_1, \ldots, H_n\}$ of hypotheses such that $\kappa_{\mathcal{H}}(S)$ is wqo-tractable for all samples $S$ that are inconsistent with all $H_i$, that is, $\kappa_{\mathcal{H}}(S) \cap \{H_1, \ldots, H_n\} = \emptyset$.*

As explained above, the interval ALF is wqo-tractable with the set $\{H_1, \ldots, H_n\}$ consisting only of the empty interval.

Combining all the previous observations, we obtain convergence for wqo-tractable ALFs (see the extended paper [31] for a proof).

**Theorem 3.** *For every ALF instance $(\mathcal{A}, \mathcal{T})$ such that $\mathcal{A}$ is wqo-tractable and $\mathcal{T}$ is realizable, there is a convergent learner.*

*A convergent learner for conjunctive linear inequality constraints.* We have illustrated wqo-tractability for intervals in Example 2. We finish this section by showing that this generalizes to higher dimensions, that is, to the domain of $n$-dimensional hyperrectangles in $(\mathbb{Z} \cup \{-\infty, \infty\})^n$, which form the hypothesis space in this example. Each such hyperrectangle is a product of intervals over $(\mathbb{Z} \cup \{-\infty, \infty\})^n$. Note that hyperrectangles can, e.g., be used to model conjunctive linear inequality constraints over a set $f_1, \ldots, f_n : \mathbb{Z}^d \to \mathbb{Z}$ of numerical attributes.

The sample space depends on the type of target specification that we are interested in. We consider here the typical sample space of positive and negative samples (however, the reasoning below also works for other sample spaces, e.g., ICE sample spaces that additionally include implications). So, samples are of the form $S = (P, N)$, where $P, N$ are sets of points in $\mathbb{Z}^n$ interpreted as positive and negative examples (as for intervals, see Example 1).

The following lemma provides the ingredients for building a convergent learner based on wqo-tractability (see the extended paper [31] for a proof).

**Lemma 3.** *(a) For each realizable sample $S = (P, N)$, there are maximal hyper-rectangles that are consistent with $S$ (possibly more than one).*
*(b) For each $p \in \mathbb{Z}^n$, the set $\mathcal{R}_p$ of hyperrectangles containing $p$ is well-quasi-ordered by inclusion.*

We conclude that the following type of learner is convergent: for the empty sample, propose the empty hyperrectangle; for every non-empty sample $S$, propose a maximal hyperrectangle consistent with $S$.

# 4   Synthesis Problems Modeled as ALFs

In this section, we list a host of existing synthesis problems and algorithms that can be seen as ALFs. Specifically, we consider examples from the areas of program verification and program synthesis. We do not go into details of each formalism; instead, we refer the reader to the extended paper [31] for a thorough discussion. We encourage the reader to look up the referenced algorithms to better understand their mapping into our framework. Moreover, we have new techniques based on ALFs to compute fixed-points in the setting of abstract interpretation using learning; due to lack of space, we again refer the reader to the extended paper [31] regarding this.

**Program Verification.** While program verification itself does not directly relate to synthesis, most program verification techniques require some form of help from the programmer before the analysis can be automated. Consequently, synthesizing objects that replace manual help has been an area of active research. We here focus on *learning loop invariants*. For the purposes of this article, let us consider while-programs with a single loop. Given a pre- and post-condition, assertions, and contracts for functions called, the problem is to find a loop invariant that proves the post-condition and assertions (assuming the program is correct).

A natural way to phrase this problem using ALFs is to model the concept space to consist of all subsets of program configurations and the hypothesis space to be the set of all logical formulas capturing the class of invariants from which we want to synthesize. For a program, the target specification would be the set $\mathcal{T}_{Inv}$ of all inductive invariants that prove the post-condition and assertions correct.

A general approach to learning invariants, called *ICE learning* (for implication counterexamples), was recently proposed by Garg et al. [16], where the learner learns from positive, negative, and implication counterexamples. The corresponding ALF is $\mathcal{A}_{\mathrm{ICE}} = (\mathcal{C}, \mathcal{H}, \gamma, \mathcal{S}, \kappa)$, where $\mathcal{C}$ is the set of all subsets of program configurations, the hypothesis space $\mathcal{H}$ is the language used to describe the invariant, and the sample space $\mathcal{S}$ is defined as follows:

- A sample is of the form $S = (P, N, I)$, where $P, N$ are sets of program configurations (interpreted as positive and negative examples), and $I$ is a set of pairs of program configurations (interpreted as implications).

- A set $C \in \mathcal{C}$ of program configurations is consistent with $(P, N, I)$ if $P \subseteq C$, $N \cap C = \emptyset$, and if $(c, c') \in I$ and $c \in C$, then also $c' \in C$.
- The order on samples is defined by component-wise set inclusion; that is, $(P, N, I) \sqsubseteq_\mathrm{s} (P', N', I')$ if $P \subseteq P'$, $N \subseteq N'$, and $I \subseteq I'$.
- The join is the component-wise union, and $\perp_\mathrm{s} = (\emptyset, \emptyset, \emptyset)$.

Based on this ALF, we can now show that there always exists a teacher since a teacher can refute any hypothesis with a positive, a negative, or an implication counterexample, depending on which property of invariants is violated. Furthermore, we can show that having only positive and negative samples precludes the existence of teachers. In fact, we can show that if $\mathcal{C} = 2^D$ (for a domain $D$) and the sample space $\mathcal{S}$ consists of only positive and negative examples in $D$, then a target set $T$ has a teacher *only if* it is defined in terms of excluding a set $B$ and including a set $G$. Proofs can be found in the extended paper [31].

Several concrete implementations of ICE framework have been proposed: Garg et al.'s original work on ICE [16], the approach proposed by Sharma and Aiken [41] (which uses a learner based on stochastic search), the work by Garg et al. [15] on synthesizing quantified invariants for linear data structures such as lists and arrays, and the algorithm described by Neider [34].

Other non-ICE learning techniques for invariant synthesis that can be modeled as ALFs are the Houdini algorithm [14], which is implemented in the Boogie program verifier [7] and widely used (e.g., in verifying device drivers [29,30] and in race-detection in GPU kernels [8]) and parts of the learning-to-verify project [46], which leverages automata learning to the verification of infinite state systems.

**Program Synthesis.** A prominent synthesis application is the sketch-based synthesis approach [42], where programmers write partial programs with holes and a system automatically synthesizes expressions or programs for these holes so that a specification (expressed using input-output pairs or logical assertions) is satisfied. The key idea is that given a sketch with a specification, we need expressions for the holes such that *for every possible input*, the specification holds. This roughly has the form $\exists e. \forall x. \psi(e, x)$, where $e$ are the expressions to synthesize and $x$ are the inputs to the program.

The Sketch system implements a CEGIS technique using SAT solving, which works in rounds: the learner proposes hypothesis expressions and the teacher checks whether $\forall x. \psi(e, x)$ holds (using SAT queries) and if not, returns a valuation for $x$ as a counterexample. Subsequently, the learner asks, again using a SAT query, whether there exists a valuation for the bits encoding the expressions such that $\psi(e, x)$ holds for every valuation of $x$ returned by the teacher thus far; the resulting expressions are the hypotheses for the next round.

The above system can be modeled as an ALF. The concept space consists of tuples of functions modeling the various expressions to synthesize, the hypothesis space is the set of expressions (or their bit encodings), the map $\gamma$ gives meaning to these expressions (or encodings), and the sample space can be seen as the set of *grounded formulae* of the form $\psi(e, v)$ where the variables $x$ have been substituted with a concrete valuation. The relation $\kappa$ maps such a sample to the set of all expressions $f$ such that the formulas in the sample all evaluate to true if $f$ is substituted for $e$. The Sketch learner can be seen as a learner in this ALF framework that uses calls to a SAT solver to find hypothesis expressions consistent with the sample.

The SyGuS format [2] is a competition format for synthesis, and extends the Sketch-based formalism above to SMT theories, with an emphasis on syntactic restrictions for expressions. More precisely, SyGuS specifications are parameterized over a background theory $T$, and an instance is a pair $(G, \psi(f))$ where $G$ is a grammar that imposes syntactic restrictions for functions (or expressions) and $\psi$ is a formula in $T$, including function symbols $f$; the functions $f$ are typed according to domains of $T$. The goal is to find functions $g$ for the symbols $f$ in the syntax $G$ such that $\psi$ holds. SyGuS further restricts $\psi$ to be of the form $\forall x. \psi'(f, x)$ where $\psi'$ is a quantifier-free formula in a decidable SMT theory.

There have been several solvers developed for SyGuS (cf. the first SyGuS competition [1,2]), and all of them are in fact learning-based (i.e., CEGIS). In particular, three solvers have been proposed: an enumerative solver, a constraint-based solver, and a stochastic solver. All these solvers can be seen as ALF instances: the concept space consists of all tuples of functions over the appropriate domains and the hypothesis space is the set of all functions allowed by the *syntax* of the problem (with the natural $\gamma$ relation giving its semantics). Note that the learners *know* $\psi$ in this scenario. However, we can model SyGuS as ALFs by taking the sample space to be grounded formulas $\psi'(f, v)$ consisting of the specification with particular values $v$ substituted for $x$. The learners can now be seen as learning from these samples, without knowledge of $\psi$ (similar to Sketch above).

We would like to emphasize that this embedding of SyGuS as an ALF clearly showcases the difference between different synthesis approaches (as mentioned in the introduction). For example, invariant generation can be done using learning either by means of ICE samples or modeled as a SyGuS problem. However, it turns out that the sample spaces (and, hence, the learners) in the two approaches are *very different*! In ICE-based learning, samples are only single configurations (labeled positive or negative) or pairs of configurations, while in a SyGuS encoding, the samples are grounded formulas that encode the entire program body, including instantiations of universally quantified variables at intermediate states in the execution of the loop.

Similarly, for synthesizing linear arithmetic expressions, there are again different kinds of solvers. The SyGuS solvers are based on the sample space of grounded formulae as above, while certain other solvers of the Alchemist variety [35,39] are based on a different sample space that involve counterexamples that encode inputs on which the hypothesis is incorrect; these two classes are consequently very different from each other (for instance, the latter use machine-learning techniques to classify inputs that cannot be achieved with the former kind of sample).

There are several algorithms that are self-described as CEGIS frameworks, and, hence, can be modeled using ALFs. For example, synthesizing loop-free programs [19], synthesizing synchronizing code for concurrent programs [10] (in this work, the sample space consists of abstract concurrent partially-ordered traces), work on using synthesis to *mine specifications* [22], synthesizing bit-manipulating programs and deobfuscating programs [21] (here, the use of separate I/O-oracle can be modeled as the teacher returning the output of the program together with a counterexample input), superoptimization [40], deductive program repair [26], synthesis of recursive functional programs over unbounded domains [27], as well as synthesis of protocols using enumerative CEGIS techniques [45]. Finally, an example for employing a human as teacher is FLASHFILL by Gulwani et al. [18], which synthesizes string manipulation macros from user-given input-output examples in the context of Microsoft Excel.

## 5   Conclusions

We have presented an abstract learning framework for synthesis that encompasses several existing techniques that use learning or counter-example guided inductive synthesis to create objects that satisfy a specification. (We refer to the extended paper [31] for a discussion of extensions and limitations of our abstract learning framework.) We were motivated by abstract interpretation [12] and how it gives a general framework and notation for verification; our formalism is an attempt at such a generalization for learning-based synthesis. The conditions we have proposed that the abstract concept spaces, hypotheses spaces, and sample spaces need to satisfy to define a learning-based synthesis domain seem to be cogent and general in forming a vocabulary for such approaches. We have also addressed various strategies for convergent synthesis that generalizes and extends existing techniques (again, in a similar vein as to how widening and narrowing in abstract interpretation give recipes for building convergent algorithms to compute fixed-points). We believe that the notation and general theorems herein will bring more clarity, understanding, and reuse of learners in synthesis algorithms.

**Acknowledgements.** This work was partially supported by NSF Expeditions in Computing ExCAPE Award #1138994.

## References

1. Alur, R., Bodík, R., Dallal, E., Fisman, D., Garg, P., Juniwal, G., Kress-Gazit, H., Madhusudan, P., Martin, M.M.K., Raghothaman, M., Saha, S., Seshia, S.A., Singh, R., Solar-Lezama, A., Torlak, E., Udupa, A.: Syntax-guided synthesis. In: Dependable Software Systems Engineering, NATO Science for Peace and Security Series, D: Information and Communication Security, vol. 40, pp. 1–25. IOS Press (2015)
2. Alur, R., Bodík, R., Juniwal, G., Martin, M.M.K., Raghothaman, M., Seshia, S.A., Singh, R., Solar-Lezama, A., Torlak, E., Udupa, A.: Syntax-guided synthesis. In: FMCAD 2013, pp. 1–8. IEEE (2013)

3. Alur, R., Cerný, P., Madhusudan, P., Nam, W.: Synthesis of interface specifications for java classes. In: POPL 2005, pp. 98–109. ACM (2005)
4. Alur, R., Fisman, D., Singh, R., Solar-Lezama, A.: Results and analysis of syguscomp 2015. Technical report, University of Pennsylvania (2015). http://www.cis.upenn.edu/fisman/documents/AFSS_SYNT15.pdf
5. Angluin, D.: Computational learning theory: survey and selected bibliography. In: STOC 1992, pp. 351–369. ACM (1992)
6. Baker, A.: Simplicity. In: Zalta, E.N. (ed.) The Stanford Encyclopedia of Philosophy. Fall 2013 edn. (2013). http://plato.stanford.edu/archives/fall2013/entries/simplicity/
7. Barnett, M., Chang, B.-Y.E., DeLine, R., Jacobs, B., M. Leino, K.R.: Boogie: a modular reusable verifier for object-oriented programs. In: de Boer, F.S., Bonsangue, M.M., Graf, S., de Roever, W.-P. (eds.) FMCO 2005. LNCS, vol. 4111, pp. 364–387. Springer, Heidelberg (2006)
8. Betts, A., Chong, N., Donaldson, A.F., Qadeer, S., Thomson, P.: Gpuverify: a verifier for GPU kernels. In: OOPSLA 2012, pp. 113–132. ACM (2012)
9. Blum, A.: Learning boolean functions in an infinite attribute space. Mach. Learn. **9**, 373–386 (1992)
10. Cerný, P., Clarke, E.M., Henzinger, T.A., Radhakrishna, A., Ryzhyk, L., Samanta, R., Tarrach, T.: From non-preemptive to preemptive scheduling using synchronization synthesis. In: Kroening, D., Păsăreanu, C.S. (eds.) CAV 2015. LNCS, vol. 9207, pp. 180–197. Springer, Heidelberg (2015)
11. Cheung, A., Madden, S., Solar-Lezama, A., Arden, O., Myers, A.C.: Using program analysis to improve database applications. IEEE Data Eng. Bull. **37**(1), 48–59 (2014)
12. Cousot, P., Cousot, R.: Abstract interpretation: a unified lattice model for static analysis of programs by construction or approximation of fixpoints. In: POPL, pp. 238–252. ACM (1977)
13. Domingos, P.M.: The role of occam's razor in knowledge discovery. Data Min. Knowl. Discov. **3**(4), 409–425 (1999)
14. Flanagan, C., Leino, K.R.M.: Houdini, an annotation assistant for ESC/Java. In: Oliveira, J.N., Zave, P. (eds.) FME 2001. LNCS, vol. 2021, pp. 500–517. Springer, Heidelberg (2001)
15. Garg, P., Löding, C., Madhusudan, P., Neider, D.: Learning universally quantified invariants of linear data structures. In: Sharygina, N., Veith, H. (eds.) CAV 2013. LNCS, vol. 8044, pp. 813–829. Springer, Heidelberg (2013)
16. Garg, P., Löding, C., Madhusudan, P., Neider, D.: ICE: a robust framework for learning invariants. In: Biere, A., Bloem, R. (eds.) CAV 2014. LNCS, vol. 8559, pp. 69–87. Springer, Heidelberg (2014)
17. Garg, P., Madhusudan, P., Neider, D., Roth, D.: Learning invariants using decision trees and implication counterexamples. In: POPL 2016 (2016, to appear)
18. Gulwani, S.: Automating string processing in spreadsheets using input-output examples. In: POPL 2011, pp. 317–330. ACM (2011)
19. Gulwani, S., Jha, S., Tiwari, A., Venkatesan, R.: Synthesis of loop-free programs. In: PLDI 2011, pp. 62–73. ACM (2011)
20. Higman, G.: Ordering by divisibility in abstract algebras. Proc. London Math. Soc. **3-2**(1), 326–336 (1952)
21. Jha, S., Gulwani, S., Seshia, S.A., Tiwari, A.: Oracle-guided component-based program synthesis. In: ICSE 2010, pp. 215–224. ACM (2010)
22. Jin, X., Donzé, A., Deshmukh, J.V., Seshia, S.A.: Mining requirements from closed-loop control models. In: HSCC 2013, pp. 43–52. ACM (2013)

23. Karaivanov, S., Raychev, V., Vechev, M.T.: Phrase-based statistical translation of programming languages. In: Onward!, SLASH 2014, pp. 173–184. ACM (2014)
24. Kearns, M.J., Vazirani, U.V.: An Introduction to Computational Learning Theory. MIT Press, Cambridge, MA, USA (1994)
25. Kitzelmann, E.: Inductive programming: a survey of program synthesis techniques. In: Schmid, U., Kitzelmann, E., Plasmeijer, R. (eds.) AAIP 2009. LNCS, vol. 5812, pp. 50–73. Springer, Heidelberg (2010)
26. Kneuss, E., Koukoutos, M., Kuncak, V.: Deductive program repair. In: Kroening, D., Păsăreanu, C.S. (eds.) CAV 2015. LNCS, vol. 9207, pp. 217–233. Springer, Heidelberg (2015)
27. Kneuss, E., Kuraj, I., Kuncak, V., Suter, P.: Synthesis modulo recursive functions. In: OOPSLA 2013, pp. 407–426. ACM (2013)
28. Kuncak, V.: Verifying and synthesizing software with recursive functions. In: Esparza, J., Fraigniaud, P., Husfeldt, T., Koutsoupias, E. (eds.) ICALP 2014. LNCS, vol. 8572, pp. 11–25. Springer, Heidelberg (2014)
29. Lal, A., Qadeer, S.: Powering the static driver verifier using corral. In: (FSE-22), pp. 202–212. ACM (2014)
30. Lal, A., Qadeer, S., Lahiri, S.K.: A solver for reachability modulo theories. In: Madhusudan, P., Seshia, S.A. (eds.) CAV 2012. LNCS, vol. 7358, pp. 427–443. Springer, Heidelberg (2012)
31. Löding, C., Madhusudan, P., Neider, D.: Abstract learning frameworks for synthesis. Technical report, University of Illinois at Urbana-Champaign (2016). http://madhu.cs.illinois.edu/tacas16b/
32. Manna, Z., Waldinger, R.: A deductive approach to program synthesis. ACM Trans. Program. Lang. Syst. 2(1), 90–121 (1980)
33. Mitchell, T.M.: Machine Learning. McGraw-Hill, New York (1997)
34. Neider, D.: Applications of Automata Learning in Verification and Synthesis. Ph.D. thesis, RWTH Aachen University (April 2014)
35. Neider, D., Saha, S., Madhusudan, P.: Synthesizing piece-wise functions by learning classifiers. In: TACAS 2016, LNCS. Springer (to appear, 2016)
36. Osera, P., Zdancewic, S.: Type-and-example-directed program synthesis. In: PLDI 2015, pp. 619–630. ACM (2015)
37. Pnueli, A., Rosner, R.: On the synthesis of a reactive module. In: POPL 1989, pp. 179–190 (1989)
38. Quinlan, J.R.: C4.5: programs for machine learning. Morgan Kaufmann, Burlington (1993)
39. Saha, S., Garg, P., Madhusudan, P.: Alchemist: learning guarded affine functions. In: Kroening, D., Păsăreanu, C.S. (eds.) CAV 2015. LNCS, vol. 9206, pp. 440–446. Springer, Heidelberg (2015)
40. Schkufza, E., Sharma, R., Aiken, A.: Stochastic superoptimization. In: ASPLOS 2013, pp. 305–316. ACM (2013)
41. Sharma, R., Aiken, A.: From invariant checking to invariant inference using randomized search. In: Biere, A., Bloem, R. (eds.) CAV 2014. LNCS, vol. 8559, pp. 88–105. Springer, Heidelberg (2014)
42. Solar-Lezama, A.: Program synthesis by sketching. Ph.D. thesis, University of California at Berkeley (2008)
43. Solar-Lezama, A., Tancau, L., Bodík, R., Seshia, S.A., Saraswat, V.A.: Combinatorial sketching for finite programs. In: ASPLOS, pp. 404–415 (2006)

44. Thakur, A., Lal, A., Lim, J., Reps, T.: PostHat and all that: Attaining most-precise inductive invariants. Technical report TR1790, University of Wisconsin, Madison (April 2013)
45. Udupa, A., Raghavan, A., Deshmukh, J.V., Mador-Haim, S., Martin, M.M.K., Alur, R.: TRANSIT: specifying protocols with concolic snippets. In: PLDI 2013, pp. 287–296. ACM (2013)
46. Vardhan, A., Sen, K., Viswanathan, M., Agha, G.: Learning to verify safety properties. In: Davies, J., Schulte, W., Barnett, M. (eds.) ICFEM 2004. LNCS, vol. 3308, pp. 274–289. Springer, Heidelberg (2004)

# Synthesizing Piece-Wise Functions by Learning Classifiers

Daniel Neider[1,2(✉)], Shambwaditya Saha[1], and P. Madhusudan[1]

[1] University of Illinois at Urbana-Champaign, Urbana, USA
{neider2,ssaha6,madhu}@illinois.edu
[2] University of California, Los Angeles, USA

**Abstract.** We present a novel general technique that uses classifier learning to synthesize piece-wise functions (functions that split the domain into *regions* and apply simpler functions to each region) against logical synthesis specifications. Our framework works by combining a synthesizer of functions for fixed concrete inputs and a synthesizer of predicates that can be used to define regions. We develop a theory of single-point refutable specifications that facilitate generating concrete counterexamples using constraint solvers. We implement the framework for synthesizing piece-wise functions in linear integer arithmetic, combining leaf expression synthesis using constraint-solving and predicate synthesis using enumeration, and tie them together using a decision tree classifier. We demonstrate that this approach is competitive compared to existing synthesis engines on a set of synthesis specifications.

## 1 Introduction

The field of synthesis is an evolving discipline in formal methods that is seeing a renaissance, mainly due to a variety of new techniques [1] to automatically synthesize small expressions or programs that are useful in niche application domains, including end-user programming [14], filling holes in program sketches [32], program transformations [7,18], automatic grading of assignments [2,30], synthesizing network configurations and migrations [21,29], as well as synthesizing annotations such as invariants or pre/post conditions for programs [12,13].

The field of machine learning [22] is close to program synthesis, especially when the specification is a set of input-output examples. The subfield of inductive programming has a long tradition in solving this problem using inductive methods that generalize from the sample to obtain programs [19]. Machine learning, which is the field of learning algorithms that can predict data from training data, is a rich field that encompasses algorithms for several problems, including classification, regression, and clustering [22].

The idea of using inductive synthesis for more general specifications than input-output examples has been explored extensively in program synthesis research. The counterexample guided inductive synthesis (CEGIS) approach to program synthesis advocates pairing inductive learning algorithms with a verification oracle: in each round, the learner learns inductively from a set of (counter-)examples and proposes an expression which the verification oracle

M. Chechik and J.-F. Raskin (Eds.): TACAS 2016, LNCS 9636, pp. 186–203, 2016.
DOI: 10.1007/978-3-662-49674-9_11

checks against the specification, and augments the set of samples with a new counterexample [32]. A majority of the current synthesis approaches rely on counter-example guided inductive synthesis [12,13,16,32].

In this paper, we consider *logical specifications* for synthesis, where the goal of synthesis is to find some expression $e$ for a function $f$, in a particular syntax, that satisfies a specification $\forall \vec{x}. \psi(\vec{x})$.[1] We will assume that $\psi$ is quantifier-free, that the satisfiability of the quantifier-free theory of the underlying logic is decidable, and that there is an effective algorithm that can produce models. The goal of this paper is to develop a framework for expression synthesis that can learn *piece-wise functions* using a *learning algorithm for classifiers* with the help of two other synthesis engines, one for synthesizing expressions for *single* inputs and another for synthesizing predicates that separate concrete inputs from each other. The framework is general in the sense that it is independent of the logic used to write specifications and the logic used to express the synthesized expressions.

A piece-wise function is a function that partitions the input domain into a finite set of regions, and then maps each region using a simpler class of functions. The framework that we build for expression synthesis is also counterexample-guided, and proceeds in the following fashion (see Fig. 1 on p. 195 and the figure on the right):

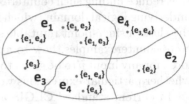

- In every round, the learner proposes a piece-wise function $H$ for $f$, and the verification oracle checks whether it satisfies the specification. If not, it returns one input $\vec{p}$ on which $H$ is incorrect. (Returning such a counterexample is nontrivial; we will discuss this issue below.)
- We show that we can now use an *expression synthesizer* for the single input $\vec{p}$ which synthesizes an expression that maps $\vec{p}$ to a correct value. This expression synthesizer will depend on the underlying theory of basic expressions, and we can use any synthesis algorithm that performs this task.
- Once we have the new expression, we compute for every counterexample input obtained thus far the set of basic expressions synthesized so far that work correctly for these inputs. This results in a set of *samples*, where each sample is of the form $(\vec{p}, Z)$, where $\vec{p}$ is a concrete input and $Z$ is the set of basic expressions that are correct for $\vec{p}$ (see points with sets of labels in figure above). The problem we need to solve now can be seen as a multi-label classification problem— that of finding a mapping from *every* input to an expression that is consistent with the set of samples.
- Since we want a classification that is a piece-wise function that divides the input domains into regions, and since the predicates needed to define regions can be arbitrarily complex and depend on the semantics of the underlying logical theory, we require a *predicate synthesizer* that synthesizes predicates that can separate concrete inputs with disjoint sets of labels. Once we have

---

[1] Note that this syntax can, of course, describe input-output examples as well.

such a set of predicates, we are equipped with an adequate number of regions to find a piece-wise function.

– The final phase uses *classification learning*, to generalize the samples to a function from all inputs to basic expressions (see figure above). The learning should be biased towards finding *simple* functions, finding few regions, or minimizing the Boolean expression that describes the piece-wise function.

The framework above requires many components, in addition to the expression synthesizer and predicate synthesizer. First, given a hypothesis function $H$ and a specification $\forall \vec{x}. \ \psi(f, \vec{x})$, we need to find a concrete counterexample input on which $H$ is wrong. It turns out that there may be *no* such input point for some specifications and even if there was, finding one may be hard. We develop a theory of *single-point definable specifications* whose definition ensures such counterexample inputs always exist, and a subclass of *single-point refutable specifications* that reduce finding such counterexample inputs to satisfiability problems over the underlying logical domain (which is decidable). Our framework works robustly for the class of singe-point refutable specifications, and we show how to extract concrete counterexamples, how to automatically synthesize a new specification tailored for any input $\vec{p}$ to be given to the expression synthesizer, and how to evaluate whether particular expressions work for particular inputs.

In current standard CEGIS approaches [1,32], when $H$ and $\forall \vec{x}. \ \psi(f, \vec{x})$ are presented, the teacher simply returns a concrete value of $\vec{x}$ for which $\neg \psi(H/f, \vec{x})$ is satisfied. We emphasize that such valuations for the universally quantified variables cannot be interpreted as inputs on which $H$ is incorrect, and hence cannot be used in our framework. The framework of single-point refutable specifications and the counterexample input generation procedures we build for them is crucial in order to be able to use classifiers to synthesize expressions.

The classifier learning algorithm can be any learning algorithm for multi-label classification (preferably with the learning bias as described above) but must ensure that the learned classifier is *consistent* with the given samples. Machine-learning algorithms more often than not make mistakes and are not consistent with the sample, often because they want to generalize assuming that the sample is noisy. In Sect. 4, we describe the second contribution of this paper— an adaptation of decision-tree learning to multi-label learning that produces classifiers that are consistent with the sample. We also explore a variety of statistical measures used within the decision-tree learning algorithm to bias the learning towards smaller trees in the presence of multi-labeled samples. The resulting decision-tree learning algorithms form one class of classifier learning algorithms that can be used to synthesize piece-wise functions over any theory that works using our framework.

The third contribution of the paper is an instantiation of our framework to build an efficient synthesizer of piece-wise linear integer arithmetic functions for specifications given in the theory of linear integer arithmetic. We implement the components of the framework for single-point refutable functions: to synthesize input counterexamples, to reformulate the synthesis problem for a single input, and to evaluate whether an expression works correctly for any input.

These problems are reduced to the satisfiability of the underlying quantifier-free theory of linear integer arithmetic, which is decidable using SMT solvers. The expression-synthesizer for single inputs is performed using an inner CEGIS-based engine using a constraint solver. The predicate synthesizer is instantiated using an enumerative synthesis algorithm. The resulting solver works extremely well on a large class of benchmarks drawn from the SyGuS 2015 synthesis competition [3] (linear integer arithmetic track) where a version of our solver fared significantly better than all the traditional SyGuS solvers (enumerative, stochastic, and symbolic constraint-based solvers). In our experience, finding an expression that satisfies a single input is a much easier problem for current synthesis engines (where constraint solvers that compute the coefficients defining such an expression are effective) than finding one that satisfies all inputs. The decision-tree based classification, on the other hand, solves the problem of generalizing this labeling to the entire input domain effectively.

**Related Work.** Our learning task is closely related to the syntax-guided synthesis framework (SyGuS) [1], which provides a language, similar to SMTLib [5], to describe synthesis problems. Several solvers following the counterexample-guided inductive synthesis approach (CEGIS) [32] for SyGuS have been developed [1], including an enumerative solver, a solver based on constraint solving, one based on stochastic search, and one based on the program synthesizer Sketch [31]. Recently, a solver based on CVC4 [26] has also been presented.

There has been several works on synthesizing piece-wise affine models of hybrid dynamical systems from input-output examples [4,6,11,34] (we refer the reader to [24] for a comprehensive survey). The setting there is to learn an affine model passively (i.e., without feedback whether the synthesized model satisfies some specification) and, consequently, only approximates the actual system. A tool for learning guarded affine functions, which uses a CEGIS approach, is Alchemist [28]. In contrast to our setting, it requires that the function to synthesize is unique.

The learning framework we develop in this paper, as well as the synthesis algorithms we use for linear-arithimetic (the outer learner, the expression synthesizer and the predicate synthesizer) can be seen as abstract learning frameworks [20] (see [23] for details).

## 2    The Synthesis Problem and Single-Point Refutable Specifications

The synthesis problem we tackle in this paper is that of finding a function $f$ that satisfies a logical specification of the form $\forall \vec{x}.\ \psi(f, \vec{x})$, where $\psi$ is a *quantifier-free* first-order formula over a logic with fixed interpretations of constants, functions, and relations (except for $f$). Further, we will assume that the quantifier-free fragment of this logic admits a *decidable* satisfiability problem and furthermore, effective procedures for producing a model that maps the variables to the domain of the logic are available. These effective procedures are required in order to generate counterexamples while performing synthesis.

For the rest of the paper, let $f$ be a function symbol with arity $n$ representing the target function that is to be synthesized. The specification logic is a formula in first-order logic, over an arbitrary set of function symbols $\mathcal{F}$, (including a special symbol $f$), constants $\mathcal{C}$, and relations/predicates $\mathcal{P}$, all of which with fixed interpretations, except for $f$. We will assume that the logic is interpreted over a countable universe $D$ and, further, and that there is a constant symbol for every element in $D$. For technical reasons, we assume that negation is pushed into atomic predicates.

The specification for synthesis is a formula of the form $\forall \vec{x}.\psi(f, \vec{x})$ where $\psi$ is a formula expressed in the following grammar (where $g \in \mathcal{F}$, $c \in \mathcal{C}$, $P \in \mathcal{P}$):

$$Term\ t ::- x \mid c \mid f(t_1, \ldots, t_n) \mid g(\vec{t})$$
$$Formula\ \varphi ::- P(\vec{t}) \mid \neg P(\vec{t}) \mid \varphi \vee \varphi \mid \varphi \wedge \varphi$$

We will assume that equality is a relation in the logic, with the standard model-theoretic interpretation.

The synthesis problem is to find, given a specification $\forall \vec{x}.\ \psi(f, \vec{x})$, a definition for the function $f$ in a particular syntax that satisfies the specification. More formally, given a subset of function symbols $\widehat{\mathcal{F}} \subseteq \mathcal{F}$ (excluding $f$) and a subset of constants $\widehat{\mathcal{C}}$ and a subset of relation/predicate symbols $\widehat{\mathcal{P}} \subseteq \mathcal{P}$, the task is to find an *expression* $e$ for $f$ that is a term with free variables $y_1, \ldots, y_n$ adhering to the following syntax (where $\widehat{g} \in \widehat{\mathcal{F}}$, $\widehat{c} \in \widehat{\mathcal{C}}$, $\widehat{P} \in \widehat{\mathcal{P}}$)

$$Expr\ t ::- \widehat{c} \mid y_i \mid \widehat{g}(\vec{t}) \mid ite(\widehat{P}(\vec{t}),\ t,\ t),$$

such that $e$ satisfies the specification, i.e., $\forall \vec{x}.\ \psi(e/f, \vec{x})$ is valid.

**Single-Point Definable Specifications.** In order to be able to define a general CEGIS algorithm for synthesizing expressions for $f$ based on learning classifiers, as described in Sect. 1, we need to be able to refute any hypothesis $H$ that does not satisfy the specification with a concrete input on which $H$ is wrong. We will now define sufficient conditions that guarantee this property. The first is a semantic property, called *single-point definable specifications*, that guarantees the existence of such concrete input counterexamples and the second is a syntactic fragment of the former, called *single-point refutable specifications*, that allows such concrete counterexamples to be found effectively using a constraint solver.

A single-point definable specification is, intuitively, a specification that restricts how each input is mapped to the output, *independent* of how other inputs are mapped to outputs. More precisely, a single-point definable specification restricts each input $\vec{p} \in D^n$ to a *set of outputs* $X_{\vec{p}} \subseteq D$ and allows any function that respects this restriction for each input. It cannot, however, restrict the output on $\vec{p}$ based on how the function behaves on other inputs. Many synthesis problems fall into this category (see Sect. 6 for several examples taken from a recent synthesis competition).

Formally, we define this concept as follows. Let $I = D^n$ be the set of inputs and $O = D$ be the set of outputs of the function being synthesized.

**Definition 1 (Single-point Definable (SPD) Specifications).** *A specification $\alpha$ is said to be* single-point definable *if the following holds. Let $\mathcal{F}$ be the class of all functions that satisfy the specification $\alpha$. Let $g : I \rightarrow O$ be a function such that for every $\vec{p} \in I$, there exists some $h \in \mathcal{F}$ such that $g(\vec{p}) = h(\vec{p})$. Then, $g \in \mathcal{F}$ (i.e., $g$ satisfies the specification $\alpha$).*

Intuitively, a specification is single-point definable if whenever we construct a function that maps each input independently according to *some* arbitrary function that satisfies the specification, the resulting function satisfies the specification as well. For each input $\vec{p}$, if $X_{\vec{p}}$ is the set of all outputs that functions that meet the specification map $\vec{p}$ to, then any function $g$ that maps every input $\vec{p}$ to some element in $X_{\vec{p}}$ will also satisfy the specification. This captures the requirement, semantically, that the specification constrains the outputs of each input independent of other inputs.

For example, the following specifications are all single-point definable specifications over the first-order theory of arithmetic:

- $f(15, 23) = 19 \wedge f(90, 20) = 91 \wedge \ldots \wedge f(28, 24) = 35$.
  More generally, any set of input-output samples can be written as a conjunction of constraints that forms a single-point definable specification.
- Any specification that is not realizable (has no function that satisfies it).
- $\forall x. \, (f(0) = 0 \wedge f(x+1) = f(x) + 1)$.
  The identity function is the only function that satisfies this specification. Any specification that has a unique solution is clearly single-point definable.

While single-point definable specifications are quite common, there are prominent specifications that are not single-point definable. For example, *inductive loop invariant synthesis* specifications for programs are not single-point definable, as counterexamples to the inductiveness constraint involve *two counterexample inputs* (the ICE learning model [12] formalizes this). Similarly, ranking function synthesis is also not single-point definable.

Note that for any SPD specification, if $H$ is some expression conjectured for $f$ that does not satisfy the specification, there will always be *one* input $\vec{p} \in D^n$ on which $H$ is *definitely wrong* in that no correct solution agrees with $H$ on $\vec{p}$. More precisely, we obtain the following directly from the definition.

**Proposition 1.** *Let $\forall \vec{x}. \, \psi(f, \vec{x})$ be a single-point definable specification and let $h : D^n \rightarrow D$ be an interpretation for $f$ such that $\forall \vec{x}. \, \psi(f, \vec{x})$ does not hold. Then there is an input $\vec{p} \in D^n$ such that for every function $h' : D^n \rightarrow D$ that satisfies the specification, $h(\vec{p}) \neq h'(\vec{p})$.*

**Single-Point Refutable Specifications.** While the above proposition ensures that there is a counterexample input for any hypothesized function that does not satisfy a single-point definable function, it does not ensure that finding such an input is tractable. We now define single-point refutable specifications, which we show to be a subclass of single-point definable specifications, and for which we can reduce the problem of finding counterexample inputs to logical satisfiability of the underlying quantifier-free logic.

Intuitively, a specification $\forall \vec{x}. \, \psi(f, \vec{x})$ is single-point refutable if for any given hypothetical interpretation $H$ to the function $f$ that does not satisfy the specification, we can find a particular input $\vec{p} \in D^n$ such that the formula $\exists \vec{x}. \, \neg \psi(f, \vec{x})$ evaluates to true, and where the truthhood is caused *solely* by the interpretation of $H$ on $\vec{p}$. The definition of single-point refutable specifications is involved as we have to define what it means for $H$ on $\vec{p}$ to solely contribute to falsifying the specification.

We first define an alternate semantics for a formula $\psi(f, \vec{x})$ that is parameterized by a set of $n$ variables $\vec{u}$ denoting an input, a variable $v$ denoting an output, and a Boolean variable $b$. The idea is that this alternate semantics evaluates the function by interpreting $f$ on $\vec{u}$ to be $v$, but "ignores" the interpretation of $f$ on all other inputs, and reports whether the formula would evaluate to $b$. We do this by expanding the domain to $D \cup \{\bot\}$, where $\bot$ is a new element, and have $f$ map all inputs other than $\vec{u}$ to $\bot$. Furthermore, when evaluating formulas, we let them evaluate to $b$ only when we are sure that the evaluation of the formula to $b$ depended only on the definition of $f$ on $\vec{u}$. We now define this alternate semantics by *transforming* a formula $\psi(f, \vec{x})$ to a formula with the usual semantics, but over the domain $D \cup \{\bot\}$. In this transformation, we will use if-then-else (*ite*) terms for simplicity.

**Definition 2 (The Isolate Transformer).** *Let $\vec{u}$ be a vector of $n$ first-order variables (where $n$ is the arity of the function to be synthesized), $v$ a first-order variable (different from ones in $\vec{u}$), and $b \in \{T, F\}$. Moreover, let $D^+ = D \cup \{\bot\}$, where $\bot \notin D$, be the extended domain, and let the functions and predicates be extended to this domain (the precise extension does not matter).*

*For a formula $\psi(f, \vec{x})$, we define the formula $Isolate_{\vec{u},v,b}(\psi(f, \vec{x}))$ over the extended domain by*

$$Isolate_{\vec{u},v,b}(\psi(f, \vec{x})) := ite\left( \bigvee_{x_i} x_i = \bot, \neg b, Isol_{\vec{u},v,b}(\psi(f, \vec{x})) \right),$$

*where $Isol_{\vec{u},v,b}$ is defined recursively as follows:*

- $Isol_{\vec{u},v,b}(x) = x$
- $Isol_{\vec{u},v,b}(c) = c$
- $Isol_{\vec{u},v,b}(g(t_1,\ldots,t_k)) =$
  $ite(\bigvee_{i=1}^{k} Isol_{\vec{u},v,b}(t_i) = \bot, \bot, g(Isol_{\vec{u},v,b}(t_1),\ldots,Isol_{\vec{u},v,b}(t_k)))$
- $Isol_{\vec{u},v,b}(f(t_1,\ldots,t_n)) = ite(\bigwedge_{i=1}^{n} Isol_{\vec{u},v,b}(t_i) = u[i], v, \bot)$
- $Isol_{\vec{u},v,b}(P(t_1,\ldots,t_k)) =$
  $ite(\bigvee_{i=1}^{k} Isol_{\vec{u},v,b}(t_i) = \bot, \neg b, P(Isol_{\vec{u},v,b}(t_1),\ldots,Isol_{\vec{u},v,b}(t_k)))$
- $Isol_{\vec{u},v,b}(\neg P(t_1,\ldots,t_k)) =$
  $ite(\bigvee_{i=1}^{k} Isol_{\vec{u},v,b}(t_i) = \bot, \neg b, \neg P(Isol_{\vec{u},v,b}(t_1),\ldots,Isol_{\vec{u},v,b}(t_k)))$

$- Isol_{\vec{u},v,b}(\varphi_1 \vee \varphi_2) = Isol_{\vec{u},v,b}(\varphi_1) \vee Isol_{\vec{u},v,b}(\varphi_2)$
$- Isol_{\vec{u},v,b}(\varphi_1 \wedge \varphi_2) = Isol_{\vec{u},v,b}(\varphi_1) \wedge Isol_{\vec{u},v,b}(\varphi_2)$

Intuitively, the function $Isolate_{\vec{u},v,b}(\psi)$ captures whether $\psi$ will evaluate to $b$ if $f$ maps $\vec{u}$ to $v$ and independent of how $f$ is interpreted on other inputs. A function of the form $f(t_1, \ldots t_n)$ is interpreted to be $v$ if the input matches $\vec{u}$ and otherwise evaluated to $\perp$. Functions on terms that involve $\perp$ are sent to $\perp$ as well. Predicates are evaluated to $b$ only if the predicate is evaluated on terms none of which is $\perp$— otherwise, they get mapped to $\neg b$, to reflect that it will not help to make the final formula $\psi$ evaluate to $b$. Note that when $Isolate_{\vec{u},v,b}(\psi)$ evaluates to $\neg b$, there is no property of $\psi$ that we claim. Also, note that $Isolate_{\vec{u},v,b}(\psi(f,\vec{x}))$ has no occurrence of $f$ in it, but has free variables $\vec{x}$, $\vec{u}$ and $v$.

We can show (using a induction over the structure of the specification) that the isolation of a specification to a particular input with $b = F$, when instantiated according to a function that satisfies a specification, cannot evaluate to false (see the full paper [23] for a proof).

**Lemma 1.** *Let $\forall \vec{x}.\ \psi(f, \vec{x})$ be a specification and $h \colon D^n \to D$ a function satisfying the specification. Then, there is no interpretation of the variables in $\vec{u}$ and $\vec{x}$ (over $D$) such that if $v$ is interpreted as $h(\vec{u})$, the formula $Isolate_{\vec{u},v,F}(\psi(f,\ \vec{x}))$ evaluates to false.*

We can also show (again using structural induction) that when the isolation of the specification with respect to $b = F$ evaluates to false, then $v$ is definitely not a correct output on $\vec{u}$ (see the full paper [23] for a proof).

**Lemma 2.** *Let $\forall \vec{x}.\ \psi(f, \vec{x})$ be a specification, $\vec{p} \in D^n$ an interpretation for $\vec{u}$, and $q \in D$ an interpretation for $v$ such that there is some interpretation for $\vec{x}$ that makes the formula $Isolate_{\vec{u},v,F}(\psi(f,\vec{x}))$ evaluate to false. Then, there exists no function $h$ satisfying the specification that maps $\vec{p}$ to $q$.*

We can now define single-point refutable specifications.

**Definition 3. (Single-point Refutable Specifications (SPR)).** *A specification $\forall \vec{x}.\ \psi(f, \vec{x})$ is said to be single-point refutable if the following holds. Let $H \colon D^n \to D$ be any interpretation for the function $f$ that does not satisfy the specification (i.e., the specification does not hold under this interpretation for $f$). Then, there exists some input $\vec{p}$ that is an interpretation for $\vec{u}$ and an interpretation for $\vec{x}$ such that when $v$ is interpreted to be $H(\vec{u})$, the isolated formula $Isolate_{\vec{u},v,F}(\psi(f,\ \vec{x}))$ evaluates to false.*

Intuitively, the above says that a specification is single-point refutable if whenever a hypothesis function $H$ does not find a specification, there is a single input $\vec{p}$ such that the specification evaluates to false independent of how the function maps inputs other than $\vec{p}$. More precisely, $\psi$ evaluates to *false* for some interpretation of $\vec{x}$ only assuming that $f(\vec{p}) = H(\vec{p})$.

We can show that single-point refutable specifications are single-point definable, which we formalize below (a proof can be found in [23]).

**Lemma 3.** *If a specification $\forall \vec{x}.\ \psi(f, \vec{x})$ is single-point refutable, then it is single-point definable.*

In the following, we list some examples and non-examples of single-point refutable specifications in the first-order theory of arithmetic:

- $f(15, 23) = 19 \wedge f(90, 20) = 91 \wedge \ldots \wedge f(28, 24) = 35$.
  More generally, any set of input-output samples can be written as a conjunction of constraints that forms a single-point refutable specification.
- $\forall x.(f(0) = 0 \wedge f(x+1) = f(x) + 1$ is *not* a single-point refutable specification thought it is single-point definable. Given a hypothesis function (e.g., $H(i) = 0$, for all $i$), the formula $f(x+1) = f(x)$ evaluates to false, but this involves the definition of $f$ on *two* inputs, and hence we cannot isolate a single input on which the function $H$ is incorrect. (In evaluating the isolated transformation of the specification parameterized with $b = F$, at least one of $f(x+1)$ and $f(x)$ will evaluate to $\perp$ and hence the whole formula never evaluate to *false*.)

When a specification $\forall \vec{x}.\ \psi(f, \vec{x})$ is single-point refutable, given an *expression* $H$ for $f$ that does not satisfy the specification, we can check satisfiability of the formula $\exists \vec{u}\, \exists v \exists \vec{x}.\ (v = H(\vec{u}) \wedge \neg Isolate_{\vec{u}, v, F}(\psi(H/f, \vec{x})))$. Assuming the underlying quantifier-free theory has a decidable satisfiability problem and can also come up with a model, the valuation of $\vec{u}$ gives a *concrete* input $\vec{p}$, and Lemma 2 shows that $H$ is definitely wrong on this input. This will form the basis of generating counterexample inputs in the synthesis framework that we outline next.

## 3    A General Synthesis Framework by Learning Classifiers

We now present our general framework for synthesizing functions over a first-order theory that uses machine-learning of classifiers. Our technique, as outlined in the introduction, is a *counterexample-guided inductive synthesis approach (CEGIS)*, and works most robustly for single-point refutable specifications.

Given a single-point refutable specification $\forall \vec{x}.\ \psi(f, \vec{x})$, the framework combines several simpler synthesizers and calls to SMT solvers to synthesize a function, as depicted in Fig. 1. The solver globally maintains a finite set of expressions $E$, a finite set of predicates $A$ (also called attributes), and a finite set $S$ of multi-labeled samples, where each sample is of the form $(\vec{p}, Z)$ consisting of an input $\vec{p} \in D^n$ and a set $Z \subseteq E$ of expressions that are correct for $\vec{p}$ (such a sample means that the specification allows mapping $\vec{p}$ to $e(\vec{p})$, for any $e \in Z$, but not to $e'(\vec{p})$, for any $e' \in E \setminus Z$).

**Phase 1:** In every round, the classifier produces a hypothesis expression $H$ for $f$. The process starts with a simple expression $H$, such as one that maps all inputs to a constant. We feed $H$ in every round to a **counterexample input finder** module, which essentially is a call to an SMT solver to check whether the formula

$$\exists \vec{u}\, \exists v\, \exists \vec{x}.\ (v = H(\vec{u}) \wedge \neg Isolate_{\vec{u}, v, F}(\psi(f, \vec{x})))$$

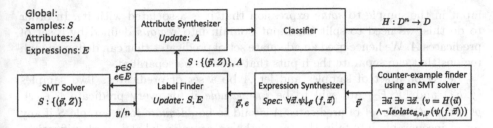

**Fig. 1.** A general synthesis framework based on learning classifiers

is satisfiable. Note that from the definition of the single-point refutable functions (see Definition 3), whenever $H$ does not satisfy the specification, we are guaranteed that this formula is satisfiable, and the valuation of $\vec{u}$ in the satisfying model gives us an input $\vec{p}$ on which $H$ is definitely wrong (see Lemma 2). If $H$ satisfies the specification, the formula would be unsatisfiable (by Lemma 1) and we can terminate, reporting $H$ as the synthesized expression.

**Phase 2:** The counterexample input $\vec{p}$ is then fed to an expression synthesizer whose goal is to find *some* correct expression that works for $\vec{p}$. We facilitate this by generating a *new specification for synthesis* that tailors the original specification to the particular input $\vec{p}$. This new specification is the formula

$$\psi\!\downarrow_{\vec{p}} (\widehat{f}, \vec{x}) := Isolate_{\vec{u}, v, T}(\psi(f, \vec{x}))[\vec{p}/\vec{u}, \widehat{f}(\vec{p})/v].$$

Intuitively, the above specification asks for a function $\widehat{f}$ that *"works"* for the input $\vec{p}$. We do this by first finding the formula that isolates the specification to $\vec{u}$ with output $v$ and demand that the specification evaluates to true; then, we substitute $\vec{p}$ for $\vec{u}$ and a new function symbol $\widehat{f}$ evaluated on $\vec{p}$ for $v$. Any expression synthesized for $\widehat{f}$ in this synthesis problem maps $\vec{p}$ to a value that is consistent with the original specification. We emphasize that we can use any expression synthesizer for this new specification.

**Phase 3:** Once we synthesize an expression $e$ that works for $\vec{p}$, we feed it to the next phase, which adds $e$ to the set of all expressions $E$ (if $e$ is new) and adds $\vec{p}$ to the set of samples. It then proceeds to find the set of *all* expressions in $E$ that work for all the inputs in the samples, and computes the new set of samples. In order to do this, we take every input $\vec{r}$ that previously existed, and ask whether $e$ works for $\vec{r}$, and if it does, add $e$ to the set of labels for $\vec{r}$. Also, we take the new input $\vec{p}$ and every expression $e' \in E$, and check whether $e'$ works for $\vec{p}$.

To compute this labeling information, we need to be able to check, in general, whether an expression $e'$ works for an input $\vec{r}$. We can do this using a call to an SMT solver that checks whether the formula $\forall \vec{x}.\ \psi\!\downarrow_{\vec{r}} (e'(\vec{r})/\widehat{f}(\vec{r}), \vec{x})$ is valid.

**Phase 4:** We now have a set of samples, where each sample consists of an input and a set of expressions that work for that input. This is when we look upon the synthesis problem as a *classification* problem— that of mapping every input in the domain to an expression that generalizes the sample (i.e., that maps every input in the sample to *some* expression that it is associated with it). In order to do this, we need to split the input domain into *regions* defined by a set of predicates $A$. We hence need an adequate set of predicates that can define enough regions that can separate the inputs that need to be separated.

Let $S$ be a set of samples and let $A$ be a set of predicates. Two samples $(\vec{j}, E_1)$ and $(\vec{j'}, E_2)$ are said to be *inseparable* if for every predicate $p \in A$, $p(\vec{j}) \equiv p(\vec{j'})$. The set of predicates $A$ is said to be *adequate* for a sample $S$ if any set of inseparable inputs in the sample has a common label as a classification. In other words, if every subset $T \subseteq S$, say $T = \{(\vec{i_1}, E_1), (\vec{i_2}, E_2), \ldots (\vec{i_t}, E_t)\}$, where every pair of inputs in $T$ is inseparable, then $\bigcap_{i=1}^{t} E_i \neq \emptyset$. We require the **attribute synthesizer** to synthesize an adequate set of predicates $A$, given the set of samples.

Intuitively, if $T$ is a set of pairwise inseparable points with respect to a set of predicates $P$, then no classifier based on these predicates can separate them, and hence they all need to be classified using the same label; this is possible only if the set of points have a common expression label.

**Phase 5:** Finally, we give the samples and the predicates to a classification learner, which divides the set of inputs into regions, and maps each region to a single expression such that the mapping is consistent with the sample. A region is a *conjunction* of predicates and the set of points in the region is the set of all inputs that satisfy all these predicates. The classification is consistent with the set of samples if for every sample $(\vec{r}, Z) \in S$, the classifier maps $\vec{r}$ to a label in $Z$. (In Sect. 4, we present a general learning algorithm based on decision trees that learns such a classifier from a set of multi-labeled samples, and which biases the classifier towards small trees.)

The classification synthesized is then converted to an expression in the logic (this will involve nested *ite* expressions using predicates to define the regions and expressions at leaves to define the function). The synthesized function is fed back to the counterexample input finder, as in Phase 1, and the process continues until we manage to synthesize a function that meets the specification.

## 4   Multi-Label Decision Tree Classifiers

In this section, we sketch a decision tree learning algorithm for a special case of the so-called multi-label learning problem, which is the problem of learning a predictive model (i.e., a classifier) from samples that are associated with multiple labels. For the purpose of learning the classifier, we assume samples to be vectors of the Boolean values $\mathbb{B} = \{F, T\}$ (these encode the values of the various attributes on the counterexample input returned). The more general case that datapoints also contain rational numbers can be handled in a straightforward manner as in Quinlan's C5.0 algorithm [25,27].

To make the learning problem precise, let us fix a finite set $L = \{\lambda_1, \ldots, \lambda_k\}$ of labels with $k \geq 2$, and let $\vec{x}_1, \ldots, \vec{x}_m$ denote $m$ individual inputs (in the following also called *datapoints*). The task we are going to solve, which we call *disjoint multi-label learning problem* (cf. Jin and Ghahramani [17]), is

---

**Algorithm 1.** Multi-label decision tree learning algorithm

---

**Input**: A finite set $S$ of datapoints $x \in \mathbb{B}^m$.

1   **return** DecTree $(S, \{1, \ldots, m\})$.

2   **Procedure** DecTree *(Set of datapoints $S$, Attributes $A$)*

3      Create a root node $r$.

4      **if** *if all datapoints in $S$ have a label in common* **then**

5         Select a common label $\lambda$ and return the single-node tree $r$ with label $\lambda$.

6      **else**

7         Select an attribute $i \in A$ that (heuristically) best splits the sample $S$.

8         Split $S$ into $S_i = \{(\vec{x}, Y) \in S \mid x_i = T\}$ and $S_{\neg i} = \{(\vec{x}, Y) \in S \mid x_i = F\}$.

9         Label $r$ with attribute $i$ and return the tree with root node $r$, left subtree
          DecTree $(S_i, A \setminus \{i\})$, and right subtree DecTree $(S_{\neg i}, A \setminus \{i\})$.

---

"Given a finite training set $S = \{(\vec{x}_1, Y_1), \ldots, (\vec{x}_m, Y_m)\}$ where $Y_i \subseteq L$ and $Y_i \neq \emptyset$ for every $i \in \{1, \ldots, m\}$, find a decision tree classifier $h \colon \mathbb{B}^m \to L$ such that $h(\vec{x}) \in Y$ for all $(\vec{x}, Y) \in S$."

Note that this learning problem is a special case of the multi-label learning problem studied in machine learning literature, which asks for a classifier that predicts all labels that are associated with a datapoint. Moreover, it is important to emphasize that we require our decision tree classifier to be consistent with the training set (i.e., it is not allowed to misclassify datapoints in the training set), in contrast to classical machine learning settings where classifier are allowed to make (small) errors.

We use a straightforward modification of Quinlan's C 5.0 algorithm [25, 27] to solve the disjoint multi-label learning problem. (We refer to standard text on machine learning [22] for more information on decision tree learning.) This modification, sketched in pseudo code as Algorithm alg:decisionspstree, is a recursive algorithm that constructs a decision tree top-down. More precisely, given a training set $S$, the algorithm heuristically selects an attribute $i \in \{1, \ldots, m\}$ and splits the set into two disjoint, nonempty subsets $S_i = \{(\vec{x}, Y) \in S \mid x_i = T\}$ and $S_{\neg i} = \{(\vec{x}, Y) \in S \mid x_i = F\}$ (we explain shortly how the attribute $i$ is chosen). Then the algorithm recurses on the two subsets, whereby it no longer considers the attribute $i$. Once the algorithm arrives at a set $S'$ in which all datapoints share at least one common label (i.e., there exists a $\lambda \in L$ such that $\lambda \in Y$ for all $(\vec{x}, Y) \in S'$), it selects a common label $\lambda$ (arbitrarily), constructs a single-node tree that is labeled with $\lambda$, and returns from the recursion. However, it might happen during construction that a set of datapoints does not have a common label and cannot be split by any (available) attribute. In this case, it returns an error, as the set of attributes is not adequate (which we make sure does not happen in our framework).

The selection of a "good" attribute to split a set of datapoints lies at the heart of the decision tree learner as it determines the size of the resulting tree and, hence, how well the tree generalizes the training data. The quality of a split can be formalized by the notion of a *measure*, which, roughly, is a measure $\mu$ mapping pairs of sets of datapoints to a set $R$ that is equipped with a total order $\preceq$ over elements of $R$ (usually, $R = \mathbb{R}_{\geq 0}$ and $\preceq$ is the natural order over $\mathbb{R}$). Given a set $S$ to split, the learning algorithm first constructs subsets $S_i$ and $S_{\neg i}$ for each available attribute $i$ and evaluates each such candidate split by computing $\mu(S_i, S_{\neg i})$. It then chooses a split that has the least value.

In the single-label setting, information theoretic measures, such as *information gain* (based on *Shannon entropy*) and *Gini*, have proven to produce successful classifiers [15]. In the case of multi-label classifiers, however, finding a good measure is still a matter of ongoing research (e.g., see Tsoumakas and Katakis [33] for an overview). Both the classical entropy and Gini measures can be adapted to the multi-label case in a straightforward way by treating datapoints with multiple labels as multiple identical datapoints with a single label (we describe these in the full paper [23]). Another modification of entropy has been proposed by Clare and King [9]. However, these approaches share a disadvantage, namely that the association of datapoints to sets of labels is lost and all measures can be high, even if all datapoints share a common label; for instance, such a situation occurs for $S = \{(\vec{x}_1, Y_1), \ldots, (\vec{x}_n, Y_n)\}$ with $\{\lambda_1, \ldots, \lambda_\ell\} \subseteq Y_i$ for every $i \in \{1, \ldots, n\}$.

Ideally, one would like to have a measure that maps to 0 if all datapoints in a set share a common label and to a value strictly greater than 0 if this is not the case. We now present a measure, based on the combinatorial problem of finding minimal hitting sets, that has this property. To the best of our knowledge, this measure is a novel contribution and has not been studied in the literature.

For a set $S$ of datapoints, a set $H \subseteq L$ is a *hitting set* if $H \cap Y \neq \emptyset$ for each $(\vec{x}, Y) \in S$. Moreover, we define the measure $hs(S) = \min_{\text{hitting set } H} |H| - 1$, i.e., the cardinality of a smallest hitting set reduced by 1. As desired, we obtain $hs(S) = 0$ if all datapoints in $S$ share a common label and $hs(S) > 0$ if this is not the case. When evaluating candidate splits, we would prefer to minimize the number of labels needed to label the datapoints in the subsets; however, if two splits agree on this number, we would like to minimize the total number of labels required. Consequently, we propose $R = \mathbb{N} \times \mathbb{N}$ with $(n, m) \preceq (n', m')$ if and only if $n < n'$ or $n = n' \wedge m \leq m'$, and as measures $\mu_{hs}(S_1, S_2) = (\max\{hs(S_1), hs(S_2)\}, hs(S_1) + hs(S_2))$. As computing $hs(S)$ is computationally hard, we implemented a standard approximate greedy algorithm (the dual of the standard greedy set cover algorithm [8]), which runs in time polynomial in the size of the sample and whose solution is at most a logarithmic factor of the optimal solution.

## 5    A Synthesis Engine for Linear Integer Arithmetic

We now describe an instantiation of our framework (described in Sect. 3) for synthesizing functions expressible in linear integer arithmetic against quantified linear integer arithmetic specifications.

The counterexample input finder (Phase 1) and the computing of labels for counterexample inputs (Phase 3) are implemented straightforwardly using an

SMT solver (note that the respective formulas will be in quantifier-free linear integer arithmetic). The *Isolate*() function works over a domain $D \cup \{\bot\}$; we can implement this by choosing a particular element $\hat{c}$ in the domain and modeling every term using a *pair* of elements, one that denotes the original term and the second that denotes whether the term is $\bot$ or not, depending on whether it is equal to $\hat{c}$. It is easy to transform the formula now to one that is on the original domain $D$ (which in our case integers) itself.

**Expression Synthesizer.** Given an input $\vec{p}$, the expression synthesizer has to find an expression that works for $\vec{p}$. Our implementation deviates slightly from the general framework.

In the first phase, it checks whether one of the existing expressions in the global set $E$ already works for $\vec{p}$. This is done by calling the label finder (as in Phase 3). If none of the expressions in $E$ work for $\vec{p}$, the expression synthesizer proceeds to the second phase, where it generates a new synthesis problem with specification $\forall \vec{x}. \ \psi \downarrow_{\vec{p}}(\hat{f}, \vec{x})$ according to Phase 2 of Sect. 3, whose solutions are expressions that work for $\vec{p}$. It solves this synthesis problem using a simple CEGIS-style algorithm, which we sketch next.

Let $\forall \vec{x}. \ \psi(f, \vec{x})$ be a specification with a function symbol $f \colon \mathbb{Z}^n \to Z$, which is to be synthesized, and universally quantified variables $\vec{x} = (x_1, \ldots, x_m)$. Our algorithm synthesizes affine expressions of the form $(\sum_{i=1}^n a_i \cdot y_i) + b$ where $y_1, \ldots, y_n$ are integer variables, $a_i \in \mathbb{Z}$ for $i \in \{1, \ldots, n\}$, and $b \in \mathbb{Z}$. The algorithm consists of two components, a *synthesizer* and a *verifier*, which implement the CEGIS principle in a similar but simpler manner as our general framework. Roughly speaking, the synthesizer maintains an (initially empty) set $V \subseteq \mathbb{Z}^m$ of valuations of the variables $\vec{x}$ and constructs an expression $H$ for the function $f$ that satisfies $\psi$ at least for each valuation in $V$ (as opposed to all possible valuations). Then, it hands this expression over to the verifier. The task of the verifier is to check whether $H$ satisfies the specification. If this is the case, the algorithm has identified a correct expression, returns it, and terminates. If this not the case, the verifier extracts a particular valuation of the variables $\vec{x}$ for which the specification is violated and hands it over to the synthesizer. The synthesizer adds this valuation to $V$, and the algorithm iterates.

**Predicate Synthesizer.** Since the decision tree learning algorithm (which is our classifier) copes extremely well with a large number of attributes, we do not spend time in generating a small set of predicates. We build an *enumerative* predicate synthesizer that simply enumerates and adds predicates until it obtains an adequate set.

More precisely, the predicate synthesizer constructs a set $A_q$ of attributes for increasing values of $q \in \mathbb{N}$. The set $A_q$ contains all predicates of the form $\sum_{i=1}^n a_i \cdot y_i \leq b$, where $y_i$ are variables corresponding to the function arguments of the function $f$ that is to be synthesized, $a_i \in \mathbb{Z}$ such that each $\Sigma_{i=1}^n |a_i| \leq q$, and $|b| \leq q^2$. If $A_q$ is already adequate for $S$ (which can be checked by recursively splitting the sample with respect to each predicate in $A_q$ and checking if all

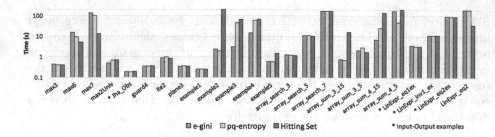

**Fig. 2.** Experimental results

samples at each leaf has a common label), we stop, else we increase the parameter
$q$ by one and iterate. Note that the predicate synthesizer is guaranteed to find
an adequate set for any sample. The reason for this is that one can separate
each input $\vec{p}$ into its own subsample (assuming each individual variable is also
an attribute) provided $q$ is large enough.

## 6   Evaluation

We implemented the framework described in Sect. 5 for specifications written in
the SyGuS format [1]. The implementation is about 5 K lines in C++ with API
calls to the Z3 SMT solver [10].

The implementations of the LIA counter-example finder and the expression
synthesizer use several heuristics. The counter-example finder prioritizes datapoints that have a single classification, and returns multiple counterexamples in
each round. The expression synthesizer uses a combination of enumeration (for
small degree expressions) and constraint-solving (for larger ones), and prioritizes
returning expressions that work for multiple neighboring inputs. More details are
in the extended version [23].

We evaluated our tool parameterized using the different measures in Sect. 4
against 43 benchmarks, and report here a representative 24 of them. These
benchmarks are predominantly from the 2014 and 2015 SyGuS competition [1,3].
Additionally, there is an example from [16] for deobfuscating C code using bitwise
operations on integers (we query this code 30 times on random inputs, record its
output and create an input-output specification, Jha_Obs, from it). The synthesis specification max2Univ reformulates the specification for max2 using universal
quantification, as

$$\forall x, r, y_1, y_2. \ (r < 0) \Rightarrow ((y_1 = x \wedge y_2 = x+r) \vee (y_1 = x+r \wedge y_2 = x)) \Rightarrow max(y_1, y_2) = x.$$

All experiments were performed on a system with an Intel Core i7-4770HQ
2.20 GHz CPU and 4 GB RAM running 64-bit Ubuntu 14.04 with a 200 seconds
timeout. The results of the 24 representative benchmarks are depicted in Fig. 2.

Figure 2 compares three measures: *e-gini*, *pq-entropy* and *hitting set*
(*pq-entropy* refers to the measure proposed by Clare and King [9]). All solvers

time-out on two benchmarks each. None of the algorithms dominates. The hitting-set measure is the only one to solve LinExpr_eq2. E-gini and pq-entropy can solve the same set of benchmarks but their performance differs on the example* specs, where e-gini performs better, and max* where pq-entropy performs better.

The CVC4 SMT-solver based synthesis tool [26] (which won the linear integer arithmetic track in the SyGuS 2015 competition [3]) worked very fast on these benchmarks, in general, but does not *generalize* from underspecifications. On specifications that list a set of input-output examples (marked with * in Fig. 2), CVC4 simply returns the precise map that the specification contains, without generalizing it. CVC4 allows restricting the syntax of target functions, but using this feature to force generalization (by disallowing large constants) renders them unsolvable. CVC4 was also not able to solve, surprisingly, the fairly simple specification max2Univ (although it has the single-invocation property [26]).

The general track SyGuS solvers (enumerative, stochastic, constraint-solver, and Sketch) [1] do not work well for these benchmarks (and did not fare well in the competition either); for example, the enumerative solver, which was the winner in 2014 can solve only 15 of the 43 benchmarks.

The above results show that the synthesis framework developed in this paper that uses theory-specific solvers for basic expressions and predicates, and combines them using a classification learner yields a competitive solver for the linear integer arithmetic domain. We believe more extensive benchmarks are needed to choose the right statistical measures for decision-tree learning.

**Acknowledgements.** This work was partially supported by NSF Expeditions in Computing ExCAPE Award #1138994.

# References

1. Alur, R. et al.: Syntax-guided synthesis. In: Dependable Software Systems Engineering. NATO Science for Peace and Security Series, D: Information and Communication Security, vol. 40, pp. 1–25. IOS Press (2015)
2. Alur, R., D'Antoni, L., Gulwani, S., Kini, D., Viswanathan, M.: Automated grading of DFA constructions. In: IJCAI 2013. IJCAI/AAAI (2013)
3. Alur, R., Fisman, D., Singh, R., Solar-Lezama, A.: Results and analysis of sygus-comp 2015. Technical report, University of Pennsylvania (2016). http://arxiv.org/abs/1602.01170
4. Alur, R., Singhania, N.: Precise piecewise affine models from input-output data. In: EMSOFT 2014, pp. 3:1–3:10. ACM (2014)
5. Barrett, C., Fontaine, P., Tinelli, C.: The SMT-LIB Standard: Version 2.5. Technical report Department of Computer Science, The University of Iowa (2015). http://www.SMT-LIB.org
6. Bemporad, A., Garulli, A., Paoletti, S., Vicino, A.: A bounded-error approach to piecewise affine system identification. IEEE Trans. Automat. Contr. 50(10), 1567–1580 (2005)

7. Cheung, A., Madden, S., Solar-Lezama, A., Arden, O., Myers, A.C.: Using program analysis to improve database applications. IEEE Data Eng. Bull. **37**(1), 48–59 (2014)
8. Chvatal, V.: A greedy heuristic for the set-covering problem. Math. Oper. Res. **4**(3), 233–235 (1979)
9. Clare, A.J., King, R.D.: Knowledge discovery in multi-label phenotype data. In: Siebes, A., De Raedt, L. (eds.) PKDD 2001. LNCS (LNAI), vol. 2168, pp. 42–53. Springer, Heidelberg (2001)
10. de Moura, L., Bjørner, N.S.: Z3: an efficient SMT solver. In: Ramakrishnan, C.R., Rehof, J. (eds.) TACAS 2008. LNCS, vol. 4963, pp. 337–340. Springer, Heidelberg (2008). http://dl.acm.org/citation.cfm?id=1792734.1792766
11. Ferrari-Trecate, G., Muselli, M., Liberati, D., Morari, M.: A clustering technique for the identification of piecewise affine systems. Automatica **39**(2), 205–217 (2003)
12. Garg, P., Löding, C., Madhusudan, P., Neider, D.: ICE: a robust framework for learning invariants. In: Biere, A., Bloem, R. (eds.) CAV 2014. LNCS, vol. 8559, pp. 69–87. Springer, Heidelberg (2014)
13. Garg, P., Madhusudan, P., Neider, D., Roth, D.: Learning invariants using decision trees and implication counterexamples. In: POPL 2016, pp. 499–512. ACM (2016)
14. Gulwani, S.: Automating string processing in spreadsheets using input-output examples. In: POPL 2011, pp. 317–330. ACM (2011)
15. Hastie, T., Tibshirani, R., Friedman, J.: The Elements of Statistical Learning. Springer Series in Statistics. Springer, New York (2001)
16. Jha, S., Gulwani, S., Seshia, S.A., Tiwari, A.: Oracle-guided component-based program synthesis. In: Proceedings of the 32nd ACM/IEEE International Conference on Software Engineering (ICSE 2010) - vol.1, pp. 215–224. ACM, New York (2010). http://doi.acm.org/10.1145/1806799.1806833
17. Jin, R., Ghahramani, Z.: Learning with multiple labels. In: NIPS 2002, pp. 897–904. MIT Press (2002)
18. Karaivanov, S., Raychev, V., Vechev, M.T.: Phrase-based statistical translation of programming languages. In: Onward! Part of SLASH 2014, pp. 173–184. ACM (2014)
19. Kitzelmann, E.: Inductive programming: a survey of program synthesis techniques. In: Schmid, U., Kitzelmann, E., Plasmeijer, R. (eds.) AAIP 2009. LNCS, vol. 5812, pp. 50–73. Springer, Heidelberg (2010)
20. Löding, C., Madhusudan, P., Neider, D. : Abstract learning frameworks for synthesis. In: Chechik, M., Raskin, J.-F., Matteescu, R., Beyer, D. (eds.) TACAS 2016. LNCS, vol. 9636, pp. 167–185. Springer, Heidelberg (2016)
21. McClurg, J., Hojjat, H., Cerný, P., Foster, N.: Efficient synthesis of network updates. In: PLDI 2015, pp. 196–207. ACM (2015)
22. Mitchell, T.M.: Machine Learning. McGraw Hill Series in Computer Science. McGraw-Hill, New York (1997)
23. Neider, D., Saha, S., Madhusudan, P.: Synthesizing piece-wise functions by learning classifiers. Technical report University of Illinois at Urbana-Champaign (2016). http://madhu.cs.illinois.edu/tacas16a/
24. Paoletti, S., Juloski, A.L., Ferrari-Trecate, G., Vidal, R.: Identification of hybrid systems: a tutorial. Eur. J. Control **13**(2–3), 242–260 (2007)
25. Quinlan, J.R.: C4.5: Programs for Machine Learning. Morgan Kaufmann, San Francisco (1993)
26. Reynolds, A., Deters, M., Kuncak, V., Tinelli, C., Barrett, C.: Counterexample-guided quantifier instantiation for synthesis in SMT. In: Kroening, D., Păsăreanu, C.S. (eds.) CAV 2015. LNCS, vol. 9207, pp. 198–216. Springer, Heidelberg (2015)

27. RuleQuest Research: Data mining tools See5 and C5.0. https://www.rulequest. com/see5-info.html. Accessed 29 December 2015
28. Saha, S., Garg, P., Madhusudan, P.: Alchemist: learning guarded affine functions. In: Kroening, D., Păsăreanu, C.S. (eds.) CAV 2015. LNCS, vol. 9206, pp. 440–446. Springer, Heidelberg (2015)
29. Saha, S., Prabhu, S., Madhusudan, P.: Netgen: synthesizing data-plane configurations for network policies. In: SOSR 2015, pp. 17:1–17:6. ACM (2015)
30. Singh, R., Gulwani, S., Solar-Lezama, A.: Automated feedback generation for introductory programming assignments. In: PLDI 2013, pp. 15–26. ACM (2013)
31. Solar-Lezama, A.: Program sketching. STTT **15**(5–6), 475–495 (2013)
32. Solar-Lezama, A., Tancau, L., Bodík, R., Seshia, S.A., Saraswat, V.A.: Combinatorial sketching for finite programs. In: ASPLOS 2006, pp. 404–415. ACM (2006)
33. Tsoumakas, G., Katakis, I.: Multi-label classification: an overview. IJDWM **3**(3), 1–13 (2007)
34. Vidal, R., Soatto, S., Ma, Y., Sastry, S.: An algebraic geometric approach to the identification of a class of linear hybrid systems. In: 42nd IEEE Conference on Decision and Control, 2003, Proceedings, vol. 1, pp. 167–172 December 2003

# An Automaton Learning Approach to Solving Safety Games over Infinite Graphs

Daniel Neider[1] and Ufuk Topcu[2(✉)]

[1] University of California, Los Angeles, USA
neider@ucla.edu
[2] The University of Texas at Austin, Austin, USA
utopcu@utexas.edu

**Abstract.** We propose a method to construct finite-state reactive controllers for systems whose interactions with their adversarial environment are modeled by infinite-duration two-player games over (possibly) infinite graphs. The method targets safety games with infinitely many states or with such a large number of states that it would be impractical—if not impossible—for conventional synthesis techniques that work on the entire state space. We resort to constructing finite-state controllers for such systems through an automata learning approach, utilizing a symbolic representation of the underlying game that is based on finite automata. Throughout the learning process, the learner maintains an approximation of the winning region (represented as a finite automaton) and refines it using different types of counterexamples provided by the teacher until a satisfactory controller can be derived (if one exists). We present a symbolic representation of safety games (inspired by regular model checking), propose implementations of the learner and teacher, and evaluate their performance on examples motivated by robotic motion planning.

## 1 Introduction

We propose an automata learning-based method to construct reactive controllers subject to safety specifications. We model the interaction between a controlled system and its possibly adversarial environment as a two-player game over a graph [16]. We consider games over *infinite graphs*. In this setting, the conventional techniques for reactive controller synthesis (e.g., fixed-point computations) are not applicable anymore. We resort to *learning* for constructing finite-state reactive controllers. The learning takes place in a setting akin to *counterexample-guided inductive synthesis* (CEGIS) [14] between a *teacher*, who has knowledge about the safety game in question, and a *learner*, whose objective is to identify a controller using information disclosed by the teacher in response to (incorrect) conjectures.

A natural context for our method is one in which the interaction between the controlled system and its environment is so complex that it can be represented only by graphs with infinitely many vertices (e.g., motion planning over unbounded grid worlds) or "practically infinitely many" states (i.e., the number

© Springer-Verlag Berlin Heidelberg 2016
M. Chechik and J.-F. Raskin (Eds.): TACAS 2016, LNCS 9636, pp. 204–221, 2016.
DOI: 10.1007/978-3-662-49674-9_12

of possible configurations is so large that the game becomes impractical for conventional techniques). Additionally, in situations in which a complete description of the game is not available in a format amenable to existing game solvers [6,9], there may still exist human experts (or automated oracles, as in Sect. 4) who acts as teacher with their insight into how the controlled system should behave.

We focus on games with safety specifications, which already capture practically interesting properties (e.g., safety and bounded-horizon reachability). However, games over infinite graphs require special attention on the representation and manipulation of the underlying graph structure. Hence, one of our main contributions is a symbolic representation of safety games, called *rational safety games*, that follows the idea of *regular model checking* [7] in that it represents sets of vertices by regular languages and edges by so-called rational relations.

We develop an iterative framework for learning winning sets—equivalently controllers—in rational safety games and particular implementations of a teacher and learner. In each iteration, the learner conjectures a winning set, represented as a deterministic finite automaton. The teacher performs a number of checks and returns, based on whether the conjecture passes the checks, a counterexample. Following the ICE learning framework [10] and partially deviating from the classical learning frameworks for regular languages [1,11], the counterexample may be one of the following four types: positive, negative, existential implication and universal implication counterexamples. Based on the response of the teacher, the learner updates his conjecture. If the conjecture passes all checks, the learning terminates with the desired controller. However, our technique is necessarily a semi-algorithm as reachability questions over rational relations are undecidable.

Even though the underlying game may be prohibitively large, a controller with a compact representation may realize the specifications. For example, depending on the given task specification in robotic motion planning, only a small subset of all possible interactions between a robot and its environment is often relevant. Based on this observation, our method possesses several desirable properties: (i) it usually identifies "small" solutions that are more likely to be interpretable by users; (ii) its runtime mainly depends on the size of the solution rather than the size of the underlying game; (iii) though the method is applicable generally, it performs particularly well when the resulting controller has a small representation; (iv) besides being applicable to infinite-state systems, the method performs well on finite-state problems by—unlike conventional techniques—avoiding potentially large intermediate artifacts. We demonstrate these properties empirically on a series of examples motivated by robotic motion planning.

**Related Work.** Games over infinite graphs have been studied, predominantly for games over pushdown graphs [15]. Also, a constraint-based approach to solving games over infinite graphs has recently been proposed [3]. Learning-based techniques for reachability games over infinite graphs were studied in [19]; in fact, our symbolic representation of safety games is a generalization of the representation proposed there. In the context of safety games, recent work [20] demonstrated the ability of learning-based approaches to extract small reactive controllers from a priori constructed controllers with a possibly large number of states. In this work, we by-pass this a priori construction of reactive controllers by learning a controller directly. Infinite (game) graphs occur often in the presence of data, and symbolic formalisms have been described for several domains, including examples such as interface automata with data [13] and modal specifications with data [2]. However, we are not aware of learning algorithms for these formalisms.

## 2   Rational Safety Games

We recap the basic notation and definitions used in the rest of the paper.

*Safety Games.* We consider safety games (i.e., infinite duration two-person games on graphs) [16]. A safety game is played on an *arena* $\mathfrak{A} = (V_0, V_1, E)$ consisting of two nonempty, disjoint sets $V_0, V_1$ of *vertices* (we denote their union by $V$) and a directed edge relation $E \subseteq V \times V$. In contrast to the classical (finite) setting, we allow $V_0$ and $V_1$ to be countable sets. As shorthand notation, we write the successors of a set $X \subseteq V$ of vertices as $E(X) = \{y \mid \exists x \in X : (x, y) \in E\}$.

We consider safety games with initial vertices, which are defined as triples $\mathfrak{G} = (\mathfrak{A}, F, I)$ consisting of an arena $\mathfrak{A} = (V_0, V_1, E)$, a set $F \subseteq V$ of *safe vertices*, and a set $I \subseteq F$ of *initial vertices*. Such safety games are played by two players, named Player 0 and Player 1, who play the game by moving a token along the edges. Formally, a *play* is an infinite sequence $\pi = v_0 v_1 \ldots \in V^\omega$ that satisfies $v_0 \in I$ and $(v_i, v_{i+1}) \in E$ for all $i \in \mathbb{N}$. The set $F$ defines the winning condition of the game in the sense that a play $v_0 v_1 \ldots$ is *winning for Player 0* if $v_i \in F$ for all $i \in \mathbb{N}$—otherwise it is *winning for Player 1* .

A strategy for Player $\sigma \in \{0, 1\}$ is a mapping $f_\sigma : V^* V_\sigma \to V$, which prescribes how to continue playing. A strategy $f_\sigma$ is called *winning* if any play $v_0 v_1 \ldots$ that is played according to the strategy (i.e., that satisfies $v_{i+1} = f_\sigma(v_0 \ldots v_i)$ for all $i \in \mathbb{N}$ and $v_i \in V_\sigma$) is winning for Player $\sigma$. A winning strategy for Player 0 translates into a controller satisfying the given safety specifications. Hence, we restrict ourselves to compute winning strategies for Player 0. Computing a winning strategy for Player 0 usually reduces to finding a so-called winning set.

**Definition 1 (Winning set).** *Let $\mathfrak{G} = (\mathfrak{A}, I, F)$ be a safety game over the arena $\mathfrak{A} = (V_0, V_1, E)$. A winning set is a set $W \subseteq V$ satisfying (1) $I \subseteq W$, (2) $W \subseteq F$, (3) $E(\{v\}) \cap W \neq \emptyset$ for all $v \in W \cap V_0$ (existential closedness), and (4) $E(\{v\}) \subseteq W$ for all $v \in W \cap V_1$ (universal closedness).*

By computing a winning set, one immediately obtains a strategy for Player 0: starting in an initial vertex, Player 0 simply moves to a successor vertex inside $W$ whenever it is his turn. A straightforward induction over the length of plays proves that every play that is played according to this strategy stays inside $F$, no matter how Player 1 plays, and, hence, is won by Player 0 (since $I \subseteq W \subseteq F$). A winning set is what we want to compute—or, more precisely, *learn*.

Algorithmically working with games over infinite arenas require symbolic representations. We follow the idea of *regular model checking* [7] and represent sets of vertices by regular languages and edges by so-called rational relations. Before we introduce our symbolic representation of safety games, however, we recap some basic concepts of automata theory.

*Basics of Automata Theory.* An *alphabet* $\Sigma$ is a nonempty, finite set, whose elements are called *symbols*. A *word* over the alphabet $\Sigma$ is a sequence $u = a_1 \ldots a_n$ of symbols $a_i \in \Sigma$ for $i \in \{1, \ldots, n\}$; the empty sequence is called *empty word* and denoted by $\varepsilon$. Given two words $u = a_1 \ldots a_m$ and $v = b_1 \ldots b_n$, the *concatenation of $u$ and $v$* is the word $u \cdot v = uv = a_1 \ldots a_m b_1 \ldots b_n$. The set of all words over the alphabet $\Sigma$ is denoted by $\Sigma^*$, and a subset $L \subseteq \Sigma^*$ is called a *language*. The set of prefixes of a language $L \subseteq \Sigma^*$ is the set $Pref(L) = \{u \in \Sigma^* \mid \exists v \in \Sigma^* : uv \in L\}$.

A *nondeterministic finite automaton (NFA)* is a tuple $\mathcal{A} = (Q, \Sigma, q_0, \Delta, F)$ consisting of a nonempty, finite set $Q$ of *states*, an *input alphabet* $\Sigma$, an *initial state* $q_0 \in Q$, a *transition relation* $\Delta \subseteq Q \times \Sigma \times Q$, and a set $F \subseteq Q$ of *final states*. A *run* of $\mathcal{A}$ on a word $u = a_1 \ldots a_n$ is a sequence of states $q_0, \ldots, q_n$ such that $(q_{i-1}, a_i, q_i) \in \Delta$ for $i \in \{1, \ldots, n\}$. We denote this run by $\mathcal{A} \colon q_0 \xrightarrow{u} q_n$. An *NFA* $\mathcal{A}$ *accepts* a word $u \in \Sigma^*$ if $\mathcal{A} \colon q_0 \xrightarrow{u} q$ with $q \in F$. The set $L(\mathcal{A}) = \{u \in \Sigma^* \mid \mathcal{A} \colon q_0 \xrightarrow{u} q, q \in F\}$ is called *language of $\mathcal{A}$*. A language $L$ is *regular* if there exists an *NFA* $\mathcal{A}$ with $L(\mathcal{A}) = L$. $NFA_\Sigma$ denotes the set of all $NFAs$ over $\Sigma$.

A *deterministic finite automaton (DFA)* is an NFA in which $(p, a, q) \in \Delta$ and $(p, a, q') \in \Delta$ imply $q = q'$. For DFAs, we replace the transition relation $\Delta$ by a transition function $\delta \colon Q \times \Sigma \to Q$.

We define infinite arenas by resorting to transducers. A *transducer* is an NFA $\mathcal{T} = (Q, \hat{\Sigma}, q_0, \Delta, F)$ over the alphabet $\hat{\Sigma} = (\Sigma \cup \{\varepsilon\}) \times (\Gamma \cup \{\varepsilon\})$—$\Sigma$ and $\Gamma$ are both alphabets—that processes pairs $(u, v) \in \Sigma^* \times \Gamma^*$ of words. The *run* of a transducer $\mathcal{T}$ on a pair $(u, v)$ is a sequence $q_0, \ldots, q_n$ of states such that $(q_{i-1}, (a_i, b_i), q_i) \in \Delta$ for all $i \in \{1, \ldots, n\}$, $u = a_1 \ldots a_n$, and $v = b_1 \ldots b_n$; note that $u$ and $v$ do not need to be of equal length since any $a_i$ or $b_i$ can be $\varepsilon$. A pair $(u, v)$ is said to be *accepted* by $\mathcal{T}$ if there exists a run of $\mathcal{T}$ on $(u, v)$ that starts in the initial state and ends in a final state. As an acceptor of pairs of words, a transducer $\mathcal{T}$ *defines* a relation, namely the relation consisting of exactly the pairs accepted by $\mathcal{T}$, which we denote by $R(\mathcal{T})$. Finally, a relation $R \subseteq \Sigma^* \times \Gamma^*$ is called *rational* if there exists a transducer $\mathcal{T}$ with $R(\mathcal{T}) = R$. (This definition is simplified from that in [5] but sufficient for our purpose.) Note that transducers as defined above do not need to preserve the length of words.

Our learning framework relies on the two facts given in Lemma 1.

**Lemma 1.** *Let $R \subseteq \Sigma^* \times \Gamma^*$ be a rational relation and $X \subseteq \Sigma^*$ a regular set. Then, (1) the relation $R^{-1} = \{(y, x) \mid (x, y) \in R\}$ is again rational, and a transducer defining this set can be constructed in linear time; and (2) the set $R(X) = \{y \in \Gamma^* \mid \exists x \in X \colon (x, y) \in R\}$, called the image of $X$ under $R$, is again regular, and an NFA accepting this set can be constructed effectively.*

*Rational Safety Games.* A rational safety game is a symbolic representation of a safety game in terms of regular languages and rational relations.

**Definition 2.** *A rational arena over the alphabet $\Sigma$ is an arena $\mathfrak{A}_\Sigma = (V_0, V_1, E)$ where $V_0, V_1 \subseteq \Sigma^*$ are regular languages and $E \subseteq V \times V$ is a rational relation.*

**Definition 3.** *A rational safety game over the alphabet $\Sigma$ is a safety game $\mathfrak{G}_\Sigma = (\mathfrak{A}_\Sigma, F, I)$ with a rational arena $\mathfrak{A}_\Sigma$ over $\Sigma$ and regular languages $F, I \subseteq \Sigma^*$.*

We assume regular languages to be given as *NFA*s and rational relations as transducers. We use these notions interchangeably; for instance, we write a rational area $\mathfrak{A}_\Sigma = (V_0, V_1, E)$ as $\mathfrak{A}_\Sigma = (\mathcal{A}_{V_0}, \mathcal{A}_{V_1}, \mathcal{T}_E)$ given that $L(\mathcal{A}_{V_0}) = V_0$, $L(\mathcal{A}_{V_1}) = V_1$, and $R(\mathcal{T}_E) = E$.

*Example 1.* Consider an example motivated by motion planning (see Fig. 1a) in which a robot moves on an infinite, one-dimensional grid that is "bounded on the left". It can move to an adjacent cell (provided that it has not reached left edge) or it stays still. The grid is partitioned into a safe (shaded in Fig. 1a) and an unsafe area. The safe area is parameterized by $k \in \mathbb{N} \setminus \{0\}$ and consists of all positions greater than or equal to $k$. The robot starts inside the safe area.

(a) A robot moving on a one-dimensional discrete grid ($k = 2$).

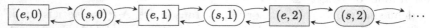

(b) The safety game $\mathfrak{G}_2$. Player 0 vertices are drawn as ellipses and Player 1 vertices are drawn as squares. Shaded vertices belong to $F$.

**Fig. 1.** Illustration of the safety game discussed in the introductory example.

The robot's movement is governed by two adversarial players, called *system* and *environment*. The system can move the robot to the right or keep it at its current position, whereas the environment can move the robot to the left (if the edge has not been reached) or keep it at its current position. The players move the robot in alternation, and the system moves first. The system's objective is to stay within the safe area, whereas the environment wants to move the robot out of it. Note that the system can win, irrespective of $k$, by always moving right.

A formalization as safety game is straightforward. Player 0 corresponds to the system and Player 1 corresponds to the environment. The arena $\mathfrak{A} = (V_0, V_1, E)$ consists of vertices $V_0 = \{s\} \times \mathbb{N}$ and $V_1 = \{e\} \times \mathbb{N}$—$s$, respectively $e$, indicates the player moving next—as well as the edge relation $E = \{((s, i), (e, i+1)) \mid i \in \mathbb{N}\} \cup \{((e, i+1), (s, i)) \mid i \in \mathbb{N}\}$. The safety game itself is the triple $\mathfrak{G}_k = (\mathfrak{A}, F, I)$ with $F = \{s, e\} \times \{i \in \mathbb{N} \mid i \geq k\}$ and $I = \{s\} \times \{i \in \mathbb{N} \mid i \geq k\}$. Figure 1b sketches the game $\mathfrak{G}_k$ for the case $k = 2$.

We now turn $\mathfrak{G}_k$ into a rational safety game. To this end, we label each vertex uniquely with a finite word. In our example, we choose $\Sigma = \{s, e, I\}$ and associate the vertex $(x, i) \in \{s, e\} \times \mathbb{N}$ with the word $xI^i$ where $I^i$ is the encoding of $i$ in unary. We represent the sets $V_0$ and $V_1$ by the following $NFAs$:

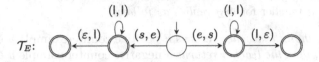

Moreover, we represent the edges by the following transducer:

$$\mathcal{T}_E: \quad \circledcirc \xleftarrow{(\varepsilon, I)} \bigcirc \xleftarrow{(I, I)} \xrightarrow{(s, e)} \bigcirc \xrightarrow{(e, s)} \bigcirc \xleftarrow{(I, I)} \xrightarrow{(I, \varepsilon)} \bigcirc$$

Finally, the NFA

$$\mathcal{A}_F: \quad \to \bigcirc \xrightarrow{s, e} \bigcirc \xrightarrow{I} \cdots \xrightarrow{I} \bigcirc \xrightarrow{I} \circledcirc \circlearrowleft I$$

with $k - 1$ states

represents the set $F$; similarly, $I$ is represented by a copy of $\mathcal{A}_F$ in which the transition labeled with $e$ is omitted.

It is worth mentioning that rational arenas not only subsume finite arenas but also a rich class of infinite arenas, including such encoding computations of Turing machines. Hence, the problem of determining the winner of a rational safety game is undecidable, and any algorithm for computing a winning set can at best be a semi-algorithm (i.e., an algorithm that, on termination, gives the correct answer but does not guarantee to halt). The algorithm we design in this paper is of this kind and guarantees to learn a winning set if one exists. For ease of presentation, we always assume that a winning set exists.

## 3   The Learning Framework

Our learning framework is an extension of the ICE framework [10] for learning loop invariants from positive and negative data as well as implications. The learning takes place between a *teacher*, who has (explicit or implicit) knowledge about the rational safety game in question, and a *learner*, whose objective is to learn a DFA accepting a winning set, but who is agnostic to the game. We assume that the teacher announces the alphabet of the game before the actual learning starts.

The learning proceeds in a CEGIS-style loop [14]. In every iteration, the learner conjectures a DFA, call it $\mathcal{C}$, and the teacher checks whether $L(\mathcal{C})$ is a winning set—this kind of query is often called *equivalence* or *correctness query*. Although the teacher does not know a winning set (the overall objective is to learn one after all), he can resort to Conditions (1)–(4) of Definition 1 in order to decide whether $L(\mathcal{C})$ is a winning set. If $L(\mathcal{C})$ satisfies Conditions (1)–(4), then the teacher replies "yes" and the learning ends. If this is not the case, the teacher returns a *counterexample* witnessing the violation of one of these conditions, and the learning continues with the next iteration. The definition below fixes the protocol between the teacher and the learner, and defines counterexamples.

**Definition 4 (Teacher for rational safety games).** *Let $\mathfrak{G}_\Sigma = (\mathfrak{A}_\Sigma, F, I)$ be a rational safety game over the rational arena $\mathfrak{A}_\Sigma = (V_0, V_1, E)$. Confronted with a DFA $\mathcal{C}$, a teacher for $\mathfrak{G}_\Sigma$ replies as follows:*

1. *If $I \not\subseteq L(\mathcal{C})$, then the teacher returns a positive counterexample $u \in I \setminus L(\mathcal{C})$.*
2. *If $L(\mathcal{C}) \not\subseteq F$, then the teacher returns a negative counterexample $u \in L(\mathcal{C}) \setminus F$.*
3. *If there exists $u \in L(\mathcal{C}) \cap V_0$ such that $E(\{u\}) \cap L(\mathcal{C}) = \emptyset$, then the teacher picks such a word $u$ and returns an existential implication counterexample $(u, \mathcal{A}) \in \Sigma^* \times NFA_\Sigma$ where $L(\mathcal{A}) = E(\{u\})$.*
4. *If there exists $u \in L(\mathcal{C}) \cap V_1$ such that $E(\{u\}) \not\subseteq L(\mathcal{C})$, then the teacher picks such a word $u$ and returns a universal implication counterexample $(u, \mathcal{A}) \in \Sigma^* \times NFA_\Sigma$ where $L(\mathcal{A}) = E(\{u\})$.*

*If $\mathcal{C}$ passes all four checks (in arbitrary order), the teacher replies "yes".*

It is easy to see that the language of a conjecture is indeed a winning set if the teacher replies "yes" (since it satisfies all conditions of Definition 1). The meaning of a positive counterexample is that any conjecture needs to accepts it but it was rejected. Similarly, a negative counterexample indicates that any conjecture has to reject it but it was accepted. An existential implication counterexample $(u, \mathcal{A})$ means that any conjecture accepting $u$ has to accept at least one $v \in L(\mathcal{A})$, which was violated by the current conjecture. Finally, a universal implication counterexample $(u, \mathcal{A})$ means that any conjecture accepting $u$ needs to accept all $v \in L(\mathcal{A})$. At this point, it is important to note that Definition 4 is sound (in particular, both types of implication counterexamples are well-defined due to Lemma 1 Part 2) and every counterexample is a finite object.

*Example 2.* We revisit Example 1 for $k = 2$ and describe how a winning set is learned. Suppose the learner conjectures the DFA $\mathcal{C}_0$ with $L(\mathcal{C}_0) = \emptyset$. As $\mathcal{C}_0$ fails Check 4 (it passes all other checks), the teacher returns a positive counterexample, say $u = s\mathsf{ll} \in I$. Next, suppose the learner conjectures the DFA $\mathcal{C}_1$ with $L(\mathcal{C}_1) = \{s\mathsf{l}^n \mid n \geq 2\}$, which passes all checks but Check 4 (as the players alternate but $L(\mathcal{C}_1)$ does not contain a vertex of the environment). The teacher replies with an existential implication counterexample, say $(s\mathsf{ll}, \mathcal{A})$ with $L(\mathcal{A}) = \{e\mathsf{ll}, e\mathsf{lll}\}$. In the next round, suppose the learner conjectures the DFA $\mathcal{C}_2$ with $L(\mathcal{C}_2) = \{s\mathsf{l}^n \mid n \geq 2\} \cup \{e\mathsf{l}^m \mid m \geq 3\}$. This conjecture passes all checks (i.e., $L(\mathcal{C}_2)$ is a winning set), the teacher replies "yes", and the learning ends.

It is important to note that classical learning frameworks for regular languages that involve learning from positive and negative data only, such as Gold's

passive learning [11] or Angluin's active learning [1], are insufficient in our setting. If the learner provides a conjecture $C$ that violates Condition (3) or (4)
of Definition 1, the teacher is stuck. For instance, if $C$ does not satisfy Conditions (4), the teacher does not know whether to exclude $u$ or to include $E(\{u\})$.
Returning an implication counterexample resolves this problem by communicating exactly why the conjecture is incorrect and, hence, allows the learner to make
progress.[1]

## 4    A Generic Teacher

We now present a generic teacher that, taking a rational safety game as input,
answers queries according to Definition 4. For the remainder of this section,
fix a rational safety game $\mathfrak{G}_\Sigma = (\mathfrak{A}_\Sigma, \mathcal{A}_F, \mathcal{A}_I)$ over the rational arena $\mathfrak{A}_\Sigma = (\mathcal{A}_{V_0}, \mathcal{A}_{V_1}, \mathcal{T}_E)$, and let $C$ be a DFA conjectured by the learner.

To answer a query, the teacher performs Checks 1 to 4 of Definition 4 as
described below. If the conjecture passes all checks, the teacher returns "yes";
otherwise, he returns a corresponding counterexample, as described next.

*Check 1 (initial vertices).* The teacher computes an NFA $\mathcal{B}$ with $L(\mathcal{B}) = L(\mathcal{A}_I) \setminus L(C)$. If $L(\mathcal{B}) \neq \emptyset$, he returns a positive counterexample $u \in L(\mathcal{B})$.

*Check 2 (safe vertices).* The teacher computes an NFA $\mathcal{B}$ with $L(\mathcal{B}) = L(C) \setminus L(\mathcal{A}_F)$. If $L(\mathcal{B}) \neq \emptyset$, he returns a negative counterexample $u \in L(\mathcal{B})$.

*Check 3 (existential closure).* The teacher successively computes three NFAs:

1. An $NFA$ $\mathcal{B}_1$ with $L(\mathcal{B}_1) = R(\mathcal{T}_E)^{-1}(L(C))$; the language $L(\mathcal{B}_1)$ contains all vertices that have a successor in $L(C)$.
2. An $NFA$ $\mathcal{B}_2$ with $L(\mathcal{B}_2) = L(\mathcal{A}_{V_0}) \setminus L(\mathcal{B}_1)$; the language $L(\mathcal{B}_2)$ contains all vertices of Player 0 that have no successor in $L(C)$.
3. An $NFA$ $\mathcal{B}_3$ with $L(\mathcal{B}_3) = L(C) \cap L(\mathcal{B}_2)$; the language $L(\mathcal{B}_3)$ contains all vertices of Player 0 that belong to $L(C)$ and have no successor in $L(C)$.

Every $u \in L(\mathcal{B}_3)$ is a witness that $C$ is not existentially closed. Hence, if $L(\mathcal{B}_3) \neq \emptyset$, the teacher picks an arbitrary $u \in L(\mathcal{B}_3)$ and returns the existential implication counterexample $(u, \mathcal{A})$ where $L(\mathcal{A}) = R(\mathcal{T}_E)(\{u\})$.

*Check 4 (universal closure).* The teacher computes three NFAs:

1. An $NFA$ $\mathcal{B}_1$ with $L(\mathcal{B}_1) = \big(L(\mathcal{A}_{V_0}) \cup L(\mathcal{A}_{V_1})\big) \setminus L(C)$; the language $L(\mathcal{B}_1)$ contains all vertices not in $L(C)$.

---

[1] Garg et al. [10] argue comprehensively in the case of learning loop invariants of
WHILE-programs why implications are in fact required. Their arguments also apply
here as one obtains a setting similar to theirs by considering a solitary game with
Player 1 as the only player.

2. An $NFA$ $\mathcal{B}_2$ with $L(\mathcal{B}_2) = R(\mathcal{T}_E)^{-1}(L(\mathcal{B}_1))$; the language $L(\mathcal{B}_2)$ contains all vertices that have a successor not belonging to $L(\mathcal{C})$.
3. An $NFA$ $\mathcal{B}_3$ with $L(\mathcal{B}_3) = L(\mathcal{A}_{V_1}) \cap L(\mathcal{C}) \cap L(\mathcal{B}_2)$; the language $L(\mathcal{B}_3)$ contains all vertices of Player 1 in $L(\mathcal{C})$ with at least one successor not in $L(\mathcal{C})$.

Every $u \in L(\mathcal{B}_3)$ is a witness that $\mathcal{C}$ is not universally closed. Hence, if $L(\mathcal{B}_3) \neq \emptyset$, the teacher picks an arbitrary $u \in L(\mathcal{B}_3)$ and returns the universal implication counterexample $(u, \mathcal{A})$ where $L(\mathcal{A}) = R(\mathcal{T}_E)(\{u\})$.

All checks can be performed using standard methods of automata theory. In our implementation, the teacher performs the checks in the order 1 to 4.

## 5   A Learner for Rational Safety Games

We design our learner with two key features: (1) it always conjectures a DFA consistent with the counterexamples received so far, and (2) it always conjectures a minimal, consistent DFA (i.e., a DFA with the least number of states among all DFAs that are consistent with the received counterexamples). The first feature prevents the learner from making the same mistake twice, while the second facilitates convergence of the overall learning (provided that a winning set exists).

Our learner stores counterexamples in a so-called *sample*, which is a tuple $\mathcal{S} = (Pos, Neg, Ex, Uni)$ consisting of a finite set $Pos \subset \Sigma^*$ of positive words, a finite set $Neg \subset \Sigma^*$ of negative words, a finite set $Ex \subset \Sigma^* \times NFA_\Sigma$ of existential implications, and a finite set $Uni \subset \Sigma^* \times NFA_\Sigma$ of universal implications. We encourage the reader to think of a sample as a finite approximation of the safety game learned thus far.

In every iteration, our learner constructs a minimal DFA *consistent* with the current sample $\mathcal{S} = (Pos, Neg, Ex, Uni)$. A DFA $\mathcal{B}$ is called *consistent* with $\mathcal{S}$ if

1. $Pos \subseteq L(\mathcal{B})$;
2. $Neg \cap L(\mathcal{B}) = \emptyset$;
3. $u \in L(\mathcal{B})$ implies $L(\mathcal{B}) \cap L(\mathcal{A}) \neq \emptyset$ for each $(u, \mathcal{A}) \in Ex$; and
4. $u \in L(\mathcal{B})$ implies $L(\mathcal{A}) \subseteq L(\mathcal{B})$ for each $(u, \mathcal{A}) \in Uni$.

Constructing a DFA that is consistent with a sample is possible only if the sample does not contain contradictory information. Contradictions can arise in two ways: first, $Pos$ and $Neg$ are not disjoint; second, the (alternating) transitive closure of the implications in $Ex$ and $Uni$ contains a pair $(u, v)$ with $u \in Pos$ and $v \in Neg$. This observation justifies the notion of *contradiction-free* samples: a sample $\mathcal{S}$ is called *contradiction-free* if a DFA that is consistent with $\mathcal{S}$ exists. If Player 0 wins from set $I$, a winning set exists and the counterexamples returned by the teacher always form contradiction-free samples.[2]

---

[2] Checking for contradictions allows detecting that a game is won by Player 1. However, since determining the winner of a rational safety game is undecidable, any sample obtained during the learning might be contradiction-free despite that Player 1 wins.

---

**Algorithm 1.** A learner for rational safety games

---

1  Initialize an empty sample $S = (Pos, Neg, Ex, Uni)$ with $Pos = \emptyset$, $Neg = \emptyset$,
   $Ex = \emptyset$, and $Uni = \emptyset$;
2  **repeat**
3  |   Construct a minimal DFA $A_S$ consistent with $S$;
4  |   Submit $A_S$ to an equivalence query;
5  |   **if** *the teacher returns a counterexample* **then**
6  |   |   Add the counterexample to $S$;
7  |   **end**
8  **until** *the teacher replies "yes" to an equivalence query*;
9  **return** $A_S$;

---

Once a minimal, consistent DFA is constructed, the learner conjectures it to the teacher. If the teacher replies "yes", the learning terminates with a winning set. If the teacher returns a counterexample, the learner adds it to $S$ and iterates. This procedure is sketched as Algorithm 1. Note that unravelling the game graph provides additional examples without the need to construct conjectures, but there is a trade-off between the number of iterations and the time needed to compute consistent DFAs. We leave an investigation of this trade-off for future work.

It is left to describe how the learner actually constructs a minimal DFA that is consistent with the current sample. However, this task, known as *passive learning*, is computationally hard (i.e., the corresponding decision problem is NP-complete) already in the absence of implications [11]. We approach this hurdle by translating the original problem into a sequence of satisfiability problems of formulas in propositional Boolean logic and use highly optimized constraint solvers as a practically effective means to solve the resulting formulas (note that a translation into a logical formulation is a popular and effective strategy). More precisely, our learner creates and solves propositional Boolean formulas $\varphi_n^S$, for increasing values of $n \in \mathbb{N}$, $n \geq 1$, with the following two properties:

1. The formula $\varphi_n^S$ is satisfiable if and only if there exists a DFA that has $n$ states and is consistent with $S$.
2. A model $\mathfrak{M}$ of (i.e., a satisfying assignment of the variables in) $\varphi_n^S$ contains sufficient information to construct a DFA $A_{\mathfrak{M}}$ that has $n$ states and is consistent with $S$.

If $\varphi_n^S$ is satisfiable, then Property 2 enables us to construct a consistent DFA from a model. However, if the formula is unsatisfiable, then the parameter $n$ has been chosen too small and the learner increments it. This procedure is summarized as Algorithm 2. We comment on its correctness later in this section. A proof can be found in the extended paper [22].

The key idea of the formula $\varphi_n^S$ is to encode a DFA with $n$ states by means of Boolean variables and to pose constraints on those variables. Our encoding relies on a simple observation: for every DFA there exists an isomorphic (hence,

---

**Algorithm 2.** Computing a minimal consistent DFA.

---

**Input**: A contradiction-free sample $\mathcal{S}$
**Output**: A minimal DFA that is consistent with $\mathcal{S}$
1  $n \leftarrow 0$;
2  **repeat**
3  $\quad$ $n \leftarrow n + 1$;
4  $\quad$ Construct and solve $\varphi_n^{\mathcal{S}}$;
5  **until** $\varphi_n^{\mathcal{S}}$ *is satisfiable, say with model* $\mathfrak{M}$;
6  **return** $\mathcal{A}_{\mathfrak{M}}$;

---

equivalent) DFA over the state set $Q = \{0, \ldots, n-1\}$ with initial state $q_0 = 0$; moreover, given that $Q$ and $q_0$ are fixed, any DFA with $n$ states is uniquely determined by its transitions and final states. Therefore, we can fix the state set of the prospective DFA as $Q = \{0, \ldots, n-1\}$ and the initial state as $q_0 = 0$; the alphabet $\Sigma$ is announced by the teacher.

Our encoding of transitions and final states follows an idea from [12,21] (similar to the approach of Biermann and Feldman [4]). We introduce Boolean variables $d_{p,a,q}$ and $f_q$ where $p, q \in Q$ and $a \in \Sigma$, which have the following meaning: setting $d_{p,a,q}$ to *true* means that the transition $\delta(p,a) = q$ exists in the prospective DFA, and setting $f_q$ to *true* means that $q$ is a final state.

To make sure that the variables $d_{p,a,q}$ encode a deterministic transition function, we impose two constraints:

$$\bigwedge_{p \in Q} \bigwedge_{a \in \Sigma} \bigwedge_{q,q' \in Q, q \neq q'} \neg d_{p,a,q} \vee \neg d_{p,a,q'} \tag{1}$$

$$\bigwedge_{p \in Q} \bigwedge_{a \in \Sigma} \bigvee_{q \in Q} d_{p,a,q} \tag{2}$$

Let $\varphi_n^{DFA}$ be the conjunction of Formulas (1) and (2). Given a model $\mathfrak{M}$ of $\varphi_n^{DFA}$ (we assume a model to be a map from the variables of a formula to the set $\{true, false\}$), deriving the encoded DFA is straightforward, as shown next.

**Definition 5 (DFA $\mathcal{A}_{\mathfrak{M}}$).** *Given a model $\mathfrak{M}$ of $\varphi_n^{DFA}$, we define the DFA $\mathcal{A}_{\mathfrak{M}} = (Q, \Sigma, q_0, \delta, F)$ by (i) $\delta(p,a) = q$ for the unique $q \in Q$ with $\mathfrak{M}(d_{p,a,q}) = true$; and (ii) $F = \{q \in Q \mid \mathfrak{M}(f_q) = true\}$. (Recall that we fixed $Q = \{0, \ldots, n-1\}$ and $q_0 = 0$.)*

To ensure that $\mathcal{A}_{\mathfrak{M}}$ is consistent with a sample $\mathcal{S} = (Pos, Neg, Ex, Uni)$, we impose further constraints, corresponding to the requirements of consistent DFAs: (i) A formula $\varphi_n^{Pos}$ asserting $Pos \subseteq L(\mathcal{A}_{\mathfrak{M}})$. (ii) A formula $\varphi_n^{Neg}$ asserting $Neg \cap L(\mathcal{A}_{\mathfrak{M}}) = \emptyset$. (iii) A formula $\varphi_n^{Ex}$ asserting that $u \in L(\mathcal{A}_{\mathfrak{M}})$ implies $L(\mathcal{A}_{\mathfrak{M}}) \cap L(\mathcal{A}) \neq \emptyset$ for each $(u, \mathcal{A}) \in Ex$. (iv) A formula $\varphi_n^{Uni}$ asserting that $u \in L(\mathcal{A}_{\mathfrak{M}})$ implies $L(\mathcal{A}_{\mathfrak{M}}) \subseteq L(\mathcal{A})$ for each $(u, \mathcal{A}) \in Uni$. Then, $\varphi_n^{\mathcal{S}} := \varphi_n^{DFA} \wedge \varphi_n^{Pos} \wedge \varphi_n^{Neg} \wedge \varphi_n^{Ex} \wedge \varphi_n^{Uni}$. We here sketch formula $\varphi_n^{Uni}$ and refer the reader to the extended paper [22] for a detailed presentation of the remaining formulas. A description of $\varphi_n^{Pos}$ and $\varphi_n^{Neg}$ can also be found in [21].

**The Formula $\varphi_n^{Uni}$.** We break the construction of $\varphi_n^{Uni}$ down into smaller parts. Roughly, we construct a formula $\varphi_n^\iota$ that asserts $L(\mathcal{A}) \subseteq L(\mathcal{A}_\mathfrak{M})$ if $u \in L(\mathcal{A}_\mathfrak{M})$ for each universal implication $\iota = (u, \mathcal{A}) \in Uni$. The formulas $\varphi_n^{Uni}$ is then the finite conjunction $\bigwedge_{\iota \in Uni} \varphi_n^\iota$. For the remainder, let us fix a universal implication $\iota \in Uni$, say $\iota = (u, \mathcal{A})$ with $\mathcal{A} = (Q_\mathcal{A}, \Sigma, q_0^\mathcal{A}, \Delta_\mathcal{A}, F_\mathcal{A})$, and let $Ante(Uni) = \{u \mid (u, \mathcal{A}) \in Uni\}$ be the set of all words occurring as antecedent of a universal implication.

As a preparatory step, we introduce auxiliary Boolean variables that track the runs of $\mathcal{A}_\mathfrak{M}$ on words of $Pref(Ante(Uni))$ in order to detect when $\mathcal{A}_\mathfrak{M}$ accepts the antecedent of a universal implication. More precisely, we introduce variables $x_{u,q}$ where $u \in Pref(Ante(Uni))$ and $q \in Q$, which have the meaning that $x_{u,q}$ is set to *true* if $\mathcal{A}_\mathfrak{M}: q_0 \xrightarrow{u} q$ (i.e., $\mathcal{A}_\mathfrak{M}$ reaches state $q$ on reading $u$):

$$x_{\varepsilon, q_0} \tag{3}$$

$$\bigwedge_{u \in Pref(Ante(Uni))} \bigwedge_{q \neq q' \in Q} \neg x_{u,q} \vee \neg x_{u,q'} \tag{4}$$

$$\bigwedge_{ua \in Pref(Ante(Uni))} \bigwedge_{p,q \in Q} (x_{u,p} \wedge d_{p,a,q}) \rightarrow x_{ua,q} \tag{5}$$

Formula (3) asserts that $x_{\varepsilon, q_0}$ is set to *true* since any run starts in the initial state $q_0$. Formula (4) enforces that for every $u \in Pref(Ante(Uni))$ there exists at most one $q \in Q$ such that $x_{u,q}$ is set to *true* (in fact, the conjunction of Formulas (2)–(5) implies that there exists a unique such state). Finally, Formula (5) prescribes how the run of $\mathcal{A}_\mathfrak{M}$ on a word $u \in Pref(Ante(Uni))$ proceeds: if $\mathcal{A}_\mathfrak{M}$ reaches state $p$ on reading $u$ (i.e., $x_{u,p}$ is set to *true*) and there exists a transition from $p$ to state $q$ on reading the symbol $a \in \Sigma$ (i.e., $d_{p,a,q}$ is set to *true*), then $\mathcal{A}_\mathfrak{M}$ reaches state $q$ on reading $ua$ and $x_{ua}$ needs to be set to *true*.

We now define $\varphi_n^\iota$. The formula ranges, in addition to $d_{p,a,q}$, $f_q$, and $x_{u,q}$, over Boolean variables $y_{q,q'}^\iota$ where $q \in Q$ and $q' \in Q_\mathcal{A}$ and $y_{q,q'}^\iota$ track runs of $\mathcal{A}$ and $\mathcal{A}_\mathfrak{M}$. More precisely, if there exists a word $u \in \Sigma^*$ with $\mathcal{A}_\mathfrak{M}: q_0 \xrightarrow{u} q$ and $\mathcal{A}: q_0^\mathcal{A} \xrightarrow{u} q'$, then $y_{q,q'}^\iota$ is set to *true*.

$$y_{q_0, q_0^\mathcal{A}}^\iota \ and \tag{6}$$

$$\bigwedge_{p,q \in Q} \bigwedge_{(p',a,q') \in \Delta_\mathcal{A}} (y_{p,p'}^\iota \wedge d_{p,a,q}) \rightarrow y_{q,q'}^\iota. \tag{7}$$

Formula (6) enforces $y_{q_0, q_0^\mathcal{A}}^\iota$ to be set to *true* because $\mathcal{A}_\mathfrak{M}: q_0 \xrightarrow{\varepsilon} q_0$ and $\mathcal{A}: q_0^\mathcal{A} \xrightarrow{\varepsilon} q_0^\mathcal{A}$. Formula (7) is similar to Formula (5) and describes how the runs of $\mathcal{A}_\mathfrak{M}$ and $\mathcal{A}$ proceed: if there exists a word $v$ such that $\mathcal{A}_\mathfrak{M}: q_0 \xrightarrow{v} p$ and $\mathcal{A}: q_0^\mathcal{A} \xrightarrow{v} p'$ (i.e., $y_{p,p'}^\iota$ is set to *true*) and there are transitions $(p', a, q') \in \Delta_\mathcal{A}$ and $\delta(p, a) = q$ in $\mathcal{A}_\mathfrak{M}$, then $\mathcal{A}_\mathfrak{M}: q_0 \xrightarrow{va} q$ and $\mathcal{A}: q_0^\mathcal{A} \xrightarrow{va} q'$, which requires $y_{q,q'}^\iota$ to be set to *true*.

Finally, the next constraint ensures that whenever $\mathcal{A}_{\mathfrak{M}}$ accepts $u$ (i.e., the antecedent is *true*), then all words that lead to an accepting state in $\mathcal{A}$ also lead to an accepting state in $\mathcal{A}_{\mathfrak{M}}$ (i.e., the consequent is *true*):

$$\left( \bigvee_{q \in Q} x_{u,q} \wedge f_q \right) \rightarrow \left( \bigwedge_{q \in Q} \bigwedge_{q' \in F_{\mathcal{A}}} y_{q,q'}^{\iota} \rightarrow f_q \right) \tag{8}$$

Let $\varphi_n^{Ante(Uni)}$ be the conjunction of Formulas (3), (4), and (5) as well as $\varphi_n^{\iota}$ the conjunction of Formulas (6), (7), and (8). Then, $\varphi_n^{Uni}$ is the (finite) conjunction $\varphi_n^{Ante(Uni)} \wedge \bigwedge_{\iota \in Uni} \varphi_n^{\iota}$.

**Correctness of the Learner.** We now sketch the technical results necessary to prove the correctness of the learner—we refer the reader to the extended paper [22] for a detailed proof. First, we state that $\varphi_n^{S}$ has the desired properties.

**Lemma 2.** *Let $S$ be a sample, $n \geq 1$, and $\varphi_n^{S}$ be as defined above. Then, the following statements hold: (1) If $\mathfrak{M} \models \varphi_n^{S}$, then $\mathcal{A}_{\mathfrak{M}}$ is a DFA with $n$ states that is consistent with $S$. (2) If there exists a DFA that has $n$ states and is consistent with $S$, then $\varphi_n^{S}$ is satisfiable.*

The next theorem states the correctness of Algorithm 2, which follows from Lemma 2 and the fact that $n$ is increased by one until $\varphi_n^{S}$ becomes satisfiable.

**Theorem 1.** *Given a contradiction free-sample $S$, Algorithm 2 returns a minimal DFA (in terms of the number of states) that is consistent with $S$. If a minimal, consistent DFA has $k$ states, then Algorithm 2 terminates after $k$ iterations.*

Finally, one can prove the correctness of our learner by using the facts that (a) the learner never conjectures a DFA twice as it always constructs minimal consistent DFAs, (b) conjectures grow in size, and (c) adding counterexamples to the sample does not rule out correct solutions.

**Theorem 2.** *Given a teacher, Algorithm 1, equipped with Algorithm 2 to construct conjectures, terminates and returns a (minimal) DFA accepting a winning set if one exists.*

## 6   Experiments

We implemented a Java prototype of our technique based on the BRICS automaton library [17] and the Z3 [18] constraint solver.[3] In addition to the learner of Sect. 5, we implemented a learner based on the popular RPNI algorithm [23], which is a polynomial time algorithm for learning DFAs from positive and negative words. For this learner, we modified the RPNI algorithm such that it

---

[3] The source code, including the games described later, is available at https://www.ae.utexas.edu/facultysites/topcu/misc/rational_safety.zip.

constructs a consistent DFA from existential and universal implications in addition to positive and negative words (a detailed presentation can be found in the extended paper [22]). In contrast to Algorithm 2, this learner cannot guarantee to find smallest consistent DFAs and, hence, the resulting learner is a fast heuristic that is sound but in general not complete. Another limitation is that it can only handle implication counterexamples $(u, \mathcal{A})$ where $L(\mathcal{A})$ is finite. To accommodate this restriction, the arenas of the games used in the experiments are of finite out-degree (i.e., each vertex of an arena has a finite, but not necessarily bounded, number of outgoing edges). We refer to the learner of Sect. 5 as *SAT learner* and the RPNI-based learner as *RPNI learner*. As teacher, we implemented the generic teacher described in Sect. 4.

We conducted three series of experiments, all of which contain games that allow for small controllers. The first series serves to asses the performance of our techniques on games over infinite arenas. The second and third series compare our prototype to existing synthesis tools, namely GAVS+ [8] and TuLiP [24], on games over finite arenas. More precisely, in the second series, we consider motion planning problem in which an autonomous robot has to follow an entity through a fairly complex 2-dimensional grid-world, while the third series compares the scalability of different approaches on games of increasing size. We conducted all experiments on an Intel Core i7-4790K CPU running at 4.00 GHz with a memory limit of 16 GiB. We imposed a runtime limit of 300 s.

**Games over Infinite Arenas.** The first series of examples consists of the following games, which are predominantly taken from the area of motion planning.

*Diagonal game:* A robot moves on a two-dimensional, infinite grid world. Player 0 controls the robot's vertical movement, whereas Player 1 controls the horizontal movement. The players move in alternation, and, stating on the diagonal, Player 0's objective is to stay inside a margin of two cells around the diagonal.

*Box game:* A version of the diagonal game in which Player 0's objective is to stay within a horizontal stripe of width three.

*Solitary box game:* A version of the box game in which Player 0 is the only player and has control over both the horizontal and the vertical movement.

*Evasion game:* Two robots, each controlled by one player, move in alternation on an infinite, two-dimensional grid. Player 0's objective is to avoid a collision.

*Follow game:* A version of the evasion game in which Player 0's objective is to keep his robot within a distance of two cells to Player 1's robot.

*Program-repair game:* A finitely-branching version of the program-repair game described by Beyene et al. [3].

Table 1 lists the overall runtimes (including the time taken by the teacher), the number of iterations, the number of states of the learned DFA, and the cardinality of each set of the final sample. As the table shows, the SAT learner computed the winning sets for all games, whereas the RPNI learner computed the winning sets for all but the Follow game. Since the RPNI learner does not compute minimal consistent DFAs, we expected that it is faster on average than

Table 1. Summary of results on games over infinite arenas.

| Game | SAT learner | | | | | | | RPNI learner | | | | | | |
|---|---|---|---|---|---|---|---|---|---|---|---|---|---|---|
| | Time in s | Iter. | Size | $|Pos|$ | $|Neg|$ | $|Ex|$ | $|Uni|$ | Time in s | Iter. | Size | $|Pos|$ | $|Neg|$ | $|Ex|$ | $|Uni|$ |
| Diagonal | 0.73 | 61 | 4 | 1 | 54 | 2 | 3 | 0.53 | 77 | 6 | 1 | 54 | 10 | 11 |
| Box | 0.29 | 32 | 4 | 1 | 30 | 0 | 0 | 0.09 | 15 | 5 | 1 | 10 | 1 | 2 |
| Solitary Box | 2.88 | 88 | 6 | 1 | 83 | 3 | 0 | 0.09 | 16 | 6 | 1 | 13 | 1 | 0 |
| Follow | 99.89 | 337 | 7 | 2 | 315 | 7 | 12 | | | —timeout ($> 300$ s)— | | | | |
| Evasion | 66.43 | 266 | 7 | 2 | 245 | 10 | 8 | 1.37 | 142 | 12 | 1 | 115 | 14 | 11 |
| Program-repair | 0.57 | 58 | 3 | 1 | 53 | 3 | 0 | 0.21 | 31 | 4 | 1 | 20 | 9 | 0 |

the SAT learner, which turned out to be the case. However, the RPNI learner fails to solve the Follow game within the time limit.

It is worth noting that the teacher replied implication counterexamples in all but one experiment. This observation highlights that classical learning algorithms, which learn from positive and negative words only, are insufficient to learn winning sets (since the learning would be stuck at that point), and one indeed requires a richer learning framework.

**Motion Planning.** The motion planning example is designed to demonstrate the applicability of our techniques to motion planning problems in a fairly complex environment and compare it to mature tools. We considered an autonomous robot that has to follow some entity that is controlled by the environment through the (randomly generated) 2-dimensional $9 \times 9$ grid-world shown  to the right (cells drawn black indicate obstacles that cannot be passed). More precisely, both the robot and the entity start at the same position and the robot's objective is to maintain a Manhattan distance of at most 1 to the entity.

We modeled this game as rational safety game as well as for the tools TuLiP and GAVS+. The SAT learner solved the game in $7.8\,s$, the RPNI learner in $2.1\,s$, and TuLiP in $5.4\,s$. GAVS+ did not solve the game (it could only solve games on a $3 \times 3$ world).

**Scalability.** We compared the scalability of our prototype, GAVS+, TuLiP, as well as a simple fixed-point algorithm (using our automaton representation) on a slightly modified and finite version of the game of Example 1. In this modified game, the one-dimensional grid world consists of $m$ cells, of which all but the rightmost cell are safe. The movement of the robot is slight changed as well: the environment can move the robot to the right or stay; the system can move the robot to the left or stay, a move to the left, however, is only allowed on the first $\ell = \lfloor \frac{m}{2} \rfloor$ cells. As a result, any winning set is a subset of the cells smaller or equal than $\ell$. (In the case of TuLiP, we had to disallow Player 1 to stay for technical reasons; however, this does not change the described properties of the game.) Note that the number of states of the automata $\mathcal{A}_{V_0}$, $\mathcal{A}_{V_1}$, and $\mathcal{A}_F$ increase when $m$ increases as the automata need to count (in unary) to track the position of the robot. Moreover, note that this game is hard for algorithms based on fixed-point computations since a fixed point is reached no sooner than after at least $\ell$ steps.

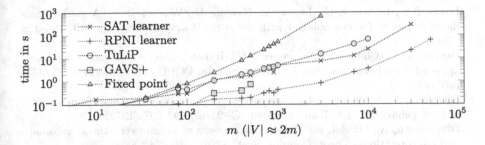

**Fig. 2.** Results of the scalability benchmark.

Figure 2 compares the runtimes of the various techniques for varying values of $m$ (the number of vertices of the resulting arena is roughly $2m$). The RPNI learner performed best and solved games up to $m = 50\,000$ (about $100\,000$ vertices), while the SAT learner ranked second and solved game up to $m = 30\,000$. TuLiP, GAVS+, and the fixed-point algorithm, which all work with the complete, large arena (explicitly or symbolically), performed worse. The third-ranked algorithm TuLiP, for instance, solved games only up to $m = 10\,000$ and was one order of magnitude slower than the RPNI learner. Though designed for games over infinite arenas, these results demonstrate that our learning-based techniques perform well even on games over large finite arenas.

## 7    Conclusion

We developed an automata learning method to construct finite-state reactive controllers for systems whose interactions with their environment are modeled by infinite-state games. We focused on the practically interesting family of safety games, introduced a symbolic representation, developed specific implementations of learners and a teacher, and demonstrated the feasibility of the method on a set of problems motivated by robotic motion planning. Our experimental results promise applicability to a wide array of practically interesting problems.

**Acknowledgements.** We thank Mohammed Alshiekh for his support with the experiments. This work has been partly funded by the awards AFRL #FA8650-15-C-2546, ONR #N000141310778, ARO #W911NF-15-1-0592, NSF #1550212, DARPA #W911NF-16-1-0001, and NSF #1138994.

# References

1. Angluin, D.: Learning regular sets from queries and counterexamples. Inf. Comput. **75**(2), 87–106 (1987)
2. Bauer, S.S., Larsen, K.G., Legay, A., Nyman, U., Wasowski, A.: A modal specification theory for components with data. Sci. Comput. Program. **83**, 106–128 (2014)
3. Beyene, T.A., Chaudhuri, S., Popeea, C., Rybalchenko, A.: A constraint-based approach to solving games on infinite graphs. In: POPL 2014, pp. 221–234. ACM (2014)
4. Biermann, A., Feldman, J.: On the synthesis of finite-state machines from samples of their behavior. IEEE Trans. Comput. **C–21**(6), 592–597 (1972)
5. Blumensath, A., Grädel, E.: Finite presentations of infinite structures: automata and interpretations. Theor. Comput. Syst. **37**(6), 641–674 (2004)
6. Bohy, A., Bruyère, V., Filiot, E., Jin, N., Raskin, J.-F.: Acacia+, a tool for LTL synthesis. In: Madhusudan, P., Seshia, S.A. (eds.) CAV 2012. LNCS, vol. 7358, pp. 652–657. Springer, Heidelberg (2012)
7. Bouajjani, A., Jonsson, B., Nilsson, M., Touili, T.: Regular model checking. In: Emerson, E.A., Sistla, A.P. (eds.) CAV 2000. LNCS, vol. 1855, pp. 403–418. Springer, Heidelberg (2000)
8. Cheng, C.-H., Knoll, A., Luttenberger, M., Buckl, C.: GAVS+: an open platform for the research of algorithmic game solving. In: Abdulla, P.A., Leino, K.R.M. (eds.) TACAS 2011. LNCS, vol. 6605, pp. 258–261. Springer, Heidelberg (2011)
9. Ehlers, R., Raman, V., Finucane, C.: Slugs GR(1) synthesizer (2014). https://github.com/LTLMoP/slugs/
10. Garg, P., Löding, C., Madhusudan, P., Neider, D.: ICE: a robust framework for learning invariants. In: Biere, A., Bloem, R. (eds.) CAV 2014. LNCS, vol. 8559, pp. 69–87. Springer, Heidelberg (2014)
11. Gold, E.M.: Complexity of automaton identification from given data. Inf. Control **37**(3), 302–320 (1978)
12. Heule, M.J.H., Verwer, S.: Exact DFA identification using SAT solvers. In: Sempere, J.M., García, P. (eds.) ICGI 2010. LNCS, vol. 6339, pp. 66–79. Springer, Heidelberg (2010)
13. Holík, L., Isberner, M., Jonsson, B.: Mediator synthesis in a component algebra with data. In: Meyer, R., Platzer, A., Wehrheim, H. (eds.) Olderog-Festschrift. LNCS, vol. 9360, pp. 238–259. Springer, Heidelberg (2015). doi:10.1007/978-3-319-23506-6_16
14. Itzhaky, S., Gulwani, S., Immerman, N., Sagiv, M.: A simple inductive synthesis methodology and its applications. In: OOPSLA 2010, pp. 36–46. ACM (2010)
15. Kupferman, O., Piterman, N., Vardi, M.Y.: An automata-theoretic approach to infinite-state systems. In: Manna, Z., Peled, D.A. (eds.) Time for Verification. LNCS, vol. 6200, pp. 202–259. Springer, Heidelberg (2010)
16. McNaughton, R.: Infinite games played on finite graphs. Ann. Pure Appl. Logic **65**(2), 149–184 (1993)
17. Møller, A.: dk.brics.automaton - finite-state automata and regular expressions for Java (2010). http://www.brics.dk/automaton/
18. de Moura, L., Bjørner, N.S.: Z3: an efficient SMT solver. In: Ramakrishnan, C.R., Rehof, J. (eds.) TACAS 2008. LNCS, vol. 4963, pp. 337–340. Springer, Heidelberg (2008)

19. Neider, D.: Reachability games on automatic graphs. In: Domaratzki, M., Salomaa, K. (eds.) CIAA 2010. LNCS, vol. 6482, pp. 222–230. Springer, Heidelberg (2011)
20. Neider, D.: Small strategies for safety games. In: Bultan, T., Hsiung, P.-A. (eds.) ATVA 2011. LNCS, vol. 6996, pp. 306–320. Springer, Heidelberg (2011)
21. Neider, D., Jansen, N.: Regular model checking using solver technologies and automata learning. In: Brat, G., Rungta, N., Venet, A. (eds.) NFM 2013. LNCS, vol. 7871, pp. 16–31. Springer, Heidelberg (2013)
22. Neider, D., Topcu, U.: An automaton learning approach to solving safety games over infinite graphs. CoRR abs/1601.01660 (2016). http://arxiv.org/abs/1601.01660
23. Oncina, J., Garcia, P.: Inferring regular languages in polynomial update time. Pattern Recogn. Image Anal. 1, 49–61 (1992)
24. Wongpiromsarn, T., Topcu, U., Ozay, N., Xu, H., Murray, R.M.: Tulip: a software toolbox for receding horizon temporal logic planning. In: HSCC 2011, pp. 313–314. ACM (2011)

# Probabilistic and Stochastic Systems II

# Uncertainty Propagation Using Probabilistic Affine Forms and Concentration of Measure Inequalities

Olivier Bouissou[2], Eric Goubault[1], Sylvie Putot[1], Aleksandar Chakarov[3], and Sriram Sankaranarayanan[3(✉)]

[1] LIX, Ecole Polytechnique, CNRS, Université Paris-Saclay, Paris-Saclay, France
[2] CEA, LIST, Gif-sur-Yvette, France
[3] University of Colorado, Boulder, USA
srirams@colorado.edu

**Abstract.** We consider the problem of reasoning about the probability of assertion violations in straight-line, nonlinear computations involving uncertain quantities modeled as random variables. Such computations are quite common in many areas such as cyber-physical systems and numerical computation. Our approach extends probabilistic affine forms, an interval-based calculus for precisely tracking how the distribution of a given program variable depends on uncertain inputs modeled as noise symbols. We extend probabilistic affine forms using the precise tracking of dependencies between noise symbols combined with the expectations and higher order moments of the noise symbols. Next, we show how to prove bounds on the probabilities that program variables take on specific values by using concentration of measure inequalities. Thus, we enable a new approach to this problem that explicitly avoids subdividing the domain of inputs, as is commonly done in the related work. We illustrate the approach in this paper on a variety of challenging benchmark examples, and thus study its applicability to uncertainty propagation.

## 1 Introduction

We consider the problem of propagating uncertainty through computation that generates random numbers with known distributions on-the-fly, and computes a variety of arithmetic operations on these numbers. Such computations are common in a wide variety of applications including systems biology, robotics, control theory and randomized algorithms. Reasoning about uncertainties involves answering *queries* about the probabilities of assertions over the program variables, expectations of expressions, and more generally, characterizing the possible probability distributions of program expressions, at the output. Often, the random number generators draw values from simple distributions such as uniform random, gaussian or exponential. However, as a result of nonlinear operations, the resulting distributions can be quite complex.

In this work, we restrict our attention to *straight line computations* involving random variables. In other words, the programs do not branch on the values

© Springer-Verlag Berlin Heidelberg 2016
M. Chechik and J.-F. Raskin (Eds.): TACAS 2016, LNCS 9636, pp. 225–243, 2016.
DOI: 10.1007/978-3-662-49674-9_13

of the random variables involved. Nevertheless, such computations are surprisingly common in many applications arising from controls, robotics and scientific computation that can generate thousands of random variables. Currently, these applications are beyond many of the existing approaches for reasoning about probabilistic programs. Our approach combines the framework of probabilistic affine forms introduced by Bouissou et al. [7] to represent program variables in terms of interval linear expressions involving uncertain *noise symbols*, and *concentration of measure* inequalities in probability theory [13] to answer queries. This approach has two main advantages: (a) probabilistic affine forms can be used to rapidly approximate several nonlinear arithmetic operations including trigonometric operations, and (b) the application of concentration of measure inequalities yields valid probability bounds without the need to perform expensive subdivisions of the set of support. In fact, in situations involving more than a few tens of noise symbols, such a subdivision is prohibitively expensive.

The contributions of this paper include (a) we extend probabilistic affine forms with precise tracking of the bounds on the expectations and higher-order moments of these forms, (b) we propose the use of concentration of measure inequalities to reason about the probabilities of queries over affine forms and (c) we demonstrate our approach on many challenging examples involving nonlinear arithmetic operations. Wherever possible, we also compare our approach with the previous use of probabilistic affine forms without concentration of measure inequalities [7]. The experimental evaluation in this paper allows us to draw two main conclusions. *(A)* Probabilistic affine forms are seen to be quite efficient even for nonlinear trigonometric and rational functions over random variables. However, this is at the cost of information lost due to linear approximation of nonlinear computations. *(B)* Concentration of measure inequalities can prove bounds on the probabilities of rare events for large affine forms, quite efficiently. Often, such bounds seem beyond the reach of related techniques. On the flip side, the bounds may sometimes be too conservative due to the abstraction.

### Related Work

Many approaches have focused on the problem of reasoning about uncertainties as they propagate through computation. These include approaches from interval arithmetic, polynomial chaos approximations, symbolic verification, and statistical approaches.

**Interval Arithmetic and Imprecise Probabilities:** Imprecise probability representations describe sets of probability distributions. These are well-suited for describing situations where some values, or events are known non-deterministically (e.g. values in an interval), whereas others are known probabilistically. Tools from this domain include P-boxes [17] and Dempster-Shafer structures [33]. These have been used to propagate both probabilistic and non-deterministic information in numerical simulation for instance, see also [8,18,21,30,37,38]. Arithmetic rules for P-boxes have been studied [39] and implemented in toolboxes such as DSI, INTLAB, and RiskCalc [3,16,31]. Our work builds on probabilistic affine forms proposed by Bouissou et al., wherein a variety of operators over these forms including meet, join and widening operators are presented [2,7].

However, these approaches rely on an explicit, finite representation of probability bounds that requires us to decompose the joint domain of distributions of these random variables. Such a decomposition rapidly becomes intractable beyond a few tens of random variables. We partly tackle this issue in our approach using concentration of measure inequalities, whose application does not require a decomposition.

Polynomial chaos approximations express the output distributions as polynomials over the input random variables [40]. However, these approximations also suffer from the curse of dimensionality. Moreover, polynomial chaos approximations focus on estimating moments, but not necessarily on providing probability bounds.

**Formal Verification Approaches:** Prism and related model checking tools have revolutionized the problem of reasoning about finite state probabilistic programs [25]. This has spurred interest in infinite state programs involving more complex random variables with distributions such as gaussian and exponential.

Related approaches include probabilistic symbolic executions that extend traditional symbolic execution over probabilistic programs and probabilistic abstract interpretation. Probabilistic symbolic execution has been explored for analyzing complex programs computing over random variables [4,19,32]. These approaches rely on expensive volume approximation techniques either off the shelf [12], or using domain decomposition [32]. Barring a few exceptions [4], they are restricted to programs with linear assignments and conditionals. However, recent work by Chistikov et al. has demonstrated a randomized approximation to volume estimation that holds the promise of scaling to larger systems involving thousands of random variables [10]. However, that approach is currently restricted to linear arithmetic SMT formulas. The ProbReach tool by Shmarov et al. also provides precise probability bounds for nonlinear continuous-time systems, building on top of the dReach tool [35]. While capable of precise reasoning for complex nonlinear systems, it relies on domain decomposition. In particular, it is currently restricted to systems with uncertainties in initial parameters as opposed to stochastic systems that are driven by noisy inputs. Similar ideas using Taylor models have been investigated by Enszer et al. [15]. Finally, the work of Abate et al. derives discrete Markov chain abstractions to compute probability of reaching unsafe states in general stochastic Markov processes [1]. The discretization also involves a subdivision of the state space of these processes with a finer subdivision providing better results. In contrast, our approach does not subdivide the state or random variables. However, our approach depends intimately on obtaining good bounds for expectations and higher-order moments for noise symbols.

Abstract domains for probabilistic programs have been investigated by Monniaux [29] and Cousot and Monereau [11]. Whereas our approach focuses on finite computations, abstract interpretation typically excels in dealing with unbounded

```
1   angles = [10, 60, 110, 160, 140, ...
2              100, 60, 20, 10, 0]
3   x := TruncGaussian(0,0.05,-0.5,0.5)
4   y := TruncGaussian(0, 0.1,-0.5,0.5)
5   for reps in range(0,100):
6   #iterate through angles
7     for theta in angles:
8       # Distance travelled variation
9       d = Uniform(0.98,1.02)
10      # Steering angle variation
11      t = deg2rad(theta) * (1 + ...
12          TruncGaussian(0,0.01,-0.05,0.05))
13      # Move distance d with angle t
14      x = x + d * cos(t)
15      y = y + d * sin(t)
16  #Probability that we went too far?
17  assert(x >= 272)
```

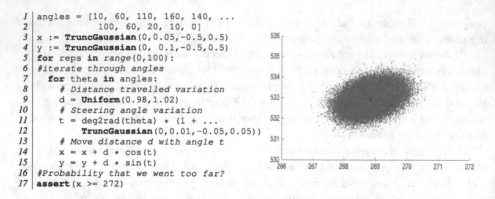

**Fig. 1. Left**: A probabilistic program capturing the final position of 2D robotic end effector. **Right**: Scatter plot showing the final $(x, y)$ values.

length computations wherein approximations such as join (see also [2]) and widening provide the ability to generalize. Previous work by Chakarov et al. also uses concentration of measure inequalities in this context to handle loops in probabilistic programs [9].

**Statistical Approaches:** Finally, statistical approaches use hypothesis testing to answer queries on uncertainties [24,41]. The main advantage lies in the ability to handle quite complex systems through simulations. However, the disadvantages often involve rare events, wherein the number of simulations required to gain a given degree of statistical confidence is simply prohibitive. In such situations, techniques like importance sampling have been applied to minimize the number of simulations [23]. However, statistical approaches provide guarantees that are fundamentally different from ours. Also, with very few exceptions [26], they do not attempt to represent the output distribution but simply answer queries by examining the evidence from simulations. As such, very little work has been undertaken to relate the two types of guarantees. A related approach by Bernholt et al. [5], introduces an explicit uncertainty data type to reason about uncertainty using Bayesian hypothesis testing. Therein, the main idea is to use Bayes networks to represent the influence of random variables over program variables and allow hypothesis testing techniques to enable programmers to deal with this uncertainty in making decisions.

## 2    Motivating Example

Figure 1 shows an example probabilistic program that models the $(x, y)$ position of a simple 2D robotic end effector that starts close to the origin and whose series of motions is specified by the list `angles`. The initial position is uncertain with a truncated normal distribution centered at the origin and with given variance as shown in lines 3, 4. At each iteration, the effector moves from its current position $(x, y)$ to $x + d_j \cos(\theta_j), y + d_j \sin(\theta_i)$, wherein $d_j$ is distributed as a uniform random number in the interval $[0.95, 1.05]$ (line 9, modeling the distance 1.0 with a 5 % uniform error). Likewise, $\theta_i$ is given by multiplying `angles` (i) with a truncated Gaussian random variable centered around 1 with variance 0.01 in the interval $[0.95, 1.05]$ (line 12). The position update is shown in lines 14 and 15. We are interested in the probability that an assertion violation is triggered in line 17.

A scatter plot (Fig. 1) of the values of $(x, y)$ at the end of the computation are shown. As noted, $10^5$ simulations do not produce any violations of the property $x \geq 272$. In fact, the largest value of $x$ seen in our simulations is around 271. Therefore, we may rightfully conclude that it is "quite rare" to reach $x \geq 272$. On the other hand, using nondeterministic semantics for the random choices concludes a potentially reachable range of $x \in [210.5, 324.3]$. We therefore, seek to know bounds on the probability that the assertion is satisfied.

**Affine Forms at Output:** Our approach uses symbolic execution to track the value of $x$ at the output as a function of random variables called *noise symbols*. The affine form for $x$ is (partially) shown below:

$$x : \begin{pmatrix} [268.78, 268.82] + [1, 1] * y_0 + [0.984, 0.985] * y_2 + [0.030, 0.031] * y_3 + [-1, -1] * y_4 + [0.030, 0.031] * y_5 \\ + [-1, -1] * y_6 + [0.49, 0.51] * y_9 + [0.90, 0.91] * y_{10} + [-1, -1] * y_{11} + [0.90, 0.91] * y_{12} + \\ \cdots \\ [0.03, 0.031] * y_{6892} + [-1, -1] * y_{6893} + [1, 1] * y_{6896} + [-1, -1] * y_{6898} + [-1, -1] * y_{6899} \end{pmatrix} .$$

Here, each $y_i$ is a noise symbol with associated information concerning it's range, dependencies with other noise symbol, expectations and higher order moments (e.g., the second moment). For instance, $y_0$ corresponds to the truncated Gaussian random variable in line 3. Using this affine form, we conclude at the end of computation that the value of $x$ has an expectation in the range $[265.9, 268.9]$ and variance in the range $[0.17, 0.23]$. This matches with the empirical evidence gathered from $10^5$ simulations. The time required for the affine form was $\sim 15\,$s and comparable to $10^5$ simulations in Matlab ($\sim 20\,$s).

**Reasoning with Affine Forms:** Finally, we utilize a concentration of measure inequality to obtain the guarantee $\mathbb{P}(x \geq 272) \leq 6.2 \times 10^{-7}$ [13]. We note that such bounds on rare events are often valuable, and hard to establish.

# 3   Probabilistic Affine Forms

In this section, we introduce probabilistic affine forms involving random variables known as *noise symbols*, and discuss the approximation of straight line computations using these affine forms.

## 3.1   Random Variables, Expectations, Moments and Independence

Let $\mathbb{R}$ represent the real numbers and $\overline{\mathbb{R}} = \mathbb{R} \cup \{\infty, -\infty\}$. Univariate random variables over reals are defined by a *cumulative density function* (CDF) $F$ : $\overline{\mathbb{R}} \mapsto [0, 1]$, wherein $F(-\infty) = 0$, $F(\infty) = 1$ and $F$ is a non-decreasing, right continuous function with left limits. The value of $F(t)$ represents the probability

$\mathbb{P}(X \le t)$ for any $t \in \mathbb{R}$. The CDF naturally extends to multivariate random variables as well [14].

The *expectation* of a function $g(X)$ for random variable $X$, denoted by $\mathbb{E}(g(X))$ is defined as the integral: $\mathbb{E}(g(X)) : \int_{\mathcal{D}} g(\boldsymbol{x}) dF(\boldsymbol{x})$. Here $\mathcal{D}$, the domain of integration, ranges over the *set of support* for the random variable $X$. The expectation exists if the integral is well-defined and yields a finite value. An important property of expectations is their *linearity*. Whenever the expectations exist, and are finite, we have $\mathbb{E}(\sum_{i=1}^{k} a_i g_i(\boldsymbol{x})) = \sum_{i=1}^{k} a_i \mathbb{E}(g_i(\boldsymbol{x}))$, for constants $a_1, \ldots, a_k$ and functions $g_1, \ldots, g_k$. Likewise, the $k^{th}$ moment for $k \ge 1$ for a random variable $X$ is defined as $\mathbb{E}(X^k)$. Its variance is defined as $\text{VAR}(X) : \mathbb{E}((X - \mathbb{E}(X))^2)$.

A pair of random variables $(X_1, X_2)$ are *independent* if and only if their CDF $F(x_1, x_2)$ can be decomposed as $F(x_1, x_2) : F_1(x_1) F_2(x_2)$. Otherwise, the random variables are called *correlated*. More generally, $(X_1, \ldots, X_n)$ are pairwise independent iff $F(x_1, \ldots, x_n) : F_1(x_1) \cdots F_n(x_n)$. If $X_1, X_2$ are independent then it follows that $\mathbb{E}(g(X_1) h(X_2)) = \mathbb{E}(g(X_1)) \mathbb{E}(h(X_2))$.

We assume that random variables that we encounter in this paper are well-behaved in the following sense: (a) Each random variable has a bounded set of support. However, we present a simple trick to handle distributions such as gaussians that have unbounded sets of support. (b) Expectations and higher moments of the random variables are finite and computable. We recall useful properties of expectations:

**Lemma 1.** *Let $X$ be a (univariate) random variable whose set of support is the interval $I \subseteq \mathbb{R}$. It follows that $\mathbb{E}(X) \in I$.*
*Let $X_1, X_2$ be two random variables. The following inequality holds:*

$$-\sqrt{\mathbb{E}(X_1^2) \mathbb{E}(X_2^2)} \le \mathbb{E}(X_1 X_2) \le \sqrt{\mathbb{E}(X_1^2) \mathbb{E}(X_2^2)}.$$

The inequality above follows from the Cauchy-Schwarz inequality.

## 3.2    Environments and Affine Forms

Before introducing affine forms, we first define noise symbols and the data associated with these symbols. Let $\boldsymbol{y} : (y_1, \ldots, y_n)$ represent a set of random variables called *noise symbols*. Each noise symbol $y_j$ is associated with an interval of support $I_j$, and a vector of moment intervals $I(y_j) = (I_j^{(1)}, \ldots, I_j^{(k)})$, wherein $\mathbb{E}(y_j^l) \in I_j^{(l)}$.

Note that in addition to storing estimates of $\mathbb{E}(y_i^l)$, we may optionally store moments of the form $\mathbb{E}(y_i y_j)$ for pairs $y_i, y_j \in \boldsymbol{y}$ for $i \ne j$. This can also extend to higher order moments of the form $\mathbb{E}(y_1^{l_1} \cdots y_n^{l_n})$ for monomials. In this presentation, we restrict ourselves to (marginal) expectations of single random variables of the form $\mathbb{E}(y_j^l)$, using Lemma 1 to conservatively estimate missing moment information.

Finally, our approach produced new noise symbols $y_j$ that are functions of other noise symbols $y_j : f(y_{j_1}, \ldots, y_{j_m})$. While we abstract away the function $f$, we remember these functional dependencies as a directed (functional) *dependence graph* $G$ with vertices $V : \{y_1, \ldots, y_n\}$ and edges $E \subseteq V \times V$ wherein the edge $(y_i, y_j)$ signifies that the random variable $y_i : f(\cdots, y_j, \cdots)$ for some function $f$. Clearly, if $(y_i, y_j) \in E$ and $(y_j, y_k) \in E$ we will also require $(y_i, y_k) \in E$. The edge relation $E$ is thus a transitive relation over $\boldsymbol{y}$. For simplicity, we also add all self-loops $(y_i, y_i) \in E$.

**Definition 1 (Environment).** *An environment $\mathcal{E} : \langle \boldsymbol{y}, \mathcal{I}, \mathcal{M}, G \rangle$ is a collection of noise symbols $\boldsymbol{y} : (y_1, \ldots, y_n)$, the sets of support for each noise symbol $\mathcal{I} : (I_1, \ldots, I_n)$, the moment intervals for each noise symbol $\mathcal{M} : (I(m_1), \ldots, I(m_n))$ and the directed functional dependence graph $G$.*

Based on the functional dependence graph, we define the notion of independence between random variables.

**Definition 2 (Probabilistic Dependence).** *Noise symbols $y_i$ and $y_j$ are probabilistically dependent random variables if there exists $y_k$ such that $(y_i, y_k)$ and $(y_j, y_k)$ belong to the graph $G$. Otherwise, they represent independent random variables.*

*The probabilistic dependence graph $\widehat{G}$ is an undirected graph where an undirected edge $(y_i, y_j)$ exists in $\widehat{G}$ iff there exists $y_k$ such that $(y_i, y_k), (y_j, y_k) \in E$ of $G$[1].*

An affine form is an interval-valued linear expression over noise symbols [7].

**Definition 3 (Affine Form).** *An affine form $f(\boldsymbol{y})$ is a linear expression $f(\boldsymbol{y}) : a_0 + \sum_{j=1}^{n} a_j y_j$, with real[2] coefficients $a_j$.*

*Example 1 (Environments and Affine Forms).* Let us consider an environment $\mathcal{E}$ with the noise symbols $y_1, y_2, y_3$. Here, $y_j$ is a random variable over the set of support $I_j : [-j, j]$, for $j = 1, 2, 3$, respectively. The moment vectors containing information up to the $4^{th}$ moments are provided below:

|  | $\mathbb{E}(y_j)$ | $\mathbb{E}(y_j^2)$ | $\mathbb{E}(y_j^3)$ | $\mathbb{E}(y_j^4)$ |  |
| --- | --- | --- | --- | --- | --- |
| $I(m_1)$ : | $([0,0],$ | $[\frac{2}{3}, \frac{2}{3}],$ | $[0,0],$ | $[\frac{2}{5}, \frac{2}{5}])$ | $\leftarrow$ Moments for $y_1$ |
| $I(m_2)$ : | $([0,0.1],$ | $[1,1.1],$ | $[-0.1,0.1],$ | $[0.1,0.2])$ | $\leftarrow$ Moments for $y_2$ |
| $I(m_3)$ : | $([-1,0.2],$ | $[0.1,1.2],$ | $[-0.5,0.5],$ | $[1.1,2.3])$ | $\leftarrow$ Moments for $y_3$ |

The graph with dependencies is shown below (without the self-loops):

As a result, the variables $y_1, y_3$ are independent. But $y_1$ and $y_2$ are dependent. The expression $f_1 : [-1,2] + [3,3.1]y_1 + [1.9,2.3]y_2 + [-0.3,-0.1]y_3$ is an affine form over $y_1, \ldots, y_3$ in the environment $\mathcal{E}$.

---

[1] The functional dependence graph is akin to the points-to graph in programs, whereas the probabilistic dependence graph is analogous to the alias graph.

[2] In the implementation, these coefficients will be safely over-approximated either by intervals of floating-point numbers, or by floating-point coefficients but with additional noise terms over-approximating the error.

**Semantics:** We briefly sketch the semantics of environments and affine forms.

An environment $\mathcal{E}$ with noise symbols $\boldsymbol{y} : (y_1, \ldots, y_n)$ corresponds to a set of possible random vectors $Y : (Y_1, \ldots, Y_n)$ that conform to the following constraints: (a) $(Y_1, \ldots, Y_n)$ must range over the set of support $I_1 \times \cdots \times I_n$. They cannot take on values outside this set. (b) The moment vectors lie in the appropriate ranges defined by $\mathcal{E} : (\mathbb{E}(Y_j), \ldots, \mathbb{E}(Y_j^k)) \in I(m_j)$. (c) If noise symbols $y_i, y_j$ are independent according to the dependence graph $G$ (Definition 2), the corresponding random variables $Y_i, Y_j$ are mutually independent. Otherwise, they are "arbitrarily" correlated while respecting the range and moment constraints above. Semantically, an affine form $f(\boldsymbol{y}) : a_0 + \sum_{i=1}^{n} a_i y_i$ represents a set of linear expressions $[\![f(\boldsymbol{y})]\!]$ over $\boldsymbol{y}$:

$$[\![f(\boldsymbol{y})]\!] := \left\{ r_0 + \sum_{i=1}^{n} r_i Y_i \mid r_i \in a_i, (Y_1, \ldots, Y_n) \in [\![\mathcal{E}]\!] \right\}.$$

We now present the basic operations over affine forms including sums, differences, products and continuous (and $k$-times differentiable) functions over affine forms.

**Sums, Differences and Products:** Let $f_1, f_2$ be affine forms in an environment $\mathcal{E}$ given by $f_1 : \boldsymbol{a}^t \boldsymbol{y} + a_0$ and $f_2 : \boldsymbol{b}^t \boldsymbol{y} + b_0$. We define the sum $f_1 \oplus f_2$ to be the affine form $(\boldsymbol{a} + \boldsymbol{b})^t \boldsymbol{y} + (a_0 + b_0)$.

Likewise, let $\lambda$ be a real number. The affine form $\lambda f_1$ is given by $(\lambda \boldsymbol{a})^t \boldsymbol{y} + \lambda a_0$. We now define the product of two forms $f_1 \otimes f_2$.

$$f_1 \otimes f_2 : a_0 b_0 + a_0 f_2 + b_0 f_1 + \mathsf{approx}\Big(\sum_{i=1}^{n} \sum_{j=1}^{n} a_i a_j y_i y_j\Big).$$

The product operation separates the affine and linear parts of this summation from the nonlinear part that must be approximated to preserve the affine form. To this end, we define a function $\mathsf{approx}$ that replaces the nonlinear terms by a collection of fresh random variables. In particular, we add a fresh random variable $y_{ij}$ to approximate the product term $y_i y_j$.

**Dependencies:** We add the dependency edges $(y_{ij}, y_i)$ and $(y_{ij}, y_j)$ to the graph $G$ to denote the functional dependence of the fresh noise symbol on $y_i$ and $y_j$.

**Set of Support:** The set of support for $y_{ij}$ is the interval product of the set of supports for $y_i, y_j$, respectively. In particular if $i = j$, we compute the set of support for $y_i^2$. Let $I_{ij}$ be the interval representing the set of support for $y_{ij}$.

**Moments:** The moments of $y_{ij}$ are derived from those of $y_i$ and $y_j$, as follows. *Case-1* $(i = j)$. If $i = j$, we have that the $\mathbb{E}(y_{ij}^p) = \mathbb{E}(y_i^{2p})$. Therefore, the even moments of $y_i$ are taken to provide the moments for $y_{ij}$. However, since we assume that only the first $k$ moments of $y_i$ are available, we have that the first $\frac{k}{2}$ moments of $y_{ij}$ are available, in general. To fill in the remaining moments, we approximate using intervals as follows: $\mathbb{E}(y_{ij}^r) \in I_{ij}^r$. While this approximation is often crude, this is a tradeoff induced by our inability to store infinitely many moments for the noise symbols.

*Case-2* $(i \neq j)$. If $i \neq j$, we have that $\mathbb{E}(y_{ij}^p) = \mathbb{E}(y_i^p y_j^p)$. If $y_i, y_j$ form an independent pair, this reduces back to $\mathbb{E}(y_i^p)\mathbb{E}(y_j^p)$. Thus, in this instance, we can fill in all $k$ moments directly as entry-wise products of the moments of $y_i$ and $y_j$. Otherwise, they are dependent, so we use the Cauchy-Schwarz inequality (see Lemma 1): $-\sqrt{\mathbb{E}(y_i^{2p})\mathbb{E}(y_j^{2p})} \leq \mathbb{E}(y_{ij}^p) \leq \sqrt{\mathbb{E}(y_i^{2p})\mathbb{E}(y_j^{2p})}$, and the interval approximation $\mathbb{E}(y_{ij}^p) \in I_{ij}^p$.

**Continuous Functions:** Let $g(\boldsymbol{y})$ be a continuous and $(m + 1)$-times differentiable function of $\boldsymbol{y}$. The Taylor expansion of $g$ around a point $\boldsymbol{y}_0$ allows us to approximate $g$ as a polynomial.

$$g(\boldsymbol{y}) = g(\boldsymbol{y}_0) + Dg(\boldsymbol{y}_0)(\boldsymbol{y} - \boldsymbol{y}_0) + \sum_{2 \leq |\alpha|_1 \leq m} \frac{D^\alpha g(\boldsymbol{y}_0)(\boldsymbol{y} - \boldsymbol{y}_0)^\alpha}{\alpha!} + R_g^{m+1},$$

wherein $Dg$ denotes the vector of partial derivatives $(\frac{\partial g}{\partial y_j})_{j=1,\ldots,n}$, $\alpha : (d_1, \ldots, d_n)$ ranges over all vector of indices where $d_i \in \mathbb{N}$ is a natural number, $|\alpha|_1 : \sum_{i=1}^n d_i$, $\alpha! = d_1! d_2! \cdots d_n!$, $D^\alpha g$ denotes the partial derivative $\frac{\partial^{d_1} g \cdots \partial^{d_n} g}{\partial y_1^{d_1} \cdots \partial y_n^{d_n}}$ and $(\boldsymbol{y} - \boldsymbol{y}_0)^\alpha :$ $\prod_{j=1}^n (y_j - y_{0,j})^{d_j}$. Finally, $R_g^{m+1}$ is an interval valued *Lagrange remainder*. Since we have discussed sums and products of affine forms, the Taylor approximation may be evaluated entirely using affine forms.

The remainder is handled using a fresh noise symbol $y_g^{(m+1)}$. Its set of support is $R_g^{m+1}$ and moments are estimated based on this interval. The newly added noise symbol is functionally dependent on all variables $\boldsymbol{y}$ that appear in $g(\boldsymbol{y})$. These dependencies are added to the graph $G$.

The Taylor expansion allows us to approximate continuous functions including rational functions and trigonometric functions of these random variables.

*Example 2.* We illustrate this by computing the sine of an affine form. Let $y_1$ be a noise symbol over the interval $[-0.2, 0.2]$ with the moments $(0, [0.004, 0.006], 0, [6 \times 10^{-5}, 8 \times 10^{-5}], 0)$. We consider the form $\sin(y_1)$. Using a Taylor series expansion around $y_1 = 0$, we obtain

$$\sin(y_1) = y_1 - \frac{1}{3!}y_1^3 + [-1.3 \times 10^{-5}, 1.4 \times 10^{-5}].$$

We introduce a fresh variable $y_2$ to replace $y_1^3$ and a fresh variable $y_3$ for the remainder interval $I_3 : [-1.3 \times 10^{-5}, 1.4 \times 10^{-5}]$.

**Dependence:** We add the edges $(y_2, y_1)$ and $(y_3, y_1)$ to $G$.
**Set of Support:** $I_2 : [-0.008, 0.008]$ and $I_3 : [-1.3 \times 10^{-5}, 1.4 \times 10^{-5}]$.
**Moments:** $\mathbb{E}(y_2) = \mathbb{E}(y_1^3) = 0$. Further moments are computed using interval arithmetic. The moment vector $I(m_2)$ is $(0, [0, 64 \times 10^{-6}], [-512 \times 10^{-9}, 512 \times 10^{-9}], \ldots)$. For $y_3$, the moment vector $I(m_3) : (I_3, \text{square}(I_3), \text{cube}(I_3), \ldots)$.

The resulting affine form for $\sin(y_1)$ is $[1, 1]y_1 - [0.16, 0.17]y_2 + [1, 1]y_3$.

### 3.3  Approximating Computations Using Affine Forms

Having developed a calculus of affine forms, we may directly apply it to propagate uncertainties across straight-line computations. Let $X = \{x_1, \ldots, x_p\}$ be a set of *program variables* collectively written as $\boldsymbol{x}$ with an initial value $\boldsymbol{x}_0$. Our semantics consist of a tuple $(\mathcal{E}, \eta)$ wherein $\mathcal{E}$ is an environment and $\eta : X \to \mathsf{AffineForms}(\mathcal{E})$ maps each variable $x_i \in X$ to an affine form over $\mathcal{E}$.

The initial environment $\mathcal{E}_0$ has no noise symbols and an empty dependence graph. The initial mapping $\eta_0$ associates each $x_i$ with the constant $x_{i,0}$. The basic operations are of two types: (a) assignment to a fresh random variable, and (b) assignment to a function over existing variables.

**Random Number Generation:** This operation is of the form $x_i := \mathsf{rand}(I, \mathbf{m})$, wherein $I$ denotes the set of support interval for the new random variable, and $\mathbf{m}$ denotes a vector of moments for the generated random variable. The operational rule is $(\mathcal{E}, \eta) \xrightarrow{x_i := \mathsf{rand}(I, \mathbf{m})} (\mathcal{E}', \eta')$, wherein the environment $\mathcal{E}'$ extends $\mathcal{E}$ by a fresh random variable $y$ whose set of support is given by $I$ and moments by $\mathbf{m}$. The dependence graph is extended by adding a new node corresponding to $y$ but without any new edges since freshly generated random numbers are assumed independent. However, if the newly generated random variable is dependent on some previous symbols, such a dependency is also easily captured in our framework.

**Assignment:** The assignment operation is of the form $x_i := g(\boldsymbol{x})$, assigning $x_i$ to a continuous and $(j + 1)$-times differentiable function $g(\boldsymbol{x})$. The operational rule has the form $(\mathcal{E}, \eta) \xrightarrow{x_i := g(\boldsymbol{x})} (\mathcal{E}', \eta')$. First, we compute an affine form $f_g$ that approximates the function $g(\eta(x_1), \ldots, \eta(x_n))$. Let $Y_g$ denote a set of fresh symbols generated by this approximation with new dependence edges $E_g$. The environment $\mathcal{E}'$ extends $\mathcal{E}$ with the addition of the new symbols $Y_g$ and and new dependence edges $E_g$. The new map is $\eta' : \eta[x_i \mapsto f_g]$.

Let $\mathcal{C}$ be a computation defined by a sequence of random number generation and assignment operations. Starting from the initial environment $(\mathcal{E}_0, \eta_0)$ and applying the rules above, we obtain a final environment $(\mathcal{E}, \eta)$. However, our main goal is to answer *queries* such as $\mathbb{P}(x_j \in I_j)$ that seek the probability that a particular variable $x_j$ belongs to an interval $I_j$. This directly translates to a query involving the affine form $\eta(x_j)$ which may involve a prohibitively large number of noise symbols that may be correlated according to the dependence graph $G$.

## 4  Concentration of Measure Inequalities

We present the use of concentration of measure inequalities to bound probabilities of the form $\mathbb{P}(f \geq c)$ and $\mathbb{P}(f \leq c)$. Let $f$ be an affine form in an environment $\mathcal{E}$.

There are numerous inequalities in probability theory that provide bounds on the probability that a particular function of random variables deviates "far" from its expected value [13]. Let $X_1, \ldots, X_n$ be a sequence of random variables that may be pairwise independent or depend on each other according to a probabilistic dependence graph $\widehat{G}$. Consider their sum $X : \sum_{j=1}^{n} X_j$ and its expected value $\mathbb{E}(X) : \sum_{j=1}^{n} \mathbb{E}(X_j)$. Under numerous carefully stated conditions, the sum "concentrates" around its average value so that the "tail" probabilities: the right tail probability $\mathbb{P}(X - \mathbb{E}(X) \geq t)$ of the sum being $t > 0$ to the right of the expectation, or the left "tail" probability $\mathbb{P}(X - \mathbb{E}(X) \leq -t)$ are bounded from above and rapidly approach zero as $t \to \infty$. We note that concentration of measure inequalities provide valid bounds on large deviations. In other words, they are more powerful than asymptotic convergence results, although they are typically used to prove convergence. A large category of concentration of measure inequalities conform to the sub-gaussian type below.

**Definition 4 (Sub-Gaussian Concentration of Measure).** *Let $X_1, \ldots, X_n$ be a set of random variables wherein each $X_i$ has a compact set of support in the interval $[a_i, b_i]$. A sub-gaussian type concentration of measure inequality is specified by two parts: (a) a condition $\Psi$ on the dependence structure between the random variables $X_i$, and (b) a constant $c > 0$. The inequality itself has the following form for any $t \geq 0$,*

$$\mathbb{P}(X - \mathbb{E}(X) \geq t) \leq exp\left(\frac{-t^2}{c \sum_{j=1}^{n}(b_i - a_i)^2}\right).$$

*The expression for the left tail probability is derived identically.*

In general, many forms of these inequalities exist under various assumptions. We focus on two important inequalities that will be used here.

*Chernoff-Hoeffding:* The condition $\Psi$ states that $X_1, \ldots, X_n$ are independent. Alternatively, the probabilistic dependence graph $\widehat{G}$ does not have any edges. In this situation, the inequality applies with a constant $c = \frac{1}{2}$.

*Chromatic Number-Based:* Janson generalizes the Chernoff-Hoeffding inequality using the chromatic number of the graph $\widehat{G}$ [22]. Let $\chi(\widehat{G})$ be an upper bound on the minimum number of colors required to color $\widehat{G}$ (i.e., it's chromatic number). The condition $\Psi$ states that the random variables depend according to $\widehat{G}$. In this situation, the inequality applies with a constant $c = \frac{\chi(\widehat{G})}{2}$. For the independent case, $\chi(\widehat{G}) = 1$ and thus, Chernoff-Hoeffding bounds are generalized.

The sub-gaussian bounds depend on the range $[a_i, b_i]$ of the individual random variables. Often, the variance $\sigma_i^2$ of each random variable is significantly smaller. In such situations, the Bernstein inequality provides useful bounds.

**Theorem 1 (Bernstein Inequality).** *Let $X_1, \ldots, X_n$ be independent random variables such that (a) there exists a constant $M > 0$ such that $|X_i - \mathbb{E}(X_i)| \leq M$ for each $i \in [1, n]$, and (b) the variance of each $X_i$ is $\sigma_i^2$. For any $t \geq 0$:*

$$\mathbb{P}(X - \mathbb{E}(X) \geq t) \leq exp\left(\frac{-t^2}{2 \sum_{i=1}^{n} \sigma_i^2 + \frac{2}{3}Mt}\right)$$

*For the left tail probability, we may derive an identical bound.*

We now illustrate how these inequalities can be used for the motivating example from Sect. 2. Let $\mathcal{E}$ be an environment and $f(\boldsymbol{y}) : a_0 + \sum_{i=1}^n a_i y_i$ be an affine form involving noise symbols $\boldsymbol{y}$.

**Chromatic Number-Based Inequality:** The application of Janson's dependent random variable inequality requires the following pieces of information: (a) An upper bound on the chromatic number of the graph $\chi(\widehat{G})$. While the precise chromatic number is often hard to compute, it is often easy to estimate upper bounds. For instance, $\chi(\widehat{G}) \leq 1 + \Delta$ wherein $\Delta$ is the maximum degree of any node in $\widehat{G}$. (b) We compute the expectation $I_E : \mathbb{E}(f(\boldsymbol{y}))$ by summing up the expectations of the individual terms. (c) Next, for each term $a_i y_i$, we compute its set of support $[c_i, d_i] := a_i I_i$ wherein $I_i$ is the range of the noise symbol $y_i$ in $\mathcal{E}$. Specifically, we calculate $C : \sum_{i=1}^n (d_i - c_i)^2$.

Since the expectation $I_E$ is an interval, we apply the concentration of measure inequality using the upper bound of $I_E$ for right tail inequalities and the lower bound for the left tail inequalities.

*Example 3.* Continuing the affine form in the 2D robotic effector model in Fig. 1, we compute the relevant constants to enable our application of the dependent random variable inequality.

The chromatic number $\chi(\widehat{G}) \leq 4$. The sum $C : \sum_{i=1}^n (d_i - c_i)^2$ was calculated as 12.2642. The expectation lies in the range $[265.9, 268.9]$. Combining, we obtain the concentration of measure inequalities: $\mathbb{P}(f \geq 268.9 + t) \leq \exp\left(\frac{-t^2}{24.53}\right)$ Similarly, $\mathbb{P}(f \leq 265.9 - t) \leq \exp\left(\frac{-t^2}{24.53}\right)$.

| $f \leq 220$ | $f \leq 235$ | $f \leq 250$ | $f \leq 260$ | $f \geq 275$ | $f \geq 285$ | $f \geq 295$ | $f \geq 310$ |
|---|---|---|---|---|---|---|---|
| $4.2E{-}35$ | $1.2E{-}13$ | $5E{-}5$ | $0.48$ | $0.21$ | $2.2E{-}7$ | $7E{-}13$ | $9.2E{-}31$ |

**Applying Chernoff-Hoeffding and Bernstein Inequalities:** The Bernstein inequality and Chernoff-Hoeffding bounds require independence of the random variables in the summation. However, the noise symbols involved in $f(\boldsymbol{y})$ may be dependent.

Suppose we compute the maximal strongly connected components (MSCC) of the graph $\widehat{G}$. Note that symbols that belong to different MSCCs are mutually independent. As a result, we decompose a given affine form $f(\boldsymbol{y})$ into *independent clusters* as $f(\boldsymbol{y}) : f_1(\boldsymbol{y}_1) + \cdots + f_k(\boldsymbol{y}_k)$. Each cluster corresponds to an affine form $f_j(\boldsymbol{y}_j)$ over noise symbols $\boldsymbol{y}_j$ involved in the $j^{th}$ MSCC of $\widehat{G}$. Note that each $f_i$ itself will be independent of $f_k$ for $k \neq i$. Thus, we may apply the Chernoff-Hoeffding bounds or the Bernstein inequality by treating each $f_j(\boldsymbol{y}_j)$ as a summand. Let $[\ell_j, u_j]$ represent the set of support for each cluster affine form $f_j(\boldsymbol{y}_j)$. To apply the Chernoff-Hoeffding bounds, we compute $C : \sum_{j=1}^k (u_j - \ell_j)^2$.

To apply the Bernstein inequality, we collect the information on the variance $\sigma_j^2$ of each $f_j$ and compute $M$ as $\max_{j=1}^n (|u_j - \mathbb{E}(f_j)|)$. The environment $\mathcal{E}$ tracks the required information to compute $\sigma^2 : \sum_{j=1}^n \sigma_j^2$ and $M$, respectively.

Since the variance is estimated over an interval, when we apply the Bernstein inequality, we always use the upper bound on $\sigma^2$.

*Example 4.* We illustrate our ideas on the example from Fig. 1. For Chernoff-Hoeffding bounds, the original form with nearly 6900 variables yields about 3000 clusters. The value of $C$ is 17.027. Combining, we obtain the concentration of measure inequalities: $\mathbb{P}(f \geq 268.9 + t) \leq \exp\left(\frac{-t^2}{8.5138}\right)$ for the right tail and $\mathbb{P}(f \leq 265.9 - t) \leq \exp\left(\frac{-t^2}{8.5138}\right)$ for the left tail. This yields much improved bounds when compared to the bounds in Example 3.

| $f \leq 220$ | $f \leq 235$ | $f \leq 250$ | $f \leq 260$ | $f \geq 275$ | $f \geq 285$ | $f \geq 295$ | $f \geq 310$ |
|---|---|---|---|---|---|---|---|
| $2.5E{-}108$ | $2E{-}49$ | $1.1E{-}13$ | $0.016$ | $0.21$ | $4E{-}14$ | $1E-35$ | $3E{-}87$ |

Applying the Bernstein inequality, we note that $\sigma^2 \in [0.1699985951, 0.2292648934]$ and $M = \max(|f_i - \mathbb{E}(f_i)|) = 0.1035521711$.

| $f \leq 220$ | $f \leq 235$ | $f \leq 250$ | $f \leq 260$ | $f \geq 275$ | $f \geq 285$ | $f \geq 295$ |
|---|---|---|---|---|---|---|
| $5E{-}253$ | $9E{-}161$ | $2.6E{-}71$ | $4E{-}18$ | $4.2E{-}19$ | $1.8E{-}72$ | $2E{-}223$ |

In particular, we obtain the result in Sect. 2: $\mathbb{P}(X \geq 272) \leq 6.2E{-}7$.

Finally, it is sometimes seen that the value of $M$ in Bernstein inequality is large but the value of $\sigma^2$ lies inside a small range. In such a situation, Chebyshev inequalities are easy to apply and prove tight bounds.

**Theorem 2 (Chebyshev-Cantelli Inequality).** *For any random variable $X$, $\mathbb{P}(X - \mathbb{E}(X) \geq k\sigma) \leq \frac{1}{1+k^2}$. A similar inequality holds for the right tail, as well.*

**Handling Unbounded Random Variables:** Finally, we mention a simple trick that allows us to bound random variables with distributions such as the normal or the exponential.

Suppose the truncated Gaussian distributions in lines 3, 4 and 12 of the program in Fig. 1 are all replaced by normal random variables. The concentration of measure inequalities no longer apply directly. However, for most distributions the probability of a large deviation from the mean is easily computed. For instance, it is known that for a normally distributed variable $X$ with mean $\mu$ and standard deviation $\sigma$, $\mathbb{P}(|X - \mu| \geq 5\sigma) \leq 6 \times 10^{-7}$. Therefore, we simply truncate the domain of each such random variable to $[\mu - 5\sigma, \mu + 5\sigma]$ and simply add $6K \times 10^{-7}$ to any probability upper bound, wherein $K$ is the number of times a Gaussian random variable is generated. Similar bounds can be obtained for other common distribution types. Even if the distribution is not known but its mean and variance are provided, a weaker Chebyshev inequality bound can be derived: $\mathbb{P}(|X - \mu| \geq k\sigma) \leq \frac{1}{k^2}$.

*Example 5.* If the random variable in line 12 of Fig. 1 were a normally distributed variable with $\sigma = 0.01$, we note that 1500 such variables are generated during the computation. The result from Example 4 is updated as $\mathbb{P}(X \geq 272) \leq 6.2 \times 10^{-7} + 1500 \times 6 \times 10^{-7} \leq 9.0062 \times 10^{-4}$.

## 5   Experiments

In this section, we report on an experimental evaluation of our ideas and a comparison the p-box based implementation of Bouissou et al. [7], wherever possible.

**Implementation:** Our prototype analyzer is built as a data-type in C++ on top of the boost interval arithmetic library with overloaded operators that make it easy to carry out sequences of computations. Our implementation includes support for nonlinear trigonometric operators such as sine and cosine. It tracks the expectation and second moments of noise symbols. Currently, we do not explicitly account for floating point/round off errors. However, as future work, we will integrate our work inside the Fluctuat analysis tool that has a sophisticated model of floating point errors [20]. The dependency $G$ and probabilistic dependency $\widehat{G}$ graphs are maintained exactly as described in Sect. 3. All concentration of measure inequalities presented in Sect. 4 have been implemented.

Table 1 reports on the results from our prototype on a collection of interesting examples taken from related work : FERSON [2], FILTER [2], TANK [2], CARTPOLE [36], TUMOR [6], RMLSWHL [36], ANESTHESIA [28] as well as new examples for this domain: DBLWELL, EULER, ARM2D, STEERING. We present for each example, the number of instructions including the random variables

**Table 1.** Experimental results at a glance: $^\dagger$: indicates a nonlinear example, #INS: total number of instructions, #RV: random variable generator calls, **n**: number of noise symbols, $\mathbf{T_{aff}}$: Time (seconds) to generate affine form, $\mathbf{T_{cmi}}$: Time (seconds) to perform concentration of measure inequality, $\chi$: Chromatic number of the probabilistic dependence graph $\widehat{G}$, #SCC: number of strongly connected components, JAN.: Jansen 2004, C-H.: Chernoff-Hoeffding, BERN.: Bernstein inequality, CHEB. Chebyshev inequality.

| ID | #INS | #RV | n | $\mathbf{T_{aff}}$ | $\mathbf{T_{cmi}}$ | $\chi$ | #SCC | END OF RANGE PROBABILITY | | | |
|---|---|---|---|---|---|---|---|---|---|---|---|
| | | | | | | | | JAN. | C-H. | BERN. | CHEB. |
| FERSON $^\dagger$ | 20 | 2 | 20 | <0.1 | <0.1 | 19 | 2 | 0.95 | 0.55 | 0.78 | 1 |
| FILTER | 182 | 32 | 32 | <0.1 | <0.1 | 1 | 32 | 0.2 | 0.2 | 0.1 | 0.1 |
| TANK | 78 | 52 | 52 | <0.1 | <0.1 | 1 | 52 | 5E-12 | 5E-12 | 5E-21 | 1E-4 |
| CARTPOLE $^\dagger$ | 180 | 40 | 164 | 0.2 | <0.1 | 92 | 71 | 0.94 | 0.30 | 0.09 | 2.5E-4 |
| TUMOR $^\dagger$ | 400 | 100 | 200 | 2.7 | 0.1 | 200 | 1 | 0.94 | 0.65 | 0.31 | 0.05 |
| DBLWELL$^\dagger$ | 400 | 100 | 200 | <0.1 | <0.1 | 99 | 102 | 0.95 | 0.63 | 0.43 | 0.34 |
| EULER | 3K | 1K | 1K | 2.7 | 0.1 | 1 | 1K | 1E-217 | 1E-217 | 3E-620 | 1E-8 |
| ARM2D$^\dagger$ | 4K | 2K | 6.9K | 5.8 | 9.5 | 5 | 3.1K | 3E-44 | 3E-160 | 1.1E-309 | 1E-4 |
| RMLSWHL $^\dagger$ | 6K | 2K | 3K | 7.4 | 2.7 | 3 | 1K | 0.32 | 0.07 | 0.02 | 0.03 |
| STEERING$^\dagger$ | 11.3K | 45 | 4.5K | 3 | 22 | 2.9K | 1.5K | 0.993 | 0.599 | 0.224 | 0.016 |
| ANESTHESIA | 22.4K | 5.6K | 5.6K | 438.2 | 12.2 | 1 | 5.6K | 9E-19 | 9E-19 | 3E-26 | 0.006 |

involved. Note that for all but one example (FERSON), this number ranges from many tens of random variables to many thousands. We also report on the number of noise symbols involved in our affine forms. Finally, the times to derive the affine form and analyze it using concentration of measure inequalities (CMI) are reported. To evaluate the performance of various CMIs at a single glance, we simply compare the probability bounds that each CMI provides for the affine form taking a value past its upper or lower bound. This probability should ideally be zero, but most CMIs will ideally report a small value close to 0. We note that Bernstein inequality is by far the most successful, thanks to our careful tracking of higher order moments as part of the affine form. The overestimation of chromatic number makes the Jansen inequality much less effective than Chernoff-Hoeffding bounds. However, for the STEERING and TUMOR examples, we find that CMIs do not yield bounds close to zero, whereas we still obtain small bounds through Chebyshev inequality. We now highlight a few examples, briefly. A detailed description of each benchmark is provided in the Appendix.

**Comparison with p-Boxes:** We directly compared our approach with the previous work of Adjé et al. on three reported examples: FERSON, TANK and FILTER [2]. At this stage, we could not handle any of the other examples using that prototype.

The FERSON example uses a large degree 5 polynomial $p(\theta_1, \theta_2)$ over two random variables $\theta_1, \theta_2$. In this example, Adjé et al. obtain a much smaller range of $[1.12, 1.17]$ for $p$ due to the subdivisions of the domain of $\theta_1, \theta_2$. In contrast, our tool reports a range of $[1.05, 1.21]$. Our approach produces a relatively narrow bound on the expectation of $p$ and is able to conclude that $\mathbb{P}(p \leq 1.13) \leq 0.5$. However, they report a much more precise bound of 0.05 for the same probability. This suggests that subdividing random variables can indeed provide us more precision. In contrast, our running time is roughly 0.01 s while Bouissou et al. report a running time of nearly 100 s.

The TANK example considers the process of filling a tank using noisy tap and measurement devices. In this example, Adjé et al. bound the probability that the tank does not fill within 20 iterations as 0.63. In fact, our approach bounds the same probability by 0.5. Likewise, they incorrectly report that the tank will always fill within 26 iterations. Our approach correctly proves a bound of at most $10^{-6}$ on the probability that the tank is not full. A simple calculation also reveals that this probability is tiny but non-zero.

Finally, we compare the filter example wherein the affine form is obtained as a linear combination of independent random variables. Bouissou et al. [7] analyze the same example and report probability bounds for the assertion $y \leq -1$ as $\mathbb{P}(y \leq -1) \leq 0.16$. Our approach on the other hand finds a bound of 0.5 for the same assertion. The difference here is a pitfall of using concentration of measure inequalities which ignore characteristics of the underlying distributions of the noise symbol. Our approach is quite fast taking less than 0.01 s whereas depending on the number of subdivisions, Bouissou et al. report between 1 s to 5 min.

We now consider models that could not be attempted by the P-Box implementation.

**Anesthesia Model:** The anesthesia model consists of a four chamber pharmacokinetic model of the anesthetic fentanyl that is administered to a surgical patient using an infusion pump [28]. This model is widely used as part of automated anesthesia delivery systems [34]. As part of this process, we model an erroneous infusion that results in varying amounts of anesthesia infused over time as truncated gaussian random noise. The target state variable $x_4$ measures the concentration of anesthesia in the blood plasma. The goal is to check the probability that the infusion errors result either in too much anesthesia $x_4 \geq 300 ng/mL$ potentially causing loss of breathing or too little anesthesia $x_4 \leq 150 ng/mL$ causing consciousness during surgery. Our approach bounds the probability $\mathbb{P}(x_4 \geq 300) \leq 7 \times 10^{-13}$ and $\mathbb{P}(x_4 \leq 150) \leq 10^{-23}$. These bounds guarantee that small infusion errors alone have a very small probability of causing safety violations.

**Tumor Model:** We examine a stochastic model of tumor growth with immunization [6]:

$$x_{n+1} = x_n + \delta(ax_n - (b_0 + \frac{\beta}{1 + x^2})x^2 + xw_n),$$

where $x_n$ denotes the fraction of tumor cells at time $t = n\delta$. We use $a = b_0 = \beta = 1$ and $w$ as a truncated normal random variable with mean 0, variance $\sigma^2 = \delta$ and range $[-10\sigma, 10\sigma]$. We ask for the probability that $x_{100} \geq 0.6$, and obtain a Chebyshev inequality bound $\mathbb{P}(x_{100} \geq 0.6) \leq 0.405$. Note that, the structure of the model leads to a situation wherein all noise symbols in our final form end up depending on each other.

**Rimless Wheel Model:** The rimless wheel model, taken from Tedrake et al. [36], models a wheel with spokes but no rims rolling down a slope. Such models are used as human gait models in robotics. Details of the model are given in the appendix. As part of this model, we wish to verify whether $P(x_{1000} \leq 0) \leq 0.5$. Our approach proves a bound of 0.07 on this probability, verifying the property.

## 6     Conclusion and Future Work

Thus far, we have presented a tractable method for answering queries on probabilities of assertions over program variables, using a combination of set-based methods (affine forms), moment propagation and concentration of measure inequalities. We showed that this method often yields precise results in a very (time and space) efficient manner, especially when tracking rare events. However, we also documented failures of this approach on some examples.

As part of the future work, we are considering extensions to programs with conditional branches and the use of concentration of measure inequalities on higher order moments. We are exploring possible improvements to our approach using the so-called "moment problem" [27].

**Acknowledgments.** This work was partially supported by the US NSF under award number 1320069, and the academic research chair "Complex Systems Engineering" of Ecole polytechnique, Thalès, FX, DGA, Dassault Aviation, DCNS Research, ENSTA ParisTech, Télécom ParisTech, Fondation ParisTech and FDO ENSTA. All opinions involved are those of the authors and not necessarily of our sponsors.

# References

1. Abate, A., Katoen, J., Lygeros, J., Prandini, M.: Approximate model checking of stochastic hybrid systems. Eur. J. Control **6**, 624–641 (2010)
2. Adje, A., Bouissou, O., Goubault-Larrecq, J., Goubault, E., Putot, S.: Static analysis of programs with imprecise probabilistic inputs. In: Cohen, E., Rybalchenko, A. (eds.) VSTTE 2013. LNCS, vol. 8164, pp. 22–47. Springer, Heidelberg (2014)
3. Auer, E., Luther, W., Rebner, G., Limbourg, P.: A verified matlab toolbox for the dempster-shafer theory. In: Workshop on the Theory of Belief Functions (2010)
4. Borges, M., Filieri, A., d'Amorim, M., Păsăreanu, C.S., Visser, W.: Compositional solution space quantification for probabilistic software analysis (2014)
5. Bornholt, J., Mytkowicz, T., McKinley, K.S.: Uncertain$<$T$>$: abstractions for uncertain hardware and software. IEEE Micro. **35**(3), 132–143 (2015)
6. Bose, T., Trimper, S.: Stochastic model for tumor growth with immunization. Phys. Rev. E **79**, 051903 (2009)
7. Bouissou, O., Goubault, E., Goubault-Larrecq, J., Putot, S.: A generalization of p-boxes to affine arithmetic. Computing **94**(2–4), 189–201 (2012)
8. Busaba, J., Suwan, S., Kosheleva, O.: A faster algorithm for computing the sum of p-boxes. J. Uncertain Syst. **4**(4), 244–249 (2010)
9. Chakarov, A., Sankaranarayanan, S.: Probabilistic program analysis with martingales. In: Sharygina, N., Veith, H. (eds.) CAV 2013. LNCS, vol. 8044, pp. 511–526. Springer, Heidelberg (2013)
10. Chistikov, D., Dimitrova, R., Majumdar, R.: Approximate counting in SMT and value estimation for probabilistic programs. In: Baier, C., Tinelli, C. (eds.) TACAS 2015. LNCS, vol. 9035, pp. 320–334. Springer, Heidelberg (2015)
11. Cousot, P., Monerau, M.: Probabilistic abstract interpretation. In: Seidl, H. (ed.) Programming Languages and Systems. LNCS, vol. 7211, pp. 169–193. Springer, Heidelberg (2012)
12. De Loera, J., Dutra, B., Koeppe, M., Moreinis, S., Pinto, G., Wu, J.: Software for Exact Integration of Polynomials over Polyhedra. ArXiv e-prints, July 2011
13. Dubhashi, D., Panconesi, A.: Concentration of Measure for the Analysis of Randomized Algorithms. Cambridge University Press, Cambridge (2009)
14. Durrett, R.: Probability. Theory and Examples. Wadsworth & Brooks/Cole, Belmont (1991)
15. Enszer, J., Lin, Y., Ferson, S., Corliss, G., Stadtherr, M.: Probability bounds analysis for nonlinear dynamic process models. AIChE J. **57**, 404–422 (2011)
16. Ferson, S.: RAMAS Risk Calc 4.0 Software: Risk Assessment with Uncertain Numbers. Lewis Publishers, Boca Raton (2002)
17. Ferson, S., Kreinovich, V., Ginzburg, L., Myers, D., Sentz, K.: Constructing probability boxes and Dempster-Shafer structures. Technical report SAND2002-4015, Sandia National Laboratories (2003)

18. Fuchs, M., Neumaier, A.: Potential based clouds in robust design optimization. J. Stat. Theo. Pract. **3**, 225–238 (2009)
19. Geldenhuys, J., Dwyer, M.B., Visser, W.: Probabilistic symbolic execution. In: ISSTA, pp. 166–176. ACM (2012)
20. Goubault, É., Putot, S.: Static analysis of numerical algorithms. In: Yi, K. (ed.) SAS 2006. LNCS, vol. 4134, pp. 18–34. Springer, Heidelberg (2006)
21. Goubault-Larrecq, J.: Continuous previsions. In: Duparc, J., Henzinger, T.A. (eds.) CSL 2007. LNCS, vol. 4646, pp. 542–557. Springer, Heidelberg (2007)
22. Janson, S.: Large deviations for sums of partly dependent random variables. Random Struct. Algorithms **24**(3), 234–248 (2004)
23. Jegourel, C., Legay, A., Sedwards, S.: Cross-entropy optimisation of importance sampling parameters for statistical model checking. In: Madhusudan, P., Seshia, S.A. (eds.) CAV 2012. LNCS, vol. 7358, pp. 327–342. Springer, Heidelberg (2012)
24. Jha, S.K., Clarke, E.M., Langmead, C.J., Legay, A., Platzer, A., Zuliani, P.: A bayesian approach to model checking biological systems. In: Degano, P., Gorrieri, R. (eds.) CMSB 2009. LNCS, vol. 5688, pp. 218–234. Springer, Heidelberg (2009)
25. Kwiatkowska, M., Norman, G., Parker, D.: PRISM 4.0: verification of probabilistic real-time systems. In: Gopalakrishnan, G., Qadeer, S. (eds.) CAV 2011. LNCS, vol. 6806, pp. 585–591. Springer, Heidelberg (2011)
26. Lassaigne, R., Peyronnet, S.: Probabilistic verification and approximation. Ann. Pure Appl. Logic **152**(1–3), 122–131 (2008)
27. Lasserre, J.B.: Moments, Positive Polynomials and Their Applications. Imperial College Press Optimization Series, vol. 1. World Scientific, Singapore (2011)
28. McClain, D.A., Hug, C.C.: Intravenous fentanyl kinetics. Clin. Pharmacol. Ther. **28**(1), 106–114 (1980)
29. Monniaux, D.: Abstract interpretation of probabilistic semantics. In: Palsberg, J. (ed.) SAS 2000. LNCS, vol. 1824, pp. 322–339. Springer, Heidelberg (2000)
30. Neumaier, A.: Clouds, fuzzy sets and probability intervals. Reliable Comput. **10**(4), 249–272 (2004)
31. Rump, S.: INTLAB - INTerval LABoratory. In: Csendes, T. (ed.) Developments in Reliable Computing, pp. 77–104. Kluwer Academic Publishers, Berlin (1999)
32. Sankaranarayanan, S., Chakarov, A., Gulwani, S.: Static analysis for probabilistic programs: inferring whole program properties from finitely many paths. In: PLDI 2013, pp. 447–458. ACM Press (2013)
33. Shafer, G.: A Mathematical Theory of Evidence. Princeton University Press, Princeton (1976)
34. Shafer, S.L., Siegel, L.C., Cooke, J.E., Scott, J.C.: Testing computer-controlled infusion pumps by simulation. Anesthesiology **68**, 261–266 (1988)
35. Shmarov, F., Zuliani, P.: Probreach: verified probabilistic delta-reachability for stochastic hybrid systems. In: HSCC 2015, pp. 134–139 (2015)
36. Steinhardt, J., Tedrake, R.: Finite-time regional verification of stochastic non-linear systems. Int. J. Robot. Res. **31**(7), 901–923 (2012)
37. Sun, J., Huang, Y., Li, J., Wang, J.M.: Chebyshev affine arithmetic based parametric yield prediction under limited descriptions of uncertainty. In: ASP-DAC, pp. 531–536. IEEE Computer Society Press (2008)
38. Terejanu, G., Singla, P., Singh, T., Scott, P.D.: Approximate interval method for epistemic uncertainty propagation using polynomial chaos and evidence theory. In: ACC 2010 (2010)

39. Williamson, R.C., Downs, T.: Probabilistic arithmetic: numerical methods for calculating convolutions and dependency bounds. J. Approximate Reasoning **4**(2), 89–158 (1990)
40. Xiu, D.: Numerical Methods for Stochastic Computation: A Spectral Method Approach. Princeton University Press, Princeton (2010)
41. Younes, H.L.S., Simmons, R.G.: Statistical probabilitistic model checking with a focus on time-bounded properties. Inform. Comput. **204**(9), 1368–1409 (2006)

# Online and Compositional Learning of Controllers with Application to Floor Heating

Kim G. Larsen, Marius Mikučionis, Marco Muñiz, Jiří Srba$^{(\boxtimes)}$, and Jakob Haahr Taankvist

Department of Computer Science, Aalborg University, Aalborg, Denmark
{kgl,marius,muniz,srba,jht}@cs.aau.dk

**Abstract.** Controller synthesis for stochastic hybrid switched systems, like e.g. a floor heating system in a house, is a complex computational task that cannot be solved by an exhaustive search though all the control options. The state-space to be explored is in general uncountable due to the presence of continuous variables (e.g. temperature readings in the different rooms) and even after digitization, the state-space remains huge and cannot be fully explored. We suggest a general and scalable methodology for controller synthesis for such systems. Instead of off-line synthesis of a controller for all possible input temperatures and an arbitrary time horizon, we propose an on-line synthesis methodology, where we periodically compute the controller only for the near future based on the current sensor readings. This computation is itself done by employing machine learning in order to avoid enumeration of the whole state-space. For additional scalability we propose and apply a compositional synthesis approach. Finally, we demonstrate the applicability of the methodology to a concrete floor heating system of a real family house.

## 1 Introduction

Home automation includes the centralized control of a number of functionalities in a house such as lighting, HVAC (heating, ventilation and air conditioning), appliances, security locks of gates and doors as well as other systems. The overall goal is to achieve improved convenience, comfort, energy efficiency as well as security. The popularity of home automation has increased significantly in recent years through affordable smartphone and tablet connectivity. Also the emergence of "Internet of Things" has tied in closely with the popularization of home automation. In particular, several devices may be connected through a home network to allow control by a personal computer, and may allow remote access from the internet.

The connectivity in the home enables new, intelligent and personalized control strategies or (and across) activities in the house. One novel approach which is being developed and applied in the on-going EU FP7 project CASSTING[1] is that of *game theory*. Empowered with efficient techniques and tools, game

---

[1] www.cassting-project.eu.

© Springer-Verlag Berlin Heidelberg 2016
M. Chechik and J.-F. Raskin (Eds.): TACAS 2016, LNCS 9636, pp. 244–259, 2016.
DOI: 10.1007/978-3-662-49674-9_14

theory comes with the promise of automatic synthesis of improved, optimal and personalized control strategies produced on demand by the user herself. In fact, the tool UPPAAL TIGA has already been successfully[2] applied to user-directed and user-demanded synthesis of control strategies for lighting in a house, and been implemented in a complete tool-chain on a Raspberry Pi [12].

Within the CASSTING project, we collaborate with the Danish company Seluxit[3] offering complete home automation solutions. The focus is on the floor-heating system of a family house, where each room of the house has its own hot-water pipe circuit. These are controlled through a number of valves based on information about room temperatures communicated wirelessly (periodically due to energy considerations) from a number of temperature sensors. In the present system, a simple "Bang-Bang"-like strategy is applied. There are though several problems with this strategy, as experienced by the house owner: it completely disregards the interaction between rooms in terms of heat-exchange, the impact of the outside temperature and weather forecast as well as information about movements in the house. Taking this knowledge into account should potentially enable the synthesis of significantly improved control strategies.

For the control synthesis of the lighting system, timed games and UPPAAL TIGA proved sufficient. However, in order to control a floor-heating system, we must take into account continuous (temperature) as well as stochastic aspects (outside temperature, movements). Hence we need to be able to (efficiently) synthesize strategies for *stochastic hybrid games*.

A promising starting point is the recent branch UPPAAL-STRATEGO [5,6], which allows for the synthesis of safe and near-optimal strategies for stochastic timed games using a combination of symbolic synthesis and reinforcement learning. The tool has recently been extended to stochastic hybrid games with a successful application to the synthesis of strategies for battery aware scheduling problems [14] as well as safe and optimal adaptive cruise controllers for cars [9].

Facing the floor heating case study of CASSTING, direct application of UPPAAL-STRATEGO does not scale: due to the enormous number of control modes it is virtually impossible to learn optimal control. Instead, we propose a novel on-line synthesis methodology, where we periodically—and *on-line*—learn the optimal controller for the near future based on the current sensor readings. For additional scalability, we propose and apply a novel compositional synthesis approach. As we shall see this combination allows us to significantly improve upon the currently applied "Bang-Bang" control strategy.

*Related Work.* In [10,11] a method and tool (PESSOA) is presented for synthesizing controllers for cyber-physical systems, represented by a set of smooth differential equations and automata given a specification in a fragment of Linear Temporal Logic (LTL). In [8] a class of hybrid systems that involve random phenomena, in addition to discrete and continuous behaviour are considered, and abstraction techniques are presented and applied to the synthesis of controllers. In [13] the authors provide an abstraction-refinement method for

---

[2] [12] won the Embedded Thesis Award 2014 of the Federation of Danish Industry.
[3] www.seluxit.com.

synthesis of controllers for discrete, stochastic dynamical systems with respect to LTL objectives. In [7] a number of benchmarks for hybrid system verification has been proposed, including a room heating benchmark. In [3] UPPAAL SMC was applied to the performance evaluation of several strategies proposed in the benchmark. In [4] a combination of UPPAAL SMC with ANOVA has been made for efficient identification of optimal parameters of the various control strategies.

Our online approach may be seen as an instance of model predictive control or receding time horizon control for hybrid systems (see e.g. [2]) where the optimal solutions are already very expensive to compute. We tackle even a more general class of systems (including stochasticity in particular) and apply a learning heuristic that is cheaper on the cost but does not guarantee optimality.

The main novelty of our work, compared to the previous research, is that we address an industrial-size case with its full complexity, where the already studied methods and approaches do not scale. It is the combination of online learning approach, employment of the very recent tool support and the compositional approach that allowed us to significantly improve upon the performance of the current controller used for the floor heating system in the existing house.

## 2    Switched Control Synthesis

We use a one-room heating control problem as a running example to demonstrate our techniques in a simple setting: we model the problem, explain the necessary theory behind the model, show how the model fits the theory and show how UPPAAL STRATEGO can be used to solve the problem.

The one-room system consists of a room with walls, a window, heater and its controller. The objective of the controller is to maintain the room temperature at the goal level (21 °C). Due to temperature sensor energy considerations the controller receives temperature readings only once every 15 min and then it has two options: either to turn the heater on (mode "HeatOn") and keep it there or switch the heater off (mode "HeatOff"). Consequently the temperature evolution will be different in these modes due to different energy supply from the heater. There is also a continuous leak of energy through the walls and the window to the outside environment. In short, the temperature dynamics can be described by the following differential equation:

$$\frac{d}{dt}T(t) = \left(T_e(t) - T(t)\right) \cdot A(t) + H(t)$$

where $T(t)$ is the room temperature at time $t$, $T_e(t)$ is the outdoor temperature, $A(t)$ is the heat exchange factor specific to the walls and windows, and $H(t)$ is the power of the heater.

Figure 1b shows such differential equation with heater step functions modelled in UPPAAL STRATEGO as hybrid automaton with two discrete modes. The continuous dynamics of $T(t)$ is typeset as an invariant constraint over the clock variable T derivative under the respective modes. The periodic behaviour of the controller is enforced by the invariant x<=P  and guard x==P over clock x with

```
const double Tg = 21.0; // goal temp. in deg.C
const double Te = 15.0; // env. temperature
const double H  = 0.04; // power of heater
const double Aclosed=0.002;// window closed
const double Aopen = 0.004;// window open
const int P = 15; // switching period, 15min
const int h = 60; // 1hour = 60min
clock t; // global time in minutes
clock T = 18.0; // room temperature in deg.C
clock D = 0.0; // distance between T and Tg
clock x; // controls switching period
clock w = 0.0; // controls window profile
int i = 0; // phase of window profile
double A = Aclosed; // heat to environment

const int L=4; // four phases in window profile:
const int closedL[L]={ 6*h, 11*h, 16*h, 19*h };
const int closedU[L]={ 7*h, 12*h, 17*h, 23*h };
const int openL[L] = { 7*h, 12*h, 18*h, 24*h };
const int openU[L] = { 8*h, 13*h, 21*h, 24*h };
```

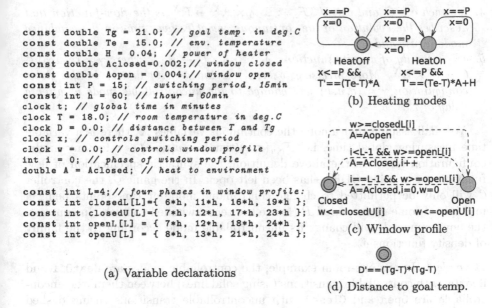

(b) Heating modes

(c) Window profile

(d) Distance to goal temp.

(a) Variable declarations

Fig. 1. UPPAAL STRATEGO model of one room with one window

default derivative of 1. For the sake of simplicity, we assume static outdoor temperature fixed to a specific value and modelled by the constant floating point variable $Te$. All model variables (their types and initial values) are declared as C structures in Fig. 1a. The window step function $A(t)$ is modelled in Fig. 1c as stochastic automaton with transitions between "Open" and "Closed" modes and changing the floating point variable $A$. Thus the window process can change the value of $A$ discretely between values $Aclosed$ and $Aopen$ at any moment with uniform probability distribution over time, but only at intervals specified by a user profile. The profile is stored in arrays $closedL/U$ and $openL/U$ denoting the lower and upper bounds of time intervals when the switch may happen. For example, one can read the profile arrays by columns: the window starts and stays closed during the night time, but it will open somewhere between 6 and 7 o'clock in the morning and close between 7 and 8 o'clock, then it will open again between 11 and 12, and close between 12 and 13, etc.

The whole system model is then a composition of the controlled heating process with the stochastic window process where temperature depends on the heating mode and the mode of the window. We use stochastic hybrid game to describe the controller synthesis formally.

**Definition 1 (Stochastic Hybrid Game).** *A stochastic hybrid game $\mathcal{G}$ is a tuple $(\mathcal{C}, \mathcal{U}, X, \mathcal{F}, \delta)$ where:*

1. *$\mathcal{C}$ is a controller with a finite set of (controllable) modes $C$,*
2. *$\mathcal{U}$ is the environment with a finite set of (uncontrollable) modes $U$,*
3. *$X = \{x_1, \ldots, x_n\}$ is a finite set of continuous (real-valued) variables,*

4. *for each $c \in C$ and $u \in U$, $\mathcal{F}_{c,u} : \mathbb{R}_{>0} \times \mathbb{R}^X \to \mathbb{R}^X$ is the flow-function that describes the evolution of the continuous variables over time in the combined mode $(c, u)$, and*

5. *$\delta$ is a family of density functions, $\delta_\gamma : \mathbb{R}_{\geq 0} \times U \to \mathbb{R}_{\geq 0}$, where $\gamma = (c, u, v) \in C \times U \times \mathbb{R}^X$. More precisely, $\delta_\gamma(\tau, u')$ is the density that $\mathcal{U}$ in the global configuration $\gamma = (c, u, v)$ will change to the uncontrollable mode $u'$ after a delay of $\tau$[4].*

We shall assume that among the continuous variables $X$, there is a variable time measuring global time, i.e. $\mathcal{F}_{c,u}(\tau, v)(\text{time}) = v(\text{time}) + \tau$ for any mode-configuration $(c, u)$. In the above definition, the syntactic specification of flow functions—e.g. using ODEs—has been left open. In the game $\mathcal{G}$, the controller $\mathcal{C}$ will only be permitted to change controllable mode at time-points being a multiple of some given period $P$ (hence the term switched control). In contrast, the environment $\mathcal{U}$ will change its uncontrollable mode according to the family of density functions $\delta_\gamma$.

*Example 1.* In our one-room example, the controllable modes are HeatOff and HeatOn with controllable transitions (using solid lines) between them, the uncontrollable are Open and Closed with uncontrollable transitions (using dashed lines). We also have a number of continuous variables: temperature T and clocks t, x and w. The differential equations together with discretely changing variables are part of the flow-function definition.                                    ◁

Now let $\mathbb{C}$ denote the set of global configurations $C \times U \times \mathbb{R}^X$ of the game $\mathcal{G}$. Then a (memoryless) strategy $\sigma$ for the controller $\mathcal{C}$ is a function $\sigma : \mathbb{C} \to C$, i.e. given the current configuration $\gamma = (c, u, v)$, the expression $\sigma(\gamma)$ is the controllable mode to be used in the next period.

Let $\gamma = (c, u, v)$ and $\gamma' = (c', u', v')$. We write $\gamma \xrightarrow{\tau} \gamma'$ in case $c' = c, u' = u$ and $v' = \mathcal{F}_{(c,u)}(\tau, v)$. We write $\gamma \xrightarrow{\tau}_u \gamma'$ in case $c' = c$, $v' = \mathcal{F}_{(c,u)}(\tau, v)$ and $\delta_\gamma(\tau, u') > 0$. Let $\sigma : \mathbb{C} \to C$ be a (memoryless) strategy. Consider an interleaved sequence $\pi$ of configurations and relative time-delays of the form:

$$\pi = \gamma_0 :: \tau_1 :: \gamma_1 :: \tau_2 :: \gamma_2 :: \tau_3 :: \gamma_3 \cdots$$

where $\gamma_i = (c_i, u_i, v_i)$, $\tau_i \in \mathbb{R}_{\geq 0}$ and for all $n$ there exist $i$ st. $\sum_{j \leq i} \tau_j = n \cdot P$. Then $\pi$ is a run according to the strategy $\sigma$ if for all $i$ either $\gamma_i \xrightarrow{\tau_{i+1}}_u \gamma_{i+1}$ or $\sum_{j \leq i+1} \tau_j$ is a multiple of $P$ and $\gamma_i \xrightarrow{\tau_{i+1}} (c_i, u_i, v_{i+1})$ with $c_{i+1} = \sigma((c_i, u_i, v_{i+1}))$ and $u_{i+1} = u_i$.

In fact, under a given strategy $\sigma$ the game $\mathcal{G}$ becomes a completely stochastic process $\mathcal{G} \restriction \sigma$, inducing a probability measure on sets of runs. Thus, if $H \in \mathbb{N}$ is a given time-horizon, and $D$ is a random variable on runs—e.g. measuring the integrated deviation of the continuous variables wrt. given target values—then $\mathbb{E}_{\sigma, H}^{\mathcal{G}, \gamma}(D) \in \mathbb{R}_{\geq 0}$ is the expected value of $D$ with respect to random runs of $\mathcal{G} \restriction \sigma$ of length $H$ starting in the configuration $\gamma$. We want to obtain a strategy $\sigma^H$ which minimizes (or maximizes) this expected value.

---

[4] Note that $\sum_{u'} \int_\tau \delta_{(c,u,v)}(\tau, u')d\tau = 1$ for all $(c, u, v)$.

*Example 2.* The one-room controller's goal is to keep the room temperature as close as possible to the goal set point, therefore a desired controller would minimize the absolute difference $T(t) - T_g$. In order to encourage the minimization even more we use a quadratic difference function to measure the distance between the room T and the goal Tg temperatures, and then integrate it to achieve a distance function over complete trajectories. Conveniently, our distance function is modelled using differential equation in Fig. 1d as a separate process. Before we synthesize anything, we can inspect how does a uniform random choice fare in Fig. 2a: the temperature curve is at the top and heating and window mode trajectories are below and they jump up when the heating is on and window is open respectively. The result is that the room temperature responds to the mode changes and varies widely, tending to overshoot above the goal, and hence the distance function after 24 h period is about 4200 on average. In order to synthesize a strategy we pose the following query in UPPAAL STRATEGO:

```
strategy opt = minE (D) [<=24*h]: <> t==24*h
```

which asks to find the strategy that will minimize the expected value of D when we reach a state with t==24*h while considering simulations of up to 24*h in duration. Once the strategy is available, we may inspect it by requesting a simulation plot:

```
simulate 1 [<=24*h] {T,Window.Open+14,Room.HeatOn+16} under opt
```

For example, the synthesized 24 h strategy using the "naive" learning method yields the distance of 2750 on average as shown in Fig. 2b. The result is even more improved by the "splitting" learning method in Fig. 2c where the temperature oscillates around the goal very closely.                                                      ◁

UPPAAL STRATEGO offers four learning methods focusing on various parts of the model, therefore we consider the quality and the cost of each method before we focus on our industrial-scale example. Table 1 shows a summary of the evaluation of various methods on two variants of a one-room example: the purely dynamical model is shown in Fig. 1 and another one that has an extra counter incremented at each period P. The result is that among the offline methods (discussed so far) the "splitting" method provides the smallest distance solution, however it is costlier than others in CPU time and memory. The right side Table 1 shows that if we add a period counter to our model, then other methods dominate and the "splitting" method is no longer as good and the "naive" computation costs significantly less. Offline-6 section (strategy for six days) requires twice as many resources as offline-3 (strategy for three days) which means that a linear number of resources is needed in terms of duration of the strategy while using the same number of runs, but the quality (distance) degraded almost four times with a period counter.

## 2.1  Online Synthesis

UPPAAL STRATEGO [5,6] provides a method for approximating $\mathbb{E}_{\sigma,H}^{\mathcal{G},\gamma}(D) \in \mathbb{R}_{\geq 0}$ by computing a near-optimal strategy $\sigma^H$ for a given horizon $H$ using

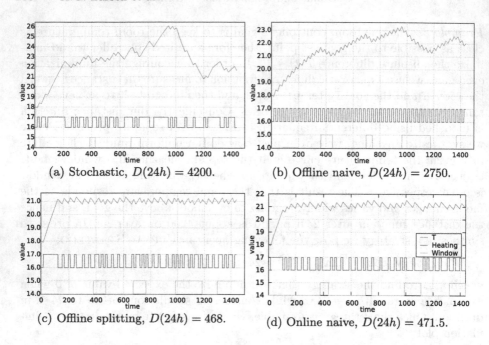

**Fig. 2.** One-room 24 h trajectories of various control strategies

reinforcement learning. However, the effort needed to learn the strategy $\sigma^H$ with a desired precision and confidence-level grows exponentially in the number of dimensions (variables). The quality of the learned control degrades sharply after the control options outnumber the number of simulation runs during learning, making this direct application of UPPAAL STRATEGO limited in the time horizon. For instance, given a realistic setting of eleven heating switches as considered in our case study, the controller is faced with $2^{11} = 2048$ distinct options at each 15 min period and thus UPPAAL STRATEGO manages to compute sensible heating configurations only for the first two periods (yielding $2048^2 = 4194304$ combinations in total) and then it simply resolves to default option of no heating at all.

Instead of learning—at great computational expense—the entire strategy $\sigma^H$, we propose a method for attentively and online (i.e. while playing the game $\mathcal{G}$ in the real setting) to compute a near-optimal strategy for controllable mode-change at the next period. More precisely, the resulting online and periodic strategy $\sigma^O$ will base the mode-change at time $n \cdot P$ not only on the configuration at that point ($\gamma_n$) but also on the configuration ($\gamma_{n-1}$) at time $(n-1) \cdot P^5$, which will be used as the basis for online learning of short-horizon ($h << H$) strategies. Formally:

$$\sigma^O(\gamma_{n-1}, \gamma_n) =^{\text{def}} \text{let } \left(\sigma^h = \text{argmin}_\sigma \mathbb{E}_{\sigma,h}^{\mathcal{G},\gamma_{n-1}}(D)\right) \text{ in } \sigma^h(\gamma_n) .$$

---

[5] Note that there may be several configurations between $\gamma_{n-1}$ and $\gamma_n$ due to the environment $\mathcal{U}$ changing the uncontrollable mode.

**Table 1.** Performance evaluation of one room controller synthesis: offline-3(-6) methods synthesize strategy for entire 72 h (144 h respectively) at once, strategy distance is evaluated on 70 simulations; online-3 methods synthesize a strategy for 5 periods of 15 min ahead and repeat synthesis and execution until 72 h are covered, the distance is averaged over 70 online simulations.

| Synthesis method | Purely dynamical model | | | Extra period counter | | |
|---|---|---|---|---|---|---|
| | Distance | cpu,s | mem,kB | Distance | cpu,s | mem,kB |
| **Offline-3** naive | 10227.8 | 1555.15 | 11884 | 3671.84 | 566.04 | 9448 |
| splitting | 517.9 | 1640.06 | 13424 | 2361.80 | 1608.48 | 90740 |
| covariance | 10227.8 | 1298.66 | 11896 | 1091.81 | 1668.45 | 22820 |
| regression | 10227.8 | 1368.34 | 11480 | 1387.84 | 1767.50 | 19196 |
| **Offline-6** naive | 19668.7 | 1855.36 | 11836 | 8032.86 | 1316.08 | 20820 |
| splitting | 593.7 | 3200.38 | 13112 | 8260.19 | 3120.03 | 167308 |
| covariance | 20234.3 | 2039.30 | 11528 | 2468.91 | 3258.09 | 39580 |
| regression | 19007.2 | 2525.13 | 12148 | 3425.62 | 3488.26 | 28416 |
| **Online-3** naive | 584.7±1.0 | 1046.5±5.0 | 7240 | 526.6±0.5 | 1227.1±3.2 | 7328 |
| splitting | 547.7±0.6 | 1136.4±3.6 | 7384 | 526.1±0.6 | 1240.8±2.5 | 7384 |
| covariance | 587.5±1.2 | 1084.0±3.9 | 7272 | 527.1±0.6 | 1158.5±2.5 | 7624 |
| regression | 585.3±1.0 | 1173.9±3.4 | 9052 | 527.9±0.5 | 1337.1±2.5 | 7380 |

We leave the formal definition of runs under the one-step-memory strategy $\sigma^O$ to the reader (slightly more complicated version of runs under a memoryless strategy given above). However, we note that $\sigma^O$ may be used for an arbitrary finite horizon $H$ or even as a strategy of infinite horizon. To maximize the quality of $\sigma^O$, the choice of the small horizon $h$ should be such that it *just* allows the learning of $\sigma^h$ to be completed between the two configurations $\gamma_{n-1}$ and $\gamma_n$, i.e. within the period $P$.

*Example 3.* We implemented the online strategy evaluation on the one-room example by repeatedly calling UPPAAL STRATEGO to synthesize and evaluate the computed strategy. The following steps are involved:

1. Synthesize a strategy capable of adapting for 5 periods ahead where LastTime starts with 0: strategy S = minE (D) [<=5*P]: <> t==LastTime+5*P
2. Simulate the system for 1 period using the strategy S and record its last state: simulate 1 [<=P] { t, T, Room.HeatOn, x, Window.Open, w, i, D }
3. Create a copy of the original model and replace the initial state with the recorded state from the simulation above.
4. Increment LastTime by P and repeat the synthesis and simulation from step 1 until a required number of periods is simulated.
5. Record the final value of the distance variable D.

The short trajectories from step 2 are then stitched together to produce a continuous trajectory of the entire 3 day simulation. An example result of the first 24 h is displayed in Fig. 2d which is also comparable to other strategies. The online-3 section of Table 1 shows the averages of the recorded distances together with the overall synthesis effort for entire 3 day emulation. The encouraging result is that the short strategy synthesis takes only 4–8 s and the overall quality of any online

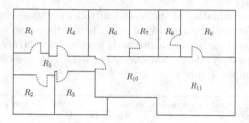

**Fig. 3.** Plan of the house

synthesis method is very close to the best and expensive offline-3 outcome (the offline "splitting" method).                                                                          ◁

## 3   Floor Heating Case Study

In Fig. 3 we see the plan of the house on which we will optimize the heating strategy.

The house consists of 11 rooms, all of them heated with a floor heating system where each room has its own pipe circuit that can be either open (hot water circulates) or closed (water does not circulate). The opening and closing of the circuits is executed by a number of valves located in room $R_7$. Every 15 min a wireless temperature sensor in each room wakes up and reports its current reading. Currently the bang-bang strategy runs every 15 min: it collects the temperatures of all rooms, if a given room temperature is below its target temperature (setup by the user) it opens the corresponding valve and similarly if the temperature is above target it closes the valve.

The problem with this controller, as experienced by the house owner, is that it completely disregards the thermodynamics of the house, the outside temperature (and weather forecast) as well as the maximal capacity of the floor heating system. We now outline the factors affecting the heating system in this house:

1. *Heating capacity of the system.* The heating system can only provide a limited water pressure to make the water circulate within the pipes. If too many valves are open, the water will only cycle in the shortest pipes. This is especially a problem in the living room $R_{11}$, as it has the longest pipe circuit, and is also the most important room for the user, meaning that the temperature of this room should be maintained close to the user's wish. A smart heating system should take the heating capacity into a consideration and never exceed it.
2. *Behaviour of the doors.* The heat exchange between rooms are significantly affected by whether doors between the rooms are open or closed. The house is not equipped with door sensors, so the position of each door is unknown. This means that the control strategy has to work under a partial observability and the status of each door can be inferred only indirectly by observing the speed of heat propagation via temperature changes in the rooms.

3. *Physical layout of the pipe circuits.* Finally, as the valves are all located in room $R_7$, the pipes leading to some of the remote rooms necessarily pass under under rooms. Hence e.g. opening a valve for the room $R_2$ will contribute also to minor increase of the room temperature in rooms $R_3$, $R_5$, $R_4$ and $R_6$ under which the pipe circuit is placed.

In our thermodynamic model of the floor heating, we take all these factors in consideration. The aim of the controller program is to optimize the user comfort and satisfaction according to some measure of how far the actual temperatures are from some goal temperature.

**Floor Heating Scenario as a Stochastic Hybrid Game.** The floor heating scenario with $n$ rooms and $m$ doors is a stochastic hybrid game $\mathcal{G}_{n,m} = (\mathcal{C}, \mathcal{U}, X, \mathcal{F}, \delta)$, where the controller $\mathcal{C}$ has a finite set of controllable modes $V = \mathbb{B}^n$ given by all possible valve opening/closing combinations. The environment $\mathcal{U}$ has a finite set of uncontrollable modes $D = \mathbb{B}^m$ given by all possible door opening/closing combinations. We assume that $\mathcal{U}$ given $\delta$ can switch among modes with equal probability at every period. The state variables in $X$ are given by the room temperatures $\{T_1, \ldots, T_n\}$ and the outside temperature $T_{\text{env}}$.

We will denote by vector $T$ the room temperatures and by $T_i$ the $i$-th room temperature. Given the current temperatures $T$, a controllable mode $v \in V$, an uncontrollable mode $d \in D$ and a time delay $\tau$, the flow function $\mathcal{F}_{v,d}(\tau, T)$ gives the room temperatures $T'$ (after $\tau$ time units passed) that are the solutions to the following differential equations:

$$\frac{d}{dt}T_i(t) = \sum_{j=1}^{n} A_{i,j}^d (T_j(t) - T_i(t)) + B_i(T_{\text{env}}(t) - T_i(t)) + H_{j,i}^v \cdot v_j \ dt$$

where $A_{i,j}^d$ contains the heat exchange coefficients between room $i$ and room $j$, given the door mode $d$. Note that there are $2^m$ matrices for the possible door modes. The vector $B$ contains the heat exchange coefficients between the outside temperature and each room, and $H^v$ contains the heat exchange coefficients for each pipe and the rooms it traverses. A pipe heats a room if it traverses it and valve $v_j$ is open. There is a capacity constraint on the water pressure, if the capacity is exceed the coefficients in $H^v$ prevent the rooms with the long pipes from been heated. Finally, $T_{\text{env}}(t)$ is the current outside temperature at time $t$. The initial conditions are given by the current temperatures $T$. Hence, for a given room $i$, the temperature $T_i'$ is influenced by the adjacent rooms, the door configuration (uncontrollable mode), the outside temperature $T_{\text{env}}$, the pipes traversing the room, and the valve configuration (controllable mode). For the thermodynamics to be realistic, the time unit is minutes.

### 3.1  Experiments

Regarding our experiments, we have two major components: a simulator written in MATLAB and a number of controllers, including the ones produced by UPPAAL

STRATEGO. The simulator implements the floor heating stochastic hybrid game $\mathcal{G}_{n,m}$. For our experiments, in the simulator we fix a time horizon $H$ of 3 days with a period $P$ of 15 min. As in the real house, every 15 min, the simulator outputs the current room temperatures $T$ which are read by the controller. Subsequently, the controller inputs the control valves $V$ which are used by the simulator for the next 15 min. The house has vectors of desired temperatures $T^g$ and weights $W$ denoting the importance of each room. Our goal is to optimize the comfort in the house. Intuitively, comfort is in proportion to the distance between the desired temperatures and the current temperatures. To measure the comfort provided by a controller (strategy) $\sigma$, we define a function dist on runs of $\mathcal{G}_{n,m} \upharpoonright \sigma$ of the form $\pi = \gamma_o \xrightarrow{t_1} \gamma_1 \xrightarrow{t_2} \ldots \xrightarrow{t_{k-1}} \gamma_{k-1} \xrightarrow{t_k} \gamma_k$ where $k = H/P$ is the number of control steps in the run $\pi$. Let $T_i(\gamma_j)$ denote the room temperature $T_i$ at configuration $\gamma_j$. Then the distance function is defined by

$$\text{dist}(\pi) = \sum_{j}^{k} \sum_{i}^{n} (T_i^g - T_i(\gamma_j))^2 \cdot W_i .$$

In our experiments, we evaluate a number of different controllers. The simulator uses the distance function dist to compare the different controllers.

**Controllers.** In the following we introduce a number of controllers which we use in our experiments. We present the current controller operating in the house, two controllers proposed by engineers and the controller synthesized using online synthesis and UPPAAL-STRATEGO.

– *Bang-Bang Controller.* The bang-bang controller is currently running in the physical house and after each reading of room temperatures $T$, it simply opens the valves of every room $i$ where $T_i < T_i^g$ and leaves the remaining valves closed.

– *Capacity Aware Bang-Bang Controller.* The main problem with the bang-bang strategy is that if all rooms are below their target temperatures, it simply opens all valves in the house, violating the restriction on the maximal capacity of the floor heating system. The capacity aware bang-bang controller, at each time where a decision is to be taken, orders in descending order all rooms according to their individual distance function, given for a room $i$ by $W_i \cdot (T_g^i - T^i)^2$ where $W_i$ is the given priority of room $i$, and then opens in this order the valves of all rooms that are below their target temperatures (as the normal bang-bang controller) but only until the maximum capacity is exceeded.

– *Brute-Force Controller.* This is an online controller with short horizon 1 that for $n$ valves by brute-force explores all possible $2^n$ valve combinations and selects a valve combination that minimizes the distance function. The controller operates as follows: after the current reading of the temperatures $T$ and the valves configuration $v$, it guesses a random door mode $d$ and using this information it computes the expected temperatures $T'$ exactly after $P$

time units (recall that in our case study we fixed the period to $P = 15$); next the controller considers all $2^n$ possible valve configurations and computes the predicted room temperatures $T''$ at time $2P$. The controller then returns the valve configuration that minimizes the distance function dist. Note that already for the short horizon 1, the computation of the brute-force controller takes over 170 seconds, so exploring by brute-force all $2^{2n}$ combinations (in our case $n = 11$) needed for the short horizon of 2 is impossible due to the 15 min duration of the period.

- *Stratego Online Controller.* (STRATEGO-ON) The controller is synthesized by UPPAAL STRATEGO using the online strategy synthesis methodology introduced in Sect. 2 with short horizon of 3. The aim is to learn the optimal valve configurations for several steps ahead using machine learning methods and hence avoid the exhaustive search done by the brute-force controller.

**Evaluation Scenarios.** In order to evaluate the performance of the different controllers described above, we fix five realistic scenarios on which we perform our experiments. We distinguish between the *stability* scenarios where the initial room temperatures are equal to the target ones ($T(0) = T^g$) and the task is to maintain these temperatures throughout the next three days relative to different weather conditions. We also study the *vacation* scenarios, where we assume that a family returns from a vacation and shortly before this the house should move from the energy-saving temperature vector $T(0)$ into the target temperature $T^g$ vector as quickly as possible.

The stability and vacation scenarios are then subject to two different weather profiles, a *mild winter* where the outside temperature behaves according to real data from the Aalborg airport from 03.02.2015, 00:20 to 07.02.2015, 23:50 where the outside temperature ranges between 2 to 5 °C, and a *tough winter* using the data from the Aalborg airport from 14.02.2015, 00:20 to 17.02.2015, 23:50 where the outside temperature ranges between -10 and 6 °C. We also consider the *spring* scenario where the outside temperature is modelled using a sinusoid $T^{env}(t) = 7 * sin(2 * pi/60 * 24 * t) + 19$ such that most of the time the outside temperature is below the target room temperatures but the peak environment temperature during the middle of the day exceeds the target room temperatures.

In all scenarios, a fixed profile when a specific door is closed or open is used, corresponding to the typical behaviour of the owner of the house. Note that none of the controllers is aware of this fixed door profile.

**Controller Evaluation for 5 Rooms.** We show the applicability of our online-synthesis methodology on the left part of the house consisting of rooms $R_1$ to $R_5$ and doors $D_1$ to $D_4$ (see Fig. 3), i.e. the stochastic hybrid game $\mathcal{G}_{5,4}$. We have restricted the maximum pressure capacity of the heating system to 50 %. In our simulator for $\mathcal{G}_{5,4}$, we executed all the above controllers and scenarios. The evaluation of the controllers is given in Table 2. Since we have fixed a door profile and the controllers are deterministic (except for STRATEGO-ON), we obtain a unique run $\pi$ for every combination of scenarios and controllers.

**Table 2.** Evaluation of controllers for 5 and 11 rooms of the house (see Fig. 3). The simulation has a horizon $H$ of 3 days, and a short horizon $h$ of 3 periods. Temperatures are read every 15 min.

| Scenario | Controller | 5 Rooms | | 11 Rooms | |
|---|---|---|---|---|---|
| | | dist | Time (sec.) | dist | Time (sec.) |
| mild winter vacation | Bang-Bang | 62704 | < 1 | 53550 | < 1 |
| | Bang-Bang-Cap-Aware | 39755 | < 1 | 31718 | < 1 |
| | Brute-Force | 36489 | ~ 2.4 | 28332 | ~ 171 |
| | STRATEGO-ON | 36418 | ~ 2.9 | 31054 | ~ 77 |
| | STRATEGO-ON-CL | — | — | 29541 | ~ 16 |
| tough winter vacation | Bang-Bang | 248367 | < 1 | 163635 | < 1 |
| | Bang-Bang-Cap-Aware | 155090 | < 1 | 82250 | < 1 |
| | Brute-Force | 137266 | ~ 2.4 | 61897 | ~ 171 |
| | STRATEGO-ON | 137223 | ~ 3.0 | 75792 | ~ 78 |
| | STRATEGO-ON-CL | — | — | 66611 | ~ 17 |
| mild winter stability | Bang-Bang | 24834 | < 1 | 9654 | < 1 |
| | Bang-Bang-Cap-Aware | 18405 | < 1 | 9430 | < 1 |
| | Brute-Force | 16765 | ~ 2.4 | 9260 | ~ 179 |
| | STRATEGO-ON | 16708 | ~ 3.0 | 9972 | ~ 76 |
| | STRATEGO-ON-CL | — | — | 9025 | ~ 16 |
| tough winter stability | Bang-Bang | 199688 | < 1 | 82849 | < 1 |
| | Bang-Bang-Cap-Aware | 121776 | < 1 | 37099 | < 1 |
| | Brute-Force | 107065 | ~ 2.2 | 33917 | ~ 192 |
| | STRATEGO-ON | 107027 | ~ 3.0 | 42229 | ~ 77 |
| | STRATEGO-ON-CL | — | — | 34585 | ~ 16 |
| spring stability | Bang-Bang | 4297 | < 1 | 4493 | < 1 |
| | Bang-Bang-Cap-Aware | 4297 | < 1 | 4419 | < 1 |
| | Brute-Force | 3875 | ~ 2.2 | 2861 | ~ 171 |
| | STRATEGO-ON | 3755 | ~ 2.8 | 3239 | ~ 50 |
| | STRATEGO-ON-CL | — | — | 2819 | ~ 16 |

For a controller, the column dist is the accumulated distance dist($\pi$) between the current temperatures and the desired temperatures during the 3 day simulation. We observe that in all scenarios, the online controller STRATEGO-ONhas the minimal distance, providing the best comfort among all the controllers. Our final goal is to synthesize a controller for the full house with 11 rooms. However, the corresponding state space hinders online strategy synthesis to scale with satisfactory quality of the produced control strategy. We address this issue in the next section.

## 4    Compositional Synthesis

Although online learning is an important step towards the scalability of our approach, it does not enable us to learn small horizon strategies of sufficient quality for the full version of the floor heating case study. Even though we have decreased the horizon, the branching factor is enormous: for each period we have to learn the optimal setting of 11 valves, i.e. the optimal of $2^{11}$ modes. Given a horizon $h$, this means that we have to learn the optimal sequence of modes out of $2^{11h}$ possible sequences. Clearly, this becomes infeasible for small $h$.

However, often the set of modes $C$ will be a product of two (or more) submodes, i.e. $C = C_1 \times C_2$; e.g. in the floor heating case study we may split the

11 valves into two subsets i.e. valves 1 to 5 and valves 6 to 11. This suggests the possibility of a compositional approach for the synthesis of $\sigma^h$ based on the synthesis of two sub-strategies $\sigma_1^h : \mathbb{C} \to C_1$ and $\sigma_2^h : \mathbb{C} \to C_2$, with $\sigma^h(\gamma) = (\sigma_1^h(\gamma), \sigma_2^h(\gamma))$.

Given an initial sub-strategy $\sigma_1^0 : \mathbb{C} \to C_1$, the game $\mathcal{G}$ becomes a reduced game $\mathcal{G} \upharpoonright \sigma_1^0$ with $C_2$ as remaining controllable modes. With the significant reduction in size, it may now be feasible to synthesize a near-optimal strategy, $\sigma_2^0 : \mathbb{C} \to C_2$, with horizon $h$ for this reduced game, i.e. $\sigma_2^0 = \operatorname{argmin}_\sigma \mathbb{E}_{\sigma, h}^{\mathcal{G} \upharpoonright \sigma_1^0, \gamma}(D)$. Now given $\sigma_2^0$, we may similarly learn an optimal sub-strategy, $\sigma_1^1 : \mathbb{C} \to C_1$, for the reduced game $\mathcal{G} \upharpoonright \sigma_2^0$ with $C_1$ as remaining controllable modes. Repeating this process will generate a sequence of sub-strategies $\sigma_1^i : \mathbb{C} \to C_1$ and $\sigma_2^i : \mathbb{C} \to C_2$, with $\sigma_1^h = \sigma_1^N$ and $\sigma_2^h = \sigma_2^N$ for some a priori chosen $N$. Clearly, this method is a heuristic, with no guarantee of converging to the optimum overall strategy, and where the quality depends on the initial sub-strategy chosen, the choice of $N$ as well as the game $\mathcal{G}$ itself. However, as we shall see, this heuristic may be with success applied to our floor heating case study.

*Stratego Online Compositional Controller.* (STRATEGO-ON-CL) This controller applies the previously introduced compositional synthesis together with online synthesis. The controller uses two UPPAAL STRATEGO models. In the first model, valves 1 to 5 are controllable and valves 6 to 11 are fixed by a Bang-Bang controller (the second model is constructed in a dual manner where the valves 1 to 5 are now fixed to the computed control strategy in the first model). At every period, distributing the valve capacity between the left and right parts of the house plays a key role. This controller dynamically assigns the maximum allowed capacity for the two parts of the house proportionally to the distance function dist of the two parts of the house.

**Experiments for 11 Rooms.** We implemented the floor heating stochastic hybrid game $\mathcal{G}_{11,8}$ with 11 rooms and 8 doors in our simulator and evaluated the Stratego compositional controller together with the previously defined controllers and all the scenarios described in Sect. 3.1. Table 2 presents the results. We observe that for all scenarios the Stratego online compositional controller obtains results comparable to the Brute-Force controller, however, by an order of magnitude faster.

In order to see how the STRATEGO-ON-CL controller can take weather information into account, consider Fig. 4 that illustrates the spring stability scenario. From points of time between 0 and 500 min, the outside temperature increases and exceeds the target temperature. We observe that since the STRATEGO-ON-CL controller is able to look at the weather forecast for the next 45 min, it shuts down the valves much earlier than the other controllers. This results in energy savings and increased comfort.

Comparing the Brute-Force controller with STRATEGO-ON-CL, we can see that in the vacation scenarios and tough winter scenario STRATEGO-ON-CL performs with a slightly larger discomfort due to the fact that the goal is to heat up all the rooms as quickly as possible and hence looking more time periods

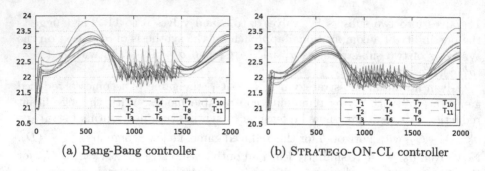

(a) Bang-Bang controller          (b) STRATEGO-ON-CL controller

**Fig. 4.** Room temperatures in the spring stability scenario

into the future does not help (there is only little risk of overshooting the target temperatures). On the other hand, in the remaining scenarios where looking more steps into the future can have an effect on the selected control strategy, STRATEGO-ON-CL has a slightly better performance. Nevertheless, STRATEGO-ON-CL is a clear winner in terms of the time needed to compute the strategy which will be particularly important when moving to even larger case studies.

## 5   Conclusion

In the floor heating case study we evaluated the existing UPPAAL STRATEGO controller synthesis techniques and showed its limitations when applied on industrial scale models. In order to solve the scalability issues, we proposed online framework to compute and combine the short-term control strategies iteratively on demand, while connected to the real house heating system. In addition, we proposed a compositional methodology in order to scale the synthesis for more rooms needed in our real scenario. The experimental evaluation showed that the resulting strategies are outperforming the presently used controller and while comparable in performance to the Brute-Force controller, our method can compute the control strategy by an order of magnitude faster. Hence the developed framework is suitable for installation at home automation systems and we have already constructed a scaled physical model of the house with the actual hardware used by the company Seluxit, as a first step towards the industrial employment of our methodology in their products.

**Acknowledgments.** The research leading to these results has received funding from the EU FP7 FET projects CASSTING and SENSATION, the project DiCyPS funded by the Innovation Fund Denmark, the Sino Danish Research Center IDEA4CPS and the ERC Advanced Grant LASSO. The fourth author is partially affiliated with FI MU, Brno, Czech Republic.

# References

1. Caccamo, M., Frazzoli, E., Grosu, R. (eds.): Proceedings of the 14th ACM International Conference on Hybrid Systems: Computation and Control, HSCC 2011, Chicago, IL, USA, 12–14 April 2011. ACM (2011)
2. Camacho, E., Ramirez, D., Limon, D., de la Pea, D.M., Alamo, T.: Model predictive control techniques for hybrid systems. Ann. Rev. Control **34**(1), 21–31 (2010). http://www.sciencedirect.com/science/article/pii/S1367578810000040
3. David, A., Du, D., Larsen, K.G., Mikučionis, M., Skou, A.: An evaluation framework for energy aware buildings using statistical model checking. SCIENCE CHINA Inf. Sci. **55**(12), 2694–2707 (2012). http://dx.doi.org/10.1007/s11432-012-4742-0
4. David, A., Du, D., Guldstrand Larsen, K., Legay, A., Mikučionis, M.: Optimizing control strategy using statistical model checking. In: Brat, G., Rungta, N., Venet, A. (eds.) NFM 2013. LNCS, vol. 7871, pp. 352–367. Springer, Heidelberg (2013)
5. David, A., Jensen, P.G., Larsen, K.G., Legay, A., Lime, D., Sørensen, M.G., Taankvist, J.H.: On time with minimal expected cost!. In: Cassez, F., Raskin, J.-F. (eds.) ATVA 2014. LNCS, vol. 8837, pp. 129–145. Springer, Heidelberg (2014)
6. David, A., Jensen, P.G., Larsen, K.G., Mikučionis, M., Taankvist, J.H.: Uppaal stratego. In: Baier, C., Tinelli, C. (eds.) TACAS 2015. LNCS, vol. 9035, pp. 206–211. Springer, Heidelberg (2015)
7. Fehnker, A., Ivančić, F.: Benchmarks for hybrid systems verification. In: Alur, R., Pappas, G.J. (eds.) HSCC 2004. LNCS, vol. 2993, pp. 326–341. Springer, Heidelberg (2004)
8. Hahn, E.M., Norman, G., Parker, D., Wachter, B., Zhang, L.: Game-based abstraction and controller synthesis for probabilistic hybrid systems. In: Eighth International Conference on Quantitative Evaluation of Systems, QEST 2011, Aachen, Germany, 5–8 September 2011, pp. 69–78. IEEE Computer Society (2011). http://dx.doi.org/10.1109/QEST.2011.17
9. Larsen, K.G., Mikucionis, M., Taankvist, J.H.: Safe and optimal adaptive cruise control. In: Meyer, R., et al. (eds.) Olderog-Festschrift. LNCS, vol. 9360, pp. 260–277. Springer, Heidelberg (2015). doi:10.1007/978-3-319-23506-6_17
10. Majumdar, R., Render, E., Tabuada, P.: Robust discrete synthesis against unspecified disturbances. In: Caccamo et al. [1], pp. 211–220. http://doi.acm.org/10.1145/1967701.1967732
11. Roy, P., Tabuada, P., Majumdar, R.: Pessoa 2.0: a controller synthesis tool for cyber-physical systems. In: Caccamo et al. [1], pp. 315–316. http://doi.acm.org/10.1145/1967701.1967748
12. Sørensen, M.G.: Automated controller synthesis in home automation. Master's thesis, Computer Science, Aalborg University (2014)
13. Svoreňová, M., Křetínský, J., Chmelík, M., Chatterjee, K., Černá, I., Belta, C.: Temporal logic control for stochastic linear systems using abstraction refinement of probabilistic games. In: Proceedings of the 18th International Conference on Hybrid Systems: Computation and Control, pp. 259–268. HSCC 2015, ACM, New York, NY, USA (2015). http://doi.acm.org/10.1145/2728606.2728608
14. Wognsen, E.R., Haverkort, B.R., Jongerden, M., Hansen, R.R., Larsen, K.G.: A score function for optimizing the cycle-life of battery-powered embedded systems. In: Sankaranarayanan, S., Vicario, E. (eds.) FORMATS 2015. LNCS, vol. 9268, pp. 305–320. Springer, Heidelberg (2015)

# Deductive Proofs of Almost Sure Persistence and Recurrence Properties

Aleksandar Chakarov[⊠], Yuen-Lam Voronin[⊠],
and Sriram Sankaranarayanan[⊠]

University of Colorado Boulder, Boulder, CO 80303, USA
{aleksandar.chakarov,yuen-lam.voronin,
sriram.sankaranarayanan}@colorado.edu

**Abstract.** Martingale theory yields a powerful set of tools that have recently been used to prove quantitative properties of stochastic systems such as stochastic safety and qualitative properties such as almost sure termination. In this paper, we examine proof techniques for establishing almost sure persistence and recurrence properties of *infinite-state* discrete time stochastic systems. A persistence property $\Diamond\Box(P)$ specifies that almost all executions of the stochastic system eventually reach $P$ and stay there forever. Likewise, a recurrence property $\Box\Diamond(Q)$ specifies that a target set $Q$ is visited infinitely often by almost all executions of the stochastic system. Our approach extends classic ideas on the use of Lyapunov-like functions to establish qualitative persistence and recurrence properties. Next, we extend known constraint-based invariant synthesis techniques to deduce the necessary supermartingale expressions to partly mechanize such proofs. We illustrate our techniques on a set of interesting examples.

**Keywords:** Temporal logic · Stochastic systems · Markov processes · Stochastic control · Sum-of-squares programming

## 1 Introduction

In this paper, we study persistence ($\Diamond\Box(\cdot)$) and recurrence ($\Box\Diamond(\cdot)$) properties for stochastic systems. Stochastic systems are commonly used to model the effect of noise or random uncertainties on systems. Examples include probabilistic programs [17,20] with random number generating constructs for modeling uncertainties, cyber-physical systems under the influence of external stochastic disturbances, financial process models, and biological models. Given a stochastic system, we attempt to find proofs that for a subset of states $T$, the behaviors of the system satisfy a persistence property $\Diamond\Box(T)$ with probability 1 (almost surely), i.e., almost every behavior of the system eventually enters $T$, and stays in $T$, forever. Similarly, we present an approach to prove $\Box\Diamond(T)$, i.e., almost every behavior of the system hits $T$ infinitely often. Such persistence properties effectively prove facts about the asymptotic behavior of these processes

© Springer-Verlag Berlin Heidelberg 2016
M. Chechik and J.-F. Raskin (Eds.): TACAS 2016, LNCS 9636, pp. 260–279, 2016.
DOI: 10.1007/978-3-662-49674-9_15

which may take many forms, including convergence towards an "equilibrium" region, or asymptotic divergence away from a particular set. Recurrence properties can be used, for instance, to show that the system keeps returning to a set of desirable configurations even if forced to leave under the influence of stochastic disturbances.

Persistence and recurrence properties are also of independent interest to the verification and control theory community [5,21]. In standard model checking approaches, we rely on showing that the system is forced to almost surely reach a strongly connected component [11,13] which is a subset of $T$, and additionally for proving $\Diamond\square(T)$, that it has no outgoing transition from it. However, Baier et al. have demonstrated that this technique is restricted to finite state stochastic transition systems [5].

In comparison, the technique we propose here can handle infinite state, discrete time, polynomial stochastic systems by automatically deriving supermartingale expressions over the system variables and leveraging properties of these supermartingale expressions. Specifically, our work extends the infinite state probabilistic transition systems used in our earlier work [8], or the probabilistic guarded command language proposed by McIver and Morgan [23] with polynomial guards and updates. However, the ideas we present here can extend to a larger class of Markov models.

In this paper, we introduce two types of proof rule arguments for proving persistence and recurrence that derive directly from classic rules for Markov chains such as the Foster-Lyapunov condition [16,24]: (a) "Geometric" rules involve finding a nonnegative function $V(\mathbf{x})$ over the state variables $\mathbf{x}$, whose expectation in the next time step is some multiplicative factor $\alpha \in (0,1)$ of its current value $V(\mathbf{x})$. These are inspired by Lyapunov functions used in control theory to prove exponential stability. (b) "Additive" rules are analogous to ranking function arguments for (nondeterministic) program termination. These conditions were studied for program termination as "supermartingale ranking functions" (SMRFs) in our previous work [8] and proven complete for certain classes of probabilistic systems by Fioriti et al. [15] and more recently by Chatterjee et al. [10]. However, SMRFs are designed to prove almost-sure termination properties of the form $\Diamond(T)$. In the current work, we show—rather counterintuitively—that SMRFs cannot in general prove $\Diamond\square(T)$ properties. We provide a suitable technical condition (of bounded increase) under which SMRFs can prove $\Diamond\square(T)$ properties. Next, we also show that both types of proofs are equivalent under some technical conditions: a proof using a geometric proof rule can be transformed into an equivalent proof using an additive rule, and vice-versa. Nevertheless, both forms are useful when searching for certificates of a given form such as a polynomial function over the state-variables.

Finally, we examine the problem of automatically synthesizing the functions $V(\mathbf{x})$ for polynomial, probabilistic transition systems to prove persistence and recurrence properties. Assuming a parameterized "template" form of this function, we derive conditions that must be satisfied over the parameters for proving a target property. We conclude by illustrating our approach on a variety of small, but interesting examples.

## 1.1   Motivating Example 1: Room Temperature Control

In [3] Abate et al. present a room temperature control problem subject to stochastic temperature perturbations. Suppose that there are two adjacent rooms, whose temperatures change according to the following stochastic difference equation:

$$x_i' := x_i + b_i(x_0 - x_i) + a \cdot \sum_{i \neq j} (x_j - x_i) + c_i\,(1 - \sigma\,(x_i)) + \nu_i, \text{ for } i \in \{1, 2\},$$

where $a = 0.0625$, $b_1 = 0.0375$, $b_2 = 0.025$ are respectively the inter-room and external heat convection constants, $x_0 = 6°C$ is the outdoor temperature, $c_1 = 0.65$, $c_2 = 0.6$ are the heat units supplied to the two rooms by the heater, and $\nu_1, \nu_2$ are i.i.d. stochastic noise. The behavior of the heater is governed by the controller unit term $\sigma$. We focus on the evolution of the room temperatures within the range $[6, 33]^2$.

Abate et al. construct a (nonlinear) sigmoidal controller $\sigma(t)$ that keeps the temperatures within a comfortable range $S : [17, 22] \times [16, 23]$ and focus on bounding the probability that the system leaves $S$ (i.e., *stochastic safety*) within finitely many steps under the influence of Gaussian noise. Figure 1 shows 100 sample executions of the system when the controller is approximated with a degree-7 polynomial:

$$\sigma(t) : 29.2 - 13.42t + 2.55t^2 - 0.26t^3 + 0.015t^4 - 5.13 \times 10^{-4}t^5 + 9.23 \times 10^{-6}t^t - 6.87 \times 10^{-8}t^7$$

under two different types of random noise: uniform $\mathcal{U}$ on a given range and normal $\mathcal{N}$.

Controller $\sigma$ was originally designed to keep the system in $S$ with finite-time (100 min) guarantees in mind. We prove that under mild stochastic disturbances (LEFT) the system satisfies the *almost sure persistence* property $\Diamond\Box S$, i.e., with probability 1 the system eventually enters $S$ and stays there forever. This is demonstrated by the proof rule PERSIST-GEOM of Sect. 3.1 and the certificate $V(x_1, x_2) : (x_1 - 18.3)^2 + (x_2 - 18.8)^2$. When the level of stochastic disturbance is increased (RIGHT) the almost sure persistence property no longer holds. This is consistent with the results in [3]; however, a weaker, almost sure *recurrence*

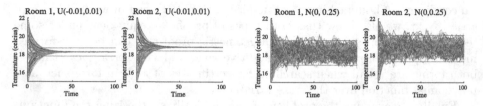

**Fig. 1.** 100 simulations of the two-room controller system, with initial temperatures $x_1$, $x_2$ uniformly drawn from $[15, 22]^2$, under two different types of stochastic noise: (LEFT) $\nu_i \sim \mathcal{U}(-0.01, 0.01)$, with the red horizontal lines indicating the intervals $[17.8, 18.7]$ (for room 1) and $[18.4, 19.3]$ (for room 2); (RIGHT) $\nu_i \sim \mathcal{N}(0, 0.25)$, with the red horizontal lines indicating the intervals $[16.9, 19.6]$ (for room 1) and $[17.3, 20.2]$ (for room 2).

property: $\Box\Diamond(16.9 \le x_1 \le 19.6 \wedge 17.3 \le x_2 \le 20.2)$ holds, i.e., with probability 1 the system visits the region infinitely often. This is demonstrated by proof rule REC of Sect. 3.2 using the same certificate function $V$.

## 1.2  Motivating Example 2: Nonlinear Markov Jump System

Figure 2 shows a nonlinear Markov jump system with two modes $q_1, q_2$ and two state variables $\mathbf{x}$ : $(x, y)$ that evolve according to the mode-dependent difference equations. The system jumps between modes with equal probability.

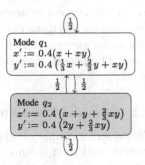

Observe that 0 is an equilibrium and $X$ : $[-0.5, 0.5]^2$ is an invariant of the system, i.e., all sample paths starting in $X$, stay in the set forever. Figure 3(a) shows the sample paths that start inside $X$ converge towards 0. We establish that the persistence property $\Diamond\Box(|x| \le 0.1 \wedge |y| \le 0.1)$ holds almost surely over all executions of the system, by synthesizing the nonnegative certificate function $V(\mathbf{x}) : 2.3x^2 + 4.15xy + 3.7y^2$. After one time step, the expected value of $V$ is at most $\frac{1}{2}$-fraction of its

**Fig. 2.** A nonlinear Markov jump system with 2 modes.

original value, i.e., $(\forall \mathbf{x} \in X)\ \mathbb{E}(V(\mathbf{x}')|\mathbf{x}) \le \frac{1}{2}V(\mathbf{x})$. Figure 3(b) plots the function $V$ over the sample paths, showing its convergence. We use the certificate $V(\mathbf{x})$ in PERSIST-GEOM (Sect. 3.1) to establish the required property.

Outside $X$, the system appears unstable as shown in Fig. 3(c), yet the behaviors approach $x = y$ asymptotically. Using the certificate $\hat{V}(\mathbf{x}) : (x - y)^2$ in SPERSIST-GEOM (Strong Persistence of Sect. 3.1) we can prove that $(\forall\ \varepsilon >$ 0) $\Diamond\Box(|x - y| \le \varepsilon)$.

**Organization.** Section 2 presents an infinite state discrete time stochastic system model and formally states the problem of proving persistence and recurrence (Sect. 2.2). Section 3 presents our main contribution in the form of proof rules for persistence and recurrence properties with the soundness results of our analysis

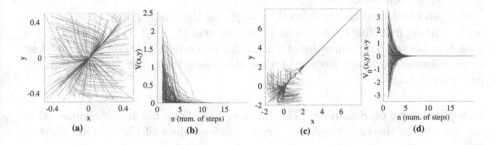

**Fig. 3.** Sample paths of the Markov jump system described in Fig. 2.

presented in Sect. 4. Section 5 presents the results of our prototype implementation on a set of benchmarks, followed by a summary of relevant related work (Sect. 6) and conclusion (Sect. 7).

## 2    Preliminaries

In this section, we present the basic computational model of discrete-time stochastic dynamical systems that we study here and introduce the notion of tail invariant properties in the form of persistence and recurrence. We formulate a problem statement for the rest of the paper and finally introduce supermartingales. The proofs of all statements can be found in the extended version of the paper.

### 2.1    Discrete Time Stochastic Systems

We present a simple yet general model of an infinite-state discrete time stochastic system, and then examine a model of polynomial stochastic transition systems. A purely deterministic system with state-space $X$ is described by a rule of the form $\mathbf{x}' := F(\mathbf{x})$ and $\mathbf{x}_0 \in X_0$, where $\mathbf{x} \in X$ and $\mathbf{x}_0$ is the initial state belonging to initial set $X_0$. Stochastic systems studied here are described by $\mathbf{x}' := F(\mathbf{x}, \mathbf{r})$ and $\mathbf{x}_0 \sim \mathcal{D}_0$, where $\mathbf{r}$ is a vector of random variables and initial state $\mathbf{x}_0$ is drawn from initial distribution $\mathcal{D}_0$.

**Definition 1 (DTSS).** *A* discrete-time stochastic system *(DTSS) $\Pi$ is defined as the tuple $\langle \Sigma, \mathcal{R}, \mathcal{F}, \mathcal{D}_0 \rangle$ with the following components:*

1. *a state space $\Sigma$ and an associated Borel $\sigma$-algebra on it,*
2. *a probability space $\mathcal{R} : \langle R, \mathcal{F}_R, P \rangle$ (with individual samples denoted by $\mathbf{r}$),*
3. *a transition function $\mathcal{F} : \Sigma \times R \to \Sigma$, wherein $\mathcal{F}(\mathbf{x}, \mathbf{r})$ denotes the next state obtained from a state $\mathbf{x} \in \Sigma$ and random sample $\mathbf{r} \in R$,*
4. *an initial probability distribution $\mathcal{D}_0$ over $\Sigma$.*

Let $\Omega$ denote the *sample set* $\Sigma \times R^\omega$, which consists of tuples $\langle \mathbf{x}_0, \mathbf{r}_0, \mathbf{r}_1, \cdots, \mathbf{r}_n, \cdots \rangle$. Here $\mathbf{x}_0 \in \Sigma$ denotes the starting state sample, and $\mathbf{r}_0, \mathbf{r}_1, \ldots, \mathbf{r}_n, \ldots$ denote successive draws of random variables from the sample set $R$ of the probability space $\mathcal{R}$. Given a discrete-time Markov process, the model maps each $\omega : \langle \mathbf{x}_0, \mathbf{r}_0, \ldots \rangle \in \Omega$ to a sample path (or trace) $\pi(\omega)$ as follows $\pi(\omega) : \ \mathbf{x}_0 \xrightarrow{\mathbf{r}_0} \mathbf{x}_1 \xrightarrow{\mathbf{r}_1} \mathbf{x}_2 \xrightarrow{\mathbf{r}_2} \cdots$.

The stochastic process is defined by applying the Kolmogorov extension theorem starting from finite-dimensional distributions $P_{t_1,\ldots,t_k}(B)$ where $B \subseteq \Sigma^k$ is a measurable set. The semantics of the stochastic system is, therefore, equivalent to an infinite-state discrete-time Markov chain (see the extended version of the paper for details).

**Independence of Samples.** The formulation above naturally assumes that the samples of the random variable $\mathbf{r}_i$ are independent of the current state $\mathbf{x}_i$ and from previous samples $\mathbf{r}_0, \ldots, \mathbf{r}_{i-1}$. While this is somewhat restrictive, in practice it encompasses nearly all example instances that we are aware of.

**No Demonic Nondeterminism.** The formulation also precludes any demonic nondeterminism since $\mathcal{F}$ is a function.

In this work, we focus on *polynomial* (stochastic) systems, which are instances of stochastic systems with piecewise polynomial update maps.

**Definition 2 (Polynomial Stochastic System).** *A polynomial stochastic system $\Pi$ is a tuple $\langle X, \mathcal{R}, \mathcal{T}, \mathcal{D}_0 \rangle$, where (a) the state-space $X \subseteq \mathbb{R}^n$ is a semialgebraic set (i.e., $X$ is the solution set of finitely many polynomial inequalities), (b) $\mathcal{R}$ is a probability space for the stochastic inputs written collectively as $\mathbf{r} : (\mathbf{r}_c, \mathbf{r}_b)$, wherein $\mathbf{r}_c$ denotes the (possibly multivariate) continuous random variable and $\mathbf{r}_b$ denote the (discrete) random variables that take on finitely many values, (c) $\mathcal{T} : \{\tau_1, \ldots, \tau_m\}$ is a finite set of transitions, and (d) $\mathcal{D}_0$ is an initial state probability distribution over $X$.*

*Each transition $\tau \in \mathcal{T}$ has two parts: a* guard *predicate $\varphi_\tau$ and an update function $f_\tau : X \times R \to X$:*

1. *The guard $\varphi_\tau(\mathbf{x})$ is a conjunction of polynomial inequalities over $\mathbf{x}$;*
2. *The update function $f_\tau(\mathbf{x}, \mathbf{r}) : X \times R \to X$ is a piecewise polynomial function of the form:*

$$
f_\tau(\mathbf{x}, \mathbf{r}) : \begin{cases} g_{\tau,1}(\mathbf{x}, \mathbf{r}_c), & \text{if } \psi_{\tau,1}(\mathbf{r}_b) \\ \quad \vdots \\ g_{\tau,j}(\mathbf{x}, \mathbf{r}_c), & \text{if } \psi_{\tau,j}(\mathbf{r}_b), \end{cases}
$$

*where $g_{\tau,1}, \ldots, g_{\tau,j}$ are multivariate polynomials over $\mathbf{x}, \mathbf{r}_c$ and $\psi_{\tau,1}(\mathbf{r}_b), \ldots,$ $\psi_{\tau,j}(\mathbf{r}_b)$ represent mutually exclusive and exhaustive predicates over the random variables with probability $p_{\tau,i} : \mathrm{Prob}(\psi_{\tau,i}(\mathbf{r}_b))$.*

We refer to each function $g_{\tau,i}$ as a *fork* of $f_\tau$ guarded by $\psi_{\tau,i}$ with corresponding *fork probability* $p_{\tau,i}$, for all $i$, $1 \le i \le j$.

For a polynomial system to represent a stochastic system over $X$ according to Definition 1, we require that transitions together form a function over the state-space $X$:

1. The guards are pairwise *mutually exclusive*: $\varphi_{\tau_i} \wedge \varphi_{\tau_j}$ is unsatisfiable for all $i \ne j$.
2. The guards are *mutually exhaustive*: $\bigvee_{j=1}^{k} \varphi_{\tau_j} \equiv true$.

With these conditions, it is easy to define an overall piecewise polynomial transition function over $\mathcal{F}$ that casts any polynomial transition system as a stochastic system.

*Example 1 (Strange Random Walk).* Let $\{Y_i\}$ be a sequence of random variables over $\mathbb{R}$ with $Y_0$ distributed uniformly over $[0, 1]$. For all $n \ge 0$, define:

$$
Y_{n+1} = \begin{cases} Y_n^2, & \text{with probability } \frac{1}{2}, \\ 2Y_n - Y_n^2, & \text{with probability } \frac{1}{2}. \end{cases}
$$

The corresponding polynomial stochastic system is $\Pi : \langle \mathbb{R}, \mathcal{R}, \{\tau\}, \mathcal{D}_0 \rangle$, where $\mathcal{R}$ is the probability space for the uniform distribution $\mathcal{U}(0, 1)$, the initial probability distribution $\mathcal{D}_0$ is $\mathcal{U}(0, 1)$, and transition $\tau : \langle true, f_\tau \rangle$, has update mapping

$$f_\tau(\mathbf{x}, \mathbf{r}) : \begin{cases} g_{\tau,1}(\mathbf{x}) : \ \mathbf{x}^2, & \text{if } \psi_{\tau,1}(\mathbf{r}_b) : \mathbf{r}_b \leq 1/2, \\ g_{\tau,2}(\mathbf{x}) : \ 2\mathbf{x} - \mathbf{x}^2, & \text{if } \psi_{\tau,2}(\mathbf{r}_b) : \mathbf{r}_b > 1/2, \end{cases}$$

and defines corresponding fork probabilities $p_1 = p_2 = 1/2$.

**Pre-Expectations.** Key to the analysis is the notion of *pre-expectation*. The definitions below are inspired by [8,19,23] and are related to drift operators of Markov processes [24]. We first formalize the notion of pre-expectations over general stochastic systems and then provide a specialized definition for polynomial stochastic systems.

Consider a stochastic system $\langle \Sigma, \mathcal{R}, \mathcal{F}, \mathcal{D}_0 \rangle$, and a function $h : \Sigma \to \mathbb{R}$ over the state-space. The *pre-expectation* of $h$ w.r.t to $\mathcal{F}$ yields another function $\hat{h} : \Sigma \to \mathbb{R}$ such that for any state $\mathbf{x} \in \Sigma$, $\hat{h}(\mathbf{x})$ yields the expected value of $h(\mathbf{x}')$, where the expectation is taken over all states $\mathbf{x}'$ reached in one step from $\mathbf{x}$. Formally, $\hat{h}(\mathbf{x}) : \ \mathbb{E}_R (h(\mathcal{F}(\mathbf{x}, \mathbf{r})))$. The pre-expectation can be difficult to compute for a stochastic system, even if $h(\mathbf{x})$ is of a simple form, for example, polynomial.

Now, we translate this definition to polynomial stochastic transition systems. We first define pre-expectations across transitions.

**Definition 3 (Pre-Expectation across a Transition).** *Given a polynomial stochastic transition system* $\langle X, \mathcal{R}, \mathcal{T}, \mathcal{D}_0 \rangle$, *a function* $h : X \to \mathbb{R}$ *and a transition* $\tau \in \mathcal{T}$ *with forks* $g_{\tau,1}, \ldots, g_{\tau,j}$ *and corresponding fork probabilities* $p_{\tau,1}, \ldots, p_{\tau,j}$, *the pre-expectation of* $h$ *across transition* $\tau$ *is a function* $\mathbf{preE}(h, \tau) : X \to \mathbb{R}$ *defined as follows:* $\forall \boldsymbol{x} \in X$, $\mathbf{preE}(h, \tau)(\boldsymbol{x}) : \mathbb{E}_R[h(f_\tau(\boldsymbol{x}, \boldsymbol{r}_c)) \,|\, \boldsymbol{x}] = \sum_{i=1}^{j} p_{\tau,i} \mathbb{E}_{Rc}[h(g_{\tau,i}(\boldsymbol{x}, \boldsymbol{r}_c))]$, *with expectation taken over* $R$ *from which the random choices* $\boldsymbol{r} = (\boldsymbol{r}_b, \boldsymbol{r}_c)$ *are drawn.*

We now define the pre-expectation transformation over an entire stochastic system.

**Definition 4.** *The* pre-expectation *of a function* $h : X \to \mathbb{R}$ *w.r.t. a polynomial stochastic system* $\Pi : \langle X, \mathcal{R}, \{\tau_1, ..., \tau_n\}, \mathcal{D}_0 \rangle$ *is a function* $\mathbf{preE}(h, \Pi) : X \to \mathbb{R}$ *defined by*

$$\mathbf{preE}(h, \Pi)(\mathbf{x}) : \ \sum_{i=1}^{n} \mathbb{1}(\varphi_i(\mathbf{x})) \cdot \mathbf{preE}(h, \tau_i)(\mathbf{x}), \quad \text{for all } \mathbf{x} \in X,$$

*where* $\varphi_i$ *is the guard of transition* $\tau_i$ *and* $\mathbb{1}(\varphi)$ *is the indicator function of predicate* $\varphi$.

Related to the pre-expectation is the notion of a drift operator.

**Definition 5 (Drift Operator).** *Let* $\Pi$ *be a stochastic transition system and* $h$ *be a function over the state-space. The* drift *of* $h$ *w.r.t.* $\Pi$ *is the function* $\mathcal{D}_\Pi h : \ \mathbf{preE}(h, \Pi) - h$.

Wherever the system $\Pi$ is clear from the context, we use $\mathcal{D}h$ to denote the drift operator $\mathcal{D}_\Pi$ applied to the function $h$.

*Example 2.* We return to Example 1 and compute the pre-expectation of $h(x) = x$:

$$\mathbf{preE}(h, \Pi) = \mathbb{1}(true) \cdot \mathbf{preE}(h, \tau) = \mathbb{E}_R[p_1 h(g_1(x)) + p_2 h(g_2(x))]$$
$$= \mathbb{E}_R[\tfrac{1}{2}(x^2) + \tfrac{1}{2}(2x - x^2)] = x.$$

It is clear that for any state $x \in X$, the value of $h$ equals the value of $\mathbf{preE}(h, \Pi)$, or equivalently, the drift $\mathcal{D}h = 0$. This function is an example of a *martingale expression* and such functions are central to our analysis. We give their definition in Sect. 2.3 and present properties of martingale expressions relevant to our analysis.

Assume that for any polynomial $p(\mathbf{r}_c)$ involving the continuous random variables $\mathbf{r}_c$ the expectation $\mathbb{E}(p(\mathbf{r}_c))$ is finite. Then the drift of a polynomial is a polynomial.

**Lemma 1.** *Assume that all cross moments exist for the random variable $\mathbf{r}_c$. For a polynomial $h(\mathbf{x})$, the pre-expectation $\mathbf{preE}(h, \tau)$ across a transition $\tau$ is also a polynomial. Moreover, the pre-expectation $\mathbf{preE}(h, \Pi)$ is a piecewise polynomial function of the form: $\sum_{j=1}^{m} \mathbb{1}(\varphi_j)q_j(\mathbf{x})$, where $\varphi_j$ is a transition guard and $q_j(\mathbf{x})$ is a polynomial.*

## 2.2   Persistence and Recurrence

Let $\Pi$ be a polynomial stochastic system with a sample set $\Omega : X \times R^\omega$ and an associated $\sigma$-algebra generated by the Borel sets over $X$ and $R$. Let Pr be the associated measure that maps a measurable subset $S \subseteq \Omega$ to its probability $\Pr(S)$. Let $\pi$ be a function that maps each sample $\omega \in \Omega$ to the corresponding sample path of the system $\pi(\omega) : \langle \mathbf{x}_0, \mathbf{x}_1, \ldots, \mathbf{x}_m, \ldots \rangle$. Likewise, let $\pi_m$ map each sample $\omega \in \Omega$ to the state encountered at time $m$, i.e., $\pi_m(\omega) : \mathbf{x}_m$.

For a predicate $\varphi$ over the system states, the persistence property $\Diamond\Box\varphi$ is a collection of sample paths: $[\![\Diamond\Box\varphi]\!] : \{\omega \in \Omega \mid \exists n \geq 0, \forall m \geq n, \pi_m(\omega) \models \varphi\}$. It is easy to show that this is a measurable set. The probability of the persistence property $\Diamond\Box\varphi$ is denoted $\Pr(\Diamond\Box\varphi)$. We say the persistence property $\Diamond\Box\varphi$ holds almost surely (a.s.) iff $\Pr(\Diamond\Box\varphi) = 1$. Such a property is also known as qualitative (probability 1) persistence property and can be stated in PCTL as $\mathbb{P}_{=1}(\Diamond\Box\ \varphi)$.

Similarly, a recurrence property $\Box\Diamond\varphi$ is a collection of sample paths: $[\![\Box\Diamond\varphi]\!]$ : $\{\omega \in \Omega \mid \forall n \geq 0,\ \exists\ m \geq n, \pi_m(\omega) \models \varphi\}$. We say that the recurrence property $\Box\Diamond\varphi$ holds almost surely iff $\Pr(\Box\Diamond\varphi) = 1$.

**Problem Statement.** Let $\Pi$ be a polynomial stochastic system with state-space $X$ and let $T \subseteq X$ be a measurable set of states. In this paper we are interested in two related problems: (i) Establish that the persistence property $\Diamond\Box(T)$ holds a.s.; and/or, (ii) Establish that the recurrence property $\Box\Diamond(T)$ holds a.s.

## 2.3　Supermartingales and Their Properties

Following [32] we recall the notion of supermartingales and some key properties.

**Definition 6.** *A discrete time real-valued stochastic process* $\mathcal{M} = \{M_i\}_{i=0}^{\infty}$ *is a supermartingale if* $\mathbb{E}(M_{n+1} | M_n = m_n, \ldots, M_0 = m_0) \leq m_n$, *for all* $n \geq 0$ *and* $m_n$.

Since our work mostly concerns Markov processes, we will write $\mathbb{E}(M_{n+1} | M_n = m_n)$ to mean $\mathbb{E}(M_{n+1} | M_n = m_n, \ldots, M_0 = m_0)$. We now propose the key definitions of additive and multiplicative supermartingales that will be used in our work.

**Definition 7 (Additive and Multiplicative Supermartingales).** *A super-martingale* $\mathcal{M} = \{M_i\}_{i=0}^{\infty}$ *is called ($\varepsilon$-)additive iff* $\mathbb{E}(M_{n+1} | M_n = m_n) \leq m_n - \varepsilon$, *for all* $n \geq 0$ *and* $m_n$, *for some* $\varepsilon > 0$. *The supermartingale* $\mathcal{M}$ *is called ($\alpha$-)multiplicative iff* $\mathbb{E}(M_{n+1} | M_n = m_n) \leq \alpha m_n$, *for all* $n \geq 0$, $m_n \geq 0$, *and for some* $0 < \alpha < 1$.

First we state the following simple result about $\alpha$-multiplicative supermartingales.

**Lemma 2.** *Let* $\mathcal{M} = \{M_i\}_{i=0}^{\infty}$ *be a nonnegative* $\alpha$-*multiplicative supermartingale for some* $\alpha \in (0, 1)$. *Then* $\widehat{\mathcal{M}} = \{\widehat{M_i} : \frac{M_i}{\alpha^i}\}_{i=0}^{\infty}$ *is a nonnegative supermartingale.*

Following [8], we relate supermartingales to polynomial stochastic systems.

**Definition 8 (Supermartingale Expressions).** *Let* $e$ *be an expression over the state variables of a polynomial transition system* $\Pi$ *(i.e.,* $e$ *is a real-valued function over the state-space* $X$ *of* $\Pi$). *The expression* $e$ *is a* supermartingale expression *for* $\Pi$ *iff*

$$(\forall \mathbf{x} \in X)\ \mathtt{preE}(e, \Pi) \leq e(\mathbf{x}),\ \text{or equivalently},\ (\forall \mathbf{x} \in X)\ \mathcal{D}e(\mathbf{x}) \leq 0.$$

*The expression* $e$ *is called ($c$-)additive or alternatively, a* supermartingale ranking function *(SMRF) iff there exists* $c > 0$ *such that*

$$(\forall \mathbf{x} \in X)\ \mathtt{preE}(e, \Pi) \leq e(\mathbf{x}) - c,\ \text{or equivalently},\ (\forall \mathbf{x} \in X)\ \mathcal{D}e(\mathbf{x}) \leq -c.$$

*Similarly,* $e$ *is an ($\alpha$-)multiplicative supermartingale expression iff*

$$(\exists \alpha \in (0, 1))(\forall \mathbf{x} \in X)\ \mathtt{preE}(e, \Pi) \leq \alpha e(\mathbf{x}).$$

By definition any ($\alpha$-)multiplicative supermartingale expression of $\Pi$ *induces* a(n) ($\alpha$-)multiplicative supermartingale when evaluated along the sample paths of $\Pi$.

# 3   Proof Rules for Persistence and Recurrence

In this section, we describe the main proof rules for persistence and recurrence properties. All proof rules involve finding a suitable "certificate" in the form of a stochastic analogue of a Lyapunov-like function over the state-space $X$. The soundness of our approach (presented in Sect. 4) relies on certificate functions behaving as supermartingale expressions over the state variables of the stochastic system.

Let $X$ be the state-space of interest and $T \subseteq X$ be a target set.

## 3.1   Proof Rules for Persistence

We provide a series of proof rules for proving persistence properties. The relation between these rules is examined in the extended version of the paper.

---

**PERSIST-GEOM: Geometric rule for persistence**

$(p1)$ $(\forall \mathbf{x} \in X)\, V(\mathbf{x}) \geq 0,$                 Positive semidef. of $V$.

$(p2)$ $(\exists\, \varepsilon > 0)\, (\forall \mathbf{x} \in X \setminus T)\, V(\mathbf{x}) \geq \varepsilon,$     Lower bnd. outside $T$.

$(p3)$ $(\forall \mathbf{x} \in T)\, \mathcal{D}V(\mathbf{x}) \leq 0,$                Drift cond. inside $T$.

$(p4)$ $(\exists\, \alpha \in (0,1))\, (\forall \mathbf{x} \in X \setminus T)\, \mathcal{D}V(\mathbf{x}) \leq (\alpha - 1)V(\mathbf{x}),$ Drift cond. outside $T$.

$\Diamond\Box(T)$ almost surely.

---

**PERSIST-ADD: Additive rule for persistence**

$(p1)$ $(\forall \mathbf{x} \in X)\, V(\mathbf{x}) \geq 0,$             Positive semidef. of $V$.

$(p2)$ $(\exists\, \varepsilon > 0)\, (\forall \mathbf{x} \in X \setminus T)\, V(\mathbf{x}) \geq \varepsilon,$     Lower bnd. outside $T$.

$(p3)$ $(\forall \mathbf{x} \in T)\, \mathcal{D}V(\mathbf{x}) \leq 0,$             Drift condition inside $T$.

$(p5)$ $(\exists\, c < 0)\, (\forall \mathbf{x} \in X \setminus T)\, \mathcal{D}V(\mathbf{x}) \leq -c,$ Drift condition outside $T$.

$\Diamond\Box(T)$ almost surely.

---

Both PERSIST-GEOM and PERSIST-ADD state that a polynomial stochastic system $\Pi$ satisfies $\Diamond\Box(T)$ almost surely if there exists a nonnegative certificate function $V$ (condition $(p1)$) whose value outside $T$ is lower bounded by some $\varepsilon > 0$ (condition $(p2)$). Moreover, the drift conditions ensure that in expected value $V$ in the next step does not increase inside $T$ (condition $(p3)$), and decreases by some fixed non-zero quantity outside $T$ (an additive constant in $(p5)$, or, a multiplicative factor in $(p4)$). Intuitively, these conditions together guarantee that $V$ is a supermartingale whose drift condition outside $T$ forces its value to decrease along almost all sample paths and eventually reach a value $\varepsilon$ at which point the sample path is "forced" to enter $T$ and persists forever.

**Applications.** We present an application of each rule and defer soundness to Sect. 4.

*Example 3.* Consider a stochastic system $\Pi$ with a single variable $x$ over $\mathbb{R}$, and a single transition: $x' := 0.1(1 + w)x$, where $w$ is a standard Gaussian random variable. We show that the almost sure persistence property $\Diamond\Box(T : |x| \leq 0.1)$ holds.

Consider the function $m(x) : x^2$, which is nonnegative on $X$ and $m(x) \geq 0.01$ for all $x \in X \backslash T$ (conditions $(p1)$, $(p2)$). Moreover, for all $x \in X$, $\mathrm{pre}\mathbb{E}(m, \Pi) = \mathbb{E}_w(m(x_{n+1})|x_n) = 0.02x_n^2$, so $\mathcal{D}m(x) \leq -0.98m(x)$. Hence, $m(x)$ defines a 0.02-multiplicative supermartingale expression (conditions $(p3)$, $(p4)$).

Applying PERSIST-GEOM, we conclude that $\Diamond\Box(-0.1 \leq x \leq 0.1)$ holds a.s.

*Example 4.* For the polynomial stochastic system of Example 1 over the state-space $X = [0, 1]$, we establish the almost sure persistence property $\Diamond\Box(x \leq 0.05 \vee x \geq 0.95)$.

Consider the certificate function $V(x) = x(1 - x)$. For all $x \in X$, $V(x) \geq 0$, and for all $x \in X \setminus T = (0.05, 0.95)$, $V(x) \geq 0.0475$ (conditions $(p1)$, $(p2)$). Next, note that $\mathrm{pre}\mathbb{E}(V, \Pi) = x(1 - x)(1 - x + x^2)$, and $\mathcal{D}V(x) = x(1 - x)(x^2 - x)$. It is easy to check that for all $x \in (0.05, 0.95)$, $\mathcal{D}V(x) \leq -0.00225625$, and for all $x \in [0, 0.05] \cup [0.95, 1]$, $\mathcal{D}V(x) \leq 0$ (conditions $(p3)$, $(p5)$).

Applying PERSIST-ADD, we conclude that $\Diamond\Box(x \leq 0.05 \vee x \geq 0.95)$ holds a.s.

*Note 1.* In both examples, the certificates $m(x)$ and $V(x)$ can be used in both PERSIST-GEOM and PERSIST-ADD: $\mathcal{D}m(x) \leq -0.98x^2 \leq -0.0098$, for all $x \in X \backslash T$, and $\mathcal{D}V(x) \leq x(1 - x)(x^2 - x) \leq -0.0475V(x)$. We expand on this point next.

**Strong Persistence.** Rules PERSIST-GEOM and PERSIST-ADD present sufficient conditions under which certificates $V$ prove that $\Diamond\Box(T)$ holds almost surely. Unfortunately, the difference in constraints inside and outside $T$ may force $V$ to be a high degree polynomial (or a piecewise polynomial function). To simplify constraints and make the search for certificates for almost sure persistence properties tractable we propose a stronger version of proof rules for persistence of the form: $(\forall\,\varepsilon > 0)\;\Diamond\Box(V(\mathbf{x}) \leq \varepsilon)$.

---

**SPERSIST-GEOM: Geometric rule for strong persistence**

$(p1)$ $(\forall\,\mathbf{x} \in X)\,V(\mathbf{x}) \geq 0$,                            Positive semidef. of $V$.
$(p6)$ $(\exists\,\alpha \in (0, 1))\,(\forall\,\mathbf{x} \in X)\,\mathcal{D}V(\mathbf{x}) \leq (\alpha - 1)V(\mathbf{x})$, Drift condition.
$\overline{\qquad(\forall\,\varepsilon > 0)\;\Diamond\Box(V(\mathbf{x}) \leq \varepsilon)\text{ almost surely.}}$

---

Similarly, we provide an additive version of strong persistence rule. We say a function $V(\mathbf{x})$ has *bounded increase* over $\Pi$ iff there is a constant $C > 0$ such that, for every possible next state $\mathbf{x}'$ reached from $\mathbf{x}$ (i.e., $\mathbf{x} \xrightarrow{\mathrm{r}} \mathbf{x}'$), $|V(\mathbf{x}') - V(\mathbf{x})| \leq C$.

---

**SPERSIST-ADD: Additive rule for strong persistence**

$(p7)$ $(\exists\,c < 0)\,(\forall\,\mathbf{x} \in X)\,\mathcal{D}V(\mathbf{x}) \leq -c$,     Drift condition.
$(p8)$ $(\forall\,\mathbf{x} \in X)\,V(\mathbf{x})$ has bounded increase,  (See above, and Def. 9 on page 273).
$\overline{\qquad(\forall\,K)\;\Diamond\Box(V(\mathbf{x}) \leq K)\text{ almost surely.}}$

SPERIST-GEOM presents a stronger, yet simpler to state and encode, version of the drift requirement dictated by PERSIST-GEOM (viz. inside the region $T$). Similarly, SPERSIST-ADD does not insist on $V$ being positive definite but only $V$ decreasing in expectation by $-c$ everywhere. The benefit of the stronger formulations of the persistence rule is that each level set of the Lyapunov-like certificate $V$ acts as a *tail invariant*: a set $S$ that almost all traces of the stochastic system reach and asymptotically confine to.

**Relations Between Proof Rules.** In Note 1 we allude to the fact that certificates for rule PERSIST-GEOM can equivalently be used for rule PERSIST-ADD to prove persistence properties of polynomial stochastic systems. We state the main result of importance here and defer all proofs and relationship between proof rules to the extended version.

**Theorem 1.** *Let $m(\mathbf{x})$ be an $\varepsilon$-additive supermartingale expression that has bounded increase in $\Pi$. Then there exist positive constants $\lambda > 1$ and $\alpha < 1$ such that $\lambda^{m(\mathbf{x})}$ is an $\alpha$-multiplicative supermartingale expression. Moreover, let $\kappa \in \mathbb{R}$ be such that $\{\mathbf{x} \in X \mid m(\mathbf{x}) \leq \kappa\}$ is nonempty. Then the system $\Pi$ satisfies the tail invariance property $m(\mathbf{x}) \leq \kappa$ almost surely.*

Under some technical conditions, it is possible to prove the converse of Theorem 1. This shows that any positive $\alpha$-multiplicative supermartingale expression used to prove a tail invariant property has an equivalent additive supermartingale (more precisely, SMRF) formulation and vice versa.

**Incompleteness.** We demonstrate that although sound, our approach is incomplete. The existence of a nonnegative $\alpha$-multiplicative supermartingale expression or a SMRF of bounded increase is sufficient but not a necessary condition for the system to almost surely satisfy a tail invariant property. Example 8 in Sect. 4.2 demonstrates this result.

## 3.2 Proof Rule for Recurrence

We now focus on proof rules for proving the almost sure recurrence property: $\square\lozenge(T)$, i.e., $T$ is visited infinitely often by almost all sample paths. The proof rule is almost identical to a related rule that establishes "positive recurrence" in Markov chains [24].

---

**REC: Rule for Recurrence**

$(r1)$ $(\forall\, \mathbf{x} \in X)\, V(\mathbf{x}) \geq 0$,            Positive semidef. of $V$.

$(r2)$ $(\exists\, \varepsilon > 0)\, (\forall\, \mathbf{x} \in X \setminus T)\, V(\mathbf{x}) \geq \varepsilon$,    Lower bnd. outside $T$.

$(r3)$ $(\exists\, H)\, (\forall\, \mathbf{x} \in T)\, \mathcal{D}V(\mathbf{x}) \leq H$,       Drift condition inside $T$.

$(r4)$ $(\exists\, c > 0)\, (\forall\, \mathbf{x} \in X \setminus T)\, \mathcal{D}V(\mathbf{x}) \leq -c$, Drift condition outside $T$.

---

$\square\lozenge(T)$ almost surely

# 4   Soundness of Proof Rules

## 4.1   Supermartingales as Certificates of Geometric Persistence Rules

We state two theorems that formally relate supermartingales and persistence properties. The first establishes the convergence of nonnegative $\alpha$-multiplicative supermartingales.

**Theorem 2.** *Let* $\mathcal{M} = \{M_i\}_{i=0}^{\infty}$ *be nonnegative* $\alpha$-*multiplicative supermartingale for some* $\alpha \in (0,1)$. *Then* $\mathcal{M}$ *converges almost surely (samplewise) to 0.*

This result can be applied directly to stochastic transition systems. Let $m(\mathbf{x})$ be a nonnegative $\alpha$-multiplicative supermartingale expression for a transition system $\Pi$ for some $\alpha \in (0,1)$. For a sample path $\{\mathbf{x}_i\}_{i=0}^{\infty}$ of $\Pi$, we say that $m(\mathbf{x}_i)$ *upcrosses* a level $\kappa > 0$ iff $m(\mathbf{x}_i) \leq \kappa$ and $m(\mathbf{x}_{i+1}) > \kappa$. If $m(\mathbf{x})$ converges almost surely to 0 on all sample paths, then the number of upcrossings of $m(\mathbf{x})$ on any sample path is a.s. finite.

**Lemma 3.** *Let* $m(\mathbf{x})$ *be a nonnegative* $\alpha$-*multiplicative supermartingale expression for a polynomial stochastic system* $\Pi$. *Then for all* $\kappa > 0$, *the number of* $\kappa$-*upcrossings of* $m(\mathbf{x})$ *is almost surely finite, i.e.,*

$$\Pr(\{\omega \in \Omega \mid \{i \mid m(\pi_i(\omega)) \leq \kappa \wedge m(\pi_{i+1}(\omega)) > \kappa\} \text{ is finite}\}) = 1.$$

*Proof.* The result follows directly from the almost sure convergence of $m(\mathbf{x})$ to zero on sample paths of $\Pi$.                                                                       □

This means that for any threshold $\kappa > 0$, $m(\mathbf{x}) \leq \kappa$ is a tail invariant property: i.e., $\Diamond\Box(\varphi : m(\mathbf{x}) \leq \kappa)$ holds almost surely.

**Theorem 3 (Soundness of PERSIST-GEOM).** *A polynomial stochastic system* $\Pi$ *satisfies the almost sure persistence property* $\Diamond\Box(T)$ *if there exists a function* $V$ *that satisfies conditions* (p1)-(p4) *of* PERSIST-GEOM.

**Necessity.** The two conditions on the multiplicative supermartingale $m(\mathbf{x})$ are $\alpha \in (0,1)$ and $m(\mathbf{x})$ nonnegative. We show their necessity through the following example.

*Example 5.* Consider a stochastic transition system with a single variable $x$ defined over the state space $[0,\infty)$ with two transitions $\tau_1$ and $\tau_2$. Transition $\tau_1$ has a guard $x \geq 1$ and does not alter the value of $x$. Transition $\tau_2$ has a guard $x < 1$ and chooses between $x' := 2x$ or $x' := \frac{x}{2}$ with equal probabilities. That is:

$$x' := \begin{cases} x & \text{if } x \geq 1, \text{ and} \\ 2x & \text{if } x < 1, \text{with prob.} \frac{1}{2} \\ \frac{x}{2} & \text{if } x < 1, \text{with prob.} \frac{1}{2} \end{cases}$$

The initial value of $x$ is exponentially distributed over $[0, \infty)$. Note that $m(x) : x$ is a nonnegative $\alpha$-multiplicative supermartingale only when $\alpha = 1$. Clearly, $m$ does not converge almost surely to zero.

Consider another transition system involving $x \in \mathbb{R}$ having two forks: $x' := x$ with probability $\frac{2}{3}$, and $x' := -x$ with probability $\frac{1}{3}$. Clearly, $m(x) : x$ is a $\frac{1}{3}$-multiplicative supermartingale. However, $m$ is not nonnegative over the state-space $\mathbb{R}$, so $m$ does not prove any persistence property. Indeed, $\Diamond\Box(x \le 1)$ is not a tail invariant for the system.

## 4.2   Supermartingales as Certificates of Additive Persistence Rules

Recall that an additive supermartingale expressions $m(\mathbf{x})$ of $\Pi$ satisfies the condition

$$(\forall\, \mathbf{x} \in X)\; \text{pre}\mathbb{E}(m(\mathbf{x}), \Pi) \le m(\mathbf{x}) - \varepsilon,$$

for some constant $\varepsilon > 0$. (See Definition 7.) Given an additive supermartingale expression $m$, let $M_\kappa : \{\mathbf{x} \in X \mid m(\mathbf{x}) \le \kappa\}$. For any $\kappa$ where $M_\kappa \ne \emptyset$, we can prove $\Diamond(M_\kappa)$ holds a.s. [8,10,15]. Yet in general, the property $\Diamond\Box(M_\kappa)$ does *not* hold a.s.

*Example 6. (*MoonWalk*)* A MoonWalk system consists of a random walk over the state-space $X : \mathbb{Z}_{\le 0}$ of the nonpositive integers:

$$x_{n+1} := \begin{cases} x_n - 1 & \text{with prob. } p(x_n), \\ 0 & \text{with prob. } 1 - p(x_n), \end{cases}$$

wherein $p(x) : \frac{x-0.5}{x-1} = 1 - \frac{0.5}{1-x}$, for $x < 0$, and $p(0) = 1$. In other words, the random walk either chooses to decrease $x$ by 1 with probability $p(x)$ or jumps to 0 with probability $1 - p(x)$. The initial state follows a negative Poisson distribution.

The function $m(x) : x$ is an additive supermartingale expression for the MoonWalk system: for $x_n < 0$, $\mathbb{E}(m(x_{n+1})|x_n) = x_n - 0.5$, and $\mathbb{E}(m(x_{n+1})|0) = x_n - 1$. Yet the sublevel sets of the function $m$ cannot be used for establishing persistence properties, because of the following result.

**Lemma 4.** *For any $\eta < 0$, the probability that a sample path of* MoonWalk *satisfies $\Diamond\Box(x \le \eta)$ is 0.*

Using an additive supermartingale expression $m$ to prove tail invariance properties of the form $\Diamond\Box(m(\mathbf{x}) \le \kappa)$ requires additional assumptions on the expression $m$. One such condition is the bounded increase (which was assumed in Theorem 1, for establishing the soundness of proving persistence properties via additive supermartingales).

**Definition 9 (Bounded Increase Expression).** *An expression $m(\mathbf{x})$ has bounded increase for a stochastic transitions system $\Pi$ iff there exists $M > 0$ so that for all possible states $\mathbf{x} \in X$ and all possible next states $\mathbf{x}'$ reachable from $\mathbf{x}$, $|m(\mathbf{x}') - m(\mathbf{x})| \le M$.*

We give an example of bounded increase expressions, which do not have to be bounded functions: whether a particular expression $m(\mathbf{x})$ has bounded increase on a system depends as much on the system itself as on the growth of $m$.

*Example 7.* Consider a stochastic system over $\mathbb{R}$, in which $x_{n+1} := x_n - 1 + w_n$, with $w_n$ a uniform random variable over $[-1, 1]$. Then the function $m(x) : x$ has bounded increase property.

If each $w_n$ is a Gaussian random variable, then $m(x)$ does not satisfy the bounded increase property. Restricting the set of support of distribution $w_n$ to a compact set (by truncation), however, allows $x$ to satisfy the bounded increase property again.

Returning to the MOONWALK system in Example 6, the additive super-martingale $m(x) : x$, whose sublevel sets do not prove any tail invariance property (due to Lemma 4), does not satisfy the bounded increase property since it is possible to move from $x = -j$, for any $j > 0$, to $x = 0$ with nonzero probability.

We close the section by demonstrating the incompleteness: an additive super-martingale does not *always* need the bounded increase property for a tail invariant property to be established.

*Example 8 (Incompleteness).* Consider the MOONWALK system with modified probability $p(x) : 1 - \frac{0.5}{(x-1)^2}$, for $x < 0$, and $p(0) = 1$. The probability of the event $\{x > \kappa\}$ is $\sum_{j=-\kappa}^{\infty} \frac{0.5}{(j+1)^2}$, which converges. By the Borel-Cantelli Lemma [14, 2.3.1], $\Pr(x > \kappa \text{ i.o.}) = 0$ holds, i.e., the tail invariant $\Diamond\Box(x < \kappa)$ holds; however, the system does not have the bounded increase property.

## 5    Implementation and Evaluation

Given a polynomial stochastic system and a semi-algebraic target set, the problem of finding "certificates" $V$ that prove persistence or recurrence properties is in general intractable. In practice, we impose several restrictions on the proof rules so that their solutions are tractable, based on sum-of-squares (SOS) optimization techniques (see e.g. [4,6] and the references therein). For illustration, we only focus on SPERSIST-GEOM and PERSIST-GEOM; the formulations for the other proof rules are similar.

Recall that for proving strong persistence properties via the geometric rule SPERSIST-GEOM, we need to find a function $V$ such that conditions $(p1), (p6)$ hold. We impose the following restrictions to make the feasibility problem tractable. First, we require that $V$ is a polynomial of degree at most some integer $d$. This means that $\mathcal{D}V$ is also a polynomial, which can be expressed in terms of the coefficients of $V$ and the moments of the random variable $\mathbf{r}_c$. Second, we replace the nonnegativity constraints by the more restrictive *sum-of-squares* (SOS) constraints, i.e., we require that both $V$ and $-\mathcal{D}V$ be sums of squares of some unknown polynomial functions. We also require that $V$ is positive definite, which is a common regularity condition assumed in semidefinite optimization and allows us to find an $\alpha \in (0, 1)$ such that the condition $(p6)$ in SPERSIST-GEOM holds. Under these two restrictions, the generally intractable feasibility problem from SPERSIST-GEOM is equivalent to a linear semidefinite feasibility problem: a polynomial being a sum of squares (of polynomial functions) is equivalent to its vector of coefficients being the image of an unknown positive semidefinite matrix under a predetermined linear transformation. (For more details on SOS relaxation techniques for solving polynomial feasibility/optimization problems, see e.g. [4,6].)

For proving persistence properties with respect to a nonempty set $T$ via the geometric rule PERSIST-GEOM, we need to find a function $V$ such that conditions $(p1)$-$(p4)$ hold. Again, we require that $V$ is a polynomial of degree at most $d$, and that $T = \{\mathbf{x} \mid g_1(\mathbf{x}) \geq 0 \land \cdots \land g_\ell(\mathbf{x}) \geq 0\}$ for some polynomials $g_1, \ldots, g_\ell$. Then we replace those constraints pertaining to the elements in $T$, by truncated *quadratic module* membership. For instance, we replace the condition $(p3)$ by the tractable constraint:

$$\mathcal{D}V = s_0 + s_1 g_1 + \cdots + s_\ell g_\ell, \quad s_0, s_1, \ldots, s_\ell \text{ SOS of degree at most some integer } \tilde{d}.$$

(The tractability is due to the fact that the polynomials $s_i$ being SOS can be phrased as semidefinite feasibility constraints.) Similar treatment can be applied on those constraints pertaining to the elements in $X \setminus T$, which is also a semialgebraic set.

Many standard semidefinite optimization solvers[1] and SOS optimization front-ends (such as SOSTOOLS [25]) are available for solving the SOS optimization problems outlined above. Below we present some simple examples on the use of SPERSIT-GEOM rules for proving persistence. In each example, an $\alpha$-multiplicative supermartingale expression is obtained using SDPT3-4.0 [31] on MATLAB R2014b, taking less than 10 seconds on a Linux machine with Intel(R) Core(TM) i7-4650U CPU @ 1.70GHz.

*Example 9 (Rimless wheel model [7,22,27]).* A rimless wheel with 8 equally spaced inelastic spokes of length $L$ rolls down a hill with stochastic slope angle $\gamma$. Let $\omega_n$ be the angular velocity at the $n$-th impact (which occurs when the stance leg is vertical). In [7,27], the dynamics of the rimless wheel is described as:

$$x_{n+1} := \cos^2 \theta \left( x_n + \tfrac{2g}{L} \left( 1 - \cos \left( \tfrac{\theta}{2} + \gamma \right) \right) \right) - \tfrac{2g}{L} \left( 1 - \cos \left( \tfrac{\theta}{2} - \gamma \right) \right),$$

where $x_n = \omega_n^2$, $g$ is the gravitational constant, $\theta = 45°$ is the angle between two consecutive spokes and $\gamma \sim \mathcal{N}(8, 1)$ (in degrees). We approximate the functions $\xi \mapsto \cos(\tfrac{\theta}{2} \pm \xi)$ over the interval $[5, 11]$ by degree 2 polynomials, and find that the angular velocity in the approximated stochastic system goes to 0 almost surely when $L = 2g$: the function $V(x) : 0.00085x^3 + x^4$ satisfies the conditions $(p1)$, $(p6)$ with $X : [0, \infty)$ and $\alpha = 0.95$: $V$ and $-\mathcal{D}V$ are nonnegative on $X$ and $\mathcal{D}V(x) \leq -0.05V(x)$ for all $x \geq 0$. Hence $V$ is a $\alpha$-multiplicative supermartingale for this system over $X$, and $\Diamond\Box(V(x) \leq \varepsilon)$ holds a.s. for any $\varepsilon > 0$. In other words, despite the randomness in the slope of the terrain, the rolling rimless wheel (with very long spokes) would eventually become stationary almost surely.

---

[1] See e.g. the list in http://plato.asu.edu/sub/nlores.html#semidef.

*Example 10* (*Room temperature control* [3]). In the two-room temperature control example from Sect. 1.1, we are interested in the evolution of the room temperatures within the range $X = [6, 33]^2$. Consider the nonnegative function $V(x_1, x_2) : (x_1 - 18.3)^2 + (x_2 - 18.8)^2$. When the noise follows the uniform distribution $\mathcal{U}(-0.01, 0.01)$, $\mathcal{D}V$ is nonpositive on $X$, and $V(x_1, x_2) \geq 0.09$ and $\mathcal{D}V(x_1, x_2) \leq -0.01V(x_1, x_2)$ for all $x \in X \setminus [17.8, 18.7] \times [18.4, 19.3]$. Hence conditions $(p1)$-$(p4)$ hold, implying the persistence property $\Diamond\Box(17.8 \leq x_1 \leq 18.7 \wedge 18.4 \leq x_2 \leq 19.3)$.

In the case of Gaussian noise $\mathcal{N}(0, 0.25)$, $\mathcal{D}V(x_1, x_2) \leq 0.25$ for all $(x_1, x_2) \in [16.9, 19.6] \times [17.3, 20.2]$, and $V(x_1, x_2) \geq 0.8$ and $\mathcal{D}V(x_1, x_2) \leq -6 \times 10^{-5}$ for all $(x_1, x_2) \in X \setminus [16.9, 19.6] \times [17.3, 20.2]$. Hence conditions $(r1)$-$(r4)$ hold, implying the recurrence property $\Box\Diamond(16.9 \leq x_1 \leq 19.6 \wedge 17.3 \leq x_2 \leq 20.2)$.

We list some additional examples in which a system is proved to satisfying a persistence or recurrence property via some of the proof rules from Sect. 3. The details of these examples can be found in the extended version of the paper.

| ADDITIONAL STOCHASTIC SYSTEMS | NOISE $u_j$ (i.i.d.) | SUPERMARTINGALE $V(x, y)$ |
|---|---|---|
| $x' := x + \frac{1}{2}y + u_1,$ $y' := \frac{1}{2}x + y - u_2$ (over $X = \mathbb{R}^2$) | $\mathcal{N}(-1, 1)$ | $\max(x - y, 0)$ (for proving recurrence) |
| $x' := 0.5(x + y) + 0.4u_1\sqrt{x^2 + y^2},$ $y' := 0.5(x - y) + 0.4u_2\sqrt{x^2 + y^2},$ (over $X = \mathbb{R}^2$) | $\mathcal{N}(0, 1)$ | $x^2 + y^2$ (0.82-multi.) |
| $x' := 0.75y^4 + 0.1u_1,$ $y' := 0.75x^4 + 0.1u_2,$ (over $X = \{(x, y) \mid x^2 + y^2 \leq 1\}$) | $\mathcal{U}(-1, 1)$ | $0.78x^2 + 1.23xy + 0.78y^2$ (0.75-multi.) |
| $x' := 0.1(y(3x^2 + 2y^2 - 0.5) + u_1\sqrt{x^2 + y^2}),$ $y' := 0.1(y(2x^2 + 4xy + 3y^2 - 0.5) + u_2\sqrt{x^2 + y^2}),$ (over $X = \{(x, y) \mid x^2 + y^2 \leq 1\}$) | $\mathcal{U}(-\sqrt{3}, \sqrt{3})$ | $1.55x^2 + 2.36xy + 1.34y^2$ (0.5-multi.) |

# 6  Related Work

Martingale analysis has been used to prove almost sure termination [8,10,15], derive inductive invariant expressions [9] in probabilistic programs, and prove stochastic reachability and safety [26,27] in the context of stochastic hybrid systems. Our paper extends this set of properties to include tail invariant, or qualitative persistence, properties.

Qualitative persistence properties are expressible in PCTL [18] and have been studied by the model-checking community [5,21] in the context of finite-state Markov processes. The approach leverages the fact that the system ends up a.s. in a *bottom strongly connected component* (BSCC [11–13], a strongly connected component with no outgoing edges), then uses a graph algorithm to efficiently check that all states in the BSCC satisfy $\varphi_{\mathrm{INV}}$. Baier et al. [5] have shown that while such results suffice for the analysis of finite-state Markov chains, they, however, do not extend to infinite-state models.

Abate [1,2] and Tkachev et al. [29] present approaches to reducing the verification problem of infinite-state Markov processes to that over finite-state Markov chains. Specifically, [1,2] presents a framework for proving probabilistic bisimulation between the original infinite-state system and its discretized (approximate) finite-state version. Guarantees on the quality of the results are proved using supermartingale bisimulation functions. Tkachev et al. [29] present a framework for analyzing infinite-horizon reach-avoid properties ($\Diamond \varphi$ and $\Box \varphi$) for Markov processes. They use locally-excessive (i.e., supermartingale) value functions to identify a subset of the state-space where discretization guarantees a precise approximate solution. In [28,30] Tkachev et al. tackle *quantitative* reachability, invariance and reach-while-avoid properties operating directly over the infinite-state model. [28] provides a characterization of the statespace based on harmonic functions defining absorbing or stochastically attractive sets. Unfortunately, the sufficient conditions for certificates in [28] define problems that in general have no analytical or computation solution. Our paper can be seen as a set of practical sufficient conditions that yield efficiently computable problems (SOS, SDP) for qualitative repeated reachability.

The problem of stability and identifying the limiting behavior of a stochastic system has been well-studied in the theory of Markov chains [24]. Similar "Foster-Lyapunov" [16] drift criteria have been derived to argue recurrence and transience for sets of states. Unfortunately, most results rely on the topological properties of the infinite-state Markov chains that may be difficult to check automatically.

# 7 Conclusion

We presented an analysis framework capable of proving that the limiting behavior of an infinite-state discrete-time polynomial stochastic system eventually settles almost surely within a region $S$ of the statespace (i.e., $\Diamond \Box (S)$). Our analysis employs constraint-based invariant generation techniques to efficiently infer polynomial functions over the states of the system: nonnegative $\alpha$-multiplicative supermartingale expressions and additive supermartingale expressions of bounded increase. We established that both types of functions constitute certificates verifying tail invariant properties and we demonstrated their equivalence. Finally, we highlighted the individual strengths of each of the two types but also the incompleteness of the general approach through the means of numerous simple, yet intricate examples.

**Acknowledgements.** We thank the anonymous reviewers for their comments. This work was supported by the US National Science Foundation (NSF) under award numbers 1527075 and 1320069. All opinions expressed are those of the authors and not necessarily of the US NSF.

# References

1. Abate, A.: A contractivity approach for probabilistic bisimulations of diffusion processes. In: Proceedings of CDC, pp. 2230–2235 (2009)
2. Abate, A.: Probabilistic bisimulations of switching and resetting diffusions. In: Proceedings of CDC, pp. 5918–5923 (2010)
3. Abate, A., Katoen, J.-P., Lygeros, J., Prandini, M.: Approximate model checking of stochastic hybrid systems. Eur. J. Control 16(6), 624–641 (2010)
4. Anjos, M.F., Lasserre, J.B.: Handbook on Semidefinite, Conic and Polynomial Optimization. International Series in Operations Research & Management Science, vol. 166. Springer, New York (2012)
5. Baier, C., Katoen, J.-P., et al.: Principles of Model Checking, vol. 26202649. MIT press, Cambridge (2008)
6. Blekherman, G., Parrilo, P.A., Thomas, R.R.: Semidefinite optimization and convex algebraic geometry. In: MOS-SIAM Series on Optimization. Society for Industrial and Applied Mathematics (SIAM), vol. 13. Mathematical Optimization Society, Philadelphia, PA (2013)
7. Byl, K., Tedrake, R.: Metastable walking machines. Int. J. Robot. Res. 28(8), 1040–1064 (2009)
8. Chakarov, A., Sankaranarayanan, S.: Probabilistic program analysis with martingales. In: Sharygina, N., Veith, H. (eds.) CAV 2013. LNCS, vol. 8044, pp. 511–526. Springer, Heidelberg (2013)
9. Chakarov, A., Sankaranarayanan, S.: Expectation invariants for probabilistic program loops as fixed points. In: Müller-Olm, M., Seidl, H. (eds.) Static Analysis. LNCS, vol. 8723, pp. 85–100. Springer, Heidelberg (2014)
10. Chatterjee, K., Fu, H., Hasheminezhad, R., Novotny, P.: Algorithmic analysis of qualitative and quantitative termination problems for affine probabilistic programs. In: Proceedings of the 43rd Annual ACM SIGPLAN-SIGACT Symposium on Principles of Programming Languages, POpPL , St. Petersburg, Florida, United States, 20–22 January 2016
11. Courcoubetis, C., Yannakakis, M.: The complexity of probabilistic verification. J. ACM (JACM) 42(4), 857–907 (1995)
12. De Alfaro, L.: Formal verification of probabilistic systems. PhD thesis, Stanford University (1997)
13. De Alfaro, L.: How to specify and verify the long-run average behaviour of probabilistic systems. In: Proceedings of LICS, pp. 454–465. IEEE (1998)
14. Durrett, R.: Probability: theory and examples. Cambridge University Press, Cambridge (2010)
15. Fioriti, L.M.F., Hartmanns, A., Hermann, H.: Probabilistic termination: Soundness, completeness, and compositionality. In: Proceedings of POPL, pp. 489–501. ACM (2015)
16. Foster, F.G.: On the stochastic matrices associated with certain queuing processes. Ann. Math. Stat. 24(3), 355–360 (1953)
17. Gordon, A.D., Henzinger, T.A., Nori, A.V., Rajamani, S.K.: Probabilistic programming. In: Proceedings of FOSE 2014, pp. 167–181 (2014)
18. Hansson, H., Jonsson, B.: A logic for reasoning about time and reliability. Formal Aspects Comput. 6(5), 512–535 (1994)
19. Katoen, J.-P., McIver, A.K., Meinicke, L.A., Morgan, C.C.: Linear-invariant generation for probabilistic programs: In: Cousot, R., Martel, M. (eds.) SAS 2010. LNCS, vol. 6337, pp. 390–406. Springer, Heidelberg (2010)

20. Kozen, D.: Semantics of probabilistic programs. J. Comput. Syst. Sci. **22**(3), 328–350 (1981)
21. Kwiatkowska, M., Norman, G., Parker, D.: PRISM 4.0: verification of probabilistic real-time systems. In: Gopalakrishnan, G., Qadeer, S. (eds.) CAV 2011. LNCS, vol. 6806, pp. 585–591. Springer, Heidelberg (2011)
22. McGeer, T.: Passive dynamic walking. Int. J. Robot. Res. **9**(2), 62–82 (1990)
23. McIver, A., Morgan, C.: Abstraction, Refinement And Proof For Probabilistic Systems (Monographs in Computer Science). SpringerVerlag, New York (2004)
24. Meyn, S.P., Tweedie, R.L.: Markov Chains and Stochastic Stability. Cambridge University Press, Cambridge (2009)
25. Papachristodoulou, A., Anderson, J., Valmorbida, G., Prajna, S., Seiler, P., Parrilo, P.A.: SOSTOOLS: Sum of squares optimization toolbox for MATLAB (2013). http://arxiv.org/abs/1310.4716
26. Prajna, S., Jadbabaie, A., Pappas, G.J.: Stochastic safety verification using barrier certificates. In: 43rd IEEE Conference on Decision and Control, CDC, vol. 1, pp. 929–934. IEEE (2004)
27. Steinhardt, J., Tedrake, R.: Finite-time regional verification of stochastic non-linear systems. Int. J. Robot. Res. **31**(7), 901–923 (2012)
28. Tkachev, I., Abate, A.: Stability and attractivity of absorbing sets for discrete-time Markov processes. In: IEEE 51st Annual Conference on Decision and Control (CDC), pp. 7652–7657. IEEE (2012)
29. Tkachev, I., Abate, A.: Characterization and computation of infinite-horizon specifications over markov processes. Theoret. Comput. Sci. **515**, 1–18 (2014)
30. Tkachev, I., Mereacre, A., Katoen, J.-P., Abate, A.: Quantitative model-checking of controlled discrete-time Markov processes (2014). arXiv preprint arXiv:1407.5449
31. Kim-Chuan, T., Todd, M.J., Tütüncü, R.H.: On the implementation and usage of SDPT3–a matlab software package for semidefinite-quadratic-linear programming, version 4.0. In: Anjos, M.F., Lasserre, J.B. (eds.) Handbook on Semidefinite, Conic and Polynomial Optimization. nternational Series in Operations Research and Management Science, vol. 166, pp. 715–754. Springer, New York (2012)
32. Williams, D.: Probability with Martingales. Cambridge University Press, Cambridge (1991)

# Probabilistic CTL*: The Deductive Way

Rayna Dimitrova[1], Luis María Ferrer Fioriti[2(✉)], Holger Hermanns[2],
and Rupak Majumdar[1]

[1] MPI-SWS, Kaiserslautern and Saarbrücken, Germany
{rayna,rupak}@mpi-sws.org
[2] Saarland University, Saarbrücken, Germany
{ferrer,hermanns}@cs.uni-saarland.de

**Abstract.** Complex probabilistic temporal behaviours need to be guaranteed in robotics and various other control domains, as well as in the context of families of randomized protocols. At its core, this entails checking infinite-state probabilistic systems with respect to quantitative properties specified in probabilistic temporal logics. Model checking methods are not directly applicable to infinite-state systems, and techniques for infinite-state probabilistic systems are limited in terms of the specifications they can handle.

This paper presents a deductive approach to the verification of countable-state systems against properties specified in probabilistic CTL*, on models featuring both nondeterministic and probabilistic choices. The deductive proof system we propose lifts the classical proof system by Kesten and Pnueli to the probabilistic setting. However, the soundness arguments are completely distinct and go via the theory of martingales. Completeness results for the finite-state case and an infinite-state example illustrate the effectiveness of our approach.

## 1 Introduction

Temporal reasoning in the presence of choice and stochastic uncertainty is a fundamental problem in many domains. In the context of finite-state systems, such reasoning can be automated and a long line of research in probabilistic model checking has culminated in efficient tools that implement automatic model checking algorithms for Markov decision processes with specifications given in probabilistic temporal logics such as PCTL and PCTL* [2,7–9,20,26]. When it comes to infinite-state systems, though, reasoning about probabilistic systems, barring a few special classes of properties such as safety or almost-sure termination, is mostly ad hoc. This is unfortunate, since many probabilistic systems are a priori infinite-state. For example, randomized distributed algorithms are often designed to work no matter how many agents participate in the system. Discrete time stochastic dynamical systems arising in control assume continuous and unbounded state spaces. More recently, probabilistic programming languages augment "normal" programming languages (with unbounded variables) with the ability to sample from probability distributions and to condition behaviors on

© Springer-Verlag Berlin Heidelberg 2016
M. Chechik and J.-F. Raskin (Eds.): TACAS 2016, LNCS 9636, pp. 280–296, 2016.
DOI: 10.1007/978-3-662-49674-9_16

observations. We would like to formally reason about the temporal behavior of these systems, but the current literature provides little direction.

In this paper, we extend the deductive approach to temporal logic verification to systems that combine non-determinism and probabilistic choice with the (quantitative) probabilistic temporal logic PCTL\*. Our central contribution is a novel set of proof rules enabling deductive proofs for PCTL and PCTL\* properties on nondeterministic probabilistic programs with possibly infinite state space. We consider both qualitative and quantitative properties, and use martingale theory as our main mathematical tool. Conceptually, the rules we present for PCTL and PCTL\* can be considered as a probabilistic enhancements of those developed by Kesten and Pnueli for CTL and CTL\* [19]. At its core, the enhancement echoes the apparent analogy between classical *termination* proofs and proofs for *almost sure termination* of probabilistic programs. The latter was first studied in the pioneering work of Hart, Sharir, and Pnueli [16] as a particular liveness property. Their 0-1 law is the foundation of several semi-automatic approaches (e.g. [12,17,21]) for proving termination of finite and parametric systems. Pnueli [22] showed that the almost sure satisfaction of liveness properties on probabilistic systems can be reduced to the non-probabilistic case adding suitable fairness constraints. Pnueli and Zuck [1,23] later extended this approach to a sound and complete characterization for finite state spaces. Almost sure properties do not depend on the actual probability values, but instead on the underlying graph structure. In contrast to this, the deductive rules developed in this paper do not rely on the graph structure. They instead reason about and deduce the "average" behaviour of the program. This makes it possible to analyse a considerably wider range of probabilistic programs and properties. We make use of Lyapunov ranking functions, a widely used technique for proving recurrence in Markov Chains. They were recently adapted to prove almost sure termination of term rewriting systems [5] and infinite-state (non)deterministic programs [6,13]. We extend these techniques to full quantitative PCTL\*.

When stretching the deductive approach of Kesten and Pnueli beyond PCTL, we must account for path formulas that describe $\omega$-regular languages. In the non-probabilistic setting, Kesten and Pnueli reduce the reasoning about $\omega$-regular properties to reasoning about safety or reachability under a *justice* assumption (justice is a form of fairness [15]). In the probabilistic setting, however, this reduction is unsound: a probabilistic program may not have any fair scheduler, thus the quantification over all fair schedulers is trivially satisfied, regardless of the original formula being invalid. The root cause of the problem is that a scheduler in the probabilistic setting generates a set of paths, opposed to just a single path in the non-probabilistic case. So, if a non-null set of paths is not fair, then the scheduler is not fair. To overcome this, we instead harvest and extend the martingale approach to checking qualitative termination [6,13] with the power to directly handle general $\omega$-regular conditions. This is achieved by a proof rule for Streett conditions which is complete in the finite-state case. The key step to prove soundness uses Levy's 0-1 law [11] to go to the limit behavior.

For finite-state systems, the proof rules we present are complete, but they are in general not complete for infinite-state systems. Technically, incompleteness is inherited from the fact that Lyapunov ranking functions are not complete for proving almost sure termination [13], in contrast to ranking functions wrt. ordinary termination. If they were complete, we would instantly obtain a completeness result, just as Kesten and Pnueli. However, even an incomplete set of proof rules can turn out to be very useful still, provided it can be effectively applied to interesting cases. For example, we can verify several parameterized randomized distributed algorithms, such as the choice coordination protocol by Rabin [24] using our proof system [10].

## 2    Probabilistic Systems and Logics

### 2.1    Probabilistic Systems

*Preliminaries.* A *probability space* [11] is a triple $(\Omega, \mathcal{F}, \mu)$ where $\Omega$ is a *sample space*, $\mathcal{F} \subseteq 2^{\Omega}$ is a $\sigma$-algebra, and $\mu : \mathcal{F} \to [0, 1]$ is a probability measure. A *random variable* $X : \mathcal{F} \to \mathbb{R}$ on a probability space $(\Omega, \mathcal{F}, \mu)$ is a Borel-measurable function; it is *discrete* if there exists a countable set $A$ such that $\mu(X^{-1}(A)) = 1$. A *random predicate* is a discrete random variable with co-domain $\{0, 1\}$.

Given a probability space $(\Omega, \mathcal{F}, \mu)$, random predicates $P_1, \ldots, P_{n+1}$, real numbers $q_1, \ldots, q_n$, and binary relations $\bowtie_1, \ldots, \bowtie_n \in \{\leq, <, \geq, >, =\}$, the predicate $P_1 \otimes_{\bowtie_1 q_1} \cdots \otimes_{\bowtie_n q_n} P_{n+1}$ is valid iff there exist disjoint measurable sets $A_1, \ldots A_{n+1}$ with $\mu(A_1 \cup \ldots \cup A_{n+1}) = 1$ such that for all $k \in \{1, \ldots, n\}$, we have $A_k \models P_k$ and $\mu(A_k) \bowtie_k q_k$, and for $n + 1$ we have $A_{n+1} \models P_{n+1}$.

In case of a countable sample space $\Omega$, the powerset $\mathcal{P}(\Omega)$ is a $\sigma$-algebra; $Distr(\Omega)$ is the set of probability measures over $\mathcal{P}(\Omega)$; and for all $\mu \in Distr(\Omega)$ $Supp(\mu)$ denotes the set $\{\omega \in \Omega \mid \mu(\omega) > 0\}$.

*Probabilistic Guarded Commands.* We model probabilistic systems as programs in a probabilistic guarded-command language. A *probabilistic program* is a tuple $P = (\mathbf{x}, C)$, where $\mathbf{x}$ is a finite set of variables with countable domains and $C$ is a finite set of guarded commands. A *deterministic guarded command* is of the form $g(\mathbf{x}) \mapsto \mathbf{x}' = \mathbf{e}(\mathbf{x})$, and a *probabilistic guarded command* has the form $g(\mathbf{x}) \mapsto \mathbf{x}' = \mathbf{e}_1(\mathbf{x}) \otimes_{=p_1} \cdots \otimes_{=p_k} \mathbf{x}' = \mathbf{e}_{k+1}(\mathbf{x})$, where $p_i \in [0, 1]$ for each $1 \leq i \leq k$. The guard $g$ is a predicate over the variables $\mathbf{x}$, and $\mathbf{e}$ and all $\mathbf{e}_i$ are expressions over $\mathbf{x}$. Intuitively, a probabilistic guarded command assigns to $\mathbf{x}$ the values of the expressions $\mathbf{e}_i$ with probability $p_i$, where $p_{k+1} = 1 - \sum_{j=1}^{k} p_j$.

*Example 1.* As a running example, we consider the probabilistic model of a robot moving on a discrete plane, starting at an arbitrary position. At each step the robot performs a diagonal jump, and its goal is to visit the origin of the grid (the point with coordinates $(0, 0)$) infinitely many times. A random force repels the robot, making the visits hard. Every time the robot performs a step, there is in each dimension a certain probability for it to go backwards a certain number of steps. The probability of going back and the number of steps is a function of the robot's position; this probability is higher when the robot is close to the origin. The program has variables $l \in \{0, 1, 2\}, x \in \mathbb{Z}, y \in \mathbb{Z}$ and guarded commands:

$$c_{NE} : l = 0 \mapsto x' = x + 1 \wedge y' = y + 1 \wedge l' = 1$$
$$c_{SE} : l = 0 \mapsto x' = x + 1 \wedge y' = y - 1 \wedge l' = 1$$
$$c_{NW} : l = 0 \mapsto x' = x - 1 \wedge y' = y + 1 \wedge l' = 1$$
$$c_{SW} : l = 0 \mapsto x' = x - 1 \wedge y' = y - 1 \wedge l' = 1$$

$$c_x : l = 1 \mapsto (x' = x + 9 \cdot \text{sign}(x) \otimes_{=\frac{1}{|x|+1}} x' = x) \wedge y' = y \wedge l' = 2$$
$$c_y : l = 2 \mapsto (y' = y + 9 \cdot \text{sign}(y) \otimes_{=\frac{1}{|y|+1}} y' = y) \wedge x' = x \wedge l' = 0$$

The first four commands, enabled in location $l = 0$, correspond to the different jump directions of the robot (which controls the non-deterministic choices) can select. Locations $l = 1$ and $l = 2$ model the effect of the random repelling forces along the $x$ and $y$ co-ordinates, respectively. We assume that the force in the $x$-axis is independent from the one in the $y$-axis. Despite its simplicity, this problem cannot be solved using probabilistic model checking (the state space is infinite), nor using current deductive proof systems based on fairness (the probability values do matter). The proof system described in this paper, on the other hand, allows us to provide a simple and *modular* correctness argument.    □

*Semantics of Probabilistic Programs.* The semantics of a probabilistic program $P = (\mathbf{x}, C)$ is a Markov decision process (MDP) $M = (S, \rho)$ [14]. The countable set of states $S$ consists of the valuations of the variables $\mathbf{x}$ and $\rho : S \to \mathcal{P}(Distr(S))$ is the transition relation defined by the guarded commands in $C$. For a state $s \in S$ we have $\mu \in \rho(s)$ iff either (1) there exists a deterministic guarded command $c : g \mapsto \mathbf{x}' = \mathbf{e}$ in $C$ such that $s \models g$, and for every $s' \in S$ it holds that $\mu(s') = 1$ if $s' = \mathbf{e}(s)$, and $\mu(s') = 0$ otherwise, where $\mathbf{e}(s)$ denotes the value of the expression $\mathbf{e}$ when the variables $\mathbf{x}$ are evaluated according to $s$, or (2) there exists a probabilistic guarded command $c : g \mapsto \mathbf{x}' = \mathbf{e}_1 \otimes_{=p_1} \ldots \otimes_{=p_k} \mathbf{x}' = \mathbf{e}_{k+1}$ in $C$ such that $s \models g$, and for every $s' \in S$ it holds that $\mu(s') = \sum_{s'=\mathbf{e}_i(s)} p_i$. We assume w.l.o.g. that all programs are deadlock-free, i.e. $\rho(s) \neq \emptyset$. Note that with each state $s$ and each command $c \in C$ with $s \models g_c$, where with $g_c$ we denote the guard of $c$, the transition relation $\rho$ associates a unique distribution $\mu_{s,c}$.

A *path* in $M$ is a finite or infinite sequence $s_0, s_1, \ldots$ of states in $S$ such that for each $i$ there exists $\mu \in \rho(s_i)$, such that $\mu(s_{i+1}) > 0$. Given a state $s \in S$, we denote with $\text{Paths}(M, s)$ the set of paths in $M$ originating in the state $s$.

*Schedulers.* A *scheduler* is a function $\alpha : S^+ \to Distr(C)$ such that $\alpha(\tau \cdot s)(c) > 0$ implies $\mu_{s,c} \in \rho(s)$. We call $\alpha$ *memoryless* if $\alpha(\tau_1 \cdot s) = \alpha(\tau_2 \cdot s)$ for all $\tau_1, \tau_2 \in S^*$ and $s \in S$. A scheduler $\alpha$ is *deterministic* if $|Supp(\alpha(\tau))| = 1$ for all $\tau \in S^+$.

Given a probabilistic program $P = (\mathbf{x}, C)$ with a corresponding MDP $M = (S, \rho)$, a scheduler $\alpha$ defines a discrete time Markov chain (DTMC) $M_\alpha = (S^\alpha, \rho^\alpha)$, where $S^\alpha = S^* \times S$ is the state space and $\rho^\alpha : S^\alpha \to Distr(S^\alpha)$

is the Markov kernel defined as $\rho^\alpha((\tau, s), (\tau', s')) = \sum \rho(s, c, s') \cdot (\alpha(\tau \cdot s)(c))$ if $\tau' = \tau \cdot s$ and $\rho^\alpha((\tau, s), (\tau', s')) = 0$ otherwise. From any initial state $s \in S$ we can define a *unique* probability measure $Prob_{s,\alpha}$ over the set of infinite measurable paths that start at $s$ and obey the probability laws of $\rho^\alpha$ [11].

*Example 2.* One possible strategy for the robot is to always choose in location $l = 0$ to decrease (when not accounting for the repelling force) the distance to the origin: if $x < 0$ and $y < 0$ then choose $c_{NE}$, if $x < 0$ and $y \geq 0$ then choose $c_{SE}$, if $x \geq 0$ and $y < 0$ then choose $c_{NW}$, and if $x \geq 0$ and $y \geq 0$ then choose $c_{SW}$. □

## 2.2   The Logics PCTL and PCTL*

We work with a simple variant of probabilistic computation tree logic (PCTL) in positive normal form [2]. Fix a set $AP$ of *assertions* from an underlying assertion language closed under Boolean operations. The set of PCTL formulas over $AP$ consists of two types of formulas: *state formulas* and *path formulas*.

State formulas are generated by the grammar $\Phi ::= a \mid \neg a \mid \Phi_1 \wedge \Phi_2 \mid \Phi_1 \vee \Phi_2 \mid \mathbb{P}^\forall_{\bowtie p}(\varphi) \mid \mathbb{P}^\exists_{\bowtie p}(\varphi)$, where $a \in AP$, $\Phi_1$ and $\Phi_2$ are state formulas, $\bowtie \in \{\leq, <, \geq, >\}$, $p \in \mathbb{R}_{\geq 0}$, and $\varphi$ is a path formula. Path formulas are generated by the grammar $\varphi ::= \bigcirc \Phi \mid \Phi_1 \mathcal{U} \Phi_2 \mid \Phi_1 \mathcal{R} \Phi_2$, where $\Phi, \Phi_1, \Phi_2$ are state formulas. $\mathcal{U}$ and $\mathcal{R}$ are the until and release operators of linear temporal logic (LTL), respectively. Recall that $\mathcal{R}$ is the dual of $\mathcal{U}$, that is, $\varphi \mathcal{R} \psi$ is equivalent to $\neg(\neg\varphi \mathcal{U} \neg\psi)$. As usual, we define the derived operators $\Diamond \varphi = \mathsf{tt} \mathcal{U} \varphi$ and $\Box \varphi = \neg \Diamond \neg \varphi = \mathsf{ff} \mathcal{R} \varphi$.

The logic PCTL* generalizes PCTL by allowing $\omega$-regular languages over state formulas as path formulas. Let $\Phi$ be a PCTL* state formula. We call $\Phi$ a *basic state formula* if it is of the form or $\mathbb{P}^\delta_{\bowtie p}(\varphi)$ where $\delta \in \{\exists, \forall\}$ and $\varphi$ is a PCTL* path formula which contains no probabilistic quantifiers (i.e. $\varphi$ is an LTL formula). In the case when $\Phi$ is a PCTL formula, $\varphi$ contains exactly one temporal operator, at the top level. We consider a presentation of PCTL* in which LTL formulas are given as *deterministic Streett automata* whose alphabet consists of sets of state formulas.[1] Recall that the set of accepting paths of a Streett automaton is measurable [7,26].

The *qualitative* versions of PCTL and PCTL* restrict the constants $p$ in $\mathbb{P}^\delta_{\bowtie p}(\varphi)$ to the set $\{0, 1\}$.

*Semantics.* Let $P = (\mathbf{x}, C)$ be a probabilistic program and $M = (S, \rho)$ be the corresponding MDP. Let $AP$ consist of assertions over the variables $\mathbf{x}$.

PCTL* state formulas are interpreted over states of $M$, while path formulas are interpreted over paths. The satisfaction relations $\models$ are defined as usual for assertions, boolean and temporal operators [2]. Formulas containing the operators $\mathbb{P}^\forall$ and $\mathbb{P}^\exists$ are interpreted using a probability measure over sets of paths. More specifically, the satisfaction of $\mathbb{P}^\forall_{\bowtie p}(\varphi)$ (resp., $\mathbb{P}^\exists_{\bowtie p}(\varphi)$)

---

[1] Usually, path formulas in PCTL* are defined using linear temporal logic (LTL) [2]. Since the analysis of PCTL* proceeds by first converting LTL to a deterministic automaton, we omit the intermediate step of converting LTL to automata and assume the path formulas are given as deterministic Streett automata.

in a state $s$ is determined by the probability measures of the sets of paths $\{\tau \in \mathsf{Paths}(M_\alpha, s) \mid M_\alpha, \tau \models \varphi\}$ where $\alpha$ ranges over all (resp., some) possible schedulers, each of which defines a DTMC in which these sets are measurable. Formally,

$$P, s \models \mathbb{P}^\forall_{\bowtie p}(\varphi) \text{ iff } Prob_{s,\alpha}(\{\tau \in \mathsf{Paths}(M_\alpha, s) \mid M_\alpha, \tau \models \varphi\}) \bowtie p$$
$$\text{for every scheduler } \alpha \text{ inducing a DTMC } M_\alpha,$$
$$P, s \models \mathbb{P}^\exists_{\bowtie p}(\varphi) \text{ iff } Prob_{s,\alpha}(\{\tau \in \mathsf{Paths}(M_\alpha, s) \mid M_\alpha, \tau \models \varphi\}) \bowtie p$$
$$\text{for some scheduler } \alpha \text{ inducing a DTMC } M_\alpha.$$

For convenience we use $P \models \Phi$ as an abbreviation for $P, s \models \Phi$ for all $s$. Finally, we note that both PCTL and PCTL* are effectively closed under negation.

# 3 A Deductive Proof System for PCTL

We now develop a deductive proof system for PCTL. We do this in three steps. First, we introduce some basic rules. Then, we show how to reason about qualitative formulas. Finally, we introduce rules for the full logic. For a probabilistic program $P$ and a PCTL state formula $\Phi$, we write the judgement $P \vdash \Phi$ to state that the proof system derives that program $P$ satisfies $\Phi$ from every state.

We assume that we can establish validities in the underlying assertion language (first order logic, or a fragment of it) plus probabilities.

## 3.1 Preliminary Rules

Figure 1 shows the preliminary rules of our proof systems for PCTL and PCTL*.

The rule BASIC-STATE allows us to reduce the verification of $\Phi$ to the verification of formulas of the form $\pi \to \Psi$, where $\pi$ is an assertion and $\Psi$ is a basic state formula. A basic state formula $\Psi$ occurring one or more times in $\Phi$ can be replaced by an assertion $\pi$ which underapproximates the set of states satisfying the state formula $\Psi$. The rule's soundness is shown by induction. By successively applying the rule BASIC-STATE, in a bottom up manner, a proof obligation $P \vdash \Phi$ reduces to a set of proof obligations that are of the form $P \vdash \pi \to \Psi$, where $\Psi$ is a basic state formula. We assume this form in subsequent rules.

The other rules lift proof rules of propositional logic to the probabilistic setting. The rule GEN concludes that a valid assertion (a tautology) holds in every state of a program $P$. The rules AND (resp. OR) formalize the distributivity of conjunction w. r. t. universal almost sure satisfaction (resp. the distributivity of disjunction w. r. t. existential satisfaction with positive probability).

*Remark 1.* For the rule MP in the existential case we must ensure that the scheduler from the second premise satisfies $\varphi$ with probability 1. With an existential quantifier in the first premise we cannot guarantee that both schedulers are the same. This problem is also present in other proof rules. For simplicity of presentation, we impose a stronger condition that requires that $\varphi$ is satisfied regardless of the resolution of the nondeterminism. Alternately, we could have a monolithic proof rule that combines the proof rules for the premises. The price would be more complex proof rules and lack of modularity.

$$\frac{\text{assertion } \pi}{P \vdash \Phi[\Psi/\pi]} \qquad \frac{\theta \text{ is a valid assertion}}{P \vdash \theta}\text{GEN}$$

$$\frac{P \vdash \pi \to \Psi}{P \vdash \Phi}\text{BASIC-STATE}$$

$$\frac{\begin{array}{c} P \vdash \pi \to \mathbb{P}^{\forall}_{=1}(\varphi) \\ P \vdash \pi \to \mathbb{P}^{\circlearrowright}_{=1}(\varphi \to \psi) \end{array}}{P \vdash \pi \to \mathbb{P}^{\circlearrowright}_{=1}(\psi)}\text{MP}$$

$$\frac{\begin{array}{c} P \vdash \pi \to \mathbb{P}^{\forall}_{=1}(\varphi_1) \\ P \vdash \pi \to \mathbb{P}^{\forall}_{=1}(\varphi_2) \end{array}}{P \vdash \pi \to \mathbb{P}^{\forall}_{=1}(\varphi_1 \wedge \varphi_2)}\text{AND} \qquad \frac{\begin{array}{c} P \vdash \pi \to \mathbb{P}^{\exists}_{>0}(\varphi_1) \\ P \vdash \pi \to \mathbb{P}^{\exists}_{>0}(\varphi_2) \end{array}}{P \vdash \pi \to \mathbb{P}^{\exists}_{>0}(\varphi_1 \vee \varphi_2)}\text{OR}$$

**Fig. 1.** Preliminary rules for $\circlearrowright \in \{\exists, \forall\}$, state formula $\Phi$ and path formulas $\varphi_1, \varphi_2, \varphi, \psi$.

## 3.2 Proof Rules for Qualitative PCTL

Figure 2 shows rules for the qualitative fragment. Since we consider basic state formulas, the formulas $\varphi$ and $\psi$ in these rules are assertions. Using the duality between $\mathbb{P}^{\forall}$ and $\mathbb{P}^{\exists}$, and the closure of PCTL and PCTL* under negation, it is sufficient to restrict attention to the operators $\mathbb{P}^{\forall}_{=1}$, $\mathbb{P}^{\forall}_{>0}$, $\mathbb{P}^{\exists}_{=1}$, and $\mathbb{P}^{\exists}_{>0}$.

The rules use (Lyapunov) ranking functions. For a DTMC $(S^{\alpha}, \rho^{\alpha})$ and a well-founded set $(A, \succ)$, a function $\delta : S^{\alpha} \to A$ is a *ranking function* if $\delta$ decreases on each step, i.e., for each path $s, s'$, we have $\delta(s) \succ \delta(s')$. A function $\delta : S^{\alpha} \to \mathbb{R}_{\geq 0}$ is a *Lyapunov ranking function* if $\delta$ decreases in expectation on each step, i.e., $\delta(s) \succ \mathbb{E}(\delta' \mid s) = \sum_{s' \in S^{\alpha}} \delta(s')\rho^{\alpha}(s, s')$ for all states $s \in S^{\alpha}$.

assertion $\theta$
Lyapunov ranking function $\delta$

$$\frac{\begin{array}{c} P \vdash \pi \wedge \neg\psi \to \theta \\ P \vdash \theta \wedge \neg\psi \to \varphi \\ P \vdash \theta \wedge \neg\psi \to \\ (\circlearrowright c \in C : g_c : \theta' \wedge \delta \succ \mathbb{E}(\delta' \mid s)) \end{array}}{P \vdash \pi \to \mathbb{P}^{\circlearrowright}_{=1}(\varphi \, \mathcal{U} \, \psi)}\text{UNTIL}^{\circlearrowright}_{=1}$$

assertion $\theta$

$$\frac{\begin{array}{c} P \vdash \pi \to \theta \\ P \vdash \theta \to \varphi \\ P \vdash \theta \wedge \neg\psi \to (\circlearrowright c \in C : g_c : \theta') \end{array}}{P \vdash \pi \to \mathbb{P}^{\circlearrowright}_{=1}(\psi \, \mathcal{R} \, \varphi)}\text{INV}^{\circlearrowright}_{=1}$$

assertion $\theta$
ranking function $\delta$

$$\frac{\begin{array}{c} P \vdash \pi \wedge \neg\psi \to \theta \\ P \vdash \theta \wedge \neg\psi \to \varphi \\ P \vdash \theta \wedge \neg\psi \to \\ (\circlearrowright c \in C : g_c : (\theta' \wedge \delta \succ \delta') \otimes_{>0} \mathsf{tt}) \end{array}}{P \vdash \pi \to \mathbb{P}^{\circlearrowright}_{>0}(\varphi \, \mathcal{U} \, \psi)}\text{UNTIL}^{\circlearrowright}_{>0}$$

assertion $\theta$

$$\frac{\begin{array}{c} P \vdash \theta \to \varphi \\ P \vdash \pi \to \mathbb{P}^{\circlearrowright}_{>0}(\varphi \, \mathcal{U} \, \theta) \\ P \vdash \theta \to \mathbb{P}^{\circlearrowright}_{=1}(\psi \, \mathcal{R} \, \theta) \end{array}}{P \vdash \pi \to \mathbb{P}^{\circlearrowright}_{>0}(\psi \, \mathcal{R} \, \varphi)}\text{INV}^{\circlearrowright}_{>0}$$

$$\frac{P \vdash \pi \to (\circlearrowright c \in C : g_c : \varphi')}{P \vdash \pi \to \mathbb{P}^{\circlearrowright}_{=1}(\bigcirc \varphi)}\text{NEXT}^{\circlearrowright}_{=1} \qquad \frac{P \vdash \pi \to (\circlearrowright c \in C : g_c : \varphi' \otimes_{>0} \mathsf{tt})}{P \vdash \pi \to \mathbb{P}^{\circlearrowright}_{>0}(\bigcirc \varphi)}\text{NEXT}^{\circlearrowright}_{>0}$$

**Fig. 2.** Proof rules for qualitative properties, where $\circlearrowright \in \{\exists, \forall\}$. The quantification $(\circlearrowright c \in C : g_c : \chi(\mathbf{x})$ stands for $\bigwedge_{c \in C}(g_c(\mathbf{x})) \to \chi(\mathbf{x}))$ if $\circlearrowright = \forall$ and for $\bigvee_{c \in C}(g_c(\mathbf{x}) \wedge \chi(\mathbf{x}))$ if $\circlearrowright = \exists$. The primed versions of assertions and expressions are obtained by replacing primed variables by the values assigned by the respective guarded command.

We extend (Lyapunov) ranking functions to MDPs by quantifying over the set of enabled commands.

The rule $\text{UNTIL}^{\circlearrowleft}_{=1}$ establishes almost sure liveness properties for states in some set of initial states described by $\pi$. The rule is standard: the premises require an assertion $\theta$ that defines an inductive invariant and a Lyapunov ranking function that decreases in expectation when taking transitions from $\theta$-states that do not satisfy the target assertion $\psi$. The rule $\text{INV}^{\circlearrowleft}_{=1}$ establishes almost sure invariance properties. In the case of universal quantification the rule corresponds to the respective rule for CTL, while the existence of a scheduler is equivalent to the existence of a winning strategy in a (non-probabilistic) safety game.

The proof rule $\text{UNTIL}^{\circlearrowleft}_{>0}$ allows us to establish liveness properties with positive probability. Here, the rule for the existential case corresponds to the one for CTL, while in the universal case the verification question is equivalent to the question about the existence of a strategy in a (non-probabilistic) reachability game. The proof rule $\text{INV}^{\circlearrowleft}_{>0}$ establishes invariance properties. The premises of this rule are rather strong: they require reaching with positive probability a set of states in which the temporal property holds almost surely. In Sect. 5.1 we give a weaker rule, for the (more general) case of satisfaction with probability at least $p$.

The rules $\text{NEXT}^{\circlearrowleft}_{=1}$ and $\text{NEXT}^{\circlearrowleft}_{>0}$ handle the next operator in the obvious way.

Consider a proof obligation $P \vdash \pi \rightarrow \Psi$, where $\pi$ is an assertion (which can be tt) and $\Psi$ is a basic state formula. By applying a rule corresponding to the temporal operator in $\Psi$ we can reduce the proof obligation to a set of state validities $P \vdash \theta$ where $\theta$ is an assertion. Such proof obligations can be discharged by applying the rule GEN using a solver for the respective logical theory.

The proof system $\mathcal{P}_{\text{qualitative}}$ consists of the proof rules GEN, BASIC-STATE, $\text{UNTIL}^{\circlearrowleft}_{=1}$, $\text{INV}^{\circlearrowleft}_{=1}$, $\text{NEXT}^{\circlearrowleft}_{=1}$, $\text{UNTIL}^{\circlearrowleft}_{>0}$, $\text{INV}^{\circlearrowleft}_{>0}$ and $\text{NEXT}^{\circlearrowleft}_{>0}$. The soundness of the proof system is proven by relatively standard reasoning. We defer the discussion about (in)completeness to Sect. 5.2.

**Proposition 1.** $\mathcal{P}_{\text{qualitative}}$ *is sound: if $P \vdash \varphi$ in $\mathcal{P}_{\text{qualitative}}$, then $P \models \varphi$.*

*Example 3.* Consider the probabilistic system $P$ from Example 1. We want to prove $P \models \text{tt} \rightarrow \mathbb{P}^{\exists}_{=1}(\Diamond \varphi_{close})$, where $\varphi_{close} \equiv |x| + |y| \leq 100$. Take the strategy which at location $l = 0$ selects the only command satisfying $x' = x - \text{sign}(x) \wedge y' = y - \text{sign}(y)$. Using rule $\text{UNTIL}^{\exists}_{=1}$, we have to find a Lyapunov ranking function $\delta$ that decreases in expectation whenever $\varphi_{close}$ is not satisfied and we execute a command from the chosen strategy. Take the following function

$$\delta(l, x, y) = \begin{cases} x^2 + y^2 & \text{if } l = 0, \\ x^2 + y^2 + 120 & \text{if } l = 1, \\ x^2 + y^2 + 60 & \text{if } l = 2. \end{cases}$$

We analyse the behaviour of $\mathbb{E}(\delta' \mid x, y)$. At $l = 0$ we have $\mathbb{E}(x'^2 + y'^2 \mid x, y) = x^2 + y^2 - 2 \cdot (|x| + |y|) + 2 \leq x^2 + y^2 - 198$. For the unique command at $l = 1$ we have $\mathbb{E}(x'^2 + y'^2 \mid x, y) = x^2 + y^2 + \frac{18|x| + 9^2}{|x| + 1} \leq x^2 + y^2 + 59$. The case $l = 2$ is similar. $\square$

## 3.3  Full PCTL

Figure 3 introduces proof rules for quantitative probabilities. The rule $\text{INV}^{\diamond}_{\bowtie p}$ for quantitative invariance is defined analogously to the respective rule for satisfaction with positive probability. The rule $\text{NEXT}^{\diamond}_{\bowtie p}$ for the next operator can be defined in the obvious way, thus it is omitted here.

The rule $\text{UNTIL}^{\diamond}_{\geq p}$ establishes quantitative liveness properties. Its premises require two auxiliary assertions $\theta$ and $\theta_{\geq p}$ such that from each $\theta_{\geq p}$-state the set $\theta$ is almost surely reachable, and every time a $\theta$-state is reached a Bernoulli trial is executed. By adapting the premises to use bound $p + \Delta$ for some $\Delta > 0$, we can easily obtain a rule for strict inequalities.

The proof rules $\text{UNTIL}^{\diamond}_{\geq p^m}$ and $\text{UNTIL}^{\diamond}_{\leq p^m}$ are slightly more complex. They allow us to prove properties of the form $\mathbb{P}^{\diamond}_{\bowtie q}(\varphi \mathcal{U} \psi)$ provided the bound $q$ has a specific form. The rule $\text{UNTIL}^{\diamond}_{\geq p^m}$ requires a ranking function which is initially bounded from above by $m$ and which decreases at each step with probability at least $p$, thus guaranteeing that the target set of states is reached with probability at least $p^m$. The rule $\text{UNTIL}^{\diamond}_{\leq p^m}$ establishes that an until formula is satisfied with probability at most $p^m$, by requiring a ranking function that is initially bounded from below by $m$ and is such that in order to reach 0 there should be at least $m$

assertions $\theta_{\geq p}, \theta$,     real number $\varepsilon > 0$
$$P \vdash \pi \wedge \neg\psi \to \theta_{\geq p}$$
$$P \vdash \theta_{\geq p} \to \neg\psi$$
$$P \vdash \theta_{\geq p} \to \mathbb{P}^{\diamond}_{=1}(\varphi \mathcal{U} \theta)$$
$$P \vdash \theta \to \varphi \wedge \theta_{\geq p}$$
$$P \vdash \theta \to (\diamond c \in C : g_c :$$
$$(\exists q : q \geq \varepsilon : \psi' \otimes_{\geq pq} \neg\theta'_{\geq p} \otimes_{=q} \text{tt}))$$
$$\overline{P \vdash \pi \to \mathbb{P}^{\diamond}_{\geq p}(\varphi \mathcal{U} \psi)} \text{UNTIL}^{\diamond}_{\geq p}$$

$$P \vdash \pi \to \mathbb{P}^{\diamond}_{\bowtie p}(\varphi \mathcal{U} \theta)$$
$$P \vdash \theta \to \mathbb{P}^{\diamond}_{=1}(\psi \mathcal{R} \varphi)$$
$$\overline{P \vdash \pi \to \mathbb{P}^{\diamond}_{\bowtie p}(\psi \mathcal{R} \varphi)} \text{INV}^{\diamond}_{\bowtie p}$$

assertion $\theta$,    ranking function $\delta$
$$P \vdash \pi \wedge \neg\psi \to \theta$$
$$P \vdash \pi \wedge \neg\psi \to \delta \leq m$$
$$P \vdash \theta \wedge \neg\psi \to \varphi$$
$$P \vdash \theta \wedge \neg\psi \to (\diamond c \in C : g_c :$$
$$(\delta' = \delta - 1 \wedge \theta') \otimes_{\geq p} \text{tt})$$
$$\overline{P \vdash \pi \to \mathbb{P}^{\diamond}_{\geq p^m}(\varphi \mathcal{U} \psi)} \text{UNTIL}^{\diamond}_{\geq p^m}$$

assertions $\theta, \overline{\theta}$,   r.f. $\delta$
$$P \vdash \pi \to \theta$$
$$P \vdash \pi \to \delta \geq m$$
$$P \vdash \overline{\theta} \to \mathbb{P}^{\diamond}_{=1}(\neg\varphi \mathcal{R} \neg\psi)$$
$$P \vdash \theta \wedge \neg\overline{\theta} \wedge \delta > 0 \to \varphi \wedge \neg\psi$$
$$P \vdash \theta \wedge \neg\overline{\theta} \to (\diamond c \in C : g_c :$$
$$(\theta' \wedge \delta \leq \delta') \vee$$
$$((\theta' \wedge \delta' = \delta - 1) \otimes_{\leq p} \overline{\theta'}))$$
$$\overline{P \vdash \pi \to \mathbb{P}^{\diamond}_{\leq p^m}(\varphi \mathcal{U} \psi)} \text{UNTIL}^{\diamond}_{\leq p^m}$$

assertion $\theta$
$$P \vdash \pi \to \mathbb{P}^{\vee}_{\leq p}(\diamond \theta)$$
$$P \vdash \pi \to \mathbb{P}^{\vee}_{=1}(\varphi \mathcal{U}(\theta \vee \psi))$$
$$\overline{P \vdash \pi \to \mathbb{P}^{\vee}_{\geq 1-p}(\varphi \mathcal{U} \psi)} \text{UNTIL}^{\vee}_{\geq 1-p}$$

assertion $\theta$
$$P \vdash \pi \to \mathbb{P}^{\diamond}_{\geq p_1}(\varphi \mathcal{U} \theta)$$
$$P \vdash \theta \to \mathbb{P}^{\diamond}_{\geq p_2}(\varphi \mathcal{U} \psi)$$
$$\overline{P \vdash \pi \to \mathbb{P}^{\diamond}_{\geq p_1 \cdot p_2}(\varphi \mathcal{U} \psi)} \text{UNTIL}^{\diamond}_{\geq p_1 \cdot p_2}$$

**Fig. 3.** Proof rules for $\mathbb{P}^{\diamond}_{\bowtie p}$ for $p > 0$ and $\diamond \in \{\exists, \forall\}$.

occurrences of a command that has probability of at least $1-p$ of going to a set of states from which the formula cannot be satisfied. Rule $\text{UNTIL}^\forall_{\geq 1-p}$ combines $\text{UNTIL}^\exists_{\geq p^m}$ and $\text{UNTIL}^\circlearrowright_{\geq 1}$. Rule $\text{UNTIL}^\circlearrowright_{\geq p_1 \cdot p_2}$ lets us "chain" reachability proofs.

The proof system $\mathcal{P}_{\text{quantitative}}$ consists of the rules in the proof system $\mathcal{P}_{\text{qualitative}}$ together with the rules in Fig. 3 and the rule $\text{NEXT}^\circlearrowright_{\bowtie p}$ (omitted here).

**Proposition 2.** $\mathcal{P}_{\text{quantitative}}$ *is sound: if* $P \vdash \varphi$ *in* $\mathcal{P}_{\text{quantitative}}$, *then* $P \models \varphi$.

*Example 4.* Consider the probabilistic system from Example 1. Here we show that $P \models \varphi_{close} \to \mathbb{P}^\exists_{\geq p}(\Diamond(x = 0 \land y = 0))$, i.e., we want to find a lower bound on the probability of reaching the origin from any state in $\varphi_{close}$. Using rule $\text{UNTIL}^\exists_{\geq p^m}$ it is enough to find a ranking function that is bounded in $\varphi_{close}$ and such that the probability of decreasing by one has a uniform lower bound in $\varphi_{close}$. For brevity, we consider a variant where the decision of the robot and the repelling disturbances occur at once, not sequentially. Then, the ranking function

$$\delta(l, x, y) = \begin{cases} \max(|x|, |y|) & \text{if } x \equiv y \mod 2 \\ \max(|x|, |y|) + 5 & \text{if } x \not\equiv y \mod 2. \end{cases}$$

fullfils the requirements. When both coordinates have the same parity and one of them is not 0, it is always possible to decrease $\delta$ by selecting a proper command and assuming that the robot is not repelled in any direction. In case that they have different parity we have to consider the case when the robot is repelled in the coordinate with the largest absolute value. The lower bound is then $p = \frac{1}{101^2}$ as we have $|x|, |y| \leq 100$ for the states satisfying $\varphi_{close}$.    □

## 4    Proof System for PCTL*

The proof rules presented in Sect. 3 are applicable to the PCTL fragment of PCTL*. We now extend the proof system $\mathcal{P}_{\text{quantitative}}$ to reason about PCTL*.

The scope of the rules in Fig. 1, and in particular BASIC-STATE, is not limited to PCTL. Thus, the rule BASIC-STATE can be applied to a PCTL* formula to arrive at a PCTL* formula $\mathbb{P}^\circlearrowright_{\bowtie p}(\varphi)$, where the formula $\varphi$ is a Streett automaton representing an $\omega$-regular language over the alphabet of sets of assertions.

*Streett Automata, Product Construction.* Let $AP$ be a finite set of assertions over **x**. A *deterministic Streett automaton* is a tuple $\mathcal{A} = (Q, \Sigma, \rho, q_0, \{(E_i, F_i)\}_{i=1}^k)$, where $Q$ is a finite set of states, $\Sigma \subseteq 2^{AP}$ is a finite input alphabet, $\rho \subseteq Q \times \Sigma \times Q$ is a transition relation, such that if $(q, \sigma_1, q_1) \in \rho$ and $(q, \sigma_2, q_2) \in \rho$ and $q_1 \neq q_2$ then $\varphi_{\sigma_1} \land \varphi_{\sigma_2}$ is unsatisfiable, where $\varphi_\sigma = (\bigwedge_{\theta \in \sigma} \theta) \land (\bigwedge_{\theta \in AP \setminus \sigma} \neg\theta)$ for $\sigma \in \Sigma$, $q_0 \in Q$ is the initial state, and for all $i = 1, \ldots, k$, $E_i \subseteq Q$ and $F_i \subseteq Q$.

A run of $\mathcal{A}$ on an infinite sequence of states (valuations of the variables **x**) $\tau \in S^\omega$ is a sequence $\eta \in Q^\omega$ of automaton states such that $\eta[0] = q_0$ and for every $i \geq 0$ there exists $\sigma \in \Sigma$ such that $(\eta[i], \sigma, \eta[i+1]) \in \rho$ and $\tau[i] \models \varphi_\sigma$. A run $\eta$ on $\tau$ is accepting if for every $i = 1, \ldots, k$ it holds that if $\text{Inf}(\eta) \cap E_k \neq \emptyset$, then also $\text{Inf}(\eta) \cap F_k \neq \emptyset$, where $\text{Inf}(\eta) \subseteq Q$ is the set of states that occur infinitely often in $\eta$. A path $\tau$ is accepted by $\mathcal{A}$ iff there exists an accepting run of $\mathcal{A}$ on $\tau$. We write $L(\mathcal{A})$ for the set of paths accepted by $\mathcal{A}$.

Consider a probabilistic program $P = (\mathbf{x}, C)$ and a deterministic Street automaton $\mathcal{A}$ with alphabet $\Sigma$ which consists of sets of assertions over $\mathbf{x}$.

The *product of $P$ and $\mathcal{A}$* is the probabilistic program $P_{\mathcal{A}} = (\mathbf{x}^{\mathcal{A}}, C^{\mathcal{A}})$, where $\mathbf{x}^{\mathcal{A}} = \mathbf{x} \mathbin{\dot\cup} \{x_q\}$, for a fresh variable $x_q$ with domain $Q$, and $C^{\mathcal{A}}$ is the set of guarded commands defined as follows. The set $C^{\mathcal{A}}$ contains one guarded command for each pair of transition $(q, \sigma, q') \in \rho$ and probabilistic guarded command $c : g \mapsto \mathbf{x}' = \mathbf{e}_1 \otimes_{=p_1} \cdots \otimes_{=p_k} \mathbf{x}' = \mathbf{e}_{k+1}$ in $C$, where $(c, q, \sigma, q')$ is the label of the product guarded command, and the assertion $\varphi_\sigma(\mathbf{x})$ represents the letter $\sigma$: $(c, q, \sigma, q') : g_c \wedge x_q = q \wedge \varphi_\sigma(\mathbf{x}) \mapsto x_q' = q' \wedge (\mathbf{x}' = \mathbf{e}_1 \otimes_{=p_1} \cdots \otimes_{=p_k} \mathbf{x}' = \mathbf{e}_{k+1})$. Similarly, for deterministic guarded commands. For a given scheduler $\alpha$ and an initial state $s$, the set of paths of $P_{\mathcal{A}}$ on which $\mathcal{A}$ has an accepting run, denoted $Acc(P, \mathcal{A})_{\alpha, s}$, is measurable [7, 26].

*Basic Path Rule.* Given a Streett automaton $\mathcal{A}$, the rule shown in Fig. 4 reduces the proof obligation $P \vdash \pi \to \mathbb{P}^{\circlearrowright}_{\bowtie p}(L(\mathcal{A}))$ to proving a statement of the form $P \vdash \pi' \to \mathbb{P}^{\circlearrowright}_{\bowtie p}(Acc(P, \mathcal{A}))$, where $\pi'$ is an assertion.

$$\dfrac{P_{\mathcal{A}} \vdash (\pi \wedge x_q = q_0) \to \mathbb{P}^{\circlearrowright}_{\bowtie p}(Acc(P, \mathcal{A}))}{P \vdash \pi \to \mathbb{P}^{\circlearrowright}_{\bowtie p}(L(\mathcal{A}))}$$

**Fig. 4.** Rule BASIC-PATH

**Proposition 3.** *If the premises of the proof rule* BASIC-PATH *are satisfied then it holds that* $P \models \pi \to \mathbb{P}^{\circlearrowright}_{\bowtie p}(L(\mathcal{A}))$.

$$\dfrac{\begin{array}{l} \text{assertions } \theta, \overline{\theta} \\ \text{constant } p > 0 \\ P \vdash \pi \to \overline{\theta} \\ P \vdash \overline{\theta} \to \mathbb{P}^{\forall}_{=1}(\Diamond \theta) \\ P \vdash \theta \to \mathbb{P}^{\forall}_{=1}(\Box \theta) \\ P \vdash \theta \wedge \varphi \to \mathbb{P}^{\forall}_{\geq p}(\Diamond \psi) \end{array}}{P \vdash \pi \to \mathbb{P}^{\forall}_{=1}(\Box \Diamond \varphi \to \Box \Diamond \psi)} \text{REC}^{\forall}_{=1} \qquad \dfrac{\begin{array}{l} \text{assertions } \theta, \overline{\theta} \\ \text{constant } p > 0 \\ P \vdash \pi \to \overline{\theta} \\ P \vdash \overline{\theta} \to \mathbb{P}^{\exists}_{=1}(\Diamond \theta) \\ P \vdash \theta \to \mathbb{P}^{\forall}_{=1}(\Box \theta) \\ \text{for all } i = 1, \ldots, m : \\ P \vdash \theta \wedge \varphi^i \to \mathbb{P}^{\exists}_{\geq p}(\Diamond \psi^i) \end{array}}{P \vdash \pi \to \mathbb{P}^{\exists}_{=1}\left(\bigwedge_{i=1}^{m}(\Box \Diamond \varphi^i \to \Box \Diamond \psi^i)\right)} \text{REC}^{\exists}_{=1}$$

**Fig. 5.** Proof rules for almost sure repeated reachability, where $\circlearrowright \in \{\exists, \forall\}$.

*Rules for Repeated Reachability.* The Streett acceptance condition of $\mathcal{A}$ can be encoded as repeated reachability formulas of the form $\bigwedge_{i=1}^{k}(\Box \Diamond \varphi_i \to \Box \Diamond \psi_i)$, where $\varphi_i$ and $\psi_i$ are assertions over $\mathbf{x}^{\mathcal{A}}$ encoding the sets $E_i$ and $F_i$ for $i = 1, \ldots, k$. Figure 5 shows the corresponding rules for the almost sure case.

**Proposition 4 (Soundness of** $\text{REC}^{\forall}_{=1}$**).** *Rules* $\text{REC}^{\forall}_{=1}$ *and* $\text{REC}^{\exists}_{=1}$ *are sound.*

*Proof (Sketch).* We prove soundness of $\text{REC}^{\forall}_{=1}$. Fix an arbitrary scheduler $\alpha$ and consider $M_\alpha$. We can restrict the proof to the infinite paths that start in a $\theta$-state since any infinite path of $P$ eventually visits only states in $\theta$. Let $S_0, S_1, \ldots$

be the random process such that $S_k$ is the state visited after executing exactly $k$ instructions, and $\mathcal{F}_k$ be the smallest $\sigma$-algebra that makes $S_k$ measurable. Let $\Diamond^{\geq n}\psi$ denote the event $\{\exists m \geq n : S_m \in \psi\}$ and $[\mathcal{E}]$ denote the indicator function for the event $\mathcal{E}$. Notice that $\lim_n \Diamond^{\geq n}\psi = \Box\Diamond\psi$.

$$[\Diamond^{\geq m}\psi] = \lim_n \mathbb{P}(\Diamond^{\geq m}\psi \mid \mathcal{F}_n) \geq \limsup_n \mathbb{P}(\Diamond^{\geq n}\psi \mid \mathcal{F}_n)$$

$$\geq \liminf_n \mathbb{P}(\Diamond^{\geq n}\psi \mid \mathcal{F}_n) \geq \lim_n \mathbb{P}(\Box\Diamond\psi \mid \mathcal{F}_n) = [\Box\Diamond\psi]$$

The equalities are a consequence of Levy's 0-1 law [11, Theorem 5.5.8] and the fact that $\Diamond^{\geq m}\psi$ and $\Box\Diamond\psi$ are measurable in $\sigma(\bigcup_n \mathcal{F}_n)$. If we let $m$ go to infinity both extremes coincide and therefore $\lim_n \mathbb{P}(\Diamond^{\geq n}\psi \mid \mathcal{F}_n) = [\Box\Diamond\psi]$.

From the last premise of the rule we have $\mathbb{P}(\Diamond^{\geq n}\psi \mid \mathcal{F}_n) \geq p[S_n \in \varphi]$, i.e. the probability of reaching a $\psi$-state from a $\varphi$-state is at least $p$. Take $\omega$ an arbitrary point event that satisfies $\Box\Diamond\varphi$, then for infinitely many $n$ we have $\mathbb{P}(\Diamond^{\geq n}\psi \mid \mathcal{F}_n)(\omega) \geq p > 0$, and therefore $[\Box\Diamond\psi](\omega) = 1$. We thus conclude that $P \models \pi \to \mathbb{P}_{=1}^{\forall}(\Box\Diamond\varphi \to \Box\Diamond\psi)$.

The soundness of the existential rule is proved in a similar way; additionally, one has to show how a witness scheduler can be constructed from the individual schedulers that guarantee reachability of each $\psi^i$ for $i = 1, \ldots, m$.     □

In the special case $\varphi := \mathrm{tt}$ in rule $\mathrm{REC}_{=1}^{\forall}$, we obtain a proof rule for unconditional recurrence as the rule given by Hart and Sharir [16, Lemma 3.3].

The rule for $\mathrm{REC}_{=1}^{\exists}$ in Fig. 5 requires that the assertion $\theta$ is invariant under all possible schedulers instead of under some scheduler. The reason is the following: the fact that there exist a scheduler that ensures the invariance and schedulers that ensure reachability does not imply that these schedulers can be combined in a scheduler that achieves both properties. Instead of referring to the rule for proving $\mathbb{P}_{\geq p}^{\exists}(\Diamond\psi^i)$ we can alternatively include the respective premises and incorporate the requirement that the scheduler should guarantee that $\theta$ is invariant. We omit this more complicated rule for simplicity of the presentation.

We can give a proof rule $\mathrm{REC}_{>0}^{\circlearrowleft}$ for repeated reachability with positive probability that is analogous to the rule $\mathrm{INV}_{>0}^{\circlearrowleft}$: Its premises require that some set of states $\theta$ is reached with positive probability and in every state in that set the repeated reachability property is satisfied almost surely. Analogously, we can obtain a rule $\mathrm{REC}_{\geq p}^{\exists}$ for the existential quantitative repeated reachability. The rule $\mathrm{REC}_{\geq p}^{\forall}$ for the universal quantitative case is a straightforward adaptation of $\mathrm{REC}_{=1}^{\forall}$: It requires that some set of states $\theta$ is invariant with probability at least $p$ and from every state in $\theta$ that satisfies $\varphi$ a $\psi$-state is reached with probability at least $q$ for some $q > 0$. Strict inequalities are handled as in the PCTL case.

*Example 5.* We want to prove that there is a strategy for the robot in Example 1 that visits infinitely often the origin regardless of the initial state. This can be specified in PCTL* as $P \models \mathrm{tt} \to \mathbb{P}_{=1}^{\exists}(\Box\Diamond(x = 0 \land y = 0))$. From Example 3 we have $P \vdash \mathsf{tt} \rightarrow \mathbb{P}^{\exists}_{=1}(\Diamond \varphi_{close})$, and from Example 4 we have $P \vdash \varphi_{close} \rightarrow \mathbb{P}^{\exists}_{\geq p}(\Diamond(x = 0 \land y = 0))$. Then, we can conclude that $P \vdash \mathsf{tt} \rightarrow \mathbb{P}^{\exists}_{\geq p}(\Diamond(x = 0 \land y = 0))$. The desired property follows immediately from the rule $\mathrm{REC}^{\exists}_{=1}$ as $P \vdash \mathsf{tt} \rightarrow \mathbb{P}^{\exists}_{=1}(\Box\Diamond\mathsf{tt})$ is a tautology.  □

Unlike the deductive proof systems for CTL* [19] and ATL* [25] here we cannot encode the accepting condition of the automaton $\mathcal{A}$ as a fairness requirement in the product system. In [19] LTL formulas are translated to temporal testers with fairness conditions, and their synchronous product with the original system yields a fair discrete system. Justice (a specific form of fairness) is then handled by specialized proof rules. Similarly, in [25] an LTL formula is transformed to a deterministic automaton, whose synchronous composition with the system yields an alternating discrete system with fairness conditions and the resulting proof condition then contains strategy quantifiers ranging over fair strategies. Subsequently, fair strategy quantifiers are transformed into unfair ones and the fairness conditions are made explicit in the resulting temporal formula, which is of a specific form and is treated by special proof rules.

The example below demonstrates that in the probabilistic case the encoding of the winning condition of the automaton as a fairness constraint is not equivalent to an explicit encoding in the temporal formula.

*Example 6.* Consider the probabilistic program $P$ over variables $s \in \{0, 1, 2\}$ and $x, y \in \mathbb{B}$. The transition relation is described by the guarded commands:

$$c_0 : s = 0 \mapsto (s' = 1 \land x' = 0 \land y' = 0) \otimes_{=\frac{1}{2}} (s' = 2 \land x' = 1 \land y' = 1),$$
$$c_1 : s = 1 \mapsto s' = 1 \land x' = 0 \land y' = 0,$$
$$c_2 : s = 2 \mapsto s' = 2 \land x' = 1 \land y' = 1.$$

Initially we have $\iota \equiv s = 0 \land x = 0 \land y = 0$. A scheduler $\alpha$ is fair w.r.t. the fairness requirement $\varphi \equiv \Box\Diamond(x = 1)$ if in the resulting DTMC starting from any $\iota$-state, $\Box\Diamond(x = 1)$ holds with probability 1. Thus, the set of schedulers that are fair w.r.t. $\varphi$ is empty and hence if quantifiers are interpreted over the set of all fair schedulers we have that $P \models \iota \rightarrow \mathbb{P}^{\exists}_{\geq 1/2}(\Box\Diamond(y = 1))$ does not hold and $P \models \iota \rightarrow \mathbb{P}^{\forall}_{\geq 1/2}(\Box\Diamond(y = 1))$ holds trivially. On the other hand, when quantifiers range over all possible schedulers, we have that $P \models \iota \rightarrow \mathbb{P}^{\exists}_{\geq 1/2}(\Box\Diamond(x = 1) \rightarrow \Box\Diamond(y = 1))$ and $P \models \iota \rightarrow \mathbb{P}^{\forall}_{\geq 1/2}(\Box\Diamond(x = 1) \rightarrow \Box\Diamond(y = 1))$ are satisfied.  □

The proof system $\mathcal{P}^{*}_{\mathrm{quantitative}}$ consists of the rules in $\mathcal{P}_{\mathrm{quantitative}}$ together with the rules MP, AND, OR, the rule BASIC-PATH and the rules for repeated reachability $\mathrm{REC}^{\forall}_{=1}, \mathrm{REC}^{\exists}_{=1}, \mathrm{REC}^{\circ}_{>0}, \mathrm{REC}^{\forall}_{\bowtie p}$ and $\mathrm{REC}^{\exists}_{\bowtie p}$.

**Proposition 5.** $\mathcal{P}^{*}_{\mathrm{quantitative}}$ *is sound: if* $P \vdash \varphi$ *in* $\mathcal{P}^{*}_{\mathrm{quantitative}}$, *then* $P \models \varphi$.

## 5    Discussion

We have presented the first deductive proof system for PCTL*. Our initial experience with the proof system has been positive: for example, we can prove the termination of Rabin's choice coordination problem with probability at least $1 - 2^{-\frac{M}{2}}$, for a parameter $M$ denoting the size of the alphabet used in the protocol, for *any* number of processes. Like with any deductive proof system, one has to come up with invariants and Lyapunov ranking functions. While we currently do this manually, it will be interesting to combine our proof system with recent automated techniques [18]. We conclude with two technical discussions: relaxations of our proof rules and completeness.

## 5.1   Variants of the Deduction Rules

Our choice of deduction rules has been driven by the intention to keep the exposition simple. We now discuss some possible relaxations to our rules, motivated by the incompleteness of some of the original rules.

*Invariant with Positive Probability.* As a first example, consider the rule for $\text{INV}^{\vee}_{\geq p}$, which checks if a set of states that each satisfy the invariant with probability one can be reached with probability at least $p$.

Consider the probabilistic program $P$ with a single variable $x$ over $\mathbb{N}$ that describes a biased random walk. The initial state is $x = 1$ and the state $x = 0$ is absorbing. At each step $x$ increases by 1 with probability $3/4$ and decreases by 1 with probability $1/4$. We have that $P \models (x = 1) \rightarrow \mathbb{P}^{\vee}_{\geq \frac{2}{3}}(\Box(x > 0))$ holds. However, from every state of $P$ the state $x = 0$ is reached with positive probability. Thus, we cannot provide an assertion $\theta$ as required by the premisses of rule $\text{INV}^{\vee}_{\geq p}$, as no subset of the set of states where $x > 0$ holds is invariant.

The rule $\overline{\text{INV}}^{\vee}_{\geq p}$ in Fig. 6 is a generalisation of $\text{INV}^{\vee}_{\geq p}$. The idea is to provide assertions, $\theta_1, \theta_2, \ldots$ such that from each $\theta_i$-state there is high enough probability to eventually move to some $\theta_j$ where $j > i$, meaning that the infinite product of these probabilities converges to the desired probability $p$ for the invariant.

We can apply the rule $\overline{\text{INV}}^{\vee}_{\geq p}$ in Fig. 6 to this random walk example as follows. Let $\theta_k = (x = k)$ for each $k > 0$. Then, clearly, $P \vdash (x = 1) \rightarrow \bigvee_{k=1}^{\infty} \theta_k$ and for all $k > 0$ we have $P \vdash \theta_k \rightarrow \varphi$. The probability of reaching $\theta_{k+1}$ from a state in $\theta_k$ is $p_k = \frac{1-3^{-k}}{1-3^{-(k+1)}}$ and thus $P \vdash \theta_k \rightarrow \mathbb{P}^{\vee}_{\geq p_k}(\Diamond \bigvee_{j=k+1}^{\infty} \theta_j)$ for all $k > 0$. Finally, $\prod_{k=1}^{\infty} p_k = 2/3$ which completes the proof. Clearly, the expressivity comes at a price of more complex premisses.

*Repeated Reachability.* As a second example, consider rule $\overline{\text{REC}}^{\vee}_{=1}$ in Fig. 6, which takes a different approach from the one in Fig. 5. Instead of ensuring that after visiting a state satisfying $\varphi$ we reach with probability at least $p$ a state satisfying $\psi$, we ensure that it is almost impossible to visit an infinite number of $\varphi$-states without visiting a single $\psi$-state. The latter is a more relaxed condition. Take any program that satisfies the former and add a self loop in a state satisfying $\neg \varphi \wedge \neg \psi$ that is reachable from a $\varphi$-state. The modified program does not satisfy the premise of the original rule, although the property still holds. The modified rule does not suffer from this.

More specifically, rule $\overline{\text{REC}}^{\vee}_{=1}$ in Fig. 6 requires the existence of a Lyapunov ranking function that decreases in expectation in states where $\varphi$ holds but $\psi$

does not hold, and cannot increase in expectation in states that do not satisfy $\psi$. Thus, the rule can be successfully applied also in cases where a $\varphi$ state is visited only finitely many times. Its completeness is discussed in Sect. 5.2.

$$
\begin{array}{l}
\text{assertions } \theta_1, \theta_2, \ldots \\
\text{constants } p_1, p_2, \ldots \\
\prod_{k=1}^{\infty} p_k \geq p \\
P \vdash \pi \to \bigvee_{k=1}^{\infty} \theta_k \\
\text{for all } k > 0 : \\
P \vdash \theta_k \to \varphi \\
\dfrac{P \vdash \theta_k \to \mathbb{P}_{\geq p_k}^{\forall}(\Diamond \bigvee_{j=k+1}^{\infty} \theta_j)}{P \vdash \pi \to \mathbb{P}_{\geq p}^{\forall}(\Box \varphi)} \; \overline{\mathrm{INV}}_{\geq p}^{\forall}
\end{array}
\qquad
\begin{array}{l}
\text{assertion } \theta, \text{ Lyapunov r. f. } \delta \\
P \vdash \pi \to \theta \\
P \vdash \theta \to \mathbb{P}_{=1}^{\forall}(\Box \theta) \\
P \vdash \theta \wedge \neg \psi \wedge \varphi \to \\
\quad (\forall c \in C : g_c : \theta' \wedge \delta \succ \mathbb{E}(\delta' \mid s)) \\
P \vdash \theta \wedge \neg \psi \quad \to \\
\dfrac{\quad (\forall c \in C : g_c : \theta' \wedge \delta \geq \mathbb{E}(\delta' \mid s))}{P \vdash \pi \to \mathbb{P}_{=1}^{\forall}(\Box \Diamond \varphi \to \Box \Diamond \psi)} \; \overline{\mathrm{REC}}_{=1}^{\forall}
\end{array}
$$

**Fig. 6.** More advanced proof rules.

## 5.2   Completeness for Finite State Systems

Our proof rules are in general incomplete for infinite-state probabilistic programs. For example, the rule $\mathrm{UNTIL}_{=1}^{\circlearrowleft}$ relies on Lyapunov ranking functions that are known to be incomplete for almost sure termination [5,13]. We focus the discussion to programs with *finite* state spaces, as most of our rules —or slight variations thereof— are complete for this class. The completeness of the rule $\mathrm{INV}_{=1}^{\circlearrowleft}$ and the rules for positive probability follows from the non-probabilistic case [19] (even for countable state spaces).

*Until.* If a program $P$ satisfies almost surely $\varphi \mathcal{U} \psi$ regardless of the scheduler, then given an initial state $s$ the expected amount of steps before reaching a $\psi$-state is bounded. Moreover, there is an optimal memoryless scheduler that maximizes this quantity for all states [3]. Then, the mapping that assigns to each state the expected time of reaching a $\psi$-state using the optimal scheduler is a valid Lyapunov ranking function. For the completeness of $\mathrm{UNTIL}_{=1}^{\exists}$ we have that there is a memoryless and deterministic scheduler that satisfies $\varphi \mathcal{U} \psi$ [4]. Then we have to take $\theta$ as the set of states visited by the scheduler, and build a Lyapunov ranking function for this sub-MDP in a similar way as above.

*Streett Condition.* The rule $\mathrm{REC}_{=1}^{\exists}$ is not complete as the premise $P \vdash \theta \to \mathbb{P}_{=1}^{\forall}(\Box \theta)$ is too strong. The monolithic proof rule (see Remark 1) that guarantees that $\theta$ is invariant w. r. t. the schedulers of the last premise is complete. We have to choose $\theta$ as the states that the scheduler visits infinitely often with non-zero probability. The set $\theta$ is almost surely reached and each of its states belongs to at least one end component [8]. If a $\varphi^i$-state is visited infinitely often, then the end component that the scheduler reaches must have a $\psi^i$-state, otherwise the property will be violated. Then, the last premise is satisfied.

The rule $\overline{\mathrm{REC}}_{=1}^{\forall}$ presented in Sect. 5.1 is complete. We need to analyze the maximal end components of the program. Consider the sub-MDP obtained from an end component $E$. From every state the maximum expected number of $\varphi$-states visited before reaching a $\psi$-state is finite, since the maximal probability of returning to a $\varphi$-state without visiting a $\psi$ state is less than one. This quantity can be used to build a Lyapunov function that decreases every time that a $\varphi \wedge \neg\psi$-state is visited. Consider now the quotient MDP that is obtained by lumping every maximal end component into a single state and removing self-loops. It has no end component except for deadlock states. Then we can build a Lyapunov ranking function that ensures that a deadlock state is reached almost surely. We can combine all these local Lyapunov functions to build a global one that satisfies the conditions of the rule $\overline{\mathrm{REC}}^{\vee}_{=1}$.

**Acknowledgements.** This work is supported by the EU FP7 projects 295261 (MEALS) and 318490 (SENSATION), by the DFG Transregional Collaborative Research Centre SFB/TR 14 AVACS, and by the CDZ project 1023 (CAP).

# References

1. Arons, T., Pnueli, A., Zuck, L.D.: Parameterized verification by probabilistic abstraction. In: Gordon, A.D. (ed.) FOSSACS 2003. LNCS, vol. 2620, pp. 87–102. Springer, Heidelberg (2003)
2. Baier, C., Katoen, J.-P.: Principles of Model Checking. MIT Press, Cambridge (2008)
3. Bertsekas, D.P., Tsitsiklis, J.N.: An analysis of stochastic shortest path problems. Math. Oper. Res. **16**(3), 580–595 (1991)
4. Bianco, A., de Alfaro, L.: Model checking of probabilistic and nondeterministic systems. In: Thiagarajan, P.S. (ed.) FSTTCS. LNCS, pp. 499–513. Springer, Heidelberg (1995)
5. Bournez, O., Garnier, F.: Proving positive almost-sure termination. In: Giesl, J. (ed.) RTA 2005. LNCS, vol. 3467, pp. 323–337. Springer, Heidelberg (2005)
6. Chakarov, A., Sankaranarayanan, S.: Probabilistic program analysis with martingales. In: Sharygina, N., Veith, H. (eds.) CAV 2013. LNCS, vol. 8044, pp. 511–526. Springer, Heidelberg (2013)
7. Courcoubetis, C., Yannakakis, M.: The complexity of probabilistic verification. J. ACM **42**(4), 857–907 (1995)
8. de Alfaro, L.: Formal verification of probabilistic systems. PhD thesis, Standford (1997)
9. de Alfaro, L., Kwiatkowska, M., Norman, G., Parker, D., Segala, R.: Symbolic model checking of probabilistic processes using MTBDDs and the Kronecker representation. In: Graf, S. (ed.) TACAS 2000. LNCS, vol. 1785, p. 395. Springer, Heidelberg (2000)
10. Dimitrova, R., Ferrer Fioriti, L.M., Hermanns, H., Majumdar, R.: PCTL*: the deductive way (extended version). Reports of SFB/TR 14 AVACS 114, (2016). http://www.avacs.org
11. Durrett, R.: Probability: Theory and Examples. Series in Statistical and Probabilistic Mathematics, 4th edn. Cambridge University Press, New York (2010)
12. Esparza, J., Gaiser, A., Kiefer, S.: Proving termination of probabilistic programs using patterns. In: Madhusudan, P., Seshia, S.A. (eds.) CAV 2012. LNCS, vol. 7358, pp. 123–138. Springer, Heidelberg (2012)

13. Ferrer Fioriti, L.M., Hermanns, H.: Probabilistic termination: soundness, completeness, and compositionality. In: POPL, pp. 489–501 (2015)
14. Filar, J., Vrieze, K.: Competitive Markov Decision Processes. Springer, Heidelberg (1997)
15. Francez, N.: Fairness. Texts and Monographs in Computer Science. Springer, Heidelberg (1986)
16. Hart, S., Sharir, M., Pnueli, A.: Termination of probabilistic concurrent program. ACM Trans. Program. Lang. Syst. **5**(3), 356–380 (1983)
17. Hurd, J.: Formal verification of probabilistic algorithms. PhD thesis, University of Cambridge (2001)
18. Katoen, J.-P., McIver, A.K., Meinicke, L.A., Morgan, C.C.: Linear-invariant generation for probabilistic programs. In: Cousot, R., Martel, M. (eds.) SAS 2010. LNCS, vol. 6337, pp. 390–406. Springer, Heidelberg (2010)
19. Kesten, Y., Pnueli, A.: A compositional approach to CTL* verification. Theor. Comput. Sci. **331**(2–3), 397–428 (2005)
20. Kwiatkowska, M.Z., Norman, G., Parker, D.: PRISM: probabilistic model checking for performance and reliability analysis. SIGMETRICS Perform. Eval. Rev. **36**(4), 40–45 (2009)
21. McIver, A., Morgan, C.: Abstraction, Refinement and Proof for Probabilistic Systems. Monographs in Computer Science. Springer, Heidelberg (2005)
22. Pnueli, A.: On the extremely fair treatment of probabilistic algorithms. In: Proceedings of the 15th Annual ACM Symposium on Theory of Computing, pp. 278–290 (1983)
23. Pnueli, A., Zuck, L.D.: Probabilistic verification. Inf. Comput. **103**(1), 1–29 (1993)
24. Rabin, M.O.: The choice coordination problem. Acta Informatica **17**, 121–134 (1982)
25. Slanina, M., Sipma, H.B., Manna, Z.: Deductive verification of alternating systems. Form. Asp. Comput. **20**(4–5), 507–560 (2008)
26. Vardi, M.Y.: Automatic verification of probabilistic concurrent finite-state programs. In: FOCS, pp. 327–338 (1985)

# Tool Papers I

# Parametric Runtime Verification of C Programs

Zhe Chen[1,2(✉)], Zhemin Wang[1], Yunlong Zhu[1], Hongwei Xi[3], and Zhibin Yang[1]

[1] College of Computer Science and Technology, Nanjing University of Aeronautics
and Astronautics, 29 Jiangjun Avenue, Nanjing 211106, Jiangsu, China
{zhechen,wangzm,zhuyl,zhibinyang}@nuaa.edu.cn
[2] Collaborative Innovation Center of Novel Software Technology and
Industrialization, Nanjing, China
[3] Computer Science Department, Boston University, 111 Cummington Street,
Boston, MA 02215, USA
hwxi@cs.bu.edu

**Abstract.** Many runtime verification tools are built based on Aspect-Oriented Programming (AOP) tools, most often AspectJ, a mature implementation of AOP for Java. Although already popular in the Java domain, there is few work on runtime verification of C programs via AOP, due to the lack of a solid language and tool support. In this paper, we propose a new general purpose and expressive language for defining monitors as an extension to the C language, and present our tool implementation of the weaver, the MOVEC compiler, which brings fully-fledged parametric runtime verification support into the C domain.

## 1 Introduction

Along with the popularity of runtime verification [16,19], many tools have been developed. These runtime verification tools automatically synthesize the code fragments of event extraction mechanisms and monitors from formal specifications, and then instrument the code into a target program, so that the monitors can extract information from the program executions at runtime, to detect and possibly react to observed behaviors satisfying or violating the specified properties. As automated program instrumentation plays a key role in monitor synthesis and weaving, many current tools are built based on Aspect-Oriented Programming (AOP), which is a programming paradigm that supports the modular implementation of crosscutting concerns [15].

By using AOP compilers, these tools are hence built in the form of specification transformers, that take an expressive high-level specification as input and produce output code written in some AOP language, most often AspectJ, a mature implementation of AOP for the Java programming language [14]. For example, among the large number of runtime verification tools, the most efficient parametric runtime verification tool JavaMOP [4,13,17] is based on AspectJ. JavaMOP transforms monitor definitions including desired properties into aspects, and then these aspects are transformed into Java code fragments and weaved into target programs using an AspectJ compiler. The desired properties can be automatically verified at runtime by running the executable file generated by AspectJ. Other tools like Tracematches [1,2] are designed in a similar way.

© Springer-Verlag Berlin Heidelberg 2016
M. Chechik and J.-F. Raskin (Eds.): TACAS 2016, LNCS 9636, pp. 299–315, 2016.
DOI: 10.1007/978-3-662-49674-9_17

Therefore, we believe that the popularity of runtime verification of Java programs is supported by the fact that a robust, reliable and efficient AOP compiler such as ajc is available.

Although already popular in the Java domain, there is few work on runtime verification of C programs via AOP, due to the lack of a solid language and tool support. For example, AspectC++ is an implementation of AOP for C++, but the generated code cannot be compiled by C compilers [20–23]. Coady et al. used "AspectC" (a hypothetical and simple subset of AspectJ) to modularize the implementation of prefetching within page fault handling in the FreeBSD OS kernel, and showed significant benefits [9,10]. But they used only a paper design for AspectC, supporting only join points of function calls and control flow, and no implementation of AspectC exists. ACC (AspeCt-oriented C) is the most advanced implementation of AOP for the C programming language at present [11], but it is currently not maintained by its developers, and the latest version is incorrect in many cases. For example, join points and pointcuts are sometimes not correctly matched, and instrumented code is possibly not semantically equivalent to its corresponding aspect. Worse, the ACC implementation is not well modularized, so fixing ACC is hard.

However, the fact is that a large number of applications is still being developed in C, especially embedded software applications such as avionics systems, which always require high dependability [7]. Thus, it is meaningful to provide a runtime verification tool or an AOP tool for the C language, so programmers can modularize the crosscutting concerns to improve maintainability, and based on AOP tools, they can also develop or use runtime verification tools to monitor and verify their programs at runtime.

In this paper, we propose a new general purpose and expressive language for defining monitors as an extension to the C language, and present our tool implementation of the weaver, the MOVEC compiler, which brings fully-fledged parametric runtime verification and AOP support into the C domain. The major contributions of our work include:

- We propose a new language for defining monitors for C programs by systematically redesigning the languages of AspectJ and JavaMOP. The main reason is that, the C language uses the procedure-oriented programming paradigm, which is very different from the object-oriented paradigm of Java, thus we have to redesign what we learned from AspectJ and JavaMOP according to the specific peculiarities of the C language. Another reason is that, the traditional AOP languages are somewhat conceptually confusing (the various types of pointcuts and advices are not systematic), not enough elegant and natural (some pointcuts and advices are written in a redundant and uncomfortable way).
- We develop a new instrumentation algorithm for the new language. In the AOP part, this is necessary because the philosophy of the C language is very different from Java, so we cannot implement aspects as classes like in AspectJ. Besides, the instrumentation algorithm of ACC, the most relevant AOP implementation, is incorrect in many cases. In the runtime verification

part, our algorithm has to implement more infrastructures than JavaMOP, because we cannot use the powerful Java class library, such as hashmaps.
- We implement an integrated tool supporting both AOP and parametric runtime verification. Getting AOP and runtime verification into the C language is a hard and tedious task, and our implementation supports all features of the new language and provides convenient user instructions. Experimental performance evaluation shows that our tool is robust, reliable and efficient.

This paper is organized as follows. Section 2 introduces the MOVEC compiler, including its software architecture, compilation process and theoretical foundations. Section 3 presents an example to show the tool's functionality, i.e., how to write monitor definitions and run MOVEC. Section 4 focuses on the design of our new language for defining monitors of C programs by introducing the semantics of each language element. Section 5 explains the tool implementation of the new language, including core data structures. Section 6 evaluates and compares the performance of MOVEC and related tools by presenting the experimental results on the same benchmark. We conclude and discuss future work in Sect. 7.

## 2    The MOVEC Compiler

MOVEC is an automated tool for runtime MOnitoring, VErification and Control of C programs as an extension to the C programming language. MOVEC is influenced by AOP and parametric runtime verification, and is an integrated implementation of these ideas for the C programming language. MOVEC aims at providing an infrastructure of AOP, runtime verification and related technologies in the context of software written in C, especially targeting embedded software such as avionics systems, leading to further explorations and investigations not possible today, as no reliable, efficient and stable implementation of these technologies for C programs exists.

MOVEC provides a source-to-source transformation that automatically weaves monitor specifications written in MOVEC into MOVEC-unaware C programs, and generates instrumented C programs which can be compiled by any compliant C compiler such as GCC and other platform-specific compilers. Note that MOVEC does not directly compile the instrumented C programs into a binary executable file, because many embedded platforms use their own C compilers which may be not compatible with each other. Thus, by using source code transformation, MOVEC can be used for all target platforms supported by C compilers.

**Software Architecture and Compilation Process.** The inputs of MOVEC are C programs and files containing monitor definitions, and the outputs are instrumented C programs. There are five major modules in MOVEC, corresponding to the five phases in the MOVEC compilation process: command line analysis (i.e., parsing the options given in a command line), parsing C programs, parsing monitor definitions, monitor generation (i.e., generating C code fragments for monitor definitions) and weaving (i.e., generating instrumented C programs).

**Theoretical Foundations.** Rosu and Chen et al. proposed the theoretical foundation of parametric runtime monitoring and verification [3,5,12,18], and implemented JavaMOP supporting parametric runtime verification of Java programs [4,13,17]. For the parametric runtime verification part, our tool implements their monitoring algorithm in the context of C programs. Our tool also implements a formal semantics of runtime monitoring, verification, enforcement and control [8], which is an instance of a more general computational model, namely control systems [6].

## 3   A Demonstration of the Tool

Generally speaking, MOVEC extends the C language with *monitor* definitions that implement crosscutting concerns in a modular way. A *monitor* definition is composed of declarations of *types*, *variables*, *pointcuts*, *actions*, *properties* and their *handlers*.

In this section, we will present a simple example to show how to write monitor definitions and run MOVEC. Suppose `malloc.c` is a C source program, which requests 10 blocks of memory from the heap by calling `malloc`, and then frees 7 of these blocks. Note that some blocks are not freed, resulting in memory leakage. We will show how to detect the memory leakage by defining monitors.

Let `monitor1.mon` be a monitor file containing the monitor named `mon` in Listing 1.1. This *parametric monitor* definition takes two parameters: `size` and `address`, and includes two parametric named pointcuts, three actions, a property and a handler. MOVEC creates a complete monitor instance for each observed value pair of `size` and `address`, both of which are specified in the creation action in this example (but not necessarily in other examples).

The first *parametric named pointcut* `cm(s)` refers to the function calls to `malloc`, and the parameter `s` binds the value of its actual argument. The second parametric named pointcut `cf(p)` refers to the function calls to `free`, and the parameter `p` binds the value of its actual argument. The symbol `%` is a wildcard character matching continuous strings of any length, e.g., any type name and any parameter identifier. The symbol `:` is a renaming operator that renames a parameter identifier to another one. The predefined pointcut `call` matches the join points of the function calls to the matched functions.

The first *parametric action* named `malloc` prints the address range of the allocated memory block, and is executed after any function call to `malloc`. The predefined pointcut `returning` assigns an identifier to the return value of the function call. The parameters `address` and `size` bind the address and size of the allocated block respectively, and the variable `tjp->loc` is a predefined variable which stores the line number of the function call. This action is also a `creation` action, which creates a new monitor instance. The second parametric action named `free` prints the address of the freed memory block, and is executed after any function call to `free`. The last action named `end` is executed after the execution of `main`. The symbol `...` is a wildcard character matching item lists of any length, e.g., any parameter list.

**Listing 1.1.** A parametric monitor

```
1  monitor mon(size_t size, void *address)
2  {
3    pointcut cm(s) = call(% malloc(% %:s));
4    pointcut cf(p) = call(% free(% %:p));
5
6    creation action malloc(address, size) after cm(size) &&
7                                  returning (address) {
8      printf("Allocated address %p-%p (size %lu) at line %d\n",
9             address, address+size, size, tjp->loc);
10   }
11
12   action free(address) after cf(address) {
13     printf("Freed address %p at line %d\n", address, tjp->loc);
14   }
15
16   action end after execution(% main(...));
17
18   ere: (malloc free)* malloc end;
19   @match {
20     printf("error: address %p (size %lu) was not"
21            "correctly freed!\n", monitor->address, monitor->size);
22   }
23 };
```

The *property* over actions `malloc`, `free` and `end` is specified in extended regular expression (ERE). It matches undesired action sequences that start with zero or more `malloc free`, followed by a `malloc`, and end with `end`. The *handler* `@match` contains a code fragment that prints a message, which will be automatically executed when an execution of the program matches the property, i.e., a memory block was allocated, but was not correctly freed. The variable `monitor` is a predefined structure variable that refers to the current monitor instance, and its member variables `monitor->address` and `monitor->size` refer to the parameters `address` and `size` of the current monitor instance, respectively.

MOVEC takes monitor files and C header/source files as inputs, and outputs instrumented header/source files, which can be compiled into monitored programs by any compliant C compiler such as GCC. For example, the following command line takes the monitor file `monitor1.mon` and the C source file `malloc.c` as inputs, automatically weaves them together, and outputs the instrumented source file `malloc.c` to the destination directory `/home/user`.

$ movec -m monitor1.mon -c malloc.c -d /home/user

Besides the instrumented source file `malloc.c`, MOVEC also outputs two additional header files `monitor.h` and `hashmap.h` to this directory. The instrumented source file `malloc.c` can be compiled into an executable file `a.out` by GCC. Running `a.out` prints a list of messages, and the last three error messages indicates that 3 allocated memory blocks were not freed, along with their addresses and sizes (the addresses may be different on your computer).

```
... (omitted) ...
error: address 0x790ad0 (size 160) was not correctly freed!
error: address 0x790cf0 (size 320) was not correctly freed!
error: address 0x792590 (size 5120) was not correctly freed!
```

In this example, MOVEC created 10 complete monitor instances, i.e., one for each value pair of `size` and `address`. Then the handler was invoked for each one of the 3 monitors that reached matching states, whereas the other 7 monitors did not invoke the handler because they did not reach matching states. Thus, the result shows that there are 3 unmatched `malloc` actions at the end.

Note that the above example only demonstrated a small portion of the language and features of MOVEC. In the following sections, we will introduce in-depth the semantics of each language element.

## 4   The Language for Defining Monitors

### 4.1   Join Points, Pointcuts and Actions

We only briefly introduce these language elements, because these concepts stem from AOP languages, although with some improvements such as more systematic design of pointcuts and advices and more concise and comfortable syntax. The reader unfamiliar with these concepts may refer to the literature on AOP languages [11,14,20].

A *join point* is a point in the execution of a program, such as function calls via function names or pointers, function executions.

A *pointcut* is an expression that matches a set of *join points* scattered in the execution of a program. Currently, MOVEC supports *match expressions* for matching program objects such as identifiers, variable declarations and function signatures, and *primitive pointcuts*, *composite pointcuts* and *named pointcuts* for matching join points.

A *literal match expression* matches a program object only if they are exactly the same, whereas a *regular expression* can match a program object by using the symbols % and ... as wildcard characters. For example, the expression % `func%(..., int x, ...)` matches any functions whose name starts with `func` and parameter list contains a parameter `int x`, but the return type and other parameters are left unspecified, e.g., `int* func1 (float foo, int x)`.

The predefined *primitive pointcuts* fall into four classes: *core* pointcut functions, *naming* pointcut functions, *dynamic scope* and *static scope* pointcut functions. The *core pointcut* functions include the following functions.

- `call`(*function-signature*) matches the join points of the function calls to the functions matched by *function-signature*. For example, the expression `call(%` `func%(..., in%, ...))` matches the function calls to any function whose name starts with `func`, parameter list contains a parameter whose type starts with `in`, but return type is left unspecified, e.g., `int* func1(float foo, int x)`.
- `callp`(*function-signature*) matches the join points of the function calls to the functions matched by *function-signature* via function pointers.
- `execution`(*function-signature*) matches the join points of executing the functions matched by *function-signature*.

The *naming pointcut* functions are used to assign names to some objects in the execution of a program, e.g., return values.

- returning(*identifier*) assigns an *identifier* to the return value of the function call matched by call or callp pointcuts, or to the return value of the function execution matched by execution pointcuts.

The *dynamic scope pointcut* functions are used to restrict the scope of matched join points at runtime.

- inexec(*function-signature*) matches the join points which are invoked during the dynamic execution of the functions matched by *function-signature*.
- condition(*boolean-expression*) matches the join points at which the condition specified by *boolean-expression* holds.

The *static scope pointcut* functions are used to restrict the scope of matched join points at compile-time.

- infunc(*function-signature*) matches the join points which statically appear in the function definitions matched by *function-signature*.
- intype(*identifier*) matches the join points which statically appear in the type definitions matched by *identifier*, such as structures, unions and enumerations.
- infile(*identifier*) matches the join points which statically appear in the files whose names are matched by *identifier*.

A *composite pointcut* is a primitive pointcut, or a logical composition of composite pointcuts with the operators: && (and), || (or), ! (not), and ( ).

To reuse pointcut declarations, we can assign a name to a pointcut by declaring a *named pointcut*, then the named pointcut can be referred by using its name in any places where a pointcut can be used. For example,

```
pointcut ppc1(x,y) = call(int foo(int x)) && returning(y);
```

An *action* declaration associates a code fragment to a pointcut, and the code fragment will be automatically executed when a join point is reached in an execution of the monitored program, such that the join point is matched by the pointcut defined inside the action declaration. Actions are also called *advices* in AOP and *events* in JavaMOP. The syntax of action declarations is as follows.

```
[creation] ("action" | "advice" | "event")
    [ACTIONID ["(" <paramids-list> ")"] ]
("before" | "after" | "around") <pc-composite>
("{" <act-action> "}" | ";")
```

An action declaration specifies a *passive action* and an *active action*. The passive action contains a composite pointcut expression pc-composite to passively match reached join points, and specifies the position where the active action shall be triggered relative to the invocations of matched join points, e.g., before, after etc. The active action act-action is a code fragment enclosed in curly braces. The active action is automatically executed if the passive action is matched.

For example, the following *parametric action* `pact` prints a message before the execution of function `foo`, which takes only one integer parameter `x`. Note that the parameter `x` is referred as a parameter of the action. As a result, the value of `x` can be accessed and printed in its active action.

```
action pact(x) before execution(int foo(int x)) {
    printf("before executing foo, x=%d\n",x);
}
```

## 4.2   Properties and Handlers

A *property* specifies the desired or undesired set of sequences of matched join points in the execution of a program, and a *handler* can be automatically executed when the property is matched or violated by an execution of the program. Currently, we can express properties using Finite State Machines (FSM) and Extended Regular Expressions (ERE).

An FSM includes a set of states, a set of actions and a set of transitions, in which one of the states is the initial state and a subset of the states is matching states (also called accepting states or final states). FSMs are also called Nondeterministic Finite Automata (NFA) in formal language theory. The syntax of FSM declarations is as follows.

```
"fsm" ":" ( STATEID1 "{"
            (ACTIONID "->" STATEID2 ";")*
            "}" )* ";"
```

An FSM declaration starts with the keyword `fsm` and a colon, possibly followed by a list of state declarations, and finally ends with a semicolon. A state declaration starts with its name `STATEID1`, followed by a list of transition declarations enclosed in curly braces. A transition declaration consists of an action name `ACTIONID`, the symbol `->`, a state name `STATEID2` and a semicolon in sequence, denoting that the action `ACTIONID` will transfer the FSM from state `STATEID1` to state `STATEID2`, where `STATEID1` and `STATEID2` could be either the same state or different states. If a state does not include a certain action, but the action appears in other states, then the action will transfer the FSM from the state to the implicit sink state, from which the FSM will never be matched. Note that the first declared state is the initial state, and the states whose name starts with `acc` are matching states.

For example, the following FSM declaration includes three states q0, q1, acc1, two actions a, b and six transitions, in which the first declared state q0 is the initial state, and state acc1 is a matching state. For each state, there are two transitions, e.g., state q0 has a transition labeled action a from q0 to q1.

```
fsm: q0 { a -> q1; b -> q2; }
     q1 { a -> q1; b -> q0; }
   acc1 { a -> q0; b -> acc1; };
```

An ERE is a sequence of identifiers and operators that defines a pattern to match sequences of identifiers. The operators in EREs include the concatenation of elements, the choice operator | which matches either the expression before or the expression after the operator, the asterisk operator * which matches the preceding element zero or more times, the plus operator + which matches the preceding element one or more times, the question mark ? which matches the preceding element zero or one time, and the parentheses () which are used to define the scope and precedence of the operators. EREs can be translated into equivalent Nondeterministic Finite Automata (NFA) in formal language theory. The syntax of ERE declarations is as follows.

```
"ere" ":" <ere> ";"
```

An ERE declaration starts with the keyword `ere` and a colon, followed by an extended regular expression `<ere>` over action names, and finally ends with a semicolon. For example, the following ERE declaration over actions `malloc`, `set`, `get` and `free` matches the action sequences that start with `malloc`, followed by zero or more `set` and `get`, and end with `free`.

```
ere: malloc  (set | get)*  free;
```

A *handler* includes a category of property (e.g., match and violation) and an active action (i.e., a code fragment). A property can be associated with several handlers, so that an active action will be automatically executed when an execution of the program transfers the property to the corresponding category. Handlers can be used for many purposes, e.g., output or logging observed information, controlling, recovering, blocking or terminating the execution. The syntax of handler declarations is as follows.

```
"@" <cate> "{" <act-action> "}"
```

A handler starts with the symbol @, followed by a predefined category name `<cate>`, and finally ends with an active action `<act-action>` enclosed in curly braces. Note that different formalisms may have different sets of predefined categories, and the active action will be automatically executed when an execution of the program transfers the property to the category. Currently MOVEC provides two predefined categories `match` and `fail` for FSMs and EREs. The category `match` means that the associated property is matched by the execution, `fail` means that the property will never be matched by any extension of the execution.

## 4.3  Monitors

A *monitor* declaration collects multiple pointcuts, actions, properties and their handlers together, to implement crosscutting concerns in a modular way. A monitor declaration can also include additional type declarations and variable declarations. The syntax of monitor declarations is as follows.

```
<modifier>* ("monitor" | "aspect")
              MONITORID ["(" <param-list> ")"] "{"
  ( <C-type-decl>    | <C-var-decl>
  | <pointcut-decl> | <action-decl>
  | <property> <handler>* )*   "}" ";"
```

A monitor declaration starts with a list of modifiers, then specifies the signature of the monitor. The signature declaration starts with one of the keywords monitor or aspect, which can be used interchangeably. The keyword is followed by a name MONITORID and possibly an enclosed parameter list param-list. If the parameter list is given, then the parameter declarations should be separated by commas in the parentheses, and the monitor is called a *parametric monitor*.

Then the monitor declaration specifies the body of the monitor enclosed in curly braces, and a semicolon denotes the end of the declaration. In the declaration body, we can declare types, variables, pointcuts, actions, properties and their handlers. Note that,

- All declared types and variables will be instrumented as global declarations.
- At least one action declaration should be preceded by the keyword creation, denoting that observing this action should create a new monitor instance with different parameter values. If the monitor is parametric, then some of the action declarations must be parametric, such that the union of all action parameters is exactly the set of monitor parameters in param-list. That is, creation actions do not necessarily contain all monitor parameters.
- Each property should be specified in one of the supported formalisms, and can refer to the declared action names. Each property may be associated with zero or more handlers.
- The handlers can access the declared types and variables, and can access the predefined variable monitor which refers to the current monitor instance, through which we can access the monitor parameters in param-list of the current monitor instance.

## 5   Implementation of Parametric Monitoring

Recall that a monitor definition may contain a set of parameters, and MOVEC may create a *monitor* (instance) for each parameter instance containing the observed values of a subset of the parameters, to store the current state of each parameter instance. That is, a monitor or parameter instance may be complete or partial (i.e., containing a strict subset of the parameters). As the literature shows, a program may create thousands of monitors during runtime monitoring, thus storing these monitors using naive structures like linked lists or arrays will significant increase runtime overhead. Therefore, developing an efficient algorithm for indexing monitors is one of the most valuable and challenging parts in implementing parametric runtime monitoring.

Indeed, thanks to the indexing algorithm of JavaMOP, it becomes the most efficient parametric runtime verification tool at present. Our indexing algorithm

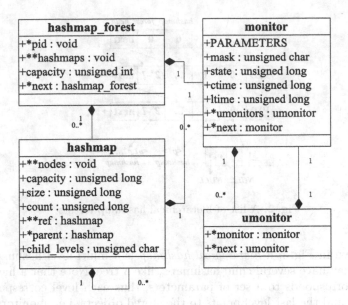

**Fig. 1.** Data structures of hierarchical hashmap forests

is inspired by JavaMOP, but our task is even more hard and tedious. We have to implement the data structures and related algorithms from scratch, because we cannot use the powerful Java class library, which includes efficient data structures such as hashmaps.

In this section, we present a new data structure, namely *hierarchical hashmap forests*, which is implemented in MOVEC for indexing monitors. Generally speaking, we maintain a list of hierarchical hashmap forests during runtime monitoring, and each created monitor is added into a hierarchical hashmap according to its corresponding property and parameter instance, so that all monitors can be efficiently retrieved. Figure 1 shows the data structures used by hierarchical hashmap forests. The `monitor` structure abstracts a monitor, including the values of `parameters`, a `mask` denoting the parameter instance, the current `state` etc. In the followings, we will present these structures from the top level.

As show in Fig. 2, we maintain a list of hierarchical hashmap forests during runtime monitoring. In the list, for each property `pid`, we create a node containing a forest of hierarchical hashmaps. The capacity of the forest depends on the number of parameters associated with the property. If a property includes $n$ parameters from $p_1$ to $p_n$, then there are $2^n$ hashmaps in the node, and each hashmap corresponds to a combination of the parameters. For example, the first location corresponds to the empty set of parameters, and the last one corresponds to the complete set. Note that the first location actually points to a monitor, instead of a hashmap, because there is only one parameter instance for this empty combination of parameters. Next we introduce the hierarchical hashmap for a set of parameters.

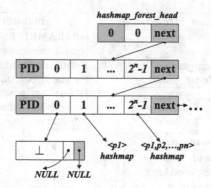

**Fig. 2.** A list of hierarchical hashmap forests

As shown in Fig. 3, a *hierarchical hashmap* is a multi-level hashmap, i.e., a hashmap may have several child hashmaps, like a tree. Note that a hierarchical hashmap corresponds to a set of parameters, thus each level corresponds to a parameter, and the last level points to the stored objects, i.e., monitors. To put these hashmaps in a tree, each hashmap contains not only the addresses of the next level hashmaps, but also a pointer *prn* to its parent and a pointer *ref* to the reference node in its parent hashmap, i.e., the pointer that refers to itself.

Recall that a hashmap maps keys to values, i.e., it uses a hash function to compute an index from which the desired value or object can be found, e.g., using modulo arithmetic. For our hierarchical hashmaps, we use parameter values as the keys for the corresponding level of hashmaps. Furthermore, we use linked lists to solve hash collisions.

For example, the hierarchical hashmap in Fig. 3 corresponds to the parameters $a$ and $b$, thus contains two levels. The first level is used to index the values of variable $a$, while the second to index the values of variable $b$. Each monitor stored in this hashmap corresponds to a parameter instance of $a$ and $b$. The monitor of the parameter instance $a_1b_2$ can be located via index 1 of the first

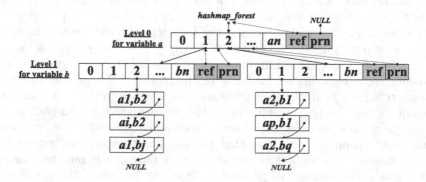

**Fig. 3.** A hierarchical hashmap

level, and then index 2 of the second level. Suppose parameter instances $a_i b_2$ and $a_1 b_j$ have the same index as $a_1 b_2$, then we put them in a linked list to solve the hash collisions. Similarly, the monitors of the parameter instances $a_2 b_1$, $a_p b_1$ and $a_2 b_q$ can be located via another path in the hierarchical hashmap.

# 6    Experimental Performance Evaluation

MOVEC uses a different weaving algorithm, compared with related tools. As Java-MOP and ACC are the most relevant and advanced tools in the runtime verification and AOP domains respectively, we compared the performance of MOVEC and the latest versions of JavaMOP and ACC on the same benchmark respectively. All experiments are done under the following platform: Intel i5-2410M CPU at 2.30 GHz, 4 GB memory, running Ubuntu 14.04 LTS 64-bit operating system.

MOVEC *vs. JavaMOP.* In our experiment, we designed a benchmark containing four projects. Note that MOVEC and JavaMOP can only process C and Java programs respectively, so each project is implemented as two equivalent versions, written in C and Java respectively, and these two versions are also very similar literally.

The first project unsafe-Enum creates a set of vectors, then creates an enumeration for each vector, and uses the enumeration to traverse the elements in the vector. But for one of these vectors, the vector is modified by adding an element while the enumeration is in use. A monitor with a regular expression property is designed to match the unsafe case where a vector with an associated enumeration is modified while the enumeration is in use. If the property is matched, a handler is invoked to print an error message.

The second project unsafe-File opens a set of files, then writes some strings into the files, and finally closes all files, except one. A monitor with a regular expression property is designed to match the unsafe case where a file was opened, but has not been closed until the program terminates. If the property is matched, a handler is invoked to increase a counter, and the count is printed when the program terminates.

The third project unsafe-Grant creates a set of tasks and a set of resources, then grants these resources to tasks, and finally these tasks release some of the granted resources, but not all. A monitor with a regular expression property is designed to match the unsafe case where a resource was granted to a task, but has not been released by the task until the program terminates. If the property is matched, a handler is invoked to increase a counter, and the count is printed when the program terminates.

The last project unsafe-MapIterator creates a map, then creates a set of collections for the map, creates an iterator for each collection, and adds an element to the map. But for two of these iterators, the iterators are used to get the next element in the collection, after the map is modified. A monitor with a regular expression property is designed to match the unsafe case where a map with an associated iterator is modified while the iterator is in use. If the property is matched, a handler is invoked to print an error message. This offers a larger challenge, because the monitor creation actions do not contain all the parameters (collections are created before iterators).

**Table 1.** Experimental performance evaluation

|  | mon. num | Movec | | | | JavaMOP | | | |
|---|---|---|---|---|---|---|---|---|---|
|  |  | orig. time | hand. num | run time | time diff. | orig. time | hand. num | run time | time diff |
| Enum | 1000 | 0.016 | 1 | 0.199 | 0.183 | 0.114 | 1 | 0.218 | **0.104** |
| Enum | 20000 | 0.141 | 1 | 21.715 | 21.574 | 0.179 | 1 | 0.817 | **0.638** |
| File | 1000 | 0.144 | 1 | 0.145 | **0.001** | 0.232 | 1 | 0.334 | 0.102 |
| File | 20000 | 2.585 | 1 | 2.793 | **0.208** | 1.867 | ~~0~~ | 2.106 | 0.239 |
| Grant | 1000 | 0.006 | 500 | 0.030 | **0.024** | 0.102 | 500 | 0.205 | 0.103 |
| Grant | 20000 | 0.010 | 10000 | 12.397 | 12.387 | 0.110 | ~~9370~~ | 0.499 | **0.389** |
| MapIter | 1000 | 0.006 | 2 | 0.079 | **0.073** | 0.104 | ~~0~~ | 0.228 | 0.124 |
| MapIter | 20000 | 0.019 | 2 | 35.735 | 35.716 | 0.118 | ~~0~~ | 22.782 | **22.664** |

Note: JavaMOP failed to correctly print the numbers of monitors and invoked handlers.

For each of the two versions of each project, we used two settings to generate different numbers of complete monitors. For each setting, we ran each version for three times, and measured in average the original run time (in seconds), the number of invoked handlers, the run time after instrumentation (in seconds) and the time difference. The data is listed in Table 1. Note that the two versions create the same number of complete monitors. Besides, JavaMOP failed to correctly print the numbers of monitors and invoked handlers, so we have to get the numbers by temporarily putting a `println` statement in the handlers.

The results show that Movec correctly invoked handlers for all projects, whereas JavaMOP failed to correctly invoke handlers in 3 projects (denoted by numbers with strikethrough lines), especially when the number of monitors is large. We considered two criteria of overhead: absolute time difference (i.e., the difference between the run time before and after instrumentation) and relative time difference (i.e., the ratio of the increased run time after instrumentation). Note that Java VM spends some time to load Java programs before execution, which is included in original run time but not in the difference, thus Java programs will benefit if we use relative time difference. In contrast, absolute time difference can avoid the effect of loading time. Indeed, absolute time difference is largely due to the algorithm for indexing and retrieving monitors, thus can more accurately reflect overhead. Hence, absolute time difference is an appropriate criterion for comparing their performance. According to this criterion, our algorithm is comparable with JavaMOP, because each tool succeeded in half of the runs. We also note that JavaMOP outperforms Movec when the number of monitors is large. The reason probably is that JavaMOP uses the efficient data structures from Java class library, such as hashmaps, whereas our data structures and algorithms are less optimized.

MOVEC *vs. ACC.* For evaluating ACC, we have to use another benchmark, because ACC does not support parametric monitoring. In our experiment, we used ten projects from MiBench, a free and commercially representative embedded benchmark suite. We evaluated the performance of MOVEC and ACC by defining exactly equivalent monitors for each project, and of course in a different syntax. Due to page limit, we do not list the data here. The results show that the instrumentation time of MOVEC is less than ACC for all projects, and MOVEC significantly outperforms ACC in reliability (the results of ACC are incorrect for 7 projects, whereas MOVEC is correct for all projects according to our manual inspection) and efficiency (the overhead introduced by ACC is greater than MOVEC for all remaining 3 correctly executed projects of ACC).

## 7    Conclusion and Future Work

The main elements of the language design and compiler implementation are now fairly stable, but the project is not nearly finished. We are focusing on fine-tuning parts of the language design (e.g., adding more pointcuts and formalisms), optimizing data structures and building the next generation compiler, to improve the quality, performance and power of the compiler. We are also working on its IDE extensions and documentation. We want to build up and support a real user community of MOVEC, and plan to work with them to empirically study the practical value of MOVEC. We are open for suggestions how to further optimize the syntax and semantics. MOVEC and a set of working code examples/benchmarks are available for download from http://svlab.nuaa.edu.cn/zchen/projects/movec.

**Acknowledgement.** This work was supported by National Natural Science Foundation of China (61100034 and 61502231), Joint Research Funds of National Natural Science Foundation of China and Civil Aviation Administration of China (U1533130), Scientific Research Foundation for the Returned Overseas Chinese Scholars of State Education Ministry (2013) and Fundamental Research Funds for the Central Universities (NS2016092).

## References

1. Allan, C., Avgustinov, P., Christensen, A.S., Hendren, L.J., Kuzins, S., Lhoták, O., de Moor, O., Sereni, D., Sittampalam, G., Tibble, J.: Adding trace matching with free variables to AspectJ. In: Johnson, R.E., Gabriel, R.P. (eds.) Proceedings of the 20th Annual ACM SIGPLAN Conference on Object-Oriented Programming, Systems, Languages, and Applications (OOPSLA 2005), pp. 345–364. ACM (2005)
2. Avgustinov, P., Tibble, J., de Moor, O.: Making trace monitors feasible. In: Gabriel, R.P., Bacon, D.F., Lopes C.V., Steele G.L. (eds.) Proceedings of the 22nd Annual ACM SIGPLAN Conference on Object-Oriented Programming, Systems, Languages, and Applications (OOPSLA 2007), pp. 589–608. ACM (2007)

3. Chen, F., Meredith, P.O., Jin, D., Rosu, G.: Efficient formalism-independent monitoring of parametric properties. In: Proceedings of the 24th IEEE/ACM International Conference on Automated Software Engineering (ASE 2009), pp. 383–394. IEEE Computer Society (2009)
4. Chen, F., Rosu, G.: MOP: an efficient and generic runtime verification framework. In: Proceedings of the 22nd Annual ACM SIGPLAN Conference on Object-Oriented Programming, Systems, Languages, and Applications (OOPSLA 2007), pp. 569–588. ACM (2007)
5. Chen, F., Roşu, G.: Parametric trace slicing and monitoring. In: Kowalewski, S., Philippou, A. (eds.) TACAS 2009. LNCS, vol. 5505, pp. 246–261. Springer, Heidelberg (2009)
6. Chen, Z.: Control systems on automata and grammars. Comput. J. **58**(1), 75–94 (2015)
7. Chen, Z., Gu, Y., Huang, Z., Zheng, J., Liu, C., Liu, Z.: Model checking aircraft controller software: a case study. Softw. Pract. Experience **45**(7), 989–1017 (2015)
8. Chen, Z., Wei, O., Huang, Z., Xi, H.: Formal semantics of runtime monitoring, verification, enforcement and control. In: Proceedings of the 9th International Symposium on Theoretical Aspects of Software Engineering (TASE 2015), pp. 63–70. IEEE Computer Society (2015)
9. Coady, Y., Kiczales, G., Feeley, M.J., Smolyn, G.: Using AspectC to improve the modularity of path-specific customization in operating system code. In: Proceedings of the 8th European Software Engineering Conference Held Jointly with 9th ACM SIGSOFT International Symposium on Foundations of Software Engineering (ESEC/FSE 2001), pp. 88–98. ACM (2001)
10. Coady, Y., Kiczales, G., Feeley, M., Hutchinson, N., Ong, J.S.: Structuring operating system aspects: using AOP to improve OS structure modularity. Commun. ACM **44**(10), 79–82 (2001)
11. Gong, W., Jacobsen, H.A.: Aspect-oriented C language specification. Working technical draft, University of Toronto, May 2010
12. Jin, D., Meredith, P.O., Griffith, D., Rosu, G.: Garbage collection for monitoring parametric properties. In: Proceedings of the 32nd ACM SIGPLAN Conference on Programming Language Design and Implementation (PLDI 2011), pp. 415–424. ACM (2011)
13. Jin, D., Meredith, P.O., Lee, C., Rosu, G.: JavaMOP: efficient parametric runtime monitoring framework. In: Proceedings of the 34th International Conference on Software Engineering (ICSE 2012), pp. 1427–1430. IEEE (2012)
14. Kiczales, G., Hilsdale, E., Hugunin, J., Kersten, M., Palm, J., Griswold, W.G.: An overview of AspectJ. In: Lindskov Knudsen, J. (ed.) ECOOP 2001. LNCS, vol. 2072, pp. 327–353. Springer, Heidelberg (2001)
15. Kiczales, G., Lamping, J., Mendhekar, A., Maeda, C., Lopes, C.V., Loingtier, J.M., Irwin, J.: Aspect-oriented programming. In: Akşit, M., Matsuoka, S. (eds.) ECOOP 1997. LNCS, vol. 1241, pp. 220–242. Springer, Heidelberg (1997)
16. Leucker, M., Schallhart, C.: A brief account of runtime verification. J. Logic Algebraic Program. **78**(5), 293–303 (2009)
17. Meredith, P.O., Jin, D., Griffith, D., Chen, F., Rosu, G.: An overview of the MOP runtime verification framework. Int. J. Softw. Tools Technol. Transf. (STTT) **14**(3), 249–289 (2012)
18. Rosu, G., Chen, F.: Semantics and algorithms for parametric monitoring. Logical Methods Comput. Sci. **8**(1), 1–47 (2012)
19. RV: The Runtime Verification workshop series (2001–2015). http://www.runtime-verification.org/

20. Spinczyk, O.: AspectC++ language reference. Version 1.10, Pure-systems GmbH, October 2012
21. Spinczyk, O.: AspectC++ compiler manual. Version 1.7, Pure-systems GmbH, September 2013
22. Spinczyk, O., Gal, A., Schröder-Preikschat, W.: AspectC++: an aspect-oriented extension to the C++ programming language. In: Proceedings of the 40th International Conference on Technology of Object-Oriented Languages and Systems (TOOLS Pacific 2002), pp. 53–60. Australian Computer Society (2002)
23. Spinczyk, O., Lohmann, D.: The design and implementation of AspectC++. Knowl. Based Syst. **20**(7), 636–651 (2007)

# Coqoon
## An IDE for Interactive Proof Development in Coq

Alexander Faithfull[1][(✉)], Jesper Bengtson[1], Enrico Tassi[2], and Carst Tankink[2]

[1] IT University of Copenhagen, Copenhagen, Denmark
alef@itu.dk
[2] Inria, Sophia Antipolis, France

**Abstract.** User interfaces for interactive proof assistants have always lagged behind those for mainstream programming languages. Whereas integrated development environments—IDEs—have support for features like project management, version control, dependency analysis and incremental project compilation, "IDE"s for proof assistants typically only operate on files in isolation, relying on external tools to integrate those files into larger projects. In this paper we present Coqoon, an IDE for Coq developments integrated into Eclipse. Coqoon manages proofs as projects rather than isolated source files, and compiles these projects using the Eclipse common build system. Coqoon takes advantage of the latest features of Coq, including asynchronous and parallel processing of proofs, and—when used together with a third-party OCaml extension for Eclipse—can even be used to work on large developments containing Coq plugins.

## 1 Introduction

In the last decade, computer-aided proof development has been gaining momentum. Interactive proof assistants allow their users to state a mathematical theorem in a language that the system understands and then prove that theorem within the system. As long as the proof assistant's verification code is free from bugs, this guarantees that all proofs are actually correct, that no details have been overlooked, and that no mistakes were made. Mechanizing proofs in this way makes very large proofs feasible and protects against subtle and hard-to-notice human errors. Two recent milestones in computer science include the verification of an optimising C compiler [6] and of a micro-kernel [17]. Proof assistants have also been used to verify advanced results in mathematics, such as the Odd Order Theorem, using Coq [12], and the proof of the Kepler conjecture, using HOL-Light and Isabelle [14].

Meanwhile, on the other side of the great chasm between theory and practice, software developers too have come to appreciate computer assistance as they work. For a developer, though, that assistance comes not in the form of a proof assistant, but of an *integrated development environment* (IDE).

C. Tankink—Funded by the Paral-ITP ANR-11-INSE-001 project.

M. Chechik and J.-F. Raskin (Eds.): TACAS 2016, LNCS 9636, pp. 316–331, 2016.
DOI: 10.1007/978-3-662-49674-9_18

The IDE combines many important tools of the trade—such as editors, compilers, refactorers, profilers, debuggers, and project and release managers—into a single unified toolbox for working with code. At a glance, the developer has an overview of every aspect of a project, and the repercussions of changes in one area can be shown in every other affected area, allowing the developer to make any necessary corrections. Many IDEs can even abstract away the build process entirely, automatically inferring the relationships between source files and libraries and rebuilding them when necessary.

The workflows of interactive proof assistants are sufficiently similar to conventional programming languages that one might expect IDEs to exist for them as well, but this is not the case. Even though proof assistants are gaining in popularity, there are still no real IDEs for them—none of them are truly *integrated*. Coq is one of the most widely-used proof assistants available, but its proofs are most often written using either Proof General or CoqIDE; these specialised text editors operate only on individual files, leaving project management entirely to developers. Projects are typically built using Makefiles, which in practice require a POSIX-like environment; file dependencies are supported via command-line tools; and complex inter-project dependencies are not supported at all, leaving the work of building and linking projects together up to the user. Moreover, both Proof General and CoqIDE have a workflow, often referred to as the *waterfall* model, in which the editor is only aware of the state at one specific point: to view the state elsewhere, the user must either execute all commands up to the desired point or explicitly revert to an earlier point in the document, throwing away all the computations back to that point in the process. This workflow is not only alien to software developers, who are used to being able to edit their files at arbitrary points and receive immediate feedback from the IDE on what effect these changes had on the rest of their development, it is also very slow (although upcoming versions of CoqIDE improve this situation somewhat).

We argue that the lack of tool support for proof assistants is to the detriment of both theoreticians and software developers with an interest in verification. Requiring that developers learn an old-fashioned workflow in order to try out formal methods is unquestionably a deterrent, but that workflow is also a waste of time and effort for those who have grown accustomed to it. Integration and automation have made life easier for programmers: why should the same not also be true for proof authors?

In this paper we present Coqoon—an Eclipse-based IDE for proof development using the Coq proof assistant. Coqoon includes support for Coq projects, much like Eclipse's built-in support for Java projects: users can create Coq projects, structure these projects using folder hierarchies, and add Coq source files to these folders, and the Eclipse automatic build system will keep track of the project dependencies behind the scenes. Whenever a file is changed, moved, or renamed, everything that depends on it is automatically recompiled, and any errors are reported to the user.

Coqoon does away with the waterfall model, instead allowing the user to make changes anywhere in a file—and automatically and asynchronously reproving only the parts that are affected by that change. In this way, Coqoon behaves a lot more like an IDE that software developers are familiar with than the tools available to Coq developers today.

Coqoon is also an *integrated* development environment in the fullest sense of the term. Eclipse has a wide variety of plugins available, ranging from version control plugins like EGit to entire development environments like OcaIDE for OCaml, which can be used alongside Coqoon. The combination of Coqoon and OcaIDE is particularly useful, as it brings support for complex Coq developments that contain both proofs and OCaml plugins.

Coqoon depends on features added to Coq in version 8.5. Architectural changes to Coq 8.5 allow it to support Wenzel's PIDE library for asynchronous proof developments [25], which powers Coqoon's replacement for the waterfall model. Coq 8.5 also adds a two-step compilation process, known as the *quick compilation chain*, that can optionally produce .vio files in place of standard Coq .vo libraries; this new format produces larger, faster files whose proofs are unchecked, but which can later be efficiently compiled into the traditional format by checking the remaining proofs in parallel.

As a test case, we have imported the mechanised proof of the Odd Order Theorem into Coqoon, which is one of the largest Coq 8.5-compatible developments available. Previous versions of this project took over two hours to compile, but, using the quick compilation chain, the project can be compiled into .vio form in just seven minutes, and then into .vo form in a further twenty minutes. Coqoon is the first IDE to include native support for the quick compilation chain—indeed, no other IDE for Coq has an integrated build system—which makes it possible to work with even the most complex projects at speeds that were hitherto unimaginable.

We have also adapted Pierce's course on Software Foundations to be compatible with this version. This development contains plenty of exercises that demonstrate a wide variety of features of Coq, and can be used to try out Coqoon's capabilities in a smaller setting than the Odd-Order Theorem.

Download links and installation instructions for Coqoon, along with pre-packaged example projects, can be found at https://coqoon.github.io/tacas2016.

## 2   Coqoon, Structured Projects, and the Build System

Coqoon is a family of plugins for the Eclipse framework that together implement an IDE for Coq developments. It has support for structuring these developments easily using Eclipse workspace projects, folders, and files, and for automatically managing the verification and build processes in the face of changed dependencies. To allow more interactive development of proof scripts, Coqoon processes them in the background, showing Coq feedback directly in the proof text editor using idioms familiar to programmers (e.g., by underlining errors in red).

As Coqoon is implemented on top of the Eclipse framework, it interoperates with other Eclipse components: version control plugins like EGit [9], for example, can be used with Coqoon projects.

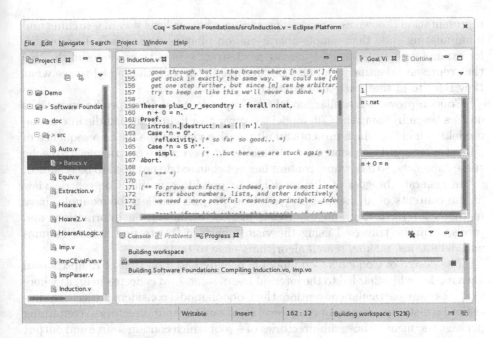

**Fig. 1.** A screenshot of Coqoon, showing the project viewer, a Coq editor with syntax highlighting, and the goal viewer. The progress bar at the bottom of the screen shows the Coq project builder at work.

## 2.1 Structured Projects

Coqoon provides a more structured environment than Coq programmers are accustomed to. From the moment the user first creates a Coq project in Coqoon, it already has a complete build system; Coq source code must be placed in designated source folders, and when files start to depend on other files, they will automatically be marked for recompilation when their dependencies are moved or changed, even if those dependencies are in other projects. A progress bar—visible at the bottom of Fig. 1—displays the state of any build operations scheduled by the builder.

This need for structure is not just the IDE being difficult: it is precisely this structure that makes more sophisticated behaviour possible. The use of the Coqoon integrated build system allows Coq projects to support dependencies on other projects, or on external developments, whilst simultaneously freeing the developer from the need to think about the build system and making it work on all operating systems supported by Eclipse.

## 2.2 The Coq Model

Replacing unstructured collections of files with structured projects is a start, but most IDEs go further. They transform source code files into a more structured representation (known as a *model*), providing a higher-level way of searching and manipulating code than simple operations on plain text. Eclipse's Java model, for example, presents Java documents as abstract syntax trees; nodes in the tree that represent identifiers can also be "resolved" through the model to see what they refer to in that particular context.

Coqoon provides a similar model for Coq code. Most Coq-specific operations on files begin by using the Coq model to convert an Eclipse file handle into a Coq model file handle, which presents an alternative view of the file as a sequence of parsed and tagged Coq sentences. The model also serves as a central place to cache these sequences, so files whose content has not changed do not need to be reparsed.

In general, the goal of this model is to provide a useful, Coq-centric view of the contents of an Eclipse project. Coq project handles, for example, have methods for retrieving and modifying project configuration information, and projects can be traversed using the visitor pattern [11] to find named lemmas and definitions, making search algorithms easy to build.

The design of Coqoon's Coq model is heavily based on that of Eclipse's own Java model, which has led to the internal use of some Java concepts in areas where Coq lacks any particular convention: the Coqoon model considers projects to consist of Java-style package roots (top-level source and output directories) containing package fragments (those subdirectories of a root which contain source and output files), for example, although the concept of a package is not one native to Coq.

## 2.3   Coq Interaction

Coqoon's integrated Coq editor communicates using the PIDE library. Originally developed for the Isabelle proof assistant, PIDE frees the user from having to explicitly direct the prover to make progress through a source file. Proofs handled by PIDE may be evaluated in parallel or out-of-order, and Coq's state after the evaluation of each sentence is saved, making it quick and easy to see how tactics affect the state of a proof. Section 3 explains the operation of the PIDE protocol in more detail.

When using PIDE, the operation of the prover in the background is transparent to the user. Any status messages and goal information associated with a command will automatically be displayed when the user moves the text cursor onto it, and errors are highlighted when the user makes a mistake.

## 2.4   The Coq Build Process

When a Coq file is added to, modified in, or removed from a Coq project, the integrated Coq builder is activated. The builder is responsible for compiling all of a project's Coq proofs into library files.

Whenever the Coqoon builder is activated, Eclipse provides it with a summary of the changes to the project since the last activation. The builder then uses the Coq model to extract the new dependency information from the changed files; it then rebuilds all the changed files and their dependents in an appropriate order, postponing the compilation of a file until its dependencies are also up-to-date.

This behaviour is common to virtually all IDEs, and—although it is not supported by existing Coq interfaces—many projects have built ad-hoc emulations of it for themselves. At the time of writing, for example, the CompCert project contains a pair of shell scripts—one for use with CoqIDE, and one for use with Proof General—which compiles the dependencies of a file, opens it in the appropriate editor, and recompiles that file when the editor is subsequently closed.

**A Second Implementation.** As the integrated build system might conceivably also be useful outside of Coqoon, we also provide a Python reimplementation of it. This reimplementation is included by default in all Coqoon projects to make it possible to work on them even in the absence of Eclipse.

## Projects and Hybrid Projects

All Eclipse projects are collections of files coupled with Eclipse build system metadata which expresses that project's specific requirements. A Coqoon project consists of Coq source code, information about the project's internal structure and its dependencies, and an instruction to the Eclipse build system explaining that the project is a Coq development under the control of the Coqoon builder.

This mechanism is sufficiently general that a project's metadata can have multiple instructions for the Eclipse build system—for example, a Coq project might declare that a bundled plugin is to be built with an OCaml builder. Indeed, a copy of Eclipse equipped with Coqoon and OcaIDE, an OCaml IDE for Eclipse[7], serves as a complete development environment for Coq projects with OCaml plugins; Sect. 4.1 describes such a scenario in more detail.

## Project Dependencies

The Coqoon builder uses a project's load path to resolve the dependencies present in that project's source code, and also provides a user interface for manipulating those dependencies. This functionality is loosely inspired by the Java class path management found in Eclipse Java projects.

Coqoon supports five different kinds of load path entries:

- folders in Eclipse projects that contain source code files;
- folders in Eclipse projects that contain compiled source code;
- other Coqoon projects in the Eclipse workspace;
- folders in the local file system containing projects neither built with nor managed by Coqoon; and
- "abstract" entries which are likely to be available everywhere but whose location cannot be known in advance, like the Coq standard library.

The builder calculates how each of these kinds of entry should be represented in the Coq load path, and uses this information to resolve the dependencies of each file in the project.

The dependency resolution process is sophisticated enough to recognize when to prefer files that have yet to be compiled to files that are already available: if a project contains a file called `List.v`, for example, then other files in that project can safely depend on its compiled form by depending on `List`, even though the Coq standard library contains an identically named file which could potentially satisfy that dependency.

**Abstract Dependencies.** When Coqoon encounters an "abstract" entry, it looks at that entry's identifier and searches an internal registry for a class that knows how to handle that identifier. These classes can then run arbitrary code to resolve the identifier; for example, the handler for the Coq standard library finds it by running a `coqtop` process with the `-where` option.

As this internal registry is also exposed through the standard Eclipse extension mechanism, it can also be used to add new kinds of dependencies to Coqoon. We discuss one possible application of this technique in Sect. 5.2.

### Aggressive Rebuilding

Coqoon's internal dependency analysis behaves like that of `make`: when a file is older than one of its dependencies, it becomes a candidate for recompilation. As a result, making changes to a file with many transitive dependencies will trigger the recompilation of many other files.

As Coq proofs do not have a clean separation between their externally-visible interface and the internal implementation, this is the only safe way of ensuring that changes to a fundamental proof are appropriately reflected throughout a project. Coqoon offers two different mitigations to make this more palatable for large developments: the builder can be configured to recompile projects only when the user explicitly requests it, or it can be told to use the Coq 8.5 quick compilation chain, speeding up compilation drastically by postponing the evaluation of proofs.

### Neatness and Namespaces

Coq developments do not typically have a clean separation between source and output folders. In a simpler setting, the resulting clutter is merely annoying; in an IDE, however, compiled libraries and other derived files are normally entirely hidden from the user, which is a much harder task when these files are not systematically separated from source code.

The Coqoon builder emulates the behaviour of the Java builder to provide this separation: the Coq source file `src/SoftwareFoundations/Basics.v`, for example, is compiled into the library `bin/SoftwareFoundations/Basics.vo`, the fully-qualified name of which would be `SoftwareFoundations.Basics`. Although there are as yet no conventions for managing the Coq library namespace, this approach is flexible enough to support any convention that might be chosen in a future version of Coq.

# 3   PIDE: Coqoon's Interaction with Coq

PIDE is a middleware layer originally developed by Wenzel [25] to bridge the gap between the Isabelle system, implemented in PolyML, and its user interface, written in Java.

For both historical and technical reasons, many proof assistants are written in a programming language that is a descendant of ML, a language conceived with that particular application in mind. IDEs, on the other hand, are more usually built atop industry-standard platforms like Java or .NET; a layer like PIDE is thus necessary to enable provers to talk to the outside world.

## 3.1   PIDE in a Nutshell

PIDE consists of a relatively prover-agnostic frontend library, implemented in Scala, and a prover-specific backend in the prover's own implementation language (i.e., PolyML for Isabelle, or OCaml for Coq). These two components co-operate to ensure that frontend and backend both agree on the content and structure of the user's document. In this model, the backend has a complete view of the document, and so is free to evaluate its commands in any order it sees fit; its half of the PIDE implementation then relays the resulting—potentially out-of-order—status and feedback messages back to the frontend (and thus to the user). The frontend can also interrupt the backend with an update to the document, or direct the backend to focus its attention on a different region.

To bring PIDE support to Coq, Tankink wrote an OCaml implementation of the PIDE backend for use with Coq 8.5, also making some minor changes to the Scala library in the process [4]. Although Coqoon has benefited greatly from this work, it was not carried out with Coqoon in mind—it was originally intended for use with jEdit, a more limited text editor used as the main interface for Isabelle.

Even though jEdit and Eclipse are two very different environments, adding PIDE support to Coqoon has required only minor changes to PIDE, which shows that the library is not tied to one particular style of frontend.

# 4   Test Cases

To assess the maturity of the tool we apply it to two Coq developments: the *Odd Order Theorem*, a large formalization that comprises both Coq theories and a Coq extension, and the widely used teaching course in *Software Foundations* by Pierce.

## 4.1   The Odd Order Theorem and the Math.Comp. Library

The Odd Order Theorem by Feit and Thompson is a masterpiece of modern mathematics for which its last author received the Fields medal in 1970 and the Abel prize in 2008. This result was not only famous because of its profound influence on the last fifty years of research in group theory, but also for its length, weighing in at more than two hundred and fifty pages. Indeed, its length and intricacy caused many to raise concerns about the correctness of its entire argument.

In 2012 a team of fifteen people, led by Gonthier [12], completed a formal verification of the proof, and of the mathematical theories it builds upon, using the Coq system. The project took six years to complete (including three years of work on the part of this paper's third author). The resulting body of formalized mathematics is divided into two main parts: the so called Mathematical Components library (Math.Comp. for short), that covers many general purpose mathematical theories (group theory, linear algebra, character theory ...) and the main proof which builds upon them.

The entire development sums up to 125 Coq modules for a total of 161,000 lines of code: 93 modules and approximately 121,000 lines for the Math.Comp. library, and 32 modules and 40,000 lines for the main proof. All Coq modules are written in a custom language, called SSReflect, that is provided by a plugin for Coq. The plugin, itself a 7,500-line OCaml program, is also part of the Math.Comp. library. The entire source code amounts to 7.4 MB.

This code base constitutes one of the largest developments for Coq, and pushes the system close to its limits; as a consequence, building it and working on it has never been a pleasant experience for the user. The dependency graph of its components, for example, is too large to be printed in this paper,[1] and building the entire project takes around two hours. This time is how long one needs to wait in order to build on top of the Math.Comp. library, or browse it comfortably, or simply to be able to go back to work after having made a minor change to one of the core modules. Despite that, other formalization projects have started depending on (parts of) the Math.Comp. library, inheriting along with it the complexity and time consumption of its build process. In particular, building the SSReflect plugin by hand has always been a source of trouble for its users, and the long time required to build the entire library eventually pushed the authors of the library to provide reduced versions of it for those users who did not need all of its power.

Importing this gargantuan project into Coqoon revealed a few deficiencies in our implementation. Coqoon's dependency resolver, for example, was overwhelmed by the size of the dependency graph, in some cases taking more than ten seconds to work out a file's dependencies. Luckily, this was easily remedied by the addition of a simple cache.

To spare the user from a prolonged compilation process, support for the quick compilation [4] chain, a new feature provided by Coq 8.5, was also added to Coqoon. This process separates Coq compilation into two phases: the first is very quick, checking only definitions and statements, while the second, slower, phase completes the compilation by checking the proofs. As the first phase produces intermediate files that can be used in place of traditional Coq libraries, it only takes around seven minutes of computation on an ordinary laptop computer before the entire set of 125 modules is usable.

---

[1] The interested reader can browse it online: http://coqfinitgroup.gforge.inria.fr/doc/.

As the user does not need to wait for the second phase in order to work with the development, it can typically be run as a background task. Unlike the first phase, it can take great advantage of parallel hardware, because each proof can be checked independently of the others: on a computer with a dozen cores, the proofs for the whole development can be completed in as few as 15 min.

In addition to that, we added support to OCaml modules to the Coq builder. Combined with the OCaml builder provided by OcaIDE, this has made it possible to build both the SSReflect plugin and the Coq modules that depend on it in a single integrated build process.

Finally, the PIDE backend for Coq was made more responsive and robust when dealing with long modules. Most of the files in the Mathematical Components library are more than a thousand lines of code in length, and some are more than four thousand lines. For comparison, in the CompCert compiler, [6] another Coq flagship project, composed of 5.2 MB of sources, more than 30 % of the modules are longer than a thousand lines.

As a result of these changes, we believe Coqoon represents the best platform for working on such large developments. In particular, at the time of writing, no other IDE for Coq can handle projects that contain both OCaml and Coq code, and Coqoon is the only one to incorporate the quick compilation chain as an integrated part of an automatic build system.

## 4.2 Software Foundations

This is a relatively small Coq development that complements the Software Foundations book by Pierce et al. It is a widely adopted course that touches on topics like logic, functional programming, interactive theorem provers, and techniques for software verification. Universities in the United States, Japan and Europe use it in their curricula.

Coqoon has been used at the IT University of Copenhagen in conjunction with the Software Foundations teaching material for three years. We have found that the use of a more familiar development environment makes Coq much more user-friendly for students, showing that building on top of an IDE brings advantages for beginners and experts alike.

# 5  Building on Coqoon

## 5.1  Embedding Coq

Our work with OcaIDE shows that Coqoon can already interoperate with other development environments built on the Eclipse platform. The next step in our work is to provide even tighter integration between the Coq and Java development environments.

Java projects can already be turned into "hybrid" projects containing both Java programs and Coq proofs about those programs, but this is only a start. There are already several tools that embed assertions and proofs directly into the source code that they describe, like Dafny [18], Spec# [3], and VeriFast [16]. The IDE seems like an obvious home for this functionality: that is, it should be possible to extend the Java editor already present in Eclipse with Coqoon-powered Coq proofs.

In fact, Coqoon's predecessor, Kopitiam, provided just such an environment. (We discuss Kopitiam in more detail in Sect. 6.1.) However, this environment was built using cruder integration techniques and predated the introduction of PIDE. A prototype inspired by Kopitiam, but built using Coqoon, PIDE, and a custom text editor more aware of the interleaving between Coq and Java code, is under development at the IT University.

## 5.2  Abstract Load Paths and OPAM

At the heart of Eclipse is an implementation of the OSGi component model [10], which provides a platform for dynamically loading and unloading Java archives. Eclipse extends these archives—known as "plugins" in the Eclipse context—with extra metadata defining *extension points*, services which plugins can declare that they contribute extensions to. Extension point definitions can require arbitrary information from extensions, but this will typically include the fully-qualified name of a class implementing a particular interface; in this way the original plugin can instantiate, configure and use code contributed by one of its extensions.

Coqoon provides a number of Coq-specific extensions to Eclipse's own core plugins: for example, it contributes the Coqoon project builder to the resource management plugin, and the PIDE document editor to the text editors plugin. However, it also defines an extension point of its own, which allows other plugins to add new handlers for abstract load path entries to Coqoon.

The Coq ecosystem has not traditionally provided any way of packaging and distributing projects, which has made building on other people's work difficult and fragile. This is, however, about to change: Coq 8.5 will be distributed alongside a repository of ready-to-install Coq projects for OPAM, the OCaml Package Manager.

Making the abstract load path mechanism extensible means that Coqoon is ready to adapt to this change. We expect to include a plugin with future versions of Coqoon that will use the abstract load path mechanism to support direct dependencies on OPAM projects, but this will not require any changes to Coqoon itself.

## 6  Related Work

Over the last thirty years, there have been multiple attempts to make the interaction with proof assistants easier. Initially, all interaction was through a Read-Eval-Print loop (REPL), a command-line interface that interprets each command typed by the user and prints out the resulting goal state (or an error) before requesting new commands. Some proof assistants, such as HOL [13] and HOL Light [15], still use this as their primary mode of interaction.

## 6.1   Waterfall Interaction

Proof General [1], based on Emacs, was the one of the first interfaces that offered more than just a REPL, and is the only one of the early interfaces that endures until today, going so far as to define the *de facto* standard method of interaction with Coq: the waterfall model. Although this still required the user to direct proof processing manually, it was nevertheless a significant improvement over the bare REPL.

The Proof General model of interaction has been duplicated by several other Coq tools, including CoqIDE, which is a GTK+-based interface bundled with Coq [23], and three Eclipse plugins. The first was created by Aspinall as an attempt to port Proof General itself to Eclipse [2]; the other by Charles and Kiniry who, as part of the Moebius project, built the plugin ProverEditor for Coq in Eclipse [8]; the third, Kopitiam [20], by Mehnert, is Coqoon's immediate predecessor.

CoqIDE is a custom cross-platform text editor. It does not add any truly new interaction features, beyond some Coq-specific code templates and the ability to invoke `make` and the Coq verifier from the interface. While it allows the user to have multiple buffers open, there is no relation between the contents of the buffers. The version of CoqIDE shipped with Coq 8.5 was improved by Tassi to support processing the waterfall in parallel. However, the fundamental interaction with Coq will not change: the user still needs to manually direct Coq to process parts of the active document.

The Proof General plugin for Eclipse was only available for Isabelle, and has not been under active development since 2010, based on its Eclipse update site at http://proofgeneral.inf.ed.ac.uk/eclipse/products/. It offered interaction based on the waterfall model, and a high-level overview of individual proofs, but did not provide any support for structured projects.

Conversely, the ProverEditor plugin for Eclipse was only available for Coq. Its project support consisted of automatic Makefile generation and support for invoking `make`—unlike Coqoon, it did not integrate into Eclipse's build system. ProverEditor was discontinued in 2009, when the last update to their GitHub page was made.

Kopitiam targeted the 8.3 series of Coq, which had no structured way of sending and receiving messages: Coq 8.4 introduced an XML-based protocol for executing commands, and Coq 8.5 allows developers to add support for entirely new protocols such as PIDE, but Coq 8.3 only supported interaction through the standard Coq REPL. This was extremely brittle, and required constant polling to read responses from Coq. Kopitiam had no support for Coq projects.

Kopitiam offered one unconventional extension to the waterfall model: it allowed Coq proofs to be interleaved with Java source code. Using aspect-oriented programming to hook into the internals of the Java editor, it added Coq-like controls to step through decorated Java programs: stepping over a Java command would cause it to be 'executed' in an environment based on a separation logic framework built by Bengtson et al. [5]. As the waterfall does not map cleanly onto any Java concepts, this was fragile and difficult to use, but it was an interesting extension—and one which we intend to reintroduce in the future using PIDE.

## 6.2  PIDE and Asynchronous Editors

With the introduction of PIDE, Wenzel ushered in the third generation of proof assistant interaction: instead of requiring the user to micromanage the system's execution, it allows asynchronous interfaces, such as Coqoon. The flagship application of the PIDE approach for Isabelle is Isabelle/jEdit [26], which is now the standard frontend to the Isabelle system.

Because PIDE and Isabelle/jEdit have been developed in tandem, the editor makes full use of the features we have described in Sect. 3: the editor allows asynchronous interaction with Isabelle, and marks up the proof document using information obtained during interpretation. Isabelle/jEdit has been partially adapted to support Coq by Tankink [4]—the resulting combination being called Coq/jEdit—but this adaptation does not have the full power of an IDE.

jEdit is an extensible text editor, not an IDE, and the way it was extended by Wenzel in order to support entire developments is Isabelle specific. Following the original design of provers of the HOL family, the Isabelle system does not provide a notion of separate compilation: files are just loaded by a single prover instance one after the other, with an option of using concurrent threads to speed up the process. The PIDE protocol is even able to multiplex multiple text buffers to the same prover instance, and expects the prover to sort that out.

The way Coq works is closer to how traditional programming languages work. The Coq compiler can deal with one file at a time, and unrelated files can be processed by different instances of the compiler, possibly in parallel. As a result Coq/jEdit can only work with a single file and relies on the user to provide their own build system for larger projects. Coqoon is able to take care of the entire build process of large developments, even when they include custom Coq plugins, as described in Sect. 2.4.

Another limitation of Coq/jEdit is that, while Isabelle/jEdit maintains a model of proof documents using PIDE, Coq/jEdit does not. The design of Isabelle's language makes it much easier to integrate that model with jEdit's syntax-and-text oriented views. Isabelle's proof language, Isar, is a two-tiered language, that consists of an outer syntax that gives structure to proof documents, the Isar language proper, and numerous inner syntaxes used for specification and proof methods, the most notable being the Higher Order Logic; HOL. The transition between these languages is syntactically indicated using quotation marks. The outer syntax has a simple structure and can easily be parsed by the Scala library of PIDE. The inner syntaxes are more versatile, and the parsing and processing is handled by the Isabelle side of PIDE. It is this outer syntax that is exposed to jEdit. In Coq's language, there is no syntactical separation between the different languages used, making it difficult to implement a Scala-side parser that exposes the structure. (Coqoon's model takes some steps in this direction, but it is necessarily full of special cases and heuristics.) This lack of a Scala-implemented parser for Coq means that jEdit plugins that rely on such a parser do not work.

Finally, because jEdit is not under active development, its plugins have also grown stale, not being updated to new models and tools. For Isabelle/jEdit,

Wenzel already had to change the core of jEdit to allow the PIDE plugin to paint text when semantic information comes in. This means that Isabelle/jEdit is a small fork of jEdit itself, and that it requires its users to install the entire client, instead of just a plugin. Coqoon works on standard Eclipse distributions.

A second client in the PIDE ecosystem is Isabelle/Eclipse [24]. The development of this Eclipse plugin is on hiatus at the moment, but the version that is available, emulates the Isabelle/jEdit interaction model in Eclipse: it does not provide any 'Eclipse-specific' features like project management or compilation of single files. In its current state, it behaves much like Isabelle/jEdit, but using Eclipse to provide the visual elements for the interface.

Clide [22] is another system that builds upon the PIDE architecture for Isabelle. It is a web interface that is mainly aimed at real time collaboration on proof documents. In a similar fashion to Google Docs, several users can work on the same document, seeing each other's modifications and the responses from Isabelle. It supports projects, but only as a way of grouping together collaborations with others; as such, files in a project are not verified when one file changes, and errors in a proof document are not shown until it is opened.

### 6.3 Another Approach: The ALF Tradition

The ALF proof assistant [19] and its modern-day descendants–chief amongst them Agda [21]—take a rather different approach to the construction of proofs. Whereas Coq proofs consist of a sequence of invocations of tactics, each of which manipulates Coq's internal representation of a proof term, a proof in the ALF tradition consists simply of the finished proof term: the indirect manipulations performed by tactics in the Coq world are replaced by direct modifications of potentially incomplete terms in source files. Compared to ALF-style proofs, Coq proofs are thus somewhat akin to an edit script: they enumerate the steps taken by the user to arrive at a complete proof term, which are analogous to the steps that the user would perform directly in ALF.

Using this approach in practice requires a more intelligent interface than a simple text editor. Agda proofs, for example, are typically written using an advanced Emacs mode equipped with the ability to rewrite regions of the document according to the transformations supported by the prover. However, this mode shares many of the other drawbacks of tools built on extensible editors: in particular, it has no support for project management.

## 7  Conclusion

This paper presents Coqoon, an IDE for the interactive proof assistant Coq in Eclipse. Coqoon moves away from traditional synchronous proof development and towards an asynchronous model that allows any part of a proof document to be modified and rechecked without having to retract unrelated proofs. It also supports Coq projects that are fully integrated into the Eclipse build system: files can be added, deleted, and moved at will, and Coqoon will track these changes and rebuild affected files whenever necessary. Coqoon can also make use of the large number of plugins already available for Eclipse, such as the OCaml plugin OcaIDE, turning Coqoon into a complete development environment for even the most complex Coq projects, or the version control plugin EGit.

Coqoon also brings support for Coq projects to other Eclipse projects and plugins, paving the way for complete IDEs for software verification where programs and proofs of their correctness can be maintained within the same project—or even in the same file.

Together, these features represent a significant advance: a truly integrated and comprehensive proof assistant IDE, bringing to the world of proof assistants a workflow that software developers have enjoyed for decades.

# References

1. Aspinall, D.: Proof general: a generic tool for proof development. In: Graf, S. (ed.) TACAS 2000. LNCS, vol. 1785, p. 38. Springer, Heidelberg (2000)
2. Aspinall, D., Lüth, C., Winterstein, D.: A framework for interactive proof. In: Kauers, M., Kerber, M., Miner, R., Windsteiger, W. (eds.) MKM/CALCULEMUS 2007. LNCS (LNAI), vol. 4573, pp. 161–175. Springer, Heidelberg (2007)
3. Barnett, M., Leino, K.R.M., Schulte, W.: The spec# programming system: an overview. In: Barthe, G., Burdy, L., Huisman, M., Lanet, J.-L., Muntean, T. (eds.) CASSIS 2004. LNCS, vol. 3362, pp. 49–69. Springer, Heidelberg (2005)
4. Barras, B., Tankink, C., Tassi, E.: Asynchronous processing of Coq documents: from the kernel up to the user interface. In: Urban, C., Zhang, X. (eds.) ITP 2015. LNCS, vol. 9236, pp. 51–66. Springer, New York (2015)
5. Bengtson, J., Jensen, J.B., Sieczkowski, F., Birkedal, L.: Verifying object-oriented programs with higher-order separation logic in Coq. In: Eekelen, M., Geuvers, H., Schmaltz, J., Wiedijk, F. (eds.) ITP 2011. LNCS, vol. 6898, pp. 22–38. Springer, Heidelberg (2011)
6. Boldo, S., Jourdan, J.-H., Leroy, X., Melquiond, G.: A formally-verified C compiler supporting floating-point arithmetic. In: ARITH, pp. 107–115. IEEE Computer Society (2013)
7. Bros, N., Cerioli, R.: OcaIDE. http://www.algo-prog.info/ocaide/
8. Charles, J., Kiniry, J.R.: A lightweight theorem prover interface for eclipse. In: UITP Workshop proceedings (2008)
9. Eclipse Foundation. EGit. http://www.eclipse.org/egit/
10. Eclipse Foundation. Equinox. http://www.eclipse.org/equinox/
11. Gamma, E., Helm, R., Johnson, R., Vlissides, J.: Design Patterns - Elements of Reusable Object-Oriented Software. Addison-Wesley, 1st edn. 20th printing (1994)
12. Gonthier, G., Asperti, A., Avigad, J., Bertot, Y., Cohen, C., Garillot, F., Le Roux, S., Mahboubi, A., O'Connor, R., Ould Biha, S., Pasca, I., Rideau, L., Solovyev, A., Tassi, E., Théry, L.: A machine-checked proof of the odd order theorem. In: Blazy, S., Paulin-Mohring, C., Pichardie, D. (eds.) ITP 2013. LNCS, vol. 7998, pp. 163–179. Springer, Heidelberg (2013)
13. Gordon, M.J.C., Melham, T.F.: Introduction to HOL: A Theorem Proving Environment for Higher Order Logic. Cambridge University Press, New York (1993)
14. Hales, T.C.: Dense Sphere Packings - a blueprint for formal proofs. Cambridge University Press (2012)

15. Harrison, J.: HOL light: an overview. In: Berghofer, S., Nipkow, T., Urban, C., Wenzel, M. (eds.) TPHOLs 2009. LNCS, vol. 5674, pp. 60–66. Springer, Heidelberg (2009)
16. Jacobs, B., Piessens, F.: The VeriFast program verifier. CW Reports CW520, Department of Computer Science, K.U.Leuven (2008)
17. Klein, G., Andronick, J., Elphinstone, K., Murray, T.C., Sewell, T., Kolanski, R., Heiser, G.: Comprehensive formal verification of an OS microkernel. ACM Trans. Comput. Syst. **32**(1), 2 (2014)
18. Leino, K.R.M.: Dafny: an automatic program verifier for functional correctness. In: Clarke, E.M., Voronkov, A. (eds.) LPAR-16 2010. LNCS, vol. 6355, pp. 348–370. Springer, Heidelberg (2010)
19. Magnusson, L., Nordström, B.: The Alf proof editor and its proof engine. In: Barendregt, H., Nipkow, T. (eds.) TYPES 1993. LNCS, vol. 806, pp. 213–237. Springer, Heidelberg (1994)
20. Mehnert, H.: Kopitiam: modular incremental interactive full functional static verification of java code. In: Bobaru, M., Havelund, K., Holzmann, G.J., Joshi, R. (eds.) NFM 2011. LNCS, vol. 6617, pp. 518–524. Springer, Heidelberg (2011)
21. Norell, U.: Towards a practical programming language based on dependent type theory. PH.D. thesis, Department of Computer Science and Engineering, Chalmers University of Technology, SE-412 96 Göteborg, Sweden, September 2007
22. Ring, M., Lüth, C.: Collaborative interactive theorem proving with clide. In: Klein, G., Gamboa, R. (eds.) ITP 2014. LNCS, vol. 8558, pp. 467–482. Springer, Heidelberg (2014)
23. The Coq Development Team. The Coq Reference Manual. http://coq.inria.fr/doc
24. Velykis, A.: Isabelle/Eclipse. http://andriusvelykis.github.io/isabelle-eclipse
25. Wenzel, M.: Asynchronous user interaction and tool integration in isabelle/PIDE. In: Klein, G., Gamboa, R. (eds.) ITP 2014. LNCS, vol. 8558, pp. 515–530. Springer, Heidelberg (2014)
26. Wenzel, M.: System description: Isabelle/jEdit in 2014. In: UITP (2014)

# Multi-core Symbolic Bisimulation Minimisation

Tom van Dijk[✉] and Jaco van de Pol

Formal Methods and Tools, University of Twente, Enschede, The Netherlands
{dijkt,vdpol}@cs.utwente.nl

**Abstract.** Bisimulation minimisation alleviates the exponential growth of transition systems in model checking by computing the smallest system that has the same behavior as the original system according to some notion of equivalence. One popular strategy to compute a bisimulation minimisation is signature-based partition refinement. This can be performed symbolically using binary decision diagrams to allow models with larger state spaces to be minimised.

This paper studies strong and branching symbolic bisimulation for labeled transition systems, continuous-time markov chains, and interactive markov chains. We introduce the notion of partition refinement with partial signatures. We extend the parallel BDD library Sylvan to parallelize the signature refinement algorithm, and develop a new parallel BDD algorithm to refine a partition, which conserves previous block numbers and uses a parallel data structure to store block assignments. We also present a specialized BDD algorithm for the computation of inert transitions. The experimental evaluation, based on benchmarks from the literature, demonstrates a speedup of up to 95x sequentially. In addition, we find parallel speedups of up to 17x due to parallelisation with 48 cores. Finally, we present the implementation of these algorithms as a versatile tool that can be customized for bisimulation minimisation in various contexts.

**Keywords:** Multi-core · Parallel · Binary decision diagrams · Bisimulation minimisation · Labeled transition systems · Continuous-time Markov chains · Interactive Markov chains

## 1 Introduction

One core challenge in model checking is the state space explosion problem. The space and time requirements of model checking increase exponentially with the size of the models. Bisimulation minimisation computes the smallest equivalent model (maximal bisimulation) under some notion of equivalence, which can significantly reduce the number of states. This technique is also used to abstract models from internal behavior, when only observable behavior is relevant.

The maximal bisimulation of a model is typically computed using partition refinement. Starting with an initially coarse partition (e.g. all states are equivalent), the partition is refined until states in each equivalence class can no

The first author is supported by the NWO project MaDriD, grant nr. 612.001.101.

M. Chechik and J.-F. Raskin (Eds.): TACAS 2016, LNCS 9636, pp. 332–348, 2016.
DOI: 10.1007/978-3-662-49674-9_19

longer be distinguished. The result is the maximal bisimulation with respect to the initial partition. Blom et al. [3] introduced a signature-based method for partition refinement, which assigns states to equivalence classes according to a characterizing signature. This method easily extends to various types of bisimulation.

Another well-known method to deal with very large state spaces is symbolic model checking, where sets of states are represented by their characteristic function, which is efficiently stored using binary decision diagrams (BDDs). In the literature, symbolic methods have been applied to bisimulation minimisation in several ways. Bouali and De Simone [5] refine the equivalence relation $R \subseteq S \times S$, by iteratively removing all "bad" pairs from $R$, i.e., pairs of states that are no longer equivalent. For strong bisimulation, Mumme and Ciardo [19] apply saturation-based methods to compute $R$. Wimmer et al. [25,26] use signatures to refine the partition, represented by the assignment to equivalence classes $P \colon S \to C$. Symbolic bisimulation based on signatures has also been applied to Markov chains by Derisavi [11] and Wimmer et al. [23,24].

The symbolic representation of the maximal bisimulation, when effective, often tends to be much larger than the original model. One particular application of symbolic bisimulation minimisation is as a bridge between symbolical models and explicit-state analysis algorithms. Such models can have very large state spaces that are efficiently encoded using BDDs. If the minimised model is sufficiently small, then it can be analyzed efficiently using explicit-state algorithms.

These techniques mainly reduce the memory requirements of model checking. To take advantage of computer systems with multiple processors, developing scalable parallel algorithms is the way forward. In [12,14], we implemented the multi-core BDD package Sylvan, applying parallelism to symbolic model checking. Parallelization has also been applied to explicit-state bisimulation minimisation. Blom et al. [2,3] introduced a parallel, signature-based algorithm for various types of bisimulation, especially strong and branching bisimulation. Also, [17] proposed a concurrent algorithm for bisimulation minimisation which combines signatures with the approach by Paige and Tarjan [20]. Recently, Wijs [22] implemented highly parallel strong and branching bisimilarity checking on GPGPUs. As far as we are aware, no earlier work combines symbolic bisimulation minimisation and parallelism.

In the current paper, we study bisimulation minimisation for labeled transition systems (LTSs), continuous-time Markov chains (CTMCs) and interactive Markov chains (IMCs), which combines the features of LTSs and CTMCs. These allow the analysis of quantitative properties, e.g. performance and dependability.

We concentrate on strong bisimulation and branching bisimulation. Strong bisimulation preserves both internal behavior ($\tau$-transitions) and observable behavior, while branching bisimulation abstracts from internal behavior. The advantage of branching bisimulation compared to other variations of weak bisimulation is that it preserves the branching structure of the LTS, thus preserving certain interesting properties such as CTL* without next-state operator [9].

The current paper contains the following contributions. We introduce the notion of partition refinement with partial signatures in Sect. 3. Section 4 discusses how we extend the multi-core BDD package Sylvan to parallelize signature-based partition refinement. In particular, we develop two specialized BDD algorithms. We implement a new `refine` algorithm, that refines a partition according to a signature, but maximally reuses the block number assignment of the previous partition (Sect. 4.3). This algorithm improves the operation cache use for the computation of the signatures of stable blocks, and enables partition refinement with partial signatures. We also present the `inert` algorithm, which, given a transition relation and a partition, removes all transitions that are not inert (Sect. 4.4). This algorithm avoids an expensive intermediate result reported in the literature [26]. Section 5 discusses experimental data based on benchmarks from the literature to demonstrate a speedup of up to 95x sequentially. In addition, we find parallel speedups of up to 17x due to parallelisation with 48 cores. Finally, we present the implementation of these algorithms as a versatile tool that can be customized for bisimulation minimisation in various contexts.

## 2 Preliminaries

We recall the basic definitions of partitions, of LTSs, of CTMCs, of IMCs, and of various bisimulations as in [3,15,25–27].

**Definition 1.** *Given a set $S$, a partition $\pi$ of $S$ is a subset $\pi \subseteq 2^S$ such that*

$$\bigcup_{C \in \pi} C = S \quad and \quad \forall C, C' \in \pi : (C = C' \lor C \cap C' = \emptyset).$$

If $\pi'$ and $\pi$ are two partitions, then $\pi'$ is a refinement of $\pi$, written $\pi' \sqsubseteq \pi$, if each block of $\pi'$ is contained in a block of $\pi$. The elements of $\pi$ are called equivalence classes or blocks. Each equivalence relation $\equiv$ is associated with a partition $\pi = S/\equiv$. In this paper, we use $\pi$ and $\equiv$ interchangeably.

**Definition 2.** *A labeled transition system (LTS) is a tuple $(S, \mathsf{Act}, \to)$, consisting of a set of states $S$, a set of labels $\mathsf{Act}$ that may contain the non-observable action $\tau$, and transitions $\to \subseteq S \times \mathsf{Act} \times S$.*

We write $s \xrightarrow{a} t$ for $(s, a, t) \in \to$. and $s \not\xrightarrow{\tau}$ when $s$ has no outgoing $\tau$-transitions. We use $\xrightarrow{a*}$ to denote the transitive reflexive closure of $\xrightarrow{a}$. Given an equivalence relation $\equiv$, we write $\xrightarrow[\equiv]{a}$ for $\xrightarrow{a} \cap \equiv$, i.e., transitions between equivalent states, called *inert* transitions. We use $\xrightarrow[\equiv]{a*}$ for the transitive reflexive closure of $\xrightarrow[\equiv]{a}$.

**Definition 3.** *A continuous-time Markov chain (CTMC) is a tuple $(S, \Rightarrow)$, consisting of a set of states $S$ and Markovian transitions $\Rightarrow \subseteq S \times \mathbb{R}^{>0} \times S$.*

We write $s \xRightarrow{\lambda} t$ for $(s, \lambda, t) \in \Rightarrow$. The interpretation of $s \xRightarrow{\lambda} t$ is that the CTMC can switch from $s$ to $t$ within $d$ time units with probability $1 - e^{-\lambda \cdot d}$. For a state $s$, let $\mathbf{R}(s)(s') = \sum \{\lambda \mid s \xRightarrow{\lambda} s'\}$ be the rate to move from state $s$ to state $s'$, and let $\mathbf{R}(s)(C) = \sum_{s' \in C} \mathbf{R}(s)(s')$ be the cumulative rate to reach a set of states $C \subseteq S$ from state $s$.

**Definition 4.** *An interactive Markov chain (IMC) is a tuple $(S, \mathsf{Act}, \rightarrow, \Rightarrow)$, consisting of a set of states $S$, a set of labels $\mathsf{Act}$ that may contain the non-observable action $\tau$, transitions $\rightarrow \subseteq S \times \mathsf{Act} \times S$, and Markovian transitions $\Rightarrow \subseteq S \times \mathbb{R}^{>0} \times S$.*

An IMC basically combines the features of an LTS and a CTMC. One feature of IMCs is the *maximal progress assumption*. Internal interactive transitions, i.e. $\tau$-transitions, can be assumed to take place immediately, while the probability that a Markovian transition executes immediately is zero. Therefore, we may remove all Markovian transitions from states that have outgoing $\tau$-transitions: $s \xrightarrow{\tau}$ implies $\mathbf{R}(s)(S) = 0$. We call IMCs to which this operation has been applied *maximal-progress-cut* (mp-cut) IMCs.

For LTSs, strong and branching bisimulation are typically defined as follows [26]:

**Definition 5.** *An equivalence relation $\equiv_S$ is a strong bisimulation on an LTS if for all states $s, t, s'$ with $s \equiv_S t$ and for all $s \xrightarrow{a} s'$, there exists a state $t'$ with $t \xrightarrow{a} t'$ and $s' \equiv_S t'$.*

**Definition 6.** *An equivalence relation $\equiv_B$ is a branching bisimulation on an LTS if for all states $s, t, s'$ with $s \equiv_B t$ and for all $s \xrightarrow{a} s'$, either*

- *$a = \tau$ and $s' \equiv_B t$, or*
- *there exist states $t', t''$ with $t \xrightarrow{\tau*} t' \xrightarrow{a} t''$ and $t \equiv_B t'$ and $s' \equiv_B t''$.*

For CTMCs, strong bisimulation is defined as follows [11, 23]:

**Definition 7.** *An equivalence relation $\equiv_S$ is a strong bisimulation on a CTMC if for all $(s, t) \in \equiv_S$ and for all classes $C \in S/\equiv_S$, $\mathbf{R}(s)(C) = \mathbf{R}(t)(C)$.*

For mp-cut IMCs, strong and branching bisimulation are defined as follows [15, 27]:

**Definition 8.** *An equivalence relation $\equiv_S$ is a strong bisimulation on an mp-cut IMC if for all $(s, t) \in \equiv_S$ and for all classes $C \in S/\equiv_S$*

- *$s \xrightarrow{a} s'$ for some $s' \in C$ implies $t \xrightarrow{a} t'$ for some $t' \in C$*
- *$\mathbf{R}(s)(C) = \mathbf{R}(t)(C)$*

**Definition 9.** *An equivalence relation $\equiv_B$ is a branching bisimulation on an mp-cut IMC if for all $(s, t) \in \equiv_B$ and for all classes $C \in S/\equiv_B$*

- *$s \xrightarrow{a} s'$ for some $s' \in C$ implies*
  - *$a = \tau$ and $(s, s') \in \equiv_B$, or*
  - *there exist states $t', t'' \in S$ with $t \xrightarrow{\tau*} t' \xrightarrow{a} t''$ and $(t, t') \in \equiv_B$ and $t'' \in C$.*
- *$\mathbf{R}(s)(C) > 0$ implies*
  - *$\mathbf{R}(s)(C) = \mathbf{R}(t')(C)$ for some $t' \in S$ such that $t \xrightarrow{\tau*} t' \xrightarrow{\tau}\!\!\!\!/\;$ and $(t, t') \in \equiv_B$.*
- *$s \xrightarrow{\tau}\!\!\!\!/\;$ implies $t \xrightarrow{\tau*} t' \xrightarrow{\tau}\!\!\!\!/\;$ for some $t'$*

## 3   Signature-Based Bisimulation

Blom and Orzan [3] introduced a signature-based approach to compute the maximal bisimulation of an LTS, which was further developed into a symbolic method by Wimmer et al. [26]. Each state is characterized by a *signature*, which is the same for all equivalent states in a bisimulation. These signatures are used to refine a partition of the state space until a fixed point is reached, which is the maximal bisimulation.

In the literature, multiple signatures are sometimes used that together fully characterize states, for example based on the state labels, based on the rates of continuous-time transitions, and based on the enabled interactive transitions. In the current paper, these multiple signatures are considered elements of a single signature that fully characterizes each state.

**Definition 10.** *A* signature *$\sigma(\pi)(s)$ is a tuple of functions $f_i(\pi)(s)$, that together characterize each state $s$ with respect to a partition $\pi$.*

Two signatures $\sigma(\pi)(s)$ and $\sigma(\pi)(t)$ are equivalent, if and only if for all $f_i$, $f_i(\pi)(s) = f_i(\pi)(t)$.

The signatures of five bisimulations from Sect. 2 are known from the literature. For all actions $a \in \mathsf{Act}$ and equivalence classes $C \in \pi$, we define

- $\mathbf{T}(\pi)(s) = \{(a, C) \mid \exists s' \in C \colon s \xrightarrow{a} s'\}$
- $\mathbf{B}(\pi)(s) = \{(a, C) \mid \exists s' \in C \colon s \xrightarrow[\pi]{\tau*} \xrightarrow{a} s' \land \neg(a = \tau \land s \in C)\}$
- $\mathbf{R}^s(\pi)(s) = C \mapsto \mathbf{R}(s)(C)$
- $\mathbf{R}^b(\pi)(s) = C \mapsto \max(\{\mathbf{R}(s')(C) \mid \exists s' \colon s \xrightarrow[\pi]{\tau*} s' \xrightarrow{\tau} \!\!\!\!\!/\,\})$

The five bisimulations are associated with the following signatures:

| | | |
|---|---|---|
| Strong bisimulation for an LTS | $(\mathbf{T})$ | [26] |
| Branching bisimulation for an LTS | $(\mathbf{B})$ | [26] |
| Strong bisimulation for a CTMC | $(\mathbf{R}^s)$ | [23] |
| Strong bisimulation for an mp-cut IMC | $(\mathbf{T}, \mathbf{R}^s)$ | [27] |
| Branching bisimulation for an mp-cut IMC | $(\mathbf{B}, \mathbf{R}^b, s\xrightarrow{\tau*}\xrightarrow{\tau}\!\!\!\!\!/\,)$ | [27] |

Functions $\mathbf{T}$ and $\mathbf{B}$ assign to each state $s$ all actions $a$ and equivalence classes $C \in \pi$, such that state $s$ can reach $C$ by an action $a$ either directly ($\mathbf{T}$) or via any number of inert $\tau$-steps ($\mathbf{B}$). $\mathbf{R}^s$ equals $\mathbf{R}$ but with the domain restricted to the equivalence classes $C \in \pi$, and represents the cumulative rate with which state $s$ can go to states in $C$. $\mathbf{R}^b$ equals $\mathbf{R}^s$ for states $s \xrightarrow{\tau}\!\!\!\!\!/\,$, and takes the highest "reachable rate" for states with inert $\tau$-transitions. In branching bisimulation for mp-cut IMCs, the "highest reachable rate" is by definition the rate that all states $s \xrightarrow{\tau}\!\!\!\!\!/\,$ in $C$ have. The element $s\xrightarrow{\tau*}\xrightarrow{\tau}\!\!\!\!\!/\,$ distinguishes time-convergent states from time-divergent states [27], and is independent of the partition.

For the bisimulations of Definitions 5–9, we state:

**Lemma 1.** *A partition $\pi$ is a bisimulation, if and only if for all $s$ and $t$ that are equivalent in $\pi$, $\sigma(\pi)(s) = \sigma(\pi)(t)$.*

For the above definitions it is fairly straightforward to prove that they are equivalent to the classical definitions of bisimulation. See e.g. [3, 26] for the bisimulations on LTSs and [27] for the bisimulations on IMCs.

## 3.1  Partition Refinement

The definition of signature-based partition refinement is as follows.

**Definition 11 (Partition refinement with full signatures)**

$$\text{sigref}(\pi, \sigma) := \{\{t \in S \mid \sigma(\pi)(s) = \sigma(\pi)(t)\} \mid s \in S\}$$
$$\pi^0 := \{S\}$$
$$\pi^{n+1} := \text{sigref}(\pi^n, \sigma)$$

The algorithm iteratively refines the initial coarsest partition $\{S\}$ according to the signatures of the states, until some fixed point $\pi^{n+1} = \pi^n$ is obtained. This fixed point is the maximal bisimulation for "monotone signatures":

**Definition 12.** *A signature is monotone if for all $\pi, \pi'$ with $\pi \sqsubseteq \pi'$, whenever $\sigma(\pi)(s) = \sigma(\pi)(t)$, also $\sigma(\pi')(s) = \sigma(\pi')(t)$.*

For all monotone signatures, the sigref operator is monotone: $\pi \sqsubseteq \pi'$ implies $\text{sigref}(\pi, \sigma) \sqsubseteq \text{sigref}(\pi', \sigma)$. Hence, following Kleene's fixed point theorem, the procedure above reaches the greatest fixed point.

In Definition 11, the full signature is computed in every iteration. We propose to apply partition refinement using parts of the signature. By definition, $\sigma(\pi)(s) = \sigma(\pi)(t)$ if and only if for all parts $f_i(\pi)(s) = f_i(\pi)(t)$.

**Definition 13 (Partition refinement with partial signatures)**

$$\text{sigref}(\pi, f_i) := \{\{t \in S \mid f_i(\pi)(s) = f_i(\pi)(t) \wedge s \equiv_\pi t\} \mid s \in S\}$$
$$\pi^0 := \{S\}$$
$$\pi^{n+1} := \text{sigref}(\pi^n, f_i) \qquad (\text{select } f_i \in \sigma)$$

We always select some $f_i$ that refines the partition $\pi$. A fixed point is reached only when no $f_i$ refines the partition further: $\forall f_i \in \sigma: \text{sigref}(\pi^n, f_i) = \pi^n$. The extra clause $s \equiv_\pi t$ ensures that every application of sigref refines the partition.

**Theorem 1.** *If all parts $f_i$ are monotone, Definition 13 yields the greatest fixed point.*

*Proof.* The procedure terminates since the chain is decreasing ($\pi^{n+1} \sqsubseteq \pi^n$), due to the added clause $s \equiv_\pi t$. We reach some fixed point $\pi^n$, since $\forall f_i \in \sigma: \text{sigref}(\pi^n, f_i) = \pi^n$ implies $\text{sigref}(\pi^n, \sigma) = \pi^n$. Finally, to prove that we get the *greatest* fixed point, assume there exists another fixed point $\xi = \text{sigref}(\xi, \sigma)$. Then also $\xi = \text{sigref}(\xi, f_i)$ for all $i$. We prove that $\xi \sqsubseteq \pi^n$ by induction on $n$. Initially, $\xi \sqsubseteq S = \pi^0$. Assume $\xi \sqsubseteq \pi^n$, then for the selected $i$, $\xi = \text{sigref}(\xi, f_i) \sqsubseteq \text{sigref}(\pi^n, f_i) = \pi^{n+1}$, using monotonicity of $f_i$. $\square$

There are several advantages to this approach due to its flexibility. First, for any $f_i$ that is independent of the partition, refinement with respect to that $f_i$ only needs to be applied once. Furthermore, refinements can be applied according to different strategies. For instance, for the strong bisimulation of an mp-cut IMC, one could refine w.r.t. $\mathbf{T}$ until there is no more refinement, then w.r.t. $\mathbf{R}^s$ until there is no more refinement, then repeat until neither $\mathbf{T}$ nor $\mathbf{R}^s$ refines the partition. Finally, computing the full signature is the most memory-intensive operation in symbolic signature-based partition refinement. If the partial signatures are smaller than the full signature, then larger models can be minimised.

## 4   Symbolic Signature Refinement

This section describes the parallel decision diagram library Sylvan, followed by the (MT)BDDs and (MT)BDD operations required for signature-based partition refinement. We describe how we encode partitions and signatures for signature-based partition refinement. We present a new parallelized **refine** function that maximally reuses block numbers from the old partition. Finally, we present a new BDD algorithm that computes inert transitions, i.e., restricts a transition relation such that states $s$ and $s'$ are in the same block.

### 4.1   Decision Diagram Algorithms in Sylvan

In symbolic model checking [7], sets of states and transitions are represented by their characteristic function, rather than stored individually. With states described by $N$ Boolean variables, a set $S \subseteq \mathbb{B}^N$ can be represented by its characteristic function $f: \mathbb{B}^N \to \mathbb{B}$, where $S = \{s \mid f(s)\}$. Binary decision diagrams (BDDs) are a concise and canonical representation of Boolean functions [6].

An (ordered) BDD is a directed acyclic graph with leaves 0 and 1. Each internal node has a variable label $x_i$ and two outgoing edges labeled 0 and 1. Variables are encountered along each path according to a fixed variable ordering. Duplicate nodes and nodes with two identical outgoing edges are forbidden. It is well known that for a fixed variable ordering, every Boolean function is represented by a unique BDD.

In addition to BDDs with leaves 0 and 1, multi-terminal binary decision diagrams have been proposed [1,8] with leaves other than 0 and 1, representing functions from the Boolean space $\mathbb{B}^N$ onto any finite set. For example, MTBDDs can have leaves representing integers (encoding $\mathbb{B}^N \to \mathbb{N}$), floating-point numbers (encoding $\mathbb{B}^N \to \mathbb{R}$) and rational numbers (encoding $\mathbb{B}^N \to \mathbb{Q}$). Partial functions are supported using a terminal leaf $\bot$.

Sylvan [12,14] implements parallelized operations on decision diagrams using parallel data structures and work-stealing. Work-stealing [4,13] is a load balancing method for task-based parallelism. Recursive operations, such as most BDD operations, implicitly form a tree of tasks. Independent subtasks are stored in queues and idle processors steal tasks from the queues of busy processors.

Algorithm 1 describes the implementation of a generic binary operation F. BDD operations mainly consist of consulting an operation cache, performing

```
1 def apply(x, y, F):
2     if (x, y, F) ∈ cache : return cache[(x, y, F)]         /* get from cache */
3     if x and y are terminals : return F(x, y)              /* apply operator F */
4     v = topVar(x,y)
5     low ← apply(x_{v=0}, y_{v=0}, F)                        /* execute in parallel */
6     high ← apply(x_{v=1}, y_{v=1}, F)
7     result ← BDDnode(v, low, high)                         /* compute result */
8     cache[(x, y, F)] ← result                              /* put in cache */
9     return result
```

**Algorithm 1.** Generic algorithm that applies a binary operator $F$ to BDDs $x$ and $y$.

some recursive step, and creating new BDD nodes using a unique table. The operation cache is required to reduce the time complexity of BDD operations from exponential to polynomial in the size of the BDDs. Sylvan uses a single shared unique table for all BDD nodes and a single shared operation cache for all operations. To obtain high performance in a multi-core environment, the datastructures for the BDD nodes and the operation cache must be highly scalable. Sylvan implements several non-blocking datastructures to enable good speedups [14].

To compute symbolic signature-based partition refinement, several basic operations must be supported by the BDD package (see also [26]). Sylvan implements basic operations such as ∧ and if-then-else, and existential quantification ∃. Negation ¬ is performed in constant time using complement edges. To compute relational products of transition systems, there are operations relnext (to compute successors) and relprev (to compute predecessors and to concatenate relations), which combine the relational product with variable renaming. Similar operations are also implemented for MTBDDs. Sylvan is designed to support custom BDD algorithms. We present two new algorithms below.

## 4.2   Encoding of Signature Refinement

We implement symbolic signature refinement similar to [26]. Unlike [26], we do not refine the partition with respect to a single block, but with respect to all blocks simultaneously. We use a binary encoding with variables $s$ for the current state, $s'$ for the next state, $a$ for the action labels and $b$ for the blocks. We order BDD variables $a$ and $b$ after $s$ and $s'$, since this is required to efficiently replace signatures $(a, b)$ by new block numbers $b$ (see below). Variables $s$ and $s'$ are interleaved, which is common in the context of transition systems.

To perform symbolic bisimulation we represent a number of sets by their characteristic functions. See also Fig. 1.

- A set of states is represented by a BDD $\mathcal{S}(s)$;
- Transitions are represented by a BDD $\mathcal{T}(s, s', a)$;
- Markovian transitions are represented by an MTBDD $\mathcal{R}(s, s')$, with leaves containing rational numbers ($\mathbb{Q}$);

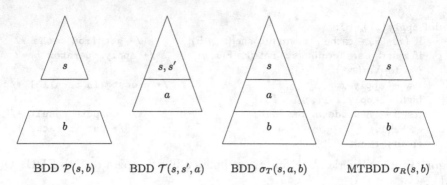

BDD $\mathcal{P}(s,b)$     BDD $\mathcal{T}(s,s',a)$     BDD $\sigma_T(s,a,b)$     MTBDD $\sigma_R(s,b)$

**Fig. 1.** Schematic overview of the BDDs in signature refinement

- Signatures $\mathbf{T}$ and $\mathbf{B}$ are represented by a BDD $\sigma_T(s,a,b)$;
- Signatures $\mathbf{R}^s$ and $\mathbf{R}^b$ are represented by an MTBDD $\sigma_R(s,b)$.

In the literature, three methods have been proposed to represent $\pi$.

1. As an equivalence relation, using a BDD $\mathcal{E}(s,s') = 1$ iff $s \equiv_\pi s'$ [5,19].
2. As a partition, by assigning each block a unique number, encoded with variables $b$, using a BDD $\mathcal{P}(s,b) = 1$ iff $s \in C_b$ [11,26,27].
3. Using $k = \lceil \log_2 n \rceil$ BDDs $\mathcal{P}_0,\ldots,\mathcal{P}_{k-1}$ such that $\mathcal{P}_i(s) = 1$ iff $s \in C_b$ and the $i^{\text{th}}$ bit of $b$ is 1. This requires significant time to restore blocks for the refinement procedure, but can require less memory [10].

We choose to use method 2, since in practice the BDD of $\mathcal{P}(s,b)$ is smaller than the BDD of $\mathcal{E}(s,s')$. Using $\mathcal{P}(s,b)$ also has the advantage of straightforward signature computation. The logarithmic representation is incompatible with our approach, since we refine all blocks simultaneously. Their approach involves restoring individual blocks to the $\mathcal{P}(s,b)$ representation, performing a refinement step, and compacting the result to the logarithmic representation. Restoring all blocks simply computes the full $\mathcal{P}(s,b)$.

We represent Markovian transitions using rational numbers, since they offer better precision than floating-point numbers. The manipulation of floating-point numbers typically introduces tiny rounding errors, resulting in different results of similar computations. This significantly affects bisimulation reduction, often resulting in finer partitions than the maximal bisimulation [23].

## 4.3  The refine Algorithm

In this section, we present a new BDD algorithm to refine partitions according to a signature, which maximally preserves previously assigned block numbers.

Partition refinement consists of two steps: computing the signatures and computing the next partition. Given the signatures $\sigma_T$ and/or $\sigma_R$ for the current partition $\pi$, the new partition can be computed as follows.

```
1  def refine(σ, P):
2      if (σ, P, iter) ∈ cache : return cache[(σ, P, iter)]
3      v = topVar(σ, P)
4      if v equals s_i for some i :
           # match paths on s in σ and P
5          low ← refine(σ_{s_i=0}, P_{s_i=0})
6          high ← refine(σ_{s_i=1}, P_{s_i=1})
7          result ← BDDnode(s_i, low, high)
8      else:
           # σ now encodes the state signature
           # P now encodes the previous block
9          B ← decodeBlock(P)
           # try to claim block B if still free
10         if blocks[B].sig = ⊥ : cas(blocks[B].sig, ⊥, σ)
11         if blocks[B].sig = σ : result ← P
12         else:
13             B ← search_or_insert(σ, B)
14             result ← encodeBlock(B)
15     cache[(σ, P, iter)] ← result
16     return result
```

**Algorithm 2.** refine, the (MT)BDD operation that assigns block numbers to signatures, given a signature $\sigma$ and the previous partition $\mathcal{P}$.

Since the chosen variable ordering has variables $s, s'$ before $a, b$, each path in $\sigma$ ends in a (MT)BDD representing the signature for the states encoded by that path. For $\sigma_T$, every path that assigns values to $s$ ends in a BDD on $a, b$. For $\sigma_R$, every path that assigns values to $s$ ends in a MTBDD on $b$ with rational leaves.

Wimmer et al. [26] present a BDD operation refine that "replaces" these sub-(MT)BDDs by the BDD representing a unique block number for each distinct signature. The result is the BDD of the next partition. They use a global counter and a hash table to associate each signature with a unique block number. This algorithm has the disadvantage that block number assignments are unstable. There is no guarantee that a stable block has the same block number in the next iteration. This has implications for the computation of the new signatures. When the block number of a stable block changes, cached results of signature computation in earlier iterations cannot be reused.

We modify the refine algorithm to use the current partition to reuse the previous block number of each state. This also allows refining a partition with respect to only a part of the signature, as described in Sect. 3. The modification is applied such that it can be parallelized in Sylvan. See Algorithm 2.

The algorithm has two input parameters: the (MT)BDD $\sigma$ which encodes the (partial) signature for the current partition, and the BDD $\mathcal{P}$ which encodes the current partition. The algorithm uses a global counter iter, which is the current iteration of partition refinement. This is necessary since the cached results of the previous iteration cannot be reused. It also uses and updates an array blocks, which contains the signature of each block in the new partition. This array is cleared between iterations of partition refinement.

The implementation is similar to other BDD operations, featuring the use of the operation cache (lines 2 and 15) and a recursion step for variables in $s$ (lines 3–7), with the two recursive operations executed in parallel. refine simultaneously descends in $\sigma$ and $\mathcal{P}$ (lines 5–6), matching the valuation of $s_i$ in $\sigma$ and $\mathcal{P}$. Block assignment happens at lines 9–14. We rely on the well-known atomic operation compare_and_swap (cas), which atomically compares and modifies a value in memory. This is necessary so the algorithm is still correct when parallelized. We use cas to claim a block number for the signature (line 10). If the block number is already used for a different signature, then this block is being refined and we call a method search_or_insert to assign a new block number.

Different implementations of search_and_insert are possible. We implemented a parallel hash table that uses a global counter for the next block number when inserting a new pair $(\sigma, B)$, similar to [26]. An alternative implementation that performed better in our experiments integrates the blocks array with a skip list. A skip list is a probabilistic multi-level ordered linked list. See [21].

## 4.4   Computing Inert Transitions

To compute the set of inert $\tau$-transitions for branching bisimulation, i.e., $s\xrightarrow{\tau}s'$, or more generally, to compute any inert transition relation $\to \cap \equiv$ where $\equiv$ is the equivalence relation corresponding to $\pi$ computed by $\mathcal{E}(s, s') = \exists b\colon \mathcal{P}(s, b) \land \mathcal{P}(s', b)$, the expression $\mathcal{T}(s, s') \land \exists b\colon \mathcal{P}(s, b) \land \mathcal{P}(s', b)$ must be computed. [26] writes that the intermediate BDD of $\exists b\colon \mathcal{P}(s, b) \land \mathcal{P}(s', b)$, obtained by first computing $\mathcal{P}(s', b)$ using variable renaming from $\mathcal{P}(s, b)$ and then $\exists b\colon \mathcal{P}(s, b) \land \mathcal{P}(s', b)$ using and_exists, is very large. This makes sense, since this intermediate result is indeed the BDD $\mathcal{E}(s, s')$, which we were avoiding by representing the partition using $\mathcal{P}(s, b)$.

The solution in [26] was to avoid computing $\mathcal{E}$ by computing the signatures and the refinement only with respect to one block at a time, which also enables several optimizations in [25].

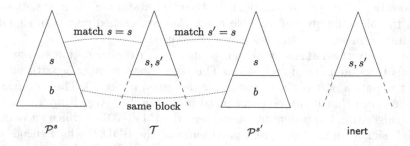

**Fig. 2.** Schematic overview of the BDDs in the inert algorithm

```
1  def inert(𝒯, 𝒫ˢ, 𝒫ˢ'):
2      if (𝒯, 𝒫ˢ, 𝒫ˢ') ∈ cache : return cache[(𝒯, 𝒫ˢ, 𝒫ˢ')]
       # find highest variable, interpreting sᵢ in 𝒫ˢ as s'ᵢ
3      v = topVar(𝒯, 𝒫ˢ, 𝒫ˢ')
4      if v equals sᵢ for some i :
          # match sᵢ in 𝒯 with 𝒫ˢ
5          low ← inert(𝒯ₛᵢ₌₀, 𝒫ˢₛᵢ₌₀, 𝒫ˢ')
6          high ← inert(𝒯ₛᵢ₌₁, 𝒫ˢₛᵢ₌₁, 𝒫ˢ')
7          result ← BDDnode(sᵢ, low, high)
8      elif v equals s'ᵢ for some i :
          # match s'ᵢ in 𝒯 with sᵢ in 𝒫ˢ'
9          low ← inert(𝒯ₛ'ᵢ₌₀, 𝒫ˢ, 𝒫ˢ'ₛ'ᵢ₌₀)
10         high ← inert(𝒯ₛ'ᵢ₌₁, 𝒫ˢ, 𝒫ˢ'ₛᵢ₌₁)
11         result ← BDDnode(s'ᵢ, low, high)
12     else:
          # match the blocks 𝒫ˢ and 𝒫ˢ'
13         if 𝒫ˢ ≠ 𝒫ˢ' : result ← False
14         else: result ← 𝒯
15     cache[(𝒯, 𝒫ˢ, 𝒫ˢ')] ← result
16     return result
```

**Algorithm 3.** Computes the inert transitions of a transition relation $\mathcal{T}$ according to the block assignments to current states ($\mathcal{P}^s$) and next states ($\mathcal{P}^{s'}$).

We present an alternative solution, which computes $\rightarrow \cap \equiv$ directly using a custom BDD algorithm. The inert algorithm takes parameters $\mathcal{T}(s, s')$ ($\mathcal{T}$ may contain other variables ordered after $s, s'$) and two copies of $\mathcal{P}(s, b)$: $\mathcal{P}^s$ and $\mathcal{P}^{s'}$. The algorithm matches $\mathcal{T}$ and $\mathcal{P}^s$ on valuations of variables $s$, and $\mathcal{T}$ and $\mathcal{P}^{s'}$ on valuations of variables $s'$. See Algorithm 3, and also Fig. 2 for a schematic overview. When in the recursive call all valuations to $s$ and $s'$ have been matched, with $S_s, S_{s'} \subseteq S$ the sets of states represented by these valuations, then $\mathcal{T}$ is the set of actions that label the transitions between states in $S_s$ and $S_{s'}$, $\mathcal{P}^s$ is the block that contains all $S_s$ and $\mathcal{P}^{s'}$ is the block that contains all $S_{s'}$. Then if $\mathcal{P}^s \neq \mathcal{P}^{s'}$, the transitions are not inert and inert returns False, removing the transition from $\mathcal{T}$. Otherwise, $\mathcal{T}$ (which may still contain other variables ordered after $s, s'$, such as action labels), is returned.

## 5   Experimental Evaluation

### 5.1   Tool Support

We implemented multi-core signature-based partition refinement in a tool called SIGREFMC, using the (MT)BDD-package Sylvan [12,14]. The tool computes the same bisimulations as the original SIGREF tool. SIGREFMC LTSs, CTMCs and IMCs delivered in two input formats, the XML format used by the original SIGREF tool, and the BDD format that the tool LTSMIN [16] generates for various model checking languages. SIGREFMC supports both the floating-point and the rational representation of rates in continuous-time transitions.

One of the design goals of this tool is to encourage researchers to extend it for their own file formats and notions of bisimulation, and to integrate it in other toolsets. Therefore, SIGREFMC is freely available online[1] and licensed with the MIT license. Documentation is available and instructions for extending the tool for different input/output formats and types of bisimulation are included.

## 5.2   Experiments

To study the improvements presented in the current paper, we compared our results (using the skip list variant of `refine`) to SIGREF 1.5 [25] for LTS and IMC models, and to a version of SIGREF used in [23] for CTMC models. For the CTMC models, we used SIGREF with rational numbers provided by the GMP library and SIGREFMC with rational number support by Sylvan. For the IMC models, version 1.5 of SIGREF does not support the GMP library and the version used in [23] does not support IMCs. We used SIGREFMC with floating points for a fairer comparison, but the tools give a slightly different number of blocks.

In the current paper, we restrict ourselves to the models presented in [23,26] and an IMC model that is part of the distribution of SIGREF. These models have been generated from PRISM benchmarks using a custom version of the PRISM toolset [18]. We refer to the literature for a description of these models.

We perform experiments on the three tools using the same 48-core machine, containing 4 AMD Opteron$^{TM}$ 6168 processors with 12 cores each. We measure the runtimes for partition refinement using SIGREF, SIGREFMC with only 1 worker, and SIGREFMC with 48 workers.

Note that apart from the new `refine` and `inert` algorithms presented in the current paper, there are several other differences. The first is that the original SIGREF uses the CUDD implementation of BDDs, while SIGREFMC obviously uses Sylvan, along with some extra BDD algorithms that avoid explicitly computing variable renaming of some BDDs. The second is that SIGREF has several optimizations [25] that are not available in SIGREFMC.

## 5.3   Results

See Table 1 for the results of these experiments. These results were obtained by repeating each benchmark at least 15 times and taking the average. The timeout was set to 3600 s. The column "States" shows the number of states before bisimulation minimisation, and "Blocks" the number of equivalence classes after bisimulation minimisation. We show the wallclock time using SIGREF ($T_w$), using SIGREFMC with 1 worker ($T_1$) and using SIGREFMC with 48 workers ($T_{48}$). We compute the sequential speedup $T_w/T_1$, the parallel speedup $T_1/T_{48}$ and the total speedup $T_w/T_{48}$.

---

[1] https://github.com/utwente-fmt/sigrefmc.

**Table 1.** Results for the benchmark experiments. Each data point is an average of at least 15 runs. The timeout was 3600 s.

| LTS models (strong) | | | Time | | | Speedups | | |
|---|---|---|---|---|---|---|---|---|
| Model | States | Blocks | $T_w$ | $T_1$ | $T_{48}$ | Seq. | Par. | Total |
| kanban03 | 1024240 | 85356 | 92.16 | 10.09 | 0.88 | 9.14 | 11.52 | 105.29 |
| kanban04 | 16020316 | 778485 | 1410.66 | 148.15 | 11.37 | 9.52 | 13.03 | 124.06 |
| kanban05 | 16772032 | 5033631 | – | 1284.86 | 73.57 | – | 17.47 | – |
| kanban06 | 264515056 | 25293849 | – | – | 2584.23 | – | – | – |
| LTS models (branching) | | | Time | | | Speedups | | |
| Model | States | Blocks | $T_w$ | $T_1$ | $T_{48}$ | Seq. | Par. | Total |
| kanban04 | 16020316 | 2785 | 8.47 | 0.52 | 0.24 | 16.39 | 2.11 | 34.60 |
| kanban05 | 16772032 | 7366 | 34.11 | 1.48 | 0.43 | 22.98 | 3.47 | 79.81 |
| kanban06 | 264515056 | 17010 | 118.19 | 3.87 | 0.83 | 30.55 | 4.65 | 142.20 |
| kanban07 | 268430272 | 35456 | 387.16 | 8.83 | 1.66 | 43.86 | 5.31 | 232.71 |
| kanban08 | 4224876912 | 68217 | 1091.67 | 17.91 | 2.98 | 60.96 | 6.02 | 366.72 |
| kanban09 | 4293193072 | 123070 | 3186.48 | 34.23 | 5.51 | 93.10 | 6.21 | 578.59 |
| CTMC models | | | Time | | | Speedups | | |
| Model | States | Blocks | $T_w$ | $T_1$ | $T_{48}$ | Seq. | Par. | Total |
| cycling-4 | 431101 | 282943 | 220.23 | 26.72 | 2.60 | 8.24 | 10.29 | 84.84 |
| cycling-5 | 2326666 | 1424914 | 1249.23 | 170.28 | 19.42 | 7.34 | 8.77 | 64.34 |
| fgf | 80616 | 38639 | 71.62 | 8.86 | 0.88 | 8.08 | 10.04 | 81.20 |
| p2p-5-6 | $2^{30}$ | 336 | 750.29 | 26.96 | 2.99 | 27.83 | 9.03 | 251.24 |
| p2p-6-5 | $2^{30}$ | 266 | 248.17 | 9.49 | 1.21 | 26.15 | 7.82 | 204.47 |
| p2p-7-5 | $2^{35}$ | 336 | 2280.76 | 24.01 | 2.97 | 94.99 | 8.08 | 767.12 |
| polling-16 | 1572864 | 98304 | 792.82 | 118.50 | 10.18 | 6.69 | 11.64 | 77.85 |
| polling-17 | 3342336 | 196608 | 1739.01 | 303.65 | 22.58 | 5.73 | 13.45 | 77.03 |
| polling-18 | 7077888 | 393216 | – | 705.22 | 49.81 | – | 14.16 | – |
| robot-020 | 31160 | 30780 | 28.15 | 3.21 | 0.60 | 8.78 | 5.36 | 47.04 |
| robot-025 | 61200 | 60600 | 78.48 | 6.78 | 0.95 | 11.58 | 7.11 | 82.39 |
| robot-030 | 106140 | 105270 | 174.30 | 12.26 | 1.47 | 14.21 | 8.33 | 118.44 |
| IMC models (strong) | | | Time | | | Speedups | | |
| Model | States | Blocks | $T_w$ | $T_1$ | $T_{48}$ | Seq. | Par. | Total |
| ftwc01 | 2048 | 1133 | 1.26 | 1.14 | 0.2 | 1.11 | 5.76 | 6.38 |
| ftwc02 | 32768 | 16797 | 154.55 | 102.07 | 15.85 | 1.51 | 6.44 | 9.75 |
| IMC models (branching) | | | Time | | | Speedups | | |
| Model | States | Blocks | $T_w$ | $T_1$ | $T_{48}$ | Seq. | Par. | Total |
| ftwc01 | 2048 | 430 | 1.12 | 0.77 | 0.13 | 1.45 | 6.07 | 8.83 |
| ftwc02 | 32786 | 3886 | 152.9 | 50.39 | 4.89 | 3.03 | 10.3 | 31.26 |

Due to space constraints, we do not include all results, but restrict ourselves to larger models. We refer to the full experimental data that is available online[2]. In the full set of results, excluding executions that take less than 1 s, SIGREFMC is always faster sequentially and always benefits from parallelism.

The results show a clear advantage for larger models. One interesting result is for the p2p-7-5 model. This model is ideal for symbolic bisimulation with a large number of states ($2^{35}$) and very few blocks after minimisation (336). For this model, our tool is 95x faster sequentially and has a parallel speedup of 8x, resulting in a total speedup of 767x. The best parallel speedup of 17x was obtained for the kanban05 model.

In almost all experiments, the signature computation dominates with 70 %–99 % of the execution time sequentially. We observe that the refinement step sometimes benefits more from parallelism than signature computation, with speedups up to

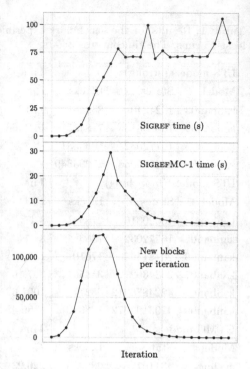

**Fig. 3.** Time per iteration for SIGREF and SIGREFMC (1 worker), and the number of new blocks per iteration for strong bisimulation of the kanban04 LTS model.

29.9x. We also find that reusing block numbers for stable blocks causes a major reduction in computation time towards the end of the procedure. The kanban LTS models and the larger polling CTMC models are an excellent case study to demonstrate this. See Fig. 3.

## 6   Conclusions

Originally we intended to investigate parallelism in symbolic bisimulation minimisation. To our surprise, we obtained a much higher sequential speedup using specialized BDD operations, as demonstrated by the results in Table 1 and Fig. 3. The specialized BDD operations offer a clear advantage sequentially and the integration with Sylvan results in decent parallel speedups. Our best result had a total speedup of 767x. Similar to our experiments in symbolic reachability [14], further parallel speedups might be obtained by disjunctively partitioning the transition relations.

---

[2] https://github.com/utwente-fmt/sigrefmc-tacas16.

# References

1. Bahar, R.I., Frohm, E.A., Gaona, C.M., Hachtel, G.D., Macii, E., Pardo, A., Somenzi, F.: Algebraic decision diagrams and their applications. In: Lightner, M.R., Jess, J.A.G. (eds.) ICCAD, pp. 188–191. IEEE Computer Society / ACM (1993)
2. Blom, S., Haverkort, B.R., Kuntz, M., van de Pol, J.: Distributed markovian bisimulation reduction aimed at CSL model checking. ENTCS **220**(2), 35–50 (2008)
3. Blom, S., Orzan, S.: Distributed branching bisimulation reduction of state spaces. ENTCS **89**(1), 99–113 (2003)
4. Blumofe, R.D.: Scheduling multithreaded computations by work stealing. In: FOCS, pp. 356–368. IEEE Computer Society (1994)
5. Bouali, A., de Simone, R.: Symbolic bisimulation minimisation. In: von Bochmann, G., Probst, D.K. (eds.) CAV 1992. LNCS, vol. 663, pp. 96–108. Springer, Heidelberg (1992)
6. Bryant, R.E.: Graph-based algorithms for boolean function manipulation. IEEE Trans. Comput. **C−35**(8), 677–691 (1986)
7. Burch, J., Clarke, E., Long, D., McMillan, K., Dill, D.: Symbolic model checking for sequential circuit verification. IEEE Trans. Comput. Aided Des. Integr. Circ. Syst. **13**(4), 401–424 (1994)
8. Clarke, E.M., McMillan, K.L., Zhao, X., Fujita, M., Yang, J.: Spectral transforms for large boolean functions with applications to technology mapping. In: DAC, pp. 54–60 (1993)
9. De Nicola, R., Vaandrager, F.W.: Three logics for branching bisimulation. J. ACM **42**(2), 458–487 (1995)
10. Derisavi, S.: A symbolic algorithm for optimal markov chain lumping. In: Grumberg, O., Huth, M. (eds.) TACAS 2007. LNCS, vol. 4424, pp. 139–154. Springer, Heidelberg (2007)
11. Derisavi, S.: Signature-based symbolic algorithm for optimal markov chain lumping. In: QEST 2007, pp. 141–150. IEEE Computer Society (2007)
12. van Dijk, T., Laarman, A.W., van de Pol, J.C.: Multi-Core BDD operations for symbolic reachability. In: 11th International Workshop on Parallel and Distributed Methods in verifiCation. ENTCS. Elsevier (2012)
13. van Dijk, T., van de Pol, J.C.: Lace: non-blocking split deque for work-stealing. In: Lopes, L., et al. (eds.) Euro-Par 2014, Part II. LNCS, vol. 8806, pp. 206–217. Springer, Heidelberg (2014)
14. van Dijk, T., van de Pol, J.C.: Sylvan: multi-core decision diagrams. In: Baier, C., Tinelli, C. (eds.) Tools and Algorithms for the Construction and Analysis of Systems. LNCS, vol. 9035, pp. 677–691. Springer, Heidelberg (2015)
15. Hermanns, H., Katoen, J.-P.: The how and why of interactive markov chains. In: de Boer, F.S., Bonsangue, M.M., Hallerstede, S., Leuschel, M. (eds.) FMCO 2009. LNCS, vol. 6286, pp. 311–337. Springer, Heidelberg (2010)
16. Kant, G., Laarman, A., Meijer, J., van de Pol, J.C., Blom, S., van Dijk, T.: LTSmin: high-performance language-independent model checking. TACAS 2015. LNCS, vol. 9035, pp. 692–707. Springer, Heidelberg (2015)
17. Kulakowski, K.: Concurrent bisimulation algorithm. CoRR abs/1311.7635 (2013)
18. Kwiatkowska, M., Norman, G., Parker, D.: PRISM 4.0: verification of probabilistic real-time systems. In: Gopalakrishnan, G., Qadeer, S. (eds.) CAV 2011. LNCS, vol. 6806, pp. 585–591. Springer, Heidelberg (2011)
19. Mumme, M., Ciardo, G.: An efficient fully symbolic bisimulation algorithm for non-deterministic systems. Int. J. Found. Comput. Sci. **24**(2), 263–282 (2013)

20. Paige, R., Tarjan, R.E.: Three partition refinement algorithms. SIAM J. Comput. **16**(6), 973–989 (1987)
21. Pugh, W.: Skip lists: a probabilistic alternative to balanced trees. Commun. ACM **33**(6), 668–676 (1990)
22. Wijs, A.: GPU accelerated strong and branching bisimilarity checking. In: Baier, C., Tinelli, C. (eds.) TACAS 2015. LNCS, vol. 9035, pp. 368–383. Springer, Heidelberg (2015)
23. Wimmer, R., Becker, B.: Correctness issues of symbolic bisimulation computation for markov chains. In: Müller-Clostermann, B., Echtle, K., Rathgeb, E.P. (eds.) MMB & DFT 2010. LNCS, vol. 5987, pp. 287–301. Springer, Heidelberg (2010)
24. Wimmer, R., Derisavi, S., Hermanns, H.: Symbolic partition refinement with automatic balancing of time and space. Perform. Eval. **67**(9), 816–836 (2010)
25. Wimmer, R., Herbstritt, M., Becker, B.: Optimization techniques for BDD-based bisimulation computation. In: 17th GLSVLSI, pp. 405–410. ACM (2007)
26. Wimmer, R., Herbstritt, M., Hermanns, H., Strampp, K., Becker, B.: SIGREF – a symbolic bisimulation tool box. In: Graf, S., Zhang, W. (eds.) ATVA 2006. LNCS, vol. 4218, pp. 477–492. Springer, Heidelberg (2006)
27. Wimmer, R., Hermanns, H., Herbstritt, M., Becker, B.: Towards Symbolic Stochastic Aggregation. Technical report, SFB/TR 14 AVACS (2007)

# Advances in Symbolic Probabilistic Model Checking with PRISM

Joachim Klein[✉], Christel Baier, Philipp Chrszon, Marcus Daum,
Clemens Dubslaff, Sascha Klüppelholz, Steffen Märcker, and David Müller

Institute of Theoretical Computer Science, Technische Universität Dresden,
01062 Dresden, Germany
klein@tcs.inf.tu-dresden.de

**Abstract.** For modeling and reasoning about complex systems, symbolic methods provide a prominent way to tackle the state explosion problem. It is well known that for symbolic approaches based on binary decision diagrams (BDD), the ordering of BDD variables plays a crucial role for compact representations and efficient computations. We have extended the popular probabilistic model checker PRISM with support for automatic variable reordering in its multi-terminal-BDD-based engines and report on benchmark results. Our extensions additionally allow the user to manually control the variable ordering at a finer-grained level. Furthermore, we present our implementation of the symbolic computation of quantiles and support for multi-reward-bounded properties, automata specifications and accepting end component computations for Streett conditions.

## 1 Introduction

One prominent approach to cope with the well-known state-explosion problem in model checking is the use of symbolic methods based on binary decision diagrams (BDDs) [8,31]. Various BDD-variants have been studied and implemented in tools for the quantitative analysis of probabilistic systems, see, e.g., [4,10,17–19,23,28,32,34]. The prominent probabilistic model-checker PRISM [26,34,35] uses symbolic approaches relying on a multi-terminal binary decision diagram (MTBDD) [3,15] representation of the model. Among others, PRISM provides support for modeling and the analysis of discrete-time Markov chains (DTMC) and Markov decision processes (MDP) as well as continuous-time Markov chains (CTMC) against temporal logical specifications. While the behavior of Markov chains is purely probabilistic, MDPs exhibit both probabilistic and nondeterministic choices. The typical task of the analysis of MDPs is to compute a scheduler for resolving the nondeterminism that maximizes or minimizes the probability for a given path property or an expectation. The symbolic implementation of

The authors are supported by the DFG through the collaborative research entre HAEC (SFB 912), the Excellence Initiative by the German Federal and State Governments (cluster of excellence cfAED and Institutional Strategy), the Research Training Groups QuantLA (GRK 1763) and RoSI (GRK 1907), the DFG/NWO-project ROCKS, and Deutsche Telekom Stiftung.

© Springer-Verlag Berlin Heidelberg 2016
M. Chechik and J.-F. Raskin (Eds.): TACAS 2016, LNCS 9636, pp. 349–366, 2016.
DOI: 10.1007/978-3-662-49674-9_20

PRISM comes in three flavors: a purely symbolic engine MTBDD and two semi-symbolic engines, called HYBRID and SPARSE. The MTBDD engine performs all computations using MTBDDs, while the HYBRID engine combines the MTBDD-based representation of the transition matrix of the model with an explicit representation of the solution state value vector in the computation [24]. The latter is motivated by the observation that the MTBDD representation of such state value vectors can be of substantive size even for models with compact MTBDD representation during probabilistic model-checking algorithms. The SPARSE engine constructs an explicit, sparse matrix from the MTBDD-based transition matrix for numerical computations and performs computations using this explicit representation. In addition to the three symbolic engines, which rely internally on the infrastructure of the C-based CUDD library [37] for MTBDD storage and manipulation, the fourth engine, EXPLICIT, is fully implemented in Java, builds an explicit representation of the reachable state space of the model and carries out all analysis on this explicit representation. Depending on the concrete model structure and size, each of the four engines has situations where it can show its particular strength.

It is well known that the variable order of the BDD variables plays a crucial role for obtaining a compact representation of the model and for model checking performance. PRISM provides limited influence on the variable order, mainly during modeling by the order in which individual modules are placed in the model file and the order of the individual state variables inside a module. While care has been taken to use a sensible variable order derived from the structure of elements in the model file [34], PRISM lacks any support for automatically identifying a good variable order using techniques such as sifting [33,36], which are routinely employed in symbolic model checkers for non-probabilistic systems (e.g., [11]). In our previous work on complex case studies, we have reached several times the point where we had to resort to manually swapping the module and variable definitions in the model file to try and find a better ordering, in particular for models where explicit approaches were infeasible (e.g., [13]).

**Contribution.** The main purpose of this paper is to present several refinements of PRISM's symbolic engines. First, we added support for the *automated variable reordering* of the MTBDD-based model representation by enabling CUDD's implementation of group sifting and by extensions of PRISM's input modeling language that allow to rearrange and interleave the orders of the bits of state variables within the same module as well as (the bits) of state variables of different modules. The impact of the automated reordering has been evaluated using the examples from the PRISM benchmark suite [27] and in the context of the symbolic quantile computations. Our second contribution are symbolic implementations of computation schemes for *cost-* or *reward-bounded reachability properties* in discrete Markovian models (DTMCs or MDPs) and corresponding *quantiles*[1]. The latter are, e.g., useful to compute the minimal energy budget required to

---

[1] While PRISM supports the computation of expected costs or rewards and probabilities for step-bounded properties, it does not contain implementations of algorithms for computing probabilities for reachability conditions with cost/reward constraints.

ensure a 90 % chance for completing a list of jobs. Algorithms for the computation of quantiles have been presented in [5,38] and prototypically implemented using (non-symbolic) explicit representations of the model. Within this paper, we report on the results of comparative experimental studies of the explicit and the new symbolic implementation. The third contribution are enhancements of PRISM's engines for the *automata-based analysis* of DTMCs and MDPs. This includes the treatment of Streett acceptance conditions in MDPs (PRISM only offers engines for Rabin acceptance and its generalized variant) and an extension of PRISM's property syntax for automata-specifications (rather than LTL-specifications).

**Outline.** Section 2 presents our new approaches for variable reordering in PRISM. Section 3 summarizes the main features of our implementations for cost/reward-bounded properties and quantiles, while Sect. 4 presents the automata-based extensions. For further details (implementation, experiments) and an extended version [21] see http://wwwtcs.inf.tu-dresden.de/ALGI/PUB/TACAS16/. We are collaborating with PRISM's authors to integrate our extensions into the main PRISM version and would like to thank David Parker for fruitful discussions.

## 2   Automatic Variable Reordering in PRISM

Here, we will briefly describe the relevant infrastructure in PRISM for dealing with variable ordering. The MTBDD variable ordering of the symbolic model representation is determined by the order of module and variable definitions in

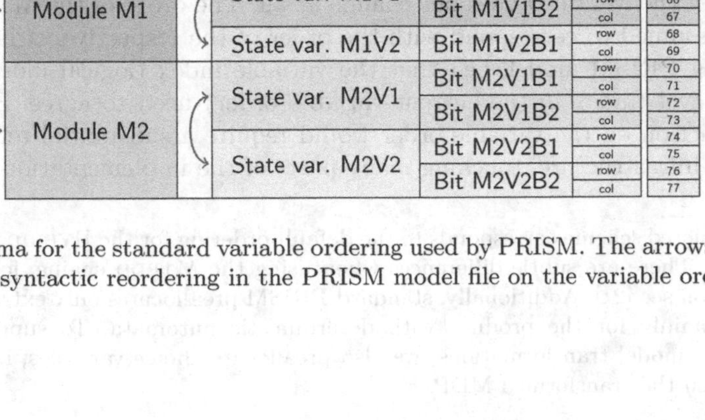

**Fig. 1.** Schema for the standard variable ordering used by PRISM. The arrows indicate the effect of syntactic reordering in the PRISM model file on the variable order.

the PRISM model file. Figure 1 sketches the general schema[2]. In a first block, MTBDD variables for nondeterministic choices are allocated. This includes a unary encoding of the synchronizing actions (i.e., one MTBDD variable for each action), scheduling variables (one MTBDD variable indicating that a given module is active) as well as several bits for representing local choices, e.g., between alternative commands for the same synchronizing action. Then, two blocks of extra variables are preallocated to serve in later model transformations, e.g., during a product construction with a deterministic $\omega$-automaton for LTL model checking. For each individual bit of a state variable in the model, two MTBDD variables are allocated, one serving in the representation of the rows and one for the columns of the transition matrix. The MTBDD variables for representing the possible values of the (integer-valued) state variables are allocated in the order in which they appear in the PRISM model file, with each state variable forming a block of row/column pairs. The bits for each state variable are ordered from most-significant to least-significant. Global state variables are treated as if they were contained in a single module located before the "real" modules.

The arrows in Fig. 1 indicate the extent of the influence that can be applied to the variable ordering by syntactically reordering the PRISM source file: At the highest level, the order of the modules can be changed. Additionally, inside each module, the order of the definition of the state variables can be changed. Note that such changes of the ordering in the PRISM model file do not lead to any semantic changes in the model, but can lead to cosmetic changes, e.g., in the order of the states for exported models. To complement the manual, trial-and-error approach for finding a good order in the model file, we detail our automatic approach in the next section.

## 2.1   Automatic Variable Reordering Using Group Sifting

PRISM internally relies on the CUDD (MT)BDD library [37] for the management of a set of BDDs that arise during probabilistic model checking. CUDD provides implementations of several heuristics for (dynamic) variable reordering which in principle should be available to be used by PRISM. Unfortunately, the implementation of PRISM heavily relies on the assumption that the variable ordering of the MTBDD does not change at all. The order of the MTBDD variables is assumed to correspond with the order of the respective variables in the underlying PRISM model, i.e., that the variable index (logical index) and the variable level (index in the current variable order) need to agree. Eliminating this restriction on the variable order would require a substantial refactoring of PRISM's infrastructure, touching many parts of the implementation.

---

[2] The depicted scheme corresponds to the default ordering for the HYBRID and SPARSE engines. There are subtle differences when using the MTBDD engine, for a detailed discussion see [21]. Additionally, standard PRISM preallocates only extra *state* variables, mainly for the product with deterministic automata. To support generic symbolic model transformations, we also preallocate choice variables, i.e., for fresh actions in the transformed MDP.

Our approach presented in this section makes automatic variable reordering available to a PRISM user while avoiding any substantial refactoring of PRISM's infrastructure. First, a symbolic, MTBDD-based representation of the model is built by PRISM as usual. After the model is built, we trigger the group sifting reordering heuristic [33,36] via the CUDD library, using several variable grouping constraints that will be detailed later. After this reordering, the MTBDD-based model representation violates PRISM's assumptions, which renders further computations in PRISM impossible. Thus, we perform an analysis of the variable ordering found by group sifting and translate the changes in variable locations back to the source level of the PRISM model. This way, we obtain a syntactically reordered PRISM model, where the placement of the PRISM modules und state variables reflects the calculated variable ordering. Our implementation then allows using this reordered model directly after the reordering computation via the following trick: After reordering, we delete the MTBDDs of the model and reset the variable ordering in CUDD to the one that PRISM expects, where each variable index corresponds to the variable level in the BDD. Then, we build the BDDs for the model a second time, this time using the syntactically reordered PRISM model. We thus obtain the reordered model again, but now with the underlying assumptions of PRISM intact, allowing to use the full PRISM machinery. This approach provides transparent and convenient access to the reordering functionality to the user. Additionally, we also support exporting the reordered model to a file, which can then be used in future PRISM runs. This way, the time for reordering can be amortized over multiple model-checking runs.

For this approach to work, it is crucial that we are able to seamlessly convert between the reordered variable ordering obtained after sifting and the variable order that is induced by syntactically reordering the elements of the PRISM model file. To achieve this, we introduce appropriate groups of MTBDD variables represented by a tree structure and used in the groups sifting. The grouping reflects the structure of the given model file: Each PRISM module forms a group of BDD variables that can be reordered as a block. This corresponds to syntactically changing the order of modules in the model file. Additionally, inside each module, the MTBDD variables for each state variable form another group. Reordering those groups corresponds to changing the order of the variable declarations inside a PRISM module. The remaining variables, e.g., those for nondeterministic choices remain in fixed positions. Hence, the above approach allows for creating all variable orders that can result from permutations of modules and state variables within the PRISM model file. In the next section we show how a more fine-grained control can be achieved.

## 2.2    Bit-Level Control over the Variable Order Using Views

Although it is well known that for some operators, e.g., the addition of two integers, an efficient representation relies on the interleaving of the individual bit-variables, there is no way of interleaving the individual bits of multiple state variables in PRISM up to now.

```
module M
    s_bit_2 : [0..1];
    s_bit_1 : [0..1];
    s_bit_0 : [0..1];

    s : view (s_bit_2,s_bit_1,s_bit_0) <=> [2..7] init 3;

    [inc] s<7 -> 1:(s'=s+1);
endmodule
```

**Fig. 2.** Defining a view s with data domain $(2, 7)$ from three single-bit state variables.

Our implementation provides the option of syntactically "exploding the bits" of all the state variables in a PRISM model file: Each multi-bit state variable $s$ is replaced with the appropriate number of single-bit variables $s_i$. To keep this transformation simple and transparent to the user we introduce a syntactic enhancement of the PRISM modeling language called a *view*. A view forms a virtual variable $s$ over bit variables $s_j$. This virtual variable can be used in guards and updates of transition definitions just as ordinary variables. Hence, exploding the bits does not affect any of the transition definitions given in the model file.

As an example, consider the PRISM module in Fig. 2. Here, the virtual state variable s with an integer data domain of $2 \leqslant s \leqslant 7$ requires three bits to represent all values, as internally integer variables are encoded by first subtracting the lower bound of the data domain (2 is internally represented as 0, etc.). The actual storage is provided by the three single-bit state variables s_bit_$i$. The order of the single-bit state variables in the view definition determines their use in the encoding, with the most-significant bit appearing first. As can be seen, the virtual view variable s is being used just like a standard PRISM state variable.

Note that "exploding the bits" of a PRISM model file alone will not change the variable ordering and MTBDD representation, as the encoding and ordering of the newly introduced single-bit state variables correspond to the standard encoding used for the original variables. When applying the automatic reordering detailed in the previous section to an "exploded" model file, the individual bits of the state variables can be now be sifted and interleaved, as their grouping is removed. However, the MTBDD variables are still restricted from crossing module boundaries. We detail how to remove this restriction in the next section.

## 2.3 Interleaving State Variables of Different Modules

To overcome the limitation that state variables cannot be interleaved across modules our implementation provides the option of "globalizing" all state variables in a PRISM model file: Each state variable inside a PRISM module is moved from the module to become a global variable, while keeping the order they appeared in the original model file. Realizing this requires to loosen some restrictions on the use of global variables imposed by PRISM. In standard PRISM, global variables cannot be updated in synchronous actions, as this has the potential of resulting in conflicting updates from multiple modules. We removed this restriction, as in

```
module M1                       global x_bit_1 : [0..1];
  x : [0..3] init 0;            global x_bit_0 : [0..1];
                                global y_bit_1 : [0..1];
  [a] true ->    0.5:(x'=0)     global y_bit_0 : [0..1];
               + 0.5:(x'=y);    global x :
endmodule                         view (x_bit_1,x_bit_0) <=> [0..3] init 0;
module M2                       global y :
  y : [0..3] init 0;              view (y_bit_1,y_bit_0) <=> [0..3] init 0;

  [a] true -> 1:(y'=0);         module M1
  [b] y<3  -> 1:(y'=y+1);         [a] true -> 0.5:(x'=0) + 0.5:(x'=y);
endmodule                       endmodule

                                module M2
                                  [a] true -> 1:(y'=0);
                                  [b] y<3  -> 1:(y'=y+1);
                                endmodule
```

**Fig. 3.** Example of both "exploding bits" and "globalizing variables" for a PRISM model file (before on the left, after on the right).

our setting only the "previous owner" of a variable, i.e., the module in which the variable was initially declared, will update the global variable in the transformed model. This ensures that there can be no conflicting updates introduced by globalizing variables. Our implementation supports such global variable updates for similar situations as well, i.e., where it is apparent by a syntactic inspection that no conflicting updates can happen.

The options for exploding the bits and globalizing the variables can be used separately and in a combined fashion (cf. Fig. 3) and the resulting model yields a starting point for group sifting. This way, fine-grained control of the variable ordering for all state variables in the model becomes possible. Within the following section we will evaluate our implementation by means of a number of case studies.

### 2.4 Benchmarking Automatic Variable Reordering of PRISM Models

To explore the effect of automatic variable reordering using our implementation, we performed benchmarks using the DTMC, CTMC and MDP models in the PRISM benchmark suite [27]. The models are parametrized in various parameters, affecting both the number of states and the size of the MTBDD representation. In total, we performed benchmarks with 208 model instances (70 DTMCs, 70 CTMCs, 68 MDPs). We present here statistics for the "top" initial variable ordering [34] used by default in the HYBRID engine. Results using the default variable ordering of the MTBDD engine were roughly similar.

Figure 4 presents statistics for the basic case, i.e., reordering without any syntactic transformations beforehand. Similar plots for reordering with the "globalize variables" (Sect. 2.3) and "explode bits" (Sect. 2.2) transformations being

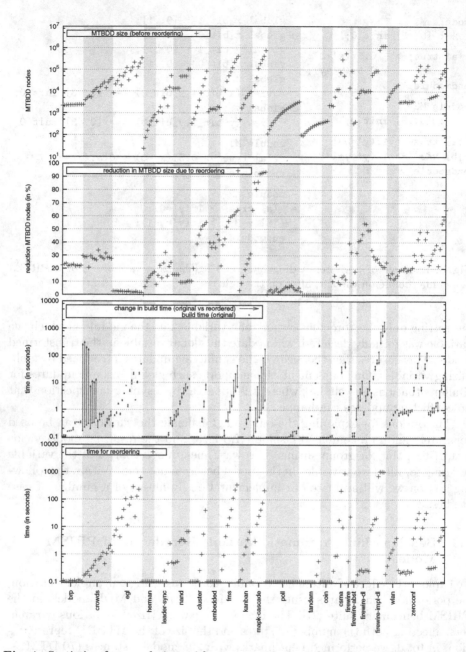

**Fig. 4.** Statistics for reordering without syntactic transformations: The number of MTBDD nodes before reordering, the reduction (larger numbers represent more reduction) in the number of MTBDD nodes, the change in time for building the model (before/after reordering) and the time spent reordering. Times below 0.1 s are clipped to 0.1 for visualization purposes. There was one timeout, reordering the "csma4_6" instance (45 min of the 1 h timeout spent on building, with 3,589,198 nodes).

applied can be found in [21][3]. In the plots, the model instances are grouped by their base model. The size of the MTBDD refers to the number of nodes in the shared MTBDD structure storing the various individual MTBDDs. Those individual MTBDDs represent the model in PRISM, i.e., its transition matrix, a 0/1-version of the transition matrix representing the underlying graph structure of the model, the set of reachable states, representations for the transition and state rewards.

As can be seen in the second plot from the top in Fig. 4, the automatic reordering was able to achieve significant reductions for many of the model instances. As a particularly striking example, the reordering was very effective for the "mapk-cascade" model, a CTMC: For the instance with parameter $N = 8$, the MTBDD size was reduced from 1,478,511 nodes to 96,718 nodes, a reduction of more than 90 %. The time for building the symbolic representation of this model instance was reduced from 174 s to 2 s for the reordered model. Most of the time, the reduction in the MTBDD size is accompanied by a reduction in the time needed for building the MTBDDs for the reordered model. The major outlier to this are several instances of the "crowds" model, where the time for building the reordered model was substantially worse compared with the original model. Our investigation revealed that this is due to the point in time at which our reordering is performed, i.e., after the symbolic transition matrix has been restricted to the reachable part of the state space, which is the symbolic representation that is then used for the actual model checking. The reordering heuristic thus produced a variable order tailored for this state space and which is not particularly suitable for the representation of the individual, not yet restricted parts of the model used during the building phase. This is a classic example of the case where an asynchronous reordering, i.e., continuously adapting the variable ordering during the construction phase, would be helpful.

In general, the time for reordering tends to be related to the size of the MTBDD before reordering, as expected. As noted above, even substantial reordering times might be worthwhile, as the reordered model can be stored and subsequently reused multiple times, profiting, e.g., from the reduced build time and more compact symbolic representation.

There were three models ("brp", "nand" and "poll"), where instances exhibited an overall reduction in the size of the MTBDD, but an increase in the size of the MTBDD for the transition matrix alone (in all cases the increase was less than 10 %). This is explained by the fact that the reordering operates on the whole shared MTBDD data structure and thus does not necessarily optimize all the individual MTBDD functions that are stored.

We have also benchmarked the effect of our syntactic transformations on the automatic reordering and present here (Table 1) some notable examples. For further, detailed statistics we refer to [21]. As already seen in Fig. 4, the "tandem"

---

[3] The benchmarks for reordering were carried out on a machine with two Intel Xeon L5630 4-core CPUs at 2.13 GHz and 192 GB RAM, with a timeout of 1 h and a CUDD memory limit of 10 GB. The max-growth factor of CUDD was set to 2, i.e., allowing a doubling in MTBDD size before sifting is abandoned.

**Table 1.** Selected statistics for the reduction achieved using reordering on the standard model instance and where the "explode bits" and "globalize variables" transformations were applied. In the last column, both transformations are applied. For reference, the MTBDD size before reordering is included as well. For full details, see [21].

| Model | instance | MTBDD before | reduction in % | | | |
|---|---|---|---|---|---|---|
| | | | standard | explode | globalize | exp.+glob. |
| tandem | c=255 | 4917 | 0.0 | 26.0 | 0.0 | 35.1 |
| tandem | c=4095 | 103233 | 0.0 | 35.7 | 0.0 | 64.3 |
| cluster | N=32 | 7391 | 45.5 | 47.9 | 52.2 | 8.3 |
| cluster | N=256 | 61749 | 53.6 | 58.7 | 24.2 | 41.4 |
| cluster | N=512 | 132908 | 55.1 | 59.3 | 61.5 | 46.2 |
| kanban | t=6 | 14001 | 27.5 | 34.0 | 1.2 | 32.3 |

model has no reduction in MTBDD size when it is reordered as-is. However, when the state variables are "exploded", reordering becomes profitable, with additional reductions when combined with the "globalize variables" transformations. Globally, for every model instance from the benchmark suite, at least one of the variants achieved some reduction. As is to be expected, no variant is uniformly best. Consider the statistics for the "cluster" model in Table 1. For $N = 32$, "exploding" and "globalizing" are individually successful, but in combination lead to only minor reductions. For $N = 256$, "exploding" is in the lead, while for $N = 512$, "globalizing" by itself leads to the most reductions. For "kanban" with $t = 6$, "globalizing" alone leads to worse reductions than reordering on the standard model. As can be seen, it remains an area of experimentation to select the reordering variant that is a good fit for a particular model and model instance. As a good first assumption, the time for model checking tends to be related in general to the compactness of the symbolic representation. We experimented with some of the properties in the benchmark suite (cf. [21] for some examples). In the next section, we will additionally report on significant reductions in model-checking time in the context of quantile computations with reordered models.

## 3    Computing Quantiles for Markov Decision Processes

Models in PRISM can be annotated with rewards (non-negative values) specifying the costs or the gain for visiting certain states or taking certain transitions. PRISM provides implementations of algorithms for reasoning about expected rewards, but lacks support for computing the probabilities for reward-bounded path properties, unless for unit-reward functions that count the number of steps. We have extended PRISM with support for the computation of (extremal) probabilities of cost-/reward-bounded simple path formulas for DTMCs and MDPs with non-negative integer rewards, e.g., of $\Pr^{\max}(\lozenge^{\leq r} \Phi)$ for a reward bound $r$.

This includes conjunctions of multiple reward bounds and step bounds [1], relying on a product transformation with a counter automaton tracking the accumulated reward. This is implemented for both the explicit and symbolic engines.

In our recent work [5,38], we addressed the computation of quantiles for probability constraints on reward-bounded reachability conditions and carried out experiments with a prototypical implementation based on PRISM's EXPLICIT engine. In the mean time, this implementation has been refined and extended by a symbolic implementation. In what follows, we describe some details of the latter. We consider here MDP with a reward function $rew : S \times Act \rightarrow \mathbb{N}_{\geq 0}$, mapping state-action pairs $(s, \alpha)$ to the non-negative integer reward $rew(s, \alpha)$. The quantiles under consideration (for details we refer to [5]) are optimal reward thresholds that guarantee that the maximal or minimal probability of a reward-bounded reachability path formula meets some probability bound. Examples are $\min\{ r : \Pr^{\max}(\lozenge^{\leq r} \Phi) > p \}$ or $\max\{ r : \Pr^{\min}(\lozenge^{\geq r} \Phi) > p \}$ where $r$ can be seen as a parametric reward bound, $\Phi$ is a state formula and $p$ a rational probability bound. Quantiles yield a useful concept for the cost-utility analysis, e.g., in terms of the minimal amount of energy $r$ required to reach some goal $\Phi$ with probability at least $p$ for some/all schedulers. The approach for computing quantiles as proposed in [5] consists of a two-step process. A precomputation step determines all states $s \in S$ for which the quantile exists, i.e., is finite. In the simplest case, this amounts to the computation of the maximal probability for unbounded reachability. In other cases, the computation requires the analysis of zero-reward and positive-reward end components [5]. For the remaining states, an iterative approach is used, which we illustrate here for a quantile of the form $\min\{ r : \Pr^{\max}(\lozenge^{\leq r} \Phi) > p \}$ where we suppose the MDP has a unique initial state $s_0$. Successively, the values $x_{s,r} = \Pr_s^{\max}(\lozenge^{\leq r} \Phi)$ for $r = 1, 2, 3, \ldots$ are computed for all states $s \in S$ until some $r$ with $x_{s_0,r} > p$ is reached, using the equation $x_{s,r} = \max\{A_s, B_s\}$ with

$$A_s = \max_{\alpha \in Act(s), rew(s,\alpha)=0} \sum_{t \in S} \Pr(s, \alpha, t) \cdot x_{t,r}$$

$$B_s = \max_{\alpha \in Act(s), rew(s,\alpha)>0} \sum_{t \in S} P(s, \alpha, t) \cdot x_{t,r-rew(s,\alpha)}$$

where $\Pr(s, \alpha, t)$ is the probability of reaching state $t$ when action $\alpha$ is chosen in state $s$. For states satisfying $\Phi$, $x_{s,r}$ is set to 1 for all $r$. The values $A_s$, handling the zero-reward actions, are computed using value iteration. The values $B_s$, handling the positive-reward actions, are determined by inserting the previously calculated values $x_{t,i}$ for $i < r$. For the other quantile variants, similar computations are performed [5]. The time complexity of this approach is exponential, meeting the complexity-theoretic optimum [16].

## 3.1 Symbolic Computation of Quantiles

We have extended PRISM with a symbolic implementation for the computation of quantiles, following the general approach outlined above. For the precomputation step, we rely on the PRISM machinery for the computation of maximal/minimal probabilities for unbounded path formulas and for the computation of (maximal) end components, adapted for identifying states in positive-reward end components and zero-reward end components by appropriate symbolic model transformations.

For the iterative computation of the values $x_{s,r}$ for $r = 1, 2, 3, \ldots$ until the probability threshold $p$ is reached, the values $x_{s,r}$ are stored symbolically, using one MTBDD per bound $r$ to represent the functions $x_r \colon S \to \mathbb{Q}$. The state-action pairs with positive reward are handled first, computing the MTBDD $B \colon S \to \mathbb{Q}$. Here, all state-action pairs with identical reward value are handled simultaneously. Consequently, this symbolic approach tends to be most efficient if there are many state-action pairs, but few distinct reward values in the model. To subsequently handle the zero-reward state-action pairs, we symbolically transform the MDP. First, all positive-reward actions are stripped and replaced by a single fresh $\tau$-action for each state. These $\tau$-actions model the choice of choosing the "best" positive-reward action in a state $s$ and go to a special *goal* trap state with probability $B(s)$ and to a *fail* trap state with probability $1 - B(s)$. The computation of $x_{s,i}$ then amounts to a standard maximal/minimal reachability probability computation in the transformed model by means of value iteration, relying on the computation engine chosen by the user, i.e., either the MTBDD, HYBRID or SPARSE engine. As the state value vectors $x_r$ are stored symbolically in all cases and the use of the semi-symbolic techniques of the HYBRID and SPARSE engines is thus limited, we denote these engines as SEMIHYBRID and SEMISPARSE in the context of our symbolic quantile implementation.

### 3.2   Benchmarks for Quantile Computations

To perform benchmarking of our implementation, we have reused several models and quantile queries that were first considered in [5] for benchmarking our quantile implementation for PRISM's EXPLICIT engine. We present here (Table 2) statistics for some noteworthy model instances, for further statistics and details on the models and quantile queries we refer to [21][4].

As can be seen in Table 2, there are model instances were the quantile implementation in the EXPLICIT engine easily outperforms our symbolic approach, e.g., for the "self-stabilizing" case study, despite a very compact MTBDD representation of the model. To put computation times such as 2153.2 s (for N=18) into context, the number of iterations in the quantile computation has to be kept in mind: Here, 392 iterations were required, with an average time per iteration of around 5 s. The large number of iterations thus amplifies the time spent in each iteration. For the "asynchronous leader-election" case study, our symbolic implementation becomes competitive for N=8 because of the time spent for model construction in the EXPLICIT engine due to the large state space. The symbolic computations still yield results for N=9, where the explicit approach times out. A similar picture is seen for query Q7 of the "energy-aware

---

[4] The benchmarks for the quantile computations were carried out on a machine with two Intel E5-2680 8-core CPUs at 2.70 GHz with 384 GB of RAM running Linux.

**Table 2.** Quantile computations for selected case studies, with statistics for the model size (reachable state space, MTBDD size of symbolic transition matrix) and times spent for model building and computing the quantile query (in seconds). The "it." column depicts the number of overall iterations in the quantile computation.

| $N$ | States | MTBDD size | it. | Explicit $t_{build}$ | Explicit $t_{query}$ | SemiHybrid $t_{build}$ | SemiHybrid $t_{query}$ | SemiSparse $t_{build}$ | SemiSparse $t_{query}$ | Mtbdd $t_{build}$ | Mtbdd $t_{query}$ |
|---|---|---|---|---|---|---|---|---|---|---|---|
| Self-stabilizing algorithm (Israeli/Jalfon), $N$ processes (query Q1) |||||||||||| |
| 11 | 2047 | 433 | 144 | 0.5 | 0.2 | <0.1 | 2.5 | <0.1 | 2.3 | <0.1 | 2.0 |
| 15 | 32767 | 729 | 271 | 1.6 | 3.9 | <0.1 | 119.1 | <0.1 | 114.7 | <0.1 | 159.3 |
| 18 | 262143 | 993 | 392 | 9.8 | 53.8 | <0.1 | 2135.2 | <0.1 | 2865.1 | <0.1 | 2240.3 |
| Asynchronous leader election, $N$ processes (query Q3) |||||||||||| |
| 7 | 2095783 | 180383 | 206 | 63.1 | 83.2 | 5.9 | 358.8 | 7.0 | 369.8 | 7.6 | 402.7 |
| 8 | 18674484 | 392093 | 238 | 1633.2 | 891.8 | 20.6 | 1228.4 | 24.6 | 1307.4 | 21.9 | 1448.8 |
| 9 | 167748115 | 868257 | 279 | – | – | 106.1 | 7751.9 | 92.3 | 5728.1 | 92.9 | 7545.6 |
| Energy-aware job scheduling, $N$ processes (query Q7) |||||||||||| |
| 5 | 6079533 | 187458 | 302 | 334.1 | 285.9 | 7.8 | 1196.2 | 7.2 | 1128.0 | 7.9 | 1142.9 |
| 6 | 44072357 | 507805 | 416 | – | – | 21.7 | 3808.4 | 22.8 | 4045.9 | 25.0 | 3962.8 |
| Energy-aware job scheduling, $N$ processes (query Q8) |||||||||||| |
| 5 | 3049471 | 25363 | 13 | 62.5 | 398.6 | 0.8 | 86.0 | 0.9 | 74.3 | 0.9 | 104.6 |
| 6 | 7901694 | 38911 | 15 | 210.0 | 2375.5 | 1.8 | 390.6 | 1.8 | 378.1 | 1.3 | 317.1 |

job scheduling" case study. For the instances of this case study and query Q8 shown in Table 2, the symbolic implementation vastly outperforms the explicit implementation. This is mainly due to the large amount of time spent there for the precomputation step (1971 s for N=6), while the symbolic engines perform this step in around 2 s. This appears to be due to inefficiencies in some of the end component computations in the Explicit engine, which we are currently investigating and working on a potential fix. For the "energy-aware job scheduling" case study, the computations were carried out in a reordered model, which lead to a significant decrease in MTBDD size and computation time. For instance, for (Q7) and N=6 we observed a reduction in the size of the transition matrix of 78.2 % and the quantile computation (SemiHybrid) took 43,832.9 s in the original model instead of 3808.4 s in the reordered model, with similar reductions for Mtbdd and SemiSparse.

**Quantiles in Feature-Oriented Systems.** In product lines, collections of systems are described through the combination of features. Thus, the systems in a product line usually share a lot of common behaviors, which makes symbolic approaches appealing. Using a family-based approach, i.e., modeling the product line in a single model, in previous work [13] we performed experiments on an energy-aware server product line eServer. There, we illustrated the benefits of symbolic representations in product-line verification and showed that variable orderings have a crucial impact on the analysis performance. However, due to

**Table 3.** Quantile computations for ESERVER, with statistics for the reachable state space and MTBDD size of the transition matrix, reduction and time for reordering, and time building the model and computing the quantile query (in seconds).

|  |  | States | MTBDD nodes | Reduction in % | $t_{reorder}$ | MTBDD $t_{build}$ | MTBDD $t_{query}$ |
|---|---|---|---|---|---|---|---|
| Instance 1 | original | 145 984 112 | 64 030 | - | - | 10.2 | 1 018.6 |
|  | reordered | " | 40 096 | 37.4 | 3.5 | 7.8 | 766.4 |
|  | with explode | " | 34 902 | 45.5 | 8.3 | 9.1 | 726.2 |
|  | with globalize | " | 36 149 | 43.5 | 2.9 | 6.3 | 704.3 |
|  | with exp.+glob. | " | 30 325 | 52.6 | 3.1 | 7.9 | 638.6 |
| Instance 2 | original | 441 704 832 | 140 556 | - | - | 27.2 | 3 664.6 |
|  | reordered | " | 72 565 | 48.4 | 68.5 | 16.6 | 3 510.5 |
|  | with explode | " | 66 874 | 52.4 | 32.3 | 17.7 | 3 204.7 |
|  | with globalize | " | 43 249 | 69.2 | 6.5 | 11.2 | 3 099.0 |
|  | with exp.+glob. | " | 37 674 | 73.3 | 8.5 | 12.1 | 2 833.0 |

the lack of a symbolic quantile implementation, an energy-utility analysis of ESERVER had to be postponed as future work.

In Table 3, we summarize statistics for the computation of quantiles on two instances of ESERVER, becoming possible due to our symbolic implementation. We computed the minimal amount of energy required to guarantee in 95 % of the cases a certain percentage of the time without any package drop. The table shows the impact of our four reorder mechanisms on the model size and the quantile computation time. We only included the results for the MTBDD engine, as the other engines struggled with the size of the model and reached a timeout after one day. Within all computations, 1476 quantile iterations were required. Interestingly, although the model presented in [13] already used heuristics to find good initial variable orderings, the fully automatic reorder mechanisms presented here allow for a further significant reduction of the model size and a speedup of the analyses.

## 4   Additional Enhancements

We report here on additional enhancements we have implemented in PRISM both for the symbolic and explicit engines, related to the support of $\omega$-automata.

**Accepting End Component Computations for Streett Conditions.** Traditionally, PRISM has relied on an internal implementation of Safra's determinization construction for generating the deterministic Rabin automata used for LTL model checking, e.g., for computing $Pr^{max}(\varphi)$ or $Pr^{min}(\varphi)$ for an LTL formula $\varphi$. Recently, support was added for automata with generalized Rabin acceptance [2,9] to benefit from advances in the construction of small deterministic automata [14,22]. This includes support for calling external tools for the transformation of LTL formulas into deterministic Muller-automata, relying on the recent Hanoi Omega Automata (HOA) format [2], which supports the concise representation of common acceptance conditions in a generic normal form.

We have extended PRISM's MDP model checking with support for Streett conditions, relying on the recursive algorithm for end-component analysis of [6]. Streett conditions are dual to Rabin conditions and are well suited for the specification of fairness constraints and for conjunctions of properties. They appear as well in the computation of conditional probabilities in MDPs [7]. It is well known, both in theory [29] and in practice [20], that for some languages, deterministic Streett automata can be significantly smaller than Rabin automata.

**Extremal Probabilities for Automata Specifications.** We have furthermore extended the property syntax of the probability operators in PRISM to allow the use of a HOA-automaton file instead of an LTL formula, providing the full power of $\omega$-regular languages. For DTMC models, the full range of acceptance conditions in the normal form of the HOA format [2] is supported. For MDPs, Rabin, generalized Rabin and Streett conditions are supported. For the computation of $\mathrm{Pr}^{\min}$, which requires the complementation of the language of the automaton, we support Rabin and Streett conditions, exploiting their duality.

## 5   Conclusion

In this paper, we have demonstrated the potential for automatic variable reordering for symbolic model checking in PRISM, including the benefits of now having fine-grained control over the variable order using our syntactic transformations. We have also shown that our symbolic implementation for quantiles is useful in practice, particularly where explicit representations of the model are infeasible.

**Future Work:** In the area of automatic variable reordering, it would be interesting to support more structured reordering: Often, models are obtained from templates with parametrization, e.g., specifying the number of copies of certain modules in the model. By swapping the variables of all copies simultaneously, it might be possible to discover good initial variable orders from instances with few copies and apply these to instances with more copies. This approach would also be interesting when the aim is to apply symmetry reduction [12,25], as all copies would remain symmetrical. While our syntactic transformations provide very fine-grained reordering for the state variables, it would be interesting to have the option of adding back some restrictions or hints for the reordering by annotating the variable declarations in the PRISM model. This would allow to state preferences which variable should be kept together, etc. In this context it would also make sense to revisit previous work on heuristics for good initial variable orderings in PRISM [30], making use of the finer-grained control that is now possible. In addition, our benchmark results serve as an indication that it would be worthwhile to attempt a refactoring of PRISM to remove the variable order assumptions and add support for asynchronous reordering.

For our symbolic quantile computations, it appears worthwhile to consider an iterative implementation that fully exploits the approach of the HYBRID engine, with a symbolic transition matrix and explicit state value vector storage. This could allow the application of several of the techniques employed by the quantile computations of the EXPLICIT engine to speed-up the computations.

The implementation of the end component computation for Streett conditions could serve as the base for supporting more complex types of fairness conditions via the approach of [6], such as fairness for the scheduling of the modules in a PRISM model. It would also be interesting to perform a detailed experimental evaluation on the use of Streett versus (generalized) Rabin automata for probabilistic model checking in practice.

# References

1. Andova, S., Hermanns, H., Katoen, J.-P.: Discrete-time rewards model-checked. In: Larsen, K.G., Niebert, P. (eds.) FORMATS 2003. LNCS, vol. 2791, pp. 88–104. Springer, Heidelberg (2003)
2. Babiak, T., Blahoudek, F., Duret-Lutz, A., Klein, J., Křetínský, J., Müller, D., Parker, D., Strejček, J.: The Hanoi omega-automata format. In: Kroening, D., Păsăreanu, C.S. (eds.) CAV 2015. LNCS, vol. 9206, pp. 479–486. Springer, Heidelberg (2015)
3. Bahar, R.I., Frohm, E.A., Gaona, C.M., Hachtel, G.D., Macii, E., Pardo, A., Somenzi, F.: Algebraic decision diagrams and their applications. Formal Methods Syst. Des. 10(2/3), 171–206 (1997)
4. Baier, C., Clarke, E.M., Hartonas-Garmhausen, V., Kwiatkowska, M.Z., Ryan, M.: Symbolic model checking for probabilistic processes. In: Degano, P., Gorrieri, R., Marchetti-Spaccamela, A. (eds.) ICALP 1997. LNCS, vol. 1256, pp. 430–440. Springer, Heidelberg (1997)
5. Baier, C., Daum, M., Dubslaff, C., Klein, J., Klüppelholz, S.: Energy-utility quantiles. In: Badger, J.M., Rozier, K.Y. (eds.) NFM 2014. LNCS, vol. 8430, pp. 285–299. Springer, Heidelberg (2014)
6. Baier, C., Groesser, M., Ciesinski, F.: Quantitative analysis under fairness constraints. In: Liu, Z., Ravn, A.P. (eds.) ATVA 2009. LNCS, vol. 5799, pp. 135–150. Springer, Heidelberg (2009)
7. Baier, C., Klein, J., Klüppelholz, S., Märcker, S.: Computing conditional probabilities in Markovian models efficiently. In: Ábrahám, E., Havelund, K. (eds.) TACAS 2014 (ETAPS). LNCS, vol. 8413, pp. 515–530. Springer, Heidelberg (2014)
8. Burch, J.R., Clarke, E.M., McMillan, K.L., Dill, D.L., Hwang, L.J.: Symbolic model checking: $10^{20}$ states and beyond. Inf. Comput. 98(2), 142–170 (1992)
9. Chatterjee, K., Gaiser, A., Křetínský, J.: Automata with generalized rabin pairs for probabilistic model checking and LTL synthesis. In: Sharygina, N., Veith, H. (eds.) CAV 2013. LNCS, vol. 8044, pp. 559–575. Springer, Heidelberg (2013)
10. Ciardo, G., Miner, A.S., Wan, M.: Advanced features in SMART: the stochastic model checking analyzer for reliability and timing. SIGMETRICS Perform. Eval. Rev. 36(4), 58–63 (2009)
11. Cimatti, A., Clarke, E., Giunchiglia, E., Giunchiglia, F., Pistore, M., Roveri, M., Sebastiani, R., Tacchella, A.: NuSMV 2: an opensource tool for symbolic model checking. In: Brinksma, E., Larsen, K.G. (eds.) CAV 2002. LNCS, vol. 2404, pp. 359–364. Springer, Heidelberg (2002)

12. Donaldson, A.F., Miller, A., Parker, D.: Language-level symmetry reduction for probabilistic model checking. In: Proceedings of the Quantitative Evaluation of Systems (QEST 2009), pp. 289–298. IEEE (2009)
13. Dubslaff, C., Baier, C., Klüppelholz, S.: Probabilistic model checking for feature-oriented systems. Trans. Aspect-Oriented Softw. Dev. **12**, 180–220 (2015)
14. Esparza, J., Křetínský, J.: From LTL to deterministic automata: a Safraless compositional approach. In: Biere, A., Bloem, R. (eds.) CAV 2014. LNCS, vol. 8559, pp. 192–208. Springer, Heidelberg (2014)
15. Fujita, M., McGeer, P.C., Yang, J.C.-Y.: Multi-terminal binary decision diagrams: An efficient data structure for matrix representation. Formal Methods Syst. Des. **10**(2/3), 149–169 (1997)
16. Haase, C., Kiefer, S.: The odds of staying on budget. In: Halldórsson, M.M., Iwama, K., Kobayashi, N., Speckmann, B. (eds.) ICALP 2015. LNCS, vol. 9135, pp. 234–246. Springer, Heidelberg (2015)
17. Hachtel, G.D., Macii, E., Pardo, A., Somenzi, F.: Markovian analysis of large finite state machines. IEEE Trans. CAD Integr. Circ., Syst. **15**(12), 1479–1493 (1996)
18. Hartonas-Garmhausen, V., Campos, S., Clarke, E.: ProbVerus: probabilistic symbolic model checking. In: Katoen, J.-P. (ed.) ARTS 1999. LNCS, vol. 1601, pp. 96–110. Springer, Heidelberg (1999)
19. Hermanns, H., Kwiatkowska, M.Z., Norman, G., Parker, D., Siegle, M.: On the use of MTBDDs for performability analysis and verification of stochastic systems. J. Logic Algebr. Program. **56**(1–2), 23–67 (2003)
20. Klein, J., Baier, C.: Experiments with deterministic ω-automata for formulas of linear temporal logic. Theoret. Comput. Sci. **363**(2), 182–195 (2006)
21. Klein, J., Baier, C., Chrszon, P., Daum, M., Dubslaff, C., Klüppelholz, S., Märcker, S., Müller, D.: Advances in symbolic probabilistic model checking with PRISM (extended version) (2016). http://wwwtcs.inf.tu-dresden.de/ALGI/PUB/TACAS16/
22. Komárková, Z., Křetínský, J.: Rabinizer 3: Safraless translation of LTL to small deterministic automata. In: Cassez, F., Raskin, J.-F. (eds.) ATVA 2014. LNCS, vol. 8837, pp. 235–241. Springer, Heidelberg (2014)
23. Kuntz, M., Siegle, M.: CASPA: symbolic model checking of stochastic systems. In: Proceedings of Measuring, Modelling and Evaluation of Computer and Communication Systems (MMB 2006), pp. 465–468. VDE Verlag (2006)
24. Kwiatkowska, M.Z., Norman, G., Parker, D.: Probabilistic symbolic model checking with PRISM: a hybrid approach. Softw. Tools Technol. Transfer **6**(2), 128–142 (2004)
25. Kwiatkowska, M., Norman, G., Parker, D.: Symmetry reduction for probabilistic model checking. In: Ball, T., Jones, R.B. (eds.) CAV 2006. LNCS, vol. 4144, pp. 234–248. Springer, Heidelberg (2006)
26. Kwiatkowska, M., Norman, G., Parker, D.: PRISM 4.0: verification of probabilistic real-time systems. In: Gopalakrishnan, G., Qadeer, S. (eds.) CAV 2011. LNCS, vol. 6806, pp. 585–591. Springer, Heidelberg (2011)
27. Kwiatkowska, M.Z., Norman, G., Parker, D., The PRISM benchmark suite. In: Proceedings of Quantitative Evaluation of Systems (QEST 2012), pp. 203–204. IEEE (2012). https://github.com/prismmodelchecker/prism-benchmarks/
28. Lampka, K.: A symbolic approach to the state graph based analysis of high-level Markov reward models. PhD thesis, Universität Erlangen-Nürnberg (2007)
29. Löding, C.: Optimal bounds for transformations of ω-automata. In: Pandu Rangan, C., Raman, V., Sarukkai, S. (eds.) FST TCS 1999. LNCS, vol. 1738, pp. 97–109. Springer, Heidelberg (1999)

30. Maisonneuve, V.: Automatic heuristic-based generation of MTBDD variable order-
    ings for PRISM models. ENS Cachan & Oxford University, Internship report
    (2009). http://www.prismmodelchecker.org/papers/vivien-bdds-report.pdf
31. McMillan, K.L.: Symbolic Model Checking. Kluwer, Norwell (1993)
32. Miner, A.S., Parker, D.: Symbolic representations and analysis of large probabilistic
    systems. In: Baier, C., Haverkort, B.R., Hermanns, H., Katoen, J.-P., Siegle, M.
    (eds.) Validation of Stochastic Systems. LNCS, vol. 2925, pp. 296–338. Springer,
    Heidelberg (2004)
33. Panda, S., Somenzi, F.: Who are the variables in your neighborhood. In: Proceed-
    ings of the Computer-Aided Design (ICCAD 1995), pp. 74–77. IEEE (1995)
34. Parker, D.: Implementation of Symbolic Model Checking for Probabilistic Systems.
    PhD thesis, University of Birmingham (2002)
35. PRISM model checker. http://www.prismmodelchecker.org/
36. Rudell, R.: Dynamic variable ordering for ordered binary decision diagrams. In:
    Proceedings of the Computer-Aided Design (ICCAD 1993), pp. 42–47. IEEE (1993)
37. Somenzi, F.: CUDD: Colorado University decision diagram package. http://vlsi.
    colorado.edu/~fabio/CUDD/
38. Ummels, M., Baier, C.: Computing quantiles in markov reward models. In: Pfen-
    ning, F. (ed.) FOSSACS 2013 (ETAPS 2013). LNCS, vol. 7794, pp. 353–368.
    Springer, Heidelberg (2013)

# PRISM-PSY: Precise GPU-Accelerated Parameter Synthesis for Stochastic Systems

Milan Češka[1]([✉]), Petr Pilař[2], Nicola Paoletti[1], Luboš Brim[2], and Marta Kwiatkowska[1]

[1] Department of Computer Science, University of Oxford, Oxford, UK
milan.ceska@cs.ox.ac.uk
[2] Faculty of Informatics, Masaryk University, Brno, Czech Republic

**Abstract.** In this paper we present PRISM-PSY, a novel tool that performs precise GPU-accelerated parameter synthesis for continuous-time Markov chains and time-bounded temporal logic specifications. We redesign, in terms of matrix-vector operations, the recently formulated algorithms for precise parameter synthesis in order to enable effective data-parallel processing, which results in significant acceleration on many-core architectures. High hardware utilisation, essential for performance and scalability, is achieved by state space and parameter space parallelisation: the former leverages a compact sparse-matrix representation, and the latter is based on an iterative decomposition of the parameter space. Our experiments on several biological and engineering case studies demonstrate an overall speedup of up to 31-fold on a single GPU compared to the sequential implementation.

## 1 Introduction

Model checking of *continuous-time Markov chains* (CTMCs) against *continuous stochastic logic* (CSL) formulae [1,27] has numerous applications in many areas of science. In biochemistry, there is an interest in analysing hypotheses (formulated using CSL) about reaction networks that can be adequately modelled as CTMCs governed by the Chemical Master Equation [9,22,28]. In engineering disciplines, CTMCs are used to study various reliability and performance aspects of computer networks [5], communication [19] and security protocols [29].

Traditionally, stochastic model checking techniques assume that model parameters – namely, the transition rate constants – are known a priori. This is often not the case and one has to consider ranges of parameter values instead, for example, when the parameters result from imprecise measurements, or when designers are interested in finding parameter values such that the model fulfils a given specification. Such problems can be effectively formulated in the framework of parameter synthesis for CTMCs [10,12,24]: given a time-bounded CSL formula and a model whose transition rates are functions of the parameters, find

This work has been supported by the ERC Advanced Grant VERIWARE, and the Czech Grant Agency grants GA16-24707Y (M. Češka) and GA15-11089S (L. Brim).

M. Chechik and J.-F. Raskin (Eds.): TACAS 2016, LNCS 9636, pp. 367–384, 2016.
DOI: 10.1007/978-3-662-49674-9_21

parameter values such that the satisfaction probability of the formula meets a given threshold, is maximised, or minimised. In [10,12] we developed synthesis algorithms that yield answers that are precise up to within an arbitrarily small tolerance value. The algorithms combine the computation of probability bounds with the refinement and sampling of the parameter space.

The complexity of the synthesis algorithms depends mainly on the size of the underlying model and on the number of parameter regions to analyse in order to achieve the desired precision. However, existing techniques do not scale with the model size and the dimensionality of the parameter space. For instance, as reported in [12], the synthesis of two parameters for a model with 5.1 K states requires the analysis of 5 K parameter regions and takes around 3.6 h.

In the last years, many-core graphical processing units (GPUs) have been utilised as general purpose, high-performance processing resources in computationally-intensive scientific applications. In light of this development, we redesign the synthesis algorithms using matrix-vector operations so as to ensure effective data-parallel processing and acceleration of the synthesis procedures on many-core architectures. The novelty of our approach is a two-level parallelisation scheme that distributes the workload for the processing of the state space and the parameter space, in order to optimally utilise the computational power of the GPU. The state space parallelisation builds on a sparse-matrix encoding of the underlying parametric CTMC. The parameter space parallelisation exploits the fact that our synthesis algorithms require the analysis of a large number of parameter regions during the parameter space refinement.

In this paper we present our new publicly available tool PRISM-PSY[1] that implements the data-parallel algorithms together with a number of optimisations of the sequential algorithms, and employs the front-end of the probabilistic model-checker PRISM [26]. We systematically evaluate the performance of PRISM-PSY and demonstrate the usefulness of our precise parameter synthesis methods on several case studies, including survivability analysis of the Google File System [2,16]. Our experiments show that the data-parallel synthesis achieves on a single GPU up to a 31-fold speedup with respect to the optimised sequential implementation and that our algorithms provide good scalability with respect to the size of the model and the number of parameter regions to analyse. As a result, PRISM-PSY enables the application of precise parameter synthesis methods to more complex problems, i.e. larger models and higher-dimensional parameter spaces.

The main contributions of this paper can be summarised as follows: (1) improvement of the sequential algorithms of [10,12], leading in some cases to more than 10-fold speedup; (2) formulation of a backward variant of the parametric transient analysis of [10] using matrix-vector operations, which enables data-parallel implementation; (3) combination of the state space and parameter space parallelisation in order to fully utilise the available computational power; (4) development of the PRISM-PSY tool that enables precise parameter synthesis on many-core architectures and (5) systematic experimental evaluation of the tool.

---

[1] http://www.prismmodelchecker.org/psy/.

**Related Work.** The parameter synthesis problem for CTMCs and bounded reachability specifications was first introduced in [24], where the authors resort to the analysis of the polynomial function describing how the reachability probability depends on the parameter values. Due to the high degree of the polynomials (determined by the number of uniformisation steps), only an approximate solution is obtained through the discretisation of the parameter space.

The function describing how the satisfaction probability of a linear time-bounded formula depends on the parameter values can be approximated through statistical methods. A technique based on Gaussian Process regression is presented in [6] and implemented in the U-check tool [7]. In contrast to our approach, statistical methods cannot provide guaranteed precision, and thus are not suitable for safety-critical applications.

Parameter synthesis has also been studied for discrete-time Markovian models and unbounded temporal properties [15,23]. The synthesis algorithms are based on constructing a rational function describing the satisfaction probability by performing state elimination. This approach is implemented in the tool PROPhESY [18] that supports incremental parameter synthesis using SMT techniques, but is not suitable for time-bounded specifications and CTMCs.

Our tool builds on methods for the efficient GPU parallelisation of matrix-vector multiplication [4] and probabilistic model checking [8,33]. In our previous work [3], we showed how the algorithms for LTL model checking can be redesigned in order to accelerate verification on GPUs.

## 2   Precise Parameter Synthesis

In this section we summarise the parameter synthesis problem for CTMCs and time-bounded CSL properties originally introduced in [12]. We also describe the sequential synthesis algorithms of [10,12] and the improvements implemented in the PRISM-PSY tool, which provide the foundation for the new data-parallel algorithms (Sect. 3) and the baseline for evaluating the parallelisation speedup.

### 2.1   Problem Formulation

*Parametric continuous-time Markov chains* (*p*CTMCs) [24] extend the notion of CTMCs by allowing transition rates to depend on parameters. We consider *p*CTMCs with a finite set of states $S$ and a finite set $K$ of parameters ranging over closed real intervals, i.e., $[k^\perp, k^\top] \subseteq \mathbb{R}$ for $k \in K$. These induce a rectangular parameter space $\mathcal{P} = \times_{k \in K} [k^\perp, k^\top]$. Subsets of $\mathcal{P}$ are referred to as *parameter regions* or *subspaces*. Given a *p*CTMC and a parameter space $\mathcal{P}$, we denote with $\mathcal{C}_\mathcal{P}$ the set $\{\mathcal{C}_p \mid p \in \mathcal{P}\}$, where $\mathcal{C}_p$ is the instantiated CTMC obtained by replacing the parameters in the parametric rate matrix $\mathbf{R}$ with the valuation $p$.

In the current implementation of the tool, we support only linear rate functions of the following two forms: for any $s, s' \in S$, $\mathbf{R}(s, s') = \sum_{k \in K} k \cdot a_{k,s,s'}$ (parametric rate) or $\mathbf{R}(s, s') = b_{s,s'}$ (constant rate) where $a_{k,s,s'}, b_{s,s'} \in \mathbb{R}_{\geq 0}$.

Such rate functions are sufficient to describe a wide range of systems, from biological to computer systems, as we will show in Sect. 4.

To specify properties over $p$CTMCs, we employ the time-bounded fragment of *Continuous Stochastic Logic (CSL)* [1] extended with time-bounded reward operators [27]. The current version of the tool considers only unnested formulae given by the following syntax: $\Phi :: = P_{\sim r}[\phi] \mid R_{\sim r}[C^{\leq t}]$ is a state formula, $\phi :: = \Psi\, U^I\, \Psi$ is a path formula, where $\Psi :: = \text{true} \mid a \mid \neg\Psi \mid \Psi \wedge \Psi$, $a$ is an atomic proposition evaluated over states, $\sim \in \{<, \leq, \geq, >\}$, r is a probability ($r \in [0,1]$) or reward ($r \in \mathbb{R}_{\geq 0}$) threshold, $t \in \mathbb{R}_{\geq 0}$ is a time bound, and $I$ is a time interval of $\mathbb{R}_{\geq 0}$. The future operator, $F^I$, can be derived as $F^I\, \Psi \equiv \text{true}\, U^I\, \Psi$. Let $\models$ denote a satisfaction relation. Intuitively, a state $s \models P_{\sim r}[\phi]$ iff the probability of the set of paths starting in $s$ and satisfying $\phi$ meets $\sim r$. A path $\omega = s_0 t_0 s_1 t_1 \ldots$ satisfies $\Phi\, U^I\, \Psi$ iff there exists a time $t \in I.(\omega@t \models \Psi \wedge \forall t' \in [0,t).\omega@t' \models \Phi)$, where $\omega@t$ denotes the state in $\omega$ at time $t$. A state $s \models R_{\sim p}[C^{\leq t}]$ iff the expected rewards over the path starting in $s$ cumulated until $t$ time units satisfies $\sim p$. We remark that the synthesis algorithms can be adapted to support the full fragment of time-bounded CSL including nested formulae, as shown in [10].

The *satisfaction function* captures how the satisfaction probability of a given property relates to the parameters and initial state. Let $\phi$ be a CSL path formula, $C_{\mathcal{P}}$ be a $p$CTMC over a space $\mathcal{P}$ and $s \in S$. We denote with $\Lambda_\phi : \mathcal{P} \to S \to [0,1]$ the satisfaction function such that $\Lambda_\phi(p)(s)$ is the probability of the set of paths (from state $s$) satisfying $\phi$ in $C_p$. The satisfaction function for reward formulae can be defined analogously and is omitted to simplify the presentation.

We consider two parameter synthesis problems: the *threshold synthesis* problem that, given a threshold $\sim r$ and a CSL path formula $\phi$, asks for the parameter region where the probability of $\phi$ meets $\sim r$; and the *max synthesis* problem that determines the parameter region where the probability of the input formula attains its maximum, together with probability bounds approximating that maximum. Solutions to the threshold synthesis problem admit parameter points left undecided, while, in the max synthesis problem, the actual set of maximising parameters is contained in the synthesised region. The min synthesis problem is defined and solved in a symmetric way to the max case.

For $C_{\mathcal{P}}$, $\phi$, an initial state $s_0$, a threshold $\sim r$ and a volume tolerance $\varepsilon > 0$, the *threshold synthesis* problem is finding a partition $\{\mathcal{T}, \mathcal{U}, \mathcal{F}\}$ of $\mathcal{P}$, such that: $\forall p \in \mathcal{T} : \Lambda_\phi(p)(s_0) \sim r$; $\forall p \in \mathcal{F} : \Lambda_\phi(p)(s_0) \nsim r$; and $\text{vol}(\mathcal{U})/\text{vol}(\mathcal{P}) \leq \varepsilon$, where $\mathcal{U}$ is an undecided subspace and $\text{vol}(A) = \int_A 1 d\mu$ is the volume of $A$.

For $C_{\mathcal{P}}$, $\phi$, $s_0$, and a probability tolerance $\epsilon > 0$, the *max synthesis* problem is finding a partition $\{\mathcal{T}, \mathcal{F}\}$ of $\mathcal{P}$ and probability bounds $\Lambda_\phi^\perp$, $\Lambda_\phi^\top$ such that: $\forall p \in \mathcal{T} : \Lambda_\phi^\perp \leq \Lambda_\phi(p)(s_0) \leq \Lambda_\phi^\top$; $\exists p \in \mathcal{T} : \forall p' \in \mathcal{F} : \Lambda_\phi(p)(s_0) > \Lambda_\phi(p')(s_0)$; and $\Lambda_\phi^\top - \Lambda_\phi^\perp \leq \epsilon$.

Figure 1 depicts an example of threshold and max synthesis problems. On the left, the satisfaction function describes the probability of the property (y-axis) depending on the values of parameter $k_1$ (x-axis). In the centre plot, we highlight the parameter regions for which the threshold $\geq r$ is met ($\mathcal{T}$, green), is not met ($\mathcal{F}$, red) and is undecided ($\mathcal{U}$, yellow). On the right, the solution to the

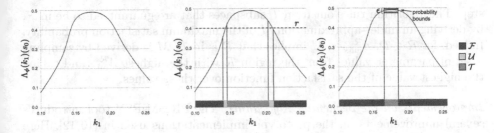

**Fig. 1. Left:** Example of a satisfaction function. **Centre:** Solution of the threshold synthesis problem for $\geq r$. **Right:** Solution of the max synthesis problem (Color figure online).

max synthesis problem is the region ($\mathcal{T}$, green) containing all the maximising parameters and whose probability bounds meet the input tolerance $\epsilon$.

## 2.2 Solution of the Synthesis Problems

The key ingredient for solving the aforementioned synthesis problems is a procedure that takes a $p$CTMC $\mathcal{C}_{\mathcal{P}}$ and CSL path formula $\phi$, and provides safe under- and over-approximations of the minimal and maximal probability that $\mathcal{C}_{\mathcal{P}}$ satisfies $\phi$: for all $s \in S$, it computes bounds $\Lambda_{\min}(s)$ and $\Lambda_{\max}(s)$ such that $\Lambda_{\min}(s) \leq \inf_{p \in \mathcal{P}} \Lambda_{\phi}(p)(s)$ and $\Lambda_{\max}(s) \geq \sup_{p \in \mathcal{P}} \Lambda_{\phi}(p)(s)$. The procedure builds on a parametric transient analysis that computes safe bounds for the parametric transient probabilities in the discrete-time process derived from the CTMC. This discretisation is obtained through standard uniformisation and the Fox and Glynn algorithm [21] that is used to derive the required number of discrete steps to consider (also called uniformisation steps or iterations) for a given time bound[2]. See [10,27] for more details.

We now summarise the algorithms for threshold and max synthesis based on the partitioning and iterative refinement of the parameter space [12]. Assume a threshold synthesis problem for a path formula $\phi$ with threshold $\geq r$. At each step, the algorithm refines the undecided parameter subspace $\mathcal{U}$, starting from $\mathcal{U} = \mathcal{P}$: it generates a partition $\mathcal{D}$ of $\mathcal{U}$ and, for each $\mathcal{R} \in \mathcal{D}$, computes the safe probability bounds $\Lambda^{\mathcal{R}}_{\min}$ and $\Lambda^{\mathcal{R}}_{\max}$ of the corresponding $p$CTMC $\mathcal{C}_{\mathcal{R}}$. If $\Lambda^{\mathcal{R}}_{\min} \geq r$, then the satisfaction of the threshold is guaranteed for the whole region $\mathcal{R}$, which is hence added to $\mathcal{T}$. Otherwise, the algorithm tests whether $\mathcal{R}$ can be added to $\mathcal{F}$ by checking if $\Lambda^{\mathcal{R}}_{\max} < r$. If $\mathcal{R}$ is neither in $\mathcal{T}$ nor in $\mathcal{F}$, it forms an undecided subspace that is added to the set $\mathcal{U}$. If the volume tolerance $\varepsilon$ is not met, the algorithm proceeds to the next iteration, where $\mathcal{U}$ is further refined. The refinement procedure guarantees termination since the over-approximation $[\Lambda^{\mathcal{R}}_{\min}, \Lambda^{\mathcal{R}}_{\max}]$ can be made arbitrarily precise by reducing the volume of $\mathcal{R}$ [13].

In the max synthesis case, the algorithm starts from $\mathcal{T} = \mathcal{P}$ and iteratively refines $\mathcal{T}$ until the tolerance $\epsilon$ is met. Let $\mathcal{D}$ be the partition of $\mathcal{T}$ at a generic

---

[2] The Fox and Glynn algorithm returns a finite bound on the number of steps needed to approximate transient probabilities up to a specified precision.

step. The algorithm rules out from $\mathcal{T}$ subspaces that are guaranteed to be in $\mathcal{F}$, by deriving an under-approximation $M$ of the maximum satisfaction probability. Indeed, for $\mathcal{R} \in \mathcal{D}$, $\Lambda_{\max}^{\mathcal{R}} < M$ implies that $\mathcal{R}$ is in $\mathcal{F}$. $M$ is derived by sampling a set of parameter values from the region $\mathcal{R}$ with the highest $\Lambda_{\min}^{\mathcal{R}}$ and taking the highest value of the satisfaction function over these values.

*Improvements on the Sequential Algorithms.* The PRISM-PSY tool introduces several improvements on the prototype implementations used in [10,12]. Here we present those having the most significant impact on performance.

*(1) Backward computation of probabilistic bounds.* In [10,12], the probability bounds $\Lambda_{\min}$ and $\Lambda_{\max}$ are computed using a forward variant of the parametric transient analysis, which requires a separate computation of the bounds for each initial state. In our tool, we also implemented a more efficient solution that requires only a single computation for all states, based on backward computation.

*(2) Adaptive Fox-Glynn.* While in previous implementations the number of uni-formisation steps was fixed and obtained using the maximum exit rate (sum of outgoing rates per a state) of the whole parameter space, the *adaptive Fox-Glynn* technique computes the number of steps for each subregion separately, using the maximum exit rate of the inspected subregion. For large parameter spaces, this technique can significantly decrease the overall number of uniformisation steps, improving the performance by more than a factor of two.

*(3) Refinement Strategies.* The tool employs improved refinement algorithms that can decrease the total number of subregions to analyse. Specifically, for threshold synthesis, at each step only the undecided subregions with the largest volume are refined while, for max synthesis, only the regions with either the lowest lower probability bound ($\Lambda_{\phi}^{\perp}$) or the highest upper bound ($\Lambda_{\phi}^{\top}$).

# 3    Data-Parallel Algorithms for Parameter Synthesis

In this section we first introduce the basic concepts of the target hardware architecture, i.e. modern general-purpose GPUs. We then formulate the backward variant of the parametric transient analysis using matrix-vector operations, and describe the sparse-matrix representation of $p$CTMCs. Finally, we present a two-level parallelisation of the synthesis algorithms. A detailed description of the data-parallel algorithms for parameter synthesis can be found in [30].

## 3.1    Computational Model for Modern GPUs

Typical GPUs consist of multiple *Streaming Multiprocessors* (SMs), with each SM following a *single instruction multiple threads* (SIMT) model. This approach establishes a hierarchy of threads prior to the actual computation. Within this hierarchy, threads are arranged into blocks that are assigned for parallel execution on SMs. Threads are hardwired into groups of 32 called warps, which form a basic scheduling unit and execute instructions in a lock-step manner. If a sufficient number of threads is dispatched, each SM maintains a set of active warps to hide the memory access latency and maximise utilisation of its functional units.

The SIMT approach supports code divergence within threads of the warp, but this usually causes significant performance degradation due to the serialisation of the execution. Another characteristic of GPUs that significantly affects their performance is the way in which simultaneous memory requests from multiple threads in a warp are handled. Requests exhibiting spatial locality are maximally *coalesced*. Simply stated, accesses to consecutive addresses are served by a single memory fetch as long as they are in the same memory segment.

A typical GPU program consists of a *host* code running on the CPU and a *device* code running on the GPU. The device code is structured into *kernels* that execute the same scalar sequential program in many independent data-parallel threads. The combination of out-of-order CPU and data-parallel processing GPU allows for heterogeneous computation.

## 3.2 Backward Computation of Probability Bounds

For a $p$CTMC $\mathcal{C}_\mathcal{R}$ over a region $\mathcal{R} = \times_{k \in K}[k^\perp, k^\top]$ and a target set $A \subseteq S$, the parametric backward analysis computes a series of vectors $\sigma_i^{\min}$ and $\sigma_i^{\max}$ such that, for all $s \in S$, $\sigma_i^{\min}(s) \leq \inf_{p \in \mathcal{P}} \sigma_{i,p}(s)$ and $\sigma_i^{\max}(s) \geq \sup_{p \in \mathcal{P}} \sigma_{i,p}(s)$, where $\sigma_{i,p}(s)$ is the probability that, starting from the state $s$, a state in $A$ is reached after $i$ discrete steps in $\mathcal{C}_p$. From these vectors, the probability bounds $\Lambda_{\min}(s)$ and $\Lambda_{\max}(s)$ are computed in a similar way to non-parametric CTMCs [27].

We define a matrix-vector operator $\diamond$ that computes the vector $\sigma_{i+1}^{\max}$ from $\sigma_i^{\max}$ and the parametric rate matrix $\mathbf{R}$ as $\sigma_{i+1}^{\max}(s) = (\mathbf{R} \diamond \sigma_i^{\max})(s)$, where $\sigma_0^{\max}(s) = 1$ if $s \in A$ and 0 otherwise. An analogous operator can be defined for $\sigma_{i+1}^{\min}$. Similarly to standard uniformisation, the definition of $\diamond$ exploits the uniformised matrix, which is, in our case, parametric. For each $s \in S$, $\sigma_{i+1}^{\max}(s)$ is first expressed by maximising the probability in $s$ stepwise, i.e. after the $i$-th step. Below, we expand the definition of the uniformised matrix using the uniformisation rate $q$ given by the maximal exit rate and the time bound [21,27]:

$$\sigma_{i+1}^{\max}(s) = \max_{p \in \mathcal{R}} \left( \sum_{s' \in S \setminus \{s\}} \sigma_i^{\max}(s') \frac{\mathbf{R}_p(s, s')}{q} + \sigma_i^{\max}(s) \left( 1 - \sum_{s' \in S \setminus \{s\}} \frac{\mathbf{R}_p(s, s')}{q} \right) \right) \quad (1)$$

where $\mathbf{R}_p$ is the rate matrix instantiated with parameter $p$. The first sum represents the probability of entering a state $s' \neq s$ and, from there, reaching $A$ in $i$ steps. The second sum is the probability of staying in $s$ and, from there, reaching $A$ in $i$ steps. By expanding the parametric rate matrix $\mathbf{R}$ in Eq. 1 we get:

$$\sigma_{i+1}^{\max}(s) = \sigma_i^{\max}(s) + \sum_{s' \in S \setminus \{s\}} \frac{\sigma_i^{\max}(s') - \sigma_i^{\max}(s)}{q} \cdot \begin{cases} \sum_{k \in K} k^\star \cdot a_{k,s,s'} & (2) \\ b_{s,s'} & (3) \end{cases}$$

where $k^\star = k^\top$ if $\sigma_i^{\max}(s') > \sigma_i^{\max}(s)$ and $k^\perp$ otherwise. These equations allow us to compute the vector $\sigma_{i+1}^{\max}$ using matrix-vector operations, as shown in the implementation of ◇ in Algorithm 1. Note that Eq. 2 is used when the transition from $s$ to $s'$ has a parametric rate, while Eq. 3 is used when it has a constant rate.

An approximation error is introduced because $\sigma_{i+1}^{\max}$ is computed by optimising $\sigma_{i+1,p}$ locally, i.e. at each step and at each state, and the error accumulates at each uniformisation step. We examine this error and its convergence in [13]. The forward variant of the parametric transient analysis can also be formulated using a vector-matrix operator [10], but the resulting code has more complex control flow and higher branch divergence, which makes parallelisation less efficient.

### 3.3   Sparse-Matrix Representation of Parametric CTMCs

We introduce a sparse-matrix representation of parametric CTMCs that allows us to implement the operator ◇ in such a way that the resulting program has a similar control flow and memory access pattern as the standard matrix-vector multiplication, for which efficient data-parallel implementations exist [4,8,33].

We represent the data in a compact format based on the *compressed sparse row* (CSR) matrix format. The CSR format stores only the non-zero values of the rate matrix $\mathbf{R}$ using three arrays: non-zero values, their column indices, and row beginnings. The CSR format is also used in the PRISM tool as the fastest explicit representation for CTMCs [26].

To handle the non-parametric transitions separately in a more efficient way, we decompose $\mathbf{R}$ into the non-parametric matrix, stored in the CSR format, and the parametric matrix. To enable an efficient data-parallel implementation of the operator ◇, for a region $\mathcal{R} = \times_{k \in K}[k^{\perp}, k^{\top}]$ and for each parametric transition rate $\mathbf{R}(s, s')$ two quantities, $r_{s,s'}^{\perp} = \sum_{k \in K} k^{\perp} \cdot a_{k,s,s'}$ and $r_{s,s'}^{\top} = \sum_{k \in K} k^{\top} \cdot a_{k,s,s'}$, are stored. From Eq. 2, it is enough to test $\sigma_i^{\max}(s') - \sigma_i^{\max}(s) > 0$ to decide whether to use $r_{s,s'}^{\top}$ or $r_{s,s'}^{\perp}$ in the multiplication, as illustrated in Algorithm 1.

In the parallel version, we provide an additional implementation using data structures based on the ELLPACK (ELL) sparse matrix representation [4]. The advantage of ELL over CSR is that it provides a single-stride aligned access to the data arrays, meaning that memory accesses within a single warp are reasonably coalesced. ELL yields better performance than CSR for some problems.

### 3.4   GPU Parallelisation

We implemented PRISM-PSY in *Open Computing Language* (OpenCL) [32]. In contrast to other programming frameworks, OpenCL supports multiple platforms and GPUs, and thus provides better portability. Moreover, its performance is comparable with that of specialised frameworks (e.g. CUDA [20]).

The synthesis algorithms are executed in a heterogeneous way. The sequential refinement procedure is executed on the CPU. For each parameter region $\mathcal{R}$ to analyse, the CPU prepares a kernel that computes the probability bounds $\Lambda_{\min}^{\mathcal{R}}$ and $\Lambda_{\max}^{\mathcal{R}}$ on the GPU, based on the backward parametric transient analysis described above. Following [4,8,33], we implement a *state space parallelisation*,

---

**Algorithm 1.** Kernel for two-level CSR parallelisation of the $\diamond$ operator

For all $0 \leq n < |S|$ and $0 \leq m <$ number of parallel regions, run in parallel:

1:  $e :=$ number of non-zero elements in $\mathbf{R}$
2:  **for** $j := \mathtt{matRowBeg}[n]$; $j < \mathtt{matRowBeg}[n+1]$; $j := j+1$ **do**
3:      $dMax := \sigma_i^{\max}[m * |S| + \mathtt{matCol}[j]] - \sigma_i^{\max}[m * |S| + n]$
4:      **if** $dMax > 0$ **then** $\sigma_{i+1}^{\max}[m * |S| + n] \mathrel{+}= dMax * \mathtt{matValTop}[m * e + j]$
5:      **else** $\sigma_{i+1}^{\max}[m * |S| + n] \mathrel{+}= dMax * \mathtt{matValBot}[m * e + j]$

---

i.e. a single row of the rate matrix (corresponding to the processing of a single state) is mapped to a single computational element. Note that the models we consider typically have a balanced distribution of the state successors, and thus yield a balanced distribution of non-zero elements in the rows of the matrix. This ensures a good load balancing within the warps and blocks.

In the case of models with small numbers of states, this parallelisation is not able to efficiently utilise all computational elements, since some of them will be idle during the kernel execution. To overcome this potential performance degradation, we combine state space parallelisation with *parameter space parallelisation* that computes the probability bounds for multiple parameter regions in parallel. As demonstrated in the experimental evaluation (Sect. 4), this *two-level* parallelisation significantly improves performance on small models. In many cases, this solution can improve the runtime of large models too, because it allows the thread scheduler to better hide memory latency.

Since parallel kernel execution is unsupported by many GPU devices or it may fundamentally decrease performance, we provide a way to perform, in a single compute kernel, multiple matrix-vector operations over multiple parameter regions. The solution exploits the fact that, in our case, the rate matrices for different regions have the same structure and only differ in the values of $r_{s,s'}^{\top}$ and $r_{s,s'}^{\perp}$. We extend the sparse-matrix representation of the $p$CTMC and store the values $r_{s,s'}^{\perp}$ and $r_{s,s'}^{\top}$ as well as $\sigma_i^{\max}(s)$ and $\sigma_{i+1}^{\max}(s)$ for all regions. This allows us to utilise $m \cdot |S|$ computational elements for $m$ parallel regions. Algorithm 1 illustrates the kernel for the two-level parallelisation using the CSR format. The vectors $\mathtt{matRowBeg}$ and $\mathtt{matCol}$, the same for all regions, keep the column indices and row beginnings, respectively. The vectors $\mathtt{matValTop}$ and $\mathtt{matValBot}$ keep the non-zero values of $r_{s,s'}^{\top}$ and $r_{s,s'}^{\perp}$, respectively. We store only the current $\sigma_i^{\max}$ and $\sigma_{i+1}^{\max}$ using two vectors and the vectors are swapped between the iterations.

Importantly, merging the computation for multiple regions requires modifying the adaptive Fox-Glynn technique to consider the highest uniformisation step among them. This means that the benefits of adaptive Fox-Glynn diminish with the number of subspaces processed in parallel.

## 4   Experimental Evaluation

In this section we evaluate the performance of the data-parallel synthesis algorithms on case studies of biological and computer systems. We discuss how model features affect parallelisation and show that parameter synthesis can be meaningfully employed to analyse various requirements, ranging from quality of service to the reliability of synthetic biochemical networks.

All the experiments were run on a 4-core Linux workstation with an AMD Phenom™ II X4 940 Processor @ 3 GHz, 8 GB DDR2 @ 1066 MHz RAM and an NVIDIA GeForce GTX 480 GPU with 1.5 GB of GPU memory. The GPU has 14 SMs, each having 32 cores and the capability to maintain up to 48 active warps. Therefore, the GPU can simultaneously maintain and schedule up to 21504 active threads to maximise the utilisation of its computational elements.

In the following, JAVA denotes the optimised sequential implementation and $CSR_n$ ($ELL_n$) the data-parallel implementation based on CSR (ELL) with $n$ subregions being processed in parallel. We report only an approximate value for the number of final subregions, since it differs slightly in some experiments due to parallel processing. We also report the results for the parameter space parallelisation only up to the best performance is reached.

### 4.1   Google File System

We consider the performance evaluation case study of the replicated file system used in the Google search engine known as Google File System (GFS). The model was first introduced as a generalised stochastic Petri net (GSPN) [16] and then translated to a CTMC [2]. Previous work on the model focused on survivability analysis, i.e. the ability of the system to recover from disturbances or disasters, and considers all model parameters to be fixed. Here, we work with a $p$CTMC model and show how parameter synthesis can be used to examine survivability.

Figure 2 illustrates the GSPN model of the GFS. Default values for stochastic rates can be found in [2, 16]. Files are divided into chunks of equal size. Each chunk exists in several copies, located in different chunk servers. There is one master server that is responsible for keeping the locations of the chunk copies, monitoring the chunk servers and replicating the chunks. The master can be: up and running (token at M_up); or failed (M1), due to a software (M_soft_d) or hardware (M_hard_d) problem. The model reproduces the life-cycle of a single chunk: the numbers of available and lost copies are given by places R_present and R_lost, respectively. Lost chunks are replicated through transition replicate. $R$ is the maximum number of copies. We consider $M$ chunk servers whose behaviour is analogous to that of the master. When a chunk server fails, a chunk copy is lost (destroy) or not (keep) depending on whether the server is storing the single chunk under consideration. We set $M = 60$ and $R = 3$, yielding a model with 21.6 K states and 145 K transitions.

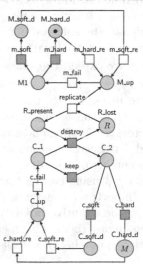

**Fig. 2.** Google File System from [2,16]. Transitions can be immediate (grey) or timed (white).

We first formulate a threshold synthesis problem for the CSL formula $\phi_{GFS_1} = F^{[0,60]}$ $SL_3$, where $SL_3 = (M\_up = 1$ and $R\_present \geq 3)$ is the QoS requirement that the master is running and at least three chunk copies are available (service level 3). The initial state models a severe hardware disaster: all the servers are down due to hardware ($C\_hard\_d = M$ and $M\_hard\_d = 1$) and all the chunk copies have been lost ($R\_lost = R$). We are interested in synthesising the values of parameter $c\_hard\_re$, that is, the rate at which chunk servers are repaired from hardware failure. Importantly, $c\_hard\_re$ can actually be controlled, e.g. by intensifying the frequency of technical interventions. Figure 3(a) illustrates the synthesis results for $c\_hard\_re \in [0.5, 2]$ and probability threshold $\geq 0.5$. The property is met for any $c\_hard\_re$ above 1, and, in particular, $SL_3$ is reached with high probability for repair rates above 1.25.

We now evaluate a property requiring that $SL_3$ is reached strictly within the time interval $[40, 60]$: $\phi_{GFS_2} = \neg SL_3$ $U^{[40,60]}$ $SL_3$. Although it is generally sought to reach the required QoS as soon as possible, this property can be

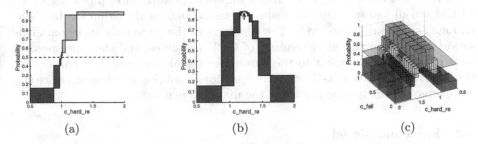

(a)                               (b)                               (c)

**Fig. 3.** Synthesis results for the GFS model. Each box denotes a parameter region (width and depth) and its probability bounds (height). Colour code is as in Fig. 1. (a) Threshold synthesis, property $\phi_{GFS_1}$, threshold $\geq 0.5$ (dashed line) and volume tolerance $\varepsilon = 0.01$. (b) Max synthesis, property $\phi_{GFS_2}$ and probability tolerance $\epsilon = 0.01$. (c) Threshold synthesis, property $\phi_{GFS_2}$, threshold $\geq 0.5$ (semi-transparent plane) and $\varepsilon = 0.1$. Parameter domains are $c\_hard\_re \in [0.5, 2]$ (a,b,c) and $c\_fail \in [0.01, 1]$ (c). Numbers of final regions are 8 (a), 24 (b) and 136 (c).

**Table 1.** Performance of the GFS model: 21.6K states, 145K transitions, and $\leq$47K iterations per subregion. Details of the synthesis problems are reported in Fig. 3.

| Threshold synthesis $\phi_{GFS_1}$ | | | Max synthesis f$\phi_{GFS_2}$ | | | Threshold synthesis $\phi_{GFS_2}$ | | |
|---|---|---|---|---|---|---|---|---|
| Impl. | Time (s) | Speedup | Impl. | Time (s) | Speedup | Impl. | Time (s) | Speedup |
| JAVA | 842 | 1.0 | JAVA | 3279 | 1.0 | JAVA | 12221 | 1.0 |
| CSR$_1$ | 56 | 15.0 | CSR$_1$ | 257 | 12.8 | CSR$_1$ | 764 | 16.0 |
| CSR$_4$ | 51 | 16.5 | CSR$_4$ | 239 | 13.7 | CSR$_8$ | 660 | 18.5 |
| CSR$_{16}$ | 51 | 16.5 | CSR$_8$ | 211 | 15.5 | CSR$_{64}$ | 636 | 19.2 |
| ELL$_{16}$ | **41** | **20.5** | ELL$_{32}$ | **207** | **15.8** | ELL$_{16}$ | **505** | **24.2** |

used in scenarios like planned downtime, where the service does not need to be up before the time scheduled for maintenance. In Fig. 3(b), we report the results of max synthesis for parameter c_hard_re. The maximising parameters (indicated with a black arrow) are found in the region approximately given by c_hard_re $\in [1.2, 1.23]$, since for high repair rates $SL_3$ is reached too early.

In the last experiment, we introduce one additional parameter, c_fail, i.e. the rate at which any failure (hardware or software) occurs in a chunk server. Since the GFS is designed to run on cheap commodity hardware, this rate can be controlled indirectly through the reliability of the machines used. We consider a threshold synthesis problem with property $\phi_{GFS_2}$ and threshold $\geq 0.5$. Results in Fig. 3(c) evidence that, interestingly, the satisfaction probability is almost independent from the failure rate, except when c_fail approaches 1, and thus slightly higher repair rates are needed.

Table 1 reports the performance of the tool on the above experiments, namely, the speedup achieved by the data-parallel algorithms. Although the state space parallelisation utilises the GPU sufficiently (enough threads are dispatched), the parameter space parallelisation further improves performance, providing up to 24-fold and 16-fold speedup with respect to the sequential algorithm for threshold and max synthesis, respectively. The efficiency of the parameter space parallelisation depends on the effective usage of GPU resources, and thus the speedup does not scale with respect to the number of regions processed in parallel. In this case the adaptive Fox-Glynn technique does not bring any benefit, since the parameters we analyse do not affect the maximal exit rate.

## 4.2    Epidemic Model

We further consider the stochastic epidemic model we analysed in [12] using the prototype implementation, in order to evaluate the enhancements of the sequential implementation presented in this paper. It describes the epidemic dynamics of susceptible $(S)$, infected $(I)$ and recovered $(R)$ individuals using the following biochemical reactions network with mass action kinetics: $S + I \xrightarrow{k_i} I + I$ and $I \xrightarrow{k_r} R$. With a total population of 100 individuals and initial state $S = 95, I = 5$ and $R = 0$, the model has 5.1 K states and 10K transitions. We consider the same max synthesis problem as in [12]: parameter space $\mathcal{P}_{SIR} = k_i \times k_r \in [0.005, 0.3] \times [0.005, 0.2]$ and property $\phi_{SIR}(t_1, t_2) = (I > 0) \ U^{[t_1, t_2]} \ (I = 0)$, expressing that the infection lasts at least $t_1$ time units but dies out before time $t_2$. As shown in [12], for $t_1 = 100$ and $t_2 = 120$, the prototype implementation produced around 5 K final parameter subspaces and required 3.6 h.

Table 2 (left) lists the results obtained with PRISM-PSY on the same synthesis problem. We can see that the optimised sequential implementation is about 14-fold faster (918 sec. vs 3.6 h.). This significant acceleration is explained by: more sophisticated refinement strategy for max/min synthesis, which reduces the number of final regions to 3K ($\sim$2-fold speedup); the adaptive Fox-Glynn technique, which reduces the number of iterations ($\sim$ 2.5-fold speedup); and more efficient data structures that accelerate the computation of the probability

**Table 2.** Max synthesis for the epidemic model: parameter space $\mathcal{P}_{SIR}$ and probability tolerance $\epsilon = 1\%$. $\phi_{SIR}(100, 120)$: 5.1K states, 10K transitions and $\leq 3.1$K iterations per region and $\sim 3.1$K final regions. $\phi_{SIR}(100, 200)$: 20K states, 40K transitions and $\leq 12$K iterations per region and $\sim 826$ final regions (depicted on the right).

| $\phi_{SIR}(100, 120)$ | | | $\phi_{SIR}(100, 200)$ | | |
|---|---|---|---|---|---|
| Impl. | Time (s) | Speedup | Impl. | Time (s) | Speedup |
| JAVA | 918 | 1.0 | JAVA | 3117 | 1.0 |
| $CSR_1$ | 363 | 2.5 | $CSR_1$ | 303 | 10.3 |
| $CSR_4$ | 269 | 3.4 | $CSR_4$ | 351 | 8.8 |
| $CSR_{16}$ | 207 | 4.4 | $CSR_{16}$ | 315 | 9.5 |
| $CSR_{128}$ | 167 | 5.5 | $CSR_{64}$ | 303 | 10.3 |
| $ELL_{128}$ | **162** | **5.6** | $ELL_{128}$ | **299** | **10.4** |

bounds as well as the refinement procedure ($\sim 3$-fold speedup). Note that the actual benefits of these enhancements essentially depend on the structure of the model and the synthesis problem. As the epidemic model is relatively small, the state space parallelisation is not able to sufficiently utilise the GPU, and thus the $CSR_1$ implementation provides only a 2.5-fold speedup. The parameter space acceleration further improves the speedup to 5.6 ($ELL_{128}$ implementation).

We now consider a more complicated variant of the problem, where we double the population size and extend the time horizon to $t_2 = 200$. Results are presented in Table 2 (middle). In this case, the state space parallelisation sufficiently utilises the GPU and for $CSR_1$, we obtain a 10.3-fold speedup. On the other hand, the parameter space parallelisation reduces the benefits of the adaptive Fox-Glynn technique, and thus overall performance is improved only slightly. Table 2 (right) depicts the results of max synthesis for the larger variant.

### 4.3 Signalling in Prokaryotic Cells

This model was introduced in [14,31] and describes a two-component signalling pathway in prokaryotic cells with two signalling components both in phosphorylated and dephosphorylated forms: the histidine kinase $H$ and $Hp$, and the response regulator $R$ and $Rp$. In this case, parameter synthesis is computationally very demanding, since the model has 116 K states and 954 K transitions. We consider a threshold synthesis problem that requires a relatively small number of refinements, in order to demonstrate the benefits of the state space parallelisation. We synthesise the production and degradation rates ($prodR$ and $degrR$) of $R$ such that the input noise of response regulators, defined as a quadratic deviation from the average population, is below 9 at least 80% of the time. This can be formalised as the cumulative reward property $\Phi_{SIG} = R_{\geq 0.8t}[C^{\leq t}]$, where the reward in state is 1 if it satisfies $(R + Rp - avg)^2 < 9$, otherwise the reward is 0. We consider $t = 10$, $avg = 30$ and parameter space $\mathcal{P}_{SIG} = prodR \times degrR \in [0.1, 0.9] \times [0.005, 0.02]$, which reflects the setting in [14].

**Table 3.** Threshold synthesis for the signalling model: property $\Phi_{\text{SIG}}$, parameter space $\mathcal{P}_{\text{SIG}}$ and $\varepsilon = 9\%$. The variant from [14]: 116K states, 954K transitions, $\leq 19K$ iterations per region and $\sim$70 final regions (depicted on the right). The larger variant: 424K states, 3.6M transitions, $\leq$ 24K iterations per region, and $\sim$67 final regions.

| The variant from [14] | | | The larger variant | | |
|---|---|---|---|---|---|
| Impl. | Time (s) | Speedup | Impl. | Time (s) | Speedup |
| JAVA | 16482 | 1.0 | JAVA | 95466 | 1.0 |
| $\text{CSR}_1$ | 868 | 19.0 | $\text{CSR}_1$ | 3870 | 24.7 |
| $\text{CSR}_2$ | 890 | 18.5 | $\text{CSR}_2$ | 3949 | 24.2 |
| $\text{CSR}_4$ | 866 | 19.0 | $\text{CSR}_4$ | 3946 | 24.2 |
| $\text{ELL}_4$ | **666** | **24.7** | $\text{ELL}_4$ | **3065** | **31.1** |

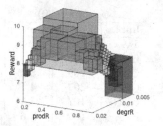

As shown in Table 3, a speedup up to 24.7 is obtained using $\text{ELL}_4$, which further improves the GPU utilisation and the memory access pattern of the pure state space parallelisation. We also consider a larger variant of the model (about 3.6-times), for which we obtain an even better speedup (up to 31.1-fold), so demonstrating good scalability of the data-parallel algorithm. Table 3 (right) depicts the synthesis results for the small variant, evidencing the non-monotonicity of the satisfaction function for the reward property.

## 4.4   Approximate Majority

The next model describes a chemical reaction network that computes the *approximate majority* – the asymptotically fastest way to approximate a common decision by all members of a population [11]. We consider the network $AM_{3,3}\#39$:

$$A+B \xrightarrow{k_1=92.9} X+X, \quad A+X \xrightarrow{k_2=26.2} A+A \text{ and } B+X \xrightarrow{k_3=23.3} B+B \text{ synthesised}$$

in [17] as the best network utilising only 3 species. The structure of the network has been synthesised using an approach based on bounded model checking and the kinetic parameters estimated by Monte Carlo-based optimisation.

As in [17], we consider small numbers of input molecules ($A = 10$, $B = 4$ and $X = 0$), and thus the model has only 120 states and 273 transitions. This

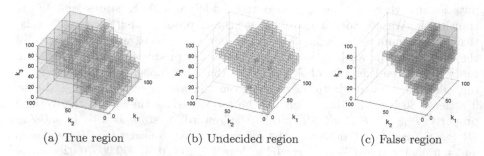

(a) True region               (b) Undecided region               (c) False region

**Fig. 4.** Threshold synthesis for the approximate majority model and property $\Phi_{\text{AM}}$.

experiment, in contrast to the previous case studies, allows us to demonstrate the performance of our tool on very small models. We synthesised the parameters such that the probability of the correct decision being made after 100 time units is at least 95 %. The property is formalised as $\Phi_{AM} = P_{\geq 0.95}[F^{[100,100]} \Psi_{correct}]$ and the parameter space is $\mathcal{P}_{AM} = k_1 \times k_2 \times k_3 \in [1, 100]^3$.

Due to the low number of states, the state space parallelisation utilises only a small portion of the computational elements of the GPU. Therefore, the GPU parallelisation using a small number of parallel parameter regions slows down the computation, as shown in Table 4. Increasing the number of parallel regions (up to 128) improves the GPU utilisation, and hence performance, yielding up to 5.7-fold speedup.

This experiment also demonstrates that, in contrast to the Monte Carlo-based optimisation, precise parameter synthesis provides detailed information about the impact of parameters on the probability of correct decision, as shown in Fig. 4. Note that the backward transient analysis implemented in our tool computes the probability bounds for all the reachable states, in this case all the inputs satisfying $A + B = 14$.

**Table 4.** Threshold synthesis for the approximate majority: property $\Phi_{AM}$, parameter space $\mathcal{P}_{AM}$ and $\varepsilon = 10\,\%$. 120 states, 273 transitions, $\leq 700K$ iterations per region and $\sim$911 final regions.

|            | Runtime (s) | Speedup |
|------------|-------------|---------|
| JAVA       | 1097        | 1.0     |
| CSR$_1$    | 11375       | 0.1     |
| CSR$_4$    | 3057        | 0.4     |
| CSR$_{16}$ | 951         | 1.2     |
| CSR$_{64}$ | 319         | 3.4     |
| CSR$_{128}$| 195         | 5.6     |
| ELL$_{128}$| **193**     | **5.7** |

### 4.5  Workstation Cluster

Finally, we consider a model describing a cluster of workstations consisting of two subclusters with $N$ workstations in each, connected in a star topology [25,34]. Both subclusters have their own switch that connects the workstations in the sub-cluster with a central backbone. The cluster maintains the minimum quality of service if at least 75 % of the workstations are operational and connected. We assume that one can control the workstation inspection (*ws_check*), repair (*ws_repair*) and failure (*ws_fail*) rates.

**Table 5.** Threshold synthesis for the cluster model: property $\Phi_{CLU}$, parameter space $\mathcal{P}_{CLU}$ and $\varepsilon = 10\,\%$. 86K states, 415K transitions, $\leq$9K iterations per region and $\sim$273 final regions.

|         | Runtime (s) | Speedup |
|---------|-------------|---------|
| JAVA    | 12074       | 1.0     |
| CSR$_1$ | **637**     | **19.0**|
| CSR$_4$ | 674         | 17.9    |
| ELL$_4$ | 672         | 18.0    |

We synthesise the parameters such that the minimum quality of service is not maintained at most 0.1 % of the time. This is formalised as $\Phi_{CLU} = R_{\leq 0.1 \cdot t} [C \leq t]$, and associating a reward of 1 to states where the minimum quality of service is not provided. In this experiment, we use $t = 100$ and parameter space $\mathcal{P}_{CLU} = ws\_check \times ws\_repair \times ws\_fail \in [5, 20] \times [0.5, 5] \times [0.001, 0.02]$.

Table 5 presents the results for $N = 48$ (85K states and 415 K transitions). In this model, the parameter space parallelisation considerably reduces the benefits of the adaptive Fox-Glynn technique, and thus the $CSR_1$ implementation provides the best performance, leading to a 19-fold speedup.

### 4.6    Result Analysis

**State space parallelisation** improves the scalability of the computation with respect to the model size. The experiments demonstrate that the speedup compared to the sequential baseline tends to improve with the number of states (see Tables 2 and 3). On the other hand, for smaller models, an insufficient number of threads is dispatched, leading to performance degradation (see Table 4). In most cases, the ELL format moderately outperforms the CSR format and it also works better with the parameter space parallelisation due to the more coalesced memory access pattern. Since the refinement procedure (running solely on CPU) is more complicated for max/min synthesis, for these instances the overall speedup is lower than that for threshold synthesis.

**Parameter space parallelisation** allows us to efficiently utilise the GPU even for small models. It scales well up to reaching the maximal number of active threads that can be dispatched (see Table 4). In practice, performance usually increases even beyond this point, since the parameter space parallelisation can improve the memory access locality. On the other hand, it mitigates the advantage of the adaptive Fox-Glynn technique, which can lead to performance degradation, as reported in Table 5. Importantly, PRISM-PSY can also be configured to perform this parallelisation using multi-core CPUs (not discussed here).

Our experiments clearly indicate that the tool is able to provide good **scalability with respect to the number of computational elements**. Since the two-level parallelisation can tune the GPU utilisation for various synthesis problems, we expect that the execution of the tool on new generations of GPUs with a larger number of cores will lead to a further improvement in acceleration.

## 5    Conclusion

We have introduced the tool PRISM-PSY that performs precise parameter synthesis for CTMCs and time-bounded specifications. In order to overcome the high computational demands, we have developed data-parallel versions of the algorithms allowing us to significantly accelerate synthesis on many-core GPUs. As a result, the tool provides up to 31-fold speedup with respect to the optimised sequential implementation, and thus considerably extends the applicability of precise parameter synthesis. In future we will extend the tool to support the full fragment of time-bounded CSL and multi-affine rate functions [13].

# References

1. Aziz, A., Sanwal, K., Singhal, V., Brayton, R.: Verifying continuous time Markov chains. In: Alur, R., Henzinger, T.A. (eds.) CAV 1996. LNCS, vol. 1102. Springer, Heidelberg (1996)
2. Baier, C., Hahn, E.M., Haverkort, B.R., Hermanns, H., Katoen, J.-P.: Model checking for performability. Math. Struct. Comput. Sci. **23**(04), 751–795 (2013)
3. Barnat, J., Bauch, P., Brim, L., Češka, M.: Designing fast LTL model checking algorithms for many-core GPUs. J. Parallel Distrib. Comput. **72**(9), 1083–1097 (2012)
4. Bell, N., Garland, M.: Efficient sparse matrix-vector multiplication on CUDA. NVIDIA Technical report NVR-2008-004, NVIDIA Corporation (2008)
5. Bolch, G., Greiner, S., de Meer, H., Trivedi, K.S.: Queueing Networks and Markov Chains: Modeling and Performance Evaluation with Computer Science Applications. Wiley, New Jersey (2006)
6. Bortolussi, L., Milios, D., Sanguinetti, G.: Smoothed model checking for uncertain continuous time markov chains. CoRR ArXiv, 1402.1450 (2014)
7. Bortolussi, L., Milios, D., Sanguinetti, G.: U-check: model checking and parameter synthesis under uncertainty. In: Campos, J., Haverkort, B.R. (eds.) QEST 2015. LNCS, vol. 9259, pp. 89–104. Springer, Heidelberg (2015)
8. Bošnački, D., Edelkamp, S., Sulewski, D., Wijs, A.: Parallel probabilistic model checking on general purpose graphics processors. Int. J. Softw. Tools Technol. Transf. **13**(1), 21–35 (2010)
9. Brim, L., Češka, M., Šafránek, D.: Model checking of biological systems. In: Bernardo, M., de Vink, E., Di Pierro, A., Wiklicky, H. (eds.) SFM 2013. LNCS, vol. 7938, pp. 63–112. Springer, Heidelberg (2013)
10. Brim, L., Češka, M., Dražan, S., Šafránek, D.: Exploring parameter space of stochastic biochemical systems using quantitative model checking. In: Sharygina, N., Veith, H. (eds.) CAV 2013. LNCS, vol. 8044, pp. 107–123. Springer, Heidelberg (2013)
11. Cardelli, L., Csikász-Nagy, A.: The cell cycle switch computes approximate majority. Scientific Reports, 2 (2012)
12. Češka, M., Dannenberg, F., Kwiatkowska, M., Paoletti, N.: Precise parameter synthesis for stochastic biochemical systems. In: Mendes, P., Dada, J.O., Smallbone, K. (eds.) CMSB 2014. LNCS, vol. 8859, pp. 86–98. Springer, Heidelberg (2014)
13. Češka, M., Dannenberg, F., Paoletti, N., Kwiatkowska, M., Brim, L.: Precise parameter synthesis for stochastic biochemical systems. Submitted to Acta Informatica (2015)
14. Česka, M., Šafránek, D., Dražan, S., Brim, L.: Robustness analysis of stochastic biochemical systems. PLoS ONE **9**(4), e94553 (2014)
15. Chen, T., Hahn, E.M., Han, T., Kwiatkowska, M., Hongyang, Q., Zhang, L.: Model repair for Markov decision processes. In: Theoretical Aspects of Software Engineering (TASE), pp. 85–92. IEEE (2013)
16. Cloth, L., Haverkort, B.R.: Model checking for survivability! In: Quantitative Evaluation of Systems (QEST), pp. 145–154. IEEE (2005)
17. Dalchau, N., Murphy, N., Petersen, R., Yordanov, B.: Synthesizing and tuning chemical reaction networks with specified behaviours. In: Phillips, A., Yin, P. (eds.) DNA 2015. LNCS, vol. 9211, pp. 16–33. Springer, Heidelberg (2015)

18. Dehnert, C., Junges, S., Jansen, N., Corzilius, F., Volk, M., Bruintjes, H., Katoen, J.-P., Ábrahám, E.: PROPhESY: a probabilistic parameter synthesis tool. In: Kroening, D., Păsăreanu, C.S. (eds.) CAV 2015. LNCS, vol. 9206, pp. 214–231. Springer, Heidelberg (2015)
19. Duflot, M., Kwiatkowska, M., Norman, G., Parker, D.: A formal analysis of bluetooth device discovery. Int. J. Softw. Tools Technol. Transfer **8**(6), 621–632 (2006)
20. Fang, J., Varbanescu, A.L., Sips, H.: A comprehensive performance comparison of CUDA and OpenCL. In: International Conference on Parallel Processing (ICCP). IEEE (2011)
21. Fox, B.L., Glynn, P.W.: Computing poisson probabilities. Commun. ACM **31**(4), 440–445 (1988)
22. Daniel, T.: Gillespie.: exact stochastic simulation of coupled chemical reactions. J. Phys. Chem. **81**(25), 2340–2361 (1977)
23. Hahn, E.M., Hermanns, H., Zhang, L.: Probabilistic reachability for parametric Markov models. Int. J. Softw. Tools Technol. Transfer (STTT) **13**(1), 3–19 (2011)
24. Han, T., Katoen, J.-P., Mereacre, A.: Approximate parameter synthesis for probabilistic time-bounded reachability. In: Real-Time Systems Symposium (RTSS), pp. 173–182. IEEE (2008)
25. Haverkort, B.R., Hermanns, H., Katoen, J.-P.: On the use of model checking techniques for dependability evaluation. In: Symposium on Reliable Distributed Systems (SRDS). IEEE (2000)
26. Kwiatkowska, M., Norman, G., Parker, D.: PRISM 4.0: verification of probabilistic real-time systems. In: Gopalakrishnan, G., Qadeer, S. (eds.) CAV 2011. LNCS, vol. 6806, pp. 585–591. Springer, Heidelberg (2011)
27. Kwiatkowska, M., Norman, G., Parker, D.: Stochastic model checking. In: Bernardo, M., Hillston, J. (eds.) SFM 2007. LNCS, vol. 4486, pp. 220–270. Springer, Heidelberg (2007)
28. Madsen, C., Myers, C.J., Roehner, N., Winstead, C., Zhang, Z.: Utilizing stochastic model checking to analyze genetic circuits. In: Computational Intelligence in Bioinformatics and Computational Biology (CIBCB), pp. 379–386. IEEE (2012)
29. Norman, G., Shmatikov, V.: Analysis of probabilistic contract signing. J. Comput. Secur. **14**(6), 561–589 (2006)
30. Pilař, P.: Accelerating parameter synthesis for stochastic models. Master's thesis, Faculty of Informatics, Masaryk University, Czech Republic (2015)
31. Steuer, R., Waldherr, S., Sourjik, V., Kollmann, M.: Robust signal processing in living cells. PLoS Comput. Biol. **7**(11), e1002218 (2011)
32. Stone, J.E., Gohara, D., Shi, G.: OpenCL: a parallel programming standard for heterogeneous computing systems. Comput. Sci. Eng. **12**(3), 66–73 (2010)
33. Wijs, A.J., Bošnački, D.: Improving GPU sparse matrix-vector multiplication for probabilistic model checking. In: Donaldson, A., Parker, D. (eds.) SPIN 2012. LNCS, vol. 7385, pp. 98–116. Springer, Heidelberg (2012)
34. PRISM - Case Studies - Workstation Cluster. http://www.prismmodelchecker.org/casestudies/cluster.php. Accessed September 2015

# Tool Papers II

# T2: Temporal Property Verification

Marc Brockschmidt[1]([✉]), Byron Cook[2], Samin Ishtiaq[1], Heidy Khlaaf[2],
and Nir Piterman[3]

[1] Microsoft Research Cambridge, Cambridge, UK
mabrocks@microsoft.com
[2] University College London, London, UK
[3] University of Leicester, Leicester, UK

**Abstract.** We present the open-source tool T2, the first public release
from the TERMINATOR project [9]. T2 has been extended over the past
decade to support automatic temporal-logic proving techniques and to
handle a general class of user-provided liveness and safety properties.
Input can be provided in a native format and in C, via the support of
the LLVM compiler framework. We briefly discuss T2's architecture, its
underlying techniques, and conclude with an experimental illustration of
its competitiveness and directions for future extensions.

## 1  Introduction

We present T2 (TERMINATOR 2), an open-source framework that implements,
combines, and extends techniques developed over the past decade aimed towards
the verification of temporal properties of programs. T2 operates on an input format that can be automatically extracted from the LLVM compiler framework's
intermediate representation, allowing T2 to analyze programs in a wide range
of programming languages (*e.g.* C, C++, Objective C, ...). T2 allows users to
(dis)prove *CTL*, *Fair-CTL*, and *CTL\** specifications via a reduction to its *safety*,
*termination* and *nontermination* analysis techniques. Furthermore, *LTL* specifications can be checked using the automata-theoretic approach for LTL verification [26] via a reduction to fair termination, which is subsumed by Fair-CTL.

In this paper we describe T2's capabilities and demonstrate its effectiveness
by an experimental evaluation against competing tools. T2 is implemented in F#
and makes heavy use of the Z3 SMT solver [11]. T2 runs on Windows, MacOS,
and Linux. It is available under the MIT license at github.com/mmjb/T2.

*Related Work.* We focus on tool features of T2 and consider only related publicly
released tools. Note that, with the exception of KITTeL [13], T2 is the only open-
source termination prover and is the first open-source temporal property prover.
Similar to T2, ARMC [23] and CProver [19], implement a TERMINATOR-style
incremental reduction to safety proving. T2 is distinguished from these tools
by its use of lexicographic ranking functions instead of disjunctive termination
arguments [10]. Other termination proving tools include FuncTion [25], KIT-
TeL [13], and Ultimate [16], which synthesize termination arguments, but have

© Springer-Verlag Berlin Heidelberg 2016
M. Chechik and J.-F. Raskin (Eds.): TACAS 2016, LNCS 9636, pp. 387–393, 2016.
DOI: 10.1007/978-3-662-49674-9_22

weak support for inferring supporting invariants in long programs with many loops. AProVE [14] is a closed-source portfolio solver implementing many successful techniques, including T2's methods. We know of only one other tool able to automatically prove CTL properties of infinite-state programs:[1] Q'ARMC [2], however Q'ARMC does not provide an automated front-end to its native input and requires a manual instantiation of the structure of the invariants. We do not know tools other than T2 that can verify Fair-CTL and CTL* for such programs.

*Limitations.* T2 only supports linear integer arithmetic fragments of C. An extension of T2 that handles heap program directly is presented in [1][2]. As in many other tools, numbers are treated as mathematical integers, not machine integers. However, our C front-end provides a transformation [12] that handles machine integers correctly by inserting explicit normalization steps at possible overflows.

## 2    Front-End

T2 improves on TERMINATOR by supporting a native input format as well as replacing the SLAM-based C interface by one based on LLVM.

*Native Format.* T2 allows input in its internal program representation to facilitate use from other tools. T2 represents programs as graphs of program locations $\mathcal{L}$ connected by transition rules with conditions and assignments to a set of integer variables $\mathcal{V}$. The location $\ell_0 \in \mathcal{L}$ is the canonical start state. An example is shown in Fig. 1(b). We assume that variables to which we do not assign values remain unchanged. For precise semantics of program evaluations, we refer to [3].
*C via LLVM.* In recent years, LLVM has become the standard basis of program analysis tools for C. We have thus chosen to extend llvm2kittel [13], which automatically translates C programs into integer term rewriting systems using LLVM,

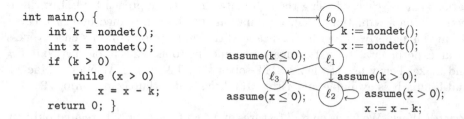

**Fig. 1.** (a) C input program. (b) T2 control-flow graph of the program in (a).

---

[1] We do not discuss tools that only support finite-state systems or pushdown automata.

[2] Alternatively, the heap-to-integer abstractions implemented in Thor [20] for C or the one implemented in AProVE [14] for C and Java can be used as a pre-processing step.

to also generate T2's native format. Our implementation uses the existing dead code elimination, constant propagation, and control-flow simplifications to simplify the input program. Figure 1(a) shows the C program from which we generate the T2 native input in Fig. 1(b). Further details can be found in [4].

## 3    Back-End

In T2, we have replaced the safety, termination, and non-termination procedures implemented in TERMINATOR by more efficient versions. In addition, we added support for temporal-logic model checking.

*Proving Safety.* To prove temporal properties, T2 repeatedly calls to a safety proving procedure on instrumented programs. For this, T2 implements the Impact [21] safety proving algorithm, and furthermore can use safety proving techniques implemented in Z3, *e.g.* generalized property directed reachability (GPDR) [17] and Spacer [18]. For this, we convert our transition systems into sets of linear Horn clauses with constraints in linear arithmetic, in which one predicate $p_\ell$ is introduced per program location $\ell$. For example, the transition from $\ell_2$ to $\ell_2$ in Fig. 1(b) is represented as $\lor x, k, x' : p_{\ell_2}(x', k) \leftarrow p_{\ell_2}(x, k) \land x' = x - k \land x > 0$.

*Proving Termination.* A schematic overview of our termination proving procedure is displayed in Fig. 2. In the initial Instrumentation phase (described in [3]), the input program is modified so that a termination proof can be constructed by a sequence of alternating safety queries and rank function synthesis steps. This reduces the check of a speculated (possibly lexicographic) rank function $f$ for a loop to asserting that the value of $f$ after one loop iteration is smaller than before that iteration. If the speculated termination argument is insufficient, our Safety check fails, and the termination argument is refined using the found counterexample in RF Synth. We follow the strategy presented in [10] to construct a lexicographic termination argument, extending a standard linear rank function synthesis procedure [22],[3] implemented as constraint solving via Z3. The overall procedure is independent of the used safety prover and rank function synthesis.

In our Preprocessing phase, a number of standard program analysis techniques are used to simplify the remaining proof. Most prominently, this includes

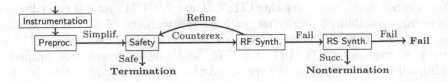

**Fig. 2.** Flowchart of the T2 termination proving procedure

---

[3] T2 can optionally also synthesize disjunctive termination arguments [24] as implemented in the original TERMINATOR [9].

the termination proving pre-processing technique presented in [3] to remove loop transitions that we can directly prove terminating, without needing further supporting invariants. In our termination benchmarks, about 80 % of program loops (*e.g.* encodings of `for i in 1 .. n` do-style loops) are eliminated at this stage.

*Disproving Termination.* When T2 cannot refine a termination argument based on a given counterexample, it tries to prove existence of a recurrent set [15] witnessing non-termination in the RS Synth. step. A recurrent set $S$ is a set of program states whose execution can eventually lead back to a state from $S$. T2 uses a variation of the techniques from [5], restricted to only take a counterexample execution into account and implemented as constraint solving via Z3.

*Proving CTL.* CTL subsumes reasoning about safety, termination, and nontermination, in addition to all state-based properties. T2 implements the bottom-up strategy for CTL verification from [7]. Given a CTL property $\varphi$, T2 first computes quantifier-free preconditions $precond_i$ for the subformulas of $\varphi$, and then verifies the formula obtained from $\varphi$ by replacing the subformulas by their preconditions. Property preconditions are computed using a counterexample-guided strategy where several preconditions for each location are computed simultaneously through the natural decomposition of the counterexample's state space.

*Proving Fair-CTL.* T2 implements the approach for verification of CTL with fairness as presented in [6]. This method reduces Fair-CTL to fairness-free CTL using prophecy variables to encode a partition of fair from unfair paths. Although CTL can express a system's interaction with inputs and nondeterminism, which linear-time temporal logics (LTL) are inadequate to express, it cannot model trace-based assumptions about the environment in sequential and concurrent settings (e.g. schedulers) that LTL can express. Fairness allows us to bridge said gap between linear-time and branching-time reasoning, in addition to allowing us to employ the automata-theoretic technique for LTL verification [26] in T2.

*Proving CTL\*.* Finally, T2 is the sole tool which supports the verification of CTL\* properties of infinite-state programs as presented in [8]. A precondition synthesis strategy is used with a program transformation that trades nondeterminism in the transition relation for nondeterminism explicit in variables predicting future outcomes when necessary. Note that Fair-CTL disallows the arbitrary interplay between linear-time and branching-time operators beyond the scope of fairness. For example, a property stating that "along *some* future an event occurs *infinitely often*" cannot be expressed in either LTL, CTL nor Fair-CTL, yet it is crucial when expressing "possibility" properties, such as the viability of a system, stating that every reachable state can spawn a fair computation. Contrarily, CTL\* is capable of expressing CTL, LTL, Fair-CTL, and the aforementioned property. Additionally, CTL\* allows us to express existential system stabilization, stating that an event can eventually become true and stay true from every reachable state. Note that for properties expressible in Fair-CTL, our Fair-CTL prover is relatively (to safety and termination subprocedures) complete, whereas our CTL\* prover is incomplete.

# 4    Experimental Evaluation and Future Work

We demonstrate T2's effectiveness compared to competing tools. We do not know of other tools supporting Fair-CTL and CTL* for infinite-state systems, thus we do not present such experiments and instead refer to [6,8]. Note that T2's performance has significantly improved since then through improvements in our back-end (e.g. by using Spacer instead of Impact). We refer to [4] for a detailed discussion of the properties and programs that these logics allowed us to verify.

*Termination Experiments.* We compare T2 as termination prover with the participants of the Termination Competition 2014 and 2015 using the collection of 1222 termination proving benchmarks used at the Termination Competition 2015 for integer transition systems. These benchmarks include manually crafted programs from the literature on termination proving, as well as many examples obtained from automatic translations from programs in higher languages such as Java (*e.g.* from java.util.HashSet) or C (*e.g.* reduced versions of Windows kernel drivers). The experiments were performed on the StarExec platform with a timeout of 300 s. Our version of T2 uses the GPDR implementation in Z3 as safety prover. Furthermore, we also consider three further versions of T2, using the three different supported safety provers. For these configurations, we use no termination proving pre-processing (NoP) step and only use our safety proving-based strategy, to better evaluate the effect of different safety back-ends. The overall number of solved instances and average runtimes are displayed in Fig. 3(a), and a detailed comparison of APROVE and T2-GPDR is shown in Fig. 3(b)[4]. All provers are assumed to be sound, and no provers returned conflicting results.

| Tool | Term | Nonterm | Fail | Avg. (s) |
|------|------|---------|------|----------|
| APROVE | 641 | 393 | 188 | 49.1 |
| CppInv | 566 | 374 | 282 | 65.5 |
| Ctrl | 445 | 0 | 777 | 80.0 |
| T2-GPDR | 627 | 442 | 153 | 23.6 |
| T2-GPDR-NoP | 589 | 438 | 195 | 31.4 |
| T2-Spacer-NoP | 591 | 429 | 202 | 33.5 |
| T2-Impact-NoP | 529 | 452 | 241 | 37.2 |

(a)

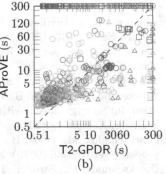

(b)

**Fig. 3.** Termination evaluation results. (a) Overview table. (b) Comparison of T2 and APROVE. Green (resp. blue) marks correspond to terminating (resp. non-terminating) examples, and gray marks examples on which both provers failed. A □ (resp. a △) indicates an example in which only T2 (resp. APROVE) succeeded, and ○ indicates an example on which both provers return the same result. (Color figure online).

---

[4] All experimental data can be viewed on https://www.starexec.org/starexec/secure/details/job.jsp?id=11121.

The results show that T2's simple architecture competes well with the port-folio approach implemented in AProVE (which subsumes T2's techniques), and is more effective than other tools. Comparing the different safety proving back-ends of T2 shows that our F# implementation of Impact is nearly as efficient as the optimized C++ implementations of GPDR and Spacer. The different exploration strategies of our safety provers yield different counterexamples, leading to differ-ences in the resulting (non)termination proofs. The impact of our pre-processing technique is visible when comparing T2-GPDR and T2-GPDR-NoP.

*CTL Experiments.* We evaluate T2's CTL verifica-tion techniques against the only other available tool, Q'ARMC [2] on the 56 benchmarks from its evaluation. These benchmarks are drawn from the I/O subsystem of the Windows OS kernel, the back-end infrastruc-ture of the PostgreSQL database server, and the Sof-tUpdates patch system. They can be found at http://www.cims.nyu.edu/~ejk/ctl/. The tools were executed on a Core i7 950 CPU with a timeout of 100 s. Both tools are able to successfully verify all examples. T2 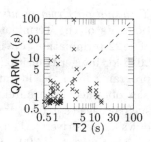 needs 2.7 s on average, whereas Q'ARMC takes 3.6 s. The scatterplot above com-pares proof times on individual examples.

*Future Work.* We wish to integrate and improve techniques for conditional ter-mination, which will improve the strength of our property verification. We also intend to support reasoning about the heap, recursion, and concurrency in T2.

# References

1. Albargouthi, A., Berdine, J., Cook, B., Kincaid, Z.: Spatial interpolants. In: Vitek, J. (ed.) ESOP 2015. LNCS, vol. 9032, pp. 634–660. Springer, Heidelberg (2015)
2. Beyene, T.A., Popeea, C., Rybalchenko, A.: Solving existentially quantified horn clauses. In: Sharygina, N., Veith, H. (eds.) CAV 2013. LNCS, vol. 8044, pp. 869–882. Springer, Heidelberg (2013)
3. Brockschmidt, M., Cook, B., Fuhs, C.: Better termination proving through cooper-ation. In: Sharygina, N., Veith, H. (eds.) CAV 2013. LNCS, vol. 8044, pp. 413–429. Springer, Heidelberg (2013)
4. Brockschmidt, M., Cook, B., Ishtiaq, S., Khlaaf, H., Piterman, N.: T2: Temporal property verification (2015). http://arxiv.org/abs/1512.08689
5. Brockschmidt, M., Ströder, T., Otto, C., Giesl, J.: Automated detection of non-termination and NullPointerExceptions for JavaBytecode. In: Beckert, B., Dami-ani, F., Gurov, D. (eds.) FoVeOOS 2011. LNCS, vol. 7421, pp. 123–141. Springer, Heidelberg (2012)
6. Cook, B., Khlaaf, H., Piterman, N.: Fairness for infinite-state systems. In: Baier, C., Tinelli, C. (eds.) TACAS 2015. LNCS, vol. 9035, pp. 384–398. Springer, Heidelberg (2015)
7. Cook, B., Khlaaf, H., Piterman, N.: Faster temporal reasoning for infinite-state programs. In: FMCAD 2014 (2014)

8.  Cook, B., Khlaaf, H., Piterman, N.: On automation of CTL* verification for infinite-state systems. In: Kroening, D., Păsăreanu, C.S. (eds.) CAV 2015. LNCS, vol. 9206, pp. 13–29. Springer, Heidelberg (2015)

9.  Cook, B., Podelski, A., Rybalchenko, A.: Termination proofs for systems code. In: PLDI 2006 (2006)

10. Cook, B., See, A., Zuleger, F.: Ramsey vs. lexicographic termination proving. In: Piterman, N., Smolka, S.A. (eds.) TACAS 2013 (ETAPS 2013). LNCS, vol. 7795, pp. 47–61. Springer, Heidelberg (2013)

11. de Moura, L., Bjørner, N.S.: Z3: an efficient SMT solver. In: Ramakrishnan, C.R., Rehof, J. (eds.) TACAS 2008. LNCS, vol. 4963, pp. 337–340. Springer, Heidelberg (2008)

12. Falke, S., Kapur, D., Sinz, C.: Termination analysis of imperative programs using bitvector arithmetic. In: Joshi, R., Müller, P., Podelski, A. (eds.) VSTTE 2012. LNCS, vol. 7152, pp. 261–277. Springer, Heidelberg (2012)

13. Falke, S., Kapur, D., Sinz, C.: Termination analysis of C programs using compiler intermediate languages. In: RTA 2011 (2011)

14. Giesl, J., Brockschmidt, M., Emmes, F., Frohn, F., Fuhs, C., Otto, C., Plücker, M., Schneider-Kamp, P., Ströder, T., Swiderski, S., Thiemann, R.: Proving termination of programs automatically with AProVE. In: Demri, S., Kapur, D., Weidenbach, C. (eds.) IJCAR 2014. LNCS, vol. 8562, pp. 184–191. Springer, Heidelberg (2014)

15. Gupta, A., Henzinger, T., Majumdar, R., Rybalchenko, A., Xu, R.: Proving non-termination. In: POPL 2008 (2008)

16. Heizmann, M., Hoenicke, J., Podelski, A.: Termination analysis by learning terminating programs. In: Biere, A., Bloem, R. (eds.) CAV 2014. LNCS, vol. 8559, pp. 797–813. Springer, Heidelberg (2014)

17. Hoder, K., Bjørner, N.: Generalized property directed reachability. In: Cimatti, A., Sebastiani, R. (eds.) SAT 2012. LNCS, vol. 7317, pp. 157–171. Springer, Heidelberg (2012)

18. Komuravelli, Λ., Gurfinkel, A., Chaki, S.: SMT-based model checking for recursive programs. In: Biere, A., Bloem, R. (eds.) CAV 2014. LNCS, vol. 8559, pp. 17–34. Springer, Heidelberg (2014)

19. Kroening, D., Sharygina, N., Tsitovich, A., Wintersteiger, C.M.: Termination analysis with compositional transition invariants. In: Touili, T., Cook, B., Jackson, P. (eds.) CAV 2010. LNCS, vol. 6174, pp. 89–103. Springer, Heidelberg (2010)

20. Magill, S., Tsai, M., Lee, P., Tsay, Y.: Automatic numeric abstractions for heap-manipulating programs. In: POPL 2010 (2010)

21. McMillan, K.L.: Lazy abstraction with interpolants. In: Ball, T., Jones, R.B. (eds.) CAV 2006. LNCS, vol. 4144, pp. 123–136. Springer, Heidelberg (2006)

22. Podelski, A., Rybalchenko, A.: A complete method for the synthesis of linear ranking functions. In: Steffen, B., Levi, G. (eds.) VMCAI 2004. LNCS, vol. 2937, pp. 239–251. Springer, Heidelberg (2004)

23. Podelski, A., Rybalchenko, A.: ARMC : The logical choice for software model checking with abstraction refinement. In: PADL 2007 (2007)

24. Podelski, A., Rybalchenko, A.: Transition invariants. In: LICS 2004 (2004)

25. Urban, C.: The abstract domain of segmented ranking functions. In: Logozzo, F., Fähndrich, M. (eds.) Static Analysis. LNCS, vol. 7935, pp. 43–62. Springer, Heidelberg (2013)

26. Vardi, M.Y., Wolper, P.: Reasoning about infinite computations. Inf. Comput. 115(1), 1–37 (1994)

# RTD-Finder: A Tool for Compositional Verification of Real-Time Component-Based Systems

Souha Ben-Rayana[1,2]([⊠]), Marius Bozga[1,2], Saddek Bensalem[1,2],
and Jacques Combaz[1,2]

[1] University Grenoble Alpes, VERIMAG, 38000 Grenoble, France
souha.benrayana@imag.fr
[2] CNRS, VERIMAG, 38000 Grenoble, France

**Abstract.** In this paper we present RTD-Finder, a tool which applies a fully compositional and automatic method for the verification of safety properties for real-time component-based systems modeled in the RT-BIP language. The core method is based on the compositional computation of a global invariant which over-approximates the set of reachable states of the system. The verification results show that when the invariant catches the safety property, the verification time for large systems is drastically reduced in comparison with exploration techniques. Nevertheless, the above method is based on an over-approximation of the reachable states set expressed by the invariant, hence false positives may occur in some cases. We completed our compositional verification method with a counterexample-based invariant refinement algorithm analyzing iteratively the generated counterexamples. The spurious counterexamples which are detected serve to strengthen incrementally the global invariant until a true counterexample is found or until it is proven that all the counterexamples are spurious.

## 1 Introduction

The synchronous model of time makes the compositional verification of real-time systems a challenging task. State-of-the-art tools [7,10,19,21] for the verification of such systems rely mostly on exploration techniques. Consequently, they suffer from the state-space explosion for systems with a large number of components. The aim of compositional verification is to avoid such limitations. The basic idea is to infer properties of a system from the properties of its components and the interactions relating them. In general, as explained in [18], the compositional verification rules concentrate on the following idea: if components $B_1$ and $B_2$ meet respectively properties $\phi_1$ and $\phi_1$, if some condition $C(B_1, B_2)$ characterizes their parallel composition, and if these properties imply conjointly a property $\Psi$, then the system resulting from their composition satisfies $\Psi$.

---

Work partially supported by the European Integrated Project STREP 318772 D-MILS.

M. Chechik and J.-F. Raskin (Eds.): TACAS 2016, LNCS 9636, pp. 394–406, 2016.
DOI: 10.1007/978-3-662-49674-9_23

In [9], a compositional verification rule was proposed for untimed systems. It is meant to prove invariance properties $\Psi$ for systems built on an n-ary composition operation via an interaction set $\gamma$ as follows:

$$\frac{B_1 \models \Box\phi_1, \quad B_2 \models \Box\phi_2, \quad II(\gamma), \quad \phi_1 \wedge \phi_2 \wedge II(\gamma) \Rightarrow \Psi}{\|_\gamma B_1, B_2 \models \Box\Psi} \quad \text{(D-Finder VR)}$$

In the above rule, $II(\gamma)$ is an interaction invariant expressing constraints on global locations resulting from the interaction structure. If the computed invariant ($\phi_1 \wedge \phi_2 \wedge II(\gamma)$) implies the safety property $\Psi$, then the system satisfies it. The above rule was implemented in the D-Finder tool [8] and was successful on several benchmarks. Nonetheless, the D-Finder tool does not handle time syntax. Furthermore, this rule is rather weak for timed systems. A straightforward adaptation of the D-Finder method to timed systems mostly yields false positives as shown in [4]. The main reason behind its weakness is that it does not capture time synchronization between components. In [4], we extended the above method precisely with the goal of offering a more successful application to timed systems. At the heart of the extension is the use of auxiliary *history clocks* (HC) in order to capture relations between the clocks of the different components. These clocks are added during the verification process and do not influence the behavior of the system. More concretely, to each action $a$, we associate an action history clock $h_a$ which is reset whenever $a$ occurs. The intuition behind this is that, on the one hand, history clocks are related to local clocks of their components thanks to the local invariants of those components and on the other hand, relations between history clocks of different components are inferred from the structure of the interactions. For ease of reference, we use $\mathcal{E}^*(\gamma)$ to denote all the additional clock constraints. Taking them all together, we obtain relations between the clocks of the different components in our global invariant. This invariant is made stronger, in case of conflicting interactions (that is, interactions which share actions) by introducing history clocks for interactions. New constraints on the interaction history clocks are gathered in the so-called $\mathcal{S}(\gamma)$ invariant. All in all, the verification rule for a system with $n$ components can be written as follows:

$$\frac{B_1^h \models \Box\phi_1, B_2^h \models \Box\phi_2, II(\gamma), \mathcal{E}^*(\gamma), \mathcal{S}(\gamma), \phi_1 \wedge \phi_2 \wedge II(\gamma) \wedge \mathcal{E}^*(\gamma) \wedge \mathcal{S}(\gamma) \Rightarrow \Psi}{\|_\gamma B_1, B_2 \models \Box\Psi} \quad \text{(VR)}$$

where $B_i^h$ represents the component $B_i$ extended with action history clocks. The tool RTD-Finder presented in this paper is an implementation of such a rule in the context of RT-BIP, a component-based framework for real-time systems where components synchronize through multi-party interactions.

## 2   Tool Structure and Main Functionalities

The structure of RTD-Finder is depicted in Fig. 1. The tool takes as input a Real-time (RT) BIP [1] source file and a safety property $\Psi$ to check for invariance.

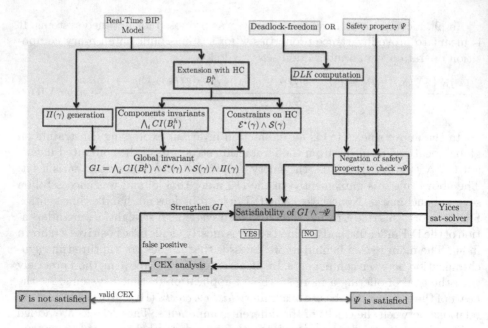

**Fig. 1.** RTD-Finder tool structure

If the property is not provided by the user, the tool proceeds by default to the verification of deadlock-freedom. Following this, it computes the predicate characterizing the set of deadlock states, the so-called DLK module. The tool extends each component $B_i$ from the input file with history clocks (HC) into $B_i^h$. It then computes the invariants of $B_i^h$ as the set of reachable symbolic states. Afterwards, it computes the interaction invariant and the inequalities on history clocks ($\mathcal{E}^*(\gamma)$ and $\mathcal{S}(\gamma)$). The combination of all the above invariants forms the global invariant $GI$. Together with the property $\Psi$, this invariant is input to Yices [12,13], an SMT solver. If $GI \wedge \neg\Psi$ is unsatisfiable, the property is valid. Else, a counter-example is generated. A guided backward analysis module is developed to decide upon their validity (the dashed box in Fig. 1).

## 2.1 The RT-BIP Framework

BIP (Behavior-Interaction-Priority) is a framework for modeling heterogeneous component-based systems. The BIP model is a superposition of three layers: the lowest layer models the behaviors of the components, the middle layer contains connectors describing interactions between the transitions of the different components and the top layer gathers priority rules to schedule among enabled interactions at a moment. Real-time (RT) BIP language extends BIP to support the continuous model of time where components are timed automata. Interested readers may refer to [1] for a detailed presentation.

## 2.2   Invariants Generation

RTD-Finder implements methods to compute components invariants, interaction invariants and the different constraints relating the history clocks:

**Component Invariant Computation.** The component invariant is a local invariant proper to the component over-approximating its reachable states set. We compute it on the component extended with history clocks $B_i^h$. Intuitevely, the possible evaluations in a location $l_i$ of component $B_i^h$ is the disjunction of zones expressing constraints on the component clocks (including the history clocks). In our framework, the local invariant $CI(B_i^h)$ of $B_i^h$ is computed as the set $Reach(B_i^h)$ of the reachable symbolic states which are computed by a depth-first-search algorithm. A symbolic state $s_i = (l_i, \zeta_i)$ of the component is defined by a location $l_i$ and a zone $\zeta_i$. In order to consider the operations and constraints on clocks during the computation of the reachability graph, we implemented various operations on zones and we included them in a DBM (Difference Bound Matrices [11, 22]) library.

**History Clocks Constraints Computation.** Constraints $\mathcal{E}^*(\gamma)$ and $\mathcal{S}(\gamma)$ relate local constraints obtained separately from the component invariants and by transitivity induce relations between inner clocks of the different components. Those constraints encode information like the fact that the history clock $h_a$ of an action $a$ is equal to the minimum among the history clocks of all the interactions to which it belongs. In fact, an action (resp. interaction) history clock is reset whenever the related action (resp. interaction) occurs. It results that the smaller the value of the history clock is, the more recent the related action (resp. interaction) is. The computation of these constraints is detailed in [4].

**Interaction Invariant Generation.** Interaction invariant $II(\gamma)$ over-approximates the set of reachable global locations. It relates locations of different components and allows to disregard some unreachable configurations. As in [9], $II(\gamma)$ is computed by static analysis of the interaction structure. In order to implement it in the RT-BIP context, we make an abstraction from all timing aspects.

## 2.3   Checking Deadlock-Freedom and Invariance Properties

**Checking Invariance Properties.** After the computation of the global invariant $GI$, we export it to Yices sat-solver to check the satisfiability of the predicate $GI \wedge \neg \Psi$. The invariance safety properties follow this grammar:

$$\Psi ::= a \mid at(l_i) \mid \Psi_1 \wedge \Psi_2 \mid \neg \Psi$$

where $a$ is an atomic clock constraint and $at(l_i)$ is a predicate expressing the presence of the component $B_i$ at its location $l_i$.

If the predicate $(GI \wedge \neg \Psi)$ is not satisfiable, then the property $\Psi$ is valid on the system and $GI$ is strong enough to detect it. However, if a counter-example is generated, then RTD-Finder cannot conclude immediately on the validity of $\Psi$ since the computed invariant is an over-approximation of the global reachable states set. A second stage of the tool aims at analyzing the generated counterexamples.

**Checking Deadlock-Freedom.** Deadlock predicate $DLK$ expresses the set of global symbolic states from which all interactions are disabled. Checking deadlock freedom is equivalent to proving invariance of $\neg DLK$.

## 2.4 Counterexample-Based Invariant Refinement

The method is proven to be sound. It is, however, incomplete: since it relies on an over-approximation of the reachable states set, a counter-example may satisfy the global invariant $GI$ and be nonetheless unreachable. The violation of the desired safety property may be the outcome of some behavior in the over-approximation which does not belong to the original model. False positives appear particularly in heavily non-deterministic systems. To remedy this, we implemented a counter-example analysis module to decide the validity of the counter-examples returned by the sat-solver. Our approach is based on a backward state space search from the raised counter-example to the initial state. The algorithm removes iteratively false positives and verifies the existence of reachable bad states. It stops when a true counter-example is found or until no suspected counter-example remains, in which case we deduce that the property is valid.

The algorithm is shown in Fig. 2. To describe it, we extend the notion of symbolic state from components to systems of parallel composition. The global location of a system is a n-tuple containing one location of each component and the zone of a global symbolic state is the conjunction of constraints relating the different components clocks.

---

1  $GI := \bigwedge CI(B_i^h) \wedge \mathcal{E}^*(\gamma) \wedge \mathcal{S}(\gamma) \wedge II(\gamma)$ ;
2  $\mathcal{V} := \emptyset$ ;
3  **while** $GI \wedge \neg\Psi$ *is satisfiable* **do**
4       Let $\theta$ a solution of $GI \wedge \neg\Psi$ ;
5       Let $(l^\theta, \zeta^\theta) := generalize(\theta, \Psi)$ ;
6       Let $\mathcal{P} := \{(l^\theta, \zeta^\theta)\}$ ;
7       **while** $\mathcal{P} \cap \mathcal{I} = \emptyset$ *and* $\mathcal{P} \neq \emptyset$ **do**
8           $\mathcal{V} := \mathcal{V} \cup \mathcal{P}$ ;
9           $\mathcal{P} := pre(\mathcal{P}) \setminus \mathcal{V}$ ;
10      **end**
11      **if** $\mathcal{P} \cap \mathcal{I} \neq \emptyset$ **then**
12          **stop** ;
13                        `// The counterexample is valid`
14      **else**
15          $GI := GI \wedge \neg(at(l^\theta) \wedge \zeta^\theta)$ ;
16                        `// The counterexample is spurious`
17      **end**
18 **end**
19 **if** $GI \wedge \neg\Psi$ *is not satisfiable* **then**
20      $\Psi$ is satisfied.
21 **end**

---

Fig. 2. Counterexample-based invariant refinement algorithm

The Yices SMT-solver generates well-defined locations of components and a precise valuation $\nu$ of clock variables of the counter-example (line 4). Therefore, a counter-example is perceived as $\theta = (l, \nu)$, where $l$ is a global location and where the clock valuation $\nu$ is the conjunction of equalities of the form $x_{ij} = c_{ij}$. The variable $x_{ij}$ is a clock of the component $B_i^h$ and $c_{ij}$ is the constant which it equals in the solution generated by the sat-solver.

As the clocks space is infinite ($\mathbb{R}$), we need to generalize the counter-example $\theta$ such that the algorithm terminates. Instead of considering only the counter example $\theta = (l, \nu)$, we analyze a set of counter-examples having the common global location $l$ and gathered in a global symbolic state whose zone is generated as follows:

$$generalize(\theta, \Psi) = (l, \bigwedge_{z_k \in \mathcal{L}.\nu \models z_k} z_k \wedge \bigwedge_{z_k \in \mathcal{L}.\nu \not\models z_k} \neg z_k)$$

where $\mathcal{L}$ stands for the set of literals constraining the clocks in the property $\Psi$. The generalization reflects which literals of the safety property are satisfied by the counterexample or not. This generalization operation is implemented in the DBM library.

The backward computation starts from a generalized counterexample and computes iteratively its preimage, resulting at each step in a set of global symbolic states $\mathcal{P}$, until the initial state $\mathcal{I}$ is reached or until the preimage is empty.

To ensure termination, at each step, the visited symbolic states set $\mathcal{V}$ relative to the previous iterations is eliminated using the subtraction operator \ in order to push the algorithm towards the initial state (line 11), else to conclude, if there is no intersection between $\mathcal{P}$ and $\mathcal{I}$ and if $\mathcal{P}$ is empty, that $(l^\theta, \zeta^\theta)$ does not contain any valid counterexample. The set $\mathcal{V}$ is cumulative: it contains the states that have been visited during the analysis of the previous counterexamples. They are all eliminated during the subtraction operation. If there exists a symbolic state $s_0 \in \mathcal{P} \cap \mathcal{I}$, then the length of the shortest path from $s_0$ to $(l^\theta, \zeta^\theta)$ is equal to the number of preimage computation operations required to reach $s_0$. For each analyzed counterexample, we note by the depth $d$ the shortest path from $(l^\theta, \zeta^\theta)$ to the first backwards reachable state belonging to $\mathcal{I}$. If such a state does not exist, that is if the backward reachability algorithm reaches a set of symbolic states that has an empty preimage and has no intersection with $\mathcal{I}$, then the counterexample is spurious and the global invariant can be refined with its negation (line 16). We note that the operators \ and $\cap$ on global symbolic states sets are slightly different from the usual set difference and conjunction operations on sets since symbolic states are defined by locations and zones. We consider the case where the zone of a symbolic state from a first set is strictly included in the zone of a symbolic state from another set and has its same location.

## 3    Experimentation

RTD-Finder is implemented in the Java programming language. It takes as input an RT-BIP file and a file where the property is expressed in Yices syntax.

The tool saves all the computed invariants to an output Yices file and displays the verification result after the satisfiability checking of $GI \wedge \neg\Psi$ with Yices. If a counter example is found, then the Yices output is parsed as a symbolic state and is generalized with respect to the safety property. If a counterexample is spurious, its negation is conjoined with the global invariant in the Yices file and the satisfiability of $GI \wedge \neg\Psi$ is further checked.

We show in this section the experimental results for four benchmarks with different properties for each of them.

**Train Gate Controller.** The first example is the classical train gate controller (TGC) system, where a controller, a gate and a number of trains interact together. We verified two properties:

1. ($P_1$) Utility property: The gate does not go down if all the trains are far from the crossing.
2. ($P_2$) Safety property: The gate is down when a train is in the crossing.

While the generated invariant was strong enough to verify the utility property, a spurious counterexample raises for the $P_2$ property. The counterexample-based refinement algorithm was necessary in this case.

**Temperature Control System.** The second example is a timed adaptation of the temperature control (TC) system in [9]. It represents a simplified model of a nuclear plant. The system consists of a controller interacting with an arbitrary number of rods in order to maintain the temperature within some bounds. When the reactor spends 900 units of time in heating, a rod must be used to cool the reactor. We verified two properties:

1. ($P_3$) At least one rod is ready to take *cool* action together with the controller when necessary.
2. ($P_4$) No rod is in cool location if the controller and the other rods are in heat position.

While ($P_3$) property is implied by the computed invariant, the counterexample analyis module is needed for ($P_4$) property.

The TGC (resp. TC) example is run with great numbers of trains (resp. rods) in order to show the scalability of the method.

**Gear Controller System.** The third benchmark is taken from [20] and models a gear controller system embedded inside vehicles. It is composed of an interface sending gear change requests to a gear controller component which interacts with an engine, a clutch and a gear-box component. In order to ensure the system correctness, some requirements have to be met. We verified the following properties after making abstraction from the data variables of the system:

1. ($P_5$) *Predictability*: When the engine is regulating the torque, the clutch should be closed.

2. ($P_6$) Error detection: The controller detects and indicates the precise errors when the clutch is not opened or closed at time and when the gear-box is unable to set or release a gear at time. ($P_6$) gathers 4 state properties.
3. ($P_7$) The gear controller system is deadlock-free.

The computed invariant was strong enough to verify all the above-mentioned correctness properties required for the gear control system.

**Dual Chamber Implantable Pacemaker.** We considered the verification of a dual chamber implantable pacemaker modeled and verified in [16]. The system is designed to manage the cardiac rhythm. In the considered pacemaker mode, both the atrium and ventricle of the heart are paced. Based on the sensing of both chambers, the pacing can be restrained or activated. For a safe operation, it is essential that the ventricles of the heart should not be paced beyond a maximum rate equal to a *TURI* constant. A ventricle pace (VP) can occur at least TURI time units after a ventricle event. This requirement expresses the *Upper rate limit* property. We summarize the verified properties in the following:

1. ($P_8$) There is a minimum time elapse *TURI* between a ventricle (VS) sense and a ventricle pace (VP) event.
2. ($P_9$) There is a minimum time elapse *TURI* between two ventricle pace (VP) events.
3. ($P_{10}$) The pacemaker system is deadlock-free.

As in [16], we verified both of ($P_8$) and ($P_9$) properties by translating them into a monitor component. Besides, our method offers another way to check the first property without resorting to the monitor as it can be expressed by means of the already introduced history clocks. In fact, the difference between the interactions history clocks relative to those two events is bigger than the desired time elapse. However, using history clocks to express the safety requirement is not possible for the second property since it compares two occurrences of the same action.

The global invariant is strong enough to catch the ($P_8$) property. Nevertheless, the counterexample analysis is necessary to eliminate 28 raised spurious counterexamples appearing during the verification of ($P_9$) property. RTD-Finder verified also deadlock-freedom ($P_{10}$) after eliminating 11 spurious counterexamples.

## Experimental Results

Table 1 gives an overview of the experimental results relative to the verification of the properties where no counterexample raises. In this table, $n$ is the number of components in the considered example, $q$ is the total number of control locations of its components and $c$ (resp. $h$) is the number of system clocks (resp. actions history clocks) and $|\gamma|$ is the number of interactions. Finally, $t$ shows the total verification time required for *GI* invariant computation and satisfiability checking of $GI \wedge \neg \Psi$ and $t_{yices}$ specifies the satisfiablity checking time required by the sat-solver.

**Table 1.** Results from experiments where no counterexample raises

| Model | Property | $n$ | $q$ | $c$ | $\lvert\gamma\rvert$ | $h$ | $t$ | $t_{yices}$ |
|---|---|---|---|---|---|---|---|---|
| Train gate controller (50 trains) | $P_1$ | 52 | 158 | 52 | 102 | 106 | 0.5 s | 0.3 s |
| Train gate controller (100 trains) | $P_1$ | 102 | 308 | 102 | 202 | 206 | 5.3 s | 0.6 s |
| Train gate controller (200 trains) | $P_1$ | 202 | 608 | 202 | 402 | 406 | 1 m 33 s | 5 s |
| Train gate controller (300 trains) | $P_1$ | 302 | 908 | 302 | 602 | 606 | 9 m 8 s | 20 s |
| Train gate controller (500 trains) | $P_1$ | 502 | 1508 | 502 | 1002 | 1006 | 1 h 13 m 20 s | 2 m 52 s |
| Temperature control (20 rods) | $P_3$ | 21 | 42 | 21 | 40 | 42 | 0.07 s | 0.01 s |
| Temperature control (50 rods) | $P_3$ | 51 | 102 | 51 | 100 | 102 | 0.35 s | 0.04 s |
| Temperature control (100 rods) | $P_3$ | 101 | 204 | 102 | 200 | 204 | 3.7 s | 0.08 s |
| Temperature control (300 rods) | $P_3$ | 301 | 602 | 302 | 600 | 602 | 5 m 47 s | 0.9 s |
| Gear controller | $P_5, P_6$ | 5 | 65 | 4 | 17 | 32 | 15.1 s | 0.14 s |
| Gear controller | $P_7$ | 5 | 65 | 4 | 17 | 32 | 17.6 s | 0.04 s |
| Pacemaker (with monitor) | $P_8$ | 7 | 19 | 11 | 6 | 21 | 0.25 s | 0.004 s |
| Pacemaker (without monitor) | $P_8$ | 6 | 16 | 9 | 6 | 19 | 0.24 s | 0.004 s |

The tool and the detailed output results are available at http://www-verimag.imag.fr/RTD-Finder. We made a comparison of RTD-Finder with the monolithic verification tool UPPAAL based on the complete method of model-checking. UPPAAL incorporates reduction techniques that are very successful on some benchmarks, like the train-gate-controller system. Yet, in general, the state-space exploration has its costs. We made a comparison with RTD-Finder on TC system. For 10 rods, UPPAAL generated no results after five hours and 436519 explored states. Nevertheless, RTD-Finder checked the property for 300 rods in a few minutes, as shown in Table 1. All the experiments are run on Linux machine Intel Core 3.20 GHz × 4 and 15.6 GiB Ram.

All of the properties shown in Table 1 are checked without resorting to the counterexample analysis module, that is the computed invariant catches them. At the opposite, the other properties are not implied by the invariant and for that the generated counterexamples have been analyzed. The results are shown in Table 2. For a spurious counterexample, $d$ is the length of the path from the suspected state $(l^\theta, \zeta^\theta)$ to the symbolic states set $\mathcal{P}$ having an empty preimage. Intuitively, the depth $d$ is the number of backward computation steps required to deduce the invalidity of the counterexample. The number $d_{max}$ is the maximum depth $d$ amongst the analyzed spurious counterexamples. By $p$, we note the total number of all the symbolic states computed and visited during the backward analysis and contained in the $\mathcal{P}$ sets, while by $k_{cex}$ we refer to the number of analyzed counterexamples. The total verification time is $t_{cex}$.

The verification time is visibly less important when the invariant is strong enough to detect the desired property, which was the case for all the properties shown in Table 1. In some cases, even when counterexample analysis is needed, RTD-Finder remains competitive to model checking using forward reachability analysis. This is for instance the case of the temperature control system and (P4) property which is verified in 3 min for 20 rods using the counterexample analysis module compared to the inability to check the property in 5 h for 10 rods with UPPAAL.

**Table 2.** Results from experiments where counterexamples analysis is needed

| Model | Property | $n$ | $|\gamma|$ | $d_{max}$ | $p$ | $k_{cex}$ | $t_{cex}$ |
|---|---|---|---|---|---|---|---|
| Train gate controller (3 trains) | $P_2$ | 5 | 8 | 22 | 440 | 1 | 0.6 s |
| Train gate controller (5trains) | $P_2$ | 7 | 12 | 22 | 2452 | 1 | 3.2 s |
| Train gate controller (10 trains) | $P_2$ | 12 | 22 | 22 | 22982 | 1 | 45 s |
| Train gate controller (20 trains) | $P_2$ | 22 | 42 | 22 | 199192 | 1 | 19 m 45 s |
| Temperature control (3 rods) | $P_4$ | 4 | 6 | 7 | 48 | 1 | 0.2 s |
| Temperature control (5 rods) | $P_4$ | 6 | 10 | 7 | 218 | 1 | 0.6 s |
| Temperature control (20 rods) | $P_4$ | 21 | 40 | 7 | 8914 | 1 | 3 m 46 s |
| Temperature control (50 rods) | $P_4$ | 51 | 100 | 7 | 128794 | 1 | 14 h 14 m |
| Pacemaker (with monitor) | $P_9$ | 7 | 3 | 6 | 126 | 28 | 0.6 s |
| Pacemaker | $P_{10}$ | 7 | 3 | 4 | 93 | 11 | 0.5 s |

It is worth noting that some symmetry reduction techniques can be applied in order to ameliorate the performances of the counterexample-guided invariant refinement algorithm. Some of them were already applied under the model-checking tool UPPAAL [14]. Symmetry reduction would notably allow to refine the global invariant not only with the negation of a given counterexample proven to be spurious, but also with a set of counterexamples to which it is symmetric. It would also serve to reduce the complexity of the backward computation.

In Table 2, we notice that for the Train-gate-controller (resp. temperature control) system, the number of backward steps $d_{max}$ necessary to deduce the invalidity of the counterexample remains the same, independently from the number of replicated trains (resp. rods) in the system. This suggests some similar behaviors among systems differing only on the copies number of the replicated component and motivates the consideration of an extension for the verification of parameterized timed systems adapted to our compositional verification method.

We propose an extension of RTD-Finder precisely with the goal of offering uniform verification for a class of parameterized timed systems.

## 4    Ongoing Extensions

Our ongoing extensions are multifold and focus mainly on the expressive power of the system properties, and the class of systems itself.

**Uniform Verification of Parameterized Timed Systems.** In [5], we proposed an extension of (VR) to the verification to parameterized timed systems. Parameterized systems are those which rely on multiple copies of a given component. Illustrative examples are satellite systems, swarm robots, ad-hoc networks, device drivers, or multi-threaded programming. The main purpose is to establish system safety independently from the number of components. It turned out that typical small model results lend themselves well to the parameterized timed systems we considered. The main idea is that it is sufficient to apply (VR) for all the systems with less than $n_0$ identical components in order to conclude correctness for the systems with any number of copies. The bound $n_0$ is computed statically from the number of quantifiers in (VR). With $n_0$ at hand, the tool computes the global invariant for any $k \leq n_0$ and checks if the property is satisfied. The steps are precisely those depicted in Fig. 1.

If we consider the TGC system and deadlock-freedom, then following the small model theorem, it suffices to check the property for all numbers of trains ranging from 1 to 5. The total RTD-Finder verification time for those *small models* is 1.4 s. We applied this method also on a timed version of a token ring system. We check that at any time, exactly one of the processes possesses the token (i.e. is in a *busy* location). The total verification time of the small models, containing from 1 to 5 processes, is 0.4 s.

The present verification approach for parameterized timed systems states that if the global invariant implies the property for the small models, then it is verified for all numbers of the replicated component. We want to complete it in order to cover the cases where the refinement of the invariant with the negation of the spurious counter examples is needed. Since the backward reachability computation is in general practical for small models, this extension of our uniform verification method would drastically reduce the verification time even when raised false positives are eliminated.

**Verification of Timed Systems with Parameters and Data.** One interesting extension of RTD-Finder is concerns parametric timed systems which contain timing constraints defined by use of parameters. These parameters may range over infinite domains and are in general related by a timing constraints set. Since the lack of restriction makes emptiness undecidable, the verification of systems composed of parametric timed automata is even harder. It requires data structures that handle efficiently and compactly the configurations that are introduced by the plentifulness of parameters. Inspired by existing work [2,15,17], a feasible approach consists in extending DBMs to parametric DBMs [3] and existentially quantifying (VR) such that the prover returns concrete values of the parameters ensuring the desired safety property for the system. As most of the existing tools are based on exploring the whole state space, they handle a relatively small number (mostly below ten) of automata, the immediate advantage of our approach is in scalability.

Another possible extension is the consideration of richer classes of models, handling data variables and urgency types on transitions [6]. This is not a trivial task since urgency does not lend itself to a compositional definition.

**Properties.** Currently, RTD-Finder handles only state safety properties but the extension to check LTL properties by use of Timed Büchi automata is possible. As for the pacemaker example, history clocks may help to express some LTL properties without resorting to the monitors.

RTD-Finder offers high scalability especially when the property to check is not combinatorial. Checking the absence of deadlock is currently more problematic. If in the untimed case one can provide an exact formalization of deadlock by means of local characterizations, this is no longer the case for timed systems. More precisely, the condition which expresses that an interaction is eventually enabled in a timed setup cannot be decided by the consideration of the involved components only, but depends also from the timing constraints of the non involved components. We are working on some approximation techniques in order to avoid its full computation.

**Acknowledgement.** The authors would like to thank Lacramioara Aştefănoaei for her contribution to the construction of the global invariant and to the verification of parameterized timed systems.

# References

1. Abdellatif, T., Combaz, J., Sifakis, J.: Model-based implementation of real-time applications. In: Proceedings of the 10th International Conference on Embedded Software, EMSOFT, pp. 229–238 (2010)
2. André, É., Soulat, R.: Synthesis of timing parameters satisfying safety properties. In: Delzanno, G., Potapov, I. (eds.) RP 2011. LNCS, vol. 6945, pp. 31–44. Springer, Heidelberg (2011)
3. Annichini, A., Asarin, E., Bouajjani, A.: Symbolic techniques for parametric reasoning about counter and clock systems. In: Emerson, E.A., Sistla, A.P. (eds.) CAV 2000. LNCS, vol. 1855, pp. 419–434. Springer, Heidelberg (2000)
4. Aştefănoaei, L., Ben Rayana, S., Bensalem, S., Bozga, M., Combaz, J.: Compositional invariant generation for timed systems. In: Ábrahám, E., Havelund, K. (eds.) TACAS 2014 (ETAPS). LNCS, vol. 8413, pp. 263–278. Springer, Heidelberg (2014)
5. Aştefănoaei, L., Ben Rayana, S., Bensalem, S., Bozga, M., Combaz, J.: Compositional verification of parameterised timed systems. In: Havelund, K., Holzmann, G., Joshi, R. (eds.) NFM 2015. LNCS, vol. 9058, pp. 66–81. Springer, Heidelberg (2015)
6. Basu, A., Bozga, M., Sifakis, J.: Modeling heterogeneous real-time components in BIP. In: Fourth IEEE International Conference on Software Engineering and Formal Methods, SEFM, pp. 3–12 (2006)
7. Behrmann, G., David, A., Larsen, K.G., Håkansson, J., Pettersson, P., Yi, W., Hendriks, M.: UPPAAL 4.0. In: Third International Conference on the Quantitative Evaluation of Systems, QEST, pp. 125–126 (2006)
8. Bensalem, S., Bozga, M., Nguyen, T.-H., Sifakis, J.: D-Finder: a tool for compositional deadlock detection and verification. In: Bouajjani, A., Maler, O. (eds.) CAV 2009. LNCS, vol. 5643, pp. 614–619. Springer, Heidelberg (2009)
9. Bensalem, S., Bozga, M., Sifakis, J., Nguyen, T.-H.: Compositional verification for component-based systems and application. In: Cha, S.S., Choi, J.-Y., Kim, M., Lee, I., Viswanathan, M. (eds.) ATVA 2008. LNCS, vol. 5311, pp. 64–79. Springer, Heidelberg (2008)
10. Bozga, M., Daws, C., Maler, O., Olivero, A., Tripakis, S., Yovine, S.: Kronos: a model-checking tool for real-time systems. In: Hu, A.J., Vardi, M.Y. (eds.) CAV 1998. LNCS, vol. 1427, pp. 546–550. Springer, Heidelberg (1998)

11. Dill, D.L.: Timing assumptions and verification of finite-state concurrent systems. In: Sifakis, J. (ed.) Automatic Verification Methods for Finite State Systems. LNCS, vol. 407, pp. 197–212. Springer, Heidelberg (1989)

12. Dutertre, B.: Yices 2.2. In: Biere, A., Bloem, R. (eds.) CAV 2014. LNCS, vol. 8559, pp. 737–744. Springer, Heidelberg (2014)

13. Dutertre, B., de Moura, L.: The Yices SMT solver. Technical report, SRI International (2006)

14. Hendriks, H., Behrmann, G., Larsen, K.G., Niebert, P., Vaandrager, F.W.: Adding symmetry reduction to UPPAAL. In: Larsen, K.G., Niebert, P. (eds.) FORMATS 2003. LNCS, vol. 2791, pp. 46–59. Springer, Heidelberg (2004)

15. Hune, T., Romijn, J., Stoelinga, M., Vaandrager, F.W.: Linear parametric model checking of timed automata. J. Log. Algebr. Program. **52–53**, 183–220 (2002)

16. Jiang, Z., Pajic, M., Moarref, S., Alur, R., Mangharam, R.: Modeling and verification of a dual chamber implantable pacemaker. In: Flanagan, C., König, B. (eds.) TACAS 2012. LNCS, vol. 7214, pp. 188–203. Springer, Heidelberg (2012)

17. Jovanović, A., Lime, D., Roux, O.H.: Integer parameter synthesis for timed automata. In: Piterman, N., Smolka, S.A. (eds.) TACAS 2013 (ETAPS 2013). LNCS, vol. 7795, pp. 401–415. Springer, Heidelberg (2013)

18. Kupferman, O., Vardi, M.Y.: Modular model checking. In: de Roever, W.-P., Langmaack, H., Pnueli, A. (eds.) COMPOS 1997. LNCS, vol. 1536, pp. 381–401. Springer, Heidelberg (1998)

19. Lime, D., Roux, O.H., Seidner, C., Traonouez, L.-M.: Romeo: a parametric model-checker for petri nets with stopwatches. In: Kowalewski, S., Philippou, A. (eds.) TACAS 2009. LNCS, vol. 5505, pp. 54–57. Springer, Heidelberg (2009)

20. Lindahl, M., Pettersson, P., Yi, W.: Formal design and analysis of a gear controller. In: Steffen, B. (ed.) TACAS 1998. LNCS, vol. 1384, pp. 281–297. Springer, Heidelberg (1998)

21. Wang, F.: Redlib for the formal verification of embedded systems. In: Second International Symposium on Leveraging Applications of Formal Methods, ISoLA, pp. 341–346 (2006)

22. Yovine, S.: Model checking timed automata. In: Rozenberg, G., Vaandrager, F.W. (eds.) Lectures on Embedded Systems. LNCS, vol. 1494, pp. 114–152. Springer, Heidelberg (1996)

# TcT: Tyrolean Complexity Tool

Martin Avanzini[1,2], Georg Moser[3], and Michael Schaper[3]($\boxtimes$)

[1] Università di Bologna, Bologna, Italy
martin.avanzini@uibk.ac.at
[2] INRIA, Sophia Antipolis, France
[3] Department of Computer Science, University of Innsbruck, Innsbruck, Austria
{georg.moser,michael.schaper}@uibk.ac.at

**Abstract.** In this paper we present TcT v3.0, the latest version of our fully automated complexity analyser. TcT implements our framework for automated complexity analysis and focuses on extensibility and automation. TcT is open with respect to the input problem under investigation and the resource metric in question. It is the most powerful tool in the realm of automated complexity analysis of term rewrite systems. Moreover it provides an expressive problem-independent strategy language that facilitates proof search. We give insights about design choices, the implementation of the framework and report different case studies where we have applied TcT successfully.

## 1 Introduction

Automatically checking programs for correctness has attracted the attention of the computer science research community since the birth of the discipline. Properties of interest are not necessarily functional, however, and among the non-functional ones, noticeable cases are bounds on the amount of resources (like time, memory and power) programs need, when executed. A variety of verification techniques have been employed in this context, like abstract interpretations, model checking, type systems, program logics, or interactive theorem provers; see [1–3, 12–16, 21, 25, 27] for some pointers.

In this paper, we present TcT v3.0, the latest version of our fully automated complexity analyser. TcT is open source, released under the BSD3 license, and available at

http://cl-informatik.uibk.ac.at/software/tct/.

TcT features a standard command line interface, an interactive interface, and a web interface. In the setup of the complexity analyser, TcT provides a *transformational approach*, depicted in Fig. 1. First, the input program in relation to the resource of interest is *transformed* to an *abstract representation*. We refer to

---

This work is partially supported by FWF (Austrian Science Fund) project P 25781-N15, FWF project J 3563 and ANR (French National Research Agency) project 14CE250005 ELICA.

M. Chechik and J.-F. Raskin (Eds.): TACAS 2016, LNCS 9636, pp. 407–423, 2016.
DOI: 10.1007/978-3-662-49674-9_24

the result of applying such a transformation as *abstract program*. It has to be guaranteed that the employed transformations are *complexity reflecting*, that is, the resource bound on the obtained abstract program reflects upon the resource usage of the input program. More precisely, the complexity analysis deals with a general *complexity problem* that consists of a program together with the resource metric of interest as input. Second, we employ problem specific techniques to derive bounds on the given problem and finally, the result of the analysis, i.e. a complexity bound or a notice of failure, is relayed to the original program. We emphasise that TcT does not make use of a *unique* abstract representation, but is designed to employ a *variety* of different representations. Moreover, different representations may interact with each other. This improves *modularity* of the approach and provides scalability and precision of the overall analysis. For now we make use of *integer transition systems* (*ITSs* for short) or various forms of *term rewrite systems* (*TRSs* for short), not necessarily first-order. Currently, we are in the process of developing dedicated techniques for the analysis of *higher-order rewrite systems* (*HRSs* for short) that once should become another abstraction subject to resource analysis (depicted as `tct-hrs` in the figure). Concretising this abstract setup, TcT currently provides a fully automated runtime complexity analysis of pure `OCaml` programs as well as a runtime analysis of object-oriented bytecode programs. Furthermore the tool provides runtime and size analysis of ITSs as well as complexity analysis of first-order rewrite systems. With respect to the latter application, TcT is the most powerful complexity analyser of its kind.[1] The latest version is a complete reimplementation of the tool that takes full advantage of the abstract *complexity framework* [6,7] introduced by the first and second author. TcT is open with respect to the complexity problem under investigation and problem specific techniques for the resource analysis. Moreover it provides an expressive problem independent *strategy language* that facilitates *proof search*. In this paper, we give insights about design choices, the implementation of the framework and report different case studies where we have applied TcT successfully.

*Development Cycle.* TcT was envisioned as a dedicated tool for the automated complexity analysis of first-order term rewrite systems. The first version was made available in 2008. Since then, TcT has successfully taken part in the complexity categories of TERMCOMP. The competition results have shown that TcT is the most powerful complexity solver for TRSs. The previous version [5] conceptually corresponds now to the `tct-trs` component depicted in Fig. 1. The reimplementation of TcT was mainly motivated by the following observations:

- automated resource analysis of programming languages is typically done by establishing complexity reflecting abstractions to formal systems
- the complexity framework is general enough to integrate those abstractions as transformations of the original program
- modularity and decomposition can be represented independently of the analysed complexity problem

---

[1] See for example the results of TcT at this year's TERMCOMP, available from http://termination-portal.org/wiki/Termination_Competition_2015/.

We have rewritten the tool from scratch to integrate and extend all the ideas that were collected and implemented in previous versions in a clean and structured way. The new tool builds upon a small core (tct-core) that provides an expressive strategy language with a clearly defined semantics, and is, as envisioned, open with respect to the type of the complexity problem.

*Structure.* The remainder of the paper is structured as follows. In the next section, we provide an overview on the design choices of the resource analysis in T$_C$T, that is, we inspect the middle part of Fig. 1. In Sect. 3 we revisit our abstract complexity framework, which is the theoretical foundation of the core of T$_C$T (tct-core). Section 4 provides details about the implementation of the complexity framework and Sect. 5 presents four different use cases that show how the complexity framework can be instantiated. Among them the instantiation for higher-order programs (tct-hoca), as well as the instantiation to complexity analysis of TRSs (tct-trs). Finally we conclude in Sect. 6.

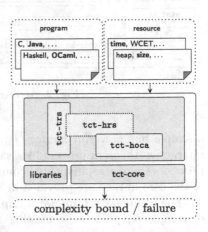

Fig. 1. Complexity Analyser T$_C$T.

## 2 Architectural Overview

In this section we give an overview of the architecture of our complexity analyser. All components of T$_C$T are written in the strongly typed, lazy functional programming language *Haskell* and released *open source* under BSD3. Our current code base consists of approximately 12.000 lines of code, excluding external libraries. The core constitutes roughly 17 % of our code base, 78 % of the code is dedicated to complexity techniques. The remaining 5 % attribute to interfaces to external tools, such as CeTA[2] and SMT solvers, and common utility functions.

As depicted in Fig. 1, the implementation of T$_C$T is divided into separate components for the different program kinds and abstractions thereof supported. These separate components are no islands however. Rather, they *instantiate* our abstract *complexity framework* for complexity analysis [6], from which T$_C$T derives its power and modularity. In short, in this framework complexity techniques are modelled as *complexity processors* that give rise to a set of inferences over *complexity proofs*. From a completed complexity proof, a complexity bound can be inferred. The theoretical foundations of this framework are given in Sect. 3.

The abstract complexity framework is implemented in T$_C$T's *core library*, termed tct-core, which is depicted in Fig. 2 at the bottom layer. Central, it provides a common notion of a proof state, viz *proof trees*, and an interface for specifying processors. Furthermore, tct-core complements the framework with

---

[2] See http://cl-informatik.uibk.ac.at/software/ceta/.

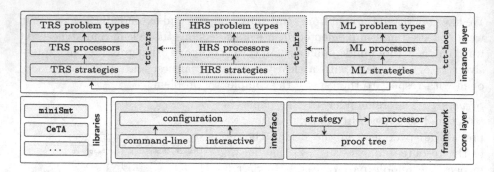

**Fig. 2.** Architectural Overview of T$_\textsf{C}$T.

a simple but powerful *strategy language*. Strategies play the role of tactics in interactive theorem provers like Isabelle or Coq. They allow us to turn a set of processors into a sophisticated complexity analyser. The implementation details of the core library are provided in Sect. 4.

The complexity framework implemented in our core library leaves the type of *complexity problem*, consisting of the analysed program together with the resource metric of interest, abstract. Rather, concrete complexity problems are provided by concrete *instances*, such as the two *instances* tct-hoca and tct-trs depicted in Fig. 2. We will look at some particular instances in detail in Sect. 5. Instances implement complexity techniques on defined problem types in the form of complexity processors, possibly relying on external libraries and tools such as e.g. SMT solvers. Optionally, instances may also specify strategies that compose the provided processors. Bridges between instances are easily specified as processors that implement conversions between problem types defined in different instances. For example our instance tct-hoca, which deals with the runtime analysis of pure OCaml programs, makes use of the instance tct-trs. Thus our system is open to the seamless integration of alternative problem types through the specification of new instances. Exemplarily, we mention the envisioned instance tct-hrs (see Fig. 1), which should incorporate dedicated techniques for the analysis of HRSs. We intend to use tct-hrs in future versions for the analysis of functional programs.

## 3   A Formal Framework for Complexity Analysis

We now briefly outline the theoretical framework upon which our complexity analyser T$_\textsf{C}$T is based. As mentioned before, both the input language (e.g. Java, OCaml, ...) as well as the resource under consideration (e.g. execution time, heap usage, ...) is kept abstract in our framework. That is, we assume that we are dealing with an abstract class of *complexity problems*, where however, each complexity problem $\mathcal{P}$ from this class is associated with a *complexity function* $\mathsf{cp}_\mathcal{P} : D \to D$, for a *complexity domain* $D$. Usually, the complexity domain $D$ will be the set of natural numbers $\mathbb{N}$, however, more sophisticated choices of complexity functions, such as e.g. those proposed by Danner et al. [11], fall into the realm of our framework.

In a concrete setting, the complexity problem $\mathcal{P}$ could denote, for instance, a Java program. If we are interested in heap usage, then $D = \mathbb{N}$ and $\mathsf{cp}_{\mathcal{P}} : \mathbb{N} \to \mathbb{N}$ denotes the function that describes the maximal heap usage of $\mathcal{P}$ in the sizes of the program inputs. As indicated in the introduction, any transformational solver converts concrete programs into abstract ones, if not already interfaced with an abstract program. Based on the possible abstracted complexity problem $\mathcal{P}$ the analysis continues using a set of *complexity techniques*. In particular, a reasonable solver will also integrate some form of *decomposition techniques*, transforming an intermediate problem into various smaller *sub-problems*, and analyse these sub-problems separately, either again by some form of decomposition method, or eventually by some *base technique* which infers a suitable resource bound. Of course, at any stage in this *transformation chain*, a solver needs to keep track of computed complexity-bounds, and relay these back to the initial problem.

To support this kind of reasoning, it is convenient to formalise the internals of a complexity analyser as an inference system over *complexity judgements*. In our framework, a complexity judgement has the shape $\vdash \mathcal{P} : B$, where $\mathcal{P}$ is a complexity problem and $B$ is a set of *bounding functions* $f : D \to D$ for a complexity domain $D$. Such a judgement is *valid* if the complexity function of $\mathcal{P}$ lies in $B$, that is, $\mathsf{cp}_{\mathcal{P}} \in B$. Complexity techniques are modelled as *processors* in our framework. A processor defines a transformation of the *input problem* $\mathcal{P}$ into a list of sub-problems $\mathcal{Q}_1, \ldots, \mathcal{Q}_n$ (if any), and it relates the complexity of the obtained sub-problems to the complexity of the input problem. Processors are given as inferences

$$\frac{Pre(\mathcal{P}) \quad \vdash \mathcal{Q}_1 : B_1 \quad \cdots \quad \vdash \mathcal{Q}_n : B_n}{\vdash \mathcal{P} : B},$$

where $Pre(\mathcal{P})$ indicates some *pre-conditions* on $\mathcal{P}$. The processor is *sound* if under $Pre(\mathcal{P})$ the validity of judgements is preserved, i.e.

$$Pre(\mathcal{P}) \wedge \mathsf{cp}_{\mathcal{Q}_1} \in B_1 \wedge \cdots \wedge \mathsf{cp}_{\mathcal{Q}_n} \in B_n \quad \Longrightarrow \quad \mathsf{cp}_{\mathcal{P}} \in B.$$

Dual, it is called *complete* if under the assumptions $Pre(\mathcal{P})$, validity of the judgement $\vdash \mathcal{P} : B$ implies validity of the judgements $\vdash \mathcal{Q}_i : B_i$.

A *proof* of a judgement $\vdash \mathcal{P} : B$ from the *assumptions* $\vdash \mathcal{Q}_1 : B_1, \ldots, \vdash \mathcal{Q}_n : B_n$ is a deduction using sound processors only. The proof is *closed* if its set of assumptions is empty. Soundness of processors guarantees that our formal system is correct. Application of complete processors on a valid judgement ensures that no invalid assumptions are derived. In this sense, the application of a complete processor is always safe.

**Proposition 1.** *If there exists a closed complexity proof $\vdash \mathcal{P} : B$, then the judgement $\vdash \mathcal{P} : B$ is valid.*

# 4    Implementing the Complexity Framework

The formal complexity framework described in the last section is implemented in the core library, termed `tct-core`. In the following we outline the two central components of this library: (i) the generation of complexity proofs, and (ii) common facilities for instantiating the framework to concrete tools, see Fig. 2.

## 4.1    Proof Trees, Processors, and Strategies

The library `tct-core` provides the verification of a valid complexity judgement $\vdash \mathcal{P} : B$ from a given input problem $\mathcal{P}$. More precise, the library provides the environment to construct a complexity proof witnessing the validity of $\vdash \mathcal{P} : B$.

Since the class $B$ of bounding-functions is a result of the analysis, and not an input, the complexity proof can only be constructed once the analysis finished successfully. For this reason, proofs are not directly represented as trees over complexity judgements. Rather, the library features *proof trees*. Conceptually, a proof tree is a tree whose leaves are labelled by *open complexity problems*, that is, problems which remain to be analysed, and whose internal nodes represent successful applications of processors. The complexity analysis of a problem $\mathcal{P}$ then amounts to the *expansion* of the proof tree whose single node is labelled by the open problem $\mathcal{P}$. *Processors* implement a single expansion step. To facilitate the expansion of proof trees, `tct-core` features a rich *strategy language*, similar to tactics in interactive theorem provers like Isabelle or Coq. Once a proof tree has been completely expanded, a complexity judgement for $\mathcal{P}$ together with the witnessing complexity proof can be computed from the proof tree.

In the following, we detail the central notions of proof tree, processor and strategy, and elaborate on important design issues.

*Proof Trees:* The first design issue we face is the representation of complexity problems. In earlier versions of TCT, we used a concrete problem type `Problem` that captured various notions of complexity problems, but all were based on term rewriting. With the addition of new kinds of complexity problem, such as runtime of functional or heap size of imperative programs, this approach became soon infeasible. In the present reimplementation, we therefore abstract over problem types, at the cost of slightly complicating central definitions. This allows concrete instantiations to precisely specify which problem types are supported. Consequently, proof trees are parameterised in the type of complexity problems.

The corresponding (generalised) algebraic data-type `ProofTree` $\alpha$ (from module `Tct.Core.Data.ProofTree`) is depicted in Fig. 3. A constructor `Open` represents a leaf labelled by an open problem of type $\alpha$. The ternary constructor `Success` represents the successful application of a processor of type $\beta$. Its first argument, a value of type `ProofNode` $\beta$, carries the applied processor, the current complexity problem under investigation as well as a proof-object of type `ProofObject` $\beta$. This information is useful for proof analysis, and allows a detailed textual representation of proof trees. Note that `ProofObject` is a type-level function, the concrete

```
data ProofTree α where
  Open    :: α → ProofTree α           -- open proof node
  Success :: Processor β ⇒             -- successful application
             ProofNode β → CertFn → [ProofTree α] → ProofTree α
  Failure :: Reason → ProofTree α      -- failed application
```

**Fig. 3.** Data-type declaration of proof trees in `tct-core`.

representation of a proof-object thus depends on the type of the applied processor. The second argument to `Success` is a *certificate-function*

$$\text{type CertFn} = [\text{Certificate}] \to \text{Certificate} ,$$

which is used to relate the estimated complexity of generated sub-problems to the analysed complexity problem. Thus currently, the set of bounding-functions $B$ occurring in the final complexity proof is fixed to those expressed by the data-type `Certificate` (module `Tct.Core.Data.Certificate`). `Certificate` includes various representations of complexity classes, such as the class of polynomials, exponential, primitive and multiple recursive functions, but also the more fine grained classes of bounding-functions $\mathcal{O}(n^k)$ for all $k \in \mathbb{N}$. The remaining argument to the constructor `Success` is a forest of proof trees, each individual proof tree representing the continuation of the analysis of a corresponding sub-problem generated by the applied processor. Finally, the constructor `Failure` indicates that the analysis failed. It results for example from the application of a processor to an open problem which does not satisfy the pre-conditions of the processor. The argument of type `Reason` allows a textual representation of the failure-condition. The analysis will always abort on proof trees containing such a *failure node*.

*Processors.* The interface for processors is specified by the type-class `Processor`, which is defined in module `Tct.Core.Data.Processor` and depicted in Fig. 4. The type of input problem and generated sub-problems are defined for processors on an individual basis, through the type-level functions `In` and `Out`, respectively. This eliminates the need for a global problem type, and facilitates the seamless combination of different instantiations of the core library. Each processor instance specifies additionally the type of proof-objects `ProofObject` $\alpha$ – the meta information provided in case of a successful application. The proof-object is constrained to instances of `ProofData`, which beside others, ensures that a textual representation can be obtained. Each instance of `Processor` has to implement a method `execute`, which given an input problem of type `In` $\alpha$, evaluates to a `TctM` action that produces a value of type `Return` $\alpha$. The monad `TctM` (defined in module `Tct.Core.Data.TctM`) extends the `IO` monad with access to runtime information, such as command line parameters and execution time. The data-type `Return` $\alpha$ specifies the result of the application of a processor to its given input problem. In case of a successful application, the return value carries the proof-object, a value of type `CertFn`, which relates complexity-bounds

```
data Return α =
  NoProgress Reason
  | Progress (ProofObject α) CertFn [ProofTree (Out α)]

class (ProofData (ProofObject α)) ⇒ Processor α where
  type In α                          -- type of input problem
  type Out α                         -- type of output problems
  type ProofObject α                 -- meta information
  execute :: α → In α → TctM (Return α)   -- implementation

-- application of processor to a problem, resulting in a proof tree
apply :: Processor α ⇒ α → In α → TctM (ProofTree (Out α))
apply p i = toProofTree <$> (execute p i 'catchError' handler)
  where
    toProofTree (NoProgress r)      = Failure r
    toProofTree (Progress ob cf ts) = Success (ProofNode p i ob) cf ts
    handler err = return (NoProgress (IOError err))
```

**Fig. 4.** Data-type and class definitions related to processors in tct-core.

on sub-problems to bounds on the input-problem and the list of generated sub-problems. In fact the type is slightly more liberal and allows for each generated sub-problem a, possibly open, proof tree. This generalisation is useful in certain contexts, for example, when the processor makes use of a second processor.

*Strategies.* To facilitate the expansion of a proof tree, tct-core features a simple but expressive *strategy language*. The strategy language is *deeply embedded*, via the generalised algebraic data-type Strategy $\alpha$ $\beta$ defined in Fig. 5. Semantics over strategies are given by the function

$$\text{evaluate} :: \text{Strategy } \alpha \ \beta \to \text{ProofTree } \alpha \to \text{TctM ( ProofTree } \beta \ ) \ ,$$

defined in module Tct.Core.Data.Strategy. A strategy of type Strategy $\alpha$ $\beta$ thus translates a proof tree with open problems of type $\alpha$ to one with open problems of type $\beta$.

The first four primitives defined in Fig. 5 constitute our tool box for modelling sequential application of processors. he strategy Id is implemented by the identity function on proof trees. The remaining three primitives traverse the given proof tree in-order, acting on all the open proof-nodes. The strategy Apply p replaces the given open proof-node with the proof tree resulting from an application of p. The strategy Abort signals that the computation should be aborted, replacing the given proof-node by a failure node. Finally, the strategy Cond predicate s1 s2 s3 implements a very specific conditional. It sequences the application of strategies s1 and s2, provided the proof tree computed by s1 satisfies the predicate predicate. For the case where the predicate is not satisfied, the conditional acts like the third strategy s3.

In Fig. 6 we showcase the definition of derived sequential strategy combinators. Sequencing s1 ≫ s2 of strategies s1 and s2 as well as a (left-biased)

```
data Strategy α β where
  -- primitives for sequential processor application
  Id          :: Strategy α α
  Apply       :: (Processor γ) ⇒ γ → Strategy (In γ) (Out γ)
  Abort       :: Strategy α β
  Cond        :: (ProofTree β → Bool) → Strategy α β → Strategy β γ
                 → Strategy α γ → Strategy α γ
  -- primitives for parallel processor application
  Par         :: Strategy α β → Strategy α β
  Race        :: Strategy α β → Strategy α β → Strategy α β
  Better      :: (ProofTree β → ProofTree β → Ordering)
                 → Strategy α β → Strategy α β → Strategy α β
  -- control operators
  Timeout     :: Time → Strategy α β → Strategy α β
  WithStatus  :: (TcTStatus α → Strategy α β) → Strategy α β
```

**Fig. 5.** Deep Embedding of our strategy language in tct-core.

```
-- auxiliary predicates on proof trees
nonFailing,progress :: ProofTree α → Bool
nonFailing t        = null [ Failure {} ← subTrees t ]
progress   Open{} = False
progress   _      = True
-- choice
(<|>) :: Strategy α β → Strategy α β → Strategy α β
s1 <|> s2 = Cond nonFailing s1 Id s2
-- composition
(≫) :: Strategy α β → Strategy β γ → Strategy α γ
s1 ≫ s2 = Cond nonFailing s1 s2 Abort
-- backtracking
try :: Strategy α α → Strategy α α
try s = s <|> Id
force :: Strategy α β → Strategy α β
force s = Cond progress s Id Abort
-- iteration
exhaustive,exhaustive+ :: Strategy α α → Strategy α α
exhaustive  s = try (exhaustive+ s)
exhaustive+ s = force s ≫ exhaustive s
```

**Fig. 6.** Derived sequential strategy combinators.

choice operator s1 <|> s2 are derived from the conditional primitive Cond. The strategy try s behaves like s, except when s fails then try s behaves as an identity. The combinator force complements the combinator try: the strategy force s enforces that strategy s produces a new proof-node. The combinator try brings *backtracking* to our strategy language, i.e. the strategy try s1 ≫ s2 first applies strategy s1, backtracks in case of failure, and applies s2 afterwards. Finally, the strategies exhaustive s applies s zero or more times, until

$$s1 \ggg (s2 \ggg s3) \equiv (s1 \ggg s2) \ggg s3 \qquad (\ggg \text{ is associative})$$

$$s1 <|> (s2 <|> s3) \equiv (s1 <|> s2) <|> s3 \qquad (<|> \text{ is associative})$$

$$s \ggg \text{Id} \equiv s \equiv \text{Id} \ggg s \qquad (\text{Id identity element of } \ggg)$$

$$s <|> \text{Abort} \equiv s \equiv \text{Abort} <|> s \qquad (\text{Abort identity element of } <|>)$$

$$s1 \ggg (s2 <|> s3) \equiv (s1 \ggg s2) <|> (s1 \ggg s3) \; (\ggg \text{ distributes over } <|>)$$

$$(s1 <|> s2) \ggg s3 \equiv (s1 \ggg s3) <|> (s2 \ggg s3)$$

$$\text{force } (s1 <|> s2) \equiv \text{force } s1 \; <|> \; \text{force } s2 \qquad (\text{force distributes over } <|>)$$

$$\text{force } (\text{try } s) \equiv \text{force } s \qquad (\text{force eliminates try})$$

**Fig. 7.** Some laws obeyed by the derived operators.

strategy s fails. The combinator `exhaustive+` behaves similarly, but applies the given strategy at least once. The obtained combinators satisfy the expected laws, compare Fig. 7 for an excerpt.

Our strategy language features also three dedicated types for parallel proof search. The strategy `Par s` implements a form of data level parallelism, applying strategy s to all open problems in the given proof tree in parallel. In contrast, the strategies `Race s1 s2` and `Better comp s1 s2` apply to each open problem the strategies s1 and s2 concurrently, and can be seen as parallel version of our choice operator. Whereas `Race s1 s2` simply returns the (non-failing) proof tree of whichever strategy returns first, `Better comp s1 s2` uses the provided comparison-function `comp` to decide which proof tree to return.

The final two strategies depicted in Fig. 5 implement timeouts, and the dynamic creation of strategies depending on the current `TctStatus`. `TctStatus` includes global state, such as command line flags and the execution time, but also proof relevant state such as the current problem under investigation.

## 4.2    From the Core to Executables

The framework is instantiated by providing a set of sound processors, together with their corresponding input and output types. At the end of the day the complexity framework has to give rise to an executable tool, which, given an initial problem, possibly provides a complexity certificate.

To ease the generation of such an executable, `tct-core` provides a default implementation of the `main` function, controlled by a `TctConfig` record (see module `Tct.Core.Main`). A minimal definition of `TctConfig` just requires the specification of a default strategy, and a parser for the initial complexity problem. Optionally, one can for example specify additional command line parameters, or a list of *declarations* for custom strategies, which allow the user to control the proof search. Strategy declarations wrap strategies with additional *meta information*, such as a *name*, a *description*, and a list of *parameters*. Firstly, this information is used for documentary purposes. If we call the default implementation with the command line flag `--list-strategies` it will present a documentation of the available processors and strategies to the user. Secondly, declarations facilitate the parser generation for custom strategies. It is noteworthy to mention that declarations and the generated parsers are type safe and are checked during compile-time. Declarations, together with usage information, are defined in module `Tct.Core.Data.Declaration`. Given a path pointing to the file holding the initial complexity problem, the generated executable will perform the following actions in order:

1. Parse the command line options given to the executable, and reflect these in the aforementioned `TctStatus`.
2. Parse the given file according to the parser specified in the `TctConfig`.
3. Select a strategy based on the command line flags, and apply the selected strategy on the parsed input problem.
4. Should the analysis succeed, a textual representation of the obtained complexity judgement and corresponding proof tree is printed to the console; in case the analysis fails, the uncompleted proof tree, including the `Reason` for failure is printed to the console.

*Interactive.* The library provides an *interactive mode* via the GHCi interpreter, similar to the one provided in TcT v2 [5]. The interactive mode is invoked via the command line flag `--interactive`. The implementation keeps track of a *proof state*, a list of proof trees that represents the history of the interactive session. We provide an interface to inspect and manipulate the proof state. Most noteworthy, the user can select individual sub-problems and apply strategies on them. The proof state is updated accordingly.

## 5   Case Studies

In this section we discuss several instantiations of the framework that have been established up to now. We keep the descriptions of the complexity problems informal and focus on the big picture. In the discussion we group abstract programs in contrast to real world programs.

### 5.1   Abstract Programs

Currently TcT provides *first-order term rewrite systems* and *integer transition systems* as abstract representations. As mentioned above, the system is open to the seamless integration of alternative abstractions.

*Term Rewrite Systems.* Term rewriting forms an abstract model of computation, which underlies much of declarative programming. Our results on pure OCaml, see below, show how we can make practical use of the clarity of the model. The `tct-trs` instance provides automated resource analysis of *first-order term rewrite systems* (*TRSs* for short) [8,26]. Complexity analysis of TRSs has received significant attention in the last decade, see [19] for details. A TRS consists of a set of rewrite rules, i.e. directed equations that can be applied from left to right. Computation is performed by *normalisation*, i.e. by successively

```
WORST_CASE(?,O(n^2))                        Orientation:
*** 1 Progress [(?,O(n^2))]  ***             mult(0(),y) = 3 + 4*y
   Considered Problem:                                   > 1
      Strict TRS Rules:                                  = 0()
         mult(0(),y)  -> 0()
         mult(s(x),y) -> plus(y,mult(x,y))    mult(s(x),y) = 3 + 3*x + 2*x*y + 4*y
         plus(x,0())  -> x                                 > 2 + 3*x + 2*x*y + 4*y
         plus(s(x),y) -> s(plus(x,y))                      = plus(y,mult(x,y))
         square(x)    -> mult(x,x)
      Signature:                              plus(x,0()) = 3 + 2*x
         {mult/2,plus/2,square/1} / {0/0,s/1}             > x
      Obligation: runtime innermost                       = x

   Applied Processor:                         plus(s(x),y) = 4 + 2*x + y
      NaturalPI {shape = Mixed 2}                         > 3 + 2*x + y
                                                          = s(plus(x,y))
   Proof:
      Polynomial Interpretation:              square(x) = 6 + 7*x + 2*x^2
            p(0)    = 1                                  > 5*x + 2*x^2
         p(mult)   = 3*x1 + 2*x1*x2 + 2*x2               = mult(x,x)
         p(plus)   = 2 + 2*x1 + x2
            p(s)   = 1 + x1
      p(square)   = 6 + 7*x1 + 2*x1^2
```

**Fig. 8.** Polynomial Interpretation Proof.

applying rewrite rules until no more rules apply. As an example, consider the following TRS $\mathcal{R}_{sq}$, which computes the squaring function on natural numbers in unary notation.

$$\mathsf{sq}(x) \to x * x \qquad x * 0 \to 0 \qquad x + 0 \to x$$

$$\mathsf{s}(x) * y \to y + (x * y) \qquad \mathsf{s}(x) + y \to \mathsf{s}(x + y).$$

The *runtime complexity* of a TRS is naturally expressed as a function that measures the length of the longest reduction, in the sizes of (normalised) starting terms. Figure 8 depicts the proof output of tct-trs when applying a polynomial interpretation [18] processor with maximum degree 2 on $\mathcal{R}_{sq}$. The resulting proof tree consists of a single progress node and returns the (optimal) quadratic asymptotic upper bound on the runtime complexity of $\mathcal{R}_{sq}$. The success of TcT as a complexity analyser, and in particular the strength of tct-trs instance is apparent from its performance at TERMCOMP.[3] It is noteworthy to mention that at this year's competition TcT not only won the combined ranking, but also the certified category. Here only those techniques are admissible that have been machine checked, so that soundness of the obtained resource bound is almost without doubt, cf. [7]. The tct-trs instance has many advantages in comparison to its predecessors. Many of them are subtle and are due to the redesign of the architecture and reimplementation of the framework. However, the practical consequences are clear: the instance tct-trs is more powerful than its predecessor, cf. the last year's TERMCOMP, where both the old and new version competed against each other. Furthermore, the actual strength of the

---

[3] See http://termination-portal.org/wiki/Termination_Competition_2015/.

latest version of TcT shows when combining different modules into bigger ones, as we are going to show in the sequent case studies.

*Integer Transition Systems.* The `tct-its` module deals with the analysis of *integer transition systems* (*ITSs* for short). An ITS can be seen as a TRS over terms $f(x_1, \ldots, x_n)$ where the variables $x_i$ range over integers, and where rules are additionally equipped with a guard $[\![\cdot]\!]$ that determines if a rule triggers. The notion of runtime complexity extends straight forward from TRSs to ITSs. ITSs naturally arise from imperative programs using loops, conditionals and integer operations only, but can also be obtained from programs with user-defined data structures using suitable size-abstractions (see e.g. [22]). Consider the following program, that computes the remainder of a natural number $m$ with respect to $n$.

```
int rem(int m,int n){ while (n > 0 && m > n){ m = m - n }; return m; }
```

This program is represented as the following ITS:

$$r(m, n) \rightarrow r(m - n, n) [\![n > 0 \wedge m > n]\!] \quad r(m, n) \rightarrow e(m, n) [\![\neg(n > 0 \wedge m > n)]\!].$$

It is not difficult to see that the runtime complexity of the ITS, i.e. the maximal length of a computation starting from $r(m, n)$, is linear in $m$ and $n$. The linear asymptotic bound is automatically derived by `tct-its`, in a fraction of a second. The complexity analysis of ITSs implemented by `tct-its` follows closely the approach by Brockschmidt et al. [10].

## 5.2   Real World Programs

One major motivation for the complexity analysis of abstract programs is that these models are well equipped to abstract over real-world programs whilst remaining conceptually simple.

*Pure* `OCaml`. For the case of higher-order functional programs, a successful application of this has been demonstrated in recent work by the first and second author in collaboration with Dal Lago [4]. In [4], we study the runtime complexity of pure `OCaml` programs. A suitable adaption of Reynold's *defunctionalisation* [24] technique translates the given program into a slight generalisation of TRSs, an *applicative term rewrite system* (*ATRS* for short). In ATRSs closures are explicitly represented as first-order structures. Evaluation of these closures is defined via a global apply function (denoted by @).

The structure of the defunctionalised program is necessarily intricate, even for simple programs. However, in conjunction with a sequence of sophisticated and in particular complexity reflecting transformations one can bring the defunctionalised program in a form which can be effectively analysed by first-order complexity provers such as the `tct-trs` instance; see [4] for the details. An example run is depicted in Fig. 9. All of this has been implemented in a prototype implementation, termed `HoCA`.[4] We have integrated the functionality

---

[4] See http://cbr.uibk.ac.at/tools/hoca/.

(a) Reversing a list, taken from Bird's textbook on functional programming [9].

```
let rec fold_left f acc = function
    [] → acc
    | x::xs → fold_left f (f acc x) xs ;;
let rev l = fold_left (fun xs x → x::xs) [] l ;;
```

(b) Defunctionalised applicative rewrite system.

$$main(x_0) \to m_1(x_0) @ f \qquad\qquad r(x_0) @ x_1 \to x_0 @ r_1 @ [\,] @ x_1$$
$$m_1(x_0) @ x_1 \to m_2(x_0) @ r(x_1) \qquad\qquad r_1 @ x_0 \to r_2(x_0)$$
$$m_2(x_0) @ x_1 \to x_1 @ x_0 \qquad\qquad r_2(x_0) @ x_1 \to x_1 :: x_0$$
$$f @ x_0 \to f_1 @ x_0 \qquad\qquad f_3(x_0, x_1) @ x_2 \to f_4(x_2, x_0, x_1)$$
$$f_1 @ x_1 \to f_2(x_1) \qquad\qquad f_4([\,], x_0, x_1) \to x_1$$
$$f_2(x_1) @ x_2 \to f_3(x_1, x_2) \qquad f_4(x_0 :: x_1, x_2, x_3) \to f @ x_1 @ (x_2 @ x_3 @ x_0) @ x_2$$

(c) Simplified first-order term rewrite system.

$$main(x_0) \to f([\,], x_0) \qquad f(x_0, [\,]) \to x_0 \qquad f(x_0, x_1 :: x_2) \to f(x_1 :: x_0, x_2)$$

**Fig. 9.** Example run of the HoCA prototype on a OCaml program.

```
hoca :: Maybe String → Strategy ML TrsProblem
hoca name = mlToAtrs name ≫ atrsToTrs ≫ toTctProblem

mlToAtrs :: Maybe String → Strategy ML ATRS
mlToAtrs name = mlToPcf name ≫ defunctionalise ≫ try simplifyAtrs

atrsToTrs :: Strategy ATRS TRS
atrsToTrs = try cfa ≫ uncurryAtrs ≫ try simplifyTrs
```

**Fig. 10.** HoCA transformation pipeline modelled in tct-hoca.

of HoCA in the instance tct-hoca. The individual transformations underlying this tool are seamlessly modelled as processors, its transformation pipeline is naturally expressed in our strategy language. The corresponding strategy, termed hoca, is depicted in Fig. 10. It takes an OCaml source fragment, of type ML, and turns it into a term rewrite system as follows. First, via mlToAtrs the source code is parsed and desugared, the resulting abstract syntax tree is turned into an expression of a typed λ-calculus with constants and fixpoints, akin to Plotkin's PCF [23]. All these steps are implemented via the strategy mlToPcf: : Maybe String → Strategy ML TypedPCF. The given parameter, an optional function name, can be used to select the analysed function. With defunctionalise : : Strategy TypedPCF ATRS this program is then turned into an ATRS, which is simplified via the strategy simplifyAtrs : : Strategy ATRS ATRS modelling the heuristics implemented in HoCA. Second, the strategy atrsToTrs uses the control-flow analysis provided by HoCA to *instantiate* occurrences of higher-order

```
jbc :: Strategy ITS () → Strategy TRS () → Strategy JBC ()
jbc its trs = toCTRS ⋙ Race (toIts ⋙ its) (toTrs ⋙ trs)
```

**Fig. 11.** `jat` transformation pipeline modelled in `tct-jbc`.

variables [4]. The instantiated ATRS is then translated into a first-order rewrite system by *uncurrying* all function calls. Further simplifications, as foreseen by the HoCA prototype at this stage of the pipeline, are performed via the strategy `simplifyTrs :: Strategy TRS TRS`.

Currently, all involved processors are implemented via calls to the library shipped with the HoCA prototype, and operate on exported data-types. The final strategy in the pipeline, `toTctProblem :: Strategy TRS TrsProblem`, converts HoCA's representation of a TRS to a complexity problem understood by `tct-trs`. Due to the open structure of T$_C$T, the integration of the HoCA prototype worked like a charm and was finalised in a couple of hours. Furthermore, essentially by construction the strength of `tct-hoca` equals the strength of the dedicated prototype. An extensive experimental assessment can be found in [4].

*Object-Oriented Bytecode Programs.* The `tct-jbc` instance provides automated complexity analysis of object-oriented bytecode programs, in particular *Jinja bytecode* (*JBC* for short) programs [17]. Given a JBC program, we measure the maximal number of bytecode instructions executed in any evaluation of the program. We suitably employ techniques from data-flow analysis and abstract interpretation to obtain a *term based* abstraction of JBC programs in terms of *constraint term rewrite systems* (*cTRSs* for short) [20]. CTRSs are a generalisation of TRSs and ITSs. More importantly, given a cTRS obtained from a JBC program, we can extract a TRS or ITS fragment. All these abstractions are complexity reflecting. We have implemented this transformation in a dedicated tool termed `jat` and have integrated its functionality in `tct-jbc` in a similar way we have integrated the functionality of HoCA in `tct-hoca`. The corresponding strategy, termed `jbc`, is depicted in Fig. 11. We then can use `tct-trs` and `tct-its` to analyse the resulting problems. Our framework is expressive enough to analyse the thus obtained problems in parallel. Note that `Race s1 s2` requires that `s1` and `s2` have the same output problem type. We can model this with transformations to a dummy problem (). Nevertheless, as intended any witness that is obtained by an successful application of `its` or `trs` will be relayed back.

# 6   Conclusion

In this paper we have presented T$_C$T v3.0, the latest version of our fully automated complexity analyser. T$_C$T is open source, released under the BSD3 license. All components of T$_C$T are written in *Haskell*. T$_C$T is open with respect to the complexity problem under investigation and problem specific techniques. It is the most powerful tool in the realm of automated complexity analysis of term rewrite systems, as for example verified at this year's TERMCOMP. Moreover it provides an expressive problem independent strategy language that facilitates the proof search, extensibility and automation.

Further work will be concerned with the finalisation of the envisioned instance `tct-hrs`, as well as the integration of current and future developments in the resource analysis of ITSs.

# References

1. Albert, E., Arenas, P., Genaim, S., Puebla, G., Román-Díez, G.: Conditional termination of loops over heap-allocated data. SCP **92**, 2–24 (2014)
2. Aspinall, D., Beringer, L., Hofmann, M., Loidl, H.W., Momigliano, A.: A program logic for resources. TCS **389**(3), 411–445 (2007)
3. Atkey, R.: Amortised resource analysis with separation logic. LMCS **7**(2), 1–33 (2011)
4. Avanzini, M., Dal Lago, U., Moser, G.: Analysing the complexity of functional programs: higher-order meets first-order. In: Proceeding of the 20th ICFP, pp. 152–164. ACM (2015)
5. Avanzini, M., Moser, G.: Tyrolean complexity tool: features and usage. In: Proceeding of the 24th RTA, LIPIcs, vol. 21, pp. 71–80 (2013)
6. Avanzini, M., Moser, G.: A combination framework for complexity. IC (to appear, 2016)
7. Avanzini, M., Sternagel, C., Thiemann, R.: Certification of complexity proofs using CeTA. In: Proceeding of the 26th RTA, LIPIcs, vol. 36, pp. 23–39 (2015)
8. Baader, F., Nipkow, T.: Term Rewriting and All That. Cambridge University Press, Cambridge (1998)
9. Bird, R.: Introduction to Functional Programming using Haskell, 2nd edn. Prentice Hall, Upper Saddle River (1998)
10. Brockschmidt, M., Emmes, F., Falke, S., Fuhs, C., Giesl, J.: Alternating runtime and size complexity analysis of integer programs. In: Ábrahám, E., Havelund, K. (eds.) TACAS 2014 (ETAPS). LNCS, vol. 8413, pp. 140–155. Springer, Heidelberg (2014)
11. Danner, N., Paykin, J., Royer, J.S.: A static cost analysis for a higher-order language. In: Proceeding of the 7th PLPV, pp. 25–34. ACM (2013)
12. Gimenez, S., Moser, G.: The complexity of interaction. In: Proceeding of the 40th POPL (to appear, 2016)
13. Hirokawa, N., Moser, G.: Automated complexity analysis based on the dependency pair method. In: Armando, A., Baumgartner, P., Dowek, G. (eds.) IJCAR 2008. LNCS (LNAI), vol. 5195, pp. 364–379. Springer, Heidelberg (2008)
14. Hoffmann, J., Aehlig, K., Hofmann, M.: Multivariate amortized resource analysis. TOPLAS **34**(3), 14 (2012)
15. Hofmann, M., Moser, G.: Multivariate amortised resource analysis for term rewrite systems. In: Proceeding of the 13th TLCA in LIPIcs Vol. 38, pp. 241–256 (2015)
16. Jost, S., Hammond, K., Loidl, H.W., Hofmann, M.: Static determination of quantitative resource usage for higher-order programs. In: Proceeding of the 37th POPL, pp. 223–236. ACM (2010)
17. Klein, G., Nipkow, T.: A machine-checked model for a java-like language, virtual machine, and compiler. TOPLAS **28**(4), 619–695 (2006)
18. Lankford, D.: On Proving Term Rewriting Systems are Noetherian. Technical Report MTP-3. Louisiana Technical University (1979)

19. Moser, G.: Proof Theory at Work: Complexity Analysis of Term Rewrite Systems. CoRR abs/0907.5527, Habilitation Thesis (2009)
20. Moser, G., Schaper, M.: A Complexity Preserving Transformation from Jinja Byte-code to Rewrite Systems (2012). CoRR, cs/PL/1204.1568, last revision: 6 May 2014
21. Noschinski, L., Emmes, F., Giesl, J.: Analyzing innermost runtime complexity of term rewriting by dependency pairs. JAR **51**(1), 27–56 (2013)
22. Hill, P.M., Payet, E., Spoto, F.: Path-length analysis of object-oriented programs. In: Proceeding of the 1st EAAI. Elsevier (2006)
23. Plotkin, G.D.: LCF considered as a programming language. TCS **5**(3), 223–255 (1977)
24. Reynolds, J.C.: Definitional interpreters for higher-order programming languages. HOSC **11**(4), 363–397 (1998)
25. Sinn, M., Zuleger, F., Veith, H.: A simple and scalable static analysis for bound analysis and amortized complexity analysis. In: Biere, A., Bloem, R. (eds.) CAV 2014. LNCS, vol. 8559, pp. 745–761. Springer, Heidelberg (2014)
26. TeReSe: Term Rewriting Systems, Cambridge Tracks in Theoretical Computer Science, vol. 55. Cambridge University Press, Cambridge (2003)
27. Wilhelm, R., Engblom, J., Ermedahl, A., Holsti, N., Thesing, S., Whalley, D., Bernat, G., Ferdinand, C., Heckmann, R., Mitra, T., Mueller, F., Puaut, I., Puschner, P., Staschulat, J., Stenstrom, P.: The worst case execution time problem - overview of methods and survey of tools. TECS **7**(3), 1–53 (2008)

# Integrated Environment for Diagnosing Verification Errors

Maria Christakis[1]($\boxtimes$), K. Rustan M. Leino[1]($\boxtimes$), Peter Müller[2]($\boxtimes$),
and Valentin Wüstholz[3]($\boxtimes$)

[1] Microsoft Research, Redmond, USA
{mchri,leino}@microsoft.com
[2] Department of Computer Science, ETH Zurich, Zurich, Switzerland
peter.mueller@inf.ethz.ch
[3] The University of Texas at Austin, Austin, USA
valentin@cs.utexas.edu

**Abstract.** A failed attempt to verify a program's correctness can result in reports of genuine errors, spurious warnings, and timeouts. The main challenge in debugging a verification failure is to determine whether the complaint is genuine or spurious, and to obtain enough information about the failed verification attempt to debug the error. To help a user with this task, this paper presents an extension of the Dafny IDE that seamlessly integrates the Dafny verifier, a dynamic symbolic execution engine, a verification debugger, and a technique for diagnosing timeouts. The paper also reports on experiments that measure the utility of the combined use of these complementary tools.

## 1 Introduction

Software developers today get more assistance than ever before from analyses running in their integrated development environment (IDE). These analyses scrutinize the code in shallow or deep ways and then display information, issue warnings, make suggestions, or rewrite the code. Examples include code formatting, intelligent code completion, semantic variable renaming, cyclomatic code complexity analysis, unit test generation, bounds checking, race detection, worst-case execution time analysis, termination checking, and functional-correctness verification. As the level of sophistication of an analysis goes up, so does the level of understanding required for a programmer to diagnose the output of the analysis and determine how to take corrective action.

In this paper, we consider the problem of diagnosing the output of a program verifier of the kind where the underlying reasoning engine, typically an SMT solver, runs without user interaction. Examples of such verifiers are Spec# [3], Frama-C [15], SPARK 2014 (for Ada) [20], AutoProof (for Eiffel) [40], and Dafny [29]. In particular, we consider three kinds of output:

(1) **Timeouts:** While SMT solvers are generally both useful and fast in practice, they occasionally time out. When they do, the information available

M. Chechik and J.-F. Raskin (Eds.): TACAS 2016, LNCS 9636, pp. 424–441, 2016.
DOI: 10.1007/978-3-662-49674-9_25

may not be the same as in cases where they output counterexamples. Moreover, a timeout can mask other error messages because it abruptly ends the counterexample search.

(2) **Spurious warnings:** The logical conditions that a program verifier needs to resolve are in general undecidable, so it would be too much to expect that every error message produced by a verifier indicates a real error. However, in practice, most warnings that are not indicative of errors in the executable code are not caused by undecidability but by the lack of strong enough auxiliary specifications (such as loop invariants) in the program.

(3) **Genuine errors:** Sometimes when the program verifier reports a real error, the programmer's response can be one of disbelief. Erroneously—perhaps by habit—assuming the error is caused by an infelicity in the verifier, the programmer spends time trying to coax the verifier into giving a different output, only to miss the blatant error that the verifier detected. Such an error can occur in either the executable code or in the program's specifications.

The main challenge in debugging verification errors is to determine which of these cases applies and to obtain enough information about the failed verification attempt to debug the error. A single tool may not support the best kind of diagnosing for each output.

In this paper, we contribute comprehensive tool support in a single verification environment. The combination of our tools covers all steps of the typical diagnosis procedures for verification.

We use as our setting the Dafny programming language, verifier, and IDE. In addition to standard (sequential) imperative and functional constructs, the language includes constructs for specifications (aka *contracts*), auxiliary specifications, and proof authoring. The verifier uses these specifications to perform *modular* verification. For example, it reasons about a method call solely in terms of the callee method's specification and about a loop solely in terms of the loop invariant.

Dafny has always had a program verifier. In this paper, we extend the Dafny IDE with a novel dynamic test generator (Delfy), the Boogie Verification Debugger (BVD) [28], and a new mode for diagnosing timeouts[1]. Using step-by-step recipes, we show how our seamless integration of these tools helps diagnose verification problems. Our paper also gives an experimental evaluation of our tool integration and its effect on diagnosing verification errors. Both Dafny and the IDE extension are available at http://dafny.codeplex.com (Delfy is currently not included).

In Sect. 2, we illustrate the use of the combination of our tools on small representative examples. We then describe in more detail the facilities that our integrated diagnosis environment offers: hover text in Sect. 3, Delfy in Sect. 4, BVD integration in Sect. 5, and timeout diagnosis in Sect. 6. We give our experimental evaluation in Sect. 7. The final sections of the paper discuss related work and conclude.

---

[1] A preliminary integration of the verifier and BVD into the Dafny IDE has previously been described in an informal workshop paper [31]. The full integration of the tools is new here, as are the test generator and the timeout-diagnosis tool.

## 2   Systematic Diagnosis of Verification Failures

In this section, we present systematic approaches to diagnosing the two forms of
verification failures: (1) verification errors, which may be spurious warnings and
genuine errors, as well as (2) timeouts. For each approach, we describe the tool
support we provide and illustrate the approach on a small example program.
Details are described in the subsequent sections.

### 2.1   Diagnosis of Verification Errors

The main challenge in debugging a verification error is to determine if the complaint is spurious or genuine, and to obtain enough information about the failed
verification attempt to debug the error. For genuine errors, this includes determining whether to fix the program or the specification. For spurious errors, it
includes determining if more auxiliary specifications are required or if the error
is caused by an incompleteness of the verifier (which happens in particular when
the SMT solver cannot discharge a verification condition even though it holds).

```
method Main(a: int) {
  var aSq := a * a;
  var r := Max(a, aSq);
  assert r = aSq;  // verification fails
}

method Max(a: int, b: int) returns (max: int)
  ensures max = a ∨ max = b
{
  if a ≤ b { max := a; }
  else     { max := b; }
}
```

**Fig. 1.** A Dafny example that asserts that an integer is never bigger than its square.
The assertion does not hold because method Max returns the minimum of its arguments;
it fails to verify because the postcondition of Max is too weak to prove it. Note that
integers in Dafny are unbounded and that calls are verified modularly, based solely on
the callee's specification.

Using the example in Fig. 1, we illustrate how we support this debugging
process. The condition stated by the assert-statement in this program does not
hold along all executions of the program, because Max erroneously computes the
*minimum* of its arguments. But even if Max had been implemented correctly, the
verifier would report a (spurious) error because the postcondition of Max is too
weak to (modularly) prove the assertion.

Diagnosing verification errors typically proceeds in the following three steps.

**Step 1: Fixing simple errors.** For certain simple verification errors (such as omitting a precondition of the method being verified), the error message of the verifier provides enough information to diagnose and debug the error. To provide easy, demand-driven access to error messages, the Dafny IDE presents them in tool tags when hovering over the error location, which is indicated by red squiggly lines. The hover text also shows inferred specifications (such as termination metrics) and parts of the counterexample provided by the SMT solver (as we shall see later in Fig. 5). In our example, the error message is simply "assertion violation", which does not point us to the source of the problem.

**Step 2: Determining whether errors are spurious.** Debugging genuine verification errors is fundamentally different from debugging spurious errors. For the former, one needs to determine which aspects of the program or specification are incorrect and fix them. For the latter, one needs to determine how to convince the verifier that the program is actually correct.

A common approach to determine if an error is spurious is to create an executable test from the counterexample given by the SMT solver [4,16]. However, this approach has two major limitations. First, the counterexample reflects the (modular) verification semantics of a method, where calls are encoded via the callee's specification, loops are encoded via loop invariants, etc. By the soundness of verification, any error in the execution semantics is also an error in the verification semantics, but not necessarily vice versa. Therefore, it is possible that a test case derived from the SMT solver's counterexample does not reveal an error even though the program fails for other inputs. A programmer might then conclude incorrectly that the verification error is spurious. Second, SMT solvers sometimes produce invalid counterexamples, that is, valuations that do not actually falsify the verification condition. This may be due to an incompleteness in the SMT solver (e.g., when reasoning about non-linear arithmetic) [33]. Executing such counterexamples does not lead to meaningful conclusions. In fact, it may not even be possible to generate a test case from such a counterexample.

To avoid these problems, we do not execute counterexamples and instead apply dynamic symbolic execution (DSE) [8,24] (also called concolic testing [35]) to generate test cases for the method that contains the verification error. We have equipped the Dafny IDE with Delfy, a DSE tool that instruments the executable code with runtime checks for assertions and then uses dynamic symbolic execution to systematically explore all paths through a Dafny method up to a given bound. DSE mitigates the limitations of counterexample execution as follows. First, it is based on the (non-modular) execution semantics, not on the verification semantics and, thus, attempts to find inputs for which the *execution* of a method leads to an assertion violation. Second, when some constraints in a proof obligation cause the SMT solver to produce an invalid counterexample during verification, the same problem may occur during DSE. However, DSE has the option of replacing symbolic inputs by concrete values, thereby simplifying the formula, which increases the chance of obtaining a valid counterexample.

Running DSE can have three different outcomes: (1) It produces a test case that leads to an assertion violation. In this case, we can conclude that the error is *definitely not spurious*. One can now use a conventional debugger to explore the execution of the test case and determine how to fix the error. (2) It is able to verify the method. This is possible when the method can be tested without exceeding the bounds of DSE (for instance, the method contains no input-dependent loops) and when the SMT solver is able to produce concrete inputs for each constraint [11]. In this case, the error is *definitely spurious*. It is now possible to communicate this verification result to the verifier. (3) If DSE neither verifies nor falsifies the method, our best guess is that the error is *spurious*, and we proceed to step 3 below.

Running Delfy on method `Main` from our example reproduces the error by generating a test case where $a \leq a * a$ (necessarily, since this is a mathematical fact, and thus the then-branch of the conditional in method `Max` is executed) and $a \neq a * a$ (such that the assertion is violated), for instance, $a = 2$. Stepping through this test case in the debugger immediately reveals that method `Max` is incorrect. After fixing the error, verification still fails. Running Delfy again verifies method `Main`. We could now communicate this result to the verifier or—as we describe next—we could try to determine what additional facts are needed by the verifier to prove the method.

**Step 3: Finding the cause of spurious errors.** When Delfy cannot reproduce a verification error, it is necessary to explore the verification semantics, which is reflected in the counterexample provided by the SMT solver. To do so in the Dafny IDE, a user can select a verification error by clicking on the red button next to the assertion (see Fig. 5). The IDE now highlights the program points along the trace leading to the error using blue buttons. By clicking on one of them, a user can bring up BVD and inspect the state at this program point as provided by the counterexample.

In our example, once method `Max` is fixed, the verification debugger shows for the program point after the call to `Max` that a is 2, aSq is 4, and r is 2. Since running Delfy did not reveal any error, we hypothesize that `Max` correctly computes the maximum of its arguments, and conclude that the counterexample values indicate that the verifier has insufficient information about the result of `Max`. We can fix this by strengthening its postcondition, and verification succeeds.

## 2.2  Diagnosis of Timeouts

The use of undecidable theories, especially quantifiers, in verification conditions can lead to a very large or even infinite search space for the SMT solver, for instance, when the verification conditions contain matching loops [19]. Therefore, Dafny and other automatic verifiers bound the time spent by the SMT solver, and report a verification failure when a timeout occurs [22]. However, if this happens, it is often unclear which fragments of a large verification condition cause the SMT solver to wander off. Moreover, because of the heuristics used in the SMT solver to instantiate quantifiers, timeouts are often caused by the interaction of different, often seemingly unrelated, terms in the program or its specification.

```
method FacUpTo(n: int) returns (f: seq⟨int⟩)
  requires 1 ≤ n
  ensures |f| = n ∧ f[0] = 1
  ensures ∀ i • 1 ≤ i < |f| ⟹ f[i] = f[i - 1] * i
⊞{...}

method Test(n: int)
  requires 1 ≤ n
{
  var f4 := FacUpTo(4);    assert f4[3] = 6;
  var f15 := FacUpTo(15);  assert f15[14] ≠ 0;

  var fn := FacUpTo(n);
  assert fn[n - 1] ≠ 0;   // verification times out
}
```

**Fig. 2.** A Dafny example that computes the factorial of the first **n** natural numbers and asserts that they are positive. The proof requires generalization and induction, which Dafny does not perform automatically. Instead, the SMT solver keeps instantiating the universal quantifier in the postcondition of the call `FacUpTo(n)`, and verification times out even though, in principle, many other assertions could be proved.

Verification of the example in Fig. 2 fails with a timeout. While trying to prove the last assertion in method `Test`, the SMT solver instantiates the universal quantifier in the postcondition of `FacUpTo` (and in the axiomatization of the sequence data type) indefinitely. For the verification to succeed, one needs to instruct Dafny to prove by induction that all elements of sequence `fn` are non-zero, for instance, by adding the following assertion after the final call in Fig. 2:

```
assert ∀ i {:induction} • 0 ≤ i < |fn| ⟹ fn[i] ≠ 0;
```

Diagnosing such timeouts typically proceeds in the following two steps.

**Step 1: Determining whether the program satisfies its specification.** Like for verification errors, it is useful to run the test case generator Delfy on the method whose verification times out. Note that the common approach of generating test cases from counterexamples is not applicable here since SMT solvers usually generate an incomplete counterexample or none at all in case of a timeout. In contrast, since Delfy relies only on the program and its specification, it can be used to diagnose timeouts. If Delfy generates a failing test, the program or its specification should be fixed before diagnosing the timeout. If Delfy manages to verify the method, Dafny can be notified such that it is no longer essential to debug the timeout. Delfy might succeed on examples that time out in the verifier because it uses a different axiomatization of data types such as sets and sequences. Moreover, Delfy's SMT queries are constraints that describe a single path through a method, whereas Dafny's verification conditions reflect all paths. Therefore, Delfy's queries might provide fewer terms that are used by the SMT solver to instantiate quantifiers.

In the example from Fig. 2, Delfy neither generates a failing test nor manages to verify method `Test`; this is due to the input-dependent loop in the body (not shown) of method `FacUpTo`, which is called. Thus, we proceed to the second step.

**Step 2: Narrowing down the cause of the timeout.** We have developed a dedicated diagnostic mode for Dafny, which splits up the verification condition into smaller fragments and invokes the SMT solver multiple times to narrow down which assertions may cause the timeout. For each invocation, this algorithm tries to prove some of the fragments, and ignores the rest. If the SMT solver fails, an error is reported. If it succeeds, the algorithm recurs and attempts to verify the fragments previously ignored. If no such fragments exist, verification succeeds. Finally, if the SMT solver still times out, the algorithm recurs on fewer fragments or, if there is just a single fragment, "blames" that fragment for the timeout.

In our example, the timeout diagnosis determines that out of the nine assertions in method `Test` (three for precondition checks, three for bounds checks, and three for assert-statements), eight verify and only the last one times out. This clearly indicates that the user should provide more hints to help the verifier in proving this assertion.

The above recipes allow a programmer to systematically diagnose and debug all three kinds of verification failures. Our recipes are supported by a novel integration of the following components into the Dafny IDE: (1) an advanced hover text mechanism, (2) the Delfy test case generator, (3) the Boogie Verification Debugger, and (4) a technique for diagnosing timeouts. We describe these components in detail in the following sections.

## 3    Hover Text

Verifiers typically accumulate a lot of information, including error messages, inferred specifications (such as termination metrics), or verification counterexamples. However, most often, the user is interested only in a small fraction of this information, and specifically, in whatever helps to diagnose verification errors.

The hover text mechanism that we have integrated in the Dafny IDE addresses this need without overwhelming the user with too much information. Our mechanism uses the parser, type checker, and verifier to collect warnings, inferred specifications, and other information, which it attaches to the relevant parts of the Dafny abstract syntax tree. As a result, the IDE displays only the most critical information at all times (that is, squiggly lines for verification errors), and the user may access all other information on demand, by hovering over the relevant parts of the program text. For instance, a warning emitted by the verifier is shown when hovering over the corresponding squiggly line, and the values of the variables in a verification counterexample are shown when hovering over the variable usages (see Fig. 5).

# 4   Delfy, the Test Case Generator

In this section, we present Delfy, a dynamic test generation tool for Dafny. In addition to handling advanced constructs of the language, Delfy is designed to exchange information with Dafny about the verification status of all assertions via annotations in the code [12]. Consequently, Dafny does not need to check assertions that have already been proven correct by Delfy and vice versa.

## 4.1   Dynamic Symbolic Execution for Dafny

Delfy implements dynamic symbolic execution, in which the concrete and symbolic executions of a method under test happen simultaneously. Given a Dafny method under test, Delfy compiles the code into .NET bytecode and runs the compiled method. The compiled code includes call-backs that trigger the symbolic execution. All constraints are solved with Z3 [18].

Delfy introduces runtime checks for Dafny specifications, including loop invariants, termination metrics, pre- and postconditions, assumptions, assertions, and frame specifications, which serve as test oracles.

Delfy has support for features of Dafny that are typically not found in mainstream programming languages, for instance, non-deterministic assignments, non-deterministic if-statements, and non-deterministic while-statements. For each non-deterministic value, the symbolic execution in Delfy introduces a fresh symbolic variable, as if they were inputs to the method under test. Consequently, the symbolic execution collects constraints on such variables and generates inputs for them, which guide execution toward all those unexplored paths.

Dafny also supports uninterpreted functions and assign-such-that-statements, which assign a value to a variable such that a condition holds. Delfy handles these by introducing a fresh symbolic variable for the return value of an uninterpreted function or the assigned variable of an assign-such-that-statement. This symbolic variable is constrained by a condition of the form $\text{ASSUME}(c)$, saying that the variable must satisfy the function specifications or the such-that-condition in each test case.

When the programmer provides a loop invariant for an input-dependent loop, Delfy can either impose a bound on the number of explored loop iterations or treat the invariant as a summary for the loop [10]. In the latter case, the symbolic execution of the loop body is turned off, and instead, the provided loop invariant serves as a symbolic description of the loop body. (Note that we abuse the term "summary" to express that reasoning about many loop iterations happens in one shot, although we do not refer to a logic formula of loop pre- and postconditions, as is typically the case in compositional symbolic execution [1, 23].) Summarization of an input-dependent loop might lead to spurious warnings when the loop invariant is too weak, in which case Delfy resembles the verifier. However, when the loop invariant is precise, this technique can be very useful in diagnosing verification errors and timeouts as it helps the exploration in covering the code after the loop.

A consequence of this approach for summarizing input-dependent loops is that the body of such a loop might not be thoroughly exercised since it is only executed concretely, and not symbolically; therefore, paths and bugs might be missed. To address this, Delfy supports a mode for thoroughly checking if an invariant is maintained by all iterations of an input-dependent loop [10].

## 4.2   Delfy in the Dafny IDE

We now present how we have integrated Delfy in the Dafny IDE. Figure 3 shows the error emitted by the verifier (denoted by the red button) for the assertion in method Main from Fig. 1. Delfy is run through a smart tag, shown in Fig. 3. Figure 4 shows how the test cases generated by Delfy are displayed for method Main from Fig. 1.

The main characteristics of this IDE integration are as follows.

**Color Coding of Assertions.** To give users a sense of where they should focus their manual diagnosis, the IDE uses colors for assertions. A green color shows that the assertion has been proven, either by Dafny or Delfy. A red color denotes that an assertion definitely does not hold, that is, Dafny has emitted a verification error, and Delfy has generated a test case that fails due to this assertion. An orange color indicates that the assertion requires the attention of the user because Dafny has emitted a verification error, and Delfy has neither verified nor falsified it. One could further refine this color scheme by reflecting how thoroughly Delfy covered an orange assertion [10].

```
method Main(a: int) {
    var a⬚ := a * a;
    var r ⚡  Analyze with Delfy
    assert r ●== aSq;  // verification fails
}
```

**Fig. 3.** A smart tag allowing the user to invoke Delfy on a method under test, and a verification error emitted by the verifier (denoted by the red button in the assertion).

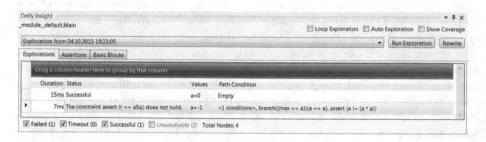

**Fig. 4.** Delfy displays the generated tests. The user can choose to inspect all generated tests, or categorize them based on their outcome.

**Selective Test Generation.** Delfy allows the user to select an assertion that has not been verified by Dafny, and explore only those paths that reach this assertion. If a programmer selects a red button in a method under test and runs Delfy, then only those test cases that exercise the corresponding unverified assertion are generated, regardless of whether there are other unverified assertions in the method under test. We determine which test cases to generate using a technique based on static symbolic execution [10].

**Debugging Failing Tests.** Delfy also makes it possible to debug the generated test cases. A smart tag allows users to run a failing test case in the .NET debugger, such that they can step through the execution and observe the values of variables.

## 5   Integration of the Verification Debugger

Counterexamples, which are provided by the verifier and the underlying solver, often include valuable information for diagnosing verification errors. Since these counterexamples reflect the verification semantics (for instance, by reasoning about method calls modularly), this holds in particular for intricate verification errors that cannot be reproduced by Delfy. (Recall that Delfy is based on the non-modular execution semantics.) BVD makes the verification counterexamples accessible through the Dafny IDE, which allows users to inspect the values of variables (including heap locations), much like in a conventional debugger. However, unlike in most runtime debuggers, a user can inspect the counterexample at any relevant point during the execution.

BVD is invoked by clicking on the red button that is associated with each verification error. Now, several blue buttons appear along the trace that leads to the error (see Fig. 5). Clicking on any of them shows the counterexample state at that program point. For instance, a user may diagnose a verification error by starting at the failing assertion and gradually moving backward in the program to understand how the failing state was reached.

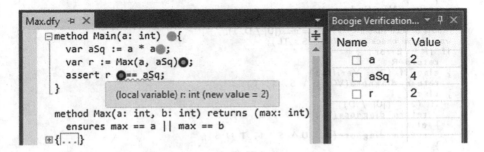

**Fig. 5.** Inspecting values from the counterexample for the error in method `Main` of Fig. 1. The hover text shows the value of variable `r` and the BVD window on the right shows the values of all variables.

## 6  Timeout Diagnosis

As discussed in Sect. 2.2, users occasionally encounter timeouts when verifying non-trivial programs. Timeouts often indicate that the verifier is unable to derive a certain fact on its own, and requires hints from the user. To detect timeouts quickly and to ensure a responsive user interaction, the Dafny IDE defaults to a time limit of ten seconds per method or function.

If this time is not enough, the user can increase the limit or use our technique for diagnosing timeouts. In the latter case, we instruct the verifier to produce slightly different verification conditions, which can be decomposed more easily and on demand. This makes it possible to split up the verification conditions and, thereby, identify those assertions that are responsible for the timeout.

Conceptually, our alternative verification conditions insert an assumption $F_k \implies A_k$ before every assertion $A_k$, where a $F_k$ is an undefined boolean function. Initially nothing is known about these functions. That is, the solver needs to consider the case that all $F_k$ functions yield false and, thus, this instrumentation does not affect verifiability of the verification condition. However, once a timeout occurs, we can define some of the $F_k$ functions to yield true, thus, *temporarily* disabling assertions and simplifying the verification task.

Figure 6 shows our algorithm for decomposing the verification task once there has been a timeout. Procedure diagnose takes four arguments: (1) the current verification condition VC, (2) the set of unverified assertions U (initially contains all assertions in the verification condition), (3) the integer D (for denominator) to determine what fraction of these assertions to check next (initially set to 2), and (4) the set of timed-out assertions T (initially empty).

If set U is empty, we are done. We return Verified if set T of timed-out assertions is empty, and TimeOut otherwise. If set U is non-empty, we choose

```
procedure diagnose(VC, U, D, T) {
   if (|U| = 0) {
      if (0 < |T|) {
         report the timed-out assertions in T;
         return TimeOut;
      }
      return Verified;
   }
   choose S, such that S ⊆ U ∧ |S| = max(|U| / D, 1);
   var R := check_some(VC, S, TL);
   if (R = Error) {
      return R;
   } else if (R = Verified) {
      return diagnose(VC, U \ S, 1, T);
   } else {
      if (2 ≤ (|U| / D)) {
         return diagnose(VC, U, 2 * D, T);
      } else {
         return diagnose(VC, U \ S, 1, T ∪ S);
      }
   }
}
```

Fig. 6. Algorithm for diagnosing timeouts.

a subset S of the unverified assertions and check only these assertions for a fixed time limit TL (set by default to 10 % of the time limit for the entire method or function). If we find a failing assertion, we terminate immediately. If the check successfully verifies the assertions in S, we recursively diagnose the timeout among the remaining assertions. Otherwise, we try to check a smaller set of assertions by invoking procedure diagnose with 2 * D. If doubling D is not possible without exceeding the cardinality of U, we have found assertions to blame for the timeout, collect them in T, and proceed to also check the remaining assertions. If the algorithm reports any blamed assertions, it is reported that each of them timed out individually, given time limit TL. This shows exactly which assertions the user should focus on in order to prevent the timeout.

The procedure check_some checks the verification condition after temporarily disabling some assertions. To do so efficiently, it makes use of scopes in the solver that push and later pop constraints about the $F_k$ functions for assertions that are not in set S.

# 7    Experimental Evaluation

In this section, we evaluate our extensions of the Dafny IDE on diagnosing both verification errors and timeouts.

## 7.1    Verification Errors

To demonstrate that even simple programming tasks exhibit different forms of verification errors, we have evaluated our extensions on Dafny solutions we developed to three challenges posed in verification competitions and benchmarks. We used the Dafny IDE to diagnose each verification error we encountered during the three verification sessions, and report the results in Table 1.

Challenge SUMMAX is taken from verification competition VSComp-2010 [27]. It consists in computing the *sum* and *max* of the elements in an array and proving that $sum \leq N * max$, where $N$ is the length of the array. Challenge MAXARRAY is taken from verification competition COST-2011 [6]. Given a non-empty integer array, MAXARRAY requires that we verify that the index returned by a given method points to an element maximal in the array. Challenge BINARYSEARCH is taken from a set of verification benchmarks [41], and consists in verifying an implementation of binary search over an array. All versions of our solutions to these challenges are numbered by a verification-error identifier, which is shown in the second column of the table, and can be provided upon request. The third column indicates that roughly half of the verification errors are spurious, which is not uncommon.

To diagnose the errors, we used hover text information about error messages and inferred specifications (fourth column), hover text information about verification counterexamples (fifth column), Delfy (sixth), and BVD (seventh). As described earlier, each of these extensions may provide complementary insights to the user about the cause of verification errors. In the table, we indicate helpful

**Table 1.** Errors diagnosed while solving three verification challenges.

| Challenge | Error ID | Spurious? | Extension | | Delfy | BVD |
|---|---|---|---|---|---|---|
| | | | Hover text (w/o CEX) | Hover text (only CEX) | | |
| SumMax | 1 | no | ✓ | ✓ | – | ✓ |
| | 2 | no | ✓ | ✓ | ✓ | ✓ |
| | 3 | yes | ✓ | ✓ | ✓ | ✓ |
| | 4 | yes | ✗ | ✓ | ✓ | ✓ |
| MaxArray | 5 | no | ✓ | ✓ | – | ✓ |
| | 6 | no | ✓ | ✓ | ✓ | ✓ |
| | 7 | yes | ✓ | ✓ | ✓ | ✓ |
| | 8 | yes | ✓ | ✓ | ✓ | ✓ |
| | 9 | yes | ✓ | ✗ | ✓ | ✓ |
| | 10 | yes | ✓ | ✓ | ✓ | ✓ |
| | 11 | yes | ✗ | ✗ | ✓ | ✓ |
| BinarySearch | 12 | no | ✓ | ✓ | – | ✓ |
| | 13 | no | ✓ | ✓ | ✓ | ✓ |
| | 14 | yes | ✓ | ✓ | ✓ | ✓ |
| | 15 | no | ✓ | ✓ | ✓ | ✓ |
| | 16 | no | ✓ | ✓ | – | ✓ |
| | 17 | no | ✓ | ✓ | ✓ | ✓ |
| | 18 | no | ✓ | ✗ | ✓ | ✓ |
| | 19 | no | ✓ | ✓ | – | ✓ |
| | 20 | yes | ✗ | ✗ | ✓ | ✓ |

insights (✓) as well as information that did not help in the diagnosis of a verification error (✗). However, note that such insights are not necessarily sufficient for diagnosing the error—multiple steps may be needed and the use of more than one of our extensions; also, different users may find some feedback more insightful than others. For instance, the counterexample information (through the hover text or the verification debugger) is perhaps more suitable for experienced users. Consequently, in particular for spurious errors, there is usually no definite answer about which extension pinpointed the source of an error.

Note that we have created a separate column for the counterexample information that is available in the hover text to highlight the difference with BVD. As shown in the table, the hover text is sufficient to diagnose most verification errors. BVD only becomes essential when inspecting values within data structures, such as arrays, which are not shown in the hover text. Fixing spurious errors without counterexample information would require significant *mental effort* and *time* from users since they would often need to resort to trial-and-error to identify which information the verifier is missing. In principle, Delfy could provide help with such cases. However, since all of our programs contained input-dependent loops, Delfy was not able to show that an error is *definitely* spurious.

In a few cases (indicated by a '–' in the table), Delfy was not applicable. This was the case when the cause of a verification error was a specification that Dafny guessed heuristically, such as a termination metric. Even though, at the moment, Delfy does not support runtime checks for such guessed specifications, it *automatically and reliably* detected all other genuine errors. Without Delfy, this would have required *manual* effort from the user, for instance, to inspect counterexamples. In other words, no extension of the Dafny IDE is absolutely indispensable, but each extension can significantly reduce the user effort for diagnosing errors.

We also found situations where the hover text about error messages and inferred specifications (fourth column of the table) provided limited support. In particular, there is no indication of how much progress a user makes in fixing a verification error. For instance, they might add one of two loop invariants that are necessary for proving a failing assertion, but the error message remains unchanged. They are, therefore, not confident that the change is a step in the right direction by only reading the hover text. In contrast, our other extensions provide better support in such cases; for instance, in this example, the counterexample state after the loop would now be different due to the additional invariant.

## 7.2 Timeouts

We have evaluated our technique for diagnosing timeouts by running it on 39 programs taken from real verification sessions, which were recorded with the Dafny IDE [32] and can be provided upon request. We compare two configurations that only differ by parameter TL from Fig. 6: (1) Low (10 % of the time limit per method/function), and (2) High (20 % of the time limit per method/function).

Table 2 demonstrates the different trade-offs. While configuration Low is significantly faster by using a larger number of short solver queries, it results in timeouts more often and is able to narrow down the set of timed-out assertions less effectively. For verification conditions that still result in a timeout, configuration Low reports on average 0.15 % (at most 10 assertions) of all assertions in that method/function as responsible. For configuration High, these numbers are significantly lower (0.11 % on average, at most 4 assertions).

Independently, both configurations are able to prevent a large number of timeouts by decomposing the verification tasks (as shown by the first three rows in Table 2). For instance, with configuration High, the algorithm from Fig. 6 returns the result Verified or Error for 50 % of the timed-out verification conditions.

**Table 2.** Comparison between two configurations for diagnosing timeouts.

| | Time limit | |
|---|---|---|
| | Low | High |
| TimeOut (in %) | 57.89 | 50.00 |
| Error (in %) | 17.11 | 20.69 |
| Verified (in %) | 25.00 | 29.31 |
| Average number of solver queries | 65.67 | 51.00 |
| Average time (relative to time limit per method/function) | 6.24 | 9.25 |
| Average number of assertions to blame | 2.67 (0.15 %) | 1.84 (0.11 %) |

Therefore, for these verification conditions, none of the assertions required more time than the limit. This suggests that the user might be able to prevent the timeout by increasing the time limit for the corresponding method or function.

# 8  Related Work

**Verification IDEs.** Several verification tools are integrated into development environments and show verification errors either continuously or at the touch of a button, e.g., [3,13–15,20,26]. Our work goes beyond the integration of a single tool, instead providing in one package a collection of tools with complementary strengths.

The Isabelle environment for mathematical formulas integrates both interactive proof assistance and automatic counterexample search [5,42].

The Eiffel Verification Environment analyzes programs in two independent ways [39]. Essentially, one way strives to fully verify the program, whereas the other cuts corners in order to provide quick turnaround with understandable error messages. This two-step verification resembles the combination of two of our tools, the Dafny verifier and Delfy.

**Dynamic Symbolic Execution.** Dynamic symbolic execution has been implemented in many popular tools over the last decade, e.g., SAGE [25], EXE [9], jCUTE [34], Pex [38], KLEE [7], BitBlaze [37], and Apollo [2]. In contrast to these tools, Delfy targets a verification language for proving functional correctness of programs and, therefore, supports specification constructs and operations that are not found in mainstream programming languages.

Delfy implements dynamic, rather than static, symbolic execution for two important reasons. First, DSE can alleviate the limitations of an underlying SMT solver by replacing complex symbolic conditions in SMT queries with their concrete values [24]. Second, the dynamic aspect has applications beyond the scope of this paper, in particular for learning specifications [17,21,36].

**Exploring Counterexamples.** BVD [28] lets one inspect counterexamples to verification conditions generated by Boogie, VCC [13], and Dafny. Besides integrating BVD into the Dafny IDE, we provide easy access to excerpts from the counterexample through hover text. OpenJML [14] also provides such hover text, but not the full BVD experience.

An alternative to a dedicated counterexample debugger is to generate an executable program that encodes the verification semantics and the counterexample, for instance, by extracting a value for a non-deterministic choice from the counterexample [33]. This approach allows one to use a conventional debugger to explore the counterexamples.

Several tools generate executable tests from counterexamples [4,16]. In contrast, Delfy lets one explore the program independently of the verification semantics that is reflected in the counterexample.

**Timeouts.** Unlike Boogie's existing verification-condition splitting [30], our technique for diagnosing timeouts is not concerned with parallelizing verification tasks. Instead of iteratively creating smaller and smaller program fragments that are fed to the verifier, our technique generates a single verification condition once and uses the SMT solver to decompose it in case of a timeout. Besides this, our technique is able to identify all assertions that time out individually after a given time limit.

## 9    Concluding Remarks

In this paper, we have enhanced the IDE of the verification-aware language Dafny with a comprehensive set of problem-diagnosing tools, including a new timeout-diagnosis tool and the novel Delfy dynamic test generator. The seamless integration of these tools, alongside the on-demand information that the IDE now provides via hover text, lets a user obtain useful feedback when trying to understand and remedy verification failures. While in this work we have made the sophisticated diagnostic information easily accessible to users, we hope in future work to also see automatic suggestions of remedies.

**Acknowledgments.** We are grateful to Patrick Emmisberger and Patrick Spettel for their contributions to Delfy.

## References

1. Anand, S., Godefroid, P., Tillmann, N.: Demand-driven compositional symbolic execution. In: Ramakrishnan, C.R., Rehof, J. (eds.) TACAS 2008. LNCS, vol. 4963, pp. 367–381. Springer, Heidelberg (2008)
2. Artzi, S., Kiezun, A., Dolby, J., Tip, F., Dig, D., Paradkar, A.M., Ernst, M.D.: Finding bugs in web applications using dynamic test generation and explicit-state model checking. TSE **36**, 474–494 (2010)
3. Barnett, M., Fähndrich, M., Leino, K.R.M., Müller, P., Schulte, W., Venter, H.: Specification and verification: the Spec# experience. CACM **54**, 81–91 (2011)
4. Beyer, D., Chlipala, A.J., Majumdar, R.: Generating tests from counterexamples. In: ICSE, pp. 326–335. IEEE Computer Society (2004)
5. Blanchette, J.C., Nipkow, T.: Nitpick: a counterexample generator for higher-order logic based on a relational model finder. In: Kaufmann, M., Paulson, L.C. (eds.) ITP 2010. LNCS, vol. 6172, pp. 131–146. Springer, Heidelberg (2010)
6. Bormer, T., et al.: The COST IC0701 verification competition 2011. In: Damiani, F., Gurov, D., Beckert, B. (eds.) FoVeOOS 2011. LNCS, vol. 7421, pp. 3–21. Springer, Heidelberg (2011)
7. Cadar, C., Dunbar, D., Engler, D.R.: KLEE: unassisted and automatic generation of high-coverage tests for complex systems programs. In: OSDI, pp. 209–224. USENIX (2008)
8. Cadar, C., Engler, D.: Execution generated test cases: how to make systems code crash itself. In: Godefroid, P. (ed.) SPIN 2005. LNCS, vol. 3639, pp. 2–23. Springer, Heidelberg (2005)
9. Cadar, C., Ganesh, V., Pawlowski, P.M., Dill, D.L., Engler, D.R.: EXE: automatically generating inputs of death. In: CCS, pp. 322–335. ACM (2006)

10. Christakis, M.: Narrowing the Gap between Verification and Systematic Testing. Ph.D. thesis, ETH Zurich (2015)

11. Christakis, M., Godefroid, P.: Proving memory safety of the ANI Windows image parser using compositional exhaustive testing. In: D'Souza, D., Lal, A., Larsen, K.G. (eds.) VMCAI 2015. LNCS, vol. 8931, pp. 373–392. Springer, Heidelberg (2015)

12. Christakis, M., Müller, P., Wüstholz, V.: Collaborative verification and testing with explicit assumptions. In: Giannakopoulou, D., Méry, D. (eds.) FM 2012. LNCS, vol. 7436, pp. 132–146. Springer, Heidelberg (2012)

13. Cohen, E., Dahlweid, M., Hillebrand, M., Leinenbach, D., Moskal, M., Santen, T., Schulte, W., Tobies, S.: VCC: a practical system for verifying concurrent C. In: Berghofer, S., Nipkow, T., Urban, C., Wenzel, M. (eds.) TPHOLs 2009. LNCS, vol. 5674, pp. 23–42. Springer, Heidelberg (2009)

14. Cok, D.R.: OpenJML: software verification for Java 7 using JML, OpenJDK, and Eclipse. In: Formal-IDE. Electronic Proceedings in Theoretical Computer Science, vol. 149, pp. 79–92. Open Publishing Association (2014)

15. Correnson, L., Cuoq, P., Kirchner, F., Prevosto, V., Puccetti, A., Signoles, J., Yakobowski, B.: Frama-C User Manual (2011). http://frama-c.com//support.html

16. Csallner, C., Smaragdakis, Y.: Check 'n' Crash: combining static checking and testing. In: ICSE, pp. 422–431. ACM (2005)

17. Csallner, C., Tillmann, N., Smaragdakis, Y.: DySy: dynamic symbolic execution for invariant inference. In: ICSE, pp. 281–290. ACM (2008)

18. de Moura, L., Bjørner, N.S.: Z3: an efficient SMT solver. In: Ramakrishnan, C.R., Rehof, J. (eds.) TACAS 2008. LNCS, vol. 4963, pp. 337–340. Springer, Heidelberg (2008)

19. Detlefs, D., Nelson, G., Saxe, J.B.: Simplify: a theorem prover for program checking. J. ACM 52, 365–473 (2005)

20. Dross, C., Efstathopoulos, P., Lesens, D., Mentré, D., Moy, Y.: Rail, space, security: three case studies for SPARK 2014. In: ERTS (2014)

21. Ernst, M.D., Perkins, J.H., Guo, P.J., McCamant, S., Pacheco, C., Tschantz, M.S., Xiao, C.: The Daikon system for dynamic detection of likely invariants. Sci. Comput. Program. 69, 35–45 (2007)

22. Flanagan, C., Leino, K.R.M., Lillibridge, M., Nelson, G., Saxe, J.B., Stata, R.: Extended static checking for Java. In: PLDI, pp. 234–245. ACM (2002)

23. Godefroid, P.: Compositional dynamic test generation. In: POPL, pp. 47–54. ACM(2007)

24. Godefroid, P., Klarlund, N., Sen, K.: DART: directed automated random testing. In: PLDI, pp. 213–223. ACM (2005)

25. Godefroid, P., Levin, M.Y., Molnar, D.A.: Automated whitebox fuzz testing. In: NDSS, pp. 151–166. The Internet Society (2008)

26. Jacobs, B., Piessens, F.: The VeriFast program verifier. Technical report CW-520, Department of Computer Science, Katholieke Universiteit Leuven (2008)

27. Klebanov, V., et al.: The 1st verified software competition: experience report. In: Schulte, W., Butler, M. (eds.) FM 2011. LNCS, vol. 6664, pp. 154–168. Springer, Heidelberg (2011)

28. Le Goues, C., Leino, K.R.M., Moskal, M.: The Boogie verification debugger (tool paper). In: Barthe, G., Pardo, A., Schneider, G. (eds.) SEFM 2011. LNCS, vol. 7041, pp. 407–414. Springer, Heidelberg (2011)

29. Leino, K.R.M.: Dafny: an automatic program verifier for functional correctness. In: Clarke, E.M., Voronkov, A. (eds.) LPAR-16 2010. LNCS, vol. 6355, pp. 348–370. Springer, Heidelberg (2010)

30. Leino, K.R.M., Moskal, M., Schulte, W.: Verification condition splitting. Technical report, Microsoft Research (2008)
31. Leino, K.R.M., Wüstholz, V.: The Dafny integrated development environment. In: Formal-IDE. Electronic Proceedings in Theoretical Computer Science, vol. 149, pp. 3–15. Open Publishing Association (2014)
32. Leino, K.R.M., Wüstholz, V.: Fine-grained caching of verification results. In: Kroening, D., Păsăreanu, C.S. (eds.) CAV 2015. LNCS, vol. 9206, pp. 380–397. Springer, Heidelberg (2015)
33. Müller, P., Ruskiewicz, J.N.: Using debuggers to understand failed verification attempts. In: Schulte, W., Butler, M. (eds.) FM 2011. LNCS, vol. 6664, pp. 73–87. Springer, Heidelberg (2011)
34. Sen, K., Agha, G.: CUTE and jCUTE: concolic unit testing and explicit path model-checking tools. In: Ball, T., Jones, R.B. (eds.) CAV 2006. LNCS, vol. 4144, pp. 419–423. Springer, Heidelberg (2006)
35. Sen, K., Marinov, D., Agha, G.: CUTE: a concolic unit testing engine for C. In ESEC, pp. 263–272. ACM (2005)
36. Sharma, R., Gupta, S., Hariharan, B., Aiken, A., Liang, P., Nori, A.V.: A data driven approach for algebraic loop invariants. In: Felleisen, M., Gardner, P. (eds.) ESOP 2013. LNCS, vol. 7792, pp. 574–592. Springer, Heidelberg (2013)
37. Song, D., Brumley, D., Yin, H., Caballero, J., Jager, I., Kang, M.G., Liang, Z., Newsome, J., Poosankam, P., Saxena, P.: BitBlaze: a new approach to computer security via binary analysis. In: Sekar, R., Pujari, A.K. (eds.) ICISS 2008. LNCS, vol. 5352, pp. 1–25. Springer, Heidelberg (2008)
38. Tillmann, N., de Halleux, J.: Pex–white box test generation for .NET. In: Beckert, B., Hähnle, R. (eds.) TAP 2008. LNCS, vol. 4966, pp. 134–153. Springer, Heidelberg (2008)
39. Tschannen, J., Furia, C.A., Nordio, M., Meyer, B.: Program checking with less hassle. In: Cohen, E., Rybalchenko, A. (eds.) VSTTE 2013. LNCS, vol. 8164, pp. 149–169. Springer, Heidelberg (2014)
40. Tschannen, J., Furia, C.A., Nordio, M., Polikarpova, N.: AutoProof: auto-active functional verification of object-oriented programs. In: Baier, C., Tinelli, C. (eds.) TACAS 2015. LNCS, vol. 9035, pp. 566–580. Springer, Heidelberg (2015)
41. Weide, B.W., Sitaraman, M., Harton, H.K., Adcock, B., Bucci, P., Bronish, D., Heym, W.D., Kirschenbaum, J., Frazier, D.: Incremental benchmarks for software verification tools and techniques. In: Shankar, N., Woodcock, J. (eds.) VSTTE 2008. LNCS, vol. 5295, pp. 84–98. Springer, Heidelberg (2008)
42. Wenzel, M.: Isabelle/jEdit–a prover IDE within the PIDE framework. In: Jeuring, J., Campbell, J.A., Carette, J., Reis, G., Sojka, P., Wenzel, M., Sorge, V. (eds.) CICM 2012. LNCS, vol. 7362, pp. 468–471. Springer, Heidelberg (2012)

# JDart: A Dynamic Symbolic Analysis Framework

Kasper Luckow[1](✉), Marko Dimjašević[2], Dimitra Giannakopoulou[3],
Falk Howar[4], Malte Isberner[5], Temesghen Kahsai[1,3], Zvonimir Rakamarić[2],
and Vishwanath Raman[6]

[1] Carnegie Mellon University Silicon Valley, Mountain View, CA, USA
kasper.luckow@sv.cmu.edu
[2] School of Computing, University of Utah, Salt Lake City, UT, USA
[3] NASA Ames Research Center, Moffett Field, CA, USA
[4] IPSSE, TU Clausthal, Goslar, Germany
[5] TU Dortmund University, Dortmund, Germany
[6] StackRox Inc., Mountain View, CA, USA

**Abstract.** We describe JDart, a dynamic symbolic analysis framework for Java. A distinguishing feature of JDart is its modular architecture: the main component that performs dynamic exploration communicates with a component that efficiently constructs constraints and that interfaces with constraint solvers. These components can easily be extended or modified to support multiple constraint solvers or different exploration strategies. Moreover, JDart has been engineered for robustness, driven by the need to handle complex NASA software. These characteristics, together with its recent open sourcing, make JDart an ideal platform for research and experimentation. In the current release, JDart supports the CORAL, SMTInterpol, and Z3 solvers, and is able to handle NASA software with constraints containing bit operations, floating point arithmetic, and complex arithmetic operations (e.g., trigonometric and nonlinear). We illustrate how JDart has been used to support other analysis techniques, such as automated interface generation and testing of libraries. Finally, we demonstrate the versatility and effectiveness of JDart, and compare it with state-of-the-art dynamic or pure symbolic execution engines through an extensive experimental evaluation.

## 1   Introduction

JDart is a dynamic symbolic analysis framework for Java, under development at CMU and NASA Ames Research Center since 2010. Our main goal in developing JDart has been to build a dynamic symbolic analysis tool that can be applied to industrial scale software, including complex NASA systems. To reach this goal, we faced challenges that required a significant amount of design and engineering effort by several researchers over multiple years.

Supported in part by NASA Contr. NNX14AI09G and NSF CCF 1421678/1422705.

M. Chechik and J.-F. Raskin (Eds.): TACAS 2016, LNCS 9636, pp. 442–459, 2016.
DOI: 10.1007/978-3-662-49674-9_26

Our main design guideline has been to strive for a modular and extensible architecture. As such, our vision has been for JDART to be a platform for experimentation not only in symbolic analysis, but also in other areas of research that may use symbolic analysis as a component. JDART has now reached a level of robustness and efficiency that makes it ready for use by a wider community of researchers and practitioners. With the opportunity of JDART's recent open sourcing[1], this paper describes the characteristics of the tool that make it unique in its field. Moreover, it presents an extensive experimental evaluation of JDART, comparing it with state-of-the-art tools on a variety of benchmarks, in order to provide interested users with an understanding of its strengths and weaknesses relative to other similar frameworks.

As mentioned, the key distinguishing feature of JDART is its modular architecture. The two main components of JDART are the *Executor* and the *Explorer*. The *Executor* executes the analyzed program and records symbolic constraints on data values. It is currently realized as an extension to the Java PathFinder framework [19,35]. The *Explorer* determines the exploration strategy to be applied. It uses the constraints library JCONSTRAINTS (developed as part of the JDART project) as an abstraction layer for efficiently encoding symbolic path constraints and provides an interface for a variety of constraint solvers. JDART's current release supports the CORAL [31], SMTInterpol [4] and Z3 [22] solvers. Furthermore, JDART provides several useful extensions, such as method summarization and JUNIT test case generation, that leverage the results of dynamic symbolic analysis. Note that all these components of JDART can be configured, extended, or replaced.

In addition to being easily extensible and configurable, JDART can also be used as a symbolic execution component within other tools. In particular, we discuss two such uses of JDART: PSYCO [13,16] and JPF-DOOP [7]. The former is a tool that uses automata learning and dynamic symbolic execution to automatically generate extended interfaces for JAVA library components. The latter is a tool that combines random feedback-directed generation of method sequences with dynamic symbolic execution for automatic testing of JAVA libraries.

Among benchmarks that we use to showcase the capabilities of JDART, we emphasize a NASA case study that has been our main challenge and driver for its development over the years. JDART has been used to generate tests for the AUTORESOLVER system — a large and complex air-traffic control tool that predicts and resolves loss of separation for commercial aircraft [9,12]. Within this context, JDART has demonstrated the capability to handle programs with more than 20 KLOC containing bit operations, floating point and non-linear arithmetic operations (e.g., trigonometric), and native methods from java.lang.Math. For the benchmarks considered in our experimental evaluation, we also demonstrate that, from the set of available and maintained symbolic execution tools, JDART is the most stable and robust.

Note that a preliminary version of JDART was presented earlier in [6]. Since then, we have added support for additional constraint solvers and exploration

---

[1] JDART is available on GitHub: https://github.com/psycopaths/jdart.

```
public class Example {                  public static void main(String[] args) {
  private int x;                          Example e = new Example(100);
  public Example(int x) {                 System.out.println(e.test(0));
    this.x = x;                         }
  }
  public int test(int i) {
    if (i > x) assert false;
    int tmp = x;
    x += i;
    return tmp;
  }
}
```

**Fig. 1.** Simple JAVA software under test (SUT) example. Method `test()` compares parameter i to field x and can lead to an assertion failure.

strategies, which are included in the open source release and discussed in this paper. We have also conducted a thorough evaluation of JDART on multiple benchmarks and compared it to state-of-the art tools.

**Synopsis.** The rest of the paper is organized as follows. Section 2 introduces dynamic symbolic execution. Section 3 describes the architecture of JDART and its usage in other analysis techniques. Section 4 discusses features of JDART and related tools. Section 5 gives an extensive experimental evaluation with benchmarks that include NASA examples. Our conclusions are discussed in Sect. 6.

## 2  Dynamic Symbolic Execution

Dynamic symbolic analysis is a program analysis technique that executes programs with *concrete* and *symbolic* inputs at the same time. It maintains a *path constraint*, i.e., a conjunction of symbolic expressions over the inputs that is updated whenever a branch instruction is executed, to encode the constraints on the inputs that reach that program point. Combined execution paths form a *constraints tree*, which is continually augmented by trying to exercise paths to unexplored branches. Concrete data values for exercising these paths are generated by a constraint solver. We explain how this works in JDART using the example shown in Fig. 1.

Dynamic symbolic execution treats some (or all) parameters of an analyzed method symbolically. This means that their values, as well as all decisions involving them, are recorded during execution. In the example of Fig. 1, parameter i is treated as a symbolic value. For the initial concrete execution of the analyzed method `test()`, JDART uses the value found on the stack, which is 0. Instance fields are not treated symbolically in the default configuration of JDART.

Executing the method with a value of 0 for i does not trigger the assertion failure because i <= 100. Since i is symbolic, we still record this check, and add it to the constraints tree. The resulting partial constraints tree is shown in

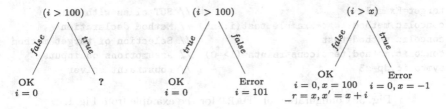

**Fig. 2.** Different constraints trees for the example in Fig. 1. Leafs show program states as well as the pre- and post-conditions of paths.

Fig. 2 (left): the *false* branch of the condition $i > 100$ (note that $x$ is not being treated symbolically) contains the result "OK", and a valuation of the symbolic variables that allows exercising the corresponding path (in this case the initial configuration, $i = 0$).

However, the constraints tree also contains an unexplored branch, namely the *true* branch. Dynamic symbolic execution now attempts to exercise this branch, by generating a valuation satisfying the *path constraint* $i > 100$, usually using an SMT solver. SMT solvers provide decision procedures for first-order logical formulas of predicates from different theories (e.g., integer numbers, bit vectors or arrays). Given a set of constraints, the solver will generate a satisfying assignment that makes the constraint satisfiable. In our example it could generate the assignment $i = 101$. The program is now rewound to the state where the analyzed method `test()` was entered. As parameter `i` is treated symbolically, the corresponding stack contents are now changed to the value 101, and the method is executed again. This time, the assertion failure is triggered. JDART augments the constraints tree by recording the outcome "Error" along with the corresponding valuation $i = 101$ (Fig. 2 (middle)). As the constraints tree now no longer contains any nodes labeled by "?", dynamic symbolic execution terminates.

By default, JDART treats only parameters symbolically. However, the symbolic treatment can be extended to *instance fields* (e.g., `this.x`) and *return values* as well. For example, Fig. 2 (right) shows the resulting constraints tree for symbolic values of `i` and `this.x`. The return value $\_r$ as well as the post-condition (the state of the instance after execution of the method) are given as symbolic expressions over $i$ and $x$.

## 3   JDART

The development of JDART has been driven by two main goals. The primary goal has been to build a symbolic analysis framework that is robust enough to handle industrial scale software. More precisely, it has to be able to execute industrial software without crashing, deal with long execution paths and complex path constraints. The second objective has been to build a modular and extensible platform that can be used for the implementation and evaluation of novel ideas in dynamic symbolic execution. For example, JDART is designed to allow for

```
target=Example                           // SUT class with main
concolic.method.test=Example.test(i:int) // Method declaration
concolic.method=test                     // Selection of target method
concolic.method.test.constraints=(i>=0)  // Assumptions on inputs
symbolic.dp=z3                           // constraint solver
```

**Fig. 3.** Configuration of JDART for the example from Fig. 1.

easy replacement of all of its components: it supports different and combined constraint solvers, and several exploration strategies and termination criteria.

This section presents the modular architecture of JDART, and discusses its main components and extension points. It subsequently describes existing uses of JDART as a component within other research tools.

### 3.1   Architecture

JDART executes JAVA Bytecode programs and performs a dynamic symbolic analysis of specific methods in these programs. JDART also implements extensions that build upon the results of a dynamic symbolic analysis:

- The *Method Summarizer* generates fully abstract method summaries for analyzed methods [16]. In the generated summaries, class members, input parameters, and return values are represented symbolically.
- The *Test Suite Generator* generates JUNIT test suites that exercise all the program paths found by JDART.

Figure 3 illustrates a basic configuration of JDART (no extensions included) for the example of Fig. 1. The configuration sets the system under test to class Example, and specifies method test(i:int) of the same class as the target of the analysis. The last two lines tell JDART to explore the target method only for parameter values $i >= 0$ and to use Z3 for solving constraints.

During dynamic symbolic analysis, JDART uses two main components to iteratively execute the target method, to record and explore symbolic constraints, and to find new concrete data values for new executions: Fig. 4 depicts the modular architecture of JDART. The basis (at the bottom) is the *Executor* that executes the analyzed program and records symbolic constraints on data values. The *Explorer* organizes recorded path constraints into a constraints tree, and decides which paths to explore next, and when to stop exploration. The Explorer uses the JCONSTRAINTS library to integrate different constraint solvers that can be used in finding concrete data values for symbolic paths constraints.

### 3.2   Executor

The Executor runs a target program and executes an analyzed method with different concrete data values for method parameters and class members. It also

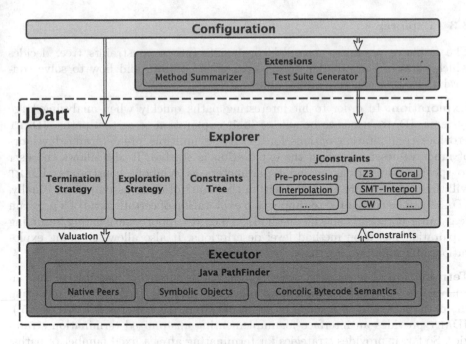

**Fig. 4.** Architecture of JDART.

records symbolic constraints for program paths. Currently, JDART uses the software model checker Java PathFinder (JPF) for the execution of JAVA Bytecode programs. JDART uses two extension points of JPF.

**Setting Concrete Values.** JPF uses "choice generators" to mark points in an execution to which JPF back tracks during state-space exploration. JDART implements a choice generator that sets parameter values of methods that are analyzed symbolically.

**Recording Symbolic Constraints.** JPF extensions can provide custom byte-code implementations. JDART adds concolic semantics to the JAVA Bytecodes that perform concrete and symbolic operations simultaneously, while also recording path constraints. Using JPF as an execution platform has several benefits. For example, is easy to integrate other JPF extensions in JDART (e.g., for dealing with native code, or for recording test coverage). Moreover, JPF provides easy access to all objects on the heap and stack, as well as to many other elements and facilities of the JVM such as stack frames and class loading. On the other hand, using a full-blown custom JVM for execution has an impact on performance. This is one of the reasons why we are keeping the integration with JPF as loose as possible. JDART has been built with the possibility of changing the underlying execution environment from JPF to more light-weight instrumentation, as is the case with other similar frameworks, such as PEX [34] or JCUTE [27].

## 3.3   Explorer

The Explorer organizes recorded constraints into a constraints tree, decides which parts of the program to explore, when to stop, and how to solve constraints for new concrete input values.

**Exploration.** In order to hit interesting paths quickly when analyzing large systems, JDART needs to be able to limit exploration to certain paths. JDART provides configuration options for specifying multiple pre-determined vectors of input values from which the exploration is started. It also allows the user to specify assumptions on input parameters as symbolic constraints. JDART will then only explore a method within the limits of those assumptions. Finally, JDART can be configured to simply skip exploration of certain parts of a program (e.g., after entering a specific method) — i.e., it supports suspending/resuming exploration based on method level descriptions. It also allows skipping exploration after a certain depth.

**Termination.** For industry-scale systems, it is often not possible to run an analysis to completion. Sometimes one may even be interested in recording the path constraint of a single program path (cf., e.g., Microsoft's SAGE [15]). JDART provides an interface for implementing customized termination strategies. So far, it provides strategies for terminating after a fixed number of paths, or for terminating after a fixed amount of time.

**Constraint Solvers.** In real world systems, path constraints can be long and complex and may contain trigonometric or elementary functions, which may challenge any state-of-the-art constraint solver. JDART provides several techniques and extension points for optimizing constraints, e.g., by simplifying path constraints, adding auxiliary definitions and/or interpolation that help solving complex constraints, and using specialized solvers. These capabilities are based on the constraints processing features of JCONSTRAINTS. For example, trigonometric constraints can be approximated by interpolation before being submitted to a solver (e.g., Z3), or they can be delegated directly to a solver that supports them (e.g., CORAL). Floating-point constraints can also be processed before submitting them to a solver. For the Z3 integration, floating-point constraints are approximated using reals. Despite this not being sound (due to the limited-precision effects), it might frequently yield valuable solutions even when they are *incorrect* — in general, JDART always analyzes the solutions and tests whether they can be used to exercise previously unexplored paths.

**Constraints Tree.** Finally, it is important to guarantee that progress is made when only approximating JAVA semantics in solvers. Sometimes a solution suggested by a solver may not be valid for a JAVA Bytecode program. JDART tests all valuations produced by a decision procedure on the constraints tree by evaluating path constraints with JAVA semantics before re-executing the program with a new valuation (this is a feature provided by JCONSTRAINTS, as explained later in this section).

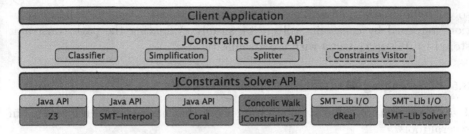

**Fig. 5.** The JCONSTRAINTS architecture.

**Potential Extensions.** In extending the explorer, we are considering to implement concolic heuristics for dealing with complex constraints, and to use coverage metrics (e.g., branch coverage or MC/DC) to prioritize exploration of decisions that may increase the selected coverage. Using JPF, in the future it will also be possible to add support for concurrent programs.

### 3.4   JConstraints

JCONSTRAINTS is a constraint solver abstraction layer for JAVA. It provides an object representation for logic expressions, unified access to different SMT and interpolation solvers, and useful tools and algorithms for working with constraints. While JCONSTRAINTS was developed for JDART, it is maintained as a stand-alone library that can be used independently. The idea has been explored by others, e.g., PYSMT [11], which has recently been developed for Python.

The architecture of JCONSTRAINTS is shown in Fig. 5: It consists of the basic library providing the object representation of logic and arithmetic expressions, the API definitions for solvers (for SMT solving and interpolation, or for incremental solving), and some basic utilities for working with expression objects (basic simplification, term replacement, and term evaluation). Plugins for connecting to different constraint solvers can be added easily by implementing a solver interface and taking care of translating between a solver-specific API and the object representation of JCONSTRAINTS.

Currently, plugins exist for connecting to the SMT solver Z3 [22], the interpolation solver SMTInterpol [4], the meta-heuristic based constraint solver CORAL [31], and a solver that implements the Concolic Walk algorithm [8]. JCONSTRAINTS uses the native interfaces for these solvers as they are much faster than file-based integration. It can also parse and export constraints in its own format and supports a subset of the SMT-LIB format [29] which enables connection to many constraint solvers that support this format. For example, through the SMT-LIB format, we were able to experiment with using the dReal solver [10] for non-linear constraints in JDART.

JCONSTRAINTS supports both JAVA and user-defined types for expressions. This enables it to record path constraints directly in terms of the analyzed program types and semantics, as opposed to the types supported by the constraint solver to be used. An advantage of this feature is that it is easy to validate solutions returned by constraint solvers by simply evaluating the path constraint stored by JCONSTRAINTS with JAVA semantics.

### 3.5 Leveraging JDART

JDART is a mature and easy to use framework that has so far been leveraged in several tools.

**Automatic Testing of Libraries.** Previous work on Randoop [23] has shown that software libraries can often be effectively explored using *feedback-directed random testing*, which generates test cases in the form of reasonable sequences of public method invocations. However, while Randoop excels at generating method sequences, its heuristic for selecting inputs for arguments of primitive data types is simplistic — these inputs are selected from a small pool of mostly randomly chosen values. This heuristic is often inadequate for reaching deep into the code of methods with many conditionals over primitive types such as integers. On the other hand, JDART's capabilities are orthogonal: it cannot generate sequences of method invocations, but it can explore deep code paths by leveraging the power of SMT solving. Hence, we implemented JPF-DOOP to combine the two approaches [7].

JPF-DOOP leverages Randoop to generate a collection of method sequences. Next, JPF-DOOP converts all primitive-type input parameters into symbolic inputs in every generated method sequence. This in turn enables JDART to be executed on such method sequences, and its dynamic symbolic execution algorithm reaches deep paths within each method in a sequence. As a result, more paths, and consequently branches and lines of code, are often explored by JPF-DOOP than by using the two tools in isolation [7].

**Generating Interfaces of Software Components.** Performing compositional software verification is key to achieving scalability to large systems. Generating interfaces for software components is an important sub-task of compositional software verification. In our previous work [13,16], we introduced an algorithm (implemented in a tool called PSYCO) for automatic generation of precise temporal interfaces of software components that include methods with parameters. PSYCO generates interfaces in the form of finite-state automata, where transitions are labeled by method names as well as guarded by symbolic constraints over their parameters. It relies on JDART's capability for computing method summaries for the public methods of the analyzed component.

## 4     JDART and Related Frameworks

Dynamic symbolic execution [14,28] is a well-known technique implemented by many automatic testing tools (e.g., [3,15,27,34]). For example, SAGE [15] is a white-box fuzzer based on dynamic symbolic execution. SAGE has been routinely

**Table 1.** Comparing the features of JDART to other symbolic analysis tools.

| Tool | Basic Technology | Primitive | Arrays | Fields | Objects | Shape | Concurrency | Retains SUT | Parallel | Native Code | Long Paths | Replay | Summaries | Test Suites[5] | String | Non-linear | Trig./Elem. |
|---|---|---|---|---|---|---|---|---|---|---|---|---|---|---|---|---|---|
| | | \multicolumn{6}{Symbolic Exploration of} | | | | | | \multicolumn{7}{Practicality} | | | | | | | \multicolumn{3}{Solvers} | | |
| JDART | Custom VM | ✓ | (✓)² | ✓ | ✓ | | | ✓ | | ✓ | ✓ | ✓ | ✓ | ✓ | ✓ | ✓ | |
| SPF | | ✓ | (✓)² | ✓ | ✓ | ✓ | ✓ | ✓ | | ✓ | ✓ | | ✓ | ✓ | ✓ | ✓ | ✓ |
| jFuzz † | | ✓ | (✓)²³ | ✓ | | | | ✓ | | ✓ | ✓ | | | ✓ | ✓ | ✓ | |
| JCute † | Code Instr. | (✓)¹ | (✓)² | | (✓)⁴ | ✓ | ✓ | | | | ✓ | ✓ | | ✓ | ✓ | | |
| CATG | | (✓)¹ | (✓)² | | (✓)⁴ | | | | | | ✓ | | | ✓ | ✓ | ✓ | |
| LCT | | (✓)¹ | (✓)² | | (✓)⁴ | ✓ | | | | ✓ | ✓ | | | ✓ | | | |

¹ No float and double.  ² Only fixed size.
³ Only char[].  ⁴ Symbolic inputs are injected by modifying SUT.
⁵ Only for sequential programs.  † No longer maintained.

applied to large Microsoft systems, such as media players and image processors, where it has been successful in finding critical security bugs.

Several symbolic execution tools specifically target JAVA Bytecode programs. A number of them implement dynamic symbolic execution via JAVA Bytecode instrumentation. JCUTE [27], the first concolic execution engine for JAVA, uses Soot [30] for instrumentation, and uses lp_solve as a constraint solver. JCUTE is no longer maintained. CATG [33] uses ASM [1] for instrumentation, and CVC4 [5] as a constraint solver. Another concolic engine, LCT [20], additionally supports distributed exploration. It uses Boolector and Yices for solving, but does not currently have support for float and double primitive types.

A drawback of instrumentation-based tools is that instrumentation at the time of class loading is confined to the SUT. LCT for example does not by default instrument the standard JAVA libraries thus limiting concolic execution to the application classes. However, the instrumentation-based tools discussed above provide the possibility of using symbolic (and/or simplified) models for non-instrumented classes or using pre-instrumented core JAVA classes.

Several dynamic symbolic execution tools for JAVA are not based on instrumentation. For example, the concolic white-box fuzzer jFuzz [18] is based on Java PathFinder (as is JDART) and can thus explore core JAVA classes without any extra prerequisites. Finally, Symbolic PathFinder [25] is a Java PathFinder extension similar to JDART. In fact, jFuzz reuses some of the core components of (albeit an older version of) SPF, notably the solver interface, and its implementations. While at its core SPF implements symbolic execution, it can also switch to concrete values in the spirit of concolic execution [24]. That enables it to deal with limitations of constraint solvers (e.g., non-linear constraints).

Table 1 summarizes the main features of the tools discussed in this section. Note that we only consider the features that are available in the official released versions of the tools. For example, parallelizing SPF has been done [32] and recently method summarization has been added too [26]. However, those features are not a part of the official release. It can be seen that JDART supports a large number of features that are desirable in symbolic execution engines to accommodate analysis of industrial scale systems. On the other hand, JDART does not currently support programs with concurrency in contrast to SPF and JCUTE. Also, JDART does not feature a mechanism for dealing with unbounded symbolic input data structures such as lists and trees. SPF supports this through its lazy initialization mechanism [21]. Finally, JDART does not currently support a parallel exploration of the constraints tree. However, JDART's architecture provides a solid basis for future extensions towards supporting such features. In particular, some of the distinctive features of SPF are relatively easy to port to JDART given the common foundation of the two tools on JPF. In general, we expect that open sourcing will expedite extensions of JDART in new directions.

## 5    Experimental Evaluation

We base our evaluation of JDART on a comparison with SPF, CATG, LCT, and random testing. For all experiments, we used a laptop with a 2.0 GHz Intel Core i7 and 8 GB RAM running Ubuntu Linux. Random testing provides a baseline, while the other tools are representative of the state-of-the-art in symbolic analysis of JAVA Bytecode. We were not able to properly set up JCUTE and JFUZZ. We note that they are no longer actively maintained. Our evaluation is performed on the following benchmarks:

**AutoResolver** is a sophisticated automated air-traffic conflict resolution system developed at the NASA Ames Research Center. It is envisioned to be part of the Next Generation Air Transportation System (NextGen). It features complex constraints arising, among others, from spherical geometry and great circle distance computations. We focus JDART on a single conflict scenario, using the test driver developed in previous work [12] that exposes a double-precision floating-point type controlling the heading difference between two aircraft at a collision point. Note that our coverage metrics take into account the entire AUTORESOLVER code base consisting of approximately 20 KLOC of JAVA code.

**MER Arbiter** is derived from a flight component for the Mars Exploration Rover developed at NASA JPL. The arbiter module is based on a Simulink/Stateflow model translated into JAVA using the Polyglot framework [2].

**TSAFE** is a flight-critical system that seeks to provide separation assurance for multiple aircraft. It features complex, nonlinear floating-point arithmetic and constraints with transcendental functions.

**TCAS** is a component of a traffic collision avoidance system installed in aircraft; its operation is controlled by 12 inputs.

**Raytracer** is a component for rendering shades on surfaces. It performs a number of calculations on 3D vectors taking into account light and color objects.

**WBS** has 18 integer and boolean inputs controlling the update operation in a wheel brake system.

**Minepump** is a classic real-time system that performs monitoring and controlling of the fluid level and methane concentration in a mine shaft.

We use the following metrics: (i) analysis time; (ii) the quality of the symbolic exploration of a benchmark in terms of multiple coverage criteria, such as general coverage metrics (branch, instruction, line, method) and *behavioral coverage*, i.e. the absolute number of paths exercised; (iii) the *quality* of the test suite produced by the tools, i.e., the ratio of paths exercised while running the suite to the number of tests. Table 2 gives our experimental results.

**Table 2.** Experimental results. Numbers in bold font denote the total number of units (e.g., instructions or branches) for the respective benchmark. "-" represents when values do not apply, e.g., when an example is not supported by a tool.

| Example | Tool | Solver | Run time [s] | Memory [MB] | Branch Cov. [%] | Instr. Cov. [%] | Line Cov. [%] | Method Cov. [%] | #Tests | #Sat. Paths | #OK | #Err. | #D/K |
|---|---|---|---|---|---|---|---|---|---|---|---|---|---|
| AutoResolver | **Totals** | | | | **10,896** | **96,304** | **19,695** | **1,941** | | **229**§ | | | |
| | JDart | Z3 | 80 | 1,483 | 15 | 24 | 27 | 35 | 3 | 3 | 3 | 0 | 6,898 |
| | SPF * | CORAL | 2 | 215 | 0 | 0 | 0 | 0 | 0 | 0 | 0 | 0 | 0 |
| | CATG † | CVC4 | - | - | - | - | - | - | - | - | - | - | - |
| | LCT † | Boolector | - | - | - | - | - | - | - | - | - | - | - |
| | Random | - | 80 | - | 16 | 24 | 27 | 35 | 1,969 | 229 | 229 | 0 | 214,982 |
| MER | **Totals** | | | | **576** | **11,047** | **2,234** | **635** | | **1,248** | | | |
| | JDart | Z3 | 69 | 340 | 50 | 81 | 79 | 77 | 1,248 | 1,248 | 1,248 | 0 | 0 |
| | SPF | Z3 | 90 | 761 | 50 | 81 | 79 | 77 | 1,248 | 1,248 | 1,248 | 0 | 0 |
| | CATG | CVC4 | crash | - | - | - | - | - | - | - | - | - | - |
| | LCT | Boolector | 2,839 | 51 | 50 | 81 | 79 | 68 | 1,256 | 1,248 | 1,248 | 0 | 0 |
| | Random | - | 69 | - | 38 | 71 | 72 | 62 | 8,259 | 81 | 81 | 0 | 231 |
| TSAFE | **Totals** | | | | **20** | **137** | **26** | **4** | | **21**§ | | | |
| | JDart | CORAL | 3 | 415 | 90 | 89 | 96 | 75 | 21 | 21 | 21 | 0 | 26 |
| | SPF | CORAL | 23 | 727 | 90 | 89 | 96 | 75 | 58 | 21 | 21 | 0 | 26 |
| | CATG † | CVC4 | - | - | - | - | - | - | - | - | - | - | - |
| | LCT† | Boolector | - | - | - | - | - | - | - | - | - | - | - |
| | Random | - | 3 | - | 70 | 85 | 92 | 75 | 54,318 | 9 | 9 | 0 | 13 |
| TCAS | **Totals** | | | | **74** | **216** | **48** | **9** | | **68** | | | |
| | JDart | Z3 | <1 | 119 | 93 | 96 | 96 | 89 | 68 | 68 | 68 | 0 | 0 |
| | SPF | Z3 | 5 | 118 | 61 | 72 | 92 | 78 | 68 | 36 | 36 | 0 | 80 |
| | CATG | CVC4 | 33 | 88 | 93 | 96 | 96 | 89 | 68 | 68 | 68 | 0 | 0 |
| | LCT | Boolector | 32 | 77 | 93 | 96 | 96 | 89 | 68 | 68 | 68 | 0 | 0 |
| | Random | - | 1 | - | 5 | 19 | 29 | 22 | 19,067 | 1 | 1 | 0 | 3 |
| Raytracer | **Totals** | | | | **44** | **798** | **119** | **18** | | **83**§ | | | |
| | JDart | CORAL | 51 | 414 | 86 | 94 | 92 | 94 | 80 | 80 | 80 | 0 | 64 |
| | SPF ‡ | CORAL | 1,524 | 350 | 82 | 94 | 92 | 94 | 548 | 83 | 83 | 0 | 158 |
| | CATG † | CVC4 | - | - | - | - | - | - | - | - | - | - | - |
| | LCT † | Boolector | - | - | - | - | - | - | - | - | - | - | - |
| | Random | - | 51 | - | 68 | 79 | 81 | 89 | 186,953 | 80 | 80 | 0 | 26 |
| WBS | **Totals** | | | | **90** | **356** | **149** | **3** | | **24** | | | |
| | JDart | Z3 | <1 | 119 | 67 | 77 | 76 | 67 | 24 | 24 | 24 | 0 | 0 |
| | SPF | Z3 | 1 | 118 | 67 | 77 | 76 | 67 | 24 | 24 | 24 | 0 | 0 |
| | CATG | CVC4 | 8 | 62 | 67 | 77 | 76 | 67 | 24 | 24 | 24 | 0 | 0 |
| | LCT | Boolector | 6 | 68 | 67 | 77 | 76 | 67 | 24 | 24 | 24 | 0 | 0 |
| | Random | - | 1 | - | 39 | 50 | 50 | 67 | 190,715 | 5 | 5 | 0 | 6 |
| Minepump | **Totals** | | | | **100** | **552** | **139** | **43** | | **1,200** | | | |
| | JDart | Z3 | 2 | 150 | 52 | 68 | 79 | 74 | 1,200 | 1,200 | 952 | 248 | 0 |
| | SPF | Z3 | 48 | 212 | 52 | 682 | 79 | 74 | 1,200 | 1,200 | 952 | 248 | 0 |
| | CATG | CVC4 | 420 | 64 | 52 | 68 | 79 | 74 | 1,200 | 1,200 | 952 | 248 | 0 |
| | LCT | Boolector | 522 | 83 | 52 | 68 | 79 | 74 | 1,729 | 1,200 | 952 | 248 | 0 |
| | Random | - | 2 | - | 52 | 68 | 79 | 74 | 39,966 | 1,200 | 952 | 248 | 0 |

*SPF with Z3 crashes. CORAL does not handle constraints with DOUBLE.ISNAN(DOUBLE), thus ignoring them.

†Does not support constraints with floating points.

‡With PSO heuristic (used with JDart), SPF does not finish <1h. Instead, the AVM heuristic is used.

§Max # of sat paths explored by any tool. The total # of sat paths might be higher due to *Don't know* paths.

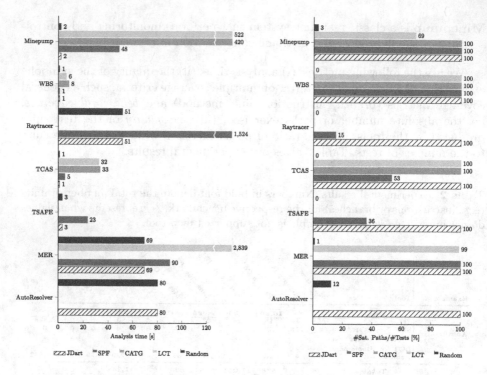

**Fig. 6.** Analysis time.                    **Fig. 7.** Test suite quality.

**Evaluation of Symbolic Analysis Tools.** With a time cap of 1 h, we monitor
the analysis time and peak memory consumption for each tool to terminate and
return input valuations. For a consistent comparison, we measure coverage of
the valuations, as opposed to using output statistics of the tools. For each tool,
we construct a JUnit test suite based on the valuations, which is then analyzed
by the JaCoCo [17] coverage measuring library. JaCoCo generates a detailed
report containing branch, instruction, line, and method coverage. Behavioral
coverage is not reported by standard code coverage libraries, so we measure
it by replaying valuations with JDart, where JDart is run without a solver.
JDART tracks the number of *unique satisfiable paths* that are exercised, as well
as whether a path yields normal termination (*OK*) or an error state (*Error*) —
assertion violation or uncaught exception. We chose to use dynamic symbolic
analysis for this purpose, because it additionally checks for validity of the valuations; as seen in the TCAS example results for SPF, 68 valuations are produced,
but only 36 of them are valid and contribute to path coverage.

We also keep track of the number of *potentially* unexplored subtrees/decisions
(*D/K*, short for *Don't Know*); *D/K*s represent decisions in the constraints tree
that are not covered by the test suite. For symbolic analysis tools, when they
terminate, it means that the used solver was *inconclusive* as to the satisfiability of
these decisions. Such situations arise due to, e.g., insufficient solver capabilities,

constraints that are computationally intractable, or constraints from undecidable theories (containing non-linear or transcendental functions).

For JDART, we select the solver and configuration that yields the best test suite defined in terms of the above coverage metrics. Unless we found a better configuration for SPF, the same configuration is used for SPF. Other tools do not expose such rich set of configuration parameters or solver options.

**Evaluation of Random Testing.** For random test case generators, we set time out to match the analysis time of JDART. Input values are randomly selected from a uniform distribution from the value range of a particular parameter's data type. Note that our implementation of random testing is rather simplistic: constraining the input ranges according to domain knowledge and picking values from non-uniform distributions (e.g., from a known "usage profile") would likely increase its applicability.

**Observation 1: Analysis Time and Path Coverage.** JDART outperforms SPF, CATG, and LCT on all benchmarks in terms of analysis time — often by an order of magnitude (see Fig. 6). Furthermore, with path coverage being the primary metric for comparison, JDART provides at least as good results as the other tools, except for the Raytracer benchmark (where SPF performed slightly better) and the AUTORESOLVER benchmark (where Random Testing performed better). Figure 9 summarizes these results. For Raytracer, SPF found three more *OK* paths. In this particular case, however, SPF was run with a slightly different configuration of CORAL that uses the Alternating Variable Method (AVM) meta-heuristic — JDART uses the Particle Swarm Optimization (PSO) meta-heuristic. If SPF is run with PSO, it does not terminate within 1 h. On the other hand, if JDART is run with AVM, it performs worse than with PSO and covers only 38 distinct paths. As a side note, the longer analysis times of SPF might be attributed to the significant number of $D/K$ paths.

**Observation 2: Random Test Case Generation.** Our experimental results demonstrate that random test case generation performs poorly on the benchmark suite. In particular, in WBS it covers only 5 different paths with a test suite containing 190,715 test cases. For AUTORESOLVER, random testing slightly outperforms JDART in terms of branch coverage (1 % point difference) at the expense of having to run 1,969 test cases (taking 80 s). In contrast, the test suite produced by JDART contains only 3 test cases (taking less than a second to run). Note that the coverage results for AUTORESOLVER are so low because large submodules are not reachable from the entry point that only deals with a single conflict scenario.

**Observation 3: Performance of Instrumentation-Based Tools.** CATG obtains similar coverage results as JDART on the benchmarks it supports, but is several orders of magnitudes slower. This might be attributed to the concolic execution approach implemented in CATG, which (similar to JCUTE) allocates a process for each execution — CATG reruns the instrumented program for each explored path. JDART, on the other hand, harnesses the JPF infrastructure and perturbation facility to efficiently restore program states and generate new

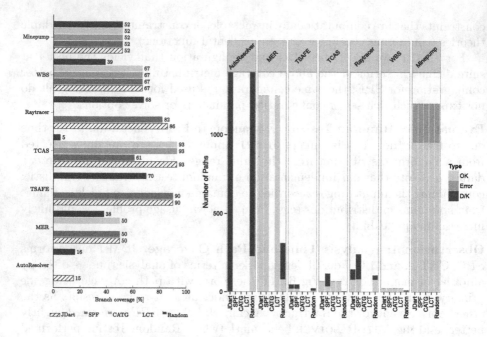

**Fig. 8.** Branch coverage.  **Fig. 9.** Path coverage. JDART and random testing on AUTORESOLVER have 6,898 and 214,982 *Don't Know* paths, respectively.

paths. LCT is also comparable to JDART on benchmarks that do not require symbolic floating-point reasoning, but like CATG it is much slower. Note that LCT supports parallel exploration that was not used in our experiments, which is a feature currently not supported in JDART.

All instrumentation-based tools employ a pre-processing step where a benchmark (and classes potentially referenced by it) need to be instrumented before the actual analysis can be performed. Our measured analysis times do not account for this step, which is often significant. For example, the instrumentation of MER with LCT takes 13 s. JDART avoids this by leveraging the JPF infrastructure to define a custom interpreter where the standard JAVA Bytecode semantics are replaced with concolic semantics.

**Observation 4: Test Suite Quality and Branch Coverage.** Figure 7 presents the quality metric for the generated test suites. Random testing, due to a very large number of generated test cases, has very low quality, often almost 0 %. On the other hand, all the dynamic symbolic execution tools typically generate minimal test suites, i.e., those with 100 % quality. SPF produces sub-optimal test suites in three cases, with as low as 15 % quality for Raytracer. We were not able to find the reason for this unexpected behavior.

We give the usual branch coverage metric in Fig. 8. No tool reaches full branch coverage on the analyzed benchmarks, which is due to infeasible paths, exemplified by TCAS where JDART achieves full path coverage (i.e., #D/K is 0).

In other words, JDART explores all possible behaviors of TCAS, and therefore 93 % is the highest possible branch coverage, thus indicating the presence of code that cannot be reached from the entry point, i.e. dead code.

# 6 Conclusions

We presented JDART, a dynamic symbolic analysis framework for JAVA Bytecode programs. We provided a detailed description of its architecture and features, as well as an experimental evaluation of the tool in comparison to other similar frameworks. After several years of development, JDART has reached a level of efficiency, robustness, and versatility that lead to its recent open sourcing by the NASA Ames Research Center. This paper is therefore meant as an introduction of the tool to the research community. We hope that the tool's current capabilities and its existing use cases within other frameworks will inspire the community to experiment and extend it in novel ways.

# References

1. ASM: A Java bytecode engineering library. http://asm.ow2.org
2. Balasubramanian, D., Păsăreanu, C.S., Whalen, M.W., Karsai, G., Lowry, M.: Polyglot: modeling and analysis for multiple statechart formalisms. In: Proceedings of the International Symposium on Software Testing and Analysis (ISSTA), pp. 45–55 (2011)
3. Cadar, C., Dunbar, D., Engler, D.: KLEE: unassisted and automatic generation of high-coverage tests for complex systems programs. In: Proceedings of the 5th USENIX Symposium on Operating Systems Design and Implementation (OSDI), pp. 209–224 (2008)
4. Christ, J., Hoenicke, J., Nutz, A.: SMTInterpol: an interpolating SMT solver. In: Donaldson, A., Parker, D. (eds.) SPIN 2012. LNCS, vol. 7385, pp. 248–254. Springer, Heidelberg (2012)
5. Deters, M., Reynolds, A., King, T., Barrett, C.W., Tinelli, C.: A tour of CVC4: how it works, and how to use it. In: Proceedings of the 14th Conference on Formal Methods in Computer-Aided Design (FMCAD), p. 7 (2014)
6. Dimjašević, M., Giannakopoulou, D., Howar, F., Isberner, M., Rakamarić, Z., Raman, V.: The dart, the psyco, and the doop: concolic execution in java pathfinder and its applications. ACM SIGSOFT Softw. Eng. Notes 40(1), 1–5 (2015). Proceedings of the 2014 Java Pathfinder Workshop (JPF)
7. Dimjašević, M., Rakamarić, Z.: JPF-Doop: combining concolic and random testing for java. In: Java Pathfinder Workshop (JPF) (2013) (Extended abstract)
8. Dinges, P., Agha, G.: Solving complex path conditions through heuristic search on induced polytopes. In: Proceedings of the 22nd ACM SIGSOFT International Symposium on Foundations of Software Engineering (FSE), pp. 425–436 (2014)
9. Erzberger, H., Lauderdale, T.A., Chu, Y.C.: Automated conflict resolution, arrival management and weather avoidance for ATM. In: International Congress of the Aeronautical Sciences (2010)
10. Gao, S., Kong, S., Clarke, E.M.: dReal: an SMT solver for nonlinear theories over the reals. In: Bonacina, M.P. (ed.) CADE 2013. LNCS, vol. 7898, pp. 208–214. Springer, Heidelberg (2013)

11. Gario, M., Micheli, A.: pysmt: a solver-agnostic library for fast prototyping of SMT-based algorithms. In: Proceedings of the 13th International Workshop on Satisfiability Modulo Theories (SMT) (2015)

12. Giannakopoulou, D., Howar, F., Isberner, M., Lauderdale, T., Rakamarić, Z., Raman, V.: Taming test inputs for separation assurance. In: Proceedings of the 29th IEEE/ACM International Conference on Automated Software Engineering (ASE), pp. 373–384 (2014)

13. Giannakopoulou, D., Rakamarić, Z., Raman, V.: Symbolic learning of component interfaces. In: Miné, A., Schmidt, D. (eds.) SAS 2012. LNCS, vol. 7460, pp. 248–264. Springer, Heidelberg (2012)

14. Godefroid, P., Klarlund, N., Sen, K.: DART: directed automated random testing. In: Proceedings of the 26th ACM SIGPLAN Conference on Programming Language Design and Implementation (PLDI), pp. 213–223 (2005)

15. Godefroid, P., Levin, M.Y., Molnar, D.: SAGE: whitebox fuzzing for security testing. Commun. ACM 55(3), 40–44 (2012)

16. Howar, F., Giannakopoulou, D., Rakamarić, Z.: Hybrid learning: interface generation through static, dynamic, and symbolic analysis. In: Proceedings of the International Symposium on Software Testing and Analysis (ISSTA), pp. 268–279 (2013)

17. JaCoCo Java code coverage library. http://www.eclemma.org/jacoco

18. Jayaraman, K., Harvison, D., Ganesh, V.: jFuzz: a concolic whitebox fuzzer for Java. In: Proceedings of the 1st NASA Formal Methods Symposium (NFM), pp. 121–125 (2009)

19. Java Pathfinder. http://jpf.byu.edu

20. Kähkönen, K., Launiainen, T., Saarikivi, O., Kauttio, J., Heljanko, K., Niemelä, I.: LCT: an open source concolic testing tool for Java programs. In: Proceedings of the 6th Workshop on Bytecode Semantics, Verification, Analysis and Transformation (BYTECODE), pp. 75–80 (2011)

21. Khurshid, S., Păsăreanu, C.S., Visser, W.: Generalized symbolic execution for model checking and testing. In: Garavel, H., Hatcliff, J. (eds.) TACAS 2003. LNCS, vol. 2619, pp. 553–568. Springer, Heidelberg (2003)

22. de Moura, L., Bjørner, N.S.: Z3: an efficient SMT solver. In: Ramakrishnan, C.R., Rehof, J. (eds.) TACAS 2008. LNCS, vol. 4963, pp. 337–340. Springer, Heidelberg (2008)

23. Pacheco, C., Lahiri, S., Ernst, M., Ball, T.: Feedback-directed random test generation. In: Proceedings of the 29th International Conference on Software Engineering (ICSE), pp. 75–84 (2007)

24. Pasareanu, C.S., Rungta, N., Visser, W.: Symbolic execution with mixed concrete-symbolic solving. In: Proceedings of the International Symposium on Software Testing and Analysis (ISSTA), pp. 34–44 (2011)

25. Păsăreanu, C.S., Mehlitz, P.C., Bushnell, D.H., Gundy-Burlet, K., Lowry, M., Person, S., Pape, M.: Combining unit-level symbolic execution and system-level concrete execution for testing NASA software. In: Proceedings of the International Symposium on Software Testing and Analysis (ISSTA), pp. 15–26 (2008)

26. Qiu, R., Yang, G., Păsăreanu, C.S., Khurshid, S.: Compositional symbolic execution with memoized replay. In: Proceedings of the 37th International Conference on Software Engineering (ICSE), pp. 632–642 (2015)

27. Sen, K., Agha, G.: CUTE and jCUTE: concolic unit testing and explicit path model-checking tools. In: Ball, T., Jones, R.B. (eds.) CAV 2006. LNCS, vol. 4144, pp. 419–423. Springer, Heidelberg (2006)

28. Sen, K., Marinov, D., Agha, G.: CUTE: a concolic unit testing engine for C. In: Proceedings of the 10th European Software Engineering Conference Held Jointly with 13th ACM SIGSOFT International Symposium on Foundations of Software Engineering (ESEC/FSE), pp. 263–272 (2005)
29. The SMT-LIB standard. http://smtlib.cs.uiowa.edu
30. Soot: A Java optimization framework. http://sable.github.io/soot
31. Souza, M., Borges, M., d'Amorim, M., Păsăreanu, C.S.: CORAL: solving complex constraints for symbolic pathfinder. In: Bobaru, M., Havelund, K., Holzmann, G.J., Joshi, R. (eds.) NFM 2011. LNCS, vol. 6617, pp. 359–374. Springer, Heidelberg (2011)
32. Staats, M., Păsăreanu, C.: Parallel symbolic execution for structural test generation. In: Proceedings of the International Symposium on Software Testing and Analysis (ISSTA), pp. 183–194 (2010)
33. Tanno, H., Zhang, X., Hoshino, T., Sen, K.: TesMa and CATG: automated test generation tools for models of enterprise applications. In: Proceedings of the 37th International Conference on Software Engineering (ICSE), pp. 717–720 (2015)
34. Tillmann, N., de Halleux, J.: Pex–White box test generation for .NET. In: Beckert, B., Hähnle, R. (eds.) TAP 2008. LNCS, vol. 4966, pp. 134–153. Springer, Heidelberg (2008)
35. Visser, W., Havelund, K., Brat, G.P., Park, S., Lerda, F.: Model checking programs. Autom. Softw. Eng. **10**(2), 203–232 (2003)

# Concurrency

# Diagnostic Information for Control-Flow Analysis of Workflow Graphs (a.k.a. Free-Choice Workflow Nets)

Cédric Favre[1,2], Hagen Völzer[1(✉)], and Peter Müller[2]

[1] IBM Research, Zurich, Switzerland
hvo@zurich.ibm.com
[2] Department of Computer Science, ETH, Zurich, Switzerland

**Abstract.** A workflow graph is a classical flow graph extended by concurrent fork and join. Workflow graphs can be used to represent the main control-flow of e.g. business process models modeled in languages such as BPMN or UML activity diagrams. They can also be seen as compact representations of free-choice Petri nets with a unique start and a unique end. A workflow graph is said to be *sound* if it is free of deadlocks and exhibits no lack of synchronization, which correspond to liveness and safeness of a slightly modified version of the corresponding Petri net. We present a new characterization of unsoundness of workflow graphs in terms of three structural, i.e., graphical error patterns. We also present a polynomial-time algorithm that decides unsoundness and returns for each unsound workflow graph, one of the three structural error patterns as diagnostic information. An experimental evaluation on over 1350 workflow graphs derived from industrial business process models suggests that our technique performs well in practice.

## 1 Introduction

Workflow graphs can capture the main control flow of processes modeled in languages such as BPMN, UML Activity Diagrams, and Event Process Chains (EPC). That is, the core routing constructs of these languages can be mapped to the routing constructs of workflow graphs: alternative split and merge, as well as concurrent fork and join. Thus, a workflow graph is a classical control-flow graph or flow chart extended by concurrent fork and join. Figure 1(a) shows a simple example of a workflow graph in BPMN notation where $f1$ and $f2$ are (concurrent) forks, $j1$ is a (concurrent) join, $d1$ is a decision (i.e., alternative split), and $m1$ and $m2$ are alternative merges. Note that Fig. 1(a) shows only the pure control-flow; representations of tasks, commands, data assignments, etc. are omitted. Those could be added to the edges of the workflow graph.

A workflow graph is equivalent to a corresponding *free-choice* Petri net [1], called a *free-choice workflow net*. The corresponding net for the workflow graph in Fig. 1(a) is shown in Fig. 1(b) where the (green) dashed part is ignored. In fact, the corresponding free-choice workflow net is in some sense isomorphic

© Springer-Verlag Berlin Heidelberg 2016
M. Chechik and J.-F. Raskin (Eds.): TACAS 2016, LNCS 9636, pp. 463–479, 2016.
DOI: 10.1007/978-3-662-49674-9_27

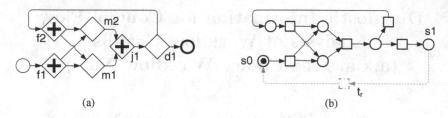

(a)                                              (b)

**Fig. 1.** (a) A workflow graph, (b) its corresponding free-choice workflow net (without dashed part) and its connected version (with dashed part)

to its workflow graph (see [1] for details) such that the workflow graph can be seen as a condensed representation of the free-choice workflow net, and all analysis information obtained on the workflow net can be easily mapped back to the workflow graph. Because of this close relationship and the rich theory available for free-choice nets [2], we will henceforth continue the technical development based on free-choice workflow nets.

A natural correctness condition for free-choice workflow nets, and the dominant one for business process modeling, called *soundness*, requires the absence of two types of control-flow errors: deadlocks and *lack of synchronization*. Lack of synchronization, called *unsafeness* in Petri net theory, occurs when there are two control-flow tokens at the same place, which gives rise to *implicit* auto-concurrency, i.e., a task executing concurrently to itself, which is usually considered a modeling error for this model class. Process languages such as BPMN have constructs for *explicit* auto-concurrency, called multiple instance tasks, where the auto-concurrency is encapsulated in a single-entry-single-exit block.

Figures 2(a) and (d) (ignore the coloring for now) show simple examples of workflow nets with deadlocks. Figures 2(b) and (c) exhibit lack of synchronization, i.e., unsafeness. In particular, Fig. 2(c) shows a special case of lack of synchronization, which causes an unbounded production of tokens, which can be a serious problem for process execution engines if undetected.

A free-choice workflow net is sound if and only if its *(strongly) connected version* is safe and live (in the Petri net sense) [3]. The connected version of the net in Fig. 1(b) is created by adding the dashed part. It can be decided in polynomial time whether a strongly connected free-choice net is safe and live using linear-algebraic techniques. However, none of the existing decision procedures [2,4–6] explicitly attempts to produce diagnostic information to support a modeler in locating, understanding and fixing the error in case the net is not live or not safe.

In this paper, we present a novel technique to detect control-flow errors and to produce diagnostic information that helps modelers to locate and fix the cause of the error. In particular, we make the following contributions:

1. We present a new characterization of unsoundness in terms of three structural error patterns, i.e., offending subgraphs (see Fig. 2) that are present in a free-choice workflow net if and only if it is unsound. This diagnostic information

is designed to be more concise and easier to consume than an error trace, which is important as many process models are created by business analysts without a strong technical background.

2. We present an algorithm that decides unsoundness in polynomial time such that one structural error pattern is returned for each unsound graph. As a byproduct, we can also generate an error trace in polynomial time to complement the main graphical diagnostic information.

3. We implemented our technique as a research prototype in the IBM WebSphere Business Modeler. An experimental evaluation on over 1350 workflow graphs derived from industrial business process models suggests that our technique is sufficiently fast to run the analysis and provide immediate concise diagnostic feedback while the process model is being developed.

Some proofs are omitted in this version. They and additional detail can be found in an extended version of this paper [7] and in a thesis [8].

**Related Work.** Our structural error patterns are similar to control-flow 'anti-patterns', which are sometimes given to modeling practitioners [9] in terms of erroneous instructive examples. However, in contrast to those anti-patterns, our structural error patterns are formally characterized as graph structures and proved to capture all situations where deadlock or lack of synchronization may occur.

Our patterns are also strongly related to a graph-theoretic characterization of live and bounded free-choice nets given by Esparza and Silva [10]. However, we are not aware of any polynomial-time decision procedure for their characterization.

An alternative approach to detect control flow errors and to provide diagnostic information is to compute an error trace through state-space exploration. An experimental study [11] has shown that whereas naive state-space exploration is not sufficient to analyze the state spaces of business process models, with appropriate reduction techniques, state space exploration can check soundness of an industrial process model in less than a second. However, the traces obtained can be large and contain many transitions that do not contribute to the actual control-flow error [12], which requires additional techniques to trim the trace [13,14], whereas our structural error patterns represent control-flow errors concisely. Moreover, many traces are difficult to visualize in the context of a process model, for instance, because they include several iterations through a cycle, whereas our structural error patterns can be displayed and understood within the process model.

The tool Woflan [15] implements a complex set of (partially exponential-time) Petri net analysis techniques. Some diagnostic hints, e.g., so-called mismatches, can be helpful in many cases to understand an error, but they do not imply unsoundness in general. For other diagnosis results, it remains unclear how they can pinpoint the cause of an error.

# 2    Preliminaries

## 2.1    Free-Choice Workflow Nets and Soundness

A *Petri net* $N = (P, T, F)$ consists of disjoint, finite and non-empty sets $P$ of places and $T$ of transitions and a relation $F \subseteq (P \times T) \cup (T \times P)$. An element of $P \cup T$ is also called an *element* of $N$. Note that $(P \cup T, F)$ is a directed (bipartite) graph and we apply well-known graph-theoretic concepts such as path and strong connectedness to it. For an element $x$ of $N$, we define $^\bullet x = \{y \mid (y, x) \in F\}$ and $x^\bullet = \{y \mid (x, y) \in F\}$ and for a set $X$ of elements, we set $^\bullet X = \bigcup_{x \in X} {}^\bullet x$ and $X^\bullet = \bigcup_{x \in X} x^\bullet$. $N$ is *free-choice* if for all transitions $t_1, t_2$, $^\bullet t_1 \cap {}^\bullet t_2 \neq \emptyset$ implies[1] $|{}^\bullet t_1| = |{}^\bullet t_2| = 1$. A *subnet* of $N$ is a Petri net $N' = (P', T', F')$ such that $P' \subseteq P$, $T' \subseteq T$ and $F' = F \cap ((P' \times T') \cup (T' \times P'))$. The *incidence matrix* of a Petri net $N$ is given by the integers $c_{t,p} = \chi_F(t, p) - \chi_F(p, t)$ for $t \in T, p \in P$ where $\chi_F$ denotes the characteristic function of $F$.

A *marking* of $N$ is a mapping $m : P \to \mathbb{N}$, i.e., a bag over $P$. If $m(p) = k$, we say that $p$ has $k$ *tokens* in $m$. If $m(p) > 0$, we say that $p$ is *marked* in $m$. We will sometimes treat a set of places $X \subseteq P$ as a marking by identifying it with its characteristic function. Addition and containment of markings is defined pointwise: $(m_1 + m_2)(p) = m_1(p) + m_2(p)$ and $m_1 \leq m_2$ if there is a marking $m$ such that $m_1 + m = m_2$. A transition $t$ is *enabled* in $m$ if $^\bullet t \leq m$. For two markings $m_1, m_2$ and a transition $t$, the relationship $m_1 \xrightarrow{t} m_2$ holds whenever $t$ is enabled in $m_1$ and $m_1 + t^\bullet = {}^\bullet t + m_2$. We write $m \to m'$ if $m \xrightarrow{t} m'$ for any $t$ and $\xrightarrow{*}$ for the reflexive and transitive closure of $\to$. We say $m'$ is *reachable* from $m$ if $m \xrightarrow{*} m'$. A transition $t$ (place $p$) is *dead* in $m$ if no marking reachable from $m$ enables $t$ (marks $p$). A transition or place $x$ is *live* in $m$ if $x$ is not dead in each marking reachable from $m$. A *local deadlock* is a marking in which a transition $t$ is dead and a place $p \in {}^\bullet t$ is marked. A *global deadlock* is a marking in which no transition is enabled. $N$ is *live* in a marking $m_0$ if every transition is live in $m_0$.

We say $N$ is *bounded* from a marking $m_0$ if there is a marking $m^*$ such that for every marking $m$ reachable from $m_0$, we have $m \leq m^*$. A marking is *safe* if each place has at most one token. $N$ is *safe* from a marking $m_0$ if every marking reachable from $m_0$ is safe.

A *workflow net* is a Petri net $N$ with a unique source $p_s$ and a unique sink $p_t \neq p_s$ such that $p_s, p_t \in P$ and every element of $N$ is on a path from $p_s$ to $p_t$. The marking $m_s$ (resp. $m_t$) of $N$ which has a single token on the source (sink) and no token elsewhere is called the *initial* (*final*) marking of $N$. An *execution sequence* of $N$ is a sequence $\sigma = m_0, m_1, m_2, \ldots$ of markings of $N$ such that $m_i \to m_{i+1}$ for each $i \geq 0$. If $\sigma = m_0, \ldots, m_n$ is finite, we also write $m_0 \xrightarrow{\sigma} m_n$. An *execution trace* of $N$ is an execution sequence $\sigma = m_0, m_1, m_2, \ldots$ of $N$ such that $m_0 = m_s$. A marking of $N$ is said to be a *reachable marking* of $N$ if it is reachable from the initial marking of $N$.

---

[1] Often, a more liberal definition is given for free-choice, which is sometimes also called *extended free-choice*. However an extended free-choice net can be converted into an equivalent free-choice net by a simple and well-known construction.

A workflow net $N$ is said to be *sound* [3] if the following three conditions are satisfied: (i) the sink is live in the initial marking, (ii) the final marking is the only reachable marking of $N$ that marks the sink, and (iii) no transition of $N$ is dead in the initial marking. Condition (ii) says that a token on the sink signals 'proper termination', i.e., there is no token left in the interior of the net. The example in Fig. 1(b) is sound. Soundness appears to be an especially natural correctness condition for free-choice workflow nets as the following theorem suggests. We define for a workflow net $N$ the *(strongly) connected* version of $N$, denoted by $\overline{N}$. $\overline{N}$ is obtained from $N$ by adding a fresh transition $t_r$, called the *return* transition and connect it such that ${}^\bullet t_r = p_t$ and $t_r^\bullet = p_s$, i.e., the return transition moves a token from the sink to the source of $N$, cf. Figure 1(b) with dashed part. Note that the underlying graph of $\overline{N}$ is indeed strongly connected.

**Theorem 1 ([3]).** *Let $N$ be a free-choice workflow net. The following five statements are equivalent: (i) $N$ is sound, (ii) $N$ is safe from the initial marking and no reachable marking is a local deadlock (iii) $N$ is safe from the initial marking and no reachable marking is a global deadlock, (iv) $\overline{N}$ is bounded and live from the initial marking, and (v) $\overline{N}$ is safe and live from the initial marking.*

It is not necessarily obvious to a modeler whether a reachable marking is a local deadlock or not. However it is fairly obvious whether a marking is a global deadlock. We could therefore call a global deadlock an *explicit* error marking and a local deadlock an *implicit* error marking. So far, we have three explicit error markings that imply unsoundness: a global deadlock, an unsafe marking, and an *improper termination*, i.e., a reachable marking that has a token on the sink and some token elsewhere. An execution trace that ends in an explicit error marking can be considered as diagnostic information for unsoundness.

## 2.2 Structural Characterizations for Safeness and Liveness in Free-Choice Nets

We will use the following concepts from Petri net and graph theory to build graphical diagnostic information: *siphons, circuits, handles and bridges*. A *siphon*[2] is a non-empty set $S$ of places such that ${}^\bullet S \subseteq S^\bullet$; $S$ is *minimal* if it does not contain another siphon. The central property of a siphon, which makes it suitable as diagnostic information, and which is an immediate consequence of its definition, is that if $S$ is not marked in a marking $m$, then each transition $t \in S^\bullet$ is dead in $m$. We will also identify a siphon $S$ with the subnet *generated* by it, which is the subnet $(P', T', F')$ such that $P' = S$ and $T' = {}^\bullet S$.

A path is said to be *trivial* if it contains only one element. A *circuit* of $N$ is a non-trivial path from an element to itself such that all other elements are pairwise distinct. A *handle* on a subnet $N'$ is a non-trivial path $H$ in $N$ from some element $x$ of $N'$ to some element $y$ of $N'$ such that $H$ is disjoint from $N'$ apart from $x$ and $y$. $H$ is a *P/T-handle* if $x \in P$ and $y \in T$ and a *T/P-handle* if $x \in T$ and $y \in P$. A *bridge* between two subnets $N'$ and $N''$ is a non-trivial

---

[2] Unfortunately, a siphon is also often called a *deadlock*.

path $B$ from an element $x$ of $N'$ to an element $y$ of $N''$ that is disjoint from $N'$ apart from $x$ and disjoint from $N''$ apart from $y$. $B$ is a *T/P-bridge* if $x \in T$ and $y \in P$.

$N$ is *structurally live* if there exists a marking from which it is live; it is *structurally bounded* if $N$ is bounded from each marking of $N$. $N$ is *SLB* if it is structurally live and structurally bounded. Note that SLB is equivalent with the notion of *well-formedness* [2] of a free-choice net, where $N$ is *well-formed* if there exists a marking from which $N$ is live and bounded. This is because a well-formed free-choice net is structurally bounded [2, Theorem 5.8].

The following propositions are directly derived from the literature. Let for the rest of this paper, $N$ denote a free-choice workflow net and $\overline{N}$ its connected version.

**Theorem 2** ([2, Theorem 6.17],[10, Theorem 4.2]). *We have: (i) $\overline{N}$ is safe and live from the initial marking iff it is SLB and every siphon contains the source and (ii) $\overline{N}$ is SLB iff it contains no circuit with a T/P-handle and for every circuit $C$ with a P/T-handle $H$, there is a T/P-bridge between $C$ and $H$.*

Imagine the connected versions for the examples in Fig. 2. Then the red part in Fig. 2(a) shows a siphon that does not contain the source. In Figs. 2(b) and (c), the red part shows a T/P-handle on a circuit (blue part + imagined return edge). Figure 2(d) shows a P/T-handle without bridges (red part) on a circuit (part of the blue plus imagined return edge). We discuss these examples in more depth in Sect. 3.1.

It can be computed in polynomial time whether every siphon is initially marked [5]. However, we do not know any way to compute Theorem 2(ii) in polynomial time. Moreover, condition (ii) of Theorem 2 has another drawback to be used directly as diagnostic information. Although a circuit with a handle is an explicit error condition as it is easily verified by a user, a circuit with a handle without bridges is less suited because the absence of bridges is not obvious to a user in a large graph.

## 3    New Diagnostic Information for Unsoundness

In this section, we present a new characterization of unsoundness in terms of the presence of three types of graph structures, which are suitable as diagnostic information. The new characterization is derived from the Esparza-Silva characterization (Theorem 2(ii)) with an essential change and some additional adaptations based on the structure of workflow nets. We present the new characterization in Sect. 3.1, and we show in Sect. 3.2 that each of the error patterns indeed indicates unsoundness.

### 3.1    A New Structural Characterization of Unsoundness

The new characterization is based on the new notion of a *DQ-siphon*:

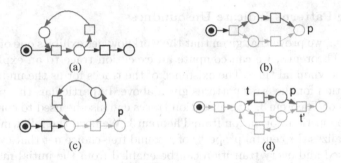

(a)          (b)

(c)          (d)

**Fig. 2.** Examples of the three error patterns: (a) A siphon (red) that does not contain the source, (b) A path to the sink (blue) with a (forward) T/P-handle (red), (c) A path to the sink (blue) with a (backward) T/P-handle (red), (d) A DQ-siphon (blue) with a P/T-handle (red).

**Definition 1.** *A decreasing quasi-component siphon, DQ-siphon for short, is a siphon $S$ such that for each transition $t$, $|t^{\bullet} \cap S| \leq 1$.*

A DQ-siphon has initially at most one token in $N$ and since the number of tokens in it cannot increase, it has never more than one token. Recall that a path in a graph is said to be *simple* if it does not visit any node twice. The new characterization is:

**Theorem 3.** *$N$ is unsound iff at least one of the following statements holds:*

1. *$N$ has a siphon that does not contain the source.*
2. *$N$ has a simple path from some element to the sink that has a T/P-handle.*
3. *$N$ has a DQ-siphon $S$ with a P/T-handle (more precisely, the subnet generated by $S$ has a P/T-handle).*

The proof of Theorem 3 is deferred to Sect. 3.3. Figure 2 shows examples for the error patterns. They indicate unsoundness as follows. As stated already above, all transitions $t \in S^{\bullet}$ are dead once the siphon $S$ is unmarked, which for Theorem 3(i), is the case already in the initial marking, cf. Figure 2(a). For a simple path with a T/P-handle, we can distinguish two cases, a *forward handle*, cf. Fig. 2(b) and a *backward handle*, cf. Fig. 2(c). The intuition of the forward handle is that we can execute, unless there is an obstruction by a deadlock, the path and the handle independently, which generates two tokens at the merging place $p$, i.e., an unsafe marking. Likewise, the intuition for the backward handle is that, if not obstructed by a deadlock, the handle and the path can be executed concurrently to produce an unbounded number of tokens at $p$. Finally, for a DQ-siphon $S$, we can assume it contains the source (otherwise we resort to Theorem 3(i)). Since $S$ has always at most one token, it becomes unmarked when the first transition of the handle occurs, which marks the handle and all transitions $t \in S^{\bullet}$ become dead. The token on the handle can be brought, unless obstructed by a deadlock, to the last place $p \in {}^{\bullet}t'$ of the handle, where $t'$ is the last transition of the handle, hence $t' \in S^{\bullet}$ and $t'$ is therefore dead, which is a local deadlock. These intuitions are substantiated in Sect. 3.2 below.

## 3.2  Error Patterns Indicate Unsoundness

In this section, we prove that given that the workflow net exhibits one of the error patterns in Theorem 3, we can compute an execution trace to an explicit error marking in polynomial time. The existence of the traces forms the underpinning for the intuition for the error patterns given above. In particular, this proves the 'if' direction of Theorem 3. The execution traces can also be used to complement the main diagnostic information from Theorem 3. We need the following lemma, which generalizes the central property of a sound free-choice net that every place can be marked and every transition can be enabled from the initial marking.

**Lemma 1.** *Let $\pi$ be a path in $N$ from a place $p_1$ to a place $p_2$, and $m$ a marking of $N$ such that $p_1$ is marked in $m$. Then, we can compute in $O(|P|^2)$ time an execution sequence from $m$ to a marking $m'$ such that $m'$ marks $p_2$ or $m'$ is an explicit error marking, i.e., a global deadlock, an improper termination, or unsafe.*

The proof of Lemma 1 is provided in the extended version of this paper [7]. The following observation will help us later: An unsafe marking or an improper termination marking are two special cases of a more general error marking:

**Lemma 2.** *Let $p_1, p_2$ be two distinct places of $N$ such that there exists a simple path from $p_1$ via $p_2$ to the sink of $N$. If there exists a reachable marking $m$ that marks both places $p_1$ and $p_2$, then $N$ is unsound. An execution sequence from $m$ to an explicit error marking can be computed in $O(|P|^2)$ time.*

By help of Lemmas 1 and 2, we can show the following:

**Theorem 4.** *If $N$ exhibits any of the three error patterns in Theorem 3, then a trace of $N$ to an explicit error marking can be computed in $O(|P|^2)$ time from the error pattern.*

A complete proof of Theorem 4 is provided in the extended version of this paper [7]. We now give a brief account of the proof for each error pattern. For any siphon that does not contain the source, there is a path from the source to a place of the siphon. As no place of an unmarked siphon can be marked, it follows directly from Lemma 1 that we can compute, in quadratic time, a trace from the initial marking to an error marking.

Consider now the case where $N$ has a simple path $\pi$ from some element $e_1$ to the sink that has a T/P-handle $H$. Applying Lemma 1 to a path from the source of $N$ to the place $p_1$ that precedes the first transition of $H$, we obtain either an error marking or a marking that marks $p_1$. In the latter case, we apply Lemma 1 to the path $H$. This will result in an error marking or, without going into the details, a marking $m$ where two places of $\pi$ are marked. By Lemma 2, we can obtain from $m$, an error trace in quadratic time.

Finally consider the case where $N$ has a DQ-siphon $S$ with a P/T-handle $H$. By the DQ-siphon property, $S$ has always at most one token. Applying Lemma 1 to a path from the source of $N$ to the first place of $H$, we obtain, in quadratic time, an execution leading to an error marking or a marking that marks a single place in $S$, viz. the first place of $H$. In the latter case, we apply Lemma 1 to the path $H$ and we obtain an execution that leads to either an error marking or a marking that marks the last place $p$ of $H$. Because $S$ became unmarked through the execution of the handle, the last transition $t'$ of $H$ is dead because $t' \in S^\bullet$, cf. Fig. 2(d). Hence we obtain an explicit error marking by once again applying Lemma 1 to a path from $p$ to the sink of $N$.

### 3.3  Proof of Theorem 3

In Theorem 4, we have shown one direction of Theorem 3. To show the other direction of Theorem 3, suppose $N$ is unsound. Due to Theorem 1, $\overline{N}$ is not safe or not live from the initial marking. Due to Theorem 2, we have either (i) some siphon of $\overline{N}$ does not contain the source, (ii) $\overline{N}$ contains a circuit with a T/P-handle, or (iii) $\overline{N}$ contains a circuit with a P/T-handle without T/P-bridges. In case (i), we conclude that $N$ has a siphon that does not contain the source because each siphon in $\overline{N}$ is also a siphon in $N$. For the cases (ii) and (iii), we use the following lemmas.

**Lemma 3.** *If $\overline{N}$ has a circuit with a T/P-handle, then $N$ has a path to the sink with a T/P-handle, which can be computed in $O(|F|)$ time.*

**Lemma 4.** *If $\overline{N}$ has a circuit with a P/T-handle without T/P-bridge, then $N$ has a minimal siphon $S$ with a P/T-handle or a siphon that does not contain the source.*

When the minimal siphon $S$ with P/T-handle that Lemma 4 returns is not a DQ-siphon, then there is a transition $t$ such that $|t^\bullet \cap S| > 1$. Then, we apply Lemma 5 below and obtain a path to the sink of $N$ with a T/P-handle, which concludes the proof of Theorem 3. Lemma 5 will be re-used in Sect. 4.

**Lemma 5.** *If $S$ is a minimal siphon of $\overline{N}$ such that there is a transition $t$ such that $|t^\bullet \cap S| > 1$, then $\overline{N}$ has a circuit with a T/P-handle, which can be computed in $O(F)$ time.*

The proofs of the lemmas are provided in the extended version of this paper [7].

## 4  Computation of Structural Diagnostic Information

In this section, we show that structural diagnostic information as given by Theorem 3 can be computed in polynomial time. We employ and extend an algorithm by Kemper and Bause [5], which in turn is based on the *rank equation* for free-choice nets. We need the following definitions. A *state machine (also called S-graph)* is a Petri net such that for each transition $t$, $|^\bullet t| = |t^\bullet| = 1$, i.e., it has no concurrency. A *P-component (also called S-component)* of $\overline{N}$ is a

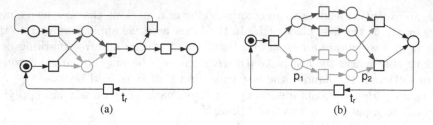

**Fig. 3.** Two nets, each decomposed into two overlapping P-components $S_1$ (green part + black part) and $S_2$ (orange part + black part) (a) is safe and live (sound), (b) is safe but not live (unsound)

subnet $(P', T', F')$ of $\overline{N}$ that is a strongly connected state machine such that $T' = {}^\bullet P' \cup P'^\bullet$. $\overline{N}$ is *state-machine decomposable (SMD)* if each element of $\overline{N}$ belongs to some P-component of $\overline{N}$. Figure 3 shows two nets that are SMD, each with a decomposition. SMD is necessary for $\overline{N}$ to be SLB but not sufficient. The net in Fig. 3(a) is SLB (sound), the net in Fig. 3(b) is not SLB (unsound). More precisely, SMD is sufficient for $\overline{N}$ being safe, but not for being live. Note that the net in Fig. 3(b) has deadlocks.

The difference between $\overline{N}$ being SMD and SLB can be captured using the *rank equation*. To this end, we need the notion of a *cluster*. For a transition $t$ of $\overline{N}$, let $[t] = \{t' \in T \mid {}^\bullet t \cap {}^\bullet t' \neq \emptyset\}$ be the *cluster* of $t$. In a free-choice net, each cluster is an equivalence class, hence clusters provide a partition of $T$. We have the following:

**Theorem 5.** ([16]) $\overline{N}$ is SLB iff $\overline{N}$ is SMD and

$$\mathrm{rank}(\overline{N}) = |\{[t] \mid t \in T\}| - 1 \tag{1}$$

where $\mathrm{rank}(\overline{N})$ is the rank of the incidence matrix of $\overline{N}$.

Note that the rank of the incidence matrix can be computed in time cubic in $\max(|P|, |T|)$. For the example net (connected version) in Fig. 3(b), the rank of the incidence matrix is 6 and the number of clusters is also 6.

We now present an algorithm that decides whether $\overline{N}$ is safe and live, which is, as stated earlier, equivalent with $N$ being sound. This algorithm, shown as Algorithm 1, returns corresponding diagnostic information for the connected net, viz. either a siphon that does not contain the source of $N$ (line 1), a circuit with a T/P-handle or a DQ-siphon with a P/T-handle (lines 2 and 10). This can then be post-processed into the desired diagnostic information for $N$ as stated in Theorem 3, which we will show below in Theorem 7.

Algorithm 1 proceeds as follows. It first checks whether $\overline{N}$ has a siphon that does not contain the source of $N$ using an algorithm by Esparza and Silva [4, Algorithm 6.6], cf. also [5]. This is denoted as *SiphonCheck($\overline{N}$)*.

Next the algorithm tries to compute a state-machine decomposition of $\overline{N}$ using an algorithm by Kemper and Bause [5, Algorithm 17], which is denoted

**Algorithm 1.** Decides whether $\overline{N}$ is safe and live and returns diagnostic information.

**CheckSafeAndLive($\overline{N}$)**

1: *SiphonCheck($\overline{N}$)*: **if** $\overline{N}$ has a siphon $S$ that does not include the source of $N$ **then return** (false, $S$) **end if**

2: *SMD-Check($\overline{N}$)*: **if** a minimal siphon $S$ of $\overline{N}$ is found that is not a state machine **then return** (false, $D$) where $D$ is either a circuit with a T/P-handle or a DQ-siphon with a P/T-handle computed from $S$ **end if**

3: *Rank-Check($\overline{N}$)*: **if** the rank Eq. (1) holds for $\overline{N}$ **then return** true **end if**

4: **loop**

5:     *Unprocessed* := the set of all places of $\overline{N}$

6:     **loop**

7:         pick $p \in$ *Unprocessed*

8:         $N' := $ delete$(p, \overline{N})$

9:         **if** $N'$ is not empty **then**

10:             *SMD-Check($N'$)*: **if** a minimal siphon $S$ of $N'$ is found that is not a state machine **then return** (false, $D$) where $D$ is either a circuit with a T/P-handle or a DQ-siphon with a P/T-handle computed from $S$ **end if**

11:             *Rank-Check($N'$)*: **if** the rank Eq. (1) does not hold for $N'$ **then** $\overline{N} := N'$; **break end if**

12:         **end if**

13:         *Unprocessed* := *Unprocessed* \ $\{p\}$

14:     **end loop**

15: **end loop**

---

as *SMD-Check($\overline{N}$)*. This algorithm computes a cover of the net with minimal siphons, i.e., a set of minimal siphons such that each place is in some minimal siphon. It then checks whether each of the computed minimal siphons is a P-component. If this is not the case, $\overline{N}$ is not SLB [5, Theorem 6]. A minimal siphon $S$ of $\overline{N}$ is not a P-component iff one of the following two conditions holds: (i) there is a transition $t$ such that $|t^{\bullet} \cap S| > 1$. In this case, we can compute a circuit with a T/P-handle as proved in Lemma 5. In the other case (ii), we have $S^{\bullet} \setminus {}^{\bullet}S \neq \emptyset$. In this case, we can compute a P/T-handle attached to $S$ as proved in Lemma 6. Note that condition (i) is checked first, so when condition (ii) is checked, we know that there is no transition $t$ such that $|t^{\bullet} \cap S| > 1$ and hence, if (ii) holds for $S$, $S$ must be a DQ-siphon.

**Lemma 6.** *If $S$ is a minimal siphon of $\overline{N}$ such that $S^{\bullet} \setminus {}^{\bullet}S \neq \emptyset$, then $S$ has a P/T-handle in $\overline{N}$, which can be computed in $O(|F|)$ time.*

In case the SMD-Check in line 2 passes, we know that each of the computed minimal siphons is a P-component and therefore, $\overline{N}$ is SMD and hence safe. The algorithm proceeds with computing the rank of the incidence matrix of $\overline{N}$ by standard techniques and checks the rank Eq. (1), denoted *Rank-Check($\overline{N}$)*. If the equation holds, then $\overline{N}$ is SLB due to Theorem 5 and safe and live due to Theorem 2. If the rank equation does not hold, we know that $\overline{N}$ is not live.

In this case, we iteratively reduce the net as described below until the SMD check for the reduced net returns diagnostic information.

For the reduction, we define $N' = \text{delete}(p, \overline{N})$ as the largest strongly connected subnet of $\overline{N}$ that does not contain $p$. Figure 4 shows in (a) the result of $\text{delete}(p_1, \overline{N})$ and (b) the result of $\text{delete}(p_2, \overline{N})$ where $\overline{N}$ is the net shown in Fig. 3(b). $N' = \text{delete}(p, \overline{N})$ can be computed in linear time. $N'$ may be empty for a particular $p$, but if $\overline{N}$ is SMD and not SLB, a place $p$ can be found such that $\text{delete}(p, \overline{N})$ is not empty (see Lemma 8). If $N'$ is not empty, we perform an SMD check on it. If the SMD check on the reduced net $N'$ (line 10) generates diagnostic information, this information is returned as diagnostic information of the original net $\overline{N}$. We argue in Lemma 7 below that this is correct.

**Lemma 7.** *Let $N' = \text{delete}(p, \overline{N})$ for some $p$ such that $N'$ is nonempty.*

(i) *If $S$ is a minimal siphon of $N'$ such that there is a transition $t$ such that $|t^\bullet \cap S| > 1$, then $S$ is also a minimal siphon of $\overline{N}$ such that there is a transition $t$ such that $|t^\bullet \cap S| > 1$.*

(ii) *If $S$ is a minimal siphon of $N'$ such that $S^\bullet \setminus {}^\bullet S \neq \emptyset$, then $S$ is also a minimal siphon of $\overline{N}$ such that $S^\bullet \setminus {}^\bullet S \neq \emptyset$.*

Otherwise, if the SMD check passes for $N'$, we check the rank equation for $N'$. If the rank equation for $N'$ does not hold, we know that $N'$ is not SLB. Hence we found a smaller net that contains an error, and, in this sense, the reduction was successful. In this case, we proceed with $N'$ as the subject of further analysis, we break from the inner loop and go into a new iteration of the outer loop to reduce the net further.

If the rank equation holds for $N'$, then $N'$ is SLB, i.e., removal of $p$ has removed the deadlock (i.e., made the net live). In this case, we try to reduce with another place $p$.

Lemma 8 below proves that, as long as a strongly connected free-choice workflow net is SMD but not SLB, we find a place $p$ such that the reduced net is not empty and not SLB, so either the SMD check or the rank check fails on the reduced net. In the former case, we are done and in the latter case, we proceed with a smaller net that is SMD but not SLB. Since this reduction can be performed at most $|P|$ many times, the SMD check must fail eventually and return diagnostic information.

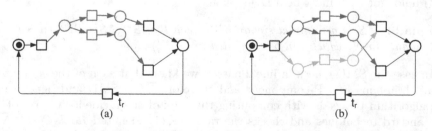

**Fig. 4.** The result of (a) $\text{delete}(p_1, \overline{N})$ and (b) $\text{delete}(p_2, \overline{N})$ where $\overline{N}$ is the net in Fig. 3(b)

**Lemma 8.** *Let $N'$ be a strongly connected subnet of $\overline{N}$ such that $N'$ is SMD. If $N'$ is not SLB then there exists a place $p$ such that* delete$(p, N')$ *is nonempty and not SLB.*

We can now conclude with the correctness of Algorithm 1.

**Theorem 6.** *Algorithm 1 decides whether $\overline{N}$ is safe and live from the initial marking. If not, it outputs either a siphon that does not include the source, a DQ-siphon with a P/T-handle, or a circuit with a T/P-handle. Algorithm 1 completes in $O(|P|^2 * max(|P|, |T|)^3)$.*

*Proof.* We have already shown the correctness of Algorithm 1. For the complexity, note that the time complexity of the Siphon Check is $O(|P|^2 * |T|)$ [5]. The complexity of the SMD Check is $O(|P| * (|P| + |T| + |F|))$ because the worst case is bounded by the need to identify $|P|$ minimal siphons and finding a minimal siphon containing a place can be done in time $O(|P| + |T| + |F|)$ [17]. Finally, checking the rank of the incidence matrix can be done in $O(max(|P|, |T|)^3)$. Thus, the complexity is dominated by the computation of the rank of the matrix. Algorithm 1 performs, at most, $|P|^2$ computations of the rank. Thus, the worst case time complexity of Algorithm 1 is $O(|P|^2 * max(|P|, |T|)^3)$.

As an example, we consider again the net from Fig. 3(b). This net passes the siphon check but might or might not pass the first SMD check, depending on the nondeterministic choice of minimal siphons in the SMD check. Suppose the algorithm finds the state machine decomposition shown in Fig. 3(b). The subsequent rank check for this net fails. If in the reduction, place $p_1$ is picked, we obtain the net shown in Fig. 4(a), which is SLB and hence passes the subsequent SMD and rank check. If however place $p_2$ is picked for reduction, we obtain the net shown in Fig. 4(b), which is not SMD and hence the SMD check must fail. Figure 5(a) shows a minimal siphon $S$ (in orange) that covers $p_3$. $S$ is not a state machine for two reasons: $|t_1^\bullet \cap S| > 1$ and $t_2 \in S^\bullet \setminus {}^\bullet S$. The first violation is picked up first, and from $S$ and $t_1$, a circuit with a T/P-handle is computed (Lemma 5), which is shown in Fig. 5(b).

The diagnostic information obtained from Algorithm 1 for $\overline{N}$ can be post-processed into diagnostic information for $N$. We obtain:

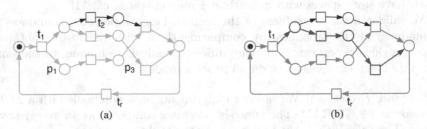

(a)                              (b)

**Fig. 5.** (a) A minimal siphon $S$ (in orange) that is not a state machine witnessed by $t_1$ (b) A circuit (in blue) with a T/P-handle (in red) computed from $S$ and $t_1$.

**Theorem 7.** *Soundness of $N$ can be decided in time $O(|P|^2 * max(|P|, |T|)^3)$ such that the algorithm returns one of the structural error patterns in Theorem 3 in case $N$ is unsound.*

*Proof.* The algorithm creates the connected version of $N$ and applies Algorithm1 to it. A siphon that does not contain the source of $N$ is returned as it is. Note that each siphon in $\overline{N}$ is a siphon in $N$. A DQ-siphon $S$ with a P/T-handle in $\overline{N}$ is a DQ-siphon with a P/T-handle in $N$ and is also returned as it is. Note that in this case, $S$ contains the source (otherwise we would return the first error pattern) and therefore the sink, because of the siphon property. Therefore, the return edge belongs to the siphon and cannot belong to the handle, so removal of the return edge retains the error pattern. A circuit with a T/P-handle in $\overline{N}$ is transformed into a path to the sink with a T/P-handle using Lemma 3. The complexity of this algorithm is dominated by the complexity of Algorithm1.

## 5     Experimental Evaluation

We implemented our technique as a research prototype in the IBM WebSphere Business Modeler and used this implementation to evaluate the performance of our technique and demonstrate that our technique provides useful diagnostic information.

Our implementation translates business process models described in the IBM WebSphere Business Modeler language into workflow graphs [11] and then applies a completion technique by Kiepuszewski et al. [18] (cf. also [11]) to obtain a workflow graph with a unique sink, as required by our technique.

*Data Set.* We ran our control flow analysis on 1353 business process models from industrial projects in the insurance and banking domain, which were also used as a benchmark in other work [11,12]. The 1353 models are organized into four libraries A, B1, B2, and B3. The libraries B1 and B2 are older releases of the library B3, where some process models were refined or changed, possibly removing or adding errors. Counting only libraries A and B3, we have 703 unique original models. Over the four libraries, the average number of nodes per derived Petri net ranges between 89 and 107. There are several large nets with up to 627 nodes. For example, 47 nets from library B3 have 200 or more nodes. Some models have state spaces with more than 1 million states, cf. [11].

We validated the correctness of the results, i.e., the detected soundness or unsoundness of the processes, by comparing them with the results obtained during previous experiments applying different analysis techniques to the same data [11]. The techniques agree on all process models.

*Performance Evaluation.* We ran our experiments on a notebook with a 2 GHz processor and 2 GB RAM. The analysis times are computed as an average over 10 runs. They also include the time spent by the tool to generate the error report for the user. The overhead for loading the process models from disk into memory during the first run is excluded.

**Table 1.** Experimental results.

| Library | A | B1 | B2 | B3 | Total |
|---|---|---|---|---|---|
| Processes | 282 | 287 | 363 | 421 | 1,353 |
| Unsound processes | 130 | 180 | 202 | 214 | 726 |
| Siphon without source | 0 | 17 | 15 | 13 | 45 |
| Path with a T/P-handle | 47 | 138 | 158 | 174 | 517 |
| DQ-siphon with a P/T-handle | 83 | 25 | 29 | 27 | 164 |
| Average library analysis time [ms] | 752 | 492 | 627 | 928 | 2799 |

Table 1 summarizes the results of our experiments for the four libraries. All three structural error patterns occurred in the data set. The average time to analyze a process model is 2ms, which is sufficiently fast to run our analysis and provide immediate feedback while the process model is being developed. In particular, our control-flow analyzer is roughly 2 to 6 times faster than existing tools that produce diagnostic information, that is, tools based on state space exploration [11].

Our implementation highlights structural error patterns inside the process model. For instance, Fig. 6 shows the error report for a path with a T/P-handle. Note that the activity 'Confirm Customer Requirement' produces a token on each of its outgoing edges according to the semantics of the used high-level language. Therefore, this activity creates a concurrent fork (as $f1$ in Fig. 1(a)) in the corresponding workflow graph. In Fig. 6, the activity 'Confirm Customer Requirement' is on a simple path (blue) to the final place and starts multiple concurrent paths including a T/P-handle (in red). Both concurrent paths join on the alternative merge (empty diamond with error flag) without being properly synchronized, which would need a concurrent join instead (as $j1$ in Fig. 1(a)). We provide examples for the other two structural patterns in the extended version of this paper [7].

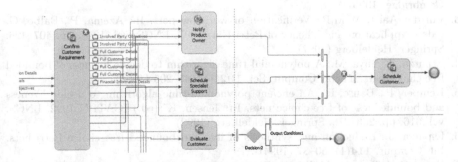

**Fig. 6.** Screenshot of the diagnostic information for a T/P-handle.

*Diagnostic Information.* As this example illustrates, our technique provides concise diagnostic information. In particular, the structural patterns have advantages over the traces computed by state space exploration. They can be displayed and understood directly in the context of the process model (which is difficult for traces that may be long and may contain iterations). Moreover, they are concise and do not contain any information that is not immediately relevant for understanding and fixing the error (in contrast to traces, which typically describe complete executions including aspects irrelevant for the error).

# 6    Conclusion

We presented a new characterization of control-flow errors in workflow graphs in terms of three structural error patterns, as well as an algorithm that decides whether one of the error patterns is present. To our knowledge, this is the first algorithm that runs in polynomial time and produces diagnostic information. It is applicable to a wide range of business process models modeled in languages such as BPMN or UML activity diagrams; features of these languages that do not translate to workflow graphs are either used rarely or orthogonal to soundness checking. Our experiments show that our technique is sufficiently fast to give instant feedback while the process model is being developed; the experiments also provide anecdotal evidence that our technique generates useful diagnostic information. Evaluating the benefit of this information in comparison, for instance, to error traces, requires a user study and involves various aspects beyond the scope of this paper, such as error visualizations and user interactions. We leave such a study for future work.

# References

1. Favre, C., Fahland, D., Völzer, H.: The relationship between workflow graphs and free-choice workflow nets. Inf. Syst. **47**, 197–219 (2015)
2. Desel, J., Esparza, J.: Free Choice Petri Nets. Cambridge University Press, Cambridge (1995)
3. van der Aalst, W.M.P.: Verification of workflow nets. In: Azéma, P., Balbo, G. (eds.) Application and Theory of Petri Nets 1997. LNCS, vol. 1248, pp. 407–426. Springer, Heidelberg (1997)
4. Esparza, J., Silva, M.: A polynomial-time algorithm to decide liveness of bounded free choice nets. Theor. Comput. Sci. **102**(1), 185–205 (1992)
5. Kemper, P., Bause, F.: An effcient polynomial-time algorithm to decide liveness and boundedness of free-choice nets. In: Jensen, K. (ed.) ICATPN 1992. LNCS, vol. 616, pp. 263–278. Springer, Heidelberg (1992)
6. Esparza, J.: Reduction and synthesis of live and bounded free choice Petri nets. Inf. Comput. **114**(1), 50–87 (1994)
7. Favre, C., Völzer, H., Müller, P.: Diagnostic information for control-flow analysis of workflow graphs (a.k.a. free-choice workflow nets). Technical Report, ETH Zurich, revised, 2015, revised (2016). http://e-citations.ethbib.ethz.ch

8. Favre, C.: Detecting, Understanding, and Fixing Control-Flow Errors in Business Process Models. Ph.D. thesis, Department of Computer Science, ETH Zurich (2014)
9. Koehler, J., Vanhatalo, J.: Process anti-patterns: How to avoid the common traps of business process modeling. Technical Report RZ 3678, IBM Research, Also published in the WebSphere Developer Technical Journal in 2007, May 2007
10. Esparza, J., Silva, M.: Circuits, handles, bridges and nets. In: Rozenberg, G. (ed.) Advances in Petri Nets 1990. LNCS, vol. 483, pp. 210–242. Springer, Heidelberg (1989)
11. Fahland, D., Favre, C., Koehler, J., Lohmann, N., Völzer, H., Wolf, K.: Analysis on demand: Instantaneous soundness checking of industrial business process models. Data Knowl. Eng. **70**(5), 448–466 (2011)
12. Lohmann, N., Fahland, D.: Where did I go wrong? In: Sadiq, S., Soffer, P., Völzer, H. (eds.) BPM 2014. LNCS, vol. 8659, pp. 283–300. Springer, Heidelberg (2014)
13. Ball, T., Naik, M., Rajamani, S.K.: From symptom to cause: Localizing errors in counterexample traces. In: POPL, Proceedings, pp. 97–105, ACM (2003)
14. Groce, A.: Error explanation with distance metrics. In: Jensen, K., Podelski, A. (eds.) TACAS 2004. LNCS, vol. 2988, pp. 108–122. Springer, Heidelberg (2004)
15. Verbeek, H.M.W.E., Basten, T., van der Aalst, W.M.P.: Diagnosing workflow processes using Woflan. Comput. J. **44**(4), 246–279 (2001)
16. Esparza, J.: Synthesis rules for Petri nets, and how they lead to new results. In: Baeten, J.C.M., Klop, J.W. (eds.) CONCUR '90 Theories of Concurrency: Unification and Extension. LNCS, vol. 458, pp. 182–198. Springer, Heidelberg (1990)
17. Kemper, P.: Linear time algorithm to find a minimal deadlock in a strongly connected free-choice net. In: Ajmone Marsan, Marco (ed.) ICATPN 1993. LNCS, vol. 691, pp. 319–338. Springer, Heidelberg (1993)
18. Kiepuszewski, B., ter Hofstede, A.H.M., van der Aalst, W.M.P.: Fundamentals of control flow in workflows. Acta Inf. **39**(3), 143–209 (2003)

# Approaching the Coverability Problem Continuously

Michael Blondin[1,2]([✉]), Alain Finkel[2], Christoph Haase[2], and Serge Haddad[2,3]

[1] DIRO, Université de Montréal, Montreal, Canada
blondimi@iro.umontreal.ca
[2] LSV, CNRS and ENS Cachan, Université Paris-Saclay, Cachan, France
haase@lsv.ens-cachan.fr
[3] Inria, Cachan, France

**Abstract.** The coverability problem for Petri nets plays a central role in the verification of concurrent shared-memory programs. However, its high EXPSPACE-complete complexity poses a challenge when encountered in real-world instances. In this paper, we develop a new approach to this problem which is primarily based on applying forward coverability in continuous Petri nets as a pruning criterion inside a backward-coverability framework. A cornerstone of our approach is the efficient encoding of a recently developed polynomial-time algorithm for reachability in continuous Petri nets into SMT. We demonstrate the effectiveness of our approach on standard benchmarks from the literature, which shows that our approach decides significantly more instances than any existing tool and is in addition often much faster, in particular on large instances.

## 1 Introduction

Counter machines and Petri nets are popular mathematical models for modeling and reasoning about distributed and concurrent systems. They provide a high level of abstraction that allows for employing them in a great variety of application domains, ranging, for instance, from modeling of biological, chemical and business processes to the formal verification of concurrent programs.

Many safety properties of real-world systems reduce to the *coverability problem* in Petri nets: Given an initial and a target configuration, does there exist a sequence of transitions leading from the initial configuration to a configuration larger than the target configuration? For instance, in an approach pioneered by German and Sistla [19] multi-threaded non-recursive finite-state programs with shared variables, which naturally occur in predicate-abstraction-based verification

M. Blondin—Supported by the Fonds québécois de la recherche sur la nature et les technologies (FQRNT), by the French Centre national de la recherche scientifique (CNRS), and by the "Chaire Digiteo, ENS Cachan — École Polytechnique".
C. Haase—Supported by Labex Digicosme, Univ. Paris-Saclay, project VERICONISS.
S. Haddad—Supported by ERC project EQualIS (FP7-308087).

M. Chechik and J.-F. Raskin (Eds.): TACAS 2016, LNCS 9636, pp. 480–496, 2016.
DOI: 10.1007/978-3-662-49674-9_28

frameworks, are modeled as Petri nets such that every program location corresponds to a place in a Petri net, and the number of tokens of a place indicates how many threads are currently at the corresponding program location. Coverability can then, for instance, be used in order to detect whether a mutual exclusion property could be violated when a potentially unbounded number of threads is executed in parallel. The coverability problem was one of the first decision problems for Petri nets that was shown decidable and EXPSPACE-complete [4,21,24]. Despite this huge worst-case complexity, over the course of the last twenty years, a plethora of tools has emerged that have shown to be able to cope with a large number of real-world instances of coverability problems in a satisfactory manner.

**Our Contribution.** We present a new approach to the coverability problem and its implementation. When run on standard benchmarks that we obtained from the literature, our approach proves more than 91 % of safe instances to be safe, most of the time much faster when compared to existing tools, and none of those tools can individually prove more than 84 % of safe instances to be safe. We additionally demonstrate that our approach is also competitive when run on unsafe instances. In particular, it decides 142 out of 176 (80 %) instances of our benchmark suite, while the best competitor only decides 122 (69 %) instances.

Our approach is conceptually extremely simple and exploits recent advances in the theory of Petri nets as well as the power of modern SMT-solvers inside a backward-coverability framework. In [14], Fraca and Haddad solved long-standing open problems about the complexity of decision problems for so-called continuous Petri nets. This class was introduced by David and Alla [5] and allows for transitions to be fired a non-negative real number of times—hence places may contain a non-negative real number of tokens. The contribution of [14] was to present polynomial-time algorithms that decide all of coverability, reachability and boundedness in this class. A further benefit of [14] is to show that continuous Petri nets over the reals are equivalent to continuous Petri nets over the rationals, and, moreover, to establish a set of simple sufficient and necessary conditions in order to decide reachability in continuous Petri nets. The first contribution of our paper is to show that these conditions can efficiently be encoded into a sentence of *linear size* in the existential theory of the non-negative rational numbers with addition and order $(FO(\mathbb{Q}_+, +, >))$. This encoding paves the way for deciding coverability in continuous Petri nets inside SMT-solvers and is particularly useful in order to efficiently answer *multiple coverability queries* on the same continuous Petri net due to caching strategies present in modern SMT-solvers. Moreover, we show that our encoding in effect *strictly subsumes* a recently introduced CEGAR-based approach to coverability described by Esparza *et al.* in [10]; in particular we can completely avoid the potentially exponentially long CEGAR-loop, cf. the related work section below. The benefit of coverability in continuous Petri nets is that it provides a way to over-approximate coverability under the standard semantics: any configuration that is not coverable in a continuous Petri net is also not coverable under the standard semantics. This observation can be exploited inside a backward-coverability framework as follows.

Starting at the target configuration to be covered, the classical backward-coverability algorithm [1] repeatedly computes the set of all minimal predecessor configurations that by application of one transition cover the target or some earlier computed configuration until a fixed point is reached, which is guaranteed to happen due to Petri nets being well-structured transition systems [13]. The crux to the performance of the algorithm lies in the size of the set of minimal elements that is computed during each iteration, which may grow exponentially.[1] This is where continuous coverability becomes beneficial. In our approach, if a minimal element is not continuously coverable, it can safely be discarded since none of its predecessors is going to be coverable either, which substantially shrinks the predecessor set. In effect, this heuristic yields a powerful pruning technique, enabling us to achieve the aforementioned advantages when compared to other approaches on standard benchmarks.

Due to space constraints, we only sketch some of the proofs in this paper. Full details can be found in [2].

**Related Work.** Our approach is primarily related to the work by Esparza *et al.* [10], by Kaiser, Kroening and Wahl [20], and by Delzanno, Raskin and van Begin [7]. In [10], Esparza *et al.* presented an implementation of a semi-decision procedure for disproving coverability which was originally proposed by Esparza and Melzer [11]. It is based on the Petri-net state equation and traps as sufficient criteria in order to witness non-coverability. As shown in [11], those conditions can be encoded into an equi-satisfiable system of linear inequalities called the *trap inequation* in [11]. This approach is, however, prone to numerical imprecision that become problematic even for instances of small size [11, Sect. 5.3]. For that reason, the authors of [10] resort to a CEGAR-based variant of the approach described in [11] which has the drawback that in the worst case, the CEGAR loop has to be executed an exponential number of times leading to an exponential number of queries to the underlying SMT-solver. We will show in Sect. 4.3 that the conditions used in [10] are strictly subsumed by a subset of the conditions required to witness coverability in continuous Petri nets: whenever the procedure described in [10] returns uncoverable then coverability does not hold in the continuous setting either, but not *vice versa*. Thus, a single satisfiability check to our formula in existential $FO(\mathbb{Q}_+, +, >)$ encoding continuous coverability that we develop in this paper completely subsumes the CEGAR-approach presented in [10]. Another difference to [10] is that here we present a sound *and* complete decision procedure.

Regarding the relationship of our work to [20], Kaiser *et al.* develop in their paper an approach to coverability in richer classes of well-structured transition systems that is also based on the classical backward-analysis algorithm. They also employ forward analysis in order to prune the set of minimal elements during the backward iteration, and in addition a widening heuristic in order to over-approximate the minimal basis. Our approach differs in that our minimal basis is always precise yet as small as possible modulo continuous coverability. Thus no

---

[1] This problem is commonly referred to as the *symbolic state explosion problem*, cf. [8].

backtracking as in [20] is needed, which is required when the widened basis turns out to be too inaccurate. Another difference is that for the forward analysis, a Karp-Miller tree is incrementally built in the approach described in [20], whereas we use the continuous coverability over-approximation of coverability.

The idea of using an over-approximation of the reachability set of a Petri net in order to prune minimal basis elements inside a backward coverability framework was first described by Delzanno *et al.* [7], who use place invariants as a pruning criterion. However, computing such invariants and checking if a minimal basis element can be pruned potentially requires exponential time.

Finally, a number of further techniques and tools for deciding Petri net coverability or more general well-structured transition systems have been described in the literature. They are, for instance, based on efficient data structures [8,12,15,16] and generic algorithmic frameworks such as EEC [17] and IC3 [22].

## 2    Preliminaries

We denote by $\mathbb{Q}$, $\mathbb{Z}$ and $\mathbb{N}$ the set of rationals, integers, and natural numbers, respectively, and by $\mathbb{Q}_+$ the set of non-negative rationals. Throughout the whole paper, numbers are encoded in binary, and rational numbers as pairs of integers encoded in binary. Let $\mathbb{D} \subseteq \mathbb{Q}$, $\mathbb{D}^E$ denotes the set of vectors indexed by a finite set $E$. A vector $\boldsymbol{u}$ is denoted by $\boldsymbol{u} = (u_i)_{i \in E}$. Given vectors $\boldsymbol{u} = (u_i)_{i \in E}$, $\boldsymbol{v} = (v_i)_{i \in E} \in \mathbb{D}^E$, addition $\boldsymbol{u} + \boldsymbol{v}$ is defined component-wise, and $\boldsymbol{u} \leq \boldsymbol{v}$ whenever $u_i \leq v_i$ for all $i \in E$. Moreover, $\boldsymbol{u} < \boldsymbol{v}$ whenever $\boldsymbol{u} \leq \boldsymbol{v}$ and $\boldsymbol{u} \neq \boldsymbol{v}$. Let $E' \subseteq E$ and $\boldsymbol{v} \in \mathbb{D}^E$, we sometimes write $\boldsymbol{v}[E']$ as an abbreviation for $(v_i)_{i \in E'}$. The *support of* $\boldsymbol{v}$ is the set $[\![\boldsymbol{v}]\!] \stackrel{\text{def}}{=} \{i \in E : \boldsymbol{v}_i \neq 0\}$.

Given finite sets of indices $E$ and $F$, and $\mathbb{D} \subseteq \mathbb{Q}$, $\mathbb{D}^{E \times F}$ denotes the set of matrices over $\mathbb{D}$ with rows and columns indexed by elements from $E$ and $F$, respectively. Let $\mathbf{M} \in \mathbb{D}^{E \times F}$, $E' \subseteq E$ and $F' \subseteq F$, we denote by $\mathbf{M}_{E' \times F'}$ the $\mathbb{D}^{E' \times F'}$ sub-matrix obtained from $\mathbf{M}$ whose row and columns indices are restricted respectively to $E'$ and $F'$.

**Petri Nets.** In what follows, we introduce the syntax and semantics of Petri nets. While we provide a single syntax for nets, we introduce a discrete (i.e. in $\mathbb{N}$) and a continuous (i.e. in $\mathbb{Q}_+$) semantics.

**Definition 1.** *A Petri net is a tuple* $\mathcal{N} = (P, T, \mathbf{Pre}, \mathbf{Post})$, *where $P$ is a finite set of* places; *$T$ is a finite set of* transitions *with $P \cap T = \emptyset$; and $\mathbf{Pre}, \mathbf{Post} \in \mathbb{N}^{P \times T}$ are the* backward *and* forward *incidence matrices, respectively.*

A (discrete) *marking* of $\mathcal{N}$ is a vector of $\mathbb{N}^P$. A *Petri net system (PNS)* is a pair $\mathcal{S} = (\mathcal{N}, \boldsymbol{m}_0)$, where $\mathcal{N}$ is a Petri net and $\boldsymbol{m}_0 \in \mathbb{N}^P$ is the *initial marking*. The *incidence matrix* $\mathbf{C}$ of $\mathcal{N}$ is the $P \times T$ integer matrix defined by $\mathbf{C} \stackrel{\text{def}}{=} \mathbf{Post} - \mathbf{Pre}$. The *reverse net* of $\mathcal{N}$ is $\mathcal{N}^{-1} \stackrel{\text{def}}{=} (P, T, \mathbf{Post}, \mathbf{Pre})$. Let $p \in P$ and

$t \in T$, the *pre-sets* of $p$ and $t$ are the sets ${}^\bullet p \overset{\text{def}}{=} \{t' \in T : \mathbf{Post}(p, t') > 0\}$ and ${}^\bullet t \overset{\text{def}}{=} \{p' \in P : \mathbf{Pre}(p', t) > 0\}$, respectively. Likewise, the *post-sets* of $p$ and $t$ are $p^\bullet \overset{\text{def}}{=} \{t' \in T : \mathbf{Pre}(p, t') > 0\}$ and $t^\bullet = \{p' \in P : \mathbf{Post}(p', t) > 0\}$, respectively. Those definitions can canonically be lifted to subsets of places and of transitions, e.g., for $Q \subseteq P$ we have ${}^\bullet Q = \bigcup_{p \in Q} {}^\bullet p$. We also introduce the *neighbors* of a subset of places/transitions by: ${}^\bullet Q^\bullet = {}^\bullet Q \cup Q^\bullet$. Let $S \subseteq T$, then $\mathcal{N}_S$ is the sub-net defined by $\mathcal{N}_S \overset{\text{def}}{=} ({}^\bullet S^\bullet, S, \mathbf{Pre}{\cdot}{}_{S^\bullet \times S}, \mathbf{Post}{\cdot}{}_{S^\bullet \times S})$.

We say that a transition $t \in T$ is *enabled* at a marking $m$ whenever $m(p) \geq \mathbf{Pre}(p, t)$ for every $p \in {}^\bullet t$. A transition $t$ that is enabled can be *fired*, leading to a new marking $m'$ such that for all places $p \in P$, $m'(p) = m(p) + \mathbf{C}(p, t)$. We write $m \overset{t}{\to} m'$ whenever $t$ is enabled at $m$ leading to $m'$, and write $m \to m'$ if $m \overset{t}{\to} m'$ for some $t \in T$. By $\to^*$ we denote the reflexive transitive closure of $\to$. A word $\sigma = t_1 t_2 \cdots t_k \in T^*$ is a *firing sequence* of $(\mathcal{N}, m_0)$ whenever there exist markings $m_1, \ldots, m_k$ such that

$$m_0 \overset{t_1}{\longrightarrow} m_1 \overset{t_2}{\longrightarrow} \cdots \overset{t_{k-1}}{\longrightarrow} m_{k-1} \overset{t_k}{\longrightarrow} m_k.$$

Given a marking $m$, the *reachability* problem asks whether $m_0 \to^* m$. The reachability problem is decidable, EXPSPACE-hard [4] and in $\mathbf{F}_{\omega^3}$ [23], a non-primitive-recursive complexity class. In this paper, however, we are interested in deciding coverability, an EXPSPACE-complete problem [4,24].

**Definition 2.** *Given a Petri net system $\mathcal{S} = (P, T, \mathbf{Pre}, \mathbf{Post}, m_0)$ and a marking $m \in \mathbb{N}^P$, the coverability problem asks whether $m_0 \to^* m'$ for some $m' \geq m$.*

*Continuous Petri nets* are Petri nets in which markings may consist of rational numbers[2], and in which transitions may be fired a fractional number of times. Formally, a marking of a continuous Petri net is a vector $m \in \mathbb{Q}_+^P$. Let $t \in T$, the *enabling degree* of $t$ with respect to $m$ is a function $enab(t, m) \in \mathbb{Q}_+ \cup \{\infty\}$ defined by:

$$enab(t, m) \overset{\text{def}}{=} \begin{cases} \min\{m(p)/\mathbf{Pre}(p, t) : p \in {}^\bullet t\} & \text{if } {}^\bullet t \neq \emptyset, \\ \infty & \text{otherwise.} \end{cases}$$

We say that $t$ is $\mathbb{Q}$-*enabled* at $m$ if $enab(t, m) > 0$. If $t$ is $\mathbb{Q}$-enabled it may be *fired* by any amount $q \in \mathbb{Q}_+$ such that $0 \leq q \leq enab(t, m)$, leading to a new marking $m'$ such that for all places $p \in P$, $m(p)' \overset{\text{def}}{=} m(p) + q \cdot \mathbf{C}(p, t)$. In this case, we write $m \overset{q \cdot t}{\longrightarrow} m'$. The definition of a $\mathbb{Q}$-*firing sequence* $\sigma = q_1 t_1 \cdots q_k t_k \in (\mathbb{Q}_+ \times T)^*$ is analogous to the standard definition of firing sequence, and so are $\to_{\mathbb{Q}}$, $\to_{\mathbb{Q}}^*$ and $\mathbb{Q}$-reachability. The $\mathbb{Q}$-*Parikh image* of the firing sequence $\sigma$ is the vector $\pi(\sigma) \in \mathbb{Q}_+^T$ such that $\pi(\sigma)(t) \overset{\text{def}}{=} \sum_{t_i = t} q_i$. We also adapt the decision problems for Petri nets.

---

[2] In fact, the original definition allows for real numbers, however for studying decidability and complexity issues, rational numbers are more convenient.

**Definition 3.** *Given a Petri net system* $\mathcal{S} = (P, T, \mathbf{Pre}, \mathbf{Post}, m_0)$ *and a marking* $m \in \mathbb{Q}_+^P$, *the* $\mathbb{Q}$-*reachability (respectively* $\mathbb{Q}$-*coverability) problem asks whether* $m_0 \to_{\mathbb{Q}}^* m$ *(respectively* $m_0 \to_{\mathbb{Q}}^* m'$ *for some* $m' \geq m$).

Recently $\mathbb{Q}$-reachability and $\mathbb{Q}$-coverability were shown to be decidable in polynomial time [14]. In Sect. 3.2, we will discuss in detail the approach from [14]. For now, observe that $m \to m'$ implies $m \to_{\mathbb{Q}} m'$, and hence $m \to^* m'$ implies $m \to_{\mathbb{Q}}^* m'$. Consequently, $\mathbb{Q}$-coverability provides an over-approximation of coverability: this fact is the cornerstone of this paper.

**Upward Closed Sets.** A set $V \subseteq \mathbb{N}^P$ is *upward closed* if for every $v \in V$ and $w \in \mathbb{N}^P$, $v \leq w$ implies $w \in V$. The *upward closure* of a vector $v \in \mathbb{N}^P$ is the set $\uparrow v \stackrel{\text{def}}{=} \{w \in \mathbb{N}^P : v \leq w\}$. This definition can be lifted to sets $V \subseteq \mathbb{N}^P$ in the obvious way, i.e., $\uparrow V \stackrel{\text{def}}{=} \bigcup_{v \in V} \uparrow v$. Due to $\mathbb{N}^P$ being well-quasi-ordered by $\leq$, any upward-closed set $V$ contains a finite set $F \subseteq V$ such that $V = \uparrow F$. Such an $F$ is called a *basis* of $V$ and allows for a finite representation of an upward-closed set. In particular, it can be shown that $V$ contains a unique *minimal basis* $B \subseteq V$ that is minimal with respect to inclusion for all bases $F \subseteq V$. We denote $minbase(F)$ this minimal basis obtained by deleting vectors $v \in F$ such that there exists $w \in F$ with $w < v$ (when $F$ is finite).

# 3   Deciding Coverability and $\mathbb{Q}$-Reachability

We now introduce and discuss existing algorithms for solving coverability and $\mathbb{Q}$-reachability which form the basis of our approach. The main reason for doing so is that it allows us to smoothly introduce some additional notations and concepts that we require in the next section. For the remainder of this section, we fix some Petri net system $\mathcal{S} = (\mathcal{N}, m_0)$ with $\mathcal{N} = (P, T, \mathbf{Pre}, \mathbf{Post})$, and some marking $m$ to be covered or $\mathbb{Q}$-reached.

## 3.1   The Backward Coverability Algorithm

The standard backward coverability algorithm, Algorithm 1, is a simple to state algorithm.

- It iteratively constructs minimal bases $M$, where in the $k$-th iteration, $M$ is the minimal basis of the (upward closed) set of markings that can cover $m$ after a firing sequence of length at most $k$. If $m_0 \in \uparrow M$, the algorithm returns true, i.e., that $m$ is coverable. Otherwise, in order to update $M$, for all $m' \in M$ and $t \in T$ it computes $m'_t(p) \stackrel{\text{def}}{=} \max\{\mathbf{Pre}(p, t), m'(p) - \mathbf{C}(p, t)\}$. The singleton $\{m'_t\}$ is the minimal basis of the set of vectors that can cover $m'$ after firing $t$.
- Thus defining $pb(M)$ as $pb(M) \stackrel{\text{def}}{=} \bigcup_{m' \in M, t \in T} \{m'_t\}$, $M \cup pb(M)$ is a (not necessarily minimal) basis of the upward closed set of markings that can cover $m$ after a firing sequence of length at most $k + 1$. This basis can be then minimized in every iteration.

---
**Algorithm 1.** Backward Coverability
---
**Require:** PNS $\mathcal{S} = (\mathcal{N}, m_0)$ and a marking $m \in \mathbb{N}^P$
1:  $M := \{m\}$;
2:  **while** $m_0 \notin \uparrow M$ **do**
3:      $B := pb(M) \setminus \uparrow M$;
4:      **if** $B = \emptyset$ **then**
5:          **return** *false*;
6:      **else**
7:          $M := minbase(M \cup B)$;
8:  **return** *true*;
---

The termination of the algorithm is guaranteed due to $\mathbb{N}^P$ being well-quasi-ordered, which entails that $M$ must stabilize and return false in this case. It can be shown that Algorithm 1 runs in 2-EXP [3]. The key point to the (empirical) performance of the algorithm is the size of the set $M$ during its computation: the smaller, the better. Even though one can establish a doubly-exponential lower bound on the cardinality of $M$ during the execution of the algorithm, in general not every element in $M$ is coverable, even when $m$ is coverable.

## 3.2    The $\mathbb{Q}$-Reachability Algorithm

We now present the fundamental concepts of the polynomial-time $\mathbb{Q}$-reachability algorithm of Fraca and Haddad [14]. The key insight underlying their algorithm is that $\mathbb{Q}$-reachability can be characterized in terms of three simple criteria. The algorithm relies on the notions of *firing set* and *maximal firing set*, denoted $fs(\mathcal{N}, m)$ and $maxfs(\mathcal{N}, m)$, and defined as follows:

$$fs(\mathcal{N}, m) \stackrel{\text{def}}{=} \{ [\![\pi(\sigma)]\!] : \sigma \in (\mathbb{Q}_+ \times T)^*, \text{ there is } m' \in \mathbb{Q}_+^P \text{ s.t. } m \xrightarrow{\sigma}_\mathbb{Q} m' \}$$

$$maxfs(\mathcal{N}, m) \stackrel{\text{def}}{=} \bigcup_{T' \in fs(\mathcal{N}, m)} T'.$$

Thus, $fs(\mathcal{N}, m)$ is the set of supports of firing sequences starting in $m$. Even though $fs(\mathcal{N}, m)$ can be of size exponential with respect to $|T|$, deciding $T' \in fs(\mathcal{N}, m)$ for some $T' \subseteq T$ can be done in polynomial time, and $maxfs(\mathcal{N}, m)$ is also computable in polynomial time [14]. The following proposition characterizes the set of $\mathbb{Q}$-reachable markings.

**Proposition 4** ([14, Theorem 20]). *A marking $m$ is $\mathbb{Q}$-reachable in $\mathcal{S} = (\mathcal{N}, m_0)$ if and only if there exists $x \in \mathbb{Q}_+^T$ such that*

(i) $m = m_0 + \mathbf{C} \cdot x$
(ii) $[\![x]\!] \in fs(\mathcal{N}, m_0)$
(iii) $[\![x]\!] \in fs(\mathcal{N}^{-1}, m)$

In this characterization, $x$ is supposed to be the Parikh image of a firing sequence. The first item expresses the state equation of $\mathcal{S}$ with respect to

---

**Algorithm 2.** $\mathbb{Q}$-reachability [14]

---

**Require:** PNS $S = (\mathcal{N}, m_0)$ with $\mathcal{N} = (P, T, \mathbf{Pre}, \mathbf{Post})$ and a marking $m$
1: **if** $m = m_0$ **then**
2:     **return** *true*;
3: $T' := T$;
4: **while** $T' \neq \emptyset$ **do**
5:     $S := \emptyset$;
6:     **for all** $t \in T'$ **do**
7:         $x := solve(\mathbf{C}_{P \times T'} \cdot x = m - m_0 \wedge x(t) > 0 \wedge x \in \mathbb{Q}_+^{T'})$;
8:         **if** $x \neq undef$ **then**
9:             $S := S \cup [\![x]\!]$;
10:    **if** $S = \emptyset$ **then**
11:       **return** *false*;
12:    $T' := maxfs(\mathcal{N}_S, m_0[{}^\bullet S^\bullet])) \cap maxfs(\mathcal{N}_S^{-1}, m[{}^\bullet S^\bullet]))$
13:    **if** $T' = S$ **then**
14:       **return** *true*;
15: **return** *false*;

---

$m_0$, $m$ and $x$. The two subsequent items express that the support of the solution of the state equation has to lie in the firing sets of $S$ and its reverse. As such, the characterization in Proposition 4 yields an NP algorithm. By employing a greatest fixed point computation, Algorithm 2, which is a decision variant of the algorithm presented in [14], turns those criteria into a polynomial-time algorithm (see [14] for a proof of its correctness). In order to use Algorithm 2 for deciding coverability, it is sufficient, for each place $p$, to add a transition to $\mathcal{N}$ that can at any time non-deterministically decrease $p$ by one token. Denote the resulting Petri net system by $S'$, it can easily checked that $m$ is $\mathbb{Q}$-coverable in $S$ if and only if $m$ is $\mathbb{Q}$-reachable in $S'$.

## 4   Backward Coverability Modulo $\mathbb{Q}$-Reachability

We now present our decision algorithm for the Petri net coverability problem.

### 4.1   Encoding $\mathbb{Q}$-Reachability into Existential $\mathrm{FO}(\mathbb{Q}_+, +, >)$

Throughout this section, when used in formulas, $w$ and $x$ are vectors of first-order variables indexed by $P$ representing markings, and $y$ is a vector of first-order variables indexed by $T$ representing the $\mathbb{Q}$-Parikh image of a transition sequence.

Condition (i) of Proposition 4, which expresses the state equation, is readily expressed as a system of linear equations and thus directly corresponds to a formula $\Phi(w, x, y)$ which holds whenever a marking $x$ is reached starting at marking $w$ by firing every transition $y(t)$ times (without any consideration whether such a firing sequence would actually be admissible):

$$\Phi_{eqn}^{\mathcal{N}}(w, x, y) \overset{\mathrm{def}}{=} x = \mathbf{C} \cdot y + w.$$

Next, we show how to encode Conditions (ii) and (iii) into suitable formulas. To this end, we require an effective characterization of membership in the firing set $fs(\mathcal{N}, \boldsymbol{w})$ defined in Sect. 3.2. The following characterization can be derived from [14, Corollary 19]. First, we define a monotonic increasing function $incfs_{\mathcal{N},\boldsymbol{w}} : 2^T \to 2^T$ as follows:

$$incfs_{\mathcal{N},\boldsymbol{w}}(S) \overset{\text{def}}{=} S \cup \{t \in T(\mathcal{N}) : {}^\bullet t \subseteq \llbracket \boldsymbol{w} \rrbracket \cup \{s^\bullet : s \in S\}\}.$$

From [14, Corollary 19], it follows that $T' \in fs(\mathcal{N}, \boldsymbol{w})$ if and only if $T' = \mathrm{lfp}(incfs_{\mathcal{N}_{T'},\boldsymbol{w}})$, where lfp is the least fixed point operator[3], i.e.,

$$T' = incfs_{\mathcal{N}_{T'},\boldsymbol{w}}(\cdots(incfs_{\mathcal{N}_{T'},\boldsymbol{w}}(\emptyset))\cdots).$$

Clearly, the least fixed point is reached after at most $|T'|$ iterations.

In order to decide whether $\llbracket \boldsymbol{y} \rrbracket \in fs(\mathcal{N}, \boldsymbol{w})$, we simulate this fixed-point computation in an existential $\mathrm{FO}(\mathbb{Q}_+, +, >)$-formula $\Phi_{fs}^{\mathcal{N}}(\boldsymbol{w}, \boldsymbol{y})$. Our approach is inspired by a technique of Verma, Seidl and Schwentick that was used to show that the reachability relation for communication-free Petri nets is definable by an existential Presburger arithmetic formula of linear size [28]. The basic idea is to introduce additional first-order variables $\boldsymbol{z}$ indexed by $P \cup T$ that, given a firing set, capture the relative order in which transitions of this set are fired and the order in which their input places are marked. This order corresponds to the computation of $\mathrm{lfp}(incfs_{\mathcal{N}_{\llbracket \boldsymbol{y} \rrbracket},\boldsymbol{w}})$ and is encoded via a numerical value $\boldsymbol{z}(t)$ (respectively $\boldsymbol{z}(p)$), representing an index that must be strictly greater than zero for a transition (respectively an input place of a transition) of this set. In addition, input places have to be marked before the firing of a transition:

$$\Phi_{dt}^{\mathcal{N}}(\boldsymbol{y}, \boldsymbol{z}) \overset{\text{def}}{=} \bigwedge_{t \in T}\left(\boldsymbol{y}(t) > 0 \to \bigwedge_{p \in {}^\bullet t} 0 < \boldsymbol{z}(p) \leq \boldsymbol{z}(t)\right).$$

Moreover, a place is either initially marked or after the firing of a transition of the firing set. So:

$$\Phi_{mk}^{\mathcal{N}}(\boldsymbol{w}, \boldsymbol{y}, \boldsymbol{z}) \overset{\text{def}}{=} \bigwedge_{p \in P}\left(\boldsymbol{z}(p) > 0 \to \left(\boldsymbol{w}(p) > 0 \vee \bigvee_{t \in {}^\bullet p} \boldsymbol{y}(t) > 0 \wedge \boldsymbol{z}(t) < \boldsymbol{z}(p)\right)\right).$$

We can now take the conjunction of the formulas above in order to obtain a logical characterization of $fs(\mathcal{N}, \boldsymbol{w})$:

$$\Phi_{fs}^{\mathcal{N}}(\boldsymbol{w}, \boldsymbol{y}) \overset{\text{def}}{=} \exists \boldsymbol{z} : \Phi_{dt}^{\mathcal{N}}(\boldsymbol{y}, \boldsymbol{z}) \wedge \Phi_{mk}^{\mathcal{N}}(\boldsymbol{w}, \boldsymbol{y}, \boldsymbol{z}).$$

Having logically characterized all conditions of Proposition 4, we can define the global $\mathbb{Q}$-reachability relation for a Petri net system $\mathcal{S} = (\mathcal{N}, \boldsymbol{w})$ as follows:

$$\Phi_{\mathcal{S}}(\boldsymbol{w}, \boldsymbol{x}) \overset{\text{def}}{=} \exists \boldsymbol{y} : \Phi_{eqn}^{\mathcal{N}}(\boldsymbol{w}, \boldsymbol{x}, \boldsymbol{y}) \wedge \Phi_{fs}^{\mathcal{N}}(\boldsymbol{w}, \boldsymbol{y}) \wedge \Phi_{fs}^{\mathcal{N}^{-1}}(\boldsymbol{x}, \boldsymbol{y}).$$

In summary, we have thus proved the following result in this section.

---

[3] In [14, Corollary 19], an algorithm is presented that basically computes $\mathrm{lfp}(incfs_{\mathcal{N}_{T'},\boldsymbol{w}})$.

---

**Algorithm 3.** Backward Coverability Modulo $\mathbb{Q}$-Reachability

---

**Require:** PNS $\mathcal{S} = (\mathcal{N}, m_0)$ and a marking $m \in \mathbb{N}^P$
1:  $M := \{m\}$; $\Phi(x) := \exists y : \Phi_{\mathcal{S}}(m_0, y) \wedge y \geq x$;
2:  **if not** $\mathbb{Q}$-*coverable*$(\mathcal{S}, m)$ **then**
3:      **return** *false*
4:  **while** $m_0 \notin \uparrow M$ **do**
5:      $B := pb(M) \setminus \uparrow M$;
6:      $D := \{v \in B : unsat(\Phi(v))\}$;
7:      $B := B \setminus D$;
8:      **if** $B = \emptyset$ **then**
9:          **return** *false*;
10:     **else**
11:         $M := minbase(M \cup B)$;
12:         $\Phi(x) := \Phi(x) \wedge \bigwedge_{v \in D} x \ngeq v$;
13: **return** *true*;

---

**Proposition 5.** *Let $\mathcal{S} = (\mathcal{N}, m_0)$ be a Petri net system and $m$ be a marking. There exists an existential $FO(\mathbb{Q}_+, +, >)$-formula $\Phi_{\mathcal{S}}(w, x)$ computable in linear time such that $m$ is $\mathbb{Q}$-reachable in $\mathcal{S}$ if and only if $\Phi_{\mathcal{S}}(m_0, m)$ is valid.*

Checking satisfiability of $\Phi_{\mathcal{S}}$ is in NP, see e.g. [26]. It is a valid question to ask why one would prefer an NP-algorithm over a polynomial-time one. We address this question in the next section. For now, note that in order to obtain an even more accurate over-approximation, we can additionally restrict $y$ to be interpreted in the natural numbers while retaining membership of satisfiability in NP, due to the following variant of Proposition 4: If a marking is reachable in $\mathcal{S}$ then there exists some $y \in \mathbb{N}^T$ such that Conditions (i), (ii) and (iii) of Proposition 4 hold.

*Remark 6.* Proposition 5 additionally allows us to improve the best known upper bound for the *inclusion problem* of continuous Petri nets, which is EXP [14]. Given two Petri net systems $\mathcal{S} = (\mathcal{N}, m_0)$ and $\mathcal{S}' = (\mathcal{N}', m_0')$ over the same set of places, this problem asks whether the set of reachable markings of $\mathcal{S}$ is included in $\mathcal{S}'$, i.e., whether $\forall m.\Phi_{\mathcal{S}}(m_0, m) \rightarrow \Phi_{\mathcal{S}'}(m_0', m)$ is valid. The latter is a $\Pi_2$-sentence of $FO(\mathbb{Q}_+, +, >)$ and decidable in $\Pi_2^P$ [26]. Hence, inclusion between continuous Petri nets is in $\Pi_2^P$.

### 4.2    The Coverability Decision Procedure

We now present Algorithm 3 for deciding coverability. This algorithm is an extension of the classical backward reachability algorithm that incorporates $\mathbb{Q}$-reachability checks during its execution in order to keep the set of minimal basis elements small.

First, on Line 1 we derive an open formula $\Phi(x)$ from $\Phi_{\mathcal{S}}$ such that $\Phi(x)$ holds if and only if $x$ is $\mathbb{Q}$-coverable in $\mathcal{S}$. Then, on Line 2, the algorithm checks whether the marking $m$ is $\mathbb{Q}$-coverable using the polynomial-time algorithm from [14] and returns that $m$ is not coverable if this is not the case. Otherwise, the algorithm enters a loop which iteratively computes a basis $M$ of the backward coverability set starting at $m$ whose elements are in addition $\mathbb{Q}$-coverable in $\mathcal{S}$. To this end, on Line 5 the algorithm computes a set $B$ of new basis elements obtained from one application of $pb$, and on Line 7 it removes from $B$ the set $D$ which contains all elements of $B$ which are not $\mathbb{Q}$-coverable. If as a result $B$ is empty the algorithm concludes that $m$ is not coverable in $\mathcal{S}$. Otherwise, on Line 11 it adds the elements of $B$ to $M$. Finally, Line 12 makes sure that in future iterations of the loop the underlying SMT solver can immediately discard elements that lie in $\uparrow D$. The latter is technically not necessary, but it provides some guidance to the SMT solver. The proof of the following proposition can be found in [2].

**Proposition 7.** *Let $\mathcal{S} = (\mathcal{N}, m_0)$ be a PNS and $m$ be a marking. Then $m$ is coverable in $\mathcal{S}$ if and only if Algorithm 3 returns true.*

*Remark 8.* In our actual implementation, we use a slight variation of Algorithm 3 in which the instruction $M := minbase(M \cup B)$ in Line 11 is replaced by $M := minbase(M \cup min_{c,k}B)$. Here, $c, k \in \mathbb{N}$ are parameters to the algorithm, and $min_{c,k}B$ is the set of the $c + |B|/k$ elements of $B$ with the smallest sum-norm. In this way, the empirically chosen parameters $c$ and $k$ create a bottleneck that gives priority to elements with small sum-norms, as they are more likely to allow for discarding elements with larger sum-norms in future iterations.

This variation of Algorithm 3 has the same correctness properties as the original one: It can be shown that using $min_{c,k}B$ instead of $B$ in Line 11 computes the same set $\uparrow M$ at the expense of delaying its stabilization.

Before we conclude this section, let us come back to the question why in our approach we choose using $\Phi_\mathcal{S}$ (whose satisfiability is in NP) over Algorithm 2 which runs in polynomial time. In Algorithm 3, we invoke Algorithm 2 only once in Line 2 in order to check if $\mathcal{S}$ is not $\mathbb{Q}$-coverable, and thereafter only employ $\Phi_\mathcal{S}$ which gets incrementally updated during each iteration of the loop. The reason is that in practice as observed in our experimental evaluation below, Algorithm 2 turns out to be often faster for a *single* $\mathbb{Q}$-coverability query. Otherwise, as soon $\Phi_\mathcal{S}$ has been checked for satisfiability once, future satisfiability queries are significantly faster than Algorithm 2, which is a desirable behavior inside a backward coverability framework. Moreover we can constraint solutions to be in $\mathbb{N}$ instead of $\mathbb{Q}$, leading to a more precise over approximation.

## 4.3   Relationship to the CEGAR-approach of Esparza Et Al

In [10], Esparza *et al.* presented a semi-decision procedure for coverability that is based on [11] and employs the Petri net state equation and traps inside a CEGAR-framework. A *trap in* $\mathcal{N}$ is a non-empty subset of places $Q \subseteq P$ such that $Q^\bullet \subseteq {}^\bullet Q$, and $Q \subseteq P$ is a *siphon in* $\mathcal{N}$ whenever ${}^\bullet Q \subseteq Q^\bullet$. Given a marking $m$, a trap (respectively siphon) is *marked in* $m$ if $\sum_{p \in Q} m(p) > 0$. An important property of traps is that if a trap is marked in $m$, it will remain marked after

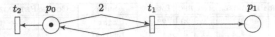

**Fig. 1.** A Petri net that cannot mark $p_1$.

any firing sequence starting in $m$. Conversely, when a siphon is unmarked in $m$ it remains so after any firing sequence starting in $m$. By definition, $Q$ is a trap in $\mathcal{N}$ if and only if $Q$ is a siphon in $\mathcal{N}^{-1}$. The coverability criteria that [10] builds upon are derived from [11] and can be summarized as follows.

**Proposition 9** ([10]). *If $m$ is $\mathbb{Q}$-reachable (respectively reachable) in $(\mathcal{N}, m_0)$ then there exists $x \in \mathbb{Q}_+^T$ (respectively $x \in \mathbb{N}^T$) such that:*

*(i) $m = m_0 + \mathbf{C} \cdot x$*
*(ii) for all traps $Q \subseteq P$, if $Q$ is marked in $m_0$ then $Q$ is marked in $m$*

As in our approach, in [10] those criteria are checked using an SMT-solver. The for-all quantifier is replaced in [10] by incrementally enumerating all traps in a CEGAR-style fashion. It is shown in [14, Proposition 18] that Condition (iii) of Proposition 4 is equivalent to requiring that $\mathcal{N}_{\llbracket x \rrbracket}^{-1}$ has no unmarked siphon in $m$, which appears to be similar to Condition (ii) of Proposition 9. In fact, we show the following.

**Proposition 10.** *Conditions (i) and (iii) of Proposition 4 strictly imply Conditions (i) and (ii) of Proposition 9 (when interpreted over $\mathbb{Q}_+$).*

*Proof.* We only show strictness, the full proof can be found in [2]. To this end, consider the Petri net $(\mathcal{N}, m_0)$ depicted in Fig. 1 with $m = (0, 1)$. Clearly $m$ is not reachable. There is a single solution to the state equation $x = (1, 0)$. There is a single trap $\{p_1\}$ which is unmarked in $m_0$. So the conditions of Proposition 9 hold, and hence the algorithm of [10] does not decide this net safe. On the contrary in $\mathcal{N}_{\llbracket x \rrbracket}^{-1}$, the reverse net without $t_2$, $\{p_0\}$ is a siphon that is unmarked in $m$. So Condition (iii) of Proposition 4 does not hold.                                                  □

This proposition shows that the single formula stated in Proposition 5 strictly subsumes the approach from [10]. Moreover, it provides a theoretical justification for why the approach of [10] performs so well in practice: the conditions are a strict subset of the conditions developed for $\mathbb{Q}$-reachability in [14].

## 5    Experimental Evaluation

We evaluate the backward coverability modulo $\mathbb{Q}$-reachability algorithm on standard benchmarks from the literature with two goals in mind. First, we demonstrate that our approach is competitive with existing approaches. In particular, we prove significantly more safe instances of our benchmarks safe in less time when compared to any other approach. Overall our algorithm decides 142 out

| Suite | QCOVER | PETRINIZER | MIST | BFC | Total |
|---|---|---|---|---|---|
| mist | **23** | 20 | 22 | 20 | 23 |
| medical | **11** | 4 | **11** | 3 | 12 |
| bfc | **2** | **2** | **2** | **2** | 2 |
| bug_tracking | **32** | **32** | 0 | 19 | 40 |
| soter | **37** | **37** | 0 | 19 | 38 |
| Total | **105** | 95 | 35 | 63 | 115 |

| Suite | QCOVER | PETRINIZER | MIST | BFC | Total |
|---|---|---|---|---|---|
| mist | 3 | — | **4** | **4** | 4 |
| medical | — | — | — | — | 0 |
| bfc | 26 | — | 29 | **42** | 44 |
| bug_tracking | 0 | — | 0 | **1** | 1 |
| soter | 8 | — | 6 | **12** | 12 |
| Total | 37 | 0 | 39 | **59** | 61 |

| Suite | QCOVER | PETRINIZER | MIST | BFC | Total |
|---|---|---|---|---|---|
| mist | **26** | 20 | **26** | 24 | 27 |
| medical | **11** | 4 | **11** | 3 | 12 |
| bfc | 28 | 2 | 31 | **44** | 46 |
| bug_tracking | **32** | **32** | 0 | 20 | 41 |
| soter | **45** | 37 | 6 | 31 | 50 |
| Total | **142** | 95 | 74 | 122 | 176 |

**Fig. 2.** Number of safe instances (top-left), unsafe instances (top-right) and total instances (bottom) decided by every tool. Bold numbers indicate the tool(s) which decide(s) the largest number of instances in the respective category.

of 176 instances, the best competitor decides 122 instances. Second, we demonstrate that $\mathbb{Q}$-coverability is a powerful pruning criterion by analyzing the relative number of minimal bases elements that get discarded during the execution of Algorithm 3.

We implemented Algorithm 3 in a tool called QCOVER in the programming language PYTHON.[4] The underlying SMT-solver is z3 [6]. For the $min_{c,k}$ heuristic mentioned in Remark 8, we empirically chose $c = 10$ and $k = 5$. We observed that any sane choice of $c$ and $k$ leads to an overall speed-up, though different values lead to different (even increasing) running times on individual instances. QCOVER takes as input coverability instances in the MIST file format.[5] The basis of our evaluation is the benchmark suite that was used in order to evaluate the tool PETRINIZER, see [10] and the references therein. This suite consists of five benchmark categories: mist, consisting of 27 instances from the MIST toolkit; bfc, consisting of 46 instances used for evaluating BFC; medical and bug_tracking, consisting of 12 and 41 instances derived from the provenance analysis of messages of a medical and a bug-tracking system, respectively; and soter, consisting of 50 instances of verification conditions derived from Erlang programs [9].

We compare QCOVER with the following tools: PETRINIZER [10], MIST [15] and BFC [20] in their latest versions available at the time of writing of this paper. MIST implements a number of algorithms, we use the backward algorithm that uses places invariant pruning [16].[6] All benchmarks were performed on a single computer equipped with four Intel® Core™ 2.00 GHz CPUs, 8 GB of memory and Ubuntu Linux 14.04 (64 bits). The execution time of the tools was limited to 2000 s (i.e. 33 min and 20 s) per benchmark instance. The running time of every tool on an instance was determined using the sum of the user and sys time reported by the Linux tool time.

---

[4] QCOVER is available at http://www-etud.iro.umontreal.ca/~blondimi/qcover/.

[5] https://github.com/pierreganty/mist/wiki#input-format-of-mist.

[6] https://github.com/pierreganty/mist/wiki#coverability-checkers-included-in-mist.

Figure 2 contains three tables which display the number of safe instances shown safe, unsafe instances shown unsafe, and the total number of instances of our benchmark suite decided by each individual tool. As expected, our algorithm outperforms all competitors on safe instances, since in this case a proof of safety (i.e. non-coverability) effectively requires the computation of the whole backward coverability set, and this is where pruning via $\mathbb{Q}$-coverability becomes most beneficial. On the other hand, QCOVER remains competitive on unsafe instances, though a tool such as BFC handles those instances better since its heuristics are more suited for proving unsafety (i.e. coverability). Nevertheless, QCOVER is the overall winner when comparing the number of safe and unsafe instances decided, being far ahead at the top of the leader-board deciding 142 out of 176 instances.

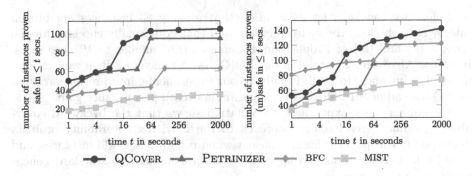

**Fig. 3.** Cumulative number of instances proven safe (left) and total number of instances decided (right) within a fixed amount of time.

QCOVER not only decides more instances, it often does so faster than its competitors. Figure 3 contains two graphs which show the cumulative number of instances proven safe and the total number of instances decided on all suites by each tool within a certain amount of time. When it comes to safety, QCOVER is always ahead of all other tools. However, when looking at all instances decided, BFC first has an advantage. We observed that this advantage occurs on instances of comparably small size. As soon as large instances come into play, QCOVER wins the race. Besides different heuristics used, one reason for this might be the choice of the implementation language (C for BFC vs. PYTHON for QCOVER). In particular, BFC can decide a non-negligible number of instances in less than 10ms, which QCOVER never achieves.

Finally, we consider the effectiveness of using $\mathbb{Q}$-coverability as a pruning criterion. To this end, consider Fig. 4 in which we plotted the number of times a certain percentage of basis elements was removed due to not being $\mathbb{Q}$-coverable. Impressively, in some cases more than 95 % of the basis elements get discarded. Overall, on average we discard 56 % of the basis elements, which substantiates the usefulness of using $\mathbb{Q}$-coverability as a pruning criterion.

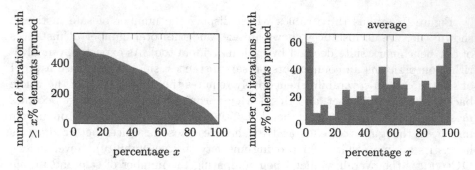

**Fig. 4.** Number of times a certain percentage of basis elements was removed due to $\mathbb{Q}$-coverability pruning.

Before we conclude, let us mention that already 83 instances are proven safe by only checking the state equation, and that additionally checking for the criteria (ii) and (iii) of Proposition 4 increases this number to 101 instances. If we use Algorithm 2 instead of our $FO(\mathbb{Q}_+, +, >)$ encoding then we can only decide 132 instances in total. Finally, in our experiments, interpreting variables over $\mathbb{Q}$ instead of $\mathbb{N}$ resulted in no measurable overall performance gain.

In summary, our experimental evaluation shows that the backward coverability modulo $\mathbb{Q}$-reachability approach to the Petri net coverability problem developed in this paper is highly efficient when run on real-world instances, and superior to existing tools and approaches when compared on standard benchmarks from the literature.

## 6    Conclusion

In this paper, we introduced backward coverability modulo $\mathbb{Q}$-reachability, a novel approach to the Petri net coverability problem that is based on using coverability in continuous Petri nets as a pruning criterion inside a backward coverability framework. A key ingredient for the practicality of this approach is an existential $FO(\mathbb{Q}_+, +, >)$-characterization of continuous reachability, which we showed to strictly subsume a recently introduced coverability semi-decision procedure [10]. Finally, we demonstrated that our approach significantly outperforms existing ones when compared on standard benchmarks.

There are a number of possible avenues for future work. It seems promising to combine the forward analysis approach based on incrementally constructing a Karp-Miller tree that is used in BFC [20] with the $\mathbb{Q}$-coverability approach introduced in this paper. In particular, recently developed minimization and acceleration techniques for constructing Karp-Miller trees should prove beneficial, see e.g. [18,25,27]. Another way to improve the empirical performance of our algorithm is to internally use more efficient data structures such as sharing trees [8]. It seems within reach that a tool which combines all of the aforementioned techniques and heuristics could decide all of the benchmark instances we used in this paper within reasonable resource restrictions.

**Acknowledgments.** We would like to thank Vincent Antaki for an early implementation of Algorithm 2. We would also like to thank Gilles Geeraerts for his support with the MIST file format.

# References

1. Cerans, K., Jonsson, B., Tsay, Y.-K.: Algorithmic analysis of programs with well quasi-ordered domains. Inf. Comput. **160**(1–2), 109–127 (2000)
2. Blondin, M., Finkel, A., Haase, C., Haddad, S.: Approaching the coverability problem continuously (2015). CoRR, abs/1510.05724
3. Bozzelli, L., Ganty, P.: Complexity analysis of the backward coverability algorithm for VASS. In: Delzanno, G., Potapov, I. (eds.) RP 2011. LNCS, vol. 6945, pp. 96–109. Springer, Heidelberg (2011)
4. Cardoza, E., Lipton, R.J., Meyer, A.R.: Exponential space complete problems for Petri nets, commutative semigroups: preliminary report. In: Symposium on Theory of Computing, STOC, pp. 50–54 (1976)
5. David, R., Alla, H.: Continuous Petri nets. In: Proceedings of the 8th European Workshop on Application and Theory of Petri nets, pp. 275–294 (1987)
6. de Moura, L., Bjørner, N.S.: Z3: an efficient SMT solver. In: Ramakrishnan, C.R., Rehof, J. (eds.) TACAS 2008. LNCS, vol. 4963, pp. 337–340. Springer, Heidelberg (2008)
7. Delzanno, G., Raskin, J.-F., Van Begin, L.: Attacking symbolic state explosion. In: Berry, G., Comon, H., Finkel, A. (eds.) CAV 2001. LNCS, vol. 2102, p. 298. Springer, Heidelberg (2001)
8. Delzanno, G., Raskin, J.-F., Van Begin, L.: Covering sharing trees: a compact data structure for parameterized verification. STTT **5**(2–3), 268–297 (2004)
9. D'Osualdo, E., Kochems, J., Ong, C.-H.L.: Automatic verification of erlang-style concurrency. In: Logozzo, F., Fähndrich, M. (eds.) Static Analysis. LNCS, vol. 7935, pp. 454–476. Springer, Heidelberg (2013)
10. Esparza, J., Ledesma-Garza, R., Majumdar, R., Meyer, P., Niksic, F.: An SMT-based approach to coverability analysis. In: Biere, A., Bloem, R. (eds.) CAV 2014. LNCS, vol. 8559, pp. 603–619. Springer, Heidelberg (2014)
11. Esparza, J., Melzer, S.: Verification of safety properties using integer programming: beyond the state equation. Formal Meth. Syst. Des. **16**(2), 159–189 (2000)
12. Finkel, A., Raskin, J.-F., Samuelides, M., Van Begin, L.: Monotonic extensions of Petri nets: forward and backward search revisited. Electr. Notes Theor. Comput. Sci. **68**(6), 85–106 (2002)
13. Finkel, A., Schnoebelen, P.: Well-structured transition systems everywhere!. Theor. Comput. Sci. **256**(1–2), 63–92 (2001)
14. Fraca, E., Haddad, S.: Complexity analysis of continuous Petri nets. Fundam. Informaticae **137**(1), 1–28 (2015)
15. Ganty, P.: Algorithmes et structures de données efficaces pour la manipulation de contraintes sur les intervalles (in French). Master's thesis, Université Libre de Bruxelles, Belgium (2002)
16. Ganty, P., Meuter, C., Delzanno, G., Kalyon, G., Raskin, J.-F., Van Begin, L.: Symbolic data structure for sets of k-uples. Technical report 570, Université Libre de Bruxelles, Belgium (2007)
17. Geeraerts, G., Raskin, J.-F., Van Begin, L.: Expand, enlarge and check: new algorithms for the coverability problem of WSTS. J. Comput. Syst. Sci. **72**(1), 180–203 (2006)

18. Geeraerts, G., Raskin, J.-F., Van Begin, L.: On the efficient computation of the minimal coverability set of petri nets. Int. J. Found. Comput. Sci. **21**(2), 135–165 (2010)
19. German, S.M., Prasad Sistla, A.: Reasoning about systems with many processes. J. ACM **39**(3), 675–735 (1992)
20. Kaiser, A., Kroening, D., Wahl, T.: A widening approach to multithreaded program verification. ACM Trans. Program. Lang. Syst. **36**(4), 1–29 (2014)
21. Karp, R.M., Miller, R.E.: Parallel program schemata: a mathematical model for parallel computation. In Switching and Automata Theory, pp. 55–61. IEEE Computer Society (1967)
22. Kloos, J., Majumdar, R., Niksic, F., Piskac, R.: Incremental, inductive coverability. In: Sharygina, N., Veith, H. (eds.) CAV 2013. LNCS, vol. 8044, pp. 158–173. Springer, Heidelberg (2013)
23. Leroux, J., Schmitz, S.: Demystifying reachability in vector addition systems. In: Logic in Computer Science, LICS, pp. 56–67. IEEE (2015)
24. Rackoff, C.: The covering and boundedness problems for vector addition systems. Theor. Comput. Sci. **6**, 223–231 (1978)
25. Reynier, P.-A., Servais, F.: Minimal coverability set for petri nets: karp and miller algorithm with pruning. Fundam. Inform. **122**(1–2), 1–30 (2013)
26. Sontag, E.D.: Real addition and the polynomial hierarchy. Inf. Process. Lett. **20**(3), 115–120 (1985)
27. Valmari, A., Hansen, H.: Old and new algorithms for minimal coverability sets. Fundam. Inform. **131**(1), 1–25 (2014)
28. Verma, K.N., Seidl, H., Schwentick, T.: On the complexity of equational horn clauses. In: Nieuwenhuis, R. (ed.) CADE 2005. LNCS (LNAI), vol. 3632, pp. 337–352. Springer, Heidelberg (2005)

# On Atomicity in Presence of Non-atomic Writes

Constantin Enea[1]([✉]) and Azadeh Farzan[2]

[1] Univ. Paris Diderot, Paris, France
cenea@liafa.univ-paris-diderot.fr
[2] University of Toronto, Toronto, Canada
azadeh@cs.toronto.edu

**Abstract.** The inherently nondeterministic semantics of concurrent programs is the root of many programming errors. Atomicity (more precisely conflict serializability) has been used to reduce the magnitude of this nondeterminism and therefore make it easier to understand the behaviour of the concurrent program. Serializability, however, has not been studied well for programs executed under memory models weaker than sequential consistency (SC), where writes are not atomic, i.e., they may be committed to the main memory later than issued. In this paper, we define the notion of conflict serializability for the Total Store Ordering (TSO) memory model, and study the relation between TSO-serializability and the well-known notions of SC-serializability and robustness. We investigate the algorithmic problem of monitoring program executions for violations of serializability, and provide lower bound complexity results for the problem, and new algorithms to perform the monitoring efficiently.

## 1  Introduction

While writing a concurrent program, a programmer often prefers to have non-interfered access to shared data that is manipulated by a thread, since this permits the reasoning about the correctness of the code to be done locally and therefore simplifies the process. *Atomicity* is a *generic* correctness criterion that is inspired by this view. Informally, an *atomic* code block has the same behaviour under interfering actions of other threads as it does when executed without interference (serially). Establishing atomicity of code blocks eases the task of reasoning about the program by substantially reducing the number of interleavings that need to be considered. Moreover, non-atomicity hints at the existence of potential bugs; a study of concurrency errors [20] shows that a majority of reported errors in concurrent programs (around 69 %) are atomicity violations.

Several notions of atomicity have been introduced in the literature. A widely recognized notion is *conflict serializability* [21], introduced as a correctness criterion with a tractable monitoring algorithm that guarantees *atomicity*. It is assumed that a program's code is divided into code blocks (such as procedures,

---

An extended version of this paper including the missing proofs can be found at [1].

© Springer-Verlag Berlin Heidelberg 2016
M. Chechik and J.-F. Raskin (Eds.): TACAS 2016, LNCS 9636, pp. 497–514, 2016.
DOI: 10.1007/978-3-662-49674-9_29

loop bodies, or even single statements) that are called *transactions*. An execution is conflict serializable if it is *equivalent* to a serial execution, i.e. an execution in which all transactions are executed in a sequential non-interleaved fashion. The key element of this definition is the notion of *equivalence* which allows permutation of non-conflicting statements to establish an equivalent serial execution.

There has been a huge body of research in the recent years that studies the problems of static and dynamic checking of atomicity, which is almost entirely based on the assumption that the programs are executed under a sequentially consistent (SC) memory model. Weak memory models have been duly getting a lot of attention in the programming languages and systems research communities, and yet the question of atomicity under a weak memory model has not been studied well. Let us start by an example to motivate why weak memory models require a carefully tailored notion of atomicity.

Consider the program with two methods in Fig. 1. Array pool implements a pool of tasks with two pointers head and tail pointing to its beginning and end. The invariant is head $\leq$ tail and the pool is empty if head = tail. The procedures (a)

```
[head++;]α
if ( head <= tail ) {
    task = pool [ head - 1 ];
    pool [ head - 1 ] = NULL;
    // Execute task
}
else
    head--;                        β
```
(a)

```
[tail--;]δ
if ( head <= tail ) {
    task = pool [ tail ];
    pool [ tail ] = NULL;
    // Execute task
}
else
    tail++;                        γ
```
(b)

**Fig. 1.** Task pool (transactions marked by brackets).

and (b) take elements from the pool's head and tail, respectively. Imagine a program that is running these two procedures in two threads (transactions are marked by brackets in the figure). Once a thread atomically modifies head/tail, interference from the other thread is tolerated. But, when it is about to modify the pool, it requires mutual exclusion. It is easy to verify that every execution of this program is conflict serializable (under sequential consistency). Even though both (a) and (b) potentially write to an element of the array pool, the conditional ensures that it is never the same element. Now consider the same program executed under the Total Store Order (TSO) memory model where writes are first stored in a thread-local buffer and non-deterministically flushed into the shared memory at a later time. When head + 1 = tail, the if condition may succeed in both (a) and (b). A write to head performed by (a) may be propagated to (b) after the condition is tested in (b), conversely a write to tail performed by (b) may be propagated to (a) after the condition is tested in (a). This is the behaviour that is strictly disallowed under SC. In that case, both threads access the same element of the array pool by first reading it and then writing to it. This is a classic violation of atomicity. Moreover, assuming that the threads are grabbing tasks from this task pool to execute, this non-atomic behaviour can lead to a real program error if a non-idempotent task ends up being executed twice by two different threads. We need a notion of atomicity that is aware of such erroneous TSO-executions, and declares them as non-atomic.

In this paper, we propose a new notion of atomicity, called *TSO-serializability*, which is inspired by the standard notion of conflict serializability under SC, in the sense that is syntactic, efficient to monitor, and helpful for the programmer to facilitate local reasoning. Yet, it makes special considerations for (i) non-atomicity of writes to the shared memory under TSO, and (ii) possible reorderings of shared memory accesses made by the same thread, allowed under TSO but not under SC. The idea is that TSO-serializability lifts the *relaxedness* of the orderings of individual statements under TSO to the level of atomic blocks (viewed as composite statements). For example, since TSO allows for two statements $write(x)read(y)$ to be reordered to $read(y)\,write(x)$ (indicating that the write is committed later), therefore we expect the two-transaction sequence $[write(x_1)write(x_2)]\,[read(y_1)read(y_2)]$ to be allowed to be reordered to $[read(y_1)read(y_2)]\,[write(x_1)write(x_2)]$ in an *equivalent* execution.

We provide a formal justification for the notion of TSO-serializability presented in this paper by stating its precise relation to SC-serializability and *robustness*. Robustness [6] is a property of a program stating that the program does not exhibit non-SC behaviour if executed on a weaker memory model such as TSO. If a program is robust, and it is SC-serializable, then for any reasonable notion of TSO-serializability, one should expect it to be serializable under TSO. That is exactly what we prove for our proposed notion of TSO-serializability. The converse, however, does not always hold. If a program exhibits strictly more behaviours under TSO (compared to SC), it is expected that some of these behaviours may not serializable, while all SC behaviours are.

Since TSO-serializability is formulated based on the concept of a syntactic conflict relation (similar to standard SC-serializability), a monitoring algorithm for TSO-serializability can be adapted from the classic algorithm for conflict serializability effortlessly; a program execution can be monitored for TSO-serializability violations using a similar algorithm as SC-serializability [21] and in the same polynomial time complexity. There is, however, a practical impediment in the way of monitoring programs for TSO-serializability violations, and that is how to obtain an execution to monitor in the first place. To obtain a detailed TSO execution (including the information about when writes were committed to memory), the monitor needs access to inner workings of the cache coherence protocol. This implies a very complicated monitor design which will likely have huge performance setbacks. Conceptually, there is a lightly distributed system that needs to be monitored, and observing global snapshots of which are costly.

We propose the notion of *traces*, as an abstraction of executions (in the form of a set of executions) which forgets information about the exact time of write commits. In a trace, once a write is issued by a thread, it can be committed at any point in the future, consistently with all the other accesses in the trace. We pose and solve the problem of monitoring a trace for TSO-serializability violations. Since a trace represents a set of executions, it is expected that this problem should be more complex than the monitoring problem of a single execution. We prove that the problem is in general NP-complete, but fixed-parameter tractable. We propose an algorithm to solve it in polynomial time if the number of threads in the program is considered to be a constant.

## 2   Multithreaded Programs and Their Executions

**Events.** A program consists of a number of threads running concurrently and communicating through shared variables. Each thread runs a sequence of transactions, which are themselves sequences of events. We fix arbitrary sets $\mathbb{T}$, $\mathbb{T}r$, $\mathbb{V}$, and $\mathbb{D}$ of thread identifiers, transaction identifiers, variable names, and values.

For a given thread identifier $t$, we fix the sets $\mathbb{R}_t = \{rd_t(x,v)_i : i \in \mathbb{T}r, x \in \mathbb{V}, v \in \mathbb{D}\}$ and $\mathbb{W}_t = \{wr_t(x,v)_i : i \in \mathbb{T}r, x \in \mathbb{V}, v \in \mathbb{D}\}$ of *read* and *write events*. Events are indexed by thread and transaction identifiers. *Fence events* (which concern the internal workings of TSO and which are explained later in this section) are denoted by $fn_t^i$. We omit the transaction identifier $i$ when it is understood from the context, or it is irrelevant. Let $\mathbb{E}_t = \mathbb{R}_t \cup \mathbb{W}_t \cup \{fn_t^i : i \in \mathbb{T}r\}$ and $\mathbb{E} = \bigcup_t \mathbb{E}_t$.

**Programs.** A sequence of events $\sigma$ is called *serial* when every two events of the same transaction are not separated by an event of another transaction, and *well-formed* when each transaction identifier is used at most once and for each thread $t$, the projection of $\sigma$ on events of thread $t$ is serial. A *program* $P$ is abstractly represented as a prefix-closed set of well-formed sequences of events (representing all possible interleavings of events of different threads). The semantics of a program $P$ for a specific memory model consists only of those sequences that are feasible under that memory model.

**Memory Models.** An *SC-execution* is a sequence of events $\eta \in \mathbb{E}^*$ where roughly, each read event reads the value written by the last preceding write. An *SC-execution of a program* $P$ is an SC-execution $\eta$ such that $\eta \in P$.

Under TSO, a write $wr_t(x,v)_i$ (called also a *write-issue*) is first stored in a thread-local FIFO buffer, called the *store buffer*, before being non-deterministically flushed into the shared memory. The written value may become visible to other threads at a later time. Flushing the store buffers introduces additional events $wr\text{-}com_t(x,v)_i$, called *write-commit* events, for removing a write $wr_t(x,v)_i$ from the store buffer of $t$ and execute it on the shared memory. We say that the write-commit $wr\text{-}com_t(x,v)_i$ *corresponds* to that write, and denote it by $wr_t(x,v)_i \sim wr\text{-}com_t(x,v)_i$. Write-commits *inherit the transaction identifier* of the corresponding write-issue (regardless of when they occur). A read $rd_t(x,v)$ prefetches the value $v$ written by the last write to $x$ in the buffer of $t$, and if no such write exists, the value $v$ is retrieved from the shared memory. A fence event $fn_t$ is enabled only when the buffer of $t$ is empty. Let $\mathbb{W}c_t = \{wr\text{-}com_t(x,v)_i : i \in \mathbb{T}r, x \in \mathbb{V}, v \in \mathbb{D}\}$, $\mathbb{E}_t^{tso} = \mathbb{E}_t \cup \mathbb{W}c_t$, and $\mathbb{E}^{tso} = \bigcup_t \mathbb{E}^{tso}{}_t$. For any $e \in \{rd_t(x,v)_i, wr_t(x,v)_i, wr\text{-}com_t(x,v)_i\}$, $th(e) = t$ and $var(e) = x$. A sequence of events $\eta \in (\mathbb{E}^{tso})^*$ satisfying this semantics is called a *TSO-execution*. A *TSO-execution of a program* $P$ is a TSO-execution $\eta$ such that the projection of $\eta$ on $\mathbb{E}$ belongs to $P$. Figure 2(a) pictures a TSO-execution of the program in Fig. 1.

# 3 Conflict Serializability

Conflict serializability was introduced in [21] as a syntactic (and tractable to monitor) notion that ensures *atomicity*. Instead of considering the data manipulated by transactions, a conservative "conflict relation", relating the individual actions of transactions, is defined which guarantees atomicity regardless of the data values read and written by individual actions. A conflict relation relates events with their values projected away, that we also call events (and inherit all the notations from Sect. 2 for sets of events). Conflict serializability is a property of a sequence of events (without values), which are also called SC/TSO-executions. Note that such a sequence represents a *set* of executions, where different values can be assigned to individual events (consistently).

Formally, a *conflict relation* is an irreflexive binary relation $\circledcirc \subseteq \mathbb{E} \times \mathbb{E}$. For a pair of events $e, e' \in \mathbb{E}$, we write $e \circledcirc e'$ to stand for $(e, e') \in \circledcirc$ and $e \not\!\!\!\circ e'$ to stand for $(e, e') \notin \circledcirc$. Intuitively, whenever $e \circledcirc e'$, the effect of executing $e$ after $e'$ *may* differ from that of executing $e$ before $e'$. The conflict relation depends on the underlying memory model. For instance, the conflict relation $\circledcirc_{SC}$ from [10] assumes sequential consistency: $e \circledcirc_{SC} e'$ whenever $e$ and $e'$ are events of the same thread (i.e., $th(e) = th(e')$) or they access the same variable, and one of them is a write (i.e., $(e, e') \in (\mathbb{R} \cup \mathbb{W})^2 \smallsetminus \mathbb{R}^2$ and $var(e) = var(e')$).

Given an execution $\eta = \eta_1 ee'\eta_2$ (where $e$ and $e'$ are events and $\eta_1$ and $\eta_2$ are executions), we say an execution $\eta' = \eta_1 e'e\eta_2$ is derived from $\eta$ by a $\circledcirc$-*valid swap* if and only if $e \not\!\!\!\circ e'$. A permutation $\eta'$ of an execution $\eta$ is $\circledcirc$-*preserving* if and only if $\eta'$ can be derived from $\eta$ through a sequence of $\circledcirc$-*valid* swaps.

An execution $\eta$ is *conflict serializable* w.r.t. the conflict relation $\circledcirc$ if and only if there exists an execution $\eta'$ that is a $\circledcirc$-preserving serial permutation of $\eta$. We call the notion of conflict serializability based on $\circledcirc_{SC}$ *SC-serializabiliy* for short. A program $P$ is *SC-serializable* iff every SC-execution of $P$ is SC-serializable.

An equivalent characterization of conflict serializability can be established through *conflict graphs* [21], where the graph was constructed for a specific conflict relation. The same definition can be easily adapted for any conflict relation.

**Definition 1 (Event-Graph).** *The* event-graph *of an execution $\eta$ is the directed graph $EG_\eta = \langle V, E \rangle$ where there is a node in $V$ for each event in $\eta$, and $E$ contains an edge from $u$ to $v$ iff $e(u) \circledcirc e(v)$ and $e(u)$ occurs before $e(v)$ in $\eta$ (where $e(v)$ is the event of execution $\eta$ corresponding to the graph node $v$).*

Intuitively, one can think of the event-graph of an execution $\eta$ as a structure that represents the order between all conflicting events in $\eta$.

The conflict-graph of an execution $\eta$ is defined based on the *event-graph* of $\eta$ by grouping all events indexed by the same transaction identifier as a new node, and considering the directed graph that is induced on these new transaction nodes. Let $tr(v)$ be the set of events that belong to a transaction node $v$.

**Definition 2 (Conflict-Graph).** *The* conflict-graph *of an execution $\eta$ is the directed graph $CG_\eta = \langle V', E' \rangle$ where $V'$ includes one node for each transaction* identifier in $\eta$, and we have $(v, v') \in E'$ iff there exists events $e \in tr(v)$ and $e' \in tr(v')$ such that $(e, e') \in E$ where $EG_\eta = (V, E)$ is the event-graph of $\eta$.

**Theorem 1** *(from [21]). For a conflict relation $\odot$, an execution $\eta$ is conflict-serializable if and only if $CG_\eta$ is acyclic.*

In [21], a polynomial time algorithm is presented that uses the conflict graph and Theorem 1 to monitor an execution under SC for violations of serializability.

Event-graphs and conflict-graphs of SC-executions are defined as in Definitions 1 and 2, respectively, using $\odot_{SC}$ instead of $\odot$.

## 4    Serializability Under TSO

In this section, we propose a conflict relation for TSO and justify the suitability of the obtained notion of conflict serializability by relating it to the classic SC serializability.

### 4.1    TSO Conflict Relation

The TSO conflict relation $\odot_{TSO}$ is formally defined as follows:

$$
e \odot_{TSO} e' \Leftrightarrow
\begin{cases}
\star\, th(e) \ne th(e') \land (e, e') \in (\mathbb{R} \cup \mathbb{W}c)^2 \smallsetminus \mathbb{R}^2 \land var(e) = var(e') \\
\quad \text{except the following cases:} \\
\quad \text{(i)} \quad e = rd_{t_1}(x) \land e' = wr\text{-}com_{t_2}(x) \land e \,\|\, e' \\
\qquad\quad e = wr\text{-}com_{t_1}(x) \land e' = rd_{t_2}(x) \land e' \,\|\, e \\
\text{(2)} \quad \star\, th(e) = th(e') \text{ except the following cases:} \\
\quad \text{(ii)} \quad e \in \mathbb{R}_t \cup \mathbb{W}_t \land e' \in \mathbb{W}c_t \land \neg e \sim e' \\
\qquad\quad e \in \mathbb{W}c_t \land e' \in \mathbb{R}_t \cup \mathbb{W}_t \land \neg e \sim e' \\
\quad \text{(iii)} \quad e = wr_t(x) \land e' = rd_t(y) \land x \ne y \\
\qquad\quad e = rd_t(x) \land e' = rd_t(y) \land x \ne y \land rd_t(x) \text{ is buffered}
\end{cases}
\tag{1}
$$

Similar to the SC conflict relation, $\odot_{TSO}$ declares events accessing the same shared memory location, where at least one of them is a *write-commit* conflicting (see (1) above). However, since under TSO, some *read* events may access values by reading from a local buffer (instead of the shared memory), there are exceptions to this general rule involving such reads.

A read $rd_{t_1}(x)$ event that occurs between a $wr_{t_1}(x)$ event and the corresponding $wr\text{-}com_{t_1}(x)$ event, and where $wr_{t_1}(x)$ is the most recent write-issue event before $rd_{t_1}(x)$, fetches its value from the store buffer that holds the value written by $wr_{t_1}(x)$. In this case, according to the TSO semantics, event $rd_{t_1}(x)$ should not be in conflict with a write-commit $wr\text{-}com_{t_2}(x)$ of another thread that

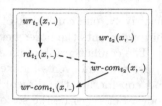

happens in parallel with it; that is, when $wr\text{-}com_{t_2}(x)$ occurs between the pair of events $wr_{t_1}(x)$ and $wr\text{-}com_{t_1}(x)$ (as illustrated in the figure on the right).

Such a pair of parallel read and write-commit events, which we denote by $rd_{t_1}(x) \parallel wr\text{-}com_{t_2}(x)$, should not be conflicting since one is a read from a local store buffer and the other a write to the shared memory (accesses to two different resources).

Similar to the SC conflict relation, $\circledcirc_{TSO}$ declares events within the *same thread* to be in conflict (see (2) above). Again, there are exceptions to this rule. A write-commit is *not* in conflict with other read and write events in the same thread (see (ii) above), except for its corresponding write issue (which must always precede it). Other exceptions (see (iii) above) are related to the relaxations of the program order allowed by the TSO semantics. There is no conflict between a write and a read event of the same thread on different variables. This exception is natural since it extrapolates the behaviour of the memory model at the level of events to the level of transactions, i.e., write-only transactions can be reordered with respect to later read-only transactions. Finally, TSO semantics relaxes the program order between a $rd_t(x)$ event that fetches its value from the store buffer and a future $rd_t(y)$ event of a different variable $y \neq x$ (see also [1]).

**Buffered Reads.** The relative ordering of $wr_t(x)/wr\text{-}com_t(x)$ events corresponding to the read event $rd_t(x)$ (of the same thread) determines whether the read fetches its value from the buffer (or the shared memory). Therefore, every read event $rd_t(x)$, that is preceded by a write $wr_t(x)$ of the same thread and no fence event $fn_t$ in between, may or may not be fetching its value from the local buffer, depending on when the write gets committed to the memory. This runtime information is unavailable when a programmer is reasoning at the level of the source code. We choose to call any such read, that *may* fetch its value from the buffer, a *buffered* read and exclude the mutual conflicts between these reads and later reads to other variables from $\circledcirc_{TSO}$ (see (iii) above). This way, we feel that the definition of conflict relation stays true to its main purpose, i.e. defining a notion atomicity that is helpful to programmers reasoning about their code.

The following proposition formally states the fact that all order relaxations introduced in the definition of $\circledcirc_{TSO}$ are consistent with the TSO semantics:

**Proposition 1.** *Any $\circledcirc_{TSO}$-preserving permutation of a TSO-execution $\eta$ is also a TSO-execution.*

The notion of conflict serializability based on $\circledcirc_{TSO}$ is called *TSO-serializability*. A program $P$ is *TSO-serializable* iff every TSO-execution of $P$ is TSO-serializable. Event/conflict-graphs of TSO-executions are defined as in Definitions 1 and 2, respectively, by replacing $\circledcirc$ with $\circledcirc_{TSO}$. An equivalent of Theorem 1 then provides an efficient (poly-time) procedure to monitor an execution for TSO-serializability violations. Figure 2(a) illustrates the event-graph of a non TSO-serializable execution of the program in Fig. 1. The conflict-graph in Fig. 2(c) contains a cycle.

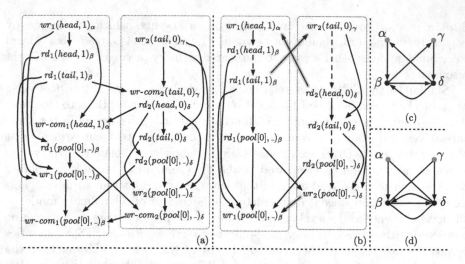

**Fig. 2.** (a) A TSO-execution $\eta$ (events are ordered from top to bottom) and its $\circledcirc_{TSO}$ event-graph $EG_\eta$. (b) Ignoring dashed edges, the write-contraction of $EG_\eta$. Dashed edges represent conflicts added by $\circledcirc_{TSO-po}$. Ignoring dashed edges and redefining the highlighted edges to be undirected, the trace event-graph $EG_\tau$ of $\tau = trace(\eta)$. (c) The conflict-graph induced by $EG_\eta$. (d) The conflict-graph induced by $EG_\tau$.

## 4.2 Connection to SC-Serializability

Beyond Proposition 1, we substantiate our definition of TSO-serializability by formally relating it to the widely accepted notion of SC-serializability. We show that SC-serializability implies TSO-serializability for *robust* programs. Intuitively, a program is robust if it does not exhibit non-SC behaviour; in other words, each of its TSO-executions is equivalent to another execution of the same program under SC. Under SC, every write-issue is immediately followed by the corresponding write-commit (i.e. no delay in propagating the write).

Let $\circledcirc_{TSO-po}$ be a strengthening of $\circledcirc_{TSO}$ in which the program order is maintained for all pairs of events in $\mathbb{E}$ in the same thread. Formally, a TSO-execution $\eta$ is *SC-equivalent* when there exists an execution $\eta'$ that is a $\circledcirc_{TSO-po}$-preserving permutation of $\eta$ and every write-issue of $\eta'$ is immediately followed by the corresponding write-commit. A program $P$ is *robust* when every TSO-execution of $P$ is SC-equivalent. One can check SC-equivalence by letting every pair of write-issue and corresponding write-commit events to form a transaction, and checking conflict serializability of the execution consisting of these transactions and all other events as single transactions (more details in [1]). The conflict graph defined this way is called a *write-contraction*. For instance, the TSO-execution in Fig. 2(a) is not SC-equivalent (since there is a cycle in Fig. 2(b)) which implies that the program in Fig. 1 is not robust.

**Theorem 2.** *A program $P$ is TSO-serializable if it is robust and SC-serializable.*

$$\begin{bmatrix} wr_1(x,1) \\ rd_1(y,0) \end{bmatrix} \quad \begin{bmatrix} wr_2(y,1) \\ rd_2(x,0) \end{bmatrix} \qquad \begin{bmatrix} wr_1(x,1) \\ rd_1(y,0) \end{bmatrix} \quad \begin{bmatrix} rd_2(x,0) \\ wr_2(y,1) \end{bmatrix}$$

The reverse of Theorem 2 doesn't hold. For instance, both programs above are TSO-serializable although the program on the left is not robust and the program on the right is not SC-serializable. The program on the left is TSO-serializable since every event is a transaction and events in the same thread are not in conflict, and it is not robust since intuitively, both reads don't see the value written by the other thread. The program on the right is TSO-serializable because the events in thread 1 are not in conflict while it is not SC-serializable since it admits only one execution where the events of thread 1 take place in between the two events of thread 2.

A program $P$ is called *transaction-fenced* when for every $\sigma \in P$, every transaction in $\sigma$, i.e., every maximal sub-sequence of events indexed by the same transaction identifier, ends with a fence[1]. For transaction-fenced programs, the converse of Theorem 2 is true:

**Theorem 3.** *A transaction-fenced program $P$ is TSO-serializable iff it is robust and SC-serializable.*

## 5 Trace TSO-Serializability

There are practical obstacles in the way of implementing a monitor that can observe a TSO-execution of a program. The monitor is subject to the same distributed nature of the memory as individual program threads, and tracking write-commits of threads requires a manipulation of the cache-coherence protocols running in the multi-core chip with potentially high performance overheads. We introduce a notion of serializability for TSO that does not require to be aware of the exact timing of write-commits. This notion applies to abstractions of TSO-executions called *traces* that forget write-commits, assuming that a write-commit can happen at any point in time after its corresponding write-issue (consistent with the TSO semantics). This effectively means that the serializability of a *set* of executions (namely those where the forgotten write-commits reappear at any of the consistent points) is monitored instead of a single execution.

The trace of an execution $\eta$, denoted by $trace(\eta)$, is the projection of $\eta$ on $\mathbb{E}$ (basically leaving out all write-commits). The set of executions $Execs(\tau)$ represented by a trace $\tau$ is the set of all TSO-executions $\eta$ such that $trace(\eta) = \tau$.

**Definition 3 (Trace TSO-Serializability).** *A trace $\tau$ is TSO-serializable iff every execution in $Execs(\tau)$ is TSO-serializable.*

The most important property of $\tau = trace(\eta)$ for some execution $\eta$ is that $\tau$ can soundly be used to check if $\eta$ is not TSO-serializable.

---

[1] Transaction-fenced programs are not necessarily robust since statements inside a transaction may not be followed by a fence.

**Proposition 2.** *If execution $\eta$ is not TSO-serializable then the trace $trace(\eta)$ is not TSO-serializable.*

We introduce a conflict relation $\overrightarrow{\circledcirc}_{TSO}$ for traces and a characterization of serializability based on that conflict relation. Intuitively, $\overrightarrow{\circledcirc}_{TSO}$ stands for the union of the conflict relations for all the individual executions of that trace, where a write event represents both the write-issue and the corresponding write-commit. The relation $\overrightarrow{\circledcirc}_{TSO}$ over traces is the union of two disjoint relations $\overrightarrow{\circledcirc}_{TSO}$ and $\overline{\circledcirc}_{TSO}$. Given $e, e' \in \mathbb{E}$,

---

$e\overrightarrow{\circledcirc}_{TSO}e'$ iff $th(e) = th(e')$ except the following cases:
$$e = wr_t(x) \;\wedge\; e' = rd_t(y) \wedge x \neq y$$
$$e = rd_t(x) \;\wedge\; e' = rd_t(y) \wedge x \neq y \wedge rd_t(x) \text{ is } a \text{ buffer read}$$

• $\quad th(e) \neq th(e')$ and $(e \circledcirc_{SC} e' \wedge fence(e, e')$

$$\text{or } e = rd_t(x) \wedge e' = wr_{t'}(x) \wedge e \text{ is not buffered})$$

$e\overline{\circledcirc}_{TSO}e'$ iff $th(e) \neq th(e') \wedge e \circledcirc_{SC} e' \wedge \neg e\overrightarrow{\circledcirc}_{TSO}e'$

---

The conflicts between events of the same thread are included in $\overrightarrow{\circledcirc}_{TSO}$ since the order between such events is fixed in all the executions of the trace. Two events of different threads are in conflict if they are so under the classic SC conflict relation, and they are related by $\overrightarrow{\circledcirc}_{TSO}$ iff they are *separated by a fence* (since the fence ensures they are ordered in the same way in all executions) or if they are a non-buffered read (reading from the shared memory) together with a write (since a read cannot see the value of a write that hasn't been issued yet). Formally, $e$ and $e'$ are *fence-separated*, denoted by $fence(e, e')$, when $e$ occurs before $e'$, $e$ is an action of thread $t$, and $\tau$ contains a fence $fn_t$ between $e$ and $e'$. In contrast, $\overline{\circledcirc}_{TSO}$ relates events that are conflicting under $\circledcirc_{SC}$ but may appear in different orders in different executions of a trace, for example two write events (of the same variable) performed by two different threads. Recall that a write represents both the write-issue and the corresponding write-commit.

Similar to the case of executions, having a graph theoretic characterization of serializability for traces is useful for algorithm design. We define the event-graph of a trace $\tau$ that contains a directed edge from event $e$ to event $e'$ iff $e\overrightarrow{\circledcirc}_{TSO}e'$ and an undirected edge between $e$ and $e'$ iff $e\overline{\circledcirc}_{TSO}e'$.

**Definition 4 (Trace Event-Graph).** *The* event-graph *of a trace $\tau$ is the graph $EG_\tau = \langle V, E, U\rangle$ where there is a node in $V$ for each event in $\tau$, $E$ is a set of directed edges $(u, v)$ such that $e(u)$ occurs before $e(v)$ in $\tau$ and $e(u)\overrightarrow{\circledcirc}_{TSO}e(v)$, and $U$ is a set of undirected edges $\{u, v\}$ such that $e(u)$ occurs before $e(v)$ in $\tau$ and $e(u)\overline{\circledcirc}_{TSO}e(v)$ (where $e(v)$ is the event of $\tau$ corresponding to the node $v$).*

Formally, an *orientation* of a graph $G = \langle V, E, U\rangle$ with a set $E$ of directed edges and a set $U$ of undirected edges is a directed graph $\langle V, E \cup E'\rangle$ such that for every undirected edge $\{u, v\} \in U$, $E'$ contains $(u, v)$ or $(v, u)$. An orientation of $EG_\tau$ is *valid* when the resulting directed graph is acyclic.

The next result relates valid orientations of the trace event-graph and write-contractions of the trace's executions event-graphs. Recall that the *write-contraction* of an event-graph $EG_\eta$ is the graph $EG_\eta^c$ where every node representing a write event $wr_t(x)$ is merged with the node representing the corresponding write-commit event $wr\text{-}com_t(x)$ (note that a contracted edge disappears and does not turn into a self-loop).

**Theorem 4.** *For an execution $\eta \in Execs(\tau)$, the write-contraction of $EG_\eta$ is a valid orientation of $EG_\tau$. Conversely, every valid orientation of $EG_\tau$ is the write-contracted event-graph $EG_\eta$ for some $\eta \in Execs(\tau)$.*

This leads to an interesting observation: $EG_\tau$ of a trace $\tau$ can be viewed as the union of the write-contractions $EG_\eta^c$ of all $\eta \in Execs(\tau)$, so that when all $EG_\eta^c$s agree on the direction of an edge between two nodes, that edge appears as a directed edge in $EG_\tau$ and when at least two $EG_\eta^c$s disagree on the direction of an edge between two nodes, that edge appears as an undirected edge in $EG_\tau$.

Also, Theorem 4 leads us to the following characterization of trace TSO-serializability based on orientations of trace event-graphs.

**Theorem 5.** *A trace $\tau$ is TSO-serializable iff every acyclic orientation of $EG_\tau$ induces an acyclic conflict-graph.*

Alternatively, one can directly define the notion of a conflict graph for traces. The event graph of a trace $EG_\tau$ induces a graph over the transactions in the same sense as the conflict graph of an execution.

**Definition 5 (Trace Conflict-Graph).** *The conflict-graph of a trace $\tau$ is the graph $CG_\tau = \langle V', E', U' \rangle$ where $V'$ includes one node for each transaction in $\tau$, and we have $(v, v') \in E'$ iff there exists actions $a \in tr(v)$ and $a \in tr(v')$ such that $(a, a') \in E$ and we have $\{v, v'\} \in U'$ iff there exists actions $b \in tr(v)$ and $b' \in tr(v')$ such that $\{b, b'\} \in U$ where $EG_\tau = (V, E, U)$ is the event-graph of $\tau$.*

For instance, the conflict-graph of the trace of the execution in Fig. 2(a) is given in Fig. 2(d). Serializability of a trace $\tau$ can be stated as a combined property of its conflict-graph $CG_\tau$ and its event-graph $EG_\tau$.

**Corollary 1.** *Trace $\tau$ is not TSO serializable iff there exists a cycle $c$ in $CG_\tau = \langle V', E', U' \rangle$ such that if $\{u_1, \dots u_m\} \subseteq U'$ participate in $c$ and $\{e_1, \dots, e_m\}$ are the same set of edges oriented in the direction of the cycle, then there exists a valid orientation $\langle V, E'' \rangle$ of the event-graph $EG_\tau = \langle V, E, U \rangle$ with $\{e_1, \dots, e_m\} \subseteq E''$.*

# 6 Monitoring TSO-serializability of Traces

In this section, we discuss the algorithmic aspect of monitoring *traces* for violations of TSO-serializability. Remember that (Sect. 3) monitoring one execution for violation of TSO-serializability is poly-time checkable.

Given a trace $\tau$, we want to check whether $\tau$ is TSO-serializable. We start by demonstrating that the general problem is NP-complete, and then propose polynomial time algorithms for approximations of this check. Specifically, we show that (i) under the assumption that the number of threads is a constant, there exists a sound and complete polynomial time algorithm that reports violations of TSO-serializability in a trace $\tau$, and (ii) if the program is *transaction-fenced*, then TSO-serializability can be checked in polynomial time.

## 6.1    NP-Completeness of Trace TSO-serializability Checking

Theorem 5 provides an equivalent characterization of trace TSO-serializability, namely that every acyclic orientation of the trace event-graph induces an acyclic conflict-graph. It turns out that this check is NP-complete. We demonstrate this by reducing the known NP-complete problem of checking for the existence of a hamiltonian path in a given graph $G$ to this problem.

**Theorem 6.** *For a trace $\tau$, the problem of checking whether $\tau$ is TSO-serializable is NP-complete.*

## 6.2    Fixed-Parameter Tractability

The good news is that there exists an algorithm for monitoring a trace for TSO-serializability violations which is polynomial time if one assumes the number of threads to be a constant. Given a trace of length $n$ with $k$ participating threads, it is easy to devise an exponential algorithm that finds a TSO-serializability violation if one exists and operates in $O(n^k)$ time. However, considering that usually $n$ (the number of events) is very large, it is desirable to have an algorithm with a running time where the exponent $k$ does not appear over $n$, but over some constant instead.

In this section, we propose an algorithm of complexity $O(n + c^k)$, where $c$ is a constant that depends on the number of shared variables in the program, $k$ is the number of threads, and $n$ is the length of the trace. The main observation that gives rise to such an algorithm is that there is a *concise witness* to violation of TSO-serializability, and it suffices to search for the existence of such a witness algorithmically. We start by defining this concise witness, which always exists if an arbitrary witness exists.

Given the event graph $EG_\tau$ of a trace $\tau$, checking serializability of $\tau$ reduces to deciding if there is a valid orientation of $EG_\tau$ that induces a cycle over the conflict graph $CG_\tau$. We will observe that if a valid orientation of $EG_\tau$ induces a cycle, then this orientation induces a *simple* cycle (to be defined) over $CG_\tau$.

Naturally, if the directed edges of the conflict graph $CG_\tau$ already form a cycle (which can be checked in polynomial time on the size of the graph), then there is nothing left to be done; we have found our TSO-serializability violation witness. Therefore, we assume that $CG_\tau$ is acyclic if it is restricted to its directed edges; let us call this graph $\overrightarrow{CG_\tau}$. Similarly, $\overrightarrow{EG_\tau}$ refers to $EG_\tau$ restricted to its directed edges. We use the notation $a <_\tau b$ to denote that $\overrightarrow{EG_\tau}$ contains a path from event $a$ to event $b$. Similarly, for transactions $tr_1$ and $tr_2$, we use the notation $tr_1 <_\tau tr_2$ iff $\overrightarrow{CG_\tau}$ contains a path from $tr_1$ to $tr_2$. The relation $<_\tau$ captures the ordering constraints between events/transactions that are imposed by the directed conflict edges. For an event $a$, we use $tr(a)$ to refer to the transaction that encloses $a$.

Let us assume that we have a cycle $c = tr_1 tr_2 \ldots tr_m$ over the conflict graph $CG_\tau$. For each pair of consecutive transactions $tr_i$ and $tr_{i+1}$, let event $b_i$ be the source and event $a_{i+1}$ be the destination of the conflict edge between $tr_i$ and $tr_{i+1}$ that participates in the cycle (rotating back from $b_m$ to $a_1$).

We say that cycle $c$ can be *simplified* if there exist two transactions $tr$ and $tr'$ on it where $tr <_\tau tr'$ and the segment of the cycle between $tr$ and $tr'$ contains at least one *undirected* conflict edge. By taking this segment of the cycle between $tr$ and $tr'$ and replacing it with the directed path (i.e. a path formed entirely of directed conflict edges) in the conflict graph from $tr$ to $tr'$, we *simplify* the cycle; we know that such a path exists by the definition of $tr <_\tau tr'$. Intuitively, during simplification we get rid of *undirected edges* and replace them by directed paths; note that undirected edges are soft constraints in a trace which reflect that the order between two events is undetermined.

**Definition 6.** *A* simple *cycle is a cycle that cannot be further simplified.*

Below, we state two properties of simple cycles that are very useful for reducing the search space of our algorithm.

**Proposition 3.** *In every* simple *cycle* $c = tr_1 tr_2 \ldots tr_m tr_1$ *over the conflict graph* $CG_\tau$ *of a trace* $\tau$ *(equivalently* $c = a_1 b_1 a_2 b_2 \ldots a_m b_m a_1$ *if the cycle is referenced by its conflict edges instead of its nodes) satisfies the following properties: (i) There exists at least one index* $k$ *such that* $a_k \not<_\tau b_k$. *(ii) Every two transactions* $tr$ *and* $tr'$ *that appear on* $c$ *with an undirected edge somewhere in the middle of them (i.e. on the segment between* $tr$ *to* $tr'$*) cannot belong to any chain (i.e. directed path) of the graph. In other words, we have* $tr \not<_\tau tr'$.

Property (ii) from the proposition above is straightforward yet significant because it implies that any simple cycle over the conflict graph can be viewed as a cycle where undirected edges connect segments of chains (i.e. directed paths) in the graph together, never visiting the same chain twice. We make use of the notion of *profiles* introduced in [11] for this algorithm. The idea is to summarize all possible entry/exits into each chain of $\overrightarrow{CG_\tau}$ (that may participate in a simple cycle) as a set of pairs (of events), and look for cycles involving those pairs only.

Consider an event $a$ of the event graph $EG_\tau$. Let
$$pair(a) = \{b \mid b \in tr(a) \lor tr(a) <_\tau tr(b))\}$$

The idea is that once a witness cycle enters $tr(a)$ through a conflict edge with destination $a$, some $b \in pair(a)$ is the event from which the cycle can leave the chain (i.e. directed path) that contains $tr(a)$ and $tr(b)$. In other words, $\{a\} \times pair(a)$ is the set of all possible path segments that start with $a$ and can be part of a simple cycle witnessing a violation of TSO-serializability.

Moreover, Proposition 3(i) states that at least for one transaction in the cycle we have a pair of events $(a, b)$ of the same transaction where $a <_\tau b$ but where $a$ and $b$ participate in the witness cycle, which is directed from $b$ back to $a$. The algorithm presented in Fig. 3 starts by enumerating all such pairs of events that

Input: $\Pi = \{\pi_1, \pi_2, \ldots, \pi_m\}$ smallest partition of $\overrightarrow{CG_\tau}$ into chains.
Output: a witness to violation of TSO-serializability, if one exists.

For all $\pi_i \in \Pi$ and each $tr \in \pi_i$
   For all events $a, b \in tr$ where $a \not<_\tau b$, and each choice of events
      For all events $a', b'$ where $tr(a'), tr(b') \in \pi_i$ and $b' \in pair(b)$ and $a \in pair(a')$
         For all $p_1 \in profile(\pi_1), \ldots, p_m \in profile(\pi_m)$
            If $(a', b')$ together with $p_1, \ldots, p_{i-1}, p_{i+1}, \ldots, p_m$ includes
            a TSO-serializability violation, then report a violation.

**Fig. 3.** Algorithm for searching for all simple cycle witnesses. The choices of events for $a, b, a', b'$ is over read and write events only. The chains $\pi_1, \ldots \pi_m$ are by definition disjoint.

$P_\pi = \varnothing$
For variables $x$, if $\exists$ events $a \in \pi$ where $a = rd(x)/wr(x)$ then $P_\pi = P_\pi \cup \{(a)\}$.
For each pair of variables $x$ and $y$ (can be equal)
   If $\exists$ events $a, b \in \pi$ where $a = rd(x)/wr(x)$ and $b = rd(y)/wr(y)$ and $b \in pair(a)$
      then $P_\pi = P_\pi \cup \{(a, b)\}$.

**Fig. 4.** Algorithm for computing the set of all profiles of a transaction chain $\pi$.

belong to a single transaction (outermost loop). It then proceeds to find the matching entry/exit events (i.e. $a'$ and $b'$) for the witness cycle in the chain containing $a$ and $b$ (the next nested loop). Finally, the innermost loop enumerates all possible choices of profiles for the remaining chains (other than the one containing $a, b, a'$ and $b'$), and then the innermost statement checks if these choices form a valid witness cycle together.

The algorithm in Fig. 3 uses a function *profile* that returns the set of all profiles for a given chain. A profile of a chain is a set of elements of the following three forms: (i) a single event $(a)$, when the witness conflict cycle enters and exits a chain at the same single event $a$, (ii) a pair of events $(a, b)$ of some transaction $tr$, where the witness cycle enters/exits a chain at two events of the same transaction $tr$, and (iii) a pair of events $(a, b)$, where a witness cycle enters a transaction in event $a$, then follows a chain of transactions on a directed path in the conflict graph and exits the chain through an event $b$ (i.e. $tr(a) <_\tau tr(b)$). The set of profiles of a chain can be computed using the algorithm in Fig. 4.

**Soundness and Completeness.** Here, we formally argue that it suffices for the algorithm to search for *simple* cycle witness to violation of TSO-serializability. The important observation is that:

**Proposition 4.** *If a trace $\tau$ is not TSO-serializable, then there exists a simple cycle witnessing the violation of TSO-serializability.*

It remains to argue that the algorithm, through the use of profiles, will definitely find a simple cycle violation of TSO-serializability if one exists.

**Proposition 5.** *For every partitioning $\Pi$ of $\overrightarrow{CG_\tau}$ into a set of chains, and every simple cycle violation of TSO-serializability $c$, we have that $c$ visits every chain in $\Pi$ at most once.*

It is important to note that the above statement is independent of the choice of partitioning of $\overrightarrow{CG_\tau}$ into chains. It is straightforward to see that a cycle's footprint in every chain can be captured through one of the three possibilities that we introduced for profiles. Finally, we conclude the soundness and completeness of the algorithm in Fig. 3:

**Theorem 7.** *Algorithm in Fig. 3 discovers a violation of TSO serializability in trace $\tau$ iff one exists.*

**Complexity Analysis.** A key observation about $\overrightarrow{EG_\tau}$ is that for any trace $\tau$, if $\overrightarrow{CG_\tau}$ is restricted to a single thread and global read and write events, then the size of the largest anti-chain of it is at most 2. In other words, in every thread, there are at most two events $a$ and $b$ such that $a \not\prec_\tau b$ and $b \not\prec_\tau a$. This is a direct implication of the definition of $\odot_{TSO}$; the only events that are not ordered in each thread are $wr(y)$ and $rd(x)$ when $x \neq y$, and the events appear in that order in the trace. Any other event that can be independent of $wr(y)$ will have to be a read event of some other variable, say $rd(z)$ which is in conflict with $rd(x)$ and therefore ordered with respect to it (similar argument for events independent of $rd(x)$). We will make use of the following well-known theorem about the width of a partial order:

**Theorem 8 (Dilworth's Theorem).** *For every partial order, there exists an anti-chain $A$, and a partition of the order into a family $P$ of chains, such that $|P| = |A|$ (which is referred to as the width of the partial order). Moreover, such an $A$ is the largest anti-chain in the order.*

Since $\overrightarrow{EG_\tau}$ is acyclic, by Dilworth's Theorem, we know that it can be partitioned into at most $p$ (maximal) chains (i.e. directed paths) where $p$ is the size of the largest anti-chain of $\overrightarrow{EG_\tau}$. The size of the largest anti-chain of $\overrightarrow{EG_\tau}$ restricted to each thread (and ignoring the buffered reads) is at most 2. If we assume that there are $k$ threads in the program, this implies that $\overrightarrow{EG_\tau}$ (ignoring the buffered reads) can be partitioned into $2k$ chains. If we have $m$ shared variables in the program, then each such chain can be summarized as at most $(2m)^2$ possible profiles (i.e. all possible combinations of $2m$ reads and $2m$ writes).

Now, let us add consideration for the *buffered* reads. In each thread, all buffered reads of the same variable are conflicting and form a chain. Therefore, in the worst case, we can account for all buffered reads of a single thread, by adding $m$ extra chains, where each consists of all buffered reads of some variable $x$ (there are at most $m$ different variables). There are in total $km$ of such chains for all $k$ threads. However, every such chain (of buffered reads of $x$) can be represented by a single trivial profile ($rd(x)$).

Our algorithm ends up enumerating all possible profiles for such partitioning of $\overrightarrow{EG_\tau}$ into a family of chains. There are at most $((2m)^2)^{2k}$ different selection of profiles to consider. It is easy to see that it takes $O(n)$ time ($n$ is the length of the trace) to compute the set of all profiles.

We need to argue that given the combination of the fixed $km$ (trivial) profiles and a choice of $2k$ profiles (from $((2m)^2)^{2k}$ many choices), a violation can be found in polynomial time, if one exists. This is equivalent to having a system of (at most) $(m+2)k$ components, where each component is a single event, a pair of events connected by an undirected edge, or a pair of components linked by a directed edge. The goal is to find a cycle in this system that obeys the direction of the directed edges. A slightly modified depth-first search algorithm can find the cycle in time polynomial in $mk$.

To summarize, the complexity of the algorithm is $O(n + c^k)$ where $n$ is the length of the trace, $c$ depends only on the number of shared variables in the program, and $k$ is the number of program threads.

**Theorem 9.** *For a program $P$ with a fixed number of threads, the algorithm in Fig. 3 discovers a witness to violation of TSO-serializability of any trace of $P$ in time polynomial on the length of the trace.*

### 6.3    Poly-time Monitor for Transaction-Fenced Programs

An alternative way of avoiding the high complexity of monitoring traces for TSO-serializability violations, for instance when there is a large number of threads in the program, is to simplify this check by ensuring that every transaction ends with a fence event (and hence making all its updates visible to other threads when it ends). As stated in Theorem 3, TSO-serializability is equivalent to the conjunction of robustness and SC-serializability for such programs.

A witness to non-robustness of a program can be discovered through a targeted search (for a specific pattern of violations) in the space of *SC-executions* of the program [6] using an algorithm that works in polynomial time for a given execution. The combination of these two monitors, a poly-time monitor for SC-serializability and a poly-time monitor for robustness, gives rise to an efficient monitor for TSO-serializability that observes only SC-executions of a program and looks for robustness or SC-serializability violations. Every violation to TSO-serializability will manifest as an SC-serializability violation or as a robustness violation for a transaction-fenced program.

The advantages of this result are twofold: (i) when transactions are naturally fenced (e.g. a lot of Java library methods are like this), it provides a poly-time algorithm for monitoring TSO-serializability, and (ii) when transactions are not naturally fenced, and the program has a large number of threads (which limits the applicability of the algorithm in Sec. 6.2), it provides the programmer with a solution: namely, to insert a fence at the end of each transaction that is not already fenced, and gain an efficient sound and complete monitor for TSO-serializability. Having a transaction-fenced program has the additional advantage that it allows to reason about the more familiar notions of SC-serializability and robustness instead of directly reasoning about TSO-serializability.

# 7    Related Work

To the best of our knowledge, this paper provides the first definition of conflict serializability under TSO. Conflict serializability was introduced in [21] for database transactions. Decision procedures for conflict serializability of finite-state concurrent models executed under an SC semantics were proposed in [10,11] and [5]. Both static [13,17,24,26] and dynamic tools [12,14,23,25] have been developed to check SC serializability, as well as transactional memory techniques that enforce serializability at run time [9,16,18,22]. The non-atomicity of writes under TSO poses new algorithmic challenges for monitoring serializability. Since observing the detailed sequence of write issues and commits is not efficiently possible (without access to the cache coherence mechanism), any dynamic analysis needs to monitor executions with missing information, that effectively stand for sets of executions. We propose a new monitoring algorithm for traces (i.e. sets of executions) that searches for certain type of cycles in graphs with both directed and undirected edges, which is more challenging than the classic serializability monitor that searches for a cycle in a directed graph [21].

Linearizability has been studied for concurrent *objects* running under TSO [7, 15,19]. This provides a means of establishing a relation between a concrete and an abstract object, which must hold in the context of *every possible client* of the object. The abstract object methods need not be atomic. In contrast, serializability is a property that is applicable to *programs* and the atomicity of a transaction is considered in the context of one specific program (in contrast to all possible clients).

Notions of robustness for TSO programs have been investigated in [2–4,6,8]. However, we are not aware of any work that establishes a relationship between robustness and atomicity under different memory models as done in this paper.

# References

1. On atomicity in presence of non-atomic writes (extended version). www.cs.toronto.edu/~azadeh/extended/tacas16-extended.pdf
2. Alglave, J., Maranget, L.: Stability in weak memory models. In: Gopalakrishnan, G., Qadeer, S. (eds.) CAV 2011. LNCS, vol. 6806, pp. 50–66. Springer, Heidelberg (2011)
3. Bouajjani, A., Meyer, R., Möhlmann, E.: Deciding robustness against total store ordering. In: Aceto, L., Henzinger, M., Sgall, J. (eds.) ICALP 2011, Part II. LNCS, vol. 6756, pp. 428–440. Springer, Heidelberg (2011)
4. Bouajjani, A., Derevenetc, E., Meyer, R.: Checking and enforcing robustness against TSO. In: Felleisen, M., Gardner, P. (eds.) ESOP 2013. LNCS, vol. 7792, pp. 533–553. Springer, Heidelberg (2013)
5. Bouajjani, A., Emmi, M., Enea, C., Hamza, J.: Verifying concurrent programs against sequential specifications. In: Felleisen, M., Gardner, P. (eds.) ESOP 2013. LNCS, vol. 7792, pp. 290–309. Springer, Heidelberg (2013)
6. Burckhardt, S., Musuvathi, M.: Effective program verification for relaxed memory models. In: Gupta, A., Malik, S. (eds.) CAV 2008. LNCS, vol. 5123, pp. 107–120. Springer, Heidelberg (2008)

7. Burckhardt, S., Gotsman, A., Musuvathi, M., Yang, H.: Concurrent library correctness on the TSO memory model. In: Seidl, H. (ed.) Programming Languages and Systems. LNCS, vol. 7211, pp. 87–107. Springer, Heidelberg (2012)

8. Burnim, J., Sen, K., Stergiou, C.: Sound and complete monitoring of sequential consistency for relaxed memory models. In: Abdulla, P.A., Leino, K.R.M. (eds.) TACAS 2011. LNCS, vol. 6605, pp. 11–25. Springer, Heidelberg (2011)

9. Dice, D., Lev, Y., Moir, M., Nussbaum, D.: Early experience with a commercial hardware transactional memory implementation. In: ASPLOS 2009, pp. 157–168 (2009)

10. Farzan, A., Madhusudan, P.: Monitoring atomicity in concurrent programs. In: Gupta, A., Malik, S. (eds.) CAV 2008. LNCS, vol. 5123, pp. 52–65. Springer, Heidelberg (2008)

11. Farzan, A., Madhusudan, P.: The complexity of predicting atomicity violations. In: Kowalewski, S., Philippou, A. (eds.) TACAS 2009. LNCS, vol. 5505, pp. 155–169. Springer, Heidelberg (2009)

12. Flanagan, C., Freund, S.N.: Atomizer: a dynamic atomicity checker for multi-threaded programs. Sci. Comput. Program. **71**(2), 89–109 (2008)

13. Flanagan, C., Freund, S.N., Lifshin, M., Qadeer, S.: Types for atomicity: static checking and inference for java. ACM Trans. Program. Lang. Syst. **30**(4), 20 (2008)

14. Flanagan, C., Freund, S.N., Yi, J.: Velodrome: a sound and complete dynamic atomicity checker for multithreaded programs. In: PLDI 2008, pp. 293–303 (2008)

15. Gotsman, A., Musuvathi, M., Yang, H.: Show no weakness: sequentially consistent specifications of TSO libraries. In: Aguilera, M.K. (ed.) DISC 2012. LNCS, vol. 7611, pp. 31–45. Springer, Heidelberg (2012)

16. Harris, T.L., Fraser, K.: Language support for lightweight transactions. In: OOPSLA 2003, pp. 388–402 (2003)

17. Hatcliff, J., Robby, Dwyer, M.B.: Verifying atomicity specifications for concurrent object-oriented software using model-checking. In: Steffen, B., Levi, G. (eds.) VMCAI 2004. LNCS, vol. 2937, pp. 175–190. Springer, Heidelberg (2004)

18. Herlihy, M., Moss, J.E.B.: Transactional memory: architectural support for lock-free data structures. In: ISCA 1993, pp. 289–300 (1993)

19. Jagadeesan, R., Petri, G., Pitcher, C., Riely, J.: Quarantining weakness. In: Felleisen, M., Gardner, P. (eds.) ESOP 2013. LNCS, vol. 7792, pp. 492–511. Springer, Heidelberg (2013)

20. Lu, S., Park, S., Seo, E., Zhou, Y.: Learning from mistakes: a comprehensive study on real world concurrency bug characteristics. In: ASPLOS, pp. 329–339 (2008)

21. Papadimitriou, C.H.: The serializability of concurrent database updates. J. ACM **26**(4), 631–653 (1979)

22. Shavit, N., Touitou, D.: Software transactional memory. Distrib. Comput. **10**(2), 99–116 (1997)

23. Sinha, A., Malik, S., Wang, C., Gupta, A.: Predicting serializability violations: SMT-based search vs. DPOR-based search. In: Eder, K., Lourenço, J., Shehory, O. (eds.) HVC 2011. LNCS, vol. 7261, pp. 95–114. Springer, Heidelberg (2012)

24. von Praun, C., Gross, T.R.: Static detection of atomicity violations in object-oriented programs. J. Object Technol. **3**(6), 103–122 (2004)

25. Wang, L., Stoller, S.D.: Runtime analysis of atomicity for multithreaded programs. IEEE Trans. Software Eng. **32**(2), 93–110 (2006)

26. Yi, J., Disney, T., Freund, S.N., Flanagan, C.: Cooperative types for controlling thread interference in java. In: ISSTA 2012, pp. 232–242 (2012)

# Formalizing and Checking Thread Refinement for Data-Race-Free Execution Models

Daniel Poetzl$^{(\boxtimes)}$ and Daniel Kroening

University of Oxford, Oxford, UK
daniel.poetzl@cs.ox.ac.uk

**Abstract.** When optimizing a thread in a concurrent program (either done manually or by the compiler), it must be guaranteed that the resulting thread is a refinement of the original thread. Most definitions of refinement are formulated in terms of valid syntactic transformations on the program code, or in terms of valid transformations on thread execution traces. We present a new theory formulated instead in terms of state transitions between synchronization operations. Our new method shows refinement in more cases and leads to more efficient and simpler procedures for refinement checking. We develop the theory for the SC-for-DRF execution model (using locks for synchronization), and show that its application in compiler testing yields speedups of on average more than two orders of magnitude compared to a previous approach.

## 1 Introduction

The refinement problem between threads appears in various contexts, such as the modular verification of concurrent programs, the validation of compiler optimization passes, or compiler testing. Informally, a thread $T'$ is a refinement of a thread $T$ if for all possible concurrent contexts $C = T_0 \parallel \ldots \parallel T_{n-1}$ (where $\parallel$ denotes parallel composition), the set of final states reachable by $T' \parallel C$ is a subset of the set of final states reachable by $T \parallel C$. We consider the problem as an instance of validating code optimization (either manual or by an optimizing compiler): the optimized thread must be a refinement of the original thread.

We focus on refinement in the "SC for DRF" execution model [1], i.e., programs behave sequentially consistent (SC) [6] if their SC executions are free of data races, and programs containing data races have undefined semantics. A program that contains data races could thus end up in any final state. Synchronization is provided via lock($l$) and unlock($l$) operations. The model is similar to, e.g., pthreads with its variety of lock operations such as pthread_mutex_lock() and pthread_mutex_unlock().

The definition of refinement given in the first paragraph is not directly useful for automated or manual reasoning, as it would require the enumeration of all possible concurrent contexts $C$. We thus develop a new theory that is based on comparing the state transitions of the original thread and the transformed thread between synchronization operations. We improve over existing work both

Supported by ERC project 280053 and SRC task 2269.002.

M. Chechik and J.-F. Raskin (Eds.): TACAS 2016, LNCS 9636, pp. 515–530, 2016.
DOI: 10.1007/978-3-662-49674-9_30

in terms of *precision* and *efficiency*. First, our theory allows to show refinement in cases where others fail. For example, we also allow the reordering of shared memory accesses out of critical sections (under certain circumstances); a transformation that is unsupported by other theories. Second, we show that applying our new specification method in a compiler testing setting leads to large performance gains. We can check whether two thread execution traces match on average 210 X as fast as a previous approach by Morisset et al. [12].

The rest of the paper is organized as follows. Section 2 introduces our state-based refinement formulation and compares it to previous event-based approaches on a concrete example. Section 3 formalizes state-based refinement. Section 4 shows that our formulation is more precise in that it supports more compiler optimizations than current theories. Section 5 evaluates our theory in the context of a compiler testing application that involves checking thread execution traces. Section 6 surveys related work. Section 7 concludes.

## 2    State-Based vs. Event-Based Refinement

Current theories of refinement for language-level memory models (such as the Java Memory Model or SC-for-DRF) are phrased in terms of transformations on thread execution traces (see e.g. [2,11,12,14,15]). We refer to this notion of refinement as *event-based refinement*. The trace transformations are then lifted to transformations on the program code. Thread traces are sequences of memory events (reads or writes) and synchronization events (lock or unlock). The valid transformations are given as descriptions of which *reorderings*, *eliminations*, and *introductions* of memory events on a trace are allowed. Checking whether a trace $t'$ is a correctly transformed version of a trace $t$ then amounts to determining whether there is a sequence of valid transformations that turns trace $t$ into trace $t'$. If each trace $t'$ of $T'$ is a transformed version of a trace $t$ of $T$, it follows that $T'$ is a refinement of $T$.

We show in the following that instead of describing refinement via a sequence of valid transformations on traces, switching to a theory based on state transitions provides several benefits. We refer to our new approach as *state-based refinement*. In essence, in the state-based approach, we only require that traces $t'$ and $t$ perform the same transformations on the shared state between corresponding synchronization operations, and that $t$ does not allow for more data races than $t$. In the next section, we illustrate the difference between the two approaches on an example.

### 2.1    Example

Consider Fig. 1, which gives an original thread $T$, a (correctly) transformed version $T'$, and a concurrent context $C$ in the form of another thread. The threads access shared variables $x, y, z$ and local variables $a, b$. The context $C$ outputs the value of variable $z$ in the final state. By inspecting $T' \parallel C$ and $T \parallel C$ (assuming initial state $\{x \mapsto 0, y \mapsto 0, z \mapsto 0\}$), we see that both combinations produce the

```
1 void thread_orig() {    1 void thread_trans() {
2    int a, b;             2    int a, b;                   1 void context() {
3    lock(l);              3    lock(l);                    2    int a;
4    x = 1;                4    x = 2;                      3    lock(l);
5    x = 2;                5    unlock(l);                  4    a = x;
6    unlock(l);            6    b = y;                      5    z = a;
7    a = x;                7    a = x;                      6    unlock(l);
8    b = y;                8    lock(l);                    7    join(thread_{orig|
9    lock(l);              9    if (b == 0)                 8                  trans});
10   if (b == 0)           10       x = 0;                  9    printf("%d\n", z);
11      x = 0;             11   b = y;                     10 }
12   unlock(l);            12   unlock(l);
13 }                       13 }                                   (c) Context
```

(a) Original thread        (b) Transformed thread

**Fig. 1.** Original thread $T$, transformed thread $T'$, and concurrent context $C$

same possible outputs (0 or 2). In fact, $T'$ and $T$ exhibit the same behavior in any concurrent context $C$ for which $T \parallel C$ is data-race-free.

Now let us look at two traces $t'$ of $T'$ and $t$ of $T$, and how a conventional event-based and our state-based theory would establish refinement. We assume for now that $T$ and $T'$ are only composed with contexts that do not write any shared memory locations accessed by them (as is the case for, e.g., the context given in Fig. 1c). Figure 2 gives the execution traces of $T$ (left trace) and $T'$ (right trace) for initial state $\{x \mapsto 0, y \mapsto 0, z \mapsto 0\}$.

A theory based on trace transformations (Fig. 2a) would establish the refinement between the two traces by noting that **write** x 1 can be removed ("overwritten write elimination"), **read** x 2 and **read** y 0 can be reordered ("non-conflicting read reordering"), and **read** y 0 can be introduced ("irrelevant read introduction"). Showing refinement this way can become significantly more complicated and costly if longer traces and more optimizations are considered.

We specify trace refinement by requiring that $t'$, $t$ perform the same state transitions from lock to subsequent unlock operations, and that $t'$ does not allow more data races than $t$. When assuming that the threads are only composed with contexts that do not write any shared memory locations, it is sufficient to check that $t'$, $t$ are in the *same state* at corresponding unlock operations. In this case, given an initial state $s_{init}$, we say a trace $t$ is in state $s$ at step $i$ if $s$ is like $s_{init}$, but updated with the values written by $t$ up to step $i$. Indeed, both traces in Fig. 2b are in state $\{x \mapsto 2, y \mapsto 0, z \mapsto 0\}$ at the first unlock($l$), and in state $\{x \mapsto 0, y \mapsto 0, z \mapsto 0\}$ at the second unlock($l$). The *key reason* for why trace refinement can be specified this way is that any context $C$ for which $T \parallel C$ is data-race-free can for each shared variable only observe the *last write* to it before an unlock operation. If it could observe any intermediate write, there would necessarily be a data race.

In addition to requiring that $t'$ and $t$ are in the same state, we also require that $t'$ does not allow more data races than $t$. This requirement is captured by the set

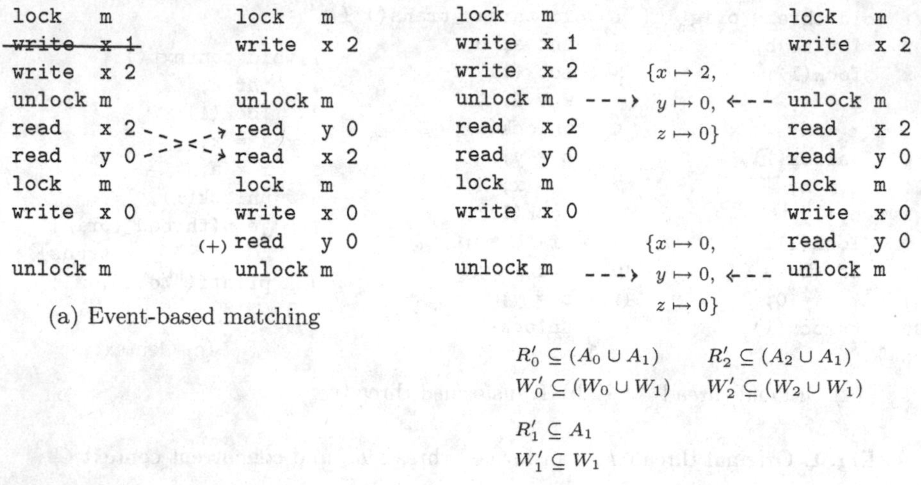

(a) Event-based matching

$$R'_0 \subseteq (A_0 \cup A_1) \qquad R'_2 \subseteq (A_2 \cup A_1)$$
$$W'_0 \subseteq (W_0 \cup W_1) \qquad W'_2 \subseteq (W_2 \cup W_1)$$

$$R'_1 \subseteq A_1$$
$$W'_1 \subseteq W_1$$

(b) State-based matching

**Fig. 2.** Trace matching

constraints in Fig. 2b. The primed sets correspond to $t'$, and the unprimed sets to $t$. The sets $R'_i, R_i$ ($W'_i, W_i$) denote the sets of memory locations read (written) between subsequent lock operations. For example, $R_1$ denotes the set of memory locations read by $t$ between the first unlock($l$) and the second lock($l$). We also use the abbreviations $A'_i = R'_i \cup W'_i$ and $A_i = R_i \cup W_i$. As an example, the condition $W'_0 \subseteq W_0 \cup W_1$ says that any memory location written by $t'$ between the first lock($l$) and the subsequent unlock($l$) must also be written by $t$ either between the first lock($l$) and the subsequent unlock($l$), or between the first unlock($l$) and the subsequent lock($l$). Since for $x \in W'_0$ we require only that $x \in W_0$ or $x \in W_1$, this allows a write to move into the critical section in $t'$ compared to $t$. We will define the set constraints more precisely in Sect. 3.

**Contexts that Write.** In the case where a thread can be put in an arbitrary context that can also write to the shared state, when generating the traces we also need to take into account that a read of a variable $x$ could yield a value that is both different from the initial value of $x$, and which the thread has not itself written (i.e., it was written by the context).

In an event-based theory this is typically handled by assuming that reads can return arbitrary values (see, e.g., [12]). However, this assumption is unnecessarily weak. For example, if a thread reads the same variable twice in a row with no intervening lock operation, and it did not itself write to the variable, then both reads need to return the same value. Otherwise, this would imply that another thread has written to the variable and thus there would be a data race.

In fact, when generating the traces of a thread, it is sufficient to assume that a thread observes the shared state only at its lock($l$) operations. The reason for this is that lock($l$) operations synchronize with preceding unlock($l$) operations of other threads. And those threads in turn make their writes available at their unlock($l$) operations.

# 3   Formalization

We now formalize the ideas from the previous section. For lack of space, we first make a few simplifying assumptions. Most notably we assume that threads do not contain nested locks (this assumption is lifted in the extended version of the paper [13]). We further assume that lock($l$) and unlock($l$) operations alternate on each thread execution, and that lock($l$) and unlock($l$) operations occur infinitely often on any infinite thread execution. This implies that a thread cannot get stuck, e.g., in an infinite loop without reaching a next lock operation. We also assume that the first operation in a thread is a lock($l$), and the last *lock* operation is an unlock($l$). We assume that the concurrent execution is the only source of nondeterminism, and that data races are the only source of undefined behavior.

## 3.1   Basics

A program $P = T_0 \| \ldots \| T_{n-1}$ is a parallel composition of threads $T_0, \ldots, T_{n-1}$. We denote by $h = (h_{T_0}, \ldots, h_{T_{n-1}})$ the vector of program counters of the threads. A program counter (pc) points at the next operation to be executed. We use the predicate lock($T, h$) (resp. unlock($T, h$)) to denote that the next operation to be executed by thread $T$ is a lock($l$) (resp. unlock($l$)). We use term($T, h$) to denote that thread $T$ has terminated.

Let $M$ be a finite, fixed-size set of shared memory locations $x_1, \ldots, x_{|M|}$. A state is a total function $s: M \to V$ from $M$ to the set of values $V$. We denote the set of all states by $S$. We assume there is a transition relation $\to$ between program configurations $(P, h, s)$. We normally omit $P$ when it is clear from context. The transition relation is generated according to interleaving semantics, and each transition step corresponds to an execution step of exactly one thread and accesses exactly one shared memory location or performs a lock operation. We denote by $h_s = (h_{s,T_0}, \ldots, h_{s,T_{n-1}})$ the initial pc vector with each thread at its entry point, and by $h_f = (h_{f,T_0}, \ldots, h_{f,T_{n-1}})$ the final pc vector with each thread having terminated.

We define a *program execution fragment* $e$ as a (finite or infinite) sequence of configurations such that successive configurations are related by $\to$. A *program execution* is an execution fragment that starts in a configuration with pc vector $h_s$, and either has infinite length (i.e., does not terminate) or ends in a configuration with pc vector $h_f$. A *program execution prefix* is a finite-length execution fragment that starts in a configuration with pc vector $h_s$. Given an execution fragment such as $e = (h_0, s_0)(h_1, s_1) \ldots (h_n, s_n)$, we use indices 0 to $n - 1$ to refer to the corresponding execution steps. For example, index 0 refers to the first execution step from $(h_0, s_0)$ to $(h_1, s_1)$.

| | | | |
|---|---|---|---|
| $\mathsf{wr}(e, i)$: | step $i$ is a shared write | $\mathsf{th}(e, i)$: | thread that performed step $i$ |
| $\mathsf{rd}(e, i)$: | step $i$ is a shared read | $\mathsf{src}(e, i)$: | source configuration of step $i$ |
| $\mathsf{mem}(e, i)$: | $\mathsf{wr}(e, i) \vee \mathsf{rd}(e, i)$ | $\mathsf{tgt}(e, i)$: | target configuration of step $i$ |
| $\mathsf{lock}(e, i)$: | step $i$ is a lock | $\mathsf{initial}(e)$: | initial state |
| $\mathsf{unlock}(e, i)$: | step $i$ is an unlock | $\mathsf{final}(e)$: | final state of execution $e$, or $\bot$ |
| $\mathsf{loc}(e, i)$: | memory location/lock accessed by step $i$ | | if $e$ is infinite |

**Fig. 3.** Notation

We next define several predicates and functions on execution fragments (Fig. 3). We usually omit the execution $e$ when it is clear from context. The expression $\mathsf{src}(e, i)$ (resp. $\mathsf{tgt}(e, i)$) refers to the configuration to the left (resp. right) of $\rightarrow$ of the transition corresponding to step $i$ of $e$.

We next define the semantics of a program according to interleaving semantics as the set of its initial/final state pairs.

**Definition 1 (Program Semantics).** $\mathbb{M}(P) = \{(s, s') \mid$ *there exists an execution $e$ of $P$ such that* $|e| < \infty \wedge \mathsf{initial}(e) = s \wedge \mathsf{final}(e) = s'\}$.

Only finite executions are relevant for the program semantics as defined above. Consequently, two programs $P'$, $P$ for which $\mathbb{M}(P') = \mathbb{M}(P)$ might have different behavior. For example, $P'$ might have a nonterminating execution while $P$ might always terminate. The programs $P'$ and $P$ are thus only *partially equivalent*.

We next define the relations sequenced-before (sb), synchronizes-with (sw), and happens-before (hb) for a given execution $e$ (with $|e| = n$). It holds that $(i, j) \in \mathsf{sb}$ if $0 \leq i < j < n$ and $\mathsf{th}(i) = \mathsf{th}(j)$. It holds that $(i, j) \in \mathsf{sw}$ if $0 \leq i < j < n$, $\mathsf{unlock}(i)$, $\mathsf{lock}(j)$, and $\mathsf{loc}(i) = \mathsf{loc}(j)$. The happens-before relation hb is then the transitive closure of $\mathsf{sb} \cup \mathsf{sw}$.

**Definition 2 (hb race).** *We say an execution $e$ (with $|e| = n$) contains an hb data race, written* $\mathsf{hb\text{-}race}(e)$, *if there are $0 \leq i < j < n$ such that $\mathsf{th}(i) \neq \mathsf{th}(j)$, $\mathsf{loc}(i) = \mathsf{loc}(j)$, $\mathsf{wr}(i)$ or $\mathsf{wr}(j)$, and $(i, j) \notin \mathsf{hb}$.*

We write $\mathsf{race}(P)$ to indicate that program $P$ has an execution that contains an hb data race, and $\mathsf{race\text{-}free}(P)$ to indicate that it does not have an execution that has an hb data race. We are now in a position to define thread refinement.

**Definition 3 (Refinement).** *We say that $T'$ is a refinement of $T$, written* $\mathsf{ref}(T', T)$, *if the following holds:*

$$\forall C: \mathsf{racefree}(T \| C) \Rightarrow (\mathsf{racefree}(T' \| C) \wedge \mathbb{M}(T' \| C) \subseteq \mathbb{M}(T \| C))$$

The above defines that $\mathsf{ref}(T', T)$ holds when for all contexts $C$ with which $T$ is data-race-free, $T'$ is also data-race-free, and the set of initial/final state pairs of $T' \| C$ is a subset of the set of initial/final state pairs of $T \| C$.

The above definition is not directly suited for automated refinement checking, as it would require implementing the $\forall$ quantifier (and hence enumerating all possible contexts $C$). We thus develop in the following our state-based refinement condition that implies $\mathsf{ref}(T', T)$, and which is more amenable to automated and manual reasoning about refinement.

## 3.2 State-Based Refinement

We next define the transition relation $\to_L$, which is more coarse-grained than $\to$. It will form the basis of the definition of our refinement condition.

**Definition 4** $(\to_L)$. $(P, h, s) \xrightarrow{l, (R_a, W_a), (R_b, W_b)}_L (P, h', s')$ *if and only if there exists an execution fragment* $e = (h_0, s_0)(h_1, s_1), \dots, (h_k, s_k), \dots, (h_n, s_n)$ *such that* $\mathsf{th}(0) = \mathsf{th}(1) = \dots = \mathsf{th}(n-1) = T$ *for some thread* $T$ *of* $P$, $\mathsf{lock}(0)$, $\mathsf{mem}(1), \dots, \mathsf{mem}(k-1), \mathsf{unlock}(k), \mathsf{mem}(k+1), \dots, \mathsf{mem}(n-1)$, *either* $\mathsf{lock}(T, h_n)$ *or* $\mathsf{term}(T, h_n)$, $\mathsf{loc}(0) = l$, $h_0 = h$ *and* $h_n = h'$. *The set* $R_a$ *(resp.* $W_a$) *is the set of memory locations read (resp. written) by steps 1 to* $k - 1$. *The set* $R_b$ *(resp.* $W_b$) *is the set of locations read (resp. written) by steps* $k + 1$ *to* $n - 1$.

We also use the abbreviations $A_a = R_a \cup W_a$ and $A_b = R_b \cup W_b$. The relation $\to_L$ embodies uninterrupted execution of a thread $T$ of $P$ from a $\mathsf{lock}(l)$ to the next $\mathsf{lock}(l)$ (or the thread terminates). Since we have excluded nested locks, this means the thread executes exactly one $\mathsf{unlock}(l)$ in between. For example, in Fig. 2b (left trace), the execution from the first lock in Line 1 to immediately before the second lock in Line 7 corresponds to a transition of $\to_L$. If we assume the thread starts in a state with all variables being 0, we have $s = \{x \mapsto 0, y \mapsto 0, z \mapsto 0\}$ and $s' = \{x \mapsto 2, y \mapsto 0, z \mapsto 0\}$. The corresponding access sets are $R_a = \{\}, W_a = \{x\}$, and $R_b = \{x, y\}, W_b = \{\}$.

We now define the semantics of a single thread $T$ as the set of its *state traces*. A state trace is a finite sequence of the form $(l_0, s_0, R_0, W_0)(R_1, W_1, s_1)(l_2, s_2, R_2, W_2)(R_3, W_3, s_3) \dots (l_{n-1}, s_{n-1}, R_{n-1}, W_{n-1})(R_n, W_n, s_n)$. Two items $i$, $i + 1$ (with $i$ being even) of a state trace belong together. The item $i$ corresponds to execution starting in state $s_i$ at a $\mathsf{lock}(l)$ and executing up to the next $\mathsf{unlock}(l)$, with the thread reading the variables in $R_i$ and writing the variables in $W_i$. The subsequent item $i + 1$ corresponds to execution continuing at the $\mathsf{unlock}(l)$ and executing until the next $\mathsf{lock}(l)$ reaching state $s_{i+1}$, with the thread reading the variables in $R_{i+1}$ and writing the variables in $W_{i+1}$.

The formal definition of the state trace set $\mathbb{S}(T)$ is given in Fig. 4. Intuitively, the state trace set of a thread $T$ embodies all interactions it could potentially have with a context $C$ for which $\mathsf{race\text{-}free}(T \parallel C)$. A thread might observe writes by the context at a $\mathsf{lock}(l)$ operation. This is modeled in $\mathbb{S}(T)$ by the state changing between transitions. For example, the target state $s_1$ of the first transition is different from the source state $s_2$ of the second transition. The last line of the definition of $\mathbb{S}(T)$ constrains how the state may change between transitions. It defines that those memory locations that the thread $T$ accesses in an execution portion from an $\mathsf{unlock}(l)$ to the next $\mathsf{lock}(l)$ (i.e., those in $A_{i-1}$) do not change at this $\mathsf{lock}(l)$. The reason for this is that if those memory locations would be written by the context, then there would be a data race. But since $\mathbb{S}(T)$ only models the potential interactions with race-free contexts, the last line excludes those state traces.

$$\mathbb{S}(T) = \{(l_0, s_0, R_0, W_0)(R_1, W_1, s_1)(l_2, s_2, R_2, W_2)(R_3, W_3, s_3) \ldots (R_n, W_n, s_n) \mid$$

$$\exists h_0, h_2, \ldots, h_{n+1}:$$

$$(T, h_0, s_0) \xrightarrow{l_0, (R_0, W_0), (R_1, W_1)}_L (T, h_2, s_1) \wedge$$

$$(T, h_2, s_2) \xrightarrow{l_2, (R_2, W_2), (R_3, W_3)}_L (T, h_4, s_3) \wedge$$

$$\ldots$$

$$(T, h_{n-1}, s_{n-1}) \xrightarrow{l_{n-1}, (R_{n-1}, W_{n-1}), (R_n, W_n)}_L (T, h_{n+1}, s_n) \wedge$$

$$h_0 = h_s \wedge$$

$$\forall i \in \mathsf{even}_n^+ : \forall x \in A_{i-1} : s_{i-1}(x) = s_i(x)\}$$

**Fig. 4.** Definition of the state trace set of a thread

Previously we stated that we are interested in the states of a thread at lock and unlock operations, but $\mathbb{S}(T)$ embodies transitions from a lock($l$) to the next lock($l$). However, since we know the state at a lock($l$), and we know the set of memory locations $W_i$ written between the previous unlock($l$) and that lock($l$), we know the state of the memory locations $M - W_i$ at the unlock($l$). This is sufficient for phrasing the refinement in the following.

We are now in a position to define the $\mathsf{match}_a(t', t)$ predicate. We will later extend it to the predicate $\mathsf{match}_b(t', t)$, which indicates whether a state trace $t' \in \mathbb{S}(T')$ matches a state trace $t \in \mathbb{S}(T)$. The formal definition of $\mathsf{match}_a(t', t)$ is given in Fig. 5. Primed symbols refer to components of $t'$, and unprimed symbols refer to components of $t$. We denote by $\mathsf{even}_n$ (resp. $\mathsf{odd}_n$) the set of all even (resp. odd) indices $i$ such that $0 \leq i \leq n$. Intuitively, the constraints in Lines 3–6 specify that $t'$ must not allow more data races than $t$. The constraints in Lines 3–4 correspond to an execution portion from a lock($l$) to the next unlock($l$), and Lines 5–6 correspond to an execution portion from the unlock($l$) to the next lock($l$). Since we have $R_i' \subseteq A_{i-1} \cup A_i \cup A_{i+1}$ and $W_i' \subseteq W_{i-1} \cup W_i \cup W_{i+1}$, the specification allows an access in $t$ to move into a critical section in $t'$ (we further investigate this in Sect. 4). The constraint in Line 7 specifies that $t'$ and $t$ receive the same new values at lock($l$) operations (modeling writes by the context). The constraint at Line 9 specifies that the values written by $t'$ and $t$ before unlock($l$) operations must be the same. The last constraint specifies that $t'$ and $t$ perform the same sequence of lock operations.

We next define the $\mathsf{match}_b(t', t)$ predicate. We denote by $t[0:i]$ the slice of a trace from index 0 to index $i$ (exclusive).

**Definition 5**

$$\mathsf{match}_b(T', T) \Leftrightarrow \mathsf{match}_a(t', t) \vee$$

$$\exists i \in \mathsf{even}^+ : \mathsf{match}_a(t'[0:i], t[0:i]) \wedge$$

$$\exists x \in (A_{i-1} - A_{i-1}') : s_{i-1}(x) \neq s_i'(x)$$

The above defines that either $t'$ and $t$ match, or there are same-length prefixes that match, and at the subsequent lock($l$) a memory location in $t'$ changes that is accessed by $t$ but not by $t'$ ($x \in A_{i-1} - A'_{i-1}$). Thus, a context that could perform the change of the memory location that $t'$ observes would have a data race with $t$. Since when $t$ is involved in a data race we have undefined behavior, any behavior of $t'$ is allowed. Thus, $t'$ and $t$ are considered matched.

$\mathsf{match}_a(t', t) \Leftrightarrow$

1   $|t'| = |t|$

2   let $n = |t|$ in

# race constraints

3   $\forall i \in \mathsf{even}_n\colon R'_i \subseteq (A_{i-1} \cup A_i \cup A_{i+1})$

4   $\forall i \in \mathsf{even}_n\colon W'_i \subseteq (W_{i-1} \cup W_i \cup W_{i+1})$

5   $\forall i \in \mathsf{odd}_n\colon R'_i \subseteq A_i$

6   $\forall i \in \mathsf{odd}_n\colon W'_i \subseteq W_i$

# state at locks constraints

7   $\forall i \in \mathsf{even}_n\colon \forall x \in M - A_{i-1}\colon s'_i(x) = s_i(x)$

8   $\forall i \in \mathsf{even}_n\colon \forall x \in A_{i-1} - A'_{i-1}\colon s'_{i-1}(x) = s'_i(x)$

# state at unlocks constraints

9   $\forall i \in \mathsf{odd}_n\colon \forall x \in M - W_i\colon s'_i(x) = s_i(x)$

# same locks constraint

10   $\forall i \in \mathsf{even}_n\colon l'_i = l_i$

**Fig. 5.** Definition of matching state traces

We can now define our refinement specification $\mathsf{check}(T', T)$, which we later show implies the refinement specification $\mathsf{ref}(T', T)$ of Definition 3.

**Definition 6 (Check)**

$$\mathsf{check}(T', T) \Leftrightarrow \forall t' \in \mathbb{S}(T')\colon \exists t \in \mathbb{S}(T)\colon \mathsf{match}_b(t', t)$$

We next state two lemmas that we use in the soundness proof of $\mathsf{check}(T', T)$. We refer to the extended version of the paper for the corresponding proofs [13].

**Lemma 1 (Coarse-Grained Interleaving).** *Let $e$ (with $|e| = n$) be an execution prefix of $P$ with $\neg\mathsf{hb\text{-}race}(e)$ and $\mathsf{final}(e) = s$. Then there is an execution prefix $e'$ of $P$ with $\neg\mathsf{hb\text{-}race}(e')$ and $\mathsf{final}(e') = s$, such that execution portions from a lock($l$) to the next lock($l$) of a thread are not interleaved with other threads. Formally:*

$$\forall 0 \le i < n\colon \mathsf{lock}(i) \Rightarrow \exists j > i\colon (\mathsf{lock}(\mathsf{th}(i), \mathsf{tgt}(j)) \lor \mathsf{term}(\mathsf{th}(i), \mathsf{tgt}(j)) \land$$
$$\forall i < k < j\colon \mathsf{th}(k) = \mathsf{th}(i))$$

**Lemma 2 (Race Refinement).** *Let* check($T', T$). *Then for all contexts* $C$, *if* $T' \parallel C$ *has an execution that has a data race, then* $T \parallel C$ *also has an execution that has a data race. Formally:*

$$\mathsf{check}(T', T) \Rightarrow \forall C \colon (\mathsf{race}(T' \parallel C) \Rightarrow \mathsf{race}(T \parallel C))$$

The following theorem establishes the soundness of our refinement condition check($T', T$).

**Theorem 1 (Soundness).** check($T', T$) $\Rightarrow$ ref($T', T$)

*Proof sketch.* Let $C$ be an arbitrary context $C$ such that race-free($T \parallel C$). Let further $(s, s')$ in $\mathbb{M}(T' \parallel C)$. Thus, there is an execution $e$ of $T' \parallel C$ that starts in state $s$ and ends in state $s'$. By Lemma 2, race-free($T' \parallel C$). Thus, by Lemma 1, there is an execution $e'$ for which portions from a lock($l$) to the next lock($l$) of a thread are not interleaved with other threads. The sequence of those execution portions of $T'$ corresponds to an element $t' \in \mathbb{S}(T')$. Then, by the definition of check($T', T$), there is an element $t \in \mathbb{S}(T)$ such that either (a) match$_a(t', t)$, or (b) $\exists i \in \mathsf{even}_n \colon \mathsf{match}_a(t'[0 \colon i], t[0 \colon i]) \land \exists x \in (A_{i-1} - A'_{i-1}) \colon s'_{i-1}(x) \neq s'_i(x)$.

(a) Then $t$ embodies the same state transitions as $t'$. This is ensured by constraints 7 and 9 of the definition of match$_a()$. Constraint 7 specifies that the starting states of a transition match, and constraint 9 specifies that the resulting states of a transition match. A closer look at constraints 7 and 9 reveals that the corresponding states of $t'$ and $t$ do not need to be completely equal (only those memory locations in $M - A_{i-1}$ resp. $M - W_i$ need to have the same value). The reason for this is that if a thread would observe those memory locations it would give rise to a data race. Since we have both race-free($T' \parallel C$) and race-free($T \parallel C$), it follows that the values of the memory locations $A_{i-1}$ resp. $W_i$ can be arbitrary. Therefore, $T$ can perform the same state transitions as $T'$. Thus, we can replace the steps of $T'$ in $e'$ by steps of $T$, and get a valid execution $e''$ of $T \parallel C$ ending in the same state. Therefore, $(s, s') \in \mathbb{M}(T \parallel C)$.

(b) Since match$_a(t'[0 \colon i], t[0 \colon i])$, the first $i$ state transitions of $t$ are the same as those of $t'$. Thus, we can replace the first $i$ execution portions of $T'$ in $e'$ by execution portions of $T$. The last execution portion of $T$ accesses a memory location $x$ that was not accessed by the corresponding execution portion of $T'$ (since we have $\exists x \in A_{i-1} - A'_{i-1}$). Moreover, by $s'_{i-1}(x) \neq s'_i(x)$ it follows that this memory location is written by the context $C$. Thus, we have race($T \parallel C$), which contradicts the premise race-free($T \parallel C$).                               □

## 4   Supported Optimizations

We now investigate which optimizations are validated by our theory. By inspecting the definition of match$_a()$ we see that it requires that $t'$ and $t$ perform the same state transitions between lock operations, and that the sets of memory locations accessed between lock operations of $t'$ must be subsets of the corresponding sets of memory locations accessed by $t$. Together with the definitions of match$_b()$

```
1 lock(1);          1 lock(1);          1 lock(1);
2 x = 1;            2 x = 1;            2 x = 1;
3 y = 1;            3 y = 1;            3 unlock(1);
4 unlock(1);        4 y = 2;            4 y = 1;
5 y = 2;            5 unlock(1);        5 y = 2;
```

(a) Original ($T$)    (b) Transformation 1 ($T'$)   (c) Transformation 2 ($T''$)

**Fig. 6.** Original, roach motel reordering, inverse roach motel reordering

and check(), this implies that if an optimization only performs transformations that do not change the state transitions between lock operations, and does not introduce accesses to new memory locations, then the optimized thread $T'$ will be a refinement of the original thread $T$. This includes all the transformations shown to be sound by Boehm [2] and Morisset et al. [12] (considering programs using lock($l$) and unlock($l$) for synchronization).

Our theory also allows the reordering of shared memory accesses into and out of critical sections (under certain circumstances). The former are called *roach motel reorderings* and have been studied for example in the context of the Java memory model (see, e.g., [15]). The latter have not been previously described in the literature. In analogy to the former we term them *inverse roach motel reorderings*. We show on an example that our theory enables the proof of both optimizations.

**Roach Motel Reorderings.** Consider Fig. 6. Both $x$ and $y$ are shared variables. Figure 6a depicts the original thread $T$, and Fig. 6b a correctly transformed version $T'$. The statement y = 2 has been moved into the critical section. This is safe as it cannot introduce data races (but might remove data races).

Let $t'$ be a state trace of $T'$ starting in some initial state $s_{init}$. Then there is a state trace $t$ of $T$ starting also in $s_{init}$. The state $s_{init}$ corresponds to the state at the first lock($l$) for both threads. At the unlock($l$) they are in states $s' = \{x \mapsto 1, y \mapsto 2\}$ resp. $s = \{x \mapsto 1, y \mapsto 1\}$. The access sets of the two state traces are $R'_0 = R'_1 = R_0 = R_1 = \{\}$ (we ignore the read sets in the following as they are empty), and $W'_0 = W_0 = \{x, y\}, W'_1 = \{\}, W_1 = \{y\}$. At the unlock($l$), according to the definition of $match_a()$, the constraint $\forall x \in M - W_1 : s'(x) = s(x)$ needs to be satisfied. This is the case as the variable $y$ for which $s'$ and $s$ differ is in $W_1$. Moreover, for $match_a()$ to be satisfied, the following must hold for the write sets: $W'_0 \subseteq W_0 \cup W_1$ and $W'_1 \subseteq W_1$. This also holds. Hence, $match_a(t', t)$ holds. Consequently, we also have $match_b(t', t)$ and thus $check(T', T)$, which implies $ref(T', T)$ according to Theorem 1. Thread $T'$ is thus a correctly transformed version of thread $T$.

**Inverse Roach Motel Reorderings.** Consider now the example in Fig. 6, which is a version $T''$ of the thread $T$. Again, it is correctly optimized. In order to get defined behavior for $T \| C$, the context $C$ must in particular avoid data races with $y = 2$. But this implies that the context cannot observe the write $y = 1$, for if it could, there would be a data race with $y = 2$. Moreover, moving $y = 1$ downwards out of the critical section cannot introduce data races, as a write to $y$ already occurs in this section. Consequently, $y = 1$ can be moved downwards out of the critical section (or in this particular case removed completely).

We can use a similar argument as in the previous section to show within our theory that $T''$ is a correctly optimized version of $T$. Let $t''$, $t$ be again two state traces starting in the same initial state $s_{init}$. At the unlock($l$) they are in states $s'' = \{x \mapsto 1, y \mapsto y_{init}\}$ resp. $s = \{x \mapsto 1, y \mapsto 1\}$, with $y_{init}$ denoting the value of $y$ in $s_{init}$. Again, the constraints $\forall x \in M - W_1 : s''(x) = s(x)$, and $W_0'' \subseteq W_0 \cup W_1$ and $W_1'' \subseteq W_1$ are satisfied, and we can conclude that $\text{match}_a(t'', t)$, $\text{match}_b(t'', t)$, $\text{check}(T'', T)$, and finally $\text{ref}(T'', T)$ hold.

## 5  Evaluation

Previously we have argued that our specification efficiently captures thread refinement in the SC-for-DRF execution model, as it abstracts over the way in which a thread implements the state transitions between lock operations. In this section, we show that with our approach we can check in linear time whether two traces match. We also provide experimental data, showing that the application of our state-based approach in a compiler testing setting leads to large performance improvements compared to using an event-based approach.

### 5.1  Compiler Testing

Eide and Regehr [4] pioneered an approach to test that a compiler correctly optimizes programs that involves repeatedly (1) generating a random C program, (2) compiling it both with and without optimizations (e.g., gcc -O0 and gcc -O3), (3) collecting a trace from both the original and the optimized program, and (4) checking whether the traces match. If two traces do not match, then a compiler bug has been found. Morisset et al. [12] extended this approach to a fragment of C11 and implemented it in their cmmtest tool.

The cmmtest tool consists of the following components: an adapted version of csmith [17] (we call it "csmith-sync" in the following) to generate random C threads, a tool to collect execution traces of a thread ("pin-interceptor"), and a tool to check whether two given traces match ("cmmtest-check"). The csmith-sync tool generates random C threads with synchronization operations such as pthread_mutex_lock(), pthread_mutex_unlock(), or the C11 primitives release() and acquire(). We only consider programs that contain lock operations. The pin-interceptor tool is based on the Pin binary instrumentation framework [10]. It executes a program and instruments the memory accesses and synchronization operations in order to collect a trace of those operations. The cmmtest-check tool takes two traces (produced by pin-interceptor) of an optimized and an unoptimized thread, and checks whether the traces match. We use the existing csmith-sync and pin-interceptor tools, and implemented our own trace checker tracecheck.

## 5.2   Complexity

Our tool tracecheck takes two traces (such as those depicted in Fig. 2b), and first determines the states of the traces at lock operations, and the sets of memory locations accessed between lock operations. That is, given a trace it constructs its corresponding state trace (i.e., an element of $\mathbb{S}(P)$). Then, it checks whether the two state traces match by evaluating the $\text{match}_b()$ predicate. This way of checking traces is very efficient as it has runtime *linear* in the trace lengths.

This can be seen as follows. The size of a state is bounded by the number of writes that have occurred so far. Moreover, it is not necessary to check the complete states for equality at each lock operation; it suffices to check the memory locations that have been written to since the last check at the previous lock operation. Thus, checking the states at lock operations (corresponding to the "states at lock" and "states at unlock" constraints of the $\text{match}_a()$ predicate) is a linear-time operation.

The race constraints can also be checked in linear time. First, the size of the sets is bounded by the number of memory locations accessed between the two corresponding lock operations. Second, subset checking between two sets $A$ and $B$ can be implemented in linear time.[1] In summary, we have a linear procedure for checking whether two traces match.

By contrast, cmmtest-check attempts to match traces by finding a sequence of valid transformations that transforms one trace into the other. Different sequences are explored in a tree-like fashion [12], suggesting exponential runtime in the worst case.

## 5.3   Experiments

We compared tracecheck to cmmtest-check on in total 40,000 randomly generated C threads. We compiled each with gcc -O0 and gcc -O3 and collected a trace from each. The length of the traces was in the range of 1 to 4,000 events. We have chosen this range such that also cmmtest-check could match all the traces within the available memory limit. On some longer traces, cmmtest-check yields a stack overflow (it is implemented in the functional language OCaml). Our tool tracecheck can also handle traces with hundreds of thousands of events. Our tool outperformed cmmtest-check on all traces and was 210 X faster on average. Both tracecheck and cmmtest-check agreed on all traces, i.e., they either both classified a trace as correct or they both classified it as buggy.

Figure 7 shows the average time it took to match two traces of a certain length, for cmmtest-check (Fig. 7a) and tracecheck (Fig. 7b). Along the x-axis, we classify the pairs of traces $t'$, $t$ into bins according to the length of the unoptimized trace $t$. Each bin $i$ contains 100 pairs $t'$, $t$ such that the length of $t$ is in the range $[250 \cdot i, 250 \cdot (i+1)]$. For example, bin 5 contains the pairs with

---

[1] If $A$ and $B$ are represented as hash sets, then $A \subseteq B$ can be checked by iterating over the elements of $A$, and for each one performing a lookup in $B$ (which has constant time). If all elements are found, $A$ is a subset of $B$.

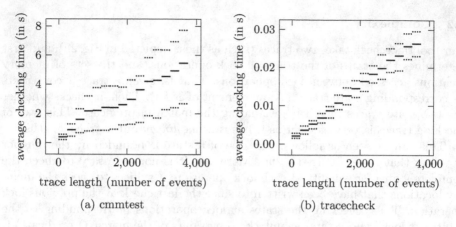

(a) cmmtest

(b) tracecheck

**Fig. 7.** Average checking time over length of traces

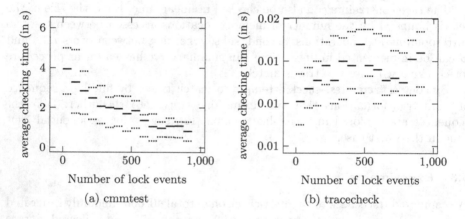

(a) cmmtest

(b) tracecheck

**Fig. 8.** Average checking time over number of locks in a trace

the length of the unoptimized trace being in the range [1250, 1500]. The y-axis shows the average time it took to match two traces $t'$, $t$ in the respective bin. The dotted lines represent the 20th and 80th percentile to indicate the spread of the times.

Figure 8 illustrates the effect of the number of lock operations in the two traces on the time it takes to check if they match. We have evaluated this on pairs of traces $t'$, $t$ with the unoptimized trace $t$ having length in the range of [1900, 2100]. Along the x-axis, we classify the pairs of traces $t'$, $t$ into bins according to the number of lock operations they contain. The y-axis again indicates the average matching time. As can be seen in Fig. 8a, cmmtest-check is sensitive to the number of locks in a trace. That is, matching traces generally takes longer the fewer locks they contain. The reason for this is that cmmtest-check considers lock operations as "barriers" against transformations: it does not try to reorder events across lock operations. Thus, the more lock operations there are in a trace, the fewer potential transformations it tries, and thus the lower the checking time. By contrast, the performance of our tool tracecheck is largely insensitive to the number of locks in a trace.

# 6  Related Work

Refinement approaches can be classified based on whether they handle language-level memory models (such as SC-for-DRF or C11) [2,11,12,14,15], hardware memory models (such as TSO) [5,16], or idealized models (typically SC) [3,9].

The approaches for language-level models typically define refinement by giving valid transformations on thread execution traces. These trace transformations are then lifted to the program code level. An example is the theory of valid optimizations of Morisset et al. [12]. They handle the fragment of C11 with lock/unlock and release/acquire operations. The theory is relatively restrictive in that they do not allow the reordering of memory accesses across synchronization operations (such as the roach motel reorderings described in Sect. 4).

The approaches of Brookes [3] (for SC) and Jagadeesan [5] (for TSO) are closer to ours in that they also specify refinement in terms of state transitions rather than transformations on traces. They provide a sound and complete denotational specification of refinement. However, their completeness proofs rely on the addition of an unrealistic await() statement, which provides strong atomicity.

Liang et al. [7] presented a rely-guarantee-based approach to reason about thread refinement. Starting from the assumption of arbitrary concurrent contexts, they allow to add constraints that capture knowledge about the context in which the threads run in. They later extended their approach to also allow reasoning about whether the original and the refined thread exhibit the same termination behavior [8].

Lochbihler [9] provides a verified non-optimizing compiler for concurrent Java guaranteeing refinement between the threads in the source program and the byte-code. It is however based on SC semantics rather than the Java memory model. Sevcik et al. [16] developed the verified CompCertTSO compiler for compilation from a C-like language with TSO semantics to x86 assembly.

The compiler testing method based on checking traces of randomly generated programs on which we evaluated our refinement specification in Sect. 5 was pioneered by Eide and Regehr [4]. They used this approach to check the correct compilation of volatile variables. It was extended to a fragment of C11 by Morisset et al. [12].

# 7  Conclusions

We have presented a new theory of thread refinement for the SC-for-DRF execution model. The theory is based on matching the state of the transformed and the original thread at lock operations, and ensuring that the former does not introduce data races that were not possible with the latter. Our theory is more precise than previous ones in that it allows to show refinement in cases where others fail. It also boosts the efficiency of reasoning about refinement. Checking whether two traces match can be done in linear time, and consequently our implementation outperformed that of a previous approach by factor 210 X.

# References

1. Adve, S.V., Hill, M.D.: Weak ordering - a new definition. In: International Symposium on Computer Architecture (ISCA), pp. 2–14. ACM (1990)
2. Boehm, H.-J.: Reordering constraints for Pthread-style locks. In: Principles and Practice of Parallel Programming (PPoPP), pp. 173–182. ACM (2007)
3. Brookes, S.: Full abstraction for a shared variable parallel language. In: Logic in Computer Science (LICS), pp. 98–109. IEEE (1993)
4. Eide, E., Regehr, J.: Volatiles are miscompiled, and what to do about it. In: Embedded Software (EMSOFT), pp. 255–264. ACM (2008)
5. Jagadeesan, R., Petri, G., Riely, J.: Brookes is relaxed, almost!. In: Birkedal, L. (ed.) FOSSACS 2012. LNCS, vol. 7213, pp. 180–194. Springer, Heidelberg (2012)
6. Lamport, L.: How to make a multiprocessor computer that correctly executes multiprocess programs. TC **100**(9), 690–691 (1979)
7. Liang, H., Feng, X., Fu, M.: A rely-guarantee-based simulation for verifying concurrent program transformations. In: Principles of Programming Languages (POPL), pp. 455–468. ACM (2012)
8. Liang, H., Feng, X., Shao, Z.: Compositional verification of termination-preserving refinement of concurrent programs. In: Logic in Computer Science (LICS), pp. 65:1–65:10. ACM (2014)
9. Lochbihler, A.: Verifying a compiler for Java threads. In: Gordon, A.D. (ed.) ESOP 2010. LNCS, vol. 6012, pp. 427–447. Springer, Heidelberg (2010)
10. Luk, C.-K., Cohn, R., Muth, R., Patil, H., Klauser, A., Lowney, G., Wallace, S., Reddi, V.J., Hazelwood, K.: Pin: Building customized program analysis tools with dynamic instrumentation. In: Programming Language Design and Implementation (PLDI), pp. 190–200. ACM (2005)
11. Manson, J., Pugh, W., Adve, S.V.: The Java memory model. In: Principles of Programming Languages (POPL), pp. 378–391. ACM (2005)
12. Morisset, R., Pawan, P., Nardelli, F.Z.: Compiler testing via a theory of sound optimisations in the C11/C++11 memory model. In: Programming Language Design and Implementation (PLDI), pp. 187–196. ACM (2013)
13. Poetzl, D., Kroening, D.: Formalizing and checking thread refinement for data-race-free execution models (extended version) (2015). CoRR, abs/1505.08581
14. Ševčík, J.: Safe optimisations for shared-memory concurrent programs. In: Programming Language Design and Implementation (PLDI), pp. 306–316. ACM (2011)
15. Ševčík, J., Aspinall, D.: On validity of program transformations in the Java memory model. In: Vitek, J. (ed.) ECOOP 2008. LNCS, vol. 5142, pp. 27–51. Springer, Heidelberg (2008)
16. Ševčík, J., Vafeiadis, V., Nardelli, F.Z., Jagannathan, S., Sewell, P.: CompCertTSO: A verified compiler for relaxed-memory concurrency. JACM **60**(3), 49 (2013)
17. X. Yang, Y. Chen, E. Eide, and J. Regehr. Finding and understanding bugs in C compilers. In Programming Language Design and Implementation (PLDI), pp. 283–294. ACM, (2011)

# Tool Demos

# The xSAP Safety Analysis Platform

Benjamin Bittner, Marco Bozzano[✉], Roberto Cavada, Alessandro Cimatti,
Marco Gario, Alberto Griggio, Cristian Mattarei, Andrea Micheli,
and Gianni Zampedri

Fondazione Bruno Kessler, Trento, Italy
bozzano@fbk.eu

**Abstract.** This paper describes the xSAP safety analysis platform.
xSAP provides several model-based safety analysis features for finite-
and infinite-state synchronous transition systems. In particular, it
supports library-based definition of fault modes, an automatic model
extension facility, generation of safety analysis artifacts such as Dynamic
Fault Trees and Failure Mode and Effects Analysis tables. Moreover,
it supports probabilistic evaluation of Fault Trees, failure propagation
analysis using Timed Failure Propagation Graphs, and Common Cause
Analysis. xSAP has been used in several industrial projects as verification back-end, and is currently being evaluated in a joint R&D Project
involving FBK and The Boeing Company.

## 1 Introduction

In recent years, there has been a growing industrial interest in model-based safety
assessment techniques (MBSA) [1–3] and their application. These methods are
based on a single safety model of a system, and analyses are carried out with
a high degree of automation, thus reducing the most tedious and error-prone
activities that today are performed manually. Formal verification tools based on
model checking have been extended to automate the generation of artifacts such
as Fault Trees, which are required for certification of safety critical systems –
see, e.g., [4,5].

xSAP is a platform for MBSA, which provides a variety of features. First,
it enables the definition of fault modes, based on a customizable fault library.
Second, it implements automatic model extension, namely the possibility to
automatically extend a system model with the fault definitions retrieved from the
library. Third, it implements a full range of safety analyses, including Fault Tree
Analysis (FTA), Failure Mode and Effects Analysis (FMEA), failure propagation
analysis using Timed Failure Propagation Graphs (TFPGs), and Common Cause
Analysis (CCA). Finally, xSAP implements a family of effective routines for such
analyses, based on state-of-the-art model checking techniques, including BDD-,
SAT- and SMT-based techniques.

xSAP is currently the core verification engine for many other tools, including
industrial ones. It has been used in several industrial projects funded by the
European Space Agency. Moreover, xSAP is currently being used in a joint

© Springer-Verlag Berlin Heidelberg 2016
M. Chechik and J.-F. Raskin (Eds.): TACAS 2016, LNCS 9636, pp. 533–539, 2016.
DOI: 10.1007/978-3-662-49674-9_31

research and development project between FBK and The Boeing Company [6]. xSAP is being developed by FBK, and it is currently distributed with a free license for academic research purposes and non-commercial applications. It can be downloaded from http://xsap.fbk.eu.

*Related Work.* xSAP is an evolution and a complete re-implementation of FSAP [7]. FSAP has been developed within the ESACS, ISAAC, and MISSA European projects. It pioneered the ideas of model extension and model-based safety assessment [2], and was applied for safety assessment of avionic systems. xSAP contains significant improvements, such as handling of infinite-state systems, more general and customizable libraries to define fault modes and their dynamics, and failure propagation analysis. Moreover, xSAP implements a family of novel routines for safety analysis: the BDD-based Fault Tree generation routines described in [8] are complemented by (different variants of) SAT-based and SMT-based routines, and routines based on IC3 [9].

Some of the safety assessment functions of xSAP are used as a back-end for the COMPASS tool [3,10] and its extensions, see e.g. [11]. There are two key differences with respect to the COMPASS tools. First, xSAP provides a wider range of routines for Fault Tree generation; second, xSAP implements a general model extension mechanism, based on a library defining fault modes and their dynamics, while in COMPASS the fault models must be modeled manually and explicitly within the SLIM language.

Other platforms for MBSA are based on Altarica/OCAS [12–14], Scade [15,16], and Statemate [17]. They support a subset of the features included in xSAP (FTA, FMEA, or some limited form of model extension), but none of them is publicly available.

*Structure of the Paper.* In Sects. 2 and 3 we describe the functionality and the architecture of xSAP. In Sect. 4 we briefly discuss its most successful applications. In Sect. 5 we draw conclusions and outline future directions.

## 2    Functionality

In this section we describe the main features of xSAP. Figure 1 illustrates the main flow.

### 2.1    Model Extension

Model extension [2,7] is an automated process that, based on a specification of the possible faults, returns a model (called *extended model*) that takes into account faulty behaviors. The model extension routine takes as input the *nominal model* (describing behavior in absence of faults), the *fault library* (containing templates for faults and their dynamics) and the *fault extension instructions* (specifying directives to instantiate the fault templates). Formal analyses can be run on the extended model, in order to assess system behavior in presence

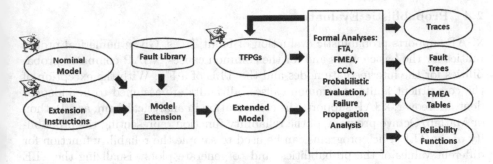

**Fig. 1.** The xSAP main flow.

of faults. The fault library of xSAP contains a comprehensive set of predefined fault modes, including, e.g., several variants of *stuck at, random, conditional, ramp down*, and can be further customized for any specific need. Moreover, a *local* and *global* dynamics libraries enable the definition of the dynamics of faults (e.g., *permanent* or *sporadic*). The fault library has been validated and extended to match the need of a significant case study of industrial size [6].

## 2.2 Safety Analysis

xSAP supports the automatic generation of artifacts that are typical of safety analysis, in particular Fault Trees and FMEA tables [4,18]. A Fault Tree (FT) is a graphical representation of the sets of possible causes of a given (undesired) event (the root of the tree – called *Top Level Event, TLE*). The TLE is linked by means of logical gates (AND, OR) to the basic events (faults). The minimal combinations of faults explaining the TLE are called *Minimal Cut Sets (MCSs)*. Finally, xSAP can generate Dynamic Fault Trees (DFTs) [19], where a *priority AND* gate is used to identify order of precedence of events. FMEA tables are a tabular representation of the causality relationships between (sets of) faults and a list of properties (undesired events). xSAP also supports the generation of Dynamic FMEA tables, where the order of the events may be imposed.

## 2.3 Common Cause Analysis

Common Cause Analysis (CCA) is a necessary step of safety assessment, that is often required by safety standards [4]. It consists in evaluating the consequences of events that may break the hypothesis of independence of different faults. CCA aims at investigating possible dependencies, and evaluates the consequences in terms of system safety/reliability. xSAP enables the definition of events named *common causes*, which may trigger the occurrence of a set of (dependent) faults. Such faults may follow a user-specified pattern, e.g., *simultaneous* or *cascading* (subject to given temporal constraints). For instance, debris caused by an engine burst (the common cause) may cause multiple components of an aircraft to fail simultaneously. xSAP enables the evaluation of reliability in presence of common causes and the generation of FTs including them.

## 2.4   Probabilistic Evaluation

xSAP supports probabilistic evaluation of Fault Trees. Given numerical probabilities for the basic events and for the common causes, xSAP computes probabilities for the intermediate nodes and the TLE of a FT. With the exception of
the constituent faults of common causes, all faults are assumed to be independent. Moreover, xSAP supports the computation in analytical form, as a Python
or Matlab/Octave program, of the reliability function representing the probability of the TLE. Such programs can be used to sample the reliability function for
different values of the probabilities, and to generate plots visualizing the TLE
probability as a function of (a subset of) the parameters.

## 2.5   Failure Propagation Analysis

xSAP supports the analysis of failure propagation using Timed Failure Propagation Graphs (TFPGs) [20,21]. A TFPG is a graph-like model that accounts
for the temporal progression of failures and for the causality between failure
effects, taking into consideration time delays, system reconfiguration and sensor failures. TFPGs support important run-time activities such as diagnosis and
prognosis [22]. The nodes of a TFPG represent either *failures* or *discrepancies*
(representing anomalous behaviors). Edges represent propagation links, labeled
with timing information (minimum and maximum propagation time) and modes
(system modes enabling the propagation). Discrepancies may be given either
AND or OR semantics – in the former case all incoming edges must be active in
order for the failure to propagate, in the latter case any of them suffices.

xSAP supports modeling of TFPGs and the following analyses: validation
of TFPG completeness (i.e., the TFPG contains at least as many behaviors as
the system it represents) and tightness (i.e., parameters of the TFPG cannot
be reduced without breaking its completeness). Moreover, xSAP implements
a procedure for the automated synthesis of tight delay parameters for a given
TFPG, and a procedure for the automated synthesis of the TFPG graph itself
from a model, given a set of failures and discrepancies. Finally, xSAP integrates
the TFPG validation features of [21].

# 3   Architecture and Implementation

The architecture of xSAP is built around the NUXMV symbolic model checker
(http://nuxmv.fbk.eu). NUXMV is an extension of NuSMV, and supports the
verification of finite- and infinite-state systems, by means of advanced SAT- and
SMT-based model checking techniques. NUXMV provides to xSAP the basic
infrastructure, e.g., the symbol table, model flattening, the Boolean encoding of
scalar variables, the representation of state machines and temporal formulae, and
the basic model checking algorithms. Moreover, xSAP relies on an interaction
shell similar to the one of NUXMV, which increases the flexibility and possibility
of integration within other tools.

On top of this, xSAP features the following blocks. *Model Extension* includes the library of fault modes, a parser for the fault extension instruction language, and the model extension. *Minimal cut sets computation* is realized by way of routines for parameterized model checking [9], using the model checking primitives of nuXmv as building blocks. *Fault Trees* can be generated/stored/retrieved either in XML or in a standard textual (tab-separated) format supported by commercial tools, such as FaultTree+. The management of *FMEA tables* is isolated in a separate module. Support for *Time Failure Propagation Graphs* is based on XML and textual formats. The textual format enables editing in a human-readable form – xSAP provides conversion from textual to XML and vice versa. *Syntax Directed Editors* (SDEs) are available for editing models, fault extension instructions, and TFPGs. Finally, the *Visualization* module contains the graphical viewers: a trace viewer, an FT Viewer and a TFPG viewer are available for displaying and analyzing traces, FTs and TFPGs, respectively.

xSAP has been developed in C and in C++ for the internal modules, while Python is used for model extension and TFPG manipulation. The viewers are based on the PyGTK, Goocanvas, PyGraphviz and Matplotlib libraries. xSAP compiles and executes on the most widely used Operating Systems (OSs) and architectures, namely: Linux, MS Windows, and MacOS X. Porting to other OSs is also possible.

# 4  Applications

The xSAP platform has been used in a wide range of applications, both industrial and academic, spanning several domains such as avionics and aerospace, railway and industrial control. xSAP has been widely used in several industrial projects with the European Space Agency (ESA), namely COMPASS, AUTO-GEF, FAME and HASDEL (see http://es.fbk.eu/projects). It is the back-end of the COMPASS family of tools [3]. Finally, xSAP has also been used in a joint project with NASA [23].

Currently, xSAP is being used by Boeing [6]. The Boeing Company has evaluated xSAP in the context of a joint research and development project in the areas of model-based safety assessment, verification and validation. The purpose of this project is to demonstrate the usefulness and suitability of model-based safety assessment techniques for improving the overall process in terms of robustness and cost-effectiveness, and for certification purposes; xSAP has been used to model an industrial-size case study [6] and thoroughly evaluated in an industrial setting.

# 5  Conclusions and Future Work

In this paper we presented xSAP, a state-of-the-art platform for model-based safety analysis, providing a full range of functionalities, based on symbolic model checking techniques. We described the architecture of xSAP and its industrial applications.

The symbolic technologies implemented in xSAP provide significant advances also in terms of scalability. We refer to [14] for a comparison with Altarica/OCAS (carried out using a license courtesy of Dassault Aviation), and to [9] for an exhaustive evaluation of the novel routines implemented in xSAP.

As future work, we intend to extend xSAP in several directions. First, we want to incorporate Contract-Based Safety Assessment (CBSA) techniques [24], enabling the generation of hierarchical FTs following the design structure. Moreover, we wish to incorporate the routines for evaluation of reliability architectures we developed in [25]. Finally, a significant extension will concern the definition of observability information in the model and the addition of related functionalities, such as diagnosability analysis and Fault Detection, Fault Isolation and Fault Recovery (FDIR) analysis [20].

# References

1. Joshi, A., Miller, S., Whalen, M., Heimdahl, M.: A proposal for model-based safety analysis. In: DASC. IEEE Computer Society (2005)
2. Bozzano, M., Villafiorita, A.: Design and Safety Assessment of Critical Systems. CRC Press (Taylor and Francis), an Auerbach Book, Boca Raton (2010)
3. Bozzano, M., Cimatti, A., Katoen, J.P., Nguyen, V., Noll, T., Roveri, M.: Safety, dependability and performance analysis of extended AADL models. Comp. J. **54**(5), 754–775 (2011)
4. SAE: ARP4761 Guidelines and Methods for Conducting the Safety Assessment Process on Civil Airborne Systems and Equipment., December 1996
5. ECSS: European Cooperation on Space Standardization. http://www.ecss.nl
6. Bozzano, M., Cimatti, A., Fernandes Pires, A., Jones, D., Kimberly, G., Petri, T., Robinson, R., Tonetta, S.: Formal design and safety analysis of AIR6110 wheel brake system. In: Kroening, D., Păsăreanu, C.S. (eds.) CAV 2015. LNCS, vol. 9206, pp. 518–535. Springer, Heidelberg (2015)
7. Bozzano, M., Villafiorita, A.: The FSAP/NuSMV-SA safety analysis platform. STTT **9**(1), 5–24 (2007)
8. Bozzano, M., Cimatti, A., Tapparo, F.: Symbolic fault tree analysis for reactive systems. In: Namjoshi, K.S., Yoneda, T., Higashino, T., Okamura, Y. (eds.) ATVA 2007. LNCS, vol. 4762, pp. 162–176. Springer, Heidelberg (2007)
9. Bozzano, M., Cimatti, A., Griggio, A., Mattarei, C.: Efficient anytime techniques for model-based safety analysis. In: Kroening, D., Păsăreanu, C.S. (eds.) CAV 2015. LNCS, vol. 9206, pp. 603–621. Springer, Heidelberg (2015)
10. Bozzano, M., Cimatti, A., Katoen, J.P., Katsaros, P., Mokos, K., Nguyen, V., Noll, T., Postma, B., Roveri, M.: Spacecraf early design validation using formal methods. Reliab. Eng. Syst. Saf. **132**, 20–35 (2014)
11. Bittner, B., Bozzano, M., Cimatti, A., de Ferluc, R., Gario, M., Guiotto, A., Yushtein, Y.: An integrated process for FDIR design in aerospace. In: IMBSA (2014)
12. Bieber, P., Castel, C., Seguin, C.: Combination of fault tree analysis and model checking for safety assessment of complex system. In: Bondavalli, A., Thévenod-Fosse, P. (eds.) EDCC 2002. LNCS, vol. 2485, pp. 19–31. Springer, Heidelberg (2002)

13. Prosvirnova, T., Batteux, M., Brameret, P.A., Cherfi, A., Friedlhuber, T., Roussel, J.M., Rauzy, A.: The altarica 3.0 project for model-based safety assessment. In: DCDS (2013)
14. Bozzano, M., Cimatti, A., Lisagor, O., Mattarei, C., Mover, S., Roveri, M., Tonetta, S.: Safety assessment of altarica models via symbolic model checking. Sci. Comput. Program. **98**(4), 464–483 (2015)
15. Deneux, J., Åkerlund, O.: A common framework for design and safety analyses using formal methods. In: PSAM7/ESREL (2004)
16. Joshi, A., Heimdahl, M.P.E.: Model-based safety analysis of simulink models using SCADE design verifier. In: Winther, R., Gran, B.A., Dahll, G. (eds.) SAFECOMP 2005. LNCS, vol. 3688, pp. 122–135. Springer, Heidelberg (2005)
17. Peikenkamp, T., Cavallo, A., Valacca, L., Böde, E., Pretzer, M., Hahn, E.M.: Towards a unified model-based safety assessment. In: Górski, J. (ed.) SAFECOMP 2006. LNCS, vol. 4166, pp. 275–288. Springer, Heidelberg (2006)
18. Vesely, W., Stamatelatos, M., Dugan, J., Fragola, J., Minarick III., J., Railsback, J.: Fault Tree Handbook with Aerospace Applications, NASA, Version 1.1. August 2002. http://www.hq.nasa.gov/office/codeq/doctree/fault_tree.htm
19. Manian, R., Dugan, J.B., Coppit, D., Sullivan, K.J.: Combining various solution techniques for dynamic fault tree analysis of computer systems. In: HASE, pp. 21–28, IEEE (1998)
20. Bozzano, M., Cimatti, A., Gario, M., Tonetta, S.: Formal design of fault detection and identification components using temporal epistemic logic. In: Ábrahám, E., Havelund, K. (eds.) TACAS 2014 (ETAPS). LNCS, vol. 8413, pp. 326–340. Springer, Heidelberg (2014)
21. Bozzano, M., Cimatti, A., Gario, M., Micheli, A.: SMT-based validation of timed failure propagation graphs. In: AAAI (2015)
22. Abdelwahed, S., Karsai, G., Mahadevan, N., Ofsthun, S.: Practical implementation of diagnosis systems using timed failure propagation graph models. IEEE Trans. Instrum. Meas. **58**(2), 240–247 (2009)
23. Mattarei, C., Cimatti, A., Gario, M., Tonetta, S., Rozier, K.: Comparing different functional allocations in automated air traffic control design. In: FMCAD, pp. 112–119. IEEE (2015)
24. Bozzano, M., Cimatti, A., Mattarei, C., Tonetta, S.: Formal safety assessment via contract-based design. In: Cassez, F., Raskin, J.-F. (eds.) ATVA 2014. LNCS, vol. 8837, pp. 81–97. Springer, Heidelberg (2014)
25. Bozzano, M., Cimatti, A., Mattarei, C.: Efficient analysis of reliability architectures via predicate abstraction. In: Bertacco, V., Legay, A. (eds.) HVC 2013. LNCS, vol. 8244, pp. 279–294. Springer, Heidelberg (2013)

# FACT: A Probabilistic Model Checker
# for Formal Verification with Confidence Intervals

Radu Calinescu[1]([✉]), Kenneth Johnson[2], and Colin Paterson[1]

[1] Department of Computer Science, University of York, York, UK
Radu.Calinescu@york.ac.uk
[2] School of Computer and Mathematical Sciences,
Auckland University of Technology, Auckland, New Zealand

**Abstract.** We introduce FACT, a probabilistic model checker that computes confidence intervals for the evaluated properties of Markov chains with unknown transition probabilities when observations of these transitions are available. FACT is unaffected by the unquantified estimation errors generated by the use of point probability estimates, a common practice that limits the applicability of quantitative verification. As such, FACT can prevent invalid decisions in the construction and analysis of systems, and extends the applicability of quantitative verification to domains in which unknown estimation errors are unacceptable.

## 1  Introduction

The development of quantitative verification [8,11] over the past fifteen years represents one of the most prominent recent advances in system modelling and analysis. Given a Markov model that captures relevant states of a system and the probabilities or rates of transition between these states, the technique can evaluate key reliability and performance properties of the system. This capability and the emergence of efficient probabilistic model checkers such as PRISM [10] and MRMC [9] have led to adoption in a wide range of applications [14].

Despite the success of quantitative verification, the usefulness of its results depends on the accuracy of the analysed models. Obtaining accurate Markov models is difficult. Although model states and transitions are typically easy to identify (e.g., through static code analysis for software systems), transition probabilities and rates need to be estimated. The common practice is to obtain these estimates through model fitting to log data or run-time observations [4,15], or from domain experts. In either case, the values used in the analysed models contain estimation errors. These errors are then propagated and may be amplified by quantitative verification (since Markov models are nonlinear), producing imprecise results that can lead to invalid design or verification conclusions.

The FACT[1] probabilistic model checker introduced in our paper is not affected by this problem. As described in Sect. 2, FACT can compute confidence intervals for the properties of a common class of parametric (discrete-time) Markov chains for which observations of the transitions associated with

---

[1] Formal verificAtion with Confidence inTervals.

© Springer-Verlag Berlin Heidelberg 2016
M. Chechik and J.-F. Raskin (Eds.): TACAS 2016, LNCS 9636, pp. 540–546, 2016.
DOI: 10.1007/978-3-662-49674-9_32

the unknown probabilities are available. The operation of FACT (presented in Sect. 3) is underpinned by recent theoretical results from [2], and the tool integrates the PRISM parametric quantitative verification engine (first introduced in version 4.2 of PRISM), the MATLAB convex optimisation toolbox YALMIP [13] and a purpose-built hill climbing optimiser. The modular architecture of the tool (discussed in Sect. 4) makes it easy to replace these components with functionally equivalent ones and to extend the tool. FACT and the models from the case studies summarised in Sect. 5 are available on our project website http:// www-users.cs.york.ac.uk/~cap/FACT.

## 2 Formal Verification with Confidence Intervals

FACT parametric Markov chains (PMCs) are specified in an extended version of the PRISM high-level modelling language [10], which models a system as the parallel composition of a set of *modules*. The state of a *module* is encoded by a set of finite-range local variables, and its state transitions are defined by probabilistic guarded commands that change these variables, and have the general form:

$$[action] \; guard \; -> e_1 : update_1 + e_2 : update_2 + \ldots + e_n : update_n; \quad (1)$$

In this command, *guard* is a boolean expression over all model variables. If *guard* evaluates to *true*, the arithmetic expression $e_i$, $1 \le i \le n$, gives the probability with which the $update_i$ change of the module variables occurs. When *action* is present, all modules comprising commands with this *action* have to synchronise (i.e., to carry out one of these commands simultaneously). In a FACT PMC, the expressions $e_1, e_2, \ldots, e_n$ can be unknown (constant) probabilities $x_1, x_2, \ldots, x_n$. These model *parameters* are associated with a declaration:

$$\textbf{param double } x = t_1 \; t_2 \; \ldots \; t_n; \quad (2)$$

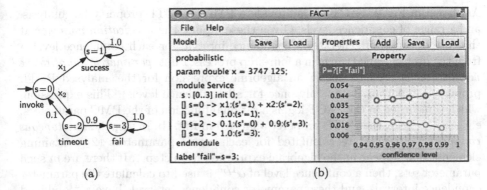

(a)    (b)

**Fig. 1.** (a) PMC model of a service whose invocations succeed with probability $x_1$ and time out with probability $x_2 = 1 - x_1$, where timed-out invocations are retried with probability 0.1; (b) FACT-generated confidence intervals for the property *'What is the probability that the service cannot be invoked successfully?'* for an instance of the service that was observed completing successfully 3747 times and timing out 125 times.

in which $t_i \in \mathbb{N}$, $1 \leq i \leq n$, represents the number of transitions associated with $update_i$ that were observed during a period of time when all outgoing transitions from states that satisfy $guard$ were monitored and recorded. An example of a simple PMC analysed using FACT is shown in Fig. 1.

FACT PMCs can have multiple sets of parameters (2). For example, the outgoing transitions from state 's = 2' in Fig. 1a could be associated with unknown probabilities $pRetry_1$ and $pRetry_2$. The only constraint is that the different sets of parameters (2) are statistically independent. This constraint is satisfied by a broad class of PMCs that includes, for instance, all the models used in the case studies of the PROPhESY tool[2] [5] for analysing parametric Markov chains.

FACT can establish confidence intervals for PMC properties expressed in probabilistic computation tree logic (PCTL) [7] extended with rewards [1]. The current version of FACT supports non-nested probabilistic PCTL properties of the form $\mathcal{P}_{=?}[\Psi]$, where the *path formula* $\Psi$ is defined by the grammar:

$$\Psi ::= X\Phi \mid \Phi \cup \Phi \mid \Phi \cup^{\leq k} \Phi$$
$$\Phi ::= true \mid a \mid \Phi \wedge \Phi \mid \neg \Phi \qquad (3)$$

with $k \in \mathbb{N}$, $a$ an *atomic proposition* associated with states that satisfy $a$ (e.g., timeout and success in Fig. 1a), $p \in [0,1]$, $\bowtie \in \{\geq, >, <, \leq\}$, and $\Phi$ is a *state formula*. FACT also supports all PCTL reward properties, i.e., the instantaneous, cumulative, reachability and steady-state reward properties defined by:

$$\Phi ::= \mathcal{R}_{=?}[I^{=k}] \mid \mathcal{R}_{=?}[C^{\leq k}] \mid \mathcal{R}_{=?}[F\Phi] \mid \mathcal{R}_{=?}[S]. \qquad (4)$$

Defining the semantics of PCTL is beyond the scope of this paper; details are available from [1,7,10].

## 3   Using FACT

As shown in Fig. 2, FACT users provide a PMC, a PCTL property for analysis, and a range of confidence levels. Given these inputs, the *verification manager* at the core of our tool generates a confidence interval for each confidence level $\alpha$ from the user-specified range in a four-step process. First, *parametric quantitative verification* is used to obtain an algebraic expression for the analysed PCTL property (step 1, executed only once for all confidence levels). This expression, which is recorded in the FACT log, is a rational function of the PMC parameters, e.g., $\frac{9x_2}{10x_1 + 9x_2}$ for the PCTL property analysed in Fig. 1b. In step 2, *simultaneous confidence intervals* are calculated for each set of parameters (2) containing elements that appear in the algebraic expression from step 1. If there are $m$ such parameter sets, then a confidence level of $\alpha^{1/m}$ is used to calculate the parameter confidence intervals, and these parameter confidence intervals have a "combined confidence level" of $(\alpha^{1/m})^m = \alpha$. Hence, step 3 uses them as input for a *convex optimisation* problem whose solution represents an $\alpha$ confidence interval for the analysed property—a formal proof of this result is available in [2].

---

[2] http://moves.rwth-aachen.de/research/tools/prophesy/#benchmarks.

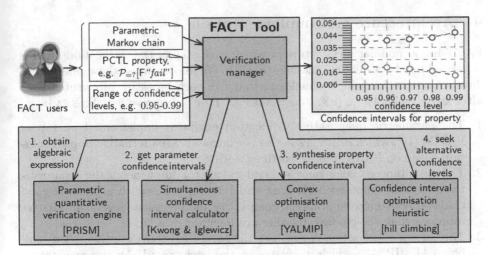

**Fig. 2.** FACT operation and architecture; the technologies used by the current version of the tool (shown in square brackets) can be replaced with alternative technologies

When $m > 1$, using $\alpha^{1/m}$ confidence intervals for each parameter set is unlikely to yield the narrowest possible $\alpha$ confidence interval for the analysed property. For two reasons, using confidence levels $\alpha_i < \alpha^{1/m} < \alpha_j$ for the confidence intervals of parameter sets $i$ and $j$ may produce a narrower $\alpha$ confidence interval:

1. If the number of state-transition observations associated with parameter set $j$ is larger than that for parameter set $i$, this choice of confidence levels may produce much narrower confidence intervals for parameter set $i$ with an insignificant widening of the confidence intervals for parameter set $j$;
2. If the analysed property is particularly sensitive to variations in the parameter set $i$, reducing $\alpha_i$ narrows the confidence intervals for parameter set $i$ and may also narrow the $\alpha$ confidence interval for the analysed property.

Therefore, step 4 uses a *confidence interval optimisation heuristic* to seek alternative confidence levels $\alpha_1, \alpha_2, \ldots, \alpha_m$ such that $\prod_{i=1}^m \alpha_i = \alpha$ and using $\alpha_i$ confidence intervals for the $i$-th parameter set, $1 \leq i \leq m$, produces a narrower $\alpha$ confidence interval for the analysed property. This optimisation can reduce the width of property confidence intervals (e.g., by up to 14% in the case studies from [2]), but is time consuming since FACT steps 2 and 3 are repeated for each $\alpha_1, \alpha_2, \ldots, \alpha_m$ combination suggested by the heuristic. Hence step 4 is by default switched off in FACT, and the user should switch it on explicitly if needed. There is one typical scenario in which this need arises. This is when FACT is used to verify whether the analysed property is above/below a threshold specified in the system requirements (with some confidence level $\alpha$), and the threshold falls inside the $\alpha$ confidence interval without the heuristic search. In this scenario, the FACT user should switch on the heuristic search by specifying a non-zero number of search iterations, which may result in a narrower $\alpha$ confidence interval that does not contain the threshold and enables a conclusion to be drawn.

# 4    Architecture and Implementation

FACT has a modular architecture in which each step of the verification process is carried out by a different module (Fig. 2). We implemented these modules in Java, using the following technologies that can each be easily substituted with alternative technologies (e.g., to extend FACT or to improve its efficiency):

1. The parametric quantitative verification engine is implemented on top of PRISM [10], which it invokes in the background. An alternative implementation based on PARAM [6] is worth exploring.
2. The simultaneous confidence interval calculator implements the (conservative) solution proposed by Kwong and Iglewicz [12], which achieves a good trade-off between computational complexity and precision. Several alternative solutions that deserve investigating are mentioned in [2].
3. The convex optimisation engine uses the MATLAB convex optimisation toolbox YALMIP [13], which it invokes in the background. An implementation based on the non-commercial GNU Octave package (https://www.gnu.org/software/octave/) is worth exploring.
4. The confidence interval optimisation heuristic currently used is hill climbing. Numerous alternative heuristics can be substituted in this module.

# 5    Case Studies and Experimental Results

To evaluate FACT, we carried out case studies involving the synthesis of confidence intervals for PCTL-encoded reliability, performance and cost properties of

**Table 1.** Experimental results for the case studies from Sect. 5

| PMC | psets[a] | params[b] | PCTL property | $t_{exp}^{c}$ | $t_{CI}^{d}$ |
|-----|------|--------|---------------|------|------|
| Web | 5 | 13 | $\mathcal{P}_{=?}[\text{F HttpResponse}]$ | 0.75s | 3.96s |
| | | | $\mathcal{P}_{=?}[\neg(\text{Database} \vee \text{FileServer})\,\text{U HttpResponse}]$ | 0.84s | 3.43s |
| | | | $\mathcal{R}_{=?}^{\text{cost}}[\text{F Done}]$ | 0.86s | 3.31s |
| | | | $\mathcal{R}_{=?}^{\text{time}}[\text{F Done}]$ | 0.89s | 3.29s |
| TAS | 3 | 6 | $\mathcal{P}_{=?}[\text{F FailedAlarm}]$ | 0.24s | 4.32s |
| | | | $\mathcal{P}_{=?}[\neg\text{Done U FailedService}]$ | 0.12s | 2.82s |
| | | | $\mathcal{P}_{=?}[\neg\text{Done U FailedAlarm}\{\text{MedicalAnalysis}\}]$ | 0.11s | 2.78s |
| LWB | 1 | 2 | $\mathcal{R}_{=?}^{\text{power}}[\text{S}]$ | 0.24s | 3.03s |
| | | | $\mathcal{R}_{=?}^{\text{energy}}[\text{F StartedUp}]$ | 0.27s | 2.98s |
| BRP | 2 | 4 | $\mathcal{P}_{=?}[\text{F SenderNoSuccessReport}]$ | 0.44s | 31.6s |
| Z | 2 | 4 | $\mathcal{R}_{=?}^{\text{numTests}}[\text{F DecisionMade}]$ | 0.15s | 5.41s |

[a]Number of parameter sets (2) in the PMC
[b]Total number of PMC parameters
[c]Time to compute algebraic expression
[d]Time to synthesise confidence interval

parametric Markov chains modelling systems from different application domains. Table 1 summarises the experimental results obtained for the PMCs of:

- a web application taken from [2] (Web);
- a tele-assistance service-based system adapted from [3,4] (TAS);
- the low-power wireless bus communication protocol taken from [2] (LWB);
- the bounded retransmission protocol from the PROPhESY [5] site (BRP);
- the Zeroconf IP address selection protocol from the PARAM [6] website (Z).

The timing results were obtained on a standard OS X 10.8.5 MacBook computer with 1.3 GHz Intel Core i5 processor and 8 GB 1600 MHz DDR3 RAM. The models, PCTL property files, results and descriptions for all case studies are available on our FACT website http://www-users.cs.york.ac.uk/~cap/FACT.

These case studies demonstrated several key benefits of our probabilistic model checker. First, FACT supports the analysis of systems for which state transition probabilities are unknown, but observations of these transitions are available from logs or run-time monitoring. Second, it enables the analysis of reliability, performance and other non-functional properties of systems at the required confidence level. This approach is better aligned with the current industrial practice than traditional quantitative verification. Third, it can prevent invalid design and verification decisions. In many scenarios, the quantitative analysis of Markov models built using point estimates of the unknown transition probabilities misleadingly suggested that requirements were met. In contrast, FACT showed that this was only the case with low confidence levels that are typically deemed unacceptable in practice. Last but not least, our case studies showed that FACT can be used to analyse systems from multiple domains.

# References

1. Andova, S., Hermanns, H., Katoen, J.-P.: Discrete-time rewards model-checked. FORMATS 2003. LNCS, vol. 2791, pp. 88–104. Springer, Heidelberg (2003)
2. Calinescu, R., Ghezzi, C., Johnson, K., Pezze, M., Rafiq, Y., Tamburrelli, G.: Formal verification with confidence intervals to establish quality of service properties of software systems. IEEE Trans. Reliab. **PP**(99), 1–16 (2015)
3. Calinescu, R., Johnson, K., Rafiq, Y.: Developing self-verifying service-based systems. In: ASE 2013, pp. 734–737 (2013)
4. Calinescu, R., Rafiq, Y., Johnson, K., Bakir, M.E.: Adaptive model learning for continual verification of non-functional properties. In: ICPE 2014, pp. 87–98 (2014)
5. Dehnert, C., Junges, S., Jansen, N., Corzilius, F., Volk, M., Bruintjes, H., Katoen, J.-P., Ábrahám, E.: PROPhESY: A PRObabilistic ParamEter SYnthesis Tool. In: Kroening, D., Păsăreanu, C.S. (eds.) CAV 2015. LNCS, vol. 9206, pp. 214–231. Springer, Heidelberg (2015)
6. Hahn, E.M., Hermanns, H., Wachter, B., Zhang, L.: PARAM: a model checker for parametric Markov models. In: Touili, T., Cook, B., Jackson, P. (eds.) CAV 2010. LNCS, vol. 6174, pp. 660–664. Springer, Heidelberg (2010)
7. Hansson, H., Jonsson, B.: A logic for reasoning about time and reliability. Formal Aspects Comput. **6**(5), 512–535 (1994)

8. Haverkort, B.R., Katoen, J.-P., Larsen, K.G.: Quantitative verification in practice. In: Margaria, T., Steffen, B. (eds.) ISoLA 2010, Part II. LNCS, vol. 6416, pp. 127–127. Springer, Heidelberg (2010)

9. Katoen, J.-P., Zapreev, I.S., Hahn, E.M., Hermanns, H., Jansen, D.N.: The ins and outs of the probabilistic model checker MRMC. Perform. Eval. **68**(2), 90–104 (2011)

10. Kwiatkowska, M., Norman, G., Parker, D.: PRISM 4.0: verification of probabilistic real-time systems. In: Gopalakrishnan, G., Qadeer, S. (eds.) CAV 2011. LNCS, vol. 6806, pp. 585–591. Springer, Heidelberg (2011)

11. Kwiatkowska, M.Z.: Quantitative verification: models, techniques and tools. In: ESEC-FSE 2007, pp. 449–458 (2007)

12. Kwong, K.-S., Iglewicz, B.: On singular multivariate normal distribution and its applications. Comput. Stat. Data Anal. **22**(3), 271–285 (1996)

13. Löfberg, J.: Automatic robust convex programming. Optim. Methods Softw. **27**(1), 115–129 (2012)

14. Norman, G., Parker, D.: Quantitative verification: formal guarantees for timeliness, reliability and performance. Technical report, London Mathematical Society and the Smith Institute for Industrial Mathematics and System Engineering (2014)

15. Su, G., Rosenblum, D.S.: Asymptotic bounds for quantitative verification of perturbed probabilistic systems. In: Groves, L., Sun, J. (eds.) ICFEM 2013. LNCS, vol. 8144, pp. 297–312. Springer, Heidelberg (2013)

# PrDK: Protocol Programming with Automata

Sung-Shik T.Q. Jongmans[1,2]([✉]) and Farhad Arbab[3]

[1] Open University, Heerlen, The Netherlands
ssj@ou.nl
[2] Radboud University Nijmegen, Nijmegen, The Netherlands
[3] Centrum Wiskunde & Informatica (CWI), Amsterdam, The Netherlands

**Abstract.** We present PrDK: a development kit for programming protocols. PrDK is based on syntactic separation of process code, presumably written in an existing general-purpose language, and protocol code, written in a domain-specific language with explicit, high-level elements of syntax for programming protocols. PrDK supports two complementary syntaxes (one graphical, one textual) with a common automata-theoretic semantics. As a tool for construction of systems, PrDK consists of syntax editors, a translator, a parser, an interpreter, and a compiler into Java. Performance in the NAS Parallel Benchmarks is promising.

## 1  Introduction

In the early 2000s, hardware manufacturers shifted their attention from manufacturing faster—yet purely sequential—unicore processors to manufacturing slower—yet increasingly parallel—multicore processors. In the wake of this shift, *concurrent programming* became essential for writing scalable programs on commodity hardware. Conceptually, concurrent programs consist of *processes*, which implement primary modules of sequential computation, and *protocols*, which implement the rules of concurrent interaction that processes must abide by.

As programmers have been writing sequential code for decades, implementing processes poses no new fundamental challenges. What *is* new—and notoriously difficult—is programming protocols. One contributing factor to the complexity of this activity is today's popular programming languages not providing programmers explicit, high-level elements of syntax for programming protocols. Instead, programmers need to use rather low-level reads/writes to shared memory protected by mutual exclusion—locks, semaphores, monitors, and the like.

In a long-term project at CWI, we study an alternative approach to concurrent programming, based on syntactic separation of processes from protocols. In this approach, programmers write their (sequential) processes in a *general-purpose language* (GPL), while they write their (concurrency) protocols in a *domain-specific language* (DSL). Paraphrasing the definition of DSLs by Van Deursen et al. [3], a DSL for protocols "is a programming language that offers, through appropriate notations and abstractions, expressive power focused on, and [..] restricted to, [programming protocols]." The semantics of our DSL is based on automata; on top of it, we have both a graphical and a textual syntax.

© Springer-Verlag Berlin Heidelberg 2016
M. Chechik and J.-F. Raskin (Eds.): TACAS 2016, LNCS 9636, pp. 547–552, 2016.
DOI: 10.1007/978-3-662-49674-9_33

```java
public interface OutputPort extends Port {        public class Processes {
  public void put(Object obj)                       public static void Producer(
    throws InterruptedException;                        OutputPort p, int id) {
  public void putUninterruptibly(Object o);           String message = id + ": Hello, World!";
  public void resume();                               while (true)
}                                                        p.putUninterruptibly(message);
                                                      }

public interface InputPort extends Port {
  public void get(Object obj)                       public static void Consumer(InputPort p) {
    throws InterruptedException;                      while (true)
  public void getUninterruptibly(Object o);           System.out.println(
  public void resume();                                 p.getUninterruptibly());
}                                                 } }
```

**Fig. 1.** API for ports (left) and example hand-written processes (right) in Java

In this paper, we present a development kit for our DSL for protocols. In Sect. 2, we briefly present the DSL. In Sect. 3, we present our development kit, available at http://www.open.ou.nl/ssj/prdk. Section 4 concludes this paper with some performance numbers and future work. We invite the reader to consult the first author's PhD thesis for details and examples [7].

## 2 The DSL

Processes, implemented in a GPL, primarily perform sequential computations. To interact with each other, in our programming model, every process also owns a set of *ports*. Ports mark the interface between processes: *output ports* let processes *offer* data to other processes, while *input ports* let processes *accept* data from other processes. Processes can perform two blocking operations on ports: put and get. When a process performs a put (get) on an output port (input port), this operation becomes *pending* on that port and the process itself becomes suspended. When a put (get) completes, its previously suspended process resumes and offers (accepts) a datum. Whenever a process offers (accepts) a datum in this way, it does not know whereto (wherefrom) this datum goes (comes); only protocols, programmed as syntactically separate modules from processes through explicit, high-level elements of syntax in a DSL, control when put/get operations may complete on which ports and how data *flow* between ports. As such, protocols effectuate only *admissible interactions* among (the ports of) the processes in a program. We stipulate that put/get have *value passing* semantics (although programmers are free to pass and interpret references to shared data as values). Figure 1 shows an API for ports and two processes in Java, defined as two static methods (*not* directly as Java threads, which programmers do not need to manually manage, or even know about, in our programming model). The actual API also has versions of put/get with timeouts (omitted here to save space).

By effectuating only admissible interactions, protocols essentially constrain the completion of put/get operations. Formally, we can represent such constraints with *automata* [7], whose every transition models a data-flow between ports with a pending put/get operation. Figure 2 shows an example. The automaton in this figure models a producers/consumer protocol involving two output ports A and B (each owned by a different producer, presumably) and an input

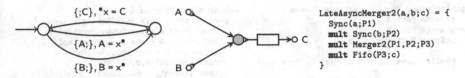

**Fig. 2.** Example automaton for a producers/consumer protocol (left), its graphical syntax (middle), and its textual syntax (right)

port C (owned by the consumer). Initially, a put by the producer owning A can complete, causing that producer to offer a datum into internal buffer x (modeled by expression A = x•). Alternatively, a put by the producer owning B can similarly complete. Subsequently, only a get by the consumer owning C can complete, causing the consumer to accept the datum previously stored in x (modeled by expression •x = C). This protocol, thus, admits asynchronous, unordered, reliable, transactional communication from two producers to a consumer.

Providing programmers syntax for writing protocols directly as automata has at least one major issue: automata quickly grow prohibitively large. A more scalable approach for defining automata is one based on their (parallel) *composition*: programmers should construct complex protocols out of simpler ones, by composing (*multiplying*) smaller automata into larger ones, starting from a predefined "core set" of primitive automata. We consider two declarative syntaxes for representing such multiplication expressions: *Reo* [1] and *Pr* [7]. Given such a core set, in Reo, programmers *draw* multiplication expressions as dataflow graphs; in Pr, programmers *write* multiplication expressions as automata signatures. Figure 2 exemplifies both Reo and Pr (for the same protocol). In the graph, every node/vertex denotes a primitive automaton in the core set; in the text, the same applies to every signature (and their multiplication is, in turn, denoted by a new signature LateAsyncMerger2).

## 3   The Development Kit

Our development kit, called PrDK, consists of tools (Eclipse plugins) for protocol programming with automata (without ever exposing programmers to automata directly): editors for Reo and Pr, an animation engine for Reo, a parser/interpreter for Pr, a Reo-to-Pr translator, and a Pr-to-Java compiler. The Reo editor and its animation engine have previously been developed as part of the ECT (http://reo.project.cwi.nl), a collection of Eclipse plugins for Reo.

In PrDK's basic workflow, programmers start by drawing a protocol as a Reo graph for a small number of processes, using the drag/drop interface of the Reo editor. The animation engine enables programmers to visualize the admissible data-flows through the graph, which is an instructive and helpful aid in protocol debugging. Subsequently, programmers can import processes, by drag/dropping Java files onto the same canvas (which appear as boxes alongside the graph, with distinct markers for their ports), and *link* (the ports of) those processes to (the nodes in the graph of) the protocol as desired. The resulting diagram

```
public class Protocol extends Thread {        public class Program {
  private Port A;                                public static void main(String[] args) {
  private Port B;                                  OutputPort A = new OutputPortImpl();
  private Port C;                                  OutputPort B = new OutputPortImpl();
                                                   InputPort C = new InputPortImpl();
  public Protocol(Port A, Port B, Port C) {        (new Protocol(A,B,C)).start();
    ...                                            (new Thread() { public void run() {
  }                                                  Process.producer(A,18); } } ).start();
                                                   (new Thread() { public void run() {
  // Event-driven code to simulate an               Process.producer(B,06); } } ).start();
  // an automaton by firing its transitions:       (new Thread() { public void run() {
  ...                                                Process.consumer(C); } } ).start();
}                                                } }
```

**Fig. 3.** Example compiler-generated protocol (partial) and main in Java

comprehensively implements a full program. By invoking the Reo-to-Pr translator, the Pr parser/interpreter, and the Pr-to-Java compiler on this diagram, PrDK generates Java code for the protocol and merges this compiler-generated code with hand-written code for processes according to their links in the diagram (detailed below). A Java compiler, then, can translate everything into an executable binary. In the basic workflow, the Pr syntax is completely hidden from programmers (i.e., the Reo-to-Pr translator, the Pr parser/interpreter, and the Pr-to-Java compiler are transparently chained, giving the programmer the illusion of a Reo-to-Java compiler).

Often, programmers need different versions of a program with different numbers of processes (e.g., depending on the number of cores of the target hardware). The Reo syntax does not conveniently support this. For instance, Reo requires programmers to draw a *specific* diagram for a protocol among two processes, another *specific* diagram for the same protocol among three processes, etc.; Reo does not support drawing a *generic* diagram for $k$ producers and one consumer. Pr, in contrast, does support such parametrization. The basic workflow can, thus, be extended with an extra step in which programmers explicitly use the Reo-to-Pr translator to translate their Reo diagram into a Pr text, which they subsequently can modify by parametrizing the protocol in its number of ports.

From a theoretical prespective, the most interesting tools in PrDK are the Pr parser/interpreter and the Pr-to-Java compiler. The parser consumes a Pr program as input and produces a syntax tree as output (if the input unambiguously satisfies Pr's concrete syntax); we implemented the parser using the ANTLR parser generator. The interpreter consumes a syntax tree (produced by the parser) as input and produces a list of automata, which represents a multiplication expression of automata, as output (if the input is well-typed). Finally, the compiler consumes a list of automata for a protocol (produced by the interpreter) and a list of method signatures for processes (in the syntax tree produced by the parser) as input and produces Java code as output.

Roughly, the compiler and its generated code work as follows. First, the compiler computes the product of the automata in its input list. Second, the compiler translates the resulting product automaton (which comprehensively models a protocol) into a singleton Java class (which effectively encapsulates a state machine for simulating that automaton). The constructor of such a class has a number of formal port parameters, to bind its single instance to actual ports at "construction-time". After construction-time, then, a thread monitors these bound ports for new put/get operations performed by processes. Whenever a put/get occurs, this thread checks if that operation—together with the already pending put/get operations—enables the firing of a transition out of the current state. If so, the thread makes that transition and completes the put/get operations involved. As the constructor of a compiler-generated "protocol class" (e.g., Fig. 3), hand-written "process methods" (e.g., Fig. 1) have formal port parameters, to bind thread-wrapped calls of those methods to actual ports at construction-time. The task of constructing ports and passing them *both* to the constructor of a protocol class *and* to process methods is performed in the main method. This main method is, as the protocol class, generated by the compiler (based on linkage information either in a Reo diagram or in its Pr equivalent).

We significantly simplified our description of the workings of the compiler and its generated code. For instance, we tacitly assumed that a program consists of only one protocol, but PrDK supports also programs with multiple protocols. Also, notably, while computing the product of automata, the compiler applies a number of provably correct (i.e., bisimulation-preserving) optimizations and automata transformations to improve the performance and scalability of its generated code. We presented these optimizations in previous work [8–11]; a comprehensive overview, including formal definitions and proofs of their correctness, appears elsewhere [7]. Also, although PrDK currently supports only Java as the target GPL, we do not use any Java-specific features; our choice for Java is, in that sense, arbitrary. Our only requirement for a target GPL is that it supports some form of multithreading. For instance, extending the compiler with support for C+Pthreads is straightforward, as already worked on by a MSc student [12].

## 4   Conclusion

To evaluate the performance of the code generated by the compiler in PrDK, we compared the Java reference implementation of the NAS Parallel Benchmarks [4]—a popular benchmark suite for parallel performance—against an implementation developed with PrDK, on a machine with 24 cores using the workflow described in Sect. 3. In seven benchmarks, we considered six numbers of processes (2, 4, 8, 16, 32, 64) for various problem sizes, yielding a total of 126 tests. Figure 4 summarizes our results, where every bar represents the percentage of times the PrDK-based implementation achieved a certain

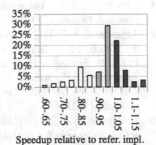

Speedup relative to refer. impl.

**Fig. 4.** Benchmark results

speedup relative to the reference implementation. In 37 % of cases (gray bars), the PrDK-based implementation is *at most* only 10 % slower than the reference implementation; in 38 % percent of cases (black bars), the PrDK-based implementation is faster. Given the high level of abstraction supported by Reo/Pr, and the consequent burden carried by the compiler—instead of the programmer—to produce efficient code, these are promising first results. Details appear elsewhere [7].

Another recent initiative based on syntactic separation of processes from protocols is *Scribble* [5,13]. In Scribble, protocols are expressed through multiparty session types [6]. One fundamental difference between Scribble and our approach is that in Scribble, all interaction is asynchronous, order-preserving, and reliable, whereas our automata allow for mixing synchrony and asynchrony (in the same protocol) and support nondeterminism (both of orderings and reliability).

Our present version of PrDK does not include previous verification tools for Reo, notably model checking [2]. We are currently investigating how to best integrate those existing tools for a seamless implementation/verification experience.

# References

1. Arbab, F.: Puff, the magic protocol. In: Agha, G., Danvy, O., Meseguer, J. (eds.) Formal Modeling: Actors, Open Systems, Biological Systems. LNCS, vol. 7000, pp. 169–206. Springer, Heidelberg (2011)
2. Baier, C., Blechmann, T., Klein, J., Klüppelholz, S., Leister, W.: Design and verification of systems with exogenous coordination using Vereofy. In: Margaria, T., Steffen, B. (eds.) ISoLA 2010, Part II. LNCS, vol. 6416, pp. 97–111. Springer, Heidelberg (2010)
3. van Deursen, A., Klint, P., Visser, J.: Domain-specific languages: an annotated bibliography. ACM SIGPLAN Not. **35**(6), 26–36 (2000)
4. Frumkin, M., Schultz, M., Jin, H., Yan, J.: Performance and scalability of the NAS parallel benchmarks in Java. In: Proceedings of IPDPS 2003, p. 139 (2003)
5. Honda, K., Mukhamedov, A., Brown, G., Chen, T.-C., Yoshida, N.: Scribbling interactions with a formal foundation. In: Natarajan, R., Ojo, A. (eds.) ICDCIT 2011. LNCS, vol. 6536, pp. 55–75. Springer, Heidelberg (2011)
6. Honda, K., Yoshida, N., Carbone, M.: Multiparty asynchronous session types. In: ACM SIGPLAN Notices, Proceedings of POPL 2008, vol. 43, no. 1, pp. 273–284 (2008)
7. Jongmans, S.S.: Automata-Theoretic Protocol Programming. Ph.D. thesis, Universiteit Leiden (2016)
8. Jongmans, S.-S.T.Q., Arbab, F.: Take command of your constraints!. In: Holvoet, T., Viroli, M. (eds.) Coordination Models and Languages. LNCS, vol. 9037, pp. 117–132. Springer, Heidelberg (2015)
9. Jongmans, S.S., Arbab, F.: Global consensus through local synchronization: a formal basis for partially-distributed coordination. Sci. Comput. Program. **115–116**, 199–224 (2016)
10. Jongmans, S.-S.T.Q., Halle, S., Arbab, F.: Automata-based optimization of interaction protocols for scalable multicore platforms. In: Kühn, E., Pugliese, R. (eds.) COORDINATION 2014. LNCS, vol. 8459, pp. 65–82. Springer, Heidelberg (2014)
11. Jongmans, S.S., Santini, F., Arbab, F.: Partially-distributed coordination with reo and constraint automata. Serv. Oriented Comput. Appl. **9**(3), 311–339 (2015)
12. van de Nes, M.: Developing Efficient Concurrent C Application Programs Using Reo. Master's thesis, Universiteit Leiden (2015)
13. Yoshida, N., Hu, R., Neykova, R., Ng, N.: The Scribble protocol language. In: Abadi, M., Lluch Lafuente, A. (eds.) TGC 2013. LNCS, vol. 8358, pp. 22–41. Springer, Heidelberg (2014)

# DLC: Compiling a Concurrent System Formal Specification to a Distributed Implementation

Hugues Evrard[✉]

Team CONVECS – Inria Grenoble Rhône-Alpes and LIG,
Montbonnot, France
hugues@hevrard.org

**Abstract.** Formal methods can verify the correctness of a concurrent system by analyzing its model. However, if the actual implementation is written by hand, subtle and hard to detect bugs may be unintentionally introduced, thus ruining the verification effort. In this paper, we present DLC (*Distributed LNT Compiler*), a tool that automatically generates distributed implementation of concurrent systems modeled in the LNT language, which can be formally verified using the CADP toolbox.

## 1 Introduction

When designing concurrent systems, the use of formal methods often consists in verifying a *model* of a system, and then writing the actual implementation by hand. The latter is tedious and error-prone, especially in the context of distributed systems, which are notoriously complex. The automatic generation of distributed implementations directly from formal models adresses both difficulties, by speeding-up the production of software, and by letting the programmer operate at the formal model level, with the benefits of formal verification tools. CADP (*Construction and Analysis of Distributed Processes*) [7] is a mature verification toolbox that can analyze concurrent systems modeled in the LNT [3] formal language. In this paper, we present DLC (*Distributed LNT Compiler*, http://hevrard.org/DLC), a tool which enables the automatic generation of distributed implementations from LNT models. DLC produces several executables that can be deployed on distinct machines. Moreover, DLC let the end user optionally define interactions between the implementation and its environment.

## 2 Formal Design with CADP and LNT

The CADP [7] toolbox gathers more than 25 years of research and development in formal methods and offers a comprehensive set of tools including a model checker and a test case generator, among others. The LNT formal language combines a syntax close to mainstream programming languages with powerful concurrency primitives inherited from process algebras. We briefly introduce LNT through a rock-paper-scissors example, illustrated in Fig. 1. For an exhaustive description of LNT including its formal operational semantics, see its manual [3].

© Springer-Verlag Berlin Heidelberg 2016
M. Chechik and J.-F. Raskin (Eds.): TACAS 2016, LNCS 9636, pp. 553–559, 2016.
DOI: 10.1007/978-3-662-49674-9_34

```
 1  type weapon is                              22          mine := any weapon;  -- random choice
 2     rock, paper, scissor with "=="           23          select
 3  end type                                    24             GAME (self, ?any nat, mine, ?hers)
 4  channel nat is (nat) end channel            25          [] GAME (?any nat, self, ?hers, mine)
 5  channel game is                             26          end select ;
 6     (nat, nat, weapon, weapon)               27          if wins_over (mine, hers) then
 7  end channel                                 28             WINNER (self)
 8                                              29          elsif wins_over (hers, mine) then
 9  function wins_over (w0, w1: weapon) : bool is  30          stop
10     case w0 in                               31          end if
11        rock   -> return w1 == scissor        32       end loop
12      | paper  -> return w1 == rock           33    end var
13      | scissor -> return w1 == paper         34  end process
14     end case                                 35
15  end function                                36  process MAIN [GAME: game, WINNER: nat] is
16                                              37     par GAME #2 in
17  process PLAYER                              38        PLAYER [GAME, WINNER] (0)
18     [GAME: game, WINNER: nat] (self: nat)    39     || PLAYER [GAME, WINNER] (1)
19  is                                          40     || PLAYER [GAME, WINNER] (2)
20     var mine, hers: weapon in                41     end par
21        loop                                  42  end process
```

**Fig. 1.** A rock-paper-scissors game modeled in LNT.

The weapon type declares the three possible weapons, and requires the equality operator to be defined on its values. Many other types are available in LNT, including array and general first-order constructor types which enable the definition of records, lists, etc. The function wins_over uses the **case** pattern matching statement to define the weapons's circular relation. Again, LNT provides many other statements, such as variable assignment, **while** and **for** loops, etc.

The PLAYER process defines a player behavior. Processes are a superset of functions, they additionally enable communication actions, non-determinism and parallel composition. The observable events of a process are *actions* on *gates*. An action contains zero or more *data offers*, whose types form a *profile*. A *channel* lists the profiles supported by a gate. Here, a player, identified by its self argument, performs actions on gates GAME and WINNER, which are restricted by channels game and nat, respectively. A player starts by assigning a random weapon to its mine variable. Then, the select nondeterministic choice statement introduces several possible behaviors, separated by "[]": a player is ready to perform either action on gate GAME—actions differ whether the player's weapon is first or second, identifiers are used for distinction. A player subsequently calls the wins_over function: if it wins, it performs an action on gate WINNER before looping on a new game; if its opponent wins, then the player stops. Otherwise, it is a draw, and both players loop on a new game.

In LNT, processes interact by *multiway rendezvous* with *value matching*, reminiscent of process algebras: one, two or more (multiway) processes synchronize on an action, with the same profile. The value of data offers in received mode (prefixed by "?") of some process is set by other processes. For instance, players can exchange values of type nat and weapon by a rendezvous on gate GAME. The **par** statement in the MAIN process defines which rendezvous are allowed in a parallel composition of three players: an action on gate WINNER can be realized by any player independently, while an action on gate GAME must synchronize any pair among the player processes ($m$-among-$n$ synchronization [8]).

# 3   Automatic Distributed Code Generation with DLC

DLC takes as input a parallel composition of LNT processes and generates a corresponding distributed implementation. Each process, also named *task*, is compiled to a distinct executable. Moreover, DLC produces one executable per gate to handle task interactions. Finally, the implementation also contains a *starter* executable that manages the deployment of other executables. For instance, when we apply DLC on our example, we obtain an executable per player, plus two executables for the gates, and the starter executable.

The starter deploys other executables according to a configuration file which associates executables to machine names. By default, DLC produces a configuration file which can be used as a template, where all executables are required to run on the local host. The configuration file adopts a classical UNIX configuration syntax, which makes it easy to be either written by hand or generated by scripts. For instance, here is a configuration file excerpt:

```
edel-12.grid5000.fr                          # machine name
    directory = /tmp/task0_PLAYER0           # working directory on the remote node
    files     = dlc_task0_PLAYER0            # name of the executable
edel-36.grid5000.fr
... etc. ...
```

## 3.1   Environment Interaction with Hook Functions

More often than not, the end user wants the generated implementation to interact with other existing systems in its environment, such as a local file system or some web service. DLC enables such interactions through *hook functions*: user-defined C functions that are called upon action events.

We want hook functions to enable not only the monitoring of actions, but also their control. Within the distributed implementation, tasks and gates use a protocol [4] to handle synchronizations while preserving the mutual exclusion of *conflicting* (i.e., targeting the same tasks) rendezvous: when a gate detects a possible action, it starts a negotiation that either succeeds and enables the action realization, or fails. Therefore, we distinguish between *pre-negotiation* hooks that are triggered before a negotiation is started, and *post-negotiation* hooks that are called once the action is achieved. Moreover, each action is both a global event of the system and a local event for each task involved in it. Accordingly, we also distinguish between *global* hooks that are executed by gate processes, and *local* hooks that are executed by task processes. From these categories, DLC provides the three following types of hook functions.

**pre-negotiation-global:** each gate has a pre-negotiation-global hook that is called before a negotiation starts for an action on that gate. This hook returns a boolean to indicate whether a negotiation must be started for this action.
**post-negotiation-global:** each gate has a post-negotiation-global hook that is called after a negotiation succeeds for an action on that gate. This hook returns a boolean to indicate whether the action must be realized.

```
1   /* Function defined in file GAME.gatehook.c */
2   bool DLC_HOOK_PRE_NEGOTIATION_GLOBAL (DLC_TYPE_ACTION *act) {
3       printf ("Allow game between %d and %d ?[y/n] ", act->offers[0], act->offers[1]);
4       switch (getchar()) {
5           case 'y': return TRUE;
6           case 'n': return FALSE;
7           default : return FALSE; /* Disallow by default */
8       }
9   }
```

```
1   /* Function defined in file WINNER.gatehook.c */
2   bool DLC_HOOK_POST_NEGOTIATION_GLOBAL (DLC_TYPE_ACTION *act) {
3       play_sound (act->offers[0]); /* Plays the winner's sound */
4       return TRUE;
5   }
```

**Fig. 2.** Hook functions enables interactions with the environment

**post-negotiation-local:** each task has a post-negotiation-local hook that is called when the task realizes an action. This hook returns nothing.

The action under consideration is passed as an argument to all the three types of hooks. Note that the pre-negotiation-global hook can decide whether a negotiation shall be started or not, but a positive response does not guarantee that the subsequent negotiation is successful. When the negotiation does succeed, it is up to the post-negotiation-global hook to eventually decide to realize the action (now that it is certain to be doable) or to abort the negotiation. All hooks can interact with the environment to make choices or perform side effects.

Hook functions are optional, as DLC can produce a stand-alone implementation without them. Hook functions for a gate $g$ (resp. a task $t$) must be defined in the file named $g$.gatehook.c (resp. $t$.taskhook.c). DLC automatically detects such files and embeds the hook functions into the implementation. Besides, DLC has an option to generate hook function templates for a particular gate or task.

Figure 2 illustrates hook functions on the rock-paper-scissors example. The pre-negotiation-global hook of gate GAME let the user decide, at runtime, which games she allows. The post-negotiation-global hook of gate WINNER is used to play some particular sound depending on which player wins a game.

## 3.2    Overview of Compilation Internals

Figure 3 gives an overview of how DLC proceeds to generate a distributed implementation. DLC relies on the EXEC/CÆSAR [9] tool of CADP to obtain a sequential implementation (in C) of each task process. However, the implementation produced by EXEC/CÆSAR is not complete: it can list the currently possible actions of a process, but does not decide which action shall be realized. This decision is made by the synchronization protocol, and DLC automatically interfaces the code generated by EXEC/CÆSAR with the protocol. Both task and gate protocol logic are implemented once for all in isolated libraries, which nonetheless require information about the specification, such as the interactions

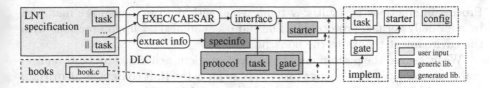

**Fig. 3.** Overview of DLC architecture.

allowed on each gate with respect to the parallel composition. DLC extracts and gathers this information into the "specinfo" library, which is also used by the starter to know who is who. Moreover, DLC detects and embeds the optional hook functions. Finally, DLC invokes a C compiler to produce the executables.

*Implementation Correctness.* The sequential implementation of each task is obtained by the existing EXEC/CÆSAR tool of CADP, which has already been employed in a formal context [9]. Interaction between tasks is achieved by a synchronization protocol [6] that we verified [4] using a formal approach that detected possible deadlocks in other protocols of the literature [5]. The actual implementation of the protocol logic is done by hand, but it is isolated in generic modules that can be thoroughly tested. The writing of these modules is a one-time effort, since they are reused in all generated implementations. Therefore, for a given LNT specification, the specific code produced by DLC comes down to the task-protocol interface which is glue code, and the "specinfo" library which only represents information in data structures. Finally, hook functions can avoid some valid actions to happen, but they cannot lead the system into an invalid action. All these considerations let us have a decent confidence in the correctness of implementations generated by DLC.

*Current Restrictions.* DLC presents two main restrictions. First, values exchanged during an action must fit into a 64bits integer, thus records, lists, and arrays must not appear in action data offers. To be removed, this restriction requires serialization primitives for any LNT types, and we look toward CADP tools to provide them. Second, an action can be *guarded* by a boolean function, i.e., the action is allowed only if its offers let the guard function evaluate to true. Since the code generated by EXEC/CÆSAR does not give access to guard functions, DLC currently ignores the restrictions on data offers possibly induced by them. To be removed, this restriction requires to modify EXEC/CÆSAR such that the generated code gives access to guard functions.

## 4   Conclusion

In this paper, we presented the DLC tool, which enables the automatic generation of a distributed implementation from the LNT formal model of a concurrent system. From an LNT parallel composition of processes, DLC produces several executables that can be easily deployed on distinct machines. We underline the fact that DLC does not require any special annotations in the LNT source.

Process interactions by multiway rendezvous with data exchange are managed by a formally verified protocol [4]. The end user can also set up interactions with the environment thanks to the hook functions.

We measured the performance of implementations generated by DLC on several examples [4,6]. Our biggest case study so far is the Raft consensus algorithm: from an LNT specification of about 500 lines, DLC produces more than 9000 lines of C code for a Raft server. Across all examples, results illustrate that implementations generated by DLC can achieve more than 1000 rendezvous in sequence per second (and of course much more when rendezvous are realized concurrently on different gates). Hence, we consider implementations generated by DLC to qualify at least for rapid prototyping.

As regards related work, BIP [11] and Chor [1] come with deadlock analysis tools and a distributed compiler. Erlang programs can be verified with McErlang [2], and Dreams [10] generates distributed implementations of Reo models.

Thanks to DLC, a concurrent system can now be modeled in LNT, formally verified with CADP, and automatically compiled to an efficient distributed implementation which is easily deployable and which can interact with its environment. In future work, we plan to get rid of the remaining restrictions of DLC, such that it can handle any LNT specification.

**Acknowledgments.** The author warmly thanks Frédéric Lang for reviews of this paper, and all other members of the CONVECS team for their support.

# References

1. Carbone, M., Montesi, F.: Deadlock-freedom-by-design: multiparty asynchronous global programming. In: POPL 2013, pp. 263–274. ACM (2013)
2. Castro, D., Gulías, V.M., Earle, C.B., Fredlund, L., Rivas, S.: A case study on verifying a supervisor component using McErlang. ENTCS **271**, 23–40 (2011)
3. Champelovier, D., Clerc, X., Garavel, H., Guerte, Y., McKinty, C., Powazny, V., Lang, F., Serwe, W., Smeding, G.: Reference Manual of the LNT to LOTOS Translator (Version 6.1). INRIA/VASY and INRIA/CONVECS, August 2014
4. Evrard, H.: Génération automatique d'implémentation distribuée à partir de modéles formels de processus concurrents asynchrones. Ph.D. thesis, Université de Grenoble, July 2015
5. Evrard, H., Lang, F.: Formal verification of distributed branching multiway synchronization protocols. In: Beyer, D., Boreale, M. (eds.) FMOODS/FORTE 2013. LNCS, vol. 7892, pp. 146–160. Springer, Heidelberg (2013)
6. Evrard, H., Lang, F.: Automatic distributed code generation from formal models of asynchronous concurrent processes. In: PDP 2015. IEEE (2015)
7. Garavel, H., Lang, F., Mateescu, R., Serwe, W.: CADP 2011: a toolbox for the construction and analysis of distributed processes. STTT **15**(2), 89–107 (2013). Springer
8. Garavel, H., Sighireanu, M.: A graphical parallel composition operator for process algebras. In: Wu, J., Chanson, S.T., Gao, Q. (eds.) FORTE/PSTV 1999. IFIP AICT, vol. 28, pp. 185–202. Springer, Heidelberg (1999)

9. Garavel, H., Viho, C., Zendri, M.: System design of a CC-NUMA multiprocessor architecture using formal specification, model-checking, co-simulation, and test generation. STTT **3**(3), 314–331 (2001). Springer
10. Proenca, J., Clarke, D., Vink, E., Arbab, F.: Dreams: a framework for distributed synchronous coordination. In: SAC. ACM (2012)
11. Quilbeuf, J.: Distributed implementations of component-based systems with prioritized multiparty interactions. Ph.D. thesis, Université de Grenoble (2013)

# PRISM-Games 2.0: A Tool for Multi-objective Strategy Synthesis for Stochastic Games

Marta Kwiatkowska[1], David Parker[2]([✉]), and Clemens Wiltsche[1]

[1] Department of Computer Science, University of Oxford, Oxford, UK
[2] School of Computer Science, University of Birmingham, Birmingham, UK
d.a.parker@cs.bham.ac.uk

**Abstract.** We present a new release of PRISM-games, a tool for verification and strategy synthesis for stochastic games. PRISM-games 2.0 significantly extends its functionality by supporting, for the first time: (i) *long-run average* (mean-payoff) and *ratio reward* objectives, e.g., to express energy consumption per time unit; (ii) strategy synthesis and Pareto set computation for *multi-objective* properties; and (iii) *compositional* strategy synthesis, where strategies for a stochastic game modelled as a composition of subsystems are synthesised from strategies for individual components using assume-guarantee contracts on component interfaces. We demonstrate the usefulness of the new tool on four case studies from autonomous transport and energy management.

## 1 Introduction

Automatic verification and strategy synthesis are techniques for analysing probabilistic systems. They can be used to produce formal guarantees with respect to quantitative properties such as safety, reliability and efficiency. For example, they can be employed to synthesise controllers in applications such as autonomous vehicles, network protocols and robotic systems. These often operate in uncertain and adverse environments, models of which require both stochasticity, e.g., to represent noise, failures or delays, and game-theoretic aspects, to model non-cooperative agents or uncontrollable events.

PRISM-games is a tool for verification and strategy synthesis for turn-based stochastic multi-player games. The original version focused on model checking for the temporal logic rPATL [7], used to express zero-sum properties in which two opposing sets of players aim to minimise or maximise a single objective: either the probability of an event or the expected reward accumulated before it occurs. It has been successfully applied to, for example, autonomous driving, self-adaptive systems, computer security and user-centric networks [16].

In this paper, we present PRISM-games 2.0, which significantly extends functionality in several directions. First, it supports strategy synthesis for *long-run* properties, such as *average* (mean-payoff) and *ratio* rewards. This provides the ability to express properties of systems that run autonomously for long periods of time, and to specify measures such as energy consumption per time unit.

© Springer-Verlag Berlin Heidelberg 2016
M. Chechik and J.-F. Raskin (Eds.): TACAS 2016, LNCS 9636, pp. 560–566, 2016.
DOI: 10.1007/978-3-662-49674-9_35

Secondly, a key new area of functionality is support for *multi-objective* properties, which enables the exploration of trade-offs, such as between performance and resource requirements. Specifically, we allow Boolean combinations of objectives expressed as expected total rewards (for *stopping games*), and expected mean-payoffs or ratios of expected mean-payoffs (in so-called *controllable multichain* games), as well as conjunctions of almost sure satisfaction for mean-payoffs and ratio rewards (in general games). The tool also performs computation and visualisation of the *Pareto sets* representing the optimal achievable trade-offs.

Thirdly, PRISM-games 2.0 facilitates *compositional* system development. This is done through *assume-guarantee* strategy synthesis, based on contracts over component interfaces that ensure cooperation between the components to achieve a common goal. For example, if one component satisfies the goal $B$ under an assumption $A$ on its environment (i.e. $A \rightarrow B$), while the other component ensures that the assumption $A$ is satisfied, we can compose strategies for the components into a strategy for the full system achieving $B$. Multi-objective strategy synthesis, e.g., for an implication $A \rightarrow B$, can be conveniently employed to realise such assume-guarantee contracts. Again, Pareto set computation can be performed to visualise the relationship between properties and across interfaces.

In this paper, we summarise the algorithms and implementation [2,3,8,9,15] behind the new functionality in PRISM-games 2.0, describe its usage in the tool, and illustrate the benefits it brings with results from four case studies drawn from autonomous systems and energy management.

**Related Tools.** For stochastic games, there is support for qualitative verification in GIST [6] and partial support in the general purpose game solver GAVS+ [10], but there are no tools for multi-objective or compositional analysis. Multi-objective verification for the simpler model of Markov decision processes is available in PRISM [13] (for LTL and expected total reward objectives) and MultiGain [4] (for mean-payoff objectives), but not for stochastic games. Analysis of Nash equilibria (which also balance contrasting objectives for different players) can be performed with EAGLE [14] or PRALINE [5], but only for non-stochastic games. Lastly, Uppaal Stratego [11] performs strategy synthesis against quantitative properties, but with a focus on real-time systems.

## 2   Modelling and Property Specification Languages

**Compositional Modelling.** PRISM-games supports action-labelled turn-based stochastic games (henceforth often simply called *games*), which are specified in an extension of the native PRISM modelling language [13]. Version 2.0 adds a compositional modelling approach to facilitate assume-guarantee strategy synthesis for 2-player stochastic games. A *top-level system* consists of several *subsystems* (component games), which are combined using the game composition operator introduced in [3]. This composition synchronises on shared actions, and actions controlled by Player 1 in subsystems are controlled by Player 1 in the composition, thus enabling composition of the synthesised Player 1 strategies.

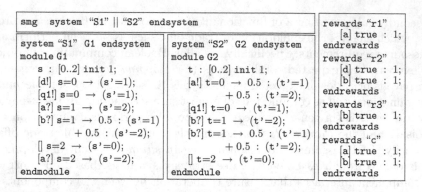

**Fig. 1.** A PRISM-games 2.0 model of a multi-component multi-objective game.

Each subsystem consists of a set of *modules*, which are combined using the original parallel composition of PRISM-games (which ignores player identity). Transitions of modules are specified using guarded commands, optionally labelled with action names (but omitted for non-synchronising transitions). Transitions may be assigned to different players in different subsystems. This is done by tagging an action name a with ! or ?, where [a!] assigns the a-transition to Player 1 and [a?] to Player 2. No state can have outgoing transitions labelled by both ! and ? since we work with turn-based games. Figure 1 shows a model for a system consisting of two subsystems.

**Property Specifications.** PRISM-games focuses on *strategy synthesis* for stochastic multi-player games, i.e., finding player strategies that satisfy some winning condition, irrespective of the (finite) strategies of any other players in the game. PRISM-games 2.0 adds *multi-objective queries* (MQs): Boolean combinations of reward-based objectives. Rewards are specified by a *reward structure* that assigns real-valued rewards to transitions of a game (see Fig. 1, right-hand side). We can reason about *total reward* (indefinitely cumulated rewards), *mean payoff* (long-run average reward), or the long-run *ratio* of two rewards. We also support ratios of expected mean-payoffs; expected ratios are synthesised soundly, but not necessarily completely using almost-sure satisfaction of ratio rewards. An *objective* sets a *target* v for a reward value to be exceeded ($\geq$) or upper-bounded ($\leq$). Objectives for the expected mean-payoff of r, expected total reward of r, and ratio of expected rewards of r and c are expressed, respectively, as $R\{\text{``}r\text{''}\}_{\geq v}[S]$, $R\{\text{``}r\text{''}\}_{\geq v}[C]$, and $R\{\text{``}r\text{''}/\text{``}c\text{''}\}_{\geq v}[S]$, where we use S and C to denote long-run and cumulative rewards. Almost-sure satisfaction objectives for mean-payoff and ratio rewards are written $P_{\geq 1}[R(\text{path})\{\text{``}r\text{''}\}_{\geq v}[S]]$ and $P_{\geq 1}[R(\text{path})\{\text{``}r\text{''}/\text{``}c\text{''}\}_{\geq v}[S]]$. Objectives in an MQ must be of the same type and are combined with the standard Boolean connectives ($\wedge$, $\vee$, $\rightarrow$, $\neg$), but almost-sure satisfaction objectives are only allowed in conjunctions. In the style of rPATL, we use $\langle\langle\text{coalition}\rangle\rangle$ to denote synthesis of strategies for the player(s) in coalition. The following are examples of MQs synthesising strategies for player 1 in a game:

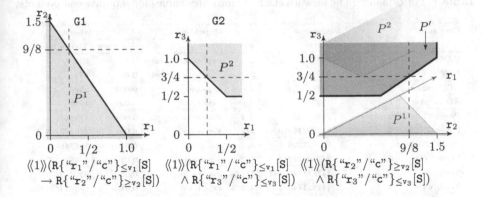

**Fig. 2.** Pareto sets for the games in Fig. 1, with property specifications beneath the respective sets. On the right is the compositional Pareto set $P'$. The global target is $(v_2, v_3) = (\frac{3}{4}, \frac{9}{8})$, and the local targets can be seen to be consistent with $v_1 = \frac{1}{4}$.

- $\langle\!\langle 1 \rangle\!\rangle (R\{\text{"packets\_in"}/\text{"time"}\}_{\leq v_1}[S] \rightarrow R\{\text{"served"}/\text{"time"}\}_{\geq v_2}[S])$ – assuming the expected rate of incoming network packets is at most $v_1$, the expected rate of serving submitted requests is guaranteed to be at least $v_2$."
- $\langle\!\langle 1 \rangle\!\rangle (R\{\text{"passengers"}\}_{\geq v_1}[C] \wedge R\{\text{"fuel"}\}_{\leq v_2}[C])$ – "the expected number of passengers transported is at least $v_1$, while simultaneously ensuring that the expected fuel consumption is at most $v_2$."

## 3 Multi-objective Strategy Synthesis

PRISM-games 2.0 implements the multi-objective strategy synthesis methods formulated in [2,8,9], at the heart of which is a fixpoint computation of the sets of achievable targets for multiple reward objectives. For expected total rewards, games must be *stopping*, i.e., terminal states with zero reward must be reached almost surely under all strategies [8]. For expected long-run objectives, games must be *controllable multichain*, i.e., the sets of states that can occur in any maximal end component are almost surely reachable [15].

MQs with objectives of all types are converted into a unified fixpoint computation. In particular, Boolean combinations of expectation objectives are converted to conjunctions by selecting appropriate *weights* for the individual objectives [8]. Then, at each state of the game we iteratively compute polytopic sets of achievable vectors, with each dimension corresponding to one objective. Performance can be improved by computing successive polytopes using in-place (i.e. Gauss-Seidel) updates, as well as rounding the corners of the polytopes at every iteration (which comes at the cost of precision) [9]. We then construct succinct strategies with *stochastic memory updates*, that win by maintaining the target below the expected value of the memory elements, which are the extreme points of the polytopes at the respective states.

**Table 1.** Performance. The forward slash (/) indicates values for separate components.

| Case study | Model | | Objectives | | Synthesis | |
|---|---|---|---|---|---|---|
| | Components | States | # | Type | Accuracy | Time[s] |
| UAV | 1 | 6251 | 2 | exp. total, Pareto | 0.1 | 652 |
| UAV | 1 | 6251 | 2 | exp. total, Pareto | 0.01 | 871 |
| AD(Charlton) | 1 | 501 | 3 | exp. total | 0.001 | 2603 |
| AD(Islip) | 1 | 1527 | 3 | exp. total | 0.001 | 1968 |
| Power(0) | 2 | 3456/3456 | 2/2 | a.s. ratio | 0.001 | 175/172 |
| Power(1) | 2 | 11400/11400 | 2/2 | a.s. ratio | 0.001 | 2261/2298 |
| Power$^+$(0) | 2 | 7296/7296 | 3/3 | a.s. ratio | 0.01 | 586/484 |
| Power$^+$(1) | 2 | 24744/24744 | 3/3 | a.s. ratio | 0.01 | 3325/2377 |
| Temp(w) | 3 | 1478/1740/1478 | 3/2/3 | exp. ratio | 0.05 | 829/69/734 |
| Temp(w) | 3 | 1478/1740/1478 | 3/2/3 | exp. ratio | 0.01 | 860/92/2480 |
| Temp(v) | 3 | 1478/1740/1478 | 3/2/3 | exp. ratio | 0.05 | 678/27/621 |
| Temp(v) | 3 | 1478/1740/1478 | 3/2/3 | exp. ratio | 0.01 | 3370/34/8605 |

The implementation uses the Parma Polyhedra Library [1] for symbolic manipulation of convex sets. Stochastic games are stored in an explicit-state fashion and analysed using an extension of PRISM's Java-based "explicit" engine.

**Pareto Sets.** An MQ is achievable for all targets in the *achievable set*; its frontier is the *Pareto set*, containing the targets that cannot be improved in any direction without degrading another. The achievable set for Boolean combinations is the union of the convex achievable sets obtained for the respective weights. The Pareto sets can be visualised by the user selecting two-dimensional *slices*.

## 4    Compositional Strategy Synthesis

We leverage assume-guarantee verification rules for probabilistic automata (i.e., games with only a single player) for assume-guarantee strategy synthesis in two-player games [3]. Given a system $\mathcal{G}$ composed of subsystems $\mathcal{G}_1$, $\mathcal{G}_2$, ..., a designer supplies respective *local property specifications* $\varphi_1$, $\varphi_2$, ... via the construct $\texttt{comp}(\varphi_1, \varphi_2, \ldots)$. By synthesising *local strategies* $\pi_i$ for $\mathcal{G}_i$ satisfying $\varphi_i$, a *global strategy* $\pi$ can be constructed for $\mathcal{G}$. Using *assume-guarantee rules*, one can then derive a *global property* $\varphi$ for $\mathcal{G}$ that is satisfied by $\pi$. The rules require *fairness* conditions, and we write $\mathcal{G}^\pi \models^u \varphi$ if the Player 1 strategy $\pi$ satisfies $\varphi$ against all unconditionally fair Player 2 strategies. For example, the rule:

$$\frac{\mathcal{G}_1^{\pi_1} \models^u \varphi^A \quad \mathcal{G}_2^{\pi_2} \models^u \varphi^A \to \varphi^G}{(\mathcal{G}_1 \parallel \mathcal{G}_2)^{\pi_1 \parallel \pi_2} \models^u \varphi^G} \quad \text{(ASYM)}$$

states that Player 1 wins with strategy $\pi_1 \parallel \pi_2$ for $\varphi^G$ in the top-level system if $\pi_2$ in $\mathcal{G}_2$ achieves $\varphi^G$ under the contract $\varphi^A \to \varphi^G$, and $\pi_1$ in $\mathcal{G}_1$ satisfies $\varphi^A$. Reward structures in shared objectives may only involve synchronised actions.

**Compositional Pareto Sets.** We compositionally compute a Pareto set for the property $\varphi$ of the top-level system, which is an under-approximation of the Pareto set computed directly on the monolithic system. For a target in the compositional Pareto set, the targets for the local property specifications $\varphi_i$ can be derived, so that the local strategies can be synthesised (see Fig. 2).

# 5 Case Studies and Tool Availability

We illustrate the new functionality in PRISM-games 2.0 with four case studies, as follows. "UAV": we compute Pareto sets for a UAV performing reconnaissance of roads, reacting to inputs from a human operator, under a conjunction of expected total rewards [12]. "AD($V$)": we synthesise a strategy to steer an autonomous car through a village $V$, reacting to its environment such as pedestrians, or traffic jams, under a conjunction of expected total rewards [9]. "Power": we maximise uptime of two components in an aircraft electrical power network, reacting to generator failures and switch delays $d$; each component has a conjunction of almost-sure satisfaction of ratio rewards. We use assume-guarantee strategy synthesis for two model variants, with (resp. without) modelling an interface, denoted $\text{Power}^+(d)$ (resp. $\text{Power}(d)$) [2]. "Temp": we control the temperature in three adjacent rooms, reacting to the outside temperature and whether windows are opened; and use Boolean combinations of expected ratios. We use assume-guarantee strategy synthesis for two model variants, denoted Temp(w) and Temp(v) [15]. Table 1 summarises the tool's performance on these case studies on a 2.8 GHz PC with 32 GB RAM. We observe that scalability mostly depends on the number of objectives, the state space size and accuracy, but our compositional approach greatly increases the viable state space sizes.

PRISM-games 2.0 is open source, released under GPL, available from [16].

**Acknowledgement.** This work has been supported by the ERC Advanced Grant VERIWARE and EPSRC Mobile Autonomy Programme Grant.

# References

1. Bagnara, R., Hill, P., Zaffanella, E.: The parma polyhedra library. Sci. Comput. Program. **72**(1–2), 3–21 (2008)
2. Basset, N., Kwiatkowska, M., Topcu, U., Wiltsche, C.: Strategy synthesis for stochastic games with multiple long-run objectives. In: TACAS 2015, pp. 256–271 (2015)
3. Basset, N., Kwiatkowska, M., Wiltsche, C.: Compositional controller synthesis for stochastic games. In: Baldan, P., Gorla, D. (eds.) CONCUR 2014. LNCS, vol. 8704, pp. 173–187. Springer, Heidelberg (2014)
4. Brázdil, T., Chatterjee, K., Forejt, V., Kučera, A.: MultiGain: a controller synthesis tool for MDPs with multiple mean-payoff objectives. In: TACAS 2015
5. Brenguier, R.: PRALINE: a tool for computing Nash equilibria in concurrent games. In: Sharygina, N., Veith, H. (eds.) CAV 2013. LNCS, vol. 8044, pp. 890–895. Springer, Heidelberg (2013)

6. Chatterjee, K., Henzinger, T.A., Jobstmann, B., Radhakrishna, A.: GIST: a solver for probabilistic games. In: Touili, T., Cook, B., Jackson, P. (eds.) CAV 2010. LNCS, vol. 6174, pp. 665–669. Springer, Heidelberg (2010)
7. Chen, T., Forejt, V., Kwiatkowska, M., Parker, D., Simaitis, A.: Automatic verification of competitive stochastic systems. FMSD **43**(1), 61–92 (2013)
8. Chen, T., Forejt, V., Kwiatkowska, M., Simaitis, A., Wiltsche, C.: On stochastic games with multiple objectives. In: Chatterjee, K., Sgall, J. (eds.) MFCS 2013. LNCS, vol. 8087, pp. 266–277. Springer, Heidelberg (2013)
9. Chen, T., Kwiatkowska, M., Simaitis, A., Wiltsche, C.: Synthesis for multi-objective stochastic games: an application to autonomous urban driving. In: QEST 2013 (2013)
10. Cheng, C.-H., Knoll, A., Luttenberger, M., Buckl, C.: GAVS+: an open platform for the research of algorithmic game solving. In: Abdulla, P.A., Leino, K.R.M. (eds.) TACAS 2011. LNCS, vol. 6605, pp. 258–261. Springer, Heidelberg (2011)
11. David, A., Jensen, P.G., Larsen, K.G., Mikučionis, M., Taankvist, J.H.: Uppaal Stratego. In: Baier, C., Tinelli, C. (eds.) TACAS 2015. LNCS, vol. 9035, pp. 206–211. Springer, Heidelberg (2015)
12. Feng, L., Wiltsche, C., Humphrey, L., Topcu, U.: Controller synthesis for autonomous systems interacting with human operators. In: ICCPS (2015)
13. Kwiatkowska, M., Norman, G., Parker, D.: PRISM 4.0: verification of probabilistic real-time systems. In: Gopalakrishnan, G., Qadeer, S. (eds.) CAV 2011. LNCS, vol. 6806, pp. 585–591. Springer, Heidelberg (2011)
14. Toumi, A., Gutierrez, J., Wooldridge, M.: A tool for the automated verification of Nash equilibria in concurrent games. In: Leucker, M., Rueda, C., Valencia, F.D. (eds.) ICTAC 2015. LNCS, vol. 9399, pp. 583–594. Springer, Heidelberg (2015)
15. Wiltsche, C.: Assume-Guarantee Strategy Synthesis for Stochastic Games. Ph.D. thesis, University of Oxford (2016, forthcoming)
16. PRISM-games website. www.prismmodelchecker.org/games/

# Cerberus: Automated Synthesis of Enforcement Mechanisms for Security-Sensitive Business Processes

Luca Compagna[2], Daniel Ricardo dos Santos[1,2,3]([✉]), Serena Elisa Ponta[2], and Silvio Ranise[1]

[1] Fondazione Bruno Kessler (FBK), Trento, Italy
dossantos@fbk.eu
[2] SAP Labs France, Mougins, France
[3] University of Trento, Trento, Italy

**Abstract.** CERBERUS is a tool to automatically synthesize run-time enforcement mechanisms for security-sensitive Business Processes (BPs). The tool is capable of guaranteeing that the execution constraints $EC$ on the tasks together with the authorization policy $AP$ and the authorization constraints $AC$ are satisfied while ensuring that the process can successfully terminate. CERBERUS can be easily integrated in many workflow management systems, it is transparent to process designers, and does not require any knowledge beyond usual BP modeling. The tool works in two phases. At design-time, the enforcement mechanism $M$, parametric in the authorization policy $AP$, is generated from $EC$ and $AC$; $M$ can thus be used with any instance of the same BP provided that $EC$ and $AC$ are left unchanged. At run-time, a specific authorization policy is added to $M$, thereby obtaining an enforcement mechanism $M^*$ dedicated to a particular instance of the security-sensitive business process. To validate our approach, we discuss the implementation and usage of CERBERUS in the SAP HANA Operational Intelligence platform.

## 1 Introduction

A security-sensitive business process (BP) [1] is a structured collection of tasks, defining a workflow, equipped with an authorization policy (AP) defining which users are entitled to execute which tasks, and authorization constraints such as Separation of Duties (SoD) defining that certain tasks must be executed by different users. The authorization policy and constraints are crucial to comply with regulations and prevent frauds. It is, however, of utmost importance to ensure that business continuity is not endangered, i.e. it must be possible to complete the process while satisfying the authorization policy and constraints.

As an example, consider the Voting process shown in Fig. 1. It is composed of four tasks (represented by rounded rectangles), *Request Voting* ($t1$), *Moderate e-mail discussion* ($t2$), *Moderate conference call* ($t3$) and *Validate Voting* ($t4$),

---

This work has been partly supported by the EU under grant 317387 SECENTIS (FP7-PEOPLE-2012-ITN).

M. Chechik and J.-F. Raskin (Eds.): TACAS 2016, LNCS 9636, pp. 567–572, 2016.
DOI: 10.1007/978-3-662-49674-9_36

and two SoD constraints (dashed lines labeled by $\neq$), which impose that the user who executes $t2$ ($t3$, resp.) cannot also execute $t3$ ($t4$, resp.). Examples of valid execution scenarios, i.e. assignments of users to tasks such that the process can terminate and constraints are satisfied, are $t1(C), t2(A), t3(B), t4(A)$ and $t1(A), t3(B), t2(C), t4(A)$. Though in this simple process it is easy to determine whether there exist valid execution scenarios, for complex BP with more constraints and expressive policies this is not the case. Establishing whether all tasks can be executed while satisfying the authorization policy and without violating any authorization constraints is known as the Workflow Satisfiability Problem (WSP), whose solution is NP-hard already in presence of one SoD constraint [9]. The problem becomes even more complex if we consider the run-time version of WSP that consists in answering user requests to execute a task while ensuring successful termination together with the satisfaction of authorization constraints. As an example consider that at run-time $t1$ has been performed by A, and B is requesting to execute $t2$. Although B is entitled to do so by the authorization policy and $t2$ is not in SoD with any task B executed in the past, granting this request would break business continuity. In fact A would be the only user entitled to execute $t3$ because of the SoD between $t2$ and $t3$, but then no user would be able to execute $t4$ without violating the SoD with $t3$. In [3] a technique was introduced to automatically synthesize, from security-sensitive BPs, enforcement mechanisms that solve the run-time WSP.

In this paper we present CERBERUS [1], a tool that relies on [3] to automatically synthesize at design-time enforcement mechanisms capable of guaranteeing at run-time that the workflow can terminate while satisfying the authorization policy and the authorization constraints. The synthesized mechanisms are parametric in the authorization policy so that they can be combined at run-time with authorization policies dedicated to different instances of the process. CERBERUS can be easily integrated in many workflow management systems, it is transparent to process designers, and does not require any knowledge beyond usual BP modeling. To demonstrate the tool, we integrated it into the SAP HANA Operational Intelligence platform [2] (OpInt) which offers a BPMN modeling and enactment environment.

## 2   Tool Architecture and Implementation

A reference architecture for Workflow Management (WFM) systems [10] is composed of the five blue elements shown in Fig. 2. *Workflow Modeling* is a graphical user interface for a *Process Designer* to create workflow models using a modeling language such as BPMN or YAWL (see, e.g., [10]). The models are stored in a *Workflow Model Repository*, while the *Workflow Engine* interprets the models

---

[1] Cerberus is a three-headed watchdog in Greek mythology, with the first head associated to the past, the second to the present and the third to the future. CERBERUS acts as a monitor that takes into account the history of executions, the current authorization relation and future executions to grant or deny requests.

[2] https://help.sap.com/hana-opint.

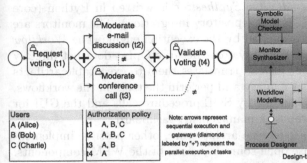

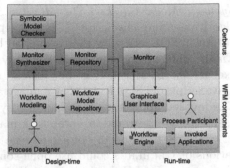

**Fig. 1.** Voting process

**Fig. 2.** Tool architecture (Color figure online)

and directs the execution to the *Invoked Applications*, in the case of system and script tasks, or to a *Graphical User Interface* (GUI), in the case of user tasks, which are performed by *Process Participants*.

On top of the WFM components, we add the CERBERUS components shown in red in Fig. 2. The *Monitor Synthesizer* is responsible for interpreting the workflow model and translating it into a transition system format accepted by a *Symbolic Model Checker* capable of computing a reachability graph whose paths are all possible executions of the workflow. Note that only the workflow model (representing the execution constraints) extended with authorization constraints is input to the monitor synthesis. This allows the synthesized monitor to support different authorization policies at run-time. The reachability graph is translated into a language such as Datalog or SQL and stored in the *Monitor Repository*. The *Monitor* itself sits between the GUI and the workflow engine and grants or denies user requests to execute tasks (users only access tasks through the GUI and automatic tasks are not part of the authorization policy or constraints[3]).

The main goals in the design of CERBERUS are usability, scalability and minimal interference with pre-existing functionalities. Usability is achieved because the tool is fully automated and all the formal details are hidden from the process designer, who only has to input the workflow model with a set of constraints that he/she wishes to be enforced (which can be done graphically). Scalability is ensured by the use of modular monitor synthesis (decomposing workflows into components, synthesizing monitors for them and combining the results [4]) and minimal interference is guaranteed by using the tool as a plug-in, so that both monitor synthesis and enforcement can be easily activated or deactivated.

The CERBERUS implementation is built on top of OpInt to synthesize, store, combine and retrieve run-time monitors for security-sensitive workflows therein modeled and enacted. HANA Studio is the IDE that acts as the *Workflow Modeling* component, while the HANA Repository implements both the *Workflow Model Repository* and the *Monitor Repository*. We added the constraint specification and monitor synthesis capabilities in the IDE and used MCMT [6] as the

---

[3] This is a limitation of the current implementation. Nonetheless the approach is able to monitor any task subject to an authorization policy.

*Symbolic Model Checker.* The *Monitor Synthesizer* is written in Python (core algorithms) and JavaScript (IDE and repository integration). The monitors are output in SQL as a view that is queried by the execution engine. The *Workflow Engine* differs from traditional WFM systems because OpInt does not directly execute the BPMN models, but instead translates them to executable artifacts (JavaScript and SQL code) that manage and perform the tasks in the workflows. The invoked applications are handled by SQL procedure calls and the GUI for user tasks is integrated in a web task management dashboard.

Since we build on top of a reference architecture, other possible implementations of CERBERUS could use open-source versions of the WFM components. The advantage of OpInt is to have all the components in the same platform.

## 3    Using Cerberus

The usage of the tool involves four steps: design-time specification, monitor synthesis, deployment, and run-time enforcement. SAP HANA is an in-memory relational database, so the BPMN artifacts and the monitors are translated to SQL. There is a long tradition of works using relational languages, such as Datalog and SQL, to express role-based access control and other authorization policies [7]. Moreover, we use database tables to store the users (USERS), authorization policy (AP) and execution history (HST).

At **design-time**, a process designer uses the HANA Studio IDE to model the control-flow and authorization constraints of a workflow. Authorization constraints are not part of standard BPMN, and there are many proposed extensions to accommodate them, but we simply use task documentation to input the constraints in textual form. This can be changed in the future so that constraints are specified as graphical elements. Authorization policies are specified by linking each task to an assignment table in the database, which is only populated at deployment-time. When design is complete, the model is translated to SQL by pressing a button in the IDE.

To model the example of Fig. 1, a process designer uses the IDE to create a new BPMN file and graphically drags, drops and connects the required elements: start and end events (the circles in the figure), user tasks (rounded rectangles), sequence flows (solid arrows) and parallel gateways (diamonds labeled by $+$). The authorization constraints are input in the documentation of the second and third tasks, the authorization policy is linked to the AP database table (which is empty at the moment) and the task UIs are linked to web pages.

The **monitor synthesis** runs in parallel with the BPMN-to-SQL compiler and is completely transparent to end users. When the monitor synthesizer receives a request to generate a monitor, the BPMN model file (in XML) is read from the repository and translated to a symbolic transition system that is fed to the SMT-based MCMT model checker. The model checker applies a backward reachability procedure and returns a reachability graph that represents all possible executions of the workflow by symbolic users, which are introduced by the model checker itself to represent placeholders for concrete users that are specified at deployment time in the USERS table. The reachability graph is composed of nodes labeled by first-order formulae representing sets of states and edges representing the execution of tasks by users, with each path representing a possible terminating execution of the system. The formulae encode the conditions that must be met for a user to execute a task and they use an interface to the authorization policy and history of execution that will be realized at run-time as the database tables AP and HST, respectively. The monitors are thus parametric in the authorization policy, which means that the same monitor needs to be generated only once for each workflow model, regardless of the run-time policy that is deployed with it. In [3], a procedure is described which takes a symbolic transition system and returns a Datalog program whose clauses are a conjunction of literals built out of the state variables in the transition system such that user $u$ can execute task $t$ and the workflow can successfully terminate iff $can\_do(u, t)$ is a logical consequence of the Datalog program with a specific authorization policy and history. The Datalog monitors are then further translated to SQL views that can be queried by the execution engine (aggregation-free SQL and non-recursive Datalog with negation are equivalent and the translation is straightforward [8]). The resulting SQL view, using the database tables representing users, authorization policy and history of execution, is stored in the repository and queried at run-time by the execution engine. The synthesized monitors are modular and can be composed to form more complex monitors, as described in [4]. This allows us to alleviate the state space explosion problem and handle large workflows by decomposing them into smaller modules.

In the example of Fig. 1, the monitor consists of an SQL view defined by a procedure containing, among others, the following query for $t2$ (simplified for the sake of clarity):

```
SELECT U2.ID FROM USERS AS U1, USERS AS U2 WHERE HST.dt1 = 1 AND HST.dt2 = 0
    AND HST.dt3 = 1 AND HST.dt4 = 0 AND (U1.ID <> U2.ID) AND NOT HST.t3by =
    U1.ID AND NOT HST.t3by = U2.ID AND U2.ID IN (SELECT ID2 FROM AP) AND U1.
    ID IN (SELECT ID4 FROM AP)
```

which encodes the fact that, to execute $t2$, the system must be in a state where $t1$ and $t3$ have been executed, but neither $t2$ nor $t4$ (dt1 = 1 AND dt2 = 0 AND dt3 = 1 AND dt4 = 0), there must be a user $u1$ who can execute $t2$ (SELECT ID2 FROM AP), and a different user $u2$ (U1.ID <> U2.ID) who can execute $t4$ (SELECT ID4 FROM AP) and neither user should have executed $t3$ because of the SoDs between $t2$ and $t3$ and between $t3$ and $t4$ (NOT t3by = U1.ID AND NOT t3by = U2.ID). Other queries for $t2$ and all queries for other tasks have been omitted for the lack of space.

For the **deployment** of a workflow it is necessary to specify the concrete authorization policy by populating the linked database tables. End users manage workflows using a generated API.

At **run-time**, there is a running job responsible for calling the next tasks based on tokens stored in the database, whose flow is specified by the control-flow in the BPMN model. When a human task is executed, the monitor associated to the workflow is called into action by the automatic invoking of a procedure from the task UI. To grant or deny a request, the monitor queries the USERS, AP and HST tables described above to ensure that the requesting user is entitled to perform the task, the user has or has not performed another conflicting task, and the execution of this task will not prevent the satisfaction of the workflow (as shown in the example query above).

Examples of valid execution scenarios and run-time enforcement for the process in Fig. 1 are given in the Introduction.

## 4   Discussion

CERBERUS is under development and it has been validated with real-world and synthetic examples [3,4]. Currently, the tool is not available for public use, but business units at SAP showed interest in the OpInt integration and discussion about pilot projects with customers is going on. It is possible to use the CERBERUS architecture with other components, as described in Sect. 2, and we already have implementations of the *Monitor Synthesizer* for Prolog, pyDatalog and MySQL, but there is no integration with other WFM systems. This work is related to runtime verification [5] and tools that address the WSP. The closest related work is [2], which presents a workflow monitor that considers policies and constraints and uses pre-existing IBM components; it does not, however, solve the WSP. As future work, we intend to encourage and study the use of the tool in more real-world scenarios and, leveraging the ideas in [4], build a repository of components with synthesized monitors that can be reused by business designers.

## References

1. Armando, A., Ponta, S.E.: Model checking of security-sensitive business processes. In: Degano, P., Guttman, J.D. (eds.) FAST 2009. LNCS, vol. 5983, pp. 66–80. Springer, Heidelberg (2010)
2. Basin, D., Burri, S.J., Karjoth, G.: Dynamic enforcement of abstract separation of duty constraints. ACM TISSeC **15**(3), 13:1–13:30 (2012)
3. Bertolissi, C., dos Santos, D.R., Ranise, S.: Automated synthesis of run-time monitors to enforce authorization policies in business processes. In: ASIACCS (2015)
4. dos Santos, D.R., Ranise, S., Ponta, S.E.: Modularity for security-sensitive workflows. In arXiv (2015)
5. Falcone, Y., Havelund, K., Reger, G.: A tutorial on runtime verification. Eng. Dependable Softw. Syst. **34**, 141–175 (2012)
6. Ghilardi, S., Ranise, S.: MCMT: a model checker modulo theories. In: Giesl, J., Hähnle, R. (eds.) IJCAR 2010. LNCS, vol. 6173, pp. 22–29. Springer, Heidelberg (2010)
7. Samarati, P., de Vimercati, S.C.: Access control: policies, models, and mechanisms. In: Focardi, R., Gorrieri, R. (eds.) FOSAD 2000. LNCS, vol. 2171, pp. 137–196. Springer, Heidelberg (2001)
8. Terracina, G., Leone, N., Lio, V., Panetta, C.: Experimenting with recursive queries in database and logic programming systems. Theory Pract. Log. Program. **8**(2), 129–165 (2008)
9. Wang, Q., Li, N.: Satisfiability and resiliency in workflow authorization systems. TISSeC **13**, 40:1–40:35 (2010)
10. Weske, M.: Business Process Management: Concepts, Languages, Architectures. Springer-Verlag New York Inc., Secaucus (2007)

# Developing and Debugging Proof Strategies by Tinkering

Yuhui Lin[⊠], Pierre Le Bras, and Gudmund Grov

Heriot-Watt University, Edinburgh, UK
{Y.Lin,PL196,G.Grov}@hw.ac.uk

**Abstract.** Previously, we have developed a graphical proof strategy language, called *PSGraph* [4], to support the development and maintenance of large and complex proof tactics for interactive theorem provers. By using labelled hierarchical graphs this formalisation improves upon tactic composition, analysis and maintenance compared with traditional tactic languages. PSGraph has been implemented as the *Tinker* system, supporting the Isabelle and ProofPower theorem provers [5]. In this paper we present *Tinker2*, a new version of Tinker, which provides enhancements in user interaction and experience, together with: novel support for controlled inspection; debugging using breakpoints and a logging mechanism; and advanced recording, exporting and reply.

## 1 PSGraph and Tinker

Most interactive theorem provers provide users with a tactic language in which they can encode common proof strategies in order to reduce user interaction. To encode proof strategies, these languages typically provide: a set of functions, called *tactics*, which reduces sub-goals into smaller and simpler sub-goals; and a set of combinators, called *tacticals*, which combines tactics in different ways.

Composition in most tacticals either relies on the number and the order of sub-goals, or is to try all tactics on all sub-goals. The former is brittle as the number and the order could be changed if any of the sub-tactics changes; and the latter is hard to debug and maintain, as if a proof fails the actual position is hard to find. It is also difficult for others to see the intuition behind tactic design.

To overcome these issues we developed *PSGraph*, a graphical proof strategy language [4], where complex tactics are represented as directed hierarchical graphs. Here, the nodes contain tactics or nested graphs, and are composed by labelled wires. The labels are called *goal types*: predicates describing expected properties of sub-goals. Each sub-goal becomes a special *goal node* on the graph, which "lives" on a wire. Evaluation is handled by applying a tactic to a goal node that is on one of its input wires. The resulting sub-goals are sent to the out wires of the tactic node. To add a goal node to a wire, the goal type must be satisfied. This mechanism is used to control that goals are sent to the right place, independent of number and order of sub-goals. For more details see [4].

This work has been supported by EPSRC grants EP/J001058 and EP/K503915.

M. Chechik and J.-F. Raskin (Eds.): TACAS 2016, LNCS 9636, pp. 573–579, 2016.
DOI: 10.1007/978-3-662-49674-9_37

In [5], we introduced the Tinker tool, which implements PSGraph with support for the *Isabelle* and *Proof-
Power* theorem provers[1]. Tinker consists of two parts: the
**CORE** and the **GUI**, each is shaded in a separated grey
boxes in Fig. 1. The core is implemented in Poly/ML, and
handles the key functionality. The GUI is implemented
in Scala. They communicate over a JSON socket protocol. In addition to the Tinker GUI, a user will work
with the GUI of the theorem prover; Tinker is only used
for the proof strategies. To achieve theorem prover independence, most functionality is implemented using ML

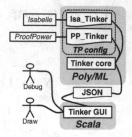

**Fig. 1.** Architecture

`functors`. Each theorem prover has a special `structure` that implements a provided `signature`, as indicated by `Isa_Tinker` and `PP_Tinker` in Fig. 1.

The main advantages of PSGraph over more traditional tactic languages (e.g.
as found in Isabelle and ProofPower) are the ability of a step-by-step inspection
of how sub-goals flow through the graph during evaluation, combined with features to debug and modify it. Such features are of great aid when debugging
and maintaining proof strategies. It also provides a more intuitive representation to understand how the proof strategy works, also for non-developers (similar
to graph visualisation of proofs in e.g. [7]). Low-level details can be hidden by
using hierarchies to improve readability. Such features rely on good GUI support, which was only partially supported by the original Tinker tool [5]. Here,
we introduce *Tinker2*, a new version of Tinker, which extends Tinker with new

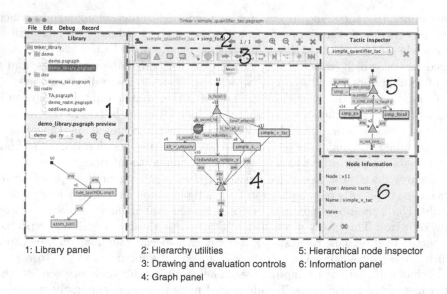

1: Library panel          2: Hierarchy utilities              5: Hierarchical node inspector
                          3: Drawing and evaluation controls  6: Information panel
                          4: Graph panel

**Fig. 2.** The Tinker2 GUI and its layout.

---

[1] A *Rodin* version is currently under development.

features, including supports for: library and hierarchical graphs; richer tactic and debugging options; and recording and replay. Figure 2 shows the Tinker2 GUI and its layout.

We will use the ProofPower instance of Tinker2 in this paper, albeit we could just as well have used Isabelle as the features are identical. In Sect. 2 we focus on how to develop proof strategies from scratch; in Sect. 3 we discuss advanced features of evaluating, debugging, recording and replaying proofs; while we conclud and briefly discuss related and further work in Sect. 4.

## 2 Developing Proof Strategies

A user can draw a PSGraph from the *Graph panel* by selecting the type of node from the *Drawing and evaluation controls* panel (see Fig. 2). Nodes are connected by dragging a line between them. When selecting an entity, the details are displayed in the *Information panel*, and they can be edited by double clicking[2]. Figure 3 shows the type of nodes that are supported by the tool.

**Fig. 3.** The node types.

**Atomic Tactics.** An atomic tactic wraps a tactic of the underlying theorem prover, which by default has the same as the name of the node. Tinker2 will automatically use all available tactics from the underlying prover. New tactics can be defined in the *tactic editor* of the Tinker2 GUI. To illustrate, the tactic definition

```
tactic all_∃_uncurry := fn [] => conv_tac all_∃_uncurry_conv;
```

creates a tactic with no argument (`fn []`). This tactic will be parsed and stored by the CORE, so that it can be used.

**Hierarchical Nodes.** Modularity is achieved by hierarchies. This can also help to reduce the complexity and size of a PSGraph by hiding parts of it. We will illustrate the new hierarchy features below.

**Identity Nodes.** Identity nodes are used to fanout and join wires. As the name suggests, they do not change the sub-goals.

**Breakpoints.** A novel feature of Tinker2 is the introduction of breakpoint nodes, which can be added/removed from wires by a simple mouse click. We return to this is in Sect. 3.

**Goal Nodes.** A goal node wraps a sub-goal of a proof, and this can not be modified by the user, i.e. these nodes can only be changed through tactic applications, and introduced by the CORE when a new proof is started.

---

[2] More details of running the tool is available from the user manual [2].

For the atomic tactics, a set of *atomic goal types* needs to be provided for each theorem prover. Tinker2 provides a Prolog-based language, with a dedicated editor, to develop these. To illustrate, the atomic goal type `top_symbol(t,s)` checks if term t has top symbol s. To declutter the graphs, we can define new goal types in the editor, which can then be used. For example:

```
is_conj() :- top_symbol(concl,conj).
```

checks if the top symbol of the conclusion (`concl`) is a conjunction ∧ (`conj`).

```
(REPEAT (CHANGED
    (REPEAT strip_∧) THEN
    (TRY (all_∃_uncurry ORELSE
        redundant_simple_∃ ORELSE
        simple_∃_equation ORELSE
        simple_∃_∧)) THEN
    (TRY (all_∀_uncurry ORELSE
        redundant_simple_∀ ORELSE
        simple_∀_∧ ORELSE
        simple_∀_tac))))
```

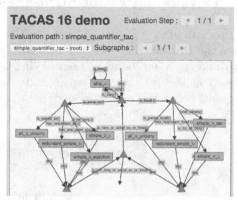

**Fig. 4.** `simple_quantifier_tac`: ProofPower (left) and PSGraph (right)

As a running example, we will use a simple tactic to eliminate quantifiers in ProofPower, called `simple_quantifier_tac`. This simplifies goals by: (1) eliminating top level conjunction (∧) as much as possible; (2) eliminating the top level existential quantifier (∃) if they are redundant or can be simplified with the one point rule[3]; (3) eliminating the top level universal quantifiers ∀. A possible implementation using ProofPower's tactic language is shown in Fig. 4 (left), where `strip_∧` eliminates ∧; `all_∃_uncurry` and `all_∀_uncurry` change paired quantifiers to uncurried versions; `redundant_simple_∃` and `redundant_simple_∀` remove the quantified variables if they are not used in the body; `simple_∃_∧` and `simple_∀_∧` distribute quantifiers over ∧; `simple_∃_equation` simplifies goals with the one point rule; and `simple_∀_tac` instantiates each ∀ quantifier with an arbitrary free variable.

The right hand side of Fig. 4 shows an encoding of the same tactic in PSGraph, developed using the described GUI[4]. This can be further simplified, by "boxing" the sub-graphs that simplifies ∃ and ∀, respectively, using hierarchical nodes. This simplified version is given in Fig. 6. Tinker2 allows such "boxing" of sub-graphs into hierarchies, by a simple mouse click. Tinker2 also supports

---

[3] In the one point rule $\exists x.P(x) \wedge x = t$ becomes $P[t/x]$.

[4] See [9] for larger view, replay and video of this and other PSGraphs in Tinker2.

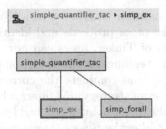

**Fig. 5.** Hierarchy utilities

a range of features to work with hierarchies. In the *Hierarchical node inspector*, users can preview the internal structure of an hierarchical node. In the *Hierarchy utilities* panel, the hierarchical path of the current graph under editing is shown, as well as a tree view of the hierarchical structure of a PSGraph. A screenshot of a tree is shown in Fig. 5. It is also easy to move between and edit hierarchical nodes.

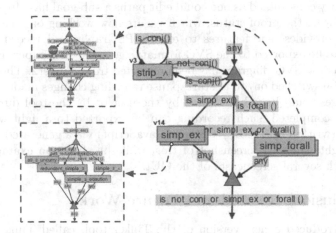

**Fig. 6.** Hierarchical PSGraph of `simple_quantifier_tac` tactic.

Reuse of PSGraphs is supported by a *library*. This feature is provided in the *Library panel* (see Fig. 2). The items in the library are PSGraphs. Therefore, the library can also be customised by simply copying PSGraph files into the library directory. When importing an item from the library to the current PSGraph, Tinker2 will copy it to the graph that the user is currently editing and merge all the required information, such as defined tactics and goal types.

## 3   Evaluating, Debugging, Exporting and Replaying

A PSGraph in Tinker2 can be applied as a normal tactic/method within an Isabelle or ProofPower proof script. This is the normal execution. However, if it fails, it can instead be run in an 'interactive mode' where the GUI is used to visualise and guide how the proof proceeds and identify where it failed. Compared with the first version of Tinker, users can now: (1) select which goal to apply; (2) choose between stepping into and stepping over the evaluation of hierarchical nodes; (3) apply and complete the current hierarchical tactic; (4) apply and finish the whole proof strategy; (5) insert a breakpoint and evaluate a graph automatically until the break point is reached by a goal. These options are illustrated in the *Drawing and evaluations controls* panel of Fig. 2 (see also [9]), which also shows a break point in the graph.

To support debugging, an *evaluation log*, which shows the details of the current proof status, can be displayed. The log uses tags that can be used to filter the log to tags of interests. It also contains a real-time development mode that allows users to develop proof strategies seamlessly during proof tasks. Here, a user can freely edit the PSGraph (except for the goal nodes), e.g. change a tactic node, and then submit the changes to continue the current evaluation with the updated PSGraph. This is achieved using a new communication protocol, with details available in the second author's UG thesis [1], Note that this is currently not sufficiently constrained as one could edit paths a sub-goal has already passed thus invalidating the proof status, which we are now working on (see Sect. 4).

Tinker2 provides new features to export PSGraphs and record proofs. A PSGraph can be exported to the SVG format, e.g. to use in a paper; Fig. 6 illustrates this as the SVG diagram has been exported from Tinker2. The recording feature can be switched on/off to start/pause recording changes made to a graph. These changes could have been made by the user or by the tool during evaluation. Once completed, such recording can be exported to a light-weight web application (written in HTML / CSS and JavaScript) via a generated JSON file. Figure 4 (right) shows a screenshot of this, while [9] shows an example of this together with several screencasts of the GUI.

## 4   Conclusion, Related and Future Work

We have introduced a new version of the Tinker tool, called Tinker2, with a range of novel features to develop, debug, maintain, record and export hierarchical proof strategies. With Tinker2, users can easily reuse existing PSGraphs to develop and debug structured and intuitive hierarchical proof strategies. The most relevant work is the first version of the Tinker tool [5], which we have compared with throughout. It is also important to note that Tinker/Tinker2 is built on top of the Quantomatic graph rewriting engine [6], which is used internally as a library function. The second author has also developed web-based version of Tinker, which supports a subset of the GUI features discussed here [1]. With the exception of simple proof visualisation (e.g. [7]), we are not familiar with any other graphical proof tools to support theorem provers. While there are tactic languages that support robust tactics (e.g. Ltac [3] for Coq), we believe that the development and debugging features of Tinker2 are novel.

With D-RisQ (www.drisq.com) we are using Tinker2 to encode their highly complex Supertac proof strategy in ProofPower [8]. Several enhancements have been motivated by this work. In the future, we would like to improve static checking of PSGraph, such as being able to validate a PSGraph before evaluation. We also plan to improve the layout algorithm, and develop and implement a better framework for combining evaluation and user edits of PSGraphs.

# References

1. Le Bras, P.: Web based interface for graphical proof strategies. Undergraduate CS Honours Thesis (2015). https://goo.gl/LWG522
2. Le Bras, P., Grov, G., Lin, Y.: Tinker: User guide. http://ggrov.github.io/tinker/userGuides.pdf
3. Delahaye, D.: A proof dedicated meta-language. Electron. Notes Theoret. Comput. Sci. **70**(2), 96–109 (2002)
4. Grov, G., Kissinger, A., Lin, Y.: A graphical language for proof strategies. In: McMillan, K., Middeldorp, A., Voronkov, A. (eds.) LPAR-19 2013. LNCS, vol. 8312, pp. 324–339. Springer, Heidelberg (2013)
5. Grov, G., Kissinger, A., Lin, Y.: Tinker, tailor, solver, proof. In: UITP 2014. ENTCS, vol. 167, pp. 23–34. Open Publishing Association (2014)
6. Kissinger, A., Zamdzhiev, V.: Quantomatic: a proof assistant for diagrammatic reasoning. In: Felty, A.P., Middeldorp, A. (eds.) CADE-25. LNCS, vol. 9195, pp. 326–336. Springer, New York (2015)
7. Libal, T., Riener, M., Rukhaia, M.: Advanced proof viewing in ProofTool. In: UITP 2014. EPTCS, vol. 167, pp. 35–47. Open Publishing Association (2014)
8. O'Halloran, C.: Automated verification of code automatically generated from Simulink. ASE **20**(2), 237–264 (2013)
9. Le Bras, P., Lin, Y., Grov, G.: Tinker2 - TACAS 16 paper resources. http://ggrov.github.io/tinker/tacas16/. Accessed 17 October 2015

# v2c – A Verilog to C Translator

Rajdeep Mukherjee[1]([⊠]), Michael Tautschnig[2], and Daniel Kroening[1]

[1] University of Oxford, Oxford, UK
{rajdeep.mukherjee,kroening}@cs.ox.ac.uk
[2] Queen Mary, University of London, London, UK
mt@eecs.qmul.ac.uk

**Abstract.** We present *v2c*, a tool for translating Verilog to C. The tool accepts synthesizable Verilog as input and generates a word-level C program as an output, which we call the *software netlist*. The generated program is cycle-accurate and bit precise. The translation is based on the synthesis semantics of Verilog. There are several use cases for *v2c*, ranging from hardware property verification, co-verification to simulation and equivalence checking. This paper gives details of the translation and demonstrates the utility of the tool.

## 1 Introduction

At the bit level, formal property verification for hardware is scalable to circuits up to the block level but runs out of capacity for SoC-level or full-chip designs. Verification at the word level promises more efficient reasoning, and thus better scalability. However, unlike the AIGER format that is used to represent bit-level netlists, there is no standard format to represent circuits at the word level. In this paper, we argue that hardware circuits given in Verilog can be represented at the word level by encoding them as C programs, which we call a *software netlist*. To this end, we present a Verilog to C translator which we name *v2c*. Given a Verilog RTL design, *v2c* applies the synthesis semantics to automatically generate an equivalent C program. The tool is available online at http://www.cprover.org/hardware/v2c/.

The primary motivation for the transition from bit level to word level is to gain scalability [5,6]. The exploitation of high-level structures for better reasoning is a standard goal in hardware verification. We propose to take one further step: the automatic translation of hardware circuits to a software netlist model in C allows us to leverage advanced software verification techniques such as abstract interpretation and loop acceleration, which have never been applied in conventional bit-level hardware verification.

Verilog and C share many common operators. However, Verilog offers a number of additional operators like part-select, bit-select from vectors, concatenation and reduction operators, which are not available in C. Additionally, Verilog statements like the initial block, the always block, the generate statement, procedural assignment (blocking, non-blocking) and continuous assignment are not

Supported by ERC project 280053 and the SRC task 2269.001.

M. Chechik and J.-F. Raskin (Eds.): TACAS 2016, LNCS 9636, pp. 580–586, 2016.
DOI: 10.1007/978-3-662-49674-9_38

supported in C. Further, Verilog offers 4-valued data-types. These non-trivial constructs, combined with parallelism, make the translation of Verilog to C challenging.

Although SoC designs are increasingly written at a higher level of abstraction [3,4], there is still a significant body of existing design IP blocks that are written in VHDL or Verilog. Our tool *v2c* allows rapid generation of software netlist models from hardware IPs given in Verilog RTL. Other tools like VTOC [2] or Verilator[1] also generate C/C++ code; however, VTOC was not obtainable; the code generated by Verilator is suitable for simulation only and is not amenable to formal analysis.

## 2   v2c – The Verilog RTL to C Translator

Figure 1 illustrates the translation steps of *v2c*. The front-end phase performs macro preprocessing, parses Verilog and checks the types. The front-end supports the 1364-2005 IEEE Standard for Verilog HDL. It generates a type-annotated parse-tree, which is passed to the translation phase. During the translation phase, the tool applies the synthesis semantics and performs a rule-based translation following the Verilog module hierarchy. The rule-based translation produces vectored assignments by mapping bit-operations to equivalent shift and mask operations and performs a global dependency analysis to determine inter-module and intra-modular dependencies. The translation phase is followed by the code-generation phase, where the intermediate vectored expressions and translated module items are converted into C expressions. Note that we refrain from any optimizations or abstractions to obtain a correct and trustworthy output.

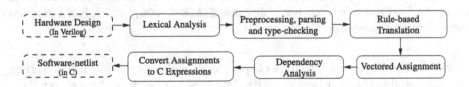

**Fig. 1.** Translation stages in *v2c*

**Software Netlist:** A *software netlist* $SN$ is a four-tuple $\langle L, A, l_0, l_e \rangle$, where $L$ is the finite set of locations for modeling the program counter in the corresponding sequential code, $l_0 \in L$ is the initial location, $l_e \in L$ is the error location and $A \subseteq L \times M \times L$ is the control flow automation. The edges in $A$ are labelled with a quantifier-free first-order formula $M$ over program variables, which encode an assignment or an assume statement. The formula $M$ is defined by five-tuples $\langle In, Out, Seq, Comb, Asgn \rangle$, where $In$, $Out$, $Seq$, $Comb$ are *input*, *output*, *sequential/state-holding* and *combinational/stateless* signals, respectively. *Asgn* is a finite set of assignments to $Out$, $Seq$ and $Comb$ where

---

[1] http://www.veripool.org/wiki/verilator.

- $Asgn ::= CAsgn|SAsgn$
- $CAsgn ::= (V_c = bvExpr)|(V_c = bool), V_c \in Comb \uplus Out$
- $SAsgn ::= (V_s = bvExpr)|(V_s = bool), V_s \in Seq$
- $bvExpr ::= bv_{const}|bv_{var}|ITE(cond, bv_1 \ldots bv_n)|bv_{op}(bv_1 \ldots bv_n), cond \in bool,$
  $bv_i \in \{bv_{const}, bv_{var}\}$
- $bool ::= true|false|\neg b|b_1 \wedge b_2|b_1 \vee b_2|bv_{rel}\{b_1 \ldots b_n\}$

## 2.1   Translating Verilog Module Items

**Data Model:** The data model in Verilog is significantly different from C. Each bit of a C integer value can have only two states, namely 0 and 1. Bits in Verilog HDL can take one of four values, namely 0, 1, $X$ and $Z$. A value of 0 represents low voltage and value of 1 represents high voltage. Further, the values $X$ and $Z$ represent an unknown logic state and a high impedance value, respectively. The simplest synthesis semantics for $X$ is treating it as a "don't-care" assignment, which allows the synthesis to choose a 0 or 1 to further improve logic minimization. v2c treats $X$ and $Z$ values to be non-deterministic.

**Registers, Wires, Parameters and Constants:** Verilog supports structural data types called *nets*, which are *wire* and *reg*. The value of wire variables changes continuously as the input value changes. By contrast, the *reg* types hold their values until another value is assigned to them. A structure containing all state holding elements of a module is declared in C to store the register variables. Wires are declared as local variables in C. Verilog parameters are constants, which are frequently used to specify the width of variables. Parameters are declared as constants in C. Verilog also allows the definition of translation unit constants using the `'define` construct, e.g., `'define STATE 2'b00;`, which is the same as the #define preprocessor directives in C.

**Variable Declaration:** Variables of specific bit-width (register, wire) in Verilog are translated to the next largest native data type in C such as `char`, `short int`, `long`, `long long`, etc.

**Always and Initial Blocks:** Always blocks are the concurrent statements, which execute when a variable in the sensitivity list changes. The statements enclosed inside the always block within *begin* . . . *end* constructs are executed in parallel or sequentially depending on whether it is a non-blocking or blocking statement, respectively. The behaviour of an initial block is the same as that of an always block, except that they are executed exactly once, before the execution of any always block. Figures 2 and 3 demonstrate the translation of Verilog always blocks. All code snippets are partial due to space limitations.

**Module Hierarchy with Input/Output Port:** The communication between modules takes place through *ports*. Ports can be input only, output only and inout. Figure 2 gives an example of a Verilog module hierarchy on the left and the translated code block in C on the right. The output ports are passed as reference to reflect the changes in the parent module. The generated C code preserves the module hierarchy of the RTL. Structurally identical code often aids debugging, as identifying corresponding C/RTL operations is easier.

| Module Hierarchy with Input/Output Ports | Data and Function definitions in C |
|---|---|
| `module top(in1 , in2);` | `struct state_elements_and {` |
| `input [3:0] in1 , in2;` | ` unsigned char c; };` |
| `wire [3:0] o1, o2;` | `struct state_elements_and sand;` |
| `and A1 (in1 , in2 , o1 , o2);` | `void and(unsigned char a, unsigned char b,` |
| `and A2 (.c(o1),.d(o2),.a(o1),.b(in2));` | `unsigned char *c, unsigned char *d) {` |
| `endmodule` | ` *d = 1; sand.c = a & b;` |
| `// Module Definition` | `}` |
| `module and1(a, b, c, d);` | `void top(unsigned char in1, unsigned char in2) {` |
| `input [3:0] a, b;` | ` unsigned char o1,o2;` |
| `output [3:0] c, d;` | ` and(in1 , in2 , &o1, &o2);` |
| `reg [3:0] c;` | ` and(o1, in2 , &o1, &o2);` |
| `always @(*) begin` | `}` |
| ` c = a & b;` | `void main() {` |
| `end` | ` unsigned char in1 ,in2;` |
| `assign d = 1;` | ` top(in1 , in2);` |
| `endmodule` | `}` |

**Fig. 2.** Handling module hierarchy with I/O ports

**Procedural Assignments:** Procedural assignments are used within Verilog always and initial blocks and are of two types: *blocking* and *non-blocking*. Blocking assignments are executed in sequential order. However, the effect of blocking assignments is visible immediately, whereas the effect of non-blocking assignments is delayed until all events triggered are processed. This form of parallelism in procedural assignments are modeled in *v2c* by first storing the value of register variables in auxiliary variables in the beginning of the clock cycle. Each read access to the register variables are then replaced by these auxiliary variables. This ensures that an assignment to a register variable do not influence subsequent procedural assignments. Figure 3 illustrates the translation of procedural assignments (given at the top) to the equivalent C semantics (given at the bottom).

**Continuous Assignment:** The continuous assignment is used to assign a value to a wire. Continuous assignments are concurrent statements, which are immediately triggered when there is any change in any of the signals used on the right-hand side. The translation of continuous assignments are discussed next.

### 2.2 Dependency Analysis

*v2c* performs intra-modular dependency analysis to correctly model the dependencies between the combinatorial and sequential blocks. Let us consider the

| Non-blocking assignment | Blocking assignment | Continuous assignment |
|---|---|---|
| `reg [7:0] x,y,z;`<br>`wire in = 1'b1;`<br>`always @(posedge clk) begin`<br>`  x <= in;`<br>`  y <= x;`<br>`  z <= y;`<br>`end` | `reg [7:0] x,y,z;`<br>`wire in = 1'b1;`<br>`always @(posedge clk) begin`<br>`  x = in;`<br>`  y = x;`<br>`  z = y;`<br>`end` | `wire in;`<br>`reg a,b,t;`<br>`wire a = in;`<br>`wire c = b; wire d = c;`<br>`always @(posedge clk) begin`<br>`  b <= a;`<br>`  t <= b;`<br>`end` |
| `struct smain {`<br>`unsigned char x,y,z; } sm;`<br>`unsigned char xs,ys,zs;`<br>`_Bool in = 1;`<br>`// save register variables`<br>`xs=sm.x;ys=sm.y;zs=sm.z;`<br>`// update register variables`<br>`sm.x = in;`<br>`sm.y = xs;`<br>`sm.z = ys;` | `struct smain {`<br>`unsigned char x,y,z;}sm;`<br>`_Bool in = 1;`<br>`// clocked block`<br>`sm.x = in;`<br>`sm.y = sm.x;`<br>`sm.z = sm.y;` | `struct smain {`<br>`_Bool a,b,t; } sm;`<br>`_Bool in,c,d,as,bs,cs,ds,ts;`<br>`sm.a = in;//continuous assign`<br>`// save register variables`<br>`as=sm.a;bs=sm.b;ts=sm.t;`<br>`// clocked block`<br>`sm.b = as; sm.t = bs;`<br>`// continuous assignment`<br>`c = sm.b; d = c;` |

**Fig. 3.** Tanslation of non-blocking, blocking and continuous assignments

following three cases for dependency analysis which are demonstrated with an example in Fig. 3.

1. A variable, say $x$, appearing in continuous assignment, say $A$, is updated directly by the input signal and the same variable is read inside an always block. The continuous assignment $A$ is placed before the always block to capture any change to the input signal and subsequently propagate the updated value of $x$ to the translated always block.
2. A variable, say $x$, assigned in a continuous assignment statement, say $A$, appears in the right-hand side of another continuous assignment statement, say $B$. In this case, the variable assignment $A$ is placed before the other assignment $B$ which reads $x$.
3. A variable, say $x$, appearing in the right-hand side of a continuous assignment, say $A$, is driven by an always block. This gives an ordering where the continuous assignment is placed after the always block to capture the updated value of $x$.

For designs with inter-modular combinatorial paths or combinatorial loops, the combinatorial signals (wire variables) may settle after several executions before the next clock cycle. The combinatorial exchanges between modules depends on the stability condition for the combinatorial signals and thus it is necessary to execute the combinatorial logic until the stability condition is reached. Determining such stability condition for large circuits is hard. An alternative way to handle combinatorial exchanges between modules is by using assumptions over the signals that encode combinatorial logic in the respective modules following synthesis semantics. An example using the latter approach is given at http://www.cprover.org/hardware/v2c/.

**Bit-Precise Code Generation:** *v2c* generates a bit-precise software netlist model in C. The tool automatically handles complex bit-level operators in Verilog like bit-select or part-select operators from a vector, concatenation operators,

| Bit-select | Part-select (SystemVerilog) | Concatenation |
|---|---|---|
| **wire** [7:0] in1,in2; <br> **reg** [7:0] out1,out2; <br> out1[7:5] = in1[4:2]; <br> out2[6] = in2[4]; | **reg** [31:0] in, out; <br> **for**(i=0;i<=3;i++) **begin** <br> out[8*i +: 8]=in[8*i +: 8]; <br> **end** | **wire** [7:0] in1, in2; <br> **reg** [9:0] out; <br> out = {in2[5:2],in1[6:1]}; |
| **unsigned char** in1,in2; <br> **struct** smain { <br> **unsigned char** out1,out2; } sm; <br> sm.out1 = sm.out1 & 0x1f \| <br> (((in1 & 0x1c)>>2)<<5); <br> sm.out2 = (sm.out2 & 0xbf)\| <br> (((in2 & 0x10)>>4)<<6); | **struct** smain { <br> **unsigned int** in,out; } sm; <br> **for**(i=0;i<=3;i++) { <br> x=8*i+(8−1); y=8*i; <br> sm.out=(sm.out&!(2^31−2^y)) <br> \|(sm.in&(2^31−2^y)); } | **unsigned char** in1,in2; <br> **struct** smain { <br> **unsigned char** out; } sm; <br> sm.out = (((in2 >> 2) <br> & 0xF) << 6)\| <br> ((in1 >> 1) & 0x3F); |

**Fig. 4.** Handling bit-select, part-select from vectors and concatenation operator

reduction OR and other operators. *v2c* retains the word-level structure of the Verilog RTL and generates vectored expressions. Figure 4 shows Verilog code (at the top) and the generated C expressions (at the bottom), which are combinations of bit-wise and arithmetic operators like bit-wise OR, AND, multiplication, subtraction, shifts and other C operators.

## 3 Equivalence of Hardware and Software Netlist

We have applied *v2c* to a range of Verilog RTL circuits, which were obtained from different sources. We have observed that the translation produces the correct output. While we do not have a formal proof of correctness, experiments have shown that for property verification, valid safety properties are proven to be $k$-inductive for the same value of $k$ in the hardware and software netlist models. Conversely, for unsafe designs, the bug is found in the same cycle for both the models.

## 4 Implementation

We have implemented *v2c* in C++ on top of the *CPROVER* framework [1]. We make a pre-compiled static-binary for Linux available at http://www.cprover. org/hardware/v2c/. We also provide several benchmarks in Verilog and the corresponding software netlist models in C, which can be used for simulation, property verification or equivalence checking. Currently, *v2c* does not support multi-clock designs, transparent latches and designs with combinatorial loops.

## 5 Conclusion and Future Work

This paper presents a tool for translating Verilog RTL to C. The generated software netlist can be used as word-level representation for hardware circuits in Verilog RTL. This design representation allows us to leverage advanced software verification techniques for hardware verification. In the future, we plan to handle combinatorial feedback between modules and also support a richer subset of SystemVerilog assertions for property specification.

# References

1. Clarke, E., Kroning, D., Lerda, F.: A tool for checking ANSI-C programs. In: Jensen, K., Podelski, A. (eds.) TACAS 2004. LNCS, vol. 2988, pp. 168–176. Springer, Heidelberg (2004)
2. Greaves, D.J.: A verilog to C compiler. In: RSP, pp. 122–127. IEEE Computer Society (2000)
3. Keating, M.: The Simple Art of SoC Design. Springer, New York (2011)
4. Liu, L., Vasudevan, S.: Scaling input stimulus generation through hybrid static and dynamic analysis of RTL. ACM TODAES **20**(1), 4:1–4:33 (2014)
5. Mukherjee, R., Kroening, D., Melham, T.: Hardware verification using software analyzers. In: ISVLSI (2015)
6. Mukherjee, R., Schrammel, P., Kroening, D., Melham, T.: Unbounded safety verification for hardware using software analyzers. In: DATE (2016)

# Abstraction and Verification II

# Parameterized Compositional Model Checking

Kedar S. Namjoshi[1]([✉]) and Richard J. Trefler[2]([✉])

[1] Bell Laboratories, Nokia, Murray Hill, NJ, USA
kedar@research.bell-labs.com
[2] University of Waterloo, Waterloo, ON, Canada
trefler@cs.uwaterloo.ca

**Abstract.** The Parameterized Compositional Model Checking Problem (PCMCP) is to decide, using compositional proofs, whether a property holds for every instance of a parameterized family of process networks. Compositional analysis focuses attention on the neighborhood structure of processes in the network family. For the verification of safety properties, the PCMCP is shown to be much more tractable than the more general Parameterized Model Checking Problem (PMCP). For example, the PMCP is undecidable for ring networks while the PCMCP is decidable in polynomial time. This result generalizes to toroidal mesh networks and related networks for describing parallel architectures. Decidable models of the PCMCP are also shown for networks of control and user processes. The results are based on the demonstration of *compositional cutoffs*; that is, small instances whose compositional proofs generalize to the entire parametric family. There are, however, control-user models where the PCMCP and the PMCP are both undecidable.

## 1  Introduction

Distributed network protocols and shared-memory concurrent programs are often parameterized by the number of processes or threads in a configured instance. State explosion generally limits model checking to protocol instances that are much smaller than those that arise in practice. It becomes important, therefore, to consider the question of determining "once and for all" if the entire unbounded family of instances satisfies a specification. This is referred to as the parameterized model checking problem (PMCP). The problem is, however, generally undecidable [5].

Faced with this obstacle, much of the work to date on the PMCP has explored two avenues. One is to restrict the structure of processes or their communication

---

K.S. Namjoshi—Supported, in part, by DARPA under agreement number FA8750-12-C-0166. The U.S. Government is authorized to reproduce and distribute reprints for Governmental purposes notwithstanding any copyright notation thereon. The views and conclusions contained herein are those of the authors and should not be interpreted as necessarily representing the official policies or endorsements, either expressed or implied, of DARPA or the U.S. Government.

R.J. Trefler—Supported in part by a Natural Sciences and Engineering Research Council of Canada Discovery Grant.

M. Chechik and J.-F. Raskin (Eds.): TACAS 2016, LNCS 9636, pp. 589–606, 2016.
DOI: 10.1007/978-3-662-49674-9_39

patterns in order to obtain decidability. Such restrictions, however, can limit applications to real protocols. The second is to analyze each protocol individually, with manually chosen abstractions applied to the global state space. In contrast, we explore a new and different form of parameterized verification, which is based instead on restricting the *shape* of a correctness proof. The formulation, which is referred to as the parametric compositional model checking problem (PCMCP), asks whether a parameterized family has a *compositional proof* that the specification is met for all instances.

Compositional analysis focuses the technical problem away from that of representing global states to one of representing local, neighborhood states. One might intuitively expect this to be easier to do. Indeed, our results show that the PCMCP is much more tractable than the PMCP. The following results are for the verification of quantified safety properties. To obtain precise statements of complexity, the internal state space of a process is assumed to be finite, and independent of the parameter $n$, the number of processes in an instance.

1. For regular network families, such as the ring, torus, and cube-connected cycles, the PCMCP is decidable in polynomial time. In contrast, the PMCP is generally undecidable and decidable only under strong restrictions [9].
2. For the synchronous control-user networks of German and Sistla [13], the PCMCP is decidable in polynomial time. In contrast, deciding the PMCP requires exponential time in the size of the processes.
3. For asynchronous shared-memory networks from [11], the PCMCP is decidable in polynomial time. The PMCP is decidable but coNP-complete.
4. For distributed memory control-user networks with an index-oblivious control process (defined later), the PCMCP is decidable in polynomial time. Decidability of the PMCP is unknown.

The positive results are based on symmetry arguments that establish the existence of *compositional cutoffs*: small instances whose compositional verification induces invariants that hold for the entire family. However, the PCMCP is not always decidable: we show that for a control-user system with a non-oblivious controller, both the PMCP and the PCMCP are undecidable.

As this is a new formulation of parameterized verification, we discuss some of the implications in more depth. First, the notion of modular proof is of intrinsic interest, practically as well as mathematically. In practice, several protocols have modular proofs, a recent example is given by a verification of the AODVv2 routing protocol by the authors [24,25]. Mathematically, modular proofs (e.g., in the Owicki-Gries or assume-guarantee sense) are interesting as they limit the state information which is correlated across processes. These limits make it possible to find neighborhood symmetries which collapse the verification for an entire family on to a smaller cutoff instance. The topology of neighborhoods is usually less complicated than that of the entire graph, which simplifies verification.

Secondly, the PCMCP is an approximate form of the PMCP and could be used as such. That is, if the PCMCP answer is "yes" (there is a modular proof), then the PMCP answer must also be "yes". Given the generally lower complexity of the PCMCP, it is advantageous to try to answer that question before attempting the PMCP. In this regard, the PCMCP is a new kind of approximation: methods for approximating the PMCP, such as counter abstraction, abstract the global state space; while the PCMCP, in contrast, restricts the structure of the proof. (Other restrictions on proof structure, such as bounding proof depth, might also be worth consideration.)

Finally, the cutoff results and modularity of the PCMCP could form a new basis for the synthesis of parameterized protocols, analogous to the application of cutoff theorems for the PMCP for that purpose (cf. [17]).

## 2  Preliminaries

We base the PCMCP on the formulation of compositional reasoning for invariance by Owicki-Gries [26] and Lamport [19] (equivalently "Modular" or "Assume-guarantee" reasoning). A compositional invariant is one where each process in a process network has its own invariant assertion, which is also guaranteed to be preserved under the actions of neighboring processes. This immunity to neighborhood "interference" (as it is called) ensures that the local per-process invariants combine to form a global program invariant.

**Processes and Inductive Invariants.** A *process* $P$ is defined by a tuple $(V, I, T)$, where $V$ is a set of (typed) variables which induce a state space $S$ that is the set of all possible valuations to $V$; $I$ is a subset of $S$, the *initial set* of states, represented in logic by a predicate $I(V)$; and $T$ is a transition relation, a subset of $S \times S$, represented by a predicate $T(V, V')$, where $V'$ is a copy of $V$ describing a valuation to $V$ in the next state. The transition relation and initial condition induce a set of *reachable* states (i.e., states which are obtained from an initial state through a sequence of transitions). An *invariant* is a *predicate* (i.e., a set of states) which holds of all reachable states.

An *inductive invariant* is a predicate that includes all initial states and is closed under the transition relation. That is[1], $\theta$ is an inductive invariant of $P = (V, I, T)$ if (1) $\theta$ includes all initial states, i.e., $[I(V) \Rightarrow \theta(V)]$, and (2) $\theta$ is closed under transitions, i.e., $[\theta(V) \wedge T(V, V') \Rightarrow \theta(V')]$. To show invariance of a predicate $f$, one determines an inductive invariant $\theta$ which is a subset of $f$, i.e., $[\theta(V) \Rightarrow f(V)]$. In the sequel, we focus on inductive invariants.

**Interleaved Composition of Processes.** An asynchronous, interleaved composition of processes $P_1 = (V_1, I_1, T_1)$ and $P_2 = (V_2, I_2, T_2)$, written $P = P_1 \,/\!/\, P_2$, is defined as the process $P = (V, I, T)$, where:

- The set of variables, $V$, is $V_1 \cup V_2$. The set of *shared* variables is $V_1 \cap V_2$.
- $I$, the set of initial states, is a predicate on $V$ such that its projection on $V_1$ is in $I_1$ and the projection on $V_2$ is in $I_2$.
- The transition relation $T$ interleaves transitions of $P_1$ and $P_2$, where transitions of one process leave the internal variables of the other process unchanged. That is, $T(V, V') = (T_1(V_1, V_1') \wedge unch(V \backslash V_1)) \vee (T_2(V_2, V_2') \wedge unch(V \backslash V_2))$.

---

[1] The notation is from Dijkstra-Scholten [8]: $[\varphi]$ means that $\varphi$ is valid.

The predicate $unch(W)$ says that the values of all variables in the set $W$ are unchanged, that is, it is the predicate $(\bigwedge w : w \in W : w' = w)$.

This definition extends to compositions $P_1 \,//\, P_2 \ldots //\, P_N$ in a similar manner.

**Compositional Invariants.** There are several formulations of compositional reasoning, but all share the crucial characteristic that the reasoning centers on a process and its neighborhood. In the formulation we use here, there is a predicate, $\theta_i$, for each process $P_i$; this is a set of *local states* of $P_i$. Each local state can be written in the form $(x, y)$, where $x$ is an internal state of $P_i$ and $y$ is the state of the neighborhood of $P_i$. The *neighborhood* of a process is the set of variables which are shared between the process and other processes. (E.g., the neighborhood of a node $i$ in a ring network of size $n$ is defined by the variables shared between that node and its left neighbor, with index $(i-1) \bmod n$, and its right neighbor, with index $(i+1) \bmod n$.)

In a network of processes, the neighborhoods of processes overlap (e.g., in a ring, nodes $i$ and $(i+1) \bmod n$ share state). Hence, the natural formulation of the constraints on the $\theta$'s is through mutual induction, often referred to as (syntactically) "circular reasoning". The constraints which the $\{\theta_i\}$ predicates must satisfy to be called a *compositional invariant* are as follows.

- (init) $\theta_i$ includes the initial states of $P_i$. That is, $[I(V) \Rightarrow \theta_i(V_i)]$, and
- (step) $\theta_i$ is inductive for $P_i$. That is, $[\theta_i(V_i) \wedge T_i(V_i, V_i') \Rightarrow \theta_i(V_i')]$, and
- (non-interference) the actions of a neighboring process, $P_j$, do not falsify $\theta_i$. That is, $[\theta_i(V_i) \wedge \theta_j(V_j) \wedge T_j(V_j, V_j') \wedge unch(V \backslash V_j) \Rightarrow \theta_i(V_i')]$.

The following theorem connects compositional to global invariance:

**Theorem 1.** *If the set $\{\theta_i\}$ is a compositional invariant, then $(\forall i : \theta_i)$ is a global inductive invariant of the program $(//\, i : P_i)$.*

*Compositionality as a Fixed Point.* Let $F_i$ be the disjunction of the predicates $I$, $(\theta_i \wedge T_i)$, and $(\theta_i \wedge \theta_j \wedge T_j \wedge unch(V \backslash V_j))$ for all neighbors $j$ of $i$. The compositional constraints can be rearranged into the set of validities $\{[F_i(\theta) \Rightarrow \theta_i]\}$. Considering $\theta = (\theta_1, \theta_2, \ldots)$ as a vector in the predicate lattice ordered by implication, $F_i$ is monotone in $\theta$. By the Knaster-Tarski theorem, there is a *least* fixpoint solution, which defines the *strongest* compositional invariant. This is the limit of the sequence $X^0 = (false, false, \ldots)$, $X^{i+1} = (F_1(X^i), F_2(X^i), \ldots)$. For finite-state processes, the limit can be computed in polynomial time in the number of processes and in the size of the state spaces of each process.

*Proving Invariance.* We focus on quantified assertions of the form $(\forall i : \xi(i))$, where $\xi(i)$ is a predicate on the local state of process $i$. To compositionally prove this assertion to be an invariant, one checks the constraints:

- (adequacy) $\theta(i)$ is a subset of $\xi(i)$, for all $i$, written as $[\theta(i) \Rightarrow \xi(i)]$.

It follows that $[(\forall i : \theta(i)) \Rightarrow (\forall i : \xi(i))]$. As $(\forall i : \theta(i))$ is a global inductive invariant of the program (by Theorem 1), $(\forall i : \xi(i))$ is a program invariant.

**Parameterized Compositional Invariants.** A compositional invariant for a parameterized family is defined using an unbounded set of compositional constraints. There is a $\theta$-component for each node $i$ in each network $N$ of the family; this is denoted as $\theta_{(i,N)}$. The components must meet the previously defined constraints for compositional invariance:

- (init) $\theta_{(i,N)}$ includes the initial states of $P_{(i,N)}$,
- (step) $\theta_{(i,N)}$ is inductive for $P_{(i,N)}$, and
- (non-interference) the actions of a neighboring process $(j, N)$ in network $N$ do not falsify $\theta_{(i,N)}$.

Although the vector $\theta$ is unbounded, there is still a strongest fixpoint solution. As processes from different instances do not influence one another, this fixpoint is the collection of strongest fixpoints for each instance. The decidability results in this paper are obtained by collapsing the unbounded collection of constraints to a bounded set through the identification of local (i.e., neighborhood) symmetries. This leads to the concept of a *compositional cutoff*.

*Compositional Cutoff.* Several of the network families examined in this paper have the following property: there is a limit, say $K$, such that the strongest compositional invariants in networks of size greater than $K$ are identical (up to neighborhood isomorphism) to the strongest compositional invariants in networks of size at most $K$. We then refer to $K$ as a *compositional cutoff*.

As a concrete illustration, any pair of nodes in the family of ring networks are locally symmetric – each has one neighbor to the left and one to the right – so that the strongest compositional solutions are isomorphic across the family, and the cutoff instance for the family is the smallest ring instance, of size 2.

## 3    Rings, Tori and Other Regular Networks

We recall results connecting compositional verification to local symmetry given in [22] and use those to show that the PCMCP is decidable in polynomial time for arbitrary protocols on rings, tori and other regular networks.

**Networks.** A *network* is formally defined as a pair $(N, E)$ where $N$ is a set of *nodes* and $E$ is a set of *edges*. Processes are placed on nodes, and shared state on edges. Each edge, $e$, is associated with a set of input nodes, $ins(e) \subseteq N$ and a set of output nodes, $outs(e) \subseteq N$. For a node $n$, the set $In(n) = \{e \mid n \in outs(e)\}$ describes the input edges to $n$ and $Out(n) = \{e \mid n \in ins(e)\}$ describes the output edges for $n$. The notation $InOut(n)$ represents the union of those sets and it forms the neighborhood of $n$. We say that node $m$ *points to* node $n$ (written $m \in pt(n)$) if there is an output edge of $m$ that is also in $InOut(n)$.

**Symmetry Groupoids.** Two nodes $m$ and $n$ are locally similar, written $m \simeq_{IO} n$, if there is a bijective function $\beta$ that maps $In(m)$ to $In(n)$, and maps $Out(m)$ to $Out(n)$. I.e., the neighborhood of $m$ is isomorphic to the neighborhood of $n$ through $\beta$. Tuples of the form $(m, \beta, n)$ where $\beta$ is a witnessing bijection for

$m \simeq_{IO} n$, are called *local symmetries*. Following [14], we call this the symmetry groupoid[2] of the network and denote it by $\mathcal{G}_{IO}$.

A groupoid induces an *orbit relation*: nodes $m$ and $n$ are related if there is a groupoid element $(m, \beta, n)$. From the groupoid properties, this is an equivalence relation. The orbit relation for the symmetry groupoid is $\simeq_{IO}$.

For a local symmetry $(m, \beta, n)$, the isomorphism $\beta$ maps the neighborhood of $m$ onto the neighborhood of $n$. We now lift this definition on structure to include the processes running at $m$ and $n$. Thus $\beta$ maps a local state $(x, y)$ of $m$ to a local state $(x, \beta(y))$ of $n$ (recall that $x$ is the internal state and $y$ is the neighborhood state), and it similarly maps a local transition $((x, y), (x', y'))$ of $m$ to a local transition $((x, \beta(y)), (x', \beta(y')))$ of $n$. This is lifted to sets of states and transitions in the standard way. An assignment of processes to nodes is *valid* for $B \subseteq \mathcal{G}_{IO}$ if it respects the local symmetries in $B$: that is, for every $(m, \beta, n) \in B$, it should hold that $[T_n \equiv \beta(T_m)]$ and $[I_n \equiv \beta(I_m)]$.

**Balance.** Intuitively, as the compositional constraints for a node refer only to its neighbors, one might expect that nodes that are locally symmetric have isomorphic invariants. This is not quite true: it is also necessary for the neighbors related by the isomorphism to be (recursively) locally symmetric. That is captured in a bisimulation-like definition of *balance*.

**Definition 1 (Balance)** *([14, 22]). A balance relation $B$ is a set of local symmetries satisfying the following properties. For any $(m, \beta, n)$ in $B$:*

1. *Its inverse, $(n, \beta^{-1}, m)$, is also in $B$, and*
2. *For any $j$ which points to $m$, there is $k$ which points to $n$ and $\delta$ such that (a) $(j, \delta, k)$ is in $B$ and (b) $\beta$ and $\delta$ agree on common edges. I.e., for every edge $f$ in $InOut(j) \cap InOut(m)$, $\delta(f) = \beta(f)$.*

We say that a vector $\theta$ of per-process predicates *respects* a balance relation $B$ if for all $(m, \beta, n)$ in $B$, $[\theta_n \equiv \beta(\theta_m)]$. We can now state the main theorem connecting balance and local symmetry to compositional reasoning.

**Theorem 2** *(Symmetry Reduction) [22]. Given a balance relation, $B$, and a valid program assignment, the strongest compositional invariant $\theta^*$ respects $B$.*

That is, balanced nodes have isomorphic strongest compositional invariants. Hence, it suffices to find a balance relation that is a groupoid (there is always one such, the greatest balance relation), pick one representative in each equivalence class of its orbit and compute an invariant for that representative. The invariants for all other nodes in the class will be isomorphic by Theorem 2.

---

[2] A groupoid is roughly a group with a *partial* composition operation. The network symmetry groupoid meets the conditions required of a groupoid: (1) $(m, \iota, m)$ is a symmetry for each node $m$, where $\iota$ is the identity map; (2) if $(m, \beta, n)$ is a symmetry so is the inverse $(n, \beta^{-1}, m)$; and (3) the composition of symmetries $(m, \beta, n)$ and $(n', \gamma, o)$, given by $(m, \gamma\beta, o)$ if $n = n'$, is also a symmetry.

For example, ring networks have only $O(n)$ global symmetries [6,10] which limits global state-space reduction. However, any two ring nodes are locally symmetric and, in fact, balanced. Thus, it suffices to compute a compositional invariant for a single node, the others will be isomorphic. To generalize this observation, we recall a result connecting global symmetry with balance.

**Theorem 3** *([22]). For a network with global symmetry group $G$, the set* $\mathsf{Local}(G) = \{(m, \beta, n) \mid \beta \in G \wedge \beta(m) = n\}$ *is a balance relation and a groupoid.*

A network with a transitive global symmetry group of automorphisms (i.e., one where any pair of nodes is connected by an automorphism) is called *vertex-transitive*. We have the following corollary.

**Corollary 1.** *In a vertex-transitive network, any pair of nodes is balanced and there is a single equivalence class.*

**Proof:** Consider any pair of nodes $m, n$. As the network has a transitive symmetry group $G$, there is an automorphism $\beta$ in $G$ such that $\beta(m) = n$. In that case, the triple $(m, \beta, n)$ is in $\mathsf{Local}(G)$ by definition. As $\mathsf{Local}(G)$ is a balance relation, $m$ and $n$ are balanced and, as it is a groupoid, the orbit relation is an equivalence, so that $m$ and $n$ are in the same equivalence class of $\mathsf{Local}(G)$. Hence, there is a single equivalence class. **EndProof.**

This corollary implies that for a vertex-transitive network, it suffices to compute a compositional invariant for a single representative node in order to obtain the compositional invariant for all other nodes. Such networks are common: rings, tori, toroidal meshes, hypercube and cube-connected-cycles (CCCs) all have transitive symmetry groups. In order to extend this symmetry reduction to a whole *family* of networks, say that a family of process networks, $\mathcal{N}$, is *uniform* if (1) each network in the family is vertex-transitive, (2) for every pair $(M, N)$ of networks, there is a pair of nodes, $m \in M$ and $n \in N$, that are locally symmetric, and (3) nodes that are locally symmetric are assigned isomorphic processes, whose state space is independent of network size. We say that a quantified assertion $(\forall n, N : n \in N : \xi_{(n,N)})$ is uniform if its components are locally symmetric. I.e., for any pair of nodes $(m, M)$ and $(n, N)$ which are locally symmetric through $\beta$, it is the case that $[\beta(\xi_{(m,M)}) \equiv \xi_{(n,N)}]$.

**Theorem 4.** *For a uniform family of networks, and a uniform quantified assertion $(\forall n, N : n \in N : \xi_{(n,N)})$, the PCMCP is decidable in polynomial time.*

**Proof:** By condition (1) of uniformity and Corollary 1, any pair of nodes in a network $N$ of the family are balanced. From condition (2), any pair of nodes in the family are locally symmetric. To see this, consider a node $n$ in network $N$ and $m$ in network $M$. Then $n$ (resp., $m$) is locally symmetric to all nodes in $N$ (resp., $M$), and condition (2) says that there is a pair of nodes from $M$ and $N$ that are locally symmetric. Thus, $m$ and $n$ are locally symmetric by transitivity.

That, in turn, implies that all nodes in the family have isomorphic neighborhoods, of a size which is a constant independent of the network size. Moreover, for a network $M$, its compositional invariant can be computed on the neighborhood of a representative node $m \in M$, and similarly for network $N$ and its representative, $n \in N$. However, as $m$ and $n$ have isomorphic neighborhoods and identical processes by condition (3), those invariants are isomorphic. Therefore, it suffices to compute the strongest compositional invariant on a single representative node from a single network of the family. As the size of the neighborhood is constant, this computation is in polynomial time in the local state space of the process on the node. Hence, the strongest per-node compositional invariant can be computed in polynomial time. As this is the *strongest* assertion, the adequacy tests succeed for some invariant if, and only if, it succeeds for the strongest one.

Consider the unbounded number of adequacy tests, each having the form $[\theta_{(n,N)} \Rightarrow \xi_{(n,N)}]$. Let $(r, R)$ be a representative node for the family. It suffices to test whether $[\theta_{(r,R)} \Rightarrow \xi_{(r,R)}]$. Assuming this holds, consider any node $(n, N)$, and let $\beta$ be the local symmetry from $(r, R)$ to $(n, N)$. From the symmetry properties, it follows that $\theta_{(n,N)} \equiv \beta(\theta_{(r,R)}) \Rightarrow \beta(\xi_{(r,R)}) \equiv \xi_{(n,N)}$, so that $[\theta_{(n,N)} \Rightarrow \xi_{(n,N)}]$ is also a validity. As the invariant computation and the adequacy test can be performed on the representative node in polynomial time, the PCMCP is decidable in polynomial time. **EndProof.**

This rather abstract result has a number of practical consequences. It implies that the PCMCP is polynomial-time decidable for ring, tori, toroidal mesh, and the hypercube-like cube-connected cycles (CCC) networks. The hypercube networks are excluded as the degree of a node increases as $\log(k)$ with network size $k$. We show below that the other networks meet the uniformity condition of the theorem. Note that for each of these networks, the PMCP is undecidable, which follows from the basic result on ring networks by Apt and Kozen [5].

**Ring Networks.** The symmetry group of a ring network is transitive, as any node can be mapped to any other by an appropriate circular rotation. Furthermore, the nodes with index 0 in ring networks of size $m$ and $n$ are locally symmetric. Hence, the family of bidirectional (and unidirectional) ring networks is uniform and its PCMCP is decidable in polynomial time.

**Mesh/Toroidal Networks.** Our next examples of regular topologies are generalizations of the mesh structure. For instance, the $\mathcal{N}(k, 2)$ meshes are the tori formed by gluing together two $k$ length cycles and wrapping the rings into a cycle of length two at every interconnection point.

This parameterized topology can be extended for any $k, a \in \mathbb{N}$, where $0 < k$ and $0 < a$ so that $\mathcal{N}(k, a)$, is the parameterized set of wrap-around toroidal meshes with $a$ ring like sections, each section having $k$ nodes, each node connected to 4 neighbors. These mesh networks are examples of torus interconnection network architectures.

Here we generalize these structures to allow regular, but fixed rectangular interconnection networks. Our first example is that of a wrap around, right rectangular toroidal mesh, that contains arbitrary, parameterized numbers of nodes. For example, in $\mathcal{N}(k_1, k_2, k_3)$, the $k_i$ range over positive elements of $\mathbb{N}$. For any fixed $k_1, k_2$, and $k_3$, there are $k_3$ toroidal mesh structures with $k_1 k_2$

nodes, stacked on top of each other. For all $a \in [0..k_1 - 1]$, $b \in [0..k_2 - 1]$, $c \in [0..k_3 - 1]$, node $(a, b, c)$ of mesh $c$ is connected to nodes $(a, b, c + 1)$ and $(a, b, c - 1)$ (where addition and subtraction are modulo $k_3$). Within mesh $c$, the nodes are connected in the standard way, node $(a, b, c)$ has neighbors $(a + 1, b, c), (a - 1, b, c), (a, b + 1, c)$, and $(a, b - 1, c)$, where the addition, respectively subtraction, are modulo $k_1$, respectively $k_2$. As in the tori of early sections we require that they be wrap-around, so that, for instance, $((k_1 - 1, b, c), (0, b, c))$ is an edge in $(N(k_1, k_2, k_3), E)$. Note that for any fixed $k_1$, $k_2$ there are an unbounded number of right rectangular tori $(N(k_1, k_2, k_3), E)$.

**Theorem 5.** *Every wrap-around toroidal mesh network, $(N(k_1, k_2, k_3), E)$, is vertex transitive.*

**Proof Sketch:** Fix any of the two dimensions. Letting the third dimensional variable vary, the edge set of $(N(k_1, k_2, k_3), E)$ forms a ring. For each pair of fixed values of the two chosen dimensions, a ring is formed by the varying third dimension. Notice that for any two pairs of values the two rings are disjoint. In each of the different rings, the nodes are related by cyclic permutations. By keeping all other dimensional relationships constant, the cyclic permutations form automorphisms of the rings, and therefore the structure as a whole. Sequential composition of the ring-like automorphisms from the different dimensions, again form automorphisms of the wrap-around, right rectangular toroidal mesh structure. Thus for any $(a, b, c)$ and $(a', b', c')$ in $N(k_1, k_2, k_3)$ there is an automorphism, $\pi$, of $(N(k_1, k_2, k_3), E)$ such that $\pi(a, b, c) = (a', b', c')$. **EndSketch.**

From the definition of the mesh, each node in an instance, regardless of the instance size, has degree 6. Hence, for a uniform family of mesh networks, all nodes in different instances are locally symmetric. Therefore it follows that the PCMCP is decidable, in polynomial time, for uniform families of mesh/toroidal networks of the form $N(k_1, k_2, k_3)$. Similarly, the PCMCP is decidable in polynomial time for uniform families of mesh/toroidal networks of the form $N(k_1, a)$ for any fixed $a$. These results also generalize to uniform families of polytopes of the form $N(k_1, \ldots, k_a)$, for fixed $a$.

**Cube-Connected Cycles (CCC).** CCC [28] are a parameterized topology used to describe interconnections of processors in parallel computing networks.

For $k \geq 3$ the $CCC(k)$ has $k2^k$ nodes. The nodes are indexed by pairs $(x, y)$ where $0 \leq x < 2^k$ and $0 \leq y < k$. Each node $(x, y)$ is connected to 3 neighbors: $(x, (y + 1) \bmod k), (x, (y - 1) \bmod k)$, and $(x \oplus 2^y, y)$. Here, $\oplus$ denotes bitwise exclusive-or on binary numbers. Nodes $(x, (y + 1) \bmod k)$ and $(x, (y - 1) \bmod k)$ are on the same cycle as node $(x, y)$, while node $(x \oplus 2^y, y)$ is on a neighboring cycle. Intuitively, a CCC is obtained by taking a hypercube and expanding each node into a cycle, so that each node has only a constant out degree of 3.

**Theorem 6** *([3]). $CCC(k)$ is vertex-transitive for all $k$.*

From the definition of the CCC, each node in an instance, regardless of the instance size, has degree 3. Hence, nodes in different instances are locally symmetric. From this, it follows that the CCC is a uniform family of networks and, therefore, its PCMCP is decidable in polynomial time.

# 4   Control-User Networks

There are several decidability results on the PMCP for networks with a single distinguished process (the "control" process) and many identical "user" processes; however, the decision procedures have high complexity. We show that the PCMCP is decidable efficiently, in polynomial time in the size of these processes for two such network types. We prove decidability for a new index-oblivious model. However, we also give an undecidability result for a stronger control process.

## 4.1   Synchronized Control-User Networks

We consider the synchronized (CCS-like) control-user formulation analyzed by German and Sistla in their pioneering paper on parameterized verification [13]. For this formulation, deciding whether the control process satisfies an invariant can be done in double exponential time in the sizes of the control and user processes. We show that the PCMCP is decidable in polynomial time in the sizes of these processes. German and Sistla also define a simpler model without a control process and show that the PMCP is decidable in polynomial time, it is interesting that their algorithm[3] is identical to the least fixpoint computation of the compositional invariant, and therefore solves the PCMCP as well.

The control and user processes synchronize with CCS semantics. That is, a step of the system consists of either an internal step by one of the processes, or a pairwise synchronization of two processes (i.e., control-user or user-user). In the simplest compositional formulation, we define two invariants: $\theta_C$, which represents local states of the control process, $C$, and $\theta_U$, which represents local states of the user processes, $U$. A compositional calculation for an instance of the system with $N$ users would have invariants $\theta_{U_i}$, for each of the user processes with $i$ ranging over $1 \ldots N$. However, we choose a formulation where the user processes in each instance, and across instances, are treated alike, and therefore have a single invariant, $\theta_U$. This choice is justified by a "compositional cutoff" result based on local symmetries showing that the user invariants for instances of size 3 or more are identical.

The states in $\theta_C$ are control states, while those in $\theta_U$ are user states. As the system is built around pairwise synchronization, the interference rules are slightly different from those given in Sect. 2.

- (Initial) All initial states of $C$ are in $\theta_C$, and all initial states of $U$ are in $\theta_U$,
- (Step) If $c \in \theta_C$ and $(c, \tau, d)$ is an internal transition of $C$, then $d \in \theta_C$. Similarly, if $u \in \theta_U$ and $(u, \tau, v)$ is an internal transition of $U$, then $v \in \theta_U$.
- (Interference) If $c \in \theta_C$ and $u \in \theta_U$ and $(c, a, d)$ and $(u, \overline{a}, v)$ are transitions in $C$ and $U$ respectively, then $d \in \theta_C$ and $v \in \theta_U$. This represents control-user interference. A similar clause applies to user-user interference.

---

[3] The algorithm in [13] considers checking Linear Temporal Logic formulae on networks of processes, in contrast we restrict attention to checking safety properties.

**Theorem 7.** *The PCMCP for the synchronous control-user system is decidable in polynomial time for uniform quantified assertions.*

**Proof:** The strongest $(\theta_C, \theta_U)$ pair can be calculated by turning the compositional rules into a simultaneous least fixpoint formulation, as described in Sect. 2, and iterating until convergence. The computation time is polynomial in the number of states of $C$ and of $U$. The target invariant has the form $(\forall n, N : n \in N : \xi_{(n,N)})$, which is uniform by assumption. With the strongest compositional invariant in hand, it suffices to check adequacy for a representative user node $(r, R)$, i.e., to check $[\theta_U \Rightarrow \xi_{(r,R))}]$, which can be done in polynomial time. This suffices as, by the cutoff theorem, all other user nodes have isomorphic values of $\theta_U$, and $\xi$ is invariant under isomorphism by the uniformity requirement. Hence, the PCMCP is decidable in polynomial time. **EndProof.**

We now consider a different control-user model analyzed in [11]. Here, a system has a single control process (a "leader" in [11]) and an unbounded number of user processes (the "contributors"), that communicate only by reading and writing to a shared memory. There are no locks or atomic test-and-set actions. If the control and user processes are finite state, the PMCP is decidable and is co-NP complete [11]. In contrast, using symmetry arguments similar to those used above, the PCMCP is decidable in polynomial time.

**Theorem 8.** *The PCMCP is decidable in polynomial time for the model of asynchronous, shared-memory control-user networks and uniform assertions.*

## 4.2   Asynchronous, Distributed Memory Networks

We consider a control-user network more akin to a client-server system. The control maintains a finite, per-user state. Each user interacts with the control process through their mutually shared state, but not directly with other users. The network structure looks like a star, the control at the center and each user at the end of a spoke, with the shared control-user state along the spoke[4].

Within this general structure, many variations are possible based on the capabilities given to the controller. We show that the PCMCP itself is *undecidable* for a rather reasonable variation. The control process has two capabilities. First, it can perform a universal (dually, existential) test on its adjacent edges of the form $(\forall i : f(e_i))$ (dually, $(\exists i : f(e_i))$). Second, it can carry out a nondeterministic guarded command on its edges, of the form $([]i : f(e_i) \rightarrow e_i := v)$. This chooses an edge-state $e_i$ for which $f(e_i)$ is true, and updates it to hold a value $v$. The command blocks if no such edge can be found. Notice that all guards and actions are fully symmetric. The user processes are finite-state. Still, both the PMCP and the PCMCP are undecidable.

---

[4] Unlike the other cases, the local state space of the control process is unbounded as it has the form $(c, x)$ where $c$ is its internal state (which is bounded), and $x$ is the vector of neighboring edge-values, which can have arbitrary length.

**Theorem 9.** *Both the PMCP and the PCMCP are undecidable for this asynchronous, distributed memory control-user system.*

**Proof Sketch:** The proof is a reduction from the undecidability of halting for two-counter machines (2CMs) [21]. We show how to simulate a 2CM using the control process alone. The user processes do nothing; they have a single internal state with a skip action. **EndSketch.**

## 4.3   A Decidable Asynchronous, Distributed Memory Network

We give a positive result for the PCMCP for a restricted control process, whose actions are "oblivious" to the user indices, i.e., one cannot target a specific index. The action either does nothing (skip) or it assigns a value $v$ to all edges, written as $(Ai : e_i := v)$ (or $(Av)$ for short). This structure is inspired by that of a specific Dining Philosophers protocol over arbitrary graphs, where nodes are assigned philosophers and edges forks. A philosopher eats if it is hungry and "owns all neighboring forks" (a universal guard); after eating, it "releases all neighboring forks" (a universal action). Its compositional analysis [23] focuses on a generic graph node with an arbitrary number of neighbors. This looks like a control-user system. We now show that the PCMCP is decidable[5].

The pair of invariants $\theta_C$ and $\theta_U$ apply to the entire family, so $\theta_C$ contains local states for the control process over all instances, and $\theta_U$ contains neighborhood states for all users in all instances. A state in $\theta_U$ is a pair $(a, k)$ where $a$ is an edge value, and $k$ is a state of the user process. A state in $\theta_C$ is a pair $(c, x)$, where $c$ is an internal state of the control process, and $x$ is a vector of values for its adjacent edges. As $\theta_C$ represents local states in all instances, the length of $x$ is unbounded. We define an abstraction of the system and show that its compositional invariant is sufficiently precise to solve the PCMCP.

The abstraction is only for the control process, user processes have finite local state and are unabstracted. The abstraction is a Galois connection $(\alpha, \gamma)$, where $\alpha(c, x) = (c, s)$, where $s$ is the *set* of edge-values which are in $x$, and $\gamma(c, s) = \{(c, x) \mid \alpha(c, x) = (c, s)\}$. In the abstract system, the transitions of the control process are abstracted to operate on sets in the standard manner: the abstract version of transition $t$ is given by $\alpha \circ t \circ \gamma$. This can be simplified as follows. For a concrete transition from internal state $c$ to $c'$ with guard $g$ and action $act$, the abstract equivalent is the following:

- If $g$ is $(\exists i : f(e_i))$, then $\overline{g}$ applied to $(c, s)$ is $(\exists a : a \in s : f(a))$. Similarly, if $g$ is $(\forall i : f(e_i))$, then $\overline{g}$ applied to $(c, s)$ is $(\forall a : a \in s : f(a))$.
- If $act$ is skip, then $\overline{act}$ is skip. If $act$ is $(Ai : e_i := v)$ then $\overline{act}$ is $s := \{v\}$.

---

[5] We do not know the status of the PMCP. The powerful WQO theory of [1] appears not to apply due to the presence of universal guards. A more general assignment action, $(Ai : e_i := h(e_i))$, also preserves the decidability of PCMCP. Allowing the dual action of assigning a value to *some* edge makes the PMCP undecidable (a reduction from 2CM). We do not know whether it also makes the PCMCP undecidable.

The abstract interference transitions operate in a similar manner. We refer to the strongest compositional invariants on the abstract system as $\Delta_C$ and $\Delta_U$.

- (control-to-user) If there is an abstract transition with action $(\mathsf{A}v)$ from $(c, s)$ to $(c', s')$, and $(a, k)$ is a state in $\Delta_U$ and $a \in s$, the interference state is $(v, k)$.
- (user-to-control) If there is an abstract user transition from $(a, k)$ to $(a', k')$, and $(c, s)$ is a state in $\Delta_C$, and $a \in s$, the interference successors are $(c, s \cup \{a'\})$ (i.e., $a'$ is added to $s$) and $(c, (s \backslash \{a\}) \cup \{a'\})$ (i.e., $a'$ replaces $a$ in $s$).

The connections between $(\theta_C, \theta_U)$ and $(\Delta_C, \Delta_U)$ are laid out in the following lemmas. The first lemma says that the compositional invariants of the abstract system over-approximate those of the concrete one. This proof is by induction on the fixpoint stages of the computation of $\theta$.

**Lemma 1.** *For each state in $\theta_C$ there is an $\alpha$-related state in $\Delta_C$. Every state in $\theta_U$ is in $\Delta_U$.*

The next lemma shows that the abstraction is not too abstract. The simpler statement $\gamma(\Delta_C) = \theta_C$ need not hold, as some abstract interference transitions are matched only by concrete states with sufficiently many components.

**Lemma 2.** *For any $k$, $\Delta_U^k \subseteq \theta_U$. For every state $(c, s)$ in $\Delta_C^k$ and any $l \geq 1$, there is a related state $(c, x)$ in $\theta_C$ where for each value $a$ in $s$, at least $l$ edges of $x$ have value $a$.*

**Proof:** By induction on $k$.

**Basis (stage 0):** $\Delta_C^0$ is just the state $(c_0, \{\bot\})$, while $\Delta_U^0$ is the state $(u_0, \bot)$, where $c_0$ and $u_0$ are the initial states of the control and user process. So $\Delta_U^0 = \theta_U^0$. By definition, $\theta_C^0$ consists of all states of the form $(c_0, x)$ where $x$ is a vector of $\bot$ entries. Hence, the hypothesis holds for $\Delta_C^0$.

**Control Step (stage $k + 1$):** Consider an abstract state $(c', s')$ of stage $k + 1$ obtained through a step by $C$ from a state $(c, s)$ at stage $k$. We consider the various step transitions separately. We use the notation $\Sigma(x)$ to represent the set of values on the edge vector $x$. First, note that for any $(c, x)$ related by $\gamma$ to $(c, s)$, a concrete transition guard is enabled at $(c, x)$ if and only if the corresponding abstract guard is enabled at $(c, s)$, because $\Sigma(x) = s$. Hence, we can focus on the effect of the actions.

(1) the action is "skip". Then $s' = s$. Consider any $l > 0$. By inductive hypothesis, there is a state $(c, x)$ related to $(c, s)$ where $x$ has at least $l$ components with value $a$ for all $a$ in $s$. Construct the state $(c', x)$. This is a step-successor of $(c, x)$ by the skip action, so it is in $\theta_C$ by closure under step. As $s' = s$, the vector $x$ in $(c', x)$ satisfies the condition required of $l$.

(2) the action is an $(\mathsf{A}v)$ action. Then $s' = \{v\}$. Consider any $l > 0$. By the inductive hypothesis, there is a state $(c, x)$ related to $(c, s)$ by $\gamma$, with at least $l$ components for $x$. Let $(c', x')$ be its successor with the $\mathsf{A}v$ action. Then this state belongs to $\theta_C$ and $x'$ is a vector of $v$-values of length at least $l$, so it satisfies the condition required.

**User Step (stage $k+1$):** Consider an abstract state $(a', m')$ of stage $k+1$ obtained through a step by $U$ from a state $(a, m)$ at stage $k$. As $(a, m)$ is in $\theta_U$ by assumption, the state $(a', m')$ is also in $\theta_U$ by closure under step transitions.

**User-to-Control Interference (stage $k+1$):** Suppose there is a user transition from $(a, m)$ to $(a', m')$, and $(c, s)$ is a state in $\Delta_C^k$ with $a \in s$. There are two interference successors: $(c, s \cup \{a'\})$ and $(c, (s \backslash \{a\}) \cup \{a'\})$.

Consider the first successor. Let $l > 0$. By the inductive hypothesis, there is a state $(c, x)$ in $\gamma(c, s)$ and in $\theta_C$, where $x$ has at least $2l$ components with value $w$ for every $w$ in $s$. Apply a sequence of $l$ concrete interference steps to $x$, each changing one of the components in $x$ with value "$a$" to "$a'$". The end state, $(c, x')$, is in $\theta_C$, by closure under interference. Notice that $\Sigma(x') = s \cup \{a'\}$ by construction, and that every value in $x'$ is replicated at least $l$ times. Hence, the inductive hypothesis holds for the first successor.

Now consider the second successor, and let $l > 0$. By the inductive hypothesis, there is a state $(c, x)$ in $\gamma(c, s)$ and in $\theta_C$, where $x$ has at least $l$ components with value $w$ for every $w$ in $S$. Apply a sequence of concrete interference steps to $x$, each changing one of the $a$ components in $x$ to $a'$ until all $a$-values are converted to $a'$. The result of this sequence, $(c, x')$, is in $\theta_C$, by closure under interference. Notice that $\Sigma(x') = s \backslash \{a\} \cup \{a'\}$ by construction, and that every value in $x'$ is replicated at least $l$ times. Hence, the inductive hypothesis holds for the second successor.

**Control-to-User Interference (stage $k+1$):** Consider an $(Av)$ abstract transition from $(c, s)$ to $(c', s')$ in $\Delta_C^k$, let $(a, k)$ be in $\Delta_U^k$, with $a \in s$. Let $(v, k)$ be the interference state. By inductive assumption, there is a state $(c, x)$ in $\gamma(c, s)$ which is in $\theta_C$, and therefore an $(Av)$ successor $(c', x')$ that is in $\gamma(c', s')$ and in $\theta_C$. Also by the inductive assumption, the state $(a, k)$ is in $\theta_U$. Hence, there is a matching interference transition in the concrete system, so that $(v, k)$ must be in $\theta_U$, by closure under interference. **EndProof.**

**Theorem 10.** *The PCMCP is decidable for this control-user system for properties on the internal state of the control process.*

**Proof:** The decision procedure is to (1) construct $\Delta_U$ and $\Delta_C$ through the standard fixpoint calculation; then (2) to check if all states of $\Delta_C$ satisfy the invariant $\varphi$. (Note that $\varphi$ is a predicate on the internal state of $C$.)

Soundness: We show that all states of $\theta_C$ also satisfy $\varphi$. By way of contradiction, suppose there is a state $(c, x)$ in $\theta_C$ for which $\varphi(c)$ is false. By Lemma 1, there is an $\alpha$-related state $(c, s)$ in $\Delta_C$, so the check in step (2) would not succeed, a contradiction.

Completeness: If there is a compositional proof of $\varphi$, then, as $\theta$ is the strongest compositional invariant, all states $(c, x)$ in $\theta_C$ must satisfy $\varphi(c)$. Consider a state $(c, s)$ in $\Delta_C$. By Lemma 2, there is a state $(c, x)$ in $\theta_C$ which is $\alpha$-related to $(c, s)$. Hence, $(c, s)$ satisfies $\varphi(c)$ as well, so step (2) succeeds. **EndProof.**

The complexity of calculating $\Delta$ is polynomial in the number of internal states of the control and user processes, and exponential in the number of edge values.

# 5    Related Work and Conclusions

Analysis questions for families of regular networks running locally symmetric progrrams were studied. In particular, the algorithms introduced here are designed to decide whether all processes in a protocol family satisfy local safety properties expressed as local invariants. This form of local invariant analysis is related to the global invariant analysis techniques studied in [20]. The focus on local reasoning allows for relatively efficient analysis, given that the processes and neighborhoods are all finite state. For the protocols studied here, the local symmetry conditions ensure that all processes of the parametrized family are locally symmetric.

The work in [29] and [30] uses satisfiability modulo theories in the design of parametrized reasoning techniques for systems of many processes. That work provides semi-decision procedures and is designed for situations where the many different process types may not be locally (or globally) symmetric.

We have shown that by restricting attention to modular proofs, parameterized verification problems become simpler and more decidable. There are several positive results on the PMCP, however they require limits on process structure or communication patterns. Examples are the requirement of a single token for a token-ring [9] – two tokens result in undecidability – and the requirement of a well-quasi-ordered global state set and monotonic transition functions in [1]. Modular proofs create a number of advantages. First, there is less need to constrain process structure or communication. Second, compositional analysis naturally splits a global state into a number of local process neighborhoods, which are considered more or less independently. As neighborhood structure is typically simpler than global structure, this suggests that the decision problem should be easier. The results in this paper show that to be the case.

The PCMCP requires a choice of the modular proof system. We have considered the Owicki-Gries kind of proof system, based on local invariance. This is known to be incomplete, in that it may be necessary to expose auxiliary state in order to obtain a correctness proof. A fascinating question for future work is to consider variants of the PCMCP which search for modular proofs with limits on auxiliary state (e.g., "at most $k$ bits of auxiliary state"). Alternative modular proof systems are based on auxiliary automata (which implicitly include auxiliary state) as in [4,18]. The shape of these proof rules is usually as follows: in order to show $P_1 || P_2 \models \varphi$, one finds auxiliary automata $A_1$ and $A_2$ such that $P_1 || A_2 \preceq A_1$, $P_2 || A_1 \preceq A_2$, and $A_1 || A_2 \models \varphi$, where $\preceq$ is usually the simulation pre-order, or language inclusion. The PCMCP formulation for this strategy would be to decide whether there are automata $A_1, A_2, \ldots$ which meet the conditions of such a rule.

Motivation for introducing the PCMCP as a decision problem also comes from results on approximate procedures for obtaining parameterized proofs, several of which are based on localized analysis. For instance, environment abstraction methods [7] analyze a process along with an abstraction of its environment;

the method of invisible invariants [27] and invisible ranking [12] generalizes invariants and rank functions from small instances to the parameterized family; and the work in [2] uses abstract interpretation on views, typically single processes or pairs of processes, to obtain a parameterized invariant. In our own work [22–24] we have used compositional methods along with localized symmetry and abstraction to build parametric proofs of protocols or families. By turning from such approximate constructions to a decision problem, the PCMCP offers a different perspective on the parameterized verification question.

Our results on the decidability of the PCMCP in the cases of mesh and CCC architectures cover two forms of parallel communication architectures. In the future, we plan to investigate PCMCP approaches for related architectures, including hypercubes (c.f. [16,31]) and Message Passing Interface designs that are built on mesh architectures (c.f. [15,32,33]).

There are several promising directions to pursue. One that has already been mentioned is to strengthen the modular reasoning methods by allowing for auxiliary state and extending the decision procedures to liveness properties. Another is to examine whether abstraction methods, such as those developed in Sect. 4.3, lead to decision procedures for regular networks such as hypercubes where the degree of a node depends on the parameter $n$. A third direction is to explore other constraints on proof structure, such as depth or context-switch bounds.

# References

1. Abdulla, P.A., Cerans, K., Jonsson, B., Tsay, Y.-K.: General decidability theorems for infinite-state systems. In: LICS, pp. 313–321. IEEE Computer Society (1996)
2. Abdulla, P.A., Haziza, F., Holík, L.: All for the price of few. In: Giacobazzi, R., Berdine, J., Mastroeni, I. (eds.) VMCAI 2013. LNCS, vol. 7737, pp. 476–495. Springer, Heidelberg (2013)
3. Akers, S.B., Krishnamurthy, B.: A group-theoretic model for symmetric interconnection networks. IEEE Trans. Comput. 38(4), 555–566 (1989)
4. Alur, R., Henzinger, T.: Reactive modules. In: IEEE LICS (1996)
5. Apt, K.R., Kozen, D.: Limits for automatic verification of finite-state concurrent systems. Inf. Process. Lett. 22(6), 307–309 (1986)
6. Clarke, E., Enders, R., Filkorn, T., Jha, S.: Exploiting symmetry in temporal logic model checking. Formal Methods Syst. Des. 9(1/2), 77–104 (1996)
7. Clarke, E., Talupur, M., Veith, H.: Environment abstraction for parameterized verification. In: Emerson, E.A., Namjoshi, K.S. (eds.) VMCAI 2006. LNCS, vol. 3855, pp. 126–141. Springer, Heidelberg (2006)
8. Dijkstra, E., Scholten, C.: Predicate Calculus and Program Semantics. Springer, New York (1990)
9. Emerson, E., Namjoshi, K.: Reasoning about rings. In: ACM Symposium on Principles of Programming Languages (1995)
10. Emerson, E., Sistla, A.: Symmetry and model checking. Formal Methods in System Design 9(1/2), 105–131 (1996)
11. Esparza, J., Ganty, P., Majumdar, R.: Parameterized verification of asynchronous shared-memory systems. In: Sharygina, N., Veith, H. (eds.) CAV 2013. LNCS, vol. 8044, pp. 124–140. Springer, Heidelberg (2013)

12. Fang, Y., Piterman, N., Pnueli, A., Zuck, L.D.: Liveness with Invisible Ranking. In: Steffen, B., Levi, G. (eds.) VMCAI 2004. LNCS, vol. 2937, pp. 223–238. Springer, Heidelberg (2004)
13. German, S., Sistla, A.: Reasoning about systems with many processes. J. ACM **39**(3), 675–735 (1992)
14. Golubitsky, M., Stewart, I.: Nonlinear dynamics of networks: the groupoid formalism. Bull. Amer. Math. Soc. **43**, 305–364 (2006)
15. Gopalakrishnan, G., Kriby, R.M., Siegel, S.F., Thakur, R., Gropp, W., Lusk, E., De Supinski, B.R., Schulz, M., Bronevetsky, G.: Formal analysis of MPI-based parallel programs. Commun. of the ACM **54**, 82–91 (2011)
16. Hayes, J.P., Mudge, T.N., Stout, Q.F., Colley, S., Palmer, J.: Architecture of a hypercube supercomputer. In: Conference on Parallel Processing, pp. 653–660 (1986)
17. Jacobs, S., Bloem, R.: Parameterized synthesis. Logical Methods Comput. Sci. **10**(1), 1–29 (2014)
18. Kurshan, R.: Computer-Aided Verification of Coordinating Processes: TheAutomata-Theoretic Approach. Princeton University Press, Princeton (1994)
19. Lamport, L.: Proving the correctness of multiprocess programs. IEEE Trans. Softw. Eng. **3**(2), 125–143 (1977)
20. Manna, Z., Pnueli, A.: Temporal Verification of Reactive Systems: Safety. Springer, New York (1995)
21. Minsky, M.: Computation: finite and infinite machines. Prentice-Hall, Englewood Cliffs (1967)
22. Namjoshi, K.S., Trefler, R.J.: Local symmetry and compositional verification. In: Kuncak, V., Rybalchenko, A. (eds.) VMCAI 2012. LNCS, vol. 7148, pp. 348–362. Springer, Heidelberg (2012)
23. Namjoshi, K.S., Trefler, R.J.: Uncovering symmetries in irregular process networks. In: Giacobazzi, R., Berdine, J., Mastroeni, I. (eds.) VMCAI 2013. LNCS, vol. 7737, pp. 496–514. Springer, Heidelberg (2013)
24. Namjoshi, K.S., Trefler, R.J.: Analysis of dynamic process networks. In: Baier, C., Tinelli, C. (eds.) TACAS 2015. LNCS, vol. 9035, pp. 164–178. Springer, Heidelberg (2015)
25. Namjoshi, K.S., Trefler, R.J.: Loop freedom in AODVv2. In: Graf, S., Viswanathan, M. (eds.) Formal Techniques for Distributed Objects, Components, and Systems. LNCS, vol. 9039, pp. 98–112. Springer, Heidelberg (2015)
26. Owicki, S.S., Gries, D.: Verifying properties of parallel programs: An axiomatic approach. Commun. ACM **19**(5), 279–285 (1976)
27. Pnueli, A., Ruah, S., Zuck, L.D.: Automatic deductive verification with invisible invariants. In: Margaria, T., Yi, W. (eds.) TACAS 2001. LNCS, vol. 2031, pp. 82–97. Springer, Heidelberg (2001)
28. Preparata, F.P., Vuillemin, J.: The cube-connected cycles: a versatile network for parallel computation. CACM **24**(5), 300–309 (1981)
29. Sánchez, A., Sánchez, C.: LEAP: a tool for the parametrized verification of concurrent datatypes. In: Biere, A., Bloem, R. (eds.) CAV 2014. LNCS, vol. 8559, pp. 620–627. Springer, Heidelberg (2014)
30. Sanchez, A., Sanchez, C.: Parametrized invariance for infinite state processes. Acta Informatica **52**(6), 525–557 (2015)
31. Seitz, C.L.: The cosmic cube. Commun. ACM **28**, 22–33 (1985)

32. Siegel, S.F., Avrunin, G.S.: Verification of MPI-based software for scientific computation. In: Graf, S., Mounier, L. (eds.) SPIN 2004. LNCS, vol. 2989, pp. 286–303. Springer, Heidelberg (2004)
33. Siegel, S.F., Gopalakrishnan, G.: Formal analysis of message passing. In: Jhala, R., Schmidt, D. (eds.) VMCAI 2011. LNCS, vol. 6538, pp. 2–18. Springer, Heidelberg (2011)

# An $O(m \log n)$ Algorithm for Stuttering Equivalence and Branching Bisimulation

Jan Friso Groote[✉] and Anton Wijs

Department of Mathematics and Computer Science, Eindhoven University of Technology, P.O. Box 513, 5600 MB Eindhoven, The Netherlands
{J.F.Groote,A.J.Wijs}@tue.nl

**Abstract.** We provide a new algorithm to determine stuttering equivalence with time complexity $O(m \log n)$, where $n$ is the number of states and $m$ is the number of transitions of a Kripke structure. This algorithm can also be used to determine branching bisimulation in $O(m(\log |Act| + \log n))$ time. Theoretically, our algorithm substantially improves upon existing algorithms which all have time complexity $O(mn)$ [2,3,9]. Moreover, it has better or equal space complexity. Practical results confirm these findings showing that our algorithm can outperform existing algorithms with orders of magnitude, especially when the sizes of the Kripke structures are large.

## 1 Introduction

Stuttering equivalence [4] and branching bisimulation [8] were proposed as alternatives to Milner's weak bisimulation [13]. They are very close to weak bisimulation, with as essential difference that all states in the mimicking sequence $\tau^* a \tau^*$ must be related to either the state before or directly after the $a$ from the first system. This means that branching bisimulation and stuttering equivalence are slightly stronger notions than weak bisimulation.

In [9] an $O(mn)$ time algorithm was proposed for stuttering equivalence and branching bisimulation, where $m$ is the number of transitions and $n$ is the number of states in either a Kripke structure (for stuttering equivalence) or a labelled transition system (for branching bisimulation). We refer to this algorithm as GV. It is based upon the $O(mn)$ algorithm for bisimulation equivalence in [11]. Both algorithms require $O(m+n)$ space. They calculate for each state whether it is bisimilar to another state.

The basic idea of the algorithms of [9,11] is to partition the set of states into blocks. States that are bisimilar always reside in the same block. Whenever there are some states in a block $B'$ from which a transition is possible to some block $B$ and there are other states in $B'$ from which such a step is not possible, $B'$ is split accordingly. Whenever no splitting is possible anymore, the partition is called stable, and two states are in the same block iff they are bisimilar.

There have been some attempts to come up with improvements of GV. The authors of [2] observed that GV only splits a block in two parts at a time.

© Springer-Verlag Berlin Heidelberg 2016
M. Chechik and J.-F. Raskin (Eds.): TACAS 2016, LNCS 9636, pp. 607–624, 2016.
DOI: 10.1007/978-3-662-49674-9_40

They proposed to split a block in as many parts as possible, reducing moving states and transitions to new blocks. Their worst case time and space complexities are worse than that of GV, especially the space complexity $O(mn)$, but in practice this algorithm can outperform GV. In [3], the space complexity is brought back to $O(m+n)$. A technique to be performed on Graphics Processing Units based on both GV and [2,3] is proposed in [19]. This improves the required runtime considerably by employing parallelism, but it does not imply any improvement to the single-threaded algorithm.

In [15] an $O(m \log n)$ algorithm is proposed for strong bisimulation as an improvement upon the algorithm of [11]. The core idea for this improvement is described as "process the smaller half" [1]. Whenever a block is split in two parts the amount of work must be contributed to the size of the smallest resulting block. In such a case a state is only involved in the process of splitting if it resides in a block at most half the size of the block it was previously in when involved in splitting. This means that a state can never be involved in more than $\log_2 n$ splittings. As the time used in each state is proportional to the number of incoming or outgoing transitions in that state, the total required time is $O(m \log n)$.

In this paper we propose the first algorithm for stuttering equivalence and branching bisimulation in which the "process the smaller half"-technique is used. By doing so, we can finally confirm the conjecture in [9] that such an improvement of GV is conceivable. Moreover, we achieve an even lower complexity, namely $O(m \log n)$, than conjectured in [9] by applying the technique twice, the second time for handling the presence of inert transitions. First we establish whether a block can be split by combining the approach regarding bottom states from GV with the detection approach in [15]. Subsequently, we use the "process the smaller half"-technique again to split a block by only traversing transitions in a time proportional to the size of the smallest subblock. As it is not known which of the two subblocks is smallest, the transitions of the two subblocks are processed alternatingly, such that the total processing time can be contributed to the smallest block. For checking behavioural equivalences, applying such a technique is entirely new. We are only aware of a similar approach for an algorithm in which the smallest bottom strongly connected component of a graph needs to be found [5].

Compared to checking other equivalences the existing algorithms for branching bisimulation/stuttering equivalence were already known to be practically very efficient. This is the reason that they are being used in multiple explicit-state model checkers, such as CADP [7], the MCRL2 toolset [10] and TVT [18]. In particular they are being used as preprocessing steps for other equivalences (weak bisimulation, trace based equivalences) that are much harder to compute. For weak bisimulation recently an $O(mn)$ algorithm has been devised [12,16], but until that time an expensive transitive closure operation of at best $O(n^{2.373})$ was required. The improvements of our new algorithm are not restricted to stuttering equivalence and branching bisimulation alone, but they can also impact the computation time of all other behavioural equivalences.

Although our algorithm theoretically outperforms its predecessors substantially, we wanted to know whether it would also do so in practice. We find that for dedicated examples our algorithm lives up to its theoretical improvement outperforming the existing algorithms in accordance with the theory. For practical examples we see that our algorithm can always match the best running times of existing algorithms, but especially when the Kripke structures and transition systems get large, our algorithm tends to outperform existing algorithms with orders of magnitude.

## 2   Preliminaries

We introduce Kripke structures and (divergence-blind) stuttering equivalence. In Sect. 6 we explain branching bisimulation and its application to labelled transition systems.

**Definition 1.** *A Kripke structure is a four tuple $K = (S, AP, \rightarrow, L)$, where*

1. *$S$ is a finite set of states.*
2. *$AP$ is a finite set of atomic propositions.*
3. *$\rightarrow \subseteq S \times S$ is a total transition relation, i.e., for each $s \in S$ there is an $s' \in S$ s.t. $s \rightarrow s'$.*
4. *$L : S \rightarrow 2^{AP}$ is a state labelling.*

We use $n = |S|$ for the number of states and $m = |\rightarrow|$ for the number of transitions. For a set of states $B \subseteq S$, we write $s \rightarrow_B s'$ for $s \rightarrow s'$ and $s' \in B$.

**Definition 2.** *Let $K = (S, AP, \rightarrow, L)$ be a Kripke structure. A symmetric relation $R \subseteq S \times S$ is a divergence-blind stuttering bisimulation iff for all $s, t \in S$ such that $sRt$:*

1. *$L(s) = L(t)$.*
2. *for all $s' \in S$ if $s \rightarrow s'$, then there are $t_0, \ldots, t_k \in S$ for some $k \in \mathbb{N}$ such that $t = t_0$, $sRt_i$, $t_i \rightarrow t_{i+1}$, and $s'Rt_k$ for all $i < k$.*

*We say that two states $s, t \in S$ are divergence-blind stuttering equivalent, notation $s \underset{dbs}{\leftrightarrow} t$, iff there is a divergence-blind stuttering equivalence relation $R$ such that $sRt$.*

An important property of divergence-blind stuttering equivalence is that if states on a loop all have the same label then all these states are divergence-blind stuttering equivalent. We define stuttering equivalence in terms of divergence-blind stuttering equivalence using the following Kripke structure.

**Definition 3.** *Let $K = (S, AP, \rightarrow, L)$ be a Kripke structure. Define the Kripke structure $K_d = (S \cup \{s_d\}, AP \cup \{d\}, \rightarrow_d, L_d)$ where $d$ is an atomic proposition not occurring in $AP$ and $s_d$ is a fresh state not occurring in $S$. Furthermore,*

1. *$\rightarrow_d = \rightarrow \cup \{\langle s, s_d \rangle \mid s$ is on a cycle of states all labelled with $L(s)$, or $s = s_d\}$.*
2. *For all $s \in S$ we define $L_d(s) = L(s)$ and $L_d(s_d) = \{d\}$.*

*States $s, t \in S$ are stuttering equivalent, notation $s \rightleftharpoons_s t$ iff there is a divergence-blind stuttering bisimulation relation $R$ on $S_d$ such that $sRt$.*

Note that an algorithm for divergence-blind stuttering equivalence can also be used to determine stuttering equivalence by employing only a linear time and space transformation. Therefore, we only concentrate on an algorithm for divergence-blind stuttering equivalence.

## 3    Partitions and Splitters: A Simple Algorithm

Our algorithms perform partition refinement of an initial partition containing the set of states $S$. A *partition* $\pi = \{B_i \subseteq S \mid 1 \leq i \leq k\}$ is a set of non empty subsets such that $B_i \cap B_j = \emptyset$ for all $1 \leq i < j \leq k$ and $S = \bigcup_{1 \leq i \leq k} B_i$. Each $B_i$ is called a *block*.

We call a transition $s \to s'$ *inert w.r.t.* $\pi$ iff $s$ and $s'$ are in the same block $B \in \pi$. We say that a partition $\pi$ *coincides* with divergence-blind stuttering equivalence when $s \rightleftharpoons_{dbs} t$ iff there is a block $B \in \pi$ such that $s, t \in B$. We say that a partition *respects* divergence-blind stuttering equivalence iff for all $s, t \in S$ if $s \rightleftharpoons_{dbs} t$ then there is some block $B \in \pi$ such that $s, t \in B$. The goal of the algorithm is to calculate a partition that coincides with divergence-blind stuttering equivalence. This is done starting with the initial partition $\pi_0$ consisting of blocks $B$ satisfying that if $s, t \in B$ then $L(s) = L(t)$. Note that this initial partition respects divergence-blind stuttering equivalence.

We say that a partition $\pi$ is *cycle-free* iff for each block $B \in \pi$ there is no state $s \in B$ such that $s \to_B s_1 \to_B \cdots \to_B s_k \to s$ for some $k \in \mathbb{N}$. It is easy to make the initial partition $\pi_0$ cycle-free by merging all states on a cycle in each block into a single state. This preserves divergence-blind stuttering equivalence and can be performed in linear time employing a standard algorithm to find strongly connected components [1].

The initial partition is refined until it coincides with divergence-blind stuttering equivalence. Given a block $B'$ of the current partition and the union $\boldsymbol{B}$ of some of the blocks in the partition, we define

$$split(B', \boldsymbol{B}) = \{s_0 \in B' \mid \exists k \in \mathbb{N}, s_1, .., s_k \in S . s_i \to s_{i+1}, s_i \in B' \text{ for all } i < k \wedge s_k \in \boldsymbol{B}\}$$
$$cosplit(B', \boldsymbol{B}) = B' \setminus split(B', \boldsymbol{B}).$$

Note that if $B' \subseteq \boldsymbol{B}$, then $split(B', \boldsymbol{B}) = B'$. It is common to split blocks under single blocks, i.e., $\boldsymbol{B}$ corresponding with a single block $B \in \pi$ [9,11]. However, as indicated in [15], it is required to split under the union of some of the blocks in $\pi$ to obtain an $O(m \log n)$ algorithm. We refer to such groups of blocks as *constellations*. In Sect. 4, we use constellations consisting of more than one block when splitting.

We say that a block $B'$ is *unstable* under $\boldsymbol{B}$ iff $split(B', \boldsymbol{B}) \neq \emptyset$ and $cosplit(B', \boldsymbol{B}) \neq \emptyset$. A partition $\pi$ is *unstable* under $\boldsymbol{B}$ iff there is at least one $B' \in \pi$ which is unstable under $\boldsymbol{B}$. If $\pi$ is not unstable under $\boldsymbol{B}$ then it is called *stable under* $\boldsymbol{B}$. If $\pi$ is stable under all $\boldsymbol{B}$, then it is simply called stable.

A *refinement* of $B' \in \pi$ under $B$ consists of two new blocks $split(B', B)$ and $cosplit(B', B)$. A partition $\pi'$ is a refinement of $\pi$ under $B$ iff all unstable blocks $B' \in \pi$ have been replaced by new blocks $split(B', B)$ and $cosplit(B', B)$.

The following lemma expresses that if a partition is stable then it coincides with divergence-blind stuttering equivalence. It also says that during refinement, the encountered partitions respect divergence-blind stuttering equivalence and remain cycle-free.

**Lemma 1.** *Let* $K = (S, AP, \rightarrow, L)$ *be a Kripke structure and* $\pi$ *a partition of* $S$.

1. *For all states* $s, t \in S$, *if* $s, t \in B$ *with* $B$ *a block of the partition* $\pi$, $\pi$ *is stable, and a refinement of the initial partition* $\pi_0$, *then* $s \underset{dbs}{\leftrightarrow} t$.
2. *If* $\pi$ *respects divergence-blind stuttering equivalence then any refinement of* $\pi$ *under the union of some of the blocks in* $\pi$ *also respects it.*
3. *If* $\pi$ *is a cycle-free partition, then any refinement of* $\pi$ *is also cycle-free.*

*Proof.* 1. We show that if $\pi$ is a stable partition, the relation $R = \{\langle s, t \rangle \mid s, t \in B, \ B \in \pi\}$ is a divergence-blind stuttering equivalence. It is clear that $R$ is symmetric. Assume $sRt$. Obviously, $L(s) = L(t)$ because $s, t \in B$ and $B$ refines the initial partition. For the second requirement of divergence-blind stuttering equivalence, suppose $s \rightarrow s'$. There is a block $B'$ such that $s' \in B'$. As $\pi$ is stable, it holds for $t$ that $t = t_0 \rightarrow t_1 \rightarrow \cdots \rightarrow t_k$ for some $k \in \mathbb{N}$, $t_0, \ldots, t_{k-1} \in B$ and $t_k \in B'$. This clearly shows that for all $i < k$ $sRt_i$, and $s'Rt_k$. So, $R$ is a divergence-blind stuttering equivalence, and therefore it holds for all states $s, t \in S$ that reside in the same block of $\pi$ that $s \underset{dbs}{\leftrightarrow} t$.
2. The second part can be proven by reasoning towards a contradiction. Let us assume that a partition $\pi'$ that is a refinement of $\pi$ under $B$ does not respect divergence-blind stuttering equivalence, although $\pi$ does. Hence, there are states $s, t \in S$ with $s \underset{dbs}{\leftrightarrow} t$ and a block $B' \in \pi$ with $s, t \in B'$ and $s$ and $t$ are in different blocks in $\pi'$. Given that $\pi'$ is a refinement of $\pi$ under $B$, $s \in split(B', B)$ and $t \in cosplit(B', B)$ (or vice versa, which can be proven similarly). By definition of $split$, there are $s_1, \ldots, s_{k-1} \in B'$ $(k \in \mathbb{N})$ and $s_k \in B$ such that $s \rightarrow s_1 \rightarrow \cdots \rightarrow s_k$. Then, either $k = 0$ and $B' \subseteq B$, but then $t \notin cosplit(B', B)$. Or $k > 0$, and since $s \underset{dbs}{\leftrightarrow} t$, there are $t_1, \ldots, t_{l-1} \in B'$ $(l \in \mathbb{N})$ and $t_l \in B$ such that $t \rightarrow t_1 \rightarrow \cdots \rightarrow t_l$ with $s_i R t_j$ for all $1 \leq i < k$, $1 \leq j < l$ and $s_k R t_l$. This means that we have $t \in split(B', B)$, again contradicting that $t \in cosplit(B', B)$.
3. If $\pi$ is cycle-free, this property is straightforward, since splitting any block of $\pi$ will not introduce cycles. $\qquad\square$

This suggests the following simple algorithm which has time complexity $O(mn)$ and space complexity $O(m+n)$, which was essentially presented in [9].

$$\boxed{\begin{array}{l} \pi := \pi_0, \text{ i.e., the initial partition;} \\ \textbf{while } \pi \text{ is unstable under some } B \in \pi \\ \quad \pi := \text{refinement of } \pi \text{ under } B; \end{array}}$$

It is an invariant of this algorithm that $\pi$ respects divergence-blind stuttering equivalence and $\pi$ is cycle-free. In particular, $\pi = \pi_0$ satisfies this invariant initially. If $\pi$ is not stable, a refinement under some block $B$ exists, splitting at least one block. Therefore, this algorithm finishes in at most $n-1$ steps as during each iteration of the algorithm the number of blocks increases by one, and the number of blocks can never exceed the number of states. When the algorithm terminates, $\pi$ is stable and therefore, two states are divergence-blind stuttering equivalent iff they are part of the same block in the final partition. This end result is independent of the order in which splitting took place.

In order to see that the time complexity of this algorithm is $O(mn)$, we must show that we can detect that $\pi$ is unstable and carry out splitting in time $O(m)$. The crucial observation to efficiently determine whether a partition is stable stems from [9] where it was shown that it is enough to look at the bottom states of a block, which always exist for each block because the partition is cycle-free. The *bottom states* of a block are those states that do not have an outgoing inert transition, i.e., a transition to a state in the same block. They are defined by

$$bottom(B) = \{s \in B \mid \text{there is no state } s' \in B \text{ such that } s \to s'\}.$$

The following lemma presents the crucial observation concerning bottom states.

**Lemma 2.** *Let $K = (S, AP, \to, L)$ be a Kripke structure and $\pi$ be a cycle-free partition of its states. Partition $\pi$ is unstable under union $\boldsymbol{B}$ of some of the blocks in $\pi$ iff there is a block $B' \in \pi$ such that*

$$split(B', \boldsymbol{B}) \neq \emptyset \text{ and } bottom(B') \cap split(B', \boldsymbol{B}) \subset bottom(B').$$

*Here $\subset$ is meant to be a strict subset.*

*Proof.* $\Rightarrow$ If $\pi$ is unstable, then $split(B', \boldsymbol{B}) \neq \emptyset$ and $split(B', \boldsymbol{B}) \neq B'$. The first conjunct corresponds with the first condition. If $split(B', \boldsymbol{B}) \neq B'$, there are states $s \notin split(B', \boldsymbol{B})$. As the blocks $B' \in \pi$ do not have cycles, consider such an $s \notin split(B', \boldsymbol{B})$ with a smallest distance to a state $s_k \in bottom(B')$, i.e., $s \to s_1 \to \cdots \to s_k$ with all $s_i \in B'$. If $s$ itself is an element of $bottom(B')$, the second part of the right hand side of the lemma follows. Assume $s \notin bottom(B')$, there is some state $s' \in B'$ closer to $bottom(B')$ such that $s \to s'$. Clearly, $s' \notin split(B', \boldsymbol{B})$ either, as otherwise $s \in split(B', \boldsymbol{B})$. But as $s'$ is closer to $bottom(B')$, the state $s$ was not a state with the smallest distance to a state in $bottom(B')$, which is a contradiction.
$\Leftarrow$ It follows from the right hand side that $split(B', \boldsymbol{B}) \neq \emptyset$, $split(B', \boldsymbol{B}) \neq B'$.
$\square$

This lemma can be used as follows to find a block to be split. Consider each $B \in \pi$. Traverse its incoming transitions and mark the states that can reach $B$ in zero or one step. If a block $B'$ has marked states, but not all of its bottom states are marked, the condition of the lemma applies, and it needs to be split. It is at most needed to traverse all transitions to carry this out, so its complexity is $O(m)$.

If $B$ is equal to $B'$, no splitting is possible. We implement it by marking all states in $B$ as each state in $B$ can reach itself in zero steps. In this case condition $bottom(B') \cap split(B', \boldsymbol{B}) \subset bottom(B')$ is not true. This is different from [9] where a block is never considered as a splitter of itself, but we require this in the algorithm in the next sections.

If a block $B'$ is unstable, and all states from which a state in $B$ can be reached in one step are marked, then a straightforward recursive procedure is required to extend the marking to all states in $split(B', B)$, and those states need to be moved to a new block. This takes time proportional to the number of transitions in $B'$, i.e., $O(m)$.

# 4    Constellations: An $O(m \log n)$ Algorithm

The crucial idea to transform the algorithm from the previous section into an $O(m \log n)$ algorithm stems from [15]. By grouping the blocks in the current partition $\pi$ into constellations such that $\pi$ is stable under the union of the blocks in such a constellation, we can determine whether a block exists under which $\pi$ is unstable by only looking at blocks that are at most half the size of the constellation, i.e., $|B| \leq \frac{1}{2}|\boldsymbol{B}|$, where $|\boldsymbol{B}| = \Sigma_{B' \in \boldsymbol{B}}|B'|$, for a block $B$ in a constellation $\boldsymbol{B}$. If a block $B' \in \pi$ is unstable under $B$, then we use a remarkable technique consisting of two procedures running alternatingly to identify the smallest block resulting from the split. The whole operation runs in time proportional to the smallest block resulting from the split. We involve the blocks in $\boldsymbol{B} \setminus B$ in the splitting without explicitly analysing the states contained therein (for convenience, we write $\boldsymbol{B} \setminus B$ instead of $\boldsymbol{B} \setminus \{B\}$).

Working with constellations in this way ensures for each state that whenever it is involved in splitting, i.e., if it is part of a block that is used to split or that is being split, this block is half the size of the previous block in which the state resided when it was involved in splitting. That ensures that each state can at most be $\log_2(n)$ times involved in splitting. When involving a state, we only analyse its incoming and outgoing transitions, resulting in an algorithm with complexity $O(m \log n)$. Although we require quite a number of auxiliary data structures, these are either proportional to the number of states or to the number of transitions. So, the memory requirement is $O(m+n)$.

In the following, the set of constellations also forms a partition, which we denote by $\mathcal{C}$. A constellation is a set of one or more blocks from the current partition $\pi$. If a constellation contains only one block, it is called *trivial*. The current partition $\pi$ is stable with respect to each constellation in $\mathcal{C}$.

If a constellation $\boldsymbol{B} \in \mathcal{C}$ contains more than one block, we select one block $B \in \boldsymbol{B}$ which is at most half the size of $\boldsymbol{B}$, and move it to a new trivial constellation $\boldsymbol{B}'$. We check whether the current partition is stable under $B$ and $\boldsymbol{B} \setminus B$ according to Lemma 2 by traversing the incoming transitions of states in $B$ and marking the encountered states that can reach $B$ in zero or one step. For all blocks $B'$ that are unstable according to Lemma 2, we calculate $split(B', B)$ and $cosplit(B', B)$, as indicated below.

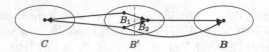

**Fig. 1.** After splitting $B'$ under $C$, $B_1$ is not stable under $B$.

As noted in [15], $cosplit(B', B)$ is stable under $B \setminus B$. Therefore, only further splitting of $split(B', B)$ under $B \setminus B$ must be investigated. If $B'$ is stable under $B$ because all bottom states of $B'$ are marked, it can be that $B'$ is not stable under $B \setminus B$, which we do not address here explicitly, as it proceeds along the same line.

There is a special list data structure to recall for any $B'$ and $B$ which transitions go from $B'$ to $B$. When investigating whether $split(B', B)$ is stable under $B$ we adapt this list to determine the transitions from $split(B', B)$ to $B \setminus B$ and we simultaneously tag the states in $B'$ that have a transition to $B \setminus B$. Therefore, we know whether there are transitions from $split(B', B)$ to $B \setminus B$ and we can traverse the bottom states of $split(B', B)$ to inspect whether there is a bottom state without a transition to $B$. Following Lemma 2, this allows us to determine whether $split(B', B)$ must be split under $B \setminus B$ in a time proportional to the size of $B$. How splitting is carried out is indicated below.

There is one aspect that complicates matters. If blocks are split, the new partition is not automatically stable under all constellations. This is contrary to the situation in [15] and was already observed in [9]. Figure 1 indicates the situation. Block $B'$ is stable under constellation $B$. But if $B'$ is split under block $C$ into $B_1$ and $B_2$, block $B_1$ is not stable under $B$. The reason is, as exemplified by the following lemma, that some states that were non-bottom states in $B'$ became bottom states in $B_1$.

**Lemma 3.** *Let $K = (S, AP, \rightarrow, L)$ be a Kripke structure with cycle free partition $\pi$ with refinement $\pi'$. If $\pi$ is stable under a constellation $B$, and $B' \in \pi$ is refined into $B'_1, \ldots, B'_k \in \pi'$, then for each $B'_i$ where the bottom states in $B'_i$ are also bottom states in $B'$, it holds that $B'_i$ is also stable under $B$.*

*Proof.* Assume $B'_i$ is not stable under $B$. This means that $B'_i$ is not an element of $B$. Hence, there is a state $s \in B'_i$ such that $s \rightarrow s'$ with $s' \in B$ and there is a bottom state $t \in B'_i$ with no outgoing transition to a state in $B$. But as $B'$ was stable under $B$, and $s$ has an outgoing transition to a state in $B$, all bottom states in $B'$ must have at least one transition to a state in $B$. Therefore, $t$ cannot be a bottom state of $B'$, and must have become a bottom state after splitting $B'$. $\qquad\square$

This means that if a block $B'$ is the result of a refinement, and some of its states became bottom states, it must be made sure that $B'$ is stable under the constellations. Typically, from the new bottom states a smaller number of blocks in the constellation can be reached. For each block we maintain a list of constellations that can be reached from states in this block. We match the outgoing transitions of the new bottom states with this list, and if there is a block $B''$ reachable from states in the constellation, but not from the bottom states, $B'$ must be split by $B''$.

The complexity of checking for additional splittings to regain stability when states become bottom states is only $O(m)$. Each state only becomes a bottom state once, and when that happens we perform calculations proportional to the number of outgoing transitions of this state to determine whether a split must be carried out.

It remains to show that splitting can be performed in a time proportional to the size of the smallest block resulting from the splitting. Consider splitting $B'$ under $B \in \mathbf{B}$. While marking $B'$ four lists of all marked and non marked, bottom and non bottom states have been constructed. We simultaneously mark states in $B'$ either red or blue. Red means that there is a path from a state in $B'$ to a state in $B$. Blue means that there is no such path. Initially, marked states are red, and non marked bottom states are blue.

This colouring is simultaneously extended to all states in $B'$, spending equal time to both. The procedure is stopped when the colouring of one of the colours cannot be enlarged. We colour states red that can reach other red states via inert transitions using a simple recursive procedure. We colour states blue for which it is determined that all outgoing inert transitions go to a blue state (for this we need to recall for each state the number of outgoing inert transitions) and there is no direct transition to $B$. The marking procedure that terminates first, provided that its number of marked states does not exceed $\frac{1}{2}|B'|$, has the smallest block that must be split. Now that we know the smallest block we move its states to a newly created block.

Splitting regarding $\mathbf{B} \setminus B$ only has to be applied to $split(B', B)$, or, if all bottom states of $B'$ were marked, to $B'$. As noted before $cosplit(B', B)$ is stable under $\mathbf{B} \setminus B$. Define $C := split(B', B)$ or $C := B'$ depending on the situation. We can traverse all bottom states of $C$ and check whether they have outgoing transitions to $\mathbf{B} \setminus B$. This provides us with the blue states. The red states are obtained as we explicitly maintained the list of all transitions from $C$ to $\mathbf{B} \setminus B$. By simultaneously extending this colouring the smallest subblock of either red or blue states is obtained and splitting can commence.

The algorithm is concisely presented in the box below. It is presented in full detail in Sect. 5 as the bookkeeping details of the algorithm are far from trivial.

---

$\pi :=$ initial partition; $\mathcal{C} := \{\pi\}$;
**while** $\mathcal{C}$ contains a non trivial constellation $\mathbf{B} \in \mathcal{C}$
    **choose** some $B \in \pi$ such that $B \in \mathbf{B}$ and $|B| \leq \frac{1}{2}|\mathbf{B}|$;
    $\mathcal{C} :=$ partition $\mathcal{C}$ where $\mathbf{B}$ is replaced by $B$ and $\mathbf{B} \setminus B$;
    **if** $\pi$ is unstable for $B$ or $\mathbf{B} \setminus B$
        $\pi' :=$ refinement of $\pi$ under $B$ and $\mathbf{B} \setminus B$;
        For each block $C \in \pi'$ with bottom states that were not bottom in $\pi$
            split $C$ until it is stable for all constellations in $\mathcal{C}$;
    $\pi := \pi'$

# 5    Detailed Algorithm

This section presents the data structures and the algorithm in more detail.

## 5.1    Data Structures

As a basic data structure, we use (singly-linked) lists. For a list $L$ of elements, we assume that for each element $e$, a reference to the position in $L$ preceding the position of $e$ is maintained, such that checking membership and removal can be done in constant time. In some cases we add extra information to the elements in the list. Moreover, for each list $L$, we maintain the size $|L|$ and pointers to its first and last element.

1. The current partition $\pi$ consists of a list of blocks. Initially, it corresponds to $\pi_0$. All blocks are part of a single, initial constellation $C_0$.
2. For each block $B$, we maintain the following:
   (a) A reference to the constellation containing $B$.
   (b) A list $B.btm\text{-}sts$ of the bottom states and a list $B.non\text{-}btm\text{-}sts$ of the other states.
   (c) A list $B.to\text{-}constlns$ of structures associated with constellations reachable via a transition from some $s \in B$. Initially, it contains one element associated with $C_0$. Each element associated with some constellation $C$ in this list also contains the following:
      – A reference $trans\text{-}list$ to a list of all transitions from states in $B$ to states in $C \setminus B$ (note that transitions between states in $B$, i.e., inert transitions, are $not$ in this list).
      – When splitting the block $B$ into $B$ and $B'$ there is a reference in each list element to the corresponding list element in $B'.to\text{-}constlns$ (which in turn refers back to the element in $B.to\text{-}constlns$).
      – In order to check for stability when splitting produces new bottom states, each element contains a list to keep track of which new bottom states can reach the associated constellation.
   (d) A reference $B.inconstln\text{-}ref$ is used to refer to the element in $B.to\text{-}constlns$ associated with the constellation of $B$. It is used when a non-inert transition becomes inert and needs to be added to the $trans\text{-}list$ of the element associated with that constellation.
   Furthermore, when splitting a block $B'$ in constellation $B'$ under a constellation $B$ and block $B \in B$, the following temporary structures are used, with $C$ the new constellation to which $B$ is moved:
   (a) A list $B'.mrkd\text{-}btm\text{-}sts$ contains marked states in $B'$ with a transition to $B$.
   (b) A list $B'.mrkd\text{-}non\text{-}btm\text{-}sts$ contains states that are marked, but are not bottom states.
   (c) A reference $B'.constln\text{-}ref$ refers to the (new) element in $B'.to\text{-}constlns$ associated with constellation $C$, i.e., the new constellation of $B$.

(d) A reference $B'.coconstln\text{-}ref$ is used to refer to the element in $B'$. $to\text{-}constlns$ associated with constellation $B$, i.e., the old constellation of $B$.

(e) A list $B'.new\text{-}btm\text{-}sts$ to keep track of the states that have become bottom states when $B'$ was split. This is required to determine whether $B'$ is stable under all constellations after a split.

3. Constellations are stored in two lists $trivial\text{-}constlns$ and $non\text{-}trivial\text{-}constlns$. The first contains constellations consisting of exactly one block, while the latter contains the other constellations. Initially, if $\pi_0$ consists of one block, $C_0$ is added to $trivial\text{-}constlns$ and nothing needs to be done, because the initial partition is already stable. Otherwise $C_0$ is added to $non\text{-}trivial\text{-}constlns$.

4. For each constellation, we maintain its list of blocks and its size (number of states).

5. Each transition $s \to s'$ refers with $to\text{-}constln\text{-}cnt$ to the number of transitions from $s$ to the constellation in which $s'$ resides. For each state and constellation, there is one such variable, provided there is a transition from this state to this constellation.

Each transition $s \to s'$ has a reference to the element associated with $B$ in the list $B.to\text{-}constlns$ where $s \in B$ and $s' \in \boldsymbol{B}$. This is denoted as $(s \to s').to\text{-}constln\text{-}ref$. Initially, it refers to the single element in $B.to\text{-}constlns$, unless the transition is inert, i.e., both $s \in B$ and $s' \in B$.

Furthermore, each transition $s \to s'$ is stored in the list of transitions from $B$ to $\boldsymbol{B}$. Initially, there is such a list for each block in the initial partition $\pi_0$. From a transition $s \to s'$, the list can be accessed via $(s \to s').to\text{-}constln\text{-}ref.trans\text{-}list$.

6. For each state $s \in B$ we maintain the following information:
   (a) A reference to the block containing $s$.
   (b) A static list $s.T_{tgt}$ of transitions of the form $s \to s'$ containing precisely all the transitions from $s$.
   (c) A static list $s.T_{src}$ of transitions $s' \to s$ containing all the transitions to $s$. We write such transitions as $s \leftarrow s'$, to stress that these move into $s$.
   (d) A counter $s.inert\text{-}cnt$ containing the number of outgoing transitions to a state in the same block as $s$. For any bottom state $s$, we have $s.inert\text{-}cnt = 0$.
   (e) Furthermore, when splitting a block $B'$ under $B$ and $B \in \boldsymbol{B}$, there are references $s.constln\text{-}cnt$ and $s.coconstln\text{-}cnt$ to the variables that are used to count how many transitions there are from $s$ to $B$ and from $s$ to $\boldsymbol{B} \setminus B$.

Figure 2 illustrates some of the used structures. A block $B_1$ in constellation $B$ contains bottom states $s_1$, $s_2'$ and non-bottom state $s_2$. For $s_1$, we have transitions $s_1 \to s_1'$, $s_1 \to s_1''$ to constellation $C$. Both have the following references:
   (a) $to\text{-}constln\text{-}cnt$ to the number of outgoing transitions from $s_1$ to $C$.
   (b) $to\text{-}constln\text{-}ref$ to the element $(C, \bullet, \bullet)$ in $B_1.to\text{-}constlns$, where the $\bullet$'s are the (now uninitialized) references that are used when splitting.
   (c) Via $(C, \bullet, \bullet)$, a reference $trans\text{-}list$ to the list of transitions from $B_1$ to $C$.

Note that for the inert transition $s_2 \to s_2'$, we only have a reference to the number of outgoing transitions from $s_2$ to $\boldsymbol{B}$.

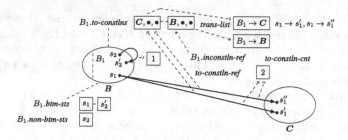

**Fig. 2.** An example showing some of the data structures used in the detailed algorithm.

## 5.2  Finding the Blocks that Must Be Split

While *non-trivial-constlns* is not empty, we perform the algorithm listed in the following sections. To determine whether the current partition $\pi$ is unstable, we select a constellation $\mathbf{B}$ in *non-trivial-constlns*, and we select a block $B$ from $\mathbf{B}$ such that $|B| \leq \frac{1}{2}|\mathbf{B}|$. We first check which blocks are unstable for $B$ and $\mathbf{B}\setminus B$.

1. Move $B$ to a new trivial constellation $\mathbf{C}$. If $|\mathbf{B}.blocks|=1$, make $\mathbf{B}$ trivial.
2. For each state $s\in B$, do the steps below for each $s'\in B'$ such that $s \leftarrow s' \in s.T_{src}$, and $B \neq B'$.
   (a) If $B'$ has no marked states, put it in a list *splittable-blks*, let $B'.coconstln\text{-}ref$ refer to $(s \leftarrow s').to\text{-}constln\text{-}ref$, $B'.constln\text{-}ref$ to a new element in $B'.to\text{-}constlns$.
   (b) Mark $s'$.
   (c) Let $s'.constln\text{-}cnt$ be the number of transitions to $B$ and $s'.coconstln\text{-}cnt$ the number of remaining outgoing transitions. All outgoing transitions of $s'$ must refer to the appropriate counter.
   (d) Move all visited transitions to $B'.constln\text{-}ref.trans\text{-}list$.
3. Next, check whether $B$ itself can be split. Mark all states, add $B$ to *splittable-blks* and reset $B.constln\text{-}ref$ and $B.coconstln\text{-}ref$. For each state $s\in B$, do the steps below for each $s'\in B'\in\mathbf{B}$ such that $s \leftarrow s' \in s.T_{src}$, and either $B'=B$ or $B'=C$.
   (a) If $\mathbf{B'}=\mathbf{B}$, let $B.coconstln\text{-}ref$ refer to $(s \rightarrow s').to\text{-}constln\text{-}ref$ and $B.constln\text{-}ref$ and $B.inconstln\text{-}ref$ to a new element for $\mathbf{C}$ in $B.to\text{-}constlns$.
   (b) Update $s.constln\text{-}cnt$ and $s.coconstln\text{-}cnt$ as in step 2(c).
4. For each $B'\in$*splittable-blks*, if all its bottom states are marked and either there is no marked bottom state $s$ with $s.coconstln\text{-}cnt=0$ or $B'.coconstln\text{-}ref.trans\text{-}list$ is empty, remove $B'$ from *splittable-blks* and remove its temporary markings, i.e. unmark all states, reset the counters and references.
5. If *splittable-blks* is not empty, start splitting (Sect. 5.3). Else, select another non-trivial constellation $\mathbf{B}$ and block $B\in\mathbf{B}$, and continuing with step 1. If there are no non-trivial constellations left, the algorithm terminates.

## 5.3   Splitting the Blocks

Splitting the splittable blocks is performed using the following steps, in which the procedures used to simultaneously mark states when splitting a block are crucial for the performance. We refer to the whole operation as the *lockstep search* and call the two procedures **detect1** and **detect2**. In the lockstep search, these procedures alternatingly process a transition. The entire operation terminates when one of the procedures terminates. If one procedure acquires more than half the number of states in the block it works on, it is stopped and the other is allowed to terminate. We present **detect1** and **detect2** below; both get a list of states, $D_1$ and $D_2$, respectively, and a block $K$ to work on as input. In addition, **detect2** takes a Boolean parameter indicating whether the splitting is a nested one, i.e., whether it directly follows an earlier split of the same block.

**detect1**$(D_1, K)$:

- Create empty stack $Q$, list $L$;
- While $|L| \leq \frac{1}{2}|K|$ and either $Q \neq \emptyset$ or end of $D_1$ not reached:
  - If $Q = \emptyset$ add next $s \in D_1$ to $Q$ and $L$;
  - Pop $s$ from $Q$. For all $s \leftarrow s' \in s.T_{src}$, if $s' \in K \wedge s' \notin L$, add $s'$ to $Q$ and $L$.

**detect2**$(D_2, K, nested)$:

- Create empty priority queue $P$, list $L'$;
- While $|L'| \leq \frac{1}{2}|K|$ and either $P$ has prio. 0 states or end of $D_2$ not reached:
  - Take a state $s$ from $D_2$ or with prio. 0 from $P$ and add it to $L'$;
  - For all $s \leftarrow s' \in s.T_{src}$, if $s' \in K \setminus (P \cup L')$, and $s' \notin$ *mrkd-non-btm-sts* or if *nested*, $s'$ does not have a transition to $B \setminus B$, add $s'$ with prio. $s'.inert\text{-}cnt$ to $P$;
  - If $s' \in P$, decrement priority of $s'$.

We walk through the blocks $B' \in \boldsymbol{B'}$ in *splittable-blks*, which must be split into two or three blocks under constellation $\boldsymbol{B}$ and block $B$. If all bottom states are marked, then we have $split(B', B) = B'$, and can start with step 3 below.

1. Launch a lockstep search with $D_1$ the list of marked states in $B'$, $D_2$ the list $B'.btm\text{-}sts$, $K = B'$, and *nested* = **false**.
2. Depending on whether **detect1** or **detect2** terminated in the previous step, one of the lists $L$ or $L'$ contains the states to be moved to a new block $B''$. Below we refer to this list as $N$. For each $s \in N$, move $s$ to $B''$, and do the following:
   (a) For each $s \rightarrow s' \in T_{tgt}$, do the following steps.
       i. If $(s \rightarrow s').to\text{-}constln\text{-}ref$ is initialized, check whether it refers to an new element in $B''.to\text{-}constlns$. If not, create it. If appropriate, set references $B''.inconstln\text{-}ref$, $B''.constln\text{-}ref$ and $B''.coconstln\text{-}ref$. Move $s \rightarrow s'$ to the *trans-list* of the new element. If the related element in $B'.to\text{-}constlns$ no longer holds transitions, remove it.

  ii. Else, if $s' \in B' \setminus N$ (a transition becomes non-inert), decrement $s.inert\text{-}cnt$. If $s.inert\text{-}cnt=0$, make $s$ bottom, add $s \to s'$ to $B''.inconstln\text{-}ref.trans\text{-}list$ (if $B''.inconstln\text{-}ref$ does not exist, create it first).

 (b) For each $s \leftarrow s' \in T_{src}$, $s' \in B' \setminus N$ (an inert transition becomes non-inert), perform steps similar to 2(a).ii.

3. Next, we split $split(B', B)$ under $B \setminus B$. Define $C = split(B', B)$. $C$ is stable under $B \setminus B$ if $C.coconstln\text{-}ref$ is uninitialized or holds an empty $trans\text{-}list$, or for all $s \in C.mrkd\text{-}btm\text{-}sts$ it holds that $s.coconstln\text{-}cnt > 0$. If this is not the case, then we launch a lockstep search with $D_1$ the list of states $s$ occurring in some $s \to s'$ in $split(B', B).coconstln\text{-}ref.trans\text{-}list$, $D_2$ the list of states $s$ with $s.coconstln\text{-}cnt = 0$ in $C.mrkd\text{-}btm\text{-}sts$, $K = C$, and $nested = \text{true}$. Finally, we split $C$ by moving the states in either $L$ or $L'$ to a new block $B'''$, depending on which list is the smallest.

4. Remove the temporary markings of each block $C$ resulting from the splitting of $B'$.

5. If the splitting of $B'$ resulted in new bottom states, check for those states whether further splitting is required, i.e., whether from some of them, not all constellations can be reached which can be reached from the block. For all $\hat{B} \in \{B', B'', B'''\}$, new bottom states $s$, $s \to s' \in s.T_{tgt}$, add $s$ to the states list of the element associated with $\bar{B}$ in $\hat{B}.to\text{-}constlns$, where $s' \in \bar{B}$, and move the element to the front of the list.

6. Perform the following steps for each block $\hat{B}$ with new bottom states, as long as there are such blocks.

 (a) Walk through the elements in $\hat{B}.to\text{-}constlns$. If the states list of an element associated with a constellation $B$ does not contain all new bottom states, further splitting is required under $B$:

  i. Launch a lockstep search with $D_1$ the list of states $s$ occurring in some $s \to s'$ with $s' \in B$ in the list $trans\text{-}list$ associated with $B \in \hat{B}.to\text{-}constlns$, $D_2$ the list of states $s \in \hat{B}.new\text{-}btm\text{-}sts$ minus the new bottom states that can reach $B$, $K = \hat{B}$, and $nested = \text{true}$.

  ii. Split $\hat{B}$ by performing step 2 to produce a new block $\hat{B}'$. Move all states in $\hat{B}.new\text{-}btm\text{-}sts$ that have moved to $\hat{B}'$ to $\hat{B}'.new\text{-}btm\text{-}sts$, and also move them from the states lists in the elements of $\hat{B}.to\text{-}constlns$ to the corresponding elements of $\hat{B}'.to\text{-}constlns$ (those elements refer to each other). If a states list becomes empty, move that element to the back of its list.

  iii. Perform step 5 for $\hat{B}$ and $\hat{B}'$.

 (b) If no further splitting was required for $\hat{B}$, empty $\hat{B}.new\text{-}btm\text{-}sts$ and clear the remaining states lists in $\hat{B}.to\text{-}constlns$.

7. If $B' \in trivial\text{-}constlns$, move it to $non\text{-}trivial\text{-}constlns$.

## 6 Application to Branching Bisimulation

We show that the algorithm can also be used to determine branching bisimulation, using the transformation from [14,17], with complexity $O(m(\log|Act| +$

$\log n$)). Branching bisimulation is typically applied to labelled transition systems (LTSs). An LTS is a three tuple $A = (S, Act, \rightarrow)$, with $S$ a finite set of states, $Act$ a finite set of actions including the internal action $\tau$, and $\rightarrow \subseteq S \times Act \times S$ a transition relation.

**Definition 4.** *Consider the LTS $A = (S, Act, \rightarrow)$. We call a symmetric relation $R \subseteq S \times S$ a branching bisimulation relation iff*

$$\forall s, t, s' \in S. \forall a \in Act. sRt \wedge s \xrightarrow{a} s' \Longrightarrow$$

$$(a = \tau \wedge s'Rt) \vee (\exists t', t'' \in S.t \twoheadrightarrow t' \xrightarrow{a} t'' \wedge sRt' \wedge s'Rt''),$$

*where $\twoheadrightarrow$ is the transitive, reflexive closure of $\xrightarrow{\tau}$.*

States are *branching bisimilar* iff there is a branching bisimulation relation $R$ relating them.

Our new algorithm can be applied to an LTS by translating it to a Kripke structure.

**Definition 5.** *Let $A = (S, Act, \rightarrow)$ be an LTS. We construct the embedding of $A$ to be the Kripke structure $K_A = (S_A, AP, \rightarrow, L)$ as follows:*

1. $S_A = S \cup \{\langle a, t \rangle \mid s \xrightarrow{a} t \text{ for some } t \in S\}$.
2. $AP = Act \cup \{\perp\}$.
3. $\rightarrow$ *is the least relation satisfying $(s, t \in S, a \in Act \backslash \tau)$: $\dfrac{s \xrightarrow{a} t}{s \rightarrow \langle a, t \rangle}$, $\overline{\langle a, t \rangle \rightarrow t}$ and* $\dfrac{s \xrightarrow{\tau} t}{s \rightarrow t}$.
4. $L(s) = \{\perp\}$ *for $s \in S$ and $L(\langle a, t \rangle) = \{a\}$.*

The following theorem stems from [14].

**Theorem 1.** *Let $A$ be an LTS and $K_A$ its embedding. Then two states are branching bisimilar in $A$ iff they are divergence-blind stuttering equivalent in $K_A$.*

If we start out with an LTS with $n$ states and $m$ transitions then its embedding has at most $m + n$ states and $2m$ transitions. Hence, the algorithm

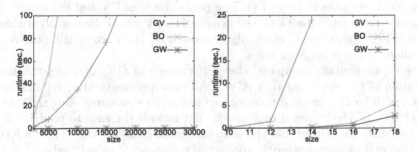

**Fig. 3.** Runtime results for $(a \cdot \tau)^{size}$ sequences (left) and trees of depth $size$ (right)

**Table 1.** Runtime (in sec.) and memory use (in MB) results for GV, BO, and GW

| Model | n | m | min. n | min. m | time GV | me. GV | time BO | me. BO | time GW | me. GW |
|---|---|---|---|---|---|---|---|---|---|---|
| vasy_40 | 40,006 | 60,007 | 20,003 | 40,004 | 142.77 | 65 | 762.69 | 62 | **0.34** | 93 |
| vasy_65 | 65,537 | 2,621,480 | 65,536 | 2,621,440 | 239.67 | 437 | 47.88 | 645 | **20.07** | 2,481 |
| vasy_66 | 66,929 | 1,302,664 | 51,128 | 1,018,692 | **7.42** | 208 | 16.16 | 356 | 9.05 | 853 |
| vasy_69 | 69,754 | 520,633 | 69,753 | 520,632 | **3.98** | 155 | 12.65 | 171 | 4.53 | 493 |
| vasy_116 | 116,456 | 368,569 | 22,398 | 87,674 | 3.84 | 95 | 15.73 | 128 | **2.68** | 142 |
| vasy_157 | 157,604 | 297,000 | 3,038 | 12,095 | 6.98 | 97 | 6.80 | 110 | **1.08** | 129 |
| vasy_164 | 164,865 | 1,619,204 | 992 | 3,456 | **3.89** | 251 | 20.20 | 316 | 5.38 | 246 |
| vasy_166 | 166,464 | 651,168 | 42,195 | 197,200 | 21.60 | 153 | 6.20 | 177 | **3.89** | 376 |
| cwi_214 | 214,202 | 684,419 | 478 | 1,612 | **0.87** | 140 | 29.92 | 197 | 2.64 | 140 |
| cwi_371 | 371,804 | 641,565 | 2,134 | 5,634 | 42.70 | 179 | 17.37 | 261 | **3.12** | 168 |
| cwi_566 | 566,640 | 3,984,157 | 198 | 791 | 1683.28 | 454 | 26.24 | 531 | **19.94** | 454 |
| vasy_574 | 574,057 | 13,561,040 | 3,577 | 16,168 | 105.10 | 1,766 | 487.01 | 2,192 | **40.18** | 1,495 |
| cwi_2165 | 2,165,446 | 8,723,465 | 4,256 | 20,880 | 80.56 | 1,403 | 387.93 | 2,409 | **59.49** | 1,948 |
| cwi_2416 | 2,416,632 | 17,605,592 | 730 | 2,899 | 1,679.55 | 1,932 | **59.29** | 2,660 | 90.69 | 1,932 |
| vasy_2581 | 2,581,374 | 11,442,382 | 704,737 | 3,972,600 | 2,592.74 | 1,690 | 463.52 | 2,344 | **76.16** | 5,098 |
| vasy_4220 | 4,220,790 | 13,944,372 | 1,186,266 | 6,863,329 | 3,643.08 | 2,054 | 863.74 | 2,951 | **119.20** | 7,287 |
| vasy_4338 | 4,338,672 | 15,666,588 | 704,737 | 3,972,600 | 5,290.54 | 2,258 | 587.87 | 3,026 | **109.21** | 6,927 |
| vasy_6020 | 6,020,550 | 19,353,474 | 256 | 510 | 130.76 | 2,045 | 95.76 | 3,482 | **45.54** | 2,045 |
| vasy_6120 | 6,120,718 | 11,031,292 | 2,505 | 5,358 | 546.11 | 1,893 | 291.30 | 2,300 | **81.05** | 3,392 |
| cwi_7838 | 7,838,608 | 59,101,007 | 62,031 | 470,230 | 745.33 | 6,319 | 11,667.98 | 11,027 | **617.46** | 14,456 |
| vasy_8082 | 8,082,905 | 42,933,110 | 290 | 680 | 288.45 | 6,098 | 677.28 | 7,824 | **200.72** | 6,108 |
| vasy_11026 | 11,026,932 | 24,660,513 | 775,618 | 2,454,834 | 5,005.61 | 3,642 | 2,555.30 | 5,235 | **225.20** | 10,394 |
| vasy_12323 | 12,323,703 | 27,667,803 | 876,944 | 2,780,022 | 5,997.26 | 4,068 | 2,068.52 | 5,770 | **256.70** | 11,575 |
| cwi_33949 | 33,949,609 | 165,318,222 | 12,463 | 71,466 | 1,684.56 | 21,951 | 11,635.09 | 42,162 | **1,459.92** | 37,437 |
| dining_14 | 18,378,370 | 164,329,284 | 228,486 | 2,067,856 | 1,264.67 | 20,155 | 3,010.17 | 31,201 | **1,100.91** | 20,155 |
| 1394-fin3 | 126,713,623 | 276,426,688 | 160,258 | 538,936 | 229,217.0 | 26,000 | 15,319.00 | 75,000 | **1,516.00** | 45,000 |

requires $O(m \log(n+m))$ time. As $m$ is at most $|Act|n^2$ this is also equal to $O(m(\log |Act| + \log n))$.

As a final note, the algorithm can also be adapted to determine divergence-sensitive branching bisimulation [8], by adding a $\tau$-self loop to those states on a $\tau$-loop.

## 7    Experiments

The new algorithm has been implemented as part of the mCRL2 toolset [6], which offers implementations of GV and the algorithm by Blom and Orzan [2] that distinguishes states by their connection to blocks via their outgoing transitions. We refer to the latter as BO. The performance of GV and BO can be very different on concrete examples. We have extensively tested the new algorithm by applying it to thousands of randomly generated LTSs and comparing the results with those of the other algorithms.

We experimentally compared the performance of GV, BO, and the implementation of the new algorithm (GW). All experiments involve the analysis of LTSs, which for GW are first transformed to Kripke structures using the translation of Sect. 6. The reported runtimes do not include the time to read the input LTS and write the output, but the time it takes to translate the LTS to a Kripke structure and to reduce strongly connected components is included.

Practically all experiments have been performed on machines running CEN-TOS LINUX, with an INTEL E5-2620 2.0 GHz CPU and 64 GB RAM. Exceptions to this are the final two entries in Table 1, which were obtained by using a machine running FEDORA 12, with an INTEL XEON E5520 2.27 GHz CPU and 1 TB RAM.

Figure 3 presents the runtime results for two sets of experiments to demonstrate that GW has the expected scalability. At the left are the results of analysing single sequences of the shape $(a \cdot \tau)^n$. As the length $2n$ of such a sequence is increased, the results show that the runtimes of both BO and GV increase at least quadratically, while the runtime of GW grows linearly. All algorithms require $n$ iterations, in which BO and GV walk over all the states in the sequence, but GW only moves two states into a new block. At the right of Fig. 3, the results are displayed of analysing trees of depth $n$ that up to level $n-1$ correspond with a binary tree of $\tau$-transitions. Each state at level $n-1$ has a uniquely labelled outgoing transition to a state in level $n$. BO only needs one iteration to obtain the stable partition. Still GW beats BO by repeatedly splitting off small blocks of size $2(k-1)$ if a state at level $k$ is the splitter.

Table 1 contains results for minimising LTSs from the VLTS benchmark set[1] and the mCRL2 toolset[2]. These experiments demonstrate that also when applied to actual state spaces of real models, GW generally outperforms the best of the other algorithms, often with a factor 10 and sometimes with a factor 100. This difference tends to grow as the LTSs get larger. GW's memory usage is only sometimes substantially higher than GV's and BO's, which surprised us given the amount of required bookkeeping.

# References

1. Aho, A., Hopcroft, J., Ullman, J.: The Design and Analysis of Computer Algorithms. Addison-Wesley, Reading (1974)
2. Blom, S.C., Orzan, S.: Distributed branching bisimulation reduction of state spaces. In: FMICS 2003. ENTCS, vol. 80, pp. 109–123. Elsevier (2003)
3. Blom, S.C., van de Pol, J.C.: Distributed branching bisimulation minimization by inductive signatures. In: PDMC 2009. EPTCS, vol. 14, pp. 32–46. Open Publ. Association (2009)
4. Browne, M.C., Clarke, E.M., Grumberg, O.: Characterizing finite Kripke structures in propositional temporal logic. Theoret. Comput. Sci. **59**(1,2), 115–131 (1988)
5. Chatterjee, K., Henzinger, M.: Faster and dynamic algorithms for maximal end-component decomposition and related graph problems in probabilistic verification. In: SODA 2011, pp. 1318–1336. SIAM (2011)
6. Cranen, S., Groote, J.F., Keiren, J.J.A., Stappers, F.P.M., de Vink, E.P., Wesselink, W., Willemse, T.A.C.: An overview of the mCRL2 toolset and its recent advances. In: Piterman, N., Smolka, S.A. (eds.) TACAS 2013 (ETAPS 2013). LNCS, vol. 7795, pp. 199–213. Springer, Heidelberg (2013)
7. Garavel, H., Lang, F., Mateescu, R., Serwe, W.: CADP 2011: a toolbox for the construction and analysis of distributed processes. Softw. Tools Technol. Transfer. **15**(2), 98–107 (2013)
8. van Glabbeek, R.J., Weijland, W.P.: Branching time and abstraction in bisimulation semantics. J. ACM **43**(3), 555–600 (1996)

---

[1] http://cadp.inria.fr/resources/vlts.
[2] http://www.mcrl2.org.

9. Groote, J.F., Vaandrager, F.W.: An efficient algorithm for branching bisimulation and stuttering equivalence. In: Paterson, M. (ed.) ICALP 1990. LNCS, vol. 443, pp. 626–638. Springer, Heidelberg (1990)

10. Groote, J.F., Mousavi, M.R.: Modeling and Analysis of Communicating Systems. The MIT Press, Cambridge (2014)

11. Kannelakis, P., Smolka, S.: CCS Expressions, Finite State Processes and Three Problems of Equivalence. Inf. Comput. **86**, 43–68 (1990)

12. Li, W.: Algorithms for computing weak bisimulation equivalence. In: TASE 2009, pp. 241–248. IEEE (2009)

13. Milner, R. (ed.): Calculus of Communicating Systems. Lecture Notes in Computer Science, vol. 92. Springer, Heidelberg (1980)

14. De Nicola, R., Vaandrager, F.W.: Three logics for branching bisimulation. Journal of the ACM **42**, 458–487 (1995)

15. Paige, R., Tarjan, R.E.: Three partition refinement algorithms. SIAM J. Comput. **16**(6), 973–989 (1987)

16. Ranzato, F., Tapparo, F.: Generalizing the Paige-Tarjan algorithm by abstract interpretation. Inf. Comput. **206**(5), 620–651 (2008)

17. Reniers, M.A., Schoren, R., Willemse, T.A.C.: Results on embeddings between state-based and event-based systems. Comput. J. **57**(1), 73–92 (2014)

18. Virtanen, H., Hansen, H., Valmari, A., Nieminen, J., Erkkilä, T.: Tampere verification tool. In: Jensen, K., Podelski, A. (eds.) TACAS 2004. LNCS, vol. 2988, pp. 153–157. Springer, Heidelberg (2004)

19. Wijs, A.: GPU accelerated strong and branching bisimilarity checking. In: Baier, C., Tinelli, C. (eds.) TACAS 2015. LNCS, vol. 9035, pp. 368–383. Springer, Heidelberg (2015)

# Interpolants in Nonlinear Theories
# Over the Reals

Sicun Gao and Damien Zufferey[(✉)]

MIT, Cambridge, USA
zufferey@csail.mit.edu

**Abstract.** We develop algorithms for computing Craig interpolants for first-order formulas over real numbers with a wide range of nonlinear functions, including transcendental functions and differential equations. We transform proof traces from $\delta$-complete decision procedures into interpolants that consist of Boolean combinations of linear constraints. The algorithms are guaranteed to find the interpolants between two formulas $A$ and $B$ whenever $A \wedge B$ is not $\delta$-satisfiable. At the same time, by exploiting $\delta$-perturbations one can parameterize the algorithm to find interpolants with different positions between $A$ and $B$. We show applications of the methods in control and robotic design, and hybrid system verification.

## 1 Introduction

Verification problems of complex embedded software can be reduced to solving logic formulas that contain continuous, typically nonlinear, real functions. The framework of $\delta$-decision procedures [19,21] establishes that, under reasonable relaxations, nonlinear SMT formulas over the reals are in principle as solvable as SAT problems. Indeed, using solvers for nonlinear theories as the algorithmic engines, straightforward bounded model checking has already shown promise on nonlinear hybrid systems [9,28]. Naturally, for enhancing performance, more advanced reasoning techniques need to be introduced, extending SMT towards general quantifier elimination. However, it is well-known that quantifier elimination is not feasible for nonlinear theories over the reals. The complexity of quantifier elimination for real arithmetic (i.e., polynomials only) has a double-exponential lower bound, which is too high for most applications; when transcendental functions are further involved, the problem becomes highly undecidable.

Craig interpolation provides a weak form of quantifier elimination. Given two formulas $A$ and $B$, such that $A \wedge B$ is unsatisfiable, an interpolant $I$ is a formula satisfying: (1) $A \Rightarrow I$, (2) $B \wedge I \Rightarrow \bot$, and (3) $I$ contains only variables common to $A$ and $B$. It has found many applications in verifications: as an heuristic to compute inductive invariant [30,33,35], for predicate discovery in abstraction

Sicun Gao was supported by NSF (Grant CCF-1161775 and CPS-1446725). Damien Zufferey was supported by NSF (Grant CCF-1138967) and DARPA (Grant FA8650-15-C-7564).

© Springer-Verlag Berlin Heidelberg 2016
M. Chechik and J.-F. Raskin (Eds.): TACAS 2016, LNCS 9636, pp. 625–641, 2016.
DOI: 10.1007/978-3-662-49674-9_41

refinement loops [32], inter procedural analysis [2,3], shape analysis [1], fault-localisation [10,17,39], and so on.

In this paper, we present methods for computing Craig interpolants in expressive nonlinear theories over the reals. To do so, we extract interpolants from proofs of unsatisfiability generated by $\delta$-decision procedures [22] that are based on Interval Constraint Propagation (ICP) [6]. The proposed algorithms are guaranteed to find the interpolants between two formulas $A$ and $B$, whenever $A \wedge B$ is not $\delta$-satisfiable.

The framework of $\delta$-decision procedures formulates a relaxed notion of logical decisions, by allowing one-sided $\delta$-bounded errors [18,19]. Instead of asking whether a formula has a satisfiable assignment or not, we ask if it is "$\delta$-satisfiable" or "unsatisfiable". Here, a formula is $\delta$-satisfiable if it would be satisfiable under some $\delta$-perturbation on the original formula [18]. On the other hand, when the algorithm determines that the formula is "unsatisfiable", it is a definite answer and no numerical error can be involved. Indeed, we can extract proofs of unsatisfiability from such answers, even though the search algorithms themselves involve numerical errors [22]. This is accomplished by analyzing the execution trace of the search tree based on the ICP algorithm.

The core ICP algorithm uses a *branch-and-prune* loop that aims to either find a small enough box that witnesses $\delta$-satisfiability, or detect that no solution exists. The loop consists of two main steps:

- (Prune) Use interval arithmetic to maintain overapproximations of the solution sets, so that one can "prune" out the part of the state space that does not contain solutions.
- (Branch) When the pruning operation does not make progress, one performs a depth-first search by "branching" on variables and restart pruning operations on a subset of the domain.

The loop is continued until either a small enough box that may contain a solution is found, or any conflict among the constraints is observed.

When a formula is unsatisfiable, the execution trace of the algorithm generates a (potentially large) proof tree that divides the space into small hypercubes and associating a constraint to each hypercube [22]. The interpolation algorithm can essentially traverse this proof tree to construct the interpolant. To each leaf in the proof, we associate $\top$ or $\bot$ depending on the source of the contradiction.

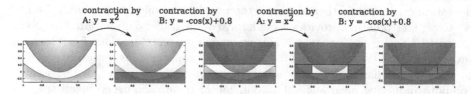

**Fig. 1.** Interval constraint propagation and interpolant construction where $A$ is $y \geq x^2$ and $B$ is $y \leq -\cos(x) + 0.8$ over the domain $x \in [-1, 1]$, $y \in [-1, 1]$. The $A$ is shown in green and $B$ in red. The final interpolant is the green part (Color figure online).

The inner nodes of the proof tree correspond to case splits and are handled in a manner reminiscent of Pudlák's algorithm [37]. Common variables are kept as branching points and $A,B$ local variables are eliminated. A simple example of the method is as follows:

*Example 1.* Let $A : y \geq x^2$ and $B : y \leq -\cos(x) + 0.8$ be two constraints over the domain $x \in [-1, 1]$, $y \in [-1, 1]$. A $\delta$-decision procedure uses $A$ and $B$ to contract the domains of $x$ and $y$ by removing the parts that be shown empty using interval arithmetic. Figure 1 shows a sequence of contraction proving the unsatisfiability of the formula. As the contraction occurs, we color the region of the space by the color of the *opposite* formula. When the interval constraint propagation has finished, the initial domain is associated to either $A$ or $B$. The interpolant $I$ is composed of the parts corresponding to $A$. We will compute that $I$ is $y \geq 0 \wedge (0.26 \leq y \vee (y \leq 0.26 \wedge -0.51 \leq x \leq 0.51))$.

We have implemented the algorithms in the SMT solver dReal [20]. We show examples of applications from various domains such as control and robotic design, and hybrid system verification.

*Related Work.* Our algorithm is very similar to the algorithm for propositional interpolation studied by Pudlák [37]. Craig interpolation for real or integer arithmetic has focused on the linear fragment with LA($\mathbb{R}$) [31,38] and LA($\mathbb{Z}$) [8,24]. Dai et al. [15] present a method to generate interpolants for polynomial formula. Their method use semi-definite programming to search for a polynomial interpolant and it is complete under the *Archimedean* condition. In fact, the Archimedean condition imposes similar restrictions as $\delta$-decidability, e.g., the variables over bounded domains and limited support for strict inequalities. Our method is more general in that it handles nonlinear fragments over $\mathbb{R}$ that include transcendental functions and solution functions of ordinary differention equations. Existing tools to compute interpolation such as MathSat5 [12], Princess [8], SmtInterpol [11], and Z3 [34] focus on linear arithmetic. We are the first to provide interpolation in nonlinear theories.

*Outline.* In Sect. 2, we review notions related to interpolation, nonlinear arithmetic over the Reals and $\delta$-decision procedures. In Sect. 3, we introduce our interpolation algorithm. In Sect. 4, we present and evaluate our implementation. We conclude and sketch future research direction in Sect. 5.

## 2   Preliminaries

*Craig Interpolation* [14]. Craig interpolants were originally defined in propositional logic, but can be easily extended to first-order logic. Given two quantifier-free first-order formulas $A$ and $B$, such that $A \wedge B$ is unsatisfiable, a Craig interpolant $I$ is a formula satisfying:

– $A \Rightarrow I$;
– $B \wedge I \Rightarrow \bot$;
– $fv(I) \subseteq fv(A) \cap fv(B)$ where $fv(\cdot)$ returns the free variables in a formula.

Intuitively, $I$ provides an overapproximation of $A$ that is still precise enough to exhibit its conflict with $B$. In particular, $I$ involves only variables (geometrically, dimensions) that are shared by $A$ and $B$.

**Notation 1.** We use the meta-level symbol $\Rightarrow$ as a shorthand for logical implications in texts. In the proof rules that we will introduce shortly, $\vdash$ is used as the formal symbol with the standard interpretation as logical derivations.

*δ-Complete Decision Procedures.* We consider first-order formulas interpreted over the real numbers. Our special focus is formulas that can contain arbitrary nonlinear functions that are *Type 2 computable* [7,40]. Intuitively, Type 2 computability corresponds to *numerical computability*. For our purpose, it is enough to note that this set of functions consist of all common elementary functions, as well as solutions of Lipschitz-continuous ordinary differential equations.

Interval Constraint Propagation (ICP) [6] finds solutions of real constraints using the *branch-and-prune* method, combining interval arithmetic and constraint propagation. The idea is to use interval extensions of functions to *prune* out sets of points that are not in the solution set and *branch* on intervals when such pruning can not be done, recursively until a small enough box that may contain a solution is found or inconsistency is observed. A high-level description of the decision version of ICP is given in Algorithm 1 [6,18]. The boxes, or interval domains, are written as $D$ and $c_i$ denotes the $i$th constraint.

*Proofs from Constraint Propagation.* A detailed description of proof extraction from δ-decision procedure is available in [22]. Here, we use a simplified version.

---

**Algorithm 1.** $\text{ICP}(c_1, ..., c_m, D = D_1 \times \cdots \times D_n, \delta)$

---

1:  $S \leftarrow D$
2:  **while** $S \neq \emptyset$ **do**
3:      $D \leftarrow S.\text{pop}()$
4:      **while** $\exists 1 \leq i \leq m, D \neq_\delta \text{Prune}(D, c_i)$ **do**
5:          $D \leftarrow \text{Prune}(D, c_i)$
6:      **end while**
7:      **if** $D \neq \emptyset$ **then**
8:          **if** $\exists 1 \leq i \leq m, |D| \geq \varepsilon$ **then**            ▷ $\varepsilon$ is some computable factor of $\delta$
9:              $\{D_1, D_2\} \leftarrow \text{Branch}(D, i)$
10:             $S.\text{push}(D_1)$
11:             $S.\text{push}(D_2)$
12:         **else**
13:             **return** sat
14:         **end if**
15:     **end if**
16: **end while**
17: **return** unsat

---

Intuitively, the proof of unsatisfiability recursively divides the solution space to small pieces, until it can prove (mostly using interval arithmetic) that every small piece of the domain contains no solution of the original system. Note that in such a proof, the difference between pruning and branching operations become blurred for the following reason.

Pruning operations show that one part of the domain can be discarded because no solution can exist there. Branching operations split the domain along one variable, and generates two sub-problems. From a proof perspective, the difference between the two kinds of operations is simply whether the emptiness in one part of domain follows from a simple properties of the functions (theory lemma), or requires further derivations. Indeed, as is shown in [22], the simple proof system in Fig. 2 is enough for establishing all theorems that can be obtained by $\delta$-decision procedures. The rules can be explained as follows.

- The Split rules divides the solution space into two disjoint subspaces.
- The theory lemmas (ThLem) are the leaves of the proof. They are used when the solver managed to prove the absence of solution in a given subspace.
- The Weakening rule extracts those conjunct out of the main formula.

We see that each step of the proof has a set of variables $x$ with a domain $D$ and $F$ is a formula. We use vector notations in the formulas, writing $x \in D$ to denote $\bigwedge_i x_i \in D_i$. The domains are intervals, i.e., each $D_i$ has the form $[l_i, u_i]$ where $l_i, u_i$ are the lower and upper bounds for $x_i$. Since we are looking at unsatisfiability proofs, each node implies $\bot$. The root of the proof is the formula $A \wedge B$, and $D$ covers the entire domain. The inner nodes are Split, and the proof's leaves are theory lemmas directly followed by weakening. To avoid duplication, we do not give a separate example here, since the full example in Fig. 5 shows the structure of some proof trees obtained from such rules.

A proof of unsatisfiability can be extracted from an execution trace of Algorithm 1 when it returns unsat. The algorithm starts at the root of the proof tree and explores the proof tree depth-first. Branching (line 9) directly corresponds

$$\frac{}{x \in D \wedge c \vdash \bot}\text{(ThLem)}$$

$$\frac{C := c \wedge \bigwedge_k C_k \qquad x \in D \wedge c \vdash \bot}{x \in D \wedge C \vdash \bot}\text{(Weakening)}$$

$$\frac{x_i \in [l_i, p] \wedge \bigwedge_{j \neq i} x_j \in D_j \wedge C \vdash \bot \qquad x_i \in [p, u_i] \wedge \bigwedge_{j \neq i} x_j \in D_j \wedge C \vdash \bot}{x_i \in [l_i, u_i] \wedge \bigwedge_{j \neq i} x_j \in D_j \wedge C \vdash \bot}\text{(Split)}$$

**Fig. 2.** Proof rules for the ICP algorithm. We use the standard notations for sequent calculus. Also, when we write an interval $[a, b]$, we always assume that it is a well-defined real interval satisfying $a \leq b$.

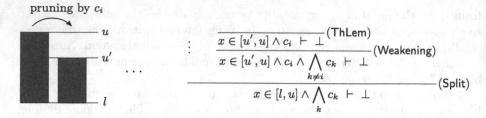

**Fig. 3.** Pruning operation and the corresponding proof. The pruning shrinks the domain of $x$ from $[l, u]$ to $[l, u']$. The corresponding proof starts with a Split around $u'$. The interval $[u', u]$ is proved empty using a ThLem and Weakening step. The remaining $[l, u']$ interval is shown empty by further operations.

to the Split rule. Pruning (line 5), on the other hand, is a combination of the three rules. Let us look at $D' = \mathrm{Prune}(D, c_i)$. The constraint $c_i$ is selected with the Weakening. For each $D'_i = [l', u']$ which is strictly smaller than $D_i = [l, u]$, the Split and ThLem rules are applied. If $u' < u$ then we split on $u'$ and a lemma shows that the interval $[u, u']$ has no solution. The same is done for the lower bounds $l', l$. Figure 3 shows a pruning step and the corresponding proof.

## 3   Interpolants in Nonlinear Theories

Intuitively, a proof of unsatisfiability is a partition of the solution space where each sub-domain is associated with a conjunct $c$ from $A \wedge B$. $c$ is a witness that shows the absence of solution in a given domain. The interpolation rules traverse the rules and selects which parts belong to the interpolant $I$. We now describe the algorithm for obtaining such interpolants for formulas $A$ and $B$ from the proof of unsatisfiability for $A \wedge B$.

### 3.1   Core Algorithms

Our method for constructing disjunctive linear interpolants takes two inputs: a proof tree and a labeling function. The labeling function maps formula and variables to either A, B, or AB. For each proof rule introduced in Fig. 2, we associate some partial interpolants, written in square bracket on the right of the conclusion of the rule. Figure 4 shows these modified versions of the rules.

- At the leaf level (rule ThLem-I), the tile is in $I$ if $c$ is not part of $A$, i.e., the contradiction originates from $B$. If $c$ is in both $A$ and $B$ then it can be considered as either part of $A$ or $B$. Both cases lead to a correct interpolant.
- The Weakening-I rule does not influence the interpolant, it is only required to pick $c$ from $A \wedge B$.
- The Split-I is the most interesting rule. Splitting the domain essentially defines the bounds of subsequent domains. Let $x$ be the variable whose domain is split at value $p$ and $I_1, I_2$ be the two interpolants for the case when $x < p$

$$\frac{}{x \in D \wedge c \vdash \bot \quad [l(c) \neq \text{A}]}\text{(ThLem-I)}$$

$$\frac{C = c \wedge \bigwedge_k C_k \quad x \in D \wedge c \vdash \bot \quad [I]}{x \in D \wedge C \vdash \bot \quad [I]}\text{(Weakening-I)}$$

$$\frac{\begin{array}{c} x_i \in [l_i, p] \wedge \bigwedge_{j \neq i} x_j \in D_j \wedge C \vdash \bot \quad [I_1] \\[2mm] x_i \in [p, u_i] \wedge \bigwedge_{j \neq i} x_j \in D_j \wedge C \vdash \bot \quad [I_2] \end{array}}{x_i \in [l_i, u_i] \wedge \bigwedge_{j \neq i} x_j \in D_j \wedge C \vdash \bot \quad \begin{bmatrix} I_1 \vee I_2 & \text{if } l(x_i)=\text{A} \\ ite(x_i<p, I_1, I_2) & \text{if } l(x_i)=\text{AB} \\ I_1 \wedge I_2 & \text{if } l(x_i)=\text{B} \end{bmatrix}}\text{(Split-I)}$$

where $ite(x, y, z)$ is a shorthand for $(x \wedge y) \vee (\neg x \wedge z)$

**Fig. 4.** Interpolant producing proof rules

and $x \geq p$. If $x$ occurs in $A$ but not $B$, then $x$ cannot occur in $I$. Since $x$ is in $A$ then we know that $A$ implies $x < p \Rightarrow I_1$ and $x \geq p \Rightarrow I_2$. Eliminating $x$ gives $I = I_1 \vee I_2$. A similar reasoning applies when $x$ occurs in $B$ but not $A$ and gives $I = I_1 \wedge I_2$. When $x$ occurs in both $A$ and $B$ then $x$ is kept in $I$ and acts as a selector for the values of $x$ smaller than $p$ $I_1$ is selected, otherwise $I_2$ applies.

The correctness of our method is shown by the following theorem:

**Theorem 1.** *The rules Split-I, ThLem-I, Weakening-I generate a Craig interpolant I from the proof of unsatisfiability of A and B.*

*Proof.* We prove correctness of the rules by induction. To express the inductive invariant, we split the domain $D$ into the domains $D_A$ and $D_B$ which contains only the intervals of the variables occurring in $A$, $B$ respectively.

At any given point in the proof, the partial interpolant $I$ is an interpolant for the formula $A$ over $D_A$ and $B$ over $D_B$. At the root of the proof tree we get an interpolant for the whole domain $D = D_A \wedge D_B$.

At the leaves of the proof, or the ThLem-I rule, one of the constraints has no solution over the domain. Let's assume that this constraint comes from $A$. Then the partial interpolant $I$ is $\bot$. We have that $A \wedge D_A \Rightarrow I$ by the semantics of the ThLem rule ($\bot \Rightarrow \bot$). Trivially, $B \wedge D_B \wedge I \Rightarrow \bot$ and $fv(I) = \emptyset \subseteq fv(A) \cap fv(B)$. When the contradiction comes from $B$, a similar reasoning applies with $I = \top$.

The Weakening-I only serves to select the constraint which causes the contradiction and does not change the invariant.

The Split-I rule is the most complex case. We have to consider whether the variable $x$ which is split come from $A$, $B$, or is shared. For instance, if $x \in fv(A)$ then the induction step has $D_{A1} = D_A \wedge x < p$ and $D_{A2} = D_A \wedge x \geq p$ and

$D_B$ is unchanged. If $x \in fv(B)$ then $D_B$ is affected and $D_A$ is unchanged. If $x$ is shared then both $D_A$ and $D_B$ are affected.

Let consider that $x \in fv(A)$ and $x \notin fv(B)$. We omit the case where $x$ is in $B$ but not $A$ as it is similar. The induction hypothesis is

$$
\begin{aligned}
& A \wedge (D_A \wedge x < p) \Rightarrow I_1 \\
& A \wedge (D_A \wedge x \geq p) \Rightarrow I_2 \\
& B \wedge D_B \wedge I_1 \Rightarrow \bot \\
& B \wedge D_B \wedge I_2 \Rightarrow \bot
\end{aligned}
\qquad \text{which simplifies to} \qquad
\begin{aligned}
& A \wedge D_A \Rightarrow I_1 \vee I_2 \\
& B \wedge D_B \wedge (I_1 \vee I_2) \Rightarrow \bot
\end{aligned}
\ .
$$

Finally, we need to consider $x \in fv(A)$ and $x \in fv(B)$. The induction hypothesis is

$$
\begin{aligned}
& A \wedge (D_A \wedge x < p) \Rightarrow I_1 \\
& A \wedge (D_A \wedge x \geq p) \Rightarrow I_2 \\
& B \wedge (D_B \wedge x < p) \wedge I_1 \Rightarrow \bot \\
& B \wedge (D_B \wedge x \geq p) \wedge I_2 \Rightarrow \bot
\end{aligned}
\qquad \text{and simplifies to} \qquad
\begin{aligned}
& A \wedge D_A \Rightarrow ite(x < p, I_1, I_2) \\
& B \wedge D_B \wedge ite(x < p, I_1, I_2) \Rightarrow \bot
\end{aligned}
\ .
$$

$\square$

*Example 2.* If we look at proof for the example in Fig. 1, we get the proof annotated with the partial interpolants shown in Fig. 5. The final interpolants $I_5$ is $0 \leq y \wedge (0.26 \leq y \vee (y \leq 0.26 \wedge -0.51 \leq x \leq 0.51))$.

*Boolean Structure.* The method we presented explain how to compute an interpolant for the conjunctive fragment of quantifier-free nonlinear theories over the reals. However, in many cases formula also contains disjunctions. To handle disjunctions, our method can be combined with the method presented by Yorsh and Musuvathi [41] for building an interpolant from a resolution proof where some of the proof's leaves carry theory interpolants.

*Handling ODE Constraints.* A special focus of $\delta$-complete decision procedures is on constraints that are defined by ordinary differential equations, which is important for hybrid system verification. In the logic formulas, the ODEs are treated simple as a class of constraints, over variables that represent both state space and time. Here we elaborate on the proofs and interpolants for the ODE constraints.

Let $t_0, T \in \mathbb{R}$ and $g : \mathbb{R}^n \to \mathbb{R}$ be a Lipschitz-continuous Type 2 computable function. Let $t_0, T \in \mathbb{R}$ satisfy $t_0 \leq T$ and $x_0 \in \mathbb{R}^n$. Consider the initial value problem

$$
\frac{dx}{dt} = g(x(t)) \text{ and } x(t_0) = x_0, \text{ where } t \in [t_0, T].
$$

It has a solution function $x : [t_0, T] \to \mathbb{R}^n$, which is itself a Type 2 computable function [40]. Thus, in the first-order language $\mathcal{L}_{\mathbb{R}_{\mathcal{F}}}$ we can write formulas like

$$
\left( ||x_0|| = 0 \right) \wedge \left( x_t = x_0 + \int_0^t g(x(s))ds \right) \wedge \left( ||x_t|| > 1 \right)
$$

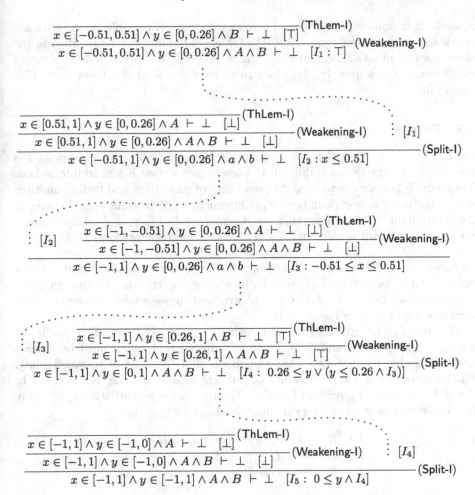

**Fig. 5.** Proof of unsatisfiability where $A$ is $y \geq x^2$, $B$ is $y \leq -\cos(x) + 0.8$ along with the corresponding interpolant

which is satisfiable when the system defined by the vector field $g$ can have a trajectory from some point $\|x(0)\| = 0$ to $\|x(t)\| = 1$ after time $t$. Note that we use first-order variable vectors $x_0$ and $x_t$ to represent the value of the solution function $x$ at time 0 and $t$. Also, the combination of equality and integration in the second conjunct simply denotes a single constraint over the variables $(x_0, x_t, t)$.

In the $\delta$-decision framework, we perform interval-based integration for ODE constraints that satisfies the following. Suppose the time domain for the ODE constraint in question is in $[t_0, T]$. Let $t_0 \leq t_1 \leq \cdots t_m \leq T$ be a sequence of time points. An interval-based integration algorithms compute boxes $D_{t_1}, ..., D_{t_m}$ such that

$$\forall i \in \{1, ..., m\}, \; \{x(t) : t_i \leq t \leq t_{i+1}, x_0 \in D_{x_0}\} \subseteq D_{t_0}.$$

Namely, it computes a sequence of boxes such that all possible trajectories are contained in them over time. Thus, the ODE constraints can be handled in the same way as non-ODE constraints, whose solution set is covered by a set of small boxes. Consequently, the proof rules from Fig. 4 apply directly to ODE constraints.

## 3.2   Extensions

For any two formulas $A,B$ which conjunction is unsatisfiable, the interpolant $I$ is not unique. In practice, it is difficult to know a priori what is a good interpolant. Therefore, it is desirable to have the possibility of generating and testing multiple interpolants. We now explain how to get interpolants of different logical strength. An interpolant $I_1$ is stronger than an interpolant $I_2$ iff $I_1 \Rightarrow I_2$. Intuitively, a stronger interpolant is closer to $A$ and a weaker interpolant closer to $B$.

*Parameterizing Interpolation Strength.* The interpolation method that we propose uses a $\delta$-decision procedure to build a Craig interpolant. $I$ being an interpolant means that $A \wedge \neg I$ and $B \wedge I$ are both unsatisfiable. However, these formulas might still be $\delta$-satisfiable.

To obtain an interpolant such that both $A \wedge \neg I$ and $B \wedge I$ are $\delta$-unsatisfiable, we can weaken both $A$ and $B$ by a factor $\delta$. However, $A$ and $B$ must be at least $3\delta$-unsatisfiable to guarantee that the solver finds a proof of unsatisfiability. Furthermore, we can also introduce perturbations only on one side in other to make the interpolant stronger of weaker. To introduce a perturbation $\delta$, we apply the following rewriting to every inequalities in $A$ and/or $B$:

$$L = R \quad \mapsto \quad L \geq R - \delta \wedge L \leq R + \delta$$
$$L \geq R \quad \mapsto \quad L \geq R - \delta$$
$$L > R \quad \mapsto \quad L > R - \delta$$

*Changing the Labelling.* Due to the similarity of our method to the interpolation of propositional formulas we can adapt the labelled interpolation system from D'Silva et al. [16] to our framework.

In the labelled interpolation system, it is possible to modify the A,B,AB labelling as long as it preserves *locality*, see [16] for the details. An additional restriction in our case is that we cannot use a projection of constraints at the proof's leaves. The projection is not computable in nonlinear theories. Therefore, the labelling must enforce that the leaves maps to the interpolants ⊤ or ⊥.

## 4   Applications and Evaluation

We have implemented the interpolation algorithm in a modified version of the dReal SMT solver.[1] The proofs produced by dReal can be very large, i.e., gigabytes. Therefore, the interpolants are built and simplified on-the-fly. The full

---

[1] Currently available in the branch https://github.com/dzufferey/dreal3/.

proof is not kept in memory. We modified the ICP loop and the contractors which are responsible for the pruning steps. The overhead induced by the interpolant generation over the solving time is smaller than 10 %.

The ICP loop (Fig. 1) builds a proof starting from the root of the proof tree and exploring the tree like a depth-first search. On the other hand, the interpolation rules build the interpolant starting from the proof's leaves. Our implementation modifies the ICP loop to keep a stack $P$ of partial interpolants alongside the stack of branching points $S$. When branching (line 9), the value used to split $D_1$ and $D_2$ is pushed on $P$. The pruning steps (line 5) are converted to a proof as shown in Fig. 3. When a contradiction is found (line 7, else branch), $P$ is popped to the branching point where the search resumes and the corresponding partial interpolant is pushed back on $P$. When the ICP loop ends, $P$ contains the final interpolant.

*Interpolant Sizes.* The ICP algorithm implemented in dReal eagerly prunes the domain by applying repeatedly *all* the constraints. Therefore, it usually generates large proofs often involving all the constraints and all the variables. Interpolation can extract more precise information from the proof. Intuitively, an interpolant which is much smaller than the proof are more likely to be useful in practice. In this test, we try to compare the size of the proof against the size of the interpolants using benchmark from the Flyspeck project [25], certificates for Lyapunov functions in powertrain control systems [27] and the other examples presented in the rest of this section.

We run dReal with a 20 min timeout and generate 1063 interpolants. Out of these, 501 are nontrivial. In Fig. 6 we plot the number of inequalities in the nontrivial interpolants against the size of the proof without the Weakening steps. For similar proofs, we see that the interpolants can be order of magnitude simpler than the proofs and other interpolants obtained by different partitions of the

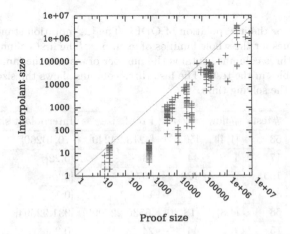

**Fig. 6.** Interpolants' size (number of inequalities) compared to the proofs' size.

formula. The trivial interpolants still bring information as they mean that the only one side is part of the unsatisfiable core.

*Hybrid System Verification.* Our method can compute interpolants for systems of ODEs. For instance, we can check that two trajectories do not intersect. Figure 7a shows an interpolant obtained for the following equations:

$$A: \quad x_t = x_0 + \int_0^t -x + cos(x)\, dx \wedge x_0 = 3 \wedge 0 \le t \le 2$$

$$B: \quad y_t = y_0 + \int_0^t -y + sin(y-1)\, dy \wedge y_0 = 2 \wedge x_t = y_t$$

A large portion, 479 out of 1063, of our examples involves differential equations. These examples include: airplane control [5], bouncing balls, networked water tanks, models of cardiac cells [29], verification of the trajectory planning and tracking stacks of autonomous vehicle (in particular, for lane change maneuver [4]), and example from dReal regression tests. Table 1 shows statistics about the interpolants for each family of examples.

*Robotic Design.* Often, hybrid system verification is used in model-based design. An expert produces a model of the system which is then analysed. However, it is also possible to extract models directly from the manufacturing designs. As part of an ongoing project about co-design of both the software and hardware component of robots [42], we extract equations from robotic designs. In the extracted models, each structural element is represented by a 3D vector for its position and a unit quaternion for the orientation. The dimension of the elements and the joints connecting them corresponds to equations that relate the position and orientation variables. Active elements, such as motors, also have specific equations associated to them.

**Table 1.** Results for the interpolation of ODEs. The [_,_] notation stands for intervals that cover the values for the whole families of examples. The first column indicates the family. The next three columns contains the number of tests in the family, the number of flows and variables in the tests. The last three columns shows the size of the proofs, interpolants, and the solving time.

| Family | #tests | #flow | #var | Proof size | Interpolant size | Time |
|---|---|---|---|---|---|---|
| Airplane control | 53 | [1,4] | [56,61] | [4213,24249] | [70,10260] | [57 s,178 s] |
| Apex | 17 | 1 | 44 | 23 | [0,22] | [5 s,9 s] |
| Bouncing ball | 165 | 2 | 128 | 857 | [0,28] | [1.6 s,5.5 s] |
| Cardiac cells | 37 | 4 | 71 | 15 | [0,1] | [15 m,20 m] |
| Water tanks | 68 | [4,8] | [18,30] | [6530,225099] | [331,92594] | [7 s,12 m] |
| Lane change | 15 | 1 | 44 | 24 | [0,23] | [19 s,20 s] |
| Other tests | 142 | 1 | 5 | 2 | [0,1] | [0.1 s,1 s] |

This approach provides models faithful to the actual robots, but it has the downside of producing large systems of equations. To verify such systems, we need to simplify them. Due to the presence of trigonometric functions we cannot use quantifier elimination for polynomial systems of equations [13]. However, we use interpolation as an approximation of quantifier elimination.

Let us consider a kinematic model, $\mathcal{K}(x, y, z)$ where $x$ is a set of design and input parameters, $y$ is the variables that represent the state of each component of the robot, and $z$ is the variables that represent the parts of the state needed to prove the property of interest. For instance, in the case of a robotic manipulator, $x$ contain the sizes of each element and the angles of the servo motors and $z$ is the position of the effector. $y$ is determined by the designed of the manipulator.

Fully controlled systems have the property that once the design and input parameters are fixed, there is a unique solution for remaining variables in the model. Therefore, we can create an interpolation query:

$$A : \quad \mathcal{K}(x, y, z) \wedge$$
$$B : \quad \mathcal{K}(x, v, w) \wedge (z - w)^2 \geq \epsilon^2 \quad \text{where } \epsilon > \delta$$

$y, v$ are two copies of the variables we want to eliminate. Since the kinematic is a function of $x$ which is the same for the two copies $z$ and $w$ should be equal. Therefore, the formula we build has no solution and we get an interpolant $I(x, z)$ which is an $\epsilon$-approximation of $\exists\, y . \mathcal{K}(x, y, z)$.

*Example 3.* Consider the simple robotic manipulator show in Fig. 7b. The manipulator has one degree of freedom. It is composed of two beams connected by a revolute joint controlled by a servo motor. The first beam is fixed.

The original system of equations describing this system has 22 variables: 7 for each beam, 7 for the effector, and 1 for the revolute joint. Using the interpolation

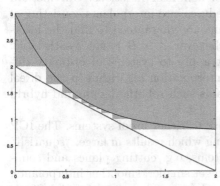

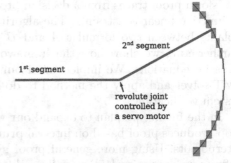

(a) Interpolant for system of nonlinear ODEs. The black and red curves are the trajectories described by $A$ and $B$. The green area is the interpolant.

(b) Model of a 1-DOF robotic manipulator composed of two 100mm long segments. The black line shows the effector's reach and the green cubes are the approximation obtained by interpolation where $\epsilon$ is 10mm.

**Fig. 7.** Application of interpolation to nonlinear systems

**Table 2.** Comparison of the original model of a 1 and 2 degrees of freedom manipulator against approximations obtained using interpolation. For the size of the formulas we report the number of theory atoms in the formula. The last column shows the time dReal takes to compute the interpolants.

| 1-DOF Model | #var | Theory | #th. atoms | time |
|---|---|---|---|---|
| original | 22 | polynomial deg. 2, trig. fct. | 24 | - |
| $\epsilon = 10$ | 4 | linear | 1073 | 0.3s |
| $\epsilon = 5$ | 4 | linear | 2757 | 0.6s |
| $\epsilon = 3$ | 4 | linear | 3307 | 0.8s |
| $\epsilon = 2$ | 4 | linear | 6137 | 1.3s |
| $\epsilon = 1$ | 4 | linear | 12485 | 2.6s |

| 2-DOF Model | #var | Theory | #th. atoms | time |
|---|---|---|---|---|
| original | 30 | polynomial deg. 2, trig. fct. | 32 | - |
| $\epsilon = 10$ | 5 | linear | 45686 | 2m 7s |
| $\epsilon = 7$ | 5 | linear | 97068 | 3m 51s |
| $\epsilon = 5$ | 5 | linear | 184762 | 6m 41s |
| $\epsilon = 3$ | 5 | linear | 547558 | 19m 4s |
| $\epsilon = 2$ | 5 | linear | 1151454 | 41m 51s |

we obtain a simpler formula with only 4 variables: 3 for the effector's position and 1 for the joint. Table 2 shows some statistics about the interpolants we obtained using different $\epsilon$ for a one and a two degrees of freedom manipulators.

# 5    Conclusion and Future Work

We present an method for computing Craig interpolants for first-order formulas over real numbers with a wide range of nonlinear functions. Our method transform proof traces from $\delta$ decision procedures into interpolants consisting of disjunctive linear constraints. The algorithms are guaranteed to find the interpolants between two formulas $A$ and $B$ whenever $A \wedge B$ is not $\delta$-satisfiable. Furthermore, we show how the framework apply to systems of ordinary differential equations. We implemented our interpolation algorithm in the dReal SMT-solver and apply the method to domains such robotic design, and hybrid system verification.

In the future, we plan to expand our work to richer proof systems. The ICP loop produces proof based on interval pruning which results in large, "squarish" interpolants. Using more general proof systems, e.g. cutting planes and semi-definite programming [15], we will be able to get smaller, smoother interpolants. CDCL-style reasoning for richer theories, e.g., LA($\mathbb{R}$) [36] and polynomial [26], is a likely basis for such extensions. Furthermore, we are interested in investigating the link between classical interpolation and Craig interpolation over the reals. Using methods like spline interpolation and radial basis functions, it maybe possible to build smoother interpolants. We also to extend the our rules to compute interpolants mixed proofs with both integer and real variables.

# References

1. Albargouthi, A., Berdine, J., Cook, B., Kincaid, Z.: Spatial interpolants. In: Vitek, J. (ed.) ESOP 2015. LNCS, vol. 9032, pp. 634–660. Springer, Heidelberg (2015)
2. Albarghouthi, A., Gurfinkel, A., Chechik, M.: WHALE: an interpolation-based algorithm for inter-procedural verification. In: Kuncak, V., Rybalchenko, A. (eds.) VMCAI 2012. LNCS, vol. 7148, pp. 39–55. Springer, Heidelberg (2012)
3. Albarghouthi, A., Li, Y., Gurfinkel, A., Chechik, M.: UFO: a framework for abstraction- and interpolation-based software verification. In: Madhusudan, P., Seshia, S.A. (eds.) CAV 2012. LNCS, vol. 7358, pp. 672–678. Springer, Heidelberg (2012)
4. Althoff, M., Dolan, J.M.: Online verification of automated road vehicles using reachability analysis. IEEE Trans. Robot. 30(4), 903–918 (2014)
5. Bae, K., Krisiloff, J., Meseguer, J., Ölveczky, P.C.: Designing and verifying distributed cyber-physical systems usingmultirate pals: an airplane turning control system case study. sci. comput. program. 103, 13–50 (2015). Selected papers from the First International Workshop on FormalTechniques for Safety-Critical Systems (FTSCS 2012)
6. Benhamou, F., Granvilliers, L.: Continuous and interval constraints. In: Rossi, F., van Beek, P., Walsh, T. (eds.) Handbook of Constraint Programming. Elsevier, Amsterdam (2006). chapter 16
7. Brattka, V., Hertling, P., Weihrauch, K.: A tutorial on computable analysis. In: Cooper, S.B., Löwe, B., Sorbi, A. (eds.) New Computational Paradigms, pp. 425–491. Springer, New York (2008)
8. Brillout, A., Kroening, D., Rümmer, P., Wahl, T.: An interpolating sequent calculus for quantifier-free presburger arithmetic. In: Giesl, J., Hähnle, R. (eds.) IJCAR 2010. LNCS, vol. 6173, pp. 384–399. Springer, Heidelberg (2010)
9. Chen, X., Ábrahám, E., Sankaranarayanan, S.: Flow*: An analyzer for non-linear hybrid systems. In: Sharygina, N., Veith, H. (eds.) CAV 2013. LNCS, vol. 8044, pp. 258–263. Springer, Heidelberg (2013)
10. Christ, J., Ermis, E., Schäf, M., Wies, T.: Flow-sensitive fault localization. In: Giacobazzi, R., Berdine, J., Mastroeni, I. (eds.) VMCAI 2013. LNCS, vol. 7737, pp. 189–208. Springer, Heidelberg (2013)
11. Christ, J., Hoenicke, J., Nutz, A.: SMTInterpol: an interpolating SMT solver. In: Donaldson, A., Parker, D. (eds.) SPIN 2012. LNCS, vol. 7385, pp. 248–254. Springer, Heidelberg (2012)
12. Cimatti, A., Griggio, A., Schaafsma, B.J., Sebastiani, R.: The mathSAT5 SMT solver. In: Piterman, N., Smolka, S.A. (eds.) TACAS 2013 (ETAPS 2013). LNCS, vol. 7795, pp. 93–107. Springer, Heidelberg (2013)
13. Collins, G., Hong, H.: Partial cylindrical algebraic decomposition for quantifier elimination. In: Caviness, B., Johnson, J. (eds.) Quantifier Elimination and Cylindrical Algebraic Decomposition, Texts and Monographs in Symbolic Computation, pp. 174–200. Springer Vienna (1998)
14. Craig, W.: Linear reasoning. A new form of the herbrand-gentzen theorem. J. Symb. Logic 22, 250–268 (1957)
15. Dai, L., Xia, B., Zhan, N.: Generating non-linear interpolants by semidefinite programming. In: Sharygina, N., Veith, H. (eds.) CAV 2013. LNCS, vol. 8044, pp. 364–380. Springer, Heidelberg (2013)
16. D'Silva, V., Kroening, D., Purandare, M., Weissenbacher, G.: Interpolant strength. In: Barthe, G., Hermenegildo, M. (eds.) VMCAI 2010. LNCS, vol. 5944, pp. 129–145. Springer, Heidelberg (2010)

17. Ermis, E., Schäf, M., Wies, T.: Error invariants. In: Méry, D., Giannakopoulou, D. (eds.) FM 2012. LNCS, vol. 7436, pp. 187–201. Springer, Heidelberg (2012)

18. Gao, S., Avigad, J., Clarke, E.M.: Delta-complete decision procedures for satisfiability over the reals. In: Gramlich et al. [23], pp. 286–300

19. Gao, S., Avigad, J., Clarke, E.M.: Delta-decidability over the reals. IEEE Computer Society, In: LICS (2012)

20. Gao, S., Kong, S., Clarke, E.M.: dReal: an SMT solver for nonlinear theories over the reals. In: Bonacina, M.P. (ed.) CADE 2013. LNCS, vol. 7898, pp. 208–214. Springer, Heidelberg (2013)

21. Gao, S., Kong, S., Clarke, E.M.: Satisfiability modulo odes. In: FMCAD, IEEE (2013)

22. Gao, S., Kong, S., Clarke, E.M.: Proof generation from delta-decisions. In: Winkler, F., Negru, V., Ida, T., Jebelean, T., Petcu, D., Watt, S.M., Zaharie, D. (eds.) SYNASC. IEEE (2014)

23. de Boer, F., Bonsangue, M., Rot, J.: Automated verification of recursive programs with pointers. In: Gramlich, B., Miller, D., Sattler, U. (eds.) IJCAR 2012. LNCS, vol. 7364, pp. 149–163. Springer, Heidelberg (2012)

24. Griggio, A., Le, T.T.H., Sebastiani, R.: Efficient interpolant generation in satisfiability modulo linear integer arithmetic. In: Abdulla, P.A., Leino, K.R.M. (eds.) TACAS 2011. LNCS, vol. 6605, pp. 143–157. Springer, Heidelberg (2011)

25. Hales, T., Adams, M., Bauer, G., Dang, D.T., Harrison, J., Hoang, T.L., Kaliszyk, C., Magron, V., McLaughlin, S., Nguyen, T.T., Nguyen, T.Q., Nipkow, T., Obua, S., Pleso, J., Rute, J., Solovyev, A., Ta, A.H.T., Tran, T.N., Trieu, D.T., Urban, J., Vu, K.K., Zumkeller, R.: A formal proof of the Kepler conjecture. ArXiv e-prints, January 2015

26. Jovanović, D., de Moura, L.: Solving non-linear arithmetic. In: Gramlich, B., Miller, D., Sattler, U. (eds.) IJCAR 2012. LNCS, vol. 7364, pp. 339–354. Springer, Heidelberg (2012)

27. Kapinski, J., Deshmukh, J.V., Sankaranarayanan, S., Arechiga, N.: Simulation-guided lyapunov analysis for hybrid dynamical systems. In: Fränzle, M., Lygeros, J. (eds.) HSCC. ACM (2014)

28. Kong, S., Gao, S., Chen, W., Clarke, E.: dReach: δ-reachability analysis for hybrid systems. In: Baier, C., Tinelli, C. (eds.) TACAS 2015. LNCS, vol. 9035, pp. 200–205. Springer, Heidelberg (2015)

29. Liu, B., Kong, S., Gao, S., Zuliani, P., Clarke, E.M.: Parameter synthesis for cardiac cell hybrid models using δ-decisions. In: Mendes, P., Dada, J.O., Smallbone, K. (eds.) CMSB 2014. LNCS, vol. 8859, pp. 99–113. Springer, Heidelberg (2014)

30. McMillan, K.L.: Interpolation and SAT-based model checking. In: Hunt Jr., W.A., Somenzi, F. (eds.) CAV 2003. LNCS, vol. 2725, pp. 1–13. Springer, Heidelberg (2003)

31. McMillan, K.L.: An interpolating theorem prover. In: Jensen, K., Podelski, A. (eds.) TACAS 2004. LNCS, vol. 2988, pp. 16–30. Springer, Heidelberg (2004)

32. McMillan, K.L.: Lazy abstraction with interpolants. In: Ball, T., Jones, R.B. (eds.) CAV 2006. LNCS, vol. 4144, pp. 123–136. Springer, Heidelberg (2006)

33. McMillan, K.L.: Interpolants and symbolic model checking. In: Cook, B., Podelski, A. (eds.) VMCAI 2007. LNCS, vol. 4349, pp. 89–90. Springer, Heidelberg (2007)

34. McMillan, K.L.: Interpolants from Z3 proofs. In: Bjesse, P., Slobodová, A. (eds.) FMCAD. FMCAD Inc. (2011)

35. McMillan, K.L.: Widening and interpolation. In: Yahav, E. (ed.) Static Analysis. LNCS, vol. 6887, p. 1. Springer, Heidelberg (2011)

36. McMillan, K.L., Kuehlmann, A., Sagiv, M.: Generalizing DPLL to richer logics. In: Bouajjani, A., Maler, O. (eds.) CAV 2009. LNCS, vol. 5643, pp. 462–476. Springer, Heidelberg (2009)
37. Pudlák, P.: Lower bounds for resolution and cutting plane proofs and monotone computations. J. Symbolic Logic **62**(3), 981–998 (1997)
38. Rybalchenko, A., Sofronie-Stokkermans, V.: Constraint solving for interpolation. In: Cook, B., Podelski, A. (eds.) VMCAI 2007. LNCS, vol. 4349, pp. 346–362. Springer, Heidelberg (2007)
39. Schäf, M., Schwartz-Narbonne, D., Wies, T.: Explaining inconsistent code. In: Meyer, B., Baresi, L., Mezini, M. (eds.) ACM SIGSOFT. ACM (2013)
40. Weihrauch, K., Analysis, C.: An Introduction (2000)
41. Yorsh, G., Musuvathi, M.: A combination method for generating interpolants. In: Nieuwenhuis, R. (ed.) CADE 2005. LNCS (LNAI), vol. 3632, pp. 353–368. Springer, Heidelberg (2005)
42. Zufferey, D., Mehta, A., DelPreto, J., Sidiroglou-Douskos, S., Rinard, M., Rus, D.: Talos: Full stack robot compilation, simulation, and synthesis.Submitted to ICRA 2016 (2016)

# Abstraction and Verification III

# PTIME Computation of Transitive Closures of Octagonal Relations

Filip Konečný[✉]

Brno, Czech Republic
filipkonecny@gmail.com

**Abstract.** Computing transitive closures of integer relations is the key to finding precise invariants of integer programs. In this paper, we study *difference bounds* and *octagonal* relations and prove that their transitive closure is a PTIME-computable formula in the existential fragment of Presburger arithmetic. This result marks a significant complexity improvement, as the known algorithms have EXPTIME worst case complexity.

## 1 Introduction

This paper gives the first polynomial-time algorithm for computing *closed forms* of *difference bounds* and *octagonal* relations. Difference bounds (DB) relations are relations defined as conjunctions over atomic propositions of the form $x - y \leq c$ where $c$ is an integer and $x, y$ range over unprimed and primed variables $\mathbf{x} \cup \mathbf{x}'$. Octagonal relations generalize difference bounds relation by allowing conjuncts of the form $\pm x \pm y \leq c$. Both classes of relations are widely used as domains in verification of software and hardware [11,12].

Given a binary relation $R$ on states (represented as a formula with primed and unprimed variables) a *closed form* of $R$ is another formula $\widehat{R}(k)$ containing primed and unprimed variables as well as a parameter variable $k$, such that substituting the parameter $k$ with any integer $n \geq 1$ gives a precise description of $R^n$, the $n$-th power of $R$. The main result of this paper is a polynomial-time algorithm that, given the formula $R$ in the form of octagonal constraints computes a closed form $\widehat{R}(k)$ as a formula in the existential fragment of Presburger arithmetic. This result immediately extends to the computation of an expression for transitive closure, because $R^+ \Leftrightarrow \exists k \geq 1 . \widehat{R}(k)$.

Approaches for computing the precise closed form of iterated relation compositions are referred to as *acceleration* algorithms. Known acceleration algorithms for the two classes of relations are based on the notion of *periodicity* and compute closed forms of the size that is polynomial in the size of the *prefix* and the *period* of a relation. Intuitively, the $n$-th power of a DB relation $R$ can be obtained by computing minimal weights of paths between pairs of vertices in

---

The results presented in this paper were established during postdoctoral research at Swiss Federal Institute of Technology in Lausanne (EPFL).

M. Chechik and J.-F. Raskin (Eds.): TACAS 2016, LNCS 9636, pp. 645–661, 2016.
DOI: 10.1007/978-3-662-49674-9_42

certain graphs (called *unfolded constraint graphs of $R$* and denoted $\mathcal{G}_R^n$). For a fixed pair of vertices, minimal weights evolve periodically as a function of $n$. However, since DB relations whose period increases super-polynomially in the binary size of the relation $\|R\|_2$ can be constructed, it follows that an algorithm for computing closed forms that runs in polynomial time must necessarily be based on a method different than explicitly computing periodicity. This paper presents the first such algorithm.

**Overview.** First, we study difference bounds relations (Sect. 3 gives a background). Our main observation is that the problem of computing a closed form of a DB relation $R$ can be reduced to the computation of closed forms of two PTIME-computable DB relations $R_{fw}$ and $R_{bw}$ such that $R_{fw}$ $(R_{bw})$ belongs to a fragment called *forward (backward) one-directional* DB relations which contains DB relations of the form

$$\bigwedge_{ij} x_i - x_j' \le c_{ij} \quad \left(\bigwedge_{ij} x_i' - x_j \le c_{ij}, \text{ respectively}\right)$$

We first study these (dual) fragments and give a PTIME algorithm which computes the closed form in the existential fragment of Presburger arithmetic (Sect. 4). The main insight of this algorithm is that the closed form can be defined by encoding polynomially many *path schemes* which can be thought of as regular patterns that capture all paths with minimal weight in unfolded constraint graphs.

Next, we observe that for a fixed pair of vertices $(u, v)$ in an unfolded constraint graph, any path $\rho$ from $u$ to $v$ can be *normalized*, i.e. replaced with another path $\rho'$ from $u$ to $v$ such that the weight of $\rho'$ is not greater than the weight of $\rho$ and $\rho'$ is in a normal form (Sect. 5).

Then, we define the relations $R_{fw}$ and $R_{bw}$ and show that there exists an integer $B$ of polynomial size such that every normalized path $\rho$ in $\mathcal{G}_R^{2B+n}$ can be viewed as a concatenation of several paths from $\mathcal{G}_{R_{fw}}^n$, $\mathcal{G}_{R_{bw}}^n$ and $\mathcal{G}_R^B$ (Sect. 6). Since paths from $\mathcal{G}_{R_{fw}}^n$ and $\mathcal{G}_{R_{bw}}^n$ are captured by closed forms $\widehat{R}_{fw}(n)$ and $\widehat{R}_{bw}(n)$ (both PTIME-computable), and since paths in $\mathcal{G}_R^B$ are captured by $R^B$ (also PTIME-computable, since $B$ is polynomially large), it follows that $\widehat{R}_{fw}(n)$, $\widehat{R}_{bw}(n)$, and $R^B$ can be combined to form a closed form $\widehat{R}(2B + n)$.

Finally, in Sect. 7, we show that these methods and results can be generalized to compute closed forms of octagonal relations in polynomial time as well. Section 8 concludes.

**Related Work.** Octagonal constraints [11] are well known in abstract interpretation as an abstract domain for over-approximating sets of reachable states. Transitive closure algorithms for octagonal relations [2] are the core of reachability analysis techniques based on computation of procedure summaries [9] or on accelerated interpolation [8].

DB and octagonal relations have been shown to have Presburger definable transitive closures [1,6,7] and to have periodic characterization [2]. An algorithm from [2] computes a transitive closure whose size is polynomial in the binary size of the relation $\|R\|_2$ and in the size of the prefix and period. The algorithm has super-polynomial complexity, since relations whose period increases exponentially in $\sqrt{\|R\|_2}$ can be constructed.

Recently, [3,5] proves that both prefix and period can also be upper-bounded by a single exponential and moreover, shows NP-completeness of the reachability problem for *flat counter systems*, a class of integer programs without nested loops where each loop (non-loop) transition is described by an octagonal relation (QFPA[1] formula). Moreover, [5] presents a non-deterministic reduction to satisfiability of QFPA formulas (an NP-complete problem), essentially by first guessing the prefix and period and then guessing one of exponentially many disjuncts of the transitive closure, for each loop. Our present result can turn this reduction into a deterministic one, since we can directly compute the transitive closure of each loop.

## 2    Preliminary Definitions

In the rest of this paper, let $N \geq 1$ and let $\mathbf{x} = \{x_1, x_2, ..., x_N\}$ be a set of variables ranging over $\mathbb{Z}$. For each $n \in \mathbb{Z}$, we define a fresh copy of variables $\mathbf{x}^{(n)} \overset{def}{=} \{x_1^{(n)}, \dots, x_N^{(n)}\}$. Similarly, $\mathbf{x}'$ denotes a fresh copy of primed variables $\mathbf{x}' = \{x_1', \dots, x_N'\}$. We assume that the reader is familiar with Presburger arithmetic (PA). For a PA formula $\phi$, let atoms($\phi$) denote the set of atomic propositions in $\phi$, and $\phi[t/x]$ denote the formula obtained by substituting the variable $x$ with the term $t$. card($S$) denotes the cardinality of a set $S$ and abs($c$) denotes the absolute value of $c \in \mathbb{Z}$. A *valuation* of $\mathbf{x}$ is a function $\nu : \mathbf{x} \to \mathbb{Z}$. The set of all such valuations is denoted by $\mathbb{Z}^{\mathbf{x}}$. Given a relation $R \subseteq \mathbb{Z}^{\mathbf{x}} \times \mathbb{Z}^{\mathbf{x}}$, we denote by $R^i$, for $i > 0$, the $i$-times composition of $R$ with itself. We denote by $R^+ = \bigcup_{i=1}^{\infty} R^i$ the *transitive closure* of $R$. If $R(\mathbf{x}, \mathbf{x}')$ defines $R$, we denote by $R^n(\mathbf{x}, \mathbf{x}')$ a formula that defines the $n$-th power $R^n$. A *closed form* of $R$ is a formula $\widehat{R}(k, \mathbf{x}, \mathbf{x}')$, where $k \notin \mathbf{x}$, such that $\widehat{R}[n/k]$ defines $R^n$, for all $n \geq 1$. For a weighted graph $G$ and a pair of vertices $u, v$, we denote by min-weight($u, v, G$) the minimal weight over all paths from $u$ to $v$ in $G$.

## 3    Difference Bounds Relations

**Definition 1.** *A formula $\phi(\mathbf{x})$ is a* difference bounds (DB) *constraint if it is a finite conjunction of atomic propositions of the form $x_i - x_j \leq \alpha_{ij}$, $1 \leq i, j \leq N$, where $\alpha_{ij} \in \mathbb{Z}$. A relation $R \subseteq \mathbb{Z}^{\mathbf{x}} \times \mathbb{Z}^{\mathbf{x}}$ is a* difference bounds relation *if it can be defined by a difference bounds constraint $\phi_R(\mathbf{x}, \mathbf{x}')$.*

---

[1] Quantifier-Free Presburger Arithmetic.

Difference bounds constraints are represented as graphs. If $\phi(\mathbf{x})$ is a difference bounds constraint, then *constraint graph* $\mathcal{G}_\phi = \langle \mathbf{x}, \rightarrow \rangle$ is a weighted graph, where each vertex corresponds to a variable, and there is an edge $x_i \xrightarrow{\alpha_{ij}} x_j$ in $\mathcal{G}_\phi$ if and only if there exists a constraint $x_i - x_j \leq \alpha_{ij}$ in $\phi$ (Fig. 1(a)). The following well known result from [10] gives means to test consistency of a DB constraint and to eliminate existential quantifiers, by analyzing weights of paths in its constraint graph:

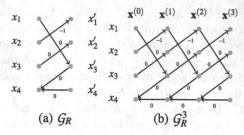

(a) $\mathcal{G}_R$       (b) $\mathcal{G}_R^3$

**Fig. 1.** The constraint graph $\mathcal{G}_R$ and its 3-times unfolding $\mathcal{G}_R^3$ for a difference bounds relation $R \Leftrightarrow x_2 - x_1' \leq -1 \wedge x_3 - x_2' \leq 0 \wedge x_1 - x_3' \leq 0 \wedge x_4' - x_4 \leq 0 \wedge x_3' - x_4 \leq 0$.

**Proposition 1.** *Let $\phi(x_0, \mathbf{x})$ be a DB constraint. Then, $\phi(x_0, \mathbf{x})$ is consistent if and only if $\mathcal{G}_\phi$ contains no cycle with negative weight. If $\phi(x_0, \mathbf{x})$ is consistent, then*

$$\exists x_0 \,.\, \phi(x_0, \mathbf{x}) \Leftrightarrow \bigwedge_{x,y \in \mathbf{x}} x - y \leq \text{min-weight}(x, y, \mathcal{G}_\phi)$$

*Moreover, consistency check and computation of $\exists x_0. \, \phi(x_0, \mathbf{x})$ is in $\mathcal{O}(\|R\|_2)$ time.*

Consequently, DB relations are closed under relational composition, i.e. $R^n(\mathbf{x}, \mathbf{x}')$ is a DB constraint for all $n \geq 1$. The $n$-th power of $R$ can be seen as a constraint graph consisting of $n$ copies of $\mathcal{G}_R$ (see Fig. 1(b)):

**Definition 2.** *Let $n \geq 1$ and $R(\mathbf{x}, \mathbf{x}')$ be a DB constraint. Then, the $n$-times unfolding of $\mathcal{G}_R$ is defined as $\mathcal{G}_R^n \stackrel{def}{=} \bigcup_{i=0}^{n-1} \mathcal{G}_{R(\mathbf{x}^{(i)}, \mathbf{x}^{(i+1)})}$.*

The vertices $\mathbf{x}^{(0)} \cup \mathbf{x}^{(n)}$ of $\mathcal{G}_R^n$ are called *extremal*. A path in $\mathcal{G}_R^n$ is said to be *extremal* if its first and last vertex are both extremal. The next lemma gives means to compute $R^n(\mathbf{x}, \mathbf{x}')$ and test its consistency, by analyzing extremal paths of $\mathcal{G}_R^n$.

**Lemma 1.** *Let $n \geq 1$ and $R(\mathbf{x}, \mathbf{x}')$ be a DB constraint. Then, $R^n(\mathbf{x}, \mathbf{x}')$ is consistent if and only if $\mathcal{G}_R^n$ contains no extremal cycle with negative weight. If $R^n(\mathbf{x}, \mathbf{x}')$ is consistent, then $R^n(\mathbf{x}, \mathbf{x}')$ can be computed as*

$$\bigwedge_{1 \leq i,j \leq N} x_i - x_j \leq \text{min-weight}(x_i^{(0)}, x_j^{(0)}, \mathcal{G}_R^n) \wedge x_i' - x_j' \leq \text{min-weight}(x_i^{(n)}, x_j^{(n)}, \mathcal{G}_R^n) \wedge$$
$$x_i - x_j' \leq \text{min-weight}(x_i^{(0)}, x_j^{(n)}, \mathcal{G}_R^n) \wedge x_i' - x_j \leq \text{min-weight}(x_i^{(n)}, x_j^{(0)}, \mathcal{G}_R^n)$$

*Moreover, consistency check and computation of $R^n(\mathbf{x}, \mathbf{x}')$ is in $\mathcal{O}(\|R\|_2 \cdot \log_2 n)$ time.*

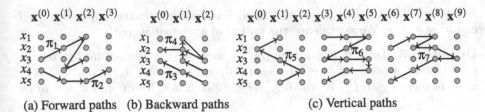

(a) Forward paths    (b) Backward paths    (c) Vertical paths

**Fig. 2.** Paths in unfolded constraint graphs. Path $\pi_1$ is repeating and essential, $\pi_2$ is repeating, $\pi_3$ is essential, $\pi_4$ is neither essential nor elementary, $\pi_5$ is essential. We have $|\pi_1| = 4, |\pi_2| = 3, \| \pi_2 \| = 3, \| \pi_1 \| = \| \pi_3 \| = \| \pi_4 \| = 2, \| \pi_5 \| = \| \pi_6 \| = \| \pi_7 \| = 0,$ positions$(\pi_6) = \{3, 4, 5\}$, vars$(\pi_2) = \{x_4, x_5\}$, vertices$(\pi_2) = \{x_4^{(0)}, x_5^{(1)}, x_5^{(2)}, x_4^{(3)}\}$.

**Paths in Unfoldings of $\mathcal{G}_R$.** In this paper, when the exact number of iterations does not matter, we sometimes consider paths in the bi-infinite unfolding $^\infty\mathcal{G}_R{}^\infty$ of $\mathcal{G}_R$, defined as

$$^\infty\mathcal{G}_R{}^\infty \stackrel{def}{=} \bigcup_{i \in \mathbb{Z}} \mathcal{G}_{R(\mathbf{x}^{(i)}, \mathbf{x}^{(i+1)})}$$

Note that each edge in $^\infty\mathcal{G}_R{}^\infty$ is either *forward* (i.e. of the form $x_i^{(p)} \stackrel{\alpha}{\to} x_j^{(p+1)}$ for some $1 \le i, j \le N$ and $p, \alpha \in \mathbb{Z}$), *backward* ($x_i^{(p+1)} \stackrel{\alpha}{\to} x_j^{(p)}$), or *vertical* ($x_i^{(p)} \stackrel{\alpha}{\to} x_j^{(p)}$). A *path* is a sequence of the form (see Fig. 2 for illustrations)

$$\rho = x_{i_0}^{(p_0)} \xrightarrow{\alpha_0} x_{i_1}^{(p_1)} \xrightarrow{\alpha_1} \ldots \xrightarrow{\alpha_{n-1}} x_{i_n}^{(p_n)}$$

for some $n \ge 0$ where $x_{i_k}^{(p_k)} \xrightarrow{\alpha_k} x_{i_{k+1}}^{(p_{k+1})}$ is an edge in $^\infty\mathcal{G}_R{}^\infty$, for each $0 \le k < n$. We say that a variable $x_{i_k}$ *occurs* on $\rho$ at *position* $p_k$, for each $0 \le k \le n$. We say that $\rho$ is *forward* (*backward, vertical*) if $p_0 < p_n$ ($p_0 > p_n$, $p_0 = p_n$, respectively). The *length* and *relative length* of $\rho$ is defined as $|\rho| = n$ and $\| \rho \| = \mathrm{abs}(p_n - p_0)$. The *weight* of $\rho$ is defined as $\omega(\rho) = \alpha_0 + \cdots + \alpha_{n-1}$. We write vars$(\rho)$ for the set $\{x_{i_0}, \ldots, x_{i_n}\}$, positions$(\rho)$ for the set $\{p_0, \ldots, p_n\}$, and vertices$(\rho)$ for the set $\{x_{i_0}^{(p_0)}, \ldots, x_{i_n}^{(p_n)}\}$. We say that $\rho$ is *repeating* if $p_0 \ne p_n$ and $i_0 = i_n$. We say that $\rho$ is *elementary* if all vertices $x_{i_0}^{(p_0)}, \ldots, x_{i_n}^{(p_n)}$ are distinct, with the exception of $x_{i_0}^{(p_0)}$ and $x_{i_n}^{(p_n)}$, which might be equal. We say that $\rho$ is *essential* if all variables $x_{i_0}, \ldots, x_{i_n}$ are distinct, with the exception of $x_{i_0}$ and $x_{i_n}$, which might be equal. Clearly, each essential path is also elementary. Note that the length of an essential path is bounded by $N$. A *subpath of* $\rho$ is any path of the form $x_{i_a}^{(p_a)} \to \ldots \to x_{i_b}^{(p_b)}$ where $0 \le a \le b \le n$. We denote by $\overrightarrow{\rho}^{(k)} : x_{i_0}^{(p_0+k)} \to \ldots \to x_{i_n}^{(p_n+k)}$ the path obtained by *shifting* $\rho$ by $k$, where $k \in \mathbb{Z}$. A path $\rho$ is said to be *isomorphic* with another path $\rho'$ if and only if $\rho' = \overrightarrow{\rho}^{(k)}$, for some $k \in \mathbb{Z}$. Consider a path $\pi = x_{j_0}^{(q_0)} \xrightarrow{\beta_0} \ldots \xrightarrow{\beta_{m-1}} x_{j_m}^{(q_m)}$. The *concatenation* $\rho \cdot \pi$ is defined if $x_{i_n}^{(p_n)} = x_{j_0}^{(q_0)}$. If $i_n = j_0$, we write $\rho \cdot \pi$ as a shorthand for $\rho \cdot \overrightarrow{\pi}^{(p_n - q_0)}$. If $\rho$ is repeating and

$k \geq 1$, we define the *k-th power of* $\rho$ as the $k$-times concatenation of $\rho$ with itself, e.g. $\rho^3 = \rho \cdot \rho \cdot \rho$. We next define the notion of a *compatible* path.

**Definition 3.** *Let* $\rho, \rho'$ *be paths in* $\mathcal{G}_R^n$ *for some* $n \geq 1$. *We say that* $\rho'$ *is compatible with* $\rho$ *(denoted* $\rho' \preceq \rho$*) if and only if (i)* $\omega(\rho') \leq \omega(\rho)$ *and (ii) there exist integers* $1 \leq i, j \leq N$ *and* $0 \leq k, \ell \leq n$ *such that both* $\rho$ *and* $\rho'$ *are of the form* $x_i^{(k)} \to \ldots \to x_j^{(\ell)}$.

**Balanced Relations.** We say that a difference bounds constraint $R(\mathbf{x}, \mathbf{x}')$ is *balanced* whenever $(x - y \leq c) \in \text{atoms}(R)$ if and only if $(x' - y' \leq c) \in \text{atoms}(R)$. Note that the relation $R_b$ (called the *balanced closure* of $R$) defined below is balanced:

$$R_b \overset{def}{=} R \wedge \bigwedge_{(x-y\leq c)\in\text{atoms}(R)} x' - y' \leq c \wedge \bigwedge_{(x'-y'\leq c)\in\text{atoms}(R)} x - y \leq c$$

We next show that the computation of the closed form for $R$ can be reduced to the computation of the closed form of its balanced closure (let $\mathbf{y}$ and $\mathbf{z}$ be fresh copies of variables in $\mathbf{x}$):

**Proposition 2.** *Let* $R(\mathbf{x}, \mathbf{x}')$ *be a DB constraint,* $R_b(\mathbf{x}, \mathbf{x}')$ *be its balanced closure, and* $\widehat{R}_b(\ell, \mathbf{x}, \mathbf{x}')$ *be the closed form of* $R_b$. *Then,* $\widehat{R}(k, \mathbf{x}, \mathbf{x}')$ *can be defined as:*

$$\bigvee_{i=1}^{2} (k = i \wedge R^i(\mathbf{x}, \mathbf{x}')) \vee \exists \mathbf{y}, \mathbf{z} \,.\, k \geq 3 \wedge R(\mathbf{x}, \mathbf{y}) \wedge \widehat{R}_b(\ell, \mathbf{y}, \mathbf{z})[k - 2/\ell] \wedge R(\mathbf{z}, \mathbf{x}')$$

Sections 5 and 6 study balanced DB relations and finally show, as a consequence of Proposition 2, that the results can be generalized to arbitrary DB relations.

## 4   Closed Forms for One-Directional Difference Bounds Relations

We say that a DB constraint $R(\mathbf{x}, \mathbf{x}')$ is *one-directional* if it is either (i) a conjunction of the form $\bigwedge_{ij} x_i - x'_j \leq c_{ij}$ (*forward* one-directional) or (ii) a conjunction of the form $\bigwedge_{ij} x'_i - x_j \leq c_{ij}$ (*backward* one-directional). Clearly, the two cases are dual: $R$ is forward one-directional if and only if its inverse $R^{-1}$ (which can be defined as $R(\mathbf{x}, \mathbf{x}')[\mathbf{x}'/\mathbf{x}, \mathbf{x}/\mathbf{x}']$) is backward one-directional. Consequently, a closed form of $R$ can be directly obtained from a closed form of $R^{-1}$ as:

$$\widehat{R}(k, \mathbf{x}, \mathbf{x}') \Leftrightarrow \widehat{R^{-1}}(k, \mathbf{x}, \mathbf{x}')[\mathbf{x}/\mathbf{x}', \mathbf{x}'/\mathbf{x}]$$

We can thus consider, without loss of generality, only forward one-directional relations. Let $R$ be such relation. Clearly, $\mathcal{G}_R^n$ contains only forwards edges for all $n \geq 1$. Hence, $|\rho| = \| \rho \|$ for each path $\rho$ in $\mathcal{G}_R^n$ and moreover, $\mathcal{G}_R^n$ contains no cycle and $R^n$ is thus consistent, for all $n \geq 1$. Then, by Proposition 1, computation of $R^n(\mathbf{x}, \mathbf{x'})$ amounts to computing, for each $1 \leq i, j \leq N$, the minimal weight over all paths in $\mathcal{G}_R^n$ of the form $x_i^{(0)} \rightarrow \ldots \rightarrow x_j^{(n)}$. We next show that minimal weight paths have, without loss of generality, regular shape in the sense that they are instances of *cubic path schemes*:

**Definition 4.** *If $\sigma, \sigma'$ are paths and $\lambda$ is an empty or an essential repeating path such that $\sigma . \lambda . \sigma'$ is a non-empty path, the expression $\theta = \sigma . \lambda^* . \sigma'$ is called a* path scheme. *A path scheme encodes the infinite set of paths $[\![\theta]\!] = \{\sigma . \lambda^n . \sigma' \mid n \geq 0\}$. We say that $\theta$ is* cubic *if $|\sigma . \sigma'| \leq N^3$.*

**Lemma 2.** *Let $R$ be a one-directional DB relation, let $n \geq 1$, and let $\rho$ be an extremal path in $\mathcal{G}_R^n$. Then, there exists a compatible path $\rho'$ and a cubic path scheme $\sigma . \lambda^* . \sigma'$, such that $\rho' \in [\![\sigma . \lambda^* . \sigma']\!]$.*

By Lemma 2, minimal weight paths can be captured by a set $\Pi$ of all cubic path schemes. For each such scheme $\sigma . \lambda^* . \sigma' \in \Pi$, we have $|\sigma . \sigma'| \leq N^3$ (by Definition 4) and $|\lambda| \leq N$ (since the length of essential paths is bounded by $N$). In the worst case, each vertex of $\mathcal{G}_R^n$ has $N$ successors and hence, there are up to $N^n$ paths in $\mathcal{G}_R^n$ of the form $x_i^{(0)} \rightarrow \ldots \rightarrow x_j^{(n)}$, for a fixed $1 \leq i, j \leq N$. Consequently, card$(\Pi)$ is of the order $2^{\mathcal{O}(N)}$. We next show that it is sufficient to consider only polynomially many representants from $\Pi$. We first partition $\Pi$ into polynomially many equivalence classes. Each class is determined by (i) first and last variables of $\sigma$, $\lambda$, and $\sigma'$, and by (ii) the length of $\lambda$ and $\sigma . \sigma'$. Formally, the partition is defined as:

$$\Xi \stackrel{def}{=} \{\Pi_{ijkpq} \mid 1 \leq i, j, k \leq N, 0 \leq p \leq N^3, 0 \leq q \leq N, p + q > 0\}$$

where each $\Pi_{ijkpq} \subseteq \Pi$ is defined as follows: $\sigma . \lambda^* . \sigma' \in \Pi_{ijkpq}$ if and only if $\sigma, \lambda, \sigma'$ are paths of the form:

$$\lambda = x_k^{(0)} \rightarrow \ldots \rightarrow x_k^{(q)} \tag{1}$$

$$\sigma = x_i^{(0)} \rightarrow \ldots \rightarrow x_k^{(r)}, \ \sigma' = x_k^{(r)} \rightarrow \ldots \rightarrow x_j^{(p)}, \text{ for some } 0 \leq r \leq p \tag{2}$$

Intuitively, $q$ ($p$) determines the length of $\lambda$ ($\sigma . \sigma'$, respectively) and $k$ determines the variable on which $\lambda$ connects with $\sigma$ and $\sigma'$. Clearly, card$(\Xi)$ is of the order $\mathcal{O}(N^7)$.

Let us fix $i, j, k, p, q$ and assume that $\Pi_{ijkpq} \neq \emptyset$. It is easy to see that if there exists a path $\lambda$ of the form (1), then there exists one with minimal weight. Similarly, if there exists a path $\sigma . \sigma'$ of the form (2), then there exists one with minimal weight. We define $\theta_{ijkpq}$ as the path scheme $\sigma . \lambda^* . \sigma'$ where $\lambda$ and $\sigma . \sigma'$ are the minimal paths. It is easy to see that $\theta_{ijkpq}$ is *minimal* in $\Pi_{ijkpq}$ in the following sense: $\omega(\sigma . \lambda^n . \sigma') \leq \omega(\nu . \mu^n . \nu')$ for each $\nu . \mu^* . \nu' \in \Pi_{ijkpq}$ and each $n \geq 0$. Hence, we can use $\theta_{ijkpq}$ as a representant of $\Pi_{ijkpq}$. The minimal representants can be computed in polynomial time:

**Lemma 3.** *The set $\{\theta_{ijkpq} \mid \Pi_{ijkpq} \neq \emptyset\}$ can be computed in PTIME.*

Next, we fix $1 \leq i, j \leq N$ and define:

$$S_{ij} \overset{def}{=} \{(|\sigma . \sigma'|, |\lambda|, \omega(\sigma . \sigma'), \omega(\lambda)) \mid \exists k, p, q . \; \theta_{ijkpq} = \sigma . \overset{*}{\lambda} . \sigma'\}$$

It follows from the previous arguments that $S_{ij}$ represents all cubic schemes which capture paths from $x_i^{(0)}$ to $x_j^{(n)}$ and moreover, $S_{ij}$ can be computed in polynomial time and its cardinality is polynomial. A closed form of the sequence $\{\text{min-weight}(x_i^{(0)}, x_j^{(n)}, \mathcal{G}_R^n)\}_{n \geq 1}$ can be then defined as:

$$\phi_{ij}(n, x_i, x_j') \Leftrightarrow n \geq 1 \wedge \bigwedge_{(p,q,a,b) \in S_{ij}} \forall \ell . \; (\ell \geq 0 \wedge n = p + q \cdot \ell) \Rightarrow (x_i - x_j' \leq a + b \cdot \ell)$$

Intuitively, each conjunct encodes a constraint of one scheme $\sigma . \lambda^* . \sigma'$: whenever the scheme captures a path of length $n$ (i.e. $n = |\sigma . \sigma'| + \ell \cdot |\lambda| = p + q \cdot \ell$ where $\ell \geq 0$), the difference $x_i - x_j'$ must be upper-bounded by the corresponding weight $\omega(\sigma . \sigma') + \ell \cdot \omega(\lambda) = a + \ell \cdot b$. Equivalently, we can write:

$$\phi_{ij}(n, x_i, x_j') \Leftrightarrow n \geq 1 \wedge \bigwedge_{(p,q,a,b) \in S_{ij}} (n \geq p \wedge q \mid n - p) \Rightarrow q \cdot (x_i - x_j') \leq q \cdot a + b \cdot (n - p) \tag{3}$$

Then, we can define the closed form of $R$ as:

$$\widehat{R}(n, \mathbf{x}, \mathbf{x}') \Leftrightarrow \bigwedge_{1 \leq i,j \leq N} \phi_{ij}(n, x_i, x_j') \tag{4}$$

Clearly, $\phi_{ij}(n, x_i, x_j')$ (and hence also $\widehat{R}(n, \mathbf{x}, \mathbf{x}')$) is a formula in the existential fragment of PA and of polynomial size, since $\text{card}(S_{ij})$ is polynomial. Thus, it follows from Lemma 3 that the whole computation of $\widehat{R}(n, \mathbf{x}, \mathbf{x}')$ is polynomial.

**Theorem 1.** *Let $R(\mathbf{x}, \mathbf{x}')$ be a one-directional DB constraint. Then, its closed form $\widehat{R}(n, \mathbf{x}, \mathbf{x}')$ can be computed in PTIME as a formula in the existential fragment of PA.*

## 5   Normalization of Paths in the Unfolded Constraint Graph

In this section, we consider only balanced DB relations and show that every extremal path in an unfolded constraint graph can be *normalized*. Intuitively, a path $\rho$ from $\mathcal{G}_R^n$ is normalized if none of its subpaths that traverses only positions in the range $\{N^2, \ldots, n - N^2\}$ is a *long corner*. Informally, a *corner* is a vertical path that stays either on the right or on the left side of the initial position. A corner is *long* if the distance between its minimal and maximal position exceeds the bound $N^2$.

**Definition 5 (Corners).** *Let $\rho$ be a vertical path of the form $\rho = x_{i_0}^{(k_0)} \to \ldots \to x_{i_m}^{(k_m)}$ for some $m \geq 1$ such that $k_0 = k_m$. If $\text{positions}(\rho) = \{k_0, \ldots, k_0 + d\}$*

*for some* $d \geq 0$, *we say that* $\rho$ *is a* right corner *of extent* $d$. *If* positions$(\rho) = \{k_0 - d, \ldots, k_0\}$ *for some* $d \geq 0$, *we say that* $\rho$ *is a* left corner *of extent* $d$. *We say that* $\rho$ *is a* corner *if it is either a left corner or a right corner. We denote the extent of a corner* $\rho$ *by* extent$(\rho)$. *We say that a corner* $\rho$ *is* basic *if* $k_0 \notin \{k_1, \ldots, k_{m-1}\}$. *We say that a corner* $\rho$ *is* long *if* extent$(\rho) > N^2$. *We say that* $\rho$ *is a* lb-corner *if it is both long and basic.*

For instance, consider vertical paths from Fig. 2(c), where $\pi_6$ is a right corner, $\pi_7$ is a right basic corner, and $\pi_5$ is not a corner. Both $\pi_6$ and $\pi_7$ are short, e.g. extent$(\pi_6) = 2 \leq 5^2 = N^2$. In the following, lb-corners$(\rho)$ (l-corners$(\rho)$, respectively) denotes the set of subpaths of $\rho$ which are lb-corners (long corners, respectively). It is easy to show that if a path contains no lb-corner, it also contains no long corner. We are now ready to formalize the notion of a *normalized* path.

**Definition 6** *(Normalized Paths). Let* $n \geq 1$ *and let* $\rho$ *be an extremal path in* $\mathcal{G}_R^n$. *We say that* $\rho$ *is* normalized *if none of its subpaths* $\theta$ *such that* positions$(\theta) \subseteq \{N^2, \ldots, n - N^2\}$ *is a long corner.*

For example, the path in Fig. 3(a) is not normalized, due to the long corner $\theta$.

**Normalization.** Given an integer $n \geq 1$ and an extremal path $\rho_1$ from $\mathcal{G}_R^n$, we construct a finite sequence $\{\rho_k\}_{k=1}^m$ of paths from $\mathcal{G}_R^n$ for some $m \geq 1$ such that $\rho_m$ is normalized and $\rho_{k+1}$ is compatible with $\rho_k$ (Definition 3), for each $1 \leq k < m$. By transitivity, we have that $\rho_m$ is compatible with $\rho_1$. For each $1 \leq k < m$, the path $\rho_{k+1}$ is obtained from $\rho_k$ by *substituting* one of its subpaths with a compatible path.

**Definition 7** *(Substitution). If* $\gamma . \theta . \gamma'$ *and* $\theta'$ *are paths in* $\mathcal{G}_R^n$ *such that* $\theta' \preceq \theta$, *the substitution of* $\theta$ *in* $\gamma . \theta . \gamma'$ *with* $\theta'$ *is defined as* $(\gamma . \theta . \gamma')[\theta' / \theta] \overset{def}{=} \gamma . \theta' . \gamma'$.

The subpaths of $\rho_1, \ldots, \rho_{m-1}$ that are substituted are certain paths called *segments*: Informally, *segments* of $\rho$ are unique subpaths of $\rho$ that traverse only positions $\{p, \ldots, q\}$ for some fixed parameters $p \leq q$.

**Definition 8** *(Path Segments). Let* $n \geq 1$ *and let* $\rho$ *be a path in* $\mathcal{G}_R^n$. *Let* $0 < p \leq q < n$ *be integers and let* $\mathcal{H}$ *be the (unique) subgraph of* $\mathcal{G}_R^n$ *obtained by removing every edge* $\tau$ *such that* positions$(\tau) \subseteq \{p, \ldots, q\}$. *We define* segments$(\rho, p, q)$ *to be the (unique) sequence* $\xi_1, \ldots, \xi_m$ *of non-empty paths, for some* $m \geq 0$, *such that*

- $\xi_i$ *is a subpath of* $\rho$ *such that* positions$(\xi_i) \subseteq \{p, \ldots, q\}$, *for each* $1 \leq i \leq m$
- *there exist non-empty paths* $\sigma_1, \ldots, \sigma_{m+1}$ *in* $\mathcal{H}$ *such that* $\rho = \sigma_1 . \xi_1 \ldots \sigma_m . \xi_m . \sigma_{m+1}$

As an example, consider the path $\rho = \sigma_1 . \gamma . \theta . \gamma' . \sigma_2$ in Fig. 3(a) for which we have segments$(\rho, N^2, n - N^2) = \gamma . \theta . \gamma'$ (i.e. $\rho$ has one segment for the parameter choice $p = N^2$ and $q = n - N^2$).

In the rest of this paper, we write segments($\rho$) as a shorthand for segments($\rho, N^2, n - N^2$). If $\xi \in$ segments($\rho$), we say that $\xi$ is a *segment* of $\rho$. It is easy to verify that each segment of an extremal path $\rho$ in $\mathcal{G}_R^n$ is of the form $\xi = x_i^{(p)} \to \ldots \to x_j^{(q)}$ for some $1 \leq i, j \leq N$ and $p, q \in \{N^2, n - N^2\}$. The next proposition allows us to use an alternative characterization of normalized paths:

**Proposition 3.** *Let $n \geq 1$ and let $\rho$ be an extremal path in $\mathcal{G}_R^n$. Then, $\rho$ is normalized if and only if* 1-corners($\xi$) $= \emptyset$ *for each $\xi \in$ segments($\rho$).*

**Termination Argument.** We next argue that the previously mentioned finite sequence $\{\rho_k\}_{k=1}^m$ exists for some $m \geq 1$, by tracking, for each segment, the distance of the *first lb-corner* from the end of the segment:

**Proposition 4 (Finding the First lb-corner).** *Let $\rho$ be a path such that* lb-corners($\rho$) $\neq \emptyset$. *Then, $\rho$ has subpaths $\rho_1, \theta, \rho_2$ such that $\rho = \rho_1 . \theta . \rho_2$,* lb-corners($\rho_1 . \theta$) $= \{\theta\}$, *and* extent($\theta$) $= N^2 + 1$. *The corner $\theta$ is called the first lb-corner of $\rho$.*

For instance, $\theta$ is the first lb-corner of the path $\sigma_1 . \gamma . \theta . \gamma' . \sigma_2$ in Fig. 3(a). We define lb-segments($\rho$) to be the subsequence of segments($\rho$) obtained by erasing every segment $\xi$ such that lb-corners($\xi$) $= \emptyset$. For each $1 \leq k < m$, we guarantee that if lb-segments($\rho_k$) $= \xi_1, \ldots, \xi_a$ for some $a \geq 1$, then either

$$
\begin{aligned}
&(1) \text{ lb-segments}(\rho_{k+1}) = \xi_2, \ldots, \xi_a, \text{ or} \\
&(2) \text{ lb-segments}(\rho_{k+1}) = \zeta, \xi_2, \ldots, \xi_a \text{ for some } \zeta
\end{aligned} \tag{5}
$$

and moreover, in case (2), $\xi_1$ and $\zeta$ are paths such that

- $\xi_1 = \gamma_1 . \theta_1 . \gamma_1'$ for some paths $\gamma_1, \theta_1, \gamma_1'$ and $\theta_1$ is the first lb-corner of $\xi_1$,
- $\zeta = \gamma_2 . \theta_2 . \gamma_2'$ for some paths $\gamma_2, \theta_2, \gamma_2'$ and $\theta_2$ is the first lb-corner of $\zeta$, and
- $|\gamma_2'| < |\gamma_1'|$

Intuitively, $\rho_k$ and $\rho_{k+1}$ have the same segments with long corners, with the exception of one segment $\xi_1$, which is either eliminated (case 1), or replaced with another segment $\zeta$ (case 2) such that the length of the unique suffix $\gamma_2'$ of $\zeta$ after its first lb-corner is strictly smaller than the length of the unique suffix $\gamma_1'$ of $\xi_1$ after its first lb-corner. Hence, the number of consecutive applications of the case 2 is bounded by $|\xi_1|$. Clearly, if $|\xi_1| = 0$, then only case 1 may happen, which decreases the number of segments with long corners, and therefore guarantees termination.

**Transforming Segments with Long Corners.** Let $n \geq 1$, let $\rho$ be an extremal path in $\mathcal{G}_R^n$, and let $\xi \in$ lb-segments($\rho$). We show how to construct a path $\rho'$ that is compatible with $\rho$ and moreover satisfies the termination properties from (5). By Proposition 4, there exists a unique corner $\theta$ (the first lb-corner of $\xi$) such that $\xi = \gamma . \theta . \gamma'$, lb-corners($\gamma . \theta$) $= \{\theta\}$, and extent($\theta$) $= N^2 + 1$, for some paths $\gamma, \gamma'$. Figure 3(a) depicts such situation. Suppose that $\xi$ starts at

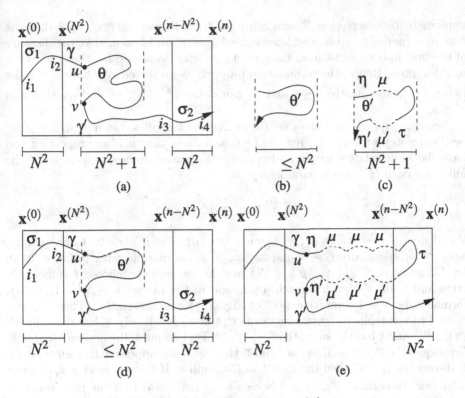

**Fig. 3.** Transformation of a segment with long corners

position $N^2$ and ends at position $n - N^2$ (the other three cases are symmetric). Then, it is not difficult to show that $\theta$ is a right corner. The following lemma states a key result which allows us to either shorten or decompose the corner $\theta$.

**Lemma 4 (Corner Shortening/Decomposition).** *Let $\rho$ be a right (left) lb-corner such that* extent$(\rho) = N^2+1$. *Then, there exists a compatible right (left) basic corner $\rho'$ such that either (i)* extent$(\rho') \leq N^2$ *or (ii)* extent$(\rho') = N^2 + 1$ *and $\rho'$ has subpaths $\eta, \mu, \tau, \mu', \eta'$ such that $\rho' = \eta.\mu.\tau.\mu'.\eta'$, $\mu$ is a forward (backward) repeating path, $\mu'$ is a backward (forward) repeating path, $\tau$ is a right (left) corner, $\|\eta\| = \|\eta'\|$, $1 \leq \|\mu\| = \|\mu'\| \leq N^2$, and $\omega(\mu) + \omega(\mu') < 0$. Moreover, for all $k \geq 0$, $\eta.\mu^k.\tau.\mu'^k.\eta'$ is a right (left) corner and* lb-corners$(\eta.\mu^k) = $ lb-corners$(\mu'^k.\eta') = \emptyset$.

Let $\theta'$ be the corner obtained by applying Lemma 4. Figure 3(b) depicts the case (i) and Fig. 3(c) the case (ii).

First, suppose that the case (i) of Lemma 4 applies. Then, one can define

$$\zeta \stackrel{def}{=} \xi[\hat{\theta}/\theta] = (\gamma.\theta.\hat{\gamma})[\hat{\theta}/\theta] = \gamma.\hat{\theta}.\hat{\gamma}$$

(see Fig. 3(d)) and prove that lb-corners$(\gamma.\theta') = \emptyset$, by using the fact from Lemma 4 that extent$(\theta') \leq N^2$. If lb-corners$(\zeta) = \emptyset$, then the case 1 in (5) applies. If lb-corners($\zeta$) $\neq \emptyset$, one can infer from lb-corners($\gamma . \theta'$) $= \emptyset$ that the first lb-corner of $\zeta$ involves at least one edge of $\gamma'$ and hence, that the distance of the first lb-corner in $\zeta$ from the end of $\zeta$ strictly decreases, i.e. that the case 2 in (5) applies. Hence, the termination property is preserved. We have $\theta' \preceq \theta$, by Lemma 4. Consequently, $\zeta \preceq \xi$ and we can define $\rho' \stackrel{def}{=} \rho[\zeta / \xi]$ and see that also $\rho' \preceq \rho$.

Second, suppose that the case (ii) of Lemma 4 applies. Let $\theta' = \eta . \mu . \tau . \mu' . \eta'$ be the decomposition of $\theta'$ given by Lemma 4. Note that $\mu, \mu'$ are repeating and have the same relative length and opposite directions. Hence, we can define the following path ($\ell \geq 1$ is a parameter):

$$\bar{\theta} \stackrel{def}{=} \eta . \mu^\ell . \tau . \mu'^\ell . \eta'$$

We define $\rho' \stackrel{def}{=} \rho[\bar{\theta} / \theta']$. By Lemma 4, $\omega(\mu) + \omega(\mu') < 0$. Consequently, $\omega(\bar{\theta}) \leq \omega(\theta')$ for any $\ell \geq 1$ and hence, $\rho'$ is compatible with $\rho$, i.e. $\rho' \preceq \rho$. By Lemma 4, $1 \leq \|\mu\| = \|\mu'\| \leq N^2$ and hence, one can choose $\ell$ sufficiently large and make the path $\bar{\theta}$ reach a position in the range $\{n - N^2 + 1, \ldots, n\}$, formally: $n - N^2 + 1 \in$ positions($\bar{\theta}$). See Fig. 3(e) for an illustration. Thus, the segment $\xi$ in $\rho$ is replaced by two segments $\zeta', \zeta$ in $\rho'$. Intuitively, $\zeta'$ has the subpath $\gamma . \eta . \mu^{\ell-1}$ and $\zeta$ has the subpath $\mu'^{\ell-1} . \eta' . \gamma'$. By Lemma 4, lb-corners($\eta . \mu^\ell$) $= \emptyset$. Consequently, $\zeta'$ has no lb-corner and $\zeta'$ thus does not appear in lb-segments($\rho'$). If lb-corners($\zeta$) $= \emptyset$, then the case 1 in (5) applies. If lb-corners($\zeta$) $\neq \emptyset$, one can infer from lb-corners($\mu'^\ell . \eta'$) $= \emptyset$ (which is by Lemma 4) that the first lb-corner of $\zeta$ involves at least one edge of $\gamma'$ and hence, that the distance of the first lb-corner in $\zeta$ from the end of $\zeta$ strictly decreases, i.e. that the case 2 in (5) applies. Hence, the termination argument holds for all cases.

We can thus conclude that every extremal path can be normalized.

**Theorem 2.** *Let $R(\mathbf{x}, \mathbf{x}')$ be a balanced DB constraint, let $n \geq 1$ be an integer, and let $\rho$ be a path between extremal vertices of $\mathcal{G}_R^n$. Then, there exists a normalized path $\rho'$ such that $\rho' \preceq \rho$.*

## 6     Closed Forms for Difference Bounds Relations

By Lemma 1, relation $R^n$ is consistent if $\mathcal{G}_R^n$ contains no extremal cycle with negative weight and moreover, a consistent relation $R^n$ can be defined as a conjunction of constraints each of which corresponds to a minimal extremal path. Hence, proving that a formula $\phi(\mathbf{x}, \mathbf{x}')$ defines $R^n$ amounts to showing that $\phi(\mathbf{x}, \mathbf{x}')$ implies exactly those constraints represented by extremal paths in $\mathcal{G}_R^n$. Consequently, a closed form $\widehat{R}(k, \mathbf{x}, \mathbf{x}')$ must satisfy the above for each $k \geq 1$. In this section, we show how to define such formula, in several steps. First, we strengthen the relation $R$ in a way that enables us to shortcut every short corner with a single vertical edge (Sect. 6.1). Second, we define a formula that encodes paths that do not contain long corners (Sect. 6.2). Third, we generalize this encoding to extremal paths (Sect. 6.3), by exploiting the fact that such paths can be decomposed into segments according to Definition 8 and that segments of extremal normalized paths contain no long corners. Finally, we show how the formula that encodes extremal paths can be used to define a closed form (Sect. 6.4).

## 6.1  Encoding Short Corners

Consider the strengthened relation $R_s$ in Fig. 4(a). We prove that for each $n \geq 1$, each short corner in $\mathcal{G}_R^n$ has a compatible vertical edge in $\mathcal{G}_{R_s}^n$ (see Fig. 4(b-c)).

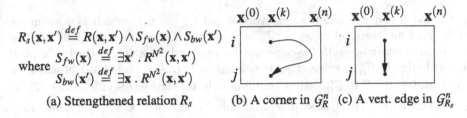

$$R_s(\mathbf{x},\mathbf{x}') \overset{def}{=} R(\mathbf{x},\mathbf{x}') \wedge S_{fw}(\mathbf{x}) \wedge S_{bw}(\mathbf{x}')$$
$$\text{where} \quad S_{fw}(\mathbf{x}) \overset{def}{=} \exists \mathbf{x}' . R^{N^2}(\mathbf{x},\mathbf{x}')$$
$$S_{bw}(\mathbf{x}') \overset{def}{=} \exists \mathbf{x} . R^{N^2}(\mathbf{x},\mathbf{x}')$$

(a) Strengthened relation $R_s$    (b) A corner in $\mathcal{G}_R^n$  (c) A vert. edge in $\mathcal{G}_{R_s}^n$

**Fig. 4.** Shortcutting a short corner by strengthening a relation

**Proposition 5** *(Encoding of Short Corners).* *Let $R(\mathbf{x},\mathbf{x}')$ be a balanced DB constraint, let $n \geq 1$ be an integer and let $\theta$ be a short corner in $\mathcal{G}_R^n$ of the form $x_i^{(k)} \rightarrow \ldots \rightarrow x_j^{(k)}$. Then:*

$$R_s(\mathbf{x},\mathbf{x}') \Rightarrow S_{fw}(\mathbf{x}) \Rightarrow x_i - x_j \leq \omega(\theta) \quad (\text{if } \theta \text{ is right})$$
$$R_s(\mathbf{x},\mathbf{x}') \Rightarrow S_{bw}(\mathbf{x}') \Rightarrow x_i' - x_j' \leq \omega(\theta) \quad (\text{if } \theta \text{ is left})$$

*Consequently, there is a compatible vertical edge $x_i^{(k)} \overset{c}{\rightarrow} x_j^{(k)}$ in $\mathcal{G}_{R_s}^n$, for some $c \leq \omega(\theta)$.*

The intuition is that if we view the above short right corner $\theta$ as an extremal path in $\mathcal{G}_R^{N^2}$ that starts at position 0, then we have, by Lemma 1, that $R^{N^2}(\mathbf{x},\mathbf{x}') \Rightarrow x_i - x_j \leq \omega(\theta)$, and hence the first implication in Proposition 5 holds, by the definition of $S_{fw}$ and $R_s$.

## 6.2  Encoding Paths Without Long Corners

The strengthening from Sect. 6.1 can be used to *straighten* paths which have only short corners. Informally, a straightened path is either (i) a sequence of forward edges, or (ii) a sequence of backward edges, or (iii) a single vertical edge. Let $\xi$ be an extremal path in $\mathcal{G}_R^n$ such that l-corners($\xi$) = $\emptyset$. First, suppose that $\xi$ is forward. Then, $\xi$ can viewed as a sequence of forward edges and right corners in $\mathcal{G}_R^n$ (Fig. 5(b)). By Proposition 5, each corner can be shortcut by a vertical

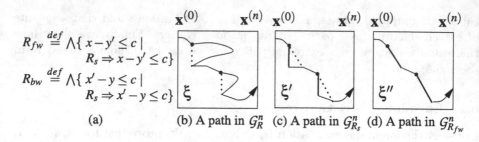

$$R_{fw} \stackrel{def}{=} \bigwedge\{\, x-y' \le c \mid$$
$$R_s \Rightarrow x-y' \le c\}$$
$$R_{bw} \stackrel{def}{=} \bigwedge\{\, x'-y \le c \mid$$
$$R_s \Rightarrow x'-y \le c\}$$

(a)    (b) A path in $\mathcal{G}_R^n$   (c) A path in $\mathcal{G}_{R_s}^n$   (d) A path in $\mathcal{G}_{R_{fw}}^n$

**Fig. 5.** Path straightening

edge, and hence we obtain an equivalent path $\xi'$ in $\mathcal{G}_{R_s}^n$ which is a sequence of forward and vertical edges in $\mathcal{G}_{R_s}^n$ (Fig. 5(c)). Then, every subpath of $\xi'$ of the form $(vertical\text{-}edge)^*.fw\text{-}edge$ can be replaced by a (transitively) implied forward edge in $\mathcal{G}_{R_{fw}}^n$ where $R_{fw}$ is defined in Fig. 5(a). and thus obtaining an equivalent path $\xi''$ in $\mathcal{G}_{R_{fw}}^n$ that contains only forward edges (Fig. 5(d)). Then, $\xi''$ is encoded by $\widehat{R}_{fw}(\ell, \mathbf{x}, \mathbf{x}')[n/\ell]$ and hence also in $\phi(\ell, \mathbf{x}, \mathbf{x}')[n/\ell]$ defined as:

$$\phi(\ell, \mathbf{x}, \mathbf{x}') \Leftrightarrow \widehat{R}_{fw}(\ell, \mathbf{x}, \mathbf{x}') \wedge \widehat{R}_{bw}(\ell, \mathbf{x}, \mathbf{x}') \wedge S_{fw}(\mathbf{x}) \wedge S_{bw}(\mathbf{x}') \tag{6}$$

If $\xi$ is an extremal right corner, then it is encoded by $S_{fw}(\mathbf{x})$ (by Proposition 5) and hence also by $\phi(\ell, \mathbf{x}, \mathbf{x}')$ (since $S_{fw}$ is its conjunct). The other cases (backward extremal path, extremal left corner) are symmetric. Hence, $\phi(\ell, \mathbf{x}, \mathbf{x}')$ encodes all extremal paths in $\mathcal{G}_R^n$ that have no long corners, in the following sense:

**Proposition 6 (Encoding of Paths Without Long Corners).** Let $R(\mathbf{x}, \mathbf{x}')$ be a balanced DB constraint, let $n \ge 1$, and let $\xi$ be an extremal path in $\mathcal{G}_R^n$, i.e. of the form $x_i^{(p)} \to \cdots \to x_j^{(q)}$ for some $1 \le i, j \le N$ and $p, q \in \{0, n\}$. If l-corners$(\xi) = \emptyset$, then:

1. $\phi(\ell, \mathbf{x}, \mathbf{x}')[n/\ell] \Rightarrow x_i - x_j' \le \omega(\xi)$   if $p = 0$, $q = n$
2. $\phi(\ell, \mathbf{x}, \mathbf{x}')[n/\ell] \Rightarrow x_i' - x_j \le \omega(\xi)$   if $p = n$, $q = 0$
3. $\phi(\ell, \mathbf{x}, \mathbf{x}')[n/\ell] \Rightarrow x_i - x_j \le \omega(\xi)$   if $p = q = 0$
4. $\phi(\ell, \mathbf{x}, \mathbf{x}')[n/\ell] \Rightarrow x_i' - x_j' \le \omega(\xi)$   if $p = q = n$

## 6.3   Encoding Extremal Paths

Consider the following formula (let $\mathbf{y}$ and $\mathbf{z}$ be fresh copies of variables in $\mathbf{x}$):

$$\psi(\ell, \mathbf{x}, \mathbf{x}') \Leftrightarrow \exists \mathbf{y}, \mathbf{z} \,.\, R^{N^2}(\mathbf{x}, \mathbf{y}) \wedge \phi(\ell, \mathbf{y}, \mathbf{z}) \wedge R^{N^2}(\mathbf{z}, \mathbf{x}') \tag{7}$$

We prove that for each $n \ge 1$, the formula $\psi(\ell, \mathbf{x}, \mathbf{x}')$ encodes every extremal path in $\mathcal{G}_R^{2N^2+n}$, in the following sense.

**Proposition 7.** (*Encoding of Extremal Paths*). *Let $R(\mathbf{x}, \mathbf{x}')$ be a balanced DB constraint, let $n \geq 1$, and let $\rho$ be an extremal normalized path in $\mathcal{G}_R^{2N^2+n}$, i.e. of the form $x_i^{(p)} \rightarrow \ldots \rightarrow x_j^{(q)}$ for some $1 \leq i, j \leq N$ and $p, q \in \{0, 2N^2+n\}$. Then:*

1. $\psi(\ell, \mathbf{x}, \mathbf{x}')[n/\ell] \Rightarrow x_i - x_j' \leq \omega(\rho)$   *if* $p = 0, q = 2N^2 + n$
2. $\psi(\ell, \mathbf{x}, \mathbf{x}')[n/\ell] \Rightarrow x_i' - x_j \leq \omega(\rho)$   *if* $p = 2N^2 + n, q = 0$
3. $\psi(\ell, \mathbf{x}, \mathbf{x}')[n/\ell] \Rightarrow x_i - x_j \leq \omega(\rho)$   *if* $p = q = 0$
4. $\psi(\ell, \mathbf{x}, \mathbf{x}')[n/\ell] \Rightarrow x_i' - x_j' \leq \omega(\rho)$   *if* $p = q = 2N^2 + n$

The intuition behind the encoding is as follows. Let $\rho$ be an extremal normalized path and let $\rho = \sigma_1 . \xi_1 \ldots \sigma_m . \xi_m . \sigma_{m+1}$ be its decomposition according to Definition 8. By Proposition 3, l-corners($\xi_i$) = $\emptyset$ for each $1 \leq i \leq m$, and hence, by Proposition 6, $\xi_i$ is encoded by $\phi(\ell, \mathbf{y}, \mathbf{z})$. For each $1 \leq i \leq m+1$, we have that $\sigma_i$ is encoded in $R^{N^2}(\mathbf{x}, \mathbf{y})$ or in $R^{N^2}(\mathbf{z}, \mathbf{x}')$. Then, since $\rho = \sigma_1 . \xi_1 \ldots \sigma_m . \xi_m . \sigma_{m+1}$, one can show, by transitivity, that (7) encodes $\rho$. For instance, consider the path $\rho = \sigma_1 . \gamma . \theta' . \gamma' . \sigma_2$ in Fig. 3(d) and denote $\xi_1 = \gamma . \theta' . \gamma'$. Supposing $\rho$ is normalized, we have:

$$\begin{pmatrix} R^{N^2}(\mathbf{x}, \mathbf{y}) & \Rightarrow x_{i_1} - y_{i_2} \leq \omega(\sigma_1) \\ \phi(\ell, \mathbf{y}, \mathbf{z})[n/\ell] \Rightarrow y_{i_2} - z_{i_3} \leq \omega(\xi_1) \\ R^{N^2}(\mathbf{z}, \mathbf{x}') & \Rightarrow z_{i_3} - x_{i_4}' \leq \omega(\sigma_2) \end{pmatrix} \Rightarrow \begin{pmatrix} \psi(\ell, \mathbf{x}, \mathbf{x}')[n/\ell] \Rightarrow \\ x_{i_1} - x_{i_4}' \leq \omega(\sigma_1 . \xi_1 . \sigma_2) = \omega(\rho) \end{pmatrix}$$

### 6.4   Defining the Closed Form

We finally prove that the formula $\widehat{R}(k, \mathbf{x}, \mathbf{x}')$ defined below is a closed form of $R$:

$$\widehat{R}(k, \mathbf{x}, \mathbf{x}') \Leftrightarrow \bigvee_{i=1}^{2N^2} (k = i \wedge R^i(\mathbf{x}, \mathbf{x}')) \vee \exists \ell \geq 1 . \ k = 2N^2 + \ell \wedge \psi(\ell, \mathbf{x}, \mathbf{x}') \quad (8)$$

Note that $R_{fw}$ and $R_{bw}$ are one-directional DB relations (see Sect. 4). Clearly, $S_{fw}$, $S_{fw}$, $R_s$, $R_{fw}$, and $R_{bw}$ are PTIME-computable DB constraints, by Lemma 1 and Proposition 1. Since $\widehat{R}_{fw}(\ell, \mathbf{x}, \mathbf{x}')$ and $\widehat{R}_{bw}(\ell, \mathbf{x}, \mathbf{x}')$ are PTIME-computable formulas in the existential fragment of PA, by Theorem 1, so is the formula $\phi(\ell, \mathbf{x}, \mathbf{x}')$ in (6), and hence also $\widehat{R}(k, \mathbf{x}, \mathbf{x}')$ in (8).

**Theorem 3.** *Let $R(\mathbf{x}, \mathbf{x}')$ be a balanced DB constraint. Then, (8) defines a closed form of $R(\mathbf{x}, \mathbf{x}')$. Moreover, $\widehat{R}(n, \mathbf{x}, \mathbf{x}')$ is a PTIME-computable formula in the existential fragment of PA.*

By Proposition 2, the result of Theorem 3 extends to arbitrary DB relation.

**Corollary 1.** *Let $R(\mathbf{x}, \mathbf{x}')$ be a difference bounds constraint. Then, its closed form is a PTIME-computable formula in the existential fragment of PA.*

# 7  Octagonal Relations

The class of integer octagonal constraints is defined as follows:

**Definition 9.** *A formula* $\phi(\mathbf{x})$ *is an* octagonal constraint *if it is a finite conjunction of terms of the form* $x_i - x_j \leq a_{ij}$, $x_i + x_j \leq b_{ij}$, *or* $-x_i - x_j \leq c_{ij}$, *where* $a_{ij}, b_{ij}, c_{ij} \in \mathbb{Z}$, *for all* $1 \leq i, j \leq N$. *A relation* $R \subseteq \mathbb{Z}^{\mathbf{x}} \times \mathbb{Z}^{\mathbf{x}}$ *is an* octagonal relation *if it can be defined by an octagonal constraint* $\phi_R(\mathbf{x}, \mathbf{x}')$.

We represent octagonal constraints as difference bounds constraints over the dual set of variables $\mathbf{y} = \{y_1, y_2, \ldots, y_{2N}\}$, with the convention that $y_{2i-1}$ stands for $x_i$ and $y_{2i}$ stands for $-x_i$, respectively. For example, the octagonal constraint $x_1 + x_2 = 3$ is represented as $y_1 - y_4 \leq 3 \wedge y_2 - y_3 \leq -3$. In order to handle the $\mathbf{y}$ variables in the following, we define $\bar{\imath} = i - 1$, if $i$ is even, and $\bar{\imath} = i + 1$ if $i$ is odd. Obviously, we have $\bar{\bar{\imath}} = i$, for all $i \in \mathbb{N}$. We denote by $\bar{\phi}(\mathbf{y})$ the difference bounds constraint over $\mathbf{y}$ that represents $\phi(\mathbf{x})$:

**Definition 10.** *Given an octagonal constraint* $\phi(\mathbf{x})$, $\mathbf{x} = \{x_1, \ldots, x_N\}$, *its difference bounds representation* $\bar{\phi}(\mathbf{y})$, *over* $\mathbf{y} = \{y_1, \ldots, y_{2N}\}$, *is a conjunction of the following difference bounds constraints, where* $1 \leq i, j \leq N$, $c \in \mathbb{Z}$.

$$(x_i - x_j \leq c) \in \mathrm{atoms}(\phi) \Leftrightarrow (y_{2i-1} - y_{2j-1} \leq c), (y_{2j} - y_{2i} \leq c) \in \mathrm{atoms}(\bar{\phi})$$
$$(-x_i + x_j \leq c) \in \mathrm{atoms}(\phi) \Leftrightarrow (y_{2j-1} - y_{2i-1} \leq c), (y_{2i} - y_{2j} \leq c) \in \mathrm{atoms}(\bar{\phi})$$
$$(-x_i - x_j \leq c) \in \mathrm{atoms}(\phi) \Leftrightarrow (y_{2i} - y_{2j-1} \leq c), (y_{2j} - y_{2i-1} \leq c) \in \mathrm{atoms}(\bar{\phi})$$
$$(x_i + x_j \leq c) \in \mathrm{atoms}(\phi) \Leftrightarrow (y_{2i-1} - y_{2j} \leq c), (y_{2j-1} - y_{2i} \leq c) \in \mathrm{atoms}(\bar{\phi})$$

The following result has been proved in [4].

**Lemma 5.** *Let* $n \geq 1$ *and let* $R(\mathbf{x}, \mathbf{x}')$ *be an octagonal relation. Then, if* $R^n(\mathbf{x}, \mathbf{x}')$ *is consistent, the following equivalence holds:*

$$R^n(\mathbf{x}, \mathbf{x}') \Leftrightarrow \overline{R}^n(\mathbf{y}, \mathbf{y}')[\sigma], \quad \text{where} \quad \sigma = [x_i/y_{2i-1}, -x_i/y_{2i}, x_i'/y_{2i-1}', x_i'/y_{2i}']_{i=1}^N$$

Hence, a consistent $n$-th power of $R(\mathbf{x}, \mathbf{x}')$ can be computed by applying the above substitution $\sigma$ on the $n$-th power of $\overline{R}(\mathbf{y}, \mathbf{y}')$.

**Checking ∗-consistency.** We say that a relation $R$ is *∗-consistent* if $R^n$ is consistent for each $n \geq 1$. If $R$ is not ∗-consistent, we define the minimal inconsistent power of $R$ as:

$$K_R \stackrel{def}{=} \min\{n \mid n \geq 1, R^n \text{ is inconsistent}\}$$

**Lemma 6.** *Checking ∗-consistency of* $R$ *and computation of* $K_R$ *can be done in PTIME.*

**Closed Form.** We prove that the closed form of an octagonal relation $R(\mathbf{x}, \mathbf{x}')$ can be defined as:

$$\widehat{R}(k, \mathbf{x}, \mathbf{x}') \Leftrightarrow \begin{cases} \widehat{\overline{R}}(k, \mathbf{y}, \mathbf{y}')[\sigma] & \text{if } R \text{ is } *\text{-consistent} \\ \widehat{\overline{R}}(k, \mathbf{y}, \mathbf{y}')[\sigma] \wedge k < K_R & \text{otherwise} \end{cases} \tag{9}$$

**Theorem 4.** *Let $R(\mathbf{x}, \mathbf{x}')$ be an octagonal constraint. Then, (9) defines its closed form and moreover, it is a PTIME-computable formula in the existential fragment of PA.*

## 8 Conclusions

We have presented a method that computes transitive closures of octagonal relations in polynomial time. This result also provides a proof of the fact that transitive closures are expressible in (the existential fragment of) Presburger arithmetic. Consequently, our result also simplifies the proof of NP-completeness of reachability checking for flat counter automata from [5], by allowing a deterministic polynomial time reduction to the satisfiability of QFPA.

## References

1. Bozga, M., Gîrlea, C., Iosif, R.: Iterating octagons. In: Kowalewski, S., Philippou, A. (eds.) TACAS 2009. LNCS, vol. 5505, pp. 337–351. Springer, Heidelberg (2009)
2. Bozga, M., Iosif, R., Konečný, F.: Fast acceleration of ultimately periodic relations. In: Touili, T., Cook, B., Jackson, P. (eds.) CAV 2010. LNCS, vol. 6174, pp. 227–242. Springer, Heidelberg (2010)
3. Bozga, M., Iosif, R., Konečný, F.: The complexity of reachability problems for flat counter machines with periodic loops. Technical Report (2013). arXiv.5321 (1307)
4. Bozga, M., Iosif, R., Konečný, F.: Deciding conditional termination. Log. Meth. Comput. Sci. **10**(3) (2014)
5. Bozga, M., Iosif, R., Konečný, F.: Safety problems are NP-complete for flat integer programs with octagonal loops. In: McMillan, K.L., Rival, X. (eds.) VMCAI 2014. LNCS, vol. 8318, pp. 242–261. Springer, Heidelberg (2014)
6. Bozga, M., Iosif, R., Lakhnech, Y.: Flat parametric counter automata. Fundamenta Informaticae **91**(2), 275–303 (2009)
7. Comon, H., Jurski, Y.: Multiple counters automata, safety analysis and presburger arithmetic. In: Hu, A.J., Vardi, M.Y. (eds.) Proceedings of CAV. LNCS, vol. 1427, pp. 268–279. Springer, Heidelberg (1998)
8. Hojjat, H., Iosif, R., Konečný, F., Kuncak, V., Rümmer, P.: Accelerating interpolants. In: Chakraborty, S., Mukund, M. (eds.) ATVA 2012. LNCS, vol. 7561, pp. 187–202. Springer, Heidelberg (2012)
9. Hojjat, H., Konečný, F., Garnier, F., Iosif, R., Kuncak, V., Rümmer, P.: A verification toolkit for numerical transition systems - tool paper. In: Proceedings of FM, pp. 247–251 (2012)
10. Miné, A.: Weakly Relational Numerical Abstract Domains (2004)
11. Miné, A.: The octagon abstract domain. High.-Ord. Symbolic Comput. **19**(1), 31–100 (2006)
12. Wang, C., Ivančić, F., Ganai, M.K., Gupta, A.: Deciding separation logic formulae by SAT and incremental negative cycle elimination. In: Sutcliffe, G., Voronkov, A. (eds.) LPAR 2005. LNCS (LNAI), vol. 3835, pp. 322–336. Springer, Heidelberg (2005)

# Scalable Verification of Linear Controller Software

Junkil Park[1]([envelope]), Miroslav Pajic[2], Insup Lee[1], and Oleg Sokolsky[1]

[1] Department of Computer and Information Science,
University of Pennsylvania, Philadelphia, USA
{park11,lee,sokolsky}@cis.upenn.edu
[2] Department of Electrical and Computer Engineering,
Duke University, Durham, USA
miroslav.pajic@duke.edu

**Abstract.** We consider the problem of verifying software implementations of linear time-invariant controllers against mathematical specifications. Given a controller specification, multiple correct implementations may exist, each of which uses a different representation of controller state (e.g., due to optimizations in a third-party code generator). To accommodate this variation, we first extract a controller's mathematical model from the implementation via symbolic execution, and then check input-output equivalence between the extracted model and the specification by similarity checking. We show how to automatically verify the correctness of C code controller implementation using the combination of techniques such as symbolic execution, satisfiability solving and convex optimization. Through evaluation using randomly generated controller specifications of realistic size, we demonstrate that the scalability of this approach has significantly improved compared to our own earlier work based on the invariant checking method.

## 1 Introduction

Control systems are at the core of many safety- and life-critical embedded applications. Ensuring the correctness of these control system implementations is an important practical problem. Modern techniques for the development of control systems are model driven. Control design is performed using a mathematical model of the system, where both the controller and the plant are represented as sets of equations, using well established tools, such as Simulink and Stateflow.

Verification of the control system and evaluation of the quality of control is typically performed at the modeling level [3]. Once the control engineer is satisfied with the design, a software implementation of the controller is produced from the model using a generator such as Simulink Coder. To ensure that the generated implementation of the controller is correct with respect to its model, we ideally would like to have verified code generators that would guarantee that any generated controller correctly implements its model. In practice, however, code generators for control software are complex tools that are not easily amenable

© Springer-Verlag Berlin Heidelberg 2016
M. Chechik and J.-F. Raskin (Eds.): TACAS 2016, LNCS 9636, pp. 662–679, 2016.
DOI: 10.1007/978-3-662-49674-9_43

to formal verification, and are typically offered as black boxes. Subtle bugs have been found in earlier versions of commercially available code generators [22].

In the absence of verified code generators, it is desirable to verify instances of generated code against their models. In this paper, we consider an approach to perform such instance verification. Our approach is based on extracting a model from the controller code and establishing equivalence between the original and the extracted models. We limit our attention to linear time-invariant (LTI) controllers, since these are the most commonly used controllers in control systems. In such controllers, relations between the values of inputs and state variables, and between state variables and outputs, are linear functions of input and state variables with constant (i.e., time-invariant) coefficients.

Our technical approach relies on symbolic execution of the generated code. Symbolic expressions for state and output variables of the control function are used to reconstruct the model of the controller. The reconstructed model is then checked for input-output equivalence between the original and reconstructed model, using the well-known necessary and sufficient condition for the equivalence of two minimal LTI models. Verification is performed using real arithmetic. We account for some numerical errors by allowing for a bounded discrepancy between the models. We compare two approaches for checking the equivalence; one reduces the equivalence problem to an SMT problem, while the other uses a convex optimization formulation. We compare equivalence checking to an alternative verification approach introduced in [23], which converts the original LTI model into input-output based code annotations for verification at the code level.

The paper is organized as follows. Section 2 provides necessary background on LTI systems. Section 3 introduces the approach based on code annotations. Section 4 presents model extraction from code, followed by the equivalence checking in Sect. 5. Section 6 evaluates the performance of the approaches. In Sects. 7 and 8, we provide a brief overview of related work and conclude the paper.

## 2 Preliminaries

In this section, we present preliminaries on linear controllers and the structure of linear controller implementations (e.g., step function generated by Embedded Coder). We also describe a couple of motivating examples and the notations used in this paper.

The role of feedback controllers is to ensure the desired behavior of the closed-loop systems by computing inputs to the plants based on previously measured plant outputs. We consider linear LTI controllers and assume that the specifications (i.e., models) of the controllers are given in the standard *state-space representation* form

$$\begin{aligned} \mathbf{z}_{k+1} &= \mathbf{A}\mathbf{z}_k + \mathbf{B}\mathbf{u}_k \\ \mathbf{y}_k &= \mathbf{C}\mathbf{z}_k + \mathbf{D}\mathbf{u}_k. \end{aligned} \tag{1}$$

where $\mathbf{u}_k \in \mathbb{R}^p$ denotes the input vector to the controller at time $k$, $\mathbf{y}_k \in \mathbb{R}^m$ denotes the output vector of the controller at time $k$, $\mathbf{z}_k \in \mathbb{R}^n$ denotes the state vector of the controller. In addition, the size of the controller state $n$ is referred to as the size of the controller and we use a common assumption that the specified controller has minimal realization [26]; this implies that $n$ is also the degree of the controller (i.e., the degree of the denominator of its characteristic polynomial). Note that the matrices $\mathbf{A} \in \mathbb{R}^{n \times n}$, $\mathbf{B} \in \mathbb{R}^{n \times p}$, $\mathbf{C} \in \mathbb{R}^{m \times n}$ and $\mathbf{D} \in \mathbb{R}^{m \times p}$ together with the initial controller state $\mathbf{z}_0$ completely specify an LTI controller. Thus, we will let $\Sigma(\mathbf{A}, \mathbf{B}, \mathbf{C}, \mathbf{D}, \mathbf{z}_0)$ denote an LTI controller, or simply write $\Sigma(\mathbf{A}, \mathbf{B}, \mathbf{C}, \mathbf{D})$ when the initial controller state $\mathbf{z}_0$ is zero.

The model of LTI controllers can be implemented in software as a function that takes as input the current state of the controller and a set of input sensor values, and computes control output (i.e., inputs applied to the plant) and the new state of the controller. We refer to this function as the *step function*. The step function is called by the control software periodically, or whenever new sensor measurements arrive. We assume that data is exchanged with the step function through global variables.[1] In other words, the input, output and state variables are declared in the global scope, and the step function reads both input and state variables, and updates both output and state variables as the effect of its execution. However, we note that this assumption does not critically limit our approach because it can be easily extended to support a different code interface for the step function.

## 2.1   Motivating Examples

We start by introducing two motivating examples that illustrate limitations of the straightforward verification based on the mathematical model from (1). This is caused by the fact that controller code might be generated by a code generator whose optimizations may potentially violate the model, while still guaranteeing the desired control functionality.

**A Scalar Linear Integrator.** We begin with an example from [23], where the controller should compute a scalar control input $u_k$ as a scaled sum of all previous measurements $y_i \in \mathbb{R}, i = 0, 1, ..., k - 1$ – i.e.,

$$u_k = \sum_{i=0}^{k-1} \alpha y_i, k > 1, \text{ and, } u_0 = 0. \tag{2}$$

If the Simulink Integrator block with Forward Euler integration is used to implement this controller, the controller will be in the form of (1) as $\Sigma(1, \alpha, 1, 0)$, – i.e., $z_{k+1} = z_k + \alpha y_k, u_k = z_k$. Note that another realization of this controller could be $\hat{\Sigma}(1, 1, \alpha, 0)$ – i.e., $z_{k+1} = z_k + y_k, u_k = \alpha z_k$, resulting in a lower computational error due to finite precision computations [10]. Thus, for controller specification (2) two different controller implementations could be produced by different code generation tools, with the same input-output behavior while maintaining scaled and unscaled sums, respectively, of the previous values for $y_k$.

---

[1] This convention is used by Embedded Coder, a code generation toolbox for Matlab/Simulink.

**Multiple-Input-Multiple-Output Controllers.** The second example we will consider is a Multiple-Input-Multiple-Output (MIMO) controller, maintaining four states with two inputs and two outputs

$$
\mathbf{z}_{k+1} = \underbrace{\begin{bmatrix}
-0.500311 & 0.16751 & 0.028029 & -0.395599 & -0.652079 \\
0.850942 & 0.181639 & -0.29276 & 0.481277 & 0.638183 \\
-0.458583 & -0.002389 & -0.154281 & -0.578708 & -0.769495 \\
1.01855 & 0.638926 & -0.668256 & -0.258506 & 0.119959 \\
0.100383 & -0.432501 & 0.122727 & 0.82634 & 0.892296
\end{bmatrix}}_{A} \mathbf{z}_k +
$$

$$
+ \underbrace{\begin{bmatrix}
1.1149 & 0.164423 \\
-1.56592 & 0.634384 \\
1.04856 & -0.196914 \\
1.96066 & 3.11571 \\
-3.02046 & -1.96087
\end{bmatrix}}_{B} \mathbf{u}_k \tag{3}
$$

$$
\mathbf{y}_k = \underbrace{\begin{bmatrix}
0.283441 & 0.032612 & -0.75658 & 0.085468 & 0.161088 \\
-0.528786 & 0.050734 & -0.681773 & -0.432334 & -1.17988
\end{bmatrix}}_{C} \mathbf{z}_k \tag{4}
$$

This controller requires $25 + 10 = 35$ multiplications to update the state $\mathbf{z}$ in each step function. Similarly, in the general case, for any controller with the model in (1), $n^2 + np = n(n + p)$ multiplications are needed to update the controller's state. On the other hand, consider the controller below that requires only $5 + 10 = 15$ multiplications to update its state

$$
\hat{\mathbf{z}}_{k+1} = \underbrace{\begin{bmatrix}
0.87224 & 0 & 0 & 0 & 0 \\
0 & 0.366378 & 0 & 0 & 0 \\
0 & 0 & -0.540795 & 0 & 0 \\
0 & 0 & 0 & -0.332664 & 0 \\
0 & 0 & 0 & 0 & -0.204322
\end{bmatrix}}_{\hat{A}} \hat{\mathbf{z}}_k +
$$

$$
+ \underbrace{\begin{bmatrix}
0.822174 & -0.438008 \\
-0.278536 & -0.824313 \\
0.874484 & 0.858857 \\
-0.117628 & -0.506362 \\
-0.955459 & -0.622498
\end{bmatrix}}_{\hat{B}} \mathbf{u}_k, \tag{5}
$$

$$
\mathbf{y}_k = \underbrace{\begin{bmatrix}
-0.793176 & 0.154365 & -0.377883 & -0.360608 & -0.142123 \\
0.503767 & -0.573538 & 0.170245 & -0.583312 & -0.56603
\end{bmatrix}}_{\hat{C}} \hat{\mathbf{z}}_k \tag{6}
$$

In general, when a matrix $\mathbf{A}$ in (1) is diagonal, only $n + np = n(p + 1)$ multiplications are performed to update $\mathbf{z}_k$ in each `step` function.

In this example, the controllers $\Sigma$ and $\hat{\Sigma}$ are *similar*,[2] meaning that if the same inputs $\mathbf{y}_k$ are delivered to both controllers, the outputs of the controllers will be identical for all $k$, although the states maintained by the controllers will most likely be different. As a result, although it does not obey the state evolution of the initial controller $\Sigma$, the 'diagonalized' controller $\hat{\Sigma}$ provides the same control functionality as $\Sigma$ at a significantly reduced computational cost – making it more suitable for embedded applications.

## 2.2    Problem Statements

The introduced examples illustrate that code generation tools for embedded systems could produce more efficient code that deviates from the initial controller model as specified in (1), while being functionally correct from the input-output perspective. Consequently, in this work we will focus on verification methods that facilitate reasoning about the correctness of linear controllers without relying on the state-space representation of the controller. We will compare our approach with a verification approach we introduced in [23] which, to enable verification at the code level, converts the original LTI model into input-output code annotations based on the controllers' transfer functions. Thus, we start by providing an overview of the code annotation method for LTI controllers introduced in [23].

## 3    Overview of Invariant-Based Approach

In [23], we introduced an approach for verification of LTI controllers using the controllers' transfer functions to provide input-output based invariants for a controller defined as $\Sigma = (\mathbf{A}, \mathbf{B}, \mathbf{C}, \mathbf{D})$. The controller's transfer function $\mathbf{G}(z)$, defined as $\mathbf{G}(z) = \frac{\mathbf{Y}(z)}{\mathbf{U}(z)} = \mathbf{C}(z\mathbf{I}_n - \mathbf{A})^{-1}\mathbf{B} + \mathbf{D}$, where $\mathbf{U}(z)$ and $\mathbf{Y}(z)$ denote the z-transforms of the signals $\mathbf{u}_k$ and $\mathbf{y}_k$ respectively, is a convenient way to capture the dependency between the controller's input and output signals. In general, $\mathbf{G}(z)$ is an $m \times p$ matrix with each element $\mathbf{G}_{i,j}(z)$ being a rational function of the complex variable $z$. To simplify the notation in this summary, we consider Single-Input-Single-Output (SISO) controllers, meaning that the transfer function $G(z)$ takes the form

$$G(z) = \frac{\beta_0 + \beta_1 z^{-1} + \cdots + \beta_n z^{-n}}{1 + \alpha_1 z^{-1} + \cdots + \alpha_n z^{-n}}, \tag{7}$$

where $n$ is the size of the initial controller model (referred also as the degree of the transfer function). This allows us to specify the dependency between the controller's input and output signals as the following difference equation [26]

$$y_k = \sum_{i=0}^{n} \beta_i u_{k-i} - \sum_{i=1}^{n} \alpha_i y_{k-i}, \tag{8}$$

---

[2] We formally define the similarity transform in Sect. 5.

with $y_k = 0, k < 0$, because $\mathbf{z}_0 = 0$ and $u_k = 0$, for $k < 0$. Thus, for any controller $\Sigma$ a linear invariant of the form in (8) can be used to specify the relationship between controller inputs and outputs, which is invariant to any similarity transformations [26].

# 4 Model Extraction from Linear Controller Implementation

In order to verify a linear controller implementation against its specification, we first extract an LTI model from the implementation (i.e., step function), and then compare it to the specification (i.e., the initial model). To obtain an LTI model from the step function, it is first necessary to identify the computation of the step function based on the program semantics. By the computation of a program, we mean how the execution of the program affects the global state.[3] This is also known as the *big-step transition relation* of a program, which is the relation between states before and after the execution of the program. In the next subsection, we explain how to identify the big-step transition relation of the step function via symbolic execution.

## 4.1 Symbolic Execution of Step Function

According to the symbolic execution semantics [6,7,18], we symbolically execute the step function with symbolic inputs and symbolic controller state. When the execution is finished, we examine the effect of the step function on the global state where output and new controller state are produced as symbolic formulas.

Model extraction via symbolic execution may not be applicable to any arbitrary program (e.g., non-terminating program, file/network IO program). However, we argue that it is feasible when focusing on the linear controller implementations which are self-contained (i.e., no dependencies on external functions) and have simple control flows (e.g., for the sake of deterministic real-time behaviors). During symbolic execution, we check if each step of the execution satisfies certain rules (i.e., restrictions), otherwise it is rejected. The rules are as follows: first of all, the conditions of conditional branches should be always evaluated to concrete boolean values. We argue that the step functions of linear controllers are unlikely necessary to branch over symbolic values such as symbolic inputs or symbolic controller states. Moreover, in many cases, the upper bound of the loops of step functions are statically fixed based on the size of the controllers, so the loop condition can be evaluated to concrete values as well. This rule results in yielding the finite and deterministic symbolic execution path of the step function. The second rule is that it is not allowed to use symbolic arguments when calling the standard mathematical functions (e.g., sin, cos, log, exp) because the use of such non-linear functions may result in non-linear input-output relation of the step function. Moreover, it is also not allowed to call external libraries

---

[3] Note that we assume that data is exchanged with the step function via global variables.

(e.g., file/network IO APIs, functions without definitions provided). This rule restricts the step function to be self-contained and to avoid using non-linear mathematical functions. Lastly, dereferencing a symbolic memory address is not allowed because the non-deterministic behavior of memory access is undesirable for controller implementations and may result in unintended information flow.

As the result of the symbolic execution of the step function, the global variables are updated with symbolic formulas. By collecting the updated variables and their new values (i.e., symbolic formulas), the big-step transition relation of the step function can be represented as a system of equations; each equation is in the following form

$$v^{(new)} = f(v_1, v_2, \ldots, v_t)$$

where $t$ is the number of variables used in the symbolic formula $f$, $v, v_i$ are the global variables, $v^{(new)}$ denotes that the variable $v$ is updated with the symbolic formula on the right-hand side of the equation, the variable without the superscript "(new)" denotes the initial symbolic value of the variable (i.e., from the initial state before symbolic execution of the step function). We call this equation *transition equation*.

For example, we consider symbolic execution for the step function in [24], obtained from the model (5), (6); we illustrate the transition equations of the step function as follows, replacing the original variable names with new shortened names for presentation purpose only, such as x for LTIS_DW.Internal_DSTATE, u for LTIS_U.u, and y for LTIS_Y.y:

$$\begin{aligned}
x[0]^{(new)} &= ((0.87224 \cdot x[0]) + ((0.822174 \cdot u[0]) + (-0.438008 \cdot u[1]))) \\
x[1]^{(new)} &= ((0.366377 \cdot x[1]) + ((-0.278536 \cdot u[0]) + (-0.824312 \cdot u[1]))) \\
x[2]^{(new)} &= ((-0.540795 \cdot x[2]) + ((0.874484 \cdot u[0]) + (0.858857 \cdot u[1]))) \\
x[3]^{(new)} &= ((-0.332664 \cdot x[3]) + ((-0.117628 \cdot u[0]) + (-0.506362 \cdot u[1]))) \\
x[4]^{(new)} &= ((-0.204322 \cdot x[4]) + ((-0.955459 \cdot u[0]) + (-0.622498 \cdot u[1]))) \quad (9) \\
y[0]^{(new)} &= (((((-0.793176 \cdot x[0]) + (0.154365 \cdot x[1])) + (-0.377883 \cdot x[2])) \\
&\quad +(-0.360608 \cdot x[3])) + (-0.142123 \cdot x[4])) \\
y[1]^{(new)} &= (((((0.503767 \cdot x[0]) + (-0.573538 * \cdot x[1])) + (0.170245 \cdot x[2])) \\
&\quad +(-0.583312 \cdot x[3])) + (-0.56603 \cdot x[4])).
\end{aligned}$$

## 4.2    Linear Time-Invariant System Model Extraction

To extract an LTI model from the obtained transition equations, we first determine which variables are used to store the controller state. To do this, we examine the data flow among the variables which appear in the equations. Let $V_{used}$ be the set of used variables which appears on the right-hand side of the transition equations. Let $V_{updated}$ be the set of updated variables which appears on the left-hand side of the transition equations. As the interface of the step function, we assume that the sets of input and output variables are given, which are denoted by $V_{input}$ and $V_{output}$, respectively. We define the set of state variables $V_{state}$ as

$$V_{state} = (V_{updated} \setminus V_{output}) \cup (V_{used} \setminus V_{input}).$$

For example, from the transition Eq. (9), x[0], x[1], x[2], x[3] and x[4] are identified as controller state variables as given the input variables u[0] and u[1], and the output variables y[0] and y[1].

The next step is to convert the transition equations into a canonical form. We fully expand the expressions on the right-hand side of the transition equations using the distributive law. The resulting expressions are represented in the form of the sum of products without containing any parentheses. We check if the expressions equations are linear (i.e., each product term should be the multiplication of a constant and a single variable), and otherwise, it is rejected. Finally, each transition equation is represented as the following canonical form

$$v^{(new)} = c_1 v_1 + c_2 v_2 + \cdots + c_t v_t$$

where $t$ is the number of product terms, $v \in V_{updated}$ is the updated variable, $v_i \in V_{used}$ are the used variables, and $c_i \in \mathbb{R}$ are the coefficients. When converting the transition equations into canonical form, we regard floating-point arithmetic expressions as real arithmetic expressions. The analysis of the discrepancy between them is left for future work. Instead, in the next section, the discrepancy issue between two LTI models due to numerical errors of floating-point arithmetic is addressed as the first step toward the full treatment of the problem.

Since the transition equations in canonical form are a system of linear equations, we finally rewrite the transition equations as matrix equations. In order to do this, we first define the input variable vector $\mathbf{u} = vec(V_{input})$, the output variable vector $\mathbf{y} = vec(V_{output})$ and the state variable vector $\mathbf{x} = vec(V_{state})$ where $vec(V)$ denotes the vectorization of the set $V$ (e.g., $vec(\{v_1, v_2, v_3\}) = [v_1, v_2, v_3]^T$). This allows for rewriting each transition equation in terms of the state variable vector $\mathbf{x}$ and the input variable vector $\mathbf{u}$ as

$$v^{(new)} = [c_1, c_2, \ldots, c_n]\mathbf{x} + [d_1, d_2, \ldots, d_p]\mathbf{u}$$

where $n$ is the length of the state variable vector, $p$ is the length of the input variable vector and $c_i, d_i \in \mathbb{R}$ are constants. Finally, we rewrite the transition equations as two matrix equations as follows

$$\mathbf{x}^{(new)} = \hat{\mathbf{A}}\mathbf{x} + \hat{\mathbf{B}}\mathbf{u}$$

$$\mathbf{y}^{(new)} = \hat{\mathbf{C}}\mathbf{x} + \hat{\mathbf{D}}\mathbf{u}$$

where $\hat{\mathbf{A}} \in \mathbb{R}^{n \times n}$, $\hat{\mathbf{B}} \in \mathbb{R}^{n \times p}$, $\hat{\mathbf{C}} \in \mathbb{R}^{m \times n}$, $\hat{\mathbf{D}} \in \mathbb{R}^{m \times p}$, and for any vector $\mathbf{v} = [v_1, \ldots v_t]^T$, we define $\mathbf{v}^{(new)} = [v_1^{(new)}, \ldots, v_t^{(new)}]^T$.

For example, consider the transition equation about $y[0]^{(new)}$ in (9), which is represented in canonical form, and then rewritten as a vector equation (i.e., equation in terms of the state and the input variable vectors) as follows

$$
\begin{aligned}
y[0]^{(new)} &= (((((-0.793176 \cdot x[0]) + (0.154365 \cdot x[1])) + (-0.377883 \cdot x[2])) \\
&\quad + (-0.360608 \cdot x[3])) + (-0.142123 \cdot x[4])) \\
&= -0.793176 \cdot x[0] + 0.154365 \cdot x[1] + -0.377883 \cdot x[2] \\
&\quad + -0.360608 \cdot x[3] + -0.142123 \cdot x[4] \\
&= [-0.793176, 0.154365, -0.377883, -0.360608, -0.142123] \cdot \mathbf{x} \ + [0, 0] \cdot \mathbf{u}
\end{aligned}
$$

where $\mathbf{x} = [\mathbf{x}[0], \mathbf{x}[1], \mathbf{x}[2], \mathbf{x}[3], \mathbf{x}[4]]^{\mathrm{T}}$, and $\mathbf{u} = [\mathbf{u}[0], \mathbf{u}[1]]^{\mathrm{T}}$. Converting each transition Eq. (9) into the corresponding vector equation, we finally reconstruct the LTI model (i.e., same as (5), (6)) from the step function of [24].

*Remark 1.* In general, the size of the extracted model $\hat{\Sigma}$ may not be equal to the size of the initial controller model $\Sigma$ from (1) (i.e., $n$). As we assume that $\Sigma$ is minimal, if the obtained model has the size less than $n$ it would clearly have to violate input-output (IO) requirements of the controller. However, if the size of $\hat{\Sigma}$ is larger than $n$, we consider a controllable and observable subsystem computed via Kalman decomposition [26] from the extracted model, as the $\hat{\Sigma}(\hat{\mathbf{A}}, \hat{\mathbf{B}}, \hat{\mathbf{C}}, \hat{\mathbf{D}})$ model extracted from the code. Note that $\hat{\Sigma}$ is minimal in this case, and thus its size has to be equal to $n$ to provide IO conformance with the initial model.

# 5    Input-Output Equivalence Checking Between Linear Controller Models

In order to verify a linear controller implementation against an LTI specification, in the previous section we described how to extract an LTI model from the implementation. This section introduces a method to check input-output (IO) equivalence between two linear controller models: (1) the original LTI specification and (2) the LTI model extracted from the implementation.

To check the IO equivalence between two LTI models, we exploit the fact that two minimal LTI models with the same size are IO equivalent if and only if they are *similar* to each other. Two LTI models $\Sigma(\mathbf{A}, \mathbf{B}, \mathbf{C}, \mathbf{D})$ and $\hat{\Sigma}(\hat{\mathbf{A}}, \hat{\mathbf{B}}, \hat{\mathbf{C}}, \hat{\mathbf{D}})$ are said to be *similar* if there exists a non-singular matrix $\mathbf{T}$ such that

$$\hat{\mathbf{A}} = \mathbf{TAT}^{-1}, \qquad \hat{\mathbf{B}} = \mathbf{TB}, \qquad \hat{\mathbf{C}} = \mathbf{CT}^{-1}, \qquad \text{and} \qquad \hat{\mathbf{D}} = \mathbf{D} \qquad (10)$$

where $\mathbf{T}$ is referred to as the *similarity transformation matrix* [26]. Thus, given two minimal LTI models, the problem of equivalence checking between the models is reduced to the problem of finding a similarity transformation matrix for the models. The rest of this section explains how to formulate this problem as a satisfiability problem and a convex optimization problem.

## 5.1    Satisfiability Problem Formulation

We start by describing an approach to formulate the problem of finding similarity transformation matrices as the satisfiability problem instance when two LTI models $\Sigma(\mathbf{A}, \mathbf{B}, \mathbf{C}, \mathbf{D})$ and $\hat{\Sigma}(\hat{\mathbf{A}}, \hat{\mathbf{B}}, \hat{\mathbf{C}}, \hat{\mathbf{D}})$ are given. Since existing SMT solvers hardly support matrices and linear algebra operations, we encode the similarity transformation matrix $\mathbf{T}$ as a set of scalar variables $\{T_{i,j} \mid 1 \leq i, j \leq n\}$ where $T_{i,j}$ is the variable to represent the element in the $i$-th row and $j$-th column of the matrix $\mathbf{T}$. The following constraints rephrase the equations of (10) in an element-wise manner

$$\bigwedge_{1\leq i\leq n}\bigwedge_{1\leq j\leq n}\left(\sum_{1\leq k\leq n}\hat{A}_{i,k}T_{k,j}=\sum_{1\leq k\leq n}T_{i,k}A_{k,j}\right)\wedge\bigwedge_{1\leq i\leq n}\bigwedge_{1\leq j\leq n}\left(\hat{B}_{i,j}=\sum_{1\leq k\leq n}T_{i,k}B_{k,j}\right)$$

$$\bigwedge_{1\leq i\leq n}\bigwedge_{1\leq j\leq n}\left(\sum_{1\leq k\leq n}\hat{C}_{i,k}T_{k,j}=C_{i,j}\right)\wedge\bigwedge_{1\leq i\leq n}\bigwedge_{1\leq j\leq n}\hat{D}_{i,j}=D_{i,j}$$

(11)

It is important to highlight that although a similarity transform always results in an IO equivalent new controller, due to finite-precision computation of the code generator performing controller optimization, it is expected that the produced controller will slightly differ from a controller that is similar to the initial controller. Consequently, there is a need to extend our input-output invariants for the case with imprecise specification of the similarity transform. To achieve this, given error bound $\epsilon$, the following constraints extends (11) to tolerate errors up to error bound $\epsilon$

$$\bigwedge_{1\leq i\leq n}\bigwedge_{1\leq j\leq n}-\epsilon\leq\left(\sum_{1\leq k\leq n}\hat{A}_{i,k}T_{k,j}\right)-\left(\sum_{1\leq k\leq n}T_{i,k}A_{k,j}\right)\leq\epsilon$$

$$\bigwedge_{1\leq i\leq n}\bigwedge_{1\leq j\leq n}-\epsilon\leq\hat{B}_{i,j}-\left(\sum_{1\leq k\leq n}T_{i,k}B_{k,j}\right)\leq\epsilon$$

(12)

$$\bigwedge_{1\leq i\leq n}\bigwedge_{1\leq j\leq n}-\epsilon\leq\left(\sum_{1\leq k\leq n}\hat{C}_{i,k}T_{k,j}\right)-C_{i,j}\leq\epsilon$$

$$\bigwedge_{1\leq i\leq n}\bigwedge_{1\leq j\leq n}-\epsilon\leq\hat{D}_{i,j}-D_{i,j}\leq\epsilon$$

For example, suppose that the original LTI model $\Sigma(\mathbf{A},\mathbf{B},\mathbf{C},\mathbf{D})$ from (3), (4), the reconstructed model from the implementation $\hat{\Sigma}(\hat{\mathbf{A}},\hat{\mathbf{B}},\hat{\mathbf{C}},\hat{\mathbf{D}})$ from (5), (6) and the error bound $\epsilon=10^{-6}$ are given. Having the problem instance formulated as (12), the similarity transformation matrix $\mathbf{T}$ for those models can be found using an SMT solver which supports the quantifier-free linear real arithmetic, QF_LRA for short. Due to the lack of space, only the first row of $\mathbf{T}$ is shown here

$$T_{1,1}=-\frac{445681907965836469807842159338}{818667375305282643804030465563}\quad(\approx-0.544399156750667)$$

$$T_{1,2}=-\frac{135442022883031921128620509482}{818667375305282643804030465563}\quad(\approx-0.165442059801384)$$

$$T_{1,3}=\frac{198172776374831449251211655628}{818667375305282643804030465563}\quad(\approx0.242067461044165)$$

$$T_{1,4}=-\frac{351256050550998919211978953100}{818667375305282643804030465563}\quad(\approx-0.429058064513855)$$

$$T_{1,5}=-\frac{476345345040634696989970420590}{818667375305282643804030465563}\quad(\approx-0.581854284748456)$$

Since, for the theory of real numbers, SMT solvers use the arbitrary-precision arithmetic when calculating answers, each element of $\mathbf{T}$ is given as a fractional number of numerous digits. For instance, although it is not displayed here, $T_{5,4}$ in this example is a fraction whose numerator and denominator are numbers with more than one hundred digits. Thus, due to the infinite precision arithmetic used by SMT solvers, the scalability of the SMT formulation-based approach is questionable. This illustrates the need for a more efficient approach for similarity checking, and in the next subsection we will present a convex optimization-based approach as an alternative method.

## 5.2   Convex Optimization Problem Formulation

The idea behind a convex optimization based approach is to use convex optimization to minimize the difference between the initial model and the model obtained via a similarity transformation from the model extracted from the code. Specifically, we formulate the equivalence checking for imprecise specifications as a convex optimization problem defined as

$$
\begin{aligned}
&\text{variables } e \in \mathbb{R}, \mathbf{T} \in \mathbb{R}^{n \times n}\\
&\text{minimize } e\\
&\text{subject to } \epsilon \le e,\\
&\qquad \left\| \hat{\mathbf{A}}\mathbf{T} - \mathbf{T}\mathbf{A} \right\|_\infty \le e, \ \left\| \hat{\mathbf{B}} - \mathbf{T}\mathbf{B} \right\|_\infty \le e,\\
&\qquad \left\| \hat{\mathbf{C}}\mathbf{T} - \mathbf{C} \right\|_\infty \le e, \ \left\| \hat{\mathbf{D}} - \mathbf{D} \right\|_\infty \le e
\end{aligned}
\tag{13}
$$

For example, given two LTI models $\mathbf{\Sigma}(\mathbf{A}, \mathbf{B}, \mathbf{C}, \mathbf{D})$ from (3), (4) and $\hat{\mathbf{\Sigma}}(\hat{\mathbf{A}}, \hat{\mathbf{B}}, \hat{\mathbf{C}}, \hat{\mathbf{D}})$ from (5), (6) and the error bound $\epsilon = 10^{-6}$, by (13), the similarity transformation matrix $\mathbf{T}$ can be found using the convex optimization solver CVX as follows

$$
\mathbf{T} = \begin{bmatrix}
-0.5443990427 & -0.1654425774 & 0.2420672805 & -0.4290576934 & -0.5818538874\\
-0.4440654044 & -0.7588435418 & 0.1765807738 & 0.2799578419 & 0.5647456751\\
-0.588433439 & -0.2004321431 & 0.6773771193 & 0.4815317446 & 0.1449186163\\
0.9314576739 & -0.0459172638 & 0.6095691172 & 0.3808322795 & 0.8653864392\\
-0.2372386619 & 0.5190687755 & 0.8165534522 & -0.1493619803 & 0.1461696487
\end{bmatrix}
$$

In addition, the original similarity transformation matrix $\mathbf{T}_{ori}$ used in the actual transformation from $\mathbf{\Sigma}$ to $\hat{\mathbf{\Sigma}}$ is

$$
\mathbf{T}_{ori} = \begin{bmatrix}
-0.5443991568 & -0.1654420598 & 0.242067461 & -0.4290580645 & -0.5818542847\\
-0.4440652236 & -0.7588431653 & 0.1765807449 & 0.279957637 & 0.564745456\\
-0.5884339121 & -0.2004321022 & 0.677376781 & 0.4815316264 & 0.144918173\\
0.9314574825 & -0.0459170889 & 0.6095698017 & 0.3808324602 & 0.8653867983\\
-0.2372380836 & 0.5190691678 & 0.816552622 & -0.1493625727 & 0.1461689364
\end{bmatrix}
$$

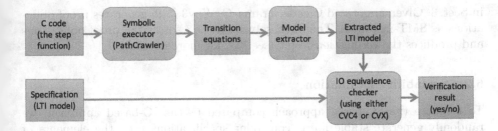

**Fig. 1.** The verification toolchain for the similarity checking-based approach.

resulting in the difference between two matrices equal to

$$|\mathbf{T}-\mathbf{T}_{ori}| = \begin{bmatrix} 0.000000114 & 0.0000005176 & 0.0000001806 & 0.0000003711 & 0.0000003973 \\ 0.0000001809 & 0.0000003766 & 0.000000029 & 0.0000002049 & 0.0000002191 \\ 0.0000004731 & 0.0000000408 & 0.0000003384 & 0.0000001182 & 0.0000004433 \\ 0.0000001914 & 0.0000001749 & 0.0000006844 & 0.0000001807 & 0.0000003591 \\ 0.0000005783 & 0.0000003923 & 0.0000008302 & 0.0000005924 & 0.0000007123 \end{bmatrix}.$$

## 6    Evaluation

To evaluate our verification approach described in Sects. 4 and 5, we compared it to our earlier work based on invariant checking [23].

### 6.1    Verification Toolchain

We implemented an automatic verification framework (presented in Fig. 1) based on the proposed approach described in Sects. 4 and 5. We refer to this approach as similarity checking (SC)-based approach. Given a step function (i.e., C code), we employ the off-the-shelf symbolic execution tool PathCrawler [32] to symbolically execute the step function and generate a set of transition equations. The model extractor which implements the method in Sect. 4.2 extracts an LTI model from the transition equations. Finally, the equivalence checker based on the method in Sect. 5 decides the similarity between the extracted LTI model and the given specification (i.e., LTI model), and produces the verification result. The equivalence checker uses either the SMT solver CVC4 [4][4] or the convex optimization solver CVX [14] depending on the formulation employed, which is described in Sect. 5.

For the invariant checking (IC)-based approach described in Sect. 3, we use the toolchain Frama-C/Why3/Z3 to verify C code with annotated controller invariants [23]. The step function is annotated with the invariants as described

---

[4] CVC4 was chosen among other SMT solvers because it showed the best performance for our QF_LRA SMT instances.

in Sect. 3. Given annotated C code, Frama-C/Why3 [5,9] generates proof obligations as SMT instances. The SMT solver Z3 [11][5] solves the proof obligations and produces the verification result (see [23] for more details).

## 6.2   Scalability Evaluation

To evaluate the SC-based approach compared to the IC-based approach, we randomly generate stable linear controller specifications (i.e., the elements of $\Sigma(\mathbf{A}, \mathbf{B}, \mathbf{C}, \mathbf{D})$). Since we observed that the controller dimension $n$ dominates the performance (i.e., running time) of both approaches, we vary $n$ from 2 to 14, and generate three controller specifications for each $n$. For each controller specification, we employ the code generator Embedded Coder to generate the step function in C. Since we use the LTI system block of Simulink for code generation, the structure of generated C code is not straightforward, having multiple loops and pointer arithmetic operations as illustrated in the step function [24]. This negatively affects the performance of the IC-based approach for reasons to be described later in this subsection. For a comparative evaluation, we use both SC-based and IC-based approaches to verify the generated step function C code against its specification. For each generated controller, we checked that IC-based and SC-based approaches give the same verification result, as long as both complete normally.

To thoroughly compare both approaches, we measure the running time of the front-end and the back-end of each approach separately. By the front-end, we refer to the process from parsing C code to generating proof obligations to be input for constraint solvers. The front-end of the SC-based approach includes the symbolic execution by PathCrawler and the model extraction, while the front-end of the IC-based approach is processing annotated code and generating proof obligations by Frama-C/Why3. On the other hand, by the back-end, we refer to the process of constraint solving. While the back-end of the SC-based approach is the IO equivalence checking based on either SMT solving using CVC4 or convex optimization solving using CVX, the back-end of the IC-based approach is proving the generated proof obligations using Z3.

We first evaluate the frond-end of both approaches (i.e., the whole verification process until constraint solving). Figure 2 shows that the average running time of the front-ends of both approaches, where missing bars indicate no data due to the lack of scalability of the utilized verification approach (e.g., the tool's abnormal termination or no termination for a prolonged time). Here, $IB'_{2n+1}$, $IB''_{3n+1}$, $IB'_{3n+1}$ and $IB'_{2n+1}$ denote the variations of annotating methods as described in [23]. We observe that the running time of the IC-based approaches exponentially increase as the controller dimension $n$ increases, while the SC-based approach remains scalable. The main reason for this is that the IC-based approach requires the preprocessing of code [23], which is unrolling the execution of the step function multiple times (e.g., $2n + 1$ or $3n + 1$ times) as well as

---

[5] Z3 was chosen among other SMT solvers because it showed the best performance for the generated proof obligations in our experiment.

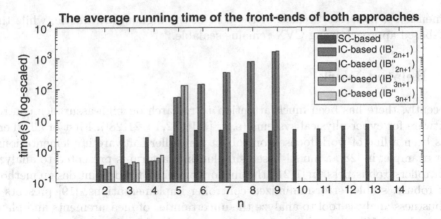

**Fig. 2.** The average running time of the front-ends of both SC-based and IC-based approaches (with the log-scaled y-axis)

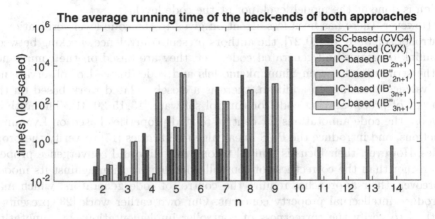

**Fig. 3.** The average running time of the back-ends of both SC-based and IC-based approaches (with the log-scaled y-axis)

unrolling each loop in the step function $(n+1)$ times. Therefore, in contrast with the SC-based approach, the IC-based approach needs to handle the significantly increased lines of code due to unrolling, so it does not scale up.

Next, we evaluate the back-end of both approaches (i.e., constraint solving). Figure 3 shows the average running time of the back-ends of both approaches, where missing bars result from the lack of scalability of either the constraint solver used at this stage or the front-end tools. "SC-based (CVC4)" denotes the SMT-based formulation while "SC-based (CVX)" denotes the convex optimization-based formulation. Recall that the SC-based approach using CVC4 and the IC-based approaches employ the SMT solvers for constraint solving, which uses the arbitrary-precision arithmetic. We observe that the running time of the back-ends of those approaches exponentially increase as the controller dimension $n$ increases because of the cost of the bignum arithmetic, while the SC-based approach using CVX remains scalable.

## 7   Related Work

Recently, there has been much attention to research on high-assurance control software for cyber physical systems (e.g., [1,10,12,19–21,28]). First of all, there has been a line of work focused on robust controller software implementations. For example, in [28], a model-based simulation platform is presented to analyze controllers' robustness. In [1,21], the authors present a fixed-point design method for robust, stable, error-minimized controller implementations. [19] presents a robustness analysis tool to analyze the uncertainties of measurements and plant states. In [10,12], the authors address the synthesis of fixed-point controller software using SMT solvers. Moreover, there exists work on verifying the control-related properties of Simulink models using theorem proving [2]. Yet, the verification is done at the model level, not at the code level.

However, there has been less attention given to the code-level verification of controller software. In [20,27], the authors present equivalence checking between Simulink diagrams and generated code. Yet, they are based on the compliance of the structures between Simulink models and code, instead of observational equivalence checking. In addition, there is a closely related work based on the concept of proof-carrying code for control software [13,15,30,31]. The authors propose the code annotations for control-related properties based on Lyapunov functions, and introduce the PVS linear algebra libraries [15] to verify the properties. However, their focus is limited to only stability and convergence properties rather than the correctness of controller implementation against its model. Moreover, their approaches require the control of code generators, which may introduce intellectual property concerns. Our own earlier work [23] presents a method to verify the correctness of controller implementations by annotating the controllers' invariants. However, the scalability of this method is challenged for real controller implementations with large state dimensions.

Finally, the model extraction technique has been used in software verification [8,16,17,25,29]. The authors in [8,16,17] extract finite state models from implementations to facilitate software model checking. [29] and [25] apply the symbolic execution technique to implemented source code to extract mathematical functional models and high-level state machine models, respectively.

## 8   Conclusion

We have presented an approach for the verification of linear controller implementations against mathematical specifications. By this, a higher degree of assurance for generated control code can be provided without trusting a code generator. We have proposed to use the symbolic execution technique to reconstruct mathematical models from linear time-invariant controller implementations. We have presented a method to check input-output equivalence between the specification model and the extracted model using the SMT formulation and the convex optimization formulation. Through the evaluation using randomly generated specification and code by Matlab, we showed that the scalability of our new approach has significantly improved compared to our own earler work. Future work includes the analysis of the effect of floating-point calculations in control code.

**Acknowledgments.** This work was supported in part by NSF CNS-1505799, NSF CNS-1505701, and the Intel-NSF Partnership for Cyber-Physical Systems Security and Privacy. This material is based on research sponsored by DARPA under agreement number FA8750-12-2-0247. The U.S. Government is authorized to reproduce and distribute reprints for Governmental purposes notwithstanding any copyright notation thereon. The views and conclusions contained herein are those of the authors and should not be interpreted as necessarily representing the official policies or endorsements, either expressed or implied, of DARPA or the U.S. Government. This research was supported in part by Global Research Laboratory Program through the National Research Foundation of Korea (NRF) funded by the Ministry of Science, ICT & Future Planning (2013K1A1A2A02078326) with DGIST.

# References

1. Anta, A., Majumdar, R., Saha, I., Tabuada, P.: Automatic verification of control system implementations. In: Proceedings of 10th ACM International Conference on Embedded Software, EMSOFT 2010, pp. 9–18 (2010)
2. Araiza-Illan, D., Eder, K., Richards, A.: Formal verification of control systems' properties with theorem proving. In: UKACC International Conference on Control (CONTROL), pp. 244–249 (2014)
3. Aström, K.J., Murray, R.M.: Feedback Systems: An Introduction for Scientists and Engineers. Princeton University Press, Princeton (2010)
4. Barrett, C., Conway, C.L., Deters, M., Hadarean, L., Jovanović, D., King, T., Reynolds, A., Tinelli, C.: CVC4. In: Gopalakrishnan, G., Qadeer, S. (eds.) CAV 2011. LNCS, vol. 6806, pp. 171–177. Springer, Heidelberg (2011)
5. Bobot, F., Filliâtre, J.C., Marché, C., Paskevich, A.: Why3: shepherd your herd of provers. In: Boogie 2011: First International Workshop on Intermediate Verification Languages, pp. 53–64 (2011)
6. Botella, B., Gotlieb, A., Michel, C.: Symbolic execution of floating-point computations. Softw. Test. Verification Reliab. **16**(2), 97–121 (2006)
7. Clarke, L.: A system to generate test data and symbolically execute programs. IEEE Trans. Softw. Eng. **3**, 215–222 (1976)
8. Corbett, J.C., Dwyer, M.B., Hatcliff, J., Laubach, S., Păsăreanu, C.S., Bby, R., Zheng, H.: Bandera: extracting finite-state models from java source code. In: Proceedings of the 2000 International Conference on Software Engineering, pp. 439–448. IEEE (2000)
9. Cuoq, P., Kirchner, F., Kosmatov, N., Prevosto, V., Signoles, J., Yakobowski, B.: Frama-C. In: Eleftherakis, G., Hinchey, M., Holcombe, M. (eds.) SEFM 2012. LNCS, vol. 7504, pp. 233–247. Springer, Heidelberg (2012)

10. Darulova, E., Kuncak, V., Majumdar, R., Saha, I.: Synthesis of fixed-point programs. In: Proceedings of 11th ACM International Conference on Embedded Software, EMSOFT 2013, pp. 22:1–22:10 (2013)
11. de Moura, L., Bjørner, N.S.: Z3: an efficient SMT solver. In: Ramakrishnan, C.R., Rehof, J. (eds.) TACAS 2008. LNCS, vol. 4963, pp. 337–340. Springer, Heidelberg (2008)
12. Eldib, H., Wang, C.: An SMT based method for optimizing arithmetic computations in embedded software code. IEEE Trans. Comput. Aided Des. Integr. Circ. Syst. **33**(11), 1611–1622 (2014)
13. Feron, E.: From control systems to control software. IEEE Control Syst. **30**(6), 50–71 (2010)
14. Grant, M., Boyd, S.: CVX: Matlab software for disciplined convex programming, version 2.1., March 2014. http://cvxr.com/cvx
15. Herencia-Zapana, H., Jobredeaux, R., Owre, S., Garoche, P.-L., Feron, E., Perez, G., Ascariz, P.: PVS linear algebra libraries for verification of control software algorithms in C/ACSL. In: Goodloe, A.E., Person, S. (eds.) NFM 2012. LNCS, vol. 7226, pp. 147–161. Springer, Heidelberg (2012)
16. Holzmann, G.J., Smith, M.H.: Software model checking: extracting verification models from source code. Softw. Test. Verification Reliab. **11**(2), 65–79 (2001)
17. Holzmann, G.J., Smith, M.H.: An automated verification method for distributed systems software based on model extraction. IEEE Trans. Softw. Eng. **28**(4), 364–377 (2002)
18. King, J.C.: Symbolic execution and program testing. Commun. ACM **19**(7), 385–394 (1976)
19. Majumdar, R., Saha, I., Shashidhar, K.C., Wang, Z.: CLSE: closed-loop symbolic execution. In: Goodloe, A.E., Person, S. (eds.) NFM 2012. LNCS, vol. 7226, pp. 356–370. Springer, Heidelberg (2012)
20. Majumdar, R., Saha, I., Ueda, K., Yazarel, H.: Compositional equivalence checking for models and code of control systems. In: 52nd Annual IEEE Conference on Decision and Control (CDC), pp. 1564–1571 (2013)
21. Majumdar, R., Saha, I., Zamani, M.: Synthesis of minimal-error control software. In: Proceedings of 10th ACM International Conference on Embedded Software, EMSOFT 2012, pp. 123–132 (2012)
22. Mathworks: Bug Reports for Incorrect Code Generation. http://www.mathworks.com/support/bugreports/?product=ALL&release=R2015b&keyword=Incorrect+Code+Generation
23. Pajic, M., Park, J., Lee, I., Pappas, G.J., Sokolsky, O.: Automatic verification of linear controller software. In: 12th International Conference on Embedded Software (EMSOFT), pp. 217–226. IEEE Press (2015)
24. Park, J.: Step function example. http://dx.doi.org/10.5281/zenodo.44338
25. Pichler, J.: Specification extraction by symbolic execution. In: 2013 20th Working Conference on Reverse Engineering (WCRE), pp. 462–466. IEEE (2013)
26. Rugh, W.J.: Linear System Theory. Prentice Hall, Upper Saddle River (1996)
27. Ryabtsev, M., Strichman, O.: Translation validation: from simulink to C. In: Bouajjani, A., Maler, O. (eds.) CAV 2009. LNCS, vol. 5643, pp. 696–701. Springer, Heidelberg (2009)
28. Sangiovanni-Vincentelli, A., Di Natale, M.: Embedded system design for automotive applications. IEEE Comput. **10**, 42–51 (2007)
29. Wang, S., Dwarakanathan, S., Sokolsky, O., Lee, I.: High-level model extraction via symbolic execution. Technical reports (CIS) Paper 967, University of Pennsylvania (2012). http://repository.upenn.edu/cis_reports/967

30. Wang, T., Jobredeaux, R., Herencia, H., Garoche, P.L., Dieumegard, A., Feron, E., Pantel, M.: From design to implementation: an automated, credible autocoding chain for control systems. arXiv preprint (2013). arxiv:1307.2641

31. Wang, T.E., Ashari, A.E., Jobredeaux, R.J., Feron, E.M.: Credible autocoding of fault detection observers. In: American Control Conference (ACC), pp. 672–677 (2014)

32. Williams, N., Marre, B., Mouy, P., Roger, M.: PathCrawler: automatic generation of path tests by combining static and dynamic analysis. In: Dal Cin, M., Kaâniche, M., Pataricza, A. (eds.) EDCC 2005. LNCS, vol. 3463, pp. 281–292. Springer, Heidelberg (2005)

# Partial Order Reduction for Event-Driven Multi-threaded Programs

Pallavi Maiya[1(✉)], Rahul Gupta[1], Aditya Kanade[1], and Rupak Majumdar[2]

[1] Indian Institute of Science, Bengaluru, India
pallavi.maiya@csa.iisc.ernet.in
[2] MPI-SWS, Kaiserslautern, Germany

**Abstract.** Event-driven multi-threaded programming is fast becoming a preferred style of developing efficient and responsive applications. In this concurrency model, multiple threads execute concurrently, communicating through shared objects as well as by posting asynchronous events. In this work, we consider partial order reduction (POR) for this concurrency model. Existing POR techniques treat event queues associated with threads as shared objects and reorder every pair of events handled on the same thread even if reordering them does not lead to different states. We do not treat event queues as shared objects and propose a new POR technique based on a backtracking set called the *dependence-covering set*. Our POR technique reorders events handled by the same thread only if necessary. We prove that exploring dependence-covering sets suffices to detect all deadlock cycles and assertion violations defined over local variables. To evaluate effectiveness of our POR scheme, we have implemented a dynamic algorithm to compute dependence-covering sets. On execution traces of some Android applications, we demonstrate that our technique explores many fewer transitions —often orders of magnitude fewer— compared to exploration based on persistent sets, in which event queues are considered as shared objects.

## 1 Introduction

Event-driven multi-threaded programming is fast becoming a preferred style of concurrent programming in many domains. In this model, multiple threads execute concurrently, and each thread may be associated with an event queue. A thread may post events to the event queue of a target thread. For each thread with an event queue, an event-loop processes the events from its event queue in the order of their arrival. The event-loop runs the handler of an event only after the previous handler finishes execution but interleaved with the execution of all the other threads. Further, threads can communicate through shared objects; even event handlers executing on the same thread may share objects. This style of programming is a staple of developing efficient and responsive smartphone applications [22]. A similar programming model is also used in distributed message-passing applications, high-performance servers, and many other settings.

Stateless model checking [12] is an approach to explore the reachable state space of concurrent programs by exploring different interleavings systematically

© Springer-Verlag Berlin Heidelberg 2016
M. Chechik and J.-F. Raskin (Eds.): TACAS 2016, LNCS 9636, pp. 680–697, 2016.
DOI: 10.1007/978-3-662-49674-9_44

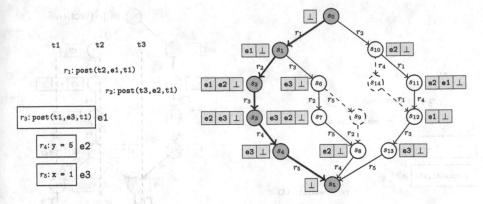

**Fig. 1.** A partial trace of an event-driven multi-threaded program

**Fig. 2.** The state space reachable through all valid permutations of operations in the trace in Fig. 1

but without storing visited states. The scalability of stateless model checking depends crucially on partial order reduction (POR) techniques [8,11,27,32]. Stateless search with POR defines an equivalence class on interleavings, and explores only a representative interleaving from each equivalence class (called a Mazurkiewicz trace [21]), while still providing certain formal guarantees *w.r.t.* exploration of the complete but possibly much larger state space. Motivated by the success of model checkers based on various POR strategies [5,6,13,14,26, 28,29,33], in this work, we propose an effective POR strategy for event-driven multi-threaded programs.

## 1.1 Motivation

We first show why existing POR techniques may not be very effective in the combined model of threads and events. Consider a partial execution trace of an event-driven multi-threaded program in Fig. 1. The operations are labeled $r_1$ to $r_5$ and execute from top to bottom. Those belonging to the same event handler are enclosed within a box labeled with the corresponding event ID. An operation $post(t, e, t')$ executed by a thread $t$ enqueues an event $e$ to the event queue of a thread $t'$. In our trace, threads t2 and t3 respectively post events e1 and e2 to thread t1. The handler of e1 posts an event e3 to t1, whereas, those of e2 and e3 respectively write to shared variables y and x.

Figure 2 shows the state space reachable through all valid permutations of operations in the trace in Fig. 1. Each node indicates a state of the program. An edge is labeled with an operation and indicates the state transition due to that operation. The interleaving corresponding to the trace in Fig. 1 is highlighted with bold lines and shaded states. For illustration purposes, we explicitly show the contents of the event queue of thread t1 at some states. Events in a queue are ordered from left to right and a box containing ⊥ indicates the rear end of the queue.

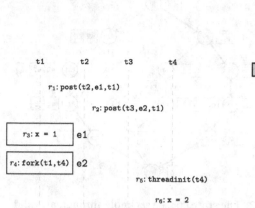

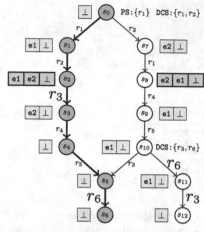

**Fig. 3.** A partial trace $w$ of a program involving a multi-threaded dependence

**Fig. 4.** A transition system for some valid permutations of operations in the trace in Fig. 3

Existing POR techniques (e.g., [5,10,11,29,31]) recognize that $r_2$ and $r_5$ (also $r_1$ and $r_4$) are independent (or non-interfering) and that it is sufficient to explore any one of them at state $s_6$ (respectively, $s_{10}$). The dashed edges indicate the unexplored transitions. However, existing POR-based model checkers will explore all other states and transitions. Since no two handlers executed on t1 modify a common object, all the interleavings reach the same state $s_5$. Thus, existing techniques explore two redundant interleavings because they treat *event queues as shared objects* and so, mark any two post operations that enqueue events to the event queue of the same thread as dependent. Consequently, they explore both $r_1$ and $r_2$ at state $s_0$, and $r_2$ and $r_3$ at state $s_1$. These result in unnecessary reorderings of events. More generally, if there are $n$ events posted to an event queue, these techniques may explore $O(n!)$ permutations among them, even if exploring only one of them may be sufficient.

## 1.2  Contributions of This Paper

Based on the observation above, we do *not* consider event queues as shared objects. Equivalently, we treat a pair of posts even to the same thread as *independent*. This enables more reductions. For example, for the state space in Fig. 2, our approach explores only the initial trace (the leftmost interleaving).

Since we shall not reorder every pair of events posted to the same thread by default, the main question is "How to determine which events to reorder and how to reorder them selectively?". Surely, if two handlers executing on the same thread contain dependent transitions then we must reorder their post operations, but this is not enough. To see this, consider a partial trace $w$ in Fig. 3. The transitions $r_3$ and $r_6$ are dependent and belong to *different* threads.

Figure 4 shows a transition system depicting a partial state space explored by different orderings of $r_3$ and $r_6$. The contents of thread t1's queue are shown next to each state. As can be seen in the rightmost interleaving, executing $r_6$ before $r_3$ requires posting e2 *before* e1 even though their handlers do not have dependent transitions. Thus, operations posting events to the same thread may have to be reordered even to reorder some multi-threaded dependences! Our first contribution is to define a relation that captures both single-threaded and multi-threaded dependences.

We now discuss what the implications of (1) treating posts as independent and (2) only selectively reordering them are. For multi-threaded programs, or when posts are considered dependent, reordering a pair of adjacent independent transitions in a transition sequence does not affect the reachable state. Hence, the existing dependence relation [11] induces equivalence classes where transition sequences differing only in the order of executing independent transitions are in the same Mazurkiewicz trace [21]. However, our new dependence relation (where posts are considered independent) may not induce Mazurkiewicz traces on an event-driven multi-threaded program. First, reordering posts to the same thread affects the order of execution of the corresponding handlers. If the handlers contain dependent transitions, it affects the reachable state. Second, one cannot rule out the possibility of *new* transitions (not present in the given transition sequence) being pulled in when independent posts are reordered, which is not admissible in a Mazurkiewicz trace. We elaborate on this in Sect. 2.3.

Our second contribution is to define a notion of *dependence-covering sequence* to provide the necessary theoretical foundation to reason about reordering posts selectively. Intuitively, a transition sequence $u$ is a dependence-covering sequence of a transition sequence $u'$ if the relative ordering of all the pairs of dependent transitions in $u'$ is preserved in $u$. While this sounds similar to the property of any pair of transition sequences in the same Mazurkiewicz trace, the constraints imposed on a dependence-covering sequence are more relaxed (as will be formalized in Definition 4), making it suitable to achieve better reductions. For instance, $u$ is permitted to have *new* transitions, that is, transitions that are not in $u'$, under certain conditions.

Given a notion of POR, a model checking algorithm such as DPOR [10] uses persistent sets [11] to explore representative transition sequences from each Mazurkiewicz trace. As we show now, DPOR based on persistent sets is *unsound* when used with the dependence relation in which posts are independent. Let us revisit Fig. 4. The set $\{r_1\}$ is persistent at state $s_0$ because exploring any other transition from $s_0$ does not reach a transition dependent with $r_1$. This set is tagged as PS in the figure. A selective exploration using this set explores only one ordering between $r_3$ and $r_6$.

Our final contribution is the notion of *dependence-covering sets* as an alternative to persistent sets. A set of transitions $L$ at a state $s$ is said to be dependence-covering if for any sequence $u'$ executed from $s$, a dependence-covering sequence $u$ starting with some transition in $L$ can be explored. We prove that selective state-space exploration based on dependence-covering sets is sufficient to detect all deadlock cycles and violations of assertions over local variables. The dependence-covering sets at certain states are marked in Fig. 4 as DCS. In contrast to PS, DCS at state $s_0$ contains *both* $r_1$ and $r_2$. Let $u'$ be the transition sequence along the rightmost interleaving in Fig. 4. The sequence $w$ (the leftmost interleaving) is not a dependence-covering sequence of $u'$ since the dependent transitions $r_3$ and $r_6$ appear in a different order. We therefore require $r_2$ to be explored at $s_0$. Note that, $\{r_2\}$ is another dependence-covering set at $s_0$ as both the orderings of $r_3$ and $r_6$ can be explored from a state $s_{10}$ reached on exploring $r_2$.

We have implemented a proof-of-concept model checking framework called EM-Explorer which simulates the non-deterministic behaviour exhibited by Android applications given individual execution traces. We implemented a dynamic algorithm to compute dependence-covering sets and a selective state-space exploration based on these sets in EM-Explorer. For comparison, we also implemented an exploration based on DPOR, where posts to the same thread are considered dependent. We performed experiments on traces obtained from 5 Android applications. Our results demonstrate that our POR explores many fewer transitions —often orders of magnitude fewer— compared to DPOR using persistent sets.

## 1.3    Related Work

Mazurkiewicz traces induced by an independence relation form the foundation for most existing work on POR, and most prior work in the event-driven setting consider operations on event queues to be dependent. For example, Sen and Agha [29] and Tasharofi et al. [31] describe dynamic POR techniques for distributed programs with actor semantics where processes (actors) communicate only by asynchronous message passing (and do not have shared variables). Both techniques explore all possible interleavings of messages sent to the same process. Basset [17], a framework for state space exploration of actor systems, uses the DPOR algorithm described in [29], resulting in exploration of all valid configurations of messages sent to the same actor. In comparison, we explore only a subset of event orderings at each thread, and doing so requires relaxing Mazurkiewicz traces to dependence-covering sequences.

Recent algorithms guarantee optimality in POR [5,28], *i.e.*, they explore at most one transition sequence per Mazurkiewicz trace. For example, POR using source sets and wakeup trees [5] enables optimal exploration. However, the notion of source sets and the corresponding algorithm assume total ordering between transitions executed on the same thread. Hence, integrating our new dependence relation with source sets will involve significant changes to the definitions and algorithms presented in [5]. Rodríguez et al. [28] describe unfolding semantics parametrized on the commutativity based classical independence relation [11], and present an unfolding based optimal POR algorithm. The unfolding semantics identifies dependent transitions with no ordering relation between them to be in conflict. Their POR algorithm backtracks and explores a new transition sequence $w$ from a state $s$ only if every prior transition explored from $s$ is in conflict with some transition in $w$. This is problematic in our setting where posts are considered independent and hence trivially non-conflicting, causing unfolding based POR to miss reordering posts when required. Establishing optimality in our setting is an interesting but non-trivial future direction.

$R^4$ [16] is a stateless model checker for event-driven programs like client-side web applications. $R^4$ adapts persistent sets and DPOR algorithm to the domain of single-threaded, event-driven programs with multiset semantics. Each event handler is atomically executed to completion without interference from other handlers, and thus an entire event handler is considered a single transition. In contrast, our work focuses on POR techniques for multi-threaded programs with event queues, and thus needs to be sensitive to interference from other threads while reordering dependent transitions.

In many domains, the event-loop works in FIFO order, as is also considered in this work. For example, Android [15,19], TinyOS [4], Java AWT [3], and Apple's Grand Central Dispatch [2], provide a default FIFO semantics. Abstracting FIFO order by the multiset semantics, as in [9,30], can lead to false positives. There is a lot of recent work on concurrency analysis for smartphone environments. For example, [7,15,19] provide algorithms for race detection for Android applications. Our work continues this line by describing a general POR technique. We note that the event dispatch semantics can be diverse in general. For example, Android applications permit posting an event with a timeout or posting a specific event to the front of the queue. We over-approximate the effect of posting with timeout by forking a new thread which does the post non-deterministically but do not address other variants in this work. We leave a more general POR approach that allows such variants to event dispatch to future work.

## 2   Formalization

We consider event-driven multi-threaded programs comprising the usual sequential and multi-threaded operations such as assignments, conditionals, synchronization through locks, and thread creation. In addition, the operation $post(t_1, e, t_2)$ posts an asynchronous event $e$ from the source thread $t_1$ to (the event queue of) a destination thread $t_2$. Each event has a handler, which runs to completion on its thread but may interleave with operations from other threads. An operation is *visible* if it accesses an object shared between at least two threads or two event handlers (possibly running on the same thread). All other operations are *invisible*. We omit the formal syntax and semantics of these operations; they can be found in [19].

The *local state of an event handler* is a valuation of the stack and the variables or heap objects that are modified only within the handler. The local state of a thread is the local state of the currently executing handler. A *global state* of the program $A$ is a valuation to the variables and heap objects that are accessed by multiple threads or multiple handlers. Even though event queues are shared objects, we do not consider them in the global state (as defined above). Instead, we define a *queue state of a thread* as an ordered sequence of events that have been posted to its event queue but are yet to be handled. This separation allows us to analyze dependence more precisely. Event queues are FIFO queues with unbounded capacity, that is, a **post** operation never blocks. For simplicity, we assume that each thread is associated with an event queue.

## 2.1   Transition System

Consider an event-driven multi-threaded program $A$. Let $L$, $G$, and $Q$ be the sets of local, global and queue states respectively. Let $T$ be the set of all threads in $A$. A *state* $s$ of $A$ is a triple $(l, g, q)$ where (1) $l$ is a partial map from $T$ to $L$, (2) $g$ is a global state and (3) $q$ is a total map from $T$ to $Q$. A *transition* by a thread $t$ updates the state of $A$ by performing one visible operation followed by a finite sequence of invisible operations ending just before the next visible operation; all of which are executed on $t$. Let $R$ be the set of all transitions in $A$. A transition $r_{t,\ell}$ of a thread $t$ at its local state $\ell$ is a partial function, $r_{t,\ell} : G \times Q \mapsto L \times G \times Q$. A transition $r_{t,\ell} \in R$ is enabled at a state $s = (l, g, q)$ if $\ell = l(t)$ and $r_{t,\ell}(g, q)$ is defined. Note that the first transition of the handler of an event $e$ enqueued to a thread $t$ is *enabled* at a state $s$, if $e$ is at the front of $t$'s queue at $s$ and $t$ is not executing any other handlers. We may use $r_{t,\ell}(s)$ to denote application of a transition $r_{t,\ell}$, instead of the more precise use $r_{t,\ell}(g, q)$.

We formalize the state space of $A$ as a *transition system* $\mathcal{S}_G = (S, s_{init}, \Delta)$, where $S$ is the set of all states, $s_{init} \in S$ is the initial state, and $\Delta \subseteq S \times S$ is the transition relation such that $(s, s') \in \Delta$ iff $\exists r \in R$ and $s' = r(s)$. We also use $s \in \mathcal{S}_G$ instead of $s \in S$. Two transitions $r$ and $r'$ *may be co-enabled* if there may exist some state $s \in S$ where they both are enabled. Two events $e$ and $e'$ handled on the same thread $t$ *may be reordered* if $\exists s, s' \in S$ reachable from $s_{init}$ such that $s = (l, g, q)$, $s' = (l', g', q')$, $q(t) = e \cdot w \cdot e' \cdot w'$ and $q'(t) = e' \cdot v \cdot e \cdot v'$. In Fig. 2, events e1 and e2 may be reordered but not e1 and e3.

In our setting, if a transition is defined for a state then it maps the state to a successor state deterministically. For simplicity, we assume that all threads and events in $A$ have unique IDs. We also assume that the transition system is *finite* and *acyclic*. This is a standard assumption for stateless model checking [10]. The transition system $\mathcal{S}_G$ collapses invisible operations and is thus already reduced when compared to the transition system in which even invisible operations are considered as separate transitions. A transition system of this form is sufficient for detecting deadlocks and assertion violations [12].

***Notation.*** Let $next(s, t)$ give the next transition of a thread $t$ in a state $s$. Let $thread(r)$ return the thread executing a transition $r$. If $r$ executes in the handler of an event $e$ on thread $t$ then the *task* of $r$ is $task(r) = (t, e)$. A transition $r$ on a thread $t$ is *blocked* at a state $s$ if $r = next(s, t)$ and $r$ is not enabled in $s$. We assume that only visible operations may block. Function $nextTrans(s)$ gives the set of next transitions of all threads at state $s$. For a transition sequence $w : r_1.r_2 \ldots r_n$ in $\mathcal{S}_G$, let $dom(w) = \{1, \ldots, n\}$. Functions $getBegin(w, e)$ and $getEnd(w, e)$ respectively return the indices of the first and the last transitions of an event $e$'s handler in $w$, provided they belong to $w$.

**Deadlock Cycles and Assertion Violations.** A pair $\langle DC, \rho \rangle$ in a state $s \in S$ is said to form a *deadlock cycle* if $DC \subseteq nextTrans(s)$ is a set of $n$ transitions blocked in $s$, and $\rho$ is a one-to-one map from $[1, n]$ to $DC$ such that each $\rho(i) \in DC$, $i \in [1, n]$, is blocked by some transition on a thread $t_{i+1} = thread(\rho(i+1))$ and may be enabled only by a transition on $t_{i+1}$, and the transition $\rho(n) \in DC$ is blocked and may be enabled by two different transitions of thread $t_1 = thread(\rho(1))$. A state $s$ in $S_G$ is a *deadlock* state if all threads are blocked in $s$ due to a deadlock cycle.

An *assertion* $\alpha$ is a predicate over local variables of a handler and is considered visible. A state $s$ *violates* an assertion $\alpha$ if $\alpha$ is enabled at $s$ and evaluates to *false*.

## 2.2 Dependence and Happens-Before Relations

The notion of dependence between transitions is well-understood for multi-threaded programs. It extends naturally to event-driven programs if event queues are considered as shared objects, thereby, marking two **posts** to the same thread as dependent. To enable more reductions, we define an alternative notion in which two **post** operations to the same thread are *not* considered dependent. One reason to selectively reorder events posted to a thread is if their handlers contain dependent transitions. This requires a new notion of dependence between transitions of event handlers executing on the same thread, which we refer to as *single-threaded dependence*.

In order to explicate single-threaded dependences, we first define an event-parallel transition system which over-approximates the transition system $S_G$. The *event-parallel transition system $\mathcal{P}_G$ of a program $A$* is a triple $(S_P, s_{init}, \Delta_P)$. In contrast to the transition system $S_G = (S, s_{init}, \Delta)$ of Sect. 2.1 where events are dispatched in their order of arrival and execute till completion, a thread with an event queue in $\mathcal{P}_G$ removes *any* event in its queue and spawns a fresh thread to execute its handler. This enables concurrent execution of events posted to the same thread. Rest of the semantics remains the same. Let $T$ and $T_P$ be the sets of all threads in $S_G$ and $\mathcal{P}_G$ respectively. For each state $(l, g, q) \in S$, there exists a state $(l', g', q') \in S_P$ such that (1) for each thread $t \in T$, if $l(t)$ is defined then there exists a thread $t' \in T_P$ where $l'(t') = l(t)$, (2) $g = g'$, and (3) for each thread $t \in T$, $q(t) = q'(t)$. Let $R_P$ be the set of transitions in $\mathcal{P}_G$ and $ep : R \to R_P$ be a total function which maps a transition $r_{t,\ell} \in R$ to an equivalent transition $r'_{t',\ell'} \in R_P$ such that $\ell = \ell'$ and either $t' = t$ or $t'$ is a fresh thread spawned by $t$ in $\mathcal{P}_G$ to handle the event to whose handler $r_{t,\ell}$ belongs in $S_G$.

We illustrate the event-parallel transition system for the example program in Fig. 5. Here, x and y are shared variables. The transitions $r_1$ and $r_2$ respectively run on threads t1 and t2. The last three lines in Fig. 5 give definitions of handlers of the events e1, e2 and e3 respectively. Figure 6 shows a partial state space of the program in Fig. 5 according to the event-parallel transition system semantics. The edges are labeled with the respective transitions. The shaded states and thick edges indicate part of the state space that is reachable in the transition system semantics of Sect. 2.1 as well, under the mapping between states and transitions described above.

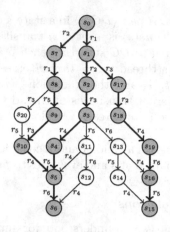

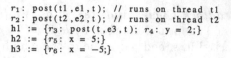

```
r1:  post(t1,e1,t); // runs on thread t1
r2:  post(t2,e2,t); // runs on thread t2
h1 := {r3: post(t,e3,t); r4: y = 2;}
h2 := {r5: x = 5;}
h3 := {r6: x = -5;}
```

**Fig. 5.** Pseudo code of an event-driven program.

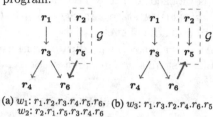

(a) $w_1$: $r_1.r_2.r_3.r_4.r_5.r_6$,   (b) $w_3$: $r_1.r_3.r_2.r_4.r_6.r_5$
$w_2$: $r_2.r_1.r_5.r_3.r_4.r_6$

**Fig. 6.** Partial event-parallel transition system for the program in Fig. 5.

**Fig. 7.** Dependence graphs of some sequences in $S_G$ of the program in Fig. 5.

**Definition 1.** Let $R_P$ be the set of transitions in the event-parallel transition system $\mathcal{P}_G$ of a program $A$. Let $D_P \subseteq R_P \times R_P$ be a binary, reflexive and symmetric relation. The relation $D_P$ is a valid **event-parallel dependence relation** iff for all $(r_1, r_2) \in R_P \times R_P$, $(r_1, r_2) \notin D_P$ implies that the following conditions hold for all states $s \in S_P$:

1. If $r_1$ is enabled in $s$ and $s' = r_1(s)$ then $r_2$ is enabled in $s$ iff it is enabled in $s'$.
2. If $r_1$ and $r_2$ are both enabled in $s$ then there exists $s' = (l', g', q') = r_1(r_2(s))$ and $s'' = (l'', g'', q'') = r_2(r_1(s))$ such that $l' = l''$ and $g' = g''$.

This definition is similar to the definition of dependence relation in [12] except that we do *not* require equality of the event states $q'$ and $q''$ in the second condition above. Clearly, any pair of post transitions, even if posting to the same event queue, are *independent* according to the event-parallel dependence relation.

**Definition 2.** Let $R$ be the set of transitions in the transition system $S_G$ of a program $A$. Let $D_P$ be a valid event-parallel dependence relation for $A$ and $D \subseteq R \times R$ be a binary, reflexive and symmetric relation. The relation $D$ is a valid **dependence relation** iff for all $(r_1, r_2) \in R \times R$, $(r_1, r_2) \notin D$ implies that the following conditions hold:

1. If $r_1$ and $r_2$ are transitions of handlers of two different events $e_1$ and $e_2$ executing on the *same thread* then the following conditions hold:
   (A) Events $e_1$ and $e_2$ may be reordered in $S_G$.
   (B) $ep(r_1)$ and $ep(r_2)$ are independent in $D_P$, i.e., $(ep(r_1), ep(r_2)) \notin D_P$.
2. Otherwise, conditions 1 and 2 in Definition 1 hold for all states $s \in S$.

Condition 1 above uses $D_P$ to define single-threaded dependence between transitions of two handlers in $\mathcal{S}_G$. Condition 2 applies the constraints in Definition 1 to states in $\mathcal{S}_G$ to define (1) dependence among transitions of the same handler and (2) multi-threaded dependence. Hence, all posts are considered *independent* of each other in $\mathcal{S}_G$.

*Example 1.* The transitions $r_5$ and $r_6$ in Fig. 5 run in two different event handlers but on the same thread t. Since the handlers execute concurrently in the event-parallel transition system, we can inspect the effect of reordering $r_5$ and $r_6$ on a state where they are co-enabled. In particular, at state $s_3$ in Fig. 6, the sequence $r_6.r_5$ reaches state $s_{14}$, whereas, $r_5.r_6$ reaches $s_{12}$ which differs from $s_{14}$ in the value of x. Therefore, $(r_5, r_6) \in D_P$ and by condition 1.B of Definition 2, $(r_5, r_6) \in D$.

The condition 1. A of Definition 2 requires that the ordering between $e_1$ and $e_2$ should not be fixed. Suppose the handler of $e_1$ posts $e_2$ but the two handlers do not have any pair of transitions that are in $D_P$. Nevertheless, since a post transition in $e_1$'s handler *enables* $e_2$, the transitions in the two handlers should be marked as dependent. This requirement is met through condition 1.A.

If $(r_i, r_j) \in D$, we simply say that $r_i$ and $r_j$ are *dependent*. In practice, we over-approximate the dependence relation, for example, by considering all conflicting accesses to shared objects as dependent. We now extend the happens-before relation defined in [10] with the FIFO rule in [15, 19].

**Definition 3.** The *happens-before relation* $\rightarrow_w$ for a transition sequence $w : r_1.r_2 \ldots r_n$ in $\mathcal{S}_G$ is the smallest relation on $dom(w)$ such that the following conditions hold:

1. If $i < j$ and $r_i$ is dependent with $r_j$ then $i \rightarrow_w j$.
2. If $r_i$ and $r_j$ are transitions posting events $e$ and $e'$ respectively to the same thread, such that $i \rightarrow_w j$ and the handler of $e$ has finished and that of $e'$ has started in $w$, then $getEnd(w, e) \rightarrow_w getBegin(w, e')$. This is the FIFO rule.
3. $\rightarrow_w$ is transitively closed.

The relation $\rightarrow_w$ is defined over transitions in $w$. We overload $\rightarrow_w$ to also relate transitions in $w$ with those in the $nextTrans$ set in the last state, say $s$, reached by $w$. For a task $(t, e)$ having a transition in $nextTrans(s)$, $i \rightarrow_w (t, e)$ if either (a) $task(r_i) = (t, e)$ or (b) $\exists k \in dom(w)$ such that $i \rightarrow_w k$ and $task(r_k) = (t, e)$.

## 2.3   Dependence-Covering Sets

Mazurkiewicz trace [21] forms the basis of POR for multi-threaded programs and event-driven programs where posts are considered dependent. Two transition sequences belong to the same Mazurkiewicz trace if they can be obtained from each other by reordering adjacent independent transitions. The objective of POR is to explore a representative sequence from each Mazurkiewicz trace. As pointed out in the Introduction, the reordering of posts (independent as per Definition 2) in a transition sequence $w$ may not yield another sequence belonging to the same Mazurkiewicz trace (denoted $[w]$) for two reasons: (1) it may reorder dependent transitions from the corresponding handlers and (2) some new transitions, not in $w$, may be pulled in.

We elaborate on the second point. Suppose in $w$, a handler $h_1$ executes before another handler $h_2$, both on the same thread, such that $h_2$ is executed only partially in $w$. Let us reorder the post operations for these two and obtain a transition sequence $w'$. Since the handlers run to completion, in order to include all the transitions of $h_1$ (executed in $w$) in $w'$, we must complete execution of $h_2$. However, as $h_2$ is only partially executed in $w$, this results in including new —previously unexplored— transitions of $h_2$ in $w'$. This renders $w$ and $w'$ inequivalent by the notion of Mazurkiewicz equivalence.

We therefore propose an alternative notion, suitable to correlate two transition sequences in event-driven multi-threaded programs, called the *dependence-covering sequence*. The objective of our reduction is to explore a dependence-covering sequence $u$ at a state $s$ for any transition sequence $w$ starting at $s$.

Let $w : r_1.r_2 \ldots r_n$ and $u : r'_1.r'_2 \ldots r'_m$ be two transition sequences from the same state $s$ in $\mathcal{S}_G$ reaching states $s_n$ and $s'_m$ respectively. Let $R_w = \{r_1, \ldots, r_n\}$ and $R_u = \{r'_1, \ldots, r'_m\}$.

**Definition 4.** The transition sequence $u$ is called a ***dependence-covering sequence*** of $w$ if (i) $R_w \subseteq R_u$ and (ii) for each pair of dependent transitions $r'_i, r'_j \in R_u$ such that $i < j$, any one among the following conditions holds:

1. $r'_i$ and $r'_j$ are executed in $w$ and their relative order in $u$ is consistent with that in $w$.
2. $r'_i$ is executed in $w$ and $r'_j \in nextTrans(s_n)$.
3. $r'_i$ is not executed in $w$, $r'_j \in nextTrans(s_n)$ and $w$ can be extended in $\mathcal{S}_G$ such that $r'_i$ executes before $r'_j$.
4. Irrespective of whether $r'_i$ is executed in $w$ or not, $r'_j$ is not in $R_w \cup nextTrans(s_n)$.

The condition (i) above allows new transitions, that are not in $w$, to be part of $u$. The condition (ii) restricts how the new transitions may interfere with the dependences exhibited in $w$ and also requires all the dependences in $w$ to be maintained in $u$. These conditions permit a dependence-covering sequence of $w$ to be a relaxation of Mazurkiewicz trace $[w]$, making it more suitable for stateless model checking of event-driven multi-threaded programs where posts may be reordered selectively.

As an example, let $w_1$, $w_2$ and $w_3$ (listed in Fig. 7) be the three transition sequences in Fig. 6 which correspond to valid sequences in the transition system $\mathcal{S}_G$ of the program in Fig. 5. To illustrate dependence-covering sequences, we visualize the dependences in these sequences as dependence graphs. The nodes in the dependence graph of a sequence $w$ represent transitions in $w$. If a transition $r_i$ executes before another transition $r_j$ in $w$ such that $r_i$ and $r_j$ are dependent then a directed edge is drawn from $r_i$ to $r_j$. Figure 7 depicts the dependence graphs of $w_1$, $w_2$ and $w_3$. Sequences $w_1$ and $w_2$ are dependence-covering sequences of each other, as their dependence graphs are identical (Fig. 7(a)). Consider a sequence $w_4 = r_2.r_5$ whose dependence graph is the subgraph $\mathcal{G}$ in Fig. 7. A dependence graph $\mathcal{G}'$ of any dependence-covering sequence $u$ of $w_4$ contains $\mathcal{G}$ as a subgraph, with no incoming edge into $\mathcal{G}$ from any node in $\mathcal{G}'$ which is not in $\mathcal{G}$. However, there are no restrictions on dependences between nodes in $\mathcal{G}'$ which are not in $\mathcal{G}$. Hence, $w_1$ and $w_2$ (see Fig. 7(a)) are dependence-covering sequences of $w_4$ even though $w_4$ and $w_1$ (or $w_2$) do not belong to the same Mazurkiewicz trace, whereas $w_3$ is not a dependence-covering sequence of $w_4$ due to the edge $r_6$ to $r_5$ (see Fig. 7(b)).

**Definition 5.** A non-empty subset $L$ of transitions enabled at a state $s$ in $\mathcal{S}_G$ is a ***dependence-covering set*** in $s$ iff, for all non-empty sequences of transitions $w : r_1 \ldots r_n$ starting at $s$, there exists a dependence-covering sequence $u : r_1' \ldots r_m'$ of $w$ starting at $s$ such that $r_1' \in L$.

*Example 2.* All the transition sequences connecting state $s_0$ to state $s_5$ in Fig. 2 are dependence-covering sequences of each other. Thus, the dependence-covering set in $s_0$ can be $\{r_1\}$, $\{r_2\}$ or $\{r_1, r_2\}$. Even if we take a prefix $\sigma$ of any of these sequences, the shaded sequence in Fig. 2 is a dependence-covering sequence of $\sigma$.

In Fig. 4, $\{r_2\}$ and $\{r_1, r_2\}$ are individually dependence-covering sets in state $s_0$, whereas, $\{r_1\}$ is not a dependence-covering set at $s_0$.

For efficient stateless model checking of event-driven multi-threaded programs, we can explore a reduced state space using dependence-covering sets.

**Definition 6.** A ***dependence-covering state space*** of an event-driven multi-threaded program $A$ is a reduced state space $\mathcal{S}_R \subseteq \mathcal{S}_G$ obtained by exploring only the transitions in a dependence-covering set at each state in $\mathcal{S}_G$ reached from $s_{init}$.

The objective of a POR approach is to show that even while exploring a reduced state space, no concurrency bug is missed *w.r.t.* the complete but possibly much larger state space. The exploration of a dependence-covering state space satisfies this objective. The following theorem states the main result of this paper.

**Theorem 1.** Let $\mathcal{S}_R$ be a dependence-covering state space of an event-driven multi-threaded program $A$ with a finite and acyclic state space $\mathcal{S}_G$. Then, all deadlock cycles in $\mathcal{S}_G$ are reachable in $\mathcal{S}_R$. If there exists a state $v$ in $\mathcal{S}_G$ which violates an assertion $\alpha$ defined over local variables then there exists a state $v'$ in $\mathcal{S}_R$ which violates $\alpha$.

The proof follows from the appropriate restrictions on allowed dependences in a dependence-covering sequence $u$ compared to the dependences in $w$ where $w$ is required to reach a deadlock cycle or an assertion violation in the complete state space. We provide a complete proof of the above theorem in Appendix A in [18]. The set $\{r_1, r_2\}$ is both a persistent set and a dependence-covering set in state $s_0$ in Fig. 2. We observe that in general, a persistent set $P$ at a state

$s \in \mathcal{S}_G$ is also a dependence-covering set at $s$. Here, persistent set is defined using the dependence relation where posts to the same event queue are dependent, whereas, dependence-covering set is defined using the dependence relation where they are not (more formally, using Definition 2). We present a proof of this claim in Appendix B in [18]. Note that a dependence-covering set need not be a persistent set. As seen in Example 2, $\{r_1\}$ and $\{r_2\}$ are both dependence-covering sets at $s_0$ in Fig. 2 but they are not persistent sets.

# 3 Implementation

This section provides a high-level sketch of our algorithm to dynamically compute dependence-covering sets. Due to lack of space, we do not present the complete algorithm and its soundness proof. We refer the readers to [18] for these details.

Android applications form a very popular class of event-driven multi-threaded programs. We further discuss the implementation of EM-Explorer, a proof-of-concept model checking framework which simulates the Android concurrency semantics given an execution trace of an Android application. We have implemented our algorithm in EM-Explorer for experimental evaluation.

## 3.1 Dynamic Algorithm for Computing Dependence-Covering Sets

DPOR [10] is an effective algorithm to dynamically compute backtracking choices for selective state-space exploration. It performs DFS traversal of the transition system of a program, but instead of exploring all the enabled transitions at a state, it only explores transitions added as backtracking choices by the steps of the algorithm. DPOR guarantees that it explores a persistent set at each of the visited states. Our algorithm, called *EM-DPOR*, extends DPOR to compute dependence-covering sets for event-driven multi-threaded programs. It differs from DPOR in the aspects of computing backtracking choices as well as the states to which the algorithm backtracks.

Let *backtrack*($s$) refer to the backtracking set computed by EM-DPOR for a state $s$. We say a task $(t, e)$ is *executable* at a state $s$ if the first transition of event $e$'s handler is enabled in $s$ (see Sect. 2.1) or the task is being executed in state $s$. Similar to DPOR, on exploring a sequence $w$ reaching a state $s'$, our algorithm identifies the nearest transition $r$ in $w$ executed at a state $s$ which is dependent with a transition $r' \in nextTrans(s')$. If $r$ and $r'$ belong to two different threads then similar to DPOR, we require that they may be co-enabled. In addition, if they belong to two different handlers on the same thread then we require that they may be reordered (see Sect. 2.1). In the latter case, we first identify a pair of post operations executed on *different* threads which need to be reordered so as to reorder $r$ and $r'$ (see [18] for the details).

We now discuss how to reorder two transitions from two different threads. Let $r$ and $r'$ be such transitions where $r$ executes before $r'$ in $w$ and $s$ be the state from which $r$ executes. In order to compute backtracking choices to reorder them, EM-DPOR computes a set of candidate tasks whose respective threads are enabled in state $s$, such that each *candidate task* contains a transition executed after $r$ that has happens-before relation with $r'$. We select a thread $t$ as a backtracking choice if $(t, e)$ is a candidate task and $t$ is not already explored from state $s$. These steps are similar to the steps of DPOR except that we use the happens-before relation of Definition 3.

A challenging case arises if the threads corresponding to all the candidate tasks are already explored from $s$. As will be illustrated in Example 3, this does not imply that $r$ and $r'$ cannot be reordered in future. Unless all candidate tasks are executable at state $s$, this also does not imply that they have been reordered in the already explored state space. Therefore, the algorithm selects some candidate task $(t', e')$ (if any) that is not executable at $s$ and attempts to reorder $e'$ with the event, say $e''$, enqueued to the same thread $t'$ and executable at $s$. This results in a *recursive* call to identify backtracking choices as well as backtracking state. Due to this, in a future run, $e''$ and $e'$ may be reordered. Suppose $r''$ is the transition in $(t', e')$ that has happens-before with $r'$. The resulting reordering of the handlers of $e''$ and $e'$ subsequently enables exploring $r''$ prior to $r$ which in turn, leads to the desired reordering of $r$ and $r'$. Example 3 illustrates the essential steps of EM-DPOR.

*Example 3.* We explain how EM-DPOR computes dependence-covering sets to explore the state space in Fig. 4 starting with transition sequence $w$ in Fig. 3. On exploring a prefix of $w$ and reaching state $s_5$, $r_3$ and $r_6$ are identified to be dependent. When attempting to compute backtracking choices at state $s_2$ (the state where $r_3$ is explored) to reorder $r_3$ and $r_6$, $r_4$ is found to have a happens-before ordering with $r_6$ and thus $r_4$'s task (t1, e2) is identified as the candidate task. However, thread t1 is already explored from state $s_2$ and task (t1, e2) is not executable (see the event queue shown at $s_2$). Hence, the algorithm tries to reorder e2 with event e1 whose task is executable at state $s_2$. This is achieved by recursively starting another backward search to identify the backtracking choices that can reorder e1 and e2. In this case, post operations $r_1$ and $r_2$ can be reordered to do so. Therefore, $r_2$ is added to the backtracking set at $s_0$, exploring which leads to $s_8$ where e2 *precedes* e1 in the event queue as required. Thus, the algorithm computes $\{r_1, r_2\}$ as a dependence-covering set at $s_0$ and eventually reaches state $s_{10}$ where $r_3$ and $r_6$ are co-enabled and can be ordered as desired.

Note that even while considering the dependence between transitions $r_3$ and $r_6$, EM-DPOR is able to identify a seemingly unrelated state $s_0$ (much prior to state $s_2$ where $r_3$ is explored) as an appropriate state to backtrack to. Also, $r_3$ and $r_6$ are transitions from two *different threads*. Even then, to reorder them, EM-DPOR had to reorder the two post transitions $r_1$ and $r_2$ to the same thread t1 at $s_0$.

Similar to DPOR, we have implemented our algorithm using a vector clocks datastructure [20]. In a multi-threaded setting where all the operations executed on the same thread are totally ordered, a clock is assigned to each thread and the components of a vector clock correspond to clock values of the threads of the program. In an event-driven program, the operations from different handlers on the same thread need not be totally ordered and hence, we assign a clock to each task in the program. In addition to the vector clock computations described in [10], we establish an order between event handlers executed on the same thread if their corresponding posts have a happens-before ordering, so as to respect the FIFO ordering of events.

## 3.2    EM-Explorer Framework

Building a full-fledged model checker for Android applications is a challenge in itself but is not the focus of this work. Tools such as JPF-Android [24] and Async-Droid [25] take promising steps in this direction. However, presently they either explore only a limited number of sources of non-determinism [25] or require a lot of framework libraries to be modeled [23,24]. We have therefore implemented a prototype exploration framework called EM-Explorer, which emulates the semantics of visible operations like post operation, memory read/write, and lock acquire/release.

EM-Explorer takes an execution trace generated by an automated testing and race detection tool for Android applications, called DroidRacer [19], as input. As DroidRacer runs on real-world applications, we can experiment on real concurrency behaviors seen in Android applications and evaluate different POR techniques on them. DroidRacer records all concurrency relevant operations and memory reads and writes. EM-Explorer *emulates* such a trace based on their operational semantics and explores all interleavings of the given execution trace permitted by the semantics. Android permits user and system-generated events apart from program-generated events. EM-Explorer only explores the non-determinism between program and system generated events while keeping the order of user events fixed. This is analogous to model checking *w.r.t.* a fixed data input. EM-Explorer does not track variable values and is incapable of evaluating conditionals on a different interleaving of the trace.

Android supports different types of component classes, e.g., Activity class for the user interface, and enforces a happens-before ordering between handlers of lifecycle events of component classes. EM-Explorer seeds the happens-before relation for such events in each trace before starting the model checking run, avoiding exploration of invalid interleavings of lifecycle events. We remove handlers with no visible operations from recorded traces before model checking.

**Table 1.** Statistics on execution traces from Android apps and their model checking runs using different POR techniques. Android apps: (A) Remind Me, (B) My Tracks, (C) Music Player, (D) Character Recognition, and (E) Aard Dictionary

| Apps | Trace length | Threads/ Events | Memory Locations | DPOR | | | EM-DPOR | | |
|------|-------|--------|-----------|----------|-------------|----------|--------|-------------|----------|
| | | | | Traces | Transitions | Time | Traces | Transitions | Time |
| A | 444 | 4/9 | 89 | 24 | 1864 | 0.18 s | 3 | 875 | 0.05 s |
| B | 453 | 10/9 | 108 | 1610684* | 113299092* | 4 h* | 405013 | 26745327 | 101 m 30 s |
| C | 465 | 6/24 | 68 | 1508413* | 93254810* | 4 h* | 266 | 34333 | 4.15 s |
| D | 485 | 4/22 | 40 | 1284788 | 67062526 | 199 m 28 s | 756 | 39422 | 6.58 s |
| E | 600 | 5/30 | 30 | 359961* | 14397143* | 4 h* | 14 | 4772 | 1.4 s |

# 4   Experimental Evaluation

We compare the performance of (1) EM-DPOR which computes dependence-covering sets with (2) DPOR which computes persistent sets. Both the algorithms are implemented in the EM-Explorer framework described in Sect. 3 and use vector clocks. The implementation of DPOR uses the dependence relation in which posts to the same thread are considered dependent.

We evaluated these POR techniques on execution traces generated by DroidRacer on 5 Android applications obtained from the Google Play Store [1]. Table 1 presents statistics like trace length (the number of *visible* operations), and the number of threads, events and (shared) memory locations in an execution trace for each of these applications. We only report the threads created by the application, and the number of events excluding events with no visible operations in their handlers.

We analyzed each of the traces described in Table 1 using both the POR techniques. Table 1 gives the number of interleavings (listed as *Traces*) and distinct transitions explored by DPOR and EM-DPOR. It also gives the time taken for exploring the reduced state space for each execution trace. If a model checking run did not terminate within 4 hours, we force-kill it and report the statistics for 4 hours. The statistics for force-killed runs are marked with * in Table 1. Since EM-Explorer does not track variable values, it cannot prune executions that are infeasible due to conditional sequential execution. However, both DPOR and EM-DPOR are implemented on top of EM-Explorer and therefore operate on the same set of interleavings. The difference in their performance thus arises from the different POR strategies.

In our experiments, DPOR's model checking run terminated only on two execution traces among the five, whereas, EM-DPOR terminated on all of them. Except for one case, EM-DPOR finished state space exploration within a few seconds. As can be seen from Table 1, DPOR explores a much larger number of interleavings and transitions, often *orders of magnitude* larger compared to EM-DPOR. While this is a small evaluation, it does show that significant reduction can be achieved for real-world event-driven multi-threaded programs by avoiding unnecessary reordering of events.

*Performance.* Both the techniques used about the same memory and the maximum peak memory consumed by EM-DPOR across all traces, as reported by Valgrind, was less than 50 MB. The experiments were performed on a machine with Intel Core i5 3.2 GHz CPU with 4 GB RAM, and running Ubuntu 12.04 OS.

# 5   Conclusions and Future Work

The event-driven multi-threaded style of programming concurrent applications is becoming increasingly popular. We considered the problem of POR-based efficient stateless model checking for this concurrency model. The key insight of our work is that more reduction is achievable by treating operations that post events to the same thread as independent and only reordering them if necessary.

We presented POR based on dependence-covering sequences and sets. Exploring only dependence-covering sets suffices to provide certain formal guarantees. Our experiments provide empirical evidence that our dynamic algorithm for computing dependence-covering sets explores orders of magnitude fewer transitions compared to DPOR for event-driven multi-threaded programs. While we evaluate our algorithm on Android applications, the general idea of dependence-covering sets is more widely applicable. As future work, we aim to achieve better reductions by defining a notion of sleep sets suitable for this concurrency model and combining it with dependence-covering sets as well as explore optimality of POR in this context.

**Acknowledgements.** P. Maiya thanks Google India for its support through a PhD Fellowship in Programming Languages and Compilers. This research was also funded in part by the Indo-German Max Planck Center in Computer Science (IMPECS).

# References

1. Google Play. https://play.google.com/store/apps
2. Grand Central Dispatch. https://developer.apple.com/library/ios/documentation/Performance/Reference/GCD_libdispatch_Ref
3. Java AWT EventQueue. http://docs.oracle.com/javase/7/docs/api/java/awt/EventQueue.html
4. TinyOS. http://www.tinyos.net
5. Abdulla, P., Aronis, S., Jonsson, B., Sagonas, K.: Optimal dynamic partial order reduction. In: POPL, pp. 373–384. ACM (2014)
6. Abdulla, P.A., Aronis, S., Atig, M.F., Jonsson, B., Leonardsson, C., Sagonas, K.: Stateless model checking for TSO and PSO. In: Baier, C., Tinelli, C. (eds.) TACAS 2015. LNCS, vol. 9035, pp. 353–367. Springer, Heidelberg (2015)
7. Bielik, P., Raychev, V., Vechev, M.T.: Scalable race detection for android applications. In: OOPSLA, pp. 332–348. ACM (2015)
8. Clarke, E.M., Grumberg, O., Minea, M., Peled, D.: State space reduction using partial order techniques. STTT **2**(3), 279–287 (1999)
9. Emmi, M., Lal, A., Qadeer, S.: Asynchronous programs with prioritized task-buffers. In: SIGSOFT FSE, pp. 48:1–48:11. ACM (2012)
10. Flanagan, C., Godefroid, P.: Dynamic partial-order reduction for model checking software. In: POPL, pp. 110–121. ACM (2005)
11. Godefroid, P. (ed.): Partial-Order Methods for the Verification of Concurrent Systems. LNCS, vol. 1032. Springer, Heidelberg (1996)
12. Godefroid, P.: Model checking for programming languages using Verisoft. In: POPL, pp. 174–186. ACM Press (1997)
13. Godefroid, P.: Software model checking: The verisoft approach. Formal Methods Syst. Des. **26**(2), 77–101 (2005)
14. Holzmann, G.: The Spin Model Checker: Primer and Reference Manual. Addison-Wesley, Reading (2004)
15. Hsiao, C.H., Yu, J., Narayanasamy, S., Kong, Z., Pereira, C.L., Pokam, G.A., Chen, P.M., Flinn, J.: Race Detection for Event-driven Mobile Applications. In: PLDI, pp. 326–336. ACM (2014)

16. Jensen, C.S., Møller, A., Raychev, V., Dimitrov, D., Vechev, M.T.: Stateless model checking of event-driven applications. In: OOPSLA, pp. 57–73. ACM (2015)
17. Lauterburg, S., Dotta, M., Marinov, D., Agha, G.A.: A framework for state-space exploration of java-based actor programs. In: ASE, pp. 468–479. IEEE Computer Society (2009)
18. Maiya, P., Gupta, R., Kanade, A., Majumdar, R.: A partial order reduction technique for event-driven multi-threaded programs. CoRR abs/1511.03213 (2015)
19. Maiya, P., Kanade, A., Majumdar, R.: Race detection for Android applications. In: PLDI, pp. 316–325. ACM (2014)
20. Mattern, F.: Virtual time and global states of distributed systems. In: Parallel and Distributed Algorithms, pp. 215–226. Elsevier (1989)
21. Mazurkiewicz, A.W.: Trace theory. In: Brauer, W., Reisig, W., Rozenberg, G. (eds.) Advances in Petri Nets 1986. LNCS, vol. 255, pp. 279–324. Springer, Heidelberg (1986)
22. Mednieks, Z., Dornin, L., Meike, G.B., Nakamura, M.: Programming Android. O'Reilly Media, Inc. (2012)
23. van der Merwe, H.: Verification of android applications. In: ICSE, vol. 2, pp. 931–934. IEEE (2015)
24. van der Merwe, H., van der Merwe, B., Visser, W.: Verifying android applications using Java PathFinder. ACM SIGSOFT Softw. Eng. Not. **37**(6), 1–5 (2012)
25. Ozkan, B.K., Emmi, M., Tasiran, S.: Systematic asynchrony bug exploration for android apps. In: Kroening, D., Păsăreanu, C.S. (eds.) CAV 2015. LNCS, vol. 9206, pp. 455–461. Springer, Heidelberg (2015)
26. Palmer, R., Gopalakrishnan, G., Kirby, R.M.: Semantics driven dynamic partial-order reduction of MPI-based Parallel Programs. In: PADTAD, pp. 43–53. ACM (2007)
27. Peled, D.: All from one, one for all: on model checking using representatives. In: Courcoubetis, C. (ed.) CAV 1993. LNCS, vol. 697, pp. 409–423. Springer, Heidelberg (1993)
28. Rodríguez, C., Sousa, M., Sharma, S., Kroening, D.: Unfolding-based partial order reduction. In: CONCUR. LIPIcs, vol. 42, pp. 456–469. Schloss Dagstuhl - Leibniz-Zentrum fuer Informatik (2015)
29. Sen, K., Agha, G.: Automated systematic testing of open distributed programs. In: Baresi, L., Heckel, R. (eds.) FASE 2006. LNCS, vol. 3922, pp. 339–356. Springer, Heidelberg (2006)
30. Sen, K., Viswanathan, M.: Model checking multithreaded programs with asynchronous atomic methods. In: Ball, T., Jones, R.B. (eds.) CAV 2006. LNCS, vol. 4144, pp. 300–314. Springer, Heidelberg (2006)
31. Tasharofi, S., Karmani, R.K., Lauterburg, S., Legay, A., Marinov, D., Agha, G.: TransDPOR: a novel dynamic partial-order reduction technique for testing actor programs. In: Giese, H., Rosu, G. (eds.) FMOODS/FORTE 2012. LNCS, vol. 7273, pp. 219–234. Springer, Heidelberg (2012)
32. Valmari, A.: Stubborn sets for reduced state space generation. In: Rozenberg, G. (ed.) APN 1990. LNCS, vol. 483, pp. 491–515. Springer, Heidelberg (1991)
33. Zhang, N., Kusano, M., Wang, C.: Dynamic partial order reduction for relaxed memory models. In: PLDI, pp. 250–259. ACM (2015)

# Acceleration in Multi-PushDown Systems

Mohamed Faouzi Atig[1]($\boxtimes$), K. Narayan Kumar[2], and Prakash Saivasan[2]

[1] Uppsala University, Uppsala, Sweden
mohamed_faouzi.atig@it.uu.se
[2] Chennai Mathematical Institute, Chennai, India
{kumar,saivasan}@cmi.ac.in

**Abstract.** Multipushdown systems (MPDS) are formal models of multi-threaded recursive programs. They are turing powerful and hence one considers under-approximation techniques in their analysis. We study the use of loop accelerations in conjunction with bounded context analysis.

## 1 Introduction

Sequential recursive programs are usually modeled as pushdown systems (PDSs) and algorithmic techniques developed for PDSs have been used to solve a number of problems related to the verification of such programs (e.g. [14, 20, 23, 26, 40, 41]). Extending this idea to multi-threaded recursive programs requires multi-pushdown systems (MPDSs), i.e. automata with multiple pushdown stores. Unfortunately, MPDSs are turing powerful. The main technique used to circumvent this problem is that of under-approximation. The idea is to identify a subset of behaviours and restrict the verification only to this subset. An underapproximation is interesting only if the verification problem when restricted to this subset is decidable and in addition the subset covers interesting behaviours. This idea came to the fore with the *bounded context analysis* proposed in [39]. A context switch occurs when the automaton switches from accessing one stack to another (or equivalently, the execution of a multi-threaded program switches from scheduling one thread to another). Placing an a priori bound on the number of context switches results in the decidability of reachability and other verification problems. Subsequently, other classes generalizing the bounded context assumption have been proposed (see [2–6, 15, 28, 32–35]).

Recall that the configuration of a PDS can be seen as a word (giving the current state and the contents of the stack). In the *global model checking problem* the aim is to compute from (a representation of) the set of initial configurations ($I$) (a representation of) the set of configurations reachable from $I$ (denoted $post^*(I)$). For PDSs if the initial set of configurations is a regular language then the set of reachable configurations is a computable regular language ([14, 26]).

The configuration of a MPDS can be represented as a tuple of words giving the current state and the contents of each of the stacks. We can then represent sets of configurations by *recognizable* or *regular* languages [10]. Given a

The authors acknowledge partial support by DST-VR Project P-02/2014, TCS PhD Fellowship, Infosys Foundation and the Linnaeus centre of excellence UPMARC.

M. Chechik and J.-F. Raskin (Eds.): TACAS 2016, LNCS 9636, pp. 698–714, 2016.
DOI: 10.1007/978-3-662-49674-9_45

recognizable language representing the set of initial configurations, the set of configurations that may be reached via runs with at most $k$-context switches is also a (computable) recognizable language [39]. Thus, the global model checking problem is decidable and this has many applications, including the obvious one — reachability can be decided.

Note that our description of global model-checking does not require that the representations of the initial set $I$ and the reachable set $post^*(I)$ to be the same. For instance, for PDSs, whether we use finite sets or regular sets for the initial set of configurations, the final set can be described effectively as a regular set. However, if both sets use the same description, then we say that the representation is stable. Stability is an useful property as it permits us to compose (and hence iterate finitely) the algorithm.

Another well known technique used in the verification of infinite state systems is that of loop accelerations. It is similar in spirit to global model checking but with different applications. The idea is to consider a loop of transitions (a finite sequence of transitions that lead from a control state back to the same control state). The aim is to determine the effect of iterating the loop. That is, to effectively construct a representation of the set of configurations that may be reached by valid iterations of the loop.

Loop accelerations turn out to be very useful in the analysis of a variety of infinite state systems (e.g., [1, 7–9, 11–13, 16, 24, 25, 29, 30, 36, 37]). In this paper, we propose to use accelerations in the verification of MPDSs. We take this further by proposing a technique that composes the iterations of such loops with context bounded runs to obtain a new decidable under-approximation for MPDSs. Observe that there is no bound on the number of context switches under loop iterations while a context bounded run permits unrestricted recursive behaviours, not permitted by loop iterations, thus complementing each other.

We begin by showing that both regular and rational sets of configurations are stable w.r.t. bounded context runs. Then, we show that this does not extend to iterations of loops. We show that under iterations of a loop, the $post^*$ of a regular set of transitions is always rational while that of a rational set need not be rational. We then address the question of a representation that is stable w.r.t. loop accelerations. Towards this we propose a new representation for configurations called $n$-CSRE inspired by the CQDDs [16] and the class of bounded semilinear languages [18]. We show that $n$-CSREs are indeed stable w.r.t iteration of loops. This result also has the pleasant feature that the construction is in polynomial time. However, $n$-CSREs are not stable w.r.t bounded context runs.

As a final step we introduce a joint generalization of both loop iterations and bounded context executions called bounded context-switch sets. We show that the class of languages defined by $n$-dimensional constrained automata (a $n$-dimensional version of Parikh automata [17,31]) is stable w.r.t accelerations via bounded context-switch sets. Since membership is decidable for this class, we obtain a decidability of reachability under this generous class of behaviours. Observe that the class of $n$-dimensional constrained automata is not closed under intersection and that the inclusion problem is undecidable.

*Related Work.* To the best of our knowledge this is the first study of accelerations in the setting of MPDSs. By using ideas from acceleration we have obtained a decidable under-approximation that significantly extends the notion of context-bounding, and which seems incomparable to many other classes considered in literature. The closest work is the pattern-based (or bounded) verification for MPDSs [21,22,27]. The pattern-based verification checks the correctness of the program for the set of the executions described as a bounded language (i.e., $w_1^* w_2^* \cdots w_n^*$). Our loop acceleration result allow to compute the set of reachable configurations induced by a bounded language and hence solving the global reachability problem for pattern-based verification for MPDSs (and providing a new proof for its decidability).

## 2   Preliminaries

Let $\mathbb{N}$ denote the set of natural numbers. For $i, j \in \mathbb{N}$ with $i \leq j$, we use $[i..j]$ to denote the set $\{k \in \mathbb{N} \mid i \leq k \leq j\}$. Let $A$ and $B$ two sets. For a partial function $g : A \rightharpoonup B$ and $a \in A$, we write $g(a) = \bot$ if $g$ is undefined on $a$. Let $\Sigma$ be a finite alphabet. As usual $\Sigma^*$ denotes the set of all finite words over $\Sigma$ and $\epsilon$ denotes the empty word. Let $u \in \Sigma^*$, we use $Parikh(u)$ to denote the mapping that associates to each letter $a$ in $\Sigma$, the number of occurrences of $a$ in $u$.

Next we extend these notions to higher dimensions. Let $\Sigma_1, \ldots, \Sigma_n$ be $n$ finite alphabets. A $n$-dim word $\mathbf{u}$ over $\Sigma_1, \ldots, \Sigma_n$ is a tuple $(u_1, u_2, \ldots, u_n)$ with $u_i \in \Sigma_i^*$. For every $j \in [1..n]$, we use $\mathbf{u}[j]$ to denote the word $u_j$. Let $i \in [1..n]$ and $w \in \Sigma_i^*$, we use $\mathbf{u}[i \leftarrow w]$ to denote the $n$-dim word $(u_1, u_2, \ldots, u_{i-1}, w, u_{i+1}, \ldots, u_n)$. A $n$-dim language is a set of $n$-dim words. Given two $n$-dim words $\mathbf{u} = (u_1, \ldots, u_n)$ and $\mathbf{v} = (v_1, \ldots, v_n)$, their concatenation is defined by $\mathbf{u}\mathbf{v} = (u_1 v_1, \ldots, u_n v_n)$. The concatenation of two $n$-dim languages $L_1, L_2$ is defined as expected to be $L_1.L_2 = \{\mathbf{u}\mathbf{v} \mid \mathbf{u} \in L_1 \wedge \mathbf{v} \in L_2\}$.

A $n$-tape finite state automaton over $\Sigma_1, \ldots, \Sigma_n$ is defined as $A = (Q, \Sigma_1, \ldots, \Sigma_n, \delta, q_0, F)$ where $Q$ is a finite set of states, $q_0$ is the initial state, $F$ is the set of final states, and $\delta \subseteq (Q \times (\Sigma_1 \cup \{\epsilon\}) \times \cdots \times (\Sigma_n \cup \{\epsilon\}) \times Q)$, is the transition relation. A run $\pi$ of $A$ over a $n$-dim word $\mathbf{w}$ over $\Sigma_1, \ldots, \Sigma_n$ is a sequence of transitions $(q_0, \mathbf{u}_1, q_1), (q_1, \mathbf{u}_2, q_2), \ldots, (q_{m-1}, \mathbf{u}_m, q_m) \in \delta$ such that $\mathbf{w} = \mathbf{u}_1 \mathbf{u}_2 \cdots \mathbf{u}_m$. The run $\pi$ is accepting if $q_m \in F$. The language of $A$, denoted by $L(A)$, is the set of $n$-dim words $\mathbf{w}$ for which there is an accepting run of $A$ over $w$. A $n$-dim language is *rational* if it is the language of some $n$-tape automaton [10]. Observe that 1-tape automata are the standard finite-state automata.

An interesting subclass of rational languages are what are called *recognizable* or *regular* languages. A $n$-dim language $L$ is *regular* if it is a finite union of products of $n$ rational 1-dim languages (i.e. $L = \bigcup_{j=1}^{m} L_{(j,1)} \times \cdots \times L_{(j,n)}$ for some $m \in \mathbb{N}$ where $L_{(j,i)}$ is an 1-dim rational language over $\Sigma_i$). Observe that if $n = 1$ rational and regular languages are the same. The language $\{(a^i, b^i) \mid i \geq 0\}$ is an example of a rational language that is not regular.

Let us recall some properties of rational and regular languages (see, e.g., [10]). First, the class of regular languages, for any dimension $n \geq 1$, is closed under boolean operations. On the other hand, for every $n \geq 2$, the class of $n$-dim rational languages is closed under union and concatenation but not under complementation, nor under intersection. However, the emptiness and membership problems for rational languages are decidable in all dimensions and further the inclusion problem is also decidable for regular languages. The inclusion problem is undecidable for rational languages (for $n \geq 2$).

We describe some additional closure properties of rational languages that will prove useful. Rational languages are effectively closed under the permutation of indices: Let $A$ be a $n$-tape automaton over $\Sigma_1, \ldots, \Sigma_n$. Given a mapping $h : [1..n] \rightarrow [1..n]$, it is possible to construct a $n$-tape automaton $h(A)$, linear in the size of $A$, such that $(w_1, \ldots, w_n) \in L(A)$ iff $(w_{h(1)}, \ldots, w_{h(n)}) \in L(h(A))$. Rational languages are also effectively closed under projection: Given a set of indices $\iota = \{i_1 < i_2 < \ldots i_m\} \subset \{1, \ldots, n\}$, we can construct an automaton $\Pi_\iota(A)$, linear in size of $A$, such that $L(\Pi_\iota(A)) = \{(w_{i_1}, w_{i_2}, \ldots, w_{i_m}) \mid (w_1, w_2, \ldots, w_n) \in L(A)\}$. Rational languages are also closed under an operation we call *composition*: Let $A$ be as before and let $A'$ be a rational language over $\Sigma_1', \Sigma_2', \ldots, \Sigma_m'$. Let $i \in \{1, \ldots, n\}$ and $j \in \{1, \ldots, m\}$ be two indices s.t. $\Sigma_j' = \Sigma_i$. Then, it is possible to construct a $(n + m - 1)$-tape automaton $A \circ_{(i,j)} A'$, whose size is $\mathcal{O}(|A|.|A'|)$, accepting $(w_1, \ldots, w_n, w_1', \ldots, w_{j-1}', w_{j+1}', \ldots, w_m')$ iff $(w_1, \ldots, w_n) \in L(A)$ and $(w_1', \ldots, w_{j-1}', w_i, w_{j+1}', \ldots, w_m') \in L(A')$, i.e. the composition corresponding to the synchronization of the $i^{th}$ tape of $A$ with the $j^{th}$ tape of $A'$.

## 3   Multi-PushDown Systems

A *Multi-PushDown System* (MPDS) is a tuple $M = (n, Q, \Gamma, \Delta)$ where: (1) $n \geq 1$ is the number of stacks, (2) $Q$ is the non-empty finite set of states, (3) $\Gamma$ is the finite set of stack symbols, and (4) $\Delta \subseteq (Q \times (\cup_{i \in [1..n]} \Omega(i)) \times Q)$ is the transition relation. For every $i \in [1..n]$, $\Omega(i)$ is the set of operations on the stack $i$ containing: $(i)$ the *push operation* $push_i(a)$ $(a \in \Gamma)$, $(ii)$ the *pop operation* $pop_i(a)$ $(a \in \Gamma)$, and $(iii)$ the *internal operation* $nop_i$. A PushDown System (PDS) can be seen as a MPDS with $n = 1$. Let $\Delta_i = \Delta \cap (Q \times \Omega_i \times Q)$.

A configuration of the MPDS $M$ is a $(n + 1)$-tuple $(q, u_1, u_2, \cdots, u_n)$ where $q \in Q$ is the current state of $M$, and for every $i \in [1..n]$, $u_i \in \Gamma^*$ is the current content of the $i$-th stack of $M$. A configuration can be seen as $(n + 1)$-word. The set of configurations of the MPDS $M$ is denoted by $Cf(M)$. Given two configurations $(q, u_1, \cdots, u_n)$ and $(q', v_1, \cdots, v_n)$ of $M$ and a transition $t \in \Delta$, we define the transition relation $\xrightarrow{t}_M$ as follows: $(q, u_1, \cdots, u_n) \xrightarrow{t}_M (q', v_1, \cdots, v_n)$ iff one of the following holds: (1) $t = (q, push_i(a), q')$, $v_i = a.u_i$ and $u_j = v_j$ for all $j \in ([1..n] \setminus \{i\})$, (2) $t = (q, pop_i(a), q')$, $u_i = a.v_i$ and $u_j = v_j$ for all $j \in ([1..n] \setminus \{i\})$, or (3) $t = (q, nop_i, q')$ and $u_j = v_j$, for all $j \in [1..n]$.

For a sequence of transitions $\sigma = t_1 t_2 \ldots t_m \in \Delta^*$ and two configurations $c, c' \in Cf(M)$, we write $c \xrightarrow{\sigma}_M c'$ to denote that one of the following two cases holds: (1) $\sigma = \epsilon$ and $c = c'$, or (2) there are configurations $c_0, \cdots, c_m \in Cf(M)$ such that $c_0 = c$, $c' = c_m$, and $c_i \xrightarrow{t_{i+1}}_M c_{i+1}$ for all $i \in [0..m - 1]$. Given a set of configurations $C \subseteq Cf(M)$ and a set of sequences of transitions $\Theta \subseteq \Delta^*$, the *acceleration problem* for $M$, with respect to $C$ and $\Theta$, consists in computing the set $Post_{\Theta^*}(C) = \{c' \mid c \xrightarrow{\sigma}_M c', c \in C, \sigma \in \Theta^*\}$.

## 4    Context-Bounding as an Acceleration Problem

In the following, we show that context-bounded analysis [33,34,38,39] for an MPDS $M = (n, Q, \Gamma, \Delta)$ can be formulated as an acceleration problem wrt. the class of rational/regular configurations. Given two configurations $c, c' \in Cf(M)$ and $k \in \mathbb{N}$, the $k$-context reachability problem consists in checking whether there is a sequence of transitions $\sigma \in \Delta_{i_1}^* \Delta_{i_2}^* \cdots \Delta_{i_k}^*$, with $i_1, i_2, \ldots, i_k \in [1..n]$, such that $c \xrightarrow{\sigma}_M c'$. The decidability of the $k$-context reachability problem can be seen as an immediate corollary of the decidability of the membership problem for rational languages and the following result:

**Theorem 1.** *Let* $i \in [1..n]$. *For every regular (rational) set of configurations* $C$, *the set* $Post_{\Delta_i^*}(C)$ *is regular (rational) and effectively constructible.*

The set $Post_{\Delta_i^*}(C)$ has been shown to be regular and effectively constructible when $C$ is regular in [39]. In the following, we prove Theorem 1 for the case when $C$ is rational. We write $M_i$ for the PDS $(1, Q, \Gamma, \Delta_i)$ simulating the behavior of $M$ only on the stack $i$. First we recall a result established in [19,35].

**Lemma 1.** *It is possible to construct, in polynomial time in the size of* $M_i$, *a 4-tape finite state automaton* $T$, *over* $Q, \Gamma, Q, \Gamma$, *such that* $(q, u, q', v) \in L(T)$ *iff* $(q, u) \xrightarrow{\pi}_{M_i} (q', v)$ *for some sequence* $\pi \in \Delta_i^*$.

Observe that Lemma 1 relates any possible starting configuration $(q, u)$ with any configuration $(q', v)$ reachable from $(q, u)$ in $M_i$. Let us assume now that we are given a $(n + 1)$-tape automaton $A = (P, Q, \Gamma, \ldots, \Gamma, \delta, p_0, F)$ accepting the set $C$. In the following, we show how to compute a $(n + 1)$-tape finite state automaton $A'$ accepting the set $Post_{\Delta_i^*}(C)$. To do that, we proceed as follows: We first compose $A$ with $T$, synchronizing the second tape of $T$ (containing the stack contents at the starting configuration) with the $(i+1)$-th tape of $A$, to construct a $(n + 4)$-tape automaton $A_1 = A \circ_{(i+1,2)} T$. We also need to synchronize the starting states (i.e. the first tape of $A$ with the first tape of $T$). This can be done by intersecting $A_1$ with the (regular) language $\bigcup_{q \in Q} \{q\} \times (\Gamma^*)^n \times \{q\} \times Q \times \Gamma^*$. Let $A_2$ be the automaton resulting from the intersection operation. Then, we project away the starting control state (occurring on tapes 1 and $n+2$) and the content of the $i + 1$-th tape to obtain the $(n + 1)$-tape automaton $A_3 = \Pi_\iota(A_2)$ where $\iota = ([1..n] \setminus \{1, i + 1, n + 2\})$. This is almost what is needed except that the new content of the stack $i$ occurs at the last position instead of position $i + 1$ and the control state occurs at penultimate position instead of the first position. We rearrange this using the permutation operation. We let $A' = h(A_3)$ where $h$ is defined as follows: (1) $h(1) = n$, (2) $h(j) = j - 1$ for all $j \leq i$, (3) $h(i + 1) = n + 1$, and (4) $h(j) = j - 2$ for all $j > i + 1$.

Observe that the size of $A'$ is polynomial in $|A|$ — this follows from Lemma 1 and the bounds on the closure operation on rational languages mentioned in Sect. 2.

# 5 Accelerating Loops: Case of Regular/Rational Sets

In this section, we address the acceleration problem for the iterative execution of a sequence of transitions in the control graph of a MPDS $M = (n, Q, \Gamma, \Delta)$. More precisely, given a sequence of transitions $\theta \in \Delta^*$ and a set of configurations $C \subseteq Cf(M)$, we are interested in characterizing the set $Post_{\theta^*}(C)$.

## 5.1 Computing the Effect of a Sequence of Transitions

Let $M = (n, Q, \Gamma, \Delta)$ be an MPDS and $\sigma \in \Delta^*$ a sequence of transitions of the form $(q_0, op_0, q_1)(q_1, op_1, q_2) \cdots (q_{m-1}, op_{m-1}, q_m)$. Intuitively, we associate to each stack $i$ a pair $(u_i, v_i)$ such that the effect of executing the sequence $\sigma$ on stack $i$ is popping the word $u_i$ and then pushing the word $v_i$ on to it (i.e. the stack content is transformed from $u_i w$ to $v_i w$ for some $w$). To this end, for every $i \in [1..n]$, we introduce a partial function $\mathtt{Eff}_i : ((\Gamma^* \times \Gamma^*) \times \Delta^*) \rightharpoonup (\Gamma^* \times \Gamma^*)$. We first define $\mathtt{Eff}_i$ when the third argument is a transition. Roughly speaking, assuming that we have already computed the effect of a transition sequence $\sigma$ on stack $i$ to be $(u, v)$, i.e. to pop $u$ and push $v$, $\mathtt{Eff}_i((u, v), t)$ computes the effect of $\sigma.t$ on stack $i$. Given $u, v \in \Gamma^*$ and $t \in \Delta$, we define $\mathtt{Eff}_i((u, v), t)$ as follows:

- if $Op(t) = pop_i(a)$ for some $a \in \Gamma$ then
  - $\mathtt{Eff}_i((u, \epsilon), t) = (u \cdot a, \epsilon)$,
  - If $v = a \cdot v'$ for some $v' \in \Gamma^*$ then $\mathtt{Eff}_i((u, v), t) = (u, v')$,
  - Otherwise $\mathtt{Eff}_i((u, v), t) = \bot$.
- if $Op(t) = push_i(a)$ for some $a \in \Gamma$, then $\mathtt{Eff}_i((u, v), t) = (u, a \cdot v)$
- If $Op(t) = nop_i$ or $t \in \Delta \setminus \Delta_i$, then $\mathtt{Eff}_i((u, v), t) = (u, v)$.

We extend the definition of $\mathtt{Eff}_i$ to sequence of transitions as expected: For every two words $u, v \in \Gamma^*$, we have (1) $\mathtt{Eff}_i((u, v), \epsilon) = (u, v)$, and (2) for every $\sigma' \in \Delta^*$ and $t \in \delta$, we have $\mathtt{Eff}_i((u, v), \sigma' \cdot t) = \mathtt{Eff}_i(\mathtt{Eff}_i((u, v), \sigma'), t)$ if $\mathtt{Eff}_i((u, v), \sigma') \neq \bot$ is defined, and $\mathtt{Eff}_i((u, v), \sigma' \cdot t) = \bot$ otherwise.

Our aim is to compute the complete effect of some sequence $\sigma$ on stack $i$ and this is given by $\mathtt{Eff}_i((\epsilon, \epsilon), \sigma)$. We shall refer to this as $\mathtt{Summ}(i, \sigma)$. The next lemma formalizes our intuition about $\mathtt{Summ}$ and characterizes precisely when a sequence of transitions $\sigma$ may be executed and computes its effect on all the stacks (if it is executable).

**Lemma 2.** Let $c = (q_0, w_1, \ldots, w_n)$ and $c' = (q_m, w'_1, \ldots, w'_n)$ be two configurations of $M$. $c \xrightarrow{\sigma} c'$ iff for every $i \in [1..n]$, we have $w_i = u_i u'_i$ and $w'_i = v_i u'_i$ for some $u_i, v_i, u'_i \in \Gamma^*$ such that $\mathtt{Summ}(i, \sigma) = (u_i, v_i)$.

Now, we will characterize $\mathtt{Summ}(i, \sigma^j)$ with $j \geq 1$, i.e., the effect of iterating the sequence $\sigma$ $j$-times, in terms of $\mathtt{Summ}(i, \sigma)$ for all $i \in [1..n]$. Observe that if $\mathtt{Summ}(i, \sigma) = \bot$, then $\mathtt{Summ}(i, \sigma^j) = \bot$ for all $j \geq 1$. Hence, let us assume that $\mathtt{Summ}(i, \sigma) = (u_i, v_i)$ for some words $u_i, v_i \in \Gamma^*$. First, let us consider the case when the sequence $\sigma$ can be iterated twice and compute its effect on all the stacks. Now, using the definition of $\mathtt{Summ}$ it is not difficult to conclude that $\mathtt{Summ}(i, \sigma\sigma)$

is defined iff either $v_i$ is a prefix of $u_i$ or $u_i$ is a prefix of $v_i$. We can in fact say more. If the former holds we let $x_i$ be the unique word such that $u_i = v_i x_i$ and $y_i = \epsilon$. In case of the latter we let $y_i$ be the unique word such that $v_i = u_i y_i$ and $x_i = \epsilon$. Then, we have $\mathrm{Summ}(i, \sigma\sigma) = (u'_i, v'_i)$ for all $i \in [1..n]$ where $u'_i = u_i x_i$ and $v'_i = v_i y_i$. We define a partial function $\mathrm{Iter} : ([1..n] \times \Delta^*) \rightharpoonup (\Gamma^* \times \Gamma^*)$ such that $\mathrm{Iter}(i, \sigma)$ is the pair $(x_i, y_i)$ as defined above when $\mathrm{Summ}(i, \sigma\sigma)$ is defined, and $\mathrm{Iter}(i, \sigma) = \bot$ otherwise. We can now generalize this computation of $\mathrm{Summ}$ to any number of iterations of $\sigma$ as shown below.

**Lemma 3.** *Let $i \in [1..n]$. If $\mathrm{Summ}(i, \sigma\sigma)$ is well-defined then $\mathrm{Summ}(i, \sigma^j)$ is well-defined for all $j \geq 1$. Furthermore, $\mathrm{Summ}(i, \sigma^j) = (u_i x_i^{j-1}, v_i y_i^{j-1})$ with $\mathrm{Summ}(i, \sigma) = (u_i, v_i)$ and $\mathrm{Iter}(i, \sigma) = (x_i, y_i)$.*

## 5.2   Acceleration of Regular/Rational Sets of Configurations by Loops

In the following, we first state that the class of regular (resp. rational) sets of configurations is not closed under $Post_{\theta*}$. Then, we show that the image by $Post_{\theta*}$ of any regular set of configurations is a rational one.

**Theorem 2.** *There is an MPDS $M = (n, Q, \Gamma, \Delta)$, a regular (resp. rational) set of its configurations $C$ and a transition sequence $\theta \in \Delta^*$ such that the set of configurations $Post_{\theta*}(C)$ is not regular (resp. rational).*

However, whenever $C$ is a regular set of configurations the set $Post_{\theta*}(C)$ has a simple description. In what follows we fix a MPDS $M = (n, Q, \Gamma, \Delta)$.

**Theorem 3.** *For every regular set of configurations $C$ and transition sequence $\theta \in \Delta^*$, the set $Post_{\theta*}(C)$ is rational and effectively constructible.*

Let $\theta$ be a sequence of transitions of the form $(q_0, op_0, q'_0)(q_1, op_1, q'_1)$ $\cdots (q_m, op_m, q'_m)$. Since $Post_{\theta*}(C_1 \cup C_2) = Post_{\theta*}(C_1) \cup Post_{\theta*}(C_2)$, we can assume w.l.o.g that $C$ is of the form $\{q\} \times L_1 \times \cdots \times L_n$ where each $L_j$ is an 1-dim rational language over $\Gamma$ accepted by a finite state automaton $A_j$ for all $j \in [1..n]$. The proof proceeds by cases.

**Case 1:** Let us assume $q'_i \neq q_{i+1}$ for some $i \in [0..m-1]$ or $q_0 \neq q$. In this case the sequence of transitions cannot be executed and hence $Post_{\theta*}(C) = C$.

**Case 2:** Let us assume $q_0 \neq q'_m$, $q_0 = q$ and $q'_i = q_{i+1}$ for all $i \in [0..m-1]$. In this case, the sequence of transitions can not be iterated more than once and so we have $Post_{\theta*}(C) = Post_{\theta}(C) \cup C$. We now examine the set $Post_{\theta}(C)$. First, let us assume that $\mathrm{Summ}(i, \theta) = \bot$ for some $i \in [1..n]$. Then $Post_{\theta}(C) = \emptyset$ and hence $Post_{\theta*}(C) = C$.

Let us assume now that $\mathrm{Summ}(i, \theta) = (u_i, v_i)$ is well-defined for all $i \in [1..n]$. We can apply Lemma 2, to show that $Post_{\theta}(C) = \{q'_m\} \times L'_1 \times \cdots \times L'_n$ where for every $i \in [1..n]$, $L'_i = \{w'_i \mid \exists w_i \in \Gamma^*. \; w'_i = v_i.w_i \wedge u_i w_i \in L_i\}$. It is easy to see that $L'_i$ is an 1-dim rational language and can be accepted by an automaton $A'_i$ whose size is polynomial in the size of $A_i$ and the length of $\theta$.

**Case 3:** Let us assume $q_0 = q'_m$, $q_0 = q$ and $q'_i = q_i$ for all $i \in [0..m-1]$. In this case, the sequence of transitions forms a loop in the control flow graph of $M$ and hence the sequence may possibly be iterated. Observe that if the function $\mathtt{Summ}(i, \theta) = \perp$ for some $i \in [1..n]$, then $Post_{\theta^*}(C) = C$. Hence, let us assume that $\mathtt{Summ}(i, \theta) = (u_i, v_i)$ for all $i \in [1..n]$ so that it is well-defined for each $i$. Lemma 3 suggests that we should examine when $\mathtt{Summ}(i, \theta\theta)$ is defined for all $i$. Indeed, if $\mathtt{Summ}(i, \theta\theta)$ is undefined for some $i \in [1..n]$, then $Post_{\theta^*}(C) = Post_{\theta}(C) \cup C$ (which can be computed as shown in the previous case). So, let us further assume that $\mathtt{Summ}(i, \theta\theta)$ is well-defined for all $i \in [1..n]$. Hence, the function $\mathtt{Iter}(i, \sigma)$ is also well-defined. Let us assume that $\mathtt{Iter}(i, \sigma) = (x_i, y_i)$.

Now, we can combine Lemma 3 with Lemma 2 to give a characterization of when a sequence $\theta$ is iterable and its effect.

**Lemma 4.** *Let $j \geq 1$ and $c = (q, w_1, \ldots, w_n)$ and $c' = (q, w'_1, \ldots, w'_n)$ be two configurations of $M$. $c \xrightarrow{\theta^j} c'$ iff for every $i \in [1..n]$, we have $w_i = u_i x_i^{j-1} w''_i$ and $w'_i = v_i y_i^{j-1} w''_i$ for some $w''_i \in \Gamma^*$ with $u_i, v_i, x_i$ and $y_i$s defined as above.*

With this lemma in place, let $L$ be the $(2n+1)$-dim language defined as the set containing the exactly the words of the form

$$(q, u_1 x_1^{j-1} w_1, v_1 y_1^{j-1} w_1, u_2 x_2^{j-1} w_2, v_2 y_2^{j-1} w_2, \ldots, u_n x_n^{j-1} w_n, v_n y_n^{j-1} w_n)$$

with $j \geq 1$ and $w_i \in \Gamma^*$ and where $u_i, v_i, x_i$ and $y_i$s are defined as above. Observe that each element of $L$ relates a pair of configurations such that from the first we can execute the sequence $\theta$ a finite number of times to reach the second. The starting configuration is given by the first and all the even numbered positions, while the ending configuration is given by all the odd numbered positions (including the first). As a matter of fact elements of $L$ relates exactly all such pairs in this manner. This language $L$ is rational and we can easily compute an $(2n+1)$-tape automaton $A$ whose size is polynomial in the size of $\theta$ and polynomial in the size of $M$. To compute an $(n+1)$-tape automaton $A'$ accepting $Post_{\theta+}(C)$, we proceed as follows: First, we define the regular language $L' = \{q\} \times L_1 \times \Gamma^* \times \cdots \times L_n \times \Gamma^*$. Then, we compute an $(2n+1)$-tape automaton $A''$ accepting precisely the language resulting from the intersection of the regular language $L'$ and $L$. This allows us to restrict the starting configurations to be precisely those from $C$. The size $A''$ is exponential in the number of stacks and polynomial in the size of $\theta$, and the finite state automata $A_1, \ldots, A_n$. Finally, we need to project away the tapes concerning the starting stack configurations. We let then $A' = \Pi_\iota(A'')$ with $\iota = \{2i+1 \mid i \in [0..n]\}$. We note that this step does not result in any blow up and thus the size of $A'$ is exponential in the number of stacks and polynomial in the size of $\theta$ and $A_1, \ldots, A_n$.

Since $Post_{\theta^*}(C) = C \cup Post_{\theta+}(C)$ and the class of rational / regular languages is closed under union, this completes the proof of Theorem 3.

# 6    Constrained Simple Regular Expressions

We now introduce the class of (1 dimensional) Constrained Simple Regular Expressions (CSRE). CSRE definable languages form an expressive class equivalent to the bounded semi-linear languages defined in [18] and the class of languages accepted by 1-CQDD introduced in [16]. To deal with configuration sets of MPDS we need $n$-dimensional CSREs and so we lift these results to that setting. We then show that the CSRE definable sets of configurations form a stable collection under acceleration by loops. However, this class is not stable w.r.t. bounded context runs. We begin by recalling some basics about *Presburger arithmetic*.

## 6.1 Presburger Arithmetic

Presburger arithmetic is the first-order theory of natural numbers with addition, subtraction and order. We recall briefly its definition. Let $\mathcal{V}$ be a set of variables. We use $x, y, \ldots$ to denote variables in $\mathcal{V}$. The set of terms in Presburger arithmetic is defined as follows: $t ::= 0 \mid 1 \mid x \mid t - t \mid t + t$. The set of formulae of the Presburger arithmetic is defined to be $\varphi ::= t \leq t \mid \neg \varphi \mid \varphi \vee \varphi \mid \exists x. \varphi$.

We use the standard abbreviations: $\varphi_1 \wedge \varphi_2 = \neg(\varphi_1 \vee \varphi_2)$, $\varphi_1 \Rightarrow \varphi_2 = \neg \varphi_1 \wedge \varphi_2$, and $\forall x. \varphi = \neg \exists x. \neg \varphi$. The notions of free and bound variables, and quantifier-free formula are as usual. An *existential* Presburger formula is one of the form $\exists x_1 \exists x_2 \ldots \exists x_n. \varphi$ where $\varphi$ is a quantifier-free formula. We shall often write positive boolean combinations of existential Presburger formulas in place of an existential Presburger formula. Clearly, by an appropriate renaming of the quantified variables, any such formula can be converted into an equivalent existential Presburger formula. We write $var(\varphi) \subseteq \mathcal{V}$ to denote the set of free variables of $\varphi$. Given a function $\mu$ from $var(\varphi)$ to $\mathbb{N}$, the meaning of $\mu$ *satisfies* $\varphi$ is as usual and we write $\mu \models \varphi$ to denote this. We write $\varphi(x_1, x_2, \ldots, x_k)$ to denote a Presburger formula $\varphi$ whose free variables are (contained in) $x_1, \ldots, x_k$. Such a formula naturally *defines* a subset of $\mathbb{N}^k$ given by $\{(i_1, i_2, \ldots, i_k) \mid \mu \models \varphi(x_1, x_2, \ldots, x_k)$ where $\mu(x_j) = i_j, 1 \leq j \leq k\}$. We say that a subset $S$ of $\mathbb{N}^k$ is definable in Presburger arithmetic if there is a formula $\varphi$ that defines it.

## 6.2 Constrained Simple Regular Expression (CSRE)

A Constrained Simple Regular Expression (CSRE) $e$ over an alphabet $\Sigma$ is defined as a tuple of the form $e = (w_1, \ldots, w_m, \varphi(x_1, x_2, \ldots, x_m))$ where $w_1, \ldots, w_m$ is a non-empty sequence of words over $\Sigma$, and $\varphi$ is an existential Presburger formula. The language defined by the CSRE $e$, denoted by $L(e)$, is the set of words of the form $w_1^{i_1} w_2^{i_2} \cdots w_m^{i_m}$ such that $\varphi$ holds for the function $\mu$ defined by $\mu(x_j) = i_j$ for all $j \in [1..m]$. The size of $e$ is defined by $|e| = |w_1 \cdots w_m| + |\varphi|$. CSREs define the same class of languages as CQDDs [16] (see [18]), however they have a much simpler presentation avoiding automata altogether and as we shall see quite amenable to a number of operations.

Next, we present some closure and decidability results for the class of CSRE definable languages. These results can be also deduced from [18] since CSREs define bounded semilinear languages.

**Lemma 5.** *The class of languages defined by CSREs is closed under intersection, union and concatenation. The emptiness, membership and inclusion problems for CSREs are decidable.*

From Lemma 4 it is clear that in order to compute the effect of the iteration of a sequence $\theta$ on the content of stack $i$ one has to *left-quotient* the content of stack $i$ by the sequence $u_i x_i^{j-1}$ and then add the sequence $v_i y_i^{j-1}$ (on the left). With this in mind we now examine left-quotients of languages defined by CSREs w.r.t. iterations of a given word. First we state a technical lemma.

**Lemma 6.** *Let $e$ be a CSRE over an alphabet $\Sigma$ and $w \in \Sigma^*$ be a word. Then, we can construct, in polynomial time in $|w| + |e|$, a CSRE $e' = (w, u_1, u_2, \ldots, u_k, \varphi(y, y_1, y_2, \ldots, y_k))$ such that for every $i \in \mathbb{N}$, $L(e_i) = \{w' \mid w^i w' \in L(e)\}$ where $e_i = (\epsilon, u_1, u_2, \ldots, u_k, (y = i \wedge \varphi(y, y_1, y_2, \ldots, y_k)))$.*

The key point about the above lemma is that the left-quotient of $L(e)$ w.r.t $w^i$, for some $i \in \mathbb{N}$, can be precisely identified as $L(e_i)$. Thus, the CSRE $(\epsilon, u_1, u_2, \ldots, u_k, \varphi(y, y_1, y_2, \ldots, y_k))$ defines the left-quotient of $L(e)$ w.r.t $\{w^i \mid i \in \mathbb{N}\}$, giving us the following corollary.

**Corollary 1.** *Let $e$ be a CSRE over an alphabet $\Sigma$ and $w \in \Sigma^*$ be a word. Then, we can construct, in polynomial time in $|w| + |e|$, a CSRE $e'$ such that $L(e') = \{w' \mid \exists i \in \mathbb{N}. \, w^i w' \in L(e)\}$.*

### 6.3   Multi-dimensional Constrained Simple Regular Expression

Let $n \geq 1$. An $n$-dim CSRE $e$ over an alphabet $\Sigma$ is a of tuple of the form $((u_1, \ldots, u_{k_1}), (u_{k_1+1}, \ldots, u_{k_2}), \ldots, (u_{k_{n-1}+1}, \ldots, u_{k_n}), \varphi(x_1, \ldots, x_{k_n}))$ where: (1) $1 \leq k_1 < k_2 < \cdots < k_n$ and (2) for every $i \in [1..k_n]$, $u_i$ is a word over $\Sigma$. An $n$-dim CSRE $\mathbf{e}$ accepts the $n$-dim language, denoted by $L(e)$, consisting of the $n$-dim words of the form $(u_1^{i_1} \cdots u_{k_1}^{i_{k_1}}, \ldots, u_{k_{n-1}+1}^{i_{k_{n-1}+1}} \cdots u_{k_n}^{i_{k_n}})$ such that $\varphi$ holds for the function $\mu$ defined by $\mu(x_j) = i_j$ for all $j \in [1..k_n]$. In order to simply the notations, we sometimes write $e$ as follows $(\mathbf{u_1}, \mathbf{u_2}, \ldots, \mathbf{u_n}, \varphi(\mathbf{x_1}, \mathbf{x_2}, \ldots, \mathbf{x_n}))$ where $\mathbf{u}_i = (u_{k_{i-1}+1}, \ldots, u_{k_i})$ and $\mathbf{x}_i = (x_{k_{i-1}+1}, \ldots, x_{k_i})$ for all $i \in [1..n]$. In the following, we show that the class of languages accepted by $n$-dim CSREs enjoys the same properties as the class of CSREs.

**Lemma 7.** *Let $n \geq 1$. The class of $n$-languages defined by $n$-CSREs is closed under intersection, union and concatenation. The emptiness problem, membership problem as well as inclusion problem are decidable for $n$-dim CSREs.*

Next, we extend Lemma 6 to $n$-dim CSREs — $n$-dim CSREs are closed under left quotienting by simultaneous iterations of a tuple of words $w_i, 1 \leq i \leq n$, one for each component. Even more, this can be achieved by constructing an $n$-CSRE in which the number of iterations may be set parametrically.

**Lemma 8.** *Let $n \geq 1$. Let $e$ be a $n$-dim CSRE over an alphabet $\Sigma$ and $\mathbf{w} = (w_1, \ldots, w_n), w_i \in \Sigma^*$. Then, we can construct, in polynomial time in $|e| + \sum_i |w_i|$, an $n$-dim CSRE $e[\mathbf{w}] = (\mathbf{u_1}, \ldots, \mathbf{u_n}, \varphi(\mathbf{x_1}, \ldots, \mathbf{x_n}))$ such that $\mathbf{u}_i[1] = w_i$, for $1 \leq i \leq n$ and for every $j \in \mathbb{N}$, $L(e[\mathbf{w}, j]) = \{\mathbf{v} \mid \mathbf{v}[i \leftarrow w_i^j \mathbf{v}[i]] \in L(e)\}$, where $e[\mathbf{w}, j] = (\mathbf{u_1}[1 \leftarrow \epsilon], \ldots, \mathbf{u_n}[1 \leftarrow \epsilon], (\bigwedge_{1 \leq i \leq n} \mathbf{x}_i[1] = j \wedge \varphi(\mathbf{x_1}, \mathbf{x_2}, \ldots, \mathbf{x_n})))$.*

We now have all the ingredients necessary to study the stability of sets of configurations defined by $n$-dim CSREs. We say that a set $C$ of configurations of the MPDS $M$ is CSRE representable if there is a function $f$ that maps any state $q \in Q$ of $M$ to an $n$-dim CSRE s.t. $(q, w_1, \ldots, w_n) \in C$ iff $(w_1, \ldots, w_n) \in L(f(q))$.

## 6.4    Acceleration of CSRE Representable Set of Configurations

Let $M = (n, Q, \Gamma, \Delta)$ be an MPDS. We now examine the sets $Post_{\Delta_i^*}(C)$ and $Post_{\theta^*}(C)$ where $\Delta_i$ is a set of transitions on the $i$-th stack of $M$ and $\theta \in \Delta^*$ where $C$ is a CSRE representable set of configurations.

**Theorem 4.** *For every transition sequence $\theta \in \Delta^*$, the class of CSRE representable sets of configurations is effectively closed under $Post_{\theta^*}$. Further post set can be computed in time polynomial in the size of $\theta$ and $|M|$.*

*Proof.* Let $\theta$ be a sequence of transitions of the form $(q_0, op_0, q_0')(q_1, op_1, q_1')$ $\cdots (q_m, op_m, q_m')$ and $C$ be a CSRE representable set of configurations. Since $Post_{\theta^*}(C_1 \cup C_2) = Post_{\theta^*}(C_1) \cup Post_{\theta^*}(C_2)$, we can assume w.l.o.g that $C$ consists of configurations of the form $(q, w_1, \ldots, w_n)$ for some fixed $q \in Q$. Let $f$ be a function from $Q$ to $n$-dim CSREs such that $L(f(p)) = \{(w_1, \ldots, w_n) \mid (q, w_1, \ldots, w_n) \in C\}$ if $p = q$ and $L(f(p)) = \emptyset$ otherwise. Next, we assume that $f(q) = (\mathbf{u_1}, \ldots, \mathbf{u_n}, \varphi(\mathbf{x_1}, \ldots, \mathbf{x_n}))$. The proof proceeds by cases.

**Case 1:** Let us assume $q_i' \neq q_i$ for some $i \in [0..m-1]$ or $q_0 \neq q$. In this case the sequence of transitions cannot be executed and hence $Post_{\theta^*}(C) = C$.

**Case 2:** Let us assume $q_0 \neq q_m'$, $q_0 = q$ and $q_i' = q_i$ for all $i \in [0..m-1]$. In this case, the sequence of transitions cannot be iterated more than once and so we have $Post_{\theta^*}(C) = Post_\theta(C) \cup C$. We now examine the set $Post_\theta(C)$. If $\mathtt{Summ}(i, \theta) = \bot$ for some $i \in [1..n]$, then $Post_\theta(C) = \emptyset$ and hence $Post_{\theta^*}(C) = C$.

Let us assume now that $\mathtt{Summ}(i, \theta) = (u_i, v_i)$ is well-defined for all $i \in [1..n]$. We can construct a $n$-CSRE $e'$ such that $(q_m', w_1, \ldots, w_n) \in Post_{\theta^*}(C)$ iff $(w_1, \ldots, w_n) \in L(e')$ in two steps: Let $e_1 = f(q)[(u_1, u_2, \cdots, u_n), 1]$. This left quotients component $i$ by $u_i$ as required and the size of $e_1$ is polynomial in the size of $\theta$, $M$ and $f(q)$. Let us assume that $e_1$ is of the form $((\epsilon, w_2, \ldots, w_{\ell_1}), \ldots, (\epsilon, w_{\ell_{n-1}+2}, \ldots, w_{\ell_n}), \varphi''(x_1, \ldots, x_{\ell_n}))$. Next, we simultaneously add the content $v_i$ to stack $i$, $1 \leq i \leq n$ as follows: Let the $n$-CSRE $e'$ be $((v_1, \epsilon, w_2, \ldots, w_{\ell_1}), \ldots, (v_n, \epsilon, w_{\ell_{n-1}+2}, \ldots, w_{\ell_n}), \varphi'(y_1, x_1, \ldots, x_{k_1}, \ldots, y_n, x_{\ell_{n-1}+1}, \ldots, x_{\ell_n}))$ where $\varphi' = \varphi'' \wedge \bigwedge_{1 \leq h \leq n} y_i = 1$.

Note that $Post_{\theta^*}(C)$ is CSRE representable by the function $f'$ s.t. $f'(q) = f(q)$, $f'(q_m') = e'$, and $L(f'(p)) = \emptyset$ for all $p \notin \{q, q_m'\}$. Observe that the construction of $Post_{\theta^*}(C)$ is done in polynomial time in the sizes of $\theta$, $M$ and $f(q)$.

**Case 3:** Let us assume $q_0 = q_m'$, $q_0 = q$ and $q_i' = q_i$ for all $i \in [0..m-1]$. In this case, the sequence of transitions forms a loop in the control flow graph of $M$ and hence the sequence may possibly be iterated. Observe that if the function $\mathtt{Summ}(i, \theta) = \bot$ for some $i \in [1..n]$, then $Post_{\theta^*}(C) = C$. Hence, let us assume that $\mathtt{Summ}(i, \theta) = (u_i, v_i)$ for all $i \in [1..n]$ so that it is well-defined for each $i$. Lemma 3 suggests that we should examine when $\mathtt{Summ}(i, \theta\theta)$ is defined for all $i$.

Indeed, if $\mathtt{Summ}(i, \theta\theta)$ is undefined for some $i \in [1..n]$, then $Post_{\theta^*}(C) = Post_{\theta}(C) \cup C$ (which can be computed as shown in the previous case). So, let us further assume that $\mathtt{Summ}(i, \theta\theta)$ is well-defined for all $i \in [1..n]$. Hence, the function $\mathtt{Iter}(i, \sigma)$ is also well-defined. Let us assume that $\mathtt{Iter}(i, \sigma) = (x_i, y_i)$

We then construct a $n$-CSRE $e'$ such that $(q'_m, w_1, \ldots, w_n) \in Post_{\theta^+}(C)$ iff $(w_1, \ldots, w_n) \in L(e')$ in a sequence of steps: First we construct the $n$-CSRE expression $e_1 = f(p)[(u_1, u_2, \cdots, u_n), 1]$. Let us assume that $e_1$ is of the form $((\epsilon, w_2, \ldots, w_{\ell_1}), \ldots, (\epsilon, w_{\ell_{n-1}+2}, \ldots, w_{\ell_n}), \varphi_1(x_1, \ldots, x_{\ell_n}))$. Observe that the size of $e_1$ is polynomial in the sizes of $\theta$, $M$ and $f(q)$ and it simultaneously left quotients component $i$ by $u_i$. Now, we must simultaneously left-quotient the $i$th component by $x_i^j$, for a fixed $j$ and then follow this by adding simultaneously $y_i^j$ to component $i$ (for the same $j$) and then add simultaneously $v_i$ to component $i$ ($1 \leq i \leq n$). To achieve this we begin by applying Lemma 8 to $e_1$ to construct the $n$-CSRE expression $e_2 = e_1[(x_1, \ldots, x_n)]$. Observe that the size of $e_2$ is also polynomial in the sizes of $\theta$, $M$ and $f(q)$. Let us assume that $e_2$ is of the form $((\epsilon, w'_2, \ldots, w'_{j_1}), \ldots, (\epsilon, w'_{j_{n-1}+2}, \ldots, w'_{j_n}), \varphi_2(z_1, \ldots, z_{j_n}))$. We now exploit the parametrized nature of $e_1[(x_1, \ldots, x_n)]$ stated in Lemma 8. We let $e' = ((v_1, y_1, \epsilon, w'_2, \ldots, w'_{j_1}), \ldots, (v_n, y_n, \epsilon, w'_{j_{n-1}+2}, \ldots, w'_{j_n}), \varphi'(t_1, t'_1, z_1, \ldots, z_{k_1}, \ldots, t_n, t'_n, z_{\ell_{n-1}+1}, \ldots, z_{j_n}))$ where $\varphi' = \varphi_2 \wedge \bigwedge_{1 \leq h \leq n} t_i = 1 \wedge (z_1 = z_{j_1+1} = \cdots = z_{z_{j_{n-1}+1}} = t'_1 = t'_2 = \cdots = t'_n)$.

Finally, it is easy to see that $Post_{\theta^*}(C)$ is CSRE representable by the function $f'$ such that $L(f'(q)) = L(f(q)) \cup L(e')$, and $\mathrm{L}(f'(p)) = \emptyset$ for all $p \notin \{q\}$. Observe that the size of $f'(q)$ is still polynomial in the sizes of $\theta$, $M$ and $f(q)$.     $\square$

Unfortunately, CSRE representable sets are not stable w.r.t. bounded context.

**Theorem 5.** *For every $i \in [1..n]$, the class of CSRE representable sets of configurations is not closed under $Post_{\Delta_i^*}(C)$.*

# 7   Acceleration of Bounded-Context Sets

In the following, we first introduce the class of *constrained* rational languages (as an extension of constrained (or Parikh) automata languages [17,31] to the settings of multi-dimensional words). Then, we present the class of bounded context-switches sets as a generalization of loops and contexts. Finally, we show that the class of constrained rational languages is stable with respect to acceleration by bounded context-switches sets.

## 7.1   Constrained Rational Languages

A constrained automaton is a finite-state automaton augmented with a semi-linear set to filter (or restrict) the accepting runs. We assume that this semi-linear set is described by an existential Presburger formula. In the following, we extend this model to multi-dimensional words. Let $n \geq 1$ and $\Sigma_1, \ldots, \Sigma_n$ be $n$ finite alphabets. Formally, a $n$-tape constrained finite-state automaton over $\Sigma_1, \ldots, \Sigma_n$

is defined as $\mathcal{C} = (A, \varphi)$ where $A = (Q, \Sigma_1, \ldots, \Sigma_n, \delta, q_0, F)$ is a $n$-tape finite-state automaton and $\varphi$ is an existential Presburger formula such that $var(\varphi) = \delta$. Furthermore, we assume w.l.o.g. that if $(q, \mathbf{u}, q')$ is in $\delta$ then $|\mathbf{u}[1] \cdot \mathbf{u}[2] \cdots \mathbf{u}[n]| \leq 1$. The language of $\mathcal{C}$, denoted by $L(\mathcal{C})$, is the set of $n$-dim words $\mathbf{w}$ for which there is an accepting run $\pi$ of $A$ over $w$ such that $Parikh(\pi) \models \varphi$. A $n$-dim language is *constrained* rational if it is the language of some $n$-tape constrained automaton. Let us state some properties about constrained rational languages. These properties can be inferred from the properties of rational languages [10] and Parikh/constrained automata [17,31,42].

**Lemma 9.** *The class of constrained rational languages is closed under union and concatenation but not under intersection. The emptiness and membership problems are decidable while the emptiness of intersection problem is undecidable.*

We can extend the permutation, projection and composition operations to the context of constrained rational languages in the straightforward manner. We also show the same closure properties as in the case of rational languages.

**Lemma 10.** *The class of constrained rational languages is closed under permutation, projection, composition and intersection with regular languages.*

The complexity of permutation, projection, composition is at most polynomial in size of input automata whereas the intersection with regular languages is at most exponential in the size of the description of the regular language and polynomial in the size of constrained rational automaton.

## 7.2   Acceleration of Bounded Context-Switches Sets

Let $M = (n, Q, \Gamma, \Delta)$ be an MPDS. A bounded context-switches set over $M$ is defined by $\Lambda = (\tau_0, \tau_1, \ldots, \tau_{2m})$ with $m \in \mathbb{N}$ where (1) for every $i \in [0..m]$, we have $\tau_{2i} \subseteq \Delta_{j_i}$ for some $j_i \in [1..n]$ with $j_0 = j_{2m}$, and (2) for every $i \in [0..(m-1)]$, $|\tau_{2i+1}| = 1$. The size of $\Lambda$ is defined as the sum of the sizes of the finite sets $\tau_j$ for all $j \in [0..2m]$. The set of sequences of transitions recognized by $\Lambda$, denoted by $L(\Lambda)$, is $\tau_0^* \tau_1 \tau_2^* \cdots \tau_{2m}^*$. Observe that when $m = 0$ and $\tau_0 = \Delta_i$ for some $i \in [1..n]$, $L(\Lambda)$ corresponds to a context associated to the stack $i$. And whenever $\tau_{2i} = \emptyset$ for all $i \in [0..m]$, $L(\Lambda)$ is a sequence of transitions. Thus, bounded context-switches sets generalize both loops and contexts. Observe that dropping one of $\tau_{2i+1}$ from the definition of $\Lambda$ will allow the simulation of unbounded unrestricted context-switch sequences and hence leads to the undecidability of the simple reachability problem. Next, we state our main theorem:

**Theorem 6.** *Let $M$ be an MPDS and $\Lambda = (\tau_0, \tau_1, \ldots, \tau_{2m})$ be a bounded context-switches set over $M$. For every constrained rational set of configurations $C$, $Post_{L(\Lambda)^*}(C)$ is a constrained rational set and effectively constructible.*

The rest of this section is dedicated to the proof of Theorem 6. First we prove an extension of Lemma 1 that shows that in addition to computing pairs of the form $(q, u, q', u)$ such that there is a run $\pi$ from $(q, u)$ to $(q', u')$ one may in addition keep track of the number iterations of $L(\Lambda)$ seen along $\pi$.

**Lemma 11.** *Let* $\mathcal{P} = (1, P, \Gamma, R)$ *be an PDS and* $\Lambda = (\tau_0, \tau_1, \ldots, \tau_{2m})$ *be a bounded context-switches set over* $\mathcal{P}$ *such that* $\tau_j \subseteq R$. *Let* $\sharp$ *be a special symbol not included in* $\Gamma$. *Then it is possible to construct, in exponential time in the sizes of* $\mathcal{P}$ *and* $\Lambda$, *an 5-tape finite-state automaton* $T = (Q_T, Q, \Gamma, Q, \Gamma, \{\sharp\}, \delta_\pi, q_0, F_T)$ *such that* $(q, u, q', v, \sharp^m) \in L(T)$ *iff* $(q, u) \xrightarrow{\pi}_\mathcal{P} (q', v)$ *for some sequence* $\pi \in (L(\Lambda))^m$. *Furthermore, the size of* $T$ *is exponential in the sizes of* $\mathcal{P}$ *and* $\Lambda$.

The proof of this lemma is based on the combination of the proof of Lemma 1 with the fact the Parikh images of context-free languages can be effectively realized as regular languages. This ability to compute the number of iterations of $L(\Lambda)$ along the run is important. It can be combined with the special structure of $L(\Lambda)$, which forces context-switches to occur at identified transitions and in a fixed sequence. This allows us to prove Lemma 12, leading to the proof of Theorem 6.

Now, one can construct a PDS $M_i$ for each stack $i$, which simulates the moves of $M$ on the $i$th stack while guessing, non-deterministically, the effect of the moves corresponding to the other stacks. Clearly, any run of $M$ can be decomposed in to a tuple of runs, one per $M_i$. However, because of the special structure of $L(\Lambda)$, a converse of this statement is true for runs of the form $L(\Lambda)^*$. Any tuple of runs, one from each $M_i$, which agree on the number of iterations of $L(\Lambda)$ seen along the run, can be composed together to give a run $M$.

Let $i \in [1..n]$. For each transition $t = (q, op, q') \in \Delta$, we represent the effect of the transition $t$ on the stack $i$ by the transition $t|_i$ defined as follows: $t|_i = t$ if $t \in \Delta_i$, and $t|_i = (q, nop_i, q')$ otherwise. We extend this operation to sets of transitions as follows: For a set $T \subseteq \Delta$, $T|_i = \{t|_i \mid t \in T\}$.

Let $M_i = (1, Q, \Gamma, \bigcup_{j \in [0..2m]} \tau_j|_i)$ be a PDS simulating the $i$-th stack while taking into account the effect transitions of the other stack operations. We define also $\Lambda|_i$ to be the bounded context-switches set defined by the tuple $(\tau_0|_i, \tau_1|_i, \ldots, \tau_{2m}|_i)$. Let $T_i$ be the 5-tape finite state automaton resulting from the application of Lemma 11 to the PDA $M_i$ and the bounded context-switches set $\Lambda|_i$. Then synchronizing the multi-tape automata $T_i$ on the number of occurrences of the special symbol $\sharp$ provides a relation between any possible starting configuration $(q, u_1, \ldots, u_n)$ with any configuration $(q', v_1, \ldots, v_n)$ reachable from $(q, u_1, \ldots, u_n)$ of $M$ by firing a sequence of transitions in $L(\Lambda)^*$.

**Lemma 12.** *Let* $m \in \mathbb{N}$. *Then,* $(q, u_1, \ldots, u_n) \xrightarrow{\pi}_M (q', v_1, \ldots, v_n)$ *for some sequence* $\pi \in (L(\Lambda))^m$ *if and only if for every* $i \in [1..n]$, $(q, u_i, q', v_i, \sharp^m) \in L(T_i)$.

Now, we are ready to prove Theorem 6. Let us assume that we are given a $(n+1)$-tape constrained automaton $\mathcal{C} = (A, \phi)$ where $A = (P, Q, \Gamma, \ldots, \Gamma, \delta, p_0, F)$ and $L(\mathcal{C}) = C$. In the following, we show how to compute a $(n + 1)$-tape constrained automaton $\mathcal{C}'$ accepting the set $Post_{(L(\Lambda))^*}(C)$. To do that, we proceed as follows: We first compose $C$ with the constrained automaton $(T_1, \text{true})$, synchronizing the second tape of $T_1$ (containing the stack contents at the starting configuration of the $M_1$) with the second tape of A, to construct a $(n+5)$-tape constrained automaton $\mathcal{C}_1 = \mathcal{C} \circ_{(2,2)} (T_1, \text{true})$. We then need to synchronize the starting states (i.e., the first tape of $A$ with the first tape of $T_1$). This can be done by intersecting $\mathcal{C}_1$ with the (regular) language $\bigcup_{q \in Q} \{q\} \times (\Gamma^*)^n \times \{q\} \times Q \times \Gamma^* \times (\{\sharp\})^*$. Let $\mathcal{C}_1'$ be the $(n+5)$-tapes resulting of this intersection. Then, we project away the starting control state occurring on the $n+2$-tape and the content of the second tape to obtain the $(n+3)$-tape constrained automaton $\mathcal{C}_1'' = \Pi_\iota(\mathcal{C}_1')$ where $\iota = ([1..n+5] \setminus \{2, n+2\})$.

Then, we need to compose $\mathcal{C}_1''$ with the constrained automaton $(T_2, \text{true})$, synchronizing the second tape of $T_2$ (containing the stack contents at the starting configuration of the $M_2$) with the second tape of $\mathcal{C}_1''$, to construct a $(n+7)$-tape constrained automaton $\mathcal{C}_2 = \mathcal{C}_1'' \circ_{(2,2)} (T_2, \text{true})$. We then need to synchronize the starting states (i.e., the first tape of $\mathcal{C}_1''$ with the first tape of $T_2$). This can be done by intersecting $\mathcal{C}_2$ with the (regular) language $\bigcup_{q \in Q} \{q\} \times (\Gamma^*)^{n-1} \times Q \times \Gamma^* \times (\{\sharp\})^* \times \{q\} \times Q \times \Gamma^* \times (\{\sharp\})^*$. Let $\mathcal{C}_2'$ be the $(n+7)$-tapes resulting of this intersection. Then, we project away the state occurring on the $n+4$-tape and the content of the second tape to obtain the $(n+5)$-tape constrained automaton $\mathcal{C}_2'' = \Pi_{\iota'}(\mathcal{C}_2')$ where $\iota' = ([1..n+6] \setminus \{2, n+4\})$.

This procedure is then repeated for all the constrained automata $(T_i, \text{true})$, with $i \in [3..n]$, to obtain at the end the $(3n+1)$-tape constrained automaton $\mathcal{C}_n''$. We can also project away the state stored at the first tape from $\mathcal{C}_n''$ since it is no longer needed. So, let $\mathcal{G} = \Pi_{[2..3n]}(\mathcal{C}_n'')$ be the resulting $(3n)$-tape constrained automaton.

Now, we need to synchronize the automata $(T_i, \text{true})$ on their final states stored respectively at the tapes $3(i-1)+1$, with $i \in [1..n]$, of $\mathcal{G}$. To do that we intersect $\mathcal{G}$ with the (regular) language $\bigcup_{q \in Q} \{q\} \times \Gamma^* \times (\{\sharp\})^* \times \{q\} \times \Gamma^* \times (\{\sharp\})^* \times \cdots \times \{q\} \times \Gamma^* \times (\{\sharp\})^*$. Let $\mathcal{G}'$ be the $(3n)$-tapes resulting of this intersection. We can then project away the copies of the final control states and only keep its first occurrence to obtain $(2n+1)$-tape constrained automaton $\mathcal{G}''$ defined as follows: $\mathcal{G}'' = \Pi_{\iota''}(\mathcal{G}')$ where $\iota'' = ([1..3n] \setminus \{3i+1 \mid i \in [1..n-1]\})$. Let us assume that $\mathcal{G}''$ is of the form $(A', \phi')$ where $A' = (P', Q, \Gamma, \{\sharp\}, \Gamma, \{\sharp\}, \ldots, \Gamma, \{\sharp\}, \delta', p_0', F')$. For every $i \in [1..n]$, let $\delta_i'$ be the subset of $\delta'$ containing only transitions of the form $(p, \mathbf{v}, p') \in \delta'$ s.t. $\mathbf{v}[2i+1] = \sharp$ (note that $\mathbf{v}[j] = \epsilon$ for all $j \neq 2i+1$).

From Lemma 12, we need to ensure the same number of the special letters $\sharp$ in all the tapes $\{2i+1 \mid i \in [1..n]\}$ by augmenting the formula $\phi'$ with additional constraints. Let $\mathcal{G}''' = (A', \phi'')$ where $\phi'' = \phi' \wedge (\sum_{t_1 \in \delta_1'} t_1 = \sum_{t_2 \in \delta_2'} t_2 = \cdots = \sum_{t_n \in \delta_n'} t_n)$. Finally, the $n+1$-tape constrained finite state automaton $\mathcal{C}'$ can be constructed from $\mathcal{G}'''$ by projecting away the tapes with symbol $\sharp$ i.e. the tapes $\{2i+1 \mid i \in [1..n]\}$. Hence, $\mathcal{C}' = \Pi_{\iota'''}(\mathcal{G}''')$ where $\iota''' = ([1..n] \setminus \{2i+1 \mid i \in [1..n]\})$.

Using the complexity results for permutation, projection, composition and the intersection with regular languages for constrained rational languages, we can show that the size of $\mathcal{C}'$ is at most double-exponential in the sizes of $M$ and $\Lambda$.

## References

1. Annichini, A., Asarin, E., Bouajjani, A.: Symbolic techniques for parametric reasoning about counter and clock systems. In: Emerson, E.A., Sistla, A.P. (eds.) CAV 2000. LNCS, vol. 1855, pp. 419–434. Springer, Heidelberg (2000)
2. Atig, M.F., Bollig, B., Habermehl, P.: Emptiness of multi-pushdown automata is 2ETIME-complete. In: Ito, M., Toyama, M. (eds.) DLT 2008. LNCS, vol. 5257, pp. 121–133. Springer, Heidelberg (2008)

3. Atig, M.F.: Model-checking of ordered multi-pushdown automata. Logical Methods Comput. Sci. **8**(3), 1–31 (2012)
4. Atig, M.F., Bouajjani, A., Narayan Kumar, K., Saivasan, P.: Linear-time model-checking for multithreaded programs under scope-bounding. In: Chakraborty, S., Mukund, M. (eds.) ATVA 2012. LNCS, vol. 7561, pp. 152–166. Springer, Heidelberg (2012)
5. Atig, M.F., Bouajjani, A., Qadeer, S.: Context-bounded analysis for concurrent programs with dynamic creation of threads. Logical Methods Comput. Sci. **7**(4), 107–123 (2011)
6. Atig, M.F., Narayan Kumar, K., Saivasan, P.: Adjacent ordered multi-pushdown systems. In: Béal, M.-P., Carton, O. (eds.) DLT 2013. LNCS, vol. 7907, pp. 58–69. Springer, Heidelberg (2013)
7. Bardin, S., Finkel, A., Leroux, J., Petrucci, L.: FAST: acceleration from theory to practice. STTT **10**(5), 401–424 (2008)
8. Bardin, S., Finkel, A., Leroux, J., Schnoebelen, P.: Flat acceleration in symbolic model checking. In: Peled, D.A., Tsay, Y.-K. (eds.) ATVA 2005. LNCS, vol. 3707, pp. 474–488. Springer, Heidelberg (2005)
9. Bérard, B., Fribourg, L.: Reachability analysis of (timed) Petri nets using real arithmetic. In: Baeten, J.C.M., Mauw, S. (eds.) CONCUR 1999. LNCS, vol. 1664, pp. 178–193. Springer, Heidelberg (1999)
10. Berstel, J.: Transductions and context-free langages. TeubnerStudienbucher Informatik. Springer, Heidelberg (1979)
11. Boigelot, B.: On iterating linear transformations over recognizable sets of integers. Theor. Comput. Sci. **309**(1–3), 413–468 (2003)
12. Boigelot, B.: Domain-specific regular acceleration. STTT **14**(2), 193–206 (2012)
13. Boigelot, B., Wolper, P.: Symbolic verification with periodic sets. In: Dill, D.L. (ed.) Computer Aided Verification. LNCS, vol. 818, pp. 55–67. Springer, Heidelberg (1994)
14. Bouajjani, A., Esparza, J., Maler, O.: Reachability analysis of pushdown automata: application to model-checking. In: Mazurkiewicz, A., Winkowski, J. (eds.) CONCUR 1997. LNCS, vol. 1243, pp. 135–150. Springer, Heidelberg (1997)
15. Bouajjani, A., Esparza, J., Schwoon, S., Strejček, J.: Reachability analysis of multithreaded software with asynchronous communication. In: Sarukkai, S., Sen, S. (eds.) FSTTCS 2005. LNCS, vol. 3821, pp. 348–359. Springer, Heidelberg (2005)
16. Bouajjani, A., Habermehl, P.: Symbolic reachability analysis of FiFo-channel systems with nonregular sets of configurations. Theor. Comput. Sci. **221**(1–2), 211–250 (1999)
17. Cadilhac, M., Finkel, A., McKenzie, P.: On the expressiveness of Parikh automata and related models. In: NCMA. books@ocg.at, vol. 282, pp. 103–119. Austrian Computer Society (2011)
18. Cadilhac, M., Finkel, A., McKenzie, P.: Bounded parikh automata. Int. J. Found. Comput. Sci. **23**(8), 1691–1710 (2012)
19. Caucal, D.: On the regular structure of prefix rewriting. Theor. Comput. Sci. **106**(1), 61–86 (1992)
20. Esparza, J., Knoop, J., Majumdar, R.: An automata-theoretic approach to interprocedural data-flow analysis. In: Thomas, W. (ed.) FOSSACS 1999. LNCS, vol. 1578, pp. 14–30. Springer, Heidelberg (1999)
21. Esparza, J., Ganty, P., Majumdar, R.: A perfect model for bounded verification. In: LICS, pp. 285–294. IEEE Computer Society (2012)
22. Esparza, J., Ganty, P., Poch, T.: Pattern-based verification for multithreaded programs. ACM Trans. Program. Lang. Syst. **36**(3), 9:1–9:29 (2014)

23. Esparza, J., Kiefer, S., Schwoon, S.: Abstraction refinement with craig interpolation and symbolic pushdown systems. In: Hermanns, H., Palsberg, J. (eds.) TACAS 2006. LNCS, vol. 3920, pp. 489–503. Springer, Heidelberg (2006)
24. Finkel, A.: A generalization of the procedure of Karp and Miller to well structured. In: Ottmann, T. (ed.) ICALP 1987. LNCS, vol. 267, pp. 499–508. Springer, Heidelberg (1987)
25. Finkel, A., Leroux, J.: How to compose Presburger-accelerations: Applications to broadcast protocols. In: Agrawal, M., Seth, A.K. (eds.) FSTTCS 2002. LNCS, vol. 2556, pp. 145–156. Springer, Heidelberg (2002)
26. Finkel, A., Willems, B., Wolper, P.: A direct symbolic approach to model checking pushdown systems. Electr. Notes Theor. Comput. Sci. **9**, 27–37 (1997)
27. Ganty, P., Majumdar, R., Monmege, B.: Bounded underapproximations. FMSD **40**(2), 206–231 (2012)
28. Heußner, A., Leroux, J., Muscholl, A., Sutre, G.: Reachability analysis of communicating pushdown systems. In: Ong, L. (ed.) FOSSACS 2010. LNCS, vol. 6014, pp. 267–281. Springer, Heidelberg (2010)
29. Karp, R.M., Miller, R.E.: Parallel program schemata. J. Comput. Syst. Sci. **3**(2), 147–195 (1969)
30. Kelly, W., Pugh, W., Rosser, E., Shpeisman, T.: Transitive closure of infinite graphs and its applications. J. Parallel Program. **24**(6), 579–598 (1996)
31. Klaedtke, F., Rueß, H.: Monadic second-order logics with cardinalities. In: Baeten, J.C.M., Lenstra, J.K., Parrow, J., Woeginger, G.J. (eds.) Automata, Languages and Programming. LNCS, vol. 2719, pp. 681–696. Springer, Heidelberg (2003)
32. La Torre, S., Madhusudan, P., Parlato, G.: Context-bounded analysis of concurrent queue systems. In: Ramakrishnan, C.R., Rehof, J. (eds.) TACAS 2008. LNCS, vol. 4963, pp. 299–314. Springer, Heidelberg (2008)
33. La Torre, S., Madhusudan, P., Parlato, G.: Reducing context-bounded concurrent reachability to sequential reachability. In: Bouajjani, A., Maler, O. (eds.) CAV 2009. LNCS, vol. 5643, pp. 477–492. Springer, Heidelberg (2009)
34. Lal, A., Reps, T.W.: Reducing concurrent analysis under a context bound to sequential analysis. FMSD **35**(1), 73–97 (2009)
35. Lal, A., Touili, T., Kidd, N., Reps, T.: Interprocedural analysis of concurrent programs under a context bound. In: Ramakrishnan, C.R., Rehof, J. (eds.) TACAS 2008. LNCS, vol. 4963, pp. 282–298. Springer, Heidelberg (2008)
36. Leroux, J.: Acceleration for Petri nets. In: Van Hung, D., Ogawa, M. (eds.) ATVA 2013. LNCS, vol. 8172, pp. 1–4. Springer, Heidelberg (2013)
37. Leroux, J., Sutre, G.: Flat counter automata almost everywhere!. In: Peled, D.A., Tsay, Y.-K. (eds.) ATVA 2005. LNCS, vol. 3707, pp. 489–503. Springer, Heidelberg (2005)
38. Musuvathi, M., Qadeer, S.: Iterative context bounding for systematic testing of multithreaded programs. In: PLDI, pp. 446–455. ACM (2007)
39. Qadeer, S., Rehof, J.: Context-bounded model checking of concurrent software. In: Halbwachs, N., Zuck, L.D. (eds.) TACAS 2005. LNCS, vol. 3440, pp. 93–107. Springer, Heidelberg (2005)
40. Reps, T., Schwoon, S., Jha, S.: Weighted pushdown systems and their application to interprocedural dataflow analysis. In: Cousot, R. (ed.) Static Analysis. LNCS, vol. 2694, pp. 189–213. Springer, Heidelberg (2003)
41. Song, F., Touili, T.: Pushdown model checking for malware detection. STTT **16**(2), 147–173 (2014)
42. Wong, K.: Parikh automata with pushdown stack. Diploma thesis, RWTH Aachen (2004)

# Languages and Automata

# Reduction of Nondeterministic Tree Automata

Ricardo Almeida[1], Lukáš Holík[2], and Richard Mayr[1(✉)]

[1] University of Edinburgh, Edinburgh, UK
rmayr@staffmail.ed.ac.uk
[2] Brno University of Technology, Brno, Czech Republic

**Abstract.** We present an efficient algorithm to reduce the size of non-deterministic tree automata, while retaining their language. It is based on new transition pruning techniques, and quotienting of the state space w.r.t. suitable equivalences. It uses criteria based on combinations of downward and upward simulation preorder on trees, and the more general downward and upward language inclusions. Since tree-language inclusion is EXPTIME-complete, we describe methods to compute good approximations in polynomial time.

We implemented our algorithm as a module of the well-known libvata tree automata library, and tested its performance on a given collection of tree automata from various applications of libvata in regular model checking and shape analysis, as well as on various classes of randomly generated tree automata. Our algorithm yields substantially smaller and sparser automata than all previously known reduction techniques, and it is still fast enough to handle large instances.

## 1 Introduction

**Background.** Tree automata are a generalization of word automata that accept trees instead of words [14]. They have many applications in model checking [5,6,12], term rewriting [15], and related areas of formal software verification, e.g., shape analysis [3,18,20]. Several software packages for manipulating tree automata have been developed, e.g., MONA [9], Timbuk [16], Autowrite [15] and libvata [22], on which other verification tools like Forester [23] are based.

For nondeterministic automata, many questions about their languages are computationally hard. The language universality, equivalence and inclusion problems are PSPACE-complete for word automata and EXPTIME-complete for tree automata [14]. However, recently techniques have been developed that can solve many practical instances fairly efficiently. For word automata there are antichain techniques [2], congruence-based techniques [10] and techniques based on generalized simulation preorders [13]. The antichain techniques have been generalized to tree automata in [11,21] and implemented in the libvata library [22]. Performance problems also arise in computing the intersection of several languages, since the product construction multiplies the numbers of states.

---

This work was supported by the Czech Science Foundation, project 16-24707Y.

M. Chechik and J.-F. Raskin (Eds.): TACAS 2016, LNCS 9636, pp. 717–735, 2016.
DOI: 10.1007/978-3-662-49674-9_46

**Automata Reduction.** Our goal is to make tree automata more computationally tractable in practice. We present an efficient algorithm for the reduction of nondeterministic tree automata, in the sense of obtaining a smaller automaton with the same language, though not necessarily with the absolute minimal possible number of states. (In general, there is no unique nondeterministic automaton with the minimal possible number of states for a given language, i.e., there can be several non-isomorphic nondeterministic automata of minimal size. This holds even for word automata.) The reason to perform reduction is that the smaller reduced automaton is more efficient to handle in a subsequent computation. Thus there is an algorithmic tradeoff between the effort for reduction and the complexity of the problem later considered for this automaton. The main applications of reduction are the following: (1) Helping to solve hard problems like language universality/equivalence/inclusion. (2) If automata undergo a long chain of manipulations/combinations by operations like union, intersection, projection, etc., then intermediate results can be reduced several times on the way to keep the automata within a manageable size. (3) There are fixed-parameter tractable problems (e.g., in model checking where an automaton encodes a logic formula) where the size of one automaton very strongly influences the overall complexity, and must be kept as small as possible.

**Our Contribution.** We present a reduction algorithm for nondeterministic tree automata. (The tool is available for download [7].) It is based on a combination of new transition pruning techniques for tree automata, and quotienting of the state space w.r.t. suitable equivalences. The pruning techniques are related to those presented for word automata in [13], but significantly more complex due to the fundamental asymmetry between the upward and downward directions in trees.

Transition pruning in word automata [13] is based on the observation that certain transitions can be removed (a.k.a pruned) without changing the language, because other 'better' transitions remain. One defines some strict partial order (p.o.) between transitions and removes all transitions that are not maximal w.r.t. this order. A strict p.o. between transitions is called *good for pruning* (GFP) iff pruning w.r.t. it preserves the language of the automaton. Note that pruning reduces not only the number of transitions, but also, indirectly, the number of states. By removing transitions, some states may become 'useless', in the sense that they are unreachable from any initial state, or that it is impossible to reach any accepting state from them. Such useless states can then be removed from the automaton without changing its language. One can obtain computable strict p.o. between transitions by comparing the possible backward- and forward behavior of their source- and target states, respectively. For this, one uses computable relations like backward/forward simulation preorder and approximations of backward/forward trace inclusion via lookahead- or multipebble simulations. Some such combinations of backward/forward trace/simulation orders on states induce strict p.o. between transitions that are GFP, while others do not [13].

However, there is always a symmetry between backward and forward, since finite words can equally well be read in either direction.

This symmetry does not hold for tree automata, because the tree branches as one goes downward, while it might 'join in' side branches as one goes upward. While downward simulation preorder (resp. downward language inclusion) between states in a tree automaton is a direct generalization of forward simulation preorder (resp. forward language inclusion) on words, the corresponding upward notions do not correspond to backward on words. Comparing upward behavior of states in tree automata depends also on the branches that 'join in' from the sides as one goes upward in the tree. Thus upward simulation/language inclusion is only defined *relative* to a given other relation that compares the downward behavior of states 'joining in' from the sides [1]. So one speaks of "upward simulation *of* the identity relation" or "upward simulation *of* downward simulation". When one studies strict p.o. between transitions in tree automata in order to check whether they are GFP, one has combinations of three relations: the source states are compared by an upward relation $X(Y)$ of some downward relation $Y$, while the target states are compared w.r.t. some downward relation $Z$ (where $Z$ can be, and often must be, different from $Y$). This yields a richer landscape, and many counter-intuitive effects.

We provide a complete picture of which combinations of upward/downward simulation/trace inclusions are GFP on tree automata; cf. Fig. 4. Since tree-(trace)language inclusion is EXPTIME-complete [14], we describe methods to compute good approximations of them in polynomial time. Finally, we also generalize results on quotienting of tree automata [19] to larger relations, such as approximations of trace inclusion.

We implemented our algorithm [7] as a module of the well-known libvata [22] tree automaton library, and tested its performance on a given collection of tree automata from various applications of libvata in regular model checking and shape analysis, as well as on various classes of randomly generated tree automata. Our algorithm yields substantially smaller automata than all previously known reduction techniques (which are mainly based on quotienting). Moreover, the thus obtained automata are also much sparser (i.e., use fewer transitions per state and less nondeterministic branching) than the originals, which yields additional performance advantages in subsequent computations.

## 2    Trees and Tree Automata

**Trees.** A *ranked alphabet* $\Sigma$ is a set of symbols together with a function $\#:\Sigma \to \mathbb{N}_0$. For $a \in \Sigma$, $\#(a)$ is called the *rank* of $a$. For $n \geq 0$, we denote by $\Sigma_n$ the set of all symbols of $\Sigma$ which have rank $n$.

We define a *node* as a sequence of elements of $\mathbb{N}$, where $\varepsilon$ is the empty sequence. For a node $v \in \mathbb{N}^*$, any node $v'$ s.t. $v = v'v''$, for some node $v''$, is said to be a *prefix* of $v$, and if $v'' \neq \varepsilon$ then $v'$ is a *strict prefix* of $v$. For a node $v \in \mathbb{N}^*$, we define the $i$-th child of $v$ to be the node $vi$, for some $i \in \mathbb{N}$. Given a ranked alphabet $\Sigma$, a *tree* over $\Sigma$ is defined as a partial mapping $t : \mathbb{N}^* \to \Sigma$

such that for all $v \in \mathbb{N}^*$ and $i \in \mathbb{N}$, if $vi \in dom(t)$ then **(1)** $v \in dom(t)$, and **(2)** $\#(t(v)) \geq i$. In this paper we consider only finite trees.

Note that the number of children of a node $v$ may be smaller than $\#(t(v))$. In this case we say that the node is *open*. Nodes which have exactly $\#(t(v))$ children are called *closed*. Nodes which do not have any children are called *leaves*. A tree is closed if all its nodes are closed, otherwise it is open. By $\mathbb{C}(\Sigma)$ we denote the set of all closed trees over $\Sigma$ and by $\mathbb{T}(\Sigma)$ the set of all trees over $\Sigma$. A tree $t$ is *linear* iff every node in $dom(t)$ has at most one child.

The *subtree* of a tree $t$ at $v$ is defined as the tree $t_v$ such that $dom(t_v) = \{v' \mid vv' \in dom(t)\}$ and $t_v(v') = t(vv')$ for all $v' \in dom(t_v)$. A tree $t'$ is a *prefix* of $t$ iff $dom(t') \subseteq dom(t)$ and for all $v \in dom(t')$, $t'(v) = t(v)$. For $t \in \mathbb{C}(\Sigma)$, the *height of a node* $v$ of $t$ is given by the function $h$: if $v$ is a leaf then $h(v) = 1$, otherwise $h(v) = 1 + max(h(v1)), \ldots, h(v\#(t(v))))$. We define the height of a tree $t \in \mathbb{C}(\Sigma)$ as $h(\epsilon)$, i.e., as the number of levels of $t$.

**Tree Automata, Top-Down.** A (finite, nondeterministic) *top-down tree automaton* (TDTA) is a quadruple $A = (\Sigma, Q, \delta, I)$ where $Q$ is a finite set of states, $I \subseteq Q$ is a set of initial states, $\Sigma$ is a ranked alphabet, and $\delta \subseteq Q \times \Sigma \times Q^+$ is the set of transition rules. A TDTA has an unique final state, which we represent by $\psi$. The transition rules satisfy that if $\langle q, a, \psi \rangle \in \delta$ then $\#(a) = 0$, and if $\langle q, a, q_1 \ldots q_n \rangle \in \delta$ (with $n > 0$) then $\#(a) = n$.

A *run* of $A$ over a tree $t \in \mathbb{T}(\Sigma)$ (or a *t-run in A*) is a partial mapping $\pi : \mathbb{N}^* \to Q$ such that $v \in dom(\pi)$ iff either $v \in dom(t)$ or $v = v'i$ where $v' \in dom(t)$ and $i \leq \#(t(v'))$. Further, for every $v \in dom(t)$, there exists either **(a)** a rule $\langle q, a, \psi \rangle$ such that $q = \pi(v)$ and $a = t(v)$, or **(b)** a rule $\langle q, a, q_1 \ldots q_n \rangle$ such that $q = \pi(v)$, $a = t(v)$, and $q_i = \pi(vi)$ for each $i : 1 \leq i \leq \#(a)$. A *leaf of a run* $\pi$ on $t$ is a node $v \in dom(\pi)$ such that $vi \in dom(\pi)$ for no $i \in \mathbb{N}$. We call it *dangling* if $v \notin dom(t)$. Intuitively, the dangling nodes of a run over $t$ are all the nodes which are in $\pi$ but are missing in $t$ due to it being incomplete. Notice that dangling leaves of $\pi$ are children of open nodes of $t$. The prefix of depth $k$ of a run $\pi$ is denoted $\pi_k$. Runs are always finite since the trees we are considering are finite.

We write $t \overset{\pi}{\Longrightarrow} q$ to denote that $\pi$ is a $t$-run of $A$ such that $\pi(\epsilon) = q$. We use $t \Longrightarrow q$ to denote that such run $\pi$ exists. A run $\pi$ is accepting if $t \overset{\pi}{\Longrightarrow} q \in I$. The *downward language of a state* $q$ in $A$ is defined by $D_A(q) = \{t \in \mathbb{C}(\Sigma) \mid t \Longrightarrow q\}$, while the *language* of $A$ is defined by $L(A) = \bigcup_{q \in I} D_A(q)$. The *upward language* of a state $q$ in $A$, denoted $U_A(q)$, is then defined as the set of open trees $t$, such that there exists an accepting $t$-run $\pi$ with exactly one dangling leaf $v$ s.t. $\pi(v) = q$. We omit the $A$ subscript notation when it is implicit which automaton we are considering.

In the related literature, it is common to define a tree automaton bottom-up, reading a tree from the leaves to the root [11,14,21]. A bottom-up tree automaton (BUTA) can be obtained from a TDTA by reversing the direction of the transition rules and by swapping the roles between the initial states and the final states. See [8] for an example of a tree automaton presented in both BUTA and TDTA form.

# 3   Simulations and Trace Inclusions

We consider different types of relations on states of a TDTA which under-approximate language inclusion. Note that words are but a special case of trees where every node has only one child, i.e., words are linear trees. *Downward* simulation/trace inclusion on TDTA corresponds to *direct forward* simulation/trace inclusion in special case of word automata, and *upward* corresponds to *backward* [13].

**Forward Simulation on Word Automata.** Let $A = (\Sigma, Q, \delta, I, F)$ be a NFA. A *direct forward simulation* $D$ is a binary relation on $Q$ such that if $q \, D \, r$, then

1. $q \in F \implies r \in F$, and
2. for any $\langle q, a, q' \rangle \in \delta$, there exists $\langle r, a, r' \rangle \in \delta$ such that $q' \, D \, r'$.

The set of direct forward simulations on $A$ contains $id$ and is closed under union and transitive closure. Thus there is a unique maximal direct forward simulation on $A$, which is a preorder. We call it *the direct forward simulation preorder on* $A$ and write $\sqsubseteq^{di}$.

**Forward Trace Inclusion on Word Automata.** Let $A = (\Sigma, Q, \delta, I, F)$ be a NFA and $w = \sigma_1 \sigma_2 \ldots \sigma_n \in \Sigma^*$ a word of length $n$. A trace of $A$ on $w$ (or a $w$-trace) starting at $q$ is a sequence of transitions $\pi = q_0 \xrightarrow{\sigma_1} q_1 \xrightarrow{\sigma_2} \cdots \xrightarrow{\sigma_n} q_n$ such that $q_0 = q$. The *direct forward trace inclusion* preorder $\subseteq^{di}$ is a binary relation on $Q$ such that $q \subseteq^{di} r$ iff

1. $(q \in F \implies r \in F)$, and
2. for every word $w = \sigma_1 \sigma_2 \ldots \sigma_n \in \Sigma^*$ and for every $w$-trace (starting at $q$) $\pi_q = q \xrightarrow{\sigma_1} q_1 \xrightarrow{\sigma_2} \cdots \xrightarrow{\sigma_n} q_n$, there exists a $w$-trace (starting at $r$) $\pi_r = r \xrightarrow{\sigma_1} r_1 \xrightarrow{\sigma_2} \cdots \xrightarrow{\sigma_n} r_n$ such that $(q_i \in F \implies r_i \in F)$ for each $i : 1 \le i \le n$.

Since $\pi_r$ is required to preserve the acceptance of the states in $\pi_q$, trace inclusion is a strictly stronger notion than language inclusion (see [8] for an example).

**Downward Simulation on Tree Automata.** Let $A = (\Sigma, Q, \delta, I)$ be a TDTA. A *downward simulation* $D$ is a binary relation on $Q$ such that if $q \, D \, r$, then

1. $(q = \psi \implies r = \psi)$, and
2. for any $\langle q, a, q_1 \ldots q_n \rangle \in \delta$, there exists $\langle r, a, r_1 \ldots r_n \rangle \in \delta$ s.t. $q_i \, D \, r_i$ for $i : 1 \le i \le n$.

Since the set of all downward simulations on $A$ is closed under union and under reflexive and transitive closure (cf. Lemma 4.1 in [19]), it follows that there is one unique maximal downward simulation on $A$, and that relation is a preorder. We call it *the downward simulation preorder on* $A$ and write $\sqsubseteq^{dw}$.

**Downward Trace Inclusion on Tree Automata.** Let $A = (\Sigma, Q, \delta, I)$ be a TDTA. The *downward trace inclusion* preorder $\subseteq^{dw}$ is a binary relation on $Q$ s.t. $q \subseteq^{dw} r$ iff for every tree $t \in \mathbb{C}(\Sigma)$ and for every $t$-run $\pi_q$ with $\pi_q(\epsilon) = q$ there exists another $t$-run $\pi_r$ s.t.

1. $\pi_r(\epsilon) = r$, and
2. $(\pi_q(v) = \psi \implies \pi_r(v) = \psi)$ for each leaf node $v \in dom(t)$.

Generally, one way of making downward language inclusion on the states of an automaton coincide with downward trace inclusion is by modifying the automaton to guarantee that **(1)** there is one unique final state which has no outgoing transitions, **(2)** from any other state, there is a path ending in that final state. Note that in a TDTA these two conditions are automatically satisfied: **(1)** since the final state is reached after reading a leaf of the tree, and **(2)** because only complete trees are in the language of the automaton. Thus, in a TDTA, downward language inclusion and downward trace inclusion coincide.

**Backward Simulation on Word Automata.** Let $A = (\Sigma, Q, \delta, I, F)$ be a NFA. A *backward simulation* $B$ is a binary relation on $Q$ s.t. if $q \mathrel{B} r$, then

1. $(q \in F \implies r \in F)$ and $(q \in I \implies r \in I)$, and
2. for any $\langle q', a, q \rangle \in \delta$, there exists $\langle r', a, r \rangle \in \delta$ s.t. $q' \mathrel{B} r'$.

Like for forward simulation, there is a unique maximal backward simulation on $A$, which is a preorder. We call it *the backward simulation preorder on $A$* and write $\subseteq^{bw}$.

**Backward Trace Inclusion on Word Automata.** Let $A = (\Sigma, Q, \delta, I, F)$ be a NFA and $w = \sigma_1 \sigma_2 \ldots \sigma_n \in \Sigma^*$ a word of length $n$. A *$w$-trace of $A$ ending at $q$* is a sequence of transitions $\pi = q_0 \xrightarrow{\sigma_1} q_1 \xrightarrow{\sigma_2} \cdots \xrightarrow{\sigma_n} q_n$ such that $q_n = q$. The *backward trace inclusion* preorder $\subseteq^{bw}$ is a binary relation on $Q$ such that $q \subseteq^{bw} r$ iff

1. $(q \in F \implies r \in F)$ and $(q \in I \implies r \in I)$, and
2. for every word $w = \sigma_1 \sigma_2 \ldots \sigma_n \in \Sigma^*$ and for every $w$-trace (ending at $q$) $\pi_q = q_0 \xrightarrow{\sigma_1} q_1 \xrightarrow{\sigma_2} \cdots \xrightarrow{\sigma_n} q$, there exists a $w$-trace (ending at $r$) $\pi_r = r_0 \xrightarrow{\sigma_1} r_1 \xrightarrow{\sigma_2} \cdots \xrightarrow{\sigma_n} r$ such that $(q_i \in F \implies r_i \in F \wedge q_i \in I \implies r_i \in I)$ for each $i : 1 \leq i \leq n$.

**Upward Simulation on Tree Automata.** Let $A = (\Sigma, Q, \delta, I)$ be a TDTA. Given a binary relation $R$ on $Q$, an *upward simulation $U(R)$ induced by $R$* is a binary relation on $Q$ such that if $q \mathrel{U(R)} r$, then

1. $(q = \psi \implies r = \psi)$ and $(q \in I \implies r \in I)$, and
2. for any $\langle q', a, q_1 \ldots q_n \rangle \in \delta$ with $q_i = q$ (for some $i : 1 \leq i \leq n$), there exists $\langle r', a, r_1 \ldots r_n \rangle \in \delta$ such that $r_i = r$, $q' \mathrel{U(R)} r'$ and $q_j \mathrel{R} r_j$ for each $j : 1 \leq j \neq i \leq n$.

Similarly to the case of downward simulation, for any given relation $R$, there is a unique maximal upward simulation induced by $R$ which is a preorder (cf. Lemma 4.2 in [19]). We call it *the upward simulation preorder on $A$ induced by $R$* and write $\sqsubseteq^{\mathsf{up}}(R)$.

**Upward Trace Inclusion on Tree Automata.** Let $A = (\Sigma, Q, \delta, I)$ be a TDTA. Given a binary relation $R$ on $Q$, the *upward trace inclusion preorder* $\subseteq^{\mathsf{up}}(R)$ *induced by $R$* is a binary relation on $Q$ such that $q \subseteq^{\mathsf{up}}(R) r$ iff ($q = \psi \implies r = \psi$) and the following holds: for every tree $t \in T(\Sigma)$ and for every $t$-run $\pi_q$ with $\pi_q(v) = q$ for some leaf $v$ of $t$, there exists a $t$-run $\pi_r$ s.t.

1. $\pi_r(v) = r$,
2. for all prefixes $v'$ of $v$, $(\pi_q(v') \in I \implies \pi_r(v') \in I)$, and
3. if $v'x \in dom(\pi_q)$, for some strict prefix $v'$ of $v$ and some $x \in \mathbb{N}$ s.t. $v'x$ is not a prefix of $v$, then $\pi_q(v'x) \, R \, \pi_r(v'x)$.

Downward trace inclusion is $\mathsf{EXPTIME}$-complete for TDTA [14], while forward trace inclusion is $\mathsf{PSPACE}$-complete for word automata. The complexity of upward trace inclusion depends on the relation $R$ (e.g., it is $\mathsf{PSPACE}$-complete for $R = id$). In contrast, downward/upward simulation preorder is computable in polynomial time [1], but typically yields only small under-approximations of the corresponding trace inclusions.

## 4  Transition Pruning Techniques

We define pruning relations on a TDTA $A = (\Sigma, Q, \delta, I)$. The intuition is that certain transitions may be deleted without changing the language, because 'better' transitions remain. We perform this pruning (i.e., deletion) of transitions by comparing their endpoints over the same symbol $\sigma \in \Sigma$. Given two binary relations $R_u$ and $R_d$ on $Q$, we define the following relation to compare transitions.

$$P(R_u, R_d) = \{(\langle p, \sigma, r_1 \cdots r_n \rangle, \langle p', \sigma, r'_1 \cdots r'_n \rangle) \mid p \, R_u \, p' \text{ and } (r_1 \cdots r_n) \, \hat{R}_d \, (r'_1 \cdots r'_n)\},$$

where $\hat{R}_d$ results from lifting $R_d \subseteq Q \times Q$ to $\hat{R}_d \subseteq Q^n \times Q^n$, as defined below. The function $P$ is monotone in the two arguments. If $t \, P \, t'$ then $t$ may be pruned because $t'$ is 'better' than $t$. We want $P(R_u, R_d)$ to be a strict partial order (p.o.), i.e., irreflexive and transitive (and thus acyclic). There are two cases in which $P(R_u, R_d)$ is guaranteed to be a strict p.o.: **(1)** $R_u$ is some strict p.o. $<_u$ and $\hat{R}_d$ is the standard lifting $\hat{\leq}_d$ of some p.o. $\leq_d$ to tuples. I.e., $(r_1 \cdots r_n) \hat{\leq}_d (r'_1 \cdots r'_n)$ iff $\forall_{1 \leq i \leq n}. r_i \leq_d r'_i$. The transitions in each pair of $P(<_u, \leq_d)$ depart from different states and therefore the transitions are necessarily different. **(2)** $R_u$ is some p.o. $\leq_u$ and $\hat{R}_d$ is the lifting $\hat{<}_d$ of some strict p.o. $<_d$ to tuples (defined below). In this case the transitions in each pair of $P(\leq_u, <_d)$ may have the same origin but must go to different tuples of states. Since for two tuples $(r_1 \cdots r_n)$ and $(r'_1 \cdots r'_n)$ to be different it suffices that $r_i \neq r'_i$ for some $1 \leq i \leq n$, we define $\hat{<}_d$ as a binary relation such that $(r_1 \cdots r_n) \hat{<}_d (r'_1 \cdots r'_n)$ iff $\forall_{1 \leq i \leq n}. r_i \leq_d r'_i$, and $\exists_{1 \leq i \leq n}. r_i <_d r'_i$.

Let $A = (\Sigma, Q, \delta, I)$ be a TDTA and let $P \subseteq \delta \times \delta$ be a strict partial order. The pruned automaton is defined as $Prune(A, P) = (\Sigma, Q, \delta', I)$ where $\delta' = \{(p, \sigma, r) \in \delta \mid \nexists(p', \sigma, r') \in \delta . (p, \sigma, r) P (p', \sigma, r')\}$. Note that the pruned automaton $Prune(A, P)$ is unique. The transitions are removed without requiring the re-computation of the relation $P$, which could be expensive. Since removing transitions cannot introduce new trees in the language, $L(Prune(A, P)) \subseteq L(A)$. If the reverse inclusion holds too (so that the language is preserved), we say that $P$ is *good for pruning* (GFP), i.e., $P$ is GFP iff $L(Prune(A, P)) = L(A)$.

We now provide a complete picture of which combinations of simulation and trace inclusion relations are GFP. Recall that simulations are denoted by square symbols $\sqsubseteq$ while trace inclusions are denoted by round symbols $\subseteq$. For every partial order $R$, the corresponding strict p.o. is defined as $R \backslash R^{-1}$.

$P(\subset^{bw}, \subset^{di})$ is not GFP for word automata (see Fig. 2(a) in [13] for a counterexample). As mentioned before, words correspond to linear trees. Thus $P(\subset^{up}(R), \subset^{dw})$ is not GFP for tree automata (regardless of the relation $R$). Figure 1 presents several more counterexamples. For word automata, $P(\subset^{bw}, \sqsubseteq^{di})$ and $P(\sqsubseteq^{bw}, \subset^{di})$ are not GFP (Fig. 1b and c) even though $P(\subseteq^{bw}, \sqsubseteq^{di})$ and $P(\sqsubseteq^{bw}, \subseteq^{di})$ are (cf. [13]). Thus $P(\subset^{up}(R), \sqsubseteq^{dw})$ and $P(\sqsubseteq^{up}(R), \subset^{dw})$ are not GFP for tree automata (regardless of the relation $R$). For tree automata, $P(\sqsubset^{up}(\sqsubseteq^{dw}), id)$ and $P(\sqsubset^{up}(\sqsubseteq^{dw}), \sqsubseteq^{dw})$ are not GFP (Fig. 1a and d). Moreover, a complex counterexample (see [8]) is needed to show that $P(\sqsubset^{up}(\sqsubseteq^{dw}), \subseteq^{dw})$ is not GFP.

The following theorems and corollaries provide several relations which are GFP.

**Theorem 1.** *For every strict partial order $R \subset \subseteq^{dw}$, it holds that $P(id, R)$ is GFP.*

**Corollary 1.** *By Theorem 1, $P(id, \subset^{dw})$ and $P(id, \sqsubset^{dw})$ are GFP.*

**Theorem 2.** *For every strict partial order $R \subset \subseteq^{up}(id)$, it holds that $P(R, id)$ is GFP.*

**Corollary 2.** *By Theorem 2, $P(\subset^{up}(id), id)$ and $P(\sqsubset^{up}(id), id)$ are GFP.*

**Definition 1.** *Given a tree automaton $A$, a binary relation $W$ on its states is called a downup-relation iff the following condition holds: If $p \, W \, q$ then for every tree $t \in \mathbb{T}(\Sigma)$ and accepting $t$-run $\pi$ from $p$ there exists an accepting $t$-run $\pi'$ from $q$ such that $\forall_{v \in \mathbb{N}^*} \, \pi(v) \sqsubseteq^{up}(W) \, \pi'(v)$.*

**Lemma 1.** *Any relation $V$ satisfying (1) $V$ is a downward simulation, and (2) $id \subseteq V \subseteq \sqsubseteq^{up}(V)$ is a downup-relation. In particular, $id$ is a downup-relation, but $\sqsubseteq^{dw}$ and $\sqsubseteq^{up}(id)$ are not.*

**Theorem 3.** *For every downup-relation $W$, it holds that $P(\sqsubset^{up}(W), \subseteq^{dw})$ is GFP.*

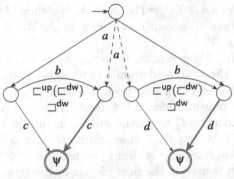

(a) $P(\sqsubset^{up}(\sqsubset^{dw}), id)$ is not GFP: if we remove the blue transitions, the automaton no longer accepts the tree $a(c,d)$. We are considering $\Sigma_0 = \{c,d\}$, $\Sigma_1 = \{b\}$ and $\Sigma_2 = \{a\}$.

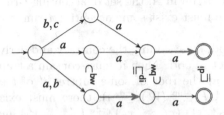

(b) $P(\sqsubset^{bw}, \sqsubseteq^{di})$ is not GFP for words: if we remove the blue transitions, the automaton no longer accepts the word $aaa$.

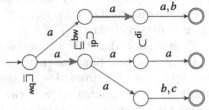

(c) $P(\sqsubseteq^{bw}, \sqsubset^{di})$ is not GFP for words: if we remove the blue transitions, the automaton no longer accepts the word $aaa$.

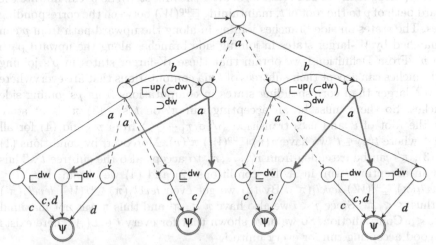

(d) $P(\sqsubset^{up}(\sqsubset^{dw}), \sqsubset^{dw})$ is not GFP: if we remove the blue transitions, the tree $a(a(c,c), a(c,c))$ is no longer accepted. We are considering $\Sigma_0 = \{c,d\}$, $\Sigma_1 = \{b\}$ and $\Sigma_2 = \{a\}$.

**Fig. 1.** GFP counterexamples. A transition is drawn in dashed when a different transition by the same symbol departing from the same state already exists. We draw a transition in thick red when it is better than another transition (drawn in thin blue).

*Proof.* Let $A' = Prune(A, P(\sqsubset^{\mathsf{up}}(W), \subseteq^{\mathsf{dw}}))$. We show $L(A) \subseteq L(A')$. If $t \in L(A)$ then there exists an accepting $t$-run $\hat{\pi}$ in $A$. We show that there is an accepting $t$-run $\hat{\pi}'$ in $A'$.

For each accepting $t$-run $\pi$ in $A$, let $level_i(\pi)$ be the tuple of states that $\pi$ visits at depth $i$ in the tree, read from left to right. Formally, let $(x_1, \ldots, x_k)$ with $x_j \in \mathbb{N}^i$ be the set of all tree positions of depth $i$ s.t. $x_j \in dom(\pi)$, in lexicographically increasing order. Then $level_i(\pi) = (\pi(x_1), \ldots, \pi(x_k)) \in Q^k$. By lifting partial orders on $Q$ to partial orders on tuples, we can compare such tuples w.r.t. $\sqsubseteq^{\mathsf{up}}(W)$. We say that an accepting $t$-run $\pi$ is $i$-good iff it does not contain any transition from $A - A'$ from any position $v \in \mathbb{N}^*$ with $|v| < i$. I.e., no pruned transition is used in the first $i$ levels of the tree.

We now define a strict partial order $<_i$ on the set of accepting $t$-runs in $A$. Let $\pi <_i \pi'$ iff $\exists k \leq i$. $level_k(\pi) \sqsubset^{\mathsf{up}}(W) level_k(\pi')$ and $\forall l < k$. $level_l(\pi) \sqsubseteq^{\mathsf{up}}(W) level_l(\pi')$. Note that $<_i$ only depends on the first $i$ levels of the run. Given $A$, $t$ and $i$, there are only finitely many different such $i$-prefixes of accepting $t$-runs. By our assumption that $\hat{\pi}$ is an accepting $t$-run in $A$, the set of accepting $t$-runs in $A$ is non-empty. Thus, for any $i$, there must exist some accepting $t$-run $\pi$ in $A$ that is maximal w.r.t. $<_i$.

We now show that this $\pi$ is also $i$-good, by assuming the contrary and deriving a contradiction. Suppose that $\pi$ is not $i$-good. Then it must contain a transition $\langle p, \sigma, r_1 \cdots r_n \rangle$ from $A - A'$ used at the root of some subtree $t'$ of $t$ at some level $j < i$. Since $A' = Prune(A, P(\sqsubset^{\mathsf{up}}(W), \subseteq^{\mathsf{dw}}))$, there must exist another transition $\langle p', \sigma, r'_1 \cdots r'_n \rangle$ in $A'$ s.t. (1) $(r_1, \ldots, r_n) \subseteq^{\mathsf{dw}} (r'_1, \ldots, r'_n)$ and (2) $p \sqsubset^{\mathsf{up}}(W) p'$.

First consider the implications of (2). Upward simulation propagates upward stepwise (though only in non-strict form after the first step). So $p'$ can imitate the upward path of $p$ to the root of $t$, maintaining $\sqsubseteq^{\mathsf{up}}(W)$ between the corresponding states. The states on side branches joining in along the upward path from $p$ can be matched by $W$-larger states in joining side branches along the upward path from $p'$. From Definition 1 we obtain that these $W$-larger states in $p'$'s joining side branches can accept their subtrees of $t$ via computations that are everywhere $\sqsubseteq^{\mathsf{up}}(W)$ larger than corresponding states in computations from $ps$ joining side branches. So there must be an accepting run $\pi'$ on $t$ s.t. (3) $\pi'$ is at state $p'$ at the root of $t'$ and uses transition $\langle p', \sigma, r'_1 \cdots r'_n \rangle$ from $p'$, and (4) for all $v \in \mathbb{N}^*$ where $t(v) \notin t'$ we have $\pi(v) \sqsubseteq^{\mathsf{up}}(W) \pi'(v)$. Moreover, by conditions (1) and (3), $\pi'$ can be extended from $r'_1, \ldots, r'_n$ to accept also the subtree $t'$. Thus $\pi'$ is an accepting $t$-run in $A$. By conditions (2) and (4) we obtain that $\forall l \leq j$. $level_l(\pi) \sqsubseteq^{\mathsf{up}}(W) level_l(\pi')$. By (2) we get even $level_j(\pi) \sqsubset^{\mathsf{up}}(W) level_j(\pi')$ and thus $\pi <_j \pi'$. Since $j < i$ we also have $\pi <_i \pi'$ and thus $\pi$ was not maximal w.r.t. $<_i$. Contradiction. So we have shown that for every $t \in L(A)$ there exists an $i$-good accepting run for every finite $i$.

If $t \in L(A)$ then there exists an accepting $t$-run $\hat{\pi}$ in $A$. Then there exists an accepting $t$-run $\hat{\pi}'$ that is $i$-good, where $i$ is the height of $t$. Thus $\hat{\pi}'$ is a run in $A'$ and $t \in L(A')$. $\qquad\square$

**Corollary 3.** *It follows from Lemma 1 and from the fact that GFP is downward closed that* $P(\sqsubseteq^{up}(V), \subseteq^{dw})$, $P(\sqsubseteq^{up}(V), \subset^{dw})$, $P(\sqsubseteq^{up}(V), \sqsubseteq^{dw})$, $P(\sqsubseteq^{up}(V), \sqsubset^{dw})$, $P(\sqsubseteq^{up}(V), id)$, $P(\sqsubseteq^{up}(id), \subseteq^{dw})$, $P(\sqsubseteq^{up}(id), \subset^{dw})$, $P(\sqsubseteq^{up}(id), \sqsubseteq^{dw})$ *and* $P(\sqsubseteq^{up}(id), \sqsubset^{dw})$ *are GFP.*

**Theorem 4.** $P(\subseteq^{up}(\sqsubseteq^{dw}), \sqsubset^{dw})$ *is GFP.*

*Proof.* Let $A' = Prune(A, P(\subseteq^{up}(\sqsubseteq^{dw}), \sqsubset^{dw}))$. We show $L(A) \subseteq L(A')$. If $t \in L(A)$ then there exists an accepting $t$-run $\hat{\pi}$ in $A$. We show that there is an accepting $t$-run $\hat{\pi}'$ in $A'$.

For each accepting $t$-run $\pi$ in $A$, let $level_i(\pi)$ be the tuple of states that $\pi$ visits at depth $i$ in the tree, read from left to right. Formally, let $(x_1, \ldots, x_k)$ with $x_j \in \mathbb{N}^i$ be the set of all tree positions of depth $i$ s.t. $x_j \in dom(\pi)$, in lexicographically increasing order. Then $level_i(\pi) = (\pi(x_1), \ldots, \pi(x_k)) \in Q^k$. By lifting partial orders on $Q$ to partial orders on tuples we can compare such tuples w.r.t. $\sqsubseteq^{dw}$. We say that an accepting $t$-run $\pi$ is $i$-good if it does not contain any transition from $A - A'$ from any position $v \in \mathbb{N}^*$ with $|v| < i$. I.e., no pruned transitions are used in the first $i$ levels of the tree.

We now show, by induction on $i$, the following property (C): For every $i$ and every accepting $t$-run $\pi$ in $A$ there exists an $i$-good accepting $t$-run $\pi'$ in $A$ s.t. $level_i(\pi) \sqsubseteq^{dw} level_i(\pi')$.

The base case is $i = 0$. Every accepting $t$-run $\pi$ in $A$ is trivially 0-good itself and thus satisfies (C).

For the induction step, let $S$ be the set of all $(i-1)$-good accepting $t$-runs $\pi'$ in $A$ s.t. $level_{i-1}(\pi) \sqsubseteq^{dw} level_{i-1}(\pi')$. Since $\pi$ is an accepting $t$-run, by induction hypothesis, $S$ is non-empty. Let $S' \subseteq S$ be the subset of $S$ containing exactly those runs $\pi' \in S$ that additionally satisfy $level_i(\pi) \sqsubseteq^{dw} level_i(\pi')$. From $level_{i-1}(\pi) \sqsubseteq^{dw} level_{i-1}(\pi')$ and the fact that $\sqsubseteq^{dw}$ is preserved downward-stepwise, we obtain that $S'$ is non-empty. Now we can select some $\pi' \in S'$ s.t. $level_i(\pi')$ is maximal, w.r.t. $\sqsubseteq^{dw}$, relative to the other runs in $S'$. We claim that $\pi'$ is $i$-good and $level_i(\pi) \sqsubseteq^{dw} level_i(\pi')$. The second part of this claim holds because $\pi' \in S'$.

We show that $\pi'$ is $i$-good by contraposition. Suppose that $\pi'$ is not $i$-good. Then it must contain a transition $\langle p, \sigma, r_1 \cdots r_n \rangle$ from $A - A'$. Since $\pi'$ is $(i-1)$-good, this transition must start at depth $(i-1)$ in the tree. Since $A' = Prune(A, P(\subseteq^{up}(\sqsubseteq^{dw}), \sqsubset^{dw}))$, there must exist another transition $\langle p', \sigma, r_1' \cdots r_n' \rangle$ in $A'$ s.t. $p \subseteq^{up}(\sqsubseteq^{dw}) p'$ and $(r_1, \ldots, r_n) \sqsubseteq^{dw} (r_1', \ldots, r_n')$. From the definition of $\subseteq^{up}(\sqsubseteq^{dw})$ we obtain that there exists another accepting $t$-run $\pi_1$ in $A$ (that uses the transition $\langle p', \sigma, r_1' \cdots r_n' \rangle$) s.t. $level_i(\pi') \sqsubseteq^{dw} level_i(\pi_1)$. The run $\pi_1$ is not necessarily $i$-good or $(i-1)$-good. However, by induction hypothesis, there exists some accepting $t$-run $\pi_2$ in $A$ that is $(i-1)$-good and satisfies $level_{i-1}(\pi_1) \sqsubseteq^{dw} level_{i-1}(\pi_2)$. Since $\sqsubseteq^{dw}$ is preserved stepwise, there also exists an accepting $t$-run $\pi_3$ in $A$ (that coincides with $\pi_2$ up-to depth $(i-1)$), which is $(i-1)$-good and satisfies $level_i(\pi_1) \sqsubseteq^{dw} level_i(\pi_3)$. In particular, $\pi_3 \in S'$.

From $level_i(\pi') \sqsubseteq^{dw} level_i(\pi_1)$ and $level_i(\pi_1) \sqsubseteq^{dw} level_i(\pi_3)$ we obtain $level_i(\pi') \sqsubset^{dw} level_i(\pi_3)$. This contradicts our condition above that $\pi'$ must be $level_i$ maximal w.r.t. $\sqsubseteq^{dw}$ in $S'$. This concludes the induction step and the proof of property (C).

If $t \in L(A)$ then there exists an accepting $t$-run $\hat{\pi}$ in $A$. By property (C), there exists an accepting $t$-run $\hat{\pi}'$ that is $i$-good, where $i$ is the height of $t$. Therefore $\hat{\pi}'$ does not use any transition from $A - A'$ and is thus also a run in $A'$. So we obtain $t \in L(A')$. $\qquad\qquad\qquad\qquad\qquad\qquad\qquad\qquad\qquad\qquad\qquad$ □

**Corollary 4.** *It follows from Theorem 4 and the fact that GFP is downward closed that* $P(\sqsubset^{up} (\sqsubseteq^{dw}), \sqsubset^{dw})$, $P(\sqsubseteq^{up} (\sqsubseteq^{dw}), \sqsubset^{dw})$, $P(\sqsubset^{up} (\sqsubseteq^{dw}), \sqsubset^{dw})$, $P(\sqsubseteq^{up} (id), \sqsubset^{dw})$, $P(\sqsubset^{up}(id), \sqsubset^{dw})$, $P(\sqsubseteq^{up}(id), \sqsubset^{dw})$ *and* $P(id, \sqsubset^{dw})$ *are GFP.*

## 5    State Quotienting Techniques

A classic method for reducing the size of automata is state quotienting. Given a suitable equivalence relation on the set of states, each equivalence class is collapsed into just one state. From a preorder $\sqsubseteq$ one obtains an equivalence relation $\equiv := \sqsubseteq \cap \sqsupseteq$. We now define quotienting w.r.t. $\equiv$. Let $A = (\Sigma, Q, \delta, I)$ be a TDTA and let $\sqsubseteq$ be a preorder on $Q$. Given $q \in Q$, we denote by $[q]$ its equivalence class w.r.t $\equiv$. For $P \subseteq Q$, $[P]$ denotes the set of equivalence classes $[P] = \{[p] \mid p \in P\}$. We define the quotient automaton w.r.t. $\equiv$ as $A/\equiv :=$ $(\Sigma, [Q], \delta_{A/\equiv}, [I])$, where $\delta_{A/\equiv} = \{\langle [q], \sigma, [q_1] \ldots [q_n]\rangle \mid \langle q, \sigma, q_1 \ldots q_n\rangle \in \delta_A\}$. It is trivial that $L(A) \subseteq L(A/\equiv)$ for any $\equiv$. If the reverse inclusion also holds, i.e., if $L(A) = L(A/\equiv)$, we say that $\equiv$ is *good for quotienting* (GFQ).

It was shown in [19] that $\sqsubseteq^{dw} \cap \sqsupseteq^{dw}$ and $\sqsubseteq^{up}(id) \cap \sqsupseteq^{up}(id)$ are GFQ. Here we generalize this result from simulation to trace equivalence. Let $\equiv^{dw} := \sqsubseteq^{dw} \cap \sqsupseteq^{dw}$ and $\equiv^{up}(R) := \sqsubseteq^{up}(R) \cap \sqsupseteq^{up}(R)$.

**Theorem 5.** $\equiv^{dw}$ *is GFQ.*

**Theorem 6.** $\equiv^{up}(id)$ *is GFQ.*

In [8] we present a counterexample showing that $\equiv := \sqsubseteq^{up}(\sqsubseteq^{dw} \cap \sqsupseteq^{dw}) \cap \sqsupseteq^{up}(\sqsubseteq^{dw} \cap \sqsupseteq^{dw})$ is not GFQ. This is an adaptation from the Example 5 in [19], where the inducing relation is referred to as the *downward bisimulation equivalence* and the automata are seen bottom-up.

One of the best methods previously known for reducing TA performs state quotienting based on a combination of downward and upward simulation [4]. However, this method cannot achieve any further reduction on an automaton which has been previously reduced with the techniques we described above [8].

## 6    Lookahead Simulations

Simulation preorders are generally not very good under-approximations of trace inclusion, since they are much smaller on many automata. Thus we consider better approximations that are still efficiently computable.

For word automata, more general *lookahead simulations* were introduced in [13]. These provide a practically useful tradeoff between the computational effort and the size of the obtained relations. Lookahead simulations can also be seen as a particular restriction of the more general (but less practically useful) *multipebble simulations* [17]. We generalize lookahead simulations to tree automata in order to compute good under-approximations of trace inclusions.

**Intuition by Simulation Games.** Normal simulation preorder on labeled transition graphs can be characterized by a game between two players, Spoiler and Duplicator. Given a pair of states $(q_0, r_0)$, Spoiler wants to show that $(q_0, r_0)$ is not contained in the simulation preorder relation, while Duplicator has the opposite goal. Starting in the initial configuration $(q_0, r_0)$, Spoiler chooses a transition $q_0 \xrightarrow{\sigma} q_1$ and Duplicator must imitate it *stepwise* by choosing a transition with the same symbol $r_0 \xrightarrow{\sigma} r_1$. This yields a new configuration $(q_1, r_1)$ from which the game continues. If a player cannot move the other wins. Duplicator wins every infinite game. Simulation holds iff Duplicator wins.

In normal simulation, Duplicator only knows Spoiler's very next step (see above), while in *k-lookahead simulation* Duplicator knows Spoiler's $k$ next steps in advance (unless Spoiler's move ends in a deadlocked state - i.e., a state with no transitions). As the parameter $k$ increases, the $k$-lookahead simulation relation becomes larger and thus approximates the trace inclusion relation better and better. Trace inclusion can also be characterized by a game. In the trace inclusion game, Duplicator knows *all* steps of Spoiler in the entire game in advance.

For every fixed $k$, $k$-lookahead simulation is computable in polynomial time, though the complexity rises quickly in $k$: it is doubly exponential for downward- and single exponential for upward lookahead simulation (due to the downward branching of trees). A crucial trick makes it possible to practically compute it for nontrivial $k$: Spoiler's moves are built incrementally, and Duplicator need not respond to all of Spoiler's announced $k$ next steps, but only to a prefix of them, after which he may request fresh information [13]. Thus Duplicator just uses the minimal lookahead necessary to win the current step.

**Lookahead Downward Simulation.** We say that a tree $t$ is $k$-bounded iff for all leaves $v$ of $t$, either (a) $|v| = k$, or (b) $|v| < k$ and $v$ is closed. Let $A = (\Sigma, Q, \delta, I)$ be a TDTA. A *k-lookahead downward simulation* $L^{k-\mathrm{dw}}$ is a binary relation on $Q$ such that if $q \, L^{k-\mathrm{dw}} \, r$, then $(q = \psi \implies r = \psi)$ and the following holds: Let $\pi_k$ be a run on a $k$-bounded tree $t_k$ with $\pi(\epsilon) = q$ s.t. every leaf node of $\pi_k$ is either at depth $k$ or downward-deadlocked (i.e., no more downward transitions exist). Then there must exist a run $\pi'_k$ over a nonempty prefix $t'_k$ of $t_k$ s.t. (1) $\pi'_k(\epsilon) = r$, and (2) for every leaf $v$ of $\pi'_k$, $\pi_k(v) \, L^{k-\mathrm{dw}} \, \pi'_k(v)$. Since, for given $A$ and $k \geq 1$, lookahead downward simulations are closed under union, there exists a unique maximal one that we call *the k-lookahead downward simulation on A*, denoted by $\sqsubseteq^{k-\mathrm{dw}}$. While $\sqsubseteq^{k-\mathrm{dw}}$ is trivially reflexive, it is not transitive in general (cf. [13], Appendix B). Since we only use it as a means to under-approximate the transitive trace inclusion relation $\subseteq^{\mathrm{dw}}$

(and require a preorder to induce an equivalence), we work with its transitive closure $\preceq^{k\text{-}dw} := (\sqsubseteq^{k\text{-}dw})^+$. In particular, $\preceq^{k\text{-}dw} \subseteq \subseteq^{dw}$.

**Lookahead Upward Simulation.** Let $A = (\Sigma, Q, \delta, I)$ be a TDTA. A *k-lookahead upward simulation* on $A$ induced by a relation $R$ is a binary relation $L^{k-up}(R)$ on $Q$ s.t. if $q\ L^{k-up}(R)\ r$, then $(q = \psi \implies r = \psi)$ and the following holds: Let $\pi$ be a run over a tree $t \in \mathbb{T}(\Sigma)$ with $\pi(v) = q$ for some bottom leaf $v$ s.t. either $|v| = k$ or $0 < |v| < k$ and $\pi(\epsilon)$ is upward-deadlocked (i.e., no more upward transitions exist).

Then there must exist $v', v''$ such that $v = v'v''$ and $|v''| \geq 1$ and a run $\pi'$ over $t_{v'}$ s.t. the following holds. (1) $\pi'(v'') = r$, (2) $\pi(v')\ L^{k-up}(R)\ \pi'(\epsilon)$, (3) $\pi(v'x) \in I \implies \pi'(x) \in I$ for all prefixes $x$ of $v''$, (4) If $v'xy \in dom(\pi)$ for some strict prefix $x$ of $v''$ and some $y \in \mathbb{N}$ where $xy$ is not a prefix of $v''$ then $\pi(v'xy)\ R\ \pi'(xy)$.

Since, for given $A$, $k \geq 1$ and $R$, lookahead upward simulations are closed under union, there exists a unique maximal one that we call *the k-lookahead upward simulation induced by $R$ on $A$*, denoted by $\sqsubseteq^{k-up}(R)$. Since both $R$ and $\sqsubseteq^{k-up}(R)$ are not necessarily transitive, we first compute its transitive closure, $R^+$, and we then compute $\preceq^{k-up}(R) := (\sqsubseteq^{k-up}(R^+))^+$, which under-approximates the upward trace inclusion $\subseteq^{up}(R^+)$.

# 7   Experiments

Our tree automata reduction algorithm (tool available [7]) combines transition pruning techniques (Sect. 4) with quotienting techniques (Sect. 5). Trace inclusions are under-approximated by lookahead simulations (Sect. 6) where higher lookaheads are harder to compute but yield better approximations. The parameters $x, y \geq 1$ describe the lookahead for downward/upward lookahead simulations, respectively. Downward lookahead simulation is harder to compute than upward lookahead simulation, since the number of possible moves is doubly exponential in $x$ (due to the downward branching of the tree) while for upward-simulation it is only single exponential in $y$. We use $(x, y)$ as $(1, 1)$, $(2, 4)$ and $(3, 7)$.

Besides pruning and quotienting, we also use the operation $RU$ that removes useless states, i.e., states that either cannot be reached from any initial state or from which no tree can be accepted. Let $Op(x, y)$ be the following sequence of operations on tree automata: $RU$, quotienting with $\preceq^{x\text{-}dw}$, pruning with $P(id, \prec^{x\text{-}dw})$, $RU$, quotienting with $\preceq^{y\text{-}up}(id)$, pruning with $P(\prec^{y\text{-}up}(id), id)$, pruning with $P(\sqsubseteq^{up}(id), \preceq^{x\text{-}dw})$, $RU$, quotienting with $\preceq^{y\text{-}up}(id)$, pruning with $P(\preceq^{y\text{-}up}(\sqsubseteq^{dw}), \sqsubseteq^{dw})$, $RU$. It is language preserving by the Theorems of Sects. 4 and 5. The order of the operations is chosen according to some considerations of efficiency. (No order is ideal for all instances.)

Our algorithm $Heavy(1, 1)$ just iterates $Op(1, 1)$ until a fixpoint is reached. For efficiency reasons, the general algorithm $Heavy(x, y)$ does not iterate $Op(x, y)$, but uses a double loop: it iterates the sequence $Heavy(1, 1)\,Op(x, y)$ until a fixpoint is reached.

We compare the reduction performance of several algorithms.

**RU:** *RU*. (Previously present in `libvata`.)
**RUQ:** *RU* and quotienting with $\sqsubseteq^{dw}$. (Previously present in `libvata`.)
**RUQP:** **RUQ**, plus pruning with $P(id, \sqsubseteq^{dw})$. (Not in `libvata`, but simple.)
**Heavy:** *Heavy*$(1,1)$, *Heavy*$(2,4)$ and *Heavy*$(3,7)$. (New.)

We tested these algorithms on three sets of automata from the `libvata` distribution. The first set are 27 moderate-sized automata (87 states and 816 transitions on avg.) derived from regular model checking applications. Heavy(1,1), on avg., reduced the number of states and transitions *to* 27 % and 14 % of the original sizes, resp. (Note the difference between 'to' and 'by'.) In contrast, RU did not perform any reduction in any case, RUQ, on avg., reduced the number of states and transitions only to 81 % and 80 % of the original sizes and RUQP reduced the number of states and transitions to 81 % and 32 % of the original sizes; cf. Fig. 2. The average computation times of Heavy(1,1), RUQP, RUQ and RU were, respectively, 0.05 s, 0.03 s, 0.006 s and 0.001 s.

The second set are 62 larger automata (586 states and 8865 transitions, on avg.) derived from regular model checking applications. Heavy(1,1), on avg., reduced the number of states and transitions *to* 4.2 % and 0.7 % of the original sizes. In contrast, RU did not perform any reduction in any case, RUQ, on avg., reduced the number of states and transitions to 75.2 % and 74.8 % of the original sizes and RUQP reduced the number of states and transitions to 75.2 % and 15.8 % of the original sizes [8]. The average computation times of Heavy(1,1), RUQP, RUQ and RU were, respectively, 2.7 s, 2.1 s, 0.2 s and 0.02 s.

The third set are 14,498 automata (57 states and 266 transitions on avg.) from the shape analysis tool Forester [23]. Heavy(1,1), on avg., reduced the number of states/transitions *to* 76.4 % and 67.9 % of the original, resp. RUQ and RUQP reduced the states and transitions only to 94 % and 88 %, resp. The average computation times of Heavy(1,1), RUQP, RUQ and RU were, respectively, 0.21 s, 0.014 s, 0.004 s, and 0.0006 s.

Due to the particular structure of the automata in these 3 sample sets, *Heavy*$(2,4)$ and *Heavy*$(3,7)$ had hardly any advantage over *Heavy*$(1,1)$. However, in general they can perform significantly better.

We also tested the algorithms on randomly generated tree automata, according to a generalization of the Tabakov-Vardi model of random word automata [24]. Given parameters $n, s$, $td$ (transition density) and $ad$ (acceptance density), it generates tree automata with $n$ states, $s$ symbols (each of rank 2), $n * td$ randomly assigned transitions for each symbol, and $n * ad$ randomly assigned leaf rules. Figure 3 shows the results of reducing automata of varying $td$ with different methods.

# 8    Summary and Conclusion

The tables in Figs. 4 and 5 summarize all our results on pruning and quotienting, respectively. Note that negative results propagate to larger relations and positive results propagate to smaller relations (i.e., GFP/GFQ is downward closed).

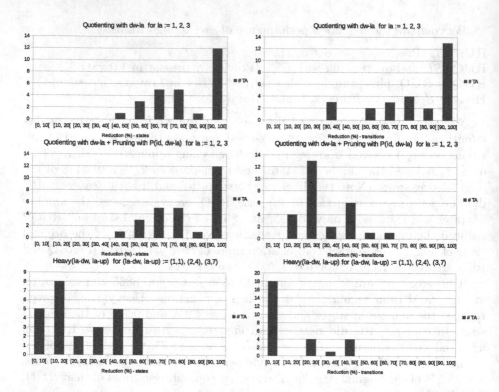

**Fig. 2.** Reduction of 27 moderate-sized tree automata by methods RUQ (top row), RUQP (middle row), and Heavy (bottom row). A bar of height $h$ at an interval $[x, x+10[$ means that $h$ of the 27 automata were reduced to a size between $x\%$ and $(x+10)\%$ of their original size. The reductions in the numbers of states/transitions are shown on the left/right, respectively. On this set of automata, the methods Heavy(2,4) and Heavy(3,7) gave exactly the same results as Heavy(1,1).

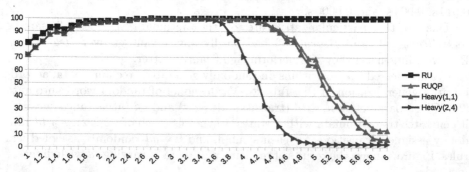

**Fig. 3.** Reduction of Tabakov-Vardi random tree automata with $n = 100, s = 2$ and $ad = 0.8$. The $x$-axis gives the transition density $td$, and the $y$-axis gives the average number of states after reduction with the various methods (smaller is better). Each data point is the average of 400 random automata. Note that Heavy(2,4) reduces much better than Heavy(1,1) for $td \geq 3.5$. Computing Heavy(x,y) for even higher $x, y$ is very slow on (some instances of) random automata.

| $R_u \backslash R_i$ | | $R_d$ | | | | |
|---|---|---|---|---|---|---|
| | | $id$ | $\sqsubset^{dw}$ | $\sqsubseteq^{dw}$ | $\subset^{dw}$ | $\subseteq^{dw}$ |
| $id$ | $id$ | − | ✓ | − | ✓ | − |
| $\sqsubset^{up}$ | $id$ | ✓ | ✓ | ✓ | ✓ | ✓ |
| | $\sqsubset^{dw}$ | × | ✓ | × | × | × |
| | $\sqsubseteq^{dw}$ | × | ✓ | × | × | × |
| | downup-rel. | ✓ | ✓ | ✓ | ✓ | ✓ |
| | $\subset^{dw}$ | × | × | × | × | × |
| | $\subseteq^{dw}$ | × | × | × | × | × |
| $\sqsubseteq^{up}$ | $id$ | − | ✓ | − | × | − |
| | $\sqsubset^{dw}$ | − | ✓ | − | × | − |
| | $\sqsubseteq^{dw}$ | − | ✓ | − | × | − |
| | $\subset^{dw}$ | − | × | − | × | − |
| | $\subseteq^{dw}$ | − | × | − | × | − |
| $\subset^{up}$ | $id$ | ✓ | ✓ | × | × | × |
| | $\sqsubset^{dw}$ | × | ✓ | × | × | × |
| | $\sqsubseteq^{dw}$ | × | ✓ | × | × | × |
| | $\subset^{dw}$ | × | × | × | × | × |
| | $\subseteq^{dw}$ | × | × | × | × | × |
| $\subseteq^{up}$ | $id$ | − | ✓ | − | × | − |
| | $\sqsubset^{dw}$ | − | ✓ | − | × | − |
| | $\sqsubseteq^{dw}$ | − | ✓ | − | × | − |
| | $\subset^{dw}$ | − | × | − | × | − |
| | $\subseteq^{dw}$ | − | × | − | × | − |

| | $R$ | |
|---|---|---|
| | $\subseteq^{dw}$ | ✓ |
| | $\sqsubseteq^{dw}$ | ✓ |
| $\sqsubseteq^{up}$ | $id$ | ✓ |
| | $\sqsubset^{dw}$ | − |
| | $\sqsubseteq^{dw}$ | × |
| | $\subset^{dw}$ | − |
| | $\subseteq^{dw}$ | × |
| $\subseteq^{up}$ | $id$ | ✓ |
| | $\sqsubset^{dw}$ | − |
| | $\sqsubseteq^{dw}$ | × |
| | $\subset^{dw}$ | − |
| | $\subseteq^{dw}$ | × |

**Fig. 4.** GFP relations $P(R_u(R_i), R_d)$ for tree automata. Relations which are GFP are marked with ✓, those which are not are marked with × and − is used to mark relations where the test does not apply due to them being reflexive (and therefore not asymmetric).

**Fig. 5.** GFQ relations $R$ for tree automata. Relations which are GFQ are marked with ✓ and those which are not are marked with ×. The relations marked with − are not even reflexive in general (unless all transitions are linear; in this case we have a word automaton and these relations are the same as $\sqsubseteq^{up}(id)$ and $\subseteq^{up}(id)$, respectively).

The experiments show that our Heavy(x,y) algorithm can significantly reduce the size of many classes of nondeterministic tree automata, and that it is sufficiently fast to handle instances with hundreds of states and thousands of transitions.

# References

1. Abdulla, P.A., Bouajjani, A., Holík, L., Kaati, L., Vojnar, T.: Computing simulations over tree automata. In: Ramakrishnan, C.R., Rehof, J. (eds.) TACAS 2008. LNCS, vol. 4963, pp. 93–108. Springer, Heidelberg (2008)
2. Abdulla, P.A., Chen, Y.-F., Holík, L., Mayr, R., Vojnar, T.: When simulation meets antichains. In: Esparza, J., Majumdar, R. (eds.) TACAS 2010. LNCS, vol. 6015, pp. 158–174. Springer, Heidelberg (2010)

3. Abdulla, P.A., Holík, L., Jonsson, B., Lengál, O., Trinh, C.Q., Vojnar, T.: Verification of heap manipulating programs with ordered data by extended forest automata. In: Van Hung, D., Ogawa, M. (eds.) ATVA 2013. LNCS, vol. 8172, pp. 224–239. Springer, Heidelberg (2013)

4. Abdulla, P.A., Holík, L., Kaati, L., Vojnar, T.: A uniform (bi-)simulation-based framework for reducing tree automata. Electr. Notes Theor. Comput. Sci. **251**, 27–48 (2009)

5. Abdulla, P.A., Legay, A., d'Orso, J., Rezine, A.: Simulation-based iteration of tree transducers. In: Halbwachs, N., Zuck, L.D. (eds.) TACAS 2005. LNCS, vol. 3440, pp. 30–44. Springer, Heidelberg (2005)

6. Abdulla, P.A., Legay, A., d'Orso, J., Rezine, A.: Tree regular model checking: a simulation-based approach. J. Log. Algebr. Program. **69**(1–2), 93–121 (2006)

7. Almeida, R., Holík, L., Mayr, R.: HeavyMinOTAut (2015). http://tinyurl.com/pm2b4qk

8. Almeida, R., Holík, L., Mayr, R.: Reduction of nondeterministic tree automata. Technical report EDI-INF-RR-1421, University of Edinburgh (2016). arXiv 1512.08823

9. Basin, D., Karlund, N., Møller, A.: Mona (2015). http://www.brics.dk/mona

10. Bonchi, F., Pous, D.: Checking NFA equivalence with bisimulations up to congruence. In: Principles of Programming Languages (POPL), Rome, Italy. ACM (2013)

11. Bouajjani, A., Habermehl, P., Holík, L., Touili, T., Vojnar, T.: Antichain-based universality and inclusion testing over nondeterministic finite tree automata. In: Ibarra, O.H., Ravikumar, B. (eds.) CIAA 2008. LNCS, vol. 5148, pp. 57–67. Springer, Heidelberg (2008)

12. Bouajjani, A., Habermehl, P., Rogalewicz, A., Vojnar, T.: Abstract regular tree model checking of complex dynamic data structures. In: Yi, K. (ed.) SAS 2006. LNCS, vol. 4134, pp. 52–70. Springer, Heidelberg (2006)

13. Clemente, L., Mayr, R.: Advanced automata minimization. In: 40th Annual ACM SIGPLAN-SIGACT Symposium on Principles of Programming Languages, POPL, pp. 63–74. ACM (2013)

14. Comon, H., Dauchet, M., Gilleron, R., Löding, C., Jacquemard, F., Lugiez, D., Tison, S., Tommasi, M.: Tree automata techniques and applications (2008). http://www.grappa.univ-lille3.fr/tata. Release 18 November 2008

15. Durand, I.: Autowrite (2015). http://dept-info.labri.fr/~idurand/autowrite

16. Genet, T., et al.: Timbuk (2015). http://www.irisa.fr/celtique/genet/timbuk/

17. Etessami, K.: A hierarchy of polynomial-time computable simulations for automata. In: Brim, L., Jančar, P., Křetínský, M., Kučera, A. (eds.) CONCUR 2002. LNCS, vol. 2421, pp. 131–144. Springer, Heidelberg (2002)

18. Habermehl, P., Holík, L., Rogalewicz, A., Šimáček, J., Vojnar, T.: Forest automata for verification of heap manipulation. In: Gopalakrishnan, G., Qadeer, S. (eds.) CAV 2011. LNCS, vol. 6806, pp. 424–440. Springer, Heidelberg (2011)

19. Holík, L.: Simulations and Antichains for Efficient Handling of Finite Automata. Ph.D. thesis, Faculty of Information Technology of Brno University of Technology (2011)

20. Holík, L., Lengál, O., Rogalewicz, A., Šimáček, J., Vojnar, T.: Fully automated shape analysis based on forest automata. In: Sharygina, N., Veith, H. (eds.) CAV 2013. LNCS, vol. 8044, pp. 740–755. Springer, Heidelberg (2013)

21. Holík, L., Lengál, O., Šimáček, J., Vojnar, T.: Efficient inclusion checking on explicit and semi-symbolic tree automata. In: Bultan, T., Hsiung, P.-A. (eds.) ATVA 2011. LNCS, vol. 6996, pp. 243–258. Springer, Heidelberg (2011)

22. Lengál, O., Simácek, J., Vojnar, T.: Libvata: highly optimised non-deterministic finite tree automata library (2015). http://www.fit.vutbr.cz/research/groups/verifit/tools/libvata/

23. Lengál, O., Simácek; J., Vojnar, T., Habermehl, P., Holík, L., Rogalewicz, A.: Forester: tool for verification of programs with pointers (2015). http://www.fit.vutbr.cz/research/groups/verifit/tools/forester/

24. Tabakov, D., Vardi, M.: Model Checking Büchi Specifications. In LATA, volume Report 35/07. Research Group on Mathematical Linguistics, Universitat Rovira i Virgili, Tarragona (2007)

# Online Timed Pattern Matching
# Using Derivatives

Dogan Ulus[1(✉)], Thomas Ferrère[1], Eugene Asarin[2], and Oded Maler[1]

[1] VERIMAG Université Grenoble-Alpes/CNRS, Grenoble, France
dogan.ulus@imag.fr
[2] IRIF, Université Paris Diderot/CNRS, Paris, France

**Abstract.** Timed pattern matching consists in finding all segments of
a dense-time Boolean signal that match a pattern defined by a timed
regular expression. This problem has been formulated and solved in [17]
via an offline algorithm that takes the signal and expression as inputs
and produces the set of all matches, represented as a finite union of
two-dimensional zones. In this work we develop an *online* version of
this approach where the input signal is presented incrementally and the
matching is computed incrementally as well.

Naturally, the concept of derivatives of regular expressions due to
Brzozowski [6] can play a role in defining what remains to match after
having read a prefix of the signal. However the adaptation of this concept
is not a straightforward for two reasons: the dense infinite-state nature of
timed behaviors and the fact that we are interested in matching, not only
in prefix acceptance. To resolve these issues we develop an alternative
theory of signals and expressions based on *absolute time* and show how
derivatives are defined and computed in this setting. We then implement
an online timed pattern matching algorithm based on these results.

## 1 Introduction

Timed regular expressions (TRE), introduced in [3,4], constitute a formalism for
expressing patterns in timed behaviors in a compact and natural way. They augment classical regular expressions with timing constraints and as such they provide
an alternative specification style to real-time temporal logics such as MTL [10]. We
believe that such expressions have numerous applications in many domains such as
runtime verification, robotics, medical monitoring and circuit analysis [7,9].

For a given expression $\varphi$ and input signal $w$, *timed pattern matching* means
computing the match set $\mathcal{M}(\varphi, w)$ consisting of all pairs $(t, t')$ of time instants
such that the segment of $w$ between $t$ and $t'$ satisfies the expression $\varphi$. In [17] we
showed how to compute $\mathcal{M}(\varphi, w)$ offline, assuming the input signal to be completely available before the matching. In this paper we develop an *online* matching
algorithm where the input is presented incrementally and matches are computed
on the fly. An online procedure can be used to monitor real systems during their
actual executions (in contrast with monitoring simulations) and alert the user in

© Springer-Verlag Berlin Heidelberg 2016
M. Chechik and J.-F. Raskin (Eds.): TACAS 2016, LNCS 9636, pp. 736–751, 2016.
DOI: 10.1007/978-3-662-49674-9_47

real time. In addition, an online procedure can reduce memory requirements, discarding signals and intermediate matches when those are no longer needed.

The online pattern matching procedure that we develop in this paper is built upon the notion of derivatives of regular expressions, introduced by Brzozowski in 1964 [6]. In essence, the derivative of an expression with respect to a letter or word, tells us what remains to be observed in order to reach acceptance. In this sense it is very similar to the tableaux construction used to build automata from temporal logic formulae. Derivatives provide an elegant solution for problems of language membership [14], pattern matching [13,16] and automaton construction [1,5,6] and have been observed to be naturally suitable for monitoring behaviors of systems [12,15]. The original notion of the derivative that we recall in Sect. 2 is based on discrete time and requires a careful adaptation to dense time. Moreover, as we will explain, matching is more complex than acceptance (of the word or its prefixes) and this has some implications on associating derivatives with rewrite rules.

In Sect. 3 we modify the definition of signals, one of the commonly-used formalisms to express timed behaviors, so as to lift the theory of derivatives to the timed setting. Signals (and sequences) are traditionally defined to start at time zero and when two signals are concatenated as in $w = u \cdot v$, the second argument $v$ is shifted forward in time, to start at the end of $u$. In contrast, we define signals in absolute time, each having its own fixed starting point. In this setting concatenation becomes a *partial* function, defined only when the domains of definition of the two signals fit. We also introduce a special place holder symbol ✓ and define extended signals where all letters in some prefix have been replaced by this symbol.

We then adapt timed regular expressions to represent sets of extended signals using the absolute time semantics. The regular expressions of [3,4,17] are obtained as a syntactic sub-class denoting "pure" ✓-free signals, used for the initial specification. The more general expressions are used to represent intermediate stages during the incremental computation of the match set.

In Sect. 4 we introduce our main technical contribution: the definition and computation of derivatives of left-reduced timed regular expressions with respect to a constant signal of arbitrary duration and all its factors. We apply this result to solve the problem of online timed pattern matching in Sect. 5 where we observe an input signal consisting of a finite concatenation of constant signals. We give a complete example of a run of our algorithm and briefly mention our implementation and its performance.

## 2    Preliminaries

Let $\Sigma^*$ be the set of all finite words over alphabet $\Sigma$ with $\epsilon$ denoting the empty word. A language $\mathcal{L}$ over $\Sigma$ is a subset of $\Sigma^*$. The syntax of regular expressions over $\Sigma$ is given by the following grammar:

$$r := \varnothing \mid \epsilon \mid a \mid r_1 \cdot r_2 \mid r_1 \vee r_2 \mid r^*$$

where $a \in \Sigma$. A regular expression $r$ specifies a regular language $[\![r]\!]$, inductively defined as follows:

$$[\![\varnothing]\!] = \varnothing \qquad [\![r_1 \cdot r_2]\!] = [\![r_1]\!] \cdot [\![r_2]\!]$$
$$[\![\epsilon]\!] = \{\epsilon\} \qquad [\![r_1 \vee r_2]\!] = [\![r_1]\!] \cup [\![r_2]\!]$$
$$[\![a]\!] = \{a\} \qquad [\![r^*]\!] = [\![r]\!]^*$$

In some cases it is important to determine whether or not the language of a regular expression $r$ contains the empty word $\epsilon$. For this purpose an empty word extraction function $\nu$ (also known as the nullability predicate) is defined such as

$$\nu(r) = \begin{cases} \epsilon & \text{if } \epsilon \in [\![r]\!] \\ \varnothing & \text{otherwise} \end{cases}$$

This function which extracts $\epsilon$ from $r$ if it exists, is computed inductively by the following rules:

$$\nu(\varnothing) = \varnothing \qquad \nu(r_1 \cdot r_2) = \nu(r_1) \cdot \nu(r_2)$$
$$\nu(\epsilon) = \epsilon \qquad \nu(r_1 \vee r_2) = \nu(r_1) \vee \nu(r_2)$$
$$\nu(a) = \varnothing \qquad \nu(r^*) = \epsilon$$

**Definition 1 (Derivative).** *The derivative of a language $\mathcal{L}$ with respect to a word $u$ is defined as*

$$D_u(\mathcal{L}) := \{ v \in \Sigma^* \mid u \cdot v \in \mathcal{L} \}.$$

In [6] Brzozowski applied the notion of derivatives to regular expressions and proved that the derivative $D_a(r)$ of an expression $r$ with respect to a letter $a$ can be computed recursively using the following syntactic rewrite rules:

$$D_a(\varnothing) = \varnothing \qquad D_a(r_1 \cdot r_2) = D_a(r_1) \cdot r_2 \vee \nu(r_1) \cdot D_a(r_2)$$
$$D_a(\epsilon) = \varnothing \qquad D_a(r_1 \vee r_2) = D_a(r_1) \vee D_a(r_2)$$
$$D_a(a) = \epsilon \qquad\qquad D_a(r^*) = D_a(r) \cdot r^*$$
$$D_a(b) = \varnothing$$

These rules are extended for words by letting $D_{a \cdot w}(r) = D_w(D_a(r))$. By definition, membership $w \in \mathcal{L}$ is equivalent to $\epsilon \in D_w(\mathcal{L})$. Hence to check, for example, whether $abc$ is in the language of the expression $\varphi = a^* \cdot (b \cdot c)^*$ we compute $D_{abc}(\varphi) = D_c(D_b(D_a(\varphi))) = (b \cdot c)^*$ as follows:

$$a^* \cdot (b \cdot c)^* \xrightarrow[D_a]{} a^* \cdot (b \cdot c)^* \xrightarrow[D_b]{} c \cdot (b \cdot c)^* \xrightarrow[D_c]{} (b \cdot c)^*,$$

and since $\nu((b \cdot c)^*) = \epsilon$, $abc \in [\![\varphi]\!]$.

It is of course not a coincidence that this procedure resembles the reading of the word by an automaton where derivatives correspond to states and those that contain $\epsilon$ correspond to accepting states. Hence we can report membership in $[\![\varphi]\!]$ of $w$ as well as the membership of all its prefixes. We can do it incrementally as new letters arrive.

Matching is more involved as we are interested in the membership of all factors of $w$, starting at arbitrary positions. Thus, having read $j$ letters of $w$, the state of a matching algorithm should contain all the derivatives by $w[i..j]$, $i \leq j$. When letter $j+1$ is read, these derivatives are updated to become derivatives by $w[i..j+1]$, new matches are extracted and a new process for matches that start at $j+1$ is spawned. Table 1 illustrates the systematic application of derivatives to find segments of $w = abcbc$ that match $\varphi = a^* \cdot (b \cdot c)^*$. The table is indexed by the start position (rows) and end position (columns) of the segments with respect to which we derive. Derivatives that contain $\epsilon$ correspond to matches and their time indices constitute the match set $\{(1,1),(1,3),(1,5),(2,3),(2,5),(4,5)\}$. In a discrete finite-state setting there are finitely many such derivatives but this is not the case for timed systems.[1]

**Table 1.** Pattern matching using derivatives for $w = abcbc$ and $\varphi = a^* \cdot (b \cdot c)^*$. Entry $(i,j)$ represents the derivative with respect to $w[i,j]$. Derivatives containing $\epsilon$ are shaded with green. The state of an online matching algorithm after reading $j$ symbols is represented in column $j$.

| Symbols | $a$ | $b$ | $c$ | $b$ | $c$ |
|---|---|---|---|---|---|
| Positions | 1 | 2 | 3 | 4 | 5 |
| 1 | $\varphi \xrightarrow{D_a} a^* \cdot (b \cdot c)^*$ | $\xrightarrow{D_b} c \cdot (b \cdot c)^*$ | $\xrightarrow{D_c} (b \cdot c)^*$ | $\xrightarrow{D_b} c \cdot (b \cdot c)^*$ | $\xrightarrow{D_c} (b \cdot c)^*$ |
| 2 | | $\varphi \xrightarrow{D_b} c \cdot (b \cdot c)^*$ | $\xrightarrow{D_c} (b \cdot c)^*$ | $\xrightarrow{D_b} c \cdot (b \cdot c)^*$ | $\xrightarrow{D_c} (b \cdot c)^*$ |
| 3 | | | $\varphi \xrightarrow{D_c} \varnothing$ | $\xrightarrow{D_b} \varnothing$ | $\xrightarrow{D_c} \varnothing$ |
| 4 | | | | $\varphi \xrightarrow{D_b} c \cdot (b \cdot c)^*$ | $\xrightarrow{D_c} (b \cdot c)^*$ |
| 5 | | | | | $\varphi \xrightarrow{D_c} \varnothing$ |

In dense time, the analogue of the arrival of a new letter is the arrival of a constant segment of the signal $w[t_1, t_2]$. When this occurs, the state of the algorithm should be updated to capture all derivatives by segments of the form $w[t, t_2]$ for $t < t_2$ and all matches ending in some $t < t_2$ should be extracted. The technique for representing and manipulating such an uncountable number of derivative together with their corresponding time segments is the main contribution of this paper.

---

[1] To keep the survey within a reasonable size and avoid tedious repetitions, the description here is not fully rigorous, using the same notation for the *semantic* notion of a left quotient, which is unique for every language and word, and the *syntactic* notion of a derivative of a regular expression. The derivation of the minimal automaton from a regular expression, for example, requires additional rewrite rules to detect equivalence between different regular expressions.

# 3   Signals, Timed Languages and Expressions

We consider an alphabet $\Sigma = \mathbb{B}^m$ which is the set of valuations of a set of propositional variables $P = \{p_1 \ldots, p_m\}$. We define signals not as free floating objects but anchor them in absolute time.

**Definition 2 (Signals).** *A signal over an alphabet $\Sigma$ is a piecewise-constant function $w : [t_1, t_2) \longrightarrow \Sigma$, where $t_1 \leq t_2 \in \mathbb{R}_{\geq 0}$ and $w$ admits a finite number of discontinuities. The time domain of the signal and its beginning and end times are denoted as*

$$\mathrm{dom}(w) = [t_1, t_2) = [\tau_1(w), \tau_2(w)).$$

*The empty signal $\epsilon$ is the unique signal satisfying $\mathrm{dom}(w) = \emptyset$. The duration of $w$ is $|w| = \tau_2(w) - \tau_1(w)$ and $|\epsilon| = 0$. We often view the boundary points of a signal as a pair, $\tau(w) = (\tau_1(w), \tau_2(w))$.*

We use $w[t, t']$ to denote the restriction of $w$ to an interval $[t, t') \subseteq dom(w)$ and let $Sub(w) = \{w[t, t'] \mid \tau_1(w) \leq t < t' \leq \tau_2(w)\}$ be the set of sub-signals (factors, segments) of $w$. Concatenation is restricted to signals that meet, that is, one ends where the other starts.

**Definition 3 (Meets and Concatenation).** *Signal $w_1$ meets signal $w_2$ when $w_1 = \epsilon$ or $w_2 = \epsilon$ or $\tau_2(w_1) = \tau_1(w_2)$. Concatenation is a partial function such that $w_1 \cdot w_2$ is defined only if $w_1$ meets $w_2$:*

$$w_1 \cdot w_2(t) = \begin{cases} w_1(t) & \text{if } t \in \mathrm{dom}(w_1) \\ w_2(t) & \text{if } t \in \mathrm{dom}(w_2) \end{cases}$$

The empty signal $\epsilon$ is the neutral element for concatenation: $\epsilon \cdot w = w \cdot \epsilon = w$. The set of signals thus defined can be made a monoid by making concatenation total by introducing a new element $\bot$ and letting $w_1 \cdot w_2 = \bot$ when the signals do not meet. The newly introduced element is an absorbing zero satisfying $\bot \cdot w = w \cdot \bot = \bot$.

The variability (logical length) of a signal $w$ is the minimal $n$ such that $w$ can be written as $w = w_1 \cdot w_2 \cdots w_n$ where each $w_i$ is a constant signal. We use notations $\Sigma^{(*)}$, $\Sigma^{(+)}$ and $\Sigma^{(n)}$ to denote the set of all signals, non-empty signals and signals of variability $n$, respectively. In particular, $\Sigma^{(1)}$ is the set of all constant signals. Sets of signals are referred to as signal languages on which Boolean operations as well as concatenation and star are defined naturally. Finally we extend the *time restriction* operation of [4] which constrains the duration of signals, to apply also to their time domains. The language ${}^K_J\langle \mathcal{L} \rangle_I$ where $I, J, K$ are intervals of non-negative reals, is a subset of $\mathcal{L}$ consisting of signals with duration in $I$, beginning in $t_1 \in J$ and ending in $t_2 \in K$. We omit the corresponding interval when there is no restriction on beginning, ending or duration.

We are interested in representing a family of sub-signals of a $n$-variability signal $w = w_1 \ldots w_n$ starting in segment $i$ and ending in segment $j$, that is,

$Sub_{[i:j]}(w) := \{w[t, t'] \mid t \in dom(w_i) \text{ and } t' \in dom(w_j)\}$. It can be easily verified that

$$Sub_{[i:j]}(w) = Sub(w_i) \cdot w_{i+1} \cdots Sub(w_j) = Sub(w_i) \cdot Sub(w_{i+1}) \cdots Sub(w_j).$$

In the classical discrete setting, the derivative $D_a$ is associated with a rewrite rule $a \to \epsilon$ and a word $w$ is accepted if it can be transformed into $\epsilon$ by successive rewritings. For the purpose of timed matching we need a more length-preserving view where reading $a$ corresponds to a rule $a \to \checkmark$ where $\checkmark$ is a special place-holder that indicates that $a$ has been processed. Acceptance then corresponds to the rewriting of $w$ into a signal $w' : dom(w) \mapsto \checkmark$. We let $\Sigma_\checkmark = \Sigma \cup \{\checkmark\}$ and define extended signals which are signals over $\Sigma_\checkmark$, as well as some subclasses of those.

**Definition 4 (Extended Signals).** *An extended signal over alphabet $\Sigma$ is a function $w : [t, t') \to \Sigma_\checkmark$. An extended signal $w$ is left-reduced if $w \in \checkmark^{(*)} \cdot \Sigma^{(*)}$. A left-reduced signal $w$ is pure if $w \in \Sigma^{(*)}$ and reduced if $w \in \checkmark^{(*)}$.*

We use initial Greek letters to denote reduced signals and hence a left-reduced signal $w$ will be written as $w = \alpha \cdot v$ where $\alpha$ is a reduced signal and $v$ is a pure signal.

**Definition 5 (Left Reduction).** *A reduction rule $R(u)$ for a signal $u \in \Sigma^{(*)}$ is a pair $(u, \gamma)$ such that $\gamma \in \checkmark^{(*)}$ and $\mathrm{dom}(u) = \mathrm{dom}(\gamma)$. The left reduction of a left-reduced signal language $\mathcal{L}$ with respect to $u$ is:*

$$\delta_u(\mathcal{L}) := \{\ \alpha\gamma w \mid \alpha uw \in \mathcal{L},\ \alpha \in \checkmark^{(*)} \text{ and } w \in \Sigma^{(*)}\}$$

We use operation $\delta_u(\mathcal{L})$ in a similar way $D_u(\mathcal{L})$ is used in the classical setting but with one important difference. When $v = D_u(w)$ the length of the word is reduced, that is, $|v| = |w| - |u|$, while when $v = \delta_u(w)$ the domains (and hence durations) of $v$ and $w$ are the same. Consequently, unlike the classical case where membership of $w$ in $\mathcal{L}$ amounts to $\epsilon \in D_w(\mathcal{L})$, here the membership is equivalent to $\gamma \in \delta_w(\mathcal{L})$ where $\gamma$ is a reduced signal of the same domain as $w$. It is not difficult to check that $\delta_{u_1 \cdot u_2}(\mathcal{L}) = \delta_{u_2}(\delta_{u_1}(\mathcal{L}))$ and sometimes we denote by $\delta_S$ the left reduction with respect to a set of signals.

*Example 1.* Consider a signal language $\mathcal{L} = \{w_1, w_2\}$ such that

$$w_1(t) = \begin{cases} a & \text{if } t \in [0, 3) \\ b & \text{if } t \in [3, 5) \end{cases} \qquad w_2(t) = \begin{cases} a & \text{if } t \in [0, 2) \\ b & \text{if } t \in [2, 5) \end{cases}$$

In Fig. 1 we illustrate a left reduction operation $\delta_{u_3}(\delta_{u_2}(\delta_{u_1}(\mathcal{L}))) = \{w_1'''\}$ with respect to $u = u_1 u_2 u_3$ with $u_1 : [0, 1) \mapsto a$, $u_2 : [1, 3) \mapsto a$ and $u_3 : [3, 5) \mapsto b$. Since $w_1'''$ is a reduced signal and $\tau(u) = \tau(w_1''')$, $u \in \mathcal{L}$.

We now introduce timed regular expressions to describe sets of signals and extended signals using the absolute time semantics. Note that the intersection operator, which is considered a syntactic sugar in the classical theory, adds expressiveness in the timed setting [4].

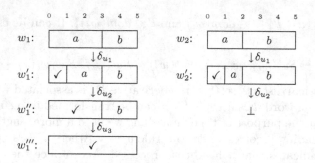

**Fig. 1.** A left reduction example.

**Definition 6 (Extended Timed Regular Expressions).** *Extended timed regular expressions are defined by the following grammar:*

$$\varphi := \varnothing \mid \epsilon \mid p \mid \checkmark \mid \varphi_1 \cdot \varphi_2 \mid \varphi_1 \vee \varphi_2 \mid \varphi_1 \wedge \varphi_2 \mid \varphi^* \mid {}^K_J \langle \varphi \rangle_I$$

*where $p$ is a proposional variable in $P$ and $I, J, K$ are intervals of $\mathbb{R}_{\geq 0}$.*

The semantics of the expressions is defined by the following rules (we use $a \models p$ to denote the fact that $p$ holds at $a$):

$$[\![\varnothing]\!] = \emptyset$$
$$[\![\epsilon]\!] = \{\epsilon\}$$
$$[\![p]\!] = \{w : [t, t') \to \Sigma \mid 0 \leq t < t' \text{ and } \forall t'' \in [t, t'). \ w(t'') \models p\}$$
$$[\![\checkmark]\!] = \{w : [t, t') \to \{\checkmark\} \mid 0 \leq t < t'\}$$
$$[\![\varphi \cdot \psi]\!] = [\![\varphi]\!] \cdot [\![\psi]\!]$$
$$[\![\varphi \vee \psi]\!] = [\![\varphi]\!] \cup [\![\psi]\!]$$
$$[\![\varphi \wedge \psi]\!] = [\![\varphi]\!] \cap [\![\psi]\!]$$
$$[\![\varphi^*]\!] = \bigcup_{i=0}^{\infty} [\![\varphi]\!]^i$$
$$[\![{}^K_J \langle \varphi \rangle_I]\!] = \{w \mid w \in [\![\varphi]\!], \ |w| \in I, \ w \neq \epsilon \to (\tau_1(w) \in J \wedge \tau_2(w) \in K)\}$$

A signal language is regular if it can be represented by a timed regular expression.

The syntax in Definition 6 allows to define sets including extended signals with arbitrary interleavings of letters and $\checkmark$. Below we define three syntactic classes of expressions. The first class, called pure (or original) timed regular expressions, corresponds almost the same syntax of expressions seen in [3,4,17]. Pure expressions are $\checkmark$-free and do not place any restriction on the absolute beginning and ending values over their sub-expressions. The second class is reduced timed regular expressions which is formed using the $\checkmark$ symbol only. Lastly we have left-reduced timed regular expressions, obtained as compositions of reduced and pure expressions satisfying some conditions.

**Definition 7 (Syntactic Classes).** *A timed regular expression $\varphi$ belongs to the classes of* reduced, pure *or* left-reduced *timed regular expressions if functions* $r?$, $p?$ *or* $lr?$, *respectively, evaluate to* true *in the following table.*

| Case | Reduced $r?(\varphi)$ | Pure $p?(\varphi)$ | Left-reduced $lr?(\varphi)$ |
|---|---|---|---|
| $\varnothing$ | $\top$ | $\top$ | $\top$ |
| $\epsilon$ | $\top$ | $\top$ | $\top$ |
| $p$ | $\bot$ | $\top$ | $\top$ |
| $\checkmark$ | $\top$ | $\bot$ | $\top$ |
| $\varphi_1 \cdot \varphi_2$ | $r?(\varphi_1) \wedge r?(\varphi_2)$ | $p?(\varphi_1) \wedge p?(\varphi_2)$ | $lr?(\varphi_1) \wedge p?(\varphi_2) \vee$ $r?(\varphi_1) \wedge lr?(\varphi_2)$ |
| $\varphi_1 \wedge \varphi_2$ | $r?(\varphi_1) \wedge r?(\varphi_2)$ | $p?(\varphi_1) \wedge p?(\varphi_2)$ | $lr?(\varphi_1) \wedge lr?(\varphi_2)$ |
| $\varphi_1 \vee \varphi_2$ | $r?(\varphi_1) \wedge r?(\varphi_2)$ | $p?(\varphi_1) \wedge p?(\varphi_2)$ | $lr?(\varphi_1) \wedge lr?(\varphi_2)$ |
| $\varphi^*$ | $r?(\varphi)$ | $p?(\varphi)$ | $r?(\varphi) \vee p?(\varphi)$ |
| $\frac{K}{J}\langle\varphi\rangle_I$ | $r?(\varphi)$ | $p?(\varphi) \wedge J = K = [0,\infty)$ | $lr?(\varphi)$ |

Trivially any reduced expression $\psi$ and any pure expression $\varphi$ represent reduced and pure signal languages such that $[\![\psi]\!] \subseteq \checkmark^{(*)}$ and $[\![\varphi]\!] \subseteq \Sigma^{(*)}$. For left-reduced expressions we do not allow concatenation and star operations on arbitrary left-reduced expressions as in Definition 7 because left-reduced languages are not closed under concatenation. By doing that we have the following result.

**Proposition 1.** *The language $[\![\varphi]\!]$ of a left-reduced timed regular expression $\varphi$ is an extended signal language such that $[\![\varphi]\!] \subseteq \checkmark^{(*)} \cdot \Sigma^{(*)}$.*

*Proof.* For the concatenation $\varphi_1 \cdot \varphi_2$ we have two possibilities: (1) $[\![\varphi_1]\!] \subset \checkmark^{(*)} \cdot \Sigma^{(*)}$ and $[\![\varphi_2]\!] \subset \Sigma^{(*)}$; (2) $[\![\varphi_1]\!] \subset \checkmark^{(*)}$ and $[\![\varphi_2]\!] \subset \checkmark^{(*)} \cdot \Sigma^{(*)}$. For both possibilities, we have $[\![\varphi_1 \cdot \varphi_2]\!] = [\![\varphi_1]\!] \cdot [\![\varphi_2]\!] \subset \checkmark^{(*)} \cdot \Sigma^{(*)}$. Other cases are straightforward by following the definitions.

A comprehensive study on regular algebra extended with intersection operation can be found in [2]. We now mention some algebraic rules relative to the time restriction operator. It is shown in [17] how the right hand side of following equations can be computed from the corresponding left hand side.

$$\frac{K_1}{J_1}\langle\checkmark\rangle_{I_1} \cdot \frac{K_2}{J_2}\langle\checkmark\rangle_{I_2} = \frac{K_3}{J_3}\langle\checkmark\rangle_{I_3} \quad \text{and} \quad \frac{K_1}{J_1}\langle\checkmark\rangle_{I_1} \wedge \frac{K_2}{J_2}\langle\checkmark\rangle_{I_2} = \frac{K_3}{J_3}\langle\checkmark\rangle_{I_3}$$

for some intervals $I_3$, $J_3$ and $K_3$, and

$$\left(\bigvee_{i=1}^{m} \frac{K_i}{J_i}\langle\checkmark\rangle_{I_i}\right)^{+} = \bigvee_{i=1}^{n} \frac{K_i'}{J_i'}\langle\checkmark\rangle_{I_i'} \quad \text{for some } m,n \in \mathbb{N}$$

Therefore we can simplify timed regular expressions further using these equations and procedures.

# 4  Derivatives of Left-Reduced Timed Regular Expressions

We now introduce, semantically and syntactically, a derivative operation for left-reduced signal languages and expressions based on the left reduction operation. Since our goal is to solve the dense time matching problem, we have to operate on sets of signals and define derivatives more symbolically. Therefore we define the derivative $\Delta_v$ to correspond to the left reduction with respect to all factors of $v$.

**Definition 8 (Dense Derivative).** *The derivative $\Delta_v(\mathcal{L})$ of a left-reduced language $\mathcal{L}$ with respect to a constant signal $v \in \Sigma^{(1)}$ is defined as follows:*

$$\Delta_v(\mathcal{L}) := \bigcup_{u \in Sub(v)} \delta_u(\mathcal{L})$$

As mentioned previously, reduced signals will provide the output of our matching procedure. Their existence will be the witness of a match and their time domains will indicate its position in the signal.

**Definition 9 (Extraction).** *The extraction $xt(\mathcal{L})$ of a left-reduced signal language $\mathcal{L}$ is*

$$xt(\mathcal{L}) := \{ \alpha \mid \alpha \in \checkmark^{(*)} \cap \mathcal{L} \}$$

The following result shows that xt can be computed syntactically for left-reduced timed regular expressions.

**Theorem 1 (Extraction Computation).** *For a given left-reduced timed regular expression $\varphi$, applying the following rules recursively yields an expression $\psi$ such that $[\![\psi]\!] = xt([\![\varphi]\!])$.*

$$
\begin{aligned}
xt(\varnothing) &= \varnothing & xt(\psi_1 \cdot \psi_2) &= xt(\psi_1) \cdot xt(\psi_2) \\
xt(\epsilon) &= \epsilon & xt(\psi_1 \vee \psi_2) &= xt(\psi_1) \vee xt(\psi_2) \\
xt(p) &= \varnothing & xt(\psi_1 \wedge \psi_2) &= xt(\psi_1) \wedge xt(\psi_2) \\
xt(\checkmark) &= \checkmark & xt(_J^K \langle \psi \rangle_I) &= {}_J^K \langle xt(\psi) \rangle_I \\
& & xt(\psi^*) &= (xt(\psi))^*
\end{aligned}
$$

*Proof.* We proceed by induction and only look at the case of concatenation, other cases are similar. For any expressions $\varphi_1$, $\varphi_2$ it holds

$$
\begin{aligned}
[\![xt(\varphi_1 \cdot \varphi_2)]\!] &= \{\alpha \mid \alpha \in \checkmark^{(*)} \text{ and } \alpha \in [\![\varphi_1 \cdot \varphi_2]\!]\} \\
&= \{\alpha_1\alpha_2 \mid \alpha_1, \alpha_2 \in \checkmark^{(*)}, \ \alpha_1 \in [\![\varphi_1]\!] \text{ and } \alpha_2 \in [\![\varphi_2]\!]\} \\
&= \{\alpha_1 \mid \alpha_1 \in \checkmark^{(*)} \text{ and } \alpha_1 \in [\![\varphi_1]\!]\} \cdot \{\alpha_2 \mid \alpha_2 \in \checkmark^{(*)} \text{ and } \alpha_2 \in [\![\varphi_2]\!]\} \\
&= [\![xt(\varphi_1)]\!] \cdot [\![xt(\varphi_2)]\!]
\end{aligned}
$$

*Example 2.* Consider a left-reduced expression $\varphi := \langle \, _{[0,3]}^{[0,3]} \langle \checkmark \rangle_{[0,3]} \cdot p^* \rangle_{[0,2]}$. Applying Theorem 1 we extract from $\varphi$ a reduced expression $\psi$ such that $\psi = \langle \, _{[0,3]}^{[0,3]} \langle \checkmark \rangle_{[0,3]} \rangle_{[0,2]}$. Expression $\psi$ can be simplified further to $_{[0,3]}^{[0,3]} \langle \checkmark \rangle_{[0,2]}$.

We now state our main result concerning derivatives of left-reduced timed regular expressions.

**Theorem 2 (Derivative Computation).** *Given a left-reduced timed regular expression $\varphi$ and a constant signal $v : [t, t') \mapsto a$, applying the following rules yields an expression $\psi$ such that $[\![\psi]\!] = \Delta_v([\![\varphi]\!])$.*

$$\Delta_v(\varnothing) = \varnothing$$
$$\Delta_v(\epsilon) = \varnothing$$
$$\Delta_v(\checkmark) = \varnothing$$
$$\Delta_v(p) = \begin{cases} \Gamma \vee \Gamma \cdot p & \text{if } a \models p \text{ where } \Gamma := {}^{[t,t']}_{[t,t']}\langle\checkmark\rangle_{[0,t'-t]} \\ \varnothing & \text{otherwise} \end{cases}$$
$$\Delta_v(\psi_1 \cdot \psi_2) = \Delta_v(\psi_1) \cdot \psi_2 \vee xt(\psi_1 \vee \Delta_v(\psi_1)) \cdot \Delta_v(\psi_2)$$
$$\Delta_v(\psi_1 \vee \psi_2) = \Delta_v(\psi_1) \vee \Delta_v(\psi_2)$$
$$\Delta_v(\psi_1 \wedge \psi_2) = \Delta_v(\psi_1) \wedge \Delta_v(\psi_2)$$
$$\Delta_v({}^K_J\langle\psi\rangle_I) = {}^K_J\langle\Delta_v(\psi)\rangle_I$$
$$\Delta_v(\psi^*) = xt(\Delta_v(\psi))^* \cdot \Delta_v(\psi) \cdot \psi^*$$

*Proof.* By semantic definition $\Delta_v(\varphi) = \{ \alpha\gamma w \mid \alpha uw \in [\![\varphi]\!] \text{ and } (u,\gamma) \in \text{RSub}(v)\}$ where $\text{RSub}(v) := \{ R(u) \mid u \in \text{Sub}(v)\}$. We proceed by induction on the structure of $\varphi$. In the following we tend to use languages and expressions interchangeably, when in the interest of readability. Consider the cases:

- For $\varphi = \varnothing$, $\varphi = \epsilon$ and $\varphi = \checkmark$ : for all cases $\alpha uw \notin [\![\varphi]\!]$ therefore $\Delta_v(\varphi) = \varnothing$.
- For $\varphi = p$ : It needs that $\alpha = \epsilon$ and $u \in [\![p]\!]$. Then, $\alpha uw \in [\![p]\!]$ can be satisfied if either $w = \epsilon$ or $w \in [\![p]\!]$. By applying definitions, we get

$$\Delta_v(p) = \{ \gamma \mid u \in [\![p]\!] \text{ and } (u,\gamma) \in \text{RSub}(v)\} \cup$$
$$\{ \gamma w \mid u \in [\![p]\!], w \in [\![p]\!] \text{ and } (u,\gamma) \in \text{RSub}(v)\}$$
$$= \Gamma \vee \Gamma \cdot \{w \mid w \in [\![p]\!]\}$$
$$= \Gamma \vee \Gamma \cdot p$$

where the expression $\Gamma$ is ${}^{[t,t']}_{[t,t']}\langle\checkmark\rangle_{[0,t'-t]}$. Hence, we have $\Delta_v(p) = \Gamma \vee \Gamma \cdot p$ if $u \in [\![p]\!]$, otherwise $\Delta_v(p) = \varnothing$. The condition $u \in [\![p]\!]$ can be easily checked by testing $a \models p$.

- For $\varphi = \varphi_1 \cdot \varphi_2$ : $\alpha uw \in [\![\varphi_1 \cdot \varphi_2]\!]$ should be satisfied. There are three possibilities to split $\alpha uw$ in dense time:
  . It can be split up into $\alpha uw_1 \in [\![\varphi_1]\!]$ and $w_2 \in [\![\varphi_2]\!]$.

$$\Delta_v(\varphi) = \{\alpha\gamma w_1 w_2 \mid \alpha uw_1 \in [\![\varphi_1]\!], w_2 \in [\![\varphi_2]\!] \text{ and } (u,\gamma) \in \text{RSub}(v)\}$$
$$= \{\alpha\gamma w_1 \mid \alpha uw_1 \in [\![\varphi_1]\!] \text{ and } (u,\gamma) \in \text{RSub}(v)\} \cdot \{w_2 \mid w_2 \in [\![\varphi_2]\!]\}$$
$$= \Delta_v(\varphi_1) \cdot \varphi_2$$

  . It can be split up into $\alpha_1 \in [\![\varphi_1]\!]$ and $\alpha_2 uw \in [\![\varphi_2]\!]$.

$$\Delta_v(\varphi) = \{\alpha_1\alpha_2\gamma w \mid \alpha_1 \in [\![\varphi_1]\!], \alpha_2 uw \in [\![\varphi_2]\!] \text{ and } (u,\gamma) \in \text{RSub}(v)\}$$
$$= \{\alpha_1 \mid \alpha_1 \in [\![\varphi_1]\!]\} \cdot \{\alpha_2\gamma w \mid \alpha_2 uw \in [\![\varphi_2]\!] \text{ and } (u,\gamma) \in \text{RSub}(v)\}$$
$$= xt(\varphi_1) \cdot \Delta_v(\varphi_2)$$

. It can be split up into $\alpha u_1 \in [\![\varphi_1]\!]$ and $u_2 w \in [\![\varphi_2]\!]$. For this case, it is required by definitions that $\varphi_1$ is a left-reduced expression and $\varphi_2$ is a pure expression. This is the most involved case requiring to split reducing signals.

$$
\begin{aligned}
\Delta_v(\varphi) &= \{\alpha\gamma_1\gamma_2 w \mid \alpha u_1 \in [\![\varphi_1]\!], \ u_2 w \in [\![\varphi_2]\!] \text{ and } (u_1 u_2, \gamma_1\gamma_2) \in \mathrm{RSub}(v)\} \\
&= \{\alpha\gamma_1\gamma_2 w \mid \alpha u_1 \in [\![\varphi_1]\!], \ u_2 w \in [\![\varphi_2]\!], \ (u_1, \gamma_1) \in \mathrm{RSub}(v), \\
&\qquad (u_2, \gamma_2) \in \mathrm{RSub}(v) \text{ and } (u_1, \gamma_1) \text{ meets } (u_2, \gamma_2)\} \\
&= \{\alpha\gamma_1 \mid \alpha u_1 \in [\![\varphi_1]\!] \text{ and } (u_1, \gamma_1) \in \mathrm{RSub}(v)\} \cdot \\
&\qquad \{\gamma_2 w \mid u_2 w \in [\![\varphi_2]\!] \text{ and } (u_2, \gamma_2) \in \mathrm{RSub}(v)\} \\
&= \mathrm{xt}(\Delta_v(\varphi_1)) \cdot \Delta_v(\varphi_2)
\end{aligned}
$$

Thus $\Delta_v(\varphi_1 \cdot \varphi_2)$ can be found by the disjunction of these three cases. Then, by rearranging the last two cases, we obtain the equality claimed in the theorem.
- For $\varphi = \psi^*$: assume without loss of generality $\epsilon \notin \psi$. Then

$$
\begin{aligned}
\Delta_v(\psi^*) &= \Delta_v(\epsilon) \vee \Delta_v(\psi \cdot \psi^*) \\
&= \Delta_v(\psi) \cdot \psi^* \vee \mathrm{xt}(\psi) \cdot \Delta_v(\psi^*) \vee \mathrm{xt}(\Delta_v(\psi)) \cdot \Delta_v(\psi^*) \\
&= \Delta_v(\psi) \cdot \psi^* \vee \mathrm{xt}(\Delta_v(\psi)) \cdot \Delta_v(\psi^*) \\
&= [\epsilon \vee X \vee X^2 \vee \cdots \vee X^\infty] \cdot \Delta_v(\psi) \cdot \psi^* \text{ where } X = \mathrm{xt}(\Delta_v(\psi)) \\
&= \mathrm{xt}(\Delta_v(\psi))^* \cdot \Delta_v(\psi) \cdot \psi^*
\end{aligned}
$$

- Time restriction and Boolean operations follow definitions straightforwardly.

**Corollary 1.** *The derivative $\Delta_v(\varphi)$ of a left-reduced timed regular expression $\varphi$ with respect to a constant signal $v$ is a left-reduced timed regular expression.*

*Proof.* Theorem 2 shows that only finite number of regular operations is required to find the derivative and these equations satisfy requirements in Definition 7.

We extend derivatives for arbitrary signals by letting $\Delta_\epsilon(\varphi) = \varphi$ and

$$
\Delta_{v \cdot w}(\varphi) = \Delta_w(\Delta_v(\varphi)).
$$

**Lemma 1.** *The derivative $\Delta_w(\varphi)$ of a left-reduced timed regular expression $\varphi$ with respect to a signal $w = w_1 \ldots w_n$ with $n$ segments is equivalent to the left reduction of $\varphi$ with respect to the set of sub-signals of $w$ beginning in $\mathrm{dom}(w_1)$ and ending in $\mathrm{dom}(w_n)$.*

$$
\Delta_w(\varphi) = \bigcup_{u \in Sub_{[1:n]}(w)} \delta_u([\![\varphi]\!])
$$

*Proof.* Using definitions we directly have

$$
\begin{aligned}
\Delta_w(\varphi) &= \Delta_{w_n}(\Delta_{w_{n-1}}(\ldots(\Delta_{w_1}(\varphi)))) \\
&= \delta_{Sub(w_n)}(\delta_{Sub(w_{n-1})}(\ldots(\delta_{Sub(w_1)}([\![\varphi]\!])))) \\
&= \delta_{Sub(w_1) \cdot Sub(w_2) \ldots Sub(w_n)}([\![\varphi]\!]) \\
&= \delta_{Sub_{[1:n]}}([\![\varphi]\!])
\end{aligned}
$$

# 5    Application to Online Timed Pattern Matching

In this section we solve the problem of online timed pattern matching by applying concepts and results introduced in previous sections. Our online matching procedure assumes the input signal $w$ to be presented incrementally as follows. Let $w = w_1 w_2 \ldots w_n$ be an $n$-variability signal and at each step $j$ we read a new segment $w_j : [t_j, t'_j] \mapsto a_j$ where $a_j \in \Sigma$. After reading a new segment $w_j$ we may have new matches ending in $\mathrm{dom}(w_j)$ in addition to previously found matches. Therefore we define an incremental match set $\mathcal{M}_j(\varphi, w)$ consisting of matches ending in $\mathrm{dom}(w_j)$ and we say that $\mathcal{M}_j(\varphi, w)$ is the output of $j^{th}$ incremental step.

$$\mathcal{M}_j(\varphi, w) := \{\, \tau(s) \mid s \in [\![\varphi]\!],\ s \in Sub_{[i:j]}(w) \text{ and } 1 \leq i \leq j\}$$

We then define the state of the online timed pattern matching procedure at the step $j$ as a left-reduced timed regular expression.

**Definition 10 (The State of Online Procedure).** *Given a pure timed regular expression $\varphi$ the state of the online timed pattern matching procedure after reading a prefix $w_{1..j}$ of the input signal is:*

$$\psi_j := \bigvee_{1 \leq i \leq j} \Delta_{w_{i..j}}(\varphi)$$

Then, starting with $\psi_0 = \varphi$, we update the state upon reading $w_{j+1}$ by letting

$$\psi_{j+1} = \Delta_{w_{j+1}}(\psi_j) \vee \Delta_{w_{j+1}}(\varphi)$$

Now we show that the extraction of reduced signals from state $\psi_j$ provides the match set $\mathcal{M}_j(\varphi, w)$. We do not make a distinction here between a reduced signal $\alpha$ and its time domain $\tau(\alpha)$ as they stand for the same thing.

**Theorem 3.** *Given a state $\psi_j$ of an online matching procedure for expression $\varphi$ and a signal $w$, the incremental match set $\mathcal{M}_j(\varphi, w)$ is found by the extraction of the state:*

$$\mathcal{M}_j(\varphi, w) = xt(\psi_j)$$

*Proof.* Following Definition 10 and Lemma 1 we know the state $\psi_j$ represents a reduced language $\delta_S(\varphi)$ of $\varphi$ with respect to a set of signals $S$ satisfying $s \in \mathrm{Sub}(w)$ and $\tau_2(s) \in \mathrm{dom}(w_j)$. A reduced signal $\alpha$ in $\delta_S(\varphi)$ indicates the existence of a signal $s \in S$ such that $\tau(s) = \tau(\alpha)$ and $s \in [\![\varphi]\!]$, thus $s$ is a match. Then we can find the match set $\mathcal{M}_j$ by extracting all reduced signals from the state $\psi_j$.

Theorem 3 allows us to have a complete procedure for online timed pattern matching for given $\varphi$ and an input signal $w = w_1 \ldots w_n$ summarized below:

1. Extract $\varphi$ to see if the empty word is a match.
2. For $1 \leq j \leq n$ repeat:

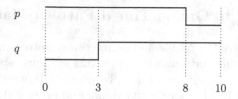

**Fig. 2.** A signal $w := w_1 w_2 w_3$ over variables $p$ and $q$.

**Table 2.** Timed pattern matching using derivatives for $w = w_1 w_2 w_3$ and $\varphi = \langle p \cdot q \rangle_I$. Entries represent the derivative with respect to $w_{i..j}$. Reduced expressions, indicating matched segments, are shaded with green. ($I = [4,7]$, $\Gamma_1 = {}^{[0,3]}_{[0,3]}\langle \checkmark \rangle_{[0,3]}$, $\Gamma_2 = {}^{[3,8]}_{[3,8]}\langle \checkmark \rangle_{[0,5]}$ and $\Gamma_3 = {}^{[8,10]}_{[8,10]}\langle \checkmark \rangle_{[0,2]}$.)

| Symbols<br>Segments | | $\{p \wedge \neg q\}$<br>$[0,3)$ | $\{p \wedge q\}$<br>$[3,8)$ | $\{\neg p \wedge q\}$<br>$[8,10)$ |
|---|---|---|---|---|
| $[0,3)$ | $\langle p \cdot q \rangle_I$ | $\xrightarrow{\Delta_{w_1}} \begin{array}{l}\langle \Gamma_1 \cdot q \rangle_I \vee \\ \langle \Gamma_1 \cdot p \cdot q \rangle_I\end{array}$ | $\xrightarrow{\Delta_{w_2}} \begin{array}{l}\boxed{\langle \Gamma_1 \cdot \Gamma_2 \rangle_I} \vee \\ \langle \Gamma_1 \cdot \Gamma_2 \cdot q \rangle_I \vee \\ \langle \Gamma_1 \cdot \Gamma_2 \cdot p \cdot q \rangle_I\end{array}$ | $\xrightarrow{\Delta_{w_3}} \begin{array}{l}\boxed{\langle \Gamma_1 \cdot \Gamma_2 \cdot \Gamma_3 \rangle_I} \vee \\ \langle \Gamma_1 \cdot \Gamma_2 \cdot \Gamma_3 \cdot q \rangle_I\end{array}$ |
| $[3,8)$ | | $\langle p \cdot q \rangle_I$ | $\xrightarrow{\Delta_{w_2}} \begin{array}{l}\boxed{\langle \Gamma_2 \rangle_I} \vee \\ \langle \Gamma_2 \cdot q \rangle_I \vee \\ \langle \Gamma_2 \cdot p \cdot q \rangle_I\end{array}$ | $\xrightarrow{\Delta_{w_3}} \begin{array}{l}\boxed{\langle \Gamma_2 \cdot \Gamma_3 \rangle_I} \vee \\ \langle \Gamma_2 \cdot \Gamma_3 \cdot q \rangle_I\end{array}$ |
| $[8,10)$ | | | $\langle p \cdot q \rangle_I$ | $\xrightarrow{\Delta_{w_3}} \varnothing$ |

(a) Update the state of the matching $\psi_j$ by deriving the previous state $\psi_{j-1}$ with respect to $w_j$ and adding a new derivation $\Delta_{w_j}(\varphi)$ to the state for matches starting in segment $j$.

(b) Extract $\psi_j$ to get matches ending in segment $j$.

We present an example of online pattern matching for the timed regular expression $\varphi := \langle p \cdot q \rangle_{[4,7]}$ and input signal $w := w_1 w_2 w_3$ with $w_1 : [0,3) \mapsto \{p \wedge \neg q\}$, $w_2 : [3,8) \mapsto \{p \wedge q\}$ and $w_3 : [8,10) \mapsto \{\neg p \wedge q\}$ over propositional variables $p$ and $q$ shown in Fig. 2. In Table 2 we depict the step-by-step computation of the match set $\mathcal{M}(\varphi, w)$ after reading the next segment from $w$. For Step 1 the state $\psi_1$ is equal to the derivative of $\varphi$ with respect to $w_1$ such that $\psi_1 = \langle \Gamma_1 \cdot q \rangle_{[4,7]} \vee \langle \Gamma_1 \cdot p \cdot q \rangle_{[4,7]}$ where $\Gamma_1 = {}^{[0,3]}_{[0,3]}\langle \checkmark \rangle_{[0,3]}$. The extraction $\mathrm{xt}(\psi_1)$ is empty therefore we do not have any match ending in $\mathrm{dom}(w_1) = [0,2)$. For Step 2 where $\Gamma_2 = {}^{[3,8]}_{[3,8]}\langle \checkmark \rangle_{[0,5]}$ the extraction of the state is equal to $\mathrm{xt}(\psi_2) = \langle \Gamma_1 \cdot \Gamma_2 \rangle_{[4,7]} \vee \langle \Gamma_2 \rangle_{[4,7]} = {}^{[4,8]}_{[0,3]}\langle \checkmark \rangle_{[4,7]} \vee {}^{[7,8]}_{[3,4]}\langle \checkmark \rangle_{[4,5]}$. Similarly, for Step 3 where $\Gamma_3 = {}^{[8,10]}_{[8,10]}\langle \checkmark \rangle_{[0,2]}$, the extraction of the state is equal to $\mathrm{xt}(\psi_3) = \langle \Gamma_1 \cdot \Gamma_2 \cdot \Gamma_3 \rangle_{[4,7]} \vee \langle \Gamma_2 \cdot \Gamma_3 \rangle_{[4,7]} = {}^{[8,9]}_{[1,3]}\langle \checkmark \rangle_{[5,7]} \vee {}^{[8,9]}_{[4,6]}\langle \checkmark \rangle_{[4,5]}$. In Fig. 3 we illustrate corresponding

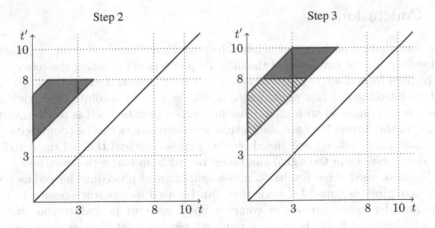

**Fig. 3.** A graphical representation of online timed pattern matching presented in Table 2 with $t$ and $t'$ denoting, respectively, the beginning and end of the match.

segments $(t, t')$ extracted in Steps 2 and 3 where solid regions show the actual outputs for the corresponding step.

We implemented our procedure using the functional term rewriting language PURE and C++. Besides derivative and extraction rules we introduced in this paper, our implementation includes some basic algebraic rewrite rules as well as simplification rules for reduced expressions given in Sect. 3. We perform our experiments on a 3.3 GHz machine for a set of test patterns and we depict performance results of the online procedure in comparison with the offline procedure in [17] in Table 3. For typical cases, experiments suggest a linear time performance with respect to the number of segments in the input for both algorithms. Although the online procedure runs slower than the offline procedure, it requires less memory and the memory usage does not depend on the input size as expected.

**Table 3.** Execution times/Memory usage (in seconds/megabytes)

| Test Patterns | Offline Algorithm Input Size | | | Online Algorithm Input Size | | |
|---|---|---|---|---|---|---|
| | 100 K | 500 K | 1 M | 100 K | 500 K | 1 M |
| $p$ | 0.06/17 | 0.27/24 | 0.51/33 | 6.74/14 | 29.16/14 | 57.87/14 |
| $p \cdot q$ | 0.08/21 | 0.42/46 | 0.74/77 | 8.74/14 | 42.55/14 | 81.67/14 |
| $\langle p \cdot q \cdot \langle p \cdot q \cdot p \rangle_I \cdot q \cdot p \rangle_J$ | 0.23/28 | 1.09/77 | 2.14/140 | 28.07/14 | 130.96/14 | 270.45/14 |
| $(\langle p \cdot q \rangle_I \cdot r) \wedge (p \cdot \langle q \cdot r \rangle_J)$ | 0.13/23 | 0.50/51 | 1.00/86 | 15.09/15 | 75.19/15 | 148.18/15 |
| $p \cdot (q \cdot r)^*$ | 0.11/20 | 0.49/37 | 0.96/60 | 11.53/15 | 52.87/15 | 110.58/15 |

# 6   Conclusions

The contribution of the paper is both theoretical and practical. From a theoretical standpoint we have tackled the difficult problem of exporting the concept of derivatives from discrete to timed behaviors, languages and expressions. To this end we introduced a new approach to handle signals in absolute time, yielding a new type of monoid with interesting properties that by itself is worth investigating in the future. We have shown that such derivatives can be computed syntactically using left-reduced timed regular expressions and that all the matches of the expressions in the signal can be extracted from this representation.

We have used these results to implement a novel procedure for online pattern matching for timed behavior that can be used to monitor systems in real time and detect occurrences of complex patterns. Our procedure consumes a constant segment from the input signal and reports a set of matches ending in that segment before processing the next segment. The algorithm can be applied, of course, to the discrete case where words are viewed as signals that can change their values only at integer times. Despite the overhead, our algorithm might be advantageous for words that have long periods of stuttering if a delay in the detection of matching can be tolerated.

We believe that this procedure has a lot of potential applications in detecting temporal patterns at different time scales. It can be used, for example to detect patterns in music as in [8], in cardiac behavior or in speech. To this end the expression should be extended with predicates over real numbers [7] as in the passage from MTL to STL (signal temporal logic) [11]. Other potential application domains could be the detection of congestions in traffic or in communication network and the analysis of execution logs of organizations information systems or web servers, for example to detect internet robots or customers who are about to abandon our web site.

**Acknowledgement.** This work was partially supported by the French ANR projects EQINOCS and CADMIDIA and benefitted from useful comments made by anonymous referees.

# References

1. Antimirov, V.M.: Partial derivatives of regular expressions and finite automaton constructions. Theor. Comput. Sci. **155**(2), 291–319 (1996)
2. Antimirov, V.M., Mosses, P.D.: Rewriting extended regular expressions. Theor. Comput. Sci. **143**(1), 51–72 (1995)
3. Asarin, E., Caspi, P., Maler, O.: A Kleene theorem for timed automata. In: Logic in Computer Science (LICS), pp. 160–171 (1997)
4. Asarin, E., Caspi, P., Maler, O.: Timed regular expressions. J. ACM **49**(2), 172–206 (2002)
5. Berry, G., Sethi, R.: From regular expressions to deterministic automata. Theor. Comput. Sci. **48**(3), 117–126 (1986)
6. Brzozowski, J.A.: Derivatives of regular expressions. J. ACM **11**(4), 481–494 (1964)

7. Ferrère, T., Maler, O., Ničković, D., Ulus, D.: Measuring with timed patterns. In: Kroening, D., Pǎsǎreanu, C.S. (eds.) CAV 2015. LNCS, vol. 9207, pp. 322–337. Springer, Heidelberg (2015)
8. Giavitto, J.-L., Echeveste, J.: Real-time matching of antescofo temporal patterns. In: Principles and Practice of Declarative Programming (PPDP), pp. 93–104 (2014)
9. Havlicek, J., Little, S.: Realtime regular expressions for analog and mixed-signal assertions. In: Formal Methods in Computer-Aided Design (FMCAD), pp. 155–162 (2011)
10. Koymans, R.: Specifying real-time properties with metric temporal logic. Real-Time Syst. **2**(4), 255–299 (1990)
11. Maler, O., Nickovic, D., Pnueli, A.: Checking temporal properties of discrete, timed and continuous behaviors. In: Avron, A., Dershowitz, N., Rabinovich, A. (eds.) Pillars of Computer Science. LNCS, vol. 4800, pp. 475–505. Springer, Heidelberg (2008)
12. Morin-Allory, K., Borrione, D.: On-line monitoring of properties built on regular expressions. In: Forum on specification and Design Languages, (FDL), pp. 249–255 (2006)
13. Owens, S., Reppy, J.H., Turon, A.: Regular-expression derivatives re-examined. J. Funct. Program. **19**(2), 173–190 (2009)
14. Rosu, G., Viswanathan, M.: Testing extended regular language membership incrementally by rewriting. In: Rewriting Techniques and Applications (RTA), pp. 499–514 (2003)
15. Sen, K., Rosu, G.: Generating optimal monitors for extended regular expressions. Electron. Notes Theor. Comput. Sci. **89**(2), 226–245 (2003)
16. Sulzmann, M., van Steenhoven, P.: A flexible and efficient ML lexer tool based on extended regular expression submatching. In: Cohen, A. (ed.) CC 2014 (ETAPS). LNCS, vol. 8409, pp. 174–191. Springer, Heidelberg (2014)
17. Ulus, D., Ferrère, T., Asarin, E., Maler, O.: Timed pattern matching. In: Legay, A., Bozga, M. (eds.) FORMATS 2014. LNCS, vol. 8711, pp. 222–236. Springer, Heidelberg (2014)

# Hybridization Based CEGAR for Hybrid Automata with Affine Dynamics

Nima Roohi[1]([⊠]), Pavithra Prabhakar[2], and Mahesh Viswanathan[1]

[1] Department of Computer Science,
University of Illinois at Urbana-Champaign, Illinois, USA
{roohi2,vmahesh}@illinois.edu
[2] Department of Computing and Information Sciences,
Kansas State University, Manhattan, USA
pprabhakar@ksu.edu

**Abstract.** We consider the problem of safety verification for hybrid systems, whose continuous dynamics in each mode is affine, $\dot{X} = AX + b$, and invariants and guards are specified using rectangular constraints. We present a counter-example guided abstraction refinement framework (CEGAR), which abstract these hybrid automata into simpler ones with rectangular inclusion dynamics, $\dot{x} \in \mathcal{I}$, where $x$ is a variable and $\mathcal{I}$ is an interval in $\mathbb{R}$. In contrast to existing CEGAR frameworks which consider discrete abstractions, our method provides highly efficient abstraction construction, though model-checking the abstract system is more expensive. Our CEGAR algorithm has been implemented in a prototype tool called HARE (Hybrid Abstraction-Refinement Engine), that makes calls to SpaceEx to validate abstract counterexamples. We analyze the performance of our tool against standard benchmark examples, and show that its performance is promising when compared to state-of-the-art safety verification tools, SpaceEx, PHAVer, SpaceEx AGAR, and HSolver.

## 1 Introduction

The safety verification of cyber-physical systems is a computationally challenging problem that is in general undecidable [1,3,21,25,33]. Thus, verifying realistic designs often involves crafting an abstract model with simpler dynamics that is amenable to automated analysis. The success of the abstraction based method depends on finding the right abstraction, which can be difficult. One approach that tries to address this issue is the counterexample guided abstraction refinement (CEGAR) technique [9] that tries to automatically discover the right abstraction through a process of progressive refinement based on analyzing spurious counterexamples in abstract models. CEGAR has been found to be useful in a number of contexts [5,12,22,23], including hybrid systems [2,10,11,14,16,24,31,32].

There are two principal CEGAR approaches in the context of verifying hybrid system that differ primarily on the space of abstract models considered. The first approach [2,10,11,29,31,32] tries to abstract hybrid models into finite state,

© Springer-Verlag Berlin Heidelberg 2016
M. Chechik and J.-F. Raskin (Eds.): TACAS 2016, LNCS 9636, pp. 752–769, 2016.
DOI: 10.1007/978-3-662-49674-9_48

discrete transition systems that have no continuous dynamics. The second approach [14,24,27] abstracts a Hybrid Automaton by another Hybrid Automaton with simpler dynamics. Using Hybrid Automata as abstractions has the advantage that constructing abstract models is computationally easier.

In this paper, we present a CEGAR framework for verifying cyber-physical systems, where the concrete and abstract models are both Hybrid Automata. We consider Hybrid Automata with Affine Dynamics and Rectangular Constraints (Affine Hybrid Automata for short) which are a subclass of Hybrid Automata, where invariants, guards, and resets are given by rectangular constraints (conjunctions of constraints comparing variables to constants), but the continuous flow in control locations is given by linear differential equations of the form $\dot{X} = AX + b$; here $X$ is the vector of continuous variables, $A$ is a rational matrix, and $b$ is a vector of rational numbers. The safety verification problem for such automata is challenging — not only is the problem undecidable, but it is even unknown whether the problem of checking if the states reachable within a time bound $t$ (without taking any discrete transitions) intersects a polyhedral unsafe region is decidable. We abstract such Affine Hybrid Automata by Rectangular Hybrid Automata. Rectangular Hybrid Automata are similar to Affine Hybrid Automata except that the continuous dynamics is given by rectangular differential inclusions (i.e., dynamics of each variable is of the form $\dot{x} \in [a, b]$) as opposed to linear differential equations. Our results extend previous Hybrid Automata based CEGAR algorithms [14,24,27] to a richer class of hybrid models (from concrete automata that have rectangular dynamics to automata that have affine dynamics).

We establish a few basic results about our CEGAR framework. First we show that any spurious counterexample will be detected during the counterexample validation step. This result is not obvious because it is unknown whether the bounded time reachability problem is decidable for Affine Hybrid Automata. Hence validation cannot be carried out "exactly". Our proof relies on the observation that the sets computed during counterexample validation are bounded, and uses the fact that continuous time bounded posts of Affine Hybrid Automata can be approximated with arbitrary precision. Next, we show that our refinement algorithm makes progress. More precisely, we prove that any abstract counterexample, if it appears sufficiently many times, is eventually eliminated. Progress is proved by observing that, for a bounded time, linear dynamics can be approximated with arbitrary precision by rectangular dynamics [29].

We have extended our CEGAR-based tool HARE (Hybrid Abstraction Refinement Engine) to verify Affine Hybrid Automata; the previous HARE implementation only handled Rectangular Hybrid Automata. Furthermore, we found existing tools for model checking Rectangular Hybrid Automata (HyTech [20], PHAVer [18], SpaceEx [19], and FLOW* [8]) inadequate for our purposes (see Sect. 5 for explanations). So we implemented a new model checker for Rectangular Hybrid Automata that uses the Parma Polyhedral Library (PPL) [4] and Z3 [13]. Counterexample validation is carried out by making calls to SpaceEx and PPL.

We have compared the performance of the new version of our tool HARE against SpaceEx with the Supp and PHAVer scenarios, SpaceEx AGAR [7], and HSolver [29] on standard benchmark examples. SpaceEx is the state-of-the-art symbolic state space explorer for Affine Hybrid Automata that over-approximates the reachable set, and may occasionally converge to a fixpoint in the process. SpaceEx AGAR is a CEGAR-based tool that merges different locations and over-approximates their dynamics. HSolver is a another CEGAR-based tool that abstracts hybrid automata into finite-state, discrete abstractions (as opposed to other hybrid automata). HSolver failed to terminate within a reasonable time on almost all of our examples. The running time of HARE was roughly comparable to SpaceEx and SpaceEx AGAR (details in Sect. 5), with each tool beating the other on different examples. But we found that HARE was more *accurate*. On quite a few examples, SpaceEx (and SpaceEx AGAR) fails to prove safety either because it does not converge to a fixpoint or because it over-approximates the reach set too much. Due to space constrains many details have been omitted, but can be found in [30].

## 2   Related Work

Doyen *et al.* consider rectangular abstractions for safety verification of affine hybrid systems in [15]. However, their refinement is not guided by counter-example analysis. Instead, a reachable unsafe location in the abstract system is determined, and the invariant of the corresponding concrete location is split to ensure certain optimality criteria on the resulting rectangular dynamics. This, in general, may not lead to abstract counter-example elimination, as in our CEGAR algorithm. We belive that the refinement algorithms of the two papers are incomparable — one may perform better than the other on certain examples. Empirical evaluations could provide some insights into the merits of the approaches, however, the implementation of the algorithm in [15] was not available for comparison at the time of writing the paper.

Bogomolov *et al.* consider polyhedral inclusion dynamics as abstract models of affine hybrid systems for CEGAR in [7]. Their abstraction merges the locations, and refinement corresponds to splitting the locations. Hence, the CEGAR loop ends with the original automaton in a finite number of steps, if safety is not proved by then. Our algorithm splits the invariants of the locations, and hence, explores finer abstractions. Our method is orthogonal to that of [7], and can be used in conjunction with [7] to further refine the abstractions.

Nellen *et al.* use CEGAR in [26] to model check chemical plants controlled by programmable logic controllers. They assume that the dynamics of the system in each location is given by *conditional* ODEs, and their abstraction consists of choosing a subset of these conditional ODEs. The refinement consists of adding some of these conditional ODEs based on a unsafe location in a counter-example. The methods does not ensure counter-example elimination in successive iterations. Their prototype tool does not automate the refinement step, in that the inputs to the refinements need to be provided manually. Hence, we did not experimentally compare with this tool.

Zutshi *et al.* propose a CEGAR-based search in [34] to find violations of safety properties. Here they consider the problem of finding a concrete counter-example and use CEGAR to guide the search of the same. We instead use CEGAR to prove safety — the absence of such concrete counter-examples.

# 3    Preliminaries

**Numbers.** Let $\mathbb{N}$, $\mathbb{Q}$, and $\mathbb{R}$ denote the set of *natural, rational,* and *real* numbers, respectively. Similarly, $\mathbb{N}_+$, $\mathbb{Q}_+$, and $\mathbb{R}_+$ are respectively the set of *positive* natural, rational, and real numbers, and $\mathbb{Q}_{\geq 0}$ and $\mathbb{R}_{\geq 0}$ are respectively the set of *non-negative* rational and real numbers. For any $n \in \mathbb{N}$ we define $[n] = \{0, 1, \ldots, n-1\}$.

**Sets and Functions.** For any sets $A$ and $B$, $|A|$ is the size of $A$ (the number of elements in $A$), $\mathcal{P}(A)$ is the power set of $A$, $A \times B$ is the Cartesian product of $A$ and $B$, and $[A \rightarrow B]$ is the set of all (total) functions from $A$ to $B$. $A^B$ is a vector of elements in $A$ indexed by elements in $B$ (we treat an element of $A^B$ as a function from $B$ to $A$). In order to make the notations simpler, for any $n, m \in \mathbb{N}$, by $A^n$ and $A^{n \times m}$, we mean $A^{[n]}$ and $A^{[n] \times [m]}$. The latter represents matrices of dimension $n \times m$ with elements from $A$. For any $f \in [A \rightarrow B]$ and set $C \subseteq A$, $f(C) = \{f(c) \mid c \in C\}$. Similarly, for any $\pi = a_1, a_2, \ldots, a_n$, a sequence of elements in $A$, we define $f(\pi)$ to be $f(a_1), f(a_2), \ldots, f(a_n)$.

**Distance and Intervals.** When $A$ and $B$ are non-empty subsets of a normed space with norm $\llbracket . \rrbracket$, we define their *Hausdorff distance* $\mathtt{dist}_\mathtt{H}(A, B)$ by

$$\max\{\sup_{a \in A} \inf_{b \in B} \llbracket a - b \rrbracket, \sup_{b \in B} \inf_{a \in A} \llbracket a - b \rrbracket\}$$

An *interval* is any subset of real numbers of the form $[a, b]$, $(a, b]$, $[a, b)$, or $(a, b)$. We denote the set of all Intervals by $\mathcal{I}$ and the set of all Closed-Bounded Intervals by $\mathcal{I}_\mathrm{o}$.

## 3.1    Hybrid Automata

In this section, we present a hybrid automaton model for representing hybrid systems.

**Definition 1.** *A Hybrid Automaton $H$ is a tuple $(\mathtt{Q}, \mathtt{X}, \mathtt{I}, \mathtt{F}, \mathtt{E}, \mathtt{Q}^\mathtt{init}, \mathtt{Q}^\mathtt{bad})$, where*

- $\mathtt{Q}$ *is a finite non-empty set of (discrete) locations.*
- $\mathtt{X}$ *is a finite set of variables. A valuation $\nu \in \mathbb{R}^\mathtt{X}$ assigns a value to each variable in $\mathtt{X}$. We denote the set of all valuations by $\mathtt{V}$.*
- $\mathtt{I} \in [\mathtt{Q} \rightarrow \mathcal{I}_\mathrm{o}^\mathtt{X}]$ *maps each location $q$ to a closed bounded rectangular region as its invariant. We denote $\mathtt{I}(q)(x)$ by $\mathtt{I}(q, x)$.*
- $\mathtt{F} \in [\mathtt{Q} \times \mathtt{V} \rightarrow \mathcal{P}(\mathtt{V})]$ *maps each location $q$ and valuation $\nu$ to a set of possible derivatives of the trajectories in that location and valuation.*
- $\mathtt{E}$ *is a finite set of edges $e$ of the form $(s, d, g, j, r)$ where:*

- $s, d \in Q$ *are* source *and* destination *locations, respectively.*
- $g \in \mathcal{I}_\circ^X$ *is* guard *of e and specifies the set of possible values for each variable in order to traverse e.*
- $j \in \mathcal{P}(X)$ *is the set of variables whose values* change *after traversing e.*
- $r \in \mathcal{I}_\circ^j$ *is* reset *of e and specifies the set of possible values for each variable in j after traversing e.*

*We write* Se, De, Ge, Je, *and* Re *to denote different elements of an edge e, respectively. Also we denote* $(Ge)(x)$ *and* $(Re)(x)$ *respectively by* $G(e, x)$ *and* $R(e, x)$.

- $Q^{init}, Q^{bad} \subseteq Q$ *are respectively the set of* initial *and* unsafe *locations.*

*For all Hybrid Automata H, we display elements of H by* $Q_H$, $X_H$, $I_H$, $F_H$, $E_H$, $S_H$, $D_H$, $G_H$, $J_H$, $R_H$, $Q_H^{init}$, $Q_H^{bad}$, *and* $V_H$. *We may omit the subscript when it is clear from the context.*

We define the semantics of a hybrid automaton by a transition system it represents. Hence, we first define transition systems.

**Definition 2.** *A* Transition System *T is a tuple* $(S, \Sigma, \rightarrow, S^{init}, S^{bad})$ *in which*

1. S *is a (possibly infinite) set of states,*
2. $\Sigma$ *is a (possibly infinite) set of labels,*
3. $\rightarrow \subseteq S \times \Sigma \times S$ *is a transition relation,*
4. $S^{init} \subseteq S$ *is the set of initial states, and*
5. $S^{bad} \subseteq S$ *is the set of unsafe states.*

*We write* $s \xrightarrow{\alpha} s'$ *instead of* $(s, \alpha, s') \in \rightarrow$. *Also, we write* $s \rightarrow s'$ *as a shorthand for* $\exists \alpha \in \Sigma \bullet s \xrightarrow{\alpha} s'$, *and* $\rightarrow^*$ *denotes the reflexive transitive closure of* $\rightarrow$. *Finally, for any* $s \in S$ *we define* $\mathsf{reach}_T(s)$ *to be the set* $\{s' \in S | s \rightarrow^* s'\}$, *and* $\mathsf{reach}(T)$ *to be* $\bigcup_{s \in S^{init}} \mathsf{reach}_T(s)$.

*For all Transition Systems T, we denote the elements of T by* $S_T$, $\Sigma_T$, $\rightarrow_T$, $S_T^{init}$, $S_T^{bad}$. *In addition, whenever it is clear, we drop the subscript T to make the notation simpler.*

The semantics of a Hybrid Automaton $H = (Q, X, I, F, E, Q^{init}, Q^{bad})$ can be defined as a Transition System $[\![H]\!] = (S, \Sigma, \rightarrow, S^{init}, S^{bad})$ in which

- $S = Q \times V$,
- $\Sigma = E \cup \mathbb{R}_{\geq 0}$,
- $\rightarrow = \rightarrow_1 \cup \rightarrow_2$ where

- $S^{init} = \{(q, \nu) \in S \mid q \in Q^{init}\}$,
- $S^{bad} = \{(q, \nu) \in S \mid q \in Q^{bad}\}$,

  - $\rightarrow_1$ is the set of time transitions and for all $t \in \mathbb{R}_{\geq 0}$ $(q, \nu) \xrightarrow{t}_1 (q', \nu')$ iff $q = q'$ and there exists a differentiable function $f \in [\![0, t]\!] \rightarrow V]$ such that 1. $f(0) = \nu$, 2. $f(t) = \nu'$, 3. $\forall t' \in [0, t] \bullet f(t') \in I(q)$, and 4. $\dot{f}(t') \in F(q, f(t'))$.
  - $\rightarrow_2$ is the set of jump transitions and $(q, \nu) \xrightarrow{e}_2 (q', \nu')$ iff 1. $q = Se$, 2. $q' = De$, 3. $\nu \in I(q) \cap Ge$, 4. $\nu' \in I(q')$, and 5. $\forall x \in X \bullet x \in Je \Rightarrow \nu'(x) \in R(e, x)$ and $x \notin Je \Rightarrow \nu(x) = \nu'(x)$.

In this paper, we deal with two subclasses of Hybrid Automata:

1. An Affine Hybrid Automaton is a Hybrid Automaton in which for every location $q \in Q$ there exists a matrix $M \in \mathbb{Q}^{x^2}$ and a vector $b \in \mathbb{Q}^x$ such that for every valuation $\nu \in V$ we have $F(q, \nu) = \{M\nu + b\}$. This is the class of Hybrid Automata we intend to analyse for safety.
2. A Rectangular Automaton is a Hybrid Automaton in which for every location $q \in Q$ there exists a rectangular region $f \in \mathcal{I}^x$ such that for every valuation $\nu \in V$ we have $F(q, \nu) = f$. We may write $F(q, x)$ to denote the set of possible flows for variable $x$ at location $q$. We use this class to represent abstract Hybrid Automata in our CEGAR algorithm.

For a Hybrid Automaton $H$, a *path* is defined to be a finite sequence $e_1, e_2, \dots, e_n$ of edges in $E$ such that $De_i = Se_{i+1}$ for all $0 < i < n$. A *timed path* $\pi$ is a finite sequence of the form $(t_1, e_1), (t_2, e_2), \dots, (t_n, e_n)$ such that $e_1, \dots, e_n$ is a path in $H$ and $t_i \in \mathbb{R}_{\geq 0}$ for all $0 < i \leq n$. A *run* $\rho$ *from* $s_0$ *to* $s_n$ is a finite sequence $s_0, (t_1, e_1), s_1, (t_2, e_2), \dots, (t_n, e_n), s_n$ such that 1. $(t_1, e_1), \dots, (t_n, e_n)$ is a timed path in $H$, 2. for all $0 \leq i \leq n$ we have $s_i \in S_{\llbracket H \rrbracket}$, and 3. for all $0 < i \leq n$ there exists a state $s'_i \in S_{\llbracket H \rrbracket}$ for which $s_{i-1} \xrightarrow{t_i} s'_i \xrightarrow{e_i} s_i$. We will denote the first and last elements of $\rho$ respectively by $\rho_0$ and $\rho_{\mathsf{lst}}$.

For any Hybrid Automaton $H$, the *reachability problem* asks whether or not $H$ has a run $\rho$ such that $\rho_0 \in S_{\llbracket H \rrbracket}^{\mathsf{init}}$ and $\rho_{\mathsf{lst}} \in S_{\llbracket H \rrbracket}^{\mathsf{bad}}$. If the answer is positive, we say the $H$ is *unsafe*. Otherwise, we say the $H$ is *safe*.

For any Hybrid Automaton $H$, set of states $S \subseteq S_{\llbracket H \rrbracket}$, and edge $e \in E_H$ we define the following functions:

- $\mathsf{dpost}_H^e(S) = \{s' \mid \exists s \in S \cdot s \xrightarrow{e} s'\}$. Discrete post of $S$ in $H$ with respect to $e$ is the set of states reachable from $S$ after taking $e$.
- $\mathsf{dpre}_H^e(S) = \{s \mid \exists s' \in S \cdot s \xrightarrow{e} s'\}$. Discrete pre of $S$ in $H$ with respect to $e$ is the set of states that can reach a state in $S$ after taking $e$.
- $\mathsf{cpost}_H(S) = \{s' \mid \exists s \in S, t \in \mathbb{R}_{\geq 0} \cdot s \xrightarrow{t} s'\}$. Continuous post of $S$ in $H$ is the set of states reachable from $S$ in an arbitrary amount of time using dynamics specified for the source states.
- $\mathsf{cpre}_H(S) = \{s \mid \exists s' \in S, t \in \mathbb{R}_{\geq 0} \cdot s \xrightarrow{t} s'\}$. Continuous pre of $S$ in $H$ is the set of states that can reach a state in $S$ in an arbitrary amount of time using dynamics specified for the source states.

## 4    CEGAR Algorithm for Safety Verification of Affine Hybrid Automata

Every CEGAR-based algorithm has four main parts [9]: 1. abstracting the concrete system, 2. model checking the abstract system, 3. validating the abstract counterexample, and 4. refining the abstract system. We explain parts of our algorithm regarding each of these parts in this section. Before that, Algorithm 1 shows at a very high level what the steps of our algorithm are.

**Algorithm 1.** High level steps of our CEGAR algorithm

| | |
|---|---|
| **Input:** $C$ an Affine Hybrid Automaton | ▷ $C$ is called concrete Hybrid Automaton. Def 1 |
| **Output:** Whether or not $C$ is safe | ▷ this is the reachability problem. Sec 3 |
| 1. Add a trivial self loop to every location of $C$ | ▷ Sec 4.2 |
| 2. $P \leftarrow$ the initial partition of invariants in $C$ | ▷ Sec 4.2 |
| 3. $A \leftarrow \alpha(C, P)$ | ▷ $A$ is called abstract Hybrid Automaton. Def 4 |
| 4. $\rho = O^{\text{RHA}}(A)$ | ▷ $O^{\text{RHA}}$ model checks Rectangular Automata. Sec 4.3 |
| 5. | ▷ $\rho$ is an annotated counterexample. Sec 4.3 |
| 6. **while** $\rho \neq \emptyset$ **do** | ▷ while abstract system is unsafe |
| 7.    **if** $\rho$ is valid in $C$ **then return** 'unsafe' | ▷ Sec 4.4 |
| 8.    $(q, p) \leftarrow$ abstract location that should be split | ▷ Sec 4.5 |
| 9.    $p_1, p_2 \leftarrow$ sets that should be separated in $(q, p)$ | ▷ Sec 4.5 |
| 10.    refine $P(q)$ such that $p_1$ and $p_2$ gets separated | ▷ Sec 4.5 |
| 11.    $A \leftarrow \alpha(C, P)$ | ▷ Sec 4.2 |
| 12.    $\rho = O^{\text{RHA}}(A)$ | ▷ Sec 4.3 |
| 13. **end while** | |
| 14. **return** 'safe' | |

## 4.1 Time-Bounded Transitions

A step of every CEGAR algorithm is to validate a counterexample of an abstract system returned by the model-checking phase (Sect. 4.4). We do validation by running the counterexample of the abstract model checker against the concrete Hybrid Automaton. In our discussion, we will assume that for Affine Hybrid Automata one can compute the continuous post of a set of states for an arbitrary amount of time. But this is not completely true. What we can do is to only compute approximations of the continuous post of a set of states. In addition, bounded error approximations can be computed only for a finite amount of time. Hence, we convert a Hybrid Automaton $H$ to another Hybrid Automaton $H'$ with the same reachability information and with the additional property that in $H'$, there is no time transition with a label larger than $t$, for some parameter $t \in \mathbb{R}_+$. With this transformation, we can compute bounded error approximations of the unbounded time post, since it is actually a continuous post over a bounded time $t$.

## 4.2 Abstraction

Input to our algorithm is an Affine Hybrid Automaton $C$ which we call the *concrete* Hybrid Automaton. The first step is to construct an *abstract* Hybrid Automaton $A$ which is a Rectangular Automaton. The abstract Hybrid Automaton $A$ is obtained from the concrete Hybrid Automaton $C$, by splitting the invariant of any location $q \in \mathbb{Q}_C$ into a finite number of cells of type $\mathcal{I}_\circ^{\mathbb{X}}$ and defining an abstract location for each of these cells which over-approximates the linear dynamics in the cell by a rectangular dynamics. Definitions 3 and 4 formalizes the way an abstraction $A$ is constructed from $C$.

**Definition 3 (Invariant Partitions).** *For any Hybrid Automaton $C$ and function $P \in [\mathbb{Q} \to \mathcal{P}(\mathcal{I}_\circ^{\mathbb{X}})]$ we say $P$ partitions invariants of $C$ iff the following conditions hold for any location $q \in \mathbb{Q}$:*

- *$\bigcup P(q) = \mathbb{I}(q)$, which means union of cells in $P(q)$ covers invariant of $q$.*
- *$\forall p_1, p_2 \in P(q), x \in \mathbb{X}$ at least one of the following conditions are true:*

- $|p_1(x) \cap p_2(x)| = 0$    • $|p_1(x) \cap p_2(x)| = 1$    • $p_1(x) = p_2(x)$

**Definition 4 (Abstraction Using Invariant Partitioning).** *For any Affine Hybrid Automaton $C$ and invariant partition $P \in [\mathsf{Q} \to \mathcal{P}(\mathcal{I}_\circ^\mathsf{x})]$, $\alpha(C, P)$ returns Rectangular Automaton $A$ which is defined below:*

- $\mathsf{Q}_A = \{(q, p) \mid q \in \mathsf{Q}_C \wedge p \in P(q)\}$,    – $\mathsf{X}_A = \mathsf{X}_C$,
- $\mathsf{Q}_A^{\mathsf{init}} = \{(q, p) \in \mathsf{Q}_A \mid q \in \mathsf{Q}_C^{\mathsf{init}}\}$,    – $\mathsf{I}_A((q, p)) = p$,
- $\mathsf{Q}_A^{\mathsf{bad}} = \{(q, p) \in \mathsf{Q}_A \mid q \in \mathsf{Q}_C^{\mathsf{bad}}\}$,
- $\mathsf{E}_A = \{((s, p_1), (d, p_2), g, j, r) \mid (s, d, g, j, r) \in \mathsf{E}_C \wedge (s, p_1), (d, p_2) \in \mathsf{Q}_A\}$, *and*
- $\mathsf{F}_A((q, p), \nu) = \mathsf{recthull}(\bigcup_{\nu \in p} \mathsf{F}_C(q, \nu))$, *where for any set $S \subset \mathbb{R}^\mathsf{x}$, $\mathsf{recthull}(S)$ is the smallest possible element of $\mathcal{I}_\circ^\mathsf{x}$ such that $\forall \nu \in S \bullet \nu \in \mathsf{recthull}(S)$.*

*In addition, we define function $\gamma_A$ to map 1. every state in $[\![A]\!]$ to a state in $[\![C]\!]$, and 2. every edge in $\mathsf{E}_A$ to an edge in $\mathsf{E}_C$. Formally, for any $s = ((q, p), \nu) \in S_{[\![A]\!]}$ and $e = ((q_1, p_1), (q_2, p_2), g, j, r) \in \mathsf{E}_A$, we define $\gamma_A(s)$ to be $(q, \nu)$ and $\gamma_A(e)$ to be $(q_1, q_2, g, j, r)$.*

For each concrete location we will have one or more abstract locations. By making invariants of abstract locations small (and thus increasing the number of abstract locations) we want to be able to make behavior of $A$ as close as required to the behavior of $C$. This requires trajectories to be always able to jump between two abstract locations when they correspond to a single concrete location. But we did not add any such edge to $A$ in Definition 4. Although defining abstract system in this way just imposes an additional initial step to our algorithm, we find it very convenient not to introduce any edge in the abstract Hybrid Automata that corresponds to no edge in the concrete Hybrid Automata. Nonetheless, it is easy to see that if for every location $q \in \mathsf{Q}_C$, $\mathsf{E}_C$ contains a trivial edge (*i.e.* an edge with no guard and no reset) from $q$ to itself, abstracting $C$ using Definition 4 will produce a trivial edge between all abstract locations corresponding to a single concrete location. One can easily add these edges to $C$ in an initial step, so in the rest of this paper, WLOG. we assume every location of $C$ has a trivial self loop. Finally, it is easy to see that these trivial self loops along with Definitions 3 and 4 introduce Zeno behavior in the abstract system (*i.e.* the abstract system can make an infinite number of discrete transitions in a finite amount of time), but our model checker can easily handle it. In fact since we check for a fixed-point, we believe our tool is not considerably affected by this type of behavior.

**Proposition 5 (Over-Approximation).** *For any Affine Hybrid Automaton $C$ and invariant partition $P$, $A = \alpha(C, P)$ is a Rectangular Automaton which over-approximates $C$, that is, $\mathsf{reach}(C) \subseteq \gamma_A(\mathsf{reach}(A))$.*

It is clear that if $A$ is safe then $C$ is also safe. Also, one can easily see that if $P$ is defined as $P(q) = \{\mathsf{I}_C(q)\}$ (for all $q \in \mathsf{Q}_C$), it is a valid invariant partition of $C$. It is actually what our algorithm always uses as the initial invariant partitioning (initially we do not partition any invariant).

### 4.3   Counterexample and Model Checking Rectangular Automata

After an abstract Hybrid Automaton is constructed (initially and after any refinement), we have to model check it. In this section we define the notion of a counterexample and annotation of a counterexample, which we assume is returned by the abstract model checker $O^{\mathrm{RHA}}$ when it finds that the input Hybrid Automaton is unsafe.

**Definition 6.** *For any Hybrid Automaton $H$, a counterexample is a path $e_1$, $\ldots, e_n$ such that $\mathsf{S}e_1 \in \mathsf{Q}^{\mathsf{init}}$ and $\mathsf{D}e_n \in \mathsf{Q}^{\mathsf{bad}}$.*

**Definition 7.** *A counterexample $\pi$ is called* valid *in $H$ iff $H$ has a run $\rho$ and $\rho$ has the same path as $\pi$. A counterexample that is not valid is called* spurious.

**Definition 8.** *An annotation for a counterexample $\pi = e_1, \ldots, e_n$ of Hybrid Automaton $H$ is a sequence $\rho = S_0 \to S_0' \xrightarrow{e_1} S_1 \to S_1' \xrightarrow{e_2} \cdots \xrightarrow{e_n} S_n \to S_n'$ such that the following conditions hold:*

1. $\forall 0 \leq i \leq n \bullet \emptyset \neq S_i, S_i' \subseteq \mathsf{S}_{[\![H]\!]}$,
2. $\forall 0 \leq i \leq n \bullet S_i = \mathsf{cpre}_H(S_i')$,

3. $\forall 0 \leq i < n \bullet S_i' = \mathsf{dpre}_H^{e_{i+1}}(S_{i+1})$,
4. $S_n' = \mathsf{S}_{[\![H]\!]}^{\mathsf{bad}} \cap (\{\mathsf{D}e_n\} \times \mathsf{V}_H)$.

Condition 1 means that each $S_i$ and $S_i'$ in $\rho$ are a non-empty set of states. Conditions 2 and 3 mean that sets of states in $\rho$ are computed using backward reachability. Finally, Condition 4 means that $S_n'$ is the set of unsafe states in destination of $e_n$. Note that these conditions completely specify $S_0, \ldots, S_n$ and $S_0', \ldots, S_n'$ from $e_1, \ldots, e_n$ and $H$. Also, every $S_i$ and $S_i'$ is a subset of states corresponding to exactly one location.

In this paper, we assume to have access to an oracle $O^{\mathrm{RHA}}$ that can correctly answer reachability problems when the Hybrid Automata are restricted to be Rectangular Automata. If no unsafe location of $A$ is reachable from an initial location of it, $O^{\mathrm{RHA}}(A)$ returns 'safe'. Otherwise, it returns an annotated counterexample of $A$.

### 4.4   Validating Abstract Counterexamples

For any invariant partition $P$ and Affine Hybrid Automaton $C$, if $O^{\mathrm{RHA}}(A)$ (for $A = \alpha(C, P)$) returns 'safe', we know $C$ is safe. So the algorithm returns $C$ is 'safe' and terminates. On the other hand, if $O^{\mathrm{RHA}}$ finds $A$ to be unsafe it returns an annotated counterexample $\rho$ of $A$. Since $A$ is an over-approximation of $C$, we cannot be certain at this point that $C$ is also unsafe. More precisely, if $\pi$ is the path in $\rho$, we do not know whether $\gamma_A(\pi)$ is a valid counterexample in $C$ or it is spurious. Therefore, we need to validate $\rho$ in order to determine if it corresponds to any actual run from an initial location to an unsafe location in $C$.

To validate $\rho$, an annotated counterexample of $A = \alpha(C, P)$, we run $\rho$ on $C$. More precisely, we create a sequence $\rho' = R_0 \to R_0' \xrightarrow{e_1'} R_1 \to \cdots \xrightarrow{e_n'} R_n \to R_n'$ where

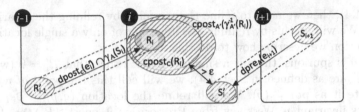

**Fig. 1.** Validation and refinement. There are three locations: $i-1$, $i$, and $i+1$. $S_{i+1}$ and $S'_i$ are elements of annotated counterexample $\rho$. $R'_{i-1}$, $R_i$, and $\mathsf{cpost}_C(R_i)$ are computed when $\rho$ is validated. $i$ is the smallest index for which $\mathsf{cpost}_C(R_i)$ and $\gamma_A(S'_i)$ are separated. Hence we need to refine $A$ in location $i$. Refinement should be done in such a way that for the result of refinement $A'$ we have $\mathsf{cpost}_{A'}(\gamma_{A'}^{-1}(R_i)) \cap \gamma_{A'}(S'_i) = \emptyset$.

1. $e'_i = \gamma_A(e_i)$,        3. $R'_i = \mathsf{cpost}_C(R_i) \cap \gamma_A(S'_i)$,
2. $R_0 = \gamma_A(S_0)$,        4. $R_i = \mathsf{dpost}_C^{e'_i}(R'_{i-1}) \cap \gamma_A(S_i)$.

Condition 1 states that edges in $\rho'$ correspond to the edges in $\rho$ as defined by the function $\gamma_A$ in Definition 4. Condition 2 states that $R_0$ is just concrete states corresponding to $S_0$. Note that $R_0$ is never empty. Condition 3 states that each $R'_i$ is the intersection of two sets: 1. concrete states corresponding to abstract states in $S'_i$, and 2. continuous post of $R_i$. Condition 4 states that each $R_i$ is the intersection of two sets: 1. concrete states corresponding to abstract states in $S_i$, and 2. discrete post of $R'_{i-1}$ using $e'_i$. It is easy to see that for any $i$ if $R_i$ or $R'_i$ becomes empty then for all $j > i$ both $R_j$ and $R'_j$ will be empty. Also, if $R_i$ is empty then $R'_i$ is empty too. Figure 1 depicts the situation when the counterexample is spurious and $R'_i$ is the first empty set we reach during our validation. Proposition 9 proves that the first empty set (if any) is always $R'_i$ for some $i$ and not $R_i$.

**Proposition 9.** $R'_n = \emptyset$ in $\rho'$ implies there exists $i$ such that 1. $R'_i = \emptyset$, 2. $R_i \neq \emptyset$, 3. $\forall j < i \bullet R_j, R'_j \neq \emptyset$, and 4. $\mathsf{cpost}_C(R_i)$ and $\gamma_A(S'_i)$ are nonempty disjoint sets.

**Lemma 10.** The counterexample $\pi' = e'_1, \ldots, e'_n$ of $C$ is valid iff $R'_n \neq \emptyset$.

Proposition 9 tells us that two sets $\mathsf{cpost}_C(R_i)$ and $\gamma_A(S'_i)$ are disjoint. Lemma 11 states a stronger result that there is a minimum distance $\epsilon > 0$ between those two sets, by exploiting the compactness of the two sets.

**Lemma 11.** There exists $\epsilon \in \mathbb{R}_+$ such that $\mathsf{dist}_H(\mathsf{cpost}_C(R_i), \gamma_A(S'_i)) > \epsilon$.

### 4.5  Refinement

Let us fix a concrete automaton $C$, an invariant partition $P$, and an abstract automaton $A = \alpha(C, P)$. Suppose model checking $A$ reveals a counterexample $\pi$ and its annotation $\rho$. If $\rho$ is found to be spurious by the validation algorithm (in Sect. 4.4), then we need to refine the model $A$ by refining the invariant partition $P$. We will do this by refining the invariant of only a single location of $A$. In this section we describe how to do this.

Since $\rho$ is spurious, there is a smallest index $i$ such that $R'_i = \emptyset$ (where the sets $R_i, R'_i$ are as defined in Sect. 4.4); we will call this the *point of refinement* and denote it as $\mathsf{por}_{C,A}(\rho)$. We will refine the location $(q,p) = \mathsf{De}_i$ of $A$ by refining its invariant $p$. We know from Proposition 9, $\mathsf{cpost}_C(R_i) \cap \gamma_A(S'_i) = \emptyset$. However, the corresponding sets in the abstract system $A$ are not disjoint, that is, $\mathsf{cpost}_A(\gamma_A^{-1}(R_i)) \cap S'_i \neq \emptyset$. Our refinement strategy is to find a partition for the location $(q,p)$ such that in the refined model $R = \alpha(C, P')$ (for some $P'$), $S'_i$ is not reachable from $R_i$. In order to define the actual refinement, and to make this condition precise, we need to introduce some definitions.

Let $C$, $A$, $R_i$, $S'_i$, and $(q,p)$ be as above. Let us denote by $C_{q,p}$ the restriction of $C$ to the single location $q$ with invariant $p$, i.e., $C_{q,p}$ has only one location $q$ whose flow and invariant is the same as that of $(q,p)$ in $A$, and only transitions whose source and destination is $q$. We will say that an invariant partition $P_r$ of $C_{q,p}$ *separates* $R_i$ from $S'_i$ iff in the automaton $A_1 = \alpha(C_{q,p}, P_r)$, $\mathsf{reach}_{A_1}(\gamma_{A_1}^{-1}(R_i)) \cap \gamma_{A_1}^{-1}(\gamma_A(S'_i)) = \emptyset$. In other words, the states corresponding to $S'_i$ in $A_1$ are not reachable from $\gamma_{A_1}^{-1}(R_i)$ in $A_1$.

**Refinement Strategy.** Let $P_r$ be an invariant partition of $C_{q,p}$ that separates $R_i$ from $S'_i$. Define the invariant partition $P'$ of $C$ as follows: $P'(q') = P(q')$ if $q' \neq q$, and $P'(q) = (P(q) \setminus \{p\}) \cup P_r(q)$. The new abstract automaton will be $R = \alpha(C, P')$. Observe that $R$ is a refinement of $A$ (since the invariant partition is refined), and the relationship between the locations and edges of the two automata is characterized by a function $\alpha_{R,A}(\cdot)$ defined as follows. For a location $(q', p')$, $\alpha_{R,A}(q', p') = (q', p')$ if either $q' \neq q$, or $p' \not\subseteq p$, and $\alpha_{R,A}(q', p') = (q, p)$ otherwise. Having defined the mapping between locations, the mapping between edges is its natural extension:

$$\alpha_{R,A}((q_1, p_1), (q_2, p_2), g, j, r) =$$
$$(\alpha_{R,A}(q_1, p_1), \alpha_{R,A}(q_2, p_2), g, j, r).$$

The goal of the refinement strategy outlined above is to ensure that a given counterexample $\pi$ is eventually eliminated, if the abstract model checker generates it sufficiently many times. To make this statement precise and to articulate the nature of progress we need to first identify when a counterexample of $R$ corresponds to a counterexample of $A$. Observe that a path $\pi$ of $A$ can "correspond" to a longer path $\pi'$ in $R$, where previous sojourn in location $(q,p)$ in $\pi$, now corresponds to a path in $\pi'$ that traverses the newly created locations by partitioning $p$. Recall that we are assuming that $\mathsf{por}_{C,A}(\rho) = i$, where $\rho$ is the annotation corresponding to $\pi$. We will say that a counterexample $\pi' = e'_1, e'_2, \ldots e'_m$ *corresponds* to counterexample $\pi = e_1, e_2, \ldots e_n$, if there exists $k$, $0 \leq k \leq m - i$, such that 1. for all $j \leq i$, $\alpha_{R,A}(e'_j) = e_j$, 2. for all $j > i + k$, $\alpha_{R,A}(e'_j) = e_{j-k}$, and 3. for all $i < j \leq i + k$, source and destination of $\alpha_{R,A}(e'_j)$ is $(q, p)$. If $\pi'$ corresponds to $\pi$, we will call $k$ its witness. Using this notion of correspondence, we are ready to state what our refinement achieves.

**Proposition 12.** *Let $\pi$ be a counterexample of $A$ and $\rho$ its annotation. Let $R$ be the refinement constructed by our strategy after $\rho$ is found to be spurious. Let $\pi'$ be a counterexample of $R$ that corresponds to $\pi$, and let $\rho'$ be its annotation. Then, $\mathrm{por}_{C,R}(\rho') < \mathrm{por}_{C,A}(\rho)$.*

The above proposition implies that a counterexample $\pi$ can appear only finitely many times in the CEGAR loop. This is because the point of refinement of any $\pi'$ in $R$ corresponding to $\pi$ in $A$ is strictly smaller.

Next, we claim that a partition satisfying the refinement strategy always exists. It relies on the following observation from [28] which states that the reach set of a linear dynamical system can be approximated to within any $\epsilon$ by a rectangular hybridization over a bounded time interval.

**Theorem 13** ([28]). *Let $H$ be a linear hybrid automaton with a single location such that there is a bound $T$ on the time for which the system can evolve in the location. Then, for any $\epsilon > 0$, there exists an invariant partition $P$ of $H$ such that $\mathrm{dist}_{\mathrm{H}}(\mathrm{reach}(H), \mathrm{reach}(\alpha(H,P))) < \epsilon$.*

**Corollary 14 (Existence of Refinement).** *There always exists a partition $P'$ that separates $R_i$ and $S_i'$.*

## 4.6   Validation Approximation

In order to validate a counterexample, we assumed to be able to exactly compute continuous post of a set of states in the Affine Hybrid Automaton for a finite amount of time. But the best one can actually hope for is computing over and under approximation of this set. In this section we show that being able to approximate the continuous post is enough for our algorithm. For any Hybrid Automaton $H$, set of states $S \subseteq \mathsf{S}_{[\![H]\!]}$, edge $e \in \mathsf{E}_H$, and parameter $\epsilon \in \mathbb{R}_+$ we define the following functions:

- $\mathsf{cpost}^{\epsilon}_{\mathsf{over}}(S)$ is an over-approximation of $\mathsf{cpost}(S)$. Formally, if $\mathsf{cpost}^{\epsilon}_{\mathsf{over}}(S)$ returns $S'$ then we know $\mathsf{cpost}(S) \subseteq S'$ and $\mathrm{dist}_{\mathrm{H}}(S', \mathsf{cpost}(S)) < \epsilon$.
- $\mathsf{cpost}^{\epsilon}_{\mathsf{under}}(S)$ is an under-approximation of $\mathsf{cpost}(S)$. Formally, if $\mathsf{cpost}^{\epsilon}_{\mathsf{under}}(S)$ returns $S'$ then we know $\mathsf{cpost}(S) \supseteq S'$ and $\mathrm{dist}_{\mathrm{H}}(S', \mathsf{cpost}(S)) < \epsilon$.

During the validation procedure, instead of computing $\rho'$ we compute $\rho_o$ and $\rho_u$. They are computed exactly as $\rho'$, except that in $\rho_o$ and $\rho_u$, instead of $\mathsf{cpost}$, we respectively use $\mathsf{cpost}^{\epsilon}_{\mathsf{over}}$ and $\mathsf{cpost}^{\epsilon}_{\mathsf{under}}$. Let us denote the last elements of $\rho_o$ and $\rho_u$ respectively by $R_n'$ and $U_n'$. If $U_n'$ is non-empty, we know $\rho$ represents at least one valid counterexample. Therefore, the algorithm outputs 'unsafe' and terminates. If $U_n'$ is empty but $R_n'$ is non-empty, it means $\epsilon$ is too big. Therefore, the algorithm repeats itself using $\frac{\epsilon}{2}$. If $R_n'$ is empty, it means all counterexamples in $\rho$ are spurious. Therefore, too much over-approximation is deployed in $A$ and it needs to be refined as stated in Sect. 4.5.

**Lemma 15.** *Given a counterexample $\pi$ of $A$, if $\gamma_A(\pi)$ is spurious, then there exists an $\epsilon > 0$ for which $R_n'$ is empty.*

The above lemma states that if the abstract counterexample is spurious, then the same will be detected by our algorithm. This is a direct consequence of Lemma 11.

## 5    Experimental Results

Our tool (Hybrid Abstraction Refinement Engine or HARE, for short) is implemented in Scala. The CEGAR framework relies on a model checker that analyzes an abstract model and produce a counterexample if the abstract model violates the safety requirement. In our case this is a model checker for Rectangular Hybrid Automata that produces counterexamples. The only model checkers for Rectangular Automata that produce counterexample that we are aware of are HyTech [20] and the old version of HARE [27][1]. Unfortunately, because HyTech is not being actively maintained, it does not have support for numbers of arbitrary size, and so in our experiments we frequently ran into overflow problems. Also, we decided not to use the old version of HARE to model check Rectangular Automata for two reasons: 1. we wanted to only study the effects of the abstraction techniques introduced in this paper, and not have our results compromised by other simplification steps introduced in [27] like merging control locations and transitions, and ignoring variables. 2. The old version of HARE internally calls HyTech, hence, the overflow error happens when the size of the automaton becomes large as a result of refinements. Therefore, we implemented a new model checker for Rectangular Hybrid Automata. Our implementation uses the Parma Polyhedral Library (PPL) [4] to compute the discrete and continuous pre in Rectangular Hybrid Automata[2], and Z3 [13] to check for fixpoints or intersection with initial states. Starting from the unsafe states, we iteratively compute pre until either a fixed point is found or we reach an initial state. Both of these libraries can handle numbers of arbitrary size. Validation of counterexamples requires computing posts in the concrete Affine Hybrid Automata. For discrete post we use the PPL library, and for the continuous post we call SpaceEx [19] with either Supp or PHAVer [18] scenario. Note that SpaceEx only computes an over-approximation of the continuous post and does not have support for computing under-approximations. Therefore, currently in our tool, we stop when an abstract counterexample is validated using the over-approximation implemented by SpaceEx. Finally, in the current implementation, in order to refine a location we simply halve its invariant along some variable at the point of refinement.

We evaluate our tool against four suites of examples that have been proposed by the community [2,6,17] as benchmarks for model checkers of hybrid systems. Each of these suites is qualitatively different and tests different aspects of the performance of a model checker. They are Tank, Satellite, Heater, and Navigation benchmarks.

---

[1] Note that FLOW* produces counterexamples and can even handle non-linear ODEs. But it does not support differential *inclusions* and therefore it is incapable of handling Rectangular Automata.

[2] Technically, we first convert the problem of computing pre to an equivalent problem of computing post, and then use PPL to find the solution.

**Table 1.** Experimental results. Columns Dim., Locs., and Trns. specify number of respectively variables (dimension), locations, and transitions in each benchmark. Five different Time columns specify amount of time each tool took to solve a problem. Times are all in seconds. '< 1' means less than a second and '> 600' means time out (more than 10 min). Also, '---' means one of the following: (1) it could not be run on HSolver because of specific features the model has, (2) it could not be run on SpaceEx AGAR because we could not find any set of locations that can be merged without causing the tool to terminate unexpectedly, (3) we do not have the data because of SpaceEx AGAR's time out. Four different Safe columns specify the output of each tool. Note that all tools perform some kind of over-approximation. Three FP. columns mean whether or not the corresponding tool reached a fixed-point in its reachability computation. No* in the FP. column of SpaceEx means that the tool reached a fixed-point, but it also generates the following warning which invalidates the reliability of its "safe" answer: WARNING (incomplete output) Reached time horizon without exhausting all states, result is incomplete.

| | Example Size | | | HARE | | SpaceEx | | | PHAVer | | | SpaceEx AGAR | | | | HSolver |
|---|---|---|---|---|---|---|---|---|---|---|---|---|---|---|---|---|
| Name | Dim. | Locs. | Trns. | Time | Safe | Time | FP. | Safe | Time | FP. | Safe | Merged Locs | Time | FP. | Safe | Time |
| Tank 14 | 7 | 7 | 12 | 4 | No | 4 | No | No | 56 | Yes | No | 3 | 10 | Yes | No | --- |
| Tank 16 | 3 | 3 | 6 | <1 | Yes | 3 | No | No | 1414 | No | Yes | 2 | 1133 | No | Yes | --- |
| Tank 17 | 3 | 3 | 6 | <1 | Yes | 5 | No* | Yes | 1309 | No | Yes | 2 | 1041 | No | Yes | --- |
| Satellite 03 | 4 | 64 | 198 | 91 | No | <1 | No | No | 1804 | No | No | 28 | >600 | --- | --- | --- |
| Satellite 04 | 4 | 100 | 307 | <1 | Yes | <1 | No* | Yes | <1 | Yes | Yes | 91 | 49 | Yes | Yes | --- |
| Satellite 11 | 4 | 576 | 1735 | 1 | Yes | <1 | No* | Yes | <1 | Yes | Yes | 449 | >600 | --- | --- | --- |
| Satellite 15 | 4 | 1296 | 3895 | 2 | Yes | <1 | No* | Yes | <1 | Yes | Yes | 264 | >600 | --- | --- | --- |
| Heater 01 | 3 | 4 | 6 | <1 | No | <1 | No* | No | <1 | Yes | No | --- | --- | --- | --- | >600 |
| Heater 02 | 3 | 4 | 6 | <1 | No | 10 | No | No | <1 | Yes | No | --- | --- | --- | --- | >600 |
| Nav 01 | 4 | 25 | 80 | 9 | Yes | <1 | Yes | Yes | <1 | Yes | Yes | 21 | 5 | Yes | Yes | >600 |
| Nav 08 | 4 | 16 | 48 | 7 | Yes | 685 | No | Yes | <1 | Yes | Yes | 10 | <1 | Yes | Yes | >600 |
| Nav 09 | 4 | 9 | 16 | 8 | Yes | <1 | No | No | <1 | Yes | No | 4 | <1 | Yes | No | >600 |
| Nav 13 | 4 | 9 | 18 | 8 | Yes | <1 | No* | Yes | <1 | Yes | Yes | 4 | <1 | Yes | Yes | >600 |
| Nav 20 | 4 | 33 | 97 | 29 | Yes | 2 | No* | Yes | <1 | Yes | Yes | 11 | <1 | Yes | Yes | >600 |

We ran different instances of the above examples on 4 different tools, in addition to HARE — SpaceEx, PHAVer (*i.e.* SpaceEx using PHAVer scenario), SpaceEx AGAR [7], and HSolver [29]. We do not compare with the older version of HARE, since it implements a CEGAR algorithm for Rectangular Hybrid Automata and not for Affine Hybrid Automata.

Table 1 shows the results on some of the instances we ran the tools on. All examples were run on a laptop with Intel i5 2.50 GHz CPU, 6 GB of RAM, and Ubuntu 14.10. The salient observations, based on the experiments reported in Table 1, are summarized below.

1. The Satellite benchmark shows that HARE scales up to automata with a large control structure.
2. HARE often beats the SpaceEx scenario in terms of proving safety or running time. For 4 problems, HARE performed faster. For 3 problems both tools have the same time, but in one of them only HARE proved safety. For 5 out of the remaining 7 problems in which SpaceEx performed faster, only HARE proved safety.
3. The PHAVer scenario is often faster but there are cases where HARE beats PHAVer. There are only 4 instances in which HARE performed faster, but in 7

examples PHAVer performed faster. Also there are 3 cases (including one in which PHAVer performed faster) where only HARE proved safety.

4. HARE often beats SpaceEx AGAR in terms of proving safety or running time. In 2 problems, we could not find any two locations such that merging them does not cause SpaceEx AGAR to encounter internal error. In 7 problems, HARE performed faster. In the remaining 5 problems SpaceEx AGAR performed faster, but there is one problem among them for which only HARE proved safety.

5. In some instances, SpaceEx, PHAVer, and SpaceEx AGAR failed to prove safety while HARE did not. There are two reasons for it. Sometimes those three tools fail to reach a fixpoint in the reachability computation. Examples of this are Tank 16-17, Satellite 4,11,15, and Nav 8,9,13,20 for SpaceEx, and Tank 16-17 for both PHAVer and SpaceEx AGAR. The other reason is that sometimes those three tools over-approximate too much. Examples of this is Nav 9 for PHAVer and SpaceEx AGAR. Furthermore, it seems merging locations is a very expensive task in SpaceEx AGAR, which we believe is the main reason for the time outs of this tool.

6. On all our examples, HSolver either timed out or the specific constraints in the model made them unamenable to analysis by HSolver. HSolver is an abstraction based tool that abstracts hybrid automata into finite state, discrete transition systems. It can handle models with non-linear dynamics, and so applies to automata more general than what HARE, SpaceEx, and PHAVer analyze. This suggests that HSolver's algorithm makes certain decisions that are not effective for Affine Hybrid Automata.

## 6 Conclusion

We presented a new algorithm for model checking safety problems of Hybrid Automata with Affine Dynamics and Rectangular Constraints in a counterexample guided abstraction refinement framework. We show that our algorithm is sound and have implemented it in a tool named HARE. We also compared the performance of our tool with a few state-of-the-art tools. Results show that performance of our tool is promising compared to the other tools (SpaceEx, PHAVer, and HSolver).

In the future, we intend to incorporate certain improvements to our implementation. In particular, we would like to integrate an algorithm for computing an under-approximation of the continuous post. The will allow us to definitively validate abstract counterexamples. Theoretically, we would like to explore the completeness of our algorithm, in terms of finding a concrete counterexample when the concrete system is unsafe. This may require a novel notion of counterexample in the abstract system, which is shortest in terms of the number of edges in the concrete system which do not correspond to self-loops. Our broad future goal is to extend the hybrid abstraction refinement method for non-linear hybrid systems.

**Acknowledgement.** The authors would like to thank Sergiy Bogolomov for help with using the SpaceEx AGAR. We gratefully acknowledge the support of the following grants — Nima Roohi was partially supported by NSF CNS 1329991; Pavithra Prabhakar was partially supported by EU FP7 Marie Curie Career Integration Grant no. 631622 and NSF CAREER 1552668; and Mahesh Viswanathan was partially supported by NSF CCF 1422798 and AFOSR FA9950-15-1-0059.

# References

1. Alur, R., Courcoubetis, C., Halbwachs, N., Henzinger, T.A., Ho, P.H., Nicollin, X., Olivero, A., Sifakis, J., Yovine, S.: The algorithmic analysis of hybrid systems. TCS **138**(1), 3–34 (1995)
2. Alur, R., Dang, T., Ivančić, F.: Predicate abstraction for reachability analysis of hybrid systems. ACM Trans. Embed. Comput. Syst. **5**(1), 152–199 (2006)
3. Asarin, E., Maler, O., Pnueli, A.: Reachability analysis of dynamical systems having piecewise-constant derivatives. TCS **138**(1), 35–65 (1995)
4. Bagnara, R., Hill, P.M., Zaffanella, E.: The parma polyhedra library: toward a complete set of numerical abstractions for the analysis and verification of hardware and software systems. Sci. Comput. Program. **72**(1–2), 3–21 (2008)
5. Ball, T., Rajamani, S.: Bebop: a symbolic model checker for boolean programs. In: Havelund, K., Penix, J., Visser, W. (eds.) SPIN 2000. LNCS, vol. 1885, pp. 113–130. Springer, Heidelberg (2000)
6. Bogomolov, S., Donze, A., Frehse, G., Grosu, R., Johnson, T.T., Ladan, H., Podelski, A., Wehrle, M.: Guided search for hybrid systems based on coarse-grained space abstractions. Int. J. Softw. Tools Technol. Transfer, October 2014
7. Bogomolov, S., Frehse, G., Greitschus, M., Grosu, R., Pasareanu, C., Podelski, A., Strump, T.: Assume-guarantee abstraction refinement meets hybrid systems. In: Yahav, E. (ed.) HVC 2014. LNCS, vol. 8855, pp. 116–131. Springer, Heidelberg (2014)
8. Chen, X., Ábrahám, E., Sankaranarayanan, S.: Flow*: an analyzer for non-linear hybrid systems. In: Sharygina, N., Veith, H. (eds.) CAV 2013. LNCS, vol. 8044, pp. 258–263. Springer, Heidelberg (2013)
9. Clarke, E., Grumberg, O., Jha, S., Lu, Y., Veith, H.: Counterexample-guided abstraction refinement. In: Emerson, E.A., Sistla, A.P. (eds.) CAV 2000. LNCS, vol. 1855, pp. 154–169. Springer, Heidelberg (2000)
10. Clarke, E., Fehnker, A., Han, Z., Krogh, B., Ouaknine, J., Stursberg, O., Theobald, M.: Abstraction and counterexample-guided refinement in model checking of hybrid systems. JFCS **14**(4), 583–604 (2003)
11. Clarke, E., Fehnker, A., Han, Z., Krogh, B.H., Stursberg, O., Theobald, M.: Verification of hybrid systems based on counterexample-guided abstraction refinement. In: Garavel, H., Hatcliff, J. (eds.) TACAS 2003. LNCS, vol. 2619, pp. 192–207. Springer, Heidelberg (2003)
12. Corbett, J., Dwyer, M., Hatcliff, J., Laubach, S., Pasareanu, C., Robby, Z.H.: Bandera: extracting finite-state models from java source code. In: ICSE, pp. 439–448 (2000)
13. de Moura, L., Bjørner, N.S.: Z3: an efficient SMT solver. In: Ramakrishnan, C.R., Rehof, J. (eds.) TACAS 2008. LNCS, vol. 4963, pp. 337–340. Springer, Heidelberg (2008)
14. Dierks, H., Kupferschmid, S., Larsen, K.G.: Automatic abstraction refinement for timed automata. In: Raskin, J.-F., Thiagarajan, P.S. (eds.) FORMATS 2007. LNCS, vol. 4763, pp. 114–129. Springer, Heidelberg (2007)

15. Doyen, L., Henzinger, T.A., Raskin, J.-F.: Automatic rectangular refinement of affine hybrid systems. In: Pettersson, P., Yi, W. (eds.) FORMATS 2005. LNCS, vol. 3829, pp. 144–161. Springer, Heidelberg (2005)
16. Fehnker, A., Clarke, E., Jha, S.K., Krogh, B.H.: Refining abstractions of hybrid systems using counterexample fragments. In: Morari, M., Thiele, L. (eds.) HSCC 2005. LNCS, vol. 3414, pp. 242–257. Springer, Heidelberg (2005)
17. Fehnker, A., Ivančić, F.: Benchmarks for hybrid systems verification. In: Alur, R., Pappas, G.J. (eds.) HSCC 2004. LNCS, vol. 2993, pp. 326–341. Springer, Heidelberg (2004)
18. Frehse, G.: PHAVer: algorithmic verification of hybrid systems past hytech. In: Morari, M., Thiele, L. (eds.) HSCC 2005. LNCS, vol. 3414, pp. 258–273. Springer, Heidelberg (2005)
19. Frehse, G., Le Guernic, C., Donzé, A., Cotton, S., Ray, R., Lebeltel, O., Ripado, R., Girard, A., Dang, T., Maler, O.: SpaceEx: scalable verification of hybrid systems. In: Gopalakrishnan, G., Qadeer, S. (eds.) CAV 2011. LNCS, vol. 6806, pp. 379–395. Springer, Heidelberg (2011)
20. Henzinger, T.A., Ho, P.H., Wong-Toi, H.: Hytech: a model checker for hybrid systems. Int. J. Softw. Tools Technol. Transfer (STTT) 1, 110–122 (1997)
21. Henzinger, T.A., Kopke, P.W., Puri, A., Varaiya, P.: What's decidable about hybrid automata? J. Comput. Syst. Sci., 373–382 (1995)
22. Henzinger, T., Jhala, R., Majumdar, R., Sutre, G.: Lazy abstraction. In: POPL 2002, pp. 58–70 (2002)
23. Holzmann, G., Smith, M.: Automating software feature verification. Bell Labs Tech. J. 5(2), 72–87 (2000)
24. Jha, S.K., Krogh, B.H., Weimer, J.E., Clarke, E.M.: Reachability for linear hybrid automata using iterative relaxation abstraction. In: Bemporad, A., Bicchi, A., Buttazzo, G. (eds.) HSCC 2007. LNCS, vol. 4416, pp. 287–300. Springer, Heidelberg (2007)
25. Mysore, V., Pnueli, A.: Refining the undecidability frontier of hybrid automata. In: Sarukkai, S., Sen, S. (eds.) FSTTCS 2005. LNCS, vol. 3821, pp. 261–272. Springer, Heidelberg (2005)
26. Nellen, J., Ábrahám, E., Wolters, B.: A CEGAR tool for the reachability analysis of PLC-Controlled plants using hybrid automata. In: Bouabana-Tebibel, T., Rubin, S.H. (eds.) Formalisms for Reuse and Systems Integration. AISC, vol. 346, pp. 55–78. Springer, Heidelberg (2015)
27. Prabhakar, P., Duggirala, P.S., Mitra, S., Viswanathan, M.: Hybrid automata-based CEGAR for rectangular hybrid systems. In: Giacobazzi, R., Berdine, J., Mastroeni, I. (eds.) VMCAI 2013. LNCS, vol. 7737, pp. 48–67. Springer, Heidelberg (2013)
28. Puri, A., Borkar, V.S., Varaiya, P.: $\epsilon$-approximation of differential inclusions. In: Alur, R., Sontag, E.D., Henzinger, T.A. (eds.) HS 1995. LNCS, vol. 1066, pp. 362–376. Springer, Heidelberg (1996)
29. Ratschan, S., She, Z.: Safety verification of hybrid systems by constraint propagation based abstraction refinement. ACM Trans. Embed. Comput. Syst. 6(1), 573–589 (2007)
30. Roohi, N., Prabhakar, P., Viswanathan, M.: Hybridization based CEGAR for hybrid automata with affine dynamics. Technical report, University of Illinois at Urbana-Champaign (2016). http://hdl.handle.net/2142/88823
31. Segelken, M.: Abstraction and counterexample-guided construction of $\omega$-Automata for model checking of step-discrete linear hybrid models. In: Damm, W., Hermanns, H. (eds.) CAV 2007. LNCS, vol. 4590, pp. 433–448. Springer, Heidelberg (2007)

32. Sorea, M.: Lazy approximation for dense real-time systems. In: Lakhnech, Y., Yovine, S. (eds.) FORMATS 2004 and FTRTFT 2004. LNCS, vol. 3253, pp. 363–378. Springer, Heidelberg (2004)
33. Vladimerou, V., Prabhakar, P., Viswanathan, M., Dullerud, G.E.: STORMED hybrid systems. In: Aceto, L., Damgård, I., Goldberg, L.A., Halldórsson, M.M., Ingólfsdóttir, A., Walukiewicz, I. (eds.) ICALP 2008, Part II. LNCS, vol. 5126, pp. 136–147. Springer, Heidelberg (2008)
34. Zutshi, A., Deshmukh, J.V., Sankaranarayanan, S., Kapinski, J.: Multiple shooting, CEGAR-based falsification for hybrid systems. In: Proceedings of the 14th International Conference on Embedded Software (2014)

# Complementing Semi-deterministic Büchi Automata

František Blahoudek[1]([⊠]), Matthias Heizmann[2], Sven Schewe[3],
Jan Strejček[1], and Ming-Hsien Tsai[4]

[1] Masaryk University, Brno, Czech Republic
[2] University of Freiburg, Freiburg, Germany
[3] University of Liverpool, Liverpool, UK
[4] Institute of Information Science, Academia Sinica, Taipei, Taiwan

**Abstract.** We introduce an efficient complementation technique for semi-deterministic Büchi automata, which are Büchi automata that are deterministic in the limit: from every accepting state onward, their behaviour is deterministic. It is interesting to study semi-deterministic automata, because they play a role in practical applications of automata theory, such as the analysis of Markov decision processes. Our motivation to study their complementation comes from the termination analysis implemented in ULTIMATE BÜCHI AUTOMIZER, where these automata represent checked runs and have to be complemented to identify runs to be checked. We show that semi-determinism leads to a simpler complementation procedure: an extended breakpoint construction that allows for symbolic implementation. It also leads to significantly improved bounds as the complement of a semi-deterministic automaton with $n$ states has less than $4^n$ states. Moreover, the resulting automaton is unambiguous, which again offers new applications, like the analysis of Markov chains. We have evaluated our construction against the semi-deterministic automata produced by the ULTIMATE BÜCHI AUTOMIZER. The evaluation confirms that our algorithm outperforms the known complementation techniques for general nondeterministic Büchi automata.

## 1 Introduction

The complementation of Büchi automata [6] is a classic problem that has been extensively studied [6,11–13,17,19,20,22,23,25–27,31–33,37] for more than half a century; see [35] for a survey. The traditional line of research has started with a proof on the existence of complementation algorithms [19,22] and continued to home in on the complexity of Büchi complementation, finally leading to matching upper [27] and lower [37] bounds for complementing Büchi automata. This line of

The research was supported through The Czech Science Foundation, grant P202/12/G061, by the German Research Council (DFG) as part of the Transregional Collaborative Research Center "Automatic Verification and Analysis of Complex Systems" (SFB/TR14 AVACS) and EPSRC grant EP/M027287/1.

M. Chechik and J.-F. Raskin (Eds.): TACAS 2016, LNCS 9636, pp. 770–787, 2016.
DOI: 10.1007/978-3-662-49674-9_49

research has been extended to more general classes of automata, notably parity [30] and generalised Büchi [29] automata.

The complementation of Büchi automata is a valuable tool in formal verification (cf. [18]), in particular when a property that all runs of a model shall have is provided as a Büchi automaton,[1] and when studying language inclusion problems of $\omega$-regular languages. With the growing understanding of the worst case complexity, the practical cost of complementing Büchi automata has become a second line of research. In particular the GOAL tool suite [33] provides a platform for comparing the behaviour of different complementation techniques on various benchmarks [32].

While these benchmarks use general Büchi automata, practical applications can produce or require subclasses of Büchi automata in specific forms. Our research is motivated by the observation that the program termination analysis in ULTIMATE BÜCHI AUTOMIZER [15] and the LTL software model checker ULTIMATE LTL AUTOMIZER [9] produce *semi-deterministic Büchi automata* (SDBA) [34,36] during their run. Semi-deterministic Büchi automata are a special class of Büchi automata that behave deterministically after traversing the first accepting state. For this reason, they are sometimes referred to as *limit deterministic* or *deterministic-in-the-limit* Büchi automata.

Program termination analysis is a model checking problem, where the aim is to prove that a given program terminates on all inputs. In other words, it tries to establish (or disprove) that all infinite execution paths in the program flowgraph are infeasible. The ULTIMATE BÜCHI AUTOMIZER uses an SDBA to represent infinite paths that are already known to be infeasible. It needs to complement the SDBA and make the product with the program flowgraph to identify the set of infinite execution paths whose infeasibility still needs to be proven. One can use off-the-shelf complementation algorithms like rank based [12,13,17,27] or determinisation based [24,25,28,29] ones, but they make no use of the special structure of SDBAs.

We show that exploiting this structure helps: while the complementation of Büchi automata with $n$ states leads to a $(cn)^n$ blow-up for a constant $c \approx 0.76$ (cf. [27] for the upper and [37] for the lower bound), an SDBA with $n$ states can be complemented to an automaton with less than $4^n$ states. More precisely, if the deterministic part (the states reachable from the accepting states) contains $d$ states, including $a$ accepting states, the complement automaton has at most $2^{n-d}3^a4^{d-a}$ states. The $2^{\Theta(n)}$ blow-up is tight as an $\Omega(2^n)$ lower bound is inherited from the complementation of nondeterministic finite automata. Another advantage of our construction is that it is suitable for the simplest class of Büchi automata: deterministic Büchi automata with $a$ accepting and $n$ non-accepting states are translated to $2n - a$ states, which meets Kurshan's construction for the complementation of deterministic Büchi automata [18].

---

[1] In model checking, one tests for emptiness the intersection of the automaton that recognises the runs of a system with the automaton that recognises the complement of the property language.

Moreover, the resulting automata have further useful properties. For example, their structure is very simple: they are merely an extended breakpoint construction [21]. Like ordinary breakpoint constructions, this provides a structure that is well suited for symbolic implementation. This is quite different from techniques based on Safra style determinisation [24, 25, 28, 29]. In addition to this, they are *unambiguous*, i.e. there is exactly one accepting run for each word accepted by such an automaton. This is notable, because disambiguation is another automata transformation that seems to be more involved than complementation, but simpler than determinisation [16], and it has proven to be useful for the quantitative analysis of Markov chains [3, 7]. For our motivating application, this is particular good news, as the connection to Markov chains implies direct applicability to model checking stochastic models as well as nondeterministic ones. The connection to stochastic models closes a cycle of applications, as they form a second source for applying semi-deterministic automata: they appear in the classic algorithm for the qualitative analysis of Markov decision processes [8] and in current model checking tools for their quantitative analysis [14] alike.

With all of these favourable properties in mind, it would be easy to think that the complementation mechanism we develop forms a class of its own. But this is not the case: when comparing it with classic rank based complementation [17] and its improvements [12, 13, 27], semi-deterministic automata prove to be automata, where all states in all runs can be assigned just three ranks, ranks 1 through 3 in the terminology of [17]. Consequently, there are only states with a single even rank, and a rank based algorithm that has to guess the rank correctly for states that are reachable from an accepting state has very similar properties. From this perspective, one could say that complementation and disambiguation are easy to obtain, as very little needs to be guessed (only the point where the rank of a state goes down to 1) and very little has to be checked.

We also motivate and present an on-the-fly modification of our complementation, which does not need to know the whole automaton before the complementation starts. The price for the on-the-fly approach is a slightly worse upper bound on the size of the produced automaton for the complement: it has less than $5^n$ states.

We have implemented our construction in the GOAL tool and the ULTIMATE AUTOMATA LIBRARY and evaluated it on semi-deterministic Büchi automata that were produced by ULTIMATE BÜCHI AUTOMIZER applied to programs of the Termination category of the software verification competition SV-COMP 2015 [4]. The evaluation confirms that the specific complementation algorithm realises its theoretical advantage and outperforms the traditional algorithms and produces smaller complement automata.

The remainder of the paper is organised as follows. After recalling some definitions and introducing our notation in Sect. 2, we present the complementation construction in Sect. 3 together with its complexity analysis and on-the-fly modification. In Sect. 4, we show a connection between our construction and rank-based constructions, followed by a correctness proof for our construction. The experimental evaluation is presented in Sect. 5.

## 2    Preliminaries

A *(nondeterministic) Büchi automaton* (NBA) is a tuple $\mathcal{A} = (Q, \Sigma, \delta, I, F)$, where

- $Q$ is a finite set of *states*,
- $\Sigma$ is a finite *alphabet*,
- $\delta : Q \times \Sigma \to 2^Q$ is a *transition function*,
- $I \subseteq Q$ is a set of *initial states*, and
- $F \subseteq Q$ is a set of *accepting states*.

A *run* of an automaton $\mathcal{A}$ over an infinite word $w = w_0 w_1 \ldots \in \Sigma^\omega$ is a finite or infinite sequence of states $\rho = q_0 q_1 q_2 \ldots \in Q^+ \cup Q^\omega$ such that $q_0 \in I$ and $q_{j+1} \in \delta(q_j, w_j)$ for each pair of adjacent states $q_j q_{j+1}$ in $\rho$. For a finite run $\rho = q_0 q_1 q_2 \ldots q_n \in Q^{n+1}$ we require that there is no transition for its last state, i.e. $\delta(q_n, w_n) = \emptyset$, and we say that the run *blocks*. A run is *accepting* if $q_j \in F$ holds for infinitely many $j$. A word $w$ is *accepted* by $\mathcal{A}$ if there exists an accepting run of $\mathcal{A}$ over $w$. The *language* of an automaton $\mathcal{A}$ is the set $L(\mathcal{A})$ of all words accepted by $\mathcal{A}$.

A *complement* of a Büchi automaton $\mathcal{A}$ is a Büchi automaton $\mathcal{C}$ over the same alphabet $\Sigma$ that accepts the complement language, $L(\mathcal{C}) = \Sigma^\omega \setminus L(\mathcal{A})$, of the language of $\mathcal{A}$.

A Büchi automaton $\mathcal{A} = (Q, \Sigma, \delta, I, F)$ is called *complete* if, for each state $q \in Q$ and for each letter $a \in \Sigma$, there exists at least one successor, i.e. $|\delta(q, a)| \geq 1$. A Büchi automaton $\mathcal{A}$ is *unambiguous* if, for each $w \in L(\mathcal{A})$, there exists only one accepting run over $w$.

A state of a Büchi automaton $\mathcal{A} = (Q, \Sigma, \delta, I, F)$ is called *reachable* if it occurs in some run for some word $w \in \Sigma^\omega$. $\mathcal{A} = (Q, \Sigma, \delta, I, F)$ is called *deterministic* if it has only one initial state, i.e. if $|I| = 1$, and if, for each reachable state $q \in Q$ and for each letter $a \in \Sigma$, there exists at most one successor, i.e. $|\delta(q, a)| \leq 1$.

We are particularly interested in semi-deterministic automata. A Büchi automaton is semi-deterministic if it behaves deterministically from the first visit of an accepting state onward. Formally, a Büchi automaton $\mathcal{A} = (Q, \Sigma, \delta, I, F)$ is a *semi-deterministic Büchi automaton* (SDBA) (also known as *deterministic-in-the-limit*) if, for each $q_f \in F$, the automaton $(Q, \Sigma, \delta, \{q_f\}, F)$ is deterministic.

Each semi-deterministic automaton can be divided into two parts: the part reachable from accepting states—which is completely deterministic—and the rest. Hence, one can alternatively define a semi-deterministic automaton such that the set of states $Q = Q_1 \cup Q_2$ consists of two disjoint sets $Q_1$ and $Q_2$, where $F \subseteq Q_2$, and the transition relation $\delta = \delta_1 \cup \delta_t \cup \delta_2$ consists of three disjoint transition functions, namely

$$\delta_1 : Q_1 \times \Sigma \to 2^{Q_1}, \qquad \delta_t : Q_1 \times \Sigma \to 2^{Q_2}, \text{ and} \qquad \delta_2 : Q_2 \times \Sigma \to 2^{Q_2},$$

where the relation $\delta_2$ is deterministic: for each $q \in Q_2$ and each $a \in \Sigma$, $|\delta_2(q, a)| \leq 1$. $\delta$ can then be defined as $\delta(q, a) = \delta_1(q, a) \cup \delta_t(q, a)$ if $q \in Q_1$ and $\delta(q, a) = \delta_2(q, a)$ if $q \in Q_2$. The elements of $\delta_t$ are called *transit edges*. This alternative definition is captured in Fig. 1 and used in the following section.

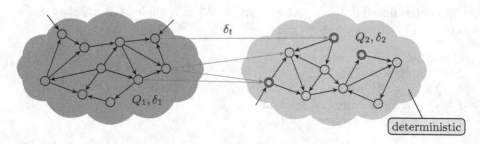

**Fig. 1.** A semi-deterministic Büchi automaton: $\delta_2$ is deterministic, accepting states are only in $Q_2$, and transit edges $(\delta_t)$ lead from $Q_1$ to $Q_2$.

# 3    Semi-deterministic Büchi Automata Complementation

First of all, we explain our complementation construction intuitively. Then we formulate it precisely and discuss the size of the resulting automata when the complementation is applied to semi-deterministic and deterministic Büchi automata. At the end, we briefly introduce the modification of our complementation construction for on-the-fly approach. The correctness is addressed in Sect. 4 after introducing the concept of level rankings and run graphs.

## 3.1    Relation of Runs to the Complement

Let $\mathcal{A} = (Q, \Sigma, \delta, I, F)$ be an SDBA, $Q_1, \delta_1, Q_2, \delta_2, \delta_t$ be the notation introduced in Fig. 1, and $w = w_0 w_1 \ldots \in \Sigma^\omega$ be an infinite word. Each run $\rho$ of $\mathcal{A}$ over $w$ has one of the following properties:

1. $\rho$ blocks,
2. $\rho$ stays forever in $Q_1$,
3. $\rho$ enters $Q_2$ and stops visiting $F$ at some point, or
4. $\rho$ is an accepting run.

Clearly, $w \notin L(\mathcal{A})$ if and only if every run of $\mathcal{A}$ over $w$ has one of the first three properties. In the third case, we say that $\rho$ is *safe* after visiting $F$ for the last time (or since the moment it enters $Q_2$ if it does not visit any accepting state at all).

In order to check whether $w \in L(\mathcal{A})$ or not, one has to track all possible runs of $\mathcal{A}$. After reading a finite prefix of $w$, the states reached by the corresponding prefixes of runs can be divided into three sets.

1. The set $N \subseteq Q_1$ represents the runs that kept out of the deterministic part ($N$ stands for *nondeterministic*) so far.
2. The set $C \subseteq Q_2$ represents the runs that have entered the deterministic part and that are not safe. One has to *check* (hence the name $C$) if some of them will be prolonged into accepting runs in the future, or if all of the runs eventually block or become safe.
3. The set $S \subseteq Q_2 \setminus F$ represents the *safe* runs.

Clearly, every accepting run of $\mathcal{A}$ stays in $C$ after leaving $N$. On the other hand, if $w \notin L(\mathcal{A})$, every infinite run either stays in $N$ or eventually leaves $C$ to $S$ and thus does not stay in $C$ forever.

## 3.2  NCSB Complementation Construction

In this section, we describe an efficient construction that produces, for a given SDBA $\mathcal{A}$, a complement automaton $\mathcal{C}$. The automaton $\mathcal{C}$ has typically a low degree of non-determinism when compared to results of other complementation algorithms, and is always unambiguous. The complementation construction proposed here tracks the runs of $\mathcal{A}$ using the well known powerset construction and guesses the right classification of runs into sets $N, C$, and $S$. Moreover, in order to check that no run stays forever in $C$, it uses one more set $B \subseteq C$. The set $B$ mimics the behaviour of $C$ with one exception: it does not adopt the runs freshly coming to $C$ via $\delta_t$. The size of $B$ never increases until it becomes empty; then we say that a *breakpoint* is reached. After each breakpoint, $B$ is set to track exactly the runs currently in $C$. To sum up, states of $\mathcal{C}$ are quadruples $(N, C, S, B)$—hence the name NCSB complementation construction.

After reading only a finite prefix of the input word $w$, the automaton cannot know whether or not some run is already safe, as this depends on the suffix of $w$. The automaton $\mathcal{C}$ uses the guess-and-check strategy. Whenever a run $\rho$ in $C$ may freshly become safe (it is leaving an accepting state or it is entering $Q_2$ via a transit edge), then the automaton $\mathcal{C}$ makes a nondeterministic decision to move $\rho$ to $S$ or to leave it in $C$. The construction punishes every wrong decision:

– in order to preserve correctness, a run of $\mathcal{C}$ is blocked if $\rho$ is moved to $S$ too early (runs in $S$ are not allowed to visit accepting states any more), and
– in order to maintain unambiguity, $\rho$ is allowed to move from $C$ to $S$ only when leaving an accepting state. Hence, if $\rho$ misses the moment when it leaves an accepting state for the last time, it will stay in $C$ forever and this particular run of $\mathcal{C}$ cannot be accepting.

Before we formally describe the NCSB construction, we first naturally extend $\delta_1, \delta_2$, and $\delta_t$ to sets. For any $\bar{\delta} \in \{\delta_1, \delta_2, \delta_t\}$, any $a \in \Sigma$, and any set $X \subseteq Q_1$ or $X \subseteq Q_2$, we set $\bar{\delta}(X, a) = \bigcup_{q \in X} \bar{\delta}(q, a)$.

With the provided intuition in mind, we define the complement automaton NBA $\mathcal{C} = (P, \Sigma, \delta', I_{\mathcal{C}}, F_{\mathcal{C}})$ as follows.

- $P \subseteq 2^{Q_1} \times 2^{Q_2} \times 2^{Q_2 \smallsetminus F} \times 2^{Q_2}$.
- $I_C = \{(Q_1 \cap I, C, S, C) \mid S \cup C = I \cap Q_2, S \cap C = \emptyset\}$.
- $F_C = \{(N, C, S, B) \in P \mid B = \emptyset\}$.
- $\delta'$ is the transition function $\delta' : P \times \Sigma \to 2^P$, such that $(N', C', S', B') \in \delta'((N, C, S, B), a)$ iff
  - $N' = \delta_1(N, a)$, $C' \cup S' = \delta_t(N, a) \cup \delta_2(C \cup S, a)$ (intuition: tracing the reachable states correctly),
  - $C' \cap S' = \emptyset$ (intuition: a run in $Q_2$ is either safe, or not),
  - $S' \supseteq \delta_2(S, a)$ (intuition: safe runs must stay safe),
  - $C' \supseteq \delta_2(C \smallsetminus F, a)$ (intuition: only runs leaving an accepting state can become safe),
  - for all $q \in C \smallsetminus F$, $\delta_2(q, a) \neq \emptyset$ (intuition: otherwise the corresponding run was safe already and should have been moved to $S$ earlier), and
  - if $B = \emptyset$ then $B' = C'$, and else $B' = \delta_2(B, a) \cap C'$ (intuition: breakpoint construction to check that no run stays in $C$ forever).

Note that the only source of nondeterminism of $\delta'$ is when $C$ has to guess correctly whether or not a run $\rho$ of $\mathcal{A}$ is safe. Such situations arise in two cases, namely when the current state $q$ of the run $\rho$ satisfies

- $q \in \delta_t(N, a) \smallsetminus (\delta_2(S, a) \cup F)$—$\rho$ is freshly entering $Q_2$, and when
- $q \in \delta_2(C \cap F, a) \smallsetminus (\delta_2(S, a) \cup F)$—$\rho$ is leaving an accepting state.

All other situations are determined, including runs that are currently in $\delta_2(S, a)$ (which belong to $S$) and runs that are currently in $F$ (which belong to $C$).

## 3.3   Complexity

Let $p = (N, C, S, B) \in P$ of $C$. Then

- for a state $q_1 \in Q_1$ of $\mathcal{A}$, $q_1$ is either present or absent in $N$;
- for $q_2 \in F$, one of the following three options holds: $q_2$ is only in $C$, $q_2$ is both in $C$ and $B$, or $q_2$ is not present in $p$ at all; and
- for $q_3 \in Q_2 \smallsetminus F$, one of the following four options holds: $q_3$ is only in $S$, $q_3$ is only in $C$, $q_3$ is both in $C$ and $B$, or $q_3$ is not present in $p$ at all.

The size of $P$ is thus bounded by $|P| \leq 2^{|Q_1|} \cdot 3^{|F|} \cdot 4^{|Q_2 \smallsetminus F|}$.

Let us note that, for deterministic automata (here we assume $\mathcal{A}$ is complete and $Q_1$ is empty), the NCSB construction leads to an automaton similar to an automaton with $2|Q| - |F|$ states produced by Kurshan's construction [18]. To see the size of the automaton produced by our construction for a DBA, recall that a state $(N, C, S, B)$ of the complement automaton encodes that exactly the states in $N \cup C \cup S$ are reachable. For a DBA, $N \cup C \cup S$ thus contains exactly one state $q$ of $Q$. Moreover, $N$ is empty and thus $B$ coincides with $C$ since $B$ becomes empty together with $C$. If $q \in F$, then it is in both $B$ and $C$. If $q \in Q_2 \smallsetminus F$, then it is either only in $S$, or in both $B$ and $C$, leading to a size $\leq 2|Q_2| - |F|$.

### 3.4  Modification Suitable for On-the-fly Implementation

Some algorithms do not need to construct the whole complement automaton. For example, in order to verify that $w \notin L(\mathcal{A})$ one only needs to built the accepting lasso in $\mathcal{C}$ for $w$. Or when building a product with some other automaton (or Markov chain), it is unnecessary to build the part of $\mathcal{C}$ which is not used in the product. Further, some tools work with implicitly encoded automata and/or query an SMT solver to check the presence of a transition in the automaton, which is expensive. ULTIMATE BÜCHI AUTOMIZER has both properties: it stores automata in an implicit form and builds a product of the complement with a program flowgraph. Such tools can greatly benefit from an *on-the-fly* complementation that does not rely on the knowledge of the whole input automaton.

Our complementation can be easily adapted for an on-the-fly implementation. Because we have no knowledge about $Q_1, Q_2$, and $\delta_t$ in this variation, the runs are held in $N$ until they reach an accepting state, only then they are moved to $\mathcal{C}$.

Technically, the "$N' = \delta_1(N, a)$" from the definition of $\delta'$ would be replaced by "$N' = \delta(N, a) \setminus F$" and for $C'$ now holds $C' \subseteq \delta(C, a) \cup (\delta(N, a) \cap F)$. The on-the-fly construction can therefore have up to $2^{|Q_1|} \cdot 3^{|F|} \cdot 5^{|Q_2 \setminus F|}$ states.

Note that the on-the-fly construction does not add any further nondeterminism to the construction. To the contrary, there is an injection of runs from the construction discussed in Sect. 3.2 to this on-the-fly construction. The correctness argument and the uniqueness argument for the accepting run which are given in Sect. 4 therefore need only very minor adjustments.

## 4  Level Rankings in Complementation and Correctness

We open this section by introduction of *run graphs* and *level rankings*. We then look at our construction through the level ranking lense and use the insights this provides for proving its correctness and unambiguity.

### 4.1  Complementation and Level Rankings

In [17], Kupferman and Vardi introduce *level rankings* as a witness for the absence of accepting runs of Büchi automata. They form the foundation of several complementation algorithms [12,13,17,27,29].

The set of all runs of a nondeterministic Büchi automaton $\mathcal{A} = (\Sigma, Q, I, \delta, F)$ over a word $w$ can be represented by a directed acyclic graph $\mathcal{G}_w = (V, E)$, called the *run graph* of $\mathcal{A}$ on $w$, with

- vertices $V \subseteq Q \times \omega$ such that $(q, i) \in V$ iff there is a run $\rho = q_0 q_1 q_2 \cdots$ over $\mathcal{A}$ on $w$ with $q_i = q$, and
- edges $E \subseteq (Q \times \omega) \times (Q \times \omega)$ such that $((q, i), (q', i')) \in E$ iff $i' = i + 1$ and there is a run $\rho = q_0 q_1 q_2 \cdots$ of $\mathcal{A}$ over $w$ with $q_i = q$ and $q_{i+1} = q'$.

The run graph $\mathcal{G}_w$ is called *rejecting* if no path in $\mathcal{G}_w$ satisfies the Büchi condition. That is, $\mathcal{G}_w$ is rejecting iff $w$ does not have any accepting run, and thus iff $w$ is not in the language of $\mathcal{A}$. $\mathcal{A}$ can be complemented to a nondeterministic Büchi automaton $\mathcal{C}$ that checks if $\mathcal{G}_w$ is rejecting.

The property that $\mathcal{G}_w$ is rejecting can be expressed in terms of *ranks* [17]. We call a vertex $(q, i) \in V$ of a graph $\mathcal{G} = (V, E)$ *safe*, if no vertex reachable from $(q, i)$ is accepting (that is, in $F \times \omega$), and *finite*, if the set of vertices reachable from $(q, i)$ in $\mathcal{G}$ is finite.

Based on these definitions, *ranks* can be assigned to the vertices of a rejecting run graph. We set $\mathcal{G}_w{}^0 = \mathcal{G}_w$, and repeat the following procedure until a fixed point is reached, starting with $i = 1$:

- Assign all safe vertices of $\mathcal{G}_w{}^{i-1}$ the rank $i$, and set $\mathcal{G}_w{}^i$ to $\mathcal{G}_w{}^{i-1}$ minus the vertices with rank $i$ (that is, minus the safe vertices in $\mathcal{G}_w{}^{i-1}$).
- Assign all finite vertices of $\mathcal{G}_w{}^i$ the rank $i+1$, and set $\mathcal{G}_w{}^{i+1}$ to $\mathcal{G}_w{}^i$ minus the vertices with rank $i+1$ (that is, minus the finite vertices in $\mathcal{G}_w{}^i$).
- Increase $i$ by 2.

A fixed point is reached in $n + 2$ steps[2], and the ranks can be used to characterise the complement language of a nondeterministic Büchi automaton:

**Proposition 1.** [17] *A nondeterministic Büchi automaton $\mathcal{A}$ with $n$ states rejects a word $w$ iff $\mathcal{G}_w{}^{2n+2}$ is empty.*    □

## 4.2   Ranks and Complementation of SDBAs

When considering the run graph for SBDAs, we only need to consider three ranks: 1, 2, and 3. What is more, the vertices $Q_2 \times \omega$ reachable from accepting vertices can only have rank 1 or rank 2 in a rejecting run graph.

**Proposition 2.** *A semi-deterministic Büchi automaton $\mathcal{A}$ rejects a word $w$ iff $\mathcal{G}_w{}^3$ is empty. This is the case iff $\mathcal{G}_w{}^2$ contains no vertex in $Q_2 \times \omega$.*

*Proof.* Let $w$ be a word rejected by $\mathcal{S}$. By construction, $\mathcal{G}_w{}^1$ contains no safe vertices. (Note that removing safe vertices does not introduce new safe vertices.)

Let us assume for contradiction that $\mathcal{G}_w{}^1$ contains a vertex $(q_i, i) \in Q_2 \times \omega$, which is not finite. As $(q_i, i)$ is not finite, there is an infinite run $\rho = q_0 q_1 q_2 \cdots q_{i-1} q_i q_{i+1} \cdots$ of $\mathcal{A}$ over $w$ such that, for all $j \geq i$, $(q_j, j)$ is a vertex in $\mathcal{G}_w{}^1$. This is because $q_i \in Q_2$, the deterministic part of the SBDA, and $\{(q_j, j) \mid j \geq i\}$ is therefore (1) determined by $w$ and $(q_i, i)$, and (2) fully in $\mathcal{G}_w{}^1$, because otherwise $(q_i, i)$ would be finite.

But if all vertices in $\{(q_j, j) \mid j \geq i\}$ are in $\mathcal{G}_w{}^1$, then none of them is safe in $\mathcal{G}_w$. Using again that the tail $q_i q_{i+1} q_{i+2} \cdots$ is unique and well defined

---

[2] It is common to use 0 as the minimal rank (i.e. to start with the finite vertices), but the correctness of the complementation does not rely on this. The proof in [17] refers to this case, and requires $n + 1$ steps. For our purpose, the minimal rank needs to be odd, i.e. we need to start with safe vertices.

(as $q_i \in Q_2$, the deterministic part of the SDBA), it follows that, for all $j \geq i$, there is a $k \geq j$ such that $q_k$ is accepting. Consequently, $\rho$ is accepting (contradiction).

We have thus shown that, if $\mathcal{S}$ rejects a word $w$, then $\mathcal{G}_w{}^2$ contains no state in $Q_2 \times \omega$. This also implies that $\mathcal{G}_w{}^2$ contains no accepting vertices. Consequently, all vertices in $\mathcal{G}_w{}^2$ are safe. Consequently, $\mathcal{G}_w{}^3$ is empty.                    □

We now consider the NCSB construction from a level ranking perspective. We start with an intuition for the *rational* run $\rho = (N_0, C_0, S_0, B_0)(N_1, C_1, S_1, B_1)(N_2, C_2, S_2, B_2)\ldots$ of $\mathcal{C}$ over a word $w$ rejected by $\mathcal{A}$, where $(V, E) = \mathcal{G}_w$. A rational run is the unique accepting run of $\mathcal{C}$ over $w$ and it guesses the ranks precisely, that is:

- $N_i = \{q \mid (q, i) \in V, q \in Q_1\}$,
- $C_i = \{q \mid (q, i) \in V, q \in Q_2$ and the rank of $(q, i)$ is 2$\}$ (we need to check that these states are finite in $\mathcal{G}_w{}^2$),
- $S_i = \{q \mid (q, i) \in V, q \in Q_2$ and the rank of $(q, i)$ is 1$\}$,
- $B_i \subseteq C_i$.

All runs of $\mathcal{C}$ that differ on some $i$ from the rational run will either block or will keep the wrongly guessed vertices with rank 1 in $C$ and thus will be not accepting.

Note that the $\mathcal{C}$ does not need to guess much. The development of the $N_i$ is deterministic. The development of $C_i \cup S_i$ is deterministic, $S_i$ and $C_i$ are disjoint, and states in $F$ cannot be in $S_i$. The $B_i$ serve as a breakpoint construction, and the development of $B_i$ is determined by the development of the $C_i$. All that needs to be guessed is the point when a vertex becomes safe, and there is only a single correct guess.

## 4.3 Correctness

After reading only a finite prefix of an input word $w$, the automaton has to use its nondeterministic power to guess which reached state in $Q_2$ should be added to $S$. We now establish that the automaton $\mathcal{C}$ is an unambiguous automaton that recognises the complement language of $\mathcal{A}$ by showing

1. $\mathcal{C}$ does not accept a word that is accepted by $\mathcal{A}$,
2. for words that are not accepted by $\mathcal{A}$, the run inferred from the level ranking discussed in Sect. 4.2 defines an accepting run, and
3. for words $w$ that are not accepted by $\mathcal{A}$, this is the only accepting run of $\mathcal{C}$ over $w$.

**Lemma 1.** *Let $\mathcal{A}$ be an SDBA, $\mathcal{C}$ be constructed by the NCSB complementation of $\mathcal{A}$, and $w \in L(\mathcal{A})$ be a word in the language of $\mathcal{A}$. Then $\mathcal{C}$ does not accept $w$.*

*Proof.* Let $\rho = q_0 q_1 \ldots$ be an accepting run of $\mathcal{A}$ over $w$, and let $i \in \omega$ be an index such that $q_i \in F$. Let us assume for contradiction that $\rho' = (N_0, C_0, S_0, B_0)(N_1, C_1, S_1, B_1)\ldots(N_n, C_n, S_n, B_n)\ldots$ is an accepting run of $\mathcal{C}$ over $w$. Clearly, $q_i \in C_i$. It therefore holds, for all $j \geq i$, that $q_j \in C_j \cup S_j$.

We look at the following case distinction.

1. For all $j \geq i$, $q_j \in C_j$. As $\rho'$ is accepting, there is a breakpoint ($B_j = \emptyset$) for some $j \geq i$. For such a $j$ we have that $q_{j+1} \in B_{j+1}$ and, moreover, that $q_k \in B_k$ for all $k \geq j+1$. Thus, $B_k \neq \emptyset$ for all $k \geq j+1$ and $\rho'$ visits only finitely many accepting states (contradiction).
2. There is a $j \geq i$ such that $q_j \in S_j$. But then $q_k \in S_k$ holds for all $k \geq j$ by construction. However, as $\rho$ is accepting, there is an $l \geq j$ such that $q_l \in F$, which contradicts $q_l \in S_l$ (contradiction). $\qquad\square$

**Lemma 2.** *Let $\mathcal{A}$ be an SDBA, $\mathcal{C}$ be the automaton constructed by the NCSB complementation of $\mathcal{A}$, $w \notin L(\mathcal{A})$, and $(V, E) = \mathcal{G}_w$ be the run graph of $\mathcal{A}$ on $w$. Then there is exactly one rational run of the form $\rho = (N_0, C_0, S_0, B_0)(N_1, C_1, S_1, B_1)(N_2, C_2, S_2, B_2)\ldots$. This run is accepting.*

*Proof.* It is easy to check that this defines exactly one infinite run: the updates of the $N$, $C$, and $S$ components follow the rules for transitions from the definition of $\mathcal{C}$, and the update of the $B$ component is fully determined by the update of $C$ and the previous value of $B$.

What remains is to show that the run is accepting. Let us assume for contradiction that there are only finitely many breakpoints reached, i.e. there is an index $i \in \omega$, for which there is no $j \geq i$, such that $B_j = \emptyset$.

Now we have $\emptyset \neq B_i \subseteq C_i = \{q \mid (q, i) \in V \text{ s.t. } q \in Q_2 \text{ and the rank of } (q, i) \text{ is } 2\}$. The construction provides that, if there is no breakpoint on or after position $i$, then $B_j$ is the set of states that correspond to vertices from $Q \times \{j\}$ reachable in $\mathcal{G}_w{}^1$ from the vertices $B_i \times \{i\}$. As there is no future breakpoint, there are infinitely many such vertices, and Königs lemma implies that there is an infinite path in $\mathcal{G}_w{}^1$ from at least one of the vertices in $B_i \times \{i\}$. This provides a contradiction to the assumption that the rank of these vertices is 2, i.e. that they are finite in $\mathcal{G}_w{}^1$. $\qquad\square$

**Lemma 3.** *Let $\mathcal{A}$ be an SDBA, $\mathcal{C}$ be the automaton constructed by the NCSB complementation of $\mathcal{A}$, $w \notin L(\mathcal{A})$, and $(V, E) = \mathcal{G}_w$ be the run graph of $\mathcal{A}$ on $w$. Let $\rho = (N_0, C_0, S_0, B_0)(N_1, C_1, S_1, B_1)(N_2, C_2, S_2, B_2)\ldots$ be an infinite, non-rational run of $\mathcal{C}$ over $w$ that is, it does not satisfy*

- $N_i = \{q \mid (q, i) \in V \text{ s.t. } q \in Q_1\}$,
- $C_i = \{q \mid (q, i) \in V \text{ s.t. } q \in Q_2 \text{ and the rank of } (q, i) \text{ is } 2\}$,
- $S_i = \{q \mid (q, i) \in V \text{ s.t. } q \in Q_2 \text{ and the rank of } (q, i) \text{ is } 1\}$,

*for some $i$. Then $\rho$ is rejecting.*

*Proof.* As the $N$ part always tracks the reachable states in $Q_1$ correctly by construction, and the $C \cup S$ part always tracks the reachable states in $Q_2$ correctly by construction, we have one of the following two cases according to Proposition 2.

The first case is that there is a safe vertex $(q, i) \in V$ such that $q \in C_i$. By construction, a unique maximal path $(q_i, i)(q_{i+1}, i+1)(q_{i+2}, i+2)(q_{i+3}, i+3)\ldots$ for $q_i = q$ exists in $\mathcal{G}_w$, and this path does not contain any accepting state. By an inductive argument, for all vertices $(q_j, j)$ on this path, $q_j \in C_j$. If the path is finite, $\rho$ blocks at the end (due to the definition of the transition function of $\mathcal{C}$), which contradicts the assumption that the run $\rho$ is infinite. Similarly, if the path is infinite, $q_k \in B_k$ for some $k \geq i$. Then $q_j \in B_j$ for all $j > k$ with $(q_j, j)$ on this path. Therefore, $\rho$ cannot be accepting.

The second case is that there is a non-safe vertex in $(q, i) \in V$ such that $q \in S_i$. (Note that this implies $q \notin F$.) By construction, we get, for $q_i = q$, a unique maximal path $(q_i, i)(q_{i+1}, i+1)(q_{i+2}, i+2)(q_{i+3}, i+3) \ldots$ in $\mathcal{G}_w$, and this path contains an accepting state $q_k$. By an inductive argument, for all vertices $(q_j, j)$ on this path, $q_j \in S_j$. But this implies $q_k \in S_k$ (contradiction). $\qquad\square$

The first two lemmas provide the correctness of our complementation algorithm. Considering that no finite run is accepting, the third lemma establishes that $\mathcal{C}$ is unambiguous.

**Theorem 1.** *Let $\mathcal{A}$ be an SDBA and $\mathcal{C}$ be the automaton constructed by the NCSB complementation of $\mathcal{A}$. Then $\mathcal{C}$ is an unambiguous Büchi automaton that recognises the complement of the language of $\mathcal{A}$.*

## 5   Experimental Evaulation

This section compares the results of the NCSB complementation with these produced by well-known complementations for nondeterministic Büchi automata. All the automata, tools, scripts and commands used in the evaluation, and some further comparisons can be found at https://github.com/xblahoud/NCSB-Complementation.

### 5.1   Implementations of the NCSB Complementation

We implemented the NCSB complementation in two tools. One implementation is available in the GOAL tool[3] [33]. GOAL is a graphical interactive tool for omega automata, temporal logics, and games. It provides several Büchi complementation algorithms and was used in an extensive evaluation of these algorithms [32]. In the commandline version, the parameter for our construction is `complement -m sdbw -a`. The partition of the set $Q$ into $Q_1$ and $Q_2$ is not a parameter, instead the implementation uses the set of all states that are reachable from some accepting state as $Q_2$.

Our second implementation is available in the ULTIMATE AUTOMATA LIBRARY. This library is used by the termination analyser ULTIMATE BÜCHI AUTOMIZER and other tools of the ULTIMATE program analysis framework[4]. The implementation uses the on-the-fly construction discussed in Sect. 3.4. The library provides a language that allows users to define automata and a sequence of commands that should be executed by the library. This language is called

---

[3] http://goal.im.ntu.edu.tw/.

[4] http://ultimate.informatik.uni-freiburg.de/.

*automata script* and an interpreter for this language is available via a web interface[5]. The operation that implements the NCSB construction has the name buchiComplementNCSB.

## 5.2   Example Automata

For our evaluation, we took automata whose complementation was a subtask while the tool ULTIMATE BÜCHI AUTOMIZER was analysing the programs from the Termination category of the software verification competition SV-COMP 2015 [4]. We wrote each Büchi automaton that was semi-deterministic but not deterministic to a file in the Hanoi omega-automata format [2]. We obtained 106 semi-deterministic Büchi automata. Using the command autfilt --unique -H from the SPOT library [10], we identified isomorphic automata and kept only the remaining 97 pairwise non-isomorphic ones.

By construction, all these automata behave deterministically only after the first visit of an accepting state. Hence the partition of the states $Q$ into $Q_1$ and $Q_2$ is unique and the results of the construction presented in Sect. 3.2 and the results of the on-the-fly modification presented in Sect. 3.4 coincide.

## 5.3   Other Complementation Constructions

The known constructions for the complementation of nondeterministic Büchi automata can be classified into the following four categories.

**Ramsey-based.** Historically the first complementation construction introduced by Büchi [6] and later improved by Sistla, Vardi, and Wolper [31] in which a Ramsey-based combinatorial argument is involved.

**Determinisation-based.** A construction proposed by Safra [25] and later enhanced by Piterman [24] in which a state of a complement is represented by a Safra tree.

**Rank-based.** A construction introduced by Kupferman and Vardi [17] for which several optimisations [12,13,17,27] have been proposed.

**Slice-based.** A construction [16] proposed by Kähler and Wilke that constructs complements accepting reduced split trees rather than run graphs.

For each of these categories, GOAL provides implementations that can be adjusted by various parameters. In our evaluation, we included one construction from each category. For the latter three categories, we took the arguments that were most successful in an extensive evaluation [32]. For the first category, we used additionally an optimisation that minimises the finite automata that are constructed during the complementation [5]. The commands that we used are listed in Table 1.

---

[5] http://ultimate.informatik.uni-freiburg.de/automata_script_interpreter.

## 5.4    Evaluation

We applied the NCSB complementation and the four complementations of Table 1 to the 97 pairwise non-isomorphic SDBAs. All complementations were run on a laptop with an Intel Core i5 2.70 GHz CPU. We restricted the maximal heap space of the JVM to 8 GB (all complementations are implemented in Java) and used a timeout of 300 s. The results are depicted in Table 2 and Fig. 2.

For 91 out of 97 SDBAs, all implementations were able to compute a result. We refer to these 91 SDBAs as easy SDBAs, while the remaining six are referenced as difficult in the Table 2. For each complementation, we provide the cumulative numbers of states and transitions of all 91 easy complements. For each of the easy SDBAs, NCSB construction produces the complement with the smallest number of states. In Fig. 2, a size of the complement produced by the NCSB construction is compared to the size of the smallest complement produced by the constructions of Table 1 for each of the easy automata.

For the difficult SDBAs, at least one construction was not able to provide the result within the given time and memory limits. We provide the number of states of the computed complements for each of them. While there are two cases where the determinisation-based construction produced an automaton with less states than the NCSB construction, the number of transition was always smaller for the NCSB construction.

A common approach to mitigate the problem of large complementation results is to apply generic size reduction algorithm. Does our NCSB construction also outperform the other constructions if we apply size reduction techniques afterwards? In order to address this question, we applied the "simplification

**Table 1.** Complementation constructions of NBAs used in our evaluation

| Construction | GOAL command |
|---|---|
| Ramsey-based | `complement -m ramsey -macc -min` |
| Determinisation-based | `complement -m piterman -macc -sim -eq` |
| Rank-based | `complement -m rank -macc -tr -ro -cp` |
| Slice-based | `complement -m slice -macc -eg -madj -ro` |

**Table 2.** Results of complementation constructions without posteriori simplifications

| Construction | 91 easy SDBAs | | 6 difficult SDBAs | | | | | |
|---|---|---|---|---|---|---|---|---|
| | States | Transitions | 1 | 2 | 3 | 4 | 5 | 6 |
| Ramsey-based | 16909 | 848969 | – | – | – | – | – | – |
| Rank-based | 2703 | 21095 | – | – | 1022 | 7460 | 8245 | – |
| Det.-based | 1841 | 24964 | – | – | 172 | 346 | 385 | 3527 |
| Slice-based | 1392 | 14783 | 66368 | – | 184 | 421 | 475 | 9596 |
| NCSB | 950 | 8003 | 20711 | 84567 | 108 | 343 | 401 | 5449 |

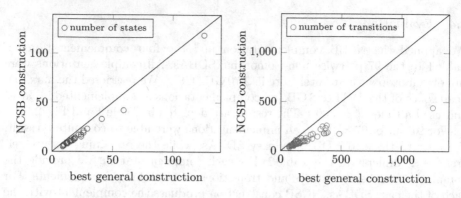

**Fig. 2.** Comparison of the NCSB construction and other complementations

routines" of the SPOT library [1] (in version 1.99.4a) to the complements. We run the command `autfilt --small --high -B -H` with a timeout of 300 s and obtained the results depicted in Table 3. For 75 SDBAs, all complements could be simplified within the timeout. For these we again provide the cumulative numbers of states and transitions before and after the simplifications. The column *min* shows how often each construction followed by simplification produced a complement with the minimal number of states. The column *failure* shows how often a timeout prevented a successful complementation or simplification. It is interesting to see that the simplifications were not able to reduce the number of transitions much for the NCSB construction, while they were able to reduce it by more than 20 % in case of the other complementations.

**Table 3.** Complementations and simplifications

| Construction | No simplifications | | With simplifications | | | Failure | |
|---|---|---|---|---|---|---|---|
| | States | Transitions | States | Transitions | min | compl. | simp. |
| Ramsey-based | 6386 | 172351 | 5223 | 90548 | 0 | 6 | 22 |
| Rank-based | 1437 | 11677 | 899 | 7657 | 4 | 3 | 14 |
| Det.-based | 1300 | 15491 | 1083 | 9589 | 0 | 2 | 11 |
| Slice-based | 892 | 8921 | 785 | 6789 | 4 | 1 | 13 |
| NCSB | 598 | 4922 | 514 | 4460 | 73 | 0 | 10 |

## 6    Conclusion

We have introduced an efficient complementation construction for semi-deterministic Büchi automata (SDBA). The results of our construction have two appealing properties: they are unambiguous and have less than $4^n$ states.

We have presented a modification of our construction suitable for implementation on-the-fly and showed that our construction can be seen as a specialised version of the rank-based construction for nondeterministic Büchi automata. We have implemented our construction in two tools and did an experimental evaluation on semi-deterministic Büchi automata produced by the termination analyser ULTIMATE BÜCHI AUTOMIZER. We have compared our construction to four known complementation constructions for (general) nondeterministic Büchi automata. The evaluation showed that our construction outperforms the existing constructions in the number of states and transitions.

# References

1. Babiak, T., Badie, T., Duret-Lutz, A., Křetínský, M., Strejček, J.: Compositional approach to suspension and other improvements to LTL translation. In: Bartocci, E., Ramakrishnan, C.R. (eds.) SPIN 2013. LNCS, vol. 7976, pp. 81–98. Springer, Heidelberg (2013)
2. Babiak, T., Blahoudek, F., Duret-Lutz, A., Klein, J., Křetínský, J., Müller, D., Parker, D., Strejček, J.: The Hanoi omega-automata format. In: Kroening, D., Păsăreanu, C.S. (eds.) CAV 2015. LNCS, vol. 9206, pp. 479–486. Springer, Heidelberg (2015)
3. Benedikt, M., Lenhardt, R., Worrell, J.: LTL model checking of interval Markov chains. In: Piterman, N., Smolka, S.A. (eds.) TACAS 2013 (ETAPS 2013). LNCS, vol. 7795, pp. 32–46. Springer, Heidelberg (2013)
4. Beyer, D.: Software verification and verifiable witnesses. In: Baier, C., Tinelli, C. (eds.) TACAS 2015. LNCS, vol. 9035, pp. 401–416. Springer, Heidelberg (2015)
5. Breuers, S., Löding, C., Olschewski, J.: Improved Ramsey-based Büchi complementation. In: Birkedal, L. (ed.) FOSSACS 2012. LNCS, vol. 7213, pp. 150–164. Springer, Heidelberg (2012)
6. Büchi, J.R.: On a decision method in restricted second order arithmetic. In: CLMpPS 1960, pp. 1–11. Stanford University Press (1962)
7. Bustan, D., Rubin, S., Vardi, M.Y.: Verifying ω-regular properties of Markov chains. In: Alur, R., Peled, D.A. (eds.) CAV 2004. LNCS, vol. 3114, pp. 189–201. Springer, Heidelberg (2004)
8. Courcoubetis, C., Yannakakis, M.: The complexity of probabilistic verification. J. ACM 42(4), 857–907 (1995)
9. Dietsch, D., Heizmann, M., Langenfeld, V., Podelski, A.: Fairness modulo theory: a new approach to LTL software model checking. In: Kroening, D., Păsăreanu, C.S. (eds.) CAV 2015. LNCS, vol. 9206, pp. 49–66. Springer, Heidelberg (2015)
10. Duret-Lutz, A., Poitrenaud, D., SPOT: An extensible model checking library using transition-based generalized Büchi automata. In: MASCOTS 2004, pp. 76–83. IEEE Computer Society (2004)
11. Fogarty, S., Kupferman, O., Wilke, T., Vardi, M.Y.: Unifying Büchi complementation constructions. Logical Methods Comput. Sci. 9(1), 1–25 (2013)
12. Friedgut, E., Kupferman, O., Vardi, M.Y.: Büchi complementation made tighter. Int. J. Found. Comput. Sci. 17(4), 851–868 (2006)
13. Gurumurthy, S., Kupferman, O., Somenzi, F., Vardi, M.Y.: On complementing nondeterministic Büchi automata. In: Geist, D., Tronci, E. (eds.) CHARME 2003. LNCS, vol. 2860, pp. 96–110. Springer, Heidelberg (2003)

14. Hahn, E.M., Li, G., Schewe, S., Turrini, A., Zhang, L.: Lazy probabilistic model checking without determinisation. In: CONCUR 2015. LIPIcs, vol. 42, pp. 354–367. Schloss Dagstuhl-Leibniz-Zentrum fuer Informatik (2015)
15. Heizmann, M., Hoenicke, J., Podelski, A.: Termination analysis by learning terminating programs. In: Biere, A., Bloem, R. (eds.) CAV 2014. LNCS, vol. 8559, pp. 797–813. Springer, Heidelberg (2014)
16. Kähler, D., Wilke, T.: Complementation, disambiguation, and determinization of Büchi automata unified. In: Aceto, L., Damgård, I., Goldberg, L.A., Halldórsson, M.M., Ingólfsdóttir, A., Walukiewicz, I. (eds.) ICALP 2008, Part I. LNCS, vol. 5125, pp. 724–735. Springer, Heidelberg (2008)
17. Kupferman, O., Vardi, M.Y.: Weak alternating automata are not that weak. ACM Trans. Comput. Logic 2(2), 408–429 (2001)
18. Kurshan, R.P.: Computer-Aided Verification of Coordinating Processes: The Automata-Theoretic Approach. Princeton University Press, Princeton (1994)
19. McNaughton, R.: Testing and generating infinite sequences by a finite automaton. Inf. Control 9(5), 521–530 (1966)
20. Michel, M.: Complementation is more difficult with automata on infinite words. Technical report, CNET, Paris (Manuscript) (1988)
21. Miyano, S., Hayashi, T.: Alternating finite automata on ω-words. Theor. Comput. Sci. 32(3), 321–330 (1984)
22. Muller, D.E.: Infinite sequences and finite machines. In: FOCS 1963, pp. 3–16. IEEE Computer Society Press (1963)
23. Pécuchet, J.-P.: On the complementation of Büchi automata. Theor. Comput. Sci. 47(3), 95–98 (1986)
24. Piterman, N.: From nondeterministic Büchi and Streett automata to deterministic parity automata. Logical Methods Comput. Sci. 3(3:5) (2007)
25. Safra, S.: On the complexity of omega-automata. In: FOCS 1988, pp. 319–327. IEEE Computer Society (1988)
26. Sakoda, W.J., Sipser, M.: Non-determinism and the size of two-way automata. In STOC 1978, pp. 274–286. ACM Press (1978)
27. Schewe, S.: Büchi complementation made tight. In: STACS 2009. LIPIcs, vol. 3, pp. 661–672. Schloss Dagstuhl - Leibniz-Zentrum fuer Informatik (2009)
28. Schewe, S.: Tighter bounds for the determinisation of Büchi automata. In: de Alfaro, L. (ed.) FOSSACS 2009. LNCS, vol. 5504, pp. 167–181. Springer, Heidelberg (2009)
29. Schewe, S., Varghese, T.: Tight bounds for the determinisation and complementation of generalised Büchi automata. In: Chakraborty, S., Mukund, M. (eds.) ATVA 2012. LNCS, vol. 7561, pp. 42–56. Springer, Heidelberg (2012)
30. Schewe, S., Varghese, T.: Tight bounds for complementing parity automata. In: Csuhaj-Varjú, E., Dietzfelbinger, M., Ésik, Z. (eds.) MFCS 2014, Part I. LNCS, vol. 8634, pp. 499–510. Springer, Heidelberg (2014)
31. Sistla, A.P., Vardi, M.Y., Wolper, P.: The complementation problem for Büchi automata with applications to temporal logic. Theor. Comput. Sci. 49(3), 217–239 (1987)
32. Tsai, M.-H., Fogarty, S., Vardi, M.Y., Tsay, Y.: State of Büchi complementation. Logical Methods Comput. Sci. 10(4:13) (2014)
33. Tsai, M.-H., Tsay, Y.-K., Hwang, Y.-S.: GOAL for Games, omega-automata, and logics. In: Sharygina, N., Veith, H. (eds.) CAV 2013. LNCS, vol. 8044, pp. 883–889. Springer, Heidelberg (2013)
34. Vardi, M.Y.: Automatic verification of probabilistic concurrent finite-state programs. In: FOCS 1985, pp. 327–338. IEEE Computer Society (1985)

35. Vardi, M.Y.: The Büchi complementation saga. In: Thomas, W., Weil, P. (eds.) STACS 2007. LNCS, vol. 4393, pp. 12–22. Springer, Heidelberg (2007)
36. Vardi, M.Y., Wolper, P.: An automata-theoretic approach to automatic program verification (preliminary report). In: LICS 1986, pp. 332–344. IEEE Computer Society (1986)
37. Yan, Q., Lower bounds for complementation of omega-automata via the full automata technique. Logical Methods Comput. Sci. 4(1: 5), 1–20 (2008)

# Security

# Reasoning About Information Flow Security of Separation Kernels with Channel-Based Communication

Yongwang Zhao[1,2]([⊠]), David Sanán[1], Fuyuan Zhang[1], and Yang Liu[1]

[1] School of Computer Engineering, Nanyang Technological University,
Singapore, Singapore
ywzhao@ntu.edu.sg, zhaoyw@buaa.edu.cn
[2] School of Computer Science and Engineering, Beihang University, Beijing, China

**Abstract.** Assurance of information flow security by formal methods is mandated in security certification of separation kernels. As an industrial standard for separation kernels, ARINC 653 has been complied with by mainstream separation kernels. Security of functionalities defined in ARINC 653 is thus very important for the development and certification of separation kernels. This paper presents the first effort to formally specify and verify separation kernels with ARINC 653 channel-based communication. We provide a reusable formal specification and security proofs for separation kernels in Isabelle/HOL. During reasoning about information flow security, we find some security flaws in the ARINC 653 standard, which can cause information leakage, and fix them in our specification. We also validate the existence of the security flaws in two open-source ARINC 653 compliant separation kernels.

## 1 Introduction

Separation kernels [26] create a secure environment by providing temporal and spatial separation of applications and ensure that there are no unintended channels for information flows between partitions other than those explicitly provided. Separation kernels decouple the verification of applications in partitions from the verification of the kernels themselves. They are often sufficiently small and straightforward to allow formal verification of their correctness. Assurance of information flow security [28] by formal methods is mandated in Separation Kernel Protection Profile (SKPP) [21] and certifying separation kernels to highest Common Criteria evaluation levels (EAL 6 or 7) is always accomplished by formally verifying information flow security.

Traditionally, security and safety of critical systems are assured and certified by using two kinds of separation kernels respectively, such as VxWorks 653 [3] for safety-critical systems and VxWorks MILS [4] for security-critical systems. A trend in this field is to integrate safe and secure functionalities into one separation kernel. For instance, PikeOS [2], LynxSecure [1] and open-source XtratuM [16] are designed to support both safety critical and security critical

© Springer-Verlag Berlin Heidelberg 2016
M. Chechik and J.-F. Raskin (Eds.): TACAS 2016, LNCS 9636, pp. 791–810, 2016.
DOI: 10.1007/978-3-662-49674-9_50

solutions. As an industrial standard for safety-critical separation kernels, ARINC 653 [5] aims at improving safety and certification process of safety-critical systems, which has been complied with by the mainstream separation kernels such as PikeOS, VxWorks 653 and XtratuM. Therefore, in order to develop ARINC 653 compliant secure separation kernels, it is necessary to assure security of the functionalities defined in ARINC 653. A security verified specification and its mechanically checked proofs of ARINC 653 are significant for the development and certification of separation kernels.

In separation kernels, Inter-Partition Communication (IPC) is a major mechanism to implement controlled information flows, but if the mechanism is not well designed, IPC can also contain covert channels [18] to leak information between applications. ARINC 653 defines the functionalities and services of a *channel-based communication* mechanism for IPC. Although formal specification [8,30–32] and verification [9,12,13,19,25,29,33] of information flow security on separation kernels have been widely studied in academia and industry, information flow security of separation kernels with ARINC 653 channel-based communication has not been studied to date. To the best of our knowledge, this paper is the first effort on this topic.

In this paper, we present a formal specification and its security proofs[1] of separation kernels with ARINC 653 channel-based communication in Isabelle/HOL [22]. In detail, the technical contributions of this work are as follows.

1. We provide a mechanically checked formal specification which comprises a generic execution model for separation kernels and an event specification for ARINC 653. We introduce two security domains: a *scheduler* and a *message transmitter*, and their security policies according to the characteristics of scheduling and IPC of separation kernels. The event specification models all IPC services defined in ARINC 653 (Sect. 3).
2. We define a set of information flow security properties and an inference framework to sketch out the implications between security properties. We provide the security proofs to indicate information flow security of the specification (Sect. 4).
3. We find some security flaws, i.e., covert channels to leak information, in the ARINC 653 standard when proving our original specification that is completely compliant with ARINC 653, and fix them by a redesign of the specification. We also validate the existence of the security flaws in two open-source ARINC 653 compliant separation kernels, i.e., XtratuM and POK [10]. The cost of this work is in total 8 person-months (Sect. 5).

## 2    Challenges and Approach Overview

This section introduces the challenges in this work and the overview of our approach.

---

[1] The specification and proofs are available at "http://securify.sce.ntu.edu.sg/skspecv1/".

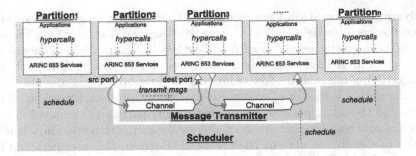

**Fig. 1.** Architecture of the Target System

**Challenges.** The challenges of this work are as follows.

1. *High complexity of the ARINC 653 standard*: The standard specifies the system functionality of separation kernels using more than 40 pages of informal descriptions and standardized services using more than 60 pages. As the core part for channel-based communication, the IPC takes more than 20 pages and defines a complicated communication mechanism including queuing and sampling modes, channel buffers and port control.
2. *Enormous efforts needed by formal verification of information flow security*: As a sort of hyperproperties [6], it is difficult to automatically verify information flow security on separation kernels so far and formal verification needs an exhausting effort. There exist different sorts of information flow security (e.g., in [20,23,27,28]) and relationship of them on ARINC 653 separation kernels has to be clarified for security assurance and certification to reduce the verification effort.

**Analysis of the Target System.** In order to address *Challenge 1*, we are more concerned on basic functionalities of separation kernels and reduce components not related to information flow security, such as hardware interface in ARINC 653. ARINC 653 uses the inter-partition flow policy [15] in which communication ports and channels are associated with partitions, and all processes in a partition can access the ports configured for this partition. Moreover, some hypervisor based separation kernels, such as XtratuM, manage partitions, but processes in a partition are invisible to the kernel. Thus, we omit the concept of "process" and intra-partition communication between processes in ARINC 653 in the formal specification. The target system to be formally specified and verified is illustrated in Fig. 1.

Since the latest version of ARINC 653 [5] is targeted at single-core processing environments, our work considers single-core separation kernels and assumes there is no in-kernel concurrency as the same as in [19]. Many separation kernel implementations only allow blocking partitions by means of invoking a "partition management" hypercall, we prohibit blocking partitions in communication events.

**Analysis of Information Flow Security.** Traditionally, language-based information flow security [28] handles only two-level domain: *High* and *Low*. The data of programs are assigned either *High* or *Low* labels. Security hereby means that variations of *High*-level data should not cause a variation of *Low*-level data. When verifying information flow security of separation kernels, the only available information is the set of configured partitions, local configurations of partitions, and the set of possible events (hypercalls) partitions can invoke. There is not any concrete information about private data of partitions. Thus, it is not possible to classify the data as *High* or *Low*. Moreover, the inter-partition flow policy of ARINC 653 is an intransitive policy [27], which cannot be addressed by traditional language-based information flow security. This problem is solved in [27], where noninterference is defined following a state-event based approach that considers intransitivity. In order to clarify different definitions on separation kernels, we formalize language-based information flow security in a state-event style and reason about the relationship of them.

Traditional formulations in the state-event based approach for information flow security assume a static mapping from actions to domains, such that the domain of an action can be determined solely from the action itself [27]. However, in separation kernels that mapping is dynamic. When a *hypercall* occurs, the kernel must consult the kernel scheduler to determine which partition is currently running, and the currently running partition is the domain of the hypercall. In our specification, we define the *scheduler* security domain for kernel scheduling, which cannot be interfered by any other domain to ensure that the scheduler security domain does not leak information via its scheduling decisions. Since ARINC 653 only defines the channel-based communication services using ports and leaves the implementation of message transmission on channels to underlying separation kernels, we define the *message transmitter* security domain, for message transmission. The transmitter also decouples message transmission from the scheduler to ensure that the scheduler is not interfered by partitions.

**Analysis of the Specification and Verification Approach.** Since separation kernels usually support the deployment of partitions which are unknown in advance, it is well suited to use logical reasoning by induction for formal verification. By following the successful experiences of applying Isabelle/HOL in seL4 [19] and PikeOS [31,32], we use Isabelle/HOL in this work.

The verification overview of our work is briefly shown in Fig. 2. In order to simplify the verification, we decompose the specification into two parts: an execution model for separation kernels with channel-based communication and an event specification for ARINC 653. The execution model defines basic components and a state machine of separation kernels. The event specification uses Isabelle/HOL functions to define the state

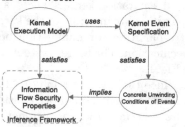

**Fig. 2.** Verification Overview

changes when an event occurs. These concrete functions are invoked by the execution model. This decomposition leads to two-step proofs of information flow security. We first define a set of information flow security properties and provide an inference framework for them on the execution model. In the second step, we define a set of *concrete unwinding conditions* on the concrete functions. Satisfaction of the concrete unwinding conditions implies that the events satisfy the classical unwinding conditions, and thus shows information flow security of our specification. The decomposition of the specification and its proofs improves their reusability for subsequent specification refinement and development of implementations, and thus reduces the verification effort.

## 3    Formal Specification

In this section, we first introduce the kernel execution model including basic components and state-based kernel execution. Then, we present the event specification. Finally, we discuss the correctness of the formal specification.

### 3.1    Basic Components

According to Fig. 1, basic components include security domains, security policies and communication components. All these components are statically configured in ARINC 653 compliant separation kernels.

**Security Domains and Policies.** As illustrated in bold and underlined in Fig. 1, the security domains are the scheduler, the transmitter, and the defined partitions. In order to discuss information flow policy, we assume a reflexive relation $\rightsquigarrow$ that specifies the allowable information flows between domains. If there is a channel from a partition a to a partition b, then a $\rightsquigarrow$ transmitter and transmitter $\rightsquigarrow$ b since we use the transmitter as the message intermediator. Since the scheduler can possibly schedule any domain, we define in the security policy that scheduler $\rightsquigarrow$ d for any domain d. The noninterference relation $\backslash\rightsquigarrow$ is the complement relation of $\rightsquigarrow$ that asserts no information flow outside of $\rightsquigarrow$.

**Communication Components.** As illustrated in Fig. 1, IPC is conducted via messages on channels, which are defined by an abstract type Message. Partitions have access to channels via *ports* which are the endpoints of channels. A *channel* links partitions and is a logical link between one source port and one or more destination ports. It also specifies the mode of transferring messages, which can be *queuing* or *sampling* mode. The datatype Channel_Type and Port_Type define these two components.

**System Configuration.** A significant characteristic of ARINC 653 compliant separation kernels is that partitions, policies and communication components are statically configured at built-time. In our specification, we use record Sys_Config to define the system configuration and fixes sysconf :: "Sys_Config" as a constant in the specification.

## 3.2    State-Based Kernel Execution

**Event and State.** We consider four types of events: *hypercalls*, *system events*, *exceptions*, and *actions in partitions*. Hypercalls cover all IPC services in ARINC 653. System events are the actions of the kernel itself and include kernel initialization, scheduling and message transmission. The other two types are abstract events that can be refined in a concrete specification. Events are illustrated in Fig. 1 as dotted line arrows and italics. Since there is no in-kernel concurrency, all these events execute atomically.

It is not that all events are enabled in a state. We use a function `event_enabled` to indicate whether an event can execute in a state. The function `exec_event` executes an event in a state and changes the state when it is enabled. In the event specification, we define functions to implement concrete communication, scheduling and message transmission. The `exec_event` function here invokes the concrete functions.

The state is defined as **record State**, which consists of information about the current running partition, partition states, communication states, created ports and current value of local variables in domains. For a state `s::State` and a sequence of events `as`, `execute as s` denotes the final state reached by executing `as` from `s`.

**Domain of Events.** Events have their own execution domains. The domain of the system events is static: the domain of the event *scheduling* is the scheduler; the domain of *message transmission* is the transmitter. On the other hand, the domain of hypercalls is dynamic and dependent on the current state of the kernel, defined as `domain_of_event s (hyperc h) = current s`, where `current s` returns the currently running partition in the state `s`.

**State Reachability.** Since not all events are enabled in a state, some states in the type `State` are not reachable from the initial state s0. Let `reachable s` ≡ ∃ `as. s = execute as s0` denote that the state `s` is reachable from the initial state s0. According to the definition of `reachable` and `execute`, we have `reachable s0` and Lemma 1.

**Lemma 1.** ∀s as. reachable s ∧ s' = execute as s ⟶ reachable s'

**State Equivalence.** A key concept for information flow security is that states are *identical* for a security domain. We define an equivalence relation ∼ d ∼ on states for each domain d such that s ∼ d ∼ t if and only if states s and t are identical for domain d, that is to say states s and t are indistinguishable for domain d. For a set of domains D, we define s ≈ D ≈ t ≡ ∀d ∈ D. s ∼ d ∼ t.

For a partition d, s ∼ d ∼ t if and only if `vpeq_part s d t`, where

```
vpeq_part s d t ≡ vpeq_vars s (the ((domv sysconf) d)) t
     ∧ (partitions s) d = (partitions t) d ∧ vpeq_part_comm s d t
```

It means that states s and t are equivalent for a partition d, when values of local variables, partition state, and communication abilities of d on these two states are the same. An example of the communication ability is that if a destination queuing port p is not empty in two states s and t, a partition d has the same ability on p in s as in t, because d has the ability to receive a message from p in these two states. The equivalence of communication abilities defines that partition d has the same set of ports, and that the number of messages is the same for all destination ports on states s and t.

Two states s and t are equivalent for the scheduler when the values of local variables of the scheduler and the current running partition on the two states are the same. The equivalence of states for the transmitter requires that all ports, states of the ports and values of local variable are the same.

## 3.3 Event Specification

The event specification defines the concrete functions to implement the execution of events. The functionalities of separation kernels in this paper include kernel initialization, scheduling, message transmission and hypercalls. The kernel initialization considers initialization of the kernel state. Since our specification does not define processes, we only consider the partition scheduling rather than the two-level scheduling on partition and process levels in ARINC 653. Because the execution of message transmission is also under the control of scheduling, we define an abstract partition scheduling that non-deterministically chooses one partition or the transmitter as the currently executing domain.

This subsection mainly discusses channel-based communication services in ARINC 653 and the message transmission. All events and their descriptions in the event specification are shown in Table 1.

**Channel-Based Communication Services.** ARINC 653 specifies the behavior of ports and the communication services via ports in detail. Programs in a partition could use IPC by invoking these services. ARINC 653 defines eleven services for sampling and queuing ports (No. 1 ∼ 11 in Table 1). The communication architecture is illustrated in Fig. 3.

In the first stage of this work, we design the event specification completely based on the service behavior specified in ARINC 653. When proving the unwinding conditions on these events, we find covert channels (Sect. 5 in detail) and change the service specification defined in ARINC 653 to avoid these covert channels. McCullough [17] provides three ways to avoid covert channels: unbounded buffer, process blocking and message loss. According to the discussion in Sect. 2, we do not allow partition blocking in communication services. Because unbounded buffer would lead to a bigger problem of denial of service (DoS), the feasible way for our specification is to allow message loss. In order to avoid covert channels, we allow message loss when sending a message to a queuing port and transmitting a message in a queuing channel.

We use a set of functions to implement one service. For instance, the Send_Queuing_Message service is implemented by function send_queuing_message_maylost as follows and a set of related functions invoked by this function.

**Table 1.** Events in Our Specification

| No | Name | Description of Event Specification |
|----|------|-----------------------------------|
| **Hypercalls** | | |
| (1) | Create_Sampling_Port | Create a sampling port. An identifier is assigned by the kernel and returned |
| (2) | Write_Sampling_Message | Write a message in the specified sampling port. The message overwrites the previous one |
| (3) | Read_Sampling_Message | Read a message from the specified sampling port |
| (4) | Get_Sampling_Portid | Return the sampling port identifier that corresponds to a sampling port name |
| (5) | Get_Sampling_Portstatus | Return the current status of the specified sampling port |
| (6) | Create_Queuing_Port | Create a queuing port. An identifier is assigned by the kernel and returned |
| (7) | Send_Queuing_Message | Send a message in the specified queuing port. If there is sufficient space in the queuing port to accept the message, the message is inserted into the port buffer. If there is insufficient space, the message is lost |
| (8) | Receive_Queuing_Message | Receive a message from the specified queuing port. If the queuing port is not empty, a message in the port buffer is removed and returned. If the queuing port is empty, None is returned |
| (9) | Get_Queuing_Portid | Return the queuing port identifier that corresponds to a queuing port name |
| (10) | Get_Queuing_Portstatus | Return the current status of the specified queuing port |
| (11) | Clear_Queuing_Port | Discard any messages in the message buffer of the specified destination port |
| **System events** | | |
| (12) | Schedule | Set one partition or the transmitter as the currently running domain |
| (13) | Transfer_Sampling_Message | Copy the message in the source sampling port to all destination sampling ports of a sampling channel, if all ports of this channel have been created |
| (14) | Transfer_Queuing_Message | Copy a message in the source queuing port to the destination queuing port of a queuing channel and remove the message from the source port, if the two ports of this channel have been created and the source port is not empty. If the destination port is full, the message is lost |
| (15) | Init | Initialize the kernel state using the system configuration |

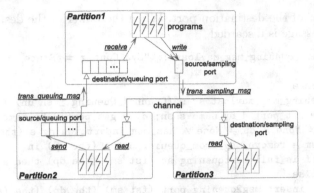

**Fig. 3.** Channel-based Communication in ARINC 653

definition send_queuing_message_maylost :: "Sys_Config ⇒ State ⇒ port_id
⇒ Message ⇒ (State × bool)" where
  "send_queuing_message_maylost sc s p m ≡
    (if(¬ is_a_queuingport s p ∨ ¬ is_source_port s p
              ∨ ¬ is_a_port_of_partition s p ) then  (s, False)
      else if is_full_portqueuing sc s p then  (s, True)
      else  (insert_msg2queuing_port s p m, True))"

As specified in the Send_Queuing_Message service in ARINC 653, when sending a message via a queuing port, it fails if either the specified port does not
exist, or it is not a source port, or it is not in current partition. When the port is
full, the calling process is blocked. Since blocking is not considered in this paper,
we just discard the message.

**Message Transmission on Channels.** ARINC 653 does not define the functionalities of message transmission and leaves its implementation to underlying
separation kernels. We design a basic specification of the message transmission
in this paper.

The message transmission on channels is shown in Fig. 3. ARINC 653 has two
modes of channel-based communication: sampling and queuing mode. The mul-
ticast message that is sent from a single source to more than one destination is
supported in sampling mode. The queuing mode only supports the unicast message. In sampling mode, a message transmission on a channel copies the message
in the source sampling port of the channel to the buffers of all destination sampling ports of the channel. Whilst in queuing mode, a message transmission on
a channel copies a message in the buffer of the source queuing port, removes it
from this buffer and stores the message into the buffer of the destination queuing
port of the channel. When the buffer of the destination queuing port is full, the
message is discarded.

For instance, the message transmission in queuing mode is defined as follows.
If the source and destination port have been created and there are messages in
the buffer of the source port, a message in the buffer is removed and inserted

into the buffer of the destination port. When the buffer of the destination port is full, the message is discarded.

```
primrec transf_queuing_msg_maylost :: "Sys_Config ⇒ State ⇒
Channel_Type
⇒ State" where
  "transf_queuing_msg_maylost sc s (Channel_Queuing _ sn dn) =
    (let sp = get_portid_by_name s sn; dp = get_portid_by_name s dn in
      if sp ≠ None ∧ dp ≠ None ∧ has_msg_inportqueuing s (the sp) then
        let sm = remove_msg_from_queuingport s (the sp) in
            if is_full_portqueuing sc (fst sm) (the dp) then s
            else
                insert_msg2queuing_port (fst sm) (the dp) (the (snd sm))
      else s )" |
  "transf_queuing_msg_maylost sc s (Channel_Sampling _ _ _) = s"
```

## 3.4   Correctness of Formal Specification

To assure the correctness of our specification, beside the manual validation by inspecting the Isabelle/HOL specification, we prove that functionalities of the specified services are correct w.r.t. the ARINC 653 informal description [5] by means of 33 lemmas for events and invariants. Due to the atomicity of event execution, the correctness of an event can be specified and proved by pre- and post-conditions of the event in Hoare logic [14], i.e., $\{P\}$ $C$ $\{Q\}$, where $C$ is the Isabelle function implementing the event, $P$ and $Q$ are the pre- and post-conditions respectively. Since the execution of events always terminate, our specification is a total correctness specification. Termination is ensured by using the **primrec** and **definition** in Isabelle/HOL to define the functions in our specification and proved automatically in Isabelle/HOL. For instance, the correctness lemma for the event Create_Sampling_Port is as follows. The pre-condition is that the port named p is configured, has not been created and is a port of the currently running partition. Under the pre-condition, the execution of create_sampling _port returns a pair of the new state and the assigned identifier of the created port. The post-condition ensures that the identifier (the (snd r)) is stored in the ports in the new state (ports (comm (fst r))).

**Lemma 2 (Correctness of Create_Sampling_Port).**
{ get_samplingport_conf sysconf p ≠ None ∧ get_portid_by_name s p = None
∧ p ∈ get_partition_cfg_ports_byid sysconf (current s) }
r = create_sampling_port sysconf s p
{ (ports (comm (fst r))) (the (snd r)) ≠ None }

Functional correctness requires to prove invariants on the data structures defining the state. An invariant is a safety property and defined on states as a predicate $\psi$ s. It is preserved in all reachable states by proving the invariant theorem: reachable s $\Longrightarrow$ $\psi$ s. A typical invariant is the predicate port_consistent s. We use a set to store created ports. The port state (e.g., the messages currently in the port) is defined as

Ports = "port_id ⇀ Port_Type". Ports belong to different partitions that is defined as part_ports :: "port_id ⇀ partition_id". The port_consistent s requires that the created port set and the domains of these two partial functions are the same in any reachable states. The invariant theorem is proved by Lemma 1 and other two lemmas: (1) ψ s0 and (2) ∀s as. ψ s ∧ s' = execute as s ⟶ ψ s'.

# 4  Information Flow Security and Proofs

This section first presents a set of information flow security properties defined on the execution model, which includes the original definitions of noninterference [27], nonleakage [23] and noninfluence [23], and their variants. Nonleakage is language-based information flow security and noninfluence is the combination of noninterference and nonleakage. Then, we present an overview of our proof structure and the proofs which include an inference framework of these properties and the security proofs of our event specification.

## 4.1  Formalizing Noninterference

Since intransitive policies could be used to specify channel control policies [27], we consider intransitive noninterference in this paper. The essence of noninterference on separation kernels is that a partition d cannot distinguish the final states between executing a sequence of events as and executing its purged sequence from the initial state. In the purged sequence, the events of partitions that are not allowed to pass information to d directly or indirectly are removed.

In order to express the allowed information flow for intransitive policies, we employ the function sources [27], which takes a sequence of events as and a target domain d and yields the set of domains that are allowed to pass information to d when as occurs. Due to the dependency of event domains on states, the sources function in our specification depends on the current state s. The sources function is used to define the classical purge function, ipurge, in terms of which security properties are formulated. The ipurge as s d yields the sequence of events as, where all events that are not allowed to pass information to d directly or indirectly when as is executed from s are removed.

We use the abbreviation s ◁ as ≅ t ◁ bs @ d for the observational equivalence. It denotes that d is identical in the two final states after executing as from s (by execute as s) and executing bs from t. Traditionally, this equivalence is defined using a projection function output which returns the observed results on a state by a domain. In this paper, we have combined the output in the state equivalence presented in Subsect. 3.2. This allows us to avoid the unwinding condition of *output consistent*. We define the classical nontransitive noninterference [27] on our execution model as follows.

noninterference ≡ ∀d as. (s0 ◁ as ≅ s0 ◁ (ipurge as s0 d) @ d)

In the definition of noninterference, the ipurge function only deletes all unsuitable events. A strong version of noninterference is introduced in

[23] to handle arbitrary insertion and deletion of secret events. Oheimb [23] says that the strong noninterference and the original one are equivalent in deterministic cases. We define this strong version of noninterference on the execution model as `weak_noninterference`, since `noninterference` implies `weak_noninterference` on our execution model.

The above definitions of noninterference are based on the initial state s0, but separation kernels usually support *warm* or *cold start* and they may start to execute from a non-initial state. Therefore, we define a more general version of noninterference as follows based on the `reachable` function. This general noninterference requires that the system starting from any reachable state is secure. It is obvious that this noninterference implies the classical noninterference due to the lemma: `reachable s0`.

```
noninterference_r ≡ ∀d as s. reachable s ⟶
                    (s ◁ as ≅ s ◁ (ipurge as s d) ⓒ d)
```

## 4.2  Formalizing Nonleakage and Noninfluence

Language-based information flow security is generalized to arbitrary multi-domain policies in [23] as a new notion *nonleakage*. *Nonleakage* and *noninterference* are also combined in [23] as a new notion *noninfluence*. Murray et al. [20] have extended the original definition of nonleakage and noninfluence and defined the general forms of them for operating systems based on the scheduler. We use Murray's definitions and define them on our execution model as follows.

```
nonleakage ≡ ∀d as s t. reachable s ∧ reachable t ⟶
            (s ∼ (scheduler sysconf) ∼ t) ⟶ (s ≈ (sources as s d) ≈ t)
            ⟶ (s ◁ as ≅ t ◁ as ⓒ d)
noninfluence ≡ ∀ d as bs s t . reachable s ∧ reachable t ⟶
            (s ≈ (sources as s d) ≈ t) ⟶ (s ∼ (scheduler sysconf) ∼ t) ⟶
            ipurge as s d = ipurge bs s d ⟶ (s ◁ as ≅ t ◁ bs ⓒ d)
```

The intuitive meaning of nonleakage is that if the secret data is not leaked initially, the secret data should not be leaked during executing a sequence of events. Separation kernels are said to preserve *nonleakage* when for any pair of reachable states s and t and observing domain d, if (1) s and t are equivalent for all domains that may (directly or indirectly) interfere with d during the run of as, i.e., s ≈ (sources as s d) ≈ t, and (2) the same domain is currently running in both states, i.e., s ∼ (scheduler sysconf) ∼ t, then s and t are observationally equivalent for d when executing as. Murray's definition of noninfluence is a weak one, we propose a strong one according to the Oheimb's noninfluence by extending the scheduler and state reachability as follows.

```
strong_noninfluence ≡ ∀ d as s t . reachable s ∧ reachable t ⟶
            (s ≈ (sources as s d) ≈ t) ⟶ (s ∼ (scheduler sysconf) ∼ t)
            ⟶ (s ◁ as ≅ t ◁ (ipurge as t d) ⓒ d)
```

## 4.3  Proof Structure

As discussed in Sect. 2, proofs of information flow security on our specification comprise two parts: an inference framework of information flow security

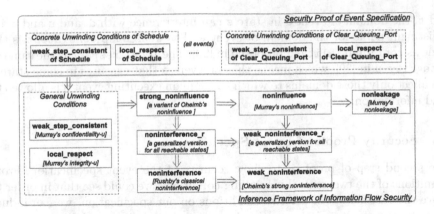

**Fig. 4.** Proof Structure

properties on the execution model and security proofs of the event specification. The proof structure of this work is shown in Fig. 4, where an arrow means the implication between properties. In the next two subsections, we discuss the two parts of proofs in turn.

## 4.4  Inference Framework of Information Flow Security

In order to clarify different properties of information flow security on our specification, we provide an inference framework on the execution model as shown in the lower part of Fig. 4. We have proven all implication relations between these properties on the execution model. We could see that the property strong_noninfluence is the strongest one and if this property is satisfied, so are all other properties.

The standard proof of information flow security properties is discharged by proving a set of unwinding conditions [27] that examine individual execution steps of the system. Our work follows this approach. In order to prove strong_noninfluence, we define two general unwinding conditions, weak_step_consistent and local_respect, as follows. As there is no output function in our specification, we do not define the classical unwinding condition of *output consistent.*

```
weak_step_consistent ≡ ∀ d a s t . reachable s ∧ reachable t ⟶
        (s ∼ d ∼ t) ∧ (s ∼ (scheduler sysconf) ∼ t) ∧
        ((domain_of_event s a) ↝ d) ∧ (s ∼ (domain_of_event s a) ∼ t)
        ⟶ ((exec_event s a) ∼ d ∼ (exec_event t a))
local_respect ≡ ∀ a d s s'. reachable s ⟶
    ((domain_of_event s a) \↝ d) ∧ (s' = exec_event s a) ⟶ (s ∼ d ∼ s')
```

The weak_step_consistent means that for any pair of reachable states s and t, and any observing domain d, the next states after executing any event a on s and t are indistinguishable for d, i.e., (exec_event s a) ∼ d ∼ (exec_event t a), if s and t are indistinguishable for d, the same domain is currently running in s and t, the domain of event a in state s can interference with d, and s and t are indistinguishable for the domain of event a. The `weak_step_consistent` is the same as `confidentiality-u` proposed in [20]. The `local_respect` is the same as `integrity-u` in [20], which means that an event a that executes in some state s can affect only those domains to which the domain executing event a is allowed to send information.

## 4.5  Security Proofs of Event Specification

The second step of proofs is to show security of the event specification. From definitions of the two general unwinding conditions, we could see that in order to prove the satisfaction of the two conditions on our specification, we can induct on each type of events in separation kernels and prove that each concrete event satisfies the two conditions. Therefore, we define a set of *concrete unwinding conditions* for all events. Satisfaction of the concrete unwinding conditions of one event implies that the event satisfies the general unwinding conditions. For instance, Lemma 3 and 4 show the concrete unwinding conditions for event `Create_Queuing_Port`.

**Lemma 3 (Local_respect of creating_queuing_port).**
`reachable s` $\wedge$ `is_a_partition sysconf (current s)` $\wedge$ `(current s)` $\backslash\leadsto$ `d` $\wedge$
`s' = fst (create_queuing_port sysconf s pname)` $\Longrightarrow$ `s ~ d ~ s'`

**Lemma 4 (Weak_step_consistent of creating_queuing_port).**
`is_a_partition sysconf (current s)` $\wedge$ `reachable s` $\wedge$ `reachable t` $\wedge$
`s ~ d ~ t` $\wedge$ `s ~ (scheduler sysconf) ~ t` $\wedge$ `(current s) ~> d` $\wedge$
`s ~ (current s) ~ t` $\wedge$ `s' = fst (create_queuing_port sysconf s pname)` $\wedge$
`t' = fst (create_queuing_port sysconf t pname)` $\Longrightarrow$ `s' ~ d ~ t'`

Finally, we conclude the satisfaction of `strong_noninfluence` on our specification and all other information flow security properties according to the inference framework.

**Table 2.** Specification and Proofs Statistics

| Specification | | | | Proofs | | | |
|---|---|---|---|---|---|---|---|
| Item | # of function/ definition | LOC | PM | Item | # of lemma/ theorem | LOP | PM |
| Execution model | 32 | ~ 200 | 2 | Inference Framework | 61 | ~ 1000 | 6 |
| Event Specification | 68 | ~ 800 | | Correctness | 33 | ~ 6000 | |
| | | | | Security | 123 | | |
| **Total** | 100 | ~ 1000 | 2 | **Total** | 217 | ~ 7000 | 6 |

# 5  Results and Discussion

**Evaluation.** We use Isabelle/HOL as the specification and verification system for separation kernels. The proofs of information flow security in our specification are conducted in the structured proof language *Isar* in Isabelle, allowing for proof text naturally understandable for both humans and computers. All derivations of our proofs have passed through the Isabelle proof kernel.

The statistics for the effort and size of the specification and proofs are shown in Table 2. We use 100 functions/definitions and $\sim$ 1000 lines of code (LOC) of Isabelle/HOL to specify the execution model and event specification. 217 lemmas/theorems in Isabelle/HOL are proved using $\sim$ 7000 lines of proof (LOP) of Isar to ensure the information flow security of our specification. The work is carried out by a total effort of roughly 8 person-months (PM).

**Validating and Fixing Covert Channels in ARINC 653.** When proving the satisfaction of unwinding conditions on the events, we find some security flaws, i.e., covert channels to leak information, in ARINC 653.

*Covert Channel 1: queuing mode channel-based communication.* If there is a queuing mode channel from partition a to b and no other channels exist, then it is secure that a $\leadsto$ transmitter, transmitter $\leadsto$ b, transmitter $\setminus\!\leadsto$ a and b $\setminus\!\leadsto$ transmitter. In fact, these security policies are violated in ARINC 653. Firstly, when a sends a message by invoking Send_Queuing_Message service of ARINC 653, the service returns NOT_AVAILABLE or TIMED_OUT when the buffer is full, and returns NO_ERROR when the buffer is not full. However, the full/empty status of the buffer in the port can be changed by message transmission executed by the transmitter. Thus, the local_respect property is not preserved on Send_Queuing_Message service, and transmitter $\setminus\!\leadsto$ a is violated. Secondly, due to no message loss required by ARINC 653, the transmitter cannot transmit a message on a channel when the destination queuing port is full. However, the full status of the destination port can be changed by Receive_Queuing_Message service executed by partition b. Thus, the local_respect property is not preserved on the event of message transmission, and b $\setminus\!\leadsto$ transmitter is violated. To avoid this covert channel, we allow message loss when sending messages to a queuing port or transmitting message on a queuing mode channel.

*Covert Channel 2: Create_Sampling_Port and Create_Queuing_Port services.* This is a potential covert channel. It is dependent on the concrete implementation of ARINC 653 and can be avoided by careful designs. In ARINC 653, the service Create_Sampling_Port and Create_Queuing_Port create a port and return a new unique identifier assigned by the kernel to the new port. In the initial specification, we use a natural number to maintain this new identifier. This number is initially assigned to one and increased by one after each port creation. We find in this design that the number becomes a covert channel that can flow information from any partition to another, and the two events do not preserve the weak_step_consistent property. This covert channel can be avoided by assigning the port identifier to each port during system initialization or in the system configuration.

**Validating and Fixing Covert Channels in Open-Source Implementations.** We have manually validated the found covert channels in two open-source separation kernels, i.e., XtratuM and POK. Covert channels are found when we validate these two implementations.

The version of XtratuM we validate is v3.7.3 for SPARC v8 architecture. Unlike that there is one buffer for each queuing port in ARINC 653, XtratuM uses one shared buffer between the source port and the destination port of a queuing mode channel as a transmitter. If the buffer is not full, the hypercall *SendQueuingPort* inserts the message into the buffer and notifies the receiver; whilst if the buffer is full, *SendQueuingPort* immediately returns *XM_OP_NOT_ALLOWED*. The hypercall *ReceiveQueuingPort* has a similar design. Thus, the found covert channel 1 exists in XtratuM. The way to avoid this security flaw is to redesign the hypercall *SendQueuingPort* to lose the message and return *XM_OK* when the buffer is full.

The version of POK we validate is the latest one released in 2014. Different from XtratuM, POK has a transmitter to transfer messages from a source port to a destination port of a channel. POK blocks processes to wait for resources. If the buffer is not full, the syscall *pok_port_queueing_send* inserts the message into the buffer; whilst if the buffer is full and *timeout* = 0, it immediately returns *POK_ERRNO_FULL*. *pok_port_transfer* responds for transmitting messages from a source port to a destination one and returns *POK_ERRNO_SIZE* when the destination port has no available space to store messages. Thus, the found covert channel 1 exists in POK. The way to avoid this security flaw is to allow message loss or block the calling process until the port buffer is not full in the syscall *pok_port_queueing_send*.

When creating a port, XtratuM and POK use the index of the port in the port array as the new identifier. Thus, they do not have the covert channel 2.

**Discussion.** The reusability of formal specification and proofs can largely alleviate the enormous efforts needed when others enforce information flow security on separation kernels. Our formal specification can be refined to the concrete specification of separation kernels. In the concrete specification, new variables and events may be introduced and some events in this paper may be refined. The state equivalence in our specification is sufficient for the abstract and concrete specification of the channel-based communication. Therefore, the new variables in the concrete specification do not change the definition of state equivalence, and thus the new variables and new events manipulating these variables do not break the information flow security of the concrete specification. Information flow security properties in this paper can be preserved on refinement of events of the channel-based communication according to the conclusion in [20]. Due to the reusability of the formal specification, the inference framework and the security proofs in this work are also reusable for the concrete specification.

# 6  Related Work and Conclusions

**Information Flow Security.** Information flow security [28] has attracted many research efforts in recent years. State-event based noninterference [27] is usually chosen for verifying general purpose operating systems and separation kernels [20]. Language-based information flow security was generalized to arbitrary multi-domain policies in [23] as a new state-event based notion nonleakage. Oheimb [23] also combined the classical noninterference and nonleakage as the notion noninfluence. These properties have been instantiated for operating systems in [20] and formally verified on seL4 [19]. In our work, all of these properties and their variants are defined in our specification. We also propose an inference framework to clarify the implications between these properties.

**Formal Specification and Verification of Separation Kernels.** Formal methods have been widely applied on separation kernels in recent years [8, 9, 12, 13, 19, 25, 29–33]. An overview is available in [34]. An Isabelle/HOL specification for a generic separation kernel was published by EURO-MILS project [31]. They provided an abstraction specification for Controlled Interruptible Separation Kernels (CISK), instantiated it to a separation kernel model, and then applied them on the PikeOS separation kernel [32]. The Isabelle/HOL specification of seL4 was extended to a separation kernel specification in [19]. Formal specification in our work provides a detailed model for ARINC 653 channel-based communication, which is not covered in related work. In particular, there is no concrete communication actions in specification of [31]. The IPC syscalls in seL4 [19] and PikeOS [32] are very different from ARINC 653 channel-based communication.

**Formalization and Verification of ARINC 653.** Formalization and verification of ARINC 653 have been considered in recent years, such as formal specification of ARINC 653 architecture [24], modeling ARINC 653 for model driven development of IMA applications [11], and verification of application software on top of ARINC 653 [7]. In [35], the system functionalities and all service requirements in ARINC 653 have been formalized in Event-B, and some inconsistencies have been found in the standard. These works aim at safety of separation kernels or applications. Our work is the first to conduct a formal security analysis of the ARINC 653 standard.

**Conclusions and Future Work.** In this paper, we applied Isabelle/HOL to formally specify and verify separation kernels with ARINC 653 channel-based communication. We provided a formal specification with mechanically checked proofs that is totally free of covert channels and therefore provided information flow security for high assurance systems. We revealed covert channels in ARINC 653 and validated their existence in XtratuM and POK. Our specification is reusable for subsequent specification refinement and development of implementations. The proofs in this work can alleviate the verification efforts on information flow security. In the next step, we will develop a formal specification of separation kernels supporting multi-core and the specification in this paper will be revised. Due to the kernel concurrency between cores, we will find a feasible way to verify multi-core separation kernels. The long-term goal of our project is to construct a compositional approach of building security verified system, which includes verification of the functional and noninterference correctness for a separation/partitioning microkernel for a multi-core architecture, and verification of the functional correctness of the underlying hardware.

**Acknowledgement.** We would like to thank Gerwin Klein and Ralf Huuck of NICTA, Australia for their suggestions. This research is supported in part by the National Research Foundation, Prime Minister's Office, Singapore under its National Cybersecurity R&D Program (Award No. NRF2014NCR-NCR001-30) and administered by the National Cybersecurity R&D Directorate.

# References

1. Lynxsecure separation kernel hypervisor. http://www.lynx.com/products/hypervisors/. Accessed July 2015
2. Sysgo pikeos hypervisor. https://www.sysgo.com/products/pikeos-rtos-and-virtualization-concept/. Accessed July 2015
3. Wind river vxworks 653 platform. http://www.windriver.com/products/vxworks/certification-profiles/. Accessed July 2015
4. Wind river vxworks mils platform. http://www.windriver.com/products/vxworks/certification-profiles/. Accessed July 2015
5. Aeronautical Radio Inc: ARINC Specification 653: Avionics Application Software Standard Interface, Part 1 - Required Services, November 2010
6. Clarkson, M.R., Schneider, F.B.: Hyperproperties. J. Comput. Secur. **18**(6), 1157–1210 (2010)
7. de la Cámara, P., Castro, J.R., Gallardo, MdM, Merino, P.: Verification support for arinc-653-based avionics software. Softw. Test. Verification Reliab. **21**(4), 267–298 (2011)
8. Craig, I.D.: Formal Refinement for Operating System Kernels. Springer, Heidelberg (2007). chap. 5
9. Dam, M., Guanciale, R., Khakpour, N., Nemati, H., Schwarz, O.: Formal verification of information flow security for a simple arm-based separation kernel. In: Proceedings of the 20th ACM Conference on Computer and Communications Security (CCS 2013). pp. 223–234. ACM, New York, NY, USA (2013)
10. Delange, J., Lec, L.: Pok, an arinc653-compliant operating system released under the bsd license. In: Proceedings of the 13th Real-Time Linux Workshop (2011)
11. Delange, J., Pautet, L., Kordon, F.: Modeling and validation of arinc653 architectures. In: Proceedings of Embedded Real-time Software and Systems Conference (ERTS 2010) (2010)
12. Freitas, L., McDermott, J.: Formal methods for security in the xenon hypervisor. Int. J. Softw. Tools Technol. Transf. **13**(5), 463–489 (2011)
13. Heitmeyer, C.L., Archer, M.M., Leonard, E.I., McLean, J.D.: Applying formal methods to a certifiably secure software system. IEEE Trans. Softw. Eng. **34**(1), 82–98 (2008)

14. Hoare, C.A.R.: An axiomatic basis for computer programming. Commun. ACM **12**(10), 576–580 (1969)
15. Levin, T.E., Irvine, C.E., Weissman, C., Nguyen, T.D.: Analysis of three multilevel security architectures. In: Proceedings of the 2007 ACM Workshop on Computer Security Architecture (CSA 2007), pp. 37–46. ACM (2007)
16. Masmano, M., Ripoll, I., Crespo, A., Metge, J.: Xtratum: a hypervisor for safety critical embedded systems. In: Proceedings of the 11th Real-Time Linux Workshop. pp. 263–272 (2009)
17. McCullough, D.: Noninterference and the composability of security properties. In: Proceedings of IEEE Symposium on Security and Privacy (S&P 1988). pp. 177–186. IEEE Computer Society (1988)
18. Millen, J.: 20 years of covert channel modeling and analysis. In: Proceedings of IEEE Symposium on Security and Privacy (S&P 1999). pp. 113–114. IEEE (1999)
19. Murray, T., Matichuk, D., Brassil, M., Gammie, P., Bourke, T., Seefried, S., Lewis, C., Gao, X., Klein, G.: sel4: from general purpose to a proof of information flow enforcement. In: Proceedings of IEEE Symposium on Security and Privacy (S&P 2013) (2013)
20. Murray, T., Matichuk, D., Brassil, M., Gammie, P., Klein, G.: Noninterference for operating system kernels. In: Hawblitzel, C., Miller, D. (eds.) CPP 2012. LNCS, vol. 7679, pp. 126–142. Springer, Heidelberg (2012)
21. National Security Agency: U.S. Government Protection Profile for Separation Kernels in Environments Requiring High Robustness (2007)
22. Nipkow, T., Wenzel, M., Paulson, L.: Isabelle/HOL: A Proof Assistant for Higher-order Logic. Springer-Verlag, Berlin, Heidelberg (2002)
23. von Oheimb, D.: Information flow control revisited: Noninfluence = Noninterference +Nonleakage. In: Samarati, P., Ryan, P.Y.A., Gollmann, D., Molva, R. (eds.) ESORICS 2004. LNCS, vol. 3193, pp. 225–243. Springer, Heidelberg (2004)
24. Oliveira Gomes, A.: Formal Specification of the ARINC 653 Architecture Using Circus. Master's thesis, University of York (2012)
25. Richards, R.J.: Modeling and security analysis of a commercial real-time operating system kernel. In: Hardin, D.S. (ed.) Design and Verification of Microprocessor Systems for High-Assurance Applications, pp. 301–322. Springer, Heidelberg (2010)
26. Rushby, J.: Design and verification of secure systems. ACM SIGOPS Oper. Syst. Rev. **15**(5), 12–21 (1981)
27. Rushby, J.: Noninterference, transitivity, and channel-control security policies. Technical report, SRI International, Computer Science Laboratory (1992)
28. Sabelfeld, A., Myers, A.C.: Language-based information-flow security. IEEE J. Sel. Areas Commun. **21**(1), 5–19 (2003)
29. Sanán, D., Butterfield, A., Hinchey, M.: Separation kernel verification: the xtratum case study. In: Giannakopoulou, D., Kroening, D. (eds.) VSTTE 2014. LNCS, vol. 8471, pp. 133–149. Springer, Heidelberg (2014)
30. Velykis, A., Freitas, L.: Formal modelling of separation kernel components. In: Cavalcanti, A., Deharbe, D., Gaudel, M.-C., Woodcock, J. (eds.) ICTAC 2010. LNCS, vol. 6255, pp. 230–244. Springer, Heidelberg (2010)
31. Verbeek, F.F., Tverdyshev, S.S., etc.: Formal specification of a generic separation kernel. Archive of Formal Proofs (2014)
32. Verbeek, F., Havle, O., Schmaltz, J., Tverdyshev, S., Blasum, H., Langenstein, B., Stephan, W., Wolff, B., Nemouchi, Y.: Formal API specification of the PikeOS separation kernel. In: Havelund, K., Holzmann, G., Joshi, R. (eds.) NFM 2015. LNCS, vol. 9058, pp. 375–389. Springer, Heidelberg (2015)

33. Wilding, M.M., Greve, D.A., Richards, R.J., Hardin, D.S.: Formal verification of partition management for the AAMP7G microprocessor. In: Hardin, D.S. (ed.) Design and Verification of Microprocessor Systems for High-Assurance Applications, pp. 175–191. Springer, Heidelberg (2010)
34. Zhao, Y.: Formal specification and verification of separation kernels: An overview. ArXiv e-prints (2015). http://arxiv.org/abs/1508.07066
35. Zhao, Y., Yang, Z., Sanan, D., Liu, Y.: Event-based formalization of safety-critical operating system standards: An experience report on arinc 653 using event-b. In: Proceedings of the 26th IEEE International Symposium on Software Reliability Engineering (ISSRE 2015). pp. 281–292. IEEE Computer Society (2015)

# Some Complexity Results for Stateful Network Verification

Yaron Velner[1], Kalev Alpernas[1]([✉]), Aurojit Panda[2], Alexander Rabinovich[1],
Mooly Sagiv[1], Scott Shenker[2], and Sharon Shoham[3]

[1] Tel Aviv University, Tel Aviv, Israel
kalevalp@post.tau.ac.il
[2] University of California Berkeley, Berkeley, USA
[3] The Academic College of Tel Aviv Yaffo, Tel Aviv, Israel

**Abstract.** In modern networks, forwarding of packets often depends on the history of previously transmitted traffic. Such networks contain *stateful* middleboxes, whose forwarding behavior depends on a mutable internal state. Firewalls and load balancers are typical examples of stateful middleboxes.

This paper addresses the complexity of verifying safety properties, such as isolation, in networks with finite-state middleboxes. Unfortunately, we show that even in the absence of forwarding loops, reasoning about such networks is undecidable due to interactions between middleboxes connected by unbounded ordered channels. We therefore abstract away channel ordering. This abstraction is sound for safety, and makes the problem decidable. Specifically, we show that safety checking is EXPSPACE-complete in the number of hosts and middleboxes in the network. We further identify two useful subclasses of finite-state middleboxes which admit better complexities. The simplest class includes, e.g., firewalls and permits polynomial-time verification. The second class includes, e.g., cache servers and learning switches, and makes the safety problem coNP-complete.

Finally, we implement a tool for verifying the correctness of stateful networks.

## 1 Introduction

Modern computer networks are extremely complex, leading to many bugs and vulnerabilities which affect our daily life. Therefore, network verification is an increasingly important topic addressed by the programming languages and networking communities (e.g., see [9,14–18,21,30]). Previous network verification tools leverage a simple network forwarding model which renders the datapath *immutable*; *i.e.,* normal packets going through the network do not change its forwarding behavior, and the control plane explicitly alters the forwarding state at relatively slow time scales. Thus, invariants can be verified before each control-plane initiated change and these invariants will be enforced until the next such change. While the notion of an immutable datapath supported by an assemblage

© Springer-Verlag Berlin Heidelberg 2016
M. Chechik and J.-F. Raskin (Eds.): TACAS 2016, LNCS 9636, pp. 811–830, 2016.
DOI: 10.1007/978-3-662-49674-9_51

of routers makes verification tractable, it does not reflect reality. Modern enterprise networks are comprised of roughly 2/3 routers and 1/3 *middleboxes* [31]. A simple example of a middlebox is a stateful firewall which permits traffic from untrusted hosts only after they have received a message from a trusted host. Middleboxes — such as firewalls, WAN optimizers, transcoders, proxies, load-balancers, intrusion detection systems (IDS) and the like — are the most common way to insert new functionality in the network datapath, and are commonly used to improve network performance and security. While useful, middleboxes are a common source of errors in the network [25], with middleboxes being responsible for over 40 % of all major incidents in networks.

This paper addresses the problem of verifying safety of networks with middleboxes, referred to as *stateful* networks. From a verification perspective, it is possible to view a middlebox as a procedure with local mutable state which is atomically changed every time a packet is transmitted. The local state determines the forwarding behavior.[1] Thus, the problem of network verification amounts to verifying the correctness of a specialized distributed system where each of the middleboxes operates atomically and the order of packet arrivals is arbitrary.

We model such a network as a finite undirected graph with two types of nodes: (i) hosts which can send packets, (ii) middleboxes which react to packet arrivals and forward modified packets. Each node in the network has a fixed number of ports, connected by network edges (links).

Real middleboxes are generally complex software programs implemented in several 100 s of thousands of lines of code. We follow [23, 24] in assuming that we are provided with middlebox models in the form of *finite-state transducers*. In our experience one can naturally model the behavior of most middleboxes this way. For every incoming packet, the transducer uses the packet header and the local state to compute the forwarding behavior (output) and to update state for future packets. The transducer can be non-deterministic to allow modelling of middleboxes like load-balancers whose behavior depends not just on state, but also on a random number source. We symbolically represent the local state of each middlebox by a fixed set of relations on finite elements, each with a fixed arity.

*The Verification Problem.* We define network safety by means of avoiding "bad" middlebox states (e.g., states from which a middlebox forwards a packet in a way that violates a network policy). Given a set of bad middlebox states, we are interested in showing that for all packet scenarios the bad states cannot be reached. This problem is hard since the number of packets is unbounded and the states of one middlebox can affect another via transmitted packets.

## 1.1   What Is Decidable About Middlebox Verification

In Sec. 3, we prove that for general stateful networks the verification problem is undecidable. This result relies on the observation that packet histories can

---

[1] Switches are a degenerate case of middleboxes, whose state is constant and hence their forwarding behavior does not change over time.

be used to count, similarly to results in model checking of infinite ordered communication channels [8]. One may believe that undecidability arises from the presence of forwarding loops in the network which are usually avoided in real networks. However, we show that the verification problem is undecidable even for networks without forwarding loops.

In order to obtain decidability, we introduce an abstract semantics of networks where the order of packet processing on each channel (connecting two middleboxes or a middlebox and a host) is arbitrary, rather than FIFO. Thus, middlebox inputs are multisets of packets which can be processed in any order. This abstraction is *conservative*, i.e., whenever we verify that the network does not reach a bad state, it is indeed the case. However, the verification may fail even in correct networks. Since packets are atomically processed, we note that network designers can impose ordering even in this abstract model by sending acknowledgments for received packets. This is useful when enforcing authentication.

In fact, this abstraction closely corresponds to assumptions made by network engineers: since packets in modern networks can traverse multiple paths, be buffered, or be chosen for more complex analysis, network software cannot assume that packets sent from a source to a server are received by a server in order. Network protocols therefore commonly build on TCP, a protocol which uses acknowledgments and other mechanisms to ensure that servers receive packets in order. Since packet ordering is enforced by causality (by sending acknowledgments) and by software on the receiving end, rather than by the network semantics, correctness of such networks typically does not rely on the order of packet processing. Therefore we can successfully verify a majority of network applications despite our abstraction.

## 1.2  Complexity of Stateful Verification

In Sec. 6, we show that the problem of network verification when assuming a nondeterministic order of packet processing is complete for exponential space, i.e., it is decidable, and in the worst case, the decision procedure can take exponential space in terms of hosts and middleboxes. This is proved by showing that the network safety problem is equivalent to the coverability problem of Petri nets, which is known to be EXPSPACE-complete [26].

Since the problem is complete, it is impossible to improve this upper-bound without further assumptions. Therefore, we also consider limited cases of middleboxes permitting more efficient verification procedures, as shown in Fig. 1. We identify four classes of middleboxes with increasing expressive power and verification complexity: (i) *stateless* middleboxes whose forwarding behavior

**Fig. 1.** Middlebox hierarchy.

is constant over time, (ii) *increasing* middleboxes whose forwarding behavior increases over time, (iii) *progressing* middleboxes whose forwarding behavior stabilizes after some fixed time, alternatively, the transition relation of the transducer does not include cycles besides self-cycles, and (iv) *arbitrary* middle-boxes without any restriction. For example, NATs, Switches and simple ACL-based firewalls are stateless; hole-punching stateful firewalls are increasing; and learning-switches and cache-proxies are progressing and not increasing.

For stateless and increasing middleboxes, we prove that any packet which arrives once can arrive any number of times, leading to a polynomial-time verification algorithm, using dynamic programming. We note that efficient near linear-time algorithms for stateless verification are known (e.g., see [17]). Our result generalizes these results to increasing networks and is in line with the recent work in [13, 19].

For progressing middleboxes, we show that verification is coNP-complete. The main insight is that if a bad state is reachable then there exists a small (polynomial) input scenario leading to a bad state. This means that tools like SAT solvers which are frequently used for verification can be used to verify large networks in many cases but it also means that we cannot hope for a general efficient solution unless P=NP.

Finally, we note that unlike the known results in stateless networks, the absence of forwarding loops does not improve the upper bound, i.e., we show that our lower bounds also hold for networks without forwarding loops.

*Packet Space Assumption.* Previous works in stateless verification [14, 16] assume that packet headers have $n$-bits, simulating realistic packet headers which can be large in practice. This makes the complexity of checking safety of stateless networks PSPACE-hard. Our model avoids packet space explosion by only supporting three fields: source, destination, and packet tags. We make this simplification since our work primarily focuses on middlebox policies (rather than routing). As demonstrated in Sec. 5.1, middlebox policies are commonly specified in terms of the source and destination hosts of a packet and the network port (service) being accessed. For example, at the application level, firewalls may decide how to handle a packet according to a small set of application types (e.g., skype, ssh, etc.). Source, destination and packet tag are thus sufficient for reasoning about safety with respect to these policies. This simplification is also supported by recent works (e.g. [17]) which suggest that in practice the forwarding behavior depends only on a small set of bits.

*Lossless Channels.* Previous works on infinite ordered communication channels have introduced *lossy channel systems* [2] as an abstraction of ordered communication that recovers decidability. Lossy channel systems allow messages to be lost in transit, making the reachability problem decidable, but with a non-elementary lower bound on time complexity. In our model, packets cannot be lost. On the other hand, the order of packets arrival becomes nondeterministic. With this abstraction, we manage to obtain elementary time complexity for verification.

*Initial Experience.* We implemented a tool which accepts symbolic representations of middleboxes and a network configuration and verifies safety. For increasing (and stateless) networks, the tool generates a Datalog program and a query which holds iff a bad state is reachable. Then, the query is evaluated using existing Datalog engines [22].

For arbitrary networks (and for progressing networks), the tool generates a petri-net and a coverability property which holds iff the network reaches a bad state. To verify the coverability property we use LOLA [1,28] — a Petri-Net model checker.

*Main Results.* The main contributions of the paper are: (i) We define a conservative abstraction of networks in which packets can be processed out of order, and show that the safety problem of stateful networks becomes decidable, but EXPSPACE-complete. (ii) We identify classes of networks, characterized by the forwarding behaviors of their middleboxes, which admit better complexity results (PTIME and coNP). We demonstrate that these classes capture real-world middleboxes. The upper bounds are made more realistic by stating them in terms of a symbolic representation of middleboxes. (iii) We present initial empirical results using Petri nets and Datalog engines to verify safety of networks. Due to space constraints, all proofs are omitted. More details and examples are provided in a technical report [34].

## 2   A Formal Model for Stateful Networks

In this section, we present a formal model of networks with stateful middleboxes.

A *network* N is a finite undirected graph of *hosts* and *middleboxes*, equipped with a *packet domain*. Formally, $N = (H \cup M, E, P)$, where $H$ is a finite set of *hosts*, $M$ is a finite set of *middleboxes*, $E \subseteq \{\{u, v\} \mid u, v \in H \cup M\}$ is the set of (undirected) edges and $P$ is a set of packets. A *host* $h \in H$ consists of a unique id and a set of packets $h_P \subseteq P$ that it can send.

*Packets.* In real networks, a packet consists of a *packet header* and a *payload*. The packet header contains a source and destination host ids and additional arbitrary stream of control bits. The payload is the content of the packet and may consist of any arbitrary sequence of bits. In particular, the set of packets need not be finite. In this work, $P$ is a set of *abstract packets*. An abstract packet $p \in P$ consists of a header only in the form of a triple $(s, d, t)$, where $s, d \in H$ are the source and destination hosts (respectively) and $t$ is a *packet tag* that ranges over a finite domain $T$. Intuitively, $T$ stands for an abstract set of services or security policies. Therefore, $P = H \times H \times T$, making it a finite set. Middlebox behavior in our model is defined with respect to abstract packets and is oblivious of the underlying concrete packets.

## 2.1   Stateful Middleboxes

A *middlebox* $m \in M$ in a network N has a set of *ports* Pr, which consists of all the adjacent edges of $m$ in the network N, and a *forwarding transducer F*.

The forwarding transducer of a middlebox is a tuple $F = (\Sigma, \Gamma, Q_m, q_m^0, \delta_m)$ where $\Sigma = P \times \mathsf{Pr}$ is the input alphabet in which each input letter consists of a packet and an input port, $\Gamma = 2^{\Sigma}$ is the output alphabet describing (possibly empty) sets of packets over the different ports, $Q_m$ is a possibly infinite set of states, $q_m^0 \in Q_m$ is the initial state, and $\delta_m : Q_m \times \Sigma \to 2^{\Gamma \times Q_m}$ is the transition relation. Note that the alphabet $\Sigma$ is finite (since abstract packets are considered). We extend $\delta_m$ to sequences $h \in (P \times \mathsf{Pr})^*$ in the natural way: $\delta_m(q, \epsilon) = \{(\epsilon, q)\}$ and $\delta_m(q, h \cdot (p, pr)) = \{(\gamma_i \cdot o', q') \mid \exists q_i \in Q_m \cdot (\gamma_i, q_i) \in \delta_m(q, h) \wedge (o', q') \in \delta_m(q_i, (p, pr))\}$. The language of a state $q \in Q_m$ is $L(q) = \{(h, \gamma) \in (P \times \mathsf{Pr})^* \times (P \times \mathsf{Pr})^* \mid (\gamma, q) \in \delta_m(q, h)\}$. The language of $F$, denoted $L(F)$, is the language of $q_m^0$. We also define the set of *histories* leading to $q \in Q_m$ as $h(q) = \{h \in (P \times \mathsf{Pr})^* \mid (\gamma, q) \in \delta_m(q_m^0, h)\}$.

If $F$ is deterministic, i.e., $|\delta_m(q, (p, pr))| \le 1$, then every history leads to at most one state and output, in which case $F$ defines a possibly partial *forwarding function* $\mathsf{f} : (P \times \mathsf{Pr})^* \times (P \times \mathsf{Pr}) \to 2^{P \times \mathsf{Pr}}$ where $\mathsf{f}(h, (p, pr)) = o$ for the (unique) output $o$ such that $(h \cdot (p, pr), \gamma \cdot o) \in L(F)$. $\mathsf{f}$ defines the (possibly empty) set of output packets (paired with output ports) that $m$ will send to its neighbors following every history $h$ of packets that $m$ received in the past and input packet $p$ arriving on input port $pr$. If $F$ is nondeterministic, a *forwarding relation* is defined in a similar way.

Note that every forwarding function $\mathsf{f}$ can be defined by an infinite-state deterministic transducer: $Q_m$ will include a state for every possible history, with $\epsilon$ as the initial state. $\delta_m$ will map a state and an input packet to the set of output packets as defined by $\mathsf{f}$, and will change the state by appending the packet to the history.

*Finite-state Middleboxes.* Arbitrary middlebox functionality, defined via infinite-state transducers, makes middleboxes Turing-complete, and hence impossible to analyze. To make the analysis tractable, we focus on abstract middleboxes, whose forwarding behavior is defined by *finite-state* transducers. Nondeterminsm can then be used to overapproximate the behavior of a concrete, possibly infinite-state, middlebox via a finite-state abstract middlebox, allowing a sound abstraction w.r.t. safety. Note that when nondeterministic transducers are considered, the correspondence between packet histories and transducer states no longer holds, as a single history might lead to multiple states.

In the sequel, unless explicitly stated otherwise, we consider abstract middleboxes. We identify a middlebox with its forwarding relation and the transducer that implements it, and use $m$ to denote each of them.

*Symbolic Representation of Middleboxes.* We use a symbolic representation of finite-state middleboxes, where a state of $m$ is described by the valuation of a finite set of relations $R_1, \ldots, R_k$ defined over finite elements (e.g., packet

**input**$(src, dst, tag, prt)$ :
    $prt = 1 \Rightarrow$ // hosts within organization
      trusted.**insert** $dst$ ;
      **output** $\{(src, dst, tag, 2)\}$
    $prt = 2 \wedge src$ **in** trusted $\Rightarrow$
      // trusted hosts outside organization
      **output** $\{(src, dst, tag, 1)\}$
    $prt = 2 \wedge \neg(src$ **in** trusted$) \Rightarrow$
      **output** $\emptyset$ // untrusted hosts

(a) A hole-punching firewall.

**input**$(src, dst, tag, prt)$ :
    $prt = 1 \wedge (dst, src, tag)$ **in** cache $\Rightarrow$
      // previously stored response
      **output** $\{(this, src, tag, 1)\}$
    $prt = 1 \Rightarrow$   // new request
      **output** $\{(this, dst, tag, 2)\}$
    $prt = 2 \Rightarrow$ // response to a request
      cache.**insert**$(src, dst, tag)$ ;
      **output**$\{(this, dst, tag, 1)\}$

(b) A Proxy.

**Fig. 2.** Symbolic representation of middleboxes.

header fields). The transition relation $\delta_m$ is also described symbolically using (nondeterministic) update operations of the relations and output. Technically, we use guarded commands, where guards are Boolean expressions over *relation membership predicates* of the form $\bar{e}$ **in** $R$ and element equalities $e_1 = e_2$. Each $e_i$ is either a constant or a variable that refers to packet fields. Commands are of the form: (i) *insert* tuple $\bar{e}$ to relation $R$, (ii) *remove* tuple $\bar{e}$ from relation $R$, and (iii) *output* set of tuples.

*Example 1.* Figure 2a contains a symbolic representation of a hole-punching Firewall which uses a unary relation trusted. It assumes that port 1 connects hosts inside a private organization to the firewall and that port 2 connects public hosts. By default, messages from public hosts are considered untrusted and are dropped. trusted stores public hosts that become trusted once they receive a packet from private hosts.

Figure 2b contains a simplified, nondeterminitic, version of a Proxy server (or cache server). A proxy stores copies of documents (packet payloads) that passed through it. Subsequent requests for those documents are provided by the proxy, rather than being forwarded. Our modelling abstracts away the packet payloads and keeps only their types. Consequently we use nondeterminism to also account for different requests with the same type. The internal relation cache stores responses for packet types.

## 2.2 Concrete (FIFO) Network Semantics

The semantics of a network is given by a transition system defined over a set of configurations. In order to define the semantics we first need to define the notion of *channels* which capture the transmission of packets in the network. Formally, each (undirected) edge $\{u, v\} \in E$ in the network induces two directed *channels*: $(u, v)$ and $(v, u)$. The channel $(v, u)$ is the *ingress channel* of $u$, as well as the *egress channel* of $v$. It consists of the sequence of packets that were sent from $v$ to $u$ and were not yet received by $u$ (and similarly for the channel $(u, v)$). The capacity of channels is unbounded, that is, the sequence of packets may be arbitrarily long.

*Configurations and Runs.* A *configuration* of a network consists of the content of each channel and the state of every middlebox. The *initial configuration* of a network consists of empty channels and initial states for all middleboxes. A configuration $c_2$ is a *successor* of configuration $c_1$ if it can be obtained by either: (i) some host $h$ sending a sequence of packets $p_1, \ldots, p_\ell \in h_P$ to a neighbor, thus appending these packets to the corresponding channel; or (ii) some middlebox $m$ processing a packet $p$ from the head of one of its ingress channels, changing its state to $q'$ and appending output $o$ to its egress channels if $(o, q') \in \delta_m(q, (p, pr))$ (where $q$ is the current state of $m$ and $pr$ is the port associated with the ingress channel). This model corresponds to asynchronous networks with non-deterministic event order.

A *run of a network from configuration* $c_0$ is a sequence of configurations $c_0, c_1, c_2, \ldots$ such that $c_{i+1}$ is a successor configuration of $c_i$. A *run* is a run from the initial configuration. The set of *reachable configurations from a configuration* $c_i$ is the set of all configurations that reside on a run from $c_i$. The set of *reachable configurations* of a network is the set of reachable configurations from the initial configuration.

## 3   Verification of Safety Properties in Stateful Networks

In this section we define the *safety* verification problem in stateful networks, as well as the special case of *isolation*. We prove their undecidability w.r.t. the FIFO semantics.

To describe safety properties, we augment middleboxes with a special *abort state* that is reached whenever $\delta_m(q, (p, pr)) = \emptyset$, i.e., the forwarding behavior is undefined (not to be confused with the case where $(\emptyset, q') \in \delta_m(q, (p, pr))$ for some $q' \in Q_m$). This lets middleboxes function as "monitors" for safety properties. If $\delta_m(q, (p, pr)) = \emptyset$, and $h \in h(q)$, we say that $m$ *aborts* on $h \cdot (p, pr)$ (and every extension thereof). Similarly, we augment the symbolic representation with an *abort* command.

We define *abort configurations* as network configurations where at least one middlebox is in an abort state.

*Safety.* The input to the *safety problem* consists of a network N (that possibly contains property middleboxes). The output is True if no abort configuration is reachable in N, and False otherwise.

*Isolation.* An important example of a safety property is isolation. In the *isolation problem*, the input is a network N, a set of hosts $H_i \subseteq H$ and a forbidden set of packets $P_i \subseteq P$. The output is True if there is no run of N in which a host from $H_i$ receives a packet from $P_i$, and False otherwise. The isolation problem can be formulated as a safety problem by introducing an *isolation middlebox* $m_{h_i}$ for every host $h_i \in H_i$. The role of $m_{h_i}$ is to monitor all traffic to $h_i$, and abort if a forbidden packet $p \in P_i$ arrives. All other packets are forwarded to $h_i$. Clearly, isolation holds if and only if the resulting network is safe.

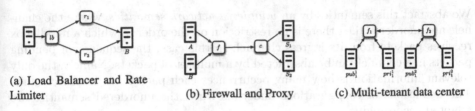

(a) Load Balancer and Rate Limiter

(b) Firewall and Proxy

(c) Multi-tenant data center

**Fig. 3.** Interesting network topologies for verification.

*Example 2.* Figure 3 shows several examples of interesting middlebox topologies for verification. In all of the topologies shown we want to verify a variant of the isolation property. In Fig. 3a we want to verify that $A$, a host, cannot send more than a fixed number of packets to $B$. Here $r_1$ and $r_2$ are rate limiters, *i.e.*, they count the number of packets they have seen going from one host to the other, and $lb$ is a load balancer that evenly spreads packets from $A$ along both paths (to minimize the load on any one path). In Fig. 3b we want to ensure that host $A$ cannot access data that originates in $S_1$, but should be allowed to access data from $S_2$, where $f$ is a firewall and $c$ is a proxy (cache) server. Finally in Fig. 3c we show a multi-tenant datacenter (e.g., Amazon EC2), where many independent tenants insert rules into firewalls ($f_1$ and $f_2$) and we want to ensure that the overall behavior of these rules is correct. For example, we would like to ensure that $pri_1^1$ cannot communicate with $pri_2^1$, and $pub_2^1$ communicates with $pri_1^1$ only if $pri_1^1$ initiates the connection.

*Undecidability of Safety w.r.t. the FIFO Semantics.* We prove undecidability even in networks with no forwarding loops. We show that undecidability holds for a network with a DAG topology (i.e., a network with uni-directional links and no directed cycles).

**Theorem 1.** *The safety problem w.r.t. the FIFO network semantics is undecidable even for networks with finite-state middleboxes and without forwarding loops.*

The proof of the theorem uses a reduction from the (undecidable) halting problem of a two-counter machine to the complement of the isolation problem. Interestingly, the reduction constructs a network with only three middleboxes, that do not change the packet header (namely, they just forward packets).

# 4    Abstract Network Semantics

In this section we define an abstract network semantics, called the *unordered semantics*, which recovers decidability of the safety problem.

In the concrete (FIFO) network semantics channels are ordered. In an ordered channel, if a packet $p_1$ precedes a packet $p_2$ in an ingress channel of some middlebox, then the middlebox will receive packet $p_1$ before it receives packet $p_2$.

We abstract this semantics by an *unordered network semantics*, where the channels are unordered, i.e., there is no restriction on the order in which a middlebox receives packets from its ingress channel. In this case, the sequence of pending packets in a channel can be abstracted by a multiset of packets. Namely, the only relevant information is how many occurrences each packet has in the channel. The definitions of configurations and runs w.r.t. the unordered semantics are adapted accordingly.

*Remark 1.* Every run w.r.t. the FIFO network semantics is also a run w.r.t. the unordered semantics. Therefore, if safety holds w.r.t. the unordered semantics, then it also holds for the FIFO semantics, making the unordered semantics a sound abstraction of the FIFO semantics w.r.t. safety. The abstraction can introduce false alarms, where a violation exists w.r.t. the unordered semantics but not w.r.t. the concrete semantics. Still, in many cases, the abstraction is precise enough to enable verification. In particular, in Lemma 4 we show that for an important class of networks, the two semantics coincide w.r.t. safety.

*Decidability of Safety w.r.t. the Unordered Semantics.* In the unordered semantics, the network forms a special case of *monotone transition systems*: We define a partial order $\leq$ between network configurations such that $c_1 \leq c_2$ if the middlebox states in $c_1$ and $c_2$ are the same and $c_2$ has at least the same packets (for every packet type) in every channel. The network is monotone in the sense that for every run from $c_1$ there is a corresponding run from any bigger $c_2$, since more packets over a channel can only add possible scenarios. The partial order is trivially a well-quasi-order (as the number of packets cannot be negative), and the predecessor relation is obviously computable. The classical results in [3,12] prove that in monotone transition systems a backward reachability algorithm always terminates and thus, the safety problem is decidable. Formal arguments and complexity bounds are provided by Theorem 4.

# 5    Classification of Stateful Middleboxes

Encouraged by the decidability of safety w.r.t. the unordered semantics, we are now interested in investigating its complexity. As a first step, in this section, we identify three special classes of forwarding behaviors of middleboxes within the class of arbitrary middleboxes. Namely, stateless, increasing, and progressing middleboxes. We show that these classes capture the behaviors of real world middleboxes. The classes naturally extend to classes of networks: a network is stateless (respectively, increasing, progressing or arbitrary) if all of its middleboxes are. As we show in Sec. 6, each of these classes results in a different complexity of the safety problem.

*Stateless Middlebox.* A middlebox $m$ is *stateless* if it can be implemented as a transducer with a single state (in addition to the abort state), i.e., its forwarding behavior does not depend on its history.

*Increasing Middlebox.* A middlebox $m$ is *increasing* if its forwarding relation is monotonically increasing w.r.t. its history, where histories are ordered by the *subsequence* relation[2], denoted by $\sqsubseteq$. Formally, a middlebox $m$ is increasing if for every two histories $h_1, h_2 \in (P \times \mathsf{Pr})^*$: if $h_1 \sqsubseteq h_2$, then for every packet $p$ and port $pr$, if $(h_1 \cdot (p, pr), \gamma_1 \cdot o_1) \in L_m$ then either $m$ aborts on $h_2 \cdot (p, pr)$ or there is $\gamma_2 \cdot o_2$ s.t. $(h_2 \cdot (p, pr), \gamma_2 \cdot o_2) \in L_m$ and $o_1 \subseteq o_2$, where $L_m$ is the language of $m$'s transducer.

*Progressing Middlebox.* In order to define progressing middleboxes, we define an equivalence relation between middlebox states based on their forwarding behavior. States $q, q'$ are equivalent, denoted $q_1 \approx q_2$, if $L(q_1) = L(q_2)$. A middlebox $m$ is *progressing* if it can be implemented by a transducer in which whenever the state is changed into a non-equivalent state, it will never return to an equivalent state. Formally, if $(o', q') \in \delta_m(q, (p, pr))$ and $q' \not\approx q$ (where $q, q'$ are reachable states of $m$) then for any history $h \in (P \times \mathsf{Pr})^*$, if $(\gamma'', q'') \in \delta_m(q', h)$ then $q'' \not\approx q$.

The next lemma summarizes the hierarchy of the classes (as illustrated by Fig. 1).

**Lemma 1.**  – *Any stateless middlebox is also increasing.*
– *Any increasing middlebox is also progressing.*

*Syntactic Characterization of Middlebox Classes.* The classes of middleboxes defined above can be characterized via syntactic restrictions on their symbolic representation.

A middlebox representation is *syntactically stateless* if its representation does not use any insert or remove command on any relation. A middlebox representation is *syntactically increasing* if its representation does not use the remove command on any relation, and does not include any insert command under guards that include negated membership predicates. A middlebox representation is *syntactically progressing* if its representation does not use the remove command on any relation.

**Lemma 2.** *A middlebox is stateless (respectively increasing, progressing) if and only if it has a stateless (respectively increasing, progressing) representation.*

## 5.1   Examples

In this subsection, we introduce several middleboxes, each of which resides in one of the classes of the hierarchy presented above.

---

[2] A subsequence is a sequence that can be derived from another sequence by deleting some elements without changing the order of the remaining elements.

*ACL Switches.* An *ACL switch* has a fixed access control list (ACL) that indicates which packets it should forward and which packets it should discard. Typically the rules in the list refer to the port number or to hosts that are allowed to use a certain service. As such, the forwarding policy of an ACL switch is based only on the source host and/or ingress port of the current packet, and does not depend on previous packets. Hence, an ACL switch can be implemented by a stateless middlebox.

*Hole-punching Firewalls.* A *hole-punching firewall* is described in Example 1. As the set of trusted hosts depends on the history of the middlebox, a hole punching firewall cannot be captured by a stateless middlebox. (Formally, the same packet is handled differently when it follows different histories.) On the other hand, it is increasing. If for a certain history a host is trusted, then any additional packets (in the past or in the future) will not make it untrusted.

*Learning Switch.* A *learning switch* dynamically learns the topology of the network and constructs a routing table accordingly. Initially, the routing table of the switch is empty. For every host $h$ the switch remembers the first port from which a packet with source $h$ has arrived. When a packet arrives, if the port of the destination host is known, then the packet is forwarded to that port; otherwise, the packet is forwarded to all connected ports excluding the input-port.

A learning switch is a progressing middlebox. Intuitively, after the middlebox's forwarding function has changed to incorporate the destination port for a certain host $h$, it will never revert to a state in which it has to flood a packet destined for $h$. A learning switch is however, not an increasing middlebox, as packets destined for a host whose location is not known are initially flooded, but after location of the host is learned, a single copy of all subsequent packets are sent.

*Proxy Server.* The *Proxy server* as described in Example 1 is an increasing middlebox. After it has stored a response, it nondeterministically replies with the stored response, or sends the request to the server again. However, in a concrete network model that does not abstract away the packet payload, a proxy is a progressing middlebox. Once a new request is responded by a proxy the forwarding behavior changes as it takes into account the new response, and it never returns to the previous forwarding behavior (as it does not "forget" the response). However, such a proxy is *not* an increasing middlebox: while it behaves in a monotonically increasing manner over its request port, it behaves in a monotonically decreasing manner over the response port.

*Round-Robin Load Balancer.* A *load balancer* is a device that distributes network traffic across a number of servers. In its simplest implementation, a round-robin balancer with $n$ out-ports (each connected to a server) forwards the $i$-th packet it receives to out-port $i \pmod n$. Round-robin load balancers are not progressing middleboxes, as the same forwarding function repeats after every cycle of $n$ packets.

*Remark 2.* In practice, middlebox behavior can also be affected by timeouts and session termination. For example, in a firewall, a trusted host may become untrusted when a session terminates (which makes the firewall behavior no longer increasing). In this work, we do not model timeouts and session termination. In many practical cases, such as firewalls, resets can only prevent packets from being forwarded and therefore restrict reachability, thus not causing safety violations.

## 6    Complexity of Safety W.r.t. the Unordered Semantics

When considering the unordered network semantics, the safety problem becomes decidable for networks with finite-state middleboxes. In this section, we analyze its complexity. We provide tight bounds, as well as algorithms with matching complexity. The complexity bounds are w.r.t the input size, namely, (i) the number of hosts; (ii) number of middleboxes; and (iii) the encoding size of the middleboxes functionality, i.e., the size of the explicit state machine (if the encoding is explicit) or the number of characters in the symbolic representation (if the encoding is symbolic).

The following lemma summarizes the obtained lower bounds:

**Lemma 3.** *The safety problem w.r.t. the unordered network semantics is coNP-hard for progressing networks, and EXPSPACE-hard for arbitrary stateful networks.*

The coNP-hardness result is proved by a reduction from the complement of the Hamiltonian Path problem. The constructed network contains only stateless middleboxes and learning switches, making the coNP-hardness result apply already to such networks, which are used in practice. The second part of the lemma is proved by a reduction from the *control state reachability problem* of *vector addition systems with states* (VASS) which is known to be EXPSPACE-complete [10].

*Upper Bounds.* The rest of this section provides complexity upper bounds for the safety problem of stateful networks w.r.t. the unordered semantics of networks. Our complexity analysis considers symbolic representations of middleboxes (which might be exponentially more succinct than explicit-state representations). The obtained upper bounds match the lower bounds from Lemma 3 (hence, the bounds are tight).

*Remark 3.* The complexity upper bounds we present are under the assumption that all relations used to define middlebox states may have at most polynomial number of elements (polynomial in the size of the network and the size of the middlebox representation). To enforce this limitation we assume that the arity of relations is constant.

$$StateData := \{m \mapsto InitialRelationValues(m) \mid m \in M\}$$
$$PacketData := \{m \mapsto NeighborHostPackets(m) \mid m \in M\}$$
**while** fixed-point not reached
    **foreach** $m \in M, (p, pr) \in PacketData(m)$
        let $q = GetState(StateData(m))$
        **if** $\delta_m(q, (p, pr)) = \emptyset$ **then return** violation // abort state reached
        let $(q', o) \in \delta_m(q, (p, pr))$
        $StateData := AddData(m, q')$
        $PacketData := AddPacketsToNeighbors(m, o)$
**return** safe

**Fig. 4.** Safety checking of increasing networks.

## 6.1 Unordered Safety of Increasing Networks is in PTIME

In this section, we show that safety of syntactically increasing networks is in PTIME. Further, we show that for increasing networks, safety w.r.t. the unordered semantics and the FIFO semantics coincide. As such, the polynomial upper bound applies to both.

Figure 4 presents a polynomial algorithm for determining safety of a syntactically increasing network. The algorithm performs a fixed-point computation of the set of all tuples present in middlebox relations in reachable middlebox states, as well as the set of all different packets transmitted in the network. For every middlebox $m \in M$, the algorithm maintains the following sets:

- $StateData(m)$: a set of pairs of the form $(R, \overline{d})$ where $R$ is a relation of $m$, and $\overline{d}$ is a tuple in the domain of $R$, indicating that there is a run in which $\overline{d} \in R$.
- $PacketData(m)$: a set of pairs of the form $(p, pr)$, where $p$ is a packet and $pr$ is a port of $m$, indicating that $p$ can reach $m$ from port $pr$.

$StateData(m)$ is initialized to reflect the initial values of all middlebox relations. $PacketData(m)$ is initialized to include the packets that can be sent from neighbor hosts. As long as a fixed-point is not reached, the algorithm iterates over all middleboxes and their packet data. For each middlebox $m$ and $(p, pr) \in PacketData(m)$, $m$ is run over $(p, pr)$ from the state $q$ in which every relation $R$ contains all the tuples $\overline{d}$ such that $(R, \overline{d}) \in StateData(m)$. The sets $StateData(m)$ and $PacketData(m')$ for every neighbor $m'$ of $m$, are updated to reflect the discovery of more elements in the relations (more reachable states), and more packets that can be transmitted.

As the algorithm only adds reachable states and packets, its running time is polynomial and bounded by $|M|(|P||Pr|\sum|R_i|)^2$.

The correctness of the algorithm relies on the property of increasing networks that if a packet is sent in some run from a reachable configuration, then a run where it is sent exists from *every* reachable configuration. The same goes for elements that are added to relations. Intuitively, this ensures that even though the algorithm considers "accumulative" middlebox states (by accumulating relation values) rather than exploring all possible reachable states, it does not miss any violation of safety. We conclude:

**Theorem 2.** *The safety problem of syntactically increasing networks w.r.t. the unordered semantics is in PTIME.*

*Remark 4.* If $n$-tag packet headers are allowed, i.e. $P = H \times H \times T_1 \ldots \times T_n$, then $|P|$ is no longer polynomial in the network representation, damaging the complexity analysis of the algorithm. In fact, in this case the safety problem w.r.t. the unordered semantics becomes PSPACE-hard even for stateless middleboxes (this is proved by reduction from the emptiness problem of the intersection of $n$ automata).

Recall that in general, safety w.r.t. the FIFO semantics and the unordered semantics do not coincide. However, the following lemma shows that for increasing networks they do, making the same algorithm and complexity analysis applicable. The proof utilizes the property that in increasing networks if a packet $p$ reaches a middlebox $m$ once (in either semantics), then it can reach $m$ again, thus enabling the simulation of unordered channels with ordered ones. The lemma applies also to infinite-state middleboxes.

**Lemma 4.** *Let* N *be an increasing network. Then the output of the safety problem in* N *w.r.t. the FIFO semantics and w.r.t. the unordered semantics is identical.*

## 6.2 Unordered Safety of Progressing Networks is in CoNP

We prove coNP-membership of the safety problem in syntactically progressing networks by proving that there exists a witness run for safety violation if and only if there exists a "short" witness run, where a witness run for safety violation is a run from the initial configuration in which at least one middlebox reaches an abort state. The key observation is formalized by the following lemma:

**Lemma 5.** *Let* N *be a syntactically progressing network whose middleboxes are defined via relations $R_1, \ldots, R_n$ (in total). Then there is a run ending in an abort state if and only if there is such a run whose length is at most $(\sum_{i=1}^{n} |R_i|)^3 |P||M|$.*

The proof of the lemma considers the *network states* that arise in a run. A *network state* consists of the values of $(R_1, \ldots, R_n)$, i.e., it captures the states of all middleboxes (not to be confused with a network configuration, which also includes the content of every channel). In order to construct a shorter run, we bound both the number of different network states in a run and the number of steps in which a run stays in the same state. The former is bounded by $\sum_{i=1}^{n} |R_i|$ due to the progress of the network. To provide a bound for the latter, we analyze the packets that "affect" the run, utilizing the property that steps that process packets that do not affect the run can be omitted.

Since the size of each relation is polynomial in the size of the network, and combined with the hardness result from Lemma 3, we conclude:

**Theorem 3.** *The safety problem of syntactically progressing networks w.r.t. the unordered semantics is coNP-complete.*

## 6.3   Unordered Safety of Arbitrary Networks is in EXPSPACE

In this section we show how to solve the non-safety problem of symbolic networks by a reduction to the *coverability problem* of *vector addition systems* (VAS), a.k.a. petri-nets, which is EXPSPACE-complete [26].

A VAS is a pair $(x_0 \in \mathbb{N}^k, X \subset \mathbb{Z}^k)$, where $x_0$ is the *initial value vector* and $X$ is a set of transition vectors, each with $k$ *dimensions*. A finite run in the VAS is a sequence of transitions $x_1, x_2, \ldots, x_\ell$, such that for every $i \in \{1, \ldots, \ell\}$ the sum $x_0 + x_1 + \cdots + x_i$ is non-negative in all dimensions. The coverability problem asks whether a VAS has a run $x_1, x_2, \ldots, x_\ell$ with $\sum_{i=0}^{\ell} x_i \geq y$, where $y$ is an input vector.

*VAS Construction.* We sketch a polynomial encoding of a network as a VAS. Roughly speaking, the transitions of the VAS are used to simulate the processing of packets in the network. Their non-deterministic nature captures the non-deterministic order of network events. We first introduce the VAS dimensions and their roles in the simulation.

*Channel Simulation:* To keep track of the packets over the unbounded channels, we assign a *packet* dimension to every packet $p \in P$ and every channel. The initial value of each packet dimension is 0, it is incremented whenever a packet is added to a channel, and decremented whenever a packet is processed.

*Relation Simulation:* To keep track of relation values, we assign two dimensions, *active* and *inactive*, to every relation $R$ and every tuple $\bar{d}$ in the domain of $R$. The active dimension indicates whether $\bar{d} \in R$ and the inactive one indicates whether $\bar{d} \notin R$. Both dimensions will have only values of 0 or 1. We need two dimensions since the VAS semantics does not allow to encode negative (e.g., non-membership) conditions.

*Single Step Simulation:* To make sure that no two packets are simultaneously processed, we introduce a *scheduler* dimension. The scheduler dimension has initial value 1, it is decremented whenever a packet processing starts, and incremented when it ends. In addition, to keep track of which command needs to be executed, we assign a *command* dimension to every guard and command, including an *abort* dimension (if an abort command exists). The guard/command dimension has value 1 when the command needs to be executed. Finally, to keep track of values of variables (e.g., *src*, *dst*, *tag*, *prt*), we assign a dimension for every possible value $d$ of variable $e_i$. The dimension of $(e_i, d)$ has value 1 if and only if $e_i$ has value $d$.

The VAS transitions increment and decrement these dimensions to simulate the start of a packet processing event, as well as the execution of each guarded command. In particular, decrements are used to enforce the execution of transitions only when the dimension has value 1 (and not 0).

Non-safety of the network then amounts to a run in the VAS where an *abort* dimension gets a positive value. The reduction, combined with the lower bound implies:

**Theorem 4.** *The safety problem of arbitrary stateful networks w.r.t. the unordered semantics is EXPSPACE-complete.*

# 7    Implementation and Case Studies

In this section, we describe a prototype implementation of a tool for verification of stateful networks, and describe our initial experience while running the tool on the networks listed in Example 2 and illustrated in Fig. 3. For the experiments we used quad core Intel Core i7-4790 CPU with 32 GB memory.

*Increasing Middleboxes.* Increasing networks are verified using LogicBlox, a Datalog based database system [5]. The Multi-Tenant Datacenter example is an increasing network. Our tool produced a datalog program with 35 predicates, 153 rules and 29 facts. LogicBlox successfully reached a fixed point in 3s, and proved all required properties.

*Arbitrary Middleboxes.* Progressing and Arbitrary networks are verified using LOLA, a Petri-Net model checker [1,28]. In the Load Balancer and Rate Limiter example our tool created a P/T net with 243 places and 663 transitions; it was successfully verified in 30ms. In the Firewall and Proxy example our tool produced a P/T net with 530 places and 4447 transitions. LOLA successfully verified the resulting petri-net in 0.2s.

# 8    Conclusion and Related Work

In this paper, we investigated the complexity of reasoning about stateful networks. We developed three algorithms and several lower bounds. In the future we hope to develop practical verification methods utilizing the results in this paper. Below we survey some of the most closely related work.

*Topology-independent Verification.* The earliest use of formal verification in networking focused on proving correctness and checking security properties for protocols [11,27]. Recent works such FlowLog [21] and VeriCon [6] also aim to verify the correctness of a given middlebox implementation w.r.t any possible network topology and configuration, e.g., flow table entries only contain forwarding rules from trusted hosts.

*Immutable Topology-dependent Verification.* Recent efforts in network verification [4,9,14,16,17,20,30,32] have focused on verifying network properties by analyzing forwarding tables. Some of these tools including HSA [15], Libra [35] and VeriFlow [17]. These tools perform near real-time verification of simple properties, but they cannot handle dynamic (mutable) datapaths.

*Mutable Topology-dependent Verification.* SymNet [33] has suggested the need to extend these mechanisms to handle mutable datapath elements. In their mechanism the mutable middlebox states are encoded in the packet header. This technique is only applicable when state is not shared across a flow (*i.e.*, the middlebox can punch holes, but do no more), and will not work for cache servers or learning switches.

The work in [24] is the most similar to our model. Their work considers Python-like syntax enriched with uninterpreted functions that model complicated functionality. However [24] do not define formal network semantic (e.g., FIFO vs ordered channels) and do not give any formal claim on the complexity of the solution.

*Channel Systems.* Channel systems, also called Finite State Communicating Machines, are systems of finite state automata that communicate via asynchronous unbounded FIFO channels [7, 8]. They are a natural model for asynchronous communication protocols. Verification of such systems in undecidable. Abdulla and Jonsson [2] introduced *lossy channel systems* where messages can be lost in transit. In their model the reachability problem is decidable but has a non-primitive lower bound [29].

In this work we use unordered (non-lossy) channels as a different relaxation for channel systems. The unordered semantics over-approximates the lossy semantics w.r.t. safety, as any violating run w.r.t. the lossy semantics can be simulated by a run w.r.t. the unordered semantics where "lost" packets are starved until the violation occurs. The unordered semantics admits verification procedures with elementary complexity, and turns out to be sufficiently precise for many network protocols.

**Acknowledgements.** The research leading to these results has received funding from the European Research Council under the European Union's Seventh Framework Programme (FP7/2007–2013) / ERC grant agreement no [321174]. Research supported by the Israel Science Foundation grant no.652/11. This research was also supported in part by NSF grants 1040838 and 1420064, and funding provided by Intel Corporation.

# References

1. Lola 2.0 sources. http://download.gna.org/service-tech/lola/lola-2.0.tar.gz
2. Abdulla, P., Jonsson, B.: Verifying programs with unreliable channels. In: Logic in Computer Science (LICS), pp. 160–170. IEEE (1993)
3. Abdulla, P.A., Čerāns, K., Jonsson, B., Tsay, Y.-K.: General decidability theorems for infinite-state systems. In: Logic in Computer Science (LICS), pp. 313–321. IEEE (1996)
4. Anderson, C.J., Foster, N., Guha, A., Jeannin, J.-B., Kozen, D., Schlesinger, C., Walker, D.: NetKAT: Semantic foundations for networks. In: POPL (2014)
5. Aref, M., ten Cate, B., Green, T.J., Kimelfeld, B., Olteanu, D., Pasalic, E., Veldhuizen, T.L., Washburn, G.: Design and implementation of the logicblox system. In: ACM SIGMOD International Conference on Management of Data, pp. 1371–1382 (2015)

6. Ball, T., Bjørner, N., Gember, A., Itzhaky, S., Karbyshev, A., Sagiv, M., Schapira, M., Valadarsky, A.: Vericon: towards verifying controller programs in software-defined networks. In: ACM SIGPLAN Conference on Programming Language Design and Implementation, PLDI, p. 31 (2014)
7. Bochmann, G.V.: Finite state description of communication protocols. Comput. Netw. 2(4–5), 361–372 (1978)
8. Brand, D., Zafiropulo, P.: On communicating finite-state machines. J. ACM (JACM) 30(2), 323–342 (1983)
9. Canini, M., Venzano, D., Peres, P., Kostic, D., Rexford, J.: A nice way to test openflow applications. In: 9th USENIX Symposium on Networked Systems Design and Implementation (NSDI 2012) (2012)
10. Cardoza, E., Lipton, R., Meyer, A.R.: Exponential space complete problems for petri nets and commutative semigroups (preliminary report). In: Proceedings of the Eighth Annual ACM Symposium on Theory of Computing, pp. 50–54. ACM (1976)
11. Clarke, E.M., Jha, S., Marrero, W.: Using state space exploration and a natural deduction style message derivation engine to verify security protocols. In: Gries, D., de Roever, W.-P. (eds.) Programming Concepts and Methods PROCOMET 1998. IFIP, pp. 87–106. Springer, Heidelberg (1998)
12. Finkel, A., Schnoebelen, P.: Well-structured transition systems everywhere!. Theoret. Comput. Sci. 256(1), 63–92 (2001)
13. Fogel, A., Fung, S., Pedrosa, L., Walraed-Sullivan, M., Govindan, R., Mahajan, R., Millstein, T.D.: A general approach to network configuration analysis. In: 12th USENIX Symposium on Networked Systems Design and Implementation, NSDI 15, Oakland, CA, USA, May 4–6, pp. 469–483 (2015)
14. Foster, N., Kozen, D., Milano, M., Silva, A., Thompson, L.: A coalgebraic decision procedure for NetKAT. In: Proceedings of the 42nd Annual ACM SIGPLAN-SIGACT Symposium on Principles of Programming Languages, POPL , Mumbai, India, 15–17 January 2015, pp. 343–355 (2015)
15. Kazemian, P., Chang, M., Zeng, H., Varghese, G., McKeown, N., Whyte, S.: Real time network policy checking using header space analysis. In: 10th USENIX Symposium on Networked Systems Design and Implementation (NSDI 2013) (2013)
16. Kazemian, P., Varghese, G., McKeown, N.: Header space analysis: Static checking for networks. In 9th USENIX Symposium on Networked Systems Design and Implementation (NSDI 2012) (2012)
17. Khurshid, A., Zhou, W., Caesar, M., Godfrey, B.: Veriflow: verifying network-wide invariants in real time. Comput. Commun. Rev. 42(4), 467–472 (2012)
18. Kuzniar, M., Peresini, P., Canini, M., Venzano, D., Kostic, D.: A soft way for openflow switch interoperability testing. In: CoNEXT, pp. 265–276 (2012)
19. Lopes, N.P., Bjørner, N., Godefroid, P., Jayaraman, K., Varghese, G.: Checking beliefs in dynamic networks. In: 12th USENIX Symposium on Networked Systems Design and Implementation, NSDI 15, Oakland, CA, USA, May 4–6, pp. 499–512 (2015)
20. Mai, H., Khurshid, A., Agarwal, R., Caesar, M., Godfrey, B., King, S.T.: Debugging the data plane with anteater. In: SIGCOMM (2011)
21. Nelson, T., Ferguson, A.D., Scheer, M.J.G., Krishnamurthi, S.: Tierless programming and reasoning for software-defined networks. In: Proceedings of the 11th USENIX Symposium on Networked Systems Design and Implementation, NSDI, Seattle, WA, USA, April 2–4, 2014, pp. 519–531 (2014)
22. OpenStack. LogicBlox. http://www.logicblox.com/. Accessed 07 July 2015

23. Panda, A., Argyraki, K.J., Sagiv, M., Schapira, M., Shenker, S.: New directions for network verification. In: 1st Summit on Advances in Programming Languages, SNAPL 3–6, 2015, Asilomar, California, USA, pp. 209–220, May 2015

24. Panda, A., Lahav, O., Argyraki, K., Sagiv, M., Shenker, S.: Verifying isolation properties in the presence of middleboxes (2014). arXiv preprint arXiv: 1409.7687

25. Potharaju, R., Jain, N.: Demystifying the dark side of the middle: a field study of middlebox failures in datacenters. In: Proceedings of the 2013 Internet Measurement Conference, IMC 2013, Barcelona, Spain, October 23–25, 2013, pp. 9–22 (2013)

26. Rackoff, C.: The covering and boundedness problems for vector addition systems. Theoret. Comput. Sci. **6**(2), 223–231 (1978)

27. Ritchey, R.W., Ammann, P.: Using model checking to analyze network vulnerabilities. In: Security and Privacy (2000)

28. Schmidt, K.: LoLA a low level analyser. In: Nielsen, M., Simpson, D. (eds.) ICATPN 2000. LNCS, vol. 1825, p. 465. Springer, Heidelberg (2000)

29. Schnoebelen, P.: Verifying lossy channel systems has nonprimitive recursive complexity. Inf. Process. Lett. **83**(5), 251–261 (2002)

30. Sethi, D., Narayana, S., Malik, S.: Abstractions for model checking SDN controllers. In: FMCAD (2013)

31. Sherry, J., Hasan, S., Scott, C., Krishnamurthy, A., Ratnasamy, S., Sekar, V.: Making middleboxes someone else's problem: Network processing as a cloud service. In: SIGCOMM (2012)

32. Skowyra, R., Lapets, A., Bestavros, A., Kfoury, A.: A verification platform for SDN-enabled applications. In: HiCoNS (2013)

33. Stoenescu, R., Popovici, M., Negreanu, L., Raiciu, C.: Symnet: static checking for stateful networks. In: Proceedings of the 2013 Workshop on Hot Topics in Middleboxes and Network Function Virtualization, pp. 31–36. ACM (2013)

34. Velner, Y., Aplernas, K., Panda, A., Rabinovich, A., Sagiv, M., Shenker, S., Shoham, S.: Some complexity results for stateful network verification. http://www.cs.tau.ac.il/~msagiv/tacas16submission.pdf

35. Zeng, H., Zhang, S., Ye, F., Jeyakumar, V., Ju, M., Liu, J., McKeown, N., Vahdat, A.: Libra: Divide and conquer to verify forwarding tables in huge networks. In: NSDI (2014)

# Optimization

# Characteristic Formulae for Session Types

Julien Lange[✉] and Nobuko Yoshida

Imperial College London, London, UK
j.lange@imperial.ac.uk

**Abstract.** Subtyping is a crucial ingredient of session type theory and
its applications, notably to programming language implementations. In
this paper, we study effective ways to check whether a session type is
a subtype of another by applying a characteristic formulae approach to
the problem. Our core contribution is an algorithm to generate a modal
$\mu$-calculus formula that characterises all the supertypes (or subtypes) of
a given type. Subtyping checks can then be off-loaded to model checkers,
thus incidentally yielding an efficient algorithm to check safety of session
types, soundly and completely. We have implemented our theory and
compared its cost with other classical subtyping algorithms.

## 1  Introduction

**Motivations.** Session types [25,26,41] have emerged as a fundamental theory
to reason about concurrent programs, whereby not only the data aspects of programs are typed, but also their *behaviours* wrt. communication. Recent applications of session types to the reverse-engineering of large and complex distributed
systems [13,30] have led to the need of handling potentially large and complex
session types. Analogously to the current trend of modern compilers to rely on
external tools such as SMT-solvers to solve complex constraints and offer strong
guarantees [17,24,32,33], state-of-the-art model checkers can be used to off-load
expensive tasks from session type tools such as [30,38,43].

A typical use case for session types in software (reverse-) engineering is to
compare the type of an existing program with a candidate replacement, so to
ensure that both are "compatible". In this context, a crucial ingredient of session type theory is the notion of *subtyping* [10,15,20] which plays a key role
to guarantee safety of concurrent programs while allowing for the refinement of
specifications and implementations. Subtyping for session types relates to many
classical theories such as simulations and pre-orders in automata and process
algebra theories; but also to subtyping for recursive types in the $\lambda$-calculus [5].
The characteristic formulae approach [1–3,12,22,39,40], which has been studied since the late eighties as a method to compute simulation-like relations in
process algebra and automata, appears then as an evident link between subtyping in session type theory and model checking theories. In this paper, we make
the first formal connection between session type and model checking theories,
to the best of our knowledge. We introduce a novel approach to session types
subtyping based on characteristic formulae; and thus establish that subtyping

© Springer-Verlag Berlin Heidelberg 2016
M. Chechik and J.-F. Raskin (Eds.): TACAS 2016, LNCS 9636, pp. 833–850, 2016.
DOI: 10.1007/978-3-662-49674-9_52

for session types can be decided in quadratic time wrt. the size of the types. This improves significantly on the classical algorithm [21]. Subtyping can then be reduced to a model checking problem and thus be discharged to powerful model checkers. Consequently, any advance in model checking technology has an impact on subtyping.

**Example.** Let us illustrate what session types are and what subtyping covers. Consider a simple protocol between a server and a client, from the point of view of the server. The client sends a message of type *request* to the server who decides whether or not the request can be processed by replying *ok* or *ko*, respectively. If the request is rejected, the client is offered another chance to send another request, and so on. This may be described by the *session type* below

$$U_1 = \mathbf{rec}\,\mathbf{x}.\,?request.\{!ok.\mathbf{end} \oplus !ko.\mathbf{x}\} \tag{1}$$

where $\mathbf{rec}\,\mathbf{x}$ binds variable $\mathbf{x}$ in the rest of the type, $?msg$ (resp. $!msg$) specifies the reception (resp. emission) of a message $msg$, $\oplus$ indicates an *internal choice* between two behaviours, and **end** signifies the termination of the conversation. An implementation of a server can then be *type-checked* against $U_1$.

The client's perspective of the protocol may be specified by the *dual* of $U_1$:

$$\overline{U}_1 = U_2 = \mathbf{rec}\,\mathbf{x}.\,!request.\{?ok.\mathbf{end}\;\&\;?ko.\mathbf{x}\} \tag{2}$$

where & indicates an *external choice*, i.e., the client expects two possible behaviours from the server. A classical result in session type theory essentially says that if the types of two programs are *dual* of each other, then their parallel composition is free of errors (e.g., deadlock).

Generally, when we say that **integer** is a subtype of **float**, we mean that one can safely use an **integer** when a **float** is required. Similarly, in session type theory, if $T$ is a *subtype* of a type $U$ (written $T \leqslant U$), then $T$ can be used whenever $U$ is required. Intuitively, a type $T$ is a *subtype* of a type $U$ if $T$ is ready to receive no fewer messages than $U$, and $T$ may not send more messages than $U$ [10,15]. For instance, we have

$$\begin{aligned} T_1 &= ?request.!ok.\mathbf{end} \leqslant U_1 \\ T_2 &= \mathbf{rec}\,\mathbf{x}.\,!request.\{?ok.\mathbf{end}\;\&\;?ko.\mathbf{x}\;\&\;?error.\mathbf{end}\} \leqslant U_2 \end{aligned} \tag{3}$$

A server of type $T_1$ can be used whenever a server of type $U_1$ (1) is required ($T_1$ is a more refined version of $U_1$, which always accepts the request). A client of type $T_2$ can be used whenever a client of type $U_2$ (2) is required since $T_2$ is a type that can deal with (strictly) more messages than $U_2$.

In Sect. 3.2, we will see that a session type can be naturally transformed into a $\mu$-calculus formula that characterises all its subtypes. The transformation notably relies on the diamond modality to make some branches mandatory, and the box modality to allow some branches to be made optional; see Example 2.

**Contribution and Synopsis.** In Sect. 2 we recall session types and give a new abstract presentation of subtyping. In Sect. 3 we present a fragment of the modal $\mu$-calculus and, following [39], we give a simple algorithm to generate a $\mu$-calculus formula from a session type that characterises either all its subtypes or all its supertypes. In Sect. 4, building on results from [10], we give a sound and complete model-checking characterisation of safety for session types. In Sect. 5, we present two other subtyping algorithms for session types: Gay and Hole's classical algorithm [21] based on inference rules that unfold types explicitly; and an adaptation of Kozen et al.'s automata-theoretic Algorithm [28]. In Sect. 6, we evaluate the cost of our approach by comparing its performances against the two algorithms from Sect. 5. Our performance analysis is notably based on a tool that generates arbitrary well-formed session types. We conclude and discuss related works in Sect. 7. Due to lack of space, full proofs are relegated to an online appendix [31]. Our tool and detailed benchmark results are available online [29].

## 2    Session Types and Subtyping

Session types are abstractions of the behaviour of a program wrt. the communication of this program on a given *session* (or conversation), through which it interacts with another program (or component).

### 2.1    Session Types

We use a two-party version of the multiparty session types in [16]. For the sake of simplicity, we focus on first order session types (that is, types that carry only simple types (sorts) or values and not other session types). We discuss how to lift this restriction in Sect. 7. Let $\mathcal{V}$ be a countable set of variables (ranged over by $\mathbf{x}, \mathbf{y}$, etc.); let $\mathbb{A}$ be a (finite) alphabet, ranged over by $a$, $b$, etc.; and $\mathcal{A}$ be the set defined as $\{!a \mid a \in \mathbb{A}\} \cup \{?a \mid a \in \mathbb{A}\}$. We let $\dagger$ range over elements of $\{!, ?\}$, so that $\dagger a$ ranges over $\mathcal{A}$. The syntax of session types is given by

$$T := \mathbf{end} \mid \bigoplus_{i \in I} !a_i . T_i \mid \underset{i \in I}{\&} ?a_i . T_i \mid \mathbf{rec\,x}.T \mid \mathbf{x}$$

where $I \neq \varnothing$ is finite, $a_i \in \mathbb{A}$ for all $i \in I$, $a_i \neq a_j$ for $i \neq j$, and $\mathbf{x} \in \mathcal{V}$. Type $\mathbf{end}$ indicates the end of a session. Type $\bigoplus_{i \in I} !a_i . T_i$ specifies an *internal* choice, indicating that the program chooses to send one of the $a_i$ messages, then behaves as $T_i$. Type $\&_{i \in I} ?a_i . T_i$ specifies an *external* choice, saying that the program waits to receive one of the $a_i$ messages, then behaves as $T_i$. Types $\mathbf{rec\,x}.T$ and $\mathbf{x}$ are used to specify recursive behaviours. We often write, e.g., $\{!a_1.T_1 \oplus \ldots \oplus !a_k.T_k\}$ for $\bigoplus_{1 \leq i \leq k} !a_i.T_i$, write $!a_1.T_1$ when $k = 1$, similarly for $\&_{i \in I} ?a_i . T_i$, and omit trailing occurrences of $\mathbf{end}$.

The sets of free and bound variables of a type $T$ are defined as usual (the unique binder is the recursion operator $\mathbf{rec\,x}.T$). For each type $T$, we assume that two distinct occurrences of a recursion operator bind different variables, and that no variable has both free and bound occurrences. In coinductive definitions, we take an equi-recursive view of types, not distinguishing between a type $\mathbf{rec\,x}.T$ and its unfolding $T[\mathbf{rec\,x}.T/\mathbf{x}]$. We assume that each type $T$ is *contractive* [35],

$$\frac{j \in I}{\bigoplus_{i \in I} !a_i.\,T_i \xrightarrow{!a_j} T_j} \text{[T-OUT]} \qquad \frac{j \in I}{\&_{i \in I} ?a_i.\,T_i \xrightarrow{?a_j} T_j} \text{[T-IN]} \qquad \frac{T[\mathbf{rec\,x}.T/x] \xrightarrow{\dagger a} T'}{\mathbf{rec\,x}.T \xrightarrow{\dagger a} T'} \text{[T-REC]}$$

**Fig. 1.** LTS for session types in $\mathcal{T}_c$

e.g., $\mathbf{rec\,x.x}$ is not a type. Let $\mathcal{T}$ be the set of all (contractive) session types and $\mathcal{T}_c \subseteq \mathcal{T}$ the set of all closed session types (i.e., which do not contain free variables).

A session type $T \in \mathcal{T}_c$ induces a (finite) *labelled transition system* (LTS) according to the rules in Fig. 1. We write $T \xrightarrow{\dagger a}$ if there is $T' \in \mathcal{T}$ such that $T \xrightarrow{\dagger a} T'$ and write $T \not\rightarrow$ if $\forall \dagger a \in \mathcal{A} : \neg(T \xrightarrow{\dagger a})$.

## 2.2 Subtyping for Session Types

Subtyping for session types was first studied in [20] and further studied in [10,15]. It is a crucial notion for practical applications of session types, as it allows for programs to be *refined* while preserving safety.

We give a definition of subtyping which is parameterised wrt. operators $\oplus$ and $\&$, so to allow us to give a common characteristic formula construction for both the subtype and the supertype relations, cf. Sect. 3.2. Below, we let $\maltese$ range over $\{\oplus, \&\}$. When writing $\maltese_{i \in I} \dagger a_i.\,T_i$, we take the convention that $\dagger$ refers to ! iff $\maltese$ refers to $\oplus$ (and vice-versa for ? and $\&$). We define the (idempotent) duality operator $\overline{\phantom{x}}$ as follows: $\overline{\oplus} \overset{\text{def}}{=} \&$, $\overline{\&} \overset{\text{def}}{=} \oplus$, $\overline{!} \overset{\text{def}}{=} ?$, and $\overline{?} \overset{\text{def}}{=} !$.

**Definition 1 (Subtyping).** Fix $\maltese \in \{\oplus, \&\}$, $\trianglelefteq^{\maltese} \subseteq \mathcal{T}_c \times \mathcal{T}_c$ is the *largest* relation that contains the rules:

$$\frac{I \subseteq J \forall i \in I : T_i \trianglelefteq^{\maltese} U_i}{\maltese_{i \in I} \dagger a_i.\,T_i \trianglelefteq^{\maltese} \maltese_{j \in J} \dagger a_j.\,U_j} \text{[S-}\maltese\text{]} \qquad \frac{}{\mathbf{end} \trianglelefteq^{\maltese} \mathbf{end}} \text{[S-END]} \qquad \frac{J \subseteq I \quad \forall j \in J : T_j \trianglelefteq^{\maltese} U_j}{\overline{\maltese}_{i \in I} \dagger a_i.\,T_i \trianglelefteq^{\maltese} \overline{\maltese}_{j \in J} \dagger a_j.\,U_j} \text{[S-}\overline{\maltese}\text{]}$$

The double line in the rules indicates that the rules should be interpreted *coinductively*. Recall that we are assuming an equi-recursive view of types.          ◇

We comment Definition 1 assuming that $\maltese$ is set to $\oplus$. Rule [S-$\maltese$] says that a type $\bigoplus_{j \in J} !a_j.\,U_j$ can be replaced by a type that offers no more messages, e.g., $!a \trianglelefteq^{\oplus} !a \oplus !b$. Rule [S-$\overline{\maltese}$] says that a type $\&_{j \in J} ?a_j.\,U_j$ can be replaced by a type that is ready to receive at least the same messages, e.g., $?a \,\&\, ?b \trianglelefteq^{\oplus} ?a$. Rule [S-END] is trivial. It is easy to see that $\trianglelefteq^{\oplus} = (\trianglelefteq^{\&})^{-1}$. In fact, we can recover the subtyping of [10,15] (resp. [20,21]) from $\trianglelefteq^{\maltese}$, by instantiating $\maltese$ to $\oplus$ (resp. $\&$).

*Example 1.* Consider the session types from (3), we have $T_1 \trianglelefteq^{\oplus} U_1$, $U_1 \trianglelefteq^{\&} T_1$, $T_2 \trianglelefteq^{\oplus} U_2$, and $U_2 \trianglelefteq^{\&} T_2$.

Hereafter, we will write $\leqslant$ (resp. $\geqslant$) for the pre-order $\trianglelefteq^{\oplus}$ (resp. $\trianglelefteq^{\&}$).

# 3   Characteristic Formulae for Subtyping

We give the core construction of this paper: a function that given a (closed) session type $T$ returns a modal $\mu$-calculus formula [27] that characterises either all the supertypes of $T$ or all its subtypes. Technically, we "translate" a session type $T$ into a modal $\mu$-calculus formula $\phi$, so that $\phi$ characterises all the supertypes of $T$ (resp. all its subtypes). Doing so, checking whether $T$ is a subtype (resp. supertype) of $U$ can be reduced to checking whether $U$ is a model of $\phi$, i.e., whether $U \models \phi$ holds.

The constructions presented here follow the theory first established in [39]; which gives a characteristic formulae approach for (bi-)simulation-like relations over finite-state processes, notably for CCS processes.

## 3.1   Modal $\mu$-calculus

In order to encode subtyping for session types as a model checking problem it is enough to consider the fragment of the modal $\mu$ calculus below:

$$\phi ::= \top \mid \bot \mid \phi \wedge \phi \mid \phi \vee \phi \mid [\dagger a]\phi \mid \langle \dagger a \rangle \phi \mid \nu \mathbf{x}.\phi \mid \mathbf{x}$$

Modal operators $[\dagger a]$ and $\langle \dagger a \rangle$ have precedence over Boolean binary operators $\wedge$ and $\vee$; the greatest fixpoint point operator $\nu \mathbf{x}$ has the lowest precedence (and its scope extends as far to the right as possible). Let $\mathcal{F}$ be the set of all (contractive) modal $\mu$-calculus formulae and $\mathcal{F}_c \subseteq \mathcal{F}$ be the set of all closed formulae. Given a set of actions $A \subseteq \mathcal{A}$, we write $\neg A$ for $\mathcal{A} \setminus A$, and $[A]\phi$ for $\bigwedge_{\dagger a \in A}[\dagger a]\phi$.

The $n^{th}$ approximation of a fixpoint formula is defined as follows:

$$(\nu \mathbf{x}.\phi)^0 \stackrel{\text{def}}{=} \top \qquad\qquad (\nu \mathbf{x}.\phi)^n \stackrel{\text{def}}{=} \phi[(\nu \mathbf{x}.\phi)^{n-1}/\mathbf{x}] \qquad \text{if } n > 0$$

A *closed* formula $\phi$ is interpreted on the labelled transition system induced by a session type $T$. The satisfaction relation $\models$ between session types and formulae is inductively defined as follows:

$$
\begin{aligned}
&T \models \top \\
&T \models \phi_1 \wedge \phi_2 &&\textit{iff}\quad T \models \phi_1 \text{ and } T \models \phi_2 \\
&T \models \phi_1 \vee \phi_2 &&\textit{iff}\quad T \models \phi_1 \text{ or } T \models \phi_2 \\
&T \models [\dagger a]\phi &&\textit{iff}\quad \forall T' \in \mathcal{T}_c : \text{if } T \xrightarrow{\dagger a} T' \text{ then } T' \models \phi \\
&T \models \langle \dagger a \rangle \phi &&\textit{iff}\quad \exists T' \in \mathcal{T}_c : T \xrightarrow{\dagger a} T' \text{ and } T' \models \phi \\
&T \models \nu \mathbf{x}.\phi &&\textit{iff}\quad \forall n \geq 0 : T \models (\nu \mathbf{x}.\phi)^n
\end{aligned}
$$

Intuitively, $\top$ holds for every $T$ (while $\bot$ never holds). Formula $\phi_1 \wedge \phi_2$ (resp. $\phi_1 \vee \phi_2$) holds if both components (resp. at least one component) of the formula hold in $T$. The construct $[\dagger a]\phi$ is a *modal* operator that is satisfied if for each $\dagger a$-derivative $T'$ of $T$, the formula $\phi$ holds in $T'$. The dual modality is $\langle \dagger a \rangle \phi$ which holds if there is an $\dagger a$-derivative $T'$ of $T$ such that $\phi$ holds in $T'$. Construct $\nu \mathbf{x}.\phi$ is the *greatest* fixpoint operator (binding $\mathbf{x}$ in $\phi$).

## 3.2 Characteristic Formulae

We now construct a $\mu$-calculus formula from a (closed) session types, parameterised wrt. a constructor ✠. This construction is somewhat reminiscent of the *characteristic functional* of [39].

**Definition 2 (Characteristic formulae).** The characteristic formulae of $T \in \mathcal{T}_c$ on ✠ is given by function $F : \mathcal{T}_c \times \{\oplus, \&\} \to \mathcal{F}_c$, defined as:

$$
F(T, ✠) \overset{\text{def}}{=}
\begin{cases}
\bigwedge_{i \in I} \langle \dagger\, a_i \rangle\, F(T_i, ✠) & \text{if } T = ✠_{i \in I}\, \dagger a_i.\, T_i \\
\bigwedge_{i \in I} [\dagger\, a_i]\, F(T_i, ✠) & \text{if } T = \overline{✠}_{i \in I}\, \dagger a_i.\, T_i \\
\quad \wedge \bigvee_{i \in I} \langle \dagger\, a_i \rangle \top \wedge [\neg\{\dagger a_i \mid i \in I\}] \bot & \\
[\mathcal{A}] \bot & \text{if } T = \mathsf{end} \\
\nu\mathbf{x}.\, F(T', ✠) & \text{if } T = \mathsf{rec}\, \mathbf{x}.T' \\
\mathbf{x} & \text{if } T = \mathbf{x}
\end{cases}
$$

◇

Given $T \in \mathcal{T}_c$, $F(T, \oplus)$ is a $\mu$-calculus formula that characterises all the *supertypes* of $T$; while $F(T, \&)$ characterises all its *subtypes*. For the sake of clarity, we comment on Definition 2 assuming that ✠ is set to $\oplus$. The first case of the definition makes every branch *mandatory*. If $T = \bigoplus_{i \in I} !a_i.\, T_i$, then every internal choice branch that $T$ can select must also be offered by a supertype, and the relation must hold after each selection. The second case makes every branch *optional* but requires at least one branch to be implemented. If $T = \&_{i \in I} ?a_i.\, T_i$, then $(i)$ for each of the $?a_i$-branch offered by a supertype, the relation must hold in its $?a_i$-derivative, $(ii)$ a supertype must offer at least one of the $?a_i$ branches, and $(iii)$ a supertype cannot offer anything else but the $?a_i$ branches. If $T = \mathsf{end}$, then a supertype cannot offer any behaviour (recall that $\bot$ does not hold for any type). Recursive types are mapped to greatest fixpoint constructions.

Lemma 1 below states the compositionality of the construction, while Theorem 1, our main result, reduces subtyping checking to a model checking problem. A consequence of Theorem 1 is that the characteristic formula of a session type precisely specifies the set of its subtypes or supertypes.

**Lemma 1.** $F(T[^U/_\mathbf{x}], ✠) = F(T, ✠)[^{F(U, ✠)}/_\mathbf{x}]$

The proof is by structural induction, see appendix [31].

**Theorem 1.** $\forall T, U \in \mathcal{T}_c : T \trianglelefteq^{✠} U \iff U \models F(T, ✠)$

The proof essentially follows the techniques of [39], see appendix [31].

**Corollary 1.** *The following holds:*

(a) $T \leqslant U \iff U \models F(T, \oplus)$
(b) $U \geqslant T \iff T \models F(U, \&)$

(c) $U \models F(T, \oplus) \iff T \models F(U, \&)$

The proof is by Theorem 1 and $\leqslant\, =\, \trianglelefteq^{\oplus}$, $\geqslant\, =\, \trianglelefteq^{\&}$, $\leqslant\, =\, \geqslant^{-1}$, and $\trianglelefteq^{\oplus} = (\trianglelefteq^{\&})^{-1}$.

**Proposition 1.** *For all $T, U \in \mathcal{T}_c$, deciding whether or not $U \models F(T, \maltese)$ holds can be done in time complexity of $\mathcal{O}(|T| \times |U|)$, in the worst case; where $|T|$ stands for the number of states in the LTS induced by $T$.*

This follows from [12], since the size of $F(T, \maltese)$ increases linearly with $|T|$.

*Example 2.* Consider session types $T_1$ and $U_1$ from (1) and (3) and fix $\mathcal{A} = \{?request, !ok, !ko\}$. Following Definition 2, we obtain:

$$F(T_1, \oplus) = [?request]\langle !ok \rangle [\mathcal{A}] \bot \;\wedge\; \langle ?request \rangle \top \;\wedge\; [\neg\{?request\}]\bot$$
$$F(U_1, \&) = \nu \mathbf{x}. \langle ?request \rangle \big( ([!ok][\mathcal{A}]\bot \;\wedge\; [!ko]\mathbf{x})$$
$$\wedge \; (\langle !ok \rangle \top \vee \langle !ko \rangle \top) \;\wedge\; [\neg\{!ok, !ko\}]\bot \big)$$

We have $U_1 \models F(T_1, \oplus)$ and $T_1 \models F(U_1, \&)$, as expected (recall tat $T_1 \leqslant U_1$).

## 4    Safety and Duality in Session Types

A key ingredient of session type theory is the notion of *duality* between types. In this section, we study the relation between duality of session types, characteristic formulae, and safety (i.e., error freedom). In particular, building on recent work [10] which studies the preciseness of subtyping for session types, we show how characteristic formulae can be used to guarantee safety. A system (of session types) is a pair of session types $T$ and $U$ that interact with each other by synchronising over messages. We write $T \mid U$ for a system consisting of $T$ and $U$ and let $S$ range over systems of session types.

**Definition 3 (Synchronous semantics).** The *synchronous* semantics of a *system* of session types $T \mid U$ is given by the rule below, in conjunction with the rules of Fig. 1.

$$\frac{T \xrightarrow{\dagger a} T' \quad U \xrightarrow{\overline{\dagger} a} U'}{T \mid U \to T' \mid U'} \; \text{[S-COM]}$$

We write $\to^*$ for the reflexive transitive closure of $\to$.                               ◇

Definition 3 says that two types interact whenever they fire dual operations.

*Example 3.* Consider the following execution of system $T_1 \mid U_2$, from (3):

$$T_1 \mid U_2 \;=\; ?request.!ok.\mathbf{end} \mid \mathbf{rec}\,\mathbf{x}.!request.\{\ldots\}$$
$$\longrightarrow !ok.\mathbf{end} \mid \{?ok.\mathbf{end} \;\&\; ?ok.\mathbf{rec}\,\mathbf{x}.?request\{\ldots\}\} \longrightarrow \mathbf{end} \mid \mathbf{end}$$

**Definition 4 (Error [10] and safety).** A system $T_1 \mid T_2$ is an *error* if, either:

(a) $T_1 = \maltese_{i \in I} \dagger a_i. T_i$ and $T_2 = \maltese_{j \in J} \dagger a_j. U_j$, with $\maltese$ fixed;
(b) $T_h = \bigoplus_{i \in I} !a_i. T_i$ and $T_g = \&_{j \in J} ?a_j. U_j$; and $\exists i \in I : \forall j \in J : a_i \neq a_j$, with $h \neq g \in \{1, 2\}$; or
(c) $T_h = \mathbf{end}$ and $T_g = \maltese_{i \in I} \dagger a_i. T_i$, with $h \neq g \in \{1, 2\}$.

We say that $S = T \mid U$ is *safe* if for all $S' : S \rightarrow^* S'$, $S'$ is not an error.     ◇

A system of the form *(a)* is an error since both types are either attempting to send (resp. receive) messages. An error of type *(b)* indicates that some of the messages cannot be received by one of the types. An error of type *(c)* indicates a system where one of the types has terminated while the other still expects to send or receive messages.

**Definition 5 (Duality).** The dual of a formula $\phi \in \mathcal{F}$, written $\overline{\phi}$ (resp. of a session type $T \in \mathcal{T}$, written $\overline{T}$), is defined recursively as follows:

$$\overline{\phi} \stackrel{\text{def}}{=} \begin{cases} \overline{\phi_1} \wedge \overline{\phi_2} & \text{if } \phi = \phi_1 \wedge \phi_2 \\ \overline{\phi_1} \vee \overline{\phi_2} & \text{if } \phi = \phi_1 \vee \phi_2 \\ [\dagger a]\overline{\phi'} & \text{if } \phi = [\dagger a]\phi' \\ \langle \dagger a \rangle \overline{\phi'} & \text{if } \phi = \langle \dagger a \rangle \phi' \\ \nu \mathbf{x}.\overline{\phi'} & \text{if } \phi = \nu \mathbf{x}.\phi' \\ \phi & \text{if } \phi = \top, \bot, \text{ or } \mathbf{x} \end{cases} \qquad \overline{T} \stackrel{\text{def}}{=} \begin{cases} \maltese_{i \in I} \dagger a_i.\overline{T_i} & \text{if } T = \maltese_{i \in I} \dagger a_i.T_i \\ \mathsf{rec}\,\mathbf{x}.\overline{T'} & \text{if } T = \mathsf{rec}\,\mathbf{x}.T' \\ \mathbf{x} & \text{if } T = \mathbf{x} \\ \mathsf{end} & \text{if } T = \mathsf{end} \end{cases}$$

◇

In Definition 5, notice that the dual of a formula only rename labels.

**Lemma 2.** *For all $T \in \mathcal{T}_c$ and $\phi \in \mathcal{F}_c$, $T \models \phi \iff \overline{T} \models \overline{\phi}$.*

The proof is direct using the definitions of $\overline{T}$ and $\overline{\phi}$.

**Theorem 2** *For all $T \in \mathcal{T} : \overline{F(T, \maltese)} = F(\overline{T}, \maltese)$.*

The proof of Theorem 2 is by structural induction on $T$, see appendix [31]. Theorem 3 follows straightforwardly from [10] and allows us to obtain a sound and complete model-checking based condition for safety, cf. Theorem 4.

**Theorem 3 (Safety).** $T \mid U$ *is safe* $\iff (T \leqslant \overline{U} \vee U \leqslant \overline{T})$.

The proof for ($\implies$) follows from [10, Table 7], while the direction ($\impliedby$) is by coinduction on the derivations of $T \leqslant \overline{U}$ and $U \leqslant \overline{T}$. See [31] for details. Theorem 4, below, is a consequence of Corollary 1 and Theorems 2 and 3.

**Theorem 4.** *The following statements are equivalent: (a) $T \mid U$ is safe*

(b) $\overline{U} \models F(T, \oplus) \vee \overline{T} \models F(U, \oplus)$      (d) $U \models F(\overline{T}, \&) \vee T \models F(\overline{U}, \&)$

(c) $T \models F(\overline{U}, \&) \vee U \models F(\overline{T}, \&)$      (e) $\overline{T} \models F(U, \oplus) \vee \overline{U} \models F(T, \oplus)$

# 5  Alternative Algorithms for Subtyping

In order to compare the cost of checking the subtyping relation via characteristic formulae to other approaches, we present two other algorithms: the original algorithm as given by Gay and Hole in [21] and an adaptation of Kozen, Palsberg, and Schwartzbach's algorithm [28] for recursive subtyping for the $\lambda$-calculus.

$$\frac{\Gamma, \mathrm{rec\,x}.T \leqslant_c U \vdash T[\mathrm{rec\,x}.T/\mathsf{x}] \leqslant_c U}{\Gamma \vdash \mathrm{rec\,x}.T \leqslant_c U} \ \text{[RL]} \qquad \frac{}{\Gamma \vdash \mathrm{end} \leqslant_c \mathrm{end}} \ \text{[END]} \qquad \frac{\Gamma, T \leqslant_c \mathrm{rec\,x}.U \vdash T \leqslant_c U[\mathrm{rec\,x}.U/\mathsf{x}]}{\Gamma \vdash T \leqslant_c \mathrm{rec\,x}.U} \ \text{[RR]}$$

$$\frac{I \subseteq J \quad \forall i \in I : \Gamma \vdash T_i \leqslant_c U_i}{\Gamma \vdash \oplus_{i \in I}\, !a_i.\,T_i \leqslant_c \oplus_{j \in J}\, !a_j.\,U_j} \ \text{[SEL]} \qquad \frac{T \leqslant_c U \in \Gamma}{\Gamma \vdash T \leqslant_c U} \ \text{[ASSUMP]} \qquad \frac{J \subseteq I \quad \forall j \in J : \Gamma \vdash T_j \leqslant_c U_j}{\Gamma \vdash \&_{i \in I}\, ?a_i.\,T_i \leqslant_c \&_{j \in J}\, ?a_j.\,U_j} \ \text{[BRA]}$$

**Fig. 2.** Algorithmic subtyping rules [21]

## 5.1 Gay and Hole's Algorithm

The inference rules of Gay and Hole's algorithm are given in Fig. 2 (adapted to our setting). The rules essentially follow those of Definition 1 but deal explicitly with recursion. They use judgments $\Gamma \vdash T \leqslant_c U$ in which $T$ and $U$ are (closed) session types and $\Gamma$ is a sequence of assumed instances of the subtyping relation, i.e., $\Gamma = T_1 \leqslant_c U_1, ..., T_k \leqslant_c U_k$, saying that each pair $T_i \leqslant_c U_i$ has been visited. To guarantee termination, rule [ASSUMP] should always be used if it is applicable.

**Theorem 5 (Correspondence** [21, Corollary 2]**).** *$T \leqslant U$ if and only if $\varnothing \vdash T \leqslant_c U$ is derivable from the rules in Fig. 2.*

Proposition 2, a contribution of this paper, states the algorithm's complexity.

**Proposition 2.** *For all $T, U \in \mathcal{T}_c$, the problem of deciding whether or not $\varnothing \vdash T \leqslant_c U$ is derivable has an $\mathcal{O}(n^{2^n})$ time complexity, in the worst case; where $n$ is the number of nodes in the parsing tree of the $T$ or $U$ (whichever is bigger).*

*Proof.* Assume the bigger session type is $T$ and its size is $n$ (the number of nodes in its parsing tree). Observe that the algorithm in Fig. 2 needs to visit every node of $T$ and relies on explicit unfolding of recursive types. Given a type of size $n$, its unfolding is of size $\mathcal{O}(n^2)$, in the worst case. Hence, we have a chain $\mathcal{O}(n) + \mathcal{O}(n^2) + \mathcal{O}(n^4) + \ldots$, or $\mathcal{O}(\sum_{1 \leqslant i \leqslant k} n^{2^i})$, where $k$ is a bound on the number of derivations needed for the algorithm to terminate. According to [21, Lemma 10], the number of derivations is bounded by the number of sub-terms of $T$, which is $\mathcal{O}(n)$. Thus, we obtain a worst case time complexity of $\mathcal{O}(n^{2^n})$. $\square$

## 5.2 Kozen, Palsberg, and Schwartzbach's Algorithm

Considering that the results of [28] *"generalise to an arbitrary signature of type constructors (. . . )"*, we adapt Kozen et al.'s algorithm, originally designed for subtyping recursive types in the $\lambda$-calculus. Intuitively, the algorithm reduces the problem of subtyping to checking the language emptiness of an automaton given by the product of two (session) types. The intuition of the theory behind the algorithm is that *"two types are ordered if no common path detects a counterexample"*. We give the details of our instantiation below.

The set of type constructors over $\mathcal{A}$, written $\mathfrak{C}_\mathcal{A}$, is defined as follows:

$$\mathfrak{C}_\mathcal{A} \overset{\text{def}}{=} \{\mathrm{end}\} \cup \{\oplus_A \mid \varnothing \subset A \subseteq \mathcal{A}\} \cup \{\&_A \mid \varnothing \subset A \subseteq \mathcal{A}\}$$

**Definition 6 (Term automata).** A term automaton over $\mathcal{A}$ is a tuple $\mathcal{M} = (Q, \mathfrak{C}_\mathcal{A}, q_0, \delta, \ell)$ where

- $Q$ is a (finite) set of states,
- $q_0 \in Q$ is the initial state,
- $\delta : Q \times \mathcal{A} \to Q$ is a (partial) function (the *transition function*), and
- $\ell : Q \to \mathfrak{C}_\mathcal{A}$ is a (total) labelling function

such that for any $q \in Q$, if $\ell(q) \in \{\oplus_A, \&_A\}$, then $\delta(q, \dagger a)$ is defined for all $\dagger a \in A$; and for any $q \in Q$ such that $\ell(q) = \mathsf{end}$, $\delta(q, \dagger a)$ is undefined for all $\dagger a \in \mathcal{A}$. We decorate $Q$, $\delta$, etc. with a superscript, e.g., $\mathcal{M}$, where necessary. ◇

We assume that session types have been "translated" to term automata, the transformation is straightforward (see, [16] for a similar transformation). Given a session type $T \in \mathcal{T}_c$, we write $\mathcal{M}(T)$ for its corresponding term automaton.

**Definition 7 (Subtyping).** $\sqsubseteq$ is the smallest binary relation on $\mathfrak{C}_\mathcal{A}$ such that:

$$\mathsf{end} \sqsubseteq \mathsf{end} \qquad \oplus_A \sqsubseteq \oplus_B \iff A \subseteq B \qquad \&_A \sqsubseteq \&_B \iff B \subseteq A \qquad ◇$$

Definition 7 essentially maps the rules of Definition 1 to type constructors. The order $\sqsubseteq$ is used in the product automaton to identify final states, see below.

**Definition 8 (Product automaton).** Given two term automata $\mathcal{M}$ and $\mathcal{N}$ over $\mathcal{A}$, their product automaton $\mathcal{M} \blacktriangleleft \mathcal{N} = (P, p_0, \Delta, F)$ is such that

- $P = Q^\mathcal{M} \times Q^\mathcal{N}$ are the states of $\mathcal{M} \blacktriangleleft \mathcal{N}$,
- $p_0 = (q_0^\mathcal{M}, q_0^\mathcal{N})$ is the initial state,
- $\Delta : P \times \mathcal{A} \to P$ is the partial function which for $q_1 \in Q^\mathcal{M}$ and $q_2 \in Q^\mathcal{N}$ gives

$$\Delta((q_1, q_2), \dagger a) = (\delta^\mathcal{M}(q_1, \dagger a), \delta^\mathcal{N}(q_2, \dagger a))$$

- $F \subseteq P$ is the set of *accepting* states: $F = \{ (q_1, q_2) \mid \ell^\mathcal{M}(q_1) \not\sqsubseteq \ell^\mathcal{N}(q_2) \}$

Note that $\Delta((q_1, q_2), \dagger a)$ is defined iff $\delta^\mathcal{M}(q_1, \dagger a)$ and $\delta^\mathcal{N}(q_2, \dagger a)$ are defined. ◇

Following [28], we obtain Theorem 6.

**Theorem 6.** *Let $T, U \in \mathcal{T}_c$, $T \leqslant U$ iff the language of $\mathcal{M}(T) \blacktriangleleft \mathcal{M}(U)$ is empty.*

Theorem 6 essentially says that $T \leqslant U$ iff one cannot find a "common path" in $T$ and $U$ that leads to nodes whose labels are not related by $\sqsubseteq$, i.e., one cannot find a counterexample for them *not* being in the subtyping relation.

*Example 4.* Below we show the constructions for $T_1$ (1) and $U_1$ (3).

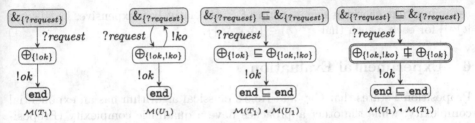

Where initial states are shaded and accepting states are denoted by a double line. Note that the language of $\mathcal{M}(T_1) \blacktriangleleft \mathcal{M}(U_1)$ is empty (no accepting states).

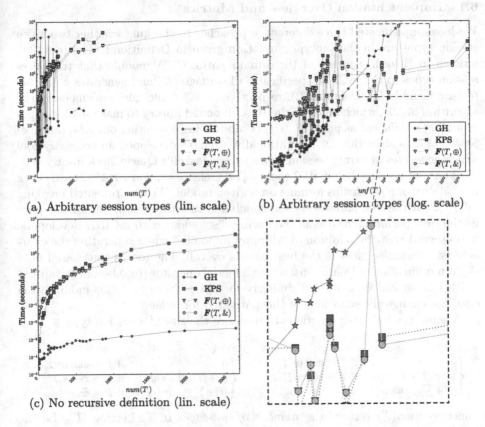

(a) Arbitrary session types (lin. scale)

(b) Arbitrary session types (log. scale)

(c) No recursive definition (lin. scale)

**Fig. 3.** Benchmarks (1)

**Proposition 3.** *For all $T, U \in \mathcal{T}_c$, the problem of deciding whether or not the language of $\mathcal{M}(T) \blacktriangleleft \mathcal{M}(U)$ is empty has a worst case complexity of $\mathcal{O}(|T| \times |U|)$; where $|T|$ stands for the number of states in the term automaton $\mathcal{M}(T)$.*

*Proof.* Follows from the fact that the algorithm in [28] has a complexity of $\mathcal{O}(n^2)$, see [28, Theorem 18]. This complexity result applies also to our instantiation, assuming that checking membership of $\sqsubseteq$ is relatively inexpensive, i.e., $|A| \ll |Q^{\mathcal{M}}|$ for each $q$ such that $\ell^{\mathcal{M}}(q) \in \{\oplus_A, \&_A\}$.          □

# 6    Experimental Evaluation

Proposition 2 states that Gay and Hole's classical algorithm has an exponential complexity; while the other approaches have a quadratic complexity (Propositions 1 and 3). The rest of this section presents several experiments that give a better perspective of the *practical* cost of these approaches.

## 6.1    Implementation Overview and Metrics

We have implemented three different approaches to checking whether two given session types are in the subtyping relation given in Definition 1. The tool [29], written in Haskell, consists of three main parts: ($i$) A module that translates session types to the mCRL2 specification language [23] and generates a characteristic formula (cf. Definition 2), respectively; ($ii$) A module implementing the algorithm of [21], which relies on the Haskell **bound** library to make session types unfolding as efficient as possible. ($iii$) A module implementing our adaptation of Kozen et al.'s algorithm [28]. Additionally, we have developed an accessory tool which generates arbitrary session types using Haskell's QuickCheck library [11].

The tool invokes the mCRL2 toolset [14] (release version 201409.1) to check the validity of a $\mu$-calculus formula on a given model. We experimented invoking mCRL2 with several parameters and concluded that the default parameters gave us the best performance overall. Following discussions with mCRL2 developers, we observed that the addition of "dummy fixpoints" while generating the characteristic formulae gave us the best results overall. The tool is thus based on a slight modification of Definition 2 where a modal operator $[\dagger a]\phi$ becomes $[\dagger a]\nu \mathbf{t}. \phi$ (with $\mathbf{t}$ fresh and unused) and similarly for $\langle \dagger a \rangle \phi$. Note that this modification does not change the semantics of the generated formulae.

We use the following functions to measure the size of a session type.

$$num(T) \stackrel{\text{def}}{=} \begin{cases} 0 & \text{if } T = \mathbf{end} \text{ or } T = \mathbf{x} \\ num(T') & \text{if } T = \mathbf{rec}\,\mathbf{x}.T' \\ |I| + \sum_{i \in I} num(T_i) & \text{if } T = \bigstar_{i \in I} \dagger a_i.T_i \end{cases} \qquad unf(T) \stackrel{\text{def}}{=} \begin{cases} 0 & \text{if } T = \mathbf{end} \text{ or } T = \mathbf{x} \\ (1 + |T'|_{\mathbf{x}}) \times unf(T') & \text{if } T = \mathbf{rec}\,\mathbf{x}.T' \\ |I| + \sum_{i \in I} unf(T_i) & \text{if } T = \bigstar_{i \in I} \dagger a_i.T_i \end{cases}$$

Function $num(T)$ returns the *number of messages* in $T$. Letting $|T|_{\mathbf{x}}$ be the number of times variable $\mathbf{x}$ appears *free* in session type $T$, function $unf(T)$ returns the number of messages in the unfolding of $T$. Function $unf(T)$ takes into account the structure of a type wrt. recursive definitions and calls (by unfolding once every recursion variable).

## 6.2    Benchmark Results

The first set of benchmarks compares the performances of the three approaches when the pair of types given are identical, i.e., we measure the time it takes

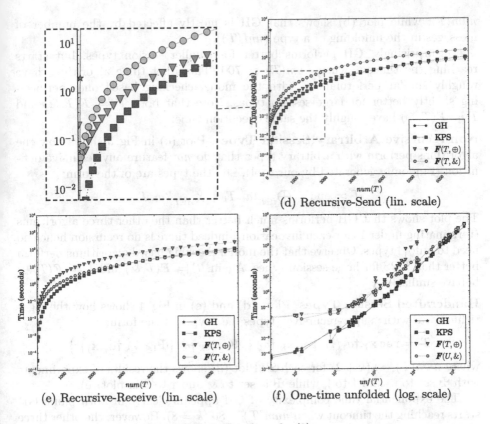

(d) Recursive-Send (lin. scale)

(e) Recursive-Receive (lin. scale)　　(f) One-time unfolded (log. scale)

**Fig. 4.** Benchmarks (2)

for an algorithm to check whether $T \leqslant T$ holds. The second set of benchmarks considers types that are "unfolded", so that types have different sizes. Note that checking whether two equal types are in the subtyping relation is one of the most costly cases of subtyping since every branch of a choice must be visited.

Our results below show the performances of four algorithms: $(i)$ our Haskell implementation of Gay and Hole's algorithm (GH), $(ii)$ our implementation of Kozen, Palsberg, and Schwartzbach's algorithm (KPS), $(iii)$ an invocation to mCRL2 to check whether $U \models \boldsymbol{F}(T, \oplus)$ holds, and $(iv)$ an invocation to mCRL2 to check whether $T \models \boldsymbol{F}(U, \&)$ holds.

All the benchmarks were conducted on a 3.40 GHz Intel i7 computer with 16 GB of RAM. Unless specified otherwise, the tests have been executed with a timeout set to 2 h (7200 s). A gap appears in the plots whenever an algorithm reached the timeout. Times ($y$-axis) are plotted on a *logarithmic* scale, the scale used for the size of types ($x$-axis) is specified below each plot.

**Arbitrary Session Types.** Plots (a) and (b) in Fig. 3 shows how the algorithms perform with randomly generated session types. Plot (a) shows clearly that the execution time of KPS, $T \models \boldsymbol{F}(T, \&)$, and $T \models \boldsymbol{F}(T, \oplus)$ mostly depends on

$num(T)$; while plot (b) shows that GH is mostly affected by the number of messages in the unfolding of a type $(unf(T))$.

Unsurprisingly, GH performs better for smaller session types, but starts reaching the timeout when $num(T) \approx 700$. The other three algorithms have roughly similar performances, with the model checking based ones performing slightly better for large session types. Note that both $T \models \boldsymbol{F}(T, \&)$ and $T \models \boldsymbol{F}(T, \oplus)$ have roughly the same execution time.

**Non-recursive Arbitrary Session Types.** Plot (c) in Fig. 3 shows how the algorithms perform with arbitrary types that do *not* feature any recursive definition (randomly generated by our tool), i.e., the types are of the form:

$$T ::= \text{end} \mid \bigoplus_{i \in I} ! a_i . T_i \mid \&_{i \in I} ? a_i . T_i$$

The plot shows that GH performs much better than the other three algorithms (terminating under 1s for each invocation), indeed there is no recursion hence no need to unfold types. Observe that the model checking based algorithms perform better than KPS for large session types. Again, $T \models \boldsymbol{F}(T, \&)$ and $T \models \boldsymbol{F}(T, \oplus)$ behave similarly.

**Handcrafted Session Types.** Plots (d) and (e) in Fig. 4 shows how the algorithms deal with "super-recursive" types, i.e., types of the form:

$$T ::= \text{rec}\, \mathsf{x}_1 . \dagger a_1 . \ldots . \text{rec}\, \mathsf{x}_k . \dagger a_k \left\{ \maltese_{1 \leq i \leq k} \dagger a_i . \{ \maltese_{1 \leq j \leq k} \dagger a_j . \mathsf{x}_j \} \right\}$$

where $num(T) = k(k+2)$ for each $T$. Plot (d) shows the results of experiments with $\maltese$ set to $\oplus$ and $\dagger$ to !; while $\maltese$ is set to $\&$ and $\dagger$ to ? in plot (e).

The exponential time complexity of GH appears clearly in both plots: GH starts reaching the timeout when $num(T) = 80$ ($k = 8$). However, the other three algorithms deal well with larger session types of this form. Interestingly, due to the nature of these session types (consisting of either only *internal* choices or only *external* choices), the two model checking based algorithms perform slightly differently. This is explained by Definition 2 where the formula generated with $\boldsymbol{F}(T, \&)$ for an internal choice is larger than for an external choice, and vice-versa for $\boldsymbol{F}(T, \oplus)$. Observe that, $T \models \boldsymbol{F}(T, \oplus)$ (resp. $T \models \boldsymbol{F}(T, \&)$) performs better than KPS for large session types in plot (d) (resp. plot (e)).

**Unfolded Types.** The last set of benchmarks evaluates the performances of the four algorithms to check whether $T = \text{rec}\, \mathsf{x}.V \leqslant \text{rec}\, \mathsf{x}. (V[V/\mathsf{x}]) = U$ holds, where $\mathsf{x}$ is fixed and $V$ (randomly generated) is of the form:

$$V ::= \bigoplus_{i \in I} ! a_i . V_i \mid \&_{i \in I} ? a_i . V_i \mid \mathsf{x}$$

Plots (f) in Fig. 4 shows the results of our experiments (with a timeout set to 6 hours). Observe that $U \models \boldsymbol{F}(T, \oplus)$ starts reaching the timeout quickly. In this case, the model (i.e., $U$) is generally much larger than the formula (i.e., $\boldsymbol{F}(T, \oplus)$). After discussing with the mCRL2 team, this discrepancy seems to originate from internal optimisations of the model checker that can be diminished (or exacerbated) by tweaking the parameters of the tool-set. The good performance of GH in this case can be explained by the fact that there is only one recursion variable in these types; hence the size of their unfolding does not grow very fast.

# 7  Related Work and Conclusions

**Related Work.** Subtyping for recursive types has been studied for many years. Amadio and Cardelli [5] introduced the first subtyping algorithm for recursive types for the $\lambda$-calculus. Kozen et al. gave a quadratic subtyping algorithm in [28], which we have adapted for session types, cf. Sect. 5.2. A good introduction to the theory and history of the field is in [19]. Pierce and Sangiori [36] introduced subtyping for IO types in the $\pi$-calculus, which later became a foundation for the algorithm of Gay and Hole who first introduced subtyping for session types in the $\pi$-calculus in [21]. The paper [15] studied an abstract encoding between linear types and session types, with a focus on subtyping. Chen et al. [10] studied the notion of *preciseness* of subtyping relations for session types. The present work is the first to study the algorithmic aspect of the problem.

Characteristic formulae for finite processes were first studied in [22], then in [39] for finite-state processes. Since then the theory has been studied extensively [1–3,12,18,34,40] for most of the van Glabbeek's spectrum [42] and in different settings (e.g., time [4] and probabilistic [37]). See [2,3] for a detailed historical account of the field. This is the first time characteristic formulae are applied to the field of session types. A recent work [3] proposes a general framework to obtain characteristic formula constructions for simulation-like relation "for free". We chose to follow [39] as it was a better fit for session types as they allow for a straightforward inductive construction of a characteristic formula.

Chaki et al. [9] propose a framework consisting of a behavioural type-and-effect system for the $\pi$-calculus and an assume-guarantee principle that allows (LTL) properties of $\pi$-calculus processes to be checked via a model checker.

**Conclusions.** In this paper, we gave a first connection between session types and model checking, through a characteristic formulae approach based on the $\mu$-calculus. We gave three new algorithms for subtyping: two are based on model checking and one is an instantiation of an algorithm for the $\lambda$-calculus [28]. All of which have a quadratic complexity in the worst case and behave well in practice.

Our approach can be easily: ($i$) adapted to types for the $\lambda$-calculus (see appendix [31]) and ($ii$) extended to session types that carry other (*closed*) session types, e.g., see [10,21], by simply applying the algorithm recursively on the carried types. For instance, to check $!a\langle?c\,\&\,?d\rangle \leqslant !a\langle?c\rangle \oplus !b\langle\mathbf{end}\rangle$ one can check the subtyping for the outer-most types, while building constraints, i.e., $\{?c\,\&\,?d \leqslant ?c\}$, to be checked later on, by re-applying the algorithm.

The present work paves the way for new connections between session types and modal fixpoint logic or model checking theories. It is a basis for upcoming connections between model checking and classical problems of session types, such as the asynchronous subtyping of [10] and multiparty compatibility checking [16,30]. We are also considering applying model checking approaches to session types with probabilistic, logical [6], or time [7,8] annotations. Finally, we remark that [10] also establishes that subtyping (cf. Definition 1) is *sound* (but not complete) wrt. the *asynchronous* semantics of session types, which models programs that communicate through FIFO buffers. Thus, our new conditions (items $(b)$-$(e)$ of Theorem 4) also imply safety $(a)$ in the asynchronous setting.

**Acknowledgements.** We would like to thank Luca Aceto, Laura Bocchi, and Alceste Scalas for their invaluable comments on earlier versions of this work. This work is partially supported by EPSRC projects EP/K034413/1, EP/K011715/1, and EP/L00058X/1; and by EU FP7 project under grant agreement 612985 (UPSCALE).

# References

1. Aceto, L., Ingólfsdóttir, A.: A characterization of finitary bisimulation. Inf. Process. Lett. **64**(3), 127–134 (1997)
2. Aceto, L., Ingólfsdóttir, A.: Characteristic formulae: from automata to logic. Bull. EATCS **91**, 58–75 (2007)
3. Aceto, L., Ingólfsdóttir, A., Levy, P.B., Sack, J.: Characteristic formulae for fixed-point semantics: a general framework. Math. Struct. Comput. Sci. **22**(2), 125–173 (2012)
4. Aceto, L., Ingólfsdóttir, A., Pedersen, M.L., Poulsen, J.: Characteristic formulae for timed automata. ITA **34**(6), 565–584 (2000)
5. Amadio, R.M., Cardelli, L.: Subtyping recursive types. ACM Trans. Program. Lang. Syst. **15**(4), 575–631 (1993)
6. Bocchi, L., Honda, K., Tuosto, E., Yoshida, N.: A theory of design-by-contract for distributed multiparty interactions. In: Gastin, P., Laroussinie, F. (eds.) CONCUR 2010. LNCS, vol. 6269, pp. 162–176. Springer, Heidelberg (2010)
7. Bocchi, L., Lange, J., Yoshida, N.: Meeting deadlines together. In: CONCUR 2015, pp. 283–296 (2015)
8. Bocchi, L., Yang, W., Yoshida, N.: Timed multiparty session types. In: Baldan, P., Gorla, D. (eds.) CONCUR 2014. LNCS, vol. 8704, pp. 419–434. Springer, Heidelberg (2014)
9. Chaki, S., Rajamani, S.K., Rehof, J.: Types as models: model checking message-passing programs. In: POPL 2002, pp. 45–57 (2002)
10. Chen, T.-C., Dezani-Ciancaglini, M., Yoshida, N.: On the preciseness of subtyping in session types. In: PPDP 2014, pp. 146–135. ACM Press (2014)
11. Claessen, K., Hughes, J.: Quickcheck: a lightweight tool for random testing of Haskell programs. In: ICFP 2000, pp. 268–279 (2000)
12. Cleaveland, R., Steffen, B.: Computing behavioural relations, logically. In: Leach Albert, J., Monien, B., Rodríguez-Artalejo, M. (eds.) ICALP 1991. LNCS, vol. 510, pp. 127–138. Springer, Heidelberg (1991)
13. Cognizant.: Zero Deviation Lifecycle. http://www.zdlc.co
14. Cranen, S., Groote, J.F., Keiren, J.J.A., Stappers, F.P.M., de Vink, E.P., Wesselink, W., Willemse, T.A.C.: An overview of the mCRL2 toolset and its recent advances. In: Piterman, N., Smolka, S.A. (eds.) TACAS 2013 (ETAPS 2013). LNCS, vol. 7795, pp. 199–213. Springer, Heidelberg (2013)
15. Demangeon, R., Honda, K.: Full abstraction in a subtyped pi-calculus with linear types. In: Katoen, J.-P., König, B. (eds.) CONCUR 2011. LNCS, vol. 6901, pp. 280–296. Springer, Heidelberg (2011)
16. Deniélou, P.-M., Yoshida, N.: Multiparty compatibility in communicating automata: characterisation and synthesis of global session types. In: Kwiatkowska, M., Peleg, D., Fomin, F.V., Freivalds, R. (eds.) ICALP 2013, Part II. LNCS, vol. 7966, pp. 174–186. Springer, Heidelberg (2013)

17. Diatchki, I.S.: Improving Haskell types with SMT. In: Haskell 2015, pp. 1–10. ACM (2015)
18. Fecher, H., Steffen, M.: Characteristic mu-calculus formulas for underspecified transition systems. Electr. Notes Theor. Comput. Sci. **128**(2), 103–116 (2005)
19. Gapeyev, V., Levin, M.Y., Pierce, B.C.: Recursive subtyping revealed. J. Funct. Program. **12**(6), 511–548 (2002)
20. Gay, S.J., Hole, M.: Types and subtypes for client-server interactions. In: Swierstra, S.D. (ed.) ESOP 1999. LNCS, vol. 1576, pp. 74–90. Springer, Heidelberg (1999)
21. Gay, S.J., Hole, M.: Subtyping for session types in the pi calculus. Acta Inf. **42**(2–3), 191–225 (2005)
22. Graf, S., Sifakis, J.: A modal characterization of observational congruence on finite terms of CCS. Inf. Control **68**(1–3), 125–145 (1986)
23. Groote, J.F., Mousavi, M.R.: Modeling and Analysis of Communicating Systems. MIT Press, Cambridge (2014)
24. Gundry, A.: A typechecker plugin for units of measure: domain-specific constraint solving in GHC Haskell. In: Haskell 2015, pp. 11–22. ACM (2015)
25. Honda, K., Vasconcelos, V.T., Kubo, M.: Language primitives and type discipline for structured communication-based programming. In: Hankin, C. (ed.) ESOP 1998. LNCS, vol. 1381, pp. 122–138. Springer, Heidelberg (1998)
26. Hüttel, H., Lanese, I., Vasconcelos, V.T., Caires, L., Carbone, M., Deniélou, P.-M., Mostrous, D., Padovani, L., Ravara, A., Tuosto, E., et al. Foundations of behavioural types. Report of the EU COST Action IC1201 (BETTY) (2014). www.behavioural-types.eu/publications/WG1-State-of-the-Art.pdf
27. Results on the propositional mu-calculus: D. Kozen. Theor. Comput. Sci. **27**, 333–354 (1983)
28. Kozen, D., Palsberg, J., Schwartzbach, M.I.: Efficient recursive subtyping. Math. Struct. Comput. Sci. **5**(1), 113–125 (1995)
29. Lange, J.: Tool and benchmark data (2015). http://bitbucket.org/julien-lange/modelcheckingsessiontypesubtyping
30. Lange, J., Tuosto, E., Yoshida, N.: From communicating machines to graphical choreographies. In: POPL 2015, pp. 221–232 (2015)
31. Lange, J., Yoshida, N.: Extended version of this paper. CoRR, abs/1510.06879 (2015)
32. Leino, K.R.M.: Dafny: an automatic program verifier for functional correctness. In: Clarke, E.M., Voronkov, A. (eds.) LPAR-16 2010. LNCS, vol. 6355, pp. 348–370. Springer, Heidelberg (2010)
33. Leino, K.R.M., Yessenov, K.: Stepwise refinement of heap-manipulating code in Chalice. Formal Asp. Comput. **24**(4–6), 519–535 (2012)
34. Müller-Olm, M.: Derivation of characteristic formulae. Electr. Notes Theor. Comput. Sci. **18**, 159–170 (1998)
35. Pierce, B.C.: Types and Programming Languages. MIT Press, Cambridge (2002)
36. Pierce, B.C., Sangiorgi, D.: Typing and subtyping for mobile processes. Math. Struct. Comput. Sci. **6**(5), 409–453 (1996)
37. Sack, J., Zhang, L.: A general framework for probabilistic characterizing formulae. In: Kuncak, V., Rybalchenko, A. (eds.) VMCAI 2012. LNCS, vol. 7148, pp. 396–411. Springer, Heidelberg (2012)
38. Scribble Project homepage. www.scribble.org
39. Steffen, B.: Characteristic formulae. In: Ronchi Della Rocca, S., Ausiello, G., Dezani-Ciancaglini, M. (eds.) ICALP 1989. LNCS, vol. 372, pp. 723–732. Springer, Heidelberg (1989)

40. Steffen, B., Ingólfsdóttir, A.: Characteristic formulae for processes with divergence. Inf. Comput. **110**(1), 149–163 (1994)
41. Takeuchi, K., Honda, K., Kubo, M.: An interaction-based language and its typing system. In: Halatsis, C., Philokyprou, G., Maritsas, D., Theodoridis, S. (eds.) PARLE 1994. LNCS, vol. 817. Springer, Heidelberg (1994)
42. van Glabbeek, R.J.: The linear time - branching time spectrum (extended abstract). In: Baeten, J.C.M., Klop, J.W. (eds.) CONCUR 1990. LNCS, vol. 458, pp. 278–297. Springer, Heidelberg (1990)
43. Yoshida, N., Hu, R., Neykova, R., Ng, N.: The scribble protocol language. In: Abadi, M., Lluch Lafuente, A. (eds.) TGC 2013. LNCS, vol. 8358, pp. 22–41. Springer, Heidelberg (2014)

# Bit-Vector Optimization

Alexander Nadel$^{(\boxtimes)}$ and Vadim Ryvchin

Intel Corporation, P.O. Box 1659, 31015 Haifa, Israel
{alexander.nadel,vadim.ryvchin}@intel.com

**Abstract.** A variety of applications of Satisfiability Modulo Theories (SMT) require finding a satisfying assignment which optimizes some user-given function. Optimization in the context of SMT is referred to as Optimization Modulo Theories (OMT). Current OMT research is mostly dedicated to optimization in arithmetic domains. This paper is about Optimization modulo Bit-Vectors (OBV). We introduce two OBV algorithms which can easily be implemented in an eager bit-vector solver. We show that an industrial problem of fixing cell placement during the physical design stage of the CAD process can be reduced to optimization modulo either Bit-Vectors (BV) or Linear Integer Arithmetic (LIA). We demonstrate that our resulting OBV tool can solve industrial instances which are out of reach of existing BV and LIA OMT solvers.

## 1 Introduction

Nowadays, Satisfiability Modulo Theories (SMT) solving is widely applied. Traditionally, SMT solvers are expected to return *any* model (satisfying assignment), given a satisfiable formula, but many applications require a model which *optimizes* some user-given function [12,13,23,24,32,38]. The problem of finding the optimal model in SMT is called *Optimization Modulo Theories (OMT)* [35].

OMT was first addressed in [32], which presented a general OMT framework, in which the minimization/maximization cost function is restricted to *Boolean* variables. The restriction of the cost function to Boolean variables was lifted in [35]. In that work, a solution for optimization modulo linear arithmetic over the rationals was proposed, where the cost function can be an arbitrary arithmetic term. The two basic approaches to optimization, given a satisfiability solver, applied in [35], are binary and linear search, respectively, for the optimal assignment. In [35], both approaches are customized and tuned to arithmetic reasoning in the context of the DPLL(T) approach to SMT [18].

Bit-vector (BV) SMT theory [5] is a highly expressive theory, where the variables are fixed-size bit-vectors and the set of operators includes arithmetic, comparison, bit-wise, and bit-propagating (e.g., extraction, concatenation, shifts) operators. BV solvers are widely applied [15,20,25,26,34,42]. Given a BV formula $F$, we define the problem of *Optimization modulo Bit-Vectors (OBV)* to be the problem of finding a satisfying assignment to $F$ which *maximizes* some user-given *target* bit-vector term $t$ in the formula, where the term is interpreted as an unsigned number. (Minimization can be modeled as maximization of the target's negation.)

© Springer-Verlag Berlin Heidelberg 2016
M. Chechik and J.-F. Raskin (Eds.): TACAS 2016, LNCS 9636, pp. 851–867, 2016.
DOI: 10.1007/978-3-662-49674-9_53

Our definition lets the cost function be as generic as possible (similarly to the approach of [35] to arithmetic optimization) as the target term can be an arbitrary function over the formula's input variables. Let our maximization target be $t = [v_{n-1}, v_{n-2}, \ldots, v_0]$, where $v_i$'s are bits and $v_0$ is the Least Significant Bit (LSB). Note that our semantics induces a strict priority for satisfying the bits of $t$ in the following sense. The solver will prefer satisfying bit $i$ while leaving the lower bits $i-1, \ldots, 0$ unsatisfied, to satisfying bits $i-1, \ldots, 0$ while leaving bit $i$ unsatisfied (since, e.g., the value $[1000] = 8$ is higher than the value $[0111] = 7$).

Surprisingly, OBV research is scarce. We are not aware of any paper dedicated to OBV. The only existing solver supporting OBV is an extension to the Z3 SMT solver, called $\nu Z$ [8,9]. $\nu Z$ solves OBV by applying the following reduction to weighted MAX-SAT, proposed in [7] (where, given a set of hard Boolean clauses and a set of soft weighted Boolean clauses, weighted MAX-SAT finds a satisfying assignment to the hard clauses maximizing the weight of the satisfied soft clauses). First, the input BV formula is translated to hard Boolean clauses. Second, for each $i \in \{0, 1, \ldots, n\}$, a soft weighted unit clause $(v_i)$ of the weight $2^i$ is added to the formula. The reduction guarantees that the solver will give a strictly higher priority to satisfying bit number $i$ than to bits $i - 1, \ldots, 0$, thus ensuring that $t$'s value is maximized. Note that applying a similar reduction with *equal* weights given to the bits of $t$ would result in maximizing the number of *satisfied bits* in $t$, rather than $t$'s *value*.

This paper proposes two new algorithms for OBV solving by leveraging binary and linear search to eager BV solving [17,21]. Both algorithms are easy to implement. Both are incremental. Both take advantage of the SAT solver's conflict analysis capabilities to prune the search space on-the-fly.

The application which triggered our OBV research emerged during the placement sub-stage of the physical design stage of the Computer-Aided Design (CAD) [39] flow at Intel. Assume that after a placement of standard cells has already been generated, a new set of design constraints of different priority, introduced late in the process, has to be taken into account by the placement flow. Re-running the placer from scratch with the new set of constraints would not satisfy backward compatibility, stability, and run-time requirements, hence a new post-processing *fixer* tool is required. The goal of the fixer is to fix as many as possible of the *violations* resulting from applying the additional design constraints, with preference being given to fixing high-priority violations. We will demonstrate that this problem can be reduced to optimization modulo either bit-vectors or linear integer arithmetic (LIA). Section 6 of this work shows that our algorithms have substantially better capacity on real-world and crafted placement fixer benchmarks than $\nu Z$ in both LIA and BV mode and OptiMath-SAT [36,37] in LIA mode (the crafted benchmarks are publicly available at [29]).

In what follows, Sect. 2 contains preliminaries. Section 3 introduces our reduction of the placement fixer problem to optimization modulo BV and LIA. Sections 4 and 5 present our OBV algorithms. Section 6 presents the experimental results, and Sect. 7 concludes our work.

## 2    Preliminaries

We start off with some basic notions. A *bit* is a Boolean variable which can be interpreted as 0 or 1. A *bit-vector* of width $n$, $v^{[n]} = [v_{n-1}, v_{n-2}, \ldots, v_0]$, is a sequence of $n$ bits, where bit $v_0$ is the Least Significant Bit (LSB) and $v_{n-1}$ is the Most Significant Bit (MSB). We consider Boolean variables and bit-vector variables of width 1 to be interchangeable. A *constant* is a bit-vector each one of whose bits is substituted by 0 or 1. A *bit-vector operation* receives one or more bit-vectors and returns a bit-vector. A *Term DAG* is a Directed Acyclic Graph (DAG), each of whose *input nodes* (that is, nodes with in-degree 0) comprises a bit-vector or a constant and each of whose *internal nodes* (that is, nodes with in-degree > 0) is an application of a bit-vector operation over previous nodes. A *BV formula* $F$ is a term DAG, where some of its Boolean terms are asserted to 1 (that is, they must be assigned 1 in every assignment which satisfies $F$).

The only assumption this paper makes about the input BV formula is that it can be translated to Conjunctive Normal Form (CNF) in propositional logic (a CNF formula is a conjunction of clauses, where each clause is a disjunction of Boolean literals, and a Boolean literal is a Boolean variable or its negation). This assumption holds for the BV language as defined in the SMT-LIB standard [5]. See [19] for a further overview of BV syntax and semantics.

Let $\mu$ be a full assignment to the variables of a BV formula $F$ and $v$ be a term in $F$. We denote by $\mu(v)$ the value assigned to $v$ in $\mu$, interpreted as an unsigned number.

A BV formula $F$ is *satisfiable* iff it has a model (where a *model* is a satisfying assignment). A model $\mu$ to $F$ is *t-maximal* iff $\mu(t) \geq \nu(t)$ for every model $\nu$ to $F$.

Given a BV formula $F$ and a term $t$ in $F$, where $t$ is called the *optimization target*, let the problem of *Bit-Vector Optimization (OBV)* be the problem of finding a $t$-maximal model to $F$.

A SAT solver [6,27,40] receives a CNF formula $F$ and returns a model, if one exists. In *incremental SAT solving under assumptions* [14,30,31], the user may invoke the SAT solver multiple times, each time with a different set of *assumption literals* and, possibly, additional clauses. The solver then checks the satisfiability of all the clauses provided so far, while enforcing the values of the current assumptions only. In the widely used Minisat's approach [14] to incremental SAT solving under assumptions, the same SAT solver instance solves the entire sequence internally. The assumptions are modeled as first decision literals in the user-given order. Each assignment to an assumption is followed by Boolean Constraint Propagation (BCP). If the solver discovers that the negation of one of the assumptions is implied by other assumptions during BCP, it halts and returns that the problem is unsatisfiable. Whenever the solver unassigns one or more of the assumptions following a backtracking or a restart, it reassigns the unassigned assumptions in the user-given order (where each assignment is followed by BCP) before picking any other decisions.

An eager BV solver [11,17] works by preprocessing the given BV formula [11, 17,28], bit-blasting it to CNF and solving with SAT.

# 3   Modeling the Placement Fixer Problem

This section details the placement fixing problem, mentioned in Sect. 1, and shows how to reduce it to an optimization problem modulo either BV or LIA.

## 3.1   Problem Formulation

We start with the problem formulation. We will be using the example in Fig. 1 for illustration.

**Initial Set Up.** We are given a grid of size $(X, Y)$ and a set of $n$ non-overlapping (but possibly touching) rectangles $r_1, \ldots, r_n$ placed on the grid. Each rectangle $r_i$'s initial placement is given as the coordinates of its bottom-left corner $(x_i, y_i)$, height $h_i$ and width $w_i$. The example in Fig. 1 has five rectangles.

A placement of rectangles in the grid might have violations between pairs of touching rectangles. A *violation* $v(b, t, \delta)$ between the *bottom* rectangle $r_b$ and the *top* rectangle $r_t$, where $1 \le b, t \le n$ and $-w_b < \delta < w_t$, occurs when $r_b$'s top side touches $r_t$'s bottom side (that is, when $y_b + h_b = y_t$) and the relative horizontal position of the rectangles is $\delta = x_b - x_t$. Each violation $v(b, t, \delta)$ has a problem-induced *unique* priority $p(b, t, \delta) \in \mathbb{N}$. In other words, the problem causes all the violations to be ranked according to their priority.

In our example shown in Fig. 1, there exist three violations of priority: $p(1, 4, -2)$, $p(4, 3, 2)$, and $p(5, 2, 0)$.

**Fixer Goal.** Given the initial placement, the fixer may *shift* the rectangles horizontally or vertically (that is, move each rectangle horizontally or vertically), so as to reduce the number of violations according to their priority. Shifting the same rectangle both horizontally and vertically is allowed. The priority is *strictly followed* in the sense that fixing one violation of priority $p$ should be preferred to fixing any number of violations of priorities lower than $p$. Note that shifting existing rectangles might create new violations.

The input problem induces additional constraints on the allowed shifts:

1. **Shift constraints:** some of the rectangles are non-shiftable (that is, they must not be shifted), while the greatest allowed horizontal and vertical shift for any shiftable rectangle is $\alpha$ and $\beta$, respectively.
2. **Parity preservation:** for each rectangle the $y$-coordinate at the new location must be even iff the original $y$-coordinate is even.

Consider our example in Fig. 1. Assume that all the rectangles are shiftable and that $\alpha = 2$ and $\beta = 2$. Violation 3 can be eliminated altogether by shifting $r_5$ down to $(6, 0)$ (shifting it down to $(6, 1)$ is disallowed by parity preservation). The other two violations $v_1$ and $v_2$ can be resolved by shifting $r_4$ to the right to $(4, 3)$. Note that if $r_4$ had been non-shiftable, violations $v_1$ and $v_2$ could have been resolved only at the expense of creating new violations, in which case the optimal solution to the problem would have depended on the actual priorities of the violations (unspecified in our example).

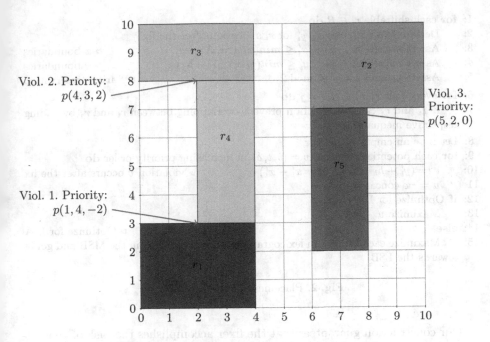

**Fig. 1.** Fixer placement problem modeling example.

## 3.2 Problem Encoding

The encoding is shown in Fig. 2. It can be applied to encode our problem into optimization modulo either BV or LIA.

First, the algorithm goes over all the shiftable rectangles. For each rectangle $r_i$, it creates two new variables $x_i'$, $y_i'$ to represent $r_i$'s location after the fix (the bit-width of the BV variables is chosen to accommodate the size of the grid). In addition, the algorithm ensures that the parity is preserved. For BV, the parity preservation constraint can be modeled by asserting $y_i \& 1 == y_i' \& 1$ (where $\&$ stands for bit-wise AND). For LIA, it can be modeled in either one of the two following ways: $(a)$ using an auxiliary variable $t$ to assert that $y_i - y_i' == 2t$, or $(b)$ using LIA's native mod operator to assert that $y_i \bmod 2 == y_j' \bmod 2$.

Second, the algorithm ensures that the rectangles will not overlap after the fix. This can easily be done for both BV and LIA by adding inequalities for each pair of rectangles over the new variables $x_i', y_i', x_j', y_j'$ to ensure there is no overlap.

Third, the algorithm creates the target term to be used for BV maximization (adjusting our construction to LIA reasoning is explained in the next paragraph). It starts by creating an empty bit-vector $u$. It then goes over all the potential violations in a loop, in order of priority, starting with the violation of the lowest priority. It formulates a condition $c$ which holds iff the violation occurs after the fix. Then the negation of $c$ is inserted into $u$ as the MSB (using concatenation).

1: **for** each shiftable $r_i \in R$ **do**
2:     Declare two variables $x_i', y_i'$ for $r_i$'s location after the fix
3:     Assert $max(0, x_i - \alpha) \leq x_i' \leq min(x_i + \alpha, X - w_j)$         ▷ $x$-boundaries
4:     Assert $max(0, y_i - \beta) \leq y_i' \leq min(y_i + \beta, Y - h_j)$         ▷ $y$-boundaries
5:     Assert $y_i$ mod 2 == $y_j'$ mod 2         ▷ Parity preservation
6: **for** every pair $r_i, r_j \in R, i \neq j$ **do**
7:     **if** $r_i$ and $r_j$ can overlap **then** prevent overlapping between $r_i$ and $r_j$ by adding respective inequalities
8: Let $u$ be an empty bit-vector
9: **for** each potential violation $v = (b, t, \delta)$ in increasing priority order **do**
10:     $c := (y_b' + h_b = y_t') \wedge (\delta = x_b' - x_t')$         ▷ violation $v$ occurs after the fix
11:     $u = \neg c$ concat $u$
12: **if** Optimize for BV **then**
13:     Maximize $u$
14: **else**         ▷ Optimize for LIA
15:     Maximize each bit of $u$ in lexicographic order starting from the MSB and going towards the LSB

**Fig. 2.** Placement fixer: encoding

Our construction guarantees that the fixer accomplishes the task of generating a placement having as few violations as possible while strictly following the priority, iff $u$ is given the maximal value. Hence, the solver is asked to maximize the value of $u$ in the case where BV reasoning is applied. To achieve the same effect for LIA, the algorithm maximizes the bits of $u$ lexicographically starting from the MSB and going towards the LSB (lexicographical maximization for LIA is available in both $\nu Z$ and OptiMathSAT).

Note that one cannot use integer linear programming (ILP) to encode our problem efficiently, since our problem requires using *disjunctive constraints* to prevent overlaps between pairs of rectangles. Specifically, given any two rectangles $r_1$ and $r_2$, it is *either* that $x_1' > x_2' + w_2$ or $x_2' > x_1' + w_1$ (similar equations must be generated for $y$ coordinates). One could, though, use Linear Disjunctive Programming (LDP) [2,3] to encode our problem. We have left the non-trivial work of reducing our problem to LDP to the future.

## 4   Optimization with Weak Assumptions

Our first OBV algorithm is based on a modification to Minisat's approach to SAT solving under assumptions, called SAT solver under *weak assumptions*. We call our algorithm OBV-WA (standing for Optimization modulo Bit-Vectors with Weak Assumptions). It can also be understood as a linear search for the $t$-maximal model starting with the highest possible value of $t$ and going towards 0, where the algorithm stops at the first satisfying assignment. Section 6 will demonstrate that OBV-WA is substantially more efficient than the Naïve Linear Search (NLS) algorithm, depicted below (given a satisfiable formula $F$ and the optimization target $t$):

1: Solve $F$ with an SMT solver
2: **while** Solve returns SAT **do**
3:     Assert $t$ is greater than $t$'s value in the last model returned by Solve
4:     Solve $F$ with an SMT solver
5: **return** last model returned by Solve

## 4.1  OBV-WA Algorithm

Assume an eager BV solver is provided with a satisfiable BV formula $F$ and an optimization target $t^{[n]}$ and is requested to find a $t$-maximal model to $F$ (one can verify that $F$ is satisfiable by invoking a BV solver before applying our algorithm). First, OBV-WA translates $F$ to CNF (following an optional invocation of word-level preprocessing). Then it applies a SAT solver, where literals corresponding to the bits $t_{n-1}, t_{n-2}, \ldots, t_0$ are provided to the solver as weak assumptions which are processed as follows. The SAT solver assigns the weak assumptions as the first decision variables in the specified order (from the MSB $t_{n-1}$ towards the LSB $t_0$), where BCP follows each assignment. If the solver discovers that the negation of one of the assumptions is implied by other assumptions during BCP, it *continues to the next assumption* (in contrast to returning that the problem is unsatisfiable, as in Minisat's approach to SAT solving under assumptions).

This simple adjustment of Minisat's algorithm guarantees that the solver returns a $t$-maximal model. Indeed, OBV-WA checks the satisfiability of $F$ under every $t$ value starting from $t = 2^n - 1$ towards $t = 0$ in decreasing order. $t$ is decreased by $\delta > 1$ only once the solver *proves* that there is no model in the range $[t, t - \delta + 1]$. Indeed, the bit $t_i$ is flipped by the solver to 0 only if there is no model to $F$ with $t_i = 1$.

The algorithm in Algorithm 1 is an implementation of OBV-WA. It contains the following three functions:

1. SOLVE: the main function invoked by the user: given a BV formula $F$ and an optimization target $t^{[n]}$, it returns a $t$-maximal model. The function initializes an index $i$, which points to the next unassigned assumption, with $n-1$. It also initializes $dl\_wa$ to 0, where $dl\_wa$ is the highest decision level where a weak assumption is assigned as a decision literal. It then invokes a SAT solver with decision and backtrack strategies modified as specified below. The algorithm returns the model found by the SAT solver (we assume an implicit conversion from the Boolean model returned by the SAT solver to the corresponding BV model to the original formula).

2. ONDECISION: invoked by the underlying SAT solver to get a decision literal when it has to take a decision. It receives the next decision level. ONDECISION returns the next unassigned assumption, if any, and decreases the index $i$ by 1. Assigned assumptions are skipped. If an unassigned assumption is found, the function stores the assumption's index in a decision level indexed array $SavedI$ and updates $dl\_wa$. This is required for proper backtracking. If all the assumptions are assigned, a standard SAT decision heuristic is applied.

3. ONBACKTRACK: invoked by the SAT solver whenever it backtracks. It receives the decision level to backtrack to. If the decision level is higher than $dl\_wa$, nothing is done. Otherwise, the function updates the assumption index $i$ so as to point to the next unassigned assumption. It also updates $dl\_wa$ accordingly.

Note that the decision level of an assigned weak assumption $i$ might be different from $n - i$, since any assumption could entail other assumptions at the same decision level. For this reason, the algorithm must maintain the mapping $SavedI$ from the decision level $dl$ of each assigned weak assumption to its index $i$.

An approach similar to SAT solving under *unordered* weak assumptions has recently been used in [10] to reduce the number of faults in model-based safety analysis. The contribution of our work is in reducing OBV to SAT solving under weak assumptions, where the assumptions must correspond to the target variable bits, ordered from the MSB towards the LSB.

## 4.2   Incrementality

OBV-WA is incremental in the same sense as Minisat's algorithm: it can be invoked multiple times with different optimization targets, where the formula can be extended between the invocations. This type of incrementality is now supported in the new SMT-LIB format SMT-LIB 2.5 [4]. To support incremental push/pop, another type of incrementality inherited by SMT-LIB 2.5 from SMT-LIB 2.0, one can use selector literals as follows: following each push, add a fresh selector literal $s$ to every clause in the bit-blasted formula and then add $\neg s$ as a (strong) assumption. To pop, add the unit clause $\neg s$. To use both strong and weak assumptions in one invocation, simply assign first the strong assumptions and then the weak ones.

## 5   Optimization with Inline Binary Search

In this section we present our second OBV algorithm, called OBV-BS (standing for Bit-Vector Optimization with Binary Search). We will see in Sect. 6 that OBV-BS's is considerably more efficient than the Naïve Binary Search (NBS) algorithm performing a binary search for the maximal $t$ value using the SMT solver as an oracle.

### 5.1   OBV-BS Algorithm

Like OBV-WA, this algorithm first translates the formula to CNF. It then applies a binary search-style algorithm implemented on top of an incremental SAT solver.

We need to extend our definitions for the subsequent discussion in the context of OBV solving given a formula $F$ and the optimization target $t$. Let the *value* of an assignment $\alpha$ to $F$ be $\alpha(t)$ (that is, the value assigned to the target $t$ in $\alpha$).

For a partial assignment $\alpha$, we define its value $\alpha(t)$ to be equal to $\alpha_0(t)$, where $\alpha_0$ extends $\alpha$ by assigning 0 to all the unassigned bits of $t$. Values of assignments

---

**Algorithm 1.** OBV-WA – OBV with Weak Assumptions

---

1: **function** SOLVE(BV Formula $F$, Optimization Target $t^{[n]}$)
**Require:**     $F$ is satisfiable
**Ensure:**     A $t$-maximal model to $F$ is returned
2:     Pre-process and bit-blast $F$ to CNF
3:     $i := n - 1$                                                   ▷ $n - 1$ is the MSB
4:     $dl\_wa := 0$
5:     $\mu := \text{SAT}()$
6:     **return** $\mu$

7: **function** ONDECISION(Decision level $dl$)
8:     **while** $i \geq 0$ and $t_i$ is assigned **do**
9:         $i := i - 1$
10:     **if** $i < 0$ **then**
11:         **return** STANDARDSATHEURISTIC($dl$)
12:     $SavedI(dl) := i$
13:     $dl\_wa := dl$
14:     **return** $t_i$

15: **function** ONBACKTRACK(Decision level $dl$)
16:     **if** $dl \leq dl\_wa$ **then**
17:         $i := SavedI(dl)$
18:         $dl\_wa := dl - 1$

---

induce an order between them. In particular, an assignment $\alpha$ is *higher*, *lower*, or *equal* to $\beta$, if $\alpha(t) > \beta(t)$, $\alpha(t) < \beta(t)$, or $\alpha(t) = \beta(t)$, respectively. We sometimes interpret assignments to $F$ as Boolean assignments, assigning values to the bits of BV variables individually. Alternatively, we sometimes interpret assignments to $F$ as sets of Boolean literals, where each assigned bit $b$ of a BV variable appears as either $b$ or $\neg b$.

Consider Algorithm 2 implementing OBV-BS. The algorithm maintains the current model $\mu$, initialized with an arbitrary model to $F$ at line 3, and a partial assignment $\alpha$, which is empty in the beginning. The main loop of the algorithm (starting at line 5) goes over all the bits of the optimization target $t$ starting from the MSB $t_{n-1}$ down to $t_0$. Each iteration extends $\alpha$ with either $t_i$ or $\neg t_i$, where $t_i$ is preferred over $\neg t_i$ iff there exists a model where $t_i$ is assigned 1 while bits higher than $i$ have already been assigned in previous iterations. In other words, $t_i$ is preferred whenever there exists a model whose value is greater than or equal to $\alpha(t) + 2^i$. Essentially, the algorithm implements a binary search over all the possible values of the optimization target $t$, where the search is automatically pruned based on the conclusions of the SAT solver's conflict analysis.

The algorithm is incremental in the same sense as OBV-WA, that is, it fully supports Minisat-style incremental solving under assumptions, while push/pop can be supported through selector variables.

## 5.2     Correctness Proof

Three invariants, which hold throughout the algorithm at the beginning of the algorithm's loop, are shown in Fig. 3. According to Inv. 1, $\mu$ must be a model. According to Inv. 2 and 3, $\alpha$ is always a subset of $\mu$ and any $t$-maximal model, respectively (where the assignments are interpreted as sets of Boolean literals). Note that if the invariants hold, then at the end of the algorithm $\mu$ is a $t$-maximal model, since: $(a)$ by the end $\alpha$ will have assigned values to every bit of $t$, $(b)$ Inv. 2 ensures that $\mu$ agrees with $\alpha$ on all bits of $t$ and $(c)$ Inv. 3 guarantees that $\alpha$ agrees on all bits of $t$ with $t$-maximal models.

The invariants clearly hold just before the first loop iteration. Consider an arbitrary iteration of the loop. We assume that the invariants hold at its beginning.

First, the algorithm checks whether the current bit $t_i$ is 1 in $\mu$ (at line 6). If it is, $\alpha$ is simply extended with $t_i$ and the algorithm goes on to the next iteration. Let us verify that the invariants hold at the end of an iteration in this case. First, $\mu$ is not changed, hence Inv. 1 still holds. Second, $\alpha$ is extended with a $\mu$ literal, thus Inv. 2 is preserved. Inv. 3 and 2 hold in the beginning of the iteration, hence any $t$-maximal model $\nu$ agrees with $\alpha$ and $\mu$ on the values of the Boolean variables $t_{n-1}, \ldots, t_{i+1}$. Any such $\nu$ must also contain $t_i$ positively, since otherwise $\mu$'s value would have been higher than that of $\nu$. Thus, Inv. 3 is preserved.

Assume now that $t_i = 0$ in $\mu$, that is $\neg t_i \in \mu$. In this case (the treatment of which starts at line 9), the algorithm checks whether there exists a model (different from $\mu$) that extends $\alpha$ with $t_i$. It does this by invoking a SAT solver and providing it $\alpha$ and $t_i$ as (strong) assumptions.

If the problem is satisfiable and a model $\tau$ is found, we update $\mu$ to $\tau$ and continue to the next iteration of the loop. Let us verify the invariants at the end of the loop for this case. $\mu$ is still a model after the update, so Inv. 1 holds. $\alpha$ still agrees with $\mu$ on all $\alpha$ values, since the $\alpha$ values have been provided to the SAT solver as assumptions, so the updated $\mu$ must contain them. Thus, Inv. 2 is preserved. Inv. 3 still holds, since $\alpha$ has not been changed.

In the only remaining case, if the SAT solver returns UNSAT, we extend $\alpha$ with $\neg t_i$. Let us verify the invariants. Inv. 1 is preserved, since $\mu$ is not changed. Inv. 2 is preserved, since $\mu$ must contain $\neg t_i$ according to our algorithm's flow (otherwise, the condition at line 6 would hold). Finally, any $t$-maximal model must still agree with $\alpha$, preserving Inv. 3 for the following reasons. The only potential disagreement could be regarding the value of $t_i$, since Inv. 3 holds at the beginning of the loop. But the outcome of our SAT query guarantees that there is no model containing $\alpha$ and $t_i$, hence any $t$-maximal model must contain $\neg t_i$.

## 5.3     Performance Optimizations

We have implemented two important performance optimizations for Algorithm 2:

1. $\mu$ is a model.
2. $\alpha \subseteq \mu$.
3. $\alpha \subseteq \nu$ for every $t$-maximal model $\nu$.

**Fig. 3.** OBV-BS invariants

---

**Algorithm 2.** OBV-BS – OBV with Inline Binary Search

---

1: **function** SOLVE(BV Formula $F$, Optimization Target $t^{[n]}$)
**Require:**    $F$ is satisfiable
**Ensure:**    A $t$-maximal model to $F$ is returned
2:    Pre-process and bit-blast $F$ to CNF
3:    $\mu := \text{SAT}()$
4:    $\alpha := \{\}$
5:    **for** $i \leftarrow n - 1$ **downto** 0 **step** 1 **do**
6:        **if** $t_i \in \mu$ **then**        $\triangleright t_i \in \mu \equiv t_i = 1$ in $\mu$
7:            $\alpha := \alpha \cup \{t_i\}$
8:        **else**
9:            $\tau := \text{SATUNDERASSUMPTIONS}(\alpha \cup \{t_i\})$
10:            **if** SAT solver returned SAT **then**
11:                $\mu := \tau$
12:            **else**
13:                $\alpha := \alpha \cup \{\neg t_i\}$
14:        **return** $\mu$

---

1. In *non-incremental mode*, one can add unit clauses instead of the assumptions at lines 7 and 13. This is expected to boost the performance, since it has been shown that using unit clauses instead of assumptions results in a substantial performance improvement in the context of incremental SAT solving under assumptions [28,30].
2. Modern SAT solvers apply phase saving [16,33,41] as their polarity selection heuristic. In phase saving, once a variable is picked by the variable decision heuristic, the literal is chosen according to its latest value, where the values are normally initialized with 0. In our implementation of OBV-BS we initialize the phase saving values of all the bits of the optimization target $t$ to 1 in each invocation, encouraging the solver to prefer a higher value for $t$'s bits by default. This optimization allows the algorithm to converge faster.

## 5.4   Comparing OBV-WA and OBV-BS

Let us compare OBV-WA and OBV-BS at a high-level. OBV-WA should work better when the $t$-optimal model's value has many 1's in it, since OBV-WA tries to assign 1's to all the bits of $t$ whenever possible. Otherwise, OBV-BS is expected to perform better. In addition, OBV-BS has the advantage that it always has an approximation of the maximal model that can be returned to the user if optimality can be traded for performance. OBV-WA does not have intermediate non-optimal solutions.

# 6  Experimental Results

We have implemented our algorithms OBV-WA and OBV-BS in Intel's eager BV solver Hazel. This section studies the performance of OBV-WA and OBV-BS on industrial placement fixer benchmarks as well as publicly available placement fixer benchmarks crafted by us [29].

The crafted benchmarks consist of diversified instances of the generic problem of placing rectangles on a grid, described in Sect. 3. First, we created a number of families, where a family is defined per grid size $g \times g$, where $g \in \{10, 25, 50, 75, 100\}$. Each family consists of 40 benchmarks. Let the *density* of a benchmark $d \in \{0.2, 0.5, 0.7, 0.9\}$ be the fraction of occupied grid cells. Each family has 10 benchmarks for each of the four possible density values. The size and coordinates of the rectangles for each benchmark are drawn randomly, where the size of rectangles' sides is drawn from the set $\{1, 2, \ldots, \lceil g/10 \rceil\}$. Second, we crafted another family of high-density instances, called *HD (High-Density)*, for grid size $50 \times 50$. Each benchmark in the HD family was created by placing rectangles on the grid until all the room was exhausted.

For the comparison we used two publicly available OMT solvers: $\nu Z$ [8,9] (version 4.3.3) in BV and LIA modes, and OptiMathSAT [36,37] (version 1.3.5) in LIA mode. $\nu Z$ and OptiMathSAT are extensions of the leading SMT solvers Z3 and MathSAT, respectively, for OMT. Note that $\nu Z$ is the only available solver that supports OBV.

Recall from Sect. 3.2 that we presented two ways of encoding the parity preservation constraint $y_i \bmod 2 == y'_j \bmod 2$: (a) using an auxiliary variable $t$ to assert that $y_i - y'_i == 2t$, or (b) using LIA's native mod operator. We experimented with $\nu Z$ in LIA mode on benchmarks generated with both encodings. $\nu Z$-BV, $\nu Z$-LIA, and $\nu Z$-LIA-m below stand for, respectively, $\nu Z$ in BV mode, $\nu Z$ in LIA mode using auxiliary variables to encode parity constraints, and $\nu Z$ in LIA mode using the LIA's native mod operator to encode parity constraints. We used OptiMathSAT with only the auxiliary variable-based encoding, since OptiMathSAT does not support the mod operator.

We have also implemented the Naïve Linear Search (NLS) and Naïve Binary Search (NBS) algorithms (recall the beginning of Sects. 4 and 5, respectively) on top of Hazel.

We used machines with 32 GB of memory running Intel® Xeon® processors with 3 GHz CPU frequency. The time-out was set to 1800 s. Detailed experimental results are available in [29].

Consider Table 1. It presents the number of instances solved within the timeout per family, where a family is defined per grid size for all crafted instances, except for the HD family. In addition, we considered a family of 50 industrial instances. The family name is shown in column 1. Column 2 shows the average number of unsatisfied bits in the optimization target $t$ (in the optimal solution), while column 3 provides the number of SAT calls within OBV-BS on average. The number of instances per family is shown in column 4. (Statistics are not available for the industrial instances because of IP considerations.) The subsequent columns present the number of instances solved for a particular solver.

**Table 1.** Comparing OBV algorithms

| Grid size | UNSAT bits in $t$ | #SAT calls in OBV-BS | # | OBV-WA | OBV-BS | Opti-MathSAT | $\nu Z$-BV | $\nu Z$-LIA | $\nu Z$-LIA-m | NLS | NBS |
|---|---|---|---|---|---|---|---|---|---|---|---|
| $10 \times 10$ | 7 | 11 | 40 | 40 | 40 | 40 | 40 | 40 | 40 | 39 | 40 |
| $25 \times 25$ | 6 | 38 | 40 | 40 | 40 | 12 | 40 | 40 | 40 | 9 | 7 |
| $50 \times 50$ | 50 | 77 | 40 | 40 | 40 | 0 | 7 | 23 | 20 | 0 | 0 |
| $75 \times 75$ | 75 | 110 | 40 | 40 | 40 | 0 | 0 | 0 | 1 | 0 | 0 |
| $100 \times 100$ | 0.025 | 182 | 40 | 40 | 40 | 0 | 0 | 0 | 0 | 0 | 0 |
| Industrial | | | 50 | 50 | 50 | 0 | 0 | 0 | 0 | 0 | 0 |
| HD | 1324 | 889 | 54 | 1 | 54 | 0 | 0 | 0 | 0 | 0 | 0 |

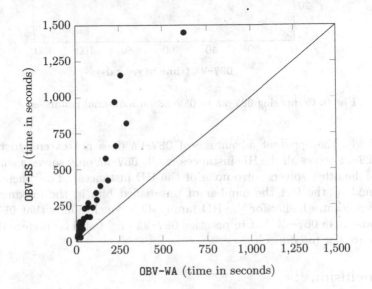

**Fig. 4.** Comparing OBV-WA to OBV-BS on $100 \times 100$ grids.

Consider the non-HD crafted instances and the industrial instances. Our algorithms clearly outperform current state-of-the-art. Both OBV-WA and OBV-BS solve all the non-HD crafted instances and all the industrial instances. None of the other solvers can solve a single industrial instance. $\nu Z$, in each one of the three modes, solves only a portion of the crafted $50 \times 50$ instances, and can solve none of the crafted $100 \times 100$ instances. OptiMathSAT is outperformed by the other solvers on the crafted instances. The naïve binary and linear search algorithms (NBS and NLS) are not competitive.

Figures 4 and 5 compare OBV-WA to OBV-BS head-to-head on $100 \times 100$ grids and industrial instances, respectively. One can see that OBV-WA consistently outperforms OBV-BS on both the crafted and the industrial instances. In light of these results, OBV-WA is now applied for the placement fixing problem at Intel.

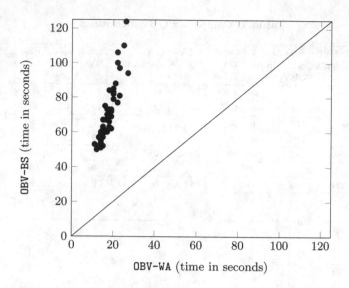

**Fig. 5.** Comparing OBV-WA to OBV-BS on industrial instances.

Strikingly, the apparent advantage of OBV-WA does not extend to the HD family. OBV-BS solves all the HD instances, while OBV-WA only solves a single HD instance (the other solvers solve none of the HD instances). This phenomenon is explained by the fact the number of unsatisfied bits in the maximal solution is significantly higher for the HD family. Our conclusion is that OBV-BS is more robust than OBV-WA, but in practice OBV-WA might still be preferred, if the instances are not too difficult.

## 7    Conclusion

This paper is the first full-blown work dedicated to the problem of Optimization modulo Bit-Vectors (OBV). We have presented two incremental OBV algorithms, which can easily be implemented in an eager Bit-Vector (BV) solver.

We have implemented our algorithms and studied their performance on real-world instances emerging in the industrial problem of fixing cell placement during the physical design stage of CAD process. The problem can be encoded as either optimization modulo BV or Linear Integer Arithmetic (LIA). We have also experimented with crafted, publicly-available instances that mimic the placement fixing problem.

Our algorithms have shown substantially better capacity than the state-of-the-art Optimization Modulo Theories (OMT) solvers $\nu Z$ and OptiMathSAT, where OptiMathSAT has been applied in LIA mode and $\nu Z$ in both BV and LIA modes.

As a future work we intend to study the integration of our algorithms with more recent approaches to incremental SAT solving under assumptions [31]. In addition, we are planning to apply our OBV algorithms to other problems.

**Acknowledgments.** The authors would like to thank Paul Inbar for editing the paper and Eran Talmor for providing useful suggestions that helped to improve this work.

# References

1. Baier, C., Tinelli, C. (eds.): TACAS 2015. LNCS, vol. 9035. Springer, Heidelberg (2015)
2. Balas, E.: Disjunctive programming: properties of the convex hull of feasible points. Discrete Appl. Math. **89**(1–3), 3–44 (1998)
3. Balas, E., Bonami, P.: New variants of lift-and-project cut generation from the LP tableau: open source implementation and testing. In: Fischetti, M., Williamson, D.P. (eds.) IPCO 2007. LNCS, vol. 4513, pp. 89–103. Springer, Heidelberg (2007)
4. Barrett, C., Fontaine, P., Stump, A., Tinelli, C.: The SMT LIB standard. Version 2.5. http://smtlib.cs.uiowa.edu/papers/smt-lib-reference-v2.5-r2015-06-28.pdf
5. Barrett, C., Stump, A., Tinelli, C.: The SMT-LIB standard: version 2.0. In: Gupta, A., Kroening, D. (eds.) Proceedings of the 8th International Workshop on Satisfiability Modulo Theories, Edinburgh, UK (2010)
6. Biere, A., Heule, M., van Maaren, H., Walsh, T. (eds.) Handbook of Satisfiability. Frontiers in Artificial Intelligence and Applications, vol. 185. IOS Press (2009)
7. Bjørner, N.: Private communication, March 2015
8. Bjørner, N., Phan, A.: $\nu z$ - maximal satisfaction with Z3. In: Kutsia, T., Voronkov, A. (eds.) 6th International Symposium on Symbolic Computation in Software Science, SCSS 2014. EPiC Series, vol. 30, Gammarth, La Marsa, Tunisia, 7–8 December 2014, pp. 1–9. EasyChair (2014)
9. Bjørner, N., Phan, A., Fleckenstein, L.: $\nu z$ - an optimizing SMT solver. In: Baier and Tinelli [1], pp. 194–199
10. Bozzano, M., Cimatti, A., Griggio, A., Mattarei, C.: Efficient anytime techniques for model-based safety analysis. In: Kroening and Pasareanu [22], pp. 603–621
11. Brummayer, R., Biere, A.: Boolector: an efficient SMT solver for bit-vectors and arrays. In: Kowalewski and Philippou [21], pp. 174–177
12. Cimatti, A., Franzén, A., Griggio, A., Sebastiani, R., Stenico, C.: Satisfiability modulo the theory of costs: foundations and applications. In: Esparza, J., Majumdar, R. (eds.) TACAS 2010. LNCS, vol. 6015, pp. 99–113. Springer, Heidelberg (2010)
13. Dillig, I., Dillig, T., McMillan, K.L., Aiken, A.: Minimum satisfying assignments for SMT. In: Madhusudan, P., Seshia, S.A. (eds.) CAV 2012. LNCS, vol. 7358, pp. 394–409. Springer, Heidelberg (2012)
14. Eén, N., Sörensson, N.: An extensible SAT-solver. In: Giunchiglia, E., Tacchella, A. (eds.) SAT 2003. LNCS, vol. 2919, pp. 502–518. Springer, Heidelberg (2004)
15. Franzén, A., Cimatti, A., Nadel, A., Sebastiani, R., Shalev, J.: Applying SMT in symbolic execution of microcode. In: Formal Methods in Computer-Aided Design (FMCAD), pp. 121–128. IEEE (2010)
16. Frost, D., Dechter, R.: In search of the best constraint satisfaction search. In: AAAI, pp. 301–306 (1994)
17. Ganesh, V., Dill, D.L.: A decision procedure for bit-vectors and arrays. In: Damm, W., Hermanns, H. (eds.) CAV 2007. LNCS, vol. 4590, pp. 519–531. Springer, Heidelberg (2007)
18. Ganzinger, H., Hagen, G., Nieuwenhuis, R., Oliveras, A., Tinelli, C.: DPLL(T): fast decision procedures. In: Alur, R., Peled, D.A. (eds.) CAV 2004. LNCS, vol. 3114, pp. 175–188. Springer, Heidelberg (2004)

19. Hadarean, L.: An Efficient and Trustworthy Theory Solver for Bit-vectors in Satisfiability Modulo Theories. Dissertation, New York University (2015)
20. Katelman, M., Meseguer, J.: vlogsl: a strategy language for simulation-based verification of hardware. In: Barner, S., Harris, I., Kroening, D., Raz, O. (eds.) HVC 2010. LNCS, vol. 504, pp. 129–145. Springer, Heidelberg (2011)
21. Kowalewski, S., Philippou, A. (eds.): TACAS 2009. LNCS, vol. 5505. Springer, Heidelberg (2009)
22. Kroening, D., Păsăreanu, C.S. (eds.): CAV 2015. LNCS, vol. 9206. Springer, Heidelberg (2015)
23. Li, Y., Albarghouthi, A., Kincaid, Z., Gurfinkel, A., Chechik, M.: Symbolic optimization with SMT solvers. In: Jagannathan, S., Sewell, P. (eds.) The 41st Annual ACM SIGPLAN-SIGACT Symposium on Principles of Programming Languages, POPL 2014, San Diego, CA, USA, 20–21 January 2014, pp. 607–618. ACM (2014)
24. Manolios, P., Papavasileiou, V.: ILP modulo theories. In: Sharygina, N., Veith, H. (eds.) CAV 2013. LNCS, vol. 8044, pp. 662–677. Springer, Heidelberg (2013)
25. Marić, F., Janičić, P.: URBiVA: uniform reduction to bit-vector arithmetic. In: Giesl, J., Hähnle, R. (eds.) IJCAR 2010. LNCS, vol. 6173, pp. 346–352. Springer, Heidelberg (2010)
26. Michel, R., Hubaux, A., Ganesh, V., Heymans, P.: An SMT-based approach to automated configuration. In: SMT Workshop 2012 10th International Workshop on Satisfiability Modulo Theories SMT-COMP 2012, p. 107 (2012)
27. Moskewicz, M.W., Madigan, C.F., Zhao, Y., Zhang, L., Malik, S.: Chaff: engineering an efficient SAT solver. In: Proceedings of the 38th Design Automation Conference, DAC 2001, Las Vegas, NV, USA, 18–22 June 2001, pp. 530–535. ACM (2001)
28. Nadel, A.: Bit-vector rewriting with automatic rule generation. In: Biere, A., Bloem, R. (eds.) CAV 2014. LNCS, vol. 8559, pp. 663–679. Springer, Heidelberg (2014)
29. Nadel, A., Ryvchin, V.: Bit-vector optimization: benchmarks and detailed results. https://goo.gl/epFbO1
30. Nadel, A., Ryvchin, V.: Efficient SAT solving under assumptions. In: Cimatti, A., Sebastiani, R. (eds.) SAT 2012. LNCS, vol. 7317, pp. 242–255. Springer, Heidelberg (2012)
31. Nadel, A., Ryvchin, V., Strichman, O.: Ultimately incremental SAT. In: Sinz, C., Egly, U. (eds.) SAT 2014. LNCS, vol. 8561, pp. 206–218. Springer, Heidelberg (2014)
32. Nieuwenhuis, R., Oliveras, A.: On SAT modulo theories and optimization problems. In: Biere, A., Gomes, C.P. (eds.) SAT 2006. LNCS, vol. 4121, pp. 156–169. Springer, Heidelberg (2006)
33. Pipatsrisawat, K., Darwiche, A.: A lightweight component caching scheme for satisfiability solvers. In: Marques-Silva, J., Sakallah, K.A. (eds.) SAT 2007. LNCS, vol. 4501, pp. 294–299. Springer, Heidelberg (2007)
34. Romano, A., Engler, D.: Expression reduction from programs in a symbolic binary executor. In: Bartocci, E., Ramakrishnan, C.R. (eds.) SPIN 2013. LNCS, vol. 7976, pp. 301–319. Springer, Heidelberg (2013)
35. Sebastiani, R., Tomasi, S.: Optimization in SMT with $\mathcal{LA}$ (Q) cost functions. In: Gramlich, B., Miller, D., Sattler, U. (eds.) IJCAR 2012. LNCS, vol. 7364, pp. 484–498. Springer, Heidelberg (2012)
36. Sebastiani, R., Tomasi, S., Trentin, P.: Optimathsat. http://optimathsat.disi.unitn.it

37. Sebastiani, R., Trentin, P.: Optimathsat: a tool for optimization modulo theories. In: Kroening and Pasareanu [22], pp. 447–454
38. Sebastiani, R., Trentin, P.: Pushing the envelope of optimization modulo theories with linear-arithmetic cost functions. In: Baier and Tinelli [1], pp. 335–349
39. Sherwani, N.A.: Algorithms for VLSI Physical Design Automation, 3rd edn. Kluwer Press, Dordrecht (1998)
40. Silva, J.P.M., Sakallah, K.A.: GRASP: a search algorithm for propositional satisfiability. IEEE Trans. Comput. 48(5), 506–521 (1999)
41. Strichman, O.: Tuning SAT checkers for bounded model checking. In: Allen Emerson, E., Sistla, A.P. (eds.) CAV 2000. LNCS, vol. 1855. Springer, Heidelberg (2000)
42. Wille, R., Große, D., Haedicke, F., Drechsler, R.: SMT-based stimuli generation in the SystemC verification library. In: Borrione, E. (ed.) Advances in Design Methods from Modeling Languages for Embedded Systems and SoCs. LNEE, vol. 63, pp. 227–244. Springer, Heidelberg (2010)

# Runtime Monitoring with Union-Find Structures

Normann Decker, Jannis Harder, Torben Scheffel, Malte Schmitz[(✉)],
and Daniel Thoma

Institute for Software Engineering and Programming Languages,
University of Lübeck, Lübeck, Germany
{decker,harder,scheffel,schmitz,thoma}@isp.uni-luebeck.de

**Abstract.** This paper is concerned with runtime verification of object-oriented software system. We propose a novel algorithm for monitoring the individual behaviour and interaction of an unbounded number of runtime objects. This allows for evaluating complex correctness properties that take runtime data in terms of object identities into account. In particular, the underlying formal model can express hierarchical interdependencies of individual objects. Currently, the most efficient monitoring approaches for such properties are based on lookup tables. In contrast, the proposed algorithm uses union-find data structures to manage individual instances and thereby accomplishes a significant performance improvement. The time complexity bounds of the very efficient operations on union-find structures transfer to our monitoring algorithm: the execution time of a single monitoring step is guaranteed logarithmic in the number of observed objects. The amortised time is bound by an inverse of Ackermann's function. We have implemented the algorithm in our monitoring tool Mufin. Benchmarks show that the targeted class of properties can be monitored extremely efficient and runtime overhead is reduced substantially compared to other tools.

## 1 Introduction

In practice, exhaustive verification of a system is often not an option because of economical or practical reasons, when third-party libraries are used or code is loaded dynamically at runtime from uncontrolled sources. In these cases, *Runtime Verification (RV)* can provide a reasonable lightweight alternative. Instead of analysing the whole behaviour of a system, RV focuses on techniques to observe a program's execution and evaluate correctness properties regarding this specific run. They allow for balancing the verification effort regarding the targeted correctness guarantees. For example, verification efforts can focus on specific, feasible parts such as low-level primitives or protocol implementations while the remaining parts are being monitored at runtime. Moreover, RV can be applied during software testing and debugging to obtain concise and specific information.

Work partially supported by the European Cooperation in Science and Technology (COST Action ARVI) and the German Federal Ministry for Education and Research (CONIRAS/01IS13029).

M. Chechik and J.-F. Raskin (Eds.): TACAS 2016, LNCS 9636, pp. 868–884, 2016.
DOI: 10.1007/978-3-662-49674-9_54

In software systems, a monitoring process is typically executed in parallel to a program under scrutiny. While this can provide a very detailed observation of the system's behaviour, it necessarily imposes runtime overhead for the whole system in terms of memory and computing resources. It is one of the main concerns in RV to keep this overhead as small as possible. This is particularly challenging for object-oriented systems. They require to track an unbounded number of runtime objects and evaluate their individual behaviour and interaction. Consider, for example, a Java collection object and iterator objects created for it. The number of iterators can become arbitrarily large. Once the collection is modified none of them is supposed to be used again, while iterators created for a different collection or after the modification have still a valid state. Thus, for each object some information, e.g. whether it is still valid to be used, may have to be stored and updated upon some program event.

The currently most efficient tools for monitoring object-oriented systems are JavaMOP [17] and MarQ [18]. They use data structures based on *lookup tables*, implemented as hash maps, to store this mapping of objects to their individual state. Unfortunately, this approach can quickly become infeasible since the number of table entries increases linearly with the number of maintained objects. A program event may affect all of them and thus require an update of the corresponding entries. Hence the cost of a *single* monitoring step can increase linearly with the length of the observed execution trace. Considering the example above, using many iterators quickly increases the lookup table. Every modification of the collection requires iterating through the table to update the entries of all derived iterator objects.

**Contribution.** We address this problem and propose a novel monitoring algorithm that uses *union-find data structures* to store the state of program objects. The essential idea is to store a mapping $c : \Delta \rightarrow Q$ from object (identifiers) $\Delta$ to monitoring information (states) $Q$ in terms of *sets* $\Delta_q \subseteq \Delta$ of objects for each state $q \in Q$. Then, changing the state of all objects in some state $q$ to some state $q'$ can be done by merging $\Delta_q$ into $\Delta_{q'}$. On union-find structures this is a constant-time operation, independent of the size of the sets. Further, our data structure allows for selecting and updating more specific subsets of program objects. The user can provide a tree-like hierarchy for the program objects and refer to it in the specification. For example, every iterator object can be filed as a direct child of its corresponding collection. The data structure then provides efficient access to the set of, e.g., all children or ancestors of a particular object. Hence, upon the modification of a collection, all corresponding valid iterator objects can be marked invalid at once. Tree-like object relations are ubiquitous in programming and employed in many algorithms, data structures and architectures. For correctness properties expressed with respect to such a hierarchy, our algorithm provides extremely efficient runtime evaluation.

*Outline.* In the following Sect. 2 we define an operational model that allows for expressing the behaviour and hierarchical dependencies between individual objects. This model provides the conceptual basis for our monitoring approach and thus characterises formally the addressed type of correctness properties.

To provide a better understanding of the properties, we also identify a corresponding fragment of first-order temporal logic. Based on the operational model, we describe our data structure in Sect. 3. Our algorithm for efficiently processing runtime events and updating the data structure is presented in Sect. 4. We discuss the performance of our approach first by providing bounds for the time complexity of a monitoring step. Then, Sect. 5 is concerned with our implementation. We present benchmarks for a collection of properties providing evidence that our approach performs well in practice and in particular in comparison with the state-of-the-art tools JavaMOP and MarQ.

**Related Work.** A monitoring approach for object-oriented systems, where the instrumentation framework AspectJ is extended by a simple expression language, was already considered in [1]. It allows for matching observed events against patterns with free variables that are bound to values provided by the observation. Data in general, of which object IDs form a special case, was intensively studied for runtime verification leading to various approaches based on different specification formalisms and execution schemes [4–7, 12, 13, 15, 19, 20]. Regarding efficient monitoring for object-oriented systems the influencial work by Chen and Rosu [19] on the *parametric trace slicing* technique is tailored specifically towards handling events carrying data in terms of object identifiers. It is implemented in the system JavaMOP [17] which is considered one of the best performing runtime verification tools. The trace slicing approach has been generalised to the concept of *quantified event automata (QEA)* [4] in order to increase expressiveness while still allowing for efficient evaluation. The tool MarQ [18] is based on QEA and can compete performance-wise even with JavaMOP. The essential idea of these frameworks is to evaluate a symbolic property on a set of projections of an input trace. Trace slicing specifically considers sequences of events which are parameterised by identifiers. A sequence is divided into sub-sequences, called slices, where all positions share common parameter values. The slices are then monitored independently. In contrast to our approach, only limited interdependencies between the different slices can be checked.

## 2    Projection Automata

The essential characteristics of an object are its *state* and *identity*. We therefore use a model that reflects both but provides a reasonable abstraction. Finite word automata are an established concept that is well suited for runtime verification because it naturally operates on sequences of inputs. Regarding identity, we employ the framework of *data words* to model observations that relate to a particular object. In this setting, an object is reduced to its mere identity and represented in terms of a so-called *data value*. Formally, we consider an infinite set $\Delta$ of such values in order to represent an arbitrary number of different objects. A finite set $\Sigma$ of *symbols* represents the type of observations, e.g., a call to a particular method or the access to a variable. A data word is now a finite sequence $w = (a_1, d_1)(a_2, d_2) \ldots (a_n, d_n) \in (\Sigma \times \Delta)^*$ of letters consisting of a symbol $a \in \Sigma$ and a value $d \in \Delta$.

For representing the hierarchical relation between objects we impose additional structure on $\Delta$ in terms of a *tree-ordering* relation $\leq$. It models the relation between all possibly occurring objects as a forest. A tree-ordering is a partial ordering where every strictly descending chain $d_1 > d_2 > \ldots$ is finite and such that for every non-minimal element $d \in \Delta$ the largest element $d' < d$ is unique. We call $d'$ the *parent* of $d$, written $\mathsf{par}(d)$. The *level* of a value $d \in \Delta$ is defined as $\mathsf{lvl}(d) = 1$ if $d$ is minimal and otherwise $\mathsf{lvl}(d) = \mathsf{lvl}(\mathsf{par}(d)) + 1$. We call $(\Delta, \leq)$ of *depth* $\ell$ if there are longest strictly descending chains of length $\ell$. Additionally, we assume that $(\Delta, \leq)$ contains infinitely many minimal elements and that every non-minimal element $d \in \Delta$ has an infinite number of siblings $d \neq d' \in \Delta$ with $\mathsf{par}(d') = \mathsf{par}(d)$.

**Definition 1 (Projection Automata).** *A* projection automaton (PA) *is a tuple* $\mathcal{A} = (Q, \Sigma, \delta, q_0, \lambda)$ *where $Q$ is a finite set of states, $\Sigma$ is a finite alphabet, $\delta : Q \times \Sigma \times \{<, =, >, \|\} \to Q$ is the transition function, $q_0 \in Q$ is the initial state and $\lambda : Q \to \mathbb{S}$ is the output labelling for some semi-lattice* $(\mathbb{S}, \sqcap)$.

*The operational semantics of PA is given in terms of configurations $c : \Delta \to Q$ that map data values to states. The run of $\mathcal{A}$ on a data word $w = (a_1, d_1) \ldots (a_n, d_n)$ is a sequence of configurations $\rho_w = c_0 \ldots c_n$ such that the initial configuration is the constant function $c_0 : \Delta \to \{q_0\}$ and for all positions $0 \leq i < n$ and all data values $d \in \Delta$ we have $c_{i+1}(d) = \delta(c_i(d), (a_{i+1}, \bowtie))$ where $\bowtie \in \{<, =, >, \|\}$ and $d_{i+1} \bowtie d$. The output of $\mathcal{A}$ for the data word $w$ is $\mathcal{A}(w) := \bigsqcap_{d \in \Delta} \lambda(c_n(d))$.*

Syntactically, a PA is a finite automaton with output (i.e., a Moore machine) over the input alphabet $\Sigma \times \{<, =, >, \|\}$ and the output alphabet $\mathbb{S}$. Intuitively, to every data value $d \in \Delta$, an instance of the automaton is associated that reads, instead of an input letter $(a, d') \in \Sigma \times \Delta$, the symbol $a \in \Sigma$ and the information how the observed value $d'$ relates to itself, in terms of one of the symbols from $\{<, =, >, \|\}$. The output of all instances is then aggregated to a single verdict, hence the semi-lattice. Note that the restriction to a deterministic transition function is not essential since non-determinism (even alternation) can be eliminated by standard constructions.

*Example.* Recall the property that modifying a collection invalidates iterators previously created for it. The data values $\Delta$ can model these two types of objects by choosing an ordering $\leq$ with two levels: collection IDs are minimal (roots) and the iterator IDs $d_I \in \Delta$ created for a collection with ID $d_C \in \Delta$ are direct children of $d_C < d_I$. Given this structure on $\Delta$, the PA in Fig. 1 (Iterator) expresses the property. Initially, all objects remain in state $q_0$. Upon the creation (c) of an iterator with ID $d_I \in \Delta$, this new iterator receives the letter (c, =) and changes its state to $q_1$. The corresponding collection receives (c, >) and all others receive (c, $\|$), thus staying in $q_0$. Upon the modification of some collection (m), all iterators for it receive (m, <) (the observed ID is strictly smaller) and if they happen to be in state $q_1$ move to state $q_2$. Finally, when $\mathtt{next}()$ is called on some iterator, this one reads the letter (n, =) and only if it happens to be in state $q_2$ it moves to the failure state. Figure 1 shows further examples to be discussed in Sect. 5.

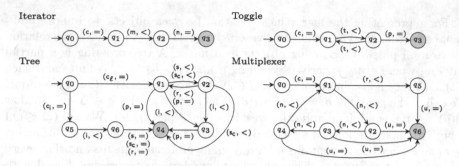

**Fig. 1.** Example properties formulated as PA with outputs ⊤ (white states) and ⊥ (grey states). Missing edges are self-loops.

Projection automata are closely related to *class automata* [11] that feature an additional transducer but use only equality on the data domain. It can easily be shown that PA (like class automata) can simulate Minsky machines.

**A Logical Perspective.** Projection automata characterise precisely the properties that our monitoring algorithm can verify since it is based on their operational semantics. On the other hand, first-order extensions of temporal logics, in particular linear-time temporal logic (LTL), received much attention in RV [8–10,13] because they provide a very generic framework for specifying properties in a declarative fashion. In the following, we therefore discuss briefly how PA relate to temporal logic with first-order constraints. We identify a fragment of first-order logic that can be translated to PA and thus allows for using the very efficient algorithm presented in Sects. 3 and 4 instead of generic techniques.

The fragment consists of a logical language that uses a single variable $x$ and a single constant $d$ as well as zero-ary predicates (propositions) $P_a$, for $a \in \Sigma$, and a binary predicate $\leq$. Formulae of that language have the form $\forall_x \varphi$ where $\varphi$ is defined by the grammar $\varphi :: = P_a \mid \varphi \wedge \varphi \mid \neg \varphi \mid X \varphi \mid \varphi U \varphi \mid t \leq t$ where $a \in \Sigma$ and $t \in \{x, d\}$ is either the variable or the constant.

Each letter $(a, d) \in \Sigma \times \Delta$ in a data word can be considered as a structure $s$ over the signature above with universe $\Delta$. Such a structure $s$ interprets the constant $d$ as the value $d \in \Delta$, the proposition $P_a$ as true, the propositions $P_b$, for $b \neq a$, as false and the binary predicate $\leq$ as the tree-order relation on $\Delta$. For simplicity, however, let us define the semantics directly over data words as follows. The semantics of the terms $d$ and $x$ is given for an interpretation $d \in \Delta$ and a valuation $d_x \in \Delta$ as $[\![d]\!](d, d_x) = d$ and $[\![x]\!](d, d_x) = d_x$. For data words $w \in (\Sigma \times \Delta)^*$, letters $(a, d) \in \Sigma \times \Delta$ and values $d_x$ we let

$$
\begin{aligned}
(w, d_x) &\models \forall_x \varphi && \text{iff } (w, d'_x) \models \varphi \text{ for all } d'_x \in \Delta \\
((a, d)w, d_x) &\models P_a \\
((a, d)w, d_x) &\models t_1 \leq t_2 && \text{iff } [\![t_1]\!](d, d_x) \leq [\![t_2]\!](d, d_x) \\
((a, d)w, d_x) &\models X \varphi && \text{iff } (w, d_x) \models \varphi \\
(w, d_x) &\models \varphi_1 U \varphi_2 && \text{iff } (w, d_x) \models \varphi_2 \vee (\varphi_1 \wedge X(\varphi_1 U \varphi_2))
\end{aligned}
$$

The semantics of Boolean operators is defined as usual. To stay close to PA we include the empty word $\epsilon$, e.g., $(\epsilon, d_x) \not\models P_a$ and $(\epsilon, d_x) \models \varphi_1 \,U(\neg P_a)$.

From formulae $\varphi$ as defined in Eq. 2 we can now construct a PA $\mathcal{A}_\varphi = (Q, \Sigma, \delta, q_0, \lambda)$ with outputs from the Boolean lattice $\mathbb{B} = \{\bot, \top\}$ such that $\mathcal{A}_\varphi(w) = \top$ if and only if $(w, d_x) \models \forall_x \varphi$ for some (hence every) $d_x \in \Delta$. Interpreting subformulae of the form $P_a$ and $t_1 \leq t_2$ as *atomic* propositions we can apply standard automata construction techniques (see, e.g., [21]) and obtain a finite automaton $\mathcal{B}$ over the alphabet $\Gamma = 2^{AP}$ for $AP = \{P_a, t_1 \leq t_2 \mid a \in \Sigma, t_1, t_2 \in \{x, d\}\}$. Due to the subset construction, the automaton $\mathcal{B}$ reads letters that cannot occur in our setting. For example, there is no letter $(a, d) \in \Sigma \times \Delta$ that induces a structure where $P_a$ and $P_b$ holds for $a \neq b$ or where $t \leq t$ does not hold for $t \in \{x, d\}$. We remove these letters and corresponding edges in $\mathcal{B}$, keeping thus only letters of the form $g_M^a = \{P_a, x \leq x, d \leq d\} \cup M \in \Gamma$ where $M \subseteq \{x \leq d, d \leq x\}$ and $a \in \Sigma$. These have a unique correspondence to the symbols from $\Sigma \times \{<, =, >, \|\}$ and we thus obtain $\mathcal{A}_\varphi$ by renaming each such $g_M^a$ to $(a, =)$ if $M = \{x \leq d, d \leq x\}$, to $(a, <)$ if $M = \{d \leq x\}$, to $(a, >)$ if $M = \{x \leq d\}$ and to $(a, \|)$ if $M = \emptyset$.

Note that this is essentially the generic construction presented in [13] instantiated for the temporal logic LTL defined accordingly and the theory of letters from $(\Sigma \times \Delta)$. Technically, removing edges with inconsistent labels can be considered as an optimisation step that is possible given the simple structure of the letters in a data word. We use LTL here due to its popularity in RV but can replace it by other logics that translate to finite automata.

## 3    Data Structure

Our monitoring algorithm is based on simulating the operational semantics of a given PA $\mathcal{A} = (Q, \Sigma, \delta, q_0, \lambda)$. It therefore operates on a data structure to represent configurations $c$ of $\mathcal{A}$ that we describe in this section. The essential idea underlying our data structure is to store such a mapping $c : \Delta \to Q$ by *partitioning* $\Delta$ into subsets of data values with the same state assigned. At the same time, this partition should also reflect the ordering relation between values. Then, updating a configuration amounts only to a few operations on subsets of $\Delta$ and we organise our data structure such that these can be performed efficiently.

When processing a letter $(a, d) \in \Sigma \times \Delta$ the successive configuration $c'$ maps every value $e \in \Delta$ to a state $\delta(c(e), (a, \bowtie))$, i.e., depending on the previous state $c(e)$ and the relation $\bowtie$ between $d$ and $e$. Our data structure therefore provides efficient access to the subsets $\Delta_q = \{d \in \Delta \mid c(d) = q\}$, $\Delta_{d\bowtie} = \{e \in \Delta \mid d \bowtie e\}$ and $\Delta_{d\bowtie, q} = \Delta_q \cap \Delta_{d\bowtie}$ for $\bowtie \in \{<, =, >, \|\}$. Then, $(\Delta_{d\bowtie, q})_{q \in Q, \bowtie \in \{<, =, >, \|\}}$ is a partition of $\Delta$ that reflects the ordering and represents the mapping $c$. It allows for characterising the partition $(\Delta'_{d\bowtie, q})_{q \in Q, \bowtie \in \{<, =, >, \|\}}$ representing $c'$ by

$$\Delta'_{d\bowtie, q} = \bigcup_{q' \mid q = \delta(q', (a, \bowtie))} \Delta_{d\bowtie, q'}.$$

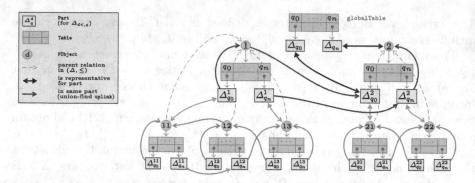

**Fig. 2.** Example for the shape of the data structure to represent PA configurations. **Part** objects are linked to the representative of their associated object collection (black and grey arrows). Non-representative elements of a collection have an uplink pointer (blue arrows) to the representative or another element. The data structure is divided into levels (indicated by colour saturation) that are only connected by the pointers between representatives and **Part** instances. Note, there is no directed connection from the global table to any of the objects within the left-hand segment of the object graph (Color figure online).

Intuitively, the input letter $(a, d)$ can be dispatched as symbol $(a, \bowtie)$ to every part $\Delta_{d\bowtie}$, for each $\bowtie \in \{<, =, >, \|\}$ and then, within $\Delta_{d\bowtie}$, the subsets $\Delta_{d\bowtie,q} \subseteq \Delta_{d\bowtie}$ for $q \in Q$ are relabelled and merged according to how the letter $(a, \bowtie)$ changes the states $q$ in $\mathcal{A}$. This is the abstract view of how our algorithm processes events.

Based on the ordering on $\Delta$ and the subsets $\Delta_{d<,q}$ and $\Delta_{d=,q}$ we can already describe the sets $\Delta_{d>,q}$ and $\Delta_{d\|,q}$ as

$$\Delta_{d>,q} = \bigcup_{i=1}^{|\mathsf{lvl}(d)|-1} \Delta_{\mathsf{par}^i(d)=,q} \quad \text{and} \quad \Delta_{d\|,q} = \Delta_q \setminus (\Delta_{d>,q} \cup \Delta_{d<,q} \cup \Delta_{d=,q}).$$

Therefore it suffices to store only $\Delta_q$, $\Delta_{d<,q}$ and $\Delta_{d=,q}$ for every $d \in \Delta$ in our data structure. We next describe a concise representation of this (infinite) collection of subsets that allows for performing the necessary operations efficiently.

**Components.** We identify data values $d \in \Delta$ with program objects and hence use the latter directly in our data structure to represent data values. The only assumption that we need to make is that we can attach additional information to every object, if needed. We represent this information in terms of a class **PObject** that provides the three fields **part**, **uplink** and **table** to store reference pointers to other objects. Technically, we assume every program object in the system to extend this class. In practice, this can be accomplished, e.g., by means of program instrumentation. In the following we therefore regard any program object simply as instance of **PObject**. Additionally, our data structure for storing a PA configuration uses the classes **Part** and **Table**. An instance of **Table** will be used to represent a partition $(\Delta_{d<,q})_{q \in Q}$ of $\Delta_{d<}$ for some particular value $d \in \Delta$. These partitions can be thought of as a (one-dimensional) table indexed by $Q$ where each cell contains a part $\Delta_{d<,q}$ of the partition. An instance of Part will in turn represent such a part.

Based on these components we store the subsets of $\Delta$ in a hierarchical fashion as depicted in Fig. 2. To every PObject corresponding to some data value $d$ we associate a Table instance that holds a Part object representing the subset $\Delta_{d<,q}$ for every state $q \in Q$. A Part object now maintains a *collection* of objects that represent subsets of $\Delta_{d<,q}$. The collection can contain both instances of Part and of PObject representing subsets $\Delta_{d'<,q}$ and $\Delta_{d'=,q}$, respectively, for direct children $d'$ of $d$. While the former in turn represent a possibly empty collection of objects, the latter indicate that the set $\Delta_{d'=,q}$ is non-empty, i.e. $c(d') = q$. Every PObject in the collection again carries a table pointing to subsets one level deeper in the data structure and every Part object is associated with a possibly empty collection of objects.

At the top of the data structure there is one designated Table instance that we refer to as globalTable. It represents the partition $(\Delta_q)_{q \in Q}$ and hence maps every state $q \in Q$ to a Part object representing the part $\Delta_q$. The collection of these Part objects now contain the program objects with minimal IDs $d$ and corresponding sup-parts $\Delta_{d<,q}$.

*Unobserved Values.* A configuration assigns a state to all (infinitely many) data values whereas only finitely many objects are actually observed during execution. We consider an object (ID) observed if it is associated to some event that occurred or it has a smaller ID (wrt. $(\Delta, \leq)$) than an observed object. The mapping of unobserved values to states is stored symbolically: every Table object holds a default field storing a state $q \in Q$. An unobserved ID is mapped to the default state of the table attached to its larges ancestor. Note that all unobserved values with the same largest observed ancestor cannot be distinguished because they always fell into the same projection class along a run.

**Union-Find.** The object collections attached to Part instances are maintained using a nesting of union-find data structures. This is the most crucial aspect regarding the performance of the monitoring algorithm. It allows for efficiently performing all operations that are necessary to update a configuration: computing the *union* of two parts, to *insert* and *delete* elements and to identify (*find*) the Part object that holds a given element.

Recall that a union-find structure represents disjoint sets of objects organised as a tree. One element (if any) of each set is appointed *representative* and used as root while all others carry a reference to one other member of the same set. For convenience we consider objects that can be inserted into a union-find structure as Findable. We assume that Part as well as PObject extend this class providing the references uplink and part. The former links an element to its parent in the union-find tree but we use the term *uplink* to avoid confusion. The part field is only used by the representative to point to the Part object that holds the set.

Classically, the operations *find* and *insert* operate on representatives of a set but since we are mostly interested in the associated Part object we assume operations with signatures

```
fun find(obj: Findable): Part
proc insert(target: Part, obj: Findable)
```
where find returns the content of the part field of the representative and insert adds an object to the collection attached to a Part object. For the same reason we use the operation
```
proc moveAll(target: Part, source: Part)
```
that is derived from the basic operation *union* and moves all elements from the collection attached to source to the collection attached to target. Moreover, we assume the union-find structure provides an operation
```
proc delete(obj: Findable)
```
which can be implemented in different ways while maintaining the worst-case complexity of the other operations [3,16].

**Helper Functions.** To facilitate the presentation of the algorithm we employ the helper functions
```
fun part(table: Table, state: Q): Part
fun state(table: Table, part: Part): Q
fun createTable(parentTable: Table, default: Q): Table
```
that can easily be implemented based on the information present in the data structure. The function part returns the Part object that the given state is mapped to by the given table. Conversely, state returns the state that the given table maps to the given Part object. It is assumed that the latter is indeed referenced by the table and that the state is unique. The function createTable creates a new Table object with the given default state. For every table index $q \in Q$ a new Part object is created and moreover inserted into the part for $q$ in parentTable. The object collection attached to itself is initially empty. Our algorithm accesses the ordering on $\Delta$ by means of par and the functions
```
fun hasParent(obj: PObject): Boolean
fun parentTable(obj: PObject): Table
```
where hasParent(obj) is true if the ID of obj is not minimal. For every program object parentTable returns the Table object associated with its parent or globalTable if it is minimal. It is assumed that the object and, if existent, its parent object have already been registered in the data structure as described below in Sect. 4. Note that the ordering is not represented in the data structure as described above. In Sect. 5 we discuss how the ordering information can be made available in our setting.

**Output.** Considering the output $v$ of the PA $\mathcal{A}$ in configuration $c$ we observe that $v = \prod_{d \in \Delta} \lambda(c(d)) = \prod_{q \mid c^{-1}(q) \neq \emptyset} \lambda(q)$ where $c^{-1}(q) = \{d \in \Delta \mid c(d) = q\}$ is the inverse of $c$. It hence suffices to evaluate which of the sets $\Delta_q$ are non-empty. Since evaluating every Part object in the data structure is not an option—in fact, Part objects are not necessarily reachable—we track the number of objects in a field counter attached to every Part object. When performing a specific operation, the local counters can easily be updated. By propagating local counter changes upwards the tree structure the counters for the parts $\Delta_q$ can invariantly provide the number of program objects mapped to a specific state.

Recall that the part corresponding to the default state $q$ in a table virtually contains unobserved objects. These cannot be distinguished and we therefore treat them as a single one and add one to the counter value of that part.

## 4    Monitor Execution Algorithm

Based on the data structure described in the previous section we now present an algorithm that simulates one step of the operational semantics of some PA $\mathcal{A} = (Q, \Sigma, \delta, q_0, \lambda)$. The main procedure $\mathtt{step}$ of the algorithm is shown in Listing 2. It takes an event name $a \in \Sigma$ and a $\mathtt{PObject}$ instance and updates the data structure such that it represents the successor configuration of $\mathcal{A}$ after reading a letter $(a, d) \in \Sigma \times \Delta$ where $d$ represents the object's ID. In the following, we identify $\mathtt{PObject}$ instances with data values from $\Delta$ representing their ID. Moreover, we identify $\mathtt{Part}$ objects with the subset of $\Delta$ they represent. The procedure $\mathtt{step}$ essentially dispatches the input letter $(a, d)$ to the parts $\Delta_{d<}$, $\Delta_{d=}$, $\Delta_{d>}$ and $\Delta_{d\|}$ as symbols $(a, <)$, $(a, =)$, $(a, >)$ and $(a, \|)$, respectively. Assume the data structure encodes a configuration $c$ of $\mathcal{A}$.

*Updating $\Delta_{d=}$.* Updating the part $\Delta_{d=}$ requires only to change the state $q = c(d)$ of the object $d$ to another state $q' = \delta(q, (a, =))$. This is implemented by the procedure $\mathtt{changeState}$ depicted in Listing 1. It removes the object $d$ from its current part $\Delta_{\mathsf{par}(d)<,q}$ and inserts it into the part $\Delta_{\mathsf{par}(d)<,q'}$. Removing $d$ amounts to deleting $d$ from the union-find structure associated with the $\mathtt{Part}$ object $\Delta_{\mathsf{par}(d)<,q}$ and consequently decrementing its counter. Subsequently, the procedure $\mathtt{setState}$ inserts $d$ into the (collection associated with the) target part $\Delta_{\mathsf{par}(d)<,q'}$ and increments its counter to update the size information. As our data structure maintains nested parts, changing the size of a part requires to propagate this change to all enclosing parts. The procedure $\mathtt{updateCounter}$ realises this functionality. It calls $\mathtt{find}$ recursively to determine all enclosing parts until a top most part $\Delta_q$ is reached and updated.

*Updating $\Delta_{d<}$.* All elements from the part $\Delta_{d<}$ need to be updated according to the symbol $(a, <)$ upon reading $(a, d)$. How this symbol changes the states of these can simply be described by the mapping $\mathtt{map} : Q \to Q$ with $\mathtt{map}(q) = \delta(q, (a, <))$. As we aim to be efficient we must not explicitly handle every element below the $\mathtt{Part}$ object $\Delta_{d<}$ in the data structure. Instead, we rearrange only the $\mathtt{Table}$ object associated to $d$: depending on $\mathtt{map}$, the parts $\Delta_{d<,q}$ are joined or moved, i.e., new $\mathtt{Part}$ objects $\Delta'_{d<,q} := \bigcup_{q'|\mathtt{map}(q')=q} \Delta_{q'}$ are created for every state $q \in$. The function $\mathtt{applyMap}$ creates these new parts and computes their counters based on the counters of the original parts. After applying the mapping, it only remains to propagate the counter changes upwards in the data structure to all enclosing parts.

Notice that this way, the data structure becomes inconsistent since the changes are not automatically propagated downward the data structure to all larger objects. In a consistent state (cf. Fig. 2) every part object $\Delta_{e<,q}$ is contained in the collection of the part object $\Delta_{\mathsf{par}(e)<,q}$ for the same state $q$. Applying the map may, e.g., effectively relabel some $\Delta_{\mathsf{par}(e)<,q}$ to $\Delta_{\mathsf{par}(e)<,q'}$ and then

**Listing 1.** Procedures operating on the data structure

```
1  proc changeState(obj: PObject, q: Q) {          38  proc changeStates(obj: PObject, map: Q → Q) {
2    updateCounter(find(obj), -1)                   39    val oldTab = obj.table
3    delete(obj)                                    40    obj.table = applyMap(oldTab, map)
4    setState(obj, q) }                             41    foreach q in Q {
                                                    42      updateCounter(part(parentTable(obj), q),
6  proc setState(obj: PObject, target: Q) {         43        part(obj.table, q).counter
7    val targetP =                                  44        - part(oldTab, q).counter) } }
8      part(parentTable(obj), target)
9    insert(targetP, obj)                           46  fun applyMap(tab: Table, map: Q → Q): Table = {
10   updateCounter(targetP, 1) }                    47    val newTab = createTable(tab, map(tab.default))
                                                    48    foreach q in Q {
12 proc updateCounter(startP: Part,                 49      val source = part(tab, q)
13                    delta: Int) {                 50      val target = part(newTab, map(q))
14   if (startP == null) return                     51      moveAll(target, source)
15   startP.counter += delta                        52      target.counter += source.counter }
16   updateCounter(find(startP), delta) }           53    return newTab }

18 proc changeStatesIncomp(obj: PObject,            55  proc register(obj: PObject) {
19          anchor: PObject, map: Q → Q) {          56    if (obj.table != null) return
20   val state = state(parentTable(obj),            57    if (hasParent(obj)) register(par(obj))
21     find(obj))                                   58    val default = parentTable(obj).default
22   if (hasParent(obj)) {                          59    obj.table =
23     changeStatesIncomp(                          60      createTable(parentTable(obj), default)
24       par(obj), anchor, map)                     61    updateCounter(part(obj.table, default), 1)
25   } else {                                       62    setState(obj, default) }
26     globalTable =
27       applyMap(globalTable, map)                 64  proc dismissUpdates(obj: PObject) {
28     if (hasParent(anchor)) {                     65    foreach q in Q {
29       pullUpdates(par(anchor)) } }               66      val displaced = part(obj.table,q)
30   changeState(obj, state) }                      67      delete(displaced)
                                                    68      insert(part(parentTable(obj), q),
32 proc pullUpdates(obj: PObject) {                 69          displaced)
33   if (hasParent(obj)) pullUpdates(par(obj))      70  }}
34   fun map(q: Q): Q = state(
35     parentTable(obj),
36     find(part(obj.table, q)))
37   obj.table = applyMap(obj.table, map) }
```

$\Delta_{e<,q}$ is enclosed by the part $\Delta_{par(e)<,q'}$, although not being a subset. However, this inconsistency only means that the parts $\Delta_{e<,q}$ did not yet receive the transition from $q$ to $q'$. We can recover the correct state by determining the outmost enclosing part and consulting the global table for its state. The procedure **pullUpdates** in Listing 1 implements this functionality. We will, however, only use it if necessary, meaning propagation of such changes is lazy. Note that, in contrast to **setStates** no counter updates must be propagated.

*Updating $\Delta_{d\|}$.* The essential idea for updating $\Delta_{d\|}$ is to save the state of $d$ and all the ancestors $e < d$ of $d$, apply the update for $(a, \|)$ to the *global* table, i.e., to all objects, and then *restore* the saved states of the ancestors and $d$. That way precisely all incomparable objects are affected. Most of this process is implemented by the recursive procedure **changeStatesIncomp** shown in Listing 1. Notice, that before restoring the states of $d$ and its ancestors, the changes made to the global table need to be propagated to $d$. Otherwise restoring would not have an effect and upon the next update the unintended modifications would still be applied. It remains to restore the state of the larger elements in the part $\Delta_{d<}$ afterwards. This is implemented independently in the procedure **dismissUpdates**. This procedure deletes for every $q$ the part associated with $q$ in the table of $d$ from its current enclosing part and inserts it into the part associated with $q$ in the parent table. Thus it corrects the inconsistency based on the information in the *local* table instead of the information in the global table, as done by **pullUpdates**.

## Listing 2. Main procedure

```
 1 proc step(obj: PObject, event: Σ) {          11   var obj2 = obj
 2   register(obj)                              12   while (hasParent(obj2)) {
 3   pullUpdates(obj)                           13     obj2 = par(obj2)
                                                14     changeState(obj2,
 5   fun mapGT(q: Q): Q = δ(q, (event, <))      15       δ(state(parentTable(obj2), find(obj2)),
 6   changeStates(obj, mapGT)                   16         (event, >))) }
                                                17   fun mapIC(q: Q): Q = δ(q, (event, ||))
 8   changeState(obj,                           18   changeStatesIncomp(obj, obj, mapIC)
 9     δ(state(parentTable(obj), find(obj)),    19   dismissUpdates(obj)
10       (event, =)))                           20 }
```

*Procedure* step. Consider the main procedure step in Listing 2 called for an event $a \in \Sigma$ and object $d \in \Delta$. It first calls register to ensure $d$ has been properly registered with our data structure. Notice that when creating a new table for the object, all parts are, technically, empty. However, the part corresponding to the default state in the table above virtually contains unobserved objects. We therefore increment its counter by one. Then, pullUpdates is used to ensure that the table associated with the observed object $d$ is consistent with respect to the global table. In lines 5–6 and 8–10 of Listing 2 the parts $\Delta_{d<}$ and $\Delta_{d=}$ are updated, respectively, as described above. The lines 11–16 update the part $\Delta_{d>}$ of smaller objects according to the symbol $(a, >)$. This case can be handled by determining all affected objects explicitly using function par. Then the corresponding target state is computed and assigned similarly as in the case of $\Delta_{d=}$. Finally, lines 17–19 handle $\Delta_{d\|}$. As before a function mapIC is defined mapping source to target states for transitions labelled by $(a, \|)$ and the procedure changeStatesIncomp is called, followed by the restore operation as described above.

**Complexity.** It is crucial to know how the performance of a monitoring algorithm depends on the behaviour of the monitored program. For the following analysis, we fix a PA $\mathcal{A}$ with $s$ control states and assume that the data domain $(\Delta, \leq)$ is of bounded depth $\ell$. Let $A_k(i)$ be Ackermann's function defined as $A_0(i) := i + 1$ and $A_{k+1}(i) := A_k^{i+1}(i)$ where $f^j(x)$ is the function $f$ iterated $j$ times on $x$. Following [2], we define the inverse of Ackermann's function as $\alpha(i, j) := \min\{k \geq 2 \mid A_k(i) > j\}$ and $\alpha(i) := \alpha(i, i)$. We observe that the execution time of step is dominated by the calls to operations on union-find data structures and that it causes $\mathcal{O}(s \cdot \ell + \ell^2)$ calls to find and $\mathcal{O}(s \cdot \ell)$ calls to union- and delete-operations. If our data structure contains $n$ program objects, the size of every union-find structure in it is bound by $s \cdot n$. Then, the find-operations can be realised in $\mathcal{O}(\log(s \cdot n))$ worst-case time and $\mathcal{O}(\alpha(s \cdot n))$ amortised time; all other operations can be realised in constant time [2]. Hence, for fixed $s$ and $\ell$, the worst-case and amortiseed execution time of step on a data structure containing $n$ program objects is in $\mathcal{O}(\log(n))$ and in $\mathcal{O}(\alpha(n))$, respectively.

Note, that our data structure only requires space linear in the number of observed objects. Furthermore, the factor $\ell^2$ for the number of find-calls arises only from the update of the set $\Delta_{d>}$ in lines 11–16 and $\Delta_{d\|}$ in lines 17–19 of Listing 2. There, setState is called at most $\ell$ times which causes in turn up to $\ell$ find-calls to adjust the counters. Updating the counters for $\ell$ consecutive `setState`-calls could be implemented accumulatively with only $\ell$ `find`-calls instead. An optimised implementation of `step` therefore provides a worst-case and amortised time complexity in $\mathcal{O}(s \cdot \ell \cdot \log(n))$ and $O(s \cdot \ell \cdot \alpha(n))$, respectively.

## 5    Implementation and Evaluation

We have implemented our approach in Java as the tool Mufin. Properties are specified in Java by defining automata using a simple Java API. In addition the required tree-ordering on data values and the mapping of program events to unary logical events has to be provided. We use AspectJ intercept program events, such as method invokations, and dispatch them to Mufin.

In the presentation of the algorithm in Sect. 4 we assumed direct access to the tree-ordering on data values and used the function `par` to obtain the parent of a program object. An implemented of such a function depends on the setting as the order used for the specification may not be directly represented in the monitored program or might be hard to access. Mufin uses special events from which this order can be observed. Consider again the example from Sect. 1. When a new iterator is created the implementation can access both, the iterator and the corresponding collection. As the collection has to be the parent of the iterator the implementation can store this information, e.g. using a pointer from the iterator to the collection. Since our monitoring algorithm requires that all smaller objects are known when an event occurs, we also require these special events to occur on an object before any other events. The implementation detects when an event occurs on an object where the parent object is not yet known or when a special event occurs that conflicts with a previously observed event.

While we assumed to use program objects directly in the conceptual presentation, our implementation adds only one additional field to program objects that points to auxiliary objects actually contained in the data-structure. As program objects are not referenced from inside the union-find structure, they can be garbage collected as soon as they are no longer referenced by the original program. Also, the `delete` operation simply marks these auxiliary objects as deleted and they are only cleaned up during `find`-operations. The obvious consequence is that unnecessary auxiliary objects might pile up within a union-find structure. However, this does not happen as long as events occur regularly involving every observed program object. The assumption that almost all program objects, that are not ready for garbage collection, will always occur in some future event seems to be reasonable for many applications. The advantage of this approach is that garbage collection does not require any additional consideration. Classical union-find structures only require upward references in direction of the representative element of a part. Efficient implementations of the `delete`-operation also require further references in the reverse direction. Assuming that `find`-operations are performed regularly on most elements, most elements will not be referenced by any other element. Once they are no longer reference by a program object they will thus be garbage collected. Using an implementation with efficient deletes would require to use the API of the Java garbage collector in order to trace when some observed program object is garbage collected which would come with some performance overhead on its own. While this is an option when requiring strict guarantees, our benchmarks show that our simpler approach works well.

Instrumenting the elementary object class requires to modify the Java Virtual Machine (JVM). To avoid this, Mufin can also use a hash table to map program objects to auxiliary objects instead of a reference. This variation, called Mufin Light, has a notable impact on runtime and memory overhead, however, the advantage of our algorithm remains as our benchmarks show.

**Evaluation.** Mufin took part in the Java track of the recent $2^{nd}$ *Competition on Runtime Verification* [14]. We selected the seven benchmarks with properties expressible in our formalism of the 14 submitted to the competition. All benchmarks comprise a property and a small program generating a sequence of events. Monitoring the given property involves keeping track of nearly all the objects of the program. Therefore, the benchmarks are very well suited to compare the performance of different tools. For real-world applications a far smaller overhead can be expected as usually only a fraction of objects and events will be observed. Projection automata for the benchmarks are depicted in Fig. 1.

*Benchmarks.* The first group of benchmarks comprises *Iterator*, already described in Sect. 1, and three variations: *SafeIterator* uses the same property but instantiates far more objects (several millions instead of about ten). *MapIterator* enforces a similar property where iterators are created for key sets of a map and modifications occur on the map, thereby requiring three instead of only two levels of objects. It also creates several millions of objects. *DelayedIterator* is a variation of *Iterator* where the next-method may be called one time after a modification of the collection without failing. These benchmarks are very common for the evaluation of online monitoring tools, e.g. in [19] only properties of this kind are considered. *Multiplexer* aims to show the effect of a property requiring more control states. It models a multiplexer with four channels where an arbitrary number of clients is connected to each channel. New clients can be attached to the active channel (c), removed (r) and used (u) and the active channel can be switched (n). Using a client attached to an inactive channel violates the property. *Toggle* is designed to demonstrate the effect of a global action affecting a large number of objects. Objects can be created (c) and the state of all existing objects can be toggled (t). Objects may only be processed (p) if they are in one of their two internal states. *Tree* provides a scenario were the maximal level of observed objects is not known in advance. Objects are created as inner nodes ($c_i$) or leafs ($c_l$) of a tree. Messages sent (s) on any node are dispatched to corresponding leafs with an input buffer of size one and processed (p) there. Conversely, a reset (r) clears the buffer of corresponding leafs. A critical send operation ($s_c$) requires the buffer of all receiving leafs to be empty. Finally, any node can be invalidated (i) effectively removing it from the tree.

*Results.* We executed the benchmarks with Mufin, Mufin Light, JavaMOP and MarQ and measured execution time and memory consumption of the complete JVM process. Figure 3 shows relative time and memory overhead, i.e. additional

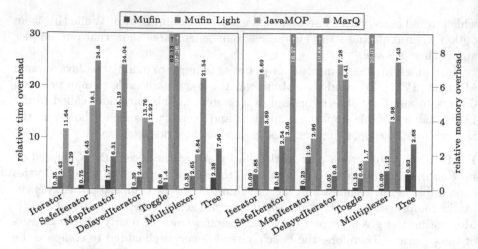

**Fig. 3.** Relative time and memory overhead of the tools Mufin, JavaMOP and MarQ while monitoring the given properties on the benchmark programs. A relative time overhead of 1 means that the absolute monitoring overhead is equal to the execution time of the non-instrumented program. (The difference between the instrumented and non-instrumented benchmark is the absolute overhead.)

time and memory consumption divided by that of the unmonitored program. Mufin (in both variants) is always multiple, often more than ten, times faster than JavaMOP and MarQ while consuming far less memory. Comparing Mufin with Mufin Light shows a notable impact of the global hash table but the performance benefit of our approach clearly persists. Comparing *Iterator*, *DelayedIterator* and *Multiplexer* shows that the number of states in a specification has only a small effect on the overhead of Mufin. Comparing *SafeIterator* and *MapIterator* shows that the impact of an addition level is small as well. The measurements for *SafeIterator* and *MapIterator* also show that Mufin handles large numbers of instantiated objects far better than the other tools. The results for *Toogle* demonstrate the massive impact of actions affecting many objects at once. In this benchmark almost every step affects around 10 000 objects rendering the previous approaches practically infeasible. The benchmark *Tree* can not be specified using the formalisms of the other tools. It shows that the overhead of Mufin grows for a greater depth of the ordering and thus of the data structure (in this case up to 7) but remains acceptable. The memory overhead of Mufin Light is significantly larger than that of Mufin, the latter remaining very small (below 1) in all cases. This is most likely due to hash tables that can only be filled up to a certain degree without becoming extremely inefficient. Some variations in memory consumption may be due to the allocation strategy of the JVM and the memory measurements therefore only show a general tendency. Mufin is available for download[1].

---

[1] http://www.isp.uni-luebeck.de/mufin.

# 6    Conclusion

Our investigations on monitoring temporal properties of object-oriented systems show that complex constraints, including hierarchical dependencies between individual objects, can be evaluated efficiently at runtime. We demonstrated that union-find data structures are a valuable algorithmic tool for runtime analysis. In the proposed monitoring algorithm they provide strict guarantees on the execution time of a monitoring step. This ensures that the accumulated runtime overhead grows effectively only linear with the execution time of the monitored program. Our benchmarks show that the conceptual benefits actually apply in practice and can outperform the currently most efficient monitoring tools Java-MOP and MarQ. Our formal model and logical characterisation provide a good understanding of the class of properties our approach can be applied to. Since we exploit their inherent hierarchical structure we clearly pay performance by expressiveness. However, since hierarchical structures are ubiquitous in computing they still cover a wide range of relevant specifications. The class of properties monitorable with our approach can be further extended. For example, some iterator implementations provide a remove method that deletes the current object from the underlying collection. It invalidates all other iterators of the same collection. To handle such constraints, further predicates are needed to address more types of subsets of objects, in this case the set of all siblings of an object. Given our data structure, the algorithm can be extended accordingly. Exploiting the ability to measure the number of objects assigned to some state provides further a basis for evaluating quantitative properties. The underlying model could easily be extended, e.g., by constraints on the number of children of an object in a certain state.

# References

1. Allan, C., Avgustinov, P., Christensen, A.S., Hendren, L.J., Kuzins, S., Lhoták, O., de Moor, O., Sereni, D., Sittampalam, G., Tibble, J.: Adding trace matching with free variables to AspectJ. In: Proceedings of Object-Oriented Programming, Systems, Languages, and Applications 2005, pp. 345–364. ACM (2005)
2. Alstrup, S., Li Gørtz, I., Rauhe, T., Thorup, M., Zwick, U.: Union-find with constant time deletions. In: Caires, L., Italiano, G.F., Monteiro, L., Palamidessi, C., Yung, M. (eds.) ICALP 2005. LNCS, vol. 3580, pp. 78–89. Springer, Heidelberg (2005)
3. Alstrup, S., Thorup, M., Gørtz, I.L., Rauhe, T., Zwick, U.: Union-find with constant time deletions. ACM Trans. Algorithms 11(1), 1–28 (2014)
4. Barringer, H., Falcone, Y., Havelund, K., Reger, G., Rydeheard, D.: Quantified event automata: towards expressive and efficient runtime monitors. In: Giannakopoulou, D., Méry, D. (eds.) FM 2012. LNCS, vol. 7436, pp. 68–84. Springer, Heidelberg (2012)
5. Barringer, H., Goldberg, A., Havelund, K., Sen, K.: Rule-based runtime verification. In: Steffen, B., Levi, G. (eds.) VMCAI 2004. LNCS, vol. 2937, pp. 44–57. Springer, Heidelberg (2004)

6. Barringer, H., Havelund, K.: TRACECONTRACT: a scala DSL for trace analysis. In: Butler, M., Schulte, W. (eds.) FM 2011. LNCS, vol. 6664, pp. 57–72. Springer, Heidelberg (2011)

7. Barringer, H., Rydeheard, D.E., Havelund, K.: Rule systems for run-time monitoring: from EAGLE to RULER. In: Sokolsky, O., Taşıran, S. (eds.) RV 2007. LNCS, vol. 4839, pp. 111–125. Springer, Heidelberg (2007)

8. Basin, D., Klaedtke, F., Müller, S.: Policy monitoring in first-order temporal logic. In: Touili, T., Cook, B., Jackson, P. (eds.) CAV 2010. LNCS, vol. 6174, pp. 1–18. Springer, Heidelberg (2010)

9. Basin, D.A., Klaedtke, F., Müller, S., Zalinescu, E.: Monitoring metric first-order temporal properties. J. ACM **62**(2), 15 (2015)

10. Bauer, A., Küster, J.-C., Vegliach, G.: From propositional to first-order monitoring. In: Legay, A., Bensalem, S. (eds.) RV 2013. LNCS, vol. 8174, pp. 59–75. Springer, Heidelberg (2013)

11. Bojańczyk, M., Lasota, S.: An extension of data automata that captures XPath. Logical Methods Comput. Sci. 8(1) (2012)

12. D'Angelo, B., Sankaranarayanan, S., Sánchez, C., Robinson, W., Finkbeiner, B., Sipma, H.B., Mehrotra, S., Manna, Z.: LOLA: runtime monitoring of synchronous systems. In: Proceedings of Temporal Representation and Reasoning 2005, pp. 166–174. IEEE Computer Society (2005)

13. Decker, N., Leucker, M., Thoma, D.: Monitoring modulo theories. Int. J. Softw. Tools Technol. Transfer 1–21 (2015)

14. Falcone, Y., Nickovic, D., Reger, G., Thoma, D.: Second international competition on runtime verification. In: Bartocci, E., et al. (eds.) RV 2015. LNCS, vol. 9333, pp. 405–422. Springer, Heidelberg (2015). doi:10.1007/978-3-319-23820-3_27

15. Havelund, K.: Rule-based runtime verification revisited. STTT **17**(2), 143–170 (2015)

16. Kaplan, H., Shafrir, N., Tarjan, R.E.: Union-find with deletions. In: Proceedings of Symposium on Discrete Algorithms 2002, pp. 19–28. ACM/SIAM (2002)

17. Meredith, P.O., Jin, D., Griffith, D., Chen, F., Rosu, G.: An overview of the MOP runtime verification framework. STTT **14**(3), 249–289 (2012)

18. Reger, G., Cruz, H.C., Rydeheard, D.: MARQ: monitoring at runtime with QEA. In: Baier, C., Tinelli, C. (eds.) TACAS 2015. LNCS, vol. 9035, pp. 596–610. Springer, Heidelberg (2015)

19. Rosu, G., Chen, F.: Semantics and algorithms for parametric monitoring. Logical Methods Comput. Sci. **8**(1), 1–47 (2012)

20. Stolz, V., Bodden, E.: Temporal assertions using AspectJ. Electr. Notes Theor. Comput. Sci. **144**(4), 109–124 (2006)

21. Vardi, M.Y.: An automata-theoretic approach to linear temporal logic. In: Moller, F., Birtwistle, G. (eds.) Logics for Concurrency. LNCS, vol. 1043, pp. 238–266. Springer, Heidelberg (1996)

# Competition on Software Verification: SV-COMP

# Reliable and Reproducible Competition Results with BenchExec and Witnesses (Report on SV-COMP 2016)

Dirk Beyer[✉]

University of Passau, Passau, Germany
dirk.beyer@sosy-lab.org

**Abstract.** The 5$^{\text{th}}$ Competition on Software Verification (SV-COMP 2016) continues the tradition of a thorough comparative evaluation of fully-automatic software verifiers. This report presents the results of the competition and includes a special section that describes how SV-COMP ensures that the experiments are reliably executed, precisely measured, and organized such that the results can be reproduced later. SV-COMP uses BENCHEXEC for controlling and measuring the verification runs, and requires violation witnesses in an exchangeable format, whenever a verifier reports that a property is violated. Each witness was validated by two independent and publicly-available witness validators. The tables report the state of the art in software verification in terms of effectiveness and efficiency. The competition used 6 661 verification tasks that each consisted of a C program and a property (reachability, memory safety, termination). SV-COMP 2016 had 35 participating verification systems (22 in 2015) from 16 countries.

## 1 Introduction

The annual Competition on Software Verification (SV-COMP)[1] is a continuous effort by the software-verification community. The effort consists of the following two parts: (1) The SV-COMP community defines and collects verification tasks that the researchers and developers of software verifiers find interesting and challenging; these verification problems should be used to evaluate the effectivity (soundness and completeness) and efficiency (performance) of modern verification tools. (2) The organizer of SV-COMP performs a systematic comparative evaluation of the relevant state-of-the-art tool implementations for automatic software verification with respect to effectiveness and efficiency; part of this is to define and explore standards for a reliable and reproducible execution of such a competition. This paper describes the rules, definitions, results, and other interesting facts about the execution of the competition experiments, in particular how to make the experiments reproducible. The main objectives that the community aims at by running yearly competitions are the following (taken from [5]):

---

[1] http://sv-comp.sosy-lab.org

© Springer-Verlag Berlin Heidelberg 2016
M. Chechik and J.-F. Raskin (Eds.): TACAS 2016, LNCS 9636, pp. 887–904, 2016.
DOI: 10.1007/978-3-662-49674-9_55

1. provide an overview of the state of the art in software-verification technology and increase visibility of the most recent software verifiers,
2. establish a repository of software-verification tasks that is publicly available for free use as standard benchmark suite for evaluating verification software,
3. establish standards that make it possible to compare different verification tools including a property language and formats for the results, and
4. accelerate the transfer of new verification technology to industrial practice.

There is consensus that (1) and (2) are already achieved, but need continuous improvement: the community of research groups and verifiers that participate in SV-COMP is increasing, and the set of verification tasks needs even more diversity, growing, and quality assurance. The repository and the issue tracker show that there was considerable effort spent on consolidating the verification tasks, in terms of consistency and quality. Regarding (3), the simple syntax of the property language works well for SV-COMP, while it would be great to increase the supported fragment of LTL. The standard witness language as a common, exchangeable format was a big step forward in terms of standardization. The requirement in SV-COMP that bug reports are counted only if the bug is reproducible, i.e., the witness can be re-played on a different machine with a different validation tool, makes it easier to understand problems. We received positive feedback in terms of Objective (4), but we cannot evaluate this here.

*Related Competitions.* SV-COMP is complemented by two other competitions in the field of software verification: RERS[2] and VerifyThis[3]. While SV-COMP performs reproducible experiments in a *controlled* environment (dedicated resources, resource limits), the RERS Challenges gives more room for exploring combinations of interactive with automatic approaches without limits on the resources, and the VerifyThis Competition focuses on evaluating approaches and ideas rather than on *fully-automatic* verification. The report on SV-COMP 2014 provides a more comprehensive list of other competitions [4].

## 2    Procedure

The procedure for the competition organization did not change in comparison to the past SV-COMP editions [2–5]. SV-COMP was again an open competition where all verification tasks were known before the submission of the participating verifiers, such that there were no surprises and developers were able to train the verifiers. In the *benchmark submission* phase, we collected and classified new verification tasks, in the *training* phase, the teams inspected verification tasks and trained their verifiers, and in the *evaluation* phase, verification runs were preformed with all competition candidates and the system descriptions were reviewed by the competition jury. As in the last years, the participants received the preliminary results of their verifier per e-mail for inspection, after which the results were publicly announced.

---

[2] http://rers-challenge.org
[3] http://etaps2015.verifythis.org

# 3   Definitions, Formats, and Rules

**Verification Task.** The definition of verification task was not changed (taken from [4]). A verification task consists of a C program and a property. A verification run is a non-interactive execution of a competition candidate on a single verification task, in order to check whether the following statement is correct: "The program satisfies the property." The result of a verification run is a triple (ANSWER, WITNESS, TIME). ANSWER is one of the following outcomes:

TRUE: The property is satisfied (i.e., no path that violates the property exists).
FALSE: The property is violated (i.e., there exists a path that violates the property) and a counterexample path is produced and reported as WITNESS.
UNKNOWN: The tool cannot decide the problem, or terminates abnormally, or exhausts the computing resources time or memory (i.e., the competition candidate does not succeed in computing an answer TRUE or FALSE).

The component WITNESS [6] was this year mandatory only for FALSE answers; in the future, witnesses are also required for TRUE answers. SV-COMP was supported by the two witness validators CPACHECKER and UAUTOMIZER. TIME is measured as consumed CPU time until the verifier terminates, including the consumed CPU time of all processes that the verifier started [8]. If the wall time was larger than the CPU time, then the TIME is set to the wall time. If TIME is equal to or larger than the time limit (15 min), then the verifier is terminated and the ANSWER is set to 'timeout' (and interpreted as UNKNOWN).

**Categories.** The collection of verification tasks, which represents the current interest and abilities of tools for software verification, is arranged into categories, according to the characteristics of the programs and the properties to be verified. The assignment was proposed and implemented by the competition chair, and approved by the competition jury.

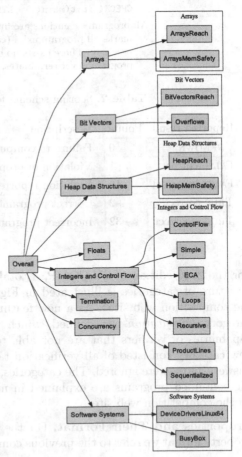

**Fig. 1.** Categories (generated by GRAPHVIZ)

**Table 1.** Properties used in the competition (cf. [5] for more details)

| Formula | Interpretation / Syntax of property |
|---|---|
| `G ! call(foo())` | A call to function `foo` is not reachable on any finite execution. `CHECK( init(main()), LTL(G ! call(__VERIFIER_error())) )` |
| `G valid-free` | All memory deallocations are valid (counterexample: invalid free). More precisely: There exists no finite execution of the program on which an invalid memory deallocation occurs. `CHECK( init(main()), LTL(G valid-free) )` |
| `G valid-deref` | All pointer dereferences are valid (counterexample: invalid dereference). More precisely: There exists no finite execution of the program on which an invalid pointer dereference occurs. `CHECK( init(main()), LTL(G valid-deref) )` |
| `G valid-memtrack` | All allocated memory is tracked, i.e., pointed to or deallocated counterexample: memory leak). More precisely: There exists no finite execution of the program on which the program lost track of some previously allocated memory. `CHECK( init(main()), LTL(G valid-memtrack) )` |
| `F end` | All program executions are finite and end on proposition `end`, which marks all program exits (counterexample: infinite loop). More precisely: There exists no execution of the program on which the program never terminates. `CHECK( init(main()), LTL(F end) )` |

**Table 2.** Scoring schema for SV-COMP 2016

| Reported result | Points | Description |
|---|---|---|
| UNKNOWN | 0 | Failure to compute verification result |
| FALSE correct | +1 | Violation of property in program was correctly found |
| FALSE incorrect | −16 | Violation reported but property holds (false alarm) |
| TRUE correct | +2 | Correct program reported to satisfy property |
| TRUE incorrect | −32 | Incorrect program reported as correct (wrong proof) |

For the 2016 edition of SV-COMP, a total of 10 categories were defined. The structure of categories is illustrated in Fig. 1 and described in more detail on the competition web site[4]. As a new feature of the competition, a new (meta) category *Falsification* was defined, which was meant to explore bug hunting capabilities of verifiers that are not able to construct correctness proofs. The new category consisted of all verification tasks with safety properties, and any answers TRUE were ignored. The categories, their defining category-set files, and the contained programs are explained in more detail under *Verification Tasks* on the competition web site.

**Properties and Their Format.** For the definition of the properties and the property format we refer to the previous competition report [5]. All specifications

---

[4] http://sv-comp.sosy-lab.org/2016/benchmarks.php

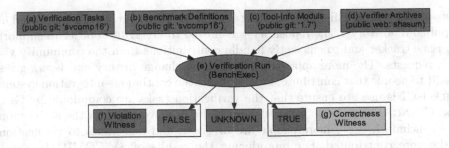

**Fig. 2.** Setup: components that support reproducibility are highlighted in green

are available as `.prp` files in the respective directories of the benchmark categories in the repository. Table 1 lists the properties and their syntax as overview.

**Evaluation by Scores and Run Time.** In order to reflect the steady progress towards completeness and soundness of verification tools, the scoring schema was again adjusted in order to increase the penalty for wrong results. Table 2 provides the overview. The ranking is decided based on the sum of points (normalized for meta categories) and for equal sum of points according to success run time, which is the total CPU time over all verification tasks for which the verifier reported a correct verification result. *Opt-out from Categories* and *Score Normalization for Meta Categories* was done as described previously [3] (page 597). The *Competition Jury* consists again of the chair and one member of each participating team. Team representatives of the jury are listed in Table 3.

## 4    Reproducibility

One of the main goals of SV-COMP is to make the competition as transparent and reproducible as possible. To achieve this goal, it is necessary to control as many as possible of the variables that might influence the results. Figure 2 gives an overview over the components that contribute to the reproducible setup of SV-COMP.

**BenchExec: Precise Controlling and Measurement of Resources (e).** For scientifically valid experiments, we require for each verification run a reliable assignment and controlling of computing resources (cores, memory, CPU time), and a precise measurement. There are several requirements that experiments of a competition such as SV-COMP have to fulfill [8]: (i) accurate measurement and reliable enforcement of limits for CPU time and memory, (ii) reliable termination of processes (including all child processes), and (iii) correct assignment of local memory (for NUMA architectures). We use BENCHEXEC[5] to perform all SV-COMP experiments, because this benchmarking framework lets us conveniently benefit from the modern resource control and measurement mechanisms that the Linux kernel offers.

---

[5] https://github.com/sosy-lab/benchexec

**Repository of Verification Tasks (a).** The verification tasks are organized in a public repository[6]. The repository was moved to GITHUB in order to support an issue tracker and to efficiently handle contributions from the community via pull requests. The more appropriate logging of change history and issues gives credit to people that contribute. Furthermore, the continuous-integration system TRAVISCI is used to ensure that the verification tasks are compilable by GCC and CLANG. The move to GITHUB also had a positive effect on the activity on the benchmark suite: more people are involved, and more fixes to verification tasks were contributed. For reproducing the results of SV-COMP, the exact versions of the verification tasks as used for SV-COMP 2016 are available via the PGP-signed tag 'svcomp16' in the git repository.

**Benchmark Definitions (b).** For executing verification runs, we need to know for each verifier, (i) which verification tasks need to be given to the verifier (derived from participation declaration) and (ii) which parameters need to be passed to the verifier (there are global parameters that are specified for all categories, and there are specific parameters such as the bit architecture and memory model). The benchmark definitions are XML files in the format that BENCHEXEC expects; they are collected in a specific repository for SV-COMP[7], in which the PGP-signed tag 'svcomp16' points to the exact versions that were used in SV-COMP 2016.

**Tool-Specific Information (c).** In order to successfully execute a verifier and correctly interpret its results, a tool-info module needs to be provided to BENCHEXEC. First, the command-line to properly invoke the verifier (including source and property file as well as the options) is assembled from the parts specified in the benchmark definition (b). Second, the (tool-specific) information that the verifier produces needs to be interpreted and translated into the uniform SV-COMP result (TRUE, FALSE(p), UNKNOWN). The tool-info modules that were used in SV-COMP 2016 are available in BENCHEXEC release 1.7.

**Verifier Archive (d).** The verifiers are provided in an archive containing a license (that permits academic use, use in SV-COMP, and reproducing the results) and all parts that are needed to execute the verifier (statically-linked executables, all components that are required in a certain version, or for which no standard Ubuntu package is available, are included). The verifiers and the above-mentioned components are provided on the systems-description page of the SV-COMP web site[8], together with the SHA1 hashes for verification of consistency.

**Violation Witnesses (f).** SV-COMP counts answers FALSE only if a valid witness according to an exchangeable, machine-readable format is part of the result triple as WITNESS. This means that each verification run must be followed by a validation run that checks if the witness adheres to the exchange format

---

[6] https://github.com/sosy-lab/sv-benchmarks
[7] https://github.com/sosy-lab/sv-comp
[8] http://sv-comp.sosy-lab.org/2016/systems.php

and can be reproduced. The time limit for a validation run was set to 10 % of the CPU time for a verification run, i.e., the witness validation was limited to 90 s. The purpose of the tighter resource limit is to avoid delegating verification work to the validator. This ensures a high quality of assignment of scores: if a verifier claims a found bug but is not able to provide a witness, then no score is assigned. The witness format and the validation process is explained on the web page[9]. More details on witness validation is given in a related research article [6].

**Correctness Witnesses (g).** Although SV-COMP requires since its second edition (2013) that each result must be accompanied by a witness, this requirement was not enforced for the answer TRUE, mainly due to the lack of validators for correctness witnesses. This year, there was a demonstration category on validation of correctness witnesses, with the purpose to get prepared for witness validation for correctness results in the future.

# 5    Results and Discussion

For the fifth time, the competition experiments represent the state of the art in fully-automatic and publicly-available software-verification tools. The report shows the improvements of the last year, in terms of effectiveness (number of verification tasks that can be solved, correctness of the results, as accumulated in the score) and efficiency (resource consumption in terms of CPU time). The results that are presented in this article were approved by the participating teams.

**Participating Verifiers.** Table 3 provides an overview of the participating competition candidates and Table 4 lists the features and technologies that are used in the verification tools.

**Computing Resources.** The resource limits were the same as last year [5]: Each verification run was limited to 8 processing units (cores), 15 GB of memory, and 15 min of CPU time. The witness validation was limited to 2 processing units, 7 GB of memory, and 1.5 min of CPU time. The machines for running the experiments were different from last year, because we had to use 24 machines instead of eight. Each machine had two Intel Xeon E5-2650 v2 CPUs, with 16 processing units each, a frequency of 3.4 GHz, 135 GB of RAM, and a GNU/Linux operating system (x86_64-linux, Ubuntu 14.04 with Linux kernel 4.2). All verification runs were executed on a dedicated CPU, i.e., 8 processing units were assigned to the verification run, while the other 8 processing units were reserved and left idle.

One complete verification execution of the competition consisted of 313 benchmarks (each verifier on each selected category according to the opt-outs), summing up to 115 761 verification runs. Witness validation required 524 benchmarks (combinations of verifier, category with witness validation, and two validators) summing up to 50 249 validation runs. The consumed total CPU time for one competition run for verification only required a total of 319 days of CPU

---

[9] http://sv-comp.sosy-lab.org/2016/witnesses/

**Table 3.** Competition candidates with their system-description references and representing jury members

| Participant | Ref. | Jury member | Affiliation |
|---|---|---|---|
| 2LS | [31] | Peter Schrammel | U Oxford, UK |
| APROVE | [33] | Jera Hensel | RWTH Aachen, Germany |
| BLAST | [32] | Vadim Mutilin | ISPRAS, Russia |
| CASCADE | [35] | Wei Wang | New York U, USA |
| CBMC | [22] | Michael Tautschnig | Queen Mary U London, UK |
| CEAGLE | | Dexi Wang | Tsinghua U, China |
| CEAGLE-ABSREF | | Guang Chen | Tsinghua U, China |
| CIVL | [36] | Stephen Siegel | U Delaware, USA |
| CPA-BAM | [14] | Karlheinz Friedberger | U Passau, Germany |
| CPA-KIND | [7] | Matthias Dangl | U Passau, Germany |
| CPA-REFSEL | [9] | Stefan Löwe | U Passau, Germany |
| CPA-SEQ | [12] | — | U Passau, Germany |
| DIVINE | [37] | Vladimír Štill | Masaryk U, Czech Republic |
| ESBMC | [24] | Mikhail Ramalho | U Southampton, UK |
| ESBMC+DEPTHK | [28] | Lucas Cordeiro | Federal U Amazonas, Brazil |
| FOREST | [13] | Pablo Sanchez | U Cantabria, Spain |
| FORESTER | [18] | Ondřej Lengál | Brno UT, Czech Republic |
| HIPREC | [23] | Quang Loc Le | National U, Singapore |
| IMPARA | | Björn Wachter | U Oxford, UK |
| LAZY-CSEQ | [19] | Omar Inverso | Gran Sasso Sc. Inst., Italy |
| LCTD | [30] | Keijo Heljanko | Aalto U, Finland |
| LPI | [20] | George Karpenkov | VERIMAG, France |
| MAP2CHECK | [29] | Herbert Rocha | Federal U Roraima, Brazil |
| MU-CSEQ | [34] | Gennaro Parlato | U Southampton, UK |
| PAC-MAN | [11] | Ming-Hsien Tsai | Academia Sinica, Taiwan |
| PREDATORHP | [21] | Tomas Vojnar | Brno UT, Czech Republic |
| SEAHORN | [15] | Jorge Navas | NASA Ames, USA |
| SKINK | | Franck Cassez | Macquarie U, Australia |
| SMACK+CORRAL | [27] | Zvonimir Rakamaric | U Utah, USA |
| SYMBIOTIC | [10] | Jan Strejček | Masaryk U, Czech Republic |
| SYMDIVINE | [1] | Jiří Barnat | Masaryk U, Czech Republic |
| UAUTOMIZER | [17] | Matthias Heizmann | U Freiburg, Germany |
| UKOJAK | [26] | Daniel Dietsch | U Freiburg, Germany |
| UL-CSEQ | [25] | Bernd Fischer | Stellenbosch U, ZA |
| VVT | [16] | Alfons Laarman | TU Vienna, Austria |

**Table 4.** Technologies and features that the verification tools offer

| Verifier | CEGAR | Predicate Abstraction | Symbolic Execution | Bounded Model Checking | k-Induction | Property-Directed Reach. | Explicit-Value Analysis | Numeric. Interval Analysis | Shape Analysis | Separation Logic | Bit-Precise Analysis | ARG-Based Analysis | Lazy Abstraction | Interpolation | Automata-Based Analysis | Concurrency Support | Ranking Functions |
|---|---|---|---|---|---|---|---|---|---|---|---|---|---|---|---|---|---|
| 2LS | | | ✓ | ✓ | | | | | | | ✓ | | | | | | |
| APROVE | | | ✓ | | | | ✓ | ✓ | | | ✓ | | | | | | ✓ |
| BLAST | ✓ | ✓ | | | | | ✓ | | | | | ✓ | ✓ | ✓ | | | |
| CASCADE | | | ✓ | ✓ | | | | | | | ✓ | | | | | | |
| CBMC | | | | ✓ | ✓ | | | | | | ✓ | | | | | ✓ | |
| CEAGLE | | | ✓ | | | | | | | | ✓ | | | | | | |
| CEAGLE-ABSREF | ✓ | ✓ | ✓ | | | | | | | | ✓ | | ✓ | ✓ | | | |
| CIVL | | | ✓ | ✓ | | | ✓ | | | | | | | | | ✓ | |
| CPA-BAM | ✓ | ✓ | | | | | ✓ | | | | ✓ | ✓ | ✓ | ✓ | | | |
| CPA-KIND | ✓ | ✓ | | ✓ | ✓ | | ✓ | ✓ | | | ✓ | ✓ | ✓ | ✓ | | | |
| CPA-REFSEL | ✓ | ✓ | | | | | ✓ | | | | ✓ | ✓ | ✓ | ✓ | | | |
| CPA-SEQ | ✓ | ✓ | ✓ | ✓ | ✓ | | ✓ | ✓ | ✓ | | ✓ | ✓ | ✓ | ✓ | | ✓ | |
| DIVINE | | | | | | | ✓ | | | | ✓ | | | | ✓ | ✓ | |
| ESBMC | | | ✓ | | | | | | | | ✓ | | | | | ✓ | |
| ESBMC+DEPTHK | | | | ✓ | ✓ | | | | | | ✓ | | | | | | |
| FOREST | | | ✓ | ✓ | | | | | | | ✓ | | | | | | |
| FORESTER | ✓ | | | | | | | | ✓ | | | | | | ✓ | | |
| HIPREC | | | | | | | | | ✓ | ✓ | | | | | | | |
| IMPARA | | | ✓ | | | | ✓ | ✓ | | | ✓ | ✓ | ✓ | ✓ | | ✓ | |
| LAZY-CSEQ | | | | ✓ | | | | | | | ✓ | | | | | ✓ | |
| LCTD | ✓ | ✓ | | | | | | | | | | | | | | | |
| LPI | ✓ | | | | ✓ | | ✓ | | | | | | ✓ | ✓ | | | |
| MAP2CHECK | | | | ✓ | | | | | | | ✓ | | | | | | |
| MU-CSEQ | | | | ✓ | | | | | | | ✓ | | | | | ✓ | |
| PAC-MAN | | | ✓ | | | | | | | | | | | | ✓ | | |
| PREDATORHP | | | | | | | | | ✓ | | | | | | | | |
| SEAHORN | | | | ✓ | | ✓ | | ✓ | | | | ✓ | ✓ | ✓ | | | ✓ |
| SKINK | ✓ | | ✓ | | | | ✓ | | | | | | ✓ | ✓ | | | |
| SMACK+CORRAL | ✓ | | | ✓ | | ✓ | | | | | ✓ | | ✓ | | | ✓ | |
| SYMBIOTIC | | | ✓ | | | | | | | | | | | | | | |
| SYMDIVINE | | | ✓ | | | | ✓ | | | | ✓ | | | | ✓ | ✓ | |
| UAUTOMIZER | ✓ | ✓ | | | | | | | | | ✓ | | ✓ | ✓ | ✓ | | |
| UKOJAK | ✓ | ✓ | | | | | | | | | ✓ | | ✓ | ✓ | | | |
| UL-CSEQ | ✓ | ✓ | | | | | | | | | | ✓ | ✓ | ✓ | | ✓ | |
| VVT | ✓ | ✓ | | ✓ | | ✓ | ✓ | | | | | | | ✓ | | ✓ | |

**Table 5.** Quantitative overview over all results

| Verifier | Arrays 316 points max. 183 tasks | BitVectors 92 points max. 60 tasks | Heap 382 points max. 239 tasks | Floats 140 points max. 81 tasks | IntegersControlFlow 3629 points max. 2331 tasks | Termination 1129 points max. 631 tasks | Concurrency 1240 points max. 1016 tasks | DeviceDriversLinux64 3977 points max. 2120 tasks | FalsificationOverall 2371 points max. 6030 tasks | Overall 10855 points max. 6661 tasks |
|---|---|---|---|---|---|---|---|---|---|---|
| 2LS | | | | **136** | 1196 | | | | -2438 | -38205 |
| APROVE | | | | | | **909** | | | | |
| BLAST | | | | | -1653 | | | 2704 | | |
| CASCADE | | | 197 | | | | | | | |
| CBMC | 62 | 46 | 8 | **134** | -1239 | | 882 | 1972 | 391 | 3386 |
| CEAGLE | | | | **136** | | | | | | |
| CEAGLE-ABSREF | | | | 124 | | | | | | |
| CIVL | | | | | | | 1240 | | | |
| CPA-BAM | -57 | 28 | -80 | 42 | 1822 | 0 | 0 | 2550 | -1218 | 1939 |
| CPA-KIND | 3 | **77** | 161 | 76 | **2095** | 0 | 0 | 2350 | **707** | 4094 |
| CPA-REFSEL | | | | 35 | 1539 | 0 | 0 | **3177** | 36 | 2157 |
| CPA-SEQ | -61 | **87** | **234** | 75 | **2652** | 0 | 282 | 2801 | 496 | **4794** |
| DIVINE | | | | | | | 951 | | | |
| ESBMC | **190** | **84** | 163 | -15 | 1217 | 0 | 742 | 1688 | 248 | 4145 |
| ESBMC+DEPTHK | 62 | 47 | 58 | 7 | 1111 | 0 | 877 | 2009 | 495 | 3110 |
| FOREST | -970 | | -1263 | | | | -20613 | | | |
| FORESTER | | | 86 | | | | | | | |
| HIPREC | | | | | | | | | | |
| IMPARA | | -592 | | 132 | -1524 | | 42 | | | |
| LAZY-CSEQ | | | | | | | **1240** | | | |
| LCTD | | | | | | | | | | |
| LPI | | | | | 1804 | | | 2107 | | |
| MAP2CHECK | | | -121 | | | | | | | |
| MU-CSEQ | | | | | | | **1240** | | | |
| PAC-MAN | | | | | -449 | | | | | |
| PREDATORHP | | | **298** | | | | | | | |
| SEAHORN | -301 | -131 | -257 | 0 | 1572 | 504 | -24659 | 1694 | -4333 | -22393 |
| SKINK | | | | | 113 | | | | | |
| SMACK+CORRAL | **146** | 44 | 155 | 0 | **2013** | 0 | 999 | 2206 | **800** | 4223 |
| SYMBIOTIC | 101 | -2 | 105 | -18 | 633 | 0 | 0 | 980 | -370 | 1223 |
| SYMDIVINE | | | | | | | -135 | | | |
| UAUTOMIZER | 83 | 69 | 169 | 2 | 1865 | 895 | | 2686 | 823 | 4843 |
| UKOJAK | 60 | 19 | 31 | 0 | 1096 | | | 937 | 339 | 1407 |
| UL-CSEQ | | | | | | | 856 | | | |
| VVT | | | | | 421 | | 1029 | | | |

**Table 6.** Overview of the top-three verifiers for each category (CPU time in h, rounded to two significant digits)

| Rank | Verifier | Score | CPU Time | Solved Tasks | False Alarms | Wrong Proofs |
|------|----------|-------|----------|--------------|--------------|--------------|
| *Arrays* | | | | | | |
| 1 | ESBMC | **190** | 3.2 | 131 | 2 | |
| 2 | SMACK+CORRAL | 146 | 2.5 | 111 | | |
| 3 | SYMBIOTIC | 101 | .61 | 77 | | |
| *Bit Vectors* | | | | | | |
| 1 | CPA-SEQ | **87** | 1.1 | 55 | | |
| 2 | ESBMC | 84 | .61 | 51 | | |
| 3 | CPA-KIND | 77 | .67 | 47 | | |
| *Heap* | | | | | | |
| 1 | PREDATORHP | **298** | .31 | 211 | 2 | |
| 2 | CPA-SEQ | 234 | 1.1 | 188 | 4 | |
| 3 | CASCADE | 197 | 2.7 | 140 | 2 | |
| *Floats* | | | | | | |
| 1 | 2LS | **136** | .98 | 79 | | |
| 2 | CEAGLE | 136 | 1.0 | 77 | | |
| 3 | CBMC | 134 | 5.0 | 78 | | |
| *Integers Control Flow* | | | | | | |
| 1 | CPA-SEQ | **2652** | 35 | 1625 | 1 | |
| 2 | CPA-KIND | 2095 | 35 | 1278 | | |
| 3 | SMACK+CORRAL | 2013 | 97 | 978 | | 4 |
| *Termination* | | | | | | |
| 1 | APROVE | **909** | 4.8 | 500 | | |
| 2 | UAUTOMIZER | 895 | 3.2 | 503 | | |
| 3 | SEAHORN | 504 | .97 | 323 | | 2 |
| *Concurrency* | | | | | | |
| 1 | MU-CSEQ | **1240** | .93 | 1016 | | |
| 2 | LAZY-CSEQ | 1240 | 2.7 | 1016 | | |
| 3 | CIVL | 1240 | 7.8 | 1016 | | |
| *Device Drivers Linux64* | | | | | | |
| 1 | CPA-REFSEL | **3177** | 24 | 1646 | 2 | |
| 2 | CPA-SEQ | 2801 | 23 | 1458 | 4 | |
| 3 | BLAST | 2704 | 5.9 | 1547 | 13 | 5 |
| *Falsification Overall* | | | | | | |
| 1 | UAUTOMIZER | **823** | 7.0 | 381 | 1 | |
| 2 | SMACK+CORRAL | 800 | 17 | 1140 | 26 | |
| 3 | CPA-KIND | 707 | 14 | 479 | 2 | |
| *Overall* | | | | | | |
| 1 | UAUTOMIZER | **4843** | 44 | 3138 | 1 | 5 |
| 2 | CPA-SEQ | 4794 | 65 | 3535 | 16 | |
| 3 | SMACK+CORRAL | 4223 | 160 | 3464 | 26 | 9 |

time. Each tool was executed several times, in order to make sure no installation issues occur during the execution.

**Quantitative Results.** Table 5 presents the quantitative overview over all tools and all categories (HIPREC participated only in subcategory *Recursive* and LCTD only in subcategory *BitVectorsReach*). The format of the table is similar to those of previous SV-COMP editions [5], with the exception that due to the volume we now omit the CPU times. The tools are listed in alphabetical order; every table row lists the scores of one verifier for each category. We indicate the top-three candidates by formatting their scores in bold face and in larger font size. An empty table cell means that the verifier opted-out from the respective category. For the calculation of the score and for the ranking, the scoring schema in Table 2 was applied, the scores for the meta categories were computed using normalized scores as defined in the report for SV-COMP'13 [3]. There were two categories for which the winner was decided based on the run time: in category *Concurrency*, all top-three verifiers achieved the maximum score of 1240 points, but the run time differed considerably; in category *Floats* the first and second both achieved a score of 136 points. More information (including formatted interactive tables, quantile plots for every category, and also the raw data in XML format) is available on the competition web-site.[10]

Table 6 reports the top-three verifiers for each category. The run time (column 'CPU Time') refers to successfully solved verification tasks (column 'Solved Tasks'). The columns 'False Alarms' and 'Wrong Proofs' report the number of verification tasks for which the tool reported wrong results: reporting an error path but the property holds (incorrect FALSE) and claiming that the program fulfills the property although it actually contains a bug (incorrect TRUE), respectively.

**Discussion of Scoring Schema and Normalization.** The SV-COMP community considers it more difficult to compute correctness proofs compared to computing error paths (cf. Table 2: TRUE yields 2 points, FALSE yields 1 point) [2]. This has consequences on the final ranking: For example, APROVE won the category *Termination* although UAUTOMIZER solved more verification tasks: APROVE solved 500, UAUTOMIZER solved 503 verification tasks. Both verifiers did not report any wrong results in this category. So the higher score of APROVE (score: 909) is due to its ability to compute more proofs than UAUTOMIZER (score: 895), while UAUTOMIZER found more violations. APROVE computed 409 proofs and found 91 property violations, while UAUTOMIZER computed 392 proofs and found 111 property violations. So in this case, the scoring schema provides a good mapping from the community's intuition to the ranking.

A similar observation can be made on the score normalization. The community considers the value of solving a verification task in a large category (many verification tasks) less than the value of solving a verification task in a small category (only a few verification tasks) [3]. The values for

---

[10] http://sv-comp.sosy-lab.org/2016/results/

category *Overall* in Table 6 illustrate the purpose of the score normalization: CPA-SEQ solved 3 535 tasks, which is about 400 solved tasks more than the winner UAUTOMIZER could solve (3 138). So why did CPA-SEQ not win the category? Because UAUTOMIZER is better in the intuitive sense of 'overall': UAUTOMIZER solved tasks more diversely, the 'overall' value of the verification work is higher. Most prominently, UAUTOMIZER solved many tasks in category *Termination* which is not supported by CPA-SEQ. Similarly, in category *FalsificationOverall*, SMACK+CORRAL solved more tasks than UAUTOMIZER, but produced also a lot of false alarms and the tasks that SMACK+CORRAL solved were considered of less value (i.e., from large categories with many tasks). In these cases, the score normalization correctly maps the community's intuition.

**Score-Based Quantile Functions for Quality Assessment.** We use score-based quantile functions [3] because these visualizations make it easier to understand the results of the comparative evaluation. The competition web-site[10] includes such a plot for each category; as example, we illustrate the category *Overall* (all verification tasks) in Fig. 3 and discuss the results below. A total of 13 verifiers participated in category *Overall* (only 6 the year before), for which the quantile plot shows the overall performance over all categories (scores for meta categories are normalized [3]).

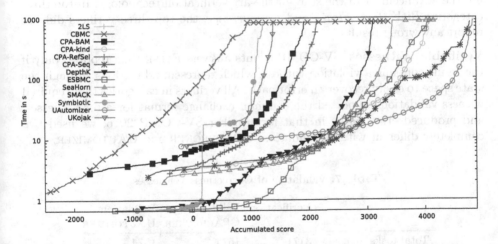

**Fig. 3.** Quantile functions for category *Overall*. Each quantile function illustrates the quantile ($x$-coordinate) of the scores obtained by correct verification runs below a certain run time ($y$-coordinate). More details are given in a previous report [3]. A logarithmic scale is used for the time range from 1 s to 1000 s, and a linear scale is used for the time range between 0 s and 1 s.

*Overall Quality Measured in Scores (Right End of Graph).* UAUTOMIZER is the winner of this category: the $x$-coordinate of the right-most data point represents the highest total score (and thus, the total value) of the completed verification work (cf. Table 6; right-most $x$-coordinates match the score values in the table).

*Amount of Incorrect Verification Work (Left End of Graph).* The left-most data points of the quantile functions represent the total negative score of a verifier ($x$-coordinate), i.e., the amount of incorrect and misleading verification work. Verifiers should start with a score close to zero; the winner UAUTOMIZER is very good in this aspect, together with the second place CPA-KIND (the two right-most columns of category *Overall* in Table 6 report the concrete numbers: only 1 and 16 false alarms, respectively, and 5 and 0 wrong proofs, for a total of 6 661 verification tasks).

*Characteristics of the Verification Tools.* Quantile plots also give hints on how a verification strategy works. For example, the horizontal lines show that some verifiers 'solve' a large quantity of verification tasks in the same run time, suggesting that an answer is given without the result being actually computed. A quick look at the wrapping execution scripts reveals that indeed a pre-mature answer is returned after 850s or 880s, respectively. This insight is one of the arguments for the community's goal to have each result supported by evidence, e.g., in the form of a verification witness.

**Robustness, Soundness, and Completeness.** Table 6 shows in the last two columns that the best verifiers of each category report a low number of wrong verification results (compared to the large number of verification tasks), indicating the advancement of the state-of-the-art verification technology. In the three categories *BitVectors*, *Floats*, and *Concurrency*, the top-three verifiers did not report any wrong results.

**Verifiable Witnesses.** SV-COMP counts answers FALSE (bug reports) only if the result contains a violation witness, which represents directions through the state space to easily recover an error path. All verifiers in categories that required witness validation supported the common exchange format for error witnesses, and produced error paths in that format. For SV-COMP 2016, we used two completely different witness validators: CPACHECKER and UAUTOMIZER.

**Table 7.** Validation of Correctness Witnesses

|  | Verification | Validation CPACHECKER | Validation UAUTOMIZER |
|---|---|---|---|
| Total tasks | 3171 | 1574 | 1574 |
| Results TRUE | 1574 | 1295 | 956 |
| Confirmed witnesses |  | 82 % | 61 % |

**Demonstration on Correctness Witnesses.** The validation of the results for answers TRUE was not yet considered, but is identified as the next open problem that the community should solve. As part of SV-COMP 2016, a demonstration category (i.e., without ranking and scores) was announced to explore the possibilities of validating correctness witnesses. Two teams participated, and the results are reported in Table 7. The table lists the results of a verification with CPACHECKER (k-induction-based configuration) and the validation results of the correctness witnesses using the validators CPACHECKER and UAUTOMIZER. The first row reports the total number of verification tasks that were given as input. The verification was performed on an SV-COMP subset of 3 171 verification tasks from the categories *IntegersControlFlow* and *DeviceDriversLinux64*. The second row reports that for 1 574 verification tasks the expected and computed verification result was TRUE. Those 1 574 verification tasks were given as input to the two validators, together with the correctness witness that the verification produced. CPACHECKER was able to validate (i.e., re-verify with the given invariants from the witness) 1 295 verification tasks (82 %) and UAUTOMIZER was able to validate 956 verification tasks (61 %). More information is given on the detailed table on the web page.[11]

# 6 Conclusion

SV-COMP 2016, the 5th edition of the Competition on Software Verification, attracted *35 participating teams* from 16 countries, which is so far the largest number of participants (2012: 10, 2013: 11, 2014: 15, 2015: 22). The repository of verification tasks was consolidated and the number of verification tasks was increased (from 5 803) to *6 661 verification tasks*. We used *verifiable witnesses* again to validate the bug reports, and the results FALSE were counted towards the score only if the witness was confirmed. The number of witness validators was increased from one to two, which contributed to the trust and neutrality of SV-COMP's evaluation. SV-COMP 2016 is the so-far broadest overview of the state of the art in software verification. The large jury and the organizer made sure that the competition follows the high quality standards of the TACAS conference, in particular with respect to the important principles of fairness, community support, and transparency. Technical accuracy was ensured by using the benchmarking framework BENCHEXEC.

# References

1. Bauch, P., Havel, V., Barnat, J.: LTL model checking of LLVM bitcode with symbolic data. In: Hliněný, P., Dvořák, Z., Jaroš, J., Kofroň, J., Kořenek, J., Matula, P., Pala, K. (eds.) MEMICS 2014. LNCS, vol. 8934, pp. 47–59. Springer, Heidelberg (2014)
2. Beyer, D.: Competition on software verification. In: Flanagan, C., König, B. (eds.) TACAS 2012. LNCS, vol. 7214, pp. 504–524. Springer, Heidelberg (2012). http://dx.doi.org/10.1007/978-3-642-28756-5_38
3. Beyer, D.: Second competition on software verification. In: Piterman, N., Smolka, S.A. (eds.) TACAS 2013 (ETAPS 2013). LNCS, vol. 7795, pp. 594–609. Springer, Heidelberg (2013). http://dx.doi.org/10.1007/978-3-642-36742-7_43

---

[11] http://sv-comp.sosy-lab.org/2016/witnesses/correctness-demo.html

4. Beyer, D.: Status report on software verification. In: Ábrahám, E., Havelund, K. (eds.) TACAS 2014 (ETAPS). LNCS, vol. 8413, pp. 373–388. Springer, Heidelberg (2014). http://dx.doi.org/10.1007/978-3-642-54862-8_25
5. Beyer, D.: Software verification and verifiable witnesses. In: Baier, C., Tinelli, C. (eds.) TACAS 2015. LNCS, vol. 9035, pp. 401–416. Springer, Heidelberg (2015). http://dx.doi.org/10.1007/978-3-662-46681-0_31
6. Beyer, D., Dangl, M., Dietsch, D., Heizmann, M., Stahlbauer, A.: Witness validation and stepwise testification across software verifiers. In: Proceedings of FSE, pp. 721–733. ACM (2015). http://dx.org/10.1145/2786805.2786867
7. Beyer, D., Dangl, M., Wendler, P.: Boosting k-induction with continuously-refined invariants. In: Kroening, D., Păsăreanu, C.S. (eds.) CAV 2015. LNCS, vol. 9206, pp. 622–640. Springer, Heidelberg (2015). http://dx.doi.org/10.1007/978-3-319-21690-4_42
8. Beyer, D., Löwe, S., Wendler, P.: Benchmarking and resource measurement. In: Fischer, B., Geldenhuys, J. (eds.) SPIN 2015. LNCS, vol. 9232, pp. 160–178. Springer, Heidelberg (2015). http://dx.doi.org/10.1007/978-3-319-23404-5_12
9. Beyer, D., Löwe, S., Wendler, P.: Refinement selection. In: Fischer, B., Geldenhuys, J. (eds.) SPIN 2015. LNCS, vol. 9232, pp. 20–38. Springer, Heidelberg (2015). http://dx.doi.org/10.1007/978-3-319-23404-5_3
10. Chalupa, M., Jonáš, M., Slaby, J., Strejček, J., Vitovská, M.: Symbiotic 3: New slicer and error-witness generation (competition contribution). In: Chechik, M., Raskin, J.-F. (eds.) TACAS 2016. LNCS, vol. 9636, pp. 946–949. Springer, Heidelberg (2016)
11. Chen, Y.-F., Hsieh, C., Lengál, O., Lii, T.-J., Tsai, M.-H., Wang, B.-Y., Wang, F.: Learning-based verification and model synthesis. In: Proceedings of ICSE (2016)
12. Dangl, M., Löwe, S., Wendler, P.: CPACHECKER with support for recursive programs and floating-point arithmetic. In: Baier, C., Tinelli, C. (eds.) TACAS 2015. LNCS, vol. 9035, pp. 423–425. Springer, Heidelberg (2015)
13. Gonzalez-de-Aledo, P., Sanchez, P.: FramewORk for embedded system verification (competition contribution). In: Baier, C., Tinelli, C. (eds.) TACAS 2015. LNCS, vol. 9035, pp. 429–431. Springer, Heidelberg (2015)
14. Friedberger, K.: CPA-BAM: Block-abstraction memoization with value analysis and predicate analysis (competition contribution). In: Chechik, M., Raskin, J.-F. (eds.) TACAS 2016. LNCS, vol. 9636, pp. 912–915. Springer, Heidelberg (2016)
15. Gurfinkel, A., Kahsai, T., Navas, J.A.: SeaHorn: a framework for verifying C programs (competition contribution). In: Baier, C., Tinelli, C. (eds.) TACAS 2015. LNCS, vol. 9035, pp. 447–450. Springer, Heidelberg (2015)
16. Günther, H., Laarman, A., Weissenbacher, G.: Vienna verification tool: IC3 for parallel software (competition contribution). In: Chechik, M., Raskin, J.-F. (eds.) TACAS 2016. LNCS, vol. 9636, pp. 954–957. Springer, Heidelberg (2016)
17. Heizmann, M., Dietsch, D., Greitschus, M., Leike, J., Musa, B., Schätzle, C., Podelski, A.: Ultimate automizer with two-track proofs (competition contribution). In: Chechik, M., Raskin, J.-F. (eds.) TACAS 2016. LNCS, vol. 9636, pp. 950–953. Springer, Heidelberg (2016)
18. Hruška, M., Holí, L., Lengál, O., Rogalewicz, A., Šimácek, J., Vojnar, T.: Run forester, run backwards! (competition contribution). In: Chechik, M., Raskin, J.-F. (eds.) TACAS 2016. LNCS, vol. 9636, pp. 923–926. Springer, Heidelberg (2016)
19. Inverso, O., Tomasco, E., Fischer, B., La Torre, S., Parlato, G.: Bounded model checking of multi-threaded C programs via lazy sequentialization. In: Biere, A., Bloem, R. (eds.) CAV 2014. LNCS, vol. 8559, pp. 585–602. Springer, Heidelberg (2014)

20. Karpenkov, E.G., Monniaux, D., Wendler, P.: Program analysis with local policy iteration. In: Jobstmann, B., et al. (eds.) VMCAI 2016. LNCS, vol. 9583, pp. 127–146. Springer, Heidelberg (2016). doi:10.1007/978-3-662-49122-5_6

21. Kotoun, M., Peringer, P., Šoková, V., Vojnar, T.: Optimized Predators and the SV-COMP heap and memory safety benchmark (competition contribution). In: Chechik, M., Raskin, J.-F. (eds.) TACAS 2016. LNCS, vol. 9636, pp. 942–945. Springer, Heidelberg (2016)

22. Kroening, D., Tautschnig, M.: CBMC – C bounded model checker (competition contribution). In: Ábrahám, E., Havelund, K. (eds.) TACAS 2014 (ETAPS). LNCS, vol. 8413, pp. 389–391. Springer, Heidelberg (2014)

23. Le, Q.L., Tran, M., Chin, W.-N.: HIPrec: Verifying recursive programs with a satisfiability solver. Technical report (2016)

24. Morse, J., Ramalho, M., Cordeiro, L., Nicole, D., Fischer, B.: ESBMC 1.22 (competition contribution). In: Ábrahám, E., Havelund, K. (eds.) TACAS 2014 (ETAPS). LNCS, vol. 8413, pp. 405–407. Springer, Heidelberg (2014)

25. Nguyen, T.L., Fischer, B., La Torre, S., Parlato, G.: Unbounded lazy-CSeq: a lazy sequentialization tool for C programs with unbounded context switches (competition contribution). In: Baier, C., Tinelli, C. (eds.) TACAS 2015. LNCS, vol. 9035, pp. 461–463. Springer, Heidelberg (2015)

26. Nutz, A., Dietsch, D., Mohamed, M.M., Podelski, A.: ULTIMATE KOJAK with memory safety checks (competition contribution). In: Baier, C., Tinelli, C. (eds.) TACAS 2015. LNCS, vol. 9035, pp. 458–460. Springer, Heidelberg (2015)

27. Rakamarić, Z., Emmi, M.: SMACK: decoupling source language details from verifier implementations. In: Biere, A., Bloem, R. (eds.) CAV 2014. LNCS, vol. 8559, pp. 106–113. Springer, Heidelberg (2014)

28. Rocha, H., Ismail, H.I., Cordeiro, L.C., Barreto, R.S.: Model checking embedded C software using k-induction and invariants. In: Proceedings of SBESC. IEEE (2015)

29. Rocha, H.O., Barreto, R., Cordeiro, L.: Hunting memory bugs in c programs with Map2Check (competition contribution). In: Chechik, M., Raskin, J.-F. (eds.) TACAS 2016. LNCS, vol. 9636, pp. 934–937. Springer, Heidelberg (2016)

30. Saarikivi, O., Heljanko, K.: LCTD: Tests-guided proofs for C programs on LLVM (competition contribution). In: Chechik, M., Raskin, J.-F. (eds.) TACAS 2016. LNCS, vol. 9636, pp. 927–929. Springer, Heidelberg (2016)

31. Schrammel, P., Kröning, D.: 2LS for program analysis (competition contribution). In: Chechik, M., Raskin, J.-F. (eds.) TACAS 2016. LNCS, vol. 9636, pp. 905–907. Springer, Heidelberg (2016)

32. Shved, P., Mandrykin, M., Mutilin, V.: Predicate analysis with BLAST 2.7 (competition contribution). In: Flanagan, C., König, B. (eds.) TACAS 2012. LNCS, vol. 7214, pp. 525–527. Springer, Heidelberg (2012)

33. Ströder, T., Aschermann, C., Frohn, F., Hensel, J., Giesl, J.: AProVE: termination and memory safety of C programs (competition contribution). In: Baier, C., Tinelli, C. (eds.) TACAS 2015. LNCS, vol. 9035, pp. 417–419. Springer, Heidelberg (2015)

34. Tomasco, E., Lam, T.N., Inverso, O., Fischer, B., Torre, S.L., Parlato, G.: MU-CSeq 0.4: Individual memory location unwindings (competition contribution). In: Chechik, M., Raskin, J.-F. (eds.) TACAS 2016. LNCS, vol. 9636, pp. 938–941. Springer, Heidelberg (2016)

35. Wang, W., Barrett, C.: Cascade. In: Baier, C., Tinelli, C. (eds.) TACAS 2015. LNCS, vol. 9035, pp. 420–422. Springer (competition contribution), Heidelberg (2015)

36. Zheng, M., Edenhofner, J.G., Luo, Z., Gerrard, M.J., Dwyer, M.B., Siegel, S.F.: CIVL: applying a general concurrency verification framework to C/Pthreads programs (competition contribution). In: Chechik, M., Raskin, J.-F. (eds.) TACAS 2016. LNCS, vol. 9636, pp. 908–911. Springer, Heidelberg (2016)
37. Štill, V., Ročkai, P., Barnat, J.: DIVINE: Explicit-state LTL model checker (competition contribution). In: Chechik, M., Raskin, J.-F. (eds.) TACAS 2016. LNCS, vol. 9636, pp. 920–922. Springer, Heidelberg (2016)

# 2LS for Program Analysis
## (Competition Contribution)

Peter Schrammel[✉] and Daniel Kroening

University of Oxford, Oxford, UK
peter.schrammel@cs.ox.ac.uk

**Abstract.** 2LS is a program analysis tool for C programs built upon the CPROVER infrastructure. 2LS is bit-precise and it can verify and refute program assertions. 2LS implements invariant generation techniques, incremental bounded model checking and incremental $k$-induction. The competition submission uses an algorithm combining all three techniques, called $k$I$k$I ($k$-invariants and $k$-induction). As a back end, the competition submission of 2LS uses Glucose 4.0.

## 1 Overview

2LS is a static analysis and verification tool for C programs that can perform interprocedural abstract interpretation, verification and refutation of assertions and termination analysis [3]. The competition version is configured for monolithic verification and refutation of assertions using an algorithm called $k$I$k$I ($k$-invariants and $k$-induction) [2], which elegantly combines bounded model checking, $k$-induction and invariant generation. The algorithm discharges these analyses to a sequence of incremental calls to a SAT or an SMT solver.

## 2 Architecture

2LS performs the following main steps, which are outlined in Fig. 1, and are explained below.

*Front end.* The *command-line front end* first configures 2LS according to user-supplied parameters, such as the bit-width. The *C parser* utilises an off-the-shelf C preprocessor (such as `gcc -E`) and builds a parse tree from the preprocessed source. Source file and line information is maintained in annotations. Being built upon the CPROVER infrastructure [4], 2LS uses *GOTO programs* as an intermediate representation. In this language, all non-linear control flow, such as if or switch-statements, loops and jumps, is translated to equivalent *guarded goto* statements. Similar to CBMC, 2LS performs a light-weight static analysis to resolve function pointers to a case split over all candidate functions, resulting in a static call graph. Furthermore, assertions guarding against invalid pointer operations or memory leaks are inserted.

© Springer-Verlag Berlin Heidelberg 2016
M. Chechik and J.-F. Raskin (Eds.): TACAS 2016, LNCS 9636, pp. 905–907, 2016.
DOI: 10.1007/978-3-662-49674-9_56

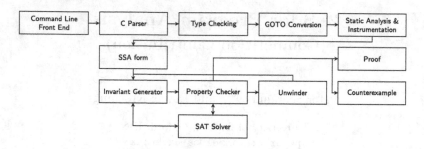

**Fig. 1.** 2LS architecture (using $k$I$k$I)

*Middle end.* 2LS performs a static analysis to derive the data flow equations for each function of the GOTO program. The result is a static single assignment (SSA) form in which loops have been cut at the back edges to the loop head. The effect of these cuts is a havocking of the variables modified in the loop at the loop head. This SSA is hence an over-approximation of the GOTO program. Subsequently, 2LS refines this over-approximation by computing invariants. 2LS performs local constant propagation and expression simplification to increase efficiency.

*Back end.* 2LS requires incremental back end solvers. Since support for incremental solving in SMT solvers is still lagging behind in comparison to SAT solvers, we use Glucose 4.0[1]. Consequently, as in CBMC, the SSA equation is translated into a CNF formula by bit-precise modelling of all expressions plus the Boolean guards. This formula is incrementally extended to perform invariant generation using template-based synthesis (see [2]; the competition version simply uses interval templates over numerical variables), to add further loop unwindings, and to the assertions for property checks. All this happens using a single solver instance so that information learned by the solver is never discarded. If a property check is satisfiable and model computed by the SAT solver does not take a path through an invariant (where over-approximation is used), then it corresponds to a path violating at least one of the assertions in the program under scrutiny. Subsequently, the model is translated back to a sequence of assignments to provide a human-readable counterexample. Conversely, if the property check is unsatisfiable, we have proven the assertions.

## 3  Strengths and Weaknesses

$k$I$k$I can provide both proofs as well as refutations using bit-precise algorithms. Refutations are essentially obtained via loop unwinding, whereas proofs are achieved by invariant generation as well as $k$-induction. This combination is quite powerful – 2LS won the gold medal in the Floats category, and is ranked

---

[1] http://www.labri.fr/perso/lsimon/glucose/#glucose-4.0.

2nd for the Loops benchmarks [1]. However, some benchmarks, e.g. those requiring reasoning about arrays contents or linked data structures, demand stronger invariants than we are currently able to infer. The monolithic analysis of the competition version does not support recursion, and there are limitations regarding irreducible control flow. Moreover, we observed issues with the counterexample witness GraphML output.

## 4   Tool Setup

The competition submission is based on 2LS version 0.3.[2] The full source code of the competition version is available at

http://www.cprover.org/svn/deltacheck/releases/2ls-0.3-sv-comp-2016.

Installation instructions are given in the file COMPILING. The executable 2ls is in the directory src/summarizer. The competition version must be given the options --k-induction and --competition-mode. For all categories with a 32-bit memory model, use --32; for those with a 64-bit memory, use --64. There is no distinction between simple and precise memory model. In order to write the counterexample to file CEX.graphml add the option --graphml-cex CEX.graphml.[3]

*Participation / Opt Out.* 2LS competes in the following categories: Bit Vectors - BitVectorsReach, Floats, Integers and Control Flow, Overall, and Falsification.

## 5   Software Project

2LS is maintained by Peter Schrammel with patches supplied by the community. It is publicly available under a BSD-style license. The source code is available at http://www.cprover.org/2LS.

## References

1. Beyer, D.: Reliable and reproducible competition results with benchexec and witnesses (report on sv-comp 2016). In: Chechik, M., Raskin, J.-F. (eds.) TACAS2016. LNCS, vol. 9636, pp. xx–yy. Springer, Heidelberg (2016)
2. Brain, M., Joshi, S., Kroening, D., Schrammel, P.: Safety verification and refutation by *k*-invariants and *k*-induction. In: Blazy, S., Jensen, T. (eds.) SAS 2015. LNCS, vol. 9291, pp. 145–161. Springer, Heidelberg (2015)
3. Chen, H.Y., David, C., Kroening, D., Schrammel, P., Wachter, B.: Synthesising interprocedural bit-precise termination proofs. In: Automated Software Engineering (ASE). ACM (2015)
4. Clarke, E., Kroning, D., Lerda, F.: A tool for checking ANSI-C programs. In: Jensen, K., Podelski, A. (eds.) TACAS 2004. LNCS, vol. 2988, pp. 168–176. Springer, Heidelberg (2004)

---

[2] All relevant information for reproducing the results (including an archive containing the executable) can be found at http://sv-comp.sosy-lab.org/2016/systems.php.

[3] See BenchExec wrapper script two_ls.py and the benchmark definition file 2ls.xml.

# CIVL: Applying a General Concurrency Verification Framework to C/Pthreads Programs (Competition Contribution)

Manchun Zheng[1]([envelope]), John G. Edenhofner[1], Ziqing Luo[1], Mitchell J. Gerrard[2], Michael S. Rogers[2], Matthew B. Dwyer[2], and Stephen F. Siegel[1]

[1] Department of Computer and Information Sciences, University of Delaware, Newark, USA
{zmanchun,johneden,ziqing,siege}@udel.edu
[2] Department of Computer Science and Engineering, University of Nebraska, Lincoln, USA
{mgerrard,mrogers,dwyer}@cse.unl.edu

**Abstract.** CIVL is a framework for the analysis and verification of concurrent programs. The front-end translates C programs that use (subsets of) Pthreads, MPI, OpenMP, or CUDA—alone or in combination—to an intermediate verification language CIVL-C. The back-end uses symbolic execution and model checking techniques to verify a number of safety properties of a CIVL-C program, such as absence of assertion violations, deadlocks, or out-of-bound indexes. We submit CIVL for verifying Pthreads programs in the concurrency category.

## 1 Verification Approach

CIVL [8] is a framework for verifying parallel programs written using various concurrency libraries or language extensions such as MPI [3], POSIX threads ("Pthreads") [2], OpenMP [6], and CUDA [5]. (Significant subsets of each of these concurrency "dialects" is supported; CUDA support excludes C++ features.) CIVL compiles programs to the CIVL-C modeling language, which extends sequential C11 with concurrency and verification primitives and linguistic features, such as nested functions and scoped memory. For each dialect, an AST "transformer" and libraries are used to express the original program as an equivalent CIVL-C program. Different transformers can work together to convert programs using multiple dialects into CIVL-C. [1]

CIVL uses a combination of explicit model checking and symbolic execution for verification. Model checking is used to explore the thread and process interleavings introduced by a concurrency model. CIVL uses state-of-the-art partial order reduction to mitigate the state space explosion problem. Symbolic execution further reduces the state space by collapsing sets of equivalent values along

---

[1] Funding for the CIVL project is provided by the U.S. National Science Foundation under awards CCF-1319571, CCF-1346769 and CCF-0953210.

© Springer-Verlag Berlin Heidelberg 2016
M. Chechik and J.-F. Raskin (Eds.): TACAS 2016, LNCS 9636, pp. 908–911, 2016.
DOI: 10.1007/978-3-662-49674-9_57

program executions. CIVL makes use of the Symbolic Analysis and Reasoning Library (SARL) [7] which is a package for normalizing, caching, and determining validity queries over logical formulae. SARL can leverage multiple Satisfiability Modulo Theories (SMT) solvers, but in general more than 99.5 % of the queries generated in a verification run are solved within SARL and do not require invocation of an SMT solver [8].

## 2   Software Architecture

The CIVL framework (Fig. 1) is distributed as open source software under the GNU General Public License and consists of several components. ABC is a C11 front-end which generates Abstract Syntax Trees (AST) from CIVL-C programs. The CIVL back-end builds a state-transition model based on the AST, then uses GMC (Generic Model Checker) and SARL to perform model checking and to manipulate symbolic state encodings to compute next states. For the competition, two theorem provers are used: CVC4 [1] and Z3 [4].

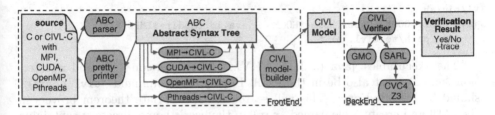

**Fig. 1.** The CIVL project architecture

CIVL is implemented in Java 7. It comes equipped with pre-built libraries to model system functions and concurrent data structures to support a variety of process and thread-level concurrency models. These libraries allow new concurrency dialects to be supported directly in the CIVL-C language, which reduces the cost of extending CIVL.

## 3   Strengths and Weaknesses

The most significant strength of CIVL is its ability to verify programs that use a variety of concurrency dialects, including "hybrid" programs that use multiple dialects, such as MPI+Pthreads. CIVL also checks a large number of generic properties, including absence of divisions by zero, reads of uninitialized variables, and out-of-bound array indexing. In fact CIVL found defects of each of these kinds in the SV-COMP suite; these defects were subsequently corrected. Additional properties include absence of memory leaks and illegal pointer dereferences, and dialect-specific properties, such as absence of "potential deadlocks" in MPI programs. In addition, CIVL can verify the functional equivalence of two versions of a C program with one or multiple of the four concurrency dialects, such as a trusted sequential version and a more complicated parallel one.

The CIVL back-end (verifier) suffers from the state explosion problem, and scalability can become an issue for programs that access shared variables frequently or have many nondeterministic choices. For the competition, small bounds were placed on the number of live threads (6). A "downscaling" transformation is performed that replaces array lengths above a certain threshold (11) with a small number (3); a similar transformation is applied to the upper bounds in for loops. These are unsound transformations, but nevertheless allowed CIVL to obtain the expected result for all of the examples in the concurrency category.

## 4    Setup and Configuration

CIVL v1.5 (available at http://vsl.cis.udel.edu/civl/svcomp16) is used for SVCOMP 2016. CIVL is distributed as a single jar file, which can be placed in any readable directory. Then an executable file named civl should be created and placed in the PATH; this file has the form

```
#!/bin/sh
java -Xmx15000M -Duser.home=$HOME -Djava.io.tmpdir=$TMPDIR \
  -jar /path/to/civl.jar $@
```

The executables java (a Java $\geq 7$ VM), cvc4 (version 1.4), and z3 (version $\geq 4.3.2$) must also be in the PATH. Finally, the command "civl config" should be executed once. This will search for appropriate theorem provers in the PATH and create a file named .sarl in the user's home directory containing information about each. The entries for CVC4 and Z3 should appear in that file.

CIVL is submitted for the concurrency category of the competition. The option -svcomp16 is used, which bundles the type and process bounds described above. The command for the competition is civl verify -svcomp16 source.i, where source.i is the file name of a target program. The wrapper script civl.py can be used to interpret verification results.

## References

1. Barrett, C., Conway, C.L., Deters, M., Hadarean, L., Jovanović, D., King, T., Reynolds, A., Tinelli, C.: CVC4. In: Gopalakrishnan, G., Qadeer, S. (eds.) CAV 2011. LNCS, vol. 6806, pp. 171–177. Springer, Heidelberg (2011)
2. IEEE: Portable Operating System Interface (POSIX) Base Specifications, IEEE Std 1003.1-2008, 2013 ed (2013). http://www.unix.org/version4/
3. Message-Passing Interface Forum: MPI: A Message-Passing Interface standard, version 3.0. http://www.mpi-forum.org/docs/docs.html
4. de Moura, L., Bjørner, N.S.: Z3: an efficient SMT solver. In: Ramakrishnan, C.R., Rehof, J. (eds.) TACAS 2008. LNCS, vol. 4963, pp. 337–340. Springer, Heidelberg (2008)
5. NVIDIA: CUDA C Programming Guide Version 7.5. http://docs.nvidia.com/cuda/cuda-c-programming-guide/. Accessed 31 Oct 2015

6. OpenMP Architecture Review Board: OpenMP API Specification for Parallel Programming. http://openmp.org/wp/. Accessed 8 Feb 2015
7. SARL: The Symbolic Algebra and Reasoning Library. http://vsl.cis.udel.edu/sarl. Accessed 6 Feb 2015
8. Siegel, S.F., Zheng, M., Luo, Z., Zirkel, T.K., Marianiello, A.V., Edenhofner, J.G., Dwyer, M.B., Rogers, M.S.: CIVL: the concurrency intermediate verification language. In: SC15 (2015). http://doi.acm.org/10.1145/2807591.2807635

# CPA-BAM: Block-Abstraction Memoization with Value Analysis and Predicate Analysis
## (Competition Contribution)

Karlheinz Friedberger

University of Passau, Passau, Germany
friedber@fim.uni-passau.de

**Abstract.** The software verification framework CPACHECKER is built
on basic approaches like CPA and CEGAR. The configuration for the
SV-COMP'16 uses the concept of block-abstraction memoization and
combines it with the parallel execution of value analysis and predicate
analysis. The CEGAR loop uses a refinement strategy that prefers to
refine the precision of the lightweight value analysis, such that the precision of the predicate analysis remains abstract and concise as long as
possible. The usage of mature analyses like value analysis and predicate
analysis allows us to bring together the potential of lazy abstraction and
interpolation and the benefits of block-abstraction memoization.

## 1 Software Architecture

CPACHECKER is a software verification framework that is build on CONFIG-
URABLE PROGRAM ANALYSIS (CPA) [1] and allows developers to easily integrate new analyses in a predefined way. CPAs are available for distinct tasks like
tracking program locations, call stacks, function pointers, and assignments to
variables. Also well-known approaches like value analysis and predicate analysis are integrated in CPACHECKER in this manner. CPAs can be combined to
form a more complex program analysis. The framework can execute a (configurable) algorithm like the CEGAR algorithm or a sequence of algorithms to
verify reachability properties. There are analyses that support checking memory-
safety properties and overflow detection, but this contribution does not use them.

CPACHECKER is written in JAVA and uses the C-parser of the Eclipse CDT
project (https://eclipse.org/cdt/). There are bindings for external libraries that
allow to use BDDs, octagons, and SMT formulas. The predicate analysis in our
configuration uses the SMT solver MathSAT5 (http://mathsat.fbk.eu/), because
it supports bit-precise reasoning and interpolation for SMT formulae.

## 2 Verification Approach

Our configuration uses block-abstraction memoization (BAM) [4] to speedup the
analysis. BAM divides the program into blocks and analyzes them separately.

© Springer-Verlag Berlin Heidelberg 2016
M. Chechik and J.-F. Raskin (Eds.): TACAS 2016, LNCS 9636, pp. 912–915, 2016.
DOI: 10.1007/978-3-662-49674-9_58

We choose functions as block size, such that a function call corresponds with a block entry and a function exit refers to a block exit, respectively. BAM aims for a modular analysis, i.e. if a block has been already analyzed, the re-analysis of this block uses the stored result from a cache.

In SV-COMP'12, BAM was used with predicate analysis [3], and in SVCOMP'15, value analysis and predicate analysis were combined in a sequential way [2]. With several improvements and extensions done in the last year, we are now able to combine BAM not only with predicate analysis, but also with value analysis, interval analysis, and combinations thereof. We have defined and implemented the operators of BAM for the corresponding domains. For this year's SV-COMP, value analysis and predicate analysis are executed in a parallel manner to leverage the advantages of both approaches within the analysis with BAM.

BAM itself does not track any assignments or predicates over variables, but delegates this task to other more precise analyses. In our submission, the value analysis tracks assignments of variables and the predicate analysis uses predicates to analyze the program. Each of these two analyses is implemented as a CPA and uses a precision that determines which facts (assignments or predicates) are important for reasoning over the program, for example, for the reachability of a property violation. Figure 1 shows the CEGAR loop that updates the precisions during the refinements of the corresponding analysis. In CPACHECKER, a reachability analysis uses the configured CPAs to examine the program until either a counterexample is reached or the program is analyzed completely. The second case refers to a program without any property violation. In the first case however, if the reachability analysis finds a counterexample, we check it for feasibility with both analyses in sequence. For a spurious counterexample one of the analyses should find the cause and perform the refinement, i.e. updating the corresponding precision. As the value analysis is more efficient in tracking many assignments, the counterexample is first checked with this analysis. As soon as one of the analyses cannot confirm the counterexample, the precision of this analysis is refined in order to exclude the spurious counterexample in the next iteration of the CEGAR loop. If both analyses confirm the counterexample, we report an error witness.

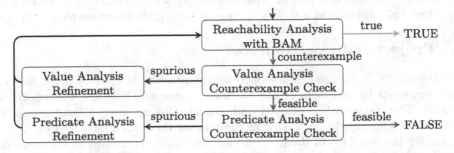

**Fig. 1.** Refinement for value analysis and predicate analysis in the CEGAR loop

Recursive tasks are analyzed by an extension of BAM that was already used in SV-COMP'15. However, last year's contribution is improved by using the parallel combination of value analysis and predicate analysis in the way described above. Additionally, if no cached block abstraction can be reused before unrolling the recursive function up to a depth of 30, we abort the analysis of any deeper recursion. This bound is sufficient for the currently available recursive tasks.

## 3   Strengths and Weaknesses

The contributed configuration of BAM is most effective for solving large programs consisting of many functions, such that the benefit of using a cache justifies the overhead of BAM itself, i.e. the reuse of block abstractions outperforms the application of special operators in BAM. We report only a few wrong results for all tasks and none of them is a wrong proof. As our approach in CPACHECKER uses its available analyses, some weaknesses are inherited. For example, value analysis and predicate analysis do not support large arrays or complex data structures. Our configuration does not check for memory-safety properties, termination or overflows, but simply ignores those cases and reports UNKNOWN.

## 4   Setup and Configuration

The CPACHECKER project is available at http://cpachecker.sosy-lab.org and needs a Java 7 runtime environment. We submit version 1.4-svcomp16c for participation in all categories. The tool can be downloaded from http://cpachecker.sosy-lab.org/CPAchecker-1.4-svcomp16c-unix.tar.bz2.
CPACHECKER has to be executed with the following command line:

```
scripts/cpa.sh -sv-comp16-bam -disable-java-assertions -heap 10000m -spec prop.prp program.i
```

The parameter -64 should be added for C programs in categories assuming a 64-bit environment. CPACHECKER will report the result of the verification to the console, including the violated property and the name of the output directory. In case of finding a property violation, the witness is written to the file witness.graphml within the output directory. CPACHECKER can be executed using the tool-info module cpachecker.py and the benchmark definition cpa-bam.xml available at http://sv-comp.sosy-lab.org/2016/systems.php.

## 5   Project and Contributors

CPACHECKER is licensed as an open-source project, headed by Dirk Beyer, and developed by members of the Software Systems Lab at the University of Passau. The framework is utilized and extended by an international group of developers. Our thanks go to all contributors for their work on CPACHECKER, especially the members of the Institute for System Programming of the Russian Academy of Sciences for reporting several bugs in our implementation of block-abstraction memoization. More information about CPACHECKER is provided at http://cpachecker.sosy-lab.org, where also a list of all contributors is available.

# References

1. Beyer, D., Henzinger, T.A., Théoduloz, G.: Configurable software verification: concretizing the convergence of model checking and program analysis. In: Damm, W., Hermanns, H. (eds.) CAV 2007. LNCS, vol. 4590, pp. 504–518. Springer, Heidelberg (2007)
2. Dangl, M., Löwe, S., Wendler, P.: CPAchecker with support for recursive programs and floating-point arithmetic. In: Baier, C., Tinelli, C. (eds.) TACAS 2015. LNCS, vol. 9035, pp. 423–425. Springer, Heidelberg (2015)
3. Wonisch, D.: Block abstraction memoization for CPAchecker. In: Flanagan, C., König, B. (eds.) TACAS 2012. LNCS, vol. 7214, pp. 531–533. Springer, Heidelberg (2012)
4. Wonisch, D., Wehrheim, H.: Predicate analysis with block-abstraction memoization. In: Aoki, T., Taguchi, K. (eds.) ICFEM 2012. LNCS, vol. 7635, pp. 332–347. Springer, Heidelberg (2012)

# CPA-RefSel: CPACHECKER with Refinement Selection
## (Competition Contribution)

Stefan Löwe(✉)

University of Passau, Passau, Germany
loewe@fim.uni-passau.de

**Abstract.** Our submission to SV-COMP'16 is based on the software verification framework CPACHECKER. We suggest to combine the value and predicate analysis of the framework, both performing CEGAR based on interpolation. The novelty of our approach is that both analyses perform intra-analysis refinement selection, with a top-level refinement component additionally employing inter-analysis refinement selection. All in all, this allows for an efficient verification process, as intra-analysis refinement selection selects a suitable refinement for an analysis and inter-analysis refinement selection selects the analysis that is best to be refined.

## 1 Verification Approach

We built our verifier using the software verification framework CPACHECKER. As framework, CPACHECKER offers a wide range of analyses, and our approach combines the value analysis (VA) and the predicate analysis (PA) in a parallel composition. This compositional approach resides inside an extension of the counterexample-guided abstraction refinement (CEGAR) approach, which in both analyses is driven by interpolation [1]. Our extension of the CEGAR algorithm is depicted in Fig. 1 (taken from [2]), and a brief outline follows.

After a short pre-analysis, which already verifies a few programs successfully, our extended CEGAR algorithm is initiated, which first closely resembles the classic CEGAR approach. The composition of the value and the predicate analysis is started with empty precisions, $\pi^{VA} = \emptyset, \pi^{PA} = \emptyset$, i.e., during the initial state-space exploration no assignments (for VA) and no predicates (for PA) are tracked. If the resulting over-approximation of the state space is free of errors, then the CEGAR loop terminates with the verdict *true*, if a real counterexample is found, then the CEGAR loop terminates with the verdict *false*. If an inconclusive error path $\sigma$ is found, here represented as sequence of pairs of an operation $op$ and a program location $l$, then the standard CEGAR algorithm would compute a *single* refinement, e.g., by inferring interpolants from the single infeasible error path to exclude this infeasible error path in future state-space explorations.

© Springer-Verlag Berlin Heidelberg 2016
M. Chechik and J.-F. Raskin (Eds.): TACAS 2016, LNCS 9636, pp. 916–919, 2016.
DOI: 10.1007/978-3-662-49674-9_59

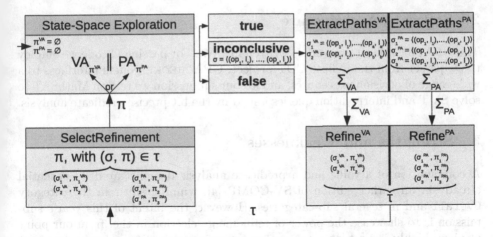

**Fig. 1.** Refinement selection for combining a value and a predicate analysis [2]

Exactly here we deviate from the standard CEGAR approach, and instead, we perform *intra-analysis refinement selection* by first calling procedure ExtractPaths to extract a set $\Sigma$ of infeasible sliced paths from the original infeasible error path [3], and then, by calling procedure Refine, to compute a set $\tau$ of individual refinements, one for each of the available infeasible sliced paths [3].

Each of the refinements makes the precision of the analysis strong enough to exclude the original infeasible error path [3]. This allows the analysis to heuristically select from a pool of available refinements, and it may pick a refinement that seems like a good fit for the further course of the analysis, while at the same time, it can avoid unsuitable ones, e.g., those that might lead to loop unrollings.

The procedures ExtractPaths and Refine are available for both the value analysis and the predicate analysis, making intra-analysis refinement selection possible for both analyses [2]. Furthermore, we can leverage refinement selection to a higher level — with intra-analysis refinement selection we have multiple refinements to select from, and we have means available to distinguish between unsuited and well-suited refinements. So we can utilize these mechanisms to enable *inter-analysis refinement selection*, i.e., we do not only select the refinement that is best for a component analysis, but we also decide whether the composite analysis should perform its refinement for the value or the predicate analysis [2].

Specifically for the SV-COMP, we made refinement selection applicable together with adjustable-block encoding. Mind that with large blocks, e.g., with abstractions computed only at loops, the number of available refinements to select from tends to be lower compared to when having small blocks, e.g. with single-block encoding. Now, we compute abstraction whenever control flow joins, as the analysis performs best with medium-sized blocks, proving that selecting suitable refinements is as important as an appropriate block-encoding strategy.

## 2 Software Architecture

The CPACHECKER framework is written in JAVA. For parsing C code we employ the C parser from the Eclipse CDT project. CPACHECKER offers interfaces to a wide range of decision procedures, and for our submission we rely on MathSAT to solve SMT and interpolation queries issued by the bit-precise predicate analysis.

## 3 Strengths and Weaknesses

A combination of a value and a predicate analysis demonstrated its potential already in an earlier edition of SV-COMP [4], winning silver in the category Overall and in several sub-categories. However, the intent of this year's submission is to showcase the power of refinement selection in the, from our point of view, highly important category DeviceDriversLinux64, where refinement selection works particularly well, allowing us to win the *gold* medal. Still, we seek for a better understanding of heuristics for inter- and intra-analysis refinement selection. Despite the fact that the CPACHECKER framework supports checking memory safety and overflows, our submission is not competitive there, while also lacking support for concurrency, termination, large arrays and explicit recursion.

## 4 Setup and Configuration

Our verifier is built from revision 18373 from the official CPACHECKER repository, branch refinementSelectionForABE. It is also archived at http://sv-comp.sosy-lab.org/2016/systems.php. To run our tool please enter this command:

```
scripts/cpa.sh -sv-comp16--refsel -disable-java-assertions -heap 12500m -spec prop.prp task.i
```

For C programs that assume a 64-bit environment add the parameter -64. The tool prints to the console the verdict, the violated property, and the name of the output directory, the latter holding the witness file witness.graphml in case a property violation is found. To reproduce the results, use Java 7, the benchmark definition cpa-refsel.xml and the tool-info module cpachecker.py, both officially archived online at http://sv-comp.sosy-lab.org/2016/systems.php.

## 5 Project and Contributors

CPACHECKER is a verification framework maintained by the Software Systems Lab at the University of Passau, made available under the Apache 2.0 license. It proofed successful in every edition of the SV-COMP, and it is used by practitioners and researchers at the Russian Academy of Science, the Universities of Darmstadt, Hamburg, Paderborn and Vienna, as well as at Verimag in Grenoble. We would like to thank all contributors for their efforts spent on CPACHECKER.

# References

1. Beyer, D., Löwe, S.: Explicit-state software model checking based on CEGAR and interpolation. In: Cortellessa, V., Varró, D. (eds.) FASE 2013 (ETAPS 2013). LNCS, vol. 7793, pp. 146–162. Springer, Heidelberg (2013)
2. Beyer, D., Löwe, S., Wendler, P.: Refinement selection. In: Fischer, B., Geldenhuys, J. (eds.) SPIN 2015. LNCS, vol. 9232, pp. 20–38. Springer, Heidelberg (2015)
3. Beyer, D., Löwe, S., Wendler, P.: Sliced path prefixes: an effective method to enable refinement selection. In: Graf, S., Viswanathan, M. (eds.) Formal Techniques for Distributed Objects, Components, and Systems. LNCS, vol. 9039, pp. 228–243. Springer, Heidelberg (2015)
4. Löwe, S.: CPACHECKER with Explicit-Value Analysis Based on CEGAR and Interpolation. In: Piterman, N., Smolka, S.A. (eds.) TACAS 2013 (ETAPS 2013). LNCS, vol. 7795, pp. 610–612. Springer, Heidelberg (2013)

# DIVINE: Explicit-State **LTL** Model Checker
## (Competition Contribution)

Vladimír Štill[(✉)], Petr Ročkai, and Jiří Barnat

Faculty of Informatics, Masaryk Universit, Brno, Czech Republic
xstill@mail.muni.cz, divine@fi.muni.cz

**Abstract.** DIVINE is an LLVM-based LTL model checker that follows the standard automata-based approach to explicit-state model checking. It aims at verification of unmodified parallel C & C++ programs without inputs. To achieve this DIVINE employs several reduction techniques combined with high-performance parallel and distributed computing.

## 1 Verification Approach and Software Architecture

As an explicit-state model checker, DIVINE is meant primarily to help detect bugs in multithreaded code [1]. As a matter of fact, the development of multithreaded code suffers from the lack of deterministic testing procedure. Therefore, concurrency related bugs, such as data races, often tend to survive in the code even beyond the release date. DIVINE provides the user with the tool to check all possible relevant executions of multithreaded code. In this way DIVINE may be used to prove the presence or absence of a bug. With this approach DIVINE requires that programs to be verified are closed, i.e. perform no input/output actions.

DIVINE is written in C++. It uses LLVM bitcode as the input formalism. Therefore, it employs Clang to translate input multithreaded C and C++ programs to LLVM bitcode prior verification. See Fig. 1. Thus the core part of DIVINE is a purpose specific LLVM bitcode interpreter. The interpreter allows to completely store and load a state of the program, and is capable of execution of LLVM instructions in order to generate new states. The program is analyzed including all the code that is executed within software libraries which has to be compiled together with the program for verification. In the standard distribution DIVINE provides bitcode with implementations of C and C++ standard libraries and pthread threading library.

## 2 Strengths and Weaknesses

The main strength of DIVINE is its ability to perform a full deterministic verification of closed piece of code. DIVINE can detect a number of issues in the code

This work has been partially supported by the Czech Science Foundation grant No. 15-08772S.

M. Chechik and J.-F. Raskin (Eds.): TACAS 2016, LNCS 9636, pp. 920–922, 2016.
DOI: 10.1007/978-3-662-49674-9_60

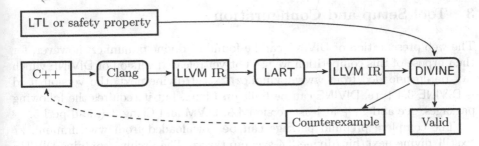

**Fig. 1.** Verification work-flow. Boxes with rounded corners represent executables.

such as invalid memory access, assertion violation, unhandled exceptions, etc. In addition, DIVINE can verify properties expressed as LTL formulas. Moreover, all the issues discovered can be witnessed with a counterexample.

The LLVM interpreter in DIVINE supports complete instruction set of LLVM bitcode including instructions for exception handling. DIVINE runtime provides almost complete implementation of C and C++ standard libraries and pthread threading library. The LLVM approach has the advantage that the behaviors that are analyzed by DIVINE are quite close to the behaviors that are actually exhibited by the program binary, for example they include most of compiler optimizations. Futhermore, with a proper runtime, DIVINE can handle other languages with LLVM-based compiler.

The ease with which LLVM-bitcode can be transformed allowed us to adapt to specifics of SV-COMP (such as atomic sections) without the need to modify DIVINE at all. For LLVM-to-LLVM transformations DIVINE employs LART— an LLVM transformation platform distributed with DIVINE.

To address the state space explosion problem in terms of both the time and memory, DIVINE offers strong $\tau$-reduction [2], efficient state-compression techniques [3] and also the ability of parallel and distributed-memory processing.

DIVINE requires the program to have finitely many states, however the program need not terminate — there is no need for loop, recursion, or context switch bounding. On the other hand, there are numerous limits of the approach. First of all, DIVINE is purely explicit-state tool, which means that simulating even a single unrestricted 32bit-wide input leads to the $2^{32}$ wide branching in the state space, making verification of open programs nearly impossible. However, since the nondeterminism in the concurrency category of SV-COMP is fairly limited, DIVINE can tackle most of the benchmarks of this category.

When preparing for SV-COMP, we also run into problems with under-specification of benchmarks — in many benchmarks there is undefined behavior with respect to reads and writes to global variables, which leads to an optimized LLVM bitcode with unexpected behavior. This is, however, not a limitation of DIVINE's approach — it is rather a bug in the benchmarks. To tackle this problem and get expected results we employ LLVM-to-LLVM transformation which adds volatile qualifier to any global variable defined in the benchmark.

## 3    Tool Setup and Configuration

The web presentation of DIVINE can be found at divine.fi.muni.cz, however, for the purpose of this competition we use not yet released version of DIVINE which can be downloaded from www.fi.muni.cz/~xstill/divine-next, the version used is DIVINE 3.4.1pre. DIVINE can be built on Linux, but it requires the following packages: gcc and g++ at least version 4.9, LLVM and Clang 3.7, and perl 5.

The complete prebuild package can be downloaded from www.fi.muni.cz/ ~xstill/divine-next/bin/divine-3.4-svcomp.tar.gz. The archive contains DIVINE and LART binaries together with all the necessary dependencies as well as Clang and LLVM otp for convenience, therefore, there is no need to install LLVM 3.7 to run DIVINE on Ubuntu 14.04.

Since the build process of C/C++ program for DIVINE has multiple steps, there is a helper script `rundivine` which handles compilation and verification automatically. The usage for SV-COMP is `rundivine <divine-bin-dir>` `--svcomp --csdr --opt=-Oz <benchmark>`. The meaning of used options is the following: `--svcomp` to run all required LART passes and setup compiler to handle input properly and DIVINE to verify assertions, use only one thread, and use compression; `--csdr` to use the Context-Switch-Directed Reachability algorithm [4]; and `--opt=-Oz` to enable optimizations using LLVM opt.

DIVINE will participate in concurrency category, with aforementioned options to the `rundivine` wrapper. The wrapper script for BenchExec is `divine.py`[1].

## 4    Software Project and Contributors

DIVINE project resides at http://divine.fi.muni.cz. The project was contributed primarily by Petr Ročkai and Vladimír Štill, with a number of other people as contributors. DIVINE is licenced under the 2-clause BSD license.

## References

1. Barnat, J., et al.: DiVinE 3.0 – an explicit-state model checker for multithreaded C & C++. In: Sharygina, N., Veith, H. (eds.) CAV 2013. LNCS, pp. 863–868. Springer, Heidelberg (2013)
2. Ročkai, P., Barnat, J., Brim, L.: Improved state space reductions for LTL model checking of C and C++ programs. In: Brat, G., Rungta, N., Venet, A. (eds.) NFM 2013. LNCS, vol. 7871, pp. 1–15. Springer, Heidelberg (2013)
3. Ročkai, P., Štill, V., Barnat, J.: Techniques for memory-efficient model checking of C and C++ code. In: Calinescu, R., Rumpe, B. (eds.) SEFM 2015. LNCS, vol. 9276, pp. 268–282. Springer, Heidelberg (2015)
4. Štill, V., Ročkai, P., Barnat, J.: Context-switch-directed verification in DIVINE. In: Hliněný, P., Dvořák, Z., Jaroš, J., Kofroň, J., Kořenek, J., Matula, P., Pala, K. (eds.) MEMICS 2014. LNCS, vol. 8934, pp. 135–146. Springer, Heidelberg (2014)

---

[1] github.com/dbeyer/benchexec/blob/master/benchexec/tools/divine.py

# Run Forester, Run Backwards!
## (Competition Contribution)

Lukáš Holík[1], Martin Hruška[1], Ondřej Lengál[2(✉)], Adam Rogalewicz[1],
Jiří Šimáček[1], and Tomáš Vojnar[1]

[1] FIT, Brno University of Technology, IT4Innovations Centre of Excellence,
Brno, Czech Republic
[2] Institute of Information Science, Academia Sinica, Taipei, Taiwan
ondra.lengal@gmail.com

**Abstract.** This paper briefly describes the Forester tree automata-based shape analyser and its participation in the SV-COMP'16 competition on software verification. In particular, it summarizes the verification approach used by Forester, its architecture and setup for the competition, as well as its strengths and weaknesses observed in the competition run. The paper highlights the newly added counterexample validation and use of refinable predicate language abstraction.

## 1 Verification Approach

**Forest Automata.** Forester implements a fully automated and sound *shape analysis* based on the notion of *forest automata* (FAs) [1]. FAs can represent sets of reachable configurations of programs with complex dynamic linked data structures (such as various kinds of lists, trees, skip lists, as well as combinations of such data structures). They have a form of tuples of *tree automata* (TAs). These tuples of TAs encode sets of heap graphs decomposed into tuples of *tree components*, whose leaves may refer back to the roots of the components (including roots of other components). The decomposition is based on cutting a heap graph at each *cut-point*, i.e., a node which is either pointed by some pointer variable or which has multiple incoming pointer edges.

In order to encode complex heap graphs, FAs may be *hierarchically structured* in such a way that a higher-level FA may use other, lower-level FAs as alphabet symbols. These nested automata, called *boxes*, encode *repetitive graph patterns* and can be automatically learned using the approach proposed in [2].

In order to be as efficient as possible, Forester never determinises the TAs it works with. All needed operations, including inclusion checking and size reduction, are therefore implemented on *non-deterministic TAs*. For that, techniques such as antichain-based inclusion checking and simulation-based reduction are used.

**Counterexample Analysis and Refinement.** In Forester, FAs are used within the framework of *abstract regular tree model checking* (ARTMC) [3].

© Springer-Verlag Berlin Heidelberg 2016
M. Chechik and J.-F. Raskin (Eds.): TACAS 2016, LNCS 9636, pp. 923–926, 2016.
DOI: 10.1007/978-3-662-49674-9_61

ARTMC accelerates the computation of sets of reachable program configurations, represented by FAs, by abstracting their component TAs, which is done by collapsing some of their states.

For deciding which TA states should be collapsed when performing ARTMC, multiple approaches have been proposed in the literature [3]. When Forester first participated in SV-COMP in 2015, it supported the simplest of these approaches based on collapsing states accepting the same *languages of trees up to some height* only. No checking of validity of counterexamples and no abstraction refinement was implemented then.

In the version of Forester participating in SV-COMP'16, an approach for checking validity of counterexamples was added. It is based on a *backward execution* of the program being verified along the suspected counterexample. For that, it was needed to add a support for *reverse execution* of all program statements over FAs. Moreover, a support for *intersection of FAs*, not needed before, had to be added. Intersection of FAs is a feature needed to either derive a concrete program trace from the forward and backward symbolic executions, or determine that no such a trace exists since the intersection gets empty at some point in the traces. It turns out that intersecting FAs is a quite complex task, which has to, e.g., deal with the fact that the two FAs being intersected may use a different decomposition of the heap graphs they represent.

Moreover, Forester has also been extended with the most advanced abstraction mechanism known in the context of ARTMC, namely *predicate language abstraction*. In its case, one collapses those TA states whose languages intersect the same predicate languages (represented also by TAs). The predicate languages to be used are learned in a *counterexample guided refinement* (CEGAR) loop from the TAs that are generated within backward executions of the program along spurious counterexample traces. Currently, the first execution of Forester uses the finite height abstraction, which is then refined in the further runs by combining it with the predicate language abstraction.

More details on the mentioned checking of validity of counterexamples and the refinable predicate language abstraction used in the context of FAs are still to be published, but a preliminary description can be found in [6].

## 2    Tool Architecture

Forester is implemented as a *GCC plugin* using the interface over GCC provided by the Code Listener infrastructure [4]. GIMPLE instructions used in the intermediate GCC code are translated to instructions of a specialised register machine that Forester uses to symbolically execute programs in the abstract domain of FAs. Forester uses the VATA [5] library to handle non-deterministic TAs from which FAs are built. Both Forester and VATA are implemented in C++.

## 3    Strengths and Weaknesses

The strengths of Forester are the following: (1) Forester is based on a sound verification approach, (2) its abstract domain allows one to analyse a large variety of classes of shape graphs, ranging from various kinds of (nested) lists, trees, to skip lists, and their combinations, (3) it can provide the user with error witnesses, (4) it newly analyses the counterexamples and refines the abstraction based one them, and (5) its internals (e.g., entailment checking) are built upon a well-understood automata theory and technology, which is constantly being developed by a wide community of researchers. Compared to the previous participation of Forester in SV-COMP in 2015, due to our enhancements, we were able to correctly mark 4 new bug-free benchmarks and 12 new erroneous benchmarks from the challenging Heap Data Structures category.

Among the main weaknesses of Forester is its weak support of handling non-pointer data such as integers or arrays. Therefore it participates in the Heap Data Structures category only, but even in this category it still loses some points due to not handling non-pointer features properly. Another weakness of Forester is that it does not support some advanced C language constructions. In particular, Forester currently loses the most points in the Heap Data Structures category by not implementing any support for pointers to functions. Due to this, Forester cannot analyse nearly 80 test cases. Another feature of C not fully supported by Forester are pointers to unstructured memory. Although a basic support for handling them is in place, Forester still has problems in tracking the size of an allocated unstructured memory block.

## 4   Tool Setup and Configuration

An archive with the SV-COMP'16 version of Forester is available at the web page of Forester[1]. The archive contains the source code of Forester and VATA. Instructions for compiling and running Forester are in the file README-FORESTER-SVCOMP-2016 in the root directory of the archive. After compilation, the directory fa_build with scripts for running Forester is created. The script for running Forester in SV-COMP is named sv_comp_run.py. It is also used in the BenchExec wrapper script of Forester.

The parameters of sv_comp_run.py are the following. The mandatory parameter of the script is the path to the file with the program under verification. The file for storing the witness leading to a counterexample is specified by the parameter --trace. The path to the property file is defined by the parameter --properties.

When Forester is run within the BenchExec framework, most of the parameters are set automatically by its wrapper script. The only exception is the parameter --trace, which must be defined manually in the forester.xml file used as the input of BenchExec. The wrapper script of Forester for BenchExec is called forester.py. Both files are available from the official page for SV-COMP'16 results reproduction (http://sv-comp.sosy-lab.org/2016/systems.php).

The output of Forester printed to the standard output has a similar format to the specification given by the rules of SV-COMP'16, specified in detail in the mentioned README file. Forester participates only in the Heap Data Structures category.

---

[1] http://www.fit.vutbr.cz/research/groups/verifit/tools/forester.

## 5    Software Project and Contributors

Forester has been developed at Brno University of Technology since 2010. The authors of this paper are currently the only people involved to development of Forester. Forester and the VATA library are both licensed under GPL.

**Acknowledgement.** This work was supported by the Czech Science Foundation under the project 14-11384S. Martin Hruška is a holder of the Brno Ph.D. Talent Scholarship, funded by the Brno City Municipality.

## References

1. Habermehl, P., Holík, L., Rogalewicz, A., Šimáček, J., Vojnar, T.: Forest automata for verification of heap manipulation. Formal Methods Syst. Des. **41**(1), 83–106 (2012). Springer
2. Holík, L., Lengál, O., Rogalewicz, A., Šimáček, J., Vojnar, T.: Fully automated shape analysis based on forest automata. In: Sharygina, N., Veith, H. (eds.) CAV 2013. LNCS, vol. 8044, pp. 740–755. Springer, Heidelberg (2013)
3. Bouajjani, A., Habermehl, P., Rogalewicz, A., Vojnar, T.: Abstract regular (tree) model checking. Int. J. Softw. Tools Technol. Transfer **14**(2), 167–191 (2012). Springer
4. Dudka, K., Peringer, P., Vojnar, T.: An easy to use infrastructure for building static analysis tools. In: Moreno-Díaz, R., Pichler, F., Quesada-Arencibia, A. (eds.) EURO-CAST 2011, Part I. LNCS, vol. 6927, pp. 527–534. Springer, Heidelberg (2012)
5. Lengál, O., Šimáček, J., Vojnar, T.: VATA: a library for efficient manipulation of non-deterministic tree automata. In: Flanagan, C., König, B. (eds.) TACAS 2012. LNCS, vol. 7214, pp. 79–94. Springer, Heidelberg (2012)
6. Hruška, M.: Verification of pointer programs based on forest automata, MSc. thesis, Brno University of Technology (2015)

# LCTD: Tests-Guided Proofs for C Programs on LLVM
## (Competition Contribution)

Olli Saarikivi[✉] and Keijo Heljanko

Helsinki Institute for Information Technology HIIT,
Department of Computer Science, Aalto University, School of Science,
PO Box 15400, FI-00076 Aalto, Finland
{olli.saarikivi,keijo.heljanko}@aalto.fi

**Abstract.** LCTD is an open source verification tool for C programs.
It uses the LLVM compiler framework to instrument programs for ver-
ification with the DASH algorithm. LCTD has been submitted to the
BitVectorsReach category of SV-COMP 2016.

## 1   Verification Approach

The DASH algorithm by Beckman et al. [1] combines dynamic symbolic execution (DSE) [2] with CEGAR. DASH attempts to generate tests based on counterexamples found in the abstraction. When test generation fails the abstraction
is refined via a splitting operation on the abstract regions to remove the counterexample. The tests can be seen as an underapproximation of the reachable
states of the program under test, which DASH tries to expand to include an
error. The abstraction on the other hand is an overapproximation which, if error
free, also proves the program under test to be so.

The flowchart in Fig. 1 provides a high-level overview of the DASH algorithm.
DASH implements a modified CEGAR loop, where instead of directly checking
whether a counterexample is spurious, DSE is used to generate a test that follows
the path to the error in the abstraction at least one step more than in previously
executed tests. When test generation fails abstraction refinement is performed
to eliminate the path from the abstraction.

We have implemented the DASH algorithm as a modification to the Lime
Concolic Tester (LCT) [3], which is an open source dynamic symbolic execution
tool for C and Java programs. Our tool LCTD extends the LLVM based C
support in LCT. For a detailed description of LCTD see [4].

## 2   Software Architecture

LCTD consists of two main parts:

- An instrumented version of the program to verify, which implements test execution and tracking, and constraint solving.
- A server component which maintains and refines the abstraction.

© Springer-Verlag Berlin Heidelberg 2016
M. Chechik and J.-F. Raskin (Eds.): TACAS 2016, LNCS 9636, pp. 927–929, 2016.
DOI: 10.1007/978-3-662-49674-9_62

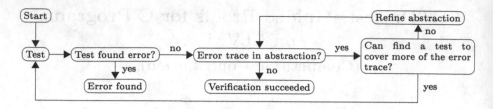

**Fig. 1.** Flowchart for the DASH algorithm

The target program is instrumented with a transformation pass in the LLVM compiler framework, which adds for all LLVM IR instructions calls to counterparts in a runtime library. These calls allow the runtime to track the execution and provide concrete values for calls to the __VERIFIER_nondet_* functions.

At startup the instrumented program connects to the server component for instructions. For test executions it receives a set of concrete inputs, which are used to execute the program. During execution tracking information will be sent to the server, which follows the execution's progress in the abstraction. For solving new input values the server sends a set of concrete inputs and a constraint to be solved at a specific point in the execution, which corresponds to generating a test that visits a desired abstract region. Constraints are solved using the Z3 4.3.2 SMT solver.

The server component initializes the abstraction to the control flow graph of the target program. It waits for the instrumented program to connect, which it then uses for executing tests and solving constraints.

## 3  Strengths and Weaknesses of the Approach

LCTD implements a bit-precise translation from LLVM IR instructions into bitvector logic making the tool very precise. The usage of a modern SMT solver allows LCTD to perform well on programs with complex bitwise logic.

LCTD leverages LLVM's optimization passes as a preprocessing step. This allows it to produce a simpler version of the program which often omits lots of inessential code and thus verify an optimized LLVM representation of the program.

One of the current challenges is that programs that rely heavily on control flow or complex loops can result in LCTD splitting the abstraction along increasingly deep paths, which results in very large region predicates that are slow to solve. Other weaknesses are limited support for floating point operations, pointer arithmetic and recursive functions.

## 4  Tool Setup and Configuration

LCTD and its benchmark definition XML can be downloaded from:
http://users.cse.aalto.fi/osaariki/lctd-svcomp/

The BenchExec script is available at:
https://github.com/OlliSaarikivi/benchexec/blob/master/benchexec/tools/
lctd.py

The version to use is "lctd-1.1.1-svcomp". To install the tool:

- Install a Java VM version 1.7.0_79 or newer. LCTD has been tested with Java 1.7.0_79 OpenJDK (IcedTea 2.5.6).
- Add the "bin/" folder inside the root directory of the tool archive to PATH.

Invoking the command "lctdsvcomp <path-to-target.c>" instruments the program and starts the verification process. Once finished it will report TRUE, FALSE or UNKNOWN and in the case of FALSE provides a path to and printout of the verification witness file. LCTD does not require any parameters apart from a path to the source code of the program to verify.

**Participation Statement:** LCTD participates in the BitVectorsReach sub-category and opts out of all other categories.

We do not participate in Overflows, the other bit vector sub-category, as LCTD currently only supports code reachability properties. Other categories were excluded mainly due to a variety of language support issues.

# 5   Software Project and Contributors

The main developer of LCTD is Olli Saarikivi. The tool was developed by Olli Saarikivi for a Master's Thesis under the supervision of Keijo Heljanko. LCTD is based on the LCT-C tool developed in the Lime project (http://www.tcs.hut.fi/Software/lime/).
LCTD is licensed under the MIT license.

# References

1. Beckman, N.E., Nori, A.V., Rajamani, S.K., Simmons, R.J.: Proofs from tests. In: Ryder, B.G., Zeller, A. (eds.) Proceedings of the ACM/SIGSOFT International Symposium on Software Testing and Analysis (ISSTA). pp. 3–14. ACM.(2008)
2. Godefroid, P., Klarlund, N., Sen, K.: DART: Directed automated random testing. In: Proceedings of the ACM SIGPLAN 2005 Conference on Programming Language Design and Implementation (PLDI). pp. 213–223. ACM.(2005)
3. Kähkönen, K., Launiainen, T., Saarikivi, O., Kauttio, J., Heljanko, K., Niemelä, I.: LCT: An open source concolic testing tool for Java programs. In: Proceedings of the 6th Workshop on Bytecode Semantics, Verification, Analysis and Transformation (BYTECODE). pp. 75–80.(2011)
4. Saarikivi, O., Heljanko, K.: LCTD: Test-guided proofs for C programs on LLVM. Journal of Logical and Algebraic Methods in Programming, NWpPT 2013 special issue..(2015)

# LPI: Software Verification with Local Policy Iteration

## (Competition Contribution)

Egor George Karpenkov[1,2(✉)]

[1] University Grenoble Alpes, VERIMAG, 38000 Grenoble, France
george@metaworld.me
[2] CNRS, VERIMAG, 38000 Grenoble, France

**Abstract.** LPI is a module for invariant generation embedded inside the CPACHECKER framework. It uses a *local policy iteration* approach, which allows it to obtain precise numerical invariants. The approach performs computations in the *template constraints domain* using *maximization modulo* SMT, and terminates with a potentially over-approximating inductive invariant.

Local policy iteration is a sound, but incomplete technique which obtains numerical, conjunctive inductive invariants for the analyzed programs. It can prove programs to be safe by finding a *separating* inductive invariant, but can not find counterexamples to safety. We supply the generated inductive invariant to the k-induction procedure, which terminates with either a counterexample or a proof of safety.

## 1 Verification Approach

LPI is a module for obtaining numeric inductive invariants on programs, which is based on the *local policy iteration* [6] approach. Local policy iteration finds an inductive invariant in the *template constraints domain* for each of the abstraction points (loop-heads for reducible programs) of the analyzed program. In this abstract domain, a set of *templates* (linear expressions over program variables) is fixed in advance, and the inductive invariant is a vector of upper bounds on the chosen templates. For example, if the selected templates are $x$ and $x + y$, a possible inductive invariant is $x \leq 5 \wedge x + y \leq 6$.

The tool includes a strategy for template synthesis. Templates are extracted from program expressions, and additionally from synthesizing simple linear expressions of a given size (e.g. $\pm x \pm y$ for all program variables $x, y$ alive at the given location). Furthermore, the set of templates is *refined*: the analysis starts with a very coarse domain (upper and lower bound on each variable, emulating the *interval* domain), and if a *separating* inductive invariant is not found

The research leading to these results has received funding from the European Research Council under the European Union's Seventh Framework Programme (FP/2007-2013) / ERC Grant Agreement nr. 306595 "STATOR".

M. Chechik and J.-F. Raskin (Eds.): TACAS 2016, LNCS 9636, pp. 930–933, 2016.
DOI: 10.1007/978-3-662-49674-9_63

(an invariant which separates the starting point from the error property), a domain is continuously refined to include more templates by increasing the size of synthesized linear expressions. However, the refinement is unguided and is not based on a target property.

Additionally, the analysis is augmented with a simple congruence module, which tracks parity (even or odd) of all variables and *simple* linear expressions (e.g. $x + y$).

The result of an LPI run is an inductive invariant, which might be an over-approximation of the reachable state space of the program. Thus pure LPI can only be used for verification, and not for finding counterexamples to the safety property. To address this, and to raise the number of programs which can be verified, an invariant produced by LPI is fed to the *k-induction* [1] procedure. For a given value of $k$, k-induction performs two checks: whether the error state is reachable from the initial one in $k$ steps (forward reachability), and whether the negation of the error property is k-inductive, subject to the strengthening by the invariant produced by LPI. LPI invariant generation (including continuous refinement) runs asynchronously to the k-induction procedure, and they are both continuously refined (number of templates is increasing, and so is the value of $k$). Counterexamples produced by k-induction are cross-checked with CBMC [5], which either verifies a counterexample or refutes it.

We have used k-induction as it is a natural fit to our invariant generation procedure due to support for continuously refined invariants. LPI improves the precision of pure k-induction, as the inductiveness check may fail due to counterexamples-to-induction which are not reachable in the selected abstract domain.

## 2   Software Architecture

The verification module is embedded inside CPACHECKER [3], an open-source framework for program analysis. CPAchecker implements the Configurable Programming Analysis [2] (CPA) concept: it runs a simple parametrized fixpoint iteration loop, and each analysis is a CPA which parametrizes this iteration. Consequently, LPI is implemented as a single CPA.

The CPA implementation of LPI relies on other CPAs to perform the splitting of the state space, namely *Location*, *Callstack* and *FunctionPointer*.

LPI analysis makes heavy use of optimization modulo SMT, which is done using $\nu Z$ solver [4]. CPAchecker is written in Java and uses the Eclipse CDT parser for dealing with C code.

## 3   Strengths and Weaknesses

As LPI is expressed in the CPA framework, it benefits from it general strength: the ability to cooperate with other analyses.

The main strength of LPI is finding complex numerical invariants, which can not be found using standard abstract interpretation methods. In the current version of SV-COMP, we have found that many programs can be efficiently analyzed using explicit case enumeration, and complex numerical invariants are usually not required. Thus it limits the applicability of LPI to the SV-COMP dataset. However, on the categories we participate in we have found that LPI obtains reasonable results.

The additional limitation is that the inductive invariant produced by LPI is only sound with respect to mathematical integers and rationals. At the moment, LPI provides no bit-precise analysis, and unsound answers result mainly from integer overflow.

## 4    Tool Setup and Configuration

LPI code is available for download at http://lpi.metaworld.me/svcomp16.tar. bz2. The only external dependency of LPI is Java 7, all others are either shipped with or downloaded automatically by ant. The tool can be run from the main directory using the command ./scripts/cpa.sh -lpi-svcomp16 -disable-java-assertions -heap 10000m -spec property.prp target_program.i. The parameter -64 should be inserted before the last argument for 64-bit environment, and -setprop cpa.predicate.handlePointerAliasing=false is inserted in case of simple memory model. If a counterexample witness is found, it is written to the file output/witness.graphml. LPI can use the same wrapping script for benchexec as CPAchecker does. This tool participates in the "Integers and Control Flow" and "Software Systems" categories and opts out from all the others.

## 5    Software Project and Contributors

The LPI code was written by George Karpenkov. The k-induction module was developed by Matthias Dangl. CPAchecker [3] is mainly developed by the Software Systems Lab at the University of Passau. The code for both is distributed under the Apache 2.0 license.

## References

1. Beyer, D., Dangl, M., Wendler, P.: Boosting k-induction with continuously-refined invariants. In: Kroening, D., Păsăreanu, C.S. (eds.) CAV 2015. LNCS, vol. 9206, pp. 622–640. Springer, Heidelberg (2015)
2. Beyer, D., Henzinger, T.A., Théoduloz, G.: Configurable software verification: concretizing the convergence of model checking and program analysis. In: Damm, W., Hermanns, H. (eds.) CAV 2007. LNCS, vol. 4590, pp. 504–518. Springer, Heidelberg (2007)
3. Beyer, D., Keremoglu, M.E.: CPAchecker: a tool for configurable software verification. In: Gopalakrishnan, G., Qadeer, S. (eds.) CAV 2011. LNCS, vol. 6806, pp. 184–190. Springer, Heidelberg (2011)

4. Bjørner, N., Phan, A.-D., Fleckenstein, L.: $\nu Z$ - an optimizing SMT solver. In: Baier, C., Tinelli, C. (eds.) TACAS 2015. LNCS, vol. 9035, pp. 194–199. Springer, Heidelberg (2015)
5. Clarke, E., Kroning, D., Lerda, F.: A tool for checking ANSI-C programs. In: Jensen, K., Podelski, A. (eds.) TACAS 2004. LNCS, vol. 2988, pp. 168–176. Springer, Heidelberg (2004)
6. Karpenkov, E.G., Monniaux, D., Wendler, P.: Code analysis with local policy iteration. In: VMCAI (to appear, 2016)

# Hunting Memory Bugs in C Programs
# with Map2Check
## (Competition Contribution)

Herbert O. Rocha[1]([✉]), Raimundo S. Barreto[2], and Lucas C. Cordeiro[2]

[1] Federal University of Roraima, Boa Vista, Brazil
herberthb12@gmail.com
[2] Federal University of Amazonas, Manaus, Brazil
rbarreto@icomp.ufam.edu.br, lucasccordeiro@gmail.com

**Abstract.** Map2Check is a tool for automatically generating and checking unit tests for C programs. The generation of unit tests is based on assertions extracted from (memory) safety properties, which are generated by the ESBMC tool. In particular, Map2Check checks for SV-COMP invalid-free, invalid-dereference, and memory-leak properties in C programs.

## 1 Overview

Map2Check automatically generates and checks unit tests for C programs [1]. The unit test generation is based on assertions, which are extracted from the memory safety properties generated by ESBMC tool [2]. In particular, Map2Check checks for SV-COMP properties "invalid-free", "invalid-dereference", and "memory-leak". Map2Check adopts source code instrumentation to create test cases from those properties, and monitors data from program's executions, in order to detect failures originating from the execution of those (generated) test cases. Map2Check supports full C99, according to the standard ISO/IEC 9899:1990, and checks programs that make use of arrays, pointers, structs, unions, and dynamic memory allocation. ESBMC is adopted as a verification condition (VC) generator, which translates a program fragment and its correctness property into a logical formula that is automatically translated into a unit test. Map2Check does not require the user to annotate C programs with pre/post-conditions to generate that VCs.

## 2 Verification Approach

Map2Check executes seven steps to generate and check test cases related to memory safety in C programs as shown in Fig. 1. In step 1, Map2Check uses ESBMC to identify memory safety properties via the option `--show-claims`, which shows all safety properties that ESBMC automatically generates from the original C program. In ESBMC, a `claim` represents a safety property; examples

© Springer-Verlag Berlin Heidelberg 2016
M. Chechik and J.-F. Raskin (Eds.): TACAS 2016, LNCS 9636, pp. 934–937, 2016.
DOI: 10.1007/978-3-662-49674-9_64

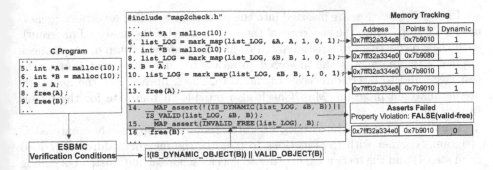

**Fig. 1.** Example of the Map2Check steps.

of claims include invalid-free, invalid-dereference, and memory-leaks; a particular claim can be violated by Map2Check if there is an execution that leads to the assertion failure.

In step 2, Map2Check analyzes the results produced in step 1 to collect several important pieces of information needed in the following steps, e.g., identification of the claim, comments about the claim, line number of the code where the claim occurred, and the property identified by that claim. For example, the particular claim !(IS_DYNAMIC_OBJECT(B)) || VALID_OBJECT(B) states a potential invalid dynamic object of "B", where an object can be represented by a pointer to a scalar variable or to a (more complex) data structure [2]. In particular, IS_DYNAMIC_OBJECT function checks whether the argument to any dereferencing operation is a dynamic object; and VALID_OBJECT(B) checks if the argument for any free or dereferencing operation is still a valid object. In Map2Check, we adopt regular expressions to find all claims information related to invalid-free, invalid-dereference, and memory-leak.

In step 3, Map2Check translates the claims provided by ESBMC into assertions written in C code, which are supported by a C library of Map2Check; this strategy is similar to that performed by Delahaye *et al.* [3], whose pre/postconditions based on formal program specification are translated into C code via assertions.

In step 4, Map2Check performs a memory tracking, which consists of two phases:

1. Track program variable operations and assignments in the analyzed source code. Map2Check performs this tracking by means of the abstract syntax tree (AST), which is generated from the analyzed C program;
2. Instrument the source code with functions that monitor the memory addresses and the addresses pointed by these variables (identified in step 1) according to the program execution. The assertions generated in step 3 are checked over the data, which are generated by the functions that monitor the memory addresses.

In step 5, test cases are inserted into the program by adding assertions (generated from step 3) into the new copy of the source code (of the analyzed program), with their respective properties related to memory safety. In step 6, Map2Check applies a template over the analyzed program to allow the validation of the test cases and to insert directives of the Map2Check library into the new copy of the analyzed program. Map2Check also provides a template for the CUnit framework [5].

Finally, in step 7, Map2Check executes that new copy of the analyzed C program, together with the functions to monitor the memory addresses (added from step 4) and the test cases, in order to check each assertion. Instead of calling a theorem-prover, Map2Check executes the code to check whether the assertions fail. Map2Check provides a program execution trace log in case of the assertion violation (i.e., if the test case fails), with data such as: the line number, memory addresses, pointer actions (e.g., allocation and deadlocation) already executed at the current point of the program.

# 3   Strengths and Weaknesses of the Approach

Map2Check participates in the Heap Data Structures category only. The strength of the tool lies in the precision of its answers based on the concrete execution of the analyzed program over the VCs generated by ESBMC, i.e., ESBMC is adopted only as a VC generator and it is not used to formally verify the properties. In preliminary experiments, Map2Check outperforms ESBMC due to timeouts or memory model limitations. Map2Check is in the initial development and there are still restrictions on the structure of the programs (*e.g.*, the C *alloca* function is not supported) that can be analyzed by our memory tracking. Most incorrect answers produced by our tool are due to bugs in the implementation. Additionally, our strategy based on random data to unwind loops and their respective loop exit condition do not allow the correct execution of the program. In particular, we implement a specific function to simulate the non-deterministic values, which are generated from the function call __nondet__int().

# 4   Architecture, Implementation and Availability

**Architecture.** Map2Check is implemented as a source-to-source transformation tool in Python (V2.7). It uses the pycparser[1] to parse a C program into an AST, and then identifies variables for tracking memory. The pyparsing[2] is used to create a parse of the ESBMC claims. It adopts uncrustify[3] as a source code beautifier. Map2Check also uses networkx[4] to generate the witness format[5] in GraphML format, and GCC compiler.

---

[1] https://github.com/eliben/pycparser.
[2] https://pyparsing.wikispaces.com.
[3] http://uncrustify.sourceforge.net.
[4] https://networkx.github.io.
[5] http://www.sosy-lab.org/~dbeyer/cpa-witnesses.

**Availability and Installation.** Map2Check source code version 6 for 64-bit Linux environment for the competition is available to freely download at https:// github.com/hbgit/Map2Check under GPL license. It must be installed as a Python script and it also requires installation of pycparser, pyparsing, networkx, uncrustify, and GCC.

**User Interface.** Map2Check is invoked via a command-line interface to SV-COMP as follows: `./map2check-wrapper.sh -c propertyFile.prpfile.i`. Map2Check accepts the property file and the verification task and provides as verification result: *FALSE + Witness* or *UNKNOWN*. For each error-path, a file that contains the violation path is generated in Map2Check root-path *graphml* folder; this file has the same name of the verification task with the extension `graphml`.

# References

1. Rocha, H., Barreto, R., Cordeiro, L.: Memory management test-case generation of C programs using bounded model checking. In: Calinescu, R., Rumpe, B. (eds.) SEFM 2015. LNCS, vol. 9276, pp. 251–267. Springer, Heidelberg (2015)
2. Cordeiro, L., Fischer, B., Marques-Silva, J.: SMT-based bounded model checking for embedded ANSI-C software. IEEE Trans. Soft. Eng. 38(4), 957–974 (2012)
3. Delahaye, M., Kosmatov, N., Signoles, J.: Common specification language for static and dynamic analysis of C programs. In: SAC, pp. 1230–1235 (2013)
4. Flanagan, C., Saxe, J.B.: Avoiding exponential explosion: generating compact verification conditions. In: POPL, pp. 193–205 (2001)
5. Rocha, H., Cordeiro, L., Barreto, R., Netto, J.: Exploiting safety properties in bounded model checking for test cases generation of C programs. In: SAST, pp. 121–130 (2010)

# MU-CSeq 0.4: Individual Memory Location Unwindings
## (Competition Contribution)

Ermenegildo Tomasco[1], Truc L. Nguyen[1], Omar Inverso[1,2], Bernd Fischer[3],
Salvatore La Torre[4], and Gennaro Parlato[1(✉)]

[1] Electronics and Computer Science, University of Southampton, Southampton, UK
gennaro@ecs.soton.ac.uk
[2] Gran Sasso Science Institute, L'Aquila, Italy
[3] Division of Computer Science, Stellenbosch University, Stellenbosch, South Africa
[4] Dipartimento di Informatica, Università di Salerno, Salerno, Italy

**Abstract.** We present the MU-CSeq tool for the verification of multi-threaded C programs with dynamic thread creation, dynamic memory allocation, and pointer arithmetic. It is based on sequentializing the programs over the new notion of *individual memory location unwinding* (IMU). IMU is derived from the notion of memory unwinding that has been implemented in the previous versions of MU-CSeq. The main concepts of IMU are: (1) the use of multiple write sequences, one for each individual shared memory location that is *effectively* used in the executions and (2) the use of memory addresses rather than variable names in the operations on the shared memory, which requires a separate table to map write sequences but supports pointer arithmetic.

## 1 Verification Approach

MU-CSeq 0.4 follows the sequentialization approach to verification. Its idea is to translate, using a code-to-code translation that preserves the verification property of interest, a concurrent program into a sequential one, which is then analyzed using a symbolic sequential verification tool.

In MU-CSeq 0.4 we have implemented a sequentialization based on the novel notion of *individual memory location unwindings* (IMU). IMU is derived from the concept of memory unwinding that has been implemented in the previous versions of MU-CSeq [2,3]. A *memory unwinding* (MU) is an explicit representation of the sequence of write operations into the shared memory performed by the threads. Each element of the sequence represents a write operation characterized by the identifier of the writing thread, the variable identifier, and the written value. The sequentialized program first guesses the values in the MU using non-determinism–supported by symbolic verification tools–and then simulates each thread against the MU. If each thread matches its memory writes in

---

Partially supported by EPSRC EP/M008991/1 grant, INDAM-GNCS 2015 grant and MIUR-FARB 2013–2015 grants.

M. Chechik and J.-F. Raskin (Eds.): TACAS 2016, LNCS 9636, pp. 938–941, 2016.
DOI: 10.1007/978-3-662-49674-9_65

the MU then their sequential simulation corresponds to a valid execution of the original concurrent program (see [2] for more details).

IMU improves on MU by providing a separate memory unwinding for each individual shared memory location corresponding to a scalar type or a pointer. To recreate a global total order over the shared memory writes we associate a *timestamp* (i.e., a distinct natural number) with each write in each individual MU. This is crucial for the correctness of the simulation since it is used to synchronize the simulation of the individual threads (otherwise the distinct MUs can give rise to many total orders).

Another important feature of the new encoding is to associate each memory location with its physical memory address. When a read or write operation is performed using a memory address, e.g., *p=3 for a pointer variable p, we first search for the location corresponding to the value of p and then simulate the read/write operation as we would do for scalar variables (for which the locations are statically known).

This new representation of the writes has several good features when used in combination with sequential BMC verification tools. In particular, the use of the individual MU simplifies the simulation of read and write operations resulting in much smaller verification conditions and verification time. In fact, for each memory access, the formula now only contains an encoding of the corresponding individual sequence and not the whole sequence of writes. Although the high level idea is simple, we observe that the underlying reasoning for IMU is more involved than MU.

Another advantage of IMU is that it gives a simple and effective way to support dynamic memory allocation and pointer arithmetics. This feature was not implemented in previous versions of MU-CSeq as it requires convoluted simulation functions resulting in a blowup of the verification time of the sequential BMC backend analysis.

IMU not only improves MU as we have mentioned above but also simplifies the development of new sequentialization schemes for other interesting properties of concurrent programs such as data-race and deadlock detection as well as weak memory models including TSO and PSO.

## 2 Software Architecture

The sequentializations in MU-CSeq 0.4 are implemented as source-to-source transformations in Python (v2.7.9), within the re-factored CSeq framework [4]. This uses the pycparser (v2.14, http://github.com/eliben/pycparser) to parse a C program into an abstract syntax tree (AST), and then traverses the AST to construct a sequentialized version, as outlined above. The resulting program can be processed independently by any verification tool for C, but we have only tested MU-CSeq 0.4 with CBMC (v5.2, www.cprover.org/cbmc/). For the competition we use a wrapper script that bundles up the translation, calls CBMC for verification, and returns its output.

Our tool takes the following options: w is the bound on the number of write operations for each location, f is the unwind bound for *for*-loops, u is the unwind bound for the remaining loops, b is the number of bits used for shared variables and memory addresses, p is the number of tracked locations that are stored on the heap, m is the maximal number of malloc invocations, v is the bound on the number of lock/unlock operations on single locations, ml is the bound on the number of lock/unlock operations on the whole memory, and thl is the bound on the number of threads that are spawned in any *while*-loop.

We use a simple syntactic analysis of the program to determine which schema and parameters we use in the competition. If the program contains more than 30 assignments but no loops, or a pthread_create inside a constant bounded *for*-loop, we use the inter-thread coarse-grained MU with parameters -w2 -f52 -u1 -b7 (for the MU scheme, w actually denotes the length of the overall sequence of writes). Otherwise we use the IMU scheme with the following parameters:

-w7 -u1 -f2 -b12 -p5 -v6 -ml7 -m3 -thl3, for programs with arrays;

-w7 -u2 -f2 -b12 -p2 -v6 -ml7 -m3 -thl3, if the program contains thread-local variables;

-w<*c1*> -u1 -f<*c1*> -b17 -p2 -v6 -ml7 -m3 -thl3, if the program's *for*-loops are upper bounded by a constant <*c1*> and do not contain pthread_create;

-w6 -u1 -f2 -b7 -p2 -v6 -ml7 -m3 -thl3, otherwise.

All parameter values were empirically determined. We use a timeout of 70 s, and interpret the cases where this timeout applies as *true*.

## 3  Tool Setup and Configuration

**Availability and Installation.** MU-CSeq 0.4 is available at http://users. ecs.soton.ac.uk/gp4/cseq/mu-cseq-0.4.zip; it also requires installation of the pycparser. CBMC must be installed in the same directory as MU-CSeq. The wrapper script for the tool on the BenchExec repository is mu-cseq.py.

**Call.** MU-CSeq should be called in the installation directory as mu-cseq.py -i *file* --spec *specfile*.

**Strengths and Weaknesses.** Since MU-CSeq 0.4 is not a full verification tool but only a concurrency preprocessor, we only competed in the Concurrency category. Here we achieved a full score, with an overall runtime of circa 45 min for all benchmarks in the category. Compared to MU-CSeq 0.3 [2], the new version achieved a substantial speedup over most of the benchmarks, as shown by the scatter plot in Fig. 1.

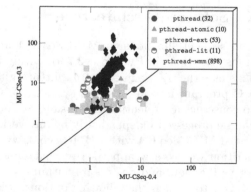

**Fig. 1.** Comparison of MU-CSeq v0.3 and v0.4.

# References

1. Inverso, O., Tomasco, E., Fischer, B., La Torre, S., Parlato, G.: Bounded model checking of multi-threaded c programs via lazy sequentialization. In: Biere, A., Bloem, R. (eds.) CAV 2014. LNCS, vol. 8559, pp. 585–602. Springer, Heidelberg (2014)
2. Tomasco, E., Inverso, O., Fischer, B., La Torre, S., Parlato, G.: Verifying concurrent programs by memory unwinding. In: Baier, C., Tinelli, C. (eds.) TACAS 2015. LNCS, vol. 9035, pp. 551–565. Springer, Heidelberg (2015)
3. Tomasco, E., Inverso, O., Fischer, B., La Torre, S., Parlato, G.: MU-CSeq 0.3: sequentialization by read-implicit and coarse-grained memory unwindings. In: Baier, C., Tinelli, C. (eds.) TACAS 2015. LNCS, vol. 9035, pp. 436–438. Springer, Heidelberg (2015)
4. Inverso, O., Nguyen, T.L., Fischer, B., La Torre, S., Parlato, G.: Lazy-CSeq: a context-bounded model checking tool for multi-threaded C-programs. In: ASE Tool Demonstration, pp. 807–812 (2015)

# Optimized PredatorHP and the SV-COMP Heap and Memory Safety Benchmark
## (Competition Contribution)

Michal Kotoun, Petr Peringer, Veronika Šoková, and Tomáš Vojnar[⊠]

FIT, IT4Innovations Centre of Excellence,
Brno University of Technology, Brno, Czech Republic
vojnar@fit.vutbr.cz

**Abstract.** This paper describes shortly the PredatorHP (Predator Hunting Party) analyzer and its participation in the SV-COMP'16 software verification competition. The paper starts by a brief sketch of the Predator shape analyzer on which PredatorHP is built, using multiple, concurrently running, specialised instances of Predator. The paper explains why the concrete mix of the different Predators was used, based on some characteristics of the SV-COMP benchmark.

## 1 Verification Approach

Predator Hunting Party (PredatorHP) uses the Predator shape analyzer, and so we first give a brief overview of Predator. Next, we discuss how Predator is used in the concurrent setting of PredatorHP, stressing changes from PredatorHP used in SV-COMP'15 together with a short analysis of the SV-COMP benchmark that motivated these changes.

### 1.1 The Predator Shape Analyzer

Predator aims at *sound* shape analysis of sequential, non-recursive C programs that use various kinds of lists implemented using low-level C pointer statements. Predator can soundly deal with various forms of pointer arithmetics, address alignment, block operations, memory contents reinterpretation, etc.

The shape analysis implemented in Predator is a form of *abstract interpretation* which uses a domain of the so-called *symbolic memory graphs* (SMGs) [1]. SMGs are oriented graphs with two main kinds of nodes and two main kinds of edges. Nodes can be divided into *objects* and *values*. Objects are further divided into *regions* (representing concrete blocks of memory allocated on the stack, on the heap, or statically) and singly- or doubly-linked *list segments*, which represent in an abstract way uninterrupted sequences of singly- or doubly-linked regions. Edges can be divided into *has-value* and *points-to* edges. The former

---

The work was supported by the Czech Science Foundation project 14-11384S.

M. Chechik and J.-F. Raskin (Eds.): TACAS 2016, LNCS 9636, pp. 942–945, 2016.
DOI: 10.1007/978-3-662-49674-9_66

represent values stored in allocated memory (which are either pointers or other kinds of data), the latter represent targets of pointer values.

Both nodes and edges are annotated by a number of *labels* that carry information such as the size of objects, offsets at which values are stored in objects, offsets with which pointers point to target objects, the type of values, offsets at which linking fields of lists are stored, the nesting level of objects (to be able to represent nested lists), or a constraint on the number of linked regions that a list segment represents. In particular, a list segment can either represent $n$ or more regions for $n \geq 0$, or 0 or 1 regions. Further, SMGs can also contain *optional regions* where a pointer to such a region either points to some allocated memory or to NULL. Sizes of blocks and offsets can have the form of *intervals* with constant bounds which allows Predator to deal with operations such as address alignment. A special kind of edges are then *disequality edges* allowing one to express that two values are for sure different (while equality of objects is expressed by representing these objects by a single node of an SMG).

Symbolic execution of C statements on SMGs uses a concept of *reinterpretation* that is able to synthesize values of previously not explicitly written fields from the known values of other fields. Currently, this concept is instantiated for dealing with blocks of nullified memory, which is quite needed for analyzing low-level programs. Another key operation on SMGs is the *join operation* that is implemented via a synchronous graph traversal of the two SMGs to be joint. The join operation is used not only to reduce the number of SMGs to deal with but also as a basis of abstraction and entailment checking. Predator uses *function summaries* to facilitate inter-procedural analysis. The support of *arithmetic* in Predator is such that Predator deals with integers exactly up to some bound (32 in SV-COMP'16) and then replaces them by an unknown value.

Compared with SV-COMP'15, not many changes were done in the Predator analyzer itself. We have just resolved several minor issues by, e.g., correcting arithmetic in the 32-bit mode or replacing error messages produced when performing so-far unsupported operations over interval-based values by producing the "unknown" verdict.

## 1.2   Predator Hunting Party

In SV-COMP'15, we started to run several variants of Predator in parallel. Among them there was one Predator *verifier* implementing the above sketched sound shape analysis. Due to its use of abstraction, the verifier could produce false alarms, and so its result was accepted only when it proved a program correct. In parallel with the verifier, three Predator *DFS hunters* without any list abstraction (though still with limited precision of the arithmetic) and with different bounds on the depth of the state space search (in particular, 400, 700, and 1000 GIMPLE instructions) were used. The verdict of these hunters was considered only when they reported an error. If neither the verifier nor the DFS hunters produced an acceptable answer, a *BFS hunter* was started to perform a breadth first search without any list abstraction and with no bound on the length of its run (other than the timeout used by SV-COMP). The BFS hunter was allowed to report errors as well as to prove a program correct in case it exhausted its state space.

For SV-COMP'16, we have decided to preserve the above concept but to revisit suitability of the concrete numbers of hunters used, their limits on the state space search, as well as the order in which they are run. First, the number of concurrently running Predators stayed at four given by the four available cores. We have, however, decided to use only two DFS hunters, with the depth of the state space search limited to 200 and 900 GIMPLE instructions, respectively. In general, this move is motivated by having one hunter that quickly searches for bugs with very short witnesses and one than searches for longer but still not very long witnesses. Moreover, we have decided to start the BFS hunter right away in place of one of the cancelled DFS hunters. Its role is to either prove correct finite-state programs (not proved correct by the verifier due to the abstraction used) or to find bugs that are not quickly found by the DFS hunters.

The above mentioned concrete DFS bounds are based on an analysis of those SV-COMP'16 programs in the heap data structures category that contain an error. In particular, it appears that: (1) In over 80 % of the cases, the error can be found in the limit of 200 instructions. (2) In about 96 % of the cases (meaning all but four of the considered programs with errors), the error can be found within 900 instructions. (3) In the remaining cases, the witness may be much longer (going up to over 50,000 instructions), which is too much for being used over all programs. Fortunately, in some of the cases, the witness may be quite long, but the search space is relatively narrow, so an error can still be found by the BFS hunter. In the end, we have programs proved correct by the verifier (but not the BFS hunter), programs proved correct by the BFS hunter (but not the verifier), programs with errors found by the DFS hunters (but not the BFS hunter), as well as programs with errors found by the BFS hunter (but not the DFS hunters).

The above change alone allowed us to prove one more program correct in the given time limit while at the same time saving around 38 % of the wall time. While the concrete numbers and bounds of hunters are tuned for the SV-COMP benchmark, the general set up of the prover and the hunters is applicable more broadly. The concrete numbers may be adjusted in a similar way for other sets of programs to be verified as common, e.g., in the world of search-based testing.

## 2   Strengths and Weaknesses

The main strength of PredatorHP is that—unlike various bounded model checkers—it treats unbounded heap manipulation in a *sound* way. At the same time, it is also quite *efficient*, and the use of various concurrently running Predator hunters greatly decreases chances of producing *false alarms* (there do not arise any due to heap manipulation, the remaining ones are due to imprecise treatment of other data types).

The main weakness of PredatorHP and also of Predator itself is its weak treatment of non-pointer data. Due to this, Predator participates in the heap data structures category only. Within this category, a weakness of Predator is that it is specialized in dealing with lists, and hence it does not handle structures such as trees or skip-lists (that is, it handles them very well in a bounded way, but our aim is to stick with sound verification).

## 3   Tool Setup and Configuration

The source code of PredatorHP used in SV-COMP'16 is freely available on the Internet[1]. The file README-SVCOMP-2016 shipped with the source code describes how to build the tool. To run it, the script predatorHP.py can be invoked. The script takes a verification task file as a single positional argument. Paths to both the property file and the desired witness file are accepted via long options. The verification outcome is printed to the standard output. The script does not impose any resource limits other than terminating its child processes when they are no longer needed. More information about the setting of PredatorHP used in the competition can be found here: http://sv-comp.sosy-lab.org/2016/systems.php.

## 4   Software Architecture, Project, and Contributors

Predator is implemented in C++ with a use of Boost libraries as a GCC plug-in based on the Code Listener framework [2]. PredatorHP is implemented as a Python script. Predator is an open source software project distributed under the GNU General Public License version 3. The main author of Predator is Kamil Dudka. Besides him and the PredatorHP team, Petr Muller and numerous other people contributed to Predator.

## References

1. Dudka, K., Peringer, P., Vojnar, T.: Byte-precise verification of low-level list manipulation. In: Logozzo, F., Fähndrich, M. (eds.) Static Analysis. LNCS, vol. 7935, pp. 215–237. Springer, Heidelberg (2013)
2. Dudka, K., Peringer, P., Vojnar, T.: An easy to use infrastructure for building static analysis tools. In: Moreno-Díaz, R., Pichler, F., Quesada-Arencibia, A. (eds.) EURO-CAST 2011, Part I. LNCS, vol. 6927, pp. 527–534. Springer, Heidelberg (2012)

---

[1] http://www.fit.vutbr.cz/research/groups/verifit/tools/predator-hp.

# Symbiotic 3: New Slicer
# and Error-Witness Generation
## (Competition Contribution)

Marek Chalupa(✉), Martin Jonáš, Jiri Slaby, Jan Strejček,
and Martina Vitovská

Faculty of Informatics, Masaryk University, Brno, Czech Republic
xchalup4@fi.muni.cz

**Abstract.** SYMBIOTIC 3 is a new generation of a bug-detection tool for
C programs. The tool sticks to the combination of program instrumentation, slicing, and symbolic execution. Large parts of the tool are rewritten, in particular the managing and instrumentation scripts and slicer
(including points-to analysis). Further, the symbolic executor KLEE has
been modified to produce error-witnesses. The changes are commented
in the description of the tool workflow.

## 1 Verification Approach and Software Architecture

As the previous versions of SYMBIOTIC [7,9], the new version also follows the
approach suggested in [8]: an analyzed program is (*i*) instrumented with code
that tracks a finite-state machine describing erroneous behaviors, (*ii*) reduced
by slicing [10] that removes code not influencing the state machine moves, and
(*iii*) symbolically executed [6] to find erroneous runs in the program.

The workflow of SYMBIOTIC 3 (together with indication of chosen programming languages and employed external tools with their respective versions) is
provided in Fig. 1. Our tool currently focuses on the *Error Function Unreachability* property (however, the approach can handle the other properties as well
and we plan to support them in near future). The *code cleanup* modifies the
C source (e.g. to bypass the known bug in CLANG where inlined functions are
omitted). The program is then translated to LLVM, checked for unsupported functionality (e.g. creation of new threads), and instrumented. As we support only
the unreachability property, the instrumentation is trivial. This step makes also
another small modifications of the program, e.g. each allocated variable is initialized to a nondeterministic value (to solve problems with uninitialized variables
appearing in some benchmarks). After linking with lib.bc (which contains our
definitions of __VERIFIER_* functions) and some optimization passes, namely
control flow graph optimization and constant propagation, we slice the program.

The slicer in SYMBIOTIC 3 is written from scratch. While the previous slicer
followed the slicing algorithm of [10], the current one implements slicing based

---

The research was supported by The Czech Science Foundation, grant GA15-17564S.

M. Chechik and J.-F. Raskin (Eds.): TACAS 2016, LNCS 9636, pp. 946–949, 2016.
DOI: 10.1007/978-3-662-49674-9_67

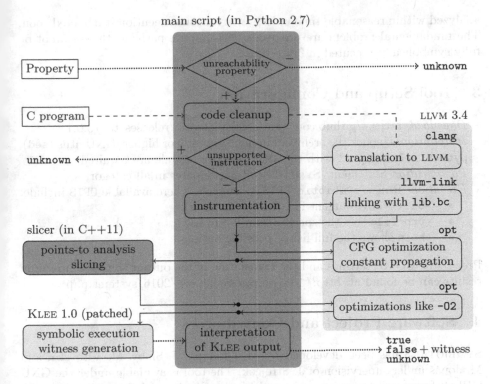

**Fig. 1.** Workflow of SYMBIOTIC 3. Dashed lines represent C programs, solid lines LLVM bytecode, and dotted lines text data.

on dependence graphs [3,5]. The slicer relies on field-sensitive, flow-insensitive points-to analysis (extended with an "unknown offset" value), which has been also reimplemented. The new slicer is substantially faster than the previous one.

The sliced program is optimized again (with passes similar to -O2 optimization level) and symbolically executed with our fork of KLEE [1]. We modified it to stop the computation when assertion violation is detected and to produce the corresponding error witness. The exact versions of KLEE and the solvers STP [4] and MINISAT [2] called by KLEE can be found in the SYMBIOTIC 3 distribution. Finally, the KLEE output is translated into the required form. In particular, a witness is translated to the GraphML format by a Perl script.

## 2   Strengths and Weaknesses

The main strengths of the approach are its soundness and universality; the approach can be applied also to the *Concurrency* benchmarks and these with more complex properties, which are currently not supported by our implementation (and thus skipped). Another advantage is the modularity of the tool architecture.

The main disadvantage is the high computational cost of symbolic execution. Especially programs with loops, recursion, or intensive branching cannot be analyzed within reasonable time unless an erroneous execution is detected soon. The fundamental problem are programs with infinite paths as these cannot be fully symbolically executed in finite time.

# 3   Tool Setup and Configuration

- *Download:* https://github.com/staticafi/symbiotic/releases/tag/3.0.1
- *Installation:* Unpack the archive. Further, gcc 4.9 or higher, GNU utils (sed), python 2.7, and perl with the XML::Writer module are required.
- *Participation Statement:* SYMBIOTIC 3 participates in all categories.
- *Execution:* Run ./symbiotic OPTS <source>, where available OPTS include:
  - --64 sets environment for 64-bit benchmarks
  - --prp=file sets the specification file to use
  - --help shows the full list of possible options

Precise SV-COMP settings and the translation of the output to the competition results can be found at: http://sv-comp.sosy-lab.org/2016/systems.php

# 4   Software Project and Contributors

SYMBIOTIC 3 has been developed by M. Chalupa, J. Slaby, M. Vitovská, and M. Jonáš under supervision of J. Strejček. The tool is available under the GNU GPLv2 License. The project is hosted by the Faculty of Informatics, Masaryk University. LLVM, KLEE, STP, and MINISAT are also available under open-source licenses. The project web page is: https://github.com/staticafi/symbiotic

# References

1. Cadar, C., Dunbar, D., Engler, D.: KLEE: unassisted and automatic generation of high-coverage tests for complex systems programs. In: OSDI, pp. 209–224. USENIX Association (2008)
2. Eén, N., Sörensson, N.: An extensible SAT-solver. In: Giunchiglia, E., Tacchella, A. (eds.) SAT 2003. LNCS, vol. 2919, pp. 502–518. Springer, Heidelberg (2004)
3. Ferrante, J., Ottenstein, K.J., Warren, J.D.: The program dependence graph and its use in optimization. In: Paul, M., Robinet, B. (eds.) International Symposium on Programming. LNCS, vol. 167, pp. 125–132. Springer, Heidelberg (1984)
4. Ganesh, V., Dill, D.L.: A decision procedure for bit-vectors and arrays. In: Damm, W., Hermanns, H. (eds.) CAV 2007. LNCS, vol. 4590, pp. 519–531. Springer, Heidelberg (2007)
5. Horwitz, S., Reps, T.W., Binkley, D.: Interprocedural slicing using dependence graphs. ACM Trans. Program. Lang. Syst. **12**(1), 26–60 (1990)
6. King, J.C.: Symbolic execution and program testing. Commun. ACM **19**(7), 385–394 (1976)
7. Slaby, J., Strejček, J.: Symbiotic 2: more precise slicing. In: Ábrahám, E., Havelund, K. (eds.) TACAS 2014 (ETAPS). LNCS, vol. 8413, pp. 415–417. Springer, Heidelberg (2014)

8. Slabý, J., Strejček, J., Trtík, M.: Checking properties described by state machines: on synergy of instrumentation, slicing, and symbolic execution. In: Stoelinga, M., Pinger, R. (eds.) FMICS 2012. LNCS, vol. 7437, pp. 207–221. Springer, Heidelberg (2012)
9. Slaby, J., Strejček, J., Trtík, M.: Symbiotic: synergy of instrumentation, slicing, and symbolic execution. In: Piterman, N., Smolka, S.A. (eds.) TACAS 2013 (ETAPS 2013). LNCS, vol. 7795, pp. 630–632. Springer, Heidelberg (2013)
10. Weiser, M.: Program slicing. In: Proceedings of ICSE, pp. 439–449. IEEE (1981)

# Ultimate Automizer with Two-track Proofs
## (Competition Contribution)

Matthias Heizmann[1(✉)], Daniel Dietsch[1], Marius Greitschus[1], Jan Leike[2],
Betim Musa[1], Claus Schätzle[1], and Andreas Podelski[1]

[1] University of Freiburg, Freiburg im Breisgau, Germany
heizmann@informatik.uni-freiburg.de
[2] The Australian National University, Canberra, Australia

**Abstract.** ULTIMATE AUTOMIZER is a software verification tool that
implements an automata-based approach for the analysis of safety and
liveness problems. The version that participates in this year's competition is able to analyze non-reachability, memory safety, termination, and
overflow problems. In this paper we present the new features of our tool
as well as the instructions how to install and use it.

## 1 Verification Approach

ULTIMATE AUTOMIZER implements an automata-based approach to software
verification that we call *trace abstraction* [4]. The key concept in this approach
is the notion of a *trace* which is a sequence of program statements. We consider
a program as a set of traces, namely the set of all traces that are labellings of
paths in the control flow graph. For the verification of a property, we start with
all traces that potentially violate the property, e.g., for checking non-reachability
of an error location we start with all traces that lead from the initial location to
the error location. Then, we iteratively prove that all these traces are infeasible,
i.e., we prove that none of these traces corresponds to a concrete program execution. In each iteration we take a sample trace $\pi$ that potentially violates the
property and analyze its feasibility. If the trace $\pi$ is feasible, we found a concrete
counterexample to the validity of the property. Otherwise, we construct a proof
for the infeasibility of $\pi$. Next, we generalize the trace $\pi$ to a set of traces that
are infeasible and whose infeasibility can be shown using the proof that was
constructed for $\pi$.

We use automata to represent sets of traces. The underlying alphabet is
the set of all program statements. The traces that potentially violate the non-
reachability property are the words that are accepted by the automaton that
resembles the control flow graph of the program and whose final state is the
node that corresponds to the error location of the program. The procedure for

This work was partly supported by the German Research Council (DFG) as part
of the Transregional Collaborative Research Center "Automatic Verification and
Analysis of Complex Systems" (SFB/TR14 AVACS).

M. Chechik and J.-F. Raskin (Eds.): TACAS 2016, LNCS 9636, pp. 950–953, 2016.
DOI: 10.1007/978-3-662-49674-9_68

obtaining sample traces is implemented as an emptiness check and in each iteration we use a difference operation on automata to ensure that we exclude all traces whose infeasibility was already shown.

In the following we present new features of this year's competition candidate.

*Two-track Proofs.* In former versions of our tool, the above mentioned infeasibility proof for a trace was an inductive sequence of state predicates. Such a sequence was obtained via Craig interpolation or via a technique that combines unsatisfiable cores, live variables and the post predicate transformer. In this year's competition contribution, we use this technique to compute two sequences of predicates. One sequence is obtained by the post predicate transformer, the other sequence is obtained by the wp predicates transformer. A second sequence of predicate is redundant to prove the infeasibility of the trace $\pi$ but it improves the generalization from one infeasible trace $\pi$ to a set of infeasible traces.

*Semi-deterministic Büchi Automata.* In our termination analysis we consider infinite traces and use Büchi automata to represent sets of traces [5]. The subtraction of traces whose infeasibility was already proven involves the complementation of Büchi automata which is known to be expensive. In order to overcome this bottleneck, we adjusted our algorithm such that the input of complementation operations is always a semi-deterministic Büchi automaton. This allows us to use a specialized complementation whose result has at most $4^n$ states [2].

*Bitprecise Analysis.* We use SMT-LIB to represent sets of program states and the transition relation of program statements. First, we try to verify a program by using the theory of (mathematical) integers. In order to soundly capture the semantics of machine integers we use modulo operations and we overapproximate bitwise operations, e.g., bitshifts, by a havoc operation. Whenever this analysis returns a counterexample that contains an overapproximated bitwise operation, we redo the analysis and use the SMT-LIB theory of bitvectors.

## 2    Software Project

ULTIMATE AUTOMIZER is one toolchain of the ULTIMATE program analysis framework. Our competition candidate uses several libraries provided by ULTIMATE, e.g., an automata library, the LASSORANKER library which is used for the termination analysis of lasso-shaped infinite traces [6], the SMT solver SMTInterpol [3], and an interface that allows us to communicate with any SMT-LIBv2 compatible SMT solver, The source code is available on Github[1] and several toolchains of ULTIMATE are available via a web interface.

## 3    Tool Setup and Configuration

A zip archive that contains the competition candidate is available at the website of ULTIMATE AUTOMIZER[2]. The archive contains a binary of Z3[3] and the

---

[1] https://github.com/ultimate-pa.

[2] https://ultimate.informatik.uni-freiburg.de/automizer/.

[3] https://github.com/Z3Prover.

installation of external tools is not required. Furthermore, the archive contains the Python script Ultimate.py, which maps the input given in the competition to the arguments that are required by the actual binary of ULTIMATE. At the SV-COMP the input to a tool is a C program inputfile, a property file prop.prp, an architecture which is either 32bit or 64bit, and a memory model which is either simple or precise. Given these arguments, the script should be invoked by the following command.

```
./Ultimate.py prop.prp inputfile 32bit|64bit simple|precise
```

The output of ULTIMATE AUTOMIZER is written to the file Ultimate.log and the result is written to stdout. When using BENCHEXEC the output can be translated by the ultimateautomizer.py tool-info module[4].

If the checked property does not hold, a human readable counterexample is written to UltimateCounterExample.errorpath and an error witness is written to witness.graphml.

## 4   Witness Validator

Verifiers that participate in the SV-COMP output an *error witness* [1] if they find a violation of the given property. An error witness is a machine readable counterexample to the validity of the property. An error witness may not represent a single program execution that violates the property, it may represent a set of program executions. The idea is that it narrows down the space in which verifiers have to search for possible violations of the property.

ULTIMATE AUTOMIZER can be used to validate error witnesses. For validating an error witness wtns.graphml we invoke the command mentioned in the preceding section and append wtns.graphml as a fifth argument.

```
./Ultimate.py prop.prp inputfile 32bit|64bit simple|precise wtns.graphml
```

The witness is confirmed if and only if ULTIMATE AUTOMIZER reports a violation of the property. I.e., the witness is confirmed if and only if a counterexample was found in the search space restricted by the witness.

## References

1. Beyer, D., Dangl, M., Dietsch, D., Heizmann, M., Stahlbauer, A.: Witness validation and stepwise testification across software verifiers. In: ESEC/FSE, pp. 721–733. ACM (2015)
2. Blahoudek, F., Heizmann, M., Schewe, S., Strejcek, J., Tsai, M.-H.: Complementing semi-deterministic Büchi automata. In: Chechik, M., Raskin, J.-F. (eds.) TACAS 2016, LNCS, vol. 9636, pp. 770–787. Springer, Heidelberg (2016)
3. Christ, J., Hoenicke, J.: Cutting the mix. In: Kroening, D., Păsăreanu, C.S. (eds.) CAV 2015. LNCS, vol. 9207, pp. 37–52. Springer, Heidelberg (2015)

---

[4] http://sv-comp.sosy-lab.org/2016/systems.php.

4. Heizmann, M., Hoenicke, J., Podelski, A.: Software model checking for people who love automata. In: Sharygina, N., Veith, H. (eds.) CAV 2013. LNCS, vol. 8044, pp. 36–52. Springer, Heidelberg (2013)
5. Heizmann, M., Hoenicke, J., Podelski, A.: Termination analysis by learning terminating programs. In: Biere, A., Bloem, R. (eds.) CAV 2014. LNCS, vol. 8559, pp. 797–813. Springer, Heidelberg (2014)
6. Leike, J., Heizmann, M.: Ranking templates for linear loops. Logical Methods Comput. Sci. **11**(1:16) (2015)

# Vienna Verification Tool:
# IC3 for Parallel Software
## (Competition Contribution)

Henning Günther, Alfons Laarman$^{(\boxtimes)}$, and Georg Weissenbacher

TU Wien, Vienna, Austria
alfons@laarman.com

**Abstract.** Recently proposed extensions of the IC3 model checking algorithm offer a powerful new way to symbolically verify software. The Vienna Verification Tool (VVT) implements these techniques with the aim to tackle the problem of parallel software verification. Its SMT-based abstraction mechanisms allow VVT to deal with infinite state systems. In addition, VVT utilizes a coarse-grained large-block encoding and a variant of Lipton's reduction to reduce the number of interleavings. This paper introduces VVT, its underlying architecture and use.

## 1 Verification Approach

VVT is an implementation of the CTIGAR approach [2], an SMT-based IC3 algorithm [3] incorporating Counterexample-Guided Abstraction Refinement (CEGAR) [5], thus enabling the verification of infinite-state systems. The underlying abstraction-refinement scheme follows the IC3 paradigm; it does not require an unwinding of the transition relation. To handle parallel programs, VVT uses a large-block encoding [8] that preserves all relevant partial interleavings by applying a novel dynamic variant of Lipton's reduction [12].

## 2 Software Architecture

VVT uses a modular approach to verification: a collection of separate tools instrument and translate the input, communicating via standard data formats such as LLVM bitcode [4] and the SMTlib format [1]. Figure 1 provides an overview.

The verification process begins by compiling the C file into LLVM bitcode using CLang. The LLVM IR has a precise semantics and comprises only a small number of instructions, thus reducing the complexity of the verifier. The increase in size resulting from the translation into bitcode is mitigated by subsequent

This work is supported by the Austrian National Research Network S11403-N23 (RiSE) of the Austrian Science Fund (FWF) and by the Vienna Science and Technology Fund (WWTF) through grant VRG11-005.

M. Chechik and J.-F. Raskin (Eds.): TACAS 2016, LNCS 9636, pp. 954–957, 2016.
DOI: 10.1007/978-3-662-49674-9_69

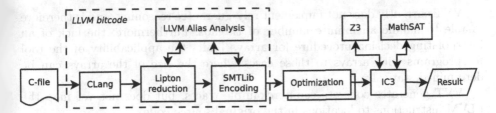

**Fig. 1.** Architecture

reduction steps. A separate tool implementing a variant of Lipton's reduction [12] identifies large blocks that can be executed atomically. These blocks are delimited by instrumenting the code with 'yield' function calls, indicating the relevant context switches. Our novel dynamic reduction method avoids static analysis[1] by expressing reduction conditions as branches. At each intermediate step the LLVM tool chain is used to optimize the bitcode (not shown in the figure).

Next, the `vvt-enc` tool translates the instrumented bitcode into an SMTlib-based format, encoding the transition relation of the program. It uses (linear) integer arithmetic to encode bit vectors to facilitate interpolation and employs alias-analysis techniques in order to keep the transition relation as small as possible. To finalize the encoding, the `vvt-opt` tool deploys a number of optimization techniques including program slicing (removing irrelevant parts of the transition relation), expression simplification and a value-set analysis (to identify constant expressions).

The last step is the actual verification with the `vvt-verify` tool. It uses Z3 [6] for IC3 consecution calls [3] and MathSAT [7] for interpolation-based refinement. To rapidly find counterexamples, VVT runs a small portfolio with the BMC tool `vvt-bmc` [11] on the same encoding (not shown in the figure), taking advantage of the modularity of the tool chain.

## 3 Strengths and Weaknesses

VVT primarily targets the verification of infinite parallel programs. Unlike BMC tools, the approach is complete and does not depend on a complete unrolling of the transition relation thanks to the underlying IC3 algorithm. The SMT-based abstraction-refinement scheme further extends the capabilities of the tool to infinite-state systems. Finally, parallelism is supported by the reductions applied to the transition relation.

Our experiments show that VVT yields good results on almost all instances of the concurrency category of the Software Verification Competition (SVCOMP) 2016. The verification results for integer/control-flow programs demonstrate that the abstraction-refinement mechanisms work well in practice.

---

[1] A lack of good static analysis is a bottleneck for obtaining powerful reductions in software model checking [9].

VVT currently does not implement rely-guarantee reasoning, and is therefore unable to handle an infinite number of threads. Furthermore, the lack of an interpolating decision procedure for arrays limits the applicability of the tool for programs with arrays to those cases where the size of the arrays can be determined statically.

VVT generates concrete counterexample traces, but does not yet map the LLVM instructions to locations in the original source code.

## 4    Tool Setup and Configuration

The Vienna Verification Tool is open source and distributed under the GPL license. Both the source code and the packaged version 0.1 submitted to SVCOMP 2016 can be found at the VVT website [10].

*Installation.* VVT v0.1 [10] requires packages LLVM 3.5 and CLang 3.5, which are available via standard package managers (APT, RPM, etc.) on many systems.

The command `vvt-svcomp-bench.sh <FILE>` starts the entire verifier tool chain (see Fig. 1), where `<FILE>` is the C or C++ file to be verified.

*Participation Statement.* For the SVCOMP 2016, we enlist VVT for participation in the categories *Integers and Control Flow* and *Concurrency*. In the former, we opt out of the sub-categories: *recursive, loops, product lines*, and *sequentialized*. We also opt out VVT of the other (unmentioned) categories.

## 5    Software Project and Contributors

VVT is developed by the Formal Methods in Systems Engineering (FORSYTE) group of the Vienna University of Technology. For more information, contact Henning Günther. Bug reports and feature requests can be submitted via the VVT website [10].

## References

1. Barrett, C., Stump, A., Tinelli, C.: The SMT-LIB standard: version 2.0. In: Gupta, A., Kroening, D. (eds,) SMT Workshopp (2010)
2. Birgmeier, J., Bradley, A.R., Weissenbacher, G.: Counterexample to induction-guided abstraction-refinement (CTIGAR). In: Biere, A., Bloem, R. (eds.) CAV 2014. LNCS, vol. 8559, pp. 829–846. Springer, Heidelberg (2014)
3. Bradley, A.R.: SAT-based model checking without unrolling. In: Jhala, R., Schmidt, D. (eds.) VMCAI 2011. LNCS, vol. 6538, pp. 70–87. Springer, Heidelberg (2011)
4. Lattner, C., Adve, V.: The LLVM Instruction Set and Compilation Strategy. Technical report UIUCDCS-R-2002-2292, University of Illinois (August 2002)
5. Clarke, E., Grumberg, O., Jha, S., Lu, Y., Veith, H.: Counterexample-guided abstraction refinement. In: Emerson, E.A., Sistla, A.P. (eds.) Computer Aided Verification. LNCS, pp. 154–169. Springer, Heidelberg (2000)

6. de Moura, L., Bjørner, N.S.: Z3: an efficient SMT solver. In: Ramakrishnan, C.R., Rehof, J. (eds.) TACAS 2008. LNCS, vol. 4963, pp. 337–340. Springer, Heidelberg (2008)
7. Cimatti, A., Griggio, A., Schaafsma, B.J., Sebastiani, R.: The MathSAT5 SMT Solver. In: Piterman, N., Smolka, S.A. (eds.) TACAS 2013 (ETAPS 2013). LNCS, vol. 7795, pp. 93–107. Springer, Heidelberg (2013)
8. Beyer, D., et al. Software model checking via large-block encoding. In: FMCAD, pp. 25–32. IEEE (2009)
9. Flanagan, C., Qadeer, S.: Transactions for software model checking. Electron. Notes Theor. Comput. Sci. **89**(3), 518–539 (2003)
10. Günther, H.: VVT website. http://vvt.forsyte.at, last visited: January 2016
11. Günther, H., Weissenbacher, G.: Incremental bounded software model checking. In: SPIN, pp. 40–47. ACM (2014)
12. Lipton, R.J.: Reduction: a method of proving properties of parallel programs. Commun. ACM **18**(12), 717–721 (1975)

# Author Index

Printed in the United States
By Bookmasters

Printed in the United States
By Bookmasters